GENERAL PRACTICE

JOHN MURTAGH

MBBS, MD, BSc, BEd,
FRACGP, DipObstRCOG

Professor of General Practice
Monash University

McGRAW-HILL BOOK COMPANY Sydney

New York San Francisco Auckland Bogotá
Caracas Lisbon London Madrid Mexico City
Milan Montreal New Delhi San Juan
Singapore Tokyo Toronto

NOTICE

Medicine is an ever-changing science. As new research and clinical experience broaden our knowledge, changes in treatment and drug therapy are required. The editors and the publisher of this work have checked with sources believed to be reliable in their efforts to provide information that is complete and generally in accord with the standards accepted at the time of publication. However, in view of the possibility of human error or changes in medical sciences, neither the editor, nor the publisher, nor any other party who has been involved in the preparation or publication of this work warrants that the information contained herein is in every respect accurate or complete. Readers are encouraged to confirm the information contained herein with other sources. For example, and in particular, readers are advised to check the product information sheet included in the package of each drug they plan to administer to be certain that the information contained in this book is accurate and that changes have not been made in the recommended dose or in the contraindications for administration. This recommendation is of particular importance in connection with new or infrequently used drugs.

National Library of Australia Cataloguing-in-Publication data:

Murtagh, John, 1936–

General practice
Includes index.
ISBN 0 07 452807 6

1. Family medicine. I. Title.

610

Published in Australia by
McGraw-Hill Book Company Australia Pty Limited
4 Barcoo Street, Roseville NSW 2069, Australia
Typeset in Australia by Midland Typesetters, Victoria
Printed in Australia by McPherson's Printing Pty Limited

Sponsoring Editor:	John Rowe
Production Editors:	Jo Rudd and Kirsten Lees
Designer:	George Sirrett
Illustrator:	Trade Wind Creations

THE AUTHOR

John Murtagh

MBBS, MD, BSc, BEd, FRACGP, DipObstRCOG
Professor of General Practice and Head of the Department of Community Medicine, Monash University.
General Practitioner, East Bentleigh Murrumbeena Medical Group.
Medical Editor, Australian Family Physician.

John Murtagh was a science master teaching chemistry, biology and physics in Victorian secondary schools when he was admitted to the first intake of the newly established medical school at Monash University. Following a comprehensive postgraduate training program, which included surgical registrarship, he practised in partnership with his medical wife, Dr Jill Rosenblatt, for ten years in the rural community of Neerim South, Victoria.

He was appointed Senior Lecturer (part-time) in the Department of Community Medicine at Monash University and eventually returned to Melbourne as a full-time Senior Lecturer. He was appointed to a professorial chair in Community Medicine at Box Hill Hospital in 1988 and subsequently as chairman of the extended department and Professor of General Practice in 1993. He has been medical editor of *Australian Family Physician* since 1986.

Contents

To my wife, Jill, and our children, Paul, Julie, Caroline, Luke and Clare, for their understanding, patience and support

and

To all my medical colleagues, past and present, who have provided the vast reservoir of knowledge from which the content of this book was made possible

Foreword

In 1960 a young schoolmaster, then teaching biology and chemistry in a secondary school in rural Victoria, decided to become a country doctor. He was admitted to the first intake of students into the Medical School of the newly established Monash University and at the end of the six year undergraduate medical course and subsequent intern and resident appointments his resolve to practise community medicine remained firm.

During his years of undergraduate and early postgraduate study Dr Murtagh continued to gather and record data relating to the diagnostic and therapeutic procedures and clinical skills he would require in solo country practice. These records, subsequently greatly expanded, were to provide at least the foundation of this book. Happily, after graduation, he married Dr Jill Rosenblatt, a young graduate from Melbourne University, who shared his vocational interests. Subsequently they also shared the fulfilment of family life and the intellectual and emotional satisfaction of serving as doctors in a rural setting.

In the meantime the Royal Australian College of General Practitioners had established postgraduate training programs that had a significant influence on standards of professional practice. At the same time Monash University established a Department of Community Medicine at one of its suburban teaching hospitals, under the Chairmanship of Professor Neil Carson and staffed by practitioners in the local community.

While in practice Dr Murtagh gained a Fellowship of the College through examination. The College recognised his unique clinical, educational and communication skills and immediately commissioned him to prepare educational programs, especially the CHECK programs. His outstanding expertise as a primary care physician led to his appointment as a senior lecturer in the University Department of Community Medicine.

The success of the initial academic development in Community Medicine at Monash University and its influence on the clinical skills of its graduates as they relate to primary care, led to a University decision to establish a further Department of Community Medicine at another suburban teaching hospital in Melbourne. It was considered by the University to be entirely appropriate that Dr Murtagh be invited to accept appointment as Professor and Head of that Department. Four years later Professor Murtagh was appointed Head of the extended Department and the first Professor of General Practice at Monash University.

John Murtagh has now become a national and international authority on the content and teaching of primary care medicine. As Medical Editor of *Australian Family Physician* he has taken that journal to a stage where it is now the most widely read medical journal in Australia.

This textbook provides a distillate of the vast experience gained by a once-upon-a-time rural doctor whose career has embraced teaching from first to last, whose interest is ensuring that disease, whether minor or life-threatening, is recognised quickly, and whose concern is that strategies to match each contingency are well understood.

General Practice is the outcome of the vision of a young schoolteacher of great talent who made a firm decision to become a country doctor; through this book his dream has become a reality for all who are privileged to practise medicine in a community setting.

G.C. Schofield
OBE, MD,ChB(NZ), DPhil(Oxon), FRACP, FRACMA, FAMA
Professor of Anatomy, Monash University 1961–77
Dean of Medicine, Monash University 1977–88

Preface

The discipline of general practice has become complex, diffuse and challenging. With the ever-burgeoning phenomenon of specialisation in medicine, with its associated complex technology and hospital basis, the need for competent, caring generalists is more important than ever before.

This textbook attempts to address the issue of the broad knowledge and skills required in modern general practice. Some of the basics of primary health care remain the same. In fact, there is an everlasting quality about many of the medical problems that affect the human being, be it a splinter under a nail, a stye of the eyelid, a terminal illness or simply stress-related anxiety. Many of the treatments and approaches to caring management are universal and timeless. Unfortunately, the modern general practitioner has lost a considerable amount of counselling and therapeutic skills compared with his or her counterpart of 50 years ago and this book encourages GPs to develop these basic skills.

General practice remains the most cost-effective health service and there is evidence that the consumer and government agencies are focusing more on general practitioners as a solution to the high-cost, high-technology, depersonalised services in the health care system. They are searching for value, satisfaction, early diagnosis and holistic management without inappropriate invasive investigations and potent medication.

This textbook of general practice attempts to take these issues into account and adopts an approach typical of western medicine: strategies for solving common problems, continuing care, basic medical skills and 'tricks of the trade'.

The discipline of general practice can be overwhelming at times, especially with patients presenting with undifferentiated problems with an overlap of organic and psychosocial aspects. There is the constant challenge to make an appropriate early diagnosis and detect the ever-lurking life-threatening illness. The approach in this book is to promote relatively fail-safe strategies to reduce the margin of error. This diagnostic model, which pervades all the chapters on problem solving, is based on my own experience, but readers can draw on their own experience to make the model work effectively for themselves.

Guidelines for early referral are included.

Another feature is the prominence given to 'masquerades' in general practice so that an increased awareness of these baffling problems will lead to improved diagnostic skills and more interesting practice. Furthermore, the preventive approach is stressed, with a particularly heavy emphasis on secondary prevention.

Such a book cannot possibly present all the medical problems likely to be encountered, but an attempt has been made to select those problems that are common, significant, preventable and treatable. I am confident that my general practice colleagues will identify with the book's content and methodology.

General practice is written with the recent graduate and the medical student in mind. It is a comprehensive textbook that focuses on the very basics of medical principles and management. However, it is hoped that all practitioners will gain useful information from the book's content.

John Murtagh

Acknowledgments

The author would like to thank the Publication Division of the Royal Australian College of General Practitioners for supporting my role as Medical Editor of *Australian Family Physician*, which has provided an excellent opportunity to gather material for this book. Acknowledgment is also due to those medical organisations that have given permission to use selected information from their publications. They include the Preventive and Community Medicine committee of the RACGP (Guidelines for Preventive Activities in General Practice), the Victorian Medical Postgraduate Foundation (Therapeutic Guidelines series), the Hypertension Guideline Committee: Research Unit RACGP (South Australian Faculty), and the *Medical Observer*, publishers of *A Manual for Primary Health Care*, for permitting reproduction of Appendices I–IV.

I am indebted to the many consultants for their help and advice after reviewing various parts of the manuscript that covered material in their particular area of expertise. They are:

Dr Roy Beran	epilepsy; fits and funny turns; neurological dilemmas
Dr Peter Berger	a diagnostic and management approach to skin problems
Professor Geoff Bishop	basic antenatal care; high-risk pregnancy
Dr John Boxall	palpitations
Dr Paul Coughlin	bruising and bleeding
Mr Rod Dalziel	common fractures and dislocations; shoulder pain
Dr Robert Dunne	common skin wounds and foreign bodies
Dr Lindsay Grayson	medical advice for travellers
Dr Michael Gribble	anaemia
Mr John Griffiths	pain in the hip and buttock
Mr Michael Grigg	pain in the leg
Dr Gary Grossbard	the painful knee
Dr Peter Hardy-Smith	the red and tender eye; visual failure
Dr Peter Holmes	cough; dyspnoea; asthma
Professor Gab Kovacs	abnormal uterine bleeding; the infertile couple
Dr Barry Lauritz	common skin problems; pigmented skin lesions
Mr Peter Lawson	disorders of the penis; prostatic disorders
Dr Peter Lothian	arthritis
Dr Ron McCoy	human immunodeficiency virus infection
Professor Barry McGrath	hypertension
Dr Michael Oldmeadow	tiredness
Dr Frank Panetta	chest pain
Dr Geoff Quail	pain in the face
Mr Ronald Quirk	pain in the foot and ankle
Dr Ian Rogers	emergency care; major trauma
Dr Jill Rosenblatt	the menopause
Associate Professor Avni Sali	abdominal pain; lumps in the breast; jaundice; constipation; dyspepsia; prevention in general practice
Dr Hugo Standish	urinary tract infection; chronic renal failure; urinary disorders
Dr Alan Yuen	fever and chills; sore throat
Dr Ronnie Yuen	diabetes mellitus; thyroid and other endocrine disorders
Dr Arthur Zulman	'nitty gritty problems'

Special thanks to Chris Sorrell, graphic designer, for his art illustration, and to Nicki Cooper for her skill and patience in typing the manuscript.

Figures 56.6, 96.7c, 96.7d were provided by Dr Levent Efe.

Thanks are also due to Jenny Green and Caroline Murtagh who helped with the preparation of the manuscript and to John Rowe and his team at McGraw-Hill Book Company for their patience and assistance in so many ways.

Abbreviations used in this text

AAA aortic abdominal aneurysm
AAFP American Academy of Family Physicians
ABC airway, breathing, circulation
ABCD airway, breathing, circulation, dextrose
AC air conduction
ACE angiotensin-converting enzyme
ACL anterior cruciate ligament
ADT adult diptheria vaccine
AFP alpha fetoprotein
AI aortic incompetence
AIDS acquired immunodeficiency syndrome
ALL acute lymphocytic leukaemia
AMI acute myocardial infarction
AML acute myeloid leukaemia
AP anterior-posterior
APF Australian pharmaceutical formulary
APTT activated partial thromboplastin time
ARC AIDS-related complex
ASD atrial septal defect
ASIS anterior superior iliac spine
AST aspartate aminotransferase
AZT azidothymidine

BC bone conduction
BCC basal cell carcinoma
BMI body mass index
BP blood pressure
BPH benign prostatic hyperplasia
BSE breast self-examination

CABG coronary artery bypass grafting
CAD coronary artery disease
CBE clinical breast examination
CCF congestive cardiac failure
CCU coronary care unit
CD_4 T helper cell
CD_8 T suppressor cell
CDH congenital dislocation of hip
CDT combined diptheria/tetanus vaccine
CFS chronic fatigue syndrome
CIN cervical intraepithelial neoplasia
CK creatinine kinase
CK-MB creatinine kinase–myocardial bound fraction
CMC carpometacarpal
CMV cytomegalovirus
CNS central nervous system
co compound
COAD chronic obstructive airways disease
COC combined oral contraceptive
COPD chronic obstructive pulmonary disease
CPA cardiopulmonary arrest
CPPD calcium pyrophosphate dihydrate
CPR cardiopulmonary resuscitation
CPS complex partial seizures
CREST calcinosis cutis; Raynaud's phenomenon; esophageal involvement; sclerodactyly; telangiectasia
CRFM chloroquine-resistant falciparum malaria
CSF cerebrospinal fluid
CSFM chloroquine-sensitive falciparum malaria
CT computerised tomography
CTS carpal tunnel syndrome
CVA cerebrovascular accident
CVS cardiovascular system
CXR chest X-ray

DA dissecting aneurysm
DBP diastolic blood pressure
DC direct current
DIC disseminated intravascular coagulation
DIP distal interphalangeal

dl	decilitre
DNA	deoxyribose-nucleic acid
drug dosage	bd — twice daily tid, tds — three times daily qid, qds — four times daily
DSM	diagnostic and statistical manual (of mental disorders)
DU	duodenal ulcer
DUB	dysfunctional uterine bleeding
DVT	deep venous thrombosis
EAR	expired air resuscitation
EBM	Epstein-Barr mononucleosis (glandular fever)
EBV	Epstein-Barr virus
ECG	electrocardiogram
ECT	electroconvulsive therapy
EDD	expected due date
EEG	electroencephalogram
ELISA	enzyme linked immunosorbent assay
EMG	electromyogram
EPL	extensor pollicus longus
EPS	expressed prostatic secretions
ER	external rotation
ERCP	endoscopic retrograde cholangiopancreatography
esp.	especially
ESR	erythrocyte sedimentation rate
ET	embryo transfer
FBE	full blood count
FDL	flexor digitorum longus
FEV_1	forced expiratory volume in 1 second
fl	femto-litre (10^{-15})
FSH	follicle stimulating hormone
FTA-ABS	fluorescent treponemal antibody absorption test
FTT	failure to thrive
FUO	fever of undetermined origin
g	gram
GA	general anaesthetic
GABHS	group A beta-haemolytic streptococcus
GBS	Guillain-Barré syndrome
GI	gastrointestinal
GIFT	gamete intrafallopian transfer
GIT	gastrointestinal tract
GO	gastro-oesophageal
G_6PD	glucose-6-phosphate dehydrogenase
GP	general practitioner
GU	gastric ulcer
HAV	hepatitis A virus
anti-HAV	hepatitis A antibody
Hb	haemoglobin
anti-HBc	hepatitis B core antibody
HBeAg	hepatitis Be antigen
anti-HBs	hepatitis B surface antibody
HBsAg	hepatitis B surface antigen
HBV	hepatitis B virus
HCV	hepatitis C virus
anti-HCV	hepatitis C virus antibody
HDL	high-density lipoprotein
HDV	hepatitis D (Delta) virus
HEV	hepatitis E virus
HIDA	hepatobiliary iminodiacetic acid
HIV	human immunodeficiency virus
HLA(B_{27})	human leucocyte antigen
HPV	human papilloma virus
HRT	hormone replacement therapy
HSV	herpes simplex viral infection
HT	hypertension
IBS	irritable bowel syndrome
IDDM	insulin dependent diabetes mellitus
IDU	injecting drug user
IgE	immunoglobulin E
IgG	immunoglobulin G
IgM	immunoglobulin M
IM IMI	intramuscular injection
INR	international normalised ratio
IOFB	intraocular foreign body
IR	internal rotation
ITP	idiopathic (or immune) thrombocytopenia purpura
IUCD	intrauterine contraceptive device
IV	intravenous
IVF	in vitro fertilisation
IVI	intravenous injection
IVP	intravenous pyelogram
IVU	intravenous urogram
JCA	juvenile chronic arthritis
kg	kilogram
KOH	potassium hydroxide
LA	local anaesthetic
LBBH	left branch bundle block
LDH/LH	lactic dehydrogenase
LFTs	liver function tests
LH	luteinising hormone
LHRH	luteinising hormone releasing hormone
LIF	left iliac fossa

LMN	lower motor neurone
LSD	lysergic acid
LUQ	left upper quadrant
LVH	left ventricular hypertrophy
mane	in morning
MAOI	monoamine oxidase inhibitor
mcg	microgram
MCL	medial collateral ligament
MG	myaesthenia gravis
MID	minor intervertebral derangement
MRI	magnetic resonance imaging
MS	multiple sclerosis
MSU	mid-stream urine
MTP	metatarsophalangeal
MVA	motor vehicle accident
NGU	non-gonococcal urethritis
NIDDM	non-insulin dependent diabetes mellitus
nocte	at night
N saline	normal saline
NSAIDs	non-steroidal anti-inflammatory drugs
NSU	non-specific urethritis
(o)	taken orally
OA	oesteoarthritis
OSA	obstructive sleep apnoea
OSD	Osgood-Schlatter disorder
OTC	over the counter
Pap	Papanicolaou
PCL	posterior cruciate ligament
PCP	pneumocystitis pneumonia
PD	Parkinson's disease
PDA	patent ductus arteriosus
PEF	peak expiratory flow
PET	pre-eclamptic toxaemia
PGL	persistent generalised lymphadenopathy
PH	past history
PID	pelvic inflammatory disease
PIP	proximal interphalangeal
PKU	phenylketonuria
PLISSIT	permission: limited information: specific suggestion: intensive therapy
PSA	prostate specific antigen
PSIS	posterior superior iliac spine
PT	prothrombin time
PUO	pyrexia of undetermined origin
PUVA	psoralen + UVA
PVC	polyvinyl chloride
PVD	peripheral vascular disease
PVST	paroxysmal supraventricular tachycardia
qds, qid	four times daily
RA	rheumatoid arthritis
RACGP	Royal Australian College of General Practitioners
RAP	recurrent abdominal pain
Rh	rhesus
RIB	rest in bed
RICE	rest, ice, compression, elevation
RPR	rapid plasma reagin
RSD	reflex sympathetic dystrophy
rt-PA	recombinant tissue plasminogen activator
SAH	subarachnoid haemorrhage
SBE	subacute bacterial endocarditis
SBO	small bowel obstruction
SBP	systolic blood pressure
SC/SCI	subcutaneous/subcutaneous injection
SCC	squamous cell carcinoma
SIJ	sacroiliac joint
SL	sublingual
SLE	systemic lupus erythematosus
SND	sensorineural deafness
SNHL	sensorineural hearing loss
SPF	sun penetration factor
SR	sustained release
SSS	sick sinus syndrome
statim	at once
STD	sexually transmitted disease
SUFE	slipped upper femoral epiphysis
SVT	supraventricular tachycardia
T_3	tri-iodothyronine
T_4	thyroxine
TA	temporal arteritis
TB	tuberculosis
tds	three times daily
TIA	transient ischaemic attack
TM	tympanic membrane
TMJ	temporomandibular joint
TORCH	toxoplasmosis, rubella, cytomegalovirus, herpes virus
TPHA	Treponema pallidum haemoglutination test
TSE	testicular self-examination
TSH	thyroid-stimulating hormone
TUIP	transurethral incision of prostate
TURP	transurethral resection of prostate
U	units

U&E	urea and electrolytes
μg	microgram
UMN	upper motor neurone
UV	ultraviolet
URTI	upper respiratory tract infection
UTI	urinary tract infection
VBI	vertebrobasilar insufficiency
VC	vital capacity
VDRL	Venereal Disease Reference Laboratory
VF	ventricular fibrillation
VMA	vanillylmandelic acid
VSD	ventricular septal defect
VT	ventricular tachycardia
WBC	white blood cells
WBR	white→blue→red
WCC	white cell count
WHO	World Health Organisation
WPW	Wolff-Parkinson-White

PART 1

THE BASIS OF GENERAL PRACTICE

1

The nature and content of general practice

General practice is a traditional method of bringing primary health care to the community. It is a medical discipline in its own right, linking the vast amount of accumulated medical knowledge with the art of communication.

Definitions

General practice can be defined as that medical discipline which provides 'community-based, continuing, comprehensive, preventive primary care', sometimes referred to as the CCCP model.

The RACGP uses the following definitions of general practice and primary care:

General practice is defined as the provision of primary continuing comprehensive whole-patient care to individuals, families and their communities.

Primary care involves the ability to take responsible action on any problem the patient presents, whether or not it forms part of an ongoing doctor-patient relationship. In managing the patient, the general/family practitioner may make appropriate referral to other doctors, health care professionals and community services. General/family practice is the point of first contact for the majority of people seeking health care. In the provision of primary care, much ill defined illness is seen; the general/family practitioner often deals with problem complexes rather than with established diseases.

The practitioner must be able to make a total assessment of the person's condition without subjecting the person to unnecessary investigations, procedure and treatment.

The American Academy of Family Physicians (AAFP)[1] and the American Board of Family Practice (ABFP) have defined family practice as:

. . . the medical specialty that provides continuing and comprehensive health care for the individual and the family. It is the specialty in breadth that integrates the biological, clinical and behavioural sciences. The scope of family practice encompasses all ages, both sexes, each organ system and disease entity.

The AAFP has emphasised that the primary objective of the specialty of family practice is to deliver primary health care, described as:

. . . a form of medical care delivery that emphasises first contact care and assumes ongoing responsibility for the patient in both health maintenance and therapy of illness. It is personal care involving a unique interaction and communication between the patient and the physician. It is comprehensive in scope and includes the overall co-ordination of care of the patient's health problems, be they biological, behavioural or social. The appropriate use of consultants and community resources is an important part of effective primary care.

The ABFP has expanded on the function of delivery of primary health care.[1,2]

Primary care is a form of delivery of medical care that encompasses the following functions:

1. *It is 'first-contact' care, serving as a point-of-entry for patients into the health care system.*
2. *It includes continuity by virtue of caring for patients over a period of time, both in sickness and in health.*

3. *It is comprehensive care, drawing from all the traditional major disciplines for its functional content.*
4. *It serves a co-ordinative function for all the health care needs of the patient.*
5. *It assumes continuing responsibility for individual patient follow-up and community health problems; and*
6. *It is a highly personalised type of care.*

Pereira Gray[3] identifies six principles—primary care, family care, domiciliary care and continuing care—all designed to achieve preventive and personal care. 'We see the patient as a whole person and this involves breadth of knowledge about each person, not just depth of disease.'

General practice is not the summation of specialties practised at a superficial level and we must avoid the temptation to become 'specialoids'. In the current climate where medicine is often fragmented there is a need greater than ever for the generalist. The patient requires a trusted focal point in the often bewildering health service jungle. Who is to do this better than the caring family doctor taking full responsibility for the welfare of the patient and intervening on his or her behalf? Specialists also need highly competent generalists to whom they can entrust ongoing care.

Unique features of general practice

Anderson, Bridges-Webb and Chancellor[4] emphasise that 'the unique and important work of the general practitioner is to provide availability and continuity of care, competence in the realm of diagnosis, care of acute and chronic illness, prompt treatment of emergencies and a preventive approach to health care'.

The features that make general practice different to hospital or specialist based medical practices include:

- first contact
- diagnostic methodology
- early diagnosis of life-threatening and serious disease
- continuity and availability of care
- personalised care
- care of acute and chronic illness
- domiciliary care
- emergency care (prompt treatment at home or in the community)
- family care
- palliative care (at home)
- preventive care
- scope for health promotion
- holistic approach
- health care co-ordination

Apart from these processes the general practitioner has to manage very common problems including a whole variety of problems not normally taught in medical school or in postgraduate programs. Many of these problems are unusual yet common and can be regarded as the 'nitty gritty' or 'bread and butter' problems of primary health care.

Continuing care

The essence of general practice is continuity of care. The doctor–patient relationship is unique in general practice in the sense that it covers a span of time which is not restricted to a specific major illness. The continuing relationship involving many separate episodes of illness provides an opportunity for the doctor to develop considerable knowledge and understanding of the patient, the family and its stresses, and the patient's work and recreational environment.

Strategies to enhance continuing care

A philosophical commitment

Underlying appropriate patient care is the attitude of the provider. A caring, responsible practitioner who is competent, available and a trusted friend is 'like gold' to his or her patients.

Medical records

An efficient medical record system is fundamental. Ideally it should include a patient profile, a database, problem lists, special investigation lists, medication lists, adverse drug reactions and 'at risk' details.

Checklists

The use of checklists or questionnaires to assemble information on presenting problems may enhance knowledge as well as assist earlier diagnosis.

Home visits

These are a goldmine of information about intrafamily dynamics. They should cement the doctor–patient relationship if used appropriately and discreetly. We are the only doctors who practise domiciliary care. We must treasure it. Sitting in the office chair practising 'conveyor belt' medicine is contrary to the ideals of general practice.

Anticipatory guidance
Unfortunately patients do not usually perceive the family doctor as a counsellor but opportunities should be taken to offer advice about anticipated problems in situations such as premarital visits, antenatal care and pre-adolescent contact.

Patient education
Whenever possible, patients should be given insight into the nature of their illness, and reasons for the treatment and prognosis. Patient education leaflets, such as those published in journals, can be used as a starting point although there is no substitute for careful personal explanation. This should lead to better compliance and an improved relationship between doctor and patient.

Personal health records
These excellent wallets which are handed to parents of newborn babies have a very important place in the ongoing care of children. Their purpose is to supply an outline of preventive health care, beginning from birth. They provide an inbuilt recall list directed at a most compliant source—mothers. In fact they provide a complete record of health care throughout a person's lifetime.

Patient register
An age and sex register of all patients in the practice is a very useful acquisition. The main strategy is to find out who are the patients, what are their basic characteristics and who suffers from chronic diseases such as cancer, diabetes and emphysema.

Recall lists
Use of recall lists based on the patient register should significantly improve health care delivery. Dentists have been using this technique successfully for some time. In Northern America and Canada doctors use recall lists regularly to remind patients that preventive items such as immunisation schedules and cancer smear tests are due.

Computers
Computers have simplified and streamlined the design and use of practice registers and patient recall systems in addition to their use for accounting purposes. Their potential for patient education and doctor education is considerable.

Common presenting symptoms

Common presenting symptoms in Australian practices are presented in Table 1.1[5], where they are compared with the United States of America.[6] The similarity is noticed but the different classification system does not permit an accurate comparison. In the third national survey of morbidity in general practice in Australia[5] the most common symptoms described by patients were cough (7.5 per 100 encounters), throat complaints (4.7 per 100), back complaints (3.8 per 100) and skin symptoms (3.6 per 100). In addition very common presentations included a check-up (13.6 per 100) and a request for prescription (8.8 per 100). McWhinney lists the ten most common presenting symptoms from representative Canadian and British practices but they are divided between males and females.[7]

For males in the Canadian study these symptoms are (in order, starting from the most common): cough, sore throat, colds, abdominal/pelvic pain, rash, fever/chills, earache, back problems, skin inflammation and chest pain.

For females the five other symptoms that are included are: menstrual disorders, depression, vaginal discharge, anxiety and headache.

In the British study the most common symptoms are virtually identical between males and females and include: cough, rash, sore throat, abdominal pain, bowel symptoms, chest pain, back pain, spots, sores and ulcers, headache.

Most frequent presenting symptoms in the author's practice[8]

The following most common symptoms were identified, with the emphasis being on pain syndromes:

- cough
- disturbance of bowel function
- pain in abdomen
- pain in back
- pain in chest
- pain in head
- pain in neck
- pain in ear
- pain in throat
- pain in joints/limbs
- rashes
- sleep problems
- tiredness/fatigue
- vaginal discomfort

Table 1.1 *Most frequent presenting problems/symptoms (excluding pregnancy, hypertension, immunisation, routine check-up)*

	Ranking in Australia		United States
Cough	1		1
Throat complaints	2		2
Back pain	3		4
Rash	4		5
Abdominal pain	5		6
Headache	6		10
Weakness/tiredness	7		
Swelling	8		
Ear pain	9		3
Fever	10		7
URTI	11		
Nasal congestion/sneeze	12		12
Diarrhoea	13		
Chest pain	14		13
Foot, toe complaints	15		
Vertigo/dizziness	16		
		Visual dysfunction	8
		Knee symptoms	9
		Head cold	11

Source: Australian figures: reference 5
United States figures (all specialties): reference 6

These symptoms should accurately reflect Australian general practice since the rural practice would represent an appropriate cross-section of the community's morbidity and the recording and classification of data from the one practitioner would be consistent.

Common managed disorders

Excluding a general medical examination, hypertension and upper respiratory tract infection (URTI) were the two most common problems encountered in both the Australian and USA[9] studies. The 23 most frequent individual disorders are listed in Table 1.2 and accounted for over 40% of all problems managed.[10]

Most commonly diagnosed disease classes

Although there is a similar general trend in the distribution of problems managed across body systems in these two Australian studies, a notable difference occurs in the diagnosis of psychological problems (Table 1.3).

The content of this textbook reflects what is fundamental to the nature and content of general practice—that which is common but is significant, relevant, preventable and treatable.

References

1. American Academy of Family Physicians. Official definition of Family Practice and Family Physician (AAFP Publication No. 303). Kansas City, Mo, AAFP, 1986.
2. Rakel RE. *Essentials of family practice.* Philadelphia: WB Saunders Company, 1993, 2–3.
3. Pereira Gray DJ. Just a GP. JR Coll Gen Pract, 1980; 30:231–239.
4. Anderson NA, Bridges-Webb C, Chancellor AHB. *General practice in Australia.* Sydney: Sydney University Press, 1986, 3–4.
5. Bridges-Webb C, Britt H, Miles D et al. Morbidity and treatment in general practice in Australia 1990–1991. Med J Aust (supplement), 19 October, 1992.

Table 1.2 *Most frequently managed disorders/diagnoses (rank order)*

	Australia	**United States**
General medical examination	1	1
Hypertension	2	3
URTI	3	2
Asthma	4	29
Osteoarthritis	5	10
Acute bronchitis	6	13
Immunisation	7	*
Anxiety	8	6†
Sprain/strain	9	5
Arthritis (excluding osteoarthritis)	10	27
Depression	11	6†
Contact dermatitis	12	9
Acute otitis media	13	18
Diabetes mellitus	14	8
Lipid metabolism disorder	15	*
Tonsillitis	16	—
Sinusitis	17	25
Urinary tract infection	18	11
Heart failure	19	—
Sleep disorders/insomnia	20	—
Female genital check-up, pap smear	21	(under 1)
Viral diseases (other)	22	—
Solar/hyper keratosis	23	—
Soft tissue injuries		4
Ischaemic heart disease		7

Source: Australian figures: reference 5
United States figures: reference 9
* not listed
† combined

Table 1.3 *Most frequently diagnosed disease classes*

	Author's country practice (1974–1978)[8]	***Australian morbidity study (1990–1991)***[5]
Respiratory	24.3%	16.7%
Psychological	12.8%	6.6%
Musculoskeletal	12.2%	12.0%
Cardiovascular	7.5%	12.5%
Skin	7.0%	12.4%
Preventive medicine	5.4%	5.6%
Digestive	4.4%	7.1%
Genitourinary	4.4%	6.7%
Reproductive	3.8%	3.4%

6. De Lozier JE, Gagnon RO. 1989 Summary: National Ambulatory Medical Care Survey. Hyattsville, Md, National Centre for Health Statistics, 1991.
7. McWhinney IR. *A textbook of family medicine.* New York: Oxford University Press, 1989, 35:42.
8. Murtagh JE. *The anatomy of a rural practice.* Melbourne: Monash University, Dept of Community Practice Publication, 1980, 8–13.
9. Rosenblatt RA, Cherkin DC, Schneeweiss R et al. The structure and content of family practice: current status and future trends. J Fam Pract, 1982; 15 (4):681–722.
10. Bridges-Webb C, Britt H, Miles D et al. Morbidity and treatment in general practice in Australia. Aust Fam Physician, 1993; 22:336–346.

2

The family

—

Working with families is the basis of family practice. Families living in relative harmony provide the basis for the good mental health of their members and also for social stability.

However, the traditional concept of the nuclear family where the wife stays at home to care for the children occurs in only about 15% of Australian families, and approximately 40% of Australian marriages end in separation. This results in many psychosocial problems that family doctors will have to address.

Family therapy is ideally undertaken by general practitioners, who are in a unique position as providers of continuing care and family care. It is important for them to work together with families in the counselling process and to avoid the common pitfalls of working in isolation and assuming personal responsibility for changing the family.

Bader[1] summarises working with families succinctly. 'From the perspective of family therapy, working with families means avoiding the trap of being too directive, too responsible for the family's welfare, with the result that the family becomes overly dependent on the general practitioner for its health and development. From the perspective of family education, working with families means developing the skills of anticipating guidance, helping families to prepare, not only for the normal changes occurring as the family develops, but also for the impact of illness on the family system.'

Characteristics of healthy families

Successful families have certain characteristics, an understanding of which can give the family doctor a basis for assessing the health of the family and a goal to help set targets for change in disrupted families. Such characteristics are:

- Healthy communication in which family members have freedom of expression for their feelings and emotions.
- Personal autonomy which includes appropriate use of power sharing between spouses.
- Flexibility so that there is appropriate 'give and take' with adaptation to individual needs and changing circumstances.
- Appreciation: this involves encouragement and praise so that members develop a healthy sense of self-esteem.
- Support networks: adequate support from within and without the family engenders security, resistance to stress and a healthy environment in general. The family doctor is part of this network.
- Family time and involvement: studies have shown that the most satisfying hallmark of a happy family is 'doing things together'.
- Spouse bonding: the importance of a sound marital relationship becomes obvious when family therapy is undertaken.

- Growth: appropriate opportunities for growth of individual family members in an encouraging atmosphere.
- Spiritual and religious values: an attachment to spiritual beliefs and values is known to be associated with positive family health, supporting the saying 'The family that prays together stays together'.

Families in crisis

Doctors are closely involved with families who experience unexpected crises which include illnesses, accidents, divorce, separation, unemployment, death of a family member, financial disasters and so on.

The effect of illness

Serious illness often precipitates crisis in individual members of the family, crises which have not previously surfaced in the apparently balanced family system. It is recognised, for example, that bereavement over the unexpected loss of a child may lead to marital breakdown, separation or divorce.

In the long term, other family members may be affected more than the patient. This may apply particularly to children and manifest as school underachievement and behaviour disturbances.

During the crisis the obvious priority of the doctor is to the patient but the less obvious needs of the family should not be ignored.

Guidelines for the doctor

- Include the family as much as possible, starting early in the acute phase of the illness. It may necessitate family conferences.
- Include the family on a continuing basis, especially if a long-term illness is anticipated. It is helpful to be alert for changes in attitudes, such as anger and resentment towards the sick member.
- Include the family in hospital discharge planning.
- If a serious change in family dynamics is observed the use of experts may be needed.

Significant presentations of family dysfunction

The following presentations may be indicators that all is not well in the family, and so the doctor needs to 'think family':

- marital or sexual difficulties
- multiple presentations of a family member—'the thick file syndrome'
- multiple presentations by multiple family members
- abnormal behaviour in a child
- the 'difficult patient'
- inappropriate behaviour in the antenatal and/or postpartum period
- drug or alcohol abuse in a family member
- evidence of physical or sexual abuse in wife or child
- psychiatric disorders
- susceptibility to illness
- increased stress/anxiety

It is important that the family doctor remain alert to the diversity of presentations and takes the responsibility for identifying an underlying family-based problem.

How to evaluate the family dynamics

- Carefully observe family members interacting.
- Invite the whole family to a counselling session (if possible).
- Visit the home: an impromptu home visit (with some pretext such as a concern about a blood test result) on the way home from work may be very revealing.

The family life cycle

Helpful in understanding the dynamics of the family is the concept of the family life cycle[2] which identifies several clearly defined stages of development (Table 2.1). Such an understanding can help the doctor form appropriate hypotheses about the problems patients are experiencing at a particular stage. Each stage brings its own tasks, happiness, crises and difficulties.

Family assessment

The assessment of families with problems can be formalised through a questionnaire which allows the collection of information in a systematic way in order to give an understanding of the functioning of the family in question.

The questionnaire[1]

1. *Family of origin*

Could each of you tell us something about the families you grew up in?
Where do you come in the family?

Table 2.1 *The family life cycle*[1]

Stage	***Tasks to be achieved***
1. Leaving home	Establishing personal independence. Beginning the emotional separation from parents.
2. Getting married	Establishing an intimate relationship with spouse. Further development of the emotional separation from parents.
3. Learning to live together	Dividing the various marital roles in an equitable way. Establishing a new more independent relationship with family.
4. Parenting the first child	Opening the family to include a new member. Dividing the parenting roles.
5. Living with the adolescent	Increasing the flexibility of the family boundaries to allow the adolescent(s) to move in and out of the family system.
6. Launching children: the empty nest phase	Accepting the multitude of exits from and entries into the family system. Adjusting to the ending of parenting roles.
7. Retirement	Adjusting to the ending of the wage-earning roles. Developing new relationships with children, grandchildren and each other.
8. Old age	Dealing with lessening abilities and greater dependence on others. Dealing with losses of friends, family members and, eventually, each other.

Were you particularly close to anyone else in the family?
Were there any severe conflicts between family members?
Did anyone abuse you in any way?
Do you have much contact with any of your family now?
Have you tried to model (or avoid) any features for your own family?

2. *History of the couple's relationship*

How did you two meet?
What attracted you to each other?
Why did you marry this person rather than someone else?
How did your families react to your choice?
How did the birth of your children affect your relationship?
When was your relationship at its best? and why?

3. *Experience in counselling and enrichment*

Have any of you been to 'marriage encounter' or similar programs?
Have any of you been to any form of counselling?
Did you go alone or with another family member?
What did you like or dislike about the experience?
In what way was it helpful or unhelpful?

4. *Expectations and goals*

Whose idea was it to come here?
What was the reaction of other family members?
Why did you come now?
Was there any particular event that triggered the decision?
What do each of you hope to gain by coming for an assessment?

5. *Family function*[1]

What is it like for each of you to live in this family? (If children are present, they should be asked first.)
Do you have any difficulty in talking to other members of the family? (Again, children first.)
Do you have any difficulty in expressing appreciation to each other? (Mention here that studies on healthy families show that both communication and appreciation rank in the top qualities.)
How do you show appreciation in this family?

How do you show affection in this family? (Again, children first.)
How satisfied are you with the present arrangement? Are there any changes you would like to see?
What ways have you used to resolve disagreements or change the way the family functions?

Assessment based on the questionnaire

Family members present in interview (names and ages)
Missing members (names and ages)
Presenting problems or reasons for family interview
Identified by whom? Any attempted solutions.
Roles—structure, organisation (who is dominant and so on)
Affect—predominant emotional tone and expressed emotions
Communication: who dominates? who talks? who listens to whom?
Stage in the family life cycle
Illness and sickness roles
Coping mechanisms

Family-based medical counselling

There are several brief counselling models to assist the family doctor in probing and counselling, using a simple infrastructure such as the BATHE model.

The BATHE technique[3]

This really represents a diagnostic technique to identify sources of disharmony which can act as a springboard for counselling.

The acronym BATHE stands for background, affect, trouble, handling, empathy, and can be summarised as follows.

Background
Enquire about possible areas of psychosocial problems to help elicit the context of the patient's visit.

'What is happening in your life?'
'Is there anything different since before you got sick?'
'How are things at home?'

Affect
Affect is the 'feeling state' and includes anxiety, so it is wise to probe potentially sensitive areas.

'How do you feel about what is going on in your life?'
'How do you feel about your home life?'
'How do you feel about work/school?'
'How do you feel about your (husband or wife or daughter or . . .)?'
'What is your mood like? Do you feel sad or happy?'

Trouble
Enquire about how the patient's problems are troubling them.

'What about the situation troubles you most?'
'What troubles or worries you most in your life?'
'What worries you most at home?'
'How stressed and upset are you about this problem?'
'How do you think this problem affects you?'

Handling

'How are you handling this problem?'
'Do you think that you have mishandled anything?'
'Do you get support at home to help handle the problem?'
'What does your support come from?'
'How do you feel that you are coping?'

Empathy
Indicate an understanding of patients' distress and legitimise their feelings.

'That must be very difficult for you.'
'That sounds really tough on you.'

Steps to bring about behaviour change

Fabb and Fleming have introduced the model of change which is fundamental to initiating therapy. The five steps are:

1. *Dissatisfaction*

There must be dissatisfaction with the present pattern of behaviour.

2. *Alternative*

There must be an acceptable alternative behaviour pattern available.

3. *Emotional commitment*

There must be an emotional commitment to the new pattern of behaviour over the old.

4. *Practice with feedback*

There must be practice of the new behaviour, with feedback, to establish the new pattern as an available behaviour.

5. *Habituation with support*

There must be installation of the new behaviour in the normal work/living situation *with support.* *All* of these must be present for change to occur. Steps 4 and 5 are often neglected with the result that change does not occur or is less successful.

Marital disharmony

Family doctors often have to provide marital counselling for one or both partners. The problems may be resolved quite simply or be so complex that marital breakdown is inevitable despite optimal opportunities for counselling.

Opportunities for prevention including anticipatory guidance about marital problems do exist and the wise practitioner will offer appropriate advice and counselling. Examples include an accident to a child attributable to neglect by a parent, or similar situation in which that parent may be the focus of blame leading to resentment and tension. The practitioner could intervene from the outset to alleviate possible feelings of guilt and anger in that marriage.

Some common causes of marital disharmony are:

- selfishness
- unrealistic expectations
- financial problems/meanness
- not listening to each other
- sickness (e.g. depression)
- drug or alcohol excess
- jealousy, especially in men
- fault finding
- 'playing games' with each other
- driving ambition
- immaturity
- poor communication

Basic counselling of couples[4]

The following text, which should be regarded as a patient education sheet, includes useful advice for couples.

The two big secrets of marital success are *caring* and *responsibility*.

Some important facts

- Research has shown that we tend to choose partners who are similar to our parents and that we may take our childish and selfish attitudes into our marriage.
- The trouble spots listed above reflect this childishness; we often expect our partners to change and meet our needs.
- If we take proper care and responsibility, we can keep these problems to a minimum.
- Physical passion is not enough to hold a marriage together—'when it burns out, only ashes will be left'.
- While a good sexual relationship is great, most experts agree that what goes on *out* of bed counts for more.
- When we do something wrong, it is most important that we feel forgiven by our partner.

Positive guidelines for success

1. *Know yourself.* The better you know yourself, the better you will know your mate. Learn about sex and reproduction.
2. *Share interests and goals.* Do not become too independent of each other. Develop mutual friends, interests and hobbies. Tell your partner 'I love you' regularly at the right moments.
3. *Continue courtship after marriage.* Spouses should continue to court and desire each other. Going out regularly for romantic evenings and giving unexpected gifts (such as flowers) are ways to help this love relationship. Engage in some high-energy fun activities such as massaging and dancing.
4. *Make love, not war.* A good sexual relationship can take years to develop, so work at making it better. Explore the techniques of lovemaking without feeling shy or inhibited. This can be helped by books such as *The Joy of Sex* and videos on lovemaking. Good grooming and a clean body are important.
5. *Cherish your mate.* Be proud of each other, not competitive or ambitious at the other's expense. Talk kindly about your spouse to others—do not put him or her down.
6. *Prepare yourself for parenthood.* Plan your family wisely and learn about child bearing and rearing. Learn about family planning methods and avoid the anxieties of an unplanned pregnancy. The best environment for a child is a happy marriage.

7. *Seek proper help when necessary.* If difficulties arise and are causing problems, seek help. Your general practitioner will be able to help. Stress-related problems and depression in particular can be lethal in a marriage—they must be 'nipped in the bud'.
8. *Do unto your mate as you would have your mate do unto you.* This gets back to the unconscious childhood needs. Be aware of each other's feelings and be sensitive to each other's needs. Any marriage based on this rule has an excellent chance of success.

The **B**e **A**ttitudes (virtues to help achieve success)

BE honest	**BE** loyal
BE loving	**BE** desiring
BE patient	**BE** fun to live with
BE forgiving	**BE** one
BE generous	**BE** caring

Making lists—a practical task

Make lists for each other to compare and discuss.

- List qualities (desirable and undesirable) of your parents.
- List qualities of each other.
- List examples of behaviour each would like the other to change.
- List things you would like the other to do for you.

Put aside special quiet times each week to share these things.

Pitfalls[1]

The general practitioner who is too closely attached to one or more members of the family can easily become trapped in the role of the 'rescuer' or 'saviour' of those members. The best defence against this trap is to respect the family's autonomy and work with the family to achieve the goals the family sets for itself, thus avoiding three major pitfalls for the general practitioner in treating families:

1. Assuming personal responsibility for changing the family.
2. Working alone, neglecting the family's assistance.
3. Becoming a 'rescuer' or 'saviour'.

Other pitfalls

- Conducting therapy with a missing member.
- Breaching confidentiality of individuals within the family.
- Failing to recognise the 'ganging-up effect'.
- Taking sides.
- Failing to use available resources.
- Overrelating to your own experiences.

Possible solutions to avoid pitfalls[1]

- Let the patients do the work.
- Share the burden with a colleague or other resources.
- Ensure that the goals for therapy are realistic.
- Point out that all family members have to work together and that therapy works best when there is openness on all sides.
- Identify any tendency to look for scapegoats within the family.
- Avoid trying to achieve quick solutions.
- Obtain clear-cut agreements on confidential matters and record this in the history.
- Keep an open mind and avoid forcing your own values on to the family.

References

1. Bader E. Working with families. Aust Fam Physician, 1990; 19:522–528.
2. Van Doorn H. *Common problems checklist for general practice*. Melbourne: Royal Australian College of General Practitioners, 1989, 19.
3. Stuart MR, Leiberman JA III. *The 15-minute hour: Applied psychotherapy for the primary care physician*. New York: Praeger, 1986.
4. Murtagh JE. Making your marriage work. In: *Patient education*, Sydney: McGraw-Hill, 1992, 3.

3

Communication skills

Hippocrates wrote: 'In the art of medicine there are three factors—the disease, the patient and the doctor . . . It is not easy for the ordinary people to understand why they are ill or why they get better or worse, but if it is explained by someone else, it can seem quite a simple matter—if the doctor fails to make himself understood he may miss the truth of the illness'.[1]

Francis Macnab, Doctor of Divinity and patient, wrote: 'The style of the doctor, the communication of the doctor and the person of the doctor at the level of primary contact and primary care can be crucial in a person's life'.[2]

Much of the art of general practice lies in the ability to communicate.

The skills of general practice

A successful outcome to the medical consultation depends on a whole array of skills required by the general practitioner. Although interrelated these skills, which can be collectively termed consulting skills, include clinical skills, diagnostic skills, management skills, communication skills, educative skills, therapeutic skills, manual skills and counselling skills.

Communication skills, which are fundamental to consulting skills, are the key to the effectiveness of the doctor as a professional and expertise with these skills is fundamental to the doctor–patient relationship. Communication skill is essential in obtaining a good history and constitutes one of the corner-stones of therapy.

A skilled interviewer will succeed in transmitting his or her findings to the patient so that they are clearly understood, are not unduly disturbing, and inspire trust and confidence in the physician.

Communication

Communication can be defined as 'the successful passing of a message from one person to another'.

There are five basic elements in the communication process:

- the communicator
- the message
- the method of communicating
- the recipient
- the response

Important principles facilitating the communication process:

- the rapport between the people involved
- the time factor: facilitated by devoting more time
- the message, which needs to be clear, correct, concise, unambiguous and in context
- the attitudes of both the communicator and the recipient

Communication in the consultation

The doctor requires appropriate communication skills for complete diagnosis (physical, emotional and social) and competent management. The majority of interaction between doctor and patient occurs in the traditional consultation. Table 3.1 shows where the communication pattern swings between being 'patient focused' or 'doctor focused'.[3]

Table 3.1 *Phases of doctor-patient communication*[3]

Phase 1 Patient focus	***Phase 2 Doctor focus***	***Phase 3 Mutual focus***
Introduction	Examination	Management discussion
Present complaint	Investigation	Follow-up
Other medical history		Sign-off
Family history		
Social history		

Important positive doctor behaviour

At first contact:

- Make the patient feel comfortable.
- Be 'unhurried' and relaxed.
- Focus firmly on the patient.
- Use open-ended questions where possible.
- Make appropriate reassuring gestures.

Active listening

Listening is the single most important skill.[3] Listening is an active process, described by Egan as follows:

One does not listen with just his ears: he listens with his eyes and with his sense of touch. He listens by becoming aware of the feelings and emotions that arise within himself because of his contact with others (that is, his own emotional resonance is another 'ear'), he listens with his mind, his heart, and his imagination. He listens to the words of others, but he also listens to the messages that are buried in the words or encoded in all the cues that surround the words. He listens to the voice, the demeanour, the vocabulary, and the gestures of the other. He listens to the context, verbal messages and linguistic pattern, and the bodily movements of others. He listens to the sounds, and to the silences.[4]

Listening includes four essential elements:

- checking facts
- checking feelings
- encouragement
- reflection

Listen with understanding, in a relaxed attentive silence. Use reflective questions, such as:

- 'You seem very sad today.'
- 'You seem upset about your husband.'
- 'It seems you're having trouble coping.'
- 'You seem to be telling me that . . .'
- 'Your main concern seems to me to . . .'

Attitudes

- caring
- empathy
- respect
- interest
- concern
- confidence
- competence
- responsibility
- trust
- sensitivity
- perceptiveness
- diligence

Communicating strategies

- modify language
- avoid jargon
- clear explanations
- clear treatment instructions
- evaluate patient's understanding
- summarise and repeat
- avoid uncertainty
- avoid inappropriate reassurance
- appropriate referral (if necessary)
- ensure patient is satisfied
- obtain informed consent

Follow-up

- Be available for phone calls.
- Ensure patients obtain results of investigations ordered, including Pap smears.
- Ensure any promised follow-up is carried out.
- Phone the patient if you have any lingering concerns (could be handled by the receptionist).
- Arrange referral if inadequate response to treatment.
- Act as an advocate if necessary, e.g. pressing for hospital admission.

Diffficulties in communication

The Victorian Medical Board lists poor communication as the most important factor causing complaints from patients and relatives against doctors.[5]

Effective communication depends on four interrelated factors concerning the message—the doctor (the sender), the patient (the recipient), the message itself, and the environment in which the message is sent (Fig. 3.1).[6]

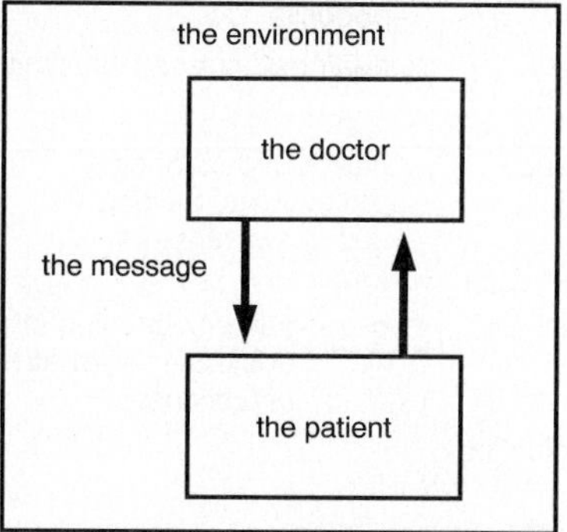

Fig. 3.1 *The four key factors affecting communication*

Environment

The physical environment is important (Table 3.2). The appearance, size and layout of consulting rooms, waiting rooms and patients' rooms will affect communication, sometimes adversely, especially if privacy is threatened by, say, leaving the consulting room door open. The doctor can create an obstacle simply by a physical 'barrier', for example, a large desk distancing the doctor from the patient (Figure 3.2).

The hospital environment will encourage the 'sick' role and generally is not conducive to good communication because of a low level of privacy.

A busy practice affected by time constraints on doctor or patient will influence communications seriously. A doctor in Wales has a notice in his waiting room: 'If the doctor is a long time with a patient don't get mad: it might be you'.

Table 3.2 *Summary of environmental factors that can adversely influence communication*

Waiting room	Poor physical layout Length of waiting time
Time pressure	'Traffic' level ? busy ? noisy ? sense of urgency
Physical factors	Desk—barriers Layout inappropriate Poor record system Substandard examination couch
Privacy	Dressing/undressing Sound Interruptions—phone

Fig. 3.2 *The physical barrier*

The message

The nature and content of the message may be uncomfortable for the doctor or the patient or both (Table 3.3). This applies to emotionally charged, complex or subtle content such as sexual problems, malignant disease, drug abuse, bereavement, malingering and psychiatric disorders.

Table 3.3 *Negative communication related to the message*

Language difficulties
Complex problems
Emotional problems
Uncertainty and doubt
Examples:
- sexuality e.g. incest, STDs
- malignancy
- multiple complaints: 'the shopping list'
- infertility
- unwanted pregnancy
- abortion

The patient may find the message difficult to comprehend because of inappropriate delivery or explanation by the doctor. Failure to use good follow-up strategies, including appointment times and appropriate patient education material, will aggravate communication breakdown. Language difficulties can distort the message and generate frustration in both parties. Good interpreters often help.

The doctor may also fail to appreciate that certain symptoms such as chronic pain or the presence of a lump mean 'cancer' to the patient. Failure to reassure the patient (where appropriate) distracts the patient.

Doctor-patient interaction

There are several general characteristics that affect communication between doctor and patient. These include:

- Poor past relationships and experiences leading to unresolved interpersonal conflict, e.g. an incorrect diagnosis or poor treatment outcome and indifferent compliance in following treatment or paying accounts.
- Personal differences, openly expressed, which may create subtle barriers, including differences in age, sex, religion, culture, social status and doctor/patient roles (occasionally influenced by political factors).
- The communication skills of doctor and patient, both as the sender and receiver of messages.
- The personal honesty and integrity of both parties in dealing with difficult messages.
- Psychosocial problems that will establish barriers, e.g. psychiatric illness or speech impediments.
- Familiarity between patient and doctor, e.g. friends or relatives.

The doctor

Although we believe that most doctors satisfactorily meet professional standards, there are times when the communication factor is adversely affected by inbuilt negative forces including chronic tiredness, stress, domestic problems and poor health (Table 3.4).

Furthermore, there are many strategies, roles, 'games', or 'hobby-horses' that some of us appear to rely on, especially when confronted with difficult or threatening circumstances, such as the management of the terminally ill.

Dare we recognise in ourselves some of the following unkind caricatures of doctors, i.e. personality types who may generate unfavourable communication.[7,8]

Dr G. Hova (Fig. 3.3) The god-like doctor (not necessarily a surgeon); aloof; omnipotent; dark suit with matching Mercedes; club tie or bow-tie; feared by medical students; partial to Scotch; pronounces certain cures; powerfully dispels doubts; no faith in the healing process before surgery but unshakeable faith after surgery; unavailable in the patient's decline.

Table 3.4 *The doctor's personal factors which influence communication*

Age	elderly, young
Sex	opposite
Senses	deafness, speech idiosyncrasy
Handicap	
Competence	health understanding professional training social awareness empathy
Attitudes	bias—patient attending other doctors or alternative practitioners
Communication style	
Differences	religion, sexual practices social class ethnic group political group dress eccentricities familiarity

Fig. 3.3 *Dr G. Hova*

Dr N. Zyme (Fig. 3.4) The scientific doctor; machine-like; cool; assured; obsessive; drives an Italian car; orders a new test and drug at every visit; conversant with the cellular biochemistry of the disease process but ignorant of its host.

Dr G. Rumble The gruff doctor; grunts in monosyllables; brilliant but appears tough and unapproachable; actually quite shy, soft and kind behind the facade; drives a Ford.

Fig. 3.4 *Dr N. Zyme*

Dr No Komento (Fig. 3.5) The secretive doctor; strong and silent, or is he weak and silent, threatened? In another world! Drives a BMW; a computer buff.

Fig. 3.5 *Dr No Komento*

Dr I. Knowall (Fig. 3.6) Glib; assured; garrulous; drives latest red sports car; drapes stethoscope around neck; accepts invitations to lecture on all subjects; rarely available on the phone; keeps patients waiting for hours.

Dr S. Winger Modern, swinging and trendy; superficial; on first name terms with patients; drives beaten-up Renault held together by political stickers; works 35 hours a week only; cavalier; undiplomatically blunt.

Fig. 3.6 *Dr I. Knowall*

Dr X. Cytabull Fanatic; madly enthusiastic about rarities; overreacts to physical abnormalities; compulsive writer to medical editors; refers patients *ad nauseam*; drives yellow Porsche.

Dr Genghis M. Pyre Longs for a mega-practice, assistants (not partners) and a pathology service; addicted to conferences and cocktail parties; also yearns for a Daimler, a halo and New Year's honours.

Dr Buzz Bee Ever busy; flits from one consulting room to another; frequent phone user during consultation; creates a sense of urgency everywhere; charming to patients but intimidates them; overservices; holds pilot's licence; drives Landcruiser when licence not suspended.

Dr Go Along Cassidy Feels comfortable when he is giving patients what they ask for; has a 'conveyor belt' type practice; rarely leaves his chair and doesn't examine his patients; drives a Colt.

Dr I. Kling Protective and possessive; hangs on to patients; refers only under pressure; overconfident; likes to be liked; indifferent medical record system; compulsive drug prescriber; still drives 1969 Volvo.

Dr Nat Ure Strong on 'alternatives'; pleasant chap; keen on Blackmore's publications and remedies; health shop (run by spouse) next door for fibre, sprouts and vitamin pills; attracts an attractive clientele; mutters audibly while writing the rare script; into massage, yoga and transcendental meditation; wears a knitted tie, rides a bicycle.

These caricatures mirror something of ourselves, hopefully so that we can understand our own attitudes and behaviour. The stereotypes portrayed may well adversely affect our relationship with our patients and colleagues.

The patient

Do we recognise, with significant emotion, these patients in our practice?

- 'Smith speaking—I insist on speaking to you directly and not to the "iron curtain" out front.'
- 'Doctor, I've lost my script again—be a good fellow and . . .'
- 'Those pills you prescribed yesterday are doing nothing for me.'
- 'Doctor, you're the only one who can help me.'

Yes, doctors are human and can harbour hostility towards the difficult patient, including the demanding patient, the seductive patient, the 'compo' patient, the difficult 'ethnic' patient, the hypochondriac, the bad debtor or the manipulative patient.

Some patients appear to have the irrepressible ability to create conflict, so often heralded by an upset receptionist, thus setting the scene for a potentially difficult consultation (Table 3.5).

However, doctors have a professional responsibility to transcend interpersonal conflict and facilitate productive communication by establishing a caring and responsible relationship even with 'difficult' patients. Not surprisingly, such patients can also be found to be warm and pleasantly human beneath their 'shoulder chip' facade and so be helped immeasurably by an empathetic doctor.

It is important to bear in mind that medical communication often occurs in an emotional environment, because 'disease' has important emotional connotations for patients and their relatives and friends. Inappropriate communication and management can generate hostility.

The doctor-become-patient in the hands of his colleagues learns fast, but possibly too late. Illness plus defective communication can bring confusion, anxiety and pain; suspicion and confinement add new dimensions to suffering.

Sooner or later we come to see ourselves as persons, both as doctor and as patient ('wearing his moccasins'). The patient in us longs for the ideal doctor who is truly professional with sound knowledge and sane judgement, who is available, unhurried, caring and responsible.

Table 3.5 *Patient characteristics that can influence communication*

Age	adolescent, elderly
Sex	opposite
Senses	deaf, blind, speech impairment
Handicapped	speech disorders, visual impairment
Illness	acutely ill/injured
Psychological	
Attitudes	aggressive, hostile, demanding, aggrieved, e.g. fees, mistakes, perception of doctor'sauthority
Anxiety/depression	
Dementia	
Fears and phobias, e.g. AIDS	
Health understanding	
Hysteria	
Hypochondriasis	
Personality disorders	
Sensitive issues, e.g. sexuality, bereavement, malignancy	
Social	
Social class	
Ethnic group	
Education	
Dress	
Political group	
Familiarity	

Non-verbal communication

Non-verbal communication or body language is a most important feature of the communication process. Birdwhistle[9] has shown that more human communication takes place by the use of gestures, postures, position and distances (non-verbal communication or 'body language') than by any other method. Albert Mehrabian showed that non-verbal cues comprise the majority of the impact of any communicated message (Table 3.6).[10]

Recognition of non-verbal cues in our communication is important especially in a doctor–patient relationship. The ability to recognise non-verbal cues improves communication, rapport

Table 3.6 *Impact of the message*

	%
Words alone	7
Tone of voice	38
Non-verbal communication	55

and understanding of the patient's fears and concerns. Recognising body language can allow doctors to modify their behaviour, thus promoting optimum communication.[11]

Interpreting body language[9,11]

The interpretation of body language, which differs between cultures, is a special study in its own right but there are certain cues and gestures which can be readily interpreted. Examples illustrated include the depressed patient (Fig. 3.7), barrier-type signals often used as a defensive mechanism to provide comfort or indicate a negative attitude (Figs. 3.8 a,b,c) and a readiness gesture indicating a desire to terminate the communication (Fig. 3.9).

Fig. 3.7 *Posture of a depressed person—head down, slumped, inanimate; position of desk and people correct*

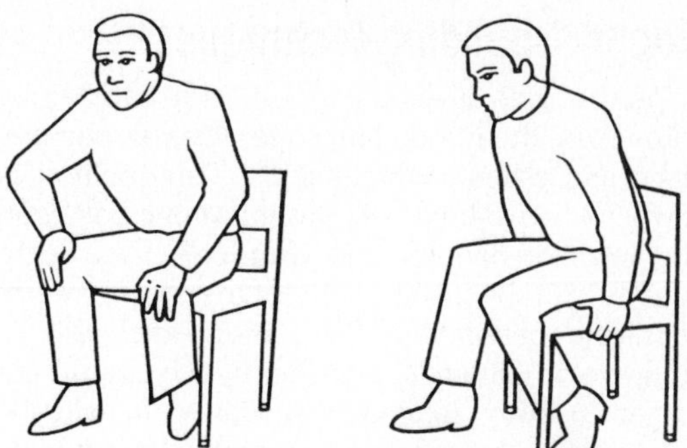

Fig. 3.9 *Body language—'readiness to go' gestures*

Having noted the non-verbal communication the doctor must then deal with it. This may require confrontation, that is, diplomatically bringing these cues to the patient's attention and exploring the associated feeling further.

It is not difficult to appreciate the importance of body language in the doctor–patient relationship. A 'hunch' or 'gut feeling' can be better understood, reinforced or corrected by skilled observation and interpretation of body language. A doctor can recognise a patient's non-verbal cues and explore the issues raised. By improving one's skills, modifying one's behaviour (and consulting room configuration) the doctor can encourage communication and a better understanding of the patient.

The skill to interpret non-verbal cues can be achieved by conscious observation of people's interaction, including our own. A technique suggested by Pease[9] is to watch television without sound for 15 minutes each day and check your interpretation each five minutes. By the end of three weeks, he suggests, you will have become a more skilled body language observer.

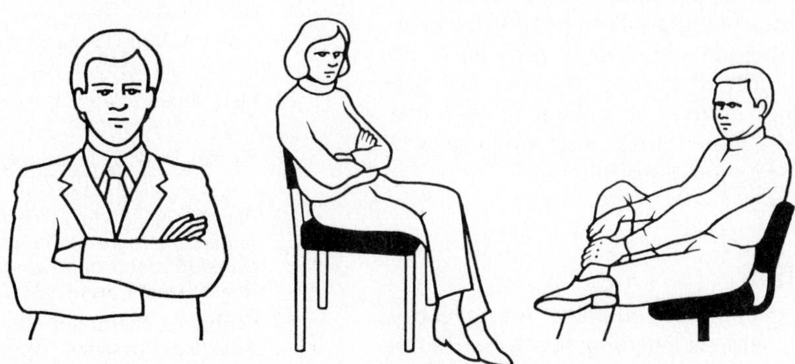

Fig. 3.8 *Body language—barrier signals:* **(a)** *arms folded;* **(b)** *legs crossed;* **(c)** *'ankle lock' pose*

Rapport-building techniques

A person can develop rapport with another by mimicking their body language, speech, posture, pace and other characteristics. This method is a type of neuro-linguistic programming based on the work of Bandler and Grinder[12]. Such techniques can be used to help the doctor communicate better with the patient and also to improve a patient's attitude by changing the patient's body language position. It will be difficult for the patient to maintain a negative attitude if the body language position isn't congruent.[11]

Mirroring

This is a useful technique whereby the limb positions and body angles of the person you are talking to can be copied. A mirror image is formed of their position so that when they look at you they see themselves as in a mirror. It is not necessary to copy uncomfortable gestures or unusual limb positions such as hands behind the head. A partial mirror is often sufficient.

Pacing

People exhibit a certain rhythm or pace which can be revealed through their breathing, talking, movements of the head, hands or feet. It you can copy the pace of another person, it will establish a sense of 'one-ness' or rapport with them. Once this pace is established you can change their pace by changing yours. This is called leading.

Vocal copying

Vocal copying is a rapid and effective way to develop rapport with people. It involves copying intonation, pitch, volume, pace, rhythm, breathing and length of the sentence before pausing.

Engaging in these strategies will bring you into such close rapport that you can intuitively pick up all kinds of things about people that were not obvious beforehand. It may also have the unfortunate effect of making you feel that you are 'drowning' in their problems. If you feel overwhelmed, then break the rapport and diplomatically go into a leading phase.[13]

Practice tips

- A fundamental prerequisite for effective communication is listening; this includes not only hearing the words but understanding their meaning in addition to being sensitive to the feelings accompanying the words.
- Undertake the strategies of paraphrasing and summarising during the consultation to emphasise that listening is occurring and to provide a basis for defining the problems.
- Associated with listening is the observation of the non-verbal language which may in many instances be the most significant part of the communication process.
- Good communication between doctors and patients decreases the chance of dissatisfaction with professional services, even with failed therapy, and the likelihood of litigation.

References

1. Elliott-Binns E. *Medicine; the forgotten art.* Tunbridge Wells, Kent: Pitman Books, 1978, 35.
2. Macnab F. Changing levels of susceptibility in sickness and in health. Aust Fam Physician, 1986; 15:1370.
3. Mansfield F. Basic communicating skills. Aust Fam Physician, 1987; 16:216–222.
4. Kidd M, Rose A. *An introduction to consulting skills.* Community Medicine student handbook. Monash University Melbourne, 1991, 15.
5. Medical Board of Victoria. Third Annual Report, 1982/3. Melbourne: FD Atkinson, Government Printers, 1983, 12.
6. Carson N, Findlay D. *Communication skills.* Student handbook. Melbourne: Monash University, Department of Community Medicine, 1986, 31.
7. Elliott CE. 'How am I doing?' Med J Aust, 1979; 2:644–645.
8. Murtagh JE, Elliott CE. Barriers to communication. Aust Fam Physician, 1987, 16:223–226.
9. Pease A. Body language. London: Camel Publishing, 1985, 1–63.
10. Mehrabian A. *Silent messages.* Belmont (Calif): Wadsworth, 1971.
11. Findlay D. Body language. Aust Fam Physician, 1987; 16:229.
12. Bandler R, Grinder J. *Re-framing: Neuro-linguistic programming and the transformation of meaning.* Maob, Utah: Real People Press, 1982, 1–203.
13. Oldham J. Neuro-linguistic programming. Aust Fam Physician, 1987; 16:237–240.

4

Counselling skills

The Macquarie Dictionary says that counselling is 'giving advice'; that it is 'opinion or instruction given in directing the judgement or conduct of another'. In the clinical context counselling can be defined as 'the therapeutic process of helping a patient to explore the nature of his or her problem in such a way that he or she determines his or her decisions about what to do, without direct advice or reassurance from the counsellor'.

The counselling process in general practice is based on the therapeutic effect of the doctor. There is an enormous and ever-increasing need for people in the community to have many of their emotional and social problems addressed by the health profession. Modern medicine has acquired a much more scientific face over recent years at the expense of its once respected humanistic one. Medicine is primarily a humanitarian pursuit, not an economic or scientific one, and uses science as a tool. Many feel that medicine is losing sight of this, at the considerable expense of its standing in the community.[1]

The public perceives that general practitioners can and do counsel people, because more people go to their GP for counselling than any other group of health workers, including psychologists, psychiatrists, social workers, marriage guidance counsellors and clergy.[1] People do not generally tell the doctor or even realise that counselling is exactly what led them to come to the doctor in the first place. The GP is therefore ideally placed in the community to make the most significant contribution to fill the community's needs in this area.

The GP as an effective counsellor

General practitioners can be effective counsellors for the following reasons:[2]

- They have the opportunity to observe and understand the patients and their environment.
- General practitioners are ideally placed to treat the whole patient.
- Their generalist skills and holistic approach permit them to have a broad grasp of the patient's problems and a multi-faceted approach to treatment.
- They can provide treatment in comfortable and familiar surroundings including the GP's rooms and the patient's home.
- They are skilled at working as a member of a professional team and directing patients to more expert members of the team as necessary.
- They can readily organise 'contracts' with the patient.
- They have an intimate knowledge of the family and the family dynamics.
- They fit comfortably into continuing patient care with appropriate follow-up treatment programs.

To be an effective counsellor the general practitioner must first prepare for this role. Following a commitment to its importance the general practitioner can acquire the knowledge and skills for basic counselling by reading, by attending workshops and by case discussion with colleagues who are skilled in counselling.[2] Well developed interviewing skills are essential, as is self-discipline to appreciate one's strengths and limitations.

Features of counselling

Doctors can respond to patients' problems and distress by a spectrum of behaviours from doctor-centred directive behaviour or advice at one end, to patient-centred non-directive behaviour at the other. In handling psychosocial problems, advice-giving is at one end of the spectrum and psychotherapy at the other.

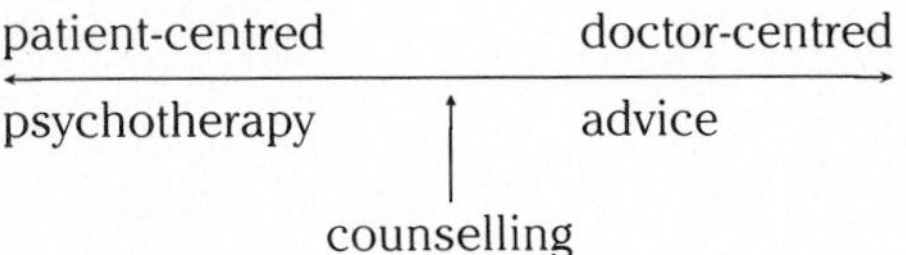

Counselling, as an activity in general practice, can be represented by a moving point between these two extremes.[1]

Counselling can be seen as having the following features:[1]

- It is a clear-cut treatment option like a course of antibiotics.
- It is a co-operative problem-solving process.
- It is an educational venture where patients learn new information and new activities.
- It is a developmental process for patients.
- It is a change process—often moving a patient from a 'stuck state'.
- It is a goal-directed activity.
- It is a process of energising patients and lifting their morale.
- It is a sensitive response to problems within a caring relationship.

A problem-solving approach

Defining the problem ('what the matter really is') is the most important step in the process of patient care. The following outline is one approach to counselling that is applicable to a general practice context.[1]

1. Listen to the problem of first presentation: this involves listening to issues, events and experiences, but also to patient's feelings and distress. The emphasis here is more on the communication skills of facilitation, silence, clarification, reflection, paraphrasing, confrontation and summary, than on questioning. In many cases this phase of the counselling constitutes the major part of the therapy; e.g. in grief or bereavement counselling, where the doctor supports the patient through a natural but distressing process.
2. Define a problem, if possible in behavioural terms:

   Beneath the feeling is the experience, beneath the experience is the event, the event is related to a problem.[3]
3. Establish a contract for counselling, with an agreed number of visits initially, e.g. weekly half hour or hour appointments for 4 to 6 weeks.
4. Define short-term and long-term goals for action.
5. Decide on one option—'experimental action'.
6. Build an action program with the patient—negotiate 'homework' for the patient between visits.
7. Evaluate progress.
8. Continue action or select another option.
9. Evaluate progress.
10. Terminate or refer.

Counselling models

The PLISSIT model

The PLISSIT model, developed by Annon (1974)[4] as an aid in therapy for sexual problems, is a very useful model for problems presented as feelings where there is limited scope for intervention by the therapist.

The mnemonic PLISSIT stands for:

- P is for permission-giving
- LI is for limited information
- SS is for specific suggestion
- IT is for intensive therapy

Annon emphasises that every primary care practitioner should be competent to offer 'permission-giving' and 'limited information'.

The Colagiuri and Craig model

The medical counselling model was developed by Colagiuri and Craig (Fig. 4.1)[5] as a useful tool for teaching contraceptive, abortion and sterilisation counselling. It can be applied in most situations as it empowers the patients to make their own decisions through facilitation as opposed to the directive and advisory learning model.

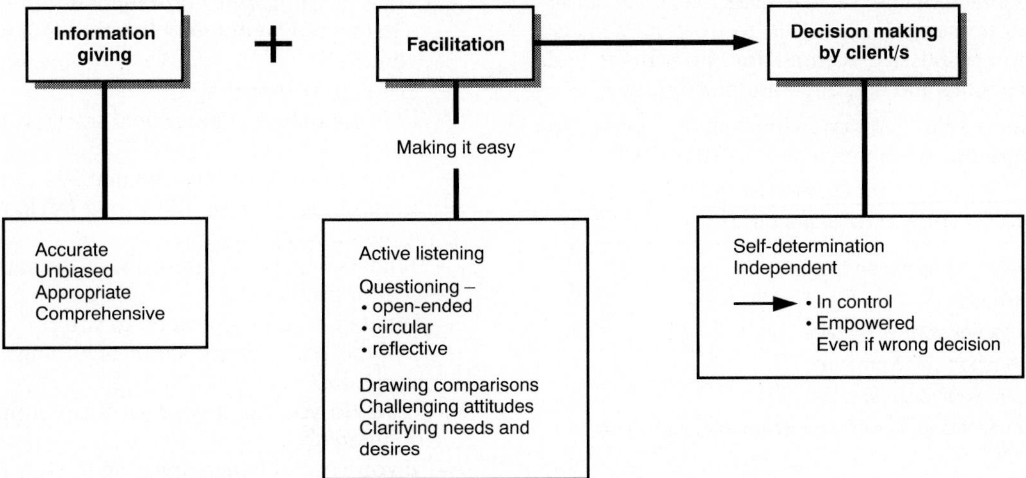

Fig. 4.1 *Medical counselling model* AFTER COLAGIURI AND CRAIG, REPRINTED WITH PERMISSION

The value of patient-centred counselling

There is evidence that the use of non-directive counselling techniques leads to more accurate diagnosis and therefore to more appropriate management and an improved outcome.[6]

Jerome Frank wrote in 1967: 'The field of counselling and psychotherapy has for years presented the puzzling spectacle of unabating enthusiasm for forms of treatment where effectiveness could not be objectively demonstrated.[7] Traux and Carkhuff[8] measured important aspects of the psychotherapeutic relationship and demonstrated what had long been recognised: the outcome was enhanced if practitioners had such qualities as accurate and sensitive awareness of the patient's feelings, deep concern for the patient's welfare (without attempting to dominate) and openness about their own reactions.

The essential feature of the patient-centred approach is that the counsellor is more like a facilitator; that is, by the asking of well-directed questions it is hoped that patients can realise their own solutions for their problems.[1] This encourages patients to attain understanding and personal growth themselves rather than just put their personal affairs in the hands of someone else. This does not mean to say that the facilitator is passive in the process of assessing the relative merit of various solutions produced by the patient. The doctor-centred approach is most applicable for patients who are so confused or distraught that their ability to reflect usefully is temporarily or permanently inaccessible. Here, taking a more active and authoritarian role may be just what is required. It is therefore important to be flexible and move between the two ends of the spectrum as needed.

Basics of counselling or psychotherapy

- Listening and empathy are the beginning of counselling.
- Good communication is the basis of counselling.
- The therapist must really care about the patient.
- Always be aware of the family context.
- It is important for therapists to handle and monitor their own feelings and emotions.
- Maintain eye contact.
- The therapist must tolerate and be comfortable with what the patient says.
- Confidentiality is essential.
- Counselling is easier if there is a good rapport with the patient, especially if a longstanding relationship exists.
- Counselling is difficult if a social relationship is present.
- Don't say to the patient, 'I'm counselling you' or 'I'm giving you psychotherapy'—make it a natural communication process.
- The therapist must be versatile and adapt a counselling style to the clinical occasion.

- Characteristics of the effective counsellor have been demonstrated to be genuineness, non-possessive warmth for the patient and accurate and empathic understanding.

Some useful interviewing skills used in counselling are summarised in Table 4.1.

Table 4.1 *Interview skills used in counselling*

Use reflected statements
Use silence
Allow expressions of emotion
Offer supportive comments
Paraphrase and summarise
Allow patients to correct your interpretations of their feelings
Observe lack of congruence
Try to understand what the patient is feeling: • anger • hostility • fear • manipulation • seduction • insecurity
Make intelligent guesses to prompt patient to continue
Don't reassure too soon

Counselling strategies[3,6]

- The therapy should be patient-centred.
- Use gentle, clever, probing questions.
- Facilitate the discussion to draw out relevant areas.
- It is important to be non-judgemental.
- Counsel through intuition and base it on common sense.
- Do not tell the patient what to do.
- Do not try to rush them into achieving a happy ending.
- Provide guidance to allow the patient to gain insight.
- Wherever possible, make therapy non-authoritarian and non-directional.
- Use appropriate 'gentle' confrontation to allow self-examination.
- Help patients to explore their own situation and express emotions such as anxiety, guilt, fear, anger, hope, sadness, self-hate, hostility to others, hurt feelings.
- Explore possible feelings of insecurity and allow free expression of such feelings.
- Explore patients' belief systems and consider and respect their spiritual aspirations and conflicts.
- Ask key searching questions such as:
  — 'What would be different in your life if you were well?'
  — 'Who are you mad at?'
  — 'If I understand you correctly you are telling me that . . .'
  — 'You seem to be telling me that . . '
  — 'Correct me if I'm on the wrong track, but you are saying that . . .'
  — 'What do you think deep down is the cause of your problem?'
  — 'What does your illness do to you?'
  — 'Do you really worry about any things in particular?'
  — 'How do you think your problem should be treated?'
  — 'If you could change anything in your life what would it be?'

Avoid

- telling patients what they must do/offering solutions
- giving basic advice on your own personal experiences and beliefs
- bringing up problems which the patient does not produce voluntarily

Counselling is not

- giving information
- giving advice
- being judgemental
- imposing one's own values, behaviour and practices
- the same as interviewing
- handing out patient education material

Cautions[1]

- Individual doctors cannot be useful to all patients, so be selective.
- We cannot solve patients' problems for them.
- Patients' problems belong to them and not to their counsellors.
- Patients often have to change by only an inch in order to move a mile.
- If a counselling relationship is no longer productive, then terminate and refer.
- Most patients in primary care need information, support and a lift in morale, not long-term psychotherapy.

Patients unlikely to benefit[1]

The following groups of patients are not likely to benefit from counselling therapy (i.e. relative contraindications):

- psychotic patients
- patients who have had an unrewarding experience with psychiatrists and other psychotherapists
- people who are antagonistic to the notion of a psychosocial diagnosis, subsequently found to be organic
- patients with little awareness or language to express emotional difficulty
- patients who don't believe doctors can treat psychosocial problems
- patients who are dependent on contact with the doctor and are willing to do almost anything to maintain the relationship
- patients with a vested interest in remaining unwell who are therefore resistant to change, e.g. patients with work-related disabilities awaiting legal settlement
- patients with chronic psychosomatic tendencies who are willing to do almost anything to maintain the relationship
- those in an intractable life situation who are unable or unwilling to change
- patients who are unwilling to examine and work on painful or uncomfortable areas of their life

Specific areas of counselling

Opportunities for basic counselling by the general practitioner are ubiquitous in medical practice. Complex problems require referral but, irrespective of that situation, the general practitioner still has an important role in continuing management.

Areas demanding counselling include:

- any crisis situation
- bereavement or grief
- terminal illness/palliative care (Chapter 6)
- marital problems (Chapter 2)
- family problems (Chapter 2)
- sexual dysfunction (Chapter 89)
- chronic pain
- anxiety and stress (Chapter 99)
- depression (Chapter 14)
- intellectual handicap in a child
- infertility (Chapter 88)
- any disease or illness, especially severe illness
- sexual abuse/child abuse (Chapter 69)
- domestic violence (Chapter 80)

Crisis management

Crisis situations are not uncommon in general practice and people in crisis are usually highly aroused and demanding. Examples include tragic deaths such as children drowning or SIDS, unexpected marital break-up and breaking bad news.

Aims of crisis intervention

- Resolve the crisis and restore psychological equilibrium as quickly and constructively as possible.
- Encourage the person in crisis to regain control and take appropriate action.

Principles of management

- Intervene early—actively and directly.
- Establish an empathic alliance.
- Be accessible.
- Attend to family and social supports.
- Be prepared for the difficult phase of 24–48 hours.
- Don't carry the burden of crisis.
- Aim for brief time-limited intervention (no more than six interviews over six weeks).
- When necessary, be prepared to provide short-term use of psychotropic drugs, e.g. a hypnotic, for two or three nights of good sleep.

Ten rules to help those in distress

The following rules are given to those in crisis (personal explanation followed by a take-home handout):

1. Give expression to your emotions.
   You simply must accept your reactions as normal and not be afraid to cry or call out. Do not bottle up feelings.
2. Talk things over with your friends.
   Do not overburden them but seek their advice and listen to them. Do not avoid talking about what has happened.
3. Focus on things as they are now—at this moment.
   Do not brood on the past and your misfortune. Concentrate on the future in a positive way.
4. Consider your problems one at a time.
   Do not allow your mind to race wildly over a wide range of problems. You can cope with one problem at a time.
5. Act firmly and promptly to solve a problem.
   Once you have worked out a way to tackle a problem, go for it. Taking positive action is a step in allowing you to get on with life.

6. Occupy yourself and your mind as much as possible.
   Any social activity—sports, theatre, cards, discussion groups, club activity—is better than sitting around alone. Many people find benefit from a holiday visit to an understanding friend or relative. Religious people usually find their faith and prayer life a great source of strength at this time.
7. Do not nurse grudges or blame other people.
   This is not easy but you must avoid getting hostile. In particular, do not get angry with yourself and your family, especially your spouse.
8. Set aside some time every day for physical relaxation.
   Make a point of doing something physical such as going for a walk, swimming or enjoying an easy exercise routine.
9. Stick to your daily routine as much as possible.
   At times of crisis a familiar pattern of regular meals and chores can bring a sense of order and security. Avoid taking your problems to bed and thus ensuring sleepless nights. Try to 'switch off' after 8p.m. Taking sleeping tablets for those few bad nights will help.
10. Consult your family doctor when you need help.
    Your doctor will clearly understand your problem because stress and crisis problems are probably the commonest he or she handles. Consult your doctor sooner rather than later.
    - Remember that there are many community resources to help you cope, e.g. ministers, social workers, community nurses, crisis centres and church organisers.
    - Take care: do drive carefully and avoid accidents, which are more common at this time.

Bereavement

Bereavement or grief may be defined as deep or intense sorrow or distress following loss.[9] Raphael uses the term to connote 'the emotional response to loss: the complex amalgam of painful affects including sadness, anger, helplessness, guilt, despair'.[10]

The general practitioner will see grief in all its forms over a wide variety of losses. Although the nature of loss and patient reaction to it varies enormously the principles of management are similar.

Stages of normal bereavement

1. *Shock or disbelief* Feelings include numbness and emptiness, searching, anxiety, fear and suicidal ideation, 'I don't believe it'. Concentration is difficult and spontaneous emotions such as crying, screaming or laughing tend to occur. There may be a sense of the deceased's presence and hallucinations (visual and auditory) may occur.
2. *Grief and despair* Feelings include anger, 'Why me?', guilt and self-blame, and yearning. Social withdrawal and memory impairment may occur. The feeling of intense grief usually lasts about six weeks and the overall stage of grief and despair for about six months, but it can resurface occasionally for a few years. The last few months involve feelings of sadness and helplessness.
3. *Adaptation and acceptance* Features of the third stage include significant feelings of apathy and depression. This phase takes a year or more. Physical illness is common and includes problems such as insomnia, asthma, bowel dysfunction, headache and appetite disturbances.

Pathological bereavement

Pathological bereavement can occur and may manifest as intense emotion, particularly anger, and multiple visits with somatic complaints; the patient often gets around to long dissertations about the deceased and the circumstances surrounding death. Extreme anger is likely when the sense of rejection is great as with divorce or sudden death. Guilt can also be intense.[9]

Raphael's classification of the patterns of pathological grief and its various resolutions are presented in Table 4.2.[10]

The GP as counsellor[9]

Important rules to bear in mind:

- The bereaved may be feeling very guilty.
- They may be angry towards their doctor or the medical profession in general.
- They need a clear explanation as to the exact cause and manner of death. Autopsy reports should be obtained and discussed.
- The bereaved tend to view an apparent lack of concern and support as disinterest or guilt.[9]
- Early intervention averts pathological grief.

The general practitioner probably had a close relationship with the deceased and the family. The GP will have a special awareness of those

Table 4.2 *Patterns and resolution of pathological grief*[10]

Morbid or pathological patterns
- Absence, inhibition or delay of bereavement
- Distorted bereavement
- Chronic grief (intense anguish continues unabated)

Outcome
- Normal resolution, satisfactory adjustment; reintegration in life, satisfying attachments
- General symptomatology (leading to increased care eliciting behaviour)
- Depression, suicidal behaviour
- Other psychiatric disorders (anxiety state, phobia, mania, alcoholism, criminal activity such as shoplifting)
- Altered relationship patterns
- Vulnerability to loss
- Anniversary phenomenon
- Death (more likely in the first 12 months)

at risk and the nature of the relationships within the family. The family is likely to maintain the relationship with the GP, expressing the physical and psychological effects of grief and consulting about intercurrent problems.[9]

Working through the stages of grief with patients will allow general practitioners to reach some acceptance of their own emotions, as well as ensure that patients feel supported and cared for, rather than distanced by embarrassment.

Help from religious sources is highly valued as it can meet both spiritual and personal needs. Other resources include funeral directors, hospice (and other) counsellors and support groups such as those for sudden infant death syndrome.[9]

At least 30 minutes should be allowed for consultations.

Long-term counselling

Normal bereavement can persist for years. Ongoing counselling is indicated if it continues unabated or psychiatric referral sought if grief is extreme. Regular enquiries during routine consultations or meetings are important if the patient appears to be coping.

Breaking bad news

Good communication skills are fundamental to giving bad news appropriately. When bad news is broken insensitively or inadequately the impact can be distressing for both giver and recipient, leaving lasting scars for the latter. Doctors should have a plan for this difficult process and learn how to cope with the recipient's reaction. Most of the circumstances described apply to unexpected death.

Optimal approach

Some basic initial rules:[11]

- If relatives have to be contacted it is preferable for the doctor (if at all possible) or a sympathetic police officer to make the contact personally, rather than a relatively matter-of-fact telephone call from the hospital or elsewhere.
- If a telephone message is necessary it should be given by an experienced person.
- The relatives or close friends should not drive to the hospital alone.

The setting for the interview:

- Use a suitable private room if possible.
- See the recipients of the news alone in the room.
- Advise that the meeting should be undisturbed.

Guidelines for the doctor

- Always ask those involved if they have heard any news or know the reasons for the consultation.
- Give information in an unhurried, honest, balanced, empathic manner.[12]
- Look directly at the person you are talking to, be honest and direct and keep information simple (avoid technical language).
- The sad news must be accompanied by positive support, understanding and encouragement.
- Give recipients time to react (offer time and moments of silence to allow the facts to sink in) and opportunities to ask questions.
- Avoid false reassurance.
- Remember that relatives appreciate the truth and genuine empathy.
- In the event of death, relatives should be given a clear explanation of the cause of death.

A list of guidelines for the interview is summarised in Table 4.3.[11]

Coping with patient responses

- The responses cover a wide range—stunned silence, disbelief, acute distress, anger, extreme guilt.
- Be prepared for any of these responses.

Table 4.3 *Breaking bad news: recommended actions during the interview (after McLauchlan[11])*

Allow
- time
- opportunities to react
- silence
- touching
- free expression of emotions
- questions
- viewing of a dead or injured body

Avoid
- rushing
- bluntness
- withholding the truth
- platitudes
- protecting own inadequacies
- euphemisms

- Appropriate training using simulated patients, video replays and skilled feedback improves communication skills.
- Give permission and encouragement for reactions such as crying and screaming.
- Have a box of facial tissues available.
- A comforting hand on the shoulder or arm or holding a hand is an acceptable comfort zone.
- Offer a cup of tea or a cool drink if available.
- Ask the patients or relatives how they feel and what they would like to do and if they want you to contact anyone.
- Arrange follow-up.
- Give appropriate patient education material.

The depressed patient

Studies have emphasised the importance and therapeutic efficacy of counselling in the management of the depressed patient.[13] The most practical approach by the general practitioner to the depressed patient is empathy, support and a logical explanation of their malaise. The author gives the following explanation to the patient.

Depression is a very real illness which affects the entire mind and body. It seriously dampens the five basic activities of humans, namely their energy for activity, sex drive, sleep, appetite and ability to cope with life. They cannot seem to lift themselves out of their misery or fight it themselves. Superficial advice to 'snap out of it' is unhelpful because the person has no control over it.

The cause is somewhat mysterious but it has been found that an important chemical is present in smaller amounts than usual in the nervous system. It is rather like a person low in iron becoming anaemic.

Depression can follow a severe loss such as the death of a loved one, a marital separation or financial loss. On the other hand it can develop for no apparent reason although it may follow an illness such as glandular fever or influenza, an operation or childbirth.

Emphasising the 'missing chemical' theory really helps patients and family come to terms with an illness that tends to have socially embarrassing connotations. It also helps compliance with therapy when antidepressant medication is prescribed.

Ongoing contact, support and availability are an important component of counselling with appropriate referral to someone with more expertise, should that be required.

Chronic pain

Patients suffering from long-term pain are a special problem, especially those with back pain who seem to be on a merry-go-round of failed multiple treatments and complex psychosocial problems. These patients are frequently treated in pain clinics. As family doctors we often observe an apparently normal, pleasant person transformed into a person who seems neurotic, pain-driven and doctor-dependent. The problem is very frustrating to the practitioner, often provoking feelings of suspicion, uncertainty and discomfort.

De Vaul et al[14] list five subgroups of patients where perplexing pain presents as the major symptom.[3]

1. Pain as a symptom of depression.
2. Pain as a delusional symptom of psychosis.
3. Pain as a conversion symptom of hysterical neurosis.
4. Pain as a symptom of an unresolved bereavement reaction.
5. Pain as a symptom of a 'need to suffer'.

Patients who somatise their symptoms present one of the most difficult challenges to our skills and usually require a multidisciplinary team approach.

Management involves:

- thorough medical assessment
- psychological assessment
- detailed explanations to the patient and family about treatment
- rational explanations about the cause of the pain
- management of associated problems, e.g. depression, sexual dysfunction

- behavioural modification to encourage increased activity and a gradual return to normality

A useful explanation

The author finds the following account a most useful method of explaining perplexing continuing back pain or neuralgia to patients (where there is no evidence of a persisting organic lesion).

Part of the problem is that psychological factors continue to aggravate and maintain the problem even though the reason for the pain in the first place may have disappeared. It is a similar problem to a person who has had a painful leg amputated. Even though it has been removed, the patient can still feel the leg and maybe even the pain. The patient has a 'phantom limb'. The nervous system, especially the brain, can play funny tricks on us in this way.

This means that even though the original disc injury has settled after several weeks, the body can still register the pain. This is more likely to occur in people who have become anxious and depressed about their problem. The pain continues. Someone once described it as a 'tension headache that has slipped down to the back'.

References

1. Hassed C. Counselling. In: Final Year Handbook. Monash University, Department of Community Medicine, 1992, 97–104.
2. Ramsay AT. The general practitioner as an effective counsellor. Aust Fam Physician, 1990, 19:473–479.
3. Harris RD, Ramsay AT. *Health care counselling*. Sydney: Williams and Wilkins, 1988, 68–95.
4. Annon JS. *The behavioural treatment of sexual problems*. Volumes 1 and 2. Honolulu: Enabling Systems Inc, 1974.
5. Craig S. A medical model for infertility counselling. Aust Fam Physician, 1990; 19:491–500.
6. Cook H. Counselling in general practice: principles and strategies. Aust Fam Physician, 1986, 15:979–981.
7. Frank JF. Foreword. In: *Towards effective counselling and psychotherapy: training in practice*. New York: Aldine, 1967:IX.
8. Traux CB, Carkhuff RR. *Towards effective counselling and psychotherapy*. New York: Aldine, 1967.
9. Williams AS. Grief counselling. Aust Fam Physician, 1986; 15:995–1002.
10. Raphael B. *The anatomy of bereavement. A handbook for the caring professions*. London: Hutchinson, 1984:33–62.
11. McLauchlan CAJ. Handling distressed relatives and breaking bad news. In: *ABC of major trauma* (ed. D. Skinner et al). London: British Medical Association, 1991, 102–106.
12. Cunningham C, Morgan P, McGucken R. Down syndrome: is dissatisfaction with disclosure of diagnosis inevitable? Devel Med Child Neurol, 1984; 26:33–39.
13. Jackson HJ, Moss JD, Solinski S. Social skills training: an effective treatment for unipolar non-psychotic depression? Australian and New Zealand Journal of Psychiatry, 1985; 19:342–353.
14. De Vaul RA, Zisook S, Stuart HJ. Patients with psychogenic pain. Journal of Family Practice, 1977; 4(1):53–55.

5

Difficult, demanding and angry patients

Weston defines a 'difficult patient' as one with whom the physician has trouble forming an effective working relationship.[1] However it is more appropriate to refer to difficult problems rather than difficult patients—it is the patients who have the problems while doctors have the difficulties.

Some characteristics of problematic patients, from the doctor's perspective, include:

- frequent attenders with trivial illness
- multiple symptomatology
- undifferentiated illness
- chronic tiredness
- negative investigations
- dissatisfaction with treatment, especially procedures
- non-compliant
- hostile or angry
- attending multiple therapists
- demanding on staff
- inconsiderate of the doctor's time
- taking multiple drugs
- seductive, then demanding

Such patients are often referred to as the 'heartsink' patients, referring to that certain sinking feeling on seeing them in the waiting room or their name on the booking list. They can provoke negative feelings in us and we have to discipline ourselves to be patient, responsible and professional.

An inevitably poor consultation will follow if we allow feelings of hostility to affect our communication with the difficult patient, especially the demanding, angry or 'compo' patient.

However it is important not to misdiagnose organic disease and also to consider the possibilities of the following disorders which may be masked.

- anxiety
- depression
- obsessive compulsive disorder
- bipolar disorder (manic depression)
- drug dependency
- alcohol abuse
- schizophrenia

It is therefore appropriate to maintain traditional standards by continual updating of the database, integrating psychosocial aspects, careful evaluation of new symptoms, conducting an appropriate physical examination and being discriminating with investigations.

Management strategies

Our professional responsibility is to rise above interpersonal conflict and facilitate productive communication by establishing a caring and responsible relationship with such patients. An appropriate strategy is to follow Professor Aldrich's precepts[2] for the 'difficult' patients who do not have an organic disorder or a psychiatric illness.

1. Give up trying to cure them—they are using their symptoms to maintain their relationship with you: accept them as they are.
2. Accept their symptoms as expressions of their neurosis. Make a primary positive diagnosis—only test if you have to.
3. Structure a program for them, e.g. 'Mrs Jones, I have decided that we should meet for 15 minutes every second Wednesday at 10 a.m.'
4. During the consultation, demonstrate your genuine interest in the person's life, garden, work and so on; show less interest, even boredom, for the litany of complaints.

Other management guidelines include:

- Use reassurance with caution—it is insufficient by itself and should be soundly based.
- Be honest and maintain trust.
- Allow the patient a fair share of your time—this is your part of the contract. At the same time indicate that there are limits to your time (set rules).
- Be polite yet assertive.
- Avoid using labels of convenience and placebo therapy.
- Be honest about your understanding (or lack of understanding) of the problems.
- Remember that the consultation is often the therapy, without a prescription.
- Don't undermine other doctors. Avoid collusion.
- Have limited objectives—zealous attempts to cure may be inappropriate.
- Do not abandon the patient however frustrating the relationship. Accept this as a legitimate role.
- Remain available if alternative therapies are sought by the patient.
- Take extra care with the 'familiar' patient and sometimes the patient who brings gifts. Maintain your professional role.
- If you are uncomfortable with counselling, consider early referral to a counsellor while maintaining contact in the future.
- You may have to accept that there are some people no one can help.

The angry patient

Anger in patients and their relatives is a common reaction in the emotive area of sickness and healing. The anger, which may be concealed or overt, might be a communication of fear and insecurity. It is important to bear in mind that many apparently calm patients may be harbouring controlled anger. The practice of our healing art is highly emotive and can provoke feelings of frustration and anger in our patients, their friends and their relatives.

Anger is a normal and powerful emotion common to every human being yet with an enormous variety of expression. The many circumstances in medicine which provoke feelings of anger include:[3]

- disappointment at unmet expectations
- crisis situations, including grief
- any illness, especially an unexpected one
- the development of a fatal illness
- iatrogenic illness
- chronic illness, such as asthma
- financial transactions, such as high cost for services
- referral to colleagues, which is often perceived as failure
- poor service, such as long waits for an appointment
- problems with medical certificates
- poor response to treatment
- inappropriate doctor behaviour, e.g. brusqueness, sarcasm, moralistic comments, aloofness, superiority

The patient's anger may manifest as a direct confrontation with the doctor or perhaps with the receptionist, with litigation or with public condemnation.

In an extreme example, a Melbourne doctor was shot and killed by an angry patient who had been denied a worker's compensation certificate for a claim considered unjustified.

When a patient expresses anger about the medical profession or our colleagues it may be directed at us personally and, conversely, if directed to us it may be displaced from someone else such as a spouse, employer or other figure of authority.

What is anger?

Anger is a person's emotional response to provocation or to a threat to his or her equilibrium. If inappropriate, it is almost always the manifestation of a deeper fear and of hidden insecurity. Angry abusive behaviour may be a veiled expression of frustration, fear, self-rejection or even guilt.

On the other hand, its expression may be a defence against the threat of feeling too close to the doctor, who could have an overfamiliar, patronising or overly friendly attitude towards the patient. Some patients cannot handle this threatening feeling.

Basically anger may be a communication of fear and insecurity. The patient could be saying, 'I am afraid there is something seriously wrong with me. Are you doing everything to help me?'

Consulting strategies[4]

When one feels attacked unfairly, to react with anger is a natural human response. This response, however, must be avoided since it will damage the doctor–patient relationship and possibly aggravate the problem.

- The initial response should be to remain calm, keep still and establish eye contact.
- 'Step back' from the emotionally charged situation and try to analyse what is happening.
- Ask the patient to sit down and try to adopt a similar position (the mirroring strategy) without any aggressive pose.
- Address the patient (or relative) with appropriate name, be it Mr or Mrs Jones or a first name.
- Appear comfortable and controlled.
- Be interested and concerned about the patient and the problem.
- Use clear, firm, non-emotive language.
- Listen intently.
- Allow patients to ventilate their feelings and help to relieve their burdens.
- Allow patients to 'be themselves'.
- Give appropriate reassurance (do not go overboard to appease the patient).
- Allow time (at least 20 minutes).

Analysing the responses

- Search for any 'hidden agenda'.
- Recognise the relationship between anger and fear.

Questions to uncover the true source of anger

The following represent some typical questions or responses that could be used during the interview.

Rapport building

'I can appreciate how you feel.'
'It concerns me that you feel so strongly about this.'
'Tell me how I can make it easier for you.'

Confrontation

'You seem very angry.'
'It's unlike you to be like this.'
'I get the feeling that you are upset with . . .'
'What is it that's upsetting you?'
'What really makes you feel this way?'

Facilitation, clarification

'I find it puzzling that you are angry with me.'
'So you feel that . . .'
'You seem to be telling me . . .'
'If I understand you correctly . . .'
'Tell me more about this . . .'
'I would like you to enlarge on this point—it seems important.'

Searching

'Do you have any special concerns about your health?'
'Tell me about things at home.'
'How are things at work?'
'How are you sleeping?'
'Do you have any special dreams?'
'Do you relate to anyone who has a problem like yours?'

Some important guidelines are summarised in Table 5.1.

Table 5.1 *Guidelines for handling the angry patient*

Do	*Don't*
Listen	Touch the patient
Be calm	Meet anger with anger
Be comfortable	Reject the patient
Show interest and concern	Be a 'wimp'
Be conciliatory	Evade the situation
Be genuine	Be overfamiliar
Allay any guilt	Talk too much
Be sincere	Be judgemental
Give time	Be patronising
Arrange follow-up	
Act as a catalyst and guide	

Management

When confronted with an angry patient the practitioner should be prepared to remain calm, interested and concerned. It is important to listen intently and allow time for the patient to ventilate his or her feelings.

A skilful consultation should provide both doctor and patient with insight into the cause of the anger and result in a contract in which both parties agree to work in a therapeutic relationship. The objective should be to come to amicable terms which, of course, may not be possible, depending on the nature of the patient's grievance.

If the problem cannot be resolved in the time available a further appointment should be made to continue the interview.

Sometimes it may be appropriate to advise the patient to seek another opinion. If the angry patient does have problems with relationships and seeks help, it would be appropriate to arrange counselling so that the patient acquires a more realistic self-image, thus leading to improved self-esteem and effectiveness in dealing with people. In addition it should lead to the ability to withstand frustration and cope with the many vicissitudes of life—a most rewarding outcome for a consultation that began with confrontation.

References

1. McWhinney I. *A textbook of family medicine*. New York: Oxford, 1989, 96–98.
2. Elliott CE. 'How am I doing?' Med J Aust, 1979; 2:644–645.
3. Murtagh JE. The angry patient. Aus Fam Physician, 1991; 20:388–389.
4. Montgomery B, Morris L. *Surviving: coping with a crisis*. Melbourne: Lothian, 1989, 179–186.

6

Palliative care

Palliative care is an approach to the management of a person with a terminal illness. It implies that at some point in the management process there is a change from the objective of curing the disease to that of controlling and alleviating symptoms.[1]

To enable a person to live in dignity, peace and comfort throughout their illnesses means responding to physical, psychological, emotional, social and spiritual needs.[1]

Palliative care is comprehensive, continuing, multidisciplinary patient care which involves the patients and their carers, consultants, domiciliary nurses, social workers, clergy and other health professionals who are able to contribute to optimal team care.

The fundamental principles of palliative care are:[2]

- good communication
- management planning
- symptom control
- emotional, social and spiritual support
- medical counselling and education
- patient involvement in decision making
- support for carers

The diseases

Palliative care applies not only to incurable malignant disease and HIV/AIDS but to several other diseases such as end-stage organ failure (heart failure, renal failure, respiratory failure and hepatic failure) and degenerative neuromuscular diseases.

The special role of the family doctor

The general practitioner is the ideal person to manage palliative care for a variety of reasons—availability, knowledge of the patient and family and the relevant psychosocial influences. A key feature is the ability to provide the patient with independence and dignity by managing palliative care at home. Someone has to take the responsibility for leadership of the team and the most appropriate professional is a trusted family doctor.

Most patients and their families require answers to six questions:[3]

- What is wrong?
- What can medical science offer?
- Will I suffer?
- Will you look after me?
- How long will I live?
- Can I be looked after at home?

Caring honesty is the best policy when discussing the answers to these questions with the patient and family.

Support for patients and carers

Studies have indicated that the most common complaints of patients are boredom and fear of the unknown. This highlights the importance for the attending doctor of the following points:

- Give emotional support.
- Listen and be receptive to unexpressed 'messages'.

- Treat the sufferer normally, openly, enthusiastically and confidently.
- Show empathy and compassion.
- Employ good communication skills.
- Give honest answers without labouring the point or giving false hope.
- Provide opportunities for questions and clarification.
- Show an understanding of the patient's needs and culture.
- Adopt a whole person approach: attend to physical, psychosocial and spiritual needs.
- Anticipate and be prepared for likely problems.

Special points worth emphasising are:

- The patient needs a feeling of security.
- Provide reassurance that the patient will not suffer unnecessarily.
- Be prepared to take the initiative and call in others who could help, e.g. clergy, cancer support group, massage therapists.
- Patients must not be made to feel isolated or be victims of the so-called 'conspiracy of silence' in which families collude with doctors to withhold information from the patient.
- The worst feeling a dying patient can sense is one of rejection and discomfort on the part of the doctor.
- Always be prepared to refer to an oncologist or appropriate therapist for another opinion about further management. The family and patient appreciate the feeling that every possible avenue is being explored.

Symptom control

Common symptoms

- boredom (the commonest symptom)
- loneliness/isolation
- pain
  - — physical
  - — emotional
  - — spiritual
  - — social
- anorexia
- nausea and vomiting
- constipation

The grief reaction

This follows five stages, as identified by Kübler-Ross:[4]

1. denial and isolation
2. anger
3. bargaining
4. depression
5. acceptance

This model provides a useful guideline in understanding the stages a patient and family will be experiencing.

The principles of symptom management are summarised in Table 6.1, and the goals of treatment according to the different stages of cancer are presented in Figure 6.1.

Table 6.1 *Principles of symptom management*[2]

Determine the cause
Treat simply
Appropriate explanation of symptoms and treatment
Regular review
Give medication regularly around the clock, not *ad hoc*
Plan 'breakthrough' pain-relieving doses.
Provide physical treatment as necessary e.g. paracentesis, pleural tap, nerve block
Provide complementary conservative therapy e.g. massage, physiotherapy, occupational therapy, dietary advice, relaxation therapy
Provide close supervision

Pain control in cancer

Achieving pain relief is one of the most important functions of palliative care and patients need reassurance that they can expect such relief. The principles of relief of cancer pain are:[1]

1. Treat the cancer.
2. Raise the pain threshold:
   - appropriate explanation
   - allow the patient to ventilate feelings and concepts
   - good psychosocial support
   - use of antidepressants or hypnotics.
3. Add analgesics according to level of pain, e.g. opioids (if necessary).
4. Use specific drugs for specific pain—not all pain responds to analgesics (refer Table 6.2).
5. Set realistic goals.
6. Organise supervision of pain control.

Note: The right drug, in the right dose, given at the right time relieves 80–90% of the pain.[1]

Use of analgesics[5]

These should be given by the clock and given according to the three-step method:

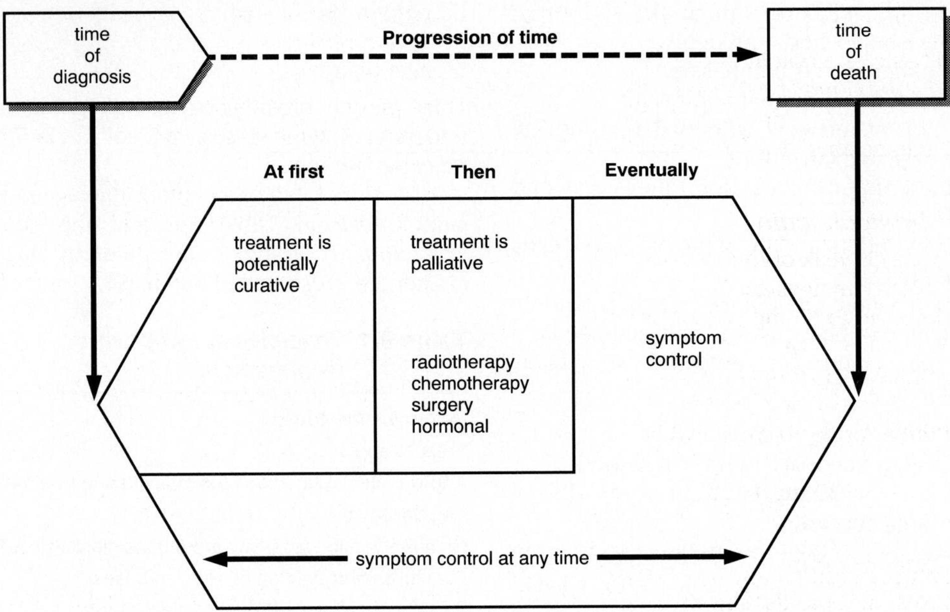

Fig. 6.1 *Stages of cancer management: the goals of treatment differ according to the different stages*
AFTER J. BUCHANAN ET AL. *SIGMA CLINICAL REVIEW* NO.18

Table 6.2 *Treatment options for cancer pain[5] (based on aetiology)*

Aetiology	*1st line treatment*	*2nd line treatment*	*Other treatment modalities to consider*
Neuropathic pain			
• Nerve involvement (nociceptive)	aspirin	opioids cortiocosteroids	radiotherapy neurosurgery e.g. cordotomy rhizotomy
• Neurogenic, e.g. sciatica, brachalgia	amitriptyline carbamazepine	opioids	spinal morphine local anaesthetic
• Dysesthesia: superficial burning pain	amitriptyline	opioids	local anaesthetic
Pressure pain			
• Tumour-associated oedema, e.g. raised intracranial pressure	corticosteroids aspirin	opioids	radiotherapy neurosurgery
Bony metastases and other tissue destruction	NSAIDs aspirin	opioids	radiotherapy hormones orthopaedic surgery
Muscle spasm pain	diazepam baclofen	opioids	
Viscus (hollow organ) obstruction, e.g. colic, tenesmus	antispasmodics	opioids chlorpromazine corticosteroids	palliative surgery radiotherapy
Metabolic effects			
• Hypercalcaemia	diphosphonates (ADP)		
Skin infiltration/ulceration	aspirin opioids	corticosteroids	treat infection dressings palliative surgery radiotherapy

Step 1: Mild pain

Start with basic non-opioid analgesics:
aspirin 600–900 mg (o) 4 hourly (preferred)
or
paracetamol 1 g (o) 4 hourly

Step 2: Moderate pain

Use low dose or weak opioids or in combination with non-opioid analgesics:
codeine up to 60 mg (o) 4 hourly
or
morphine 5 to 10 mg (o) 4 hourly
or
oxycodone up to 10 mg (o) 4 hourly
or
30 mg, rectally, 8 hourly

Step 3: Severe pain

Larger doses of opioids should be used and morphine is the drug of choice:
morphine 10 mg (o) 4 hourly
or
morphine SR tablets (MS Contin) (o) 12 hourly

- Give dosage according to individual needs (MS Contin comes in 10, 30, 60, 100 mg tablets).
- The proper dosage is that which is sufficient to alleviate pain.
- Give usual morphine 10 mg with first dose of morphine SR and then as necessary for 'rescue dosing'.
- Gauge the probable dose of the long-acting morphine from the standard dosage.
- To convert to MS Contin calculate the daily oral dose of regular morphine and divide by 2 to get the 12 hourly dose.
- Do not crush, chew or divide the tablets.

Guidelines

- Ensure that pain is likely to be opioid-sensitive.
- Give morphine orally (if possible) either by mixture or tablets.
- Starting doses are usually in the range of 5–20 mg (average 10 mg).
- If analgesia is inadequate, the next dose should be increased by 50% until pain control is achieved.
- Give it regularly, usually 4 hourly, before the return of the pain.
- Many patients find a mixture easier to swallow than tablets, e.g. 10 mg/10 ml solution.
- Constipation is a problem so treat prophylactically with regular laxatives and carefully monitor bowel function.
- Order a 'rescue dose' (usually 5 mg) for breakthrough pain or anticipated pain (e.g. going to toilet).
- Order antiemetics, e.g. haloperidol prn at first (usually can discontinue in 1 to 2 weeks as tolerance develops).
- Reassure the patient and family about the safety and efficacy of morphine (see Table 6.3).
- Using morphine as a mixture with other substances, e.g. Brompton's cocktail, has no particular advantage.
- Pethidine is not recommended (short half-life, toxic metabolites).
- Other opioids are sometimes used instead of morphine (Table 6.4).

Table 6.3 *Common myths about morphine*[5]

- Morphine is a last resort
  This is not so, and there is no maximum dose.
- The patient will become addicted
  This is rare and probably irrelevant in the context of palliative care.
- The patient will need ever-increasing amounts
  The drug does not lose its effect but is usually increased according to disease progression.
- Morphine will cause respiratory depression
  This is rarely a problem and may even help those with dyspnoea. An overdose can be reversed with an injection of naloxone.
- Morphine will shorten life
  The reverse may in fact apply. It is not being used for euthanasia but to control pain.

Parenteral morphine

This is generally given subcutaneously (not IV or IM).

Indications[6]

1. Unable to swallow, e.g. severe oral mucositis; dysphagia; oesophageal obstruction
2. Bowel obstruction
3. Severe nausea and vomiting
4. At high oral dose, i.e. above 100–200 mg dose, there appears to be no additional benefit from further dose increments.

Adjuvant therapy (refer Table 6.2)

Pain control

Bone pain

- aspirin, paracetamol, NSAIDs are helpful co-analgesics

Table 6.4 *Non-morphine opioids used in pain control*[1]

Opioid	*Duration of action (Hours)*	*Dose equivalent to oral morphine 10 mg*
Codeine	3–5	60 mg
Oxycodone		
Endone (oral)	3–5	10 mg
Proladone (rectal)	6–12	10 mg
Methadone	variable 8–24	15 mg
Dextromoramide (Palfium)	2	20 mg

Neuropathic pain

- antidepressants, e.g. amitriptyline
- anticonvulsants, e.g. carbamazepine

Neurological pressure

- corticosteroids for spinal cord compression and raised intracranial pressure
  e.g. dexamethasone 4–16 mg (o) daily
  or
  prednisolone 25–100 mg (o) daily

Continuous subcutaneous infusion of morphine

When the oral and/or rectal routes are not possible or ineffective a subcutaneous infusion with a syringe pump can be used.

It is also useful for symptom control when there is a need for a combination of drugs, e.g. for pain, nausea and agitation. It may avoid bolus peak effects (sedation, nausea or vomiting) or trough effects (breakthrough pain) with intermittent parenteral morphine injections.

Practical aspects

- Access to the subcutaneous space is via a 21 g butterfly needle which is replaced regularly (1, 2, 3 or 4 days).
- Most regions are suitable. The more convenient are the abdomen, the anterior thigh, and the anterior upper arm (usually the anterior abdominal wall is used).
- The infusion can be managed at home.
- About one-half to two-thirds of the 24 hour oral morphine requirement is placed in the syringe.
- The syringe is placed into the pump driver, which is set for 24 hour delivery.
- Areas of oedema are not suitable.

Spinal morphine

Epidural or intrathecal morphine is sometimes indicated for pain below the head and neck, where oral or parenteral opioids have been ineffective. It is necessary to insert an epidural or intrathecal catheter (anaesthetist or neurosurgeon).[5]

Common symptom control[1]

Anorexia

metoclopramide 10 mg tds
or
corticosteroids, e.g. dexamethasone 2–8 mg tds
high-energy drink supplements

Constipation

If opioids need to be maintained, the laxatives need to be peristaltic stimulants, not bulk-forming agents. Aim for firm faeces with bowels open about every third day.

e.g. senna (Senokot) 2 daily or bd
bisacodyl (Durolax) 5–10 mg bd

Rectal suppositories, microenemas or enemas may be required, e.g. Microlax.

Death rattles

Hyoscine 0.4–0.8 mg, 4–8 hourly, can be used to dry secretions and stop the 'death rattle'.

Dyspnoea

Identify the cause, such as a pleural effusion, and treat as appropriate. Pleural taps can be performed readily in the home. Corticosteroids can be given for lung metastases. Oxygen may be necessary to help respiratory distress in the terminal stages and bedside oxygen can be readily obtained. Morphine can be used for intractable dyspnoea, together with haloperidol or a phenothiazine for nausea.

Nausea and vomiting

If due to morphine:

haloperidol 1.5–5 mg daily[1]
can be reduced after 10 days
or
prochlorperazine (Stemetil)
5–10 mg (o) qid
or
25 mg rectally bd

Consider ondansetron (Zofran) for nausea and vomiting induced by cytotoxic chemotherapy and radiotherapy.

Cerebral metastases

Common symptoms are headache and nausea. Consider corticosteroid therapy. Analgesics and antiemetics such as haloperidol are effective.

Paraplegia

Paraplegia is especially prone to occur with carcinoma of the prostate, even when treated with LH–RH analogues. The warning signs are the development of new back pain, paraesthesia in limbs or the recent development of urinary retention.[1] The objective is to prevent paraplegia developing. High-dose corticosteroids are given while arranging urgent hospital admission.

Hiccoughs

Try a starting dose of
chlorpromazine 25 mg tds
or
haloperidol 25 mg bd

Swallowing granulated sugar with or without vinegar does not appear to be effective.

Weakness and weight loss

This problem may be assisted by a high-calorie and high-protein diet. A list of high-energy drink supplements is provided in *Palliative care: the nitty gritty handbook*[1].

Examples

Banana Sustagen milk

- milk — 2 cups
- banana — one
- egg — one
- Sustagen powder — 3 dessertspoons
- skim milk powder — 1 dessertspoon
- Glucodin — 1 dessertspoon
- ice — crushed

(Vitamise all together.)

Egg flip

- egg — one
- milk — one cup
- vanilla syrup or essence — to taste (1–3 drops)
- sugar — 1 teaspoon
- brandy — (optional)

(Vitamise all together, strain, sprinkle with nutmeg.)

High-energy cordial

- cordial — 1 tablespoon
- Glucodin — 1 teaspoon
- water — 1 cup
- ice — crushed

(Blend cordial and Glucodin till smooth, stir in water.)

High-energy juice

- juice — 1 cup
- Glucodin — 1 dessertspoon

(Blend Glucodin with a little juice till smooth. Stir in remaining juice.)

Dying and grieving

The stages of the grieving process as described by Kübler-Ross may be experienced by both the patient and family, albeit not exactly according to the five stages. The grieving process following the death of a loved one can vary enormously but many people are devastated.

The principles of care and counselling include:[1]

- Be available and be patient.
- Allow them to talk while you listen.
- Reassure them that their feelings are normal.
- Accept any show of anger passively.
- Avoid inappropriate reassurance.
- Encourage as much companionship as possible, if desired.

(See guidelines for crisis counselling in Chapter 4.)

Communicating with the dying patient

Good communication is essential between the doctor and patient in order to inform, explain, encourage and show empathy. However, it can be very difficult, especially with the cancer patient.

Good communication is dependent on honesty and integrity in the relationship. Telling the truth can be painful and requires sensitivity, but it builds trust which enables optimal sharing of other difficult concerns and decisions such as abandoning curative treatment, explaining the dying process and perhaps addressing thoughts on euthanasia.

Improved communication will lead not only to better 'spiritual' care but also to better symptom control.[1] Give patients every opportunity to talk about their illness and future expectations and be available and patient in offering help and support.

Spiritual issues

Spirituality is an important issue for all people, especially when faced with inevitable death. Many people are innately spiritual or religious and those with deep faith and a belief in 'paradise' appear to cope better with the dying process. Others begin to reflect seriously about spirituality and search for a meaning for life in this situation; carers, including the attending doctor, should be sensitive to their needs and turmoil and reach out a helping hand which may simply involve contacting a minister of religion.

Spiritual care builds on patients' existing resources to enable them to rise above the physical, emotional and social effects of their terminal illness.[1]

The question of euthanasia[3]

It should be a rare experience to be confronted with a request for the use of euthanasia, especially as the media clichés of 'suffering' and 'agonising death' are rarely encountered in the context of attentive whole-person continuing care. The non-use of life support systems, the use of 'round the clock' morphine, cessation of cytotoxic drugs, the use of ancillary drugs such as antidepressants and antiemetics, various nerve blocks and loving attention almost always help the patient cope without undue pain and suffering.

Practice tips

- Consider prescribing tricyclic antidepressants routinely for patients in pain.
- Remember the 'sit down rule' whereby the home visit is treated as a social visit—sitting down with the patient and family, having a 'cuppa' and sharing medical and social talk.[3]

References

1. Fairbank E, Banks T. *Palliative care: the nitty gritty handbook.* Melbourne: RACGP Services Division, 1993, 1–18.
2. McGuckin R, Currow D, Redelman P. Palliative care: your role. Medical Observer, 27 November 1992, 41–42.
3. Carson NE, Miller C. *Care of the terminally ill.* Monash University: Department of Community Medicine Handbook, 1993, 107–115.
4. Kübler-Ross E. *On death and dying.* London: Tavistock, 1970.
5. Moulds RFW et al. *Analgesic guidelines.* Melbourne: Victorian Medical Postgraduate Foundation, 1992-3, 39–48.
6. Buchanan J et al. *Management of pain in cancer.* Melbourne: Sigma Clinical Review, 1991, 18:8–10.

7

The elderly patient

—

The ageing (over 65 years) are the fastest growing section of the Australian population. The number of 'old-old' (over 85 years) is increasing at an even faster rate.[1]

The over 65s in 1988 made up 10.8% of the Australian population (12% in the United States). It is expected that this group will make up 13.4% in 2011 and 20% in the year 2031. A similar trend is expected in the United States with 13% by the year 2000 and 18% in 2040.[2]

The over 65s use twice the number of health services per head of population. They account for 25% of all hospital costs and 75% of all nursing home costs. They represent 25% of all general practice consultations.[1] Many are affected by multisystem disease. All are affected to a greater or lesser extent by the normal physiological changes of organ ageing.

Ageing is characterised by the following:[1]

- decrease in metabolic mass
- reduction in the functional capacity of organs
- reduced capacity to adapt to stress
- increased vulnerability to disease
- increased probability of death

Age-associated deterioration occurs with:

hearing, vision, glucose tolerance, systolic blood pressure, renal function, pulmonary function, immune function, bone density, cognitive function, mastication, bladder function.

Ageing and disease

Degenerative cardiovascular disease emerges with ageing according to the following approximate guidelines:

aged 40 — obesity
50 — diabetes
55 — ischaemic heart disease
65 — myocardial infarction
70 — cardiac arrhythmias
75 — heart failure
80 — cerebrovascular accidents

Deterioration in health and the 'masquerades'

Unexpected illness including mental confusion (one of the major hallmarks of disease in the elderly) can be caused commonly by any of the so-called masquerades outlined in Chapter 13:

- depression
- drugs, including alcohol
- diabetes mellitus
- anaemia
- thyroid disease
- urinary tract infection
- neurological dilemmas
  — Parkinson's disease
  — cerebrovascular accident
- infections, e.g. bronchopneumonia
- neoplasia
- giant cell arteritis/polymyalgia rheumatica

Common significant management disorders encountered in the elderly include:

- hypertension
- ischaemic heart disease and heart failure
- depression
- diabetes (NIDDM)
- dementia
- social and physical isolation
- osteoarthritis
- disorders of the prostate

- urinary incontinence
- locomotive (lower limb) disorders
  - — neurological
    - peripheral neuropathy
    - ataxia
  - — claudication due to vascular insufficiency
  - — other peripheral vascular disease
  - — claudication due to spinal canal stenosis
  - — sciatica/nerve root paresis
  - — osteoarthritis: hips, knees, feet
  - — foot disorders, e.g. ingrown toenails
  - — leg ulceration

Important problems affecting the elderly are presented in Figure 7.1.

Changes in sensory thresholds and homeostasis

A clinically significant feature in some elderly patients is the raising of the pain threshold and changes in homeostatic mechanisms such as temperature control. Consequently these patients may have an abnormal response to diseases such as appendicitis, pyelonephritis, internal abscess, pneumonia and septicaemia. There may be no complaints of pain and no significant fever but simply general malaise and abnormal behaviour such as delirium, agitation and restlessness.

Establishing rapport with the elderly patient

The elderly patient especially requires considerable support, understanding, caring and attention from a general practitioner who can instil confidence and security in a patient who is likely to be lonely, insecure and fragile. This means taking time, showing a genuine interest, a modicum of humour and always leaving detailed instructions.

One of the best ways to generate a good relationship is through home visitation. The value of home visits can be considered under the concepts of the Royal Australian College of General Practitioners.[3]

1. Assessment, both initial and continuing: 'You don't know your patient until you've visited their home'.
2. Continuing care:
   - security to the patient
   - support for 'caring' family
   - effective monitoring/intervention role
   - effective liaison with patient/family
   - checking medication

Home visits can be considered in three categories:

1. an 'unexpected' visit (especially to a new patient)
2. a patient-initiated but routine request for a 'check-up and tablets'
3. the regular call—usually 2 to 4 weeks

These home visits are a 'security gesture' to the patient, evidence that they are supported in their desire to remain independent for as long as possible in their own home. They strengthen the patient–doctor relationship as a position of trust, which is of special importance to frail, elderly people feeling increasingly insecure and threatened.

If the patient is being supported by a spouse or relative the doctor can provide continuous reassurance and support to all concerned as well as continual assessment, both physical and mental. Finally, the home visit may become part of the terminal care of a dying patient, something that is very important to the elderly patient. Home visits can enhance the quality of life, both physical and mental, of an ageing person.

Doctor behaviour that can irritate and confuse elderly patients

Ellard[4] has written a most interesting paper, based on a compendium of complaints by the elderly about their doctors, on behaviour that upsets the elderly.

- Having a consulting room with slippery steps, poor lighting and inadequate handrails
- Non-attention to simple courtesies by receptionist staff
- Keeping them waiting
- Having low soft chairs in the waiting room and surgery
- Being overfamiliar, with addresses such as 'Pop' or first names for elderly females
- Shouting at them on the assumption that they are deaf
- Appearing rushed and keen to get the consultation over quickly
- Forgetting their psychosocial problems and concentrating only on their physical problems, i.e. not treating the whole person
- Forgetting that they have several things wrong with them and using a different priority list to theirs

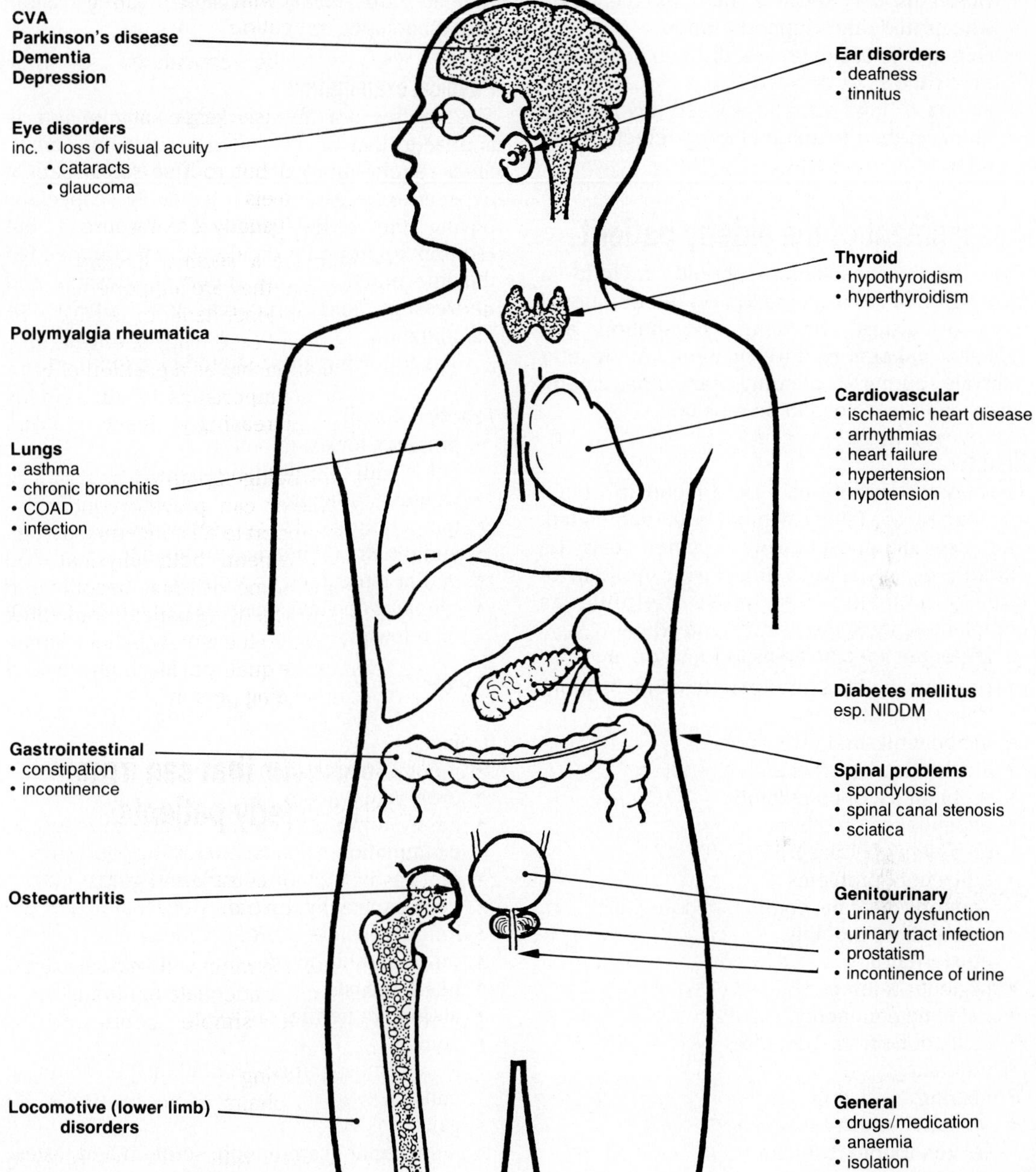

Fig. 7.1 *Significant problems affecting the elderly*

- Being unaware that they may have seen other practitioners or may be taking additional medication
- Failing to ask patients to give their understanding of what is wrong
- Omitting to give printed patient education handouts about their problems and medications
- Omitting to explain how the medication will work
- Treating them as though they would have little comprehension of their health and treatment
- Failing to respect their privacy such as not knocking before entering the examination room
- Failing to provide appropriate advice on

various social services such as meals on wheels and other support groups
- Failing to re-evaluate carefully their health and medication
- Failing to take steps to reverse any deterioration in their health including reluctance to refer

Assessment of the elderly patient

The initial consultation should include a thorough clinical examination on the traditional lines of history, physical examination and selective laboratory investigation. At regular intervals during continuing care this careful assessment may need to be repeated.

History

The medical history may be difficult to obtain and the help of a family member is recommended. The use of questionnaires, which can be completed at leisure at home with the help of family members, is most helpful as complementary to the medical interview.

Important specific areas to focus on are:

- previous medical history and hospitalisation
- immunisation status
- medications and OTC drugs
- alcohol intake, smoking
- problem list of complaints
- dependence on others
- members of household
- household problems
- comforts: heating, cooling, bedding, etc.
- ambulation/mobility
- meals: diet
- hygiene: bathing
- toileting: continence
- teeth: condition, ? dentures
- vision
- hearing
- systems review, especially:
  - — genitourinary function
  - — gastrointestinal
  - — cardiorespiratory
- locomotion including feet
- Nervous system, ? falls, giddiness, faints
- emotional and mental health
- evidence of depression
- history of bereavement

A thorough family history and psychosocial history is of prime importance. At all times concentrate on a general assessment of the patients' ability to communicate by evaluating mental status, comprehension, hearing, vision, mood and speech.

Physical examination

The routine for the physical examination is similar to that of the younger adult but certain areas require more attention. The elderly patient expects to be examined adequately (especially having the blood pressure measured) but requires appropriate dignity. It is recommended that the practice nurse supervise dressing and undressing and prepares the patient for examination.

The following areas should be examined.

Practice nurse

- prepares for examination
- helps with questionnaire
- weight and height
- temperature, pulse and respiration
- audiometry (if hearing problem)
- ocular tension (if appropriate)
- prepares cervical smear tray for female patient (if relevant)

Doctor

- general appearance including skin, hair and face
- mental status examination (Fig. 7.2)[5]
- eyes: visual acuity
- ears: simple hearing test; auroscopic examination
- oral cavity, including teeth and gums
- neck especially thyroid
- lungs: consider peak flow meter
- pulse and blood pressure (repeat)
- heart; breasts
- abdomen; hernial orifices
- spine
- lower limbs: joints; circulation; feet including nails
- gait
- men: rectal examination; scrotum and testes
- women: cervical smear if appropriate

The mini-mental status examination

Evidence of memory difficulty remains the best single indicator of dementia and should always be evaluated by formal memory testing. However, memory problems may be due to factors other than dementia and demonstrating failure in other areas of cognitive functioning (language, spatial ability, reasoning) is necessary to confirm the diagnosis of dementia.[5] A number of screening

Introduction

'I'd like to ask you some questions about your health.'
'What's your sleep been like?'_________ 'Your appetite?' _________
'Your interest?'_________ 'Your energy?' _________ 'Your concentration?' _________
'What's your memory like these days? Do you mind if I test it?'

Memory registration

'What I want to do is give you three things I want you to try to remember for me. First I want you to repeat them, then in a few minutes I'll ask you how many you can recall. Here are the three things I want you to remember for me.'
'MELBOURNE, CRICKET, BLUE.'

—/3 'Can you repeat them for me?' (Score number of attempts required —/3, for example, CORRECT FIRST TRY = 3; SECOND TRY = 2; THIRD TRY = 1)
'Good, now can you try to remember those three things for me, because I'm going to ask you to recall them shortly. But first I'd like to get you to do some things that might interfere with your memory.'

Attention and concentration

'First I'd like you to count out loud from 1 to 20.' _________
'Now could you count backwards from 20 to 1.' _________
'Next can I get you to spell the word WORLD for me?' _________ WORLD
—/5 'Now can you try to spell WORLD backwards for me?' _D_L_R_O_W

Memory recall

'Now what were those three words I asked you to remember for me?'
—/3 SPONTANEOUS RECALL: _____ MELBOURNE, _____ CRICKET, _____ BLUE
Optional: Cued recall (____ City, ____ Sport, ____ Colour)
Recognition (List four cities, four sports, four colours)

Language

'Sometimes as people get older they have trouble remembering words, the right word, does that ever happen to you?'
'Well, let's see. What do you call this?'
—/1 ____ PEN (Optional more difficult items ____ Cap ____ Point)
—/1 ____ WATCH (Optional difficult items ____ Strap ____ Winder)
'Can I get you to repeat a sentence, exactly as I say it?'
—/1 NO IFS, ANDS OR BUTS ____________________
'Can I get you to do three things with this envelope?'
—/3 'PICK IT UP WITH YOUR LEFT HAND ____ , FOLD THE ENVELOPE IN HALF ____ and PUT THE ENVELOPE ON THE FLOOR' ____
'Can you read what's written on the envelope and do what it says?'
—/1 'CLOSE YOUR EYES' (Written in large letters)
'Can you write a sentence for me on the back?'
—/1 SENTENCE (should contain subject and object and make sense)

Orientation

'Can you put your address on the envelope?
—/5 NUMBER ____ , STREET ______ , SUBURB/CITY ______ , STATE ______ , COUNTRY ______ .
'Can you put today's date on the back?'
—/5 DATE _____ , MONTH ______ , YEAR _____ , DAY ______ , SEASON ______ .

Visuospatial skills

'Can you make a COPY of this figure for me?'
—/1
—/30 *Total score:* Probable cognitive impairment < 24
Definite cognitive impairment < 17

Fig. 7.2 *A practical adaptation of the mini-mental state examination* ADAPTED FROM M.F. FOLSTEIN, S.E. FOLSETIN AND P.R. McHUGH. 'MINI-MENTAL STATE', J PSYCH RESEARCH 1975; 12:189

tests are available but the mini-mental status examination depicted in Figure 7.2 can be used.

Laboratory investigations

The laboratory tests should be selected according to the evaluation of the patient and to costs versus potential benefits.

Recommended investigations for suspected dementia include:[7]

- renal function
- hepatic function
- thyroid function
- full blood screen
- blood glucose
- serum electrolytes (especially if on diuretics)
- urinalysis
- serum B_{12} and folate
- syphilis serology
- chest X-ray
- computerised tomography

Behavioural changes in the elderly

As general practitioners we are often called to assess abnormal behaviour in the elderly patient, with the question being asked, 'Is it dementia?' or 'Is it Alzheimer's, doctor?'

There are many other causes of behavioural changes in people over the age of 65 years and dementia must be regarded as a diagnosis of exclusion. The clinical presentation of some of these conditions can be virtually identical to early dementia.

The clinical features of early dementia include:

- poor recent memory
- impaired acquisition of new information
- mild anomia (cannot remember names)
- personality change, e.g. withdrawn, irritable
- minimal visuospatial impairment, e.g. tripping easily
- inability to perform sequential tasks

The differential diagnosis for behavioural changes apart from dementia include several other common and important problems (which must be excluded) and can be considered under a mnemonic for dementia.[6]

D drugs and alcohol
depression
E ears
eyes
M metabolic, e.g. hyponatraemia
diabetes mellitus
hypothyroidism
E emotional problems, e.g. loneliness
N nutrition: diet, e.g. Vitamin B group deficiency, teeth problems
T tumours } of CNS
trauma }
I infection
A arteriovascular disease → cerebral insufficiency

All these conditions should be considered with the onset of deterioration in health of the elderly person. Even apparently minor problems such as the onset of deafness (e.g. wax in ears), visual deterioration (e.g. cataracts), diuretic therapy, poor mastication and diet, urinary tract, intercurrent infection, boredom and anxiety can precipitate abnormal behaviour.

Depression and dementia

The main differential diagnosis of dementia is depression, especially major depression which is termed pseudodementia. The mode of onset is one way in which it may be possible to distinguish between depression and dementia. Dementia has a slow and surreptitious onset that is not clear-cut, while depression has a more definable and clear-cut onset which may be precipitated by a specific incident. Patients with dementia have no insight while those with depression have insight, readily give up tasks, complain bitterly and become distressed by their inability to perform their normal enjoyable tasks.

In response to cognitive testing, the typical response of the depressed patient is 'don't know', while making an attempt with a near miss typifies the patient with dementia.

It is vital to detect depression in the elderly as they are prone to suicide. 'Nothing to look back on with pride and nothing to look forward to.' The middle-aged and elderly may not complain of depression, which can be masked. They may present with somatic symptoms or delusions.

Dementia (chronic organic brain syndrome)

The incidence of dementia increases with age, affecting about one person in 10 over 65 years and 1 in 5 over 80 years. The important causes of dementia are:

- degenerative cerebral diseases including Alzheimer's disease (60%)
- vascular (15%)
- alcohol excess[7]

The characteristic feature is impairment of memory. Abstract thinking, judgement, verbal fluency and the ability to perform complex tasks also become impaired. Personality may change, impulse control may be lost and personal care deteriorates.[7]

The DSM-III (R) criteria for dementia are presented in Table 7.1 and clinical clues suggesting dementia in Table 7.2.

The many guises of dementia can be considered in terms of four major symptom groups.[5]

1. Deficit presentations: due to loss of cognitive abilities, including
   - forgetfulness
   - confusion and restlessness
   - apathy (usually a late change)
   - self-neglect with no insight
   - poor powers of reasoning and understanding

Table 7.1 *DSM-III (R) criteria for dementia*

Diagnosis of dementia requires evidence of:

A Memory impairment

B At least one of the following:
1. Abstract thinking impairment
2. Impaired judgement
3. Disturbed higher cortical functions:
   - Language = aphasia
   - Motor actions = apraxia
   - Recognition = agnosia
   - Constructional difficulties

C Personality change

D Disturbance significantly interferes with work, social interactions or relationships

E Not due to delirium or other disorders, e.g. major depression

Source: Diagnostic and Statistical Manual (3rd ed. Revised). Washington, DCA: American Psychiatric Association, 1987.

Table 7.2 *Clinical clues suggesting dementia (after McLean[5])*

1. Patient presentations
   - new psychological problems in old age
   - ill-defined and muddled complaints
   - uncharacteristic behaviour
   - relapse of physical disorders
   - recurrent episodes of confusion
2. Problems noted by carers
   - 'not themselves'—change in personality, e.g. humourless
   - domestic accidents especially with cooking and heating
   - unsafe driving
   - false accusations
   - emotional, irritable outbursts
   - tendency to wander
   - misplacing or losing items, e.g. keys, money, tablets, glasses
   - muddled on awakening at night
3. Mental state observations
   - vague, rambling or disorganised conversation
   - difficulty dating or sequencing past events
   - repeating stock phrases or comments
   - plays down obvious, perhaps serious, problems
   - deflects or evades memory testing

2. Unsociable presentations: based on personality change, including
   - uninhibited behaviour
   - risk taking and impulsive behaviour
   - suspicious manner
   - withdrawn behaviour
3. Dysphoric presentations: based on disturbed mood and personal distress, including
   - depression (hopeless and helpless)
   - irritability with emotional outbursts
   - lack of co-operation
   - insecurity
4. Disruptive presentations: causing distress and disturbance to others, including
   - aggressive, sometimes violent behaviour
   - agitation with restlessness

The problem occasionally results in marked emotional and physical instability. It is sad and difficult for relatives to watch their loved ones develop aggressive and antisocial behaviour, such as poor table manners, poor personal cleanliness, rudeness and a lack of interest in others. Sometimes severe problems such as violent behaviour, sexual promiscuity and incontinence will eventuate.

There is always the likelihood of accidents with household items such as fire, gas, kitchen knives and hot water. Accidents at the toilet, in the bath and crossing roads may be a problem, especially if combined with failing sight and hearing. Such people should not drive motor vehicles.

Without proper supervision they are likely to eat poorly, neglect their bodies and develop medical problems such as skin ulcers and infections. They can also suffer from malnutrition and incontinence of urine or faeces.

Management of suspected dementia

Exclude reversible or arrestable causes of dementia.

- full medical history (including drug and alcohol intake)
- mental state examination
- physical examination
- investigations (see page 498)

Management of dementia

There is no cure for dementia—the best that can be offered to the patient is tender loving care.

Education, support and advice should be given to both patient and family. Multidisciplinary evaluation and assistance are needed. Regular home visits by caring sympathetic people are important. Such people include relatives, friends, general practitioners, district nurses, home help, members of a dementia self-help group, religious ministers and meals on wheels. The sufferers tend to manage much better in the familiar surroundings of their own home and this assists in preventing behaviour disturbance.

Special attention should be paid to organising memory aids such as lists, routines and medication, and to hygiene, diet and warmth. Adequate nutrition, including vitamin supplements if necessary, has been shown to help.

Associated problems[7]

Depression can occur early in dementia and requires intervention. Demented patients are vulnerable to superimposed delirium which is often due to:

- urinary tract infection
- other febrile illness
- prescribed medication
- drug withdrawal

Delirium should be suspected if a stable patient becomes acutely disturbed.

Medication[7]

Demented patients often do not require any psychotropic medication. Antidepressant drugs can be prescribed for depression.

To control psychotic symptoms or disturbed behaviour probably due to psychosis:

haloperidol 1.5–10 mg (o) daily

or

thioridazine 25–50 mg (o) 1 to 4 times daily

To control symptoms of anxiety and agitation use:

oxazepam 15 mg (o) 1 to 4 times daily

but benzodiazepines should only be used for short periods as they tend to exacerbate cognitive impairment in dementia.

Adverse drug reactions

Ageing is associated with increased rates of adverse drug reactions.[1] The rate of adverse drug reactions for a single medication rises from about 6% at age 20 years to about 20% at age 70 years.

For less than six medications taken concurrently the rate of adverse drug reactions is about 6%. For greater than six medications taken concurrently the rate of adverse drug reactions jumps to 20%.[1]

Factors predisposing to adverse drug reactions in the elderly[1]

Most adverse drug reactions in the elderly are entirely predictable. Most are merely an extension of the pharmacological action of the drug, e.g. all antihypertensives will reduce blood pressure and have the capacity to cause hypotension and falls in a person with impaired baroreceptor function or poor homeostasis in their vascular tree. Very few adverse reactions are idiosyncratic or unexpected.

The five mechanisms of adverse drug reactions in the elderly are:

1. Drug–drug interaction
   e.g. beta-blockers given concomitantly with digoxin increases the risk of heart block and bradycardia.

   Alcohol used in combination with antidepressants increases the risk of sedation.
2. Drug–disease interaction
   e.g. in the presence of renal impairment, tetracyclines carry an increased risk of renal deterioration.
3. Age-related changes leading to increases in drug plasma concentration
   Decreased renal excretion can extend the half-life of medication, leading to accumulation and toxicity.
4. Age-related changes leading to increased drug sensitivity
   e.g. there is some suggestion that the pharmacological response to warfarin, narcotics and benzodiazepines is increased in the elderly. Conversely the pharmacological response to insulin, theophylline and beta adrenergic blocking agents is thought to be decreased.
5. Patient error
   Multiple medications can lead to patient error. The incidence and prevalence of dementia also increases with age.

Increasing the number of simultaneous medications increases the risk for all five mechanisms of adverse drug reactions.

In a study on adverse drug reaction in elderly patients the drugs most frequently causing admission to hospital were:[8]

- digoxin
- diuretics
- antihypertensives (including beta-blockers)
- psychotropics and hypnotics
- analgesics and NSAIDs

The same study showed that drugs regularly prescribed without revision were:

- barbiturates
- benzodiazepines
- antidepressants
- antihypertensives
- beta-blockers
- digoxin
- diuretics

Drug regimens should be kept as simple as possible to aid compliance and avoid or minimise drug interactions.

The elderly may need much lower doses of anxiolytics and hypnotics than younger patients to produce the same effect, thus rendering them more susceptible to adverse effects and toxicity. The elderly are especially liable to accumulate the longer-acting benzodiazepines.

In particular, any drug or combination of drugs with anticholinergic properties, e.g. tricyclic antidepressants, antiparkinsonian agents, antihistamines, phoenthiazines and some cold remedies, can precipitate a central anticholinergic syndrome.[7]

Starting medications[7]

The starting dose of a drug in the aged should be at the lower end of recommended ranges. Dosage increments should be gradual and reviewed regularly.

That is, start low, go slow and monitor frequently. It is important to individualise doses for the elderly.

References

1. Harris E. *Prescribing for the ageing population.* Monash University Medical School: Update Course Proceedings handbook, 1992.
2. Sloane PD, Slatt LM, Baker RM. *Essentials of family medicine.* Baltimore: Williams and Wilkins, 1988, 49–56.
3. Lang D. Home visits to the elderly. Aust Fam Physician, 1993; 22:264.
4. Ellard J. How to irritate and confuse your elderly patients—20 simple rules. Modern Medicine of Australia, 1990; 7:66–68.
5. McLean S. Is it dementia? Aust Fam Physician, 1992; 21:1762–1776.
6. Turnbull JM. *Dementia and depression in the elderly.* California: AUDIO DIGEST family practice, 1993; 41:10.
7. Mashford ML (Chairman). *Psychotropic drug guidelines.* Victorian Medical Postgraduate Foundation, 1993–94, 56–57.
8. Briant RH. Medication problems of old age. Patient Management, 1988; 5:27–31.

8

Prevention in general practice

Definitions[1]

Prevention may be defined as the means of promoting and maintaining health or averting illness.

It is concerned with removal or reduction of risks, early diagnosis, early treatment, limitation of complications, including those of iatrogenic origin, and maximum adaptation to disability.

The promotion of health concerns helping well people to learn healthy behaviours and to accept responsibility for their own well-being.

A preventive attitude implies that the doctor understands and can utilise the preventive potential in each primary care consultation by an 'opportunistic approach'. In addition to the traditional management of both presenting and continuing problems, the doctor takes the opportunity to modify the patient's health-seeking behaviour, to provide education about the illness, and to promote health by relating the patient's present condition to previous unhealthy behaviour.

Primary prevention

Primary prevention includes action taken to avert the occurrence of disease. As a result there is no disease. Primary preventive strategies include:

1. Sanitation, keeping our water supplies clean and disposing efficiently of sewage and industrial wastes.
2. Sterilisation of surgical instruments and other medical equipment.
3. Eradication as with vector control of mosquitoes to prevent malaria.
4. Immunisation against infective diseases.
5. Education to bring about changes in lifestyle factors known to be associated with diseases, e.g. smoking cessation, healthily balanced diets, reduction in alcohol intake, exercise.
6. Legislation exists to ensure that some of these primary preventive measures are carried out.

Secondary prevention

Secondary prevention includes actions taken to stop or delay the progression of disease.

The term is usually applied to measures for the detection of disease at its earliest stage, i.e. in the presymptomatic phase, so that treatment can be started before irreversible pathology is present. The early recognition of hypertension through routine testing (screening) of patients allows treatment during the presymptomatic phase of the illness process. Screening for cervical cancer allows the treatment of cervical dysplasia, a premalignant condition.

Tertiary prevention

Tertiary prevention includes the management of established disease so as to minimise disability.

The term is usually applied to the rehabilitation process necessary to restore the patient to the best level of adaptation possible when there has been damage of an irreversible nature. A patient who has suffered a stroke because of hypertension may be restored to a useful lifestyle with appropriate rehabilitation.

It can be seen that there is a clearer demarcation between primary and secondary prevention than between secondary and tertiary prevention, although the latter term is particularly useful in dealing with the elderly and the handicapped. Conceptually, curative medicine falls within the definitions of secondary and tertiary prevention while public health measures are mainly concerned with primary prevention. Prevention is really wider than medical practice but because of the success of public health practices in the past, more attention is now being focused on prevention by doctors (see Fig. 8.1).[2]

As general practitioners our role in prevention is twofold:

1. First, we can recognise the preventable factors that are involved in an illness process and determine appropriate interventions.
2. Second, we can act to implement the preventive measure. In cases where the responsibility rests with the individual or the community, doctors can support prevention through education, applying political pressure or working with community agencies.

The practice of preventive medicine by the doctor

What is preventable?

The first step in the implementation of prevention is to define which specific diseases can be prevented and to what extent, given certain restraints such as manpower, technology and the cost to the community. All diseases have a potential preventability but it may be unrealistic to try to achieve this.

Diseases which can be prevented can be grouped according to their aetiology. They fall into the following broad categories:

- genetic disorders
- conditions occurring during pregnancy and the puerperium
- developmental disorders
- accidents
- infections
- addictions
- behavioural disorders
- occupational disorders
- premature vascular disease
- neoplasms
- handicap in the disabled
- certain 'other' diseases, e.g. diverticular disease

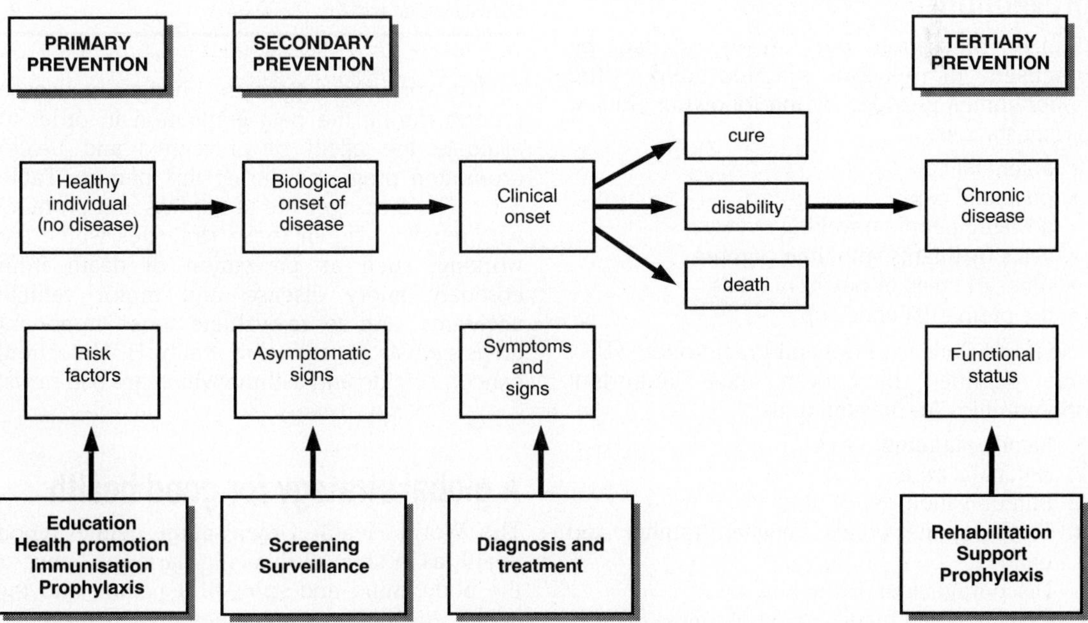

Fig. 8.1 *The phases of prevention in relation to the natural history of disease*

Mortality is the only reliable index by which the outcome of preventive activities can be judged. Conditions can be ranked in importance as causes of premature death according to the 'person years of life lost before 70 years' as follows:[1]

accidents, poisoning and violence	29%
neoplasms	19%
circulatory diseases	17%
perinatal conditions	10%
congenital conditions	7%

This gives quite a different perspective to prevention and explains why the efforts of public health authorities and practising doctors do not always coincide.

The interventions available to us in medical practice are as follows:

1. Educational—health promotion, health education and illness education
2. Screening
3. Surveillance
4. Interventional care—immunisation, behaviour modification and drug prophylaxis
5. Rehabilitation

Optimal opportunities for prevention

Primary prevention *par excellence* can be practised in general practice under the opportunities provided by the following clinical circumstances:

- antenatal care
- postnatal care
- advising people travelling overseas
- visits by infants with their parents
- times of crisis or potential crisis
- the premarital check-up

The Royal College of General Practitioners (UK) has identified the seven most important opportunities for prevention as:

1. Family planning
2. Antenatal care
3. Immunisation
4. Fostering the bonds between mother and child
5. Discouragement of smoking
6. Detection and management of raised BP
7. Helping the bereaved

Mortality and morbidity considerations

An understanding of the mortality and morbidity patterns in the modern human being is essential to the planning of preventive programs. The great infectious diseases of the past, such as tuberculosis, syphilis, smallpox, influenza, diphtheria and streptococcal infections, have been largely contained but other diseases have become prominent as life expectancy increases. The great modern diseases are atherosclerosis (hardening of the arteries), malignant disease (cancer), HIV infection and iatrogenesis (doctor-induced illness).

These diseases and the common causes of mortality (Table 8.1) act as a focus for our energies in addressing preventive programs.

Tale 8.1 *Common causes of deaths in Australia*

		%
Circulatory disease		
Ischaemic heart disease	32	
Cerebrovascular disease	14	
		46
Malignant disease		24
Respiratory disease		8
Accidents, poisoning and violence		8
Digestive disease		3

It is worth focusing on the changes in disease indices during the past generation in order to evaluate the effect of preventive and health promotion programs during this period (Table 8.2)[3]. The messages are to harness and promote with renewed vigour those strategies which are working, such as prevention of death from coronary artery disease and motor vehicle accidents, and to re-evaluate those important areas such as Aboriginal mortality, HIV infection, cancer, suicide and asthma which are bad news!

A global strategy for good health

The World Health Organisation defines good health as 'a state of dynamic harmony between the body, mind and spirit of a person and the social and cultural influences which make up his or her environment'.

Table 8.2 *Apparent changes in disease indices 1960–1988*

Improvements	***No change or deterioration***
Overall mortality	Aboriginal mortality (minor improvement)
Heart attack	Cancers
Stroke	—pancreas
Unintentional Injuries/ poisonings	—breast
—motor vehicle	—skin
—drownings	—lung (women)
—falls	AIDS
—occupational injury	Alcohol-related diseases
Most infectious diseases	Drug abuse
Cancer of lung (men)	Asthma
Cervical cancer (women)	Senile dementia
Cancer of stomach	STDs
Unintentional pregnancies	Suicide in the young
Violence/homicide	Cirrhosis
Pregnancy complications	Musculoskeletal disorders
Congenital abnormalities	
Dental health	
Perinatal complications	
Chronic bronchitis	

Source: Egger 1992

A considerable amount of epidemiological information has emerged to support what general practitioners have known for a long time—that a common-sense healthy lifestyle not only promotes good health but reduces the risk of the main causes of mortality and morbidity in this country, including cardiovascular disease and cancer.

The common theme for virtually all disease is to follow the guidelines below.

Diet

- Keep to ideal weight.
- Take a high-fibre diet.
- Eat more fruits and vegetables, breads and cereals (preferably wholegrain).
- Eat fish at least twice a week.
- Eat less saturated fat, refined sugar and salt.
- Avoid 'fast foods' and deep-fried foods.
- Do not eat animal meat every day and then eat small portions.
- Always trim fat off meat.
- Use olive oil for cooking in preference to polyunsaturated oils.
- Drink more water.
- Limit caffeine intake: 0–3 drinks a day (maximum).
- Check plasma cholesterol and if elevated aim to reduce it with diet.

Lifestyle and mental health

- Do not smoke.
- Do not imbibe alcohol or, if one must, limit it to no more than two standard drinks a day—reserve alcohol for special occasions and to only one occasion in the day.
- Take regular exercise, e.g. 30 minutes per day for three days per week.
- Practise relaxation.
- Partake in ample recreational activities.
- Encourage a circle of friends who can offer emotional support.
- Give expression to feelings rather than suppressing them.
- Discuss problems regularly with someone with a listening ear.

Behaviour modification

Lifestyle habits which have developed over many years can be very difficult to change even when the individual is well motivated to change. There are a variety of instructional, motivational and behavioural techniques that can be used to initiate a lifestyle change program; GPs should be aware of these and use the resources of a multidisciplinary team to give support to motivated people who as a rule find behaviour modification difficult.

Vascular disease

Risk factors for vascular disease (atherosclerosis) are:

- hypertension
- smoking
- high cholesterol
- diabetes
- obesity
- sedentary lifestyle
- stress
- alcohol excess
- poor diet
- family history

The preceding guidelines for good health, if followed, will help prevent the development of cardiovascular and cerebrovascular disease.

It is worth noting that the death rate from coronary heart disease is about 70% higher for smokers than for non-smokers and for very heavy smokers the risk is almost 200% higher. It has been shown that the incidence of heart disease falls in those who have ceased smoking.

Malignant disease

Primary prevention of cancer is an important objective and there is a need to focus on this vital factor as much as on secondary prevention. The interesting statistics on the five year survival rate for specific cancers is shown in Table 8.3.

Table 8.3 *Cancer prognosis: 5 year survival (after Sali)*[8]

Cancer	*1960* %	*1985* %
Lung	10	10
Bowel	35	35
Breast	60	60
Pancreas	2	2
Stomach	10	10

That environmental factors are involved in the aetiology of colorectal cancer and other cancers is indicated by wide variations in incidence between different countries.

Suspicion falls on diet and there is epidemiological evidence implicating diets high in animal fats and low in fibre, fruits and vegetables; and also high alcohol consumption. It is noted that there are higher incidence rates in people migrating from low- to high-risk countries, e.g. Japanese to Hawaii[4] and Greeks and Italians to Australia.[5]

Studies in the United States indicate that at least 35% of all cancer deaths are related to diet. Obese individuals have increased risk of colon, breast and uterine cancers. High-fat diets are a risk factor for prostate, breast and colon cancers. Salt-cured, smoked and nitrate-cured foods increase the risk of upper GI cancers. Foods rich in vitamin A (dark green and deep yellow vegetables and fruits) and vitamin C and cruciferous vegetables (cabbage, brussels sprouts, broccoli and cauliflower) are all considered to have protective effects for various cancers.[6]

Overall, diet, smoking, alcohol and occupational exposures (5%) appear to account for over 73% of all cancer mortality.[6]

Doll and Peto[7] consider that environmental factors are responsible for 80–90% of cancers and estimate that diet is a major factor in the cause of cancer in 40% of men and 60% of women.

The role of immunity in cancer

The development of a number of cancers appears to be related to a depression of the individual's immune system, particularly in relation to cellular immunity, in a similar way albeit on a different scale to the effect of HIV infection. Studies have shown that the immune system is adversely influenced by:[8]

- stress, especially bereavement
- depression
- ageing
- drugs
- pollutants
- cigarette smoke
- inappropriate diet
- alcohol
- radiation

On the other hand, a protective effect on the immune system is provided by:

- food antioxidants (Table 8.4)
- tranquillity
- meditation

Table 8.4 *Food antioxidants (after Sali)*[8]

Vitamin A, esp. beta-carotene
Vitamin C
Vitamin E
Selenium
Zinc
Manganese
Copper

Of particular interest is the major role of micronutrients in immunity and their protective effect against cancer, especially of the gastrointestinal tract.[9,10]

Food antioxidants (Table 8.4) appear to protect against free radicals that can suppress immunity. Free radicals, which are usually a toxic form of oxygen containing an odd number of electrons, are produced by a variety of toxins as mentioned above.[8,9] Apart from the possible toxicity to immunity from free radicals, they may also damage body tissues such as the liver in alcoholics as well as increasing susceptibility to degenerative diseases.[11]

A medical practitioner is forced to re-evaluate fixed beliefs when confronted with first-hand anecdotal accounts of how macular degeneration of the retina was arrested and reversed by ophthalmologists using antioxidants such as

Vitamin C, Vitamin E and selenium, and how malignancies can go into unpredictable long remissions with patients following an optimal diet, taking antioxidants, changing their lifestyle and practising meditation. Diet certainly appears to be a most important factor in the primary prevention of disease.

If immune deficient diseases can respond in such a way, imagine what a powerful primary preventive force such a lifestyle represents for all disease.

Asthma and other respiratory diseases

The death rate and morbidity rate for asthma and other respiratory diseases is unacceptable and much of it can be prevented.[12] A recent report claims that at an estimated cost of $585 to $720 million per year the cost of asthma to the Australian community compares with the total cost of coronary artery disease ($623 million).[12] The report also claimed that there is evidence that a significant proportion of diagnosed asthmatics are currently receiving treatment which does not provide the best possible control of the disease.

Prevention means being better informed and treating such an 'irritable' disease as bronchial asthma aggressively. It means focusing on better assessment and monitoring (e.g. home use of the mini peak flow meter), better delivery of medication to the airways (e.g. use of spacers attached to inhalers and/or use of pumps and nebulisers) and appropriate management of the cause (inflammation of the bronchial tree) by the use of inhaled corticosteroids or sodium cromoglycate as first-line treatment for significant asthma. Following the six-step asthma management plan (Table 8.5) of the National Asthma Campaign would certainly promote prevention in this fickle disease.

Table 8.5 *The six-step asthma management plan (National Asthma Campaign: Australia)*

1. Establish the severity of the asthma
2. Achieve best lung function
3. Maintain best lung function—avoid trigger factors
4. Maintain best lung function—follow an optimal medication program
5. Develop an action plan
6. Educate and review regularly

Periodic health examination

Since 86% of the population visit a general practitioner at some stage of the year[3], and these people visit about five times each year (on average), GPs are in an ideal position to develop strategies for a periodic health examination. An emphasis should be placed on the history in addition to the physical examination and related basic investigations.

As for any smooth-running quality professional program, it is important to be organised with prepared practice staff, checklists and record systems. The Royal Australian College of General Practitioners has developed a College Record System, which has several leaflets covering all approaches to the patient 'check-up'.[13]

The following guidelines for the periodic health examination are adapted from those recommended by the Preventive and Community Medicine Committee of the RACGP.[13] This represents appropriate screening at the front line of primary health care.

Aims of screening

In practice, screening is not only to detect disease at its earliest stage, but also to find individuals at risk or those with established disease who are not receiving adequate care. There are three levels at which screening can be applied in general practice:

1. 'Well' individuals with risk factors which predispose to disease, e.g. obesity, uncomplicated essential hypertension, hyperlipidaemia.
2. Asymptomatic individuals with signs of early disease or illness, e.g. congenital dislocation of the hip, ectopic testis, glaucoma, bacteriuria of pregnancy, carcinoma *in situ* of cervix.
3. Symptomatic individuals whose irreversible abnormalities are unreported but the effects can be controlled or assisted, e.g. visual defects, deafness, mental handicap.

The history[13]

An appropriate history will allow the recognition of certain risk factors that may foreshadow future disease. Though established patients will have a previously acquired database, their history should be reviewed and updated. It is recommended that the following items be included in history taking in the appropriate age groups.

Family history In particular, cardiovascular disease, some cancers (breast, bowel, melanoma with dysplastic naevi), diabetes, asthma, genetic disorders, and bowel disease will alert the doctor to specific risk factors (and psychological factors) for these patients.

Suicide and accidents Consider the risk factors predisposing to suicide and accidents, which are the major preventable causes of death in children and young adults.

Substance abuse Tobacco and alcohol are the major causes of preventable death in adults, although other drugs contribute to a lesser extent. Counselling by general practitioners, about smoking in particular, has been shown to be effective.

Exercise and nutrition These factors have a role to play in preventing cardiovascular disease and to a lesser extent in blood pressure control, cancer, diabetes and constipation. They have an even greater role to play in improving general well-being and preventing morbidity.

Occupational health hazards Consider these in working adults, as occupational health hazards can significantly contribute to morbidity and mortality, e.g. exposure to toxic substances, unsafe work practices.

Physical functioning, home conditions and social supports Consider these in elderly people, as physical function and social supports are of crucial importance in determining whether they can care for themselves—intervention can prevent accidents and death.

Sexuality/contraception Sexually transmitted diseases are all preventable, as are unwanted pregnancies. Opportunities should be sought to ask young people, in particular, about their sexuality, and to counsel them. The question 'Do you have any concerns about sex?' is very useful in this context.

Osteoporosis Osteoporosis affects nearly a third of all postmenopausal women, most of whom suffer osteoporotic fractures. Fractures of the femoral neck have a particularly poor prognosis, with up to a third of these women dying within six months, and many more requiring continuing nursing home care. Bone loss accelerates at the time of the menopause, and can be reduced by hormone replacement therapy.

Women at risk of osteoporosis are: short, slim, Caucasian, drink coffee and alcohol, smoke, eat a high-protein and high-salt diet, and don't exercise.

Masquerades in general practice It is worth considering the 'masquerades' (Chapter 13, Tables 13.4 and 13.5), which may present as undifferentiated illness, as a means of following the important medical principle of early detection of disease: engendering a certain awareness.

Primary masquerades to consider are:

- depression
- diabetes mellitus
- drug problems
- anaemia
- thyroid disorders, especially hypothyroidism
- urinary tract infection
- vertebral (spinal) dysfunction

Hypothyroidism has been estimated to exist in up to 15% of women aged 60 and above, and searching for clues may elicit subtle symptoms and signs previously attributed to ageing.

Relationships and psychosocial health Consider the mental health of patients, particularly the elderly, by enquiring about how they are coping with life, how they are coping financially, about their peace of mind and how things are at home. Focus on the quality of their close relationships, e.g. husband–wife, father–son, mother–daughter, employer–employee. Enquire about losses in their life, especially family bereavements.

Examination screening specific to children[13]

Childhood health record books provide an excellent opportunity for communication between different health care givers; parents should be provided with the record books and encouraged to bring them to every visit. Various recommendations for screening are made under the following headings.

Height/weight/head circumference Record height from age 3 and weight at regular intervals to age 5 years. Record head circumference up to six months. The adequacy of a child's growth cannot be assessed on one measurement and serial recordings on growth charts are recommended. Head circumference recordings may provide further data about a child's growth.

Hips Screen for congenital dislocation at birth, 6–8 weeks, 6–9 months and 12–24 months.

The flexed hips are abducted, checking for movement and a 'clunk' of the femoral head forwards (the test is most likely to be positive at 3–6 weeks and usually negative after 8 weeks). Shortening or limited abduction is also abnormal. Ultrasound examination is more sensitive than the clinical examination especially up to 3 to 4 months. Observe gait when starting to walk.

Strabismus Strabismus should be sought in all infants and toddlers by occlusion testing (not very sensitive), examining light reflexes and questioning parents, which must be taken very seriously. Amblyopia can be prevented by early recognition and treatment of strabismus by occlusion and surgery. Early referral is essential.

Visual acuity At birth and 2 months, eyes should be inspected and examined with an ophthalmoscope with a 3+ lens at a distance of 20–30 cm to detect cataracts and red reflexes. At 9 months gross vision should be determined by assessing ability to see common objects. Visual acuity should be formally assessed at school entry using Sheridan Gardiner charts.

Hearing Hearing should be tested by distraction at 9 months; also by pure tone audiometry at 1000 and 4000 Hertz when child is 4 years (pre-school entry) and 12 years.

Note: Formal audiological evaluation should be carried out at any time if there is clinical suspicion or parental concern. No simple screening test is very reliable for sensorineural or conductive deafness.

Testes Screen at birth, and 6–8 weeks, 6–9 months and 3–5 years for absence or maldescent. Those who have been treated for maldescent have a higher risk of neoplastic development in adolescence.

Dental assessment/fluoride Advise daily fluoride drops or tablets, if water supply is not fluoridated. Children's teeth should be checked regularly, particularly if a school dental service is not available. Advice should be given on sugar consumption, especially night-time bottles, and tooth cleaning to prevent plaque.

Scoliosis Screening of females by the forward flexion test, which is carried out around 12 years of age, is of questionable value because of poor sensitivity and specificity.

Femoral pulses Testing for absence of femoral pulses or delay between brachial/femoral pulses at birth and 8 weeks will exclude coarctation of the aorta. Refer the child immediately if concerned.

Speech and language A child's speech should be intelligible to strangers by three years.

Screening for adults[13]

The following recommendations apply for adults.

Weight Weight should be recorded at least every few years. Obesity is a major reversible health risk for adults contributing to many diseases, e.g. heart disease, diabetes, arthritis. Body Mass Index (BMI) should be between 20 and 25.

$$\text{BMI} = \frac{\text{Wt(kg)}}{\text{Ht(m)}^2}$$

Blood pressure Blood pressure should be recorded at least every 2 years on all adults aged under 50, and annually thereafter. There is no dispute that control of blood pressure results in reduced mortality from cerebrovascular accidents and, to a lesser extent, heart disease, renal failure and retinopathy.

Cholesterol All adults aged 18 and over should have a five yearly estimation of serum cholesterol. Total cholesterol is adequate for screening purposes. HDL levels give additional information. The National Heart Foundation recommends keeping cholesterol levels below 5.5 mmol/L. For most, dietary modification is sufficient to achieve these levels; some may require drug treatment.

Carcinoma of the cervix Women aged 18–70 who have ever been sexually active should have a Pap smear every two years. Those over 70 who have never been screened should have two or three successive tests before screening is ceased. After consideration of the relative risks to the individual woman, she and her physician may choose to increase the interval between smears, but not greater than three years.

Risk factors include:

- all women who are or ever have been sexually active
- early age at first sexual intercourse
- multiple sexual partners
- genital wart virus infection
- cigarette smoking

Carcinoma of the breast Mammography should be performed at least every two years on women aged 50–70 years. It is not useful for screening prior to age 40 years due to difficulty in discriminating malignant lesions from dense tissue. Mammography must not be used alone to exclude cancer if a lump is palpable. Such lesions require a complete appraisal since, even in the best hands, mammography still has a false negative rate of at least 10%.

Colorectal cancer A history should be taken, with specific enquiry as to family history of adenomas or colorectal cancer, past history of inflammatory bowel disease, rectal bleeding. Rectal examination should be performed as part of an examination. Faecal occult blood screening is not recommended for screening nor for investigation of rectal bleeding.

Should a positive history be elicited, then the following are recommended:

- past history or large bowel cancer or colonic adenomas—colonoscopy
- past or present history of ulcerative colitis—sigmoidoscopy and rectal biopsy, colonoscopy
- familial polyposis, Gardner's syndrome—prophylactic colectomy.

It is unfortunate that faecal occult blood testing cannot be recommended as a screening test in the standard-risk, asymptomatic individual. False positive rate can be up to 50%, and a false negative rate of up to 30% is reported.

Skin cancer All patients should be informed regularly about the need for protection of the skin from solar radiation, using clothing and sunscreens, and avoiding exposure during midday hours.

Skin cancer, which is increasing in incidence, is common in Australia, particularly in more northern areas. Squamous cell carcinoma, and melanoma in particular, may be lethal. Detection and treatment of early lesions prevents mortality and morbidity. Prevention of skin cancer by reduction of sun exposure should be taught to all patients.

Oral hygiene/cancer Patients should be counselled about cessation of smoking and alcohol consumption, and dental hygiene should be taught. The oral cavity should be inspected annually in patients over the age of 40.

Although oral cancer has a relatively low incidence, premalignant lesions may be detected by inspection of the oral cavity. Its incidence is highest in elderly people with a history of heavy smoking or drinking. Poor dental hygiene may result in poor nutrition, particularly among the elderly.

Immunisation

Basic diseases (diphtheria, tetanus, polio, whooping cough, measles, mumps, rubella) should be covered. Children should be immunised according to the NH&MRC recommendation.

Age of child	*Immunisation*
2 months	Triple antigen and Sabin vaccine
4 months	Triple antigen and Sabin vaccine
6 months	Triple antigen and Sabin vaccine
2 months or later	Haemophilus influenza b (varies by vaccine)
12 months	Measles/mumps/rubella
18 months	Triple antigen
5 years	Combined diphtheria/tetanus vaccine (CDT) and Sabin vaccine
12 years	Measles/mumps/rubella
15 years	Adult diphtheria/tetanus vaccine (ADT) and Sabin vaccine

All adults should receive an Adult Diphtheria & Tetanus (ADT) booster *each* 10 years.

All women of child-bearing years should have their rubella antibody status reviewed.

The general immunisation summary is presented in Table 8.6.

Paracetamol prophylaxis: Consider giving paracetamol to children at the time of immunisation and then a further dose in four hours, to reduce the side effects of the vaccines.

Influenza Influenza immunisation is recommended on an annual basis for persons of all ages with chronic debilitating diseases, especially chronic cardiac, pulmonary, renal and metabolic diseases, persons over 65 years of age and persons receiving immnosuppressant therapy. Health care personnel may wish to consider it for their own use.

Hepatitis B Immunisation is recommended for all ages of individuals who, through work or lifestyle, may be exposed to hepatitis B and have been shown to be susceptible. Such groups would include health care personnel, personnel and residents of institutions, prisoners and prison staff, persons with frequent and/or close contact with high-risk groups, persons at increased risk due to their sexual practices. Household contacts of any of the above groups should be considered for immunisation. Booster doses may be appropriate. This is currently under consideration.

Table 8.6 *Childhood immunisation summary (as recommended by the NH&MRC)*

Initial courses			
Diphtheria, tetanus and pertussis	Intramuscular	Triple antigen	2, 4, 6, 18 months
Poliomyelitis	Oral	Sabin	2, 4, 6 months
Measles, mumps and rubella	Subcutaneous	MMR	12 months
Haemophilus Influenzae b	Intramuscular	various	varies by vaccine: from 2 months or at 18 months; usually 2, 4, 2–15 months
Hepatitis B (for those at risk)	Intramuscular	HBsAg subunit	0, 1, 6 months
Booster doses			
Diphtheria and tetanus	Intramuscular	Combined diph/tetanus (CDT)	5 years or prior to school entry
Poliomyelitis	Oral	Sabin	5 years
Measles, mumps and rubella	Subcutaneous	MMR	12 years
Hepatitis B	Intramuscular	HBsAg subunit	consider at 3–5 years after initial course
Diphtheria and tetanus	Intramuscular	Adult diph/tetanus (ADT)	15 years or prior to school leaving

Haemophilus influenza type b Hib immunisation is recommended for all children, especially those in child care. It is ideal to achieve immunity by the age of 18 months and preferably commencing at 2 months. Risk factors for Hib disease include day care attendance, presence of ill siblings under 6 years of age in the home, household crowding.

Q fever People at reasonable risk from Q fever, particularly abattoir workers, should be given this vaccine which is virtually 100% effective.

Measles–mumps–rubella Both females and males should be immunised against measles, mumps and rubella at age 12 months using the trivalent vaccine. All should also be re-immunised during the years between age 10 and 16.

All women of child-bearing years should have their rubella antibody status reviewed, preferably prior to consideration of pregnancy.

Measles vaccine should be given to non-immune children as young as 5 months during an epidemic, and repeated at the usual time to ensure high serological response.

References

1. Piterman L, Sommer SJ. *Preventive care.* Monash University, Department of Community Medicine. Final year handbook, 1993, 75–85.
2. Silagy C. Prevention in general practice. In: McNeil J et al, eds. *A textbook of preventive medicine*, Melbourne: Edward Arnold, 1990, 269–277.
3. National Health Strategy. *The future of general practice.* Issues paper No. 3 (1992), AGPS Canberra: 54–169.
4. Locke FB, King H. Cancer Mortality Risk among Japanese in the United States. Journal of the National Cancer Institute, 1980; 65:1149.
5. Potter JD, McMichael AJ. Diet and cancer of the colon and rectum: A case control study. Journal of the National Cancer Institute, 1986; 76:557–69.
6. Rakel RE. *Essentials of family practice.* Philadelphia: Saunders, 1993, 126–127.
7. Doll R, Peto R. *The causes of cancer.* New York: Oxford University Press, 1981, 1197–1219.
8. Sali A. Strategies for cancer prevention. Aust Fam Physician, 1987; 16:1603–1613.
9. Beisel WR. Single nutrients and immunity. Am J Clin Nutrition, 1982; 35(supp):147–148.
10. Meyskens FZ, Prasad KN. *Vitamins and cancer: Human cancer prevention by vitamins and micronutrients.* Clifton: Humana Press, 1986:3–478.
11. Dormandy TL. An approach to free radicals. Lancet 1983; 2:1010–1014.
12. Antic R. *Report on the cost of asthma in Australia.* Melbourne: National Asthma Campaign, 1992,14–33.
13. Royal Australian College of General Practitioners. *Guidelines for preventive activities in general practice.* (2nd edition), 1993.

9

Health promotion and patient education

Health promotion[1]

Health promotion is the motivation and encouragement of individuals and the community to see good health as a desirable state which should be maintained by the adoption of healthy practices. It is also the process of helping people obtain their optimal health.

For those who feel healthy, the message may have little meaning, but it is reinforced by contact with others who become ill, particularly within the family.

Health education

Health education is the provision of information about how to maintain or attain good health.

There are many methods including the advertising of health practices; the provision of written information, e.g. about diet and exercise, immunisation, accident prevention and the symptoms of disease; and methods to avoid disease, e.g. sexually transmitted disease.

Illness education

A great deal of so-called 'health' education is in reality information about the cause of particular illnesses. Clearly the medical practitioner is in a pre-eminent position to provide his or her patients with specific information about the cause of an illness at the time either individually or to the family. This educative strategy has a preventive objective which is often the modification of help-seeking behaviour.

Every consultation is an opportunity to provide information about the condition under care and this can be reinforced in written, diagrammatic or printed form. Patients' own X-rays can be similarly used to illustrate the nature of the problem.

Health promotion in general practice

General practitioners are ideally placed to undertake health promotion and prevention, mainly due to opportunity.

There are several reasons for this health promotion role:

- Population access: over 80% of the population visit a GP at least once a year.[2]
- On average people visit a GP about 5 times each year.
- GPs have a knowledge of the patient's personal and family health history.
- The GP can act as leader or co-ordinator of preventive health services in his or her local area.
- The GP can participate in community education programs.
- GPs should undertake opportunistic health promotion—the ordinary consultation can be

used not just to treat the presenting problem, but also to manage ongoing problems, co-ordinate care with other health professionals, check whether health services are being used appropriately and undertake preventive health activities.[2]

Opportunistic health promotion

The classic model by Stott and Davis (Table 9.1) highlights the opportunities for health promotion in each consultation.[3] Since the consultation is patient-initiated, it is the doctor who needs to be the initiator of preventive health care. The potential in the consultation involves reactive and proactive behaviour by the doctor (Fig. 9.1).[4]

Table 9.1 *The potential in each primary care consultation: an aide memoire—by Stott and Davis*

A Management of presenting problems	*B* Modification of help-seeking behaviour
C Management of continuing problems	*D* Opportunistic health promotion

Reactive professional behaviour deals only with the presenting complaint. It may be performed with skill but if the practitioner is only trained to perform reactively then the opportunity for preventive and promotive health care will be lost.

Proactive behaviour is defined as professional behaviour that is necessary for the patient's well-being, but performed not merely as a response to the presenting problem, and it is initiated by the doctor.[4] It includes health promotion, preventive care and screening and the early detection of disease before it becomes symptomatic. Other aspects of proactive care are seen in Figure 9.1.

Proactive behaviour also includes:[4]

- Continuing care of a previously treated problem, e.g. rechecking blood pressure, checking diabetic control, follow-up bereavement counselling.
- Co-ordination of care by organising referral to appropriate agencies or specialists and maintaining adequate medical records.
- The modification of abnormal or inappropriate help-seeking behaviour: e.g. the person who never attends is at risk from 'silent disease'; the too frequent attender wastes

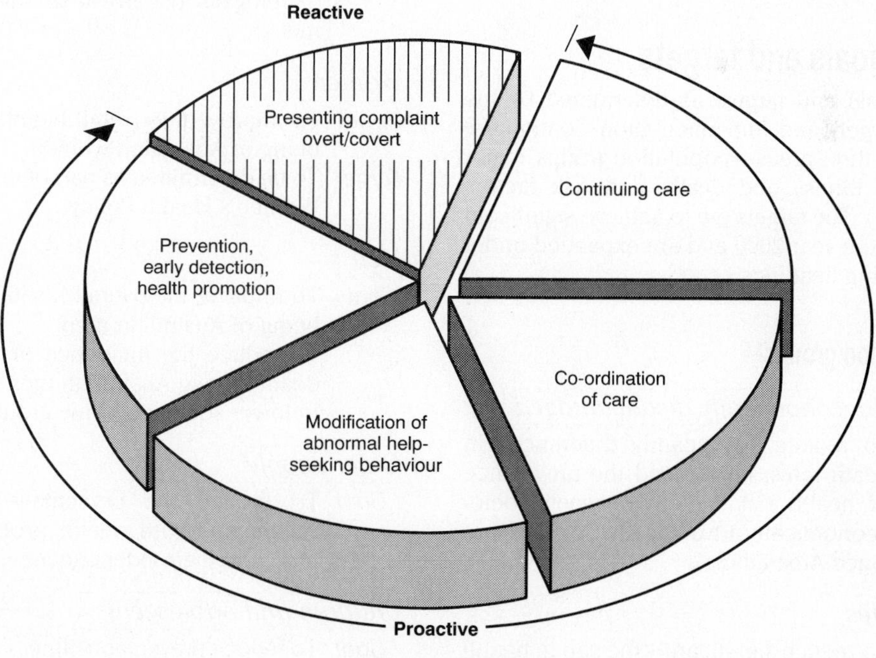

Fig. 9.1 *The potential in every general practice consultation* REPRODUCED WITH PERMISSION FROM M.SALES

resources and serious illness may be overlooked.

This mix of reactive and proactive behaviour is not appropriate in every consultation. It requires counselling skills and training in the delivery of quality general practice.

Methods

- Being informed and updated by maintaining continuing medical education, especially in preventive roles.
- Using health promotional material for patient education:
  - handouts
  - waiting room posters
  - waiting room video systems
- Having an efficient medical record system.
- Operating a patient register and recall system.
- Encouraging regular health checks for at-risk groups.
- Providing regular advice on:
  - nutrition
  - exercise
  - stress management
  - weight control
- Providing personal health records to the parents of newborn babies.

Health goals and targets

Health goals and targets as determined by the Health Targets and Implementation Committee[5] were set in three areas—population groups, major causes of illness and death, and risk factors (Table 9.2). The targets are to achieve significant results by the year 2000 and are expanded under the following headings.

Table 9.2 *Health promotion areas in which goals and targets have been set*

Population groups
The socioeconomically disadvantaged, Aborigines, migrants, women, men, older people, children and adolescents.

Major causes of illness and death
Heart disease and stroke, cancers (including lung, breast, cervical and skin cancer), injury, communicable diseases, musculoskeletal disease, diabetes, disability, dental disease, mental illness, asthma.

Risk factors
Drugs (including tobacco smoking, alcohol misuse, pharmaceutical misuse or abuse, illicit drugs and substance abuse), nutrition, physical inactivity, high blood pressure, high blood cholesterol, occupational health hazards, unprotected sexual activity, environmental health hazards.

Source: HTIC 1988[5]

1. Population groups[2,5]

The socioeconomically disadvantaged

Goal To reduce significantly differences in death rates, illness and the prevalence of health risk factors between socio-economically advantaged and disadvantaged Australians.

Aborigines

Goal To reduce significantly the gap in health status between Aborigines and the rest of the Australian population.

Migrants

Goals To ensure that the health advantage of migrants on arrival in Australia is not eroded by the adoption of less healthy lifestyles or environments.
To ensure that the special health needs of refugees on arrival in Australia are met.

Women

Goal To improve the overall health and well-being of Australian women.

Target To be determined as part of the National Women's Health Policy.

Men

Goals To improve the overall health and well-being of Australian men.
To reduce the incidence of premature death among Australian men especially in lower socioeconomic groups.

Older people

Goal To reduce the percentage of older Australians with health problems that preclude their independence.

Children and adolescents

Goal To reduce preventable illness, injury and death among Australian children and adolescents.

2. Major causes of sickness and death

Heart disease and stroke

Goal To reduce avoidable illness and premature death from heart disease and stroke.

Targets By the year 2000 to achieve a significant reduction in:
- the death rate from heart disease
- the death rate from stroke
- the prevalence of smokers (15% or less)
- the proportion of adults who persistently have a diastolic blood pressure of greater than 90 millimetres of mercury
- the prevalence of plasma cholesterol levels of 6.5 millimoles per litre or more in people aged 25–64 years
- the mean fasting plasma cholesterol level from 5.6 millimoles per litre to 4.8 millimoles per litre or less in people aged 25-64 years
- the prevalence of overweight and obesity in people aged 25–64 years
- the contribution of fat to dietary energy
- dietary sodium intake to 100 millimoles (2.3 grams) or less per day.

To increase participation in sufficient activity to achieve and maintain physical fitness and health.

Lung cancer

Goal To reduce the incidence of death from lung cancer.

Breast cancer

Goal To reduce illness and death from breast cancer.

Target To increase participation in breast cancer screening to 70% or more of eligible women by the year 1995.

Cervical cancer

Goal To reduce the incidence of death from cervical cancer.

Targets To increase triennial participation in Pap smear screening of women aged 18–69 years.

To establish organised population-based cervical neoplasia screening programs in each state and territory.

Skin cancer

Goals To reduce illness and death from melanoma and other skin cancers through early detection.

To reduce the incidence of all forms of skin cancer through protection against ultraviolet exposure.

Targets To reduce exposure to ultraviolet radiation.

To reduce exposure to ultraviolet radiation for people at high risk of skin cancer.

Injury

Goal To reduce preventable death and disability from injury and poisoning.

Targets To reduce:
- the death rate from drowning to 2 per 100 000 per annum or less in children aged 1–4 years.
- fractures related to playground equipment
- the incidence of poisoning severe enough to require hospitalisation
- the incidence of burns and scalds severe enough to require hospitalisation
- the incidence of injury severe enough to require medical attention
- death and injury due to motor vehicle accidents in children aged 0–4 years
- the incidence of motor vehicle injury, including 'whiplash', due to rear-end collisions involving passenger cars
- illness and death due to alcohol-related motor vehicle accidents.

Communicable diseases

Goals To reduce the incidence of death and disability caused by communicable diseases for which immunisation is available.

To eradicate measles, hepatitis B, and rubella embryopathy.

To minimise illness due to communicable diseases not preventable through immunisation by promoting accurate diagnosis and effective infection control procedures.

Targets To ensure that evidence of a completed immunisation schedule is used as a condition of primary school enrolment,

with exemptions being granted for defined medical, personal or religious reasons.
To eradicate indigenous measles.
To ensure use of a combined measles/mumps/rubella (MMR) vaccine in all immunisation programs for children.
To increase immunity against rubella to 90% or more of women aged 15 to 34 years.
To increase participation in screening for hepatitis B surface antigen just before childbirth, of individuals at a high risk of being infected.
To ensure that hepatitis B immunoglobulin and a complete course of vaccination is given to all newborn infants of women identified as carriers.
To increase vaccination against hepatitis B of newborn infants in populations which have 10% or more of their individuals identified as carriers.
To ensure that a contingency plan for the control of epidemics of Australian encephalitis and other mosquito-transmitted diseases is developed.
To ensure that maps of the mosquito breeding sites associated with the spread of viral diseases are prepared.
To ensure that knowledge of the avoidance of sexually transmitted diseases is gained by adolescents aged 15 years.

Musculoskeletal diseases

Goal To reduce the prevalence of musculoskeletal diseases.

Diabetes

Goal To reduce preventable illness, handicap and premature death due to diabetes.

Targets To establish a national database to record the incidence of diabetes and its complications.
To slow down the increase in the prevalence of diabetes in Australia.

Disability

Goal To reduce the proportion of handicapped people having insufficient social, emotional and physical support to maintain independence.

Dental disease

Goals To reduce the incidence of dental disease.
To reduce inequalities in dental health status.

Mental illness

Goal To reduce the levels of psychiatric illness and psychosocial problems.

Asthma

Goal To reduce illness and death from asthma.

3. Risk factors

Drugs

Goal To minimise the harmful effects of drugs.

Tobacco smoking

Goals To prevent the onset of smoking in non-smokers, especially children.
To reduce the number of smokers.
To reduce the exposure of smokers to tobacco-derived carcinogens.
To reduce involuntary exposure to tobacco smoke.

Targets To reduce the prevalence of smokers to 15% or less.
To reduce the difference in the prevalence of smokers between upper white and lower blue collar men.
To reduce the prevalence of regular smokers in adolescents aged 15 years.
To introduce regulations to prohibit the sale of tobacco products to minors in all states and territories.
To introduce legislation or regulations to prohibit smoking on government controlled or regulated public transport and associated buildings in all states and territories.
To ensure that all government buildings are smoke-free.
To ensure that all enclosed public spaces are smoke-free.

Alcohol misuse

Goals To reduce the incidence and prevalence of alcohol dependence and other alcohol-related problems.
To reduce consumption of alcohol per capita.

Pharmaceutical misuse or abuse

Goals To reduce the incidence of misuse of pharmaceuticals.
To ensure appropriate use of pharmaceutical drugs.

Targets To develop a comprehensive medicinal drug policy pursuant to the recommendations of the World Health Organisation Conference of Experts on the Rational Use of Drugs.

Illicit drugs and substance abuse

Goal To reduce the use of illicit drugs and substance abuse.

Nutrition

Goal To reduce the incidence and prevalence of diet-related health disorders.

Targets To reduce the prevalence of overweight and obesity in people aged 25–64 years.
To reduce the contribution of fat to dietary energy.
To reduce the contribution of refined sugars to dietary energy.
To reduce dietary sodium intake to 100 millimoles (2.3 grams) per day or less.
To reduce the contribution of alcoholic beverages to dietary energy.
To increase dietary fibre intake to 30 grams per day or more.
To increase the level of breast-feeding at 3 months of life.

Physical inactivity

Goal To increase participation by adults in sufficient activity to achieve and maintain physical fitness and health.

Target: To increase participation in sufficient activity to achieve and maintain physical fitness and health.

High blood pressure

Goal To reduce the incidence and prevalence of high blood pressure.

Targets To reduce the proportion of adults who persistently have a diastolic blood pressure greater than 90 millimetres of mercury.
To increase the proportion of adults who have had their blood pressure accurately measured within the last two years.

High blood cholesterol

Goal To reduce the incidence and prevalence of high blood cholesterol levels.

Targets These targets are based on the work of the Better Health Commission Cardiovascular Taskforce (see under 'Heart disease and stroke').

Occupational health hazards

Goals To reduce the incidence of occupational illness, injury and death.
To provide all workers with a safe and healthy working environment.

Unprotected sexual activity

Goal To reduce the number of unwanted pregnancies among teenagers.

Targets: To reduce both the birth rate and total pregnancy rate for females aged 15 years or less.

Environmental health hazards

Goal To increase protection against and reduce exposure to environmental hazards posing a threat to health.

Targets To ensure an adequate supply of good quality drinking water to the whole population.
To reduce the number of deaths and injuries caused by the use of hazardous chemicals in the home.
To safely dispose of the intractable chemical wastes at present stored in Australia.

Psychosocial health promotion

The preceding health goals and targets focus mainly on physical illness and do not emphasise mental health. However, this area represents an enormous opportunity for anticipatory guidance. It includes the important problems of stress and anxiety, chronic pain, depression, crisis and bereavement, sexual problems, adolescent problems, child behavioural problems, psychotic disorders and several other psychosocial problems.

Time spent in counselling, giving advice, stressing ways of coping with potential problems such as suicide and deterioration in relationships is rewarding. GPs need to pay more attention to promoting health in this area, which at times can be quite complex.

Patient education

Evidence has shown that intervention by general practitioners can have a significant effect on patients' attitudes to a change to a healthier lifestyle. If we are to make an impact on improving the health of the community, we must encourage our patients to take responsibility for their own health and thus change to a healthier lifestyle. They must be supported however by a caring doctor who follows the same guidelines and maintains a continuing interest. Examples include modifying diet, cessation of smoking, reduction of alcohol intake and undertaking exercise.

In an American survey of 360 patients, 90% reported wanting a pamphlet at some or all of their office visits. Overall, 67% reported reading or looking through and saving pamphlets received, 30% read or looked through them and then threw them away, and only 2% threw them away without review. Only 11% of males and 26% of females reported ever asking a doctor for pamphlets. More patients desire pamphlets than are receiving them.[6]

Patient educational materials have been shown to have a beneficial effect. Giving patients a handout about tetanus increased the rate of immunisation against tetanus among adults threefold.[7] An educational booklet on back pain for patients reduced the number of consultations made by patients over the following year and 84% said that they found it useful.[8] The provision of systematic patient education on cough significantly changed the behaviour of patients to follow practice guidelines and did not result in patients delaying consultation when they had a cough lasting longer than three weeks or one with 'serious' symptoms.[9]

There is no evidence that patient education has a harmful effect. Patient education about drug side effects has been shown not to have any detectable adverse effects.[10]

One form of patient education is giving handouts (either prepared or printed from a computer at the time of the consultation) to the patient as an adjunct to the verbal explanation which, it must be emphasised, is more important than the printed handout.

The patient education leaflets should be in non-technical language and focus on the key points of the illness or problem. The objectives are to improve the quality of care, reduce costs and encourage a greater input by patients in the management of their own illness. In modern society where informed consent and better education about health and disease is expected, this information is very helpful from a medicolegal viewpoint.

The author has produced a book called *Patient Education* which has a one-page summary of each of 154 common medical conditions.[11] The concept is to photocopy the relevant problem or preventive advice and hand it to the patient or relative. Over the years the greatest demand (following a survey of requests for prints of the sheets) has been for the following (in order):

- exercises for your back (Fig. 9.2)
- backache (Fig. 9.3)
- exercises for your neck
- your painful neck
- exercises for your knee
- breast-feeding and milk supply
- how to lower cholesterol
- breast self-examination
- testicular self-examination
- vaginal thrush
- menopause
- anxiety
- coping with stress
- depression
- bereavement

Summary

Recommended target areas for health promotion in general practice include:

- nutrition
- weight control
- substance abuse and control
  - — smoking
  - — alcohol
  - — other drugs
- exercise practices
- appropriate sleep, rest and recreation
- safe sexual practices
- promotion of self-esteem and personal growth
- stress management

Important health promotion recommendations are to encourage patients:[12]

- to cease smoking
- to reduce alcohol intake to safe levels
  - — women no more than two standard drinks per day
  - — men no more than three standard drinks per day
  - — three alcohol-free days per week

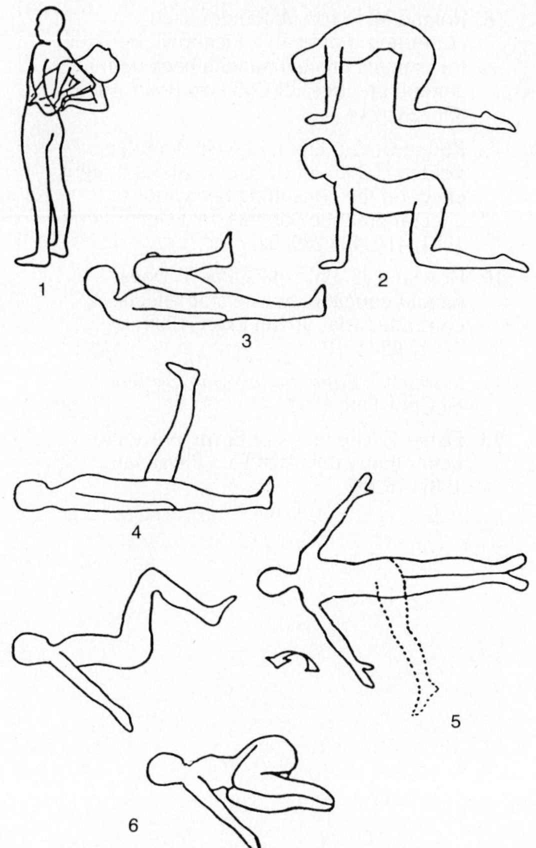

Fig. 9.2 *Patient education leaflet: exercises for your lower back*

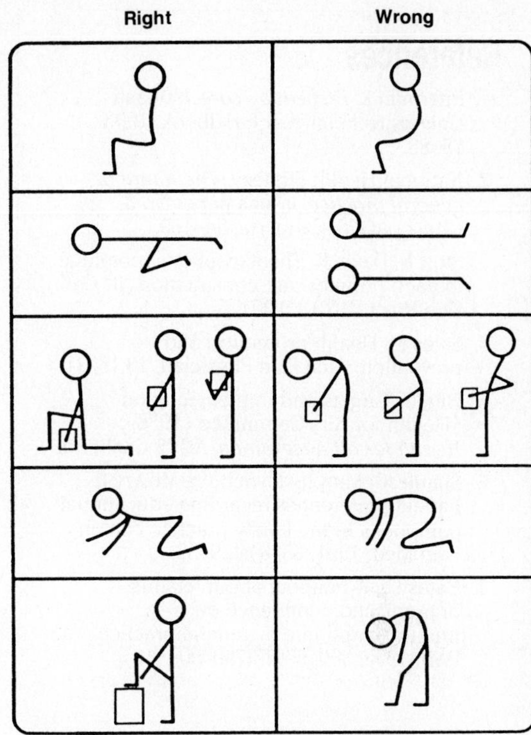

Fig. 9.3 *Patient education leaflet on backache: rules of care for sitting, lying, lifting and bending*

- to limit caffeine intake to three drinks per day
- to increase regular physical activity
  — 30 minutes per day for three days per week, sufficient to produce a sweat
- to reduce fasting plasma cholesterol to 4.8 mmol per litre
- to have a diastolic BP of less than 90mm of mercury
- to have a body mass index of between 20 and 25

$$\text{BMI} = \frac{(\text{weight in kg})}{(\text{height in metres})^2}$$

- to reduce fat, refined sugar and salt intake in all food
- to increase dietary fibre to 30 grams per day
- to build up their circle of friends who offer emotional support
- to express their feelings rather than suppress them
- to discuss their problems regularly with some other person
- to work continuously to improve their relationships with people
- not to drive a car when angry, upset or after drinking
- to have a two yearly Pap smear
- to avoid casual sex
- to practise safe sex
- to have an HIV antibody check before entering a relationship.

References

1. Piterman L. *Preventive care*. Monash University: Final year handbook, 1993, 75–85.
2. National Health Strategy. *The future of general practice*. Issues paper No 3. (1992) AGPS, Canberra, 54–169.
3. Stott N, Davis R. The exceptional potential in each primary care consultation. JR Coll Gen Pract, 1979; 29:201–5.
4. Sales M. Health promotion and prevention. Aust Fam Physician, 18:18–21.
5. Health Targets and Implementation (Health for All) Committee (1988), *Health for all Australians*. AGPS Canberra.
6. Shank JC, Murphy M, Schulte-Mowry L. Patient preferences regarding educational pamphlets in the family practice center. Fam Med, 1991; 23(6):429–32.
7. Cates CJ. A handout about tetanus immunisation: influence on immunisation rate in general practice. BMJ, 1990; 300(6727):789–90.
8. Roland M, Dixon M. Randomised controlled trial of an educational booklet for patients presenting with back pain in general practice. JR Coll Gen Pract, 1989; 39(323):244–6.
9. Rutten G, Van Eijk J, Beek M, Van der Velden H. Patient education about cough: effect on the consulting behaviour of general practice patients. Br J Gen Pract, 1991, 41(348):289–92.
10. Howland JS, Baker MG, Poe T. Does patient education cause side effects? A controlled trial. J Fam Pract, 1990; 31(1):62–4.
11. Murtagh J. *Patient education*, Sydney: McGraw-Hill, 1992.
12. Fisher E. The botch of Egypt: prevention better than cure. Aust Fam Physician, 1987; 16:187.

10

Whole person approach to management

The management of the whole person, or the holistic approach, is an important approach to patient care in modern medicine. Whole person diagnosis is based on two components:[1]

1. the disease-centred diagnosis
2. the patient-centred diagnosis

The disease-centred consultation is the traditional medical model based on the history, examination and special investigations, with the emphasis being on making a diagnosis and treating the disease. The disease-centred diagnosis, which is typical of hospital-based medicine, is defined in terms of pathology and does not focus significantly on the feelings of the person suffering from the disease.

The patient-centred consultation not only takes into account the diagnosed disease and its management but adds another dimension—that of the psychosocial hallmarks of the patient (Table 10.1) including details about:[1]

- the patient as a person
- emotional reactions to the illness
- the family
- the effect on relationships
- work and leisure
- lifestyle
- the environment

Dimensions to whole person management

In the diagnostic model presented in Chapter 13 the fifth and final question is: 'What is the patient trying to tell me?' and this self-posed question should be scrutinised and answered in most instances. This presupposes being tuned in to the patient, watching for cues and listening.

An efficient medical record system also helps the process, since following a set routine generally ensures that important facets of the patient's psychosocial history are not omitted.

The answer to the above question takes into account the patient's:

- feelings
- fears or concerns
- expectations of the doctor
- future aspirations

Such an approach may determine whether there is a 'hidden agenda' in the presentation and whether various stressors including interpersonal conflicts are significant factors in the illness.

Illustrative case history

The patient: John R, aged 47, bus driver
Disease-centred problem: low back pain for 5 months, after sudden onset of left sciatica (now settled) and low back pain (see Fig. 10.1).

Back pain analysis

History of injury:	Yes—lifting a large suitcase out of the bus.
Site and radiation:	Low lumbar—central and unilateral (left), left buttock.

Table 10.1 *Whole person diagnosis and management*

WHOLE PERSON DIAGNOSIS AND MANAGEMENT

Disease-centred diagnosis

- aetiology of disease

Patient-centred diagnosis

- significance of illness to patient
- effect on family and relationships
- efffect on work and income
- psychological effects
  - stress and anxiety
  - abnormal illness/behaviour
  - sleep
  - depression
- effect on sexuality
- effect on attitudes and spirituality

Disease-centred management

- rest
- drugs
- intervention
- surgery
- other invasive techniques

Patient-centred management

- psychological support
- appropriate reassurance
- patient education
- empowering self-responsibility
- anticipatory guidance/special hazards
- prevention
- health promotion
- lifestyle recommendations/modifications
  - diet/nutrition
  - exercise
  - alcohol
  - smoking
  - stress management
- family and social supports
- self-help groups
- alternative options
- consultation and referral
- follow-up

Type of pain: Dull ache (severe at times). Has changed from a throbbing burning pain to a deep ache.

Onset: Present after sitting for long periods and provoked by various activities such as gardening and lifting.

Offset: Fluctuates throughout day—better with restricted activity.

Aggravation: Sitting, car travel, coughing and sneezing, soft beds, sex and more strenuous activity.

Relief: Walking, gentle activity, swimming, massage.

Associations: Stiffness in the back, headache, tiredness, insomnia.

Current management of the problem: Visited another doctor at first, then an allied health professional; referred to a consultant who diagnosed a disc prolapse and considered surgical removal of the disc was the only appropriate treatment. Patient has 'played a waiting game' and is taking analgesics only.

Past history: Haemorrhoidectomy, mild episodes of back pain, appendicectomy.

Family history: Non insulin dependent diabetes, coronary artery disease.

Drug history: Piroxicam 20 mg daily (prescribed by consultant); OTC analgesics; allergic to penicillin and indomethacin; alcohol—average 4 standard drinks a day; smoking—20 cigarettes a day.

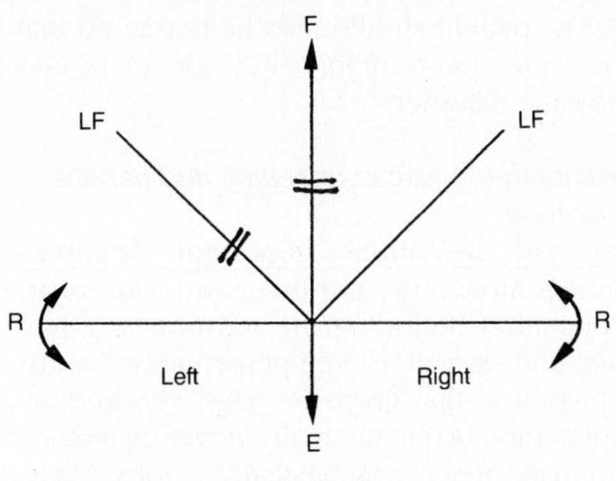

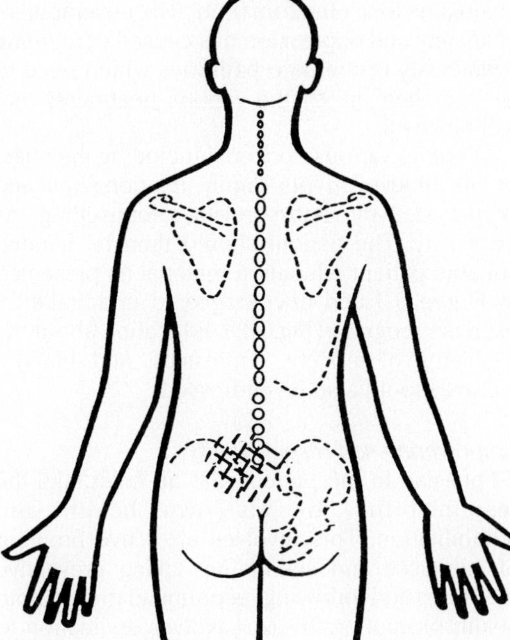

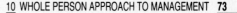

Fig. 10.1 *Mr JR: site of low back pain and illustration of painful limitation of movement on direction of movement diagram*

Physical examination

General: Overweight middle-aged man with stiff gait.

Examination of lumbar spine

Inspection: Gait and movement—stiff, cautious.
Posture: normal, no muscle spasm.

Palpation: Tender over spinous process L4, over the L4–L5 interspinous space, and unilaterally to left between L4 and L5.

Movement: Restricted left lateral flexion and forward flexion (Fig. 10.1).

General: Lower limbs normal.
No neurological abnormalities.
Urine analysis: NAD

Investigations

(Past) plain X-ray—slight narrowing L4–L5 disc, minimal degenerative changes in facet joints.

CT scan: mild spondylosis (facet joints) and L4–L5 disc degeneration: nerve roots unaffected.

Disease-centred diagnosis: L4–L5 disc degeneration

Disease-centred management:

- back brace
- piroxicam 20 mg daily
- codeine and paracetamol compound tablets prn

Patient-centred problems

A more detailed history about the effect of the back disorder on the patient revealed the following:

- humiliation about being on worker's compensation
- boredom and frustration leading to irritable behaviour ('not like me')
- anxious about his future, particularly occupation
- fears of being a cripple 'in a wheelchair'
- conflicts with family members
- concern about reduction of sexual performance
- anger with lack of response from medical management
- anger with lack of interest in his problem
- concerns about something more serious (he admitted to a fear of cancer)
- feels depressed: unable to cope, sleep disturbance
- concerned about taking drugs, especially NSAIDs

Patient-centred physical examination (additional)

General: tense and anxious man looking older than his years, senile arcus.

Cardiovascular examination: blood pressure 165/100.

Weight: 85 kg Height: 1.67 metres Body mass index: 30.5

Problem list

- chronic back pain
- hypertension
- obesity
- anxiety
- depression
- concerns about
  - serious disease
  - future employment
  - finances
  - sexual performance
  - drug taking
- family disruption
- problem drinking
- nicotine excess
- NIDDM risk and inappropriate use
- ischaemic heart disease risk

Discussion

JR (a real patient) is representative of many patients encountered in general practice with the common problem of chronic back pain. His case serves to illustrate the importance of managing the whole person.

Approaches to management

Psychological support

Factors that make patients feel supported and generate their confidence in the doctor include:

- showing an interest in all aspects
- examining the problematic area
- more thorough examination
- picking up 'cues' and drawing attention to them

It is noteworthy just how impressed some patients are when they are physically examined. It is appreciated particularly by those who say 'The other doctor did not get me to take off my clothes nor examine me'.

Support includes acting as the patient's advocate during the complex process of coping with the red tape of worker's compensation formalities, examinations by other doctors and any medicolegal issues.

Appropriate reassurance

Reassurance should be given from an appropriate knowledge base. It should be emphasised to the patient that on the law of averages the chronic back pain should eventually resolve and the patient can look forward to resuming a relatively normal life.

The patient should also be reassured that he does not have malignancy or a physically crippling disorder.

Explanation, basic counselling and patient education

One of the most important features of management is careful and appropriate explanation including the reasons why he has pain and why it is self-perpetuating. A useful approach is that given on page 31 whereby the explanation is that the main triggering factor (the prolapsed disc) has basically resolved but the central nervous system is still registering the pain, analogous to a 'phantom limb'. The development of anxiety and depression has caused continuing overactivity of the pain pathways which need to be 'switched off' by the various treatments that will be given.

Explore various concerns including the effect of his illness on his family relationships and sexual activity and provide counselling as necessary. The patient should then be handed suitable patient education material as presented in Figure 9.3 and encouraged to undertake an exercise program (Fig. 9.2). Education about the problems of anxiety, depression and lifestyle factors should also be addressed.

Empowering self-responsibility

Emphasise to the patient that he must take the responsibility for his own health and rehabilitation. This involves an active program of exercises and swimming, taking preventive measures and following recommendations about health promotion. It also involves dedication to restoration of ideal weight since his obesity (BMI > 30) would be contributing to his back pain.

Medication

Explain tactfully that since there is no clinical evidence of inflammation, his NSAIDs can be ceased.

Because he is depressed with an anxiety component and insomnia, an antidepressant can be prescribed to be taken at night (see explanation for the patient on page 30). He can be assured that not only will this help his psychological state but it should help 'shut the pain pathway gate' and reverse the overactivity of the nervous system.

Patient education including patient education handouts about possible side effects and how to cope with them would be appropriate.

Prevention and health promotion

The patient should be informed in a supportive way that he has the following risk factors:

- family history of cardiovascular disease
- family history of diabetes
- hypertension (related to obesity, NSAIDs, alcohol excess and smoking)
- smoking
- obesity
- possible hypercholesterolaemia (senile arcus noted)
- stress and anxiety

It would be important to stress (despite the fact that he might not be receptive during a depressed state) that for the sake of his future health it was time to change his lifestyle to try to reverse the risk factor process.

Advice on the prevention of recurrence of his back problem is important with advice on daily activities, lifting, bending and so on. The use of a brace is not generally recommended as dependency on the supportive device tends to lead to aggravation of the chronicity of the back.

Lifestyle recommendation

In JR's case, and indeed for many patients, he should receive advice, education, guidelines and support in the basic lifestyle factors, namely:

- diet control
  - — weight reduction
  - — low fat/cholesterol diet
  - — high fibre
  - — alcohol restriction
- smoking
- exercise and suitable physical activities
- interesting hobbies
- relaxation techniques

Family support and counselling

It would be ideal to include Mrs JR in the next consultation or, better still, arrange a home visit to discuss the role the family can take in his rehabilitation. Explanations and seeking family support would be very helpful.

Other positive suggestions would be to encourage Mrs JR to perform massage (as instructed) on the aching back and co-operate with his diet and other lifestyle issues; and to assess the state of the bed and the chairs as a possible aggravation factor for the back pain.

Anticipatory guidance and special hazards

Possible problems for JR include aggravation of his back pain by inappropriate physical and emotional stressors, marital break-up, loss of job and even suicide. These issues should be diplomatically discussed with the patient in a positive way. Hopefully the interest, encouragement and support he receives can help avert these serious problems.

Recommended treatment for JR

- attention to lifestyle factors
- antidepressant medication
  - — amitriptyline 100 mg nocte
- referral for therapy
  - — hydrotherapy
  - — mobilisation
  - — active exercises
- therapeutic massage

Alternative options

There are many alternative therapies which can be used to help alleviate his painful condition. It is important for GPs to keep abreast of these therapies and their relative success rate based on scientific evidence. (Where known, the relative success rate, based on research by the author, is indicated.[2]) If the response is slow, one or more of these treatment modalities can be selected and the patient referred to a reputable therapist experienced in the therapy.

- spinal mobilisation and manipulation (64%)
- manipulation under general anaesthesia (34%)
- transcutaneous electrical nerve stimulation (TENS)
- acupuncture
- biofeedback
- meditation
- facet joint injections (20%)
- nerve blockage (48% after 6 months)
- epidural injections
- neurofasciotomy (42%)
- radiofrequency denervation (65%)
- electrotherapy
  for superficial heating
  - — radiant heat lamps
  - — infra-red lamps

  for deep heating
  - — short-wave diathermy
  - — ultrasound

Consultation and referral

One of the skills of a responsible general practitioner is to sum up his or her own limitations with a particular problem and consult with and/or refer to a colleague if it is in the patient's best interests. Effective communication and advice is only a phone call away. Patients with a chronic illness should be referred to an expert in the discipline to satisfy patient, family and GP that everything possible is being attempted to help the patient. Patients and their families often judge us by the quality of the referral process and its outcome, so considerable thought has to be given to the most outstanding consultant for that particular problem at a given time. The GP should remain in charge of the team and direct management.

JR could be referred to medical consultants such as an orthopaedic surgeon, an orthopaedic physician or a rheumatologist. It would be inappropriate to refer him to a psychiatrist in the early stage of his pain but if a psychological problem intervened and complicated management (as in this case) referral should be strongly considered. As a rule depression and anxiety can be managed well by a caring family doctor.

Probably the best option for a patient like JR is referral to a pain clinic which is staffed by a multidisciplinary team of specialists including psychiatrists, social workers, physiotherapists, occupational therapists and other medical specialists. They look at the total problem and the whole person. As a patient similar to JR said after attending a pain clinic: 'For the first time all my problems—physical, psychological, drug dependency and other disturbed fragments of my life—have been dealt with by the whole team'.

Follow-up

Careful instructions to ensure follow-up visits by the patient is important as there is a tendency for some dissatisfied and emotional patients to seek attention elsewhere and thus get on the chronic disorder 'merry-go-round'.

Outcome

JR gradually improved, presumably because depression had complicated the problem. The aphorism 'acute pain = acute anxiety and chronic pain = depression' applied to JR and relief of his depression, combined with supportive measures such as physiotherapy, hydrotherapy, physical therapy and strong psychological support from his family and GP, provided the 'holistic' approach to healing.

The holistic approach to management[3]

In a healing profession obsessed with interventionism, invasive technology and drug management, the general practitioner has an obligation to his or her patients to use natural healing methods wherever possible and be very discerning and conservative with investigatory medicine.

Patients appreciate natural remedies and taking responsibility for their own management wherever possible and appropriate. Examples include relative rest, exercise, swimming, stress management, meditation, spiritual awareness, antioxidant therapy (e.g. vitamin C, vitamin E, selenium), weight control, optimal healthy nutrition, avoidance of toxins (e.g. illicit drugs, nicotine, caffeine and alcohol) and sexual fulfilment.

Underlying a successful outcome is motivation and the healing factor of the physician in being the motivator, teacher and facilitator should never be underestimated.

References

1. Carson N. The diagnostic process. In: Monash University, Department of Community Medicine Final Year handbook, 1990, 9–25.
2. Murtagh J. Back pain in general practice: an MD thesis, Monash University, 1988, 160–165.
3. Hetzel R. *The new physician: tapping the potential for true health.* Melbourne: Houghton Mifflin, 1991.

11

Medical advice for travellers

—

If you can't peel it, boil it or cook it—don't eat it.
Anon

Emporiatics—the science of travel medicine

With over 400 million international trips being taken annually the health problems faced by travellers are considerable and variable depending on the countries visited and the lifestyle adopted by the traveller.[1] There is evidence that many travellers are receiving inaccurate predeparture travel advice.[2] Travellers to North America, Europe and Australasia are usually at no greater risk of getting an infectious disease than they would be at home, but those visiting the less developed tropical and subtropical countries of Africa, Central and South America and South-East Asia are at significant risk of contracting infectious diseases.

Problems range in complexity from the most frequent and usually benign problems, such as traveller's diarrhoea, to more exotic and potentially fatal infections such as malaria, Japanese encephalitis and HIV. It must also be remembered that in some countries with volatile political changes there is the possibility of injury, incarceration or being left stranded. Travel means transport and thus the potential for accidents and crippled body and bank balance. Insurance for such contingencies is as important as preventive health measures.

Key facts and checkpoints

- The main diseases facing the international traveller are traveller's diarrhoea (relatively mild) and malaria, especially the potentially lethal chloroquine-resistant falciparum malaria (CRFM).
- Most cases of traveller's diarrhoea are caused by enterotoxigenic *E.coli* (up to 75%).
- Enteroinvasive *E.coli* (a different serotype) produces a dysentery-like illness similar to *Shigella*.
- Traveller's diarrhoea is contracted mainly from contaminated water and ice used for beverages, washing food or utensils or cleaning teeth.
- One bite from an infected mosquito during a single overnight stop in a malaria area can result in a possible lethal infection.
- Infections transmitted by mosquitoes include malaria, yellow fever, Rift Valley fever, Japanese encephalitis and dengue fever. Preventing their bites is excellent prevention.
- Every year over 500 Australians catch malaria while travelling overseas.
- Malaria is a dusk till dawn risk only, but bites from daytime mosquitoes can cause dengue.
- CRFM is steadily increasing, as is resistance to newer antimalarials.

Principles of pre-travel health care

- Advise the patient to plan early—at least eight weeks beforehand.
- Advise a dental check.

- Allow adequate time for consultation, e.g. 30–45 minutes.
- Individualise advice.
- Provide current information.
- Provide written as well as verbal advice.
- Provide a letter concerning existing medical illness and treatment.
- Encourage personal responsibility.

Gastrointestinal infections

The commonest problem facing travellers is traveller's diarrhoea but other important diseases caused by poor sanitation include hepatitis A, and worm infestations such as hookworm and schistosomiasis.

Contamination of food and water is a major problem especially in Third World countries.

Reputable soft drinks, such as Coca Cola, should be recommended for drinking. Indian-style tea, in which the milk is boiled with tea, is usually safe, but tea with added milk is not. The food handlers can be infected and the water used to wash food may be contaminated.

Traveller's diarrhoea

Traveller's diarrhoea is a special problem in Mexico, Nepal, India, Pakistan, Latin America, the Middle East and central Africa and its many colourful labels include 'Bali Belly', 'Gippy Tummy', 'Rangoon Runs', 'Tokyo Trots' and 'Montezuma's Revenge'. It occurs about 6–12 hours after taking infected food or water.

The illness is usually mild and lasts only two or three days. It is unusual for it to last longer than five days. Symptoms include abdominal cramps, frequent diarrhoea with loose watery bowel motions and possible vomiting. Very severe diarrhoea, especially if associated with the passing of blood or mucus, may be a feature of a more serious bowel infection such as amoebiasis.

Most traveller's diarrhoea is caused by an *Escherichia coli (E. coli)*. Travellers are infected because they are exposed to slightly different types or strains of *E. coli* from the ones they are used to at home.[3]

The possible causes of diarrhoeal illness are listed in Table 11.1.

Treatment (refer to Figure 11.1)[3]

Mild diarrhoea

- maintain fluid intake—cordial or diluted soft drink
- antimotility agents (judicious use: if no blood in stools)
  loperamide (Imodium) 2 caps statim then 1 after each unformed stool (max: 8 caps/day)
  or
  diphenoxylate with atropine (Lomotil) 2 tablets statim
  then 1–2 (o) 8 hourly
  Imodium is the preferred agent.

Table 11.1 *Causes of diarrhoea in travellers*

	Causative organism	*Type of illness*
Bacteria	*Escherichia coli*	Traveller's diarrhoea
	Shigella species	Dysentery
	Salmonella species	Typhoid fever, food poisoning
	Campylobacter jejuni	Traveller's diarrhoea, dysentery
	Vibrio cholerae	Cholera
	Yersinia enterocolitica	Traveller's diarrhoea
	Aeromonas hydrophilia	Traveller's diarrhoea
	Staphylococcus aureus (toxin)	Food poisoning
	Clostridium perfringens	Food poisoning
	Bacillus cereus	Food poisoning
Viruses	Rotavirus	Children's diarrhoea
	Norwalk virus	Traveller's diarrhoea
Protozoa parasites	Cryptosporidium	
	Entamoeba histolytica	Amoebiasis
	Giardia lamblia	Giardiasis
	Strongyloides stercoralis	Strongyloidiasis
Chemicals	Capsicum (chilli)	

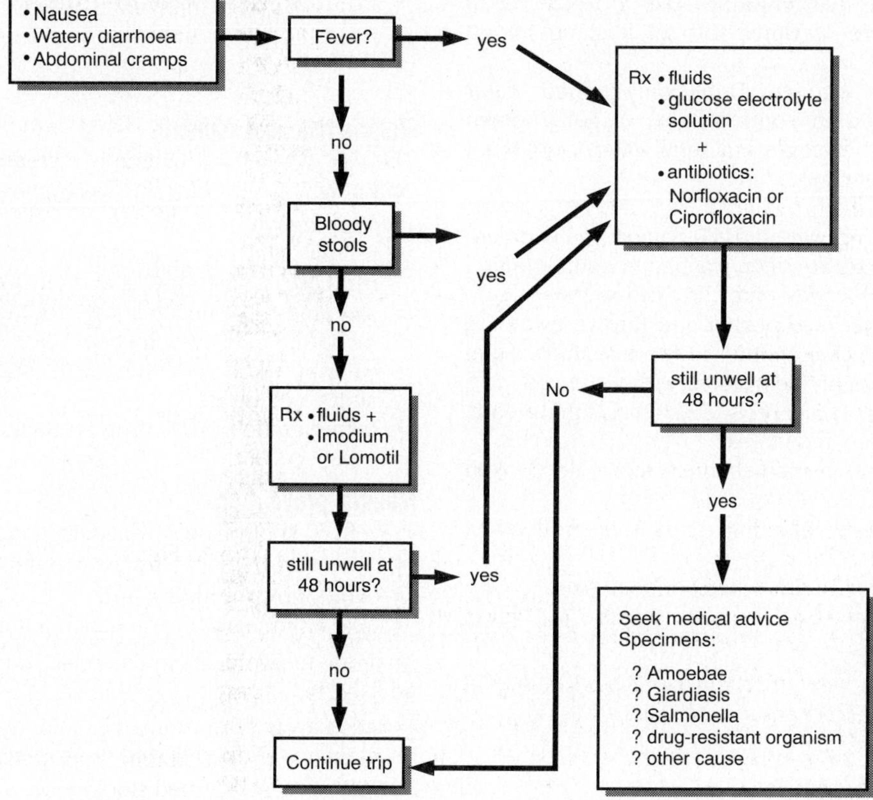

Fig. 11.1 *Algorithm for adult travellers with acute diarrhoea* AFTER LOOKE

Moderate diarrhoea

- attend to hydration
- patient can self-administer antibiotic—e.g. norfloxacin 400 mg bd for 3 days, or ciprofloxacin; use co-trimoxazole in children
- avoid Lomotil or Imodium

Severe diarrhoea (patient toxic and febrile)

- ? admit to hospital
- attend to hydration—use an oral hydrate solution, e.g. Gastrolyte or WHO formulation
- avoid Lomotil and Imodium
- antibiotic: norfloxacin or ciprofloxacin.

Note There is increasing resistance to doxycycline and co-trimoxazole, especially in SE Asia.

Persistent diarrhoea

Any travellers with persistent diarrhoea after visiting less developed countries, especially India and China, may have a protozoal infection such as amoebiasis or giardiasis. If the patient has a fever and mucus or blood in the stools, suspect amoebiasis. Giardiasis is characterised by abdominal cramps, flatulence, and bubbly, foul-smelling diarrhoea persisting beyond 2 to 4 days.

Treatment

Giardiasis: tinidazole or metronidazole
Amoebiasis: metronidazole or tinidazole
Patient can self-administer these drugs and carry them if visiting areas at risk.

Preventive advice

The following advice will help prevent diseases caused by contaminated food and water. These 'rules' need only be followed in areas of risk such as Africa, South America, India and other parts of Asia.

- Purify all water by boiling for 10 minutes. Adding purifying tablets is not so reliable but if the water cannot be boiled some protection is provided by adding Puratabs (chlorine) or iodine (2% tincture of iodine) which is more effective than chlorine—use 4 drops iodine to 1 litre of water and let it stand for 30 minutes.

- Do not use ice. Drink only boiled water (supplied in some hotels) or well known bottled beverages (mineral water, 7-up, Coca Cola, beer).
- Avoid fresh salads or raw vegetables (including watercress). Salads or uncooked vegetables are often washed in contaminated water. Bananas and fruit with skins are safe once you have peeled and thrown away the skin but care should be taken with fruit that may possibly be injected with water.
- Be wary of dairy products such as milk, cream, ice-cream and cheese.
- Avoid eating raw shellfish and cold cooked meats.
- Avoid food, including citrus fruits, from street vendors.
- Drink hot liquids wherever possible.
- Use disposable moist towels for hand washing.

The golden rule is: *If you can't peel it, boil it or cook it—don't eat it.*

Malaria

General aspects:

- Travellers to all tropical countries are at some risk.
- Malaria is endemic in 102 countries.[4]
- The risk is very low in the major cities of Central and Southern America and South-East Asia.
- Malaria is either benign (vivax, ovale) or malignant (falciparum).
- Resistance to many drugs is increasing:
  - the lethal *Plasmodium falciparum* is developing resistance to chloroquine and the antifolate malarials (Fansidar and Maloprim)[4]
  - resistance is now reported to mefloquine
  - CRFM is common in South-East Asia, Northern South America and parts of Africa.
- Chloroquine is still effective against *P.ovale* and *P.vivax* (the most common forms).
- The long-awaited vaccine will make all the complex drug management much simpler. However, it still appears to be many years away despite considerable research.
- Practitioners should follow updated recommended guidelines, e.g. NH&MRC, WHO.

Malaria risk assessment

The risk of catching malaria is increased by:

- being in a malaria area, especially during and after the wet season
- a prolonged stay in a malaria area especially rural areas, small towns and city fringes
- sleeping in unscreened rooms without mosquito nets over the bed
- wearing dark clothing with short-sleeved shirts and shorts
- taking inappropriate drug prophylaxis

Malarial prevention

Travellers should be advised that malaria may be prevented by following two simple rules:

- avoid mosquito bites; and
- take antimalarial medicines regularly

In order to avoid mosquito bites, travellers are advised to:

- keep away from rural areas after dusk
- sleep in air-conditioned or properly screened rooms
- use insecticide sprays to kill any mosquitoes in the room or use mosquito coils at night
- smear an insect repellent on exposed parts of the body; an effective repellent is diethyl-m-toluamide (Muskol, Repellem, Rid)
- use mosquito nets (tuck under mattress; check for tears)
- impregnate nets with permethrin (Ambush) or deltamethrin
- wear sufficient light-coloured clothing, long sleeves and long trousers, to protect whole body and arms and legs when in the open after sunset
- avoid using perfumes, cologne and after shave lotion (also attracts insects)

Important considerations in malaria prophylaxis

1. Minimise exposure to mosquitoes and avoid bites.
2. Known areas of risk:
   - tropical South America (southern Mexico to northern half South America)
   - tropical Africa (sub-Sahara to northern South Africa)
   - Nile region including Egypt
   - Southern Asia especially tropical areas

3. Know areas of widespread chloroquine resistance:
   - Asia, tropical South America (rare north of Panama Canal), sub-Sahara, East Africa
4. Consider several factors:
   - intensity of transmission
   - season and length of stay
   - itinerary urban—hotel
urban—non-hotel
rural—housing
rural—backpacking
   - resistance patterns
   - host factors — age
— pregnancy
— associated illness
— compliance
5. Know the antimalarial drugs (Table 11.2).
6. Balance risk benefit of drug prophylaxis: drug side effects *v* risk of CRFM.
7. Visiting areas of CRFM does not automatically require the use of potentially harmful drugs.[1]
8. Those at special risk are pregnant women, young children and the immunocompromised.

Drug prophylaxis

Guidelines

- Accommodation in large air-conditioned hotels in most cities of SE Asia (dusk–dawn) for < 2 weeks: no prophylaxis required.

> *Summary of recommendations*
>
> 1. CSFM area: chloroquine
> 2. CRFM area:
mefloquine
or
doxycycline
> 3. Multi-drug resistant area
doxycycline 100 mg/day
for stays > 8 weeks
chloroquine
+
doxycycline 50 mg/day
>
> CSFM = chloroquine-sensitive falciparum malaria
> CRFM = chloroquine-resistant falciparum malaria

Table 11.2 *Common drugs used for malarial prophylaxis*

	Adult dosage	*Children's dose*	*Comments*
Chloroquine (Chloroquine) (Nivaquine)	300 mg base (2 tabs) same day each week 2 wk before, during 4 wk after exposure	5 mg base/kg up to maximum adult dose	Only antimalarial approved for pregnancy Aggravates psoriasis Beware of retinopathy
Doxycycline	100 mg each day, 1 to 2 days before, during, 2 weeks after	> 8 years only 2 mg/kg/day up to 100 mg	Photosensitivity reactions
Mefloquine (Lariam)	250 mg (1 tab) same day each week, 1 week before, during, 4 weeks after	Not recommended < 45 kg > 45 kg as for adults	Side effects: dizziness, 'fuzzy' head, blurred vision Beware of beta-blockers

Table 11.3 *Drugs used for treatment of chloroquine-resistant malaria (presumptive breakthrough where professional medical care unavailable)*[5]

	Adult dose	*Children's dose*
Melfoquine (Lariam)	500 mg (2 tablets) statim Repeat after 8–12 hours	only recommended if weight > 45 kg (as for adults)
Fansidar	3 tablets as a single dose	2–11 months: ¼ tablet 1–3 years: ½ tablet 4–8 years: 1 tablet 9–14 years: 2 tablets > 14 years: 3 tablets

- For low-risk travel (urban: dusk–dawn) in areas of high resistance for < 2 weeks: chloroquine adequate, use a treatment course of mefloquine if necessary (Table 11.3).
- For short- and long-term travel to rural areas of high resistance, e.g. SE Asia including Thailand, Kenya, Tanzania, Ecuador, Venezuela, Brazil: doxycycline daily alone or mefloquine (once a week).

Specific infectious diseases and immunisation

Protection from many types of infection is available through immunisation. All travellers should be immunised against tetanus, polio and diphtheria and measles. Protection against tetanus requires an initial course of three injections followed by a booster every 10 years.

Vaccinations are required for special circumstances. Yellow fever vaccination is a legal requirement for any travellers returning from a yellow fever endemic area. Cholera is not usually required.

Some travellers may be exposed to tuberculosis, hepatitis, plague, rabies, typhoid, typhus, and meningococcal infection. Immunisation against these is available and recommended for those at risk. Smallpox has now been eradicated from the world and therefore smallpox vaccination is no longer required for any traveller.

Japanese B encephalitis presents as a special problem to the traveller. Table 11.4 outlines a summary of recommendations to consider.[6]

Table 11.4 *Summary of preventive measures and vaccinations*

All travellers, all destinations
Tetanus toxoid booster
if > 10 years since last dose if > 5 years for Third World travel
All travellers to developing countries free of malaria
Tetanus toxoid booster
Polio immunisation if > 10 years
Measles immunisation
Yellow fever and cholera vaccine (if compulsory)
Preventive measures against: • gastrointestinal infections • sexually transmitted diseases • mosquito bites
Travellers to developing and other countries at high risk of infection
As above plus:
Malaria prophylaxis
Hepatitis A—vaccine or immunoglobulin
Typhoid
Other vaccinations: consider • hepatitis B • meningococcus • Japanese B encephalitis • rabies • typhus

Compulsory immunisations

The two vaccinations that may be required before visiting 'at risk' areas are cholera and yellow fever.

Cholera

Cholera vaccination is not recommended by the World Health Organisation (WHO) because it has only limited effectiveness. Notwithstanding this recommendation, the following countries still require a cholera vaccination from travellers arriving from endemic areas: Pakistan, Pitcairn. Cholera is given in two injections 7 to 28 days apart. It is not recommended in children under five years or pregnant women.

Yellow fever

Yellow fever is a serious viral infection spread by mosquitoes and, like malaria, is a tropical disease. Yellow fever vaccination is essential for travel to or through equatorial Africa and northern parts of South America, and for re-entry to Australia from those countries.

One injection only is required and the immunisation is valid for 10 years. Children aged less than nine months should not be given this vaccine. It should not be given within three weeks of cholera vaccine.

Note: It is important to check specific country requirements in the World Health Organisation book on vaccination requirements.[8]

According to WHO a certificate against yellow fever is the only certificate that should be required for international travel. The requirements of some countries are in excess of International Health Regulations. However, vaccination against yellow fever is strongly recommended to all travellers who intend to visit places other than the major cities in the countries where the disease occurs in humans.

Voluntary immunisation

Precautions against the following diseases are recommended for those travellers who may be at special risk.

Hepatitis A, B, E

Hepatitis A is a common problem in rural areas of developing countries. There is a declining level of antibodies to hepatitis A in developed countries and adults are at special risk. A vaccine is now available and the 3-dose course should be given. If there is insufficient time a single injection of human immunoglobulin (IG) can give protection for 3 to 6 months. It is safe for all age groups but children under 8 years should not need it. A blood test for hepatitis A antibodies should be carried out to determine a person's immunity.

Prevention

- The rules of avoiding contaminated food and water apply (as for traveller's diarrhoea).

Hepatitis B is endemic in South-East Asia, South America and other developing countries. Vaccination is recommended especially for people working in such countries, especially those in the health care area or those who may expect to have sexual or drug contact. If patients have a 'negative' HB core IgG titre, then vaccination would be worthwhile (3 doses: 0, 1 and 6 months).

Typhoid

Typhoid immunisation is not required for entry into any country but is recommended for travel to Third World countries where the standards of sanitation are low. It should be considered for travellers to smaller cities, village and rural areas in Africa, Asia, Central and South America and Southern Europe.

The parenteral (subcutaneous) vaccine can be used but the new oral vaccine which has fewer side effects is generally preferred. The oral vaccine which is given as a series of four capsules appears to afford protection for about five years.

Japanese B encephalitis

This mosquito-borne infection presents a real dilemma to the traveller and doctor because it is a very severe infection (mortality rate 20–40%) with high infectivity and high prevalence in endemic countries. The vaccine is prone to give anaphylaxis and is unlicensed in Australia and the United States. It may be obtained only in very restricted circumstances but can be obtained more readily abroad.

The disease is prevalent during summer in the region bound in the west by Nepal and Siberian Russia and in the east by Japan and Singapore, especially in Nepal, Burma, Korea, Thailand, China, Eastern Soviet Union and the lowlands of India. Rice paddies and pig farms are areas of risk. The usual preventive measures against mosquito bites are important.

Meningococcal infection

Meningitis due to this organism is a contagious lethal disease. It is common in Nepal and parts of Africa and Asia, especially in the dry season. Travellers trekking through the Kathmandu valley of Nepal and those attending the Haj pilgrimage to Saudi Arabia are at special risk and should have the vaccine.

Rabies

A preventive vaccine should be considered for people going to high-risk areas to work with animals. The vaccination can be effective after the bite of a rabid animal, so routine vaccination is not recommended for the traveller. Affected animals include dogs, cats, monkeys and feral (wild) animals. A traveller who sustains a bite or scratch or even is licked by an animal in countries at risk should wash the site immediately with soap or a detergent, and then seek medical help. The pre-bite vaccination does not remove the need for post-exposure vaccination.

Typhus

Typhus is transmitted to humans by bites from lice, fleas or ticks. Immunisation against typhus is desirable for doctors, nurses, agricultural and technical advisers whose work takes them to remote areas of Bolivia, Burundi, Ethiopia, Mexico, Rwanda and mountainous regions of Asia. A booster injection should be given at 12 months if the traveller is still in an area of risk.

Plague

Plague is still prevalent in rodents in several countries such as Vietnam, Brazil, Peru, Ecuador, Kenya and Malagasy Republic. Although not compulsory, vaccination is recommended for those engaged in field operations in plague areas and rural health workers who may be exposed to infected patients. Two doses are given to adults (3 to children < 12 years) and a booster every 6 months.

Special problems

Prevention of sexually transmitted diseases

Casual sexual contacts place the traveller at risk of contracting a serious, perhaps fatal, sexually transmitted disease (STD). The common STDs especially prevalent in South-East Asia and Africa are non-specific urethritis, gonorrhoea (especially penicillin-resistant strains), hepatitis B, and syphilis. HIV infection is a rapidly increasing problem, with heterosexual transmission common in Africa and in South-East Asia. Unusual STDs such as lymphogranuloma venerum, chancroid and donovanosis are encountered more commonly in tropical developing countries. A practical rule is to assume that all 'at risk' travellers are both ignorant and irresponsible and advise accordingly.

Prevention

Abstinence or take your partner
(condoms and diaphragms do not give absolute protection)

Drugs

Possession of and trafficking in drugs is very hazardous and many people are held in foreign prisons for various drug offences. The penalty for carrying drugs can be death!

Countries that currently may enforce the death penalty are Burma, Indonesia, Malaysia, Singapore, Thailand and Turkey. Travellers should be warned about taking cannabis while in a foreign country, as it can cause profound personality changes in the user.

Drug addicts should under no circumstances travel. Young travellers should be wary about accepting lifts or hitch-hiking in countries 'at risk'.

Problems in the returned traveller

- Most will present within 2 weeks except HIV infection.
- Common infections encountered are giardiasis, amoebiasis, hepatitis A,B or E, gonorrhoea or *Chlamydia trachomatis*, malaria and helminthic infestations.
- An important non-infected problem requiring vigilance is deep venous thrombosis and thromboembolism.
- The asymptomatic traveller may present for advice about an illness acquired or about exposure (without illness) such as rabies, malaria, schistosomiasis and sexually transmitted diseases.

Exposure to STDs

If a patient has had unprotected intercourse and is at definite risk of acquiring an STD such as penicillin-resistant gonorrhoea or NSU, the following may be appropriate:[1]

ceftriaxone 250 mg IM (as a single dose)
doxycycline 100 mg (o) for 10 days

Gastrointestinal symptoms

Mild diarrhoea

- stool microscopy and culture
- look for and treat associated helminthic infestation, e.g. roundworms, hookworms

Moderate or prolonged (> 3 weeks) diarrhoea

Usually due to *Giardia lamblia, Entamoeba histolytica, Campylobacter jejuni*, salmonella, *Yersinia enterocolitica* or Cryptosporidium.

- stool examination (3 fresh specimens)
  - — microscopy
  - — wet preparation
  - — culture
- treat pathogen (see guidelines under diarrhoea p. 79)

Non-pathogens such as *E.coli* and *Endolimax nana* are often reported but do not treat specifically.

Note: Consider exotic causes such as schistosomiasis, strongyloidiasis and ciguatera in unusual chronic post-travel 'gastroenteritis'.

Persistent abdominal discomfort

This common syndrome includes bloating, intestinal hurry and borborygmi, and often follows an episode of diarrhoea. Usually no pathogens are found on stool examination. However, giardiasis can be difficult to detect and an empirical course of tinidazole (2 g statim) is worthwhile. Any persistent problem then is a type of postinfective bowel dysfunction or irritable bowel. Reassurance is important.

Fever

- Causes range from mild viral infections to potentially fatal cerebral malaria (Table 11.5) and meningococcal septicaemia.
- The common serious causes are malaria, typhoid, hepatitis (especially A and B), dengue fever and amoebiasis.
- Most deaths from malaria have occurred after at least 3 or 4 days of symptoms which may be mild. Death can occur within 24 hours.

Factors responsible for death from malaria include delayed presentation, missed or delayed diagnosis (most cases), no chemoprophylaxis and old age.

- Refer immediately to a specialist unit if the patient is unwell.
- Be vigilant for meningitis and encephalitis.
- Be vigilant for amoebiasis—can present with a toxic megacolon, especially if antimotility drugs given.
- If well but febrile: *First line screening tests*
  full blood examination and ESR
  thick and thin films
  liver function tests
  urine for micro and culture
- Refer immediately if malaria is proven or if fever persists after a further 24 hours.

Malaria (see Figure 11.2)

- incubation period: *P. falciparum* 7–14 days; others 12–40 days
- most present within 2 months of return
- can present up to 2 or more years
- can masquerade as several other illnesses

Symptoms

- high fever, chills, rigor, sweating
- usually abrupt onset
- can have atypical presentations, e.g. diarrhoea, abdominal pain, cough

Other features

- beware of modified infection
- must treat within 4 days
- typical relapsing patterns often absent
- thick smear allows detection of parasites (some laboratories are poorly skilled with thick films)
- thin smear helps diagnose malaria type

If index of suspicion high, repeat the smear ('No evidence of malaria' = 3 negative daily thick films). Monocytosis is a helpful diagnostic clue. Cerebral malaria and blackwater fever are severe and dramatic.

Treatment

- admit to hospital with infectious disease expertise
- supportive measures

Table 11.5 *Fever and malaise in the returned traveller: diagnostic strategy model*

NB 'All fever in a returned traveller is malaria until proved otherwise!'

Q. *Probability diagnosis*
A. Viral respiratory illness, e.g. influenza
Hepatitis (may be subclinical)
Gastroenteritis

Q. *Serious disorders not to be missed*
A. Malaria
Typhoid
Japanese B encephalitis
Meningococcal meningitis
Meliodiosis
Amoebiasis (liver abscess)

Q. *Pitfalls (often missed)*
A. Ascending cholangitis
Infective endocarditis
Dengue fever
Lyme disease
Bronchopneumonia
Rarities
Legionnaire's disease
Schistosomiasis
African trypanosomiasis
Yellow fever
Rift Valley fever
Spotted fever
Lasa fever

NB *Three causes of a dry cough (in absence of chest signs) are malaria, typhoid, amoebic liver abscess.*

Q. *Seven masquerades checklist*
A. Drugs ✓ (reaction to antimalarials)
Urinary infection ✓

Investigations (if no obvious cause)
Full blood examination
Thick and thin blood films
Blood culture
Liver function tests
Urine—micro and culture
Stool—micro and culture
ESR

- *P. vivax, P. ovale, P.malariae*
  chloroquine + primaquine: 14 days (check G6PD first)

  P. falciparum
  uncomplicated: quinine + doxycycline or mefloquine (alone)
  complicated: quinine IV
  then
  quinine + Fansidar (o)

  NB: Check for hypoglycaemia.
  Beware if antimalarial use in previous 48 hours.

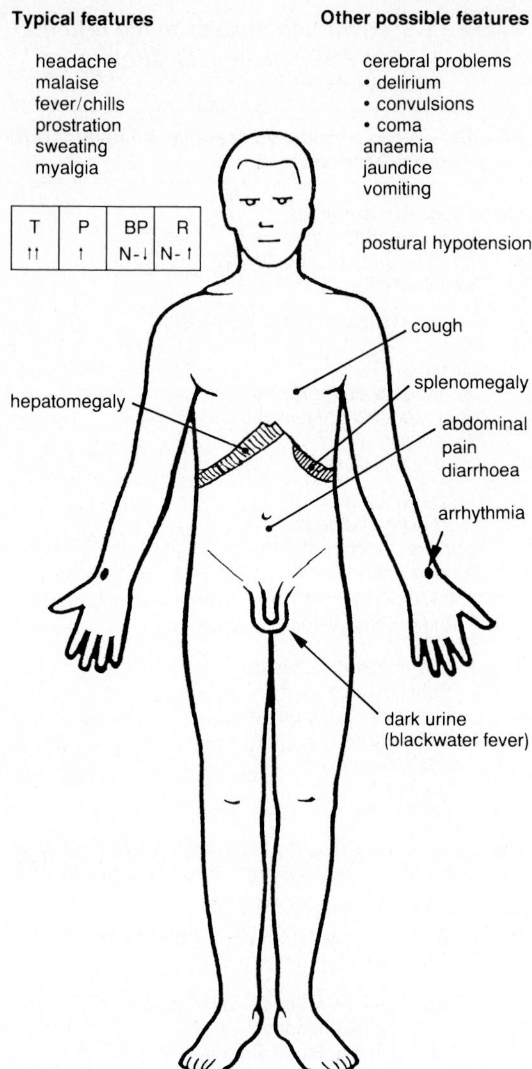

Fig. 11.2 *Clinical features of malaria*

Typhoid fever

Incubation period 10–14 days.

Clinical presentation

- insidious onset
- headache prominent
- dry cough
- fever gradually increases in 'stepladder' manner over 4 days or so
- abdominal pain and constipation (early)
- diarrhoea and rash (late)

Diagnosis on suspicion → blood culture serology not very helpful

Treatment ciprofloxacin

Dengue fever

Also known as 'breakbone' fever.

Features

- mosquito-borne viral infection
- incubation period 5–6 days
- abrupt onset fever, malaise, headache, pain behind eyes, severe backache
- severe aching of muscles and joints
- fever subsides for about 2 days then returns
- maculopapular rubelliform rash on limbs → trunk
- the rare haemorrhagic form is very severe; may present with shock
- later severe fatigue and depression (prone to suicide)

Diagnosis clinical suspicion → isolation of virus

Treatment is symptomatic with supportive follow-up

Prevention avoid mosquito bites—no vaccine available

Japanese B encephalitis and meningococcal meningitis

Consider these serious infections in a patient presenting with headache, fever and malaise before neurological symptoms such as delirium, convulsions and coma develop.

Unusual or exotic infections

Most of these infections are contracted through contaminated food and water, insect bites and walking barefoot on contaminated soil. The risk of such infections is highest in rural areas of countries other than Europe, North America and Australasia.

African trypanosomiasis (sleeping sickness)

Clinical features

- incubation period about 3 weeks
- fever, headache and a skin chancre or nodule
- lymphadenopathy, hepatosplenomegaly

Diagnosis demonstrating trypomastiogotes in peripheral blood smear or chancre aspirate

Treatment suramin IV
infectious disease consultation essential

Prevention Avoid bites of the tsetse fly. If visiting areas of East, Central and West Africa especially, the 'safari game parks' travellers should use insect repellent and wear protective light-coloured clothing including long sleeves and trousers.

Cutaneous leishmaniasis

This may be encountered in travellers and servicemen returning from the Middle East, especially the Persian Gulf. The protozoa is transmitted by a sandfly and has an average incubation period of 9 weeks. The key clinical finding is an erythematous papule. Diagnosis is made by performing a punch biopsy and culturing tissue in a special medium. Treatment for extensive lesions is with high dosage ketoconazole for 1 month. Smaller lesions should be treated topically with 15% paromomycin and 12% methyl benzethonium chloride ointment applied bd for 10 days.[7] A special vaccine is available in Israel.

Schistosomiasis (bilharzia)

The first clinical sign is a local skin reaction at the site of penetration of the parasite (it then invades liver, bowel and bladder). This site is known as 'swimmer's itch'. Within a week or so there is a generalised allergic response usually with fever, malaise, myalgia and urticaria. A gastroenteritis-like syndrome can occur (nausea, vomiting, diarrhoea) and respiratory symptoms, particularly cough. Clinical findings, like trypanosomiasis, include lymphadenopathy and hepatosplenomegaly.

The infestation is caused by parasite organisms (schistosomes) whose eggs are passed in human excreta which contaminates water courses (notably stagnant water) and irrigation channels in Egypt, Africa, South America and some parts of South-East Asia, e.g. China. Freshwater snails are the carriers (vectors).

Diagnosis detecting eggs in the stools, the urine or in a rectal biopsy.

Treatment praziquantel.

Prevention Travellers should be warned against drinking from, or swimming and wading in dams, watercourses or irrigation channels especially in Egypt and Africa.

Hookworm and strongyloidiasis

Hookworm and *Strongyloides* are parasites that are acquired by walking barefoot (or wearing thongs or sandals) on earth contaminated by faeces. The larvae penetrate the skin, travel through the lungs and settle in the small intestine. The first sign is local irritation or 'creeping eruption' at the point of entry known as 'ground itch', which is often unnoticed. This subsides within two days or so and is followed 1–2 weeks later by respiratory symptoms which may be associated with bronchitis and bronchopneumonia. Eventually a severe and chronic anaemia may develop. Hookworm infection is the commonest cause of iron deficiency anaemia in the world. Strongyloidiasis, which usually does not present with anaemia, is an important pathogen since it remains undetected for decades and presents as a severe infection such as septicaemia when the host becomes immunocompromised for any reason.

Diagnosis detecting larvae or ova in the stool.

Treatment Hookworm—mebendazole 100 mg bd for 3 days
Strongyloidiasis—thiabendazole 1.5 g bd for 2 days (or more)
Adverse effects are common.

Prevention Travellers should be warned to wear shoes and socks in endemic areas to prevent entry of the larvae into the skin of the feet.

Lyme disease

Lyme disease is a spirochaetal infection transmitted by tick bites. Cases have been reported in many countries including developed first and second world countries such as the United Kingdom, the United States of America, Europe and possibly Australia.

Clinical features (first stage)

- characteristic skin rash—erythema chronicum migrans (soon after bite)

- headache, fever, myalgia, arthralgia
- lymphadenopathy

Refer page 184.

Diagnosis positive serology (specific 1gM antibodies)

Treatment penicillin or tetracycline

Prevention Avoid tick bites in endemic areas by protective clothing and personal insect repellents.

Melioidosis

This serious disease with a high mortality is caused by the Gram-negative bacillus, *Pseudomonas pseudomallei*, a soil saprophyte which infects humans mainly by penetrating through skin wounds, especially abrasions. It is mostly acquired while wading in rice paddies. It is mainly a disease of Third World countries and occurs between 20° North and 20° South of the equator, mainly in South-East Asia and including Northern Australia. It may manifest as a focal infection or as septicaemia with abscesses in the lung, kidney, liver or spleen. It presents with fever, cough and myalgia. It is called the 'Vietnamese time bomb' because it can present years after the initial infection in Vietnamese war veterans.

Diagnosis blood culture, swabs from focal lesions, haemagglutination test

Treatment ceftazidime IV

Prevention traumatised people with open wounds (especially diabetics) in endemic areas (tropical South-East Asia) should be carefully nursed.

Ciguatera

This is a type of fish food poisoning caused by eating tropical fish, especially large coral trout and large cod, in tropical waters, e.g. the Caribbean and tropical Pacific. The problem is caused by a type of poison which concentrates in the fish after they feed on certain micro-organisms around reefs. Ciguatera poisoning presents as a bout of 'gastroenteritis' (vomiting, diarrhoea and stomach pains) and then symptoms affecting the nervous system such as muscle aching and weakness, paraesthesia and burning sensations of the skin particularly of the fingers and lips. There is no cure for the problem but it can be treated with gammaglobulin. It is unwise to eat large predatory reef fish especially their offal (mainly the liver).

Pregnancy and travel

Most international airlines do not allow passengers to travel after the thirty-sixth week of pregnancy and may require a doctor's certificate after twenty-eight weeks. Air travel is contraindicated in the last month of pregnancy and until the seventh day after delivery. The past obstetric history should be taken into account. The same health risks apply except that most antimalarial tablets and vaccinations are not recommended. Only chloroquine is definitely safe. Live vaccinations (measles, rubella, influenza) are generally contraindicated[8] but the WHO considers it safe to have polio vaccine. Administration of killed or inactivated vaccines, toxoids and polysaccharides is permitted during pregnancy. Yellow fever vaccine is considered safe after the sixth month. As a general rule pregnancy and travel to Third World countries do not mix and pregnant women should be advised not to travel to these countries.

Tetanus immunisation is important as protection is passed on to the child during early infancy. Immunoglobin can be safely given as prevention against hepatitis.

The antimalarial drugs chloroquine, quinine and proguanil may be given to pregnant women but all others mentioned in Table 11.2 are contraindicated.

Children and travel

Although children including infants are good travellers and adapt well their resistance, especially to heat and infections, is lower. A child can suffer from acute dehydration very rapidly.[8] Air travel is not recommended for infants of less than seven days or premature infants.

The change in atmospheric pressure on landing can cause distressing ear pain so taking a bottle during descent is recommended.

In tropical areas it is important to keep children well hydrated and wear loose cotton clothing. A good guide to the health of a child is the amount and colour of their urine. If it is scanty and concentrated they are not getting sufficient fluid.

Most vaccines (diphtheria, tetanus, poliomyelitis, BCG) can safely be given in the first few weeks of life. Measles is common overseas and it is worthwhile considering it even under 12 months. Yellow fever vaccine should not be given under 12 months. Hence the importance of protection against mosquito bites. Malaria prophylaxis is important. Chloroquine, proguanil and quinine may be given safely to infants. However, as a rule young children should be discouraged from travel.

Air travel

Air travel is safe and comfortable but jet lag and air sickness are problems that face many travellers.

Jet lag

This is the uncomfortable aftermath of a long flight in which the person feels exhausted and disoriented, has poor concentration, insomnia and anxiety. The problem on arrival is poor concentration and judgement during the daytime.

Other symptoms that may occur include anorexia, weakness, headache, blurred vision and dizziness.

Jet lag is a feature of flying long distances east–west or west–east through several time zones, causing the person's routine daily rhythm of activity and sleep to get out of phase. The worst cases appear to be in those travelling eastbound from England to Australia. It can occur with travel in any direction, but the north–south flights are not so bothersome.

Factors influencing jet lag

Personal factors These include age, state of health, tolerance to change, preparation for the long trip and, very importantly, the emotional and mental state.

General factors Noise, vibration, air humidity and sitting still for long periods can influence jet lag.

Specific factors Duration of the flight, time of departure, changes in climate and culture at the destination affect the severity of jet lag. The problem is aggravated by:

- stress of the pre-trip planning
- last minute rushing and anxiety
- lack of sleep during the trip
- overeating and excessive alcohol during the flight
- smoking

How to minimise the problem (advice to patients)

Before the flight

- Allow plenty of time for planning.
- Plan a stopover if possible.
- If possible arrange the itinerary so that you are flying into the night.
- Ensure a good sleep the night before flying.
- Ensure a relaxed trip to the airport.
- Take along earplugs if noise (75–100 decibels) is bothersome.

During the flight

- *Fluids* Avoid alcohol and coffee. Drink plenty of non-alcoholic drinks such as orange juice and mineral water.
- *Food* Eat only when hungry and even skip a meal or two. Eat the lighter, more digestible parts of your meals and avoid fatty foods and rich carbohydrate foods.
- *Dress* Women should wear loose clothes (e.g. long skirts, comfortable jeans, light jumpers) and avoid girdles or restrictive clothing. Wear comfortable (not tight) shoes and take them off during flight.
- *Smoking* Reduce smoking to a minimum. Non-smokers should seek a non-smoking zone.
- *Sleep* Try to sleep on longer sections of the flight (give the movies a miss). Close the blinds, wear special eye masks and ask for a pillow. Sedatives such as temazepam (Euhypnos or Normison) or antihistamines can help sleep.
- *Activity* Try to take regular walks around the aircraft and exercise at airport stops. Keep feet up when resting, and exercise by flexing the major muscles of the legs. Avoid resting the calves of legs against the seat for long periods. Rest without napping during daylight sectors.
- *Special body care* Continually wet the face and eyes. A wetting agent such as hydromellose 0.5% eye drops can help those with a tendency to sore eyes.

At the destination

Take a nap for 1–2 hours if possible.

Wander around until you are tired and go to bed at the usual time. It is good to have a full day's convalescence and avoid big decision making soon after arrival. Allow about three days for adjustment after the London to Australia flight.

Who is fit to fly?

Patients with these problems should avoid flying:[9]

- upper airways congested by infection, including influenza
- acute gastroenteritis
- severe respiratory disease (emphysema, chronic bronchitis, pneumothorax)
- unstable heart failure
- severe anaemia (below 8 g/dl)
- pregnancy beyond 200 days (28 weeks) (up to 36 weeks if necessary)
- previous violent or unpredictable behaviour
- within 4 weeks of a myocardial infarction
- within 14 days of a cerebrovascular accident
- within 14 days of major surgery
- brain tumour or recent skull fracture
- recent eye surgery
- severe or poorly controlled hypertension
- poorly controlled epilepsy

Special precautions are required by travellers with the following problems:

- *Colostomy* Patients should wear a large colostomy bag and take extra bags.
- *Varicose veins* Such patients should wear supportive stockings and exercise frequently.
- *Plaster casts* Those with broken limbs in plaster should be careful of swelling.
- *Pacemakers* Those with pacemakers may have a problem with X-rays at some overseas airports. Mention it to security officials before passing through security equipment.
- *Epilepsy* Medication should be increased on the day of travel.
- *Diabetics* Diabetics should discuss their therapy and control with their doctor. They should carry sweets.

Travel sickness

Almost everyone is sick when sailing on rough seas. However, some people especially children suffer sickness from the effect of motion on a boat, in a car or plane. The larger the boat, plane or car, the less the likelihood of sickness; travel by train rarely causes sickness. Nearly all children grow out of the tendency to have travel sickness, but many adults remain 'bad' sailors.

The problem is caused by sensitivity of the semicircular canals of the inner ear. They are affected by the movement and vibration of travel. Some people have sensitive inner ear canals and are prone to sickness, especially on certain types of journeys (e.g. winding roads through hills) and in certain vehicles.

The main symptoms of travel sickness are nausea, vomiting, dizziness, weakness and lethargy. Early signs are pallor and drowsiness, and sudden silence from an active, talkative child.

How to minimise the problem

1. Keep calm and relaxed before and during travel. With children avoid excitement and apprehension about the travelling. Encourage activities such as looking at distant objects; discourage activities such as reading and games that require close visual concentration.
2. Lie down, if possible, because this rests the inner ear canals and reduces the urge to vomit. If travelling by car, stop regularly for breaks. Passengers should use the front seat if possible.
3. Do not have a large meal a few hours before the journey or during it; avoid milk and fried or greasy foods. Do not travel with an empty stomach: have a light simple meal about an hour before and do not drink too much. Glucose drinks such as lemonade are suitable, as are glucose sweets and biscuits while travelling.

Medication for travel sickness

Many medicines are available for travel sickness. They include hyoscine, various antihistamines and other phenothiazine derivatives, all of which can cause drowsiness; although a problem to drivers this sedative effect may be helpful for children or for those travelling long distances by plane.

Phenothiazine derivatives which provide appropriate anti-labyrinthine activity include prochlorperazine (Compazine, Stemetil), promethazine hydrochloride (Phenergan, Prothazine), promethazine theoclate (Avomine) and thiethylperazine (Torecan).

Combination antihistamine and hyoscine preparations for travel sickness include Travacalm and Benacine (Table 11.6).

Hyoscine comes in tablet form, either alone or in combination and in the now popular adhesive patches.

Recommended medications

Car travel: adult passengers and children

Dimenhydrinate (Andrumin, Dramamine)

or

Promethazine theoclate (Avomine)

or

Hyoscine (Kwells)

Table 11.6 *Medication to consider for motion sickness*

Drug (genre)	Brand names and formulations	Dosage: Adults	Dosage: Children
Antihistamines			
Dimenhydrinate	Andrumin 25 mg, 50 mg Dramamine 25 mg, 50 mg syrup 12.5 mg/5 ml	50 mg statim then 4 hourly prn (max 300 mg/24 hours)	avoid < 2 years 2-6 years: 6.25 mg 6-8 years: 12.5 mg 8-12 years: 25 mg > 12 years: 50 mg tds (max: 3-4 doses/24 hours)
Melcozine	Ancolan 25 mg	25 mg bd	< 12 years: 12.5 mg bd
Pheniramine	Avil, 10 mg, 50 mg syrup 3 mg/ml Fenamine 50 mg syrup 3 mg/ml	25-50 mg tds	infants 10 mg bd < 10 years: 10 mg tds > 10 years: 10-20 mg tds
Promethazine theoclate	Avomine 25 mg	25 mg statim or nocte for long journeys	< 5 years: ¼ tab 5-10 years: ½ tab > 10 years: 1 tab
Promethazine hydrochloride	Phenergan 10 mg, 25 mg syrup 1 mg/ml	25 mg bd	1-5 years: 5 mg bd 5-12 years: 10 mg bd
Related phenothiazines			
Prochlorperazine	Compazine 5 mg Stemetil 5 mg suppositories 5 mg, 25 mg	5-15 mg tds	0.2 mg/kg bd or tds < 10 kg: avoid
Hyoscine			
Hyoscine hydrobromide	Kwells 0.3 mg tab	1-2 tab statim then 1 tab 4-6 hour prn (max 4/24 hours)	2-7 years: ¼ tab > 7 years: ½ tab (max 4 doses/24 hours)
	Scop 1.5 mg transdermal	1 patch per 72 hours	avoid < 10 years
Combinations			
Hyoscine (0.33 mg) diphenhydramine (25 mg)	Benacine	1 tab statim then 4 hours prn	3-7 years: ¼ tab 7-14 years: ½ tab (max 4 doses/24 hours)
Hyoscine (0.2 mg) + dimenhydrinate (50 mg) + caffeine (20 mg)	Travacalm	1-2 tabs statim (max 4/24 hours)	< 2 years: avoid 2-3 years: ¼ tab 4-7 years: ¼-½ tab 8-13 years: ½-1 tab (max 4 doses/24 hours)

General rules All tablets should be taken 30-60 minutes before departure and repeated 4-6 hourly as necessary (aim for maximum of 4 doses per 24 hours). Antihistamines should be used less frequently and some may be used once a day. Take care with drowsiness, pregnancy, the elderly and prostatic problems. Common adverse effects are drowsiness, irritability, dry mouth, dizziness and blurred vision which are compounded by alcohol, antidepressants and tranquillisers. Hyoscine overdosage (from skin discs) can include confusion, memory loss, giddiness and hallucinations.

These preventive oral preparations should ideally be taken 30–60 minutes before the trip and can be repeated 4–6 hourly during the trip (maximum 4 tablets in 24 hours).

Hyoscine dermal discs (Scop)

One of these adhesive patches should be applied to dry unbroken hairless skin behind the ear, 5–6 hours before travel and left on for 3 days. Wash the hands thoroughly after applying and removing the disc—be careful of accidental finger to eye contact.

Sea travel

Sea travel generally poses no special problems apart from motion sickness and the possibility of injuries in the aged. The larger the ship the less likely the problem. Those prone to sea sickness are advised to take antiemetics 60 minutes before sailing and for the first two days at sea until they obtain their 'sea legs'. However the use of hyoscine transdermal delivery systems is recommended for convenience.

Severe sea sickness The standard treatment is promethazine (Phenergan) 25 mg IM injection. If injections are not possible prochlorperazine (Stemetil) suppositories can be used.

The aged Generally the elderly travel well but should take safeguards to avoid falls. The Chief Surgeon on P&O's ship *Canberra* recommends that elderly people should bring the following:

- a letter from their doctor stating diagnosis and medication
- a spare set of spectacles
- a spare set of dentures
- a walking stick (if appropriate)

Altitude sickness

High altitudes pose special problems for people who live at low altitude especially if they have heart and lung disease. The severity depends on altitude, the speed of ascent, the temperature and level of activity. The high altitudes of Africa (Kilimanjaro, Kenya), India, Nepal (Himalayas), Rockies of Canada and the United States and South America provide such problems. It is usually safe to trek under 2500 metres altitude but problems may occur over 3000 metres.

Forms

1. acute mountain sickness (mild → severe)
2. high-altitude pulmonary oedema
3. high-altitude cerebral oedema

Clinical features

- usually within 8–24 hours of exposure
- frontal headache (worse in morning and when supine)
- malaise, fatigue, anorexia, nausea, insomnia

More severe: fluid retention, dyspnoea, vomiting, dry cough, dizziness.

Serious: marked dyspnoea, neurological symptoms and signs.

Management

Prevention

careful acclimatisation with gradual ascent[10]
spend 2–3 days at intermediate altitudes
ascent rate less than 300 metres per day above 3000 metres
ample fluid intake
acetazolamide (Diamox) 250 mg 8 hourly the day before ascent; continue 3–6 days (deaths from mountain sickness have occurred while on this drug)

Treatment

immediate (urgent and rapid) descent to below 2000 metres
oxygen
dexamethasone e.g. 4 mg, 6 hourly

Travellers' medical kit

If a person intends to travel for a long time the following represents a comprehensive medical kit. It should not be regarded as an alternative to seeking appropriate medical help if it is available. Typical examples of general items are included in brackets.

Materials

bandaids and elastoplast dressing strip
bandages (2 cotton gauze, 2 crepe x 10 cm)
pocket torch
steristrips or 'butterfly strips' (to patch small cuts)
sterile gauze and cotton wool
thermometer
scissors and tweezers
safety pins

Topical items

antifungal cream
cetrimide antiseptic cream (Savlon)
insect repellent containing diethyl-m-toluamide (Muskol, Repellem or Rid)
insecticide spray
mosquito net repellent solution: permethrin (Ambush—ICI)
nasal spray or drops
Stingose spray (for bites and stings)
Strepsils
UV anti-sunburn cream

Medication checklist

Those items marked with * usually require a prescription.

* Antibiotics—norfloxacin 400 mg (6 tablets for 3 days)
—co-trimoxazole (for children)
Antacid tablets—for heartburn or indigestion
* Antimalarials—where appropriate
* Diamox tablets for acute mountain sickness

* Fasigyn 2 g or Flagyl 2.4 g—for amoebiasis or giardiasis
Laxative (Senokot)
* Imodium or Lomotil—for diarrhoea
Motion sickness tablets (Avomine, Kwells or Phenergan)
Paracetamol tablets—for fever or pain
* Sleeping tablets (Euhypnos, Normison, Serepax or Phenergan)
Rehydration mixture (Gastrolyte)

General tips for the traveller

Checklist for 'at risk' countries:

- 'If you can't peel, boil or cook it, don't eat it.'
- Boil or purify water, avoid dairy products, ice-cream, shellfish, food left in open, salads, watercress, ice and recooked or reheated food.
- Never walk around barefoot at night in snake areas (and use a torch).
- Always shake your shoes before putting them on.
- Never wear nylon items in hot tropical areas.
- Never bathe, wade or drink in rivers, lakes or harbours unless you know they are bilharzia-free.
- Keep yourself well covered after dark and use a mosquito net.
- Use insect repellent on skin frequently.
- Use an insecticide spray in your bedroom.
- Seek medical help if bitten by an excited dog, after washing bite.

Other tips

- Organise a dental check before departure.
- Arrange stopovers on a long flight (if possible).
- Take along a spare pair of spectacles and adequate medication.
- Arrange health and travel insurance.
- Check out your nearest embassy/consulate when visiting remote areas or politically unstable countries.
- Consider a traveller's medical kit.
- Never carry a parcel or luggage through Customs to oblige a stranger or recent acquaintance.
- Abstain from sex with a stranger.
- Have a credit card that allows a quick cash advance or an airline ticket purchase (for many countries a policy of 'if you get sick, then get out' is necessary).
- Most death and injury among travellers is caused by motor accidents. Avoid buses in India (and elsewhere)—trains are safer.

References

1. Oldmeadow M. *Travel medicine*. Monash University: Proceedings of Update Course for General Practitioners, 1991, 4.
2. Grayson L, McNeill J. Preventive health advice for Australian travellers to Bali. Med J Aust, 1988; 149: 462–466.
3. Locke DM. Traveller's diarrhoea. Aust Fam Physician, 1990; 19:194–203.
4. Currie B. Malaria. MIMS Disease Index. Sydney: IMS Publishing, 1991–2, 317–320.
5. Brown GV, Biggs BA. Malaria: Advice to travellers. Aust Fam Physician, 1990; 19:177–192.
6. Munro R, Macleod C. Recommendations for international travellers. Mod Medicine Aust, August 1991, 50–57.
7. Amichai B, Finkelstein et al. Think cutaneous leishmaniasis. Aust Fam Physician, 1993; 22:1213–1217.
8. World Health Organisation. International Health for Travellers, 1992.
9. Schroeder S. *Current medical diagnosis and treatment*. East Norwalk: Appleton and Lange, 1990, 1090-1092.
10. McDonnell L. Altitude sickness. Aust Fam Physician, 1990; 19:205–208.

PART 2

DIAGNOSTIC PERSPECTIVE IN GENERAL PRACTICE

12

Inspection as a clinical skill

—

More mistakes, many more, are made by not looking than by not knowing

Sir William Jenner

General practitioners have an ideal opportunity to practise the art of careful observation and to notice all the signs and features characteristic of a patient from the time seen in the waiting room until the physical examination. We should be 'like Sherlock Holmes' in our analysis of the patient and accept the challenge of being astute diagnosticians and proud members of a noble profession.

It is important to stand back (so to speak) and look at the patient's general appearance and demeanour. We should be assessing their mood and affect as much as their physical appearance.

First impressions

The first impression of the patient is always striking in some way and we should discipline ourselves to be as analytical as possible.

A rapid inspection from a trained observer may be all that is necessary to allow the observer to pinpoint specific disorders such as anaemia, hyperthyroidism, jaundice, acromegaly and alcohol abuse. Such 'spot' diagnosis is not justifiable unless the original signs are supported by further examination, which must be comprehensive.

The following observations should therefore be made:

1. facial characteristics
2. abnormalities of the head and neck
3. examination of the mouth
4. character and distribution of hair
5. examination of the skin (in general)
6. height and weight
7. posture and gait
8. genitalia
9. examination of extremities (hands, feet, nails, etc.)

Physiognomy

Physiognomy, which is the art of judging character from the features of the face, flourished in the Middle Ages. According to Addison, 'everyone is in some degree a master of that art which is physiognomy; and naturally forms to themselves the character of a stranger from the features of the face'. In reality, all doctors use a physiognomical approach to diagnose many medical conditions although we may not be as expert at the art as we should be.

The face is a person's most immediate means of communicating with others, it is a shield and banner, a mask and a mirror. It reveals mental faculties and emotional turmoil. It is the first perspective gained of patients as they walk into the consulting room.

The face as a mirror of disease

A fascinating aspect of the art of clinical medicine is the clinical interpretation of the patient's facies. Not only are specific skin lesions common on the face but the face may mirror endocrine disorders and organ failure such as respiratory, cardiac, renal and liver failure.

Jaundice may be masked by the natural colour of the cheeks but the yellow conjunctivae will be distinctive. A marked plethoric complexion may be seen in chronic alcoholics (alcohol may produce a pseudo-Cushing's syndrome), in Cushing's disease or in polycythaemia. Thickening of the subcutaneous tissues may be seen in chronic alcoholism, acromegaly and myxoedema, and the puffiness of the eyelids in the latter condition may simulate the true subcutaneous oedema of renal disease

An individual's personality and mood rarely fail to leave an impression on the facial characteristics. This is partly due to the alteration in facial lines and wrinkles which may become modified in anger, irritability, anxiety and stress. More profound changes occur with mental disease. Various CNS diseases such as Parkinson's disease and myopathies can affect facial expression, e.g. the immobile face of the patient with Parkinson's disease.

The appearance of the eyes can also be very significant and may reflect underlying systemic disease.

Diagnostic facies

Acromegalic

The enlarged characteristic face is due to a large supraorbital ridge which causes frontal bossing, a broad nose and a prominent broad and square lower jaw. Other features include an enlarged tongue and soft tissue swelling of the nose, lips and ears.

Alcoholic (due to chronic use)

It is important to recognise the characteristic changes as early as possible—a plethoric face, thickened 'greasy' skin, telangiectasia, suffused conjunctivae and rosacea. Other features may include rhinophyma, parotid swelling and characteristic changes to the lips and corners of the mouth.

Bird-like (systemic sclerosis: CREST syndrome)

The bird-like features, beaking of the nose, limitation of mouth opening, puckering or furrowing of the lips and a fixed facial expression, are due to binding down of facial skin. Other features include telangiectasia on the face and hands.

Chipmunk (thalassaemia minor)

There is bossing of the skull, hypertrophy of the maxillae (which tends to expose the upper teeth), prominent malar eminences and depression of the bridge of the nose. The major haemoglobinopathies cause hyperplasia of the skull and facial bones because of an increase in the bone marrow cavity.

Cushignoid

The face has a typical 'moon shape', plethora, hirsutism (more obvious in women), acne.

Facial nerve palsy

Features include unilateral drooping of the corner of the mouth and flattening of the nasolabial fold.
UMN type: the forehead movement is spared.
LMN type: e.g. Bell's palsy, Ramsay Hunt syndrome: lack of forehead muscle tone.

Obese

The distinguishing feature from the 'moon face' of Cushing's disease is the general roundness and uniform fatness of the face.

Thyrotoxic (hyperthyroidism)

The prominent eyes (sclera may not be covered by the lower eyelid) and conjunctivitis are features of the thyrotoxic patient. The thyroid stare (a frightened expression) may also be present.

Myxoedemic (hypothyroidism)

The face usually has an apathetic look and is 'puffy' with possible periorbital oedema. There is broadening of the lower part of the face. The skin (not the sclera) may appear yellow (due to hypercarotenaemia) and is generally dry and coarse. Other features may include thin, coarse, listless hair and loss or thinning of the outer third of the eyebrows. The tongue is usually enlarged and the patient speaks with a 'thickened', croaking, slow speech.

Marfanoid (Marfan's syndrome)

The typical tall stature, arachnydactyly and chest deformities, combined with the facial features of a subluxation of the lens of the eye and high arched palate, help to pinpoint the diagnosis.

Mongoloid (Down syndrome)

The facial features include a flat profile, with crowded features, a round head, dysplastic low-set ears, protruding tongue, mongoloid slant of the eyes with epicanthic folds, mouth hanging open and peripheral silver iris spots (Brushfield's spots).

Mitral (mitral valve disease, especially mitral stenosis)

This is typically shown in flushed or rosy cheeks with a bluish tinge due to dilatation of the malar capillaries. It is associated with pulmonary hypertension.

Myotonic (dystrophia myotonia)

Typical features include frontal baldness, expressionless triangular facies, partial ptosis, cataracts and temporal muscle atrophy.

Myopathic (myopathy/myasthaenia gravis)

Facial characteristics include an expressionless, 'tired' looking face with bilateral ptosis.

Pagetic (Paget's disease)

The main feature is skull enlargement, notably of the frontal and parietal areas (the head circumference is usually greater than 55 cm, which is abnormal)—the 'hat doesn't fit any more' hallmark. Other features include increased bony warmth and deafness.

Parkinsonian

Characteristic is the mask-like facies with lack of facial expression and fixed unblinking stare. There is immobility of the facial muscles.

Turner's syndrome

The facial characteristics include ptosis—'fish-like' mouth, small chin (micrognathia), low-set ears and deafness. Webbing of the neck is the classic sign.

Specific characteristics

Various facial signs may be present. The causes of these signs are listed below.

Butterfly 'rash'

• SLE	Erythema, scaling with a discrete red advancing edge on the cheeks and bridge of the nose. The sharp border, lack of pustules and adherent scale makes it differ from rosacea.
• Rosacea	Papules, pustules and telangiectasia on an erythematous background on cheeks, forehead and chin.
• Erysipelas	Painful, erythematous, indurated skin infection with a well-defined raised edge.
• Seborrhoeic dermatitis	Red and scaly rash involving eyebrows, eyelids, nasolabial folds.
• Photosensitivity eruptions	Erythematous on sun-exposed area

Cloasma/melasma

Increased browning pigmentation, usually confined to symmetrical areas of the cheeks. Caused by drugs:

- combined oral contraceptive pill
- hydroxyquinolones (Plaquenil)
- diphenylhydramine

Malar flush

- mitral stenosis
- pulmonary stenosis
- rosacea
- SLE
- mesenteric adenitis

Spider naevi

- pregnancy
- liver disease
- vitamin B deficiency, in normal people

Enlarged tongue

- acromegaly
- hypothyroidism
- amyloidosis

Cataracts

- senility
- corticosteroid therapy
- diabetes
- hypoparathyroidism
- dystrophia myotonia
- trauma
- ocular disease, e.g. glaucoma

Telangiectasia

- systemic sclerosis
- CREST syndrome
- liver disease, e.g. alcoholism

Cyanosis

Cyanosis is a bluish discolouration of the skin and mucous membranes due to deoxygenated haemoglobin concentrated in the superficial blood vessels. It is classified as central or peripheral.

Central

Cyanosis is present in parts of the body with good circulation such as the lips and tongue. The areas feel warm. The main causes are pulmonary disease, cyanotic congenital heart disease (right to left shunt), respiratory depression, polycythaemia.

Peripheral

Cyanosis is in the extremities such as the outer surface of the lips, nose and ears. The areas feel cold. The main causes are peripheral vascular disease, cardiac failure, exposure to cold, left ventricular failure and all causes of central cyanosis.

Increased pigmentation

Increased pigmentation is not common but if obvious in areas exposed to the sun look for 'hidden' areas such as the inner aspect of the forearms. Causes include those listed below.

Increased melanocyte-stimulating hormone (MSH)

- Addison's disease
- Cushing's disease
- Ectopic ACTH syndrome

Metabolic

- Hyperthyroidism
- Haemocharomatosis
- Cirrhosis of the liver
- Porphyria
- Chronic renal failure
- Malnutrition/malabsorption
- Pregnancy

Drugs

- Oral contraceptive pill
- Psoralens
- Photochemotherapy (PUVA)
- Arsenic, gold, silver
- Phenothiazines
- Antimalarials (chloroquine/Plaquenil)
- Dapsone
- Antibiotics (busulphan, bleomycin)
- Amiodarone

Tumours

- Lymphomas
- Acanthosis nigricans
- Metastatic melanoma

13

A safe diagnostic strategy

The discipline of general practice is probably the most difficult, complex and challenging of the healing arts. Our field of endeavour is at the very front line of medicine and as practitioners we shoulder the responsibility of the early diagnosis of very serious, perhaps life-threatening, illness in addition to the recognition of anxiety traits in our patients.

The teaching of our craft is also an exciting challenge and presupposes that we have a profound comprehension of our discipline.

Our area is characterised by a wide kaleidoscope of presenting problems, often foreign to the classical textbook presentation and sometimes embellished by a 'shopping list' of seemingly unconnected problems—the so-called undifferentiated illness syndrome.[1] Common undifferentiated symptoms include tiredness or fatigue, sleeping problems, anxiety and stress, dizziness, headache, indigestion, anorexia and nausea, sexual dysfunction, weight loss, loss of interest, flatulence, abdominal discomfort and chest discomfort.[2] It is important, especially in a busy practice, to adopt a fail-safe strategy to analyse such presenting problems. Such an approach is even more important in a world of increasing medical litigation and specialisation.

To help bring order to the jungle of general practice problems the author has developed a simple model to facilitate diagnosis and reduce the margin of error.

The basic model

The use of the diagnostic model requires a disciplined approach to the problem with the medical practitioner quickly answering five self-posed questions. The questions are contained in Table 13.1.

Table 13.1 *The diagnostic model for a presenting problem*

1. What is the probability diagnosis?
2. What serious disorders must not be missed?
3. What conditions are often missed (the pitfalls)?
4. Could this patient have one of the 'masquerades' in medical practice?
5. Is this patient trying to tell me something else?

This approach, which is based on considerable experience, requires the learning of a predetermined plan which, naturally, would vary in different parts of the world but would have a certain universal application in the so-called developed world.

Each of the above five questions will be expanded.

1. The probability diagnosis

The probability diagnosis is based on the doctor's perspective and experience with regard to prevalence, incidence and the natural history of disease. General practitioners acquire first-hand epidemiological knowledge about the patterns of illness apparent in individuals and in the community, which enables them to view illness from a perspective that is not available to doctors in any other disciplines. Thus, during the medical interview, the doctor is not only gathering information, allocating priorities and making hypotheses, but is also developing a probability diagnosis based on acquired epidemiological knowledge.

2. What serious disorders must not be missed?

While epidemiological knowledge is a great asset to the general practitioner it can be a disadvantage in that he or she is so familiar with what is common that the all-important rare cause of a presenting symptom may be overlooked. On the other hand, the doctor in the specialist clinic, where a different spectrum of disease is encountered, is more likely to focus on the rare at the expense of the common cause. However, it is vital, especially working in the modern framework of a litigation-conscious society, not to miss serious, life-threatening disorders.

To achieve early recognition of serious illness the general practitioner needs to develop a 'high index of suspicion'. This is generally regarded as largely intuitive, but this is probably not so, and it would be more accurate to say that it comes with experience.

The serious disorders that should always be considered 'until proven otherwise' include malignant disease, acquired immunodeficiency syndrome (AIDS), coronary disease and life-threatening infections such as meningitis, Haemophilus influenza b infections, septicaemia and infective endocarditis (Table 13.2).

Table 13.2 *Serious 'not to be missed' conditions*

Neoplasia, esp. malignancy

HIV infection / AIDS

Asthma

Severe infections, esp.
- meningoencephalitis
- septicaemia
- epiglottitis
- infective endocarditis

Coronary disease
- myocardial infarction
- unstable angina
- arrhythmias

Imminent or potential suicide

Myocardial infarction or ischaemia is extremely important to consider because it is so potentially lethal and at times can be overlooked by the busy practitioner. It does not always manifest as the classical presentation of crushing central pain but can present as pain of varying severity and quality in a wide variety of sites. These sites include the jaw, neck, arm, epigastrium and interscapular region. Coronary artery disease may manifest as life-threatening arrhythmias which may present as palpitations and/or dizziness. A high index of suspicion is necessary to diagnose arrhythmias.

3. What conditions are often missed?

This question refers to the common 'pitfalls' so often encountered in general practice. This area is definitely related to the experience factor and includes rather simple non-life-threatening problems that can be so easily overlooked unless doctors are prepared to include them in their diagnostic framework.

Classic examples include smoking or dental caries as a cause of abdominal pain; allergies to a whole variety of unsuspected everyday contacts; foreign bodies; occupational or environmental hazards as a cause of headache, respiratory discomfort or malaise; and faecal impaction as a cause of diarrhoea. We have all experienced the 'red face syndrome' from a urinary tract infection whether it is the cause of fever in a child, lumbar pain in a pregnant woman or malaise in an older person. The dermatomal pain pattern caused by herpes zoster prior to the eruption of the rash (or if only a few sparse vesicles erupt) is a real trap.

Menopausal symptoms can also be overlooked as we focus on a particular symptom. Some important pitfalls are given in Table 13.3.

4. The masquerades

It is important to utilise a type of fail-safe mechanism to avoid missing the diagnosis of these disorders. Some practitioners refer to consultations that make their 'head spin' in confusion and bewilderment, with patients presenting with a 'shopping list' of problems. It is in these patients that a checklist is useful. Consider the apparently neurotic patient who presents with headache, lethargy, tiredness, constipation, anorexia, indigestion, shortness of breath on exertion, pruritus, flatulence, sore tongue and backache. In such a patient we must

Table 13.3 *Classic pitfalls*

Allergies
Candida infection
Domestic abuse inc. child abuse
Drugs (see Table 13.4)
Herpes zoster
Faecal impaction
Foreign bodies
Lead poisoning
Menopause syndrome
Migraine (atypical variants)
Paget's disease
Pregnancy (early)
Urinary infection

consider a diagnosis that links all these symptoms, especially if the physical examination is inconclusive; this includes iron deficiency anaemia, depression, diabetes mellitus, hypothyroidism and drug abuse.

Table 13.4 *The seven primary masquerades*

1. Depression
2. Diabetes mellitus
3. Drugs
   - iatrogenic
   - self-abuse
   - alcohol
   - narcotics
   - nicotine
   - others
4. Anaemia
5. Thyroid and other endocrine disorders
   - hyperthyroidism
   - hypothyroidism
6. Spinal dysfunction
7. Urinary infection

A century ago it was important to consider diseases such as syphilis and tuberculosis as the great common masquerades, but these infections have been replaced by iatrogenesis, malignant disease, alcoholism, endocrine disorders and the various manifestations of atherosclerosis, particularly coronary insufficiency and cerebrovascular insufficiency.

If the patient has pain anywhere it is possible that it could originate from the spine, so the possibility of spinal pain (radicular or referred) should be considered as the cause for various pain syndromes such as headache, arm pain, leg pain, chest pain, pelvic pain and even abdominal pain. The author's experience is that spondylogenic pain is one of the most underdiagnosed problems in general practice.

Table 13.5 *The seven other masquerades*

1. Chronic renal failure
2. Malignant disease
   - lymphomas
   - lung
   - caecum/colon
   - kidney
   - multiple myeloma
   - ovary
   - metastasis
3. HIV infection/AIDS
4. Baffling bacterial infections
   - syphilis
   - tuberculosis
   - infective endocarditis
   - the zoonoses
   - chlamydia infections
   - others
5. Baffling viral (and protozoal) infections
   - Epstein-Barr mononucleosis
   - TORCH organisms, e.g. cytomegalovirus
   - hepatitis A,B,C,D,E
   - mosquito-borne infections
     - malaria
     - Ross River fever
     - others
6. Neurological dilemmas
   - Parkinson's disease
   - Guillain-Barré syndrome
   - seizure disorders
   - multiple sclerosis
   - myasthenia gravis
   - space-occupying lesion of skull
   - migraine
7. Connective tissue disorders and the vasculitides
   - Connective tissue disorders
     - SLE
     - systemic sclerosis
     - dermatomyositis
     - overlap syndrome
   - Vasculitides
     - polyarteritis nodosa
     - giant cell arteritis/polymyalgia rheumatica
     - granulomatous disorders

A checklist that has been divided into two groups of seven disorders is presented (Tables 13.4 and 13.5). The first list, 'the seven primary masquerades', represents the more common disorders encountered in general practice; the second list includes less common masquerades although some, such as Epstein-Barr mononucleosis, can be very common masquerades in general practice.

Neoplasia, especially malignancy of the so-called 'silent areas', can be an elusive diagnostic problem. Typical examples are carcinoma of the nasopharynx and sinuses, ovary, caecum, kidney and lymphoietic tissue. Sarcoidosis is another disease that can be a real masquerade (page 394).

As a practical diagnostic ploy, the author has both lists strategically placed on the surgery wall immediately behind the patient. The lists are rapidly perused for inspiration should the diagnosis for a particular patient prove elusive.

Is the patient trying to tell me something?

The doctor has to consider, especially in the case of undifferentiated illness, whether the patient has a 'hidden agenda' for the presentation.[3] Of course, the patient may be depressed (overt or masked) or may have a true anxiety state. However, a presenting symptom such as tiredness may represent a 'ticket of entry' to the consulting room. It may represent a plea for help in a stressed or anxious patient. We should be sensitive to patients' needs and feelings and as listening, caring, empathetic practitioners provide the right opportunity for the patient to communicate freely.

Deep sexual anxieties and problems, poor self-esteem, and fear of malignancy or some other medical catastrophe are just some of the reasons patients present to doctors. The author has another checklist (Table 13.6) to help identify the psychosocial reasons for a patient's malaise.

In the author's experience of counselling patients and families the number of problems caused by interpersonal conflict is quite amazing and makes it worthwhile specifically exploring the quality of close relationships, such as those between husband–wife, mother–daughter and father–son.

Table 13.6 *Underlying fears or image problems that cause stress and anxiety*

1.	Interpersonal conflict in the family
2.	Identification with sick or deceased friends
3.	Fear of malignancy
4.	STDs especially AIDS
5.	Impending 'coronary' or 'stroke'
6.	Sexual problem
7.	Drug-related problem
8.	Crippling arthritis

Identification and transference of illness, symptoms and death, in particular, are important areas of anxiety to consider. Patients often identify their problems with relatives, friends or public personalities who have malignant disease. Other somatoform disorders and the factitious disorders, including the fascinating Munchausen's syndrome, may be obvious or extremely complex and difficult to recognise.

The bottom line is that patients are often desperately searching for security and we have an important role to play in helping them.

Some examples of application of the model

HICCUP

Summary of diagnostic strategy model for abnormal hiccup

1. Q. *Probability diagnosis*
   A. Food and alcohol excess
   Psychogenic/functional
   Postoperative
   - gastric distension
   - phrenic nerve irritation
2. Q. *Serious disorders not to be missed*
   A. Neoplasia
   - CNS
   - neck
   - oesophagus
   - lung

   Subphrenic abscess
   Myocardial infarction/pericarditis
   CNS disorders, e.g. CVA; infection
3. Q. *Pitfalls*
   A. Alcohol excess
   Smoking
   Aerophagy
   GIT disorders
   - oesophagitis
   - peptic ulcer
   - hiatus hernia
   - cholecystitis
   - hepatomegaly

   Rarities
   Sudden temperature change
   Neck cysts and vascular abnormalities

6-15-97

To Darling Melanie,

Here's a keepsake photo of me looking at my best at 15 wks old during my baptism. Judge for yourself - ha! ha!

Lots of love,
Emily Margaret
Marin

4. Q. *Seven masquerades checklist*
   A. Depression –
   Diabetes –
   Drugs ✓
   Anaemia –
   Thyroid disease –
   Spinal dysfunction possible
   UTI –
5. Q. *Is the patient trying to tell me something?*
   A. Emotional causes always to be considered.

HALITOSIS

Summary of diagnostic strategy model

1. Q. *Probability diagnosis*
   A. Dietary habits
   Orodental disease
   Dry mouth, e.g. on waking
   Smoking/alcohol
2. Q. *Serious disorders not to be missed*
   A. Malignancy:
   lung, oropharynx, larynx, stomach, nose, leukaemia
   Pulmonary tuberculosis
   Quinsy
   Lung abscess
   Blood dyscrasias/leukaemia
   Uraemia
   Hepatic failure
3. Q. *Pitfalls*
   A. Nasal and sinus infection
   Systemic infection
   Appendicitis
   Bronchiectasis
   Hiatus hernia
   Rarities
   Pharyngeal and oesophageal diverticula
   Sjögren's syndrome
   Scurvy
4. Q. *Seven masquerades checklist*
   A. Depression ✓
   Diabetes ✓ acetone
   Drugs ✓
   Anaemia –
   Thyroid disease –
   Spinal dysfunction –
   UTI –
5. Q. *Is the patient trying to tell me something?*
   A. Possible manifestation of psychogenic disorder.

References

1. Murtagh J. Common problems: a safe diagnostic strategy. Aust Fam Physician, 1990; 19:733–742.
2. Frith J, Knowlden S. Undifferentiated illness. Med J Aust, 1992; 156:472–476.
3. Levenstein JH, McCracken EC, McWhinney IR et al. The patient centred method. I. A model for the doctor-patient interaction in family medicine. Fam Pract, 1986; 3:24–30.

14

Depression

Depressive illness, which is probably *the* greatest masquerade of general practice, is one of the commonest illnesses in medicine and is often confused with other illnesses. It is a very real illness that affects the entire mind and body. Unfortunately, there is a social stigma associated with depression and many patients tend to deny that they are depressed.

It is a useful working rule to consider depression as an illness that seriously dampens the five basic activities of humans:

- energy for activity
- sex drive
- sleep
- appetite
- ability to cope with life

Many episodes of depression are transient and should be regarded as normal but 10% of the population have significant depressive illness. The lifetime risk of being treated for depression is approximately 12% for men and 15% for women.[1]

Classifications

- Affective or mood disorders refer to those conditions in which there is a disturbance of affect or mood.
- The DSM-III-R classification divides the disorder into the depressive disorders and bipolar disorders (both manic and depressive episodes).
- The depressive disorders include major depression, adjustment disorders with depressive mood, and dysthymia.
  - — Major depression includes those disorders with one or more major depressive episodes.[1]
  - — Dysthymia refers to longstanding (2 years or more) depression of mild severity ('neurotic depression').[1]
  - — Adjustment disorder with depressed mood is a less severe form of depression without sufficient criteria for major depression. It is very common and occurs in response to identifiable stressors ('reactive depression'). Its duration is usually no longer than 6 months.

Major depression

The patient can experience many symptoms, both physical and mental. The DSM-III-R diagnostic criteria for depression are outlined in the next column.

These criteria can be extended to include:

- a feeling of not being able to cope with life
- continual tiredness
- loss of sense of humour
- tension and anxiety
- irritability, anger or fearfulness
- somatic symptoms such as headache, constipation, indigestion, weight loss, dry mouth and unusual pains or sensations in the chest or abdomen

The symptoms may vary during the day, but are usually worse on waking in the morning. Some patients have psychotic features, usually only

DSM-III-R Diagnostic Criteria
for Major Depression
At least 5 of the following symptoms for 2 weeks
(criterion 1 or 2 essential)

1. Depressed mood
2. Loss of interest or pleasure
3. Significant appetite or weight loss or gain (usually poor appetite)
4. Insomnia or hypersomnia (usually early morning waking)
5. Psychomotor agitation and retardation
6. Fatigue or loss of energy
7. Feelings of worthlessness or excessive guilt
8. Impaired thinking or concentration; indecisiveness
9. Suicidal thoughts/thoughts of death

delusions, but sometimes also hallucinations, and may be misdiagnosed as schizophrenic.

In practice the DSM-III-R classification seems too rigid and the experienced doctor has to consider the global constellation of symptoms. Better management follows early diagnosis and intervention before the formal criteria for major depression develop.

Important points

- The essential feature of depression is mood change which can vary in intensity from despondency to intense despair.[1]
- The other major feature is loss of interest or pleasure, including loss of interest in family, hobbies, sexual activity and personal appearance.

Minor depression

Minor depression is basically a condition where fluctuations of symptoms occur with some vague somatic symptoms and a transient lowering of mood that can respond to environmental influences. Suicidal feelings are fleeting and delusions and hallucinations are absent. These patients usually respond in time to simple psychotherapy, reassurance and support. However, care should be taken lest they move into major depression.

Masked depression

This is a difficult yet common type of depression in practice and tends to be misdiagnosed. Patients do not complain of the classic symptoms and tend to deny depression which is perceived as a social stigma and a sign of weakness. They usually have multiple minor complaints of the 'ticket of entry' type. Mood changes may be elicited only after careful questioning.

The classic affective features of depression are masked by a complex of somatic complaints. Such symptoms include fatigue, anorexia, weight loss, menstrual changes, unusual sensations in the abdomen, chest or head, bodily aches and pain, dry mouth and difficulty in breathing.

If depression is not considered many fruitless, expensive and distressing investigations may be performed. According to Davies[2], nearly half of patients with depressive illness report to the doctor with complaints that suggest physical illness. The family doctor has to suspect masked depression in a patient with a multitude of physical complaints or with complaints that do not fit any definite pattern of organic disease.

The differential diagnoses of depression are presented in Table 14.1.

An Australian study on masked depression[3] concluded: 'It must be stressed that the masking of the depressive state occurs on the doctor's side as well as the patient's, and an awareness that this may be so leads us to recommend that, once organic lesions have been excluded, there is a place for the use of an adequate therapeutic trial of antidepressants'.

The following additional points were made by a panel of psychiatrists at a symposium entitled 'Depression: Masked or Missed?' in Dallas, Texas:[4]

- Some patients dismissed as 'crocks' may go on to suicide if their depression is not treated.
- Masked depression would be missed much less frequently if the physician would look beneath symptoms that do not quite ring true.
- The patient with the 'tired blood syndrome' deserves something other than an iron tonic.
- Depression frequently accompanies organic diseases that are associated with nausea and other illness.
- A complete work-up may help to rule out organic disease but may result in iatrogenic disease if pursued overzealously.
- Alcoholism should be suspected as a cause of depression.

Table 14.1 *Differential diagnoses of depression*

Psychiatric conditions
- anxiety disorder
- schizophrenia
- drug and alcohol abuse
- dementia

Organic disorders
- malignancy, e.g. lung, pancreas, lymphoma
- hypothyroidism
- hyperparathyroidism
- other endocrine disorders, e.g. Cushing's, Addison's anaemia, especially pernicious anaemia
- postinfective states, e.g. Epstein-Barr mononucleosis
- cerebrovascular disease
- Parkinson's disease
- congestive cardiac failure
- systemic lupus erythematosus
- drugs (which may cause depression)
  - antihypertensives
  - antiparkinson drugs
  - corticosteroids
  - cytotoxic agents
  - NSAIDs
  - oral contraceptives/progestogen

Depression in the elderly

Depression can have bizarre features in the elderly and may be misdiagnosed as dementia or psychosis. Agitated depression is the most frequent type of depression in the aged.[1] Features may include histrionic behaviour, delusions and disordered thinking.

A useful clue is a change in sleep pattern so a request for sleeping tablets may lead to the prescription for a more sedating antidepressant. Medical illness is an important precipitant of depression in the elderly. Tricyclic antidepressants have to be used with caution in the elderly and most have some contraindications to their use.

Depression in children

Sadness is common in children but depression, although not as common, does occur and is characterised by feelings of helplessness, worthlessness and despair. Parents and doctors both tend to be unaware of depression in children.[5]

Major depression in children and adolescents may be diagnosed using the same criteria as for adults, namely loss of interest in usual activities and the presence of a sad or irritable mood, persisting for two weeks or more.[6] The other constellation of depressive symptoms including somatic complaints may be present. Although suicidal thoughts are common, suicide is rare before adolescence. Referral of these patients to an experienced child psychiatrist is advisable.

The diagnostic approach

Depression can be associated with many illnesses but it is important to realise that the somatic symptoms may be the presentation of depressive illness and thus 'undifferentiated illness' is a feature. The patient tends to complain of aches and pains, gastrointestinal symptoms and other similar symptoms rather than emotional problems.

There is a relationship between anxiety and depression so that many depressed patients are agitated and anxious—a feature that may mask the underlying depression.[7]

Questions to assess level of depression

What do you think is the matter with you?
Do you think that your feelings are possibly caused by nerves, anxiety or depression?
Can you think of any reason why you feel this way?
Do you feel down in the dumps?
Do you feel that you are coping well?
Do you have any good times?
Has anything changed in your life?
How do you sleep? Do you wake early?
What time of the day do you feel at your worst?
Where would you put yourself between 0 and 100%?
Have you felt hopeless?
Do you brood about the past?
What is your energy like?
What is your appetite like?
Are you as interested in sex as before?
Do you feel guilty about anything?
Do you feel that life is worthwhile?
Has the thought of ending your life occurred to you?
Do you cry when no one is around? (especially for children)

Management

Important considerations from the outset are:

- Is the patient a suicide risk?

- Does the patient require inpatient assessment?
- Is referral to a specialist psychiatrist indicated?

If the symptoms are major and the patient appears in poor health or is a suicide risk, referral is appropriate.

The basic treatments are:

- Psychotherapy, including education, reassurance and support. All patients require minor psychotherapy. More sophisticated techniques such as cognitive or behavioural therapy may be used for selected patients. Cognitive therapy basically involves teaching patients new ways of positive thinking, which have to be relevant and achievable for the patient.
- Pharmacological agents.
- Electroconvulsive treatment.

Useful guidelines

- mild depression: psychotherapy alone may suffice but keep medication in mind
- moderate to severe depression: psychotherapy plus antidepressants.

Explanatory supportive notes for patients and relatives

Most people feel unhappy or depressed every now and again, but there is a difference between this feeling and the illness of depression.

Depression is a very real illness that affects the entire mind and body. People cannot seem to lift themselves out of their misery or 'fight it themselves'. Superficial advice like 'snap out of it' is unhelpful, because the person has no control over it.

What is the cause?

The cause is somewhat mysterious, but it has been found that an important chemical is present in smaller amounts than usual in the nervous system. It is rather like a person low in iron becoming anaemic.

Depression can follow a severe loss, such as the death of a loved one, a marital separation or financial loss. On the other hand it can develop for no apparent reason, although it may follow an illness such as glandular fever or influenza, an operation or childbirth. Depression is seen more commonly in late adolescence, middle age (both men and women), retirement age and in the elderly.

What is the treatment?

The basis of treatment is to replace the missing chemicals with antidepressant medication. Antidepressants are not drugs of addiction and are very effective but take about two weeks before an improvement is noticed. Alcohol can interact with the tablets so it is important not to drink and drive. If the person is very seriously depressed and there is a risk of suicide, admission to hospital will most likely be advised. Other more effective treatments can be used if needed. The depressed person needs a lot of understanding, support and therapy. Once treatment is started, the outlook is very good (an 80% cure rate).

Important points

- Depression is an illness.
- It is more common than realised.
- It just happens; no one is to blame.
- It affects the basic functions of energy, sex, appetite and sleep.
- It can be lethal if untreated.
- It can destroy relationships.
- The missing chemical needs to be replaced.
- It responds well to treatment.

Recommended reading

Paul Hauck, *Overcoming Depression*. The Westminster Press, London, 1987.

Antidepressant medication

The initial choice of an antidepressant depends on the age and sex of the patient and the side effect profile. All antidepressants are equally efficacious. The tricyclics and tetracyclics are the first-line drugs but the newer drugs, fluoxetine (a serotonin reuptake inhibitor) and moclobemide (a reversible monoamine oxide inhibitor (MAOI) antidepressant) are equally effective.

Tricyclic antidepressants[6]

I. amitriptyline and imipramine
   - the first generation tricyclics
   - the most sedating: valuable if marked anxiety and insomnia
   - strongest anticholinergic side effects, e.g. constipation, blurred vision, prostatism

II. nortriptyline, desipramine, doxepin, dothiepin
   - less sedating and anticholinergic activity
   - nortriptyline is the least hypotensive of the tricyclics

Dosage: 50–75 mg (o) nocte, increasing every 2 to 3 days to 150 mg (o) nocte by day 7

If no response after 2 to 3 weeks, increase by 25–50 mg daily at 2 to 3 week intervals (depending on adverse effects) to 200–250 mg (o) nocte.

General side effects

- dry mouth, weight gain, constipation, sedation
- glaucoma, urinary retention, tremor
- confusion and delirium in the elderly (caution in the elderly)
- sexual dysfunction
- postural hypotension
- cardiac conduction impairment (caution in heart disease)
- lowered seizure threshold

Tetracyclic antidepressants[6]

Mianserin 30–60 mg (o) nocte increasing to 60–120 mg (o) nocte by day 7

Side effects

- polyarthritis
- neutropenia (reversible) especially > 65 years
- less anticholinergic effects than tricyclics
- fewer cardiovascular side effects

Fluoxetine[6]

Fluoxetine 20 mg (o) mane

This dose is usually sufficient for most patients.

If no response after 2 to 3 weeks, increase by 20 mg at 2 to 3 week intervals to 40–80 mg (o) daily in divided doses.

This new drug has a similar efficacy profile to the tricyclics. It does not appear to cause weight gain, interact with alcohol or cause serious cardiovascular effects.

Adverse effects: Nausea, nervousness, diarrhoea, headaches, insomnia. Possible effects include sexual dysfunction, mainly ejaculatory disturbances.

Fluoxetine should not be used with MAOIs or the tricyclics.

Moclobemide

Moclobemide 150 mg (o) bd

If no response after 2–3 weeks, increase by 50 mg daily to maximum 300 mg (o) bd.

- This is a reversible MAOI which is less toxic than the irreversible MAOIs.
- It has minimal interaction with tyramine-containing foodstuffs, so that no dietary restrictions are necessary.
- Adverse effects include nausea, headache, dizziness and insomnia.
- The irreversible MAOIs, which should be reserved for second-line MAOI therapy, include phenelzine and tranylcypromine.

Notes about antidepressants[6]

- Tricyclics can be given once daily (usually in the evening).
- There is a delay in onset of action of 1 to 2 weeks after a therapeutic dose (equivalent to 150 mg imipramine at least) is reached.
- Each drug should have a clinical trial at an adequate dose for at least 3 weeks before treatment is changed.
- Consider referral if there is a failed (adequate) trial.
- Full recovery may take up to 6 weeks or longer (in those who respond).
- Continue treatment at maintenance levels for at least 6 to 9 months.[1] There is a high risk of relapse.
- MAOIs are often the drugs of choice for neurotic depression or atypical depression.[1]

Electroconvulsive therapy (ECT)

ECT is safe, effective and rapidly acting.[1,6,9]

Indications

- psychotic depression, e.g. delusions, hallucinations
- melancholic depression unresponsive to antidepressants
- substantial suicide risk
- ineffective antidepressant medication
- severe psycomotor depression
  - — refusal to eat or drink
  - — depressive stupor
  - — severe personal neglect

Immediate referral for hospital admission is necessary in most of these circumstances. The usual course is 6–8 treatments over three weeks. Tricyclic antidepressants can be used in combination with ECT and after ECT to prevent relapse.

Suicide

The risk of suicide is a concern in all depressed patients. Between 11 and 17% of people who have suffered a severe depressive disorder at any time will eventually commit suicide.[9] Referral for hospital admission should be arranged for patients who are at great risk for suicide. There is a distinction between patients who are determined to suicide and those who attempt suicide (parasuicide).

Risk factors for suicide include:

- male sex
- older age > 55 years
- immigrant status
- isolation/living alone
- recent divorce, separation or bereavement
- recent loss of employment or retirement
- family history of psychiatric illness (including suicide)
- impulsive, hostile personality
- previous suicide attempt
- severe depression
- financial difficulties
- alcohol or drug addiction
- early dementia
- physical illness, especially if chronic pain

If there is concern about suicide risk and treatment is supervised outside hospital, provide closer supervision and considerable support and prescribe drugs which are less toxic in overdosage, e.g. mianserin or fluoxetine. If tricyclics are prescribed, useful guidelines are that dangerous medical complications occur with an equivalent dosage of 1000 mg (40 tablets) of imipramine and a high risk of death with 2000 mg (80 tablets).[6]

When to refer[1]

- Inpatient care obviously necessary.
- Severe depression.
- Substantial suicide risk.
- Failure of response to routine antidepressant therapy.
- Associated psychiatric or physical disorders.
- Difficult problem in the elderly—where diagnosis including 'dementia' is doubtful.
- Children with apparent major depression.

References

1. Burrows GD. Depressive disorders. In: MIMS Disease Index. Sydney: IMS Publishing, 1991–2, 133–135.
2. Davies B. *An introduction to clinical psychiatry*. University of Melbourne, 1977, 76–77.
3. Serry DK, Serry M. Masked depression and the use of antidepressants in general practice. Med J Australia, 15 February 1969, 35–37.
4. Depression: Masked or missed? Patient Care, vol 1, no 3: October 1972, 6–14.
5. Robinson MJ. *Practical paediatrics* (2nd edition), Melbourne: Churchill Livingstone, 1990, 552–553.
6. Mashford ML. *Psychotropic drug guidelines* (2nd edition), Melbourne: Victorian Medical Postgraduate Foundation, 1993/4, 74–82.
7. Davis A, Bolin T, Ham J. *Symptom analysis and physical diagnosis* (2nd edition), London: Bailliere Tindall, 1990, 983.
8. Murtagh J. *Patient education*. Sydney: McGraw-Hill, 1992, 117.
9. Kumar PJ, Clark ML. *Clinical medicine* (2nd edition), London: Bailliere Tindall, 1990, 983.

15

Diabetes mellitus

Diabetes comes from a Greek word meaning 'to pass or flow through' (i.e. excessive urination) and mellitus means 'sweet'. Its diagnosis is confirmed by an elevated fasting venous plasma glucose level greater than 7.8 mmol/L. A non-fasting glucose level greater than 11.1 mmol/L strongly suggests diabetes mellitus.

There are two main types of diabetes (see Table 15.1).

Type I is known as juvenile onset diabetes or insulin dependent diabetes mellitus (IDDM).

Type II is known as maturity onset diabetes or non-insulin dependent diabetes mellitus (NIDDM).

Key facts and checkpoints

- The prevalence of diabetes is about 3% of the adult population (includes about 1% undiagnosed).[1]
- A further 3% will have impaired glucose tolerance.[1]
- About 30% of these people will develop clinical diabetes within 10 years.[1]
- Many type II diabetics are asymptomatic.
- Diabetes can exist for years before detection and complications may be evident.
- Type II diabetes is not a mild disease. About one-third of those surviving 15 years will require insulin injections to control symptoms

Table 15.1 *Clinical differentiation between type I and type II diabetes*

	Type I IDDM	*Type II NIDDM*
Relative frequency (approx)	15%	85%
Peak age incidence	10–30 years	> 40 years
Age of onset	usually < 20	> 40
Onset	rapid	insidious
Weight at onset	low (thin)	high (obese)
Ketoacidosis	yes	no
Familial	weak	strong
Insulin status	deficient	resistant
Complications	yes	yes

Note These are generalisations and the clinical features may vary, e.g. type II may be thin and have a rapid onset; type I may exhibit a weak genetic link.

or complications.[2] Complications occur in type II diabetes as well as in type I.

- There are several causes of secondary diabetes which are very uncommon (see Table 15.2).

Table 15.2 *Causes of secondary diabetes*

Endocrine disorders
- Cushing's syndrome
- acromegaly
- phaeochromocytoma

Pancreatic disorders
- haemochromatosis
- chronic pancreatitis

Drug-induced diabetes (transient)
- thiazide diuretics
- oestrogen therapy (high dose—not with low-dose HRT)
- corticosteroids

Other transient causes
- gestational diabetes
- medical or surgical stress

Clinical features

The classical symptoms of uncontrolled diabetes are:

- polyuria (every hour or so)
- polydypsia
- loss of weight (type I)
- tiredness and fatigue
- propensity for infections, especially of the skin and genitals

The young insulin dependent diabetic typically presents with a brief 2–4 week history of the classic triad of symptoms:

Thirst
Polyuria
Weight loss

Other symptoms are:

- vulvovaginitis } due to candida albicans
- pruritus vulvae } due to candida albicans
- balanitis } due to candida albicans
- nocturnal enuresis (type I)
- blurred vision

Symptoms of complications (may be presenting feature)

- staphylococcal skin infections
- polyneuropathy
  — tingling or numbness in feet
- impotence
- arterial disease
  — myocardial ischaemia
  — peripheral vascular disease

The clinical examination should follow the guidelines under the heading 'Examinations' in Table 15.7.

Diagnosis of diabetes

The diagnosis is simply made on measuring the random or fasting plasma glucose (FPG). In symptomatic patients, a single elevated reading indicates diabetes. In asymptomatic or mildly symptomatic patients, the diagnosis is made on two separate elevated readings.

Diagnosis of diabetes:

Fasting plasma glucose ≥ 7.8 mmol/L in any person

Random plasma glucose ≥ 11.1 mmol/L in a symptomatic person

In routine practice the patient has a random reading and if it is greater than 11 mmol/L a fasting level is ordered. If greater than (round figure of) 8 mmol/L the patient is a diabetic.

A glucose tolerance test (GTT) is an overused test and unnecessary when the criteria are satisfied. It is never necessary to diagnose type I diabetes. The GTT should be reserved for true borderline cases and for gestational diabetes. A screening test at 26–30 weeks gestation is recommended.

The diagnostic criteria after a 75 g load of glucose are:

Venous plasma glucose	*Fasting*	*2 hours later*
Normal	< 5.5	< 7.8
Impaired tolerance	< 7.8	≥ 7.8–11.1
Diabetes	> 7.8	> 11.1
Gestational diabetes		≥ 7.8

Urinalysis is unreliable in diagnosis since glycosuria occurs at different plasma glucose values in patients with different renal thresholds.

Management principles

- Provide detailed and comprehensive patient education, support and reassurance.
- Achieve control of presenting symptoms.

- Emphasise the importance of the diet: good nutrition, adequate complex carbohydrates, restricted fats and sugars.
- Promptly diagnose and treat urinary tract infection.
- Treat and prevent life-threatening complications of ketoacidosis or hyperosmolar coma.
- Treat and prevent hypoglycaemia in those having insulin and oral hypoglycaemic agents.
- Organise self-testing techniques, preferably blood glucose monitoring.
- Detect and treat complications of diabetes—neuropathy, nephropathy, retinopathy, vascular disease.
- Beware of the deadly quartet:
  1. upper truncal obesity
  2. hyperlipidaemia
     ↑ triglycerides
     ↓ HDL
  3. glucose intolerance, i.e. NIDDM
  4. hypertension

  These are all risk factors for coronary atherosclerosis.

Monitoring techniques

- blood glucose estimation (fasting and postprandial)
- urine glucose (of limited usefulness)
- urine ketones (for type I diabetes)
- glycosylated haemoglobin (HbAlc) or fructosamine
- microalbuminuria (regarded as an early and reversible sign of nephropathy)
- blood pressure
- serum lipids
- renal function (serum urea/creatinine)

Control guidelines are summarised in Figure 15.1 and Table 15.3.

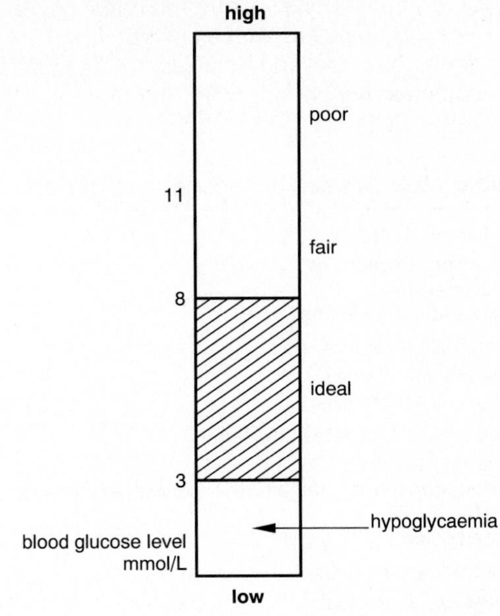

Fig. 15.1 *Control guidelines for diabetic management*

Blood glucose monitoring at home

This can be done using visual strips or a glucose meter (glucometer). Patients should be advised about the most appropriate glucometer to obtain.

Method

- Obtain capillary blood by pricking the finger with a lancet.
- Place a large drop of blood to cover both colour strips (avoid smearing).
- At 60 seconds blot off excess blood with tissue paper. (Time can vary from 30–60 seconds depending on the brand used.)
- The strip is read by comparing the colour with a colour chart or by using an electronic meter (glucometer).

Table 15.3 *Suggested guidelines for glycaemic control (plasma glucose mmol/L)*

	Ideal	*Acceptable (fair)*	*Suboptimal or Unacceptable*
Before meals (fasting)	< 6	6–8	> 8
After meals (2 hours postprandial)	< 8	8–11	> 11
Glycohaemoglobin (HbAlc) %*	< 8	8–11	> 11

* HbAlc is an index of the mean plasma glucose levels over the preceding 2–3 months (assume a reference range of 4.5–8%). The reference ranges vary in different laboratories.

How often and when?

- Type I diabetes: twice a day (at least once)
  four times a day at first and for problems
  may settle for 1–2 times a week (if good control)
  Fasting (before meals and before bedtime)
- Type II diabetes: twice a day (fasting and 2–3 hours postprandial)
  if good control—once a week or every 2 weeks

Note

- Capillary blood glucose is approximately 7% higher than venous blood.
- Glucometer error is usually ± 5%.

Glycosylated haemoglobin

Glycosylated haemoglobin is abnormally high in diabetics with persistent hyperglycaemia and is reflective of their metabolic control. The major form of glycohaemoglobin is haemoglobin AIc, which normally comprises 4–6% of the total haemoglobin.[3] Glycohaemoglobins have a long half-life and its measure reflects the mean plasma glucose levels over the past 2 to 3 months and hence provides a good method of assessing overall diabetic control. It should be checked every 3–6 months.

Insulin dependent diabetes mellitus

The three main objectives of treatment of IDDM are:[4]

1. Maintain good health, free from the problems of hyperglycaemia and hypoglycaemia.
2. Achieve proper growth and maturation for children and protect the foetus and mother in a mother with IDDM.
3. Prevent, arrest or delay long-term macrovascular and microvascular complications.

Insulin regimens for type I diabetes

Preferred insulin regimens (Table 15.4).[4]

1. A short-acting or neutral (regular) insulin before each meal with a long-acting insulin before the evening meal or before bed.
2. A 'split and mix' of short-acting and long-acting insulin (isophane or insulin zinc suspension), twice daily before breakfast and before the evening meal.

Maintenance insulin therapy requires an average daily insulin dose for adults of about 0.7 units (± 0.3 units) per kg body-weight, although it is wise to commence with a portion of this dose, e.g. 40 units a day (Table 15.5).

Insulin requirements often vary significantly even in the same individual under different lifestyle conditions.

Methods of giving insulin injections

When: Get the patient to develop a set routine such as eating meals on time and giving the injections about 30 minutes before the meal.

Where: Into subcutaneous tissue—the best place is the abdomen below the umbilicus (Fig. 15.2). It is advisable to keep to one area such as the abdomen and avoid injections into the arms, near joints and the groin. The injection should be given at a different place each time keeping

Table 15.4 *Insulin regimes and timing of their main effect on blood glucose*[4]

	Insulin	***Affects blood glucose at these times***	
A.	'Split and mixed' system—two injections a day		
	Quick-acting before breakfast	from breakfast →	before lunch
	Long-acting before breakfast	from lunch →	before evening meal
	Quick-acting before evening meal	from evening meal →	before bed
	Long-acting before evening meal	overnight →	early morning and before breakfast
B.	Multiple injection system—four injections a day, e.g. using the insulin pen (basal/bolus regime)		
	Quick-acting before breakfast	from breakfast →	before lunch
	Quick-acting before lunch	from lunch →	before evening meal
	Quick-acting before evening meal	from evening meal →	before bed
	Long-acting before bed	overnight →	early morning and before breakfast

Table 15.5 *Starting insulin: specific examples*[4]

This table presents an example of specific regimens for a 30 year old, 70 kg patient with newly diagnosed IDDM requiring 40 units per day initially.

Split and mixed regimen (twice daily)		
Velosulin	8 units	before breakfast
Insulatard	20 units	
Velosulin	6 units	before dinner (evening meal)
Insulatard	6 units	
Multiple injection regimen (four daily)		
Actrapid insulin	10 units	before breakfast (6 am)
Actrapid insulin	10 units	before lunch (12 pm)
Actrapid insulin	10 units	before dinner (6 pm)
Protaphane, or ultratard, or monotard insulin	10 units	before bed (10 pm)

a distance of 3 cm or more from the previous injection. This reduces the risk of development of lipodystrophy.

How: Pinch a large area of skin on the abdomen between the thumb and fingers and insert the needle straight in. After withdrawing the needle, press down firmly (do not rub or massage) over the injection site for 60 seconds.

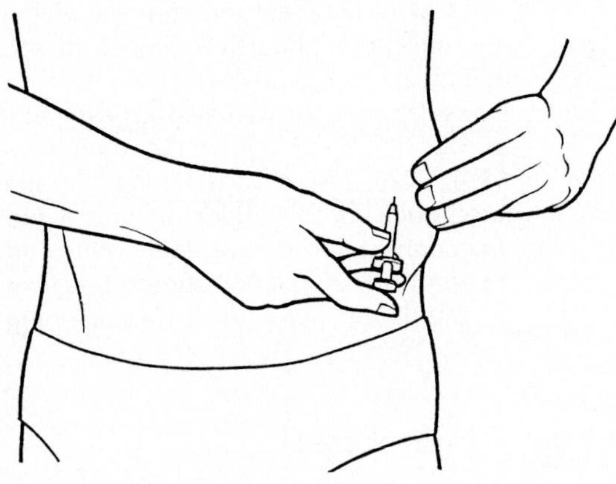

Fig. 15.2 *Method of giving insulin injections; use the abdomen below the umbilicus*

Guidelines for the patient[5]

The proper injection of insulin is very important to allow your body, which lacks natural insulin, to function as normally as possible. You should be very strict about the way you manage your insulin injections and have your technique down to a fine art.

Common mistakes:

- poor mixing technique when mixing insulin
- wrong doses (because of poor eyesight)
- poor injection technique—into the skin or muscle rather than the soft, fatty layer
- not taking insulin when you feel ill

Drawing up the insulin

Make sure your technique is checked by an expert. You may be using either a single insulin or a mixed insulin. A mixed insulin is a combination of shorter and longer acting insulin and is cloudy.

Rules for mixing

- Always draw up clear insulin first.
- Do not permit any of the cloudy insulin to get into the clear insulin bottle.
- Do not push any of the clear insulin into the cloudy insulin bottle.

Golden rules

- Take your insulin every day, even if you feel ill.
- Do not change your dose unless instructed by your doctor or you are competent to do so yourself.

Problems

Injection sites should be inspected regularly because lipo-hypertrophy or lipo-atrophy can occur.

Type II (NIDDM) diabetes

First-line treatment: * diet therapy
(especially if obese) * exercise program

Most symptoms improve dramatically within 1 to 4 weeks on diet alone.[2] The secret to success is patient compliance through good education and supervision. The role of a diabetic education service, especially with a dietician, can be invaluable. If unsatisfactory control persists after 3–6 months, consider adding an oral hypoglycaemic agent (Table 15.6).

One of the sulphonylureas is selected: they are effective and have a low side effect profile. They should be introduced with care and in a low dose in the elderly. Metformin, which has moderate antidiabetic potential, has less tendency to weight gain and is often used for obese patients.

When oral hypoglycaemics fail (secondary failure) insulin is required. The classic symptom of hyperglycaemia may be present but more commonly patients experience general disability.

The importance of diet

Type I patients often require three meals and regular snacks each day.

Type II patients usually require less food intake and restriction of total intake.

Principles of dietary management

- keep to a regular nutritious diet
- achieve ideal body weight
- reduce calories (kilojoules)
  added sugar
  dietary fat
- increase proportions of vegetables, fresh fruit, cereal foods
- special diabetic foods are not necessary
- qualitative diets, rather than quantitative diets such as 'exchanges' or 'portions', are now used

Patient education

The following handout is helpful to patients:

The importance of diet

All diabetics require a special diet in which refined carbohydrate and fat intake is controlled. The objectives of the diet are:

- to keep to ideal weight (neither fat nor thin)
- to keep the blood sugar level as near normal as possible

This is achieved by:

- eating good food regularly (not skimping)
- spacing the meals throughout the day (three main meals and three snacks) for many type I diabetics
- cutting down fat to a minimum
- avoiding sugar and refined carbohydrates (e.g. sugar, jam, honey, chocolates, sweets, pastries, cakes, soft drinks)
- eating a balance of more complex carbohydrates (starchy foods such as wholemeal bread, potatoes and cereals)
- eating a good variety of fruit and vegetables
- cutting out alcohol or drinking only a little

Table 15.6 *Commonly prescribed oral hypoglycaemic agents*

Drug	*Duration of action (hours)*	*Maximum effective daily dose*	*Notes*
Sulphonylureas			Hypoglycaemia most common side effect
Tolbutamide	6–10	1 g, tds	Preferred in elderly
Gliclazide	6–12	160 mg, bd	Strong and equipotent, caution in elderly (Gliclazide and Glipizide)
Glipizide	6–12	20 mg, bd	
Glibenclamide	16–24	10 mg, bd	Potent—unsuitable first-line therapy in elderly
Chlorpropamide	24–72	500 mg, mane	Usually unsuitable in elderly
Biguanides			Reserved usually for obese
Metformin	6–10	1 g, tds	Side effects: GIT disturbances; Avoid in cardiac, renal and hepatic disease; Vitamin B depletion

The importance of exercise

Exercise is very beneficial to your health. Exercise is any physical activity that keeps you fit. Good examples are brisk walking (e.g. 2 km per day), jogging, tennis, skiing and aerobics. Aim for at least 30 minutes three times a week, but daily is ideal. Go slow when you start and increase your pace gradually.

> *Good advice*
>
> - Exercise is important.
> - Do not get overweight.
> - A proper diet is the key to success.
> - A low-fat, no-sugar diet is needed.
> - Do not smoke.
> - Minimise alcohol.
> - Take special care of your feet.
> - Self-discipline will help make your life normal.

Psychosocial considerations

The psychological and social factors involving the patient are very influential on outcome. Considerable support and counselling is necessary to help both patient and family cope with the 'distress' of the diagnosis and the rigid discipline required for optimal control of their blood glucose. Reasons for poor dietary compliance and insulin administration must be determined and mobilisation of a supportive multidisciplinary network (where practical) is most helpful. The general practitioner should be the pivot of the team. Joining a self-support group can be very helpful.

Foot care

Foot problems are one of the commonest complications that need special attention, so prevention is the appropriate approach. Pressure sores can develop on the soles of the feet from corns, calluses, ill-fitting footwear and stones and nails. Minor injuries such as cuts can become a major problem through poor healing. Infection of the wound is a major problem.

Advice to the diabetic patient

1. Keep your diabetes under good control and do not smoke.
2. Check your feet daily. Report any sores, infection or unusual signs.
3. Wash your feet daily:
   - Use lukewarm water (beware of scalds).
   - Dry thoroughly, especially between the toes.
   - Soften dry skin, especially around the heels, with lanoline.
   - Applying methylated spirits between the toes helps stop dampness.
4. Attend to your toe-nails regularly:
   - Clip them straight across.
   - Do not cut them deep into the corners or too short across.
5. Wear clean cotton or wool socks daily; avoid socks with elastic tops.
6. Exercise the feet each day to help the circulation in them.

How to avoid injury

- Wear good-fitting, comfortable leather shoes.
- The shoes must not be too tight.
- Do not walk barefoot, especially out of doors.
- Do not cut your own toe-nails if you have difficulty reaching them or have poor eyesight.
- Avoid home treatments and corn pads that contain acid.
- Be careful when you walk around the garden and in the home.
- Do not use hot water bottles or heating pads on your feet.
- Do not test the temperature of water with your feet.
- Take extra care when sitting in front of an open fire or heater.

Complications of diabetes

Complications occur in both type I and type II diabetes even with early diagnosis and treatment (Fig. 15.3). Insulin dependent diabetics still have a significantly reduced life expectancy. Those diagnosed before the age of 20 have only a 20–60% chance of surviving beyond the age of 45.[7] The main causes of death are diabetic nephropathy and vascular disease (myocardial infarction and stroke).

Diabetes causes both macrovascular and microvascular complications but microvascular disease is specific to diabetes. Complications are illustrated in Figure 15.3. Special attention should be paid to the 'deadly quartet' associated with type II diabetes.

Microvascular disease

The small vessels most affected from a clinical viewpoint are the retina, nerve sheath and renal

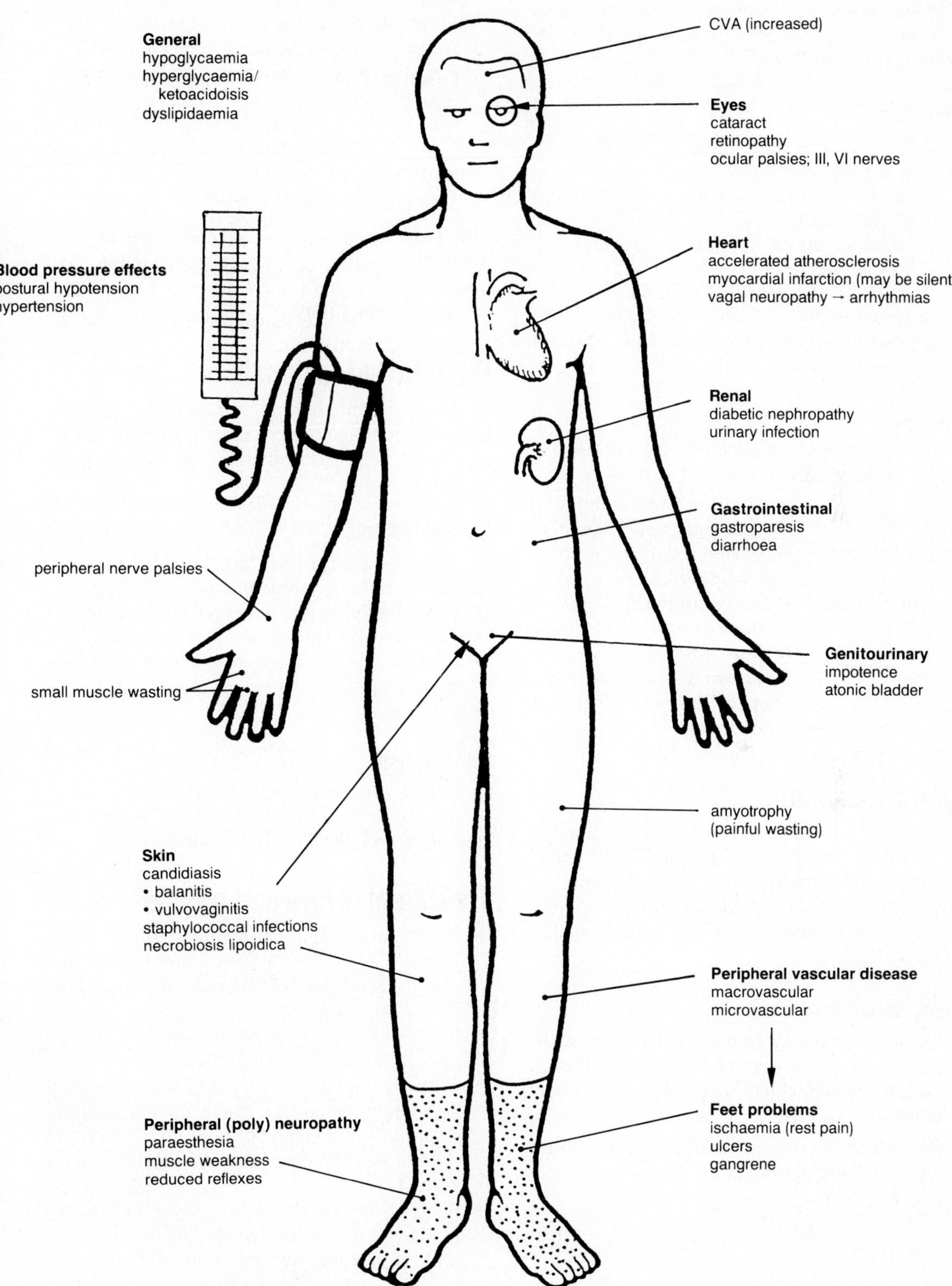
General
hypoglycaemia
hyperglycaemia/
ketoacidoisis
dyslipidaemia
CVA (increased)
Eyes
cataract
retinopathy
ocular palsies; III, VI nerves
Blood pressure effects
postural hypotension
hypertension
Heart
accelerated atherosclerosis
myocardial infarction (may be silent)
vagal neuropathy → arrhythmias
Renal
diabetic nephropathy
urinary infection
Gastrointestinal
gastroparesis
diarrhoea
peripheral nerve palsies
small muscle wasting
Genitourinary
impotence
atonic bladder
amyotrophy
(painful wasting)
Skin
candidiasis
• balanitis
• vulvovaginitis
staphylococcal infections
necrobiosis lipoidica
Peripheral vascular disease
macrovascular
microvascular
Feet problems
ischaemia (rest pain)
ulcers
gangrene
Peripheral (poly) neuropathy
paraesthesia
muscle weakness
reduced reflexes

Fig. 15.3 *The complications of diabetes*

glomerulus. In younger patients it takes about 10 to 20 years after diagnosis for the problems of diabetic retinopathy, neuropathy and nephropathy to manifest.

Neuropathy

The following types of neuropathy may occur:

- sensory polyneuropathy
- isolated mononeuropathy and multiple mononeuropathy
  - — isolated peripheral nerve lesions, e.g. median nerve
  - — cranial nerve palsies, e.g. III, VI
  - — amyotrophy
- autonomic neuropathy, especially postural hypotension and impotence

Infections

Poorly controlled diabetics are prone to infections, especially:

- skin — mucocutaneous candidiasis, e.g. balanitis, vulvovaginitis
  — staphylococcal infections, e.g. folliculitis
- urinary tract — cystitis (women)
  — pyelonephritis and peri-nephric abscess
- lungs — pneumonia: staphylococcal, strep. pneumonia, others
  — tuberculosis

Hypoglycaemia[4]

Hypoglycaemia occurs when blood glucose levels fall to less than 3.0 mmol/L. It is more common with treated IDDM but can occur in NIDDM on oral hypoglycaemic drugs, notably sulphonylureas (biguanides hardly ever cause hypoglycaemia).

Clinical variations

1. Classic warning symptoms: sweating, tremor, palpitations, hunger, perioral paraesthesia. Usually treated with refined carbohydrate, e.g. glucose.
2. Rapid loss of consciousness, usually without warning—hypoglycaemic unawareness is less common.
3. Coma: stuporose, comatose or 'strange' behaviour.

For mild cases give something sweet by mouth, followed by a snack.

Treatment of severe cases or patient unconscious

Treatment of choice

- 10–25 ml 50% Dextrose IV
  (instil rectally using the nozzle of the syringe if IV access difficult)

or

Alternative

- 1 ml glucagon IM

Admit to hospital if concerned (rarely necessary). Ascertain cause of the hypoglycaemia and instruct the patient how to avoid a similar situation in the future.

Diabetic ketoacidosis

This life-threatening emergency requires intensive management. It usually occurs during an illness (e.g. gastroenteritis) when insulin is omitted.

Clinical features

- develops over a few days, but may occur in a few hours in 'brittle' diabetics
- preceding polyuria, polydipsia, drowsiness
- vomiting and abdominal pain
- hyperventilation—severe acidosis (acidotic breathing)
- ketonuria

Management

- arrange urgent hospital admission
- give 10 units rapid-acting insulin IM (not SC)
- commence IV infusion of normal saline

Treatment errors and pitfalls[2]

- Avoid prescribing oral hypoglycaemic agents prematurely. Allow a substantial trial of diet and exercise for NIDDM patients, especially if they are overweight.
- Review the need for continued oral therapy after three months of treatment.
- Glucose tolerance tests should be avoided if the diagnosis can be made on the basis of symptoms and fasting or random blood sugar (a glucose load carries a risk of hyperosmolar coma).
- Keep an eye on the development of ketones in IDDM patients by checking urinary ketones and if present watch carefully because diabetic ketoacidosis is a life-threatening emergency.

When to refer[2]

- Type I diabetic patients for specialist evaluation and then 1 to 2 yearly review.
- Type II diabetic patients:
  - — all young patients
  - — those requiring education
  - — those requiring insulin
  - — those with complications
- For ophthalmological screening: every 1 to 3 years to inspect retina.
- Diabetics with treatable complications, including:
  - — overt retinopathy
  - — nephropathy
  - — neuropathy

Shared care

The management of the diabetic patient provides an ideal opportunity for shared care between a co-operative team comprising the patient, the general practitioner and the specialist diabetic team. The objective is to encourage patients to attend their own doctor for primary care and be less reliant on hospital outpatient services or the diabetic clinics. A well co-ordinated arrangement with good communication strategies provides optimal opportunities for the ongoing education of the patient, the general practitioner and the specialist diabetic team.

Practice tips

- For every diagnosed diabetic there is an undiagnosed diabetic, so vigilance for diagnosing diabetes is important.
- Follow-up programs should keep to a prepared format. A format that can be used for IDDM is presented in Table 15.7. This can be modified for NIDDM.
- Hyperglycaemia is a common cause of tiredness. If elderly type II diabetic patients are very tired, think of hyperglycaemia and consider giving insulin to improve their symptoms.
- The management of the diabetic patient is a team effort involving family members, a nurse education centre, podiatrists, domiciliary nursing service, general practitioner and consultant.
- If a diabetic patient (particularly IDDM) is very drowsy and looks sick, consider first the diagnosis of ketoacidosis.
- Foot care is vital: always examine the feet when the patient comes in for review.
- Treat associated hypertension with ACE inhibitors or a calcium channel blocker.

Table 15.7 *Type I (IDDM): A follow-up program[4]*

1. *History*
   Smoking and alcohol use
   Symptoms of hypoglycaemia, hyperglycaemia
   Check symptoms relating to eyes, circulation, feet*
2. *Examinations*
   Weight, height; BMI
   Blood pressure—standing and lying
   Examine heart*
   Carotid and peripheral pulses*
   Eyes
   - visual acuity (Snellen chart)
   - ? cataracts
   - optic fundi (or ophthalmologist referral)*

   Tendon reflexes and sensation for peripheral neuropathy*
   Skin (general)
   Foot examination*
   Check injection sites
   Urine examination: protein, ketones, glucose, nitrites
3. *Biochemistry*
   Blood glucose
   Glycosylated haemoglobin
   Lipids
   Urine microalbumin*
4. *Education on self-management*
   Diet—or dietary review by dietician
   Self-monitoring of blood glucose. Check patterns of use of blood glucose test strips and examine test profiles.
   Exercise program
5. *Review insulin regimen and dose*
6. *Consider other specialist referrals*
7. Schedule review appointment—forgetting to do this is a frequent cause of failure to return.

Items marked * comprise a program for detection of long-term complications. They should be conducted annually, commencing 5 years after diagnosis.

References

1. Phillips P. *Diabetes*. CHECK Programme, unit 236. Melbourne: RACGP, 1991, 5–20.
2. Welborn TA. Diabetic mellitus. In: MIMS Disease Index. Sydney: IMS Publishing, 1991–2, 145–149.
3. Schroeder SA et al. *Current medical diagnosis and treatment*. East Norwalk: Appleton and Lange, 1990, 821–830.

4. Cohen M. Management of insulin dependent diabetes. Aust Fam Physician, 1990, 19:1201–1214.
5. Murtagh J. Diabetes: insulin injections. In: *Patient education*. Sydney: McGraw-Hill, 1992, 121.
6. Murtagh J. Diabetes: Foot care for diabetics. In *Patient education*. Sydney: McGraw-Hill, 1992, 120.
7. Kumar PJ, Clark ML. *Clinical medicine* (2nd edition), London: Bailliere Tindall, 1990, 835–845

16

Drug problems

Drug-related problems are true masquerades in family practice. This includes prescribed drugs, over the counter drugs and social or illegal street drugs. It is important therefore that all prescribing doctors maintain a high index of suspicion that any clinical problem may be associated with their treatment of the patient.

Adverse drug reactions

An adverse drug effect is defined as 'any unwanted effect of treatment from the medical use of drugs that occurs at a usual therapeutic dose'. Almost every drug can cause an adverse reaction which must be elicited in the history. Any substance that produces beneficial therapeutic effects may also produce unwanted, adverse or toxic effects. The severity of the reaction may range from a mild skin rash or nausea to sudden death from anaphylaxis. A study has shown that the incidence of adverse reactions increases from about 3% in patients 10–20 years of age to about 20% in patients 80–89 years of age.[1]

Reactions can be classified in several ways, e.g. side effects, overdosage, intolerance, hypersensitivity and idiosyncrasy. However, a useful classification of unwanted effects is divided into type A and type B.

Type A reactions are the most common and involve Augmented pharmacology, i.e. they are caused by unwanted albeit predictable effects of the drug.

Examples

- constipation due to verapamil
- blurred vision and urinary outflow problems due to tricyclic antidepressants
- hyperuricaemia due to thiazide diuretics

Type A reactions are dose-dependent.

Type B reactions are by definition Bizarre. The reactions are unpredictable from known properties of the drug. Examples include hepatotoxicity and blood dyscrasias.

Golden rules for prevention of adverse effects

Before prescribing any drug the prescriber should consider the following rules:

1. Is the drug really necessary?
2. What will happen if it is not used?
3. What good do I hope to achieve?
4. What harm may result from this treatment?

Common adverse effects

There is an extensive list of clinical problems caused by drugs as side effects or interactions which are highlighted throughout this book. Common side effects include:

CNS	malaise, drowsiness, fatigue/tiredness, headache, dizziness
CVS	palpitations, peripheral oedema, hypotension
GIT	nausea, vomiting, dyspepsia, change in bowel habit (diarrhoea, constipation)

SKIN	rash, pruritus, flushing
PSYCHIATRIC/ EMOTIONAL	insomnia, irritability, anxiety, depression, agitation

Drugs that commonly produce adverse effects

Antimicrobials	• penicillin/cephalosporins • sulphonamides • tetracyclines • streptomycin • ketoconazole
Anticonvulsants	• carbamazepine • phenobarbitone • phenytoin • sodium valproate
Antidepressants	• tricyclics • MAO inhibitors
Anti-inflammatories and analgesics	• aspirin/salicylates • codeine/morphine, etc. • NSAIDs • gold salts
Antihyper-tensive agents	• (several)
Cardiac agents	• digoxin • quinidine • amiodarone • other antiarrhythmics
Diuretics	• thiazides • frusemide
Tranquillisers	• phenothiazines • benzodiazepines • barbiturates • chlordiazepoxide
Other drugs include	• cytotoxics • hormones • allopurinol • warfarin

Nicotine

'Smoking is good for you', according to an old Arab proverb. 'The dogs will not bite you because you smell so bad; thieves will not rob you at night because you cough in your sleep and you will not suffer the indignities of old age because you will die when you are relatively young.'

Tobacco smoking is the largest single, preventable cause of death and disease in Australia. It has been estimated to have caused approximately 20 000 deaths in 1991, over six times the number of deaths from road accidents.[2] Diseases attributed to smoking are summarised in Figure 16.1.

Getting patients to quit

Several studies have highlighted the value of opportunistic intervention by the family doctor. Not only is it important to encourage people to quit but also to organise a quitting program and follow-up. 80% of smokers in Australia (representing about 30% of the adult population) have indicated that they wish to stop smoking. Point out that it is not easy and requires strong will power. As Mark Twain said, 'Quitting is easy—I've done it a thousand times.'

Methods

- Educate patients about the risks to their health and the many advantages of giving up smoking, with an emphasis on the improvement in *health, longevity, money savings, looks* and *sexuality.*

Facts to point out

- — food tastes better
- — sense of smell improves
- — better exercise tolerance
- — improved sexual pleasure
- — bad breath improves
- — risk of lung cancer drops: after 10–15 years of quitting it is as low as someone who has never smoked
- — reversibility of COAD
- — decreases URTIs and bronchitis
- — less chance of premature skin wrinkling and stained teeth
- — removes effects of passive smoking on family and friends
- — removes problem of effects on pregnancy

- Ask them to keep a smoker's diary.
- If they say no to quitting, give them motivational literature and ask them to reconsider.
- If they say yes, make a contract (example below).

> *A contract to quit*
>
> *'I .... agree to stop smoking on ....*
> *I understand that stopping smoking is the single best thing I can do for my health and that my doctor has strongly encouraged me to quit.'*
>
> .... *(Patient's signature)*
>
> .... *(Doctor's signature)*

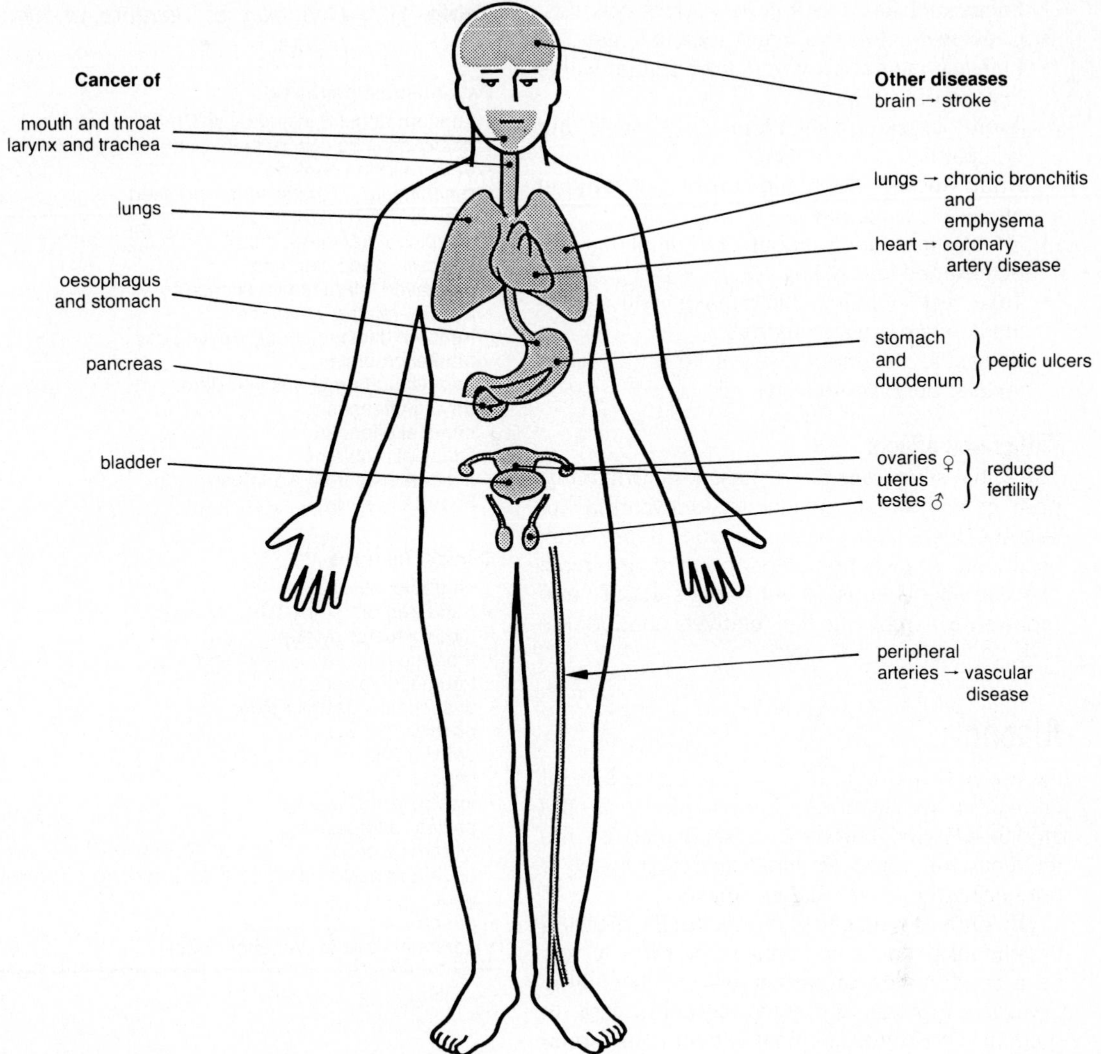

Fig. 16.1 *Possible serious adverse effects of nicotine smoking*

- Arrange follow-up (very important), especially during first 3 months.
- *Nicotine education* Nicotine can be used to help withdrawal from cigarette nicotine dependence. It is a temporary measure and should not be used for longer than 3–4 months.

  Formulations Nicotine gum (Nicorette)
  Nicotine polacrix
  Nicotine transdermal patches

  NB: ongoing support and counselling (including anticipatory guidance) is essential.
- *Going 'cold turkey'* Stopping completely is preferable but before making the final break it can be made easier by changing to a lighter brand, inhaling less, stubbing out earlier, reducing the number. Changing to cigars or pipes is best avoided.

Quitting tips (advice to patient)

- Make a definite date to stop (e.g. during a holiday).

After quitting

- Eat more fruit and vegetables (e.g. munch carrots, celery and dried fruit).

- Foods such as citrus fruit can reduce cravings.
- Chew low-calorie gum and suck lozenges.
- Increase your activity (e.g. take regular walks instead of watching TV).
- Avoid smoking situations and seek the company of non-smokers.
- Drink more water and avoid substituting alcohol for cigarettes.
- Be single-minded about not smoking—be determined and strong.
- Take up hobbies that make you forget smoking (e.g. water sports).
- Put aside the money you save and have a special treat. You deserve it!!

Withdrawal effects

The initial symptoms are restlessness, irritability, poor concentration, headache, tachycardia, insomnia, increased cough, tension, depression, tiredness and sweating. After about 10 days most of these effects subside but it takes about three months for a smoker to feel relatively comfortable with not smoking any more.

Alcohol

Excessive drinking of alcohol can cause several clinical manifestations. Identification of the alcohol-affected person is complicated by the tendency of some to hide, underestimate or understate the extent of their intake.

In order to diagnose and classify alcohol-dependent people, the family doctor has to rely on a combination of parameters which include clinical symptoms and signs, available data on quantity consumed, clinical intuition, personal knowledge of the social habits of patients, and information (usually unsolicited) from relatives, friends or other health workers.

A checklist of pointers to the adverse effects of chronic alcohol abuse is presented in Table 16.1. In a study by the author the outstanding clinical problems are the psychogenic disorders (anxiety, depression and insomnia) and hypertension.[4] Susceptibility to work and domestic accidents were also significant findings.

The challenge to the family doctor is early recognition of the alcohol problem. This is achieved by developing a special interest in the problem and a knowledge of the early clinical and social pointers, and being ever alert to the telltale signs of alcohol dependence (refer to Chapter 98).

Table 16.1 *Checklist of pointers of alcohol abuse*

Psychosocial features

- concern about drinking by self, family or others
- heavy drinking—more than six glasses per day
- early morning drinking
- reaching for the bottle when stressed
- regular hotel patron
- skipping meals/poor diet
- cancelling appointments
- increased tolerance to alcohol
- alcohol-related accidents
- frequent drinking during working day
- marital problems
- behavioural problems in children
- driving offences
- criminal offences
- financial problems
- absenteeism from work/loss of job
- heavy smoking

Clinical features

- characteristic facies
- hand tremor
- alcohol foetor by day
- morning nausea and vomiting
- traumatic episodes
- dyspepsia—gastritis/ulcer
- obesity
- palpitations
- impotence
- insomnia/nightmares
- anxiety/depression
- hypertension
- hepatomegaly
- gout
- pancreatitis
- personal neglect, 'vagabond' look

Hard addictive street drugs

There are several psychotropic substances that are used for their effects on mood and other mental functions. Many of the severe problems are due to withdrawal of the drug. Symptomatic behaviour common to the hard addictive drugs includes:

- Rapid disappearance of clothing, personal belongings from home.
- Signs of unusual activity around hangouts and other buildings.
- Loitering in hallways or in areas frequented by addicts.
- Spending unusual amounts of time in locked bathrooms.
- Inability to hold a job or stay in school.

- Rejection of old friends.
- Using jargon of addicts.

Newer drugs include 'crack' which is a cocaine base where the hydrochloride has mostly been removed, usually in a microwave oven. Crack can be inhaled or smoked. It is the crude form of methamphetamine, a derivative of amphetamine.

A summary of the effects of 'hard' street drugs is presented in Table 16.2.

Narcotic dependence

This section will focus on heroin dependence.

Typical profile of a heroin-dependent person[5]

- Male or female: 16–30 years.
- Family history: often severely disrupted, e.g. parental problems, early death, separation, divorce, alcohol or drug abuse, sexual abuse, mental illness, lack of affection.

Table 16.2 *Illicit substance abuse: A summary of hallmarks*

Drug	*Physical symptoms*	*Look for*	*Dangers*
LSD	Severe hallucinations. Feelings of detachment. Incoherent speech. Cold hands and feet. Vomiting. Laughing and crying.	Cube sugar with discolouration in centre. Strong body odour. Small tube of liquid.	Suicidal tendencies. Unpredictable behaviour. Chronic exposure causes brain damage. LSD causes chromosomal breakdown.
Amphetamines	Aggressive or overactive behaviour. Giggling. Silliness. Euphoria. Rapid speech. Confused thinking. No appetite. Extreme fatigue. Dry mouth. Shakiness.	Jars of pills of varying colours. Chain smoking.	Death from overdose. Hallucinations. Methamphetamines sometimes cause temporary psychosis.
Barbiturates	Drowsiness. Stupor. Dullness. Slurred speech. Drunk appearance. Vomiting.	Pills of various colours.	Death from overdose or as a result of withdrawal. Addictions. Convulsions.
Narcotics (a) opiates, e.g. heroin	Stupor/drowsiness. Marks on body. Watery eyes. Loss of appetite. Blood stain on shirt sleeve. Running nose.	Needle or hypodermic syringe. Cotton. Tourniquet—string. Rope, belt, burnt bottle, caps or spoons. Glassine envelopes.	Death from overdose. Mental deterioration. Destruction of brain and liver. Hepatitis. Embolisms.
(b) cocaine	Similar effects to amphetamines—muscle pains, irritability, paranoia, hyperactive, jerky movements.	Powder: in microwave ovens	Death from overdose—sudden death from arrhythmias. Seizures, mental disorders. Severe respiratory problems.
Phencycidine (Angel Dust)	Lack of co-ordination. Feeling of increased physical strength. Hallucinations. Mood disorders.	White powder. Tablets—unbranded. Syringes. Smoked in conjunction with marijuana.	Suicidal tendencies. Death from overdose. Mental disorder. Self-injury.
Marijuana	Initial euphoria, floating feeling, sleepiness, wandering mind, enlarged eye pupils, lack of co-ordination, craving for sweets, changes of appetite.	Strong odour of burnt leaves. Small seeds in pocket lining. Cigarette paper. Discoloured fingers.	Inducement to take stronger narcotics. Recent medical findings reveal that prolonged usage causes cerebral lesions.
Glue sniffing	Aggression and violence. Drunk appearance, slurred speech. Dreamy or blank expression.	Tubes of glue, glue smears. Large paper or plastic bags or handkerchiefs.	Lung/brain/liver damage. Death through suffocation or choking.

- Personal history: low threshold for toleration, unpleasant emotions, poor academic record, failure to fulfil aims, poor self-esteem.
- First experiments with drugs are out of curiosity, then regular use follows with loss of job, alienation from family, finally moving into a 'drug scene' type of lifestyle.

Methods of intake

1. Oral ingestion
2. Inhalation — intranasal
   — smoking
3. Parenteral — subcutaneous
   — intramuscular
   — intravenous

Withdrawal effects

These develop within 12 hours of ceasing regular usage. Maximum withdrawal symptoms usually between 36–72 hours.

- anxiety and panic
- irritability
- chills and shivering
- excessive sweating
- 'gooseflesh' (cold turkey)
- loss of appetite, nausea (possibly vomiting)
- lacrimation/rhinorrhoea
- tiredness/insomnia
- muscle aches and cramps
- abdominal colic
- diarrhoea

A secondary abstinence syndrome is identified[5] at 2 to 3 months and includes irritability, depression and insomnia.

Complications

Medical

- Acute heroin reaction: respiratory depression—may include fatal cardiopulmonary collapse.
- Injection site: scarring, pigmentation, thrombosis, abscesses, ulceration (especially with barbiturates).
- Distal septic complications: septicaemia, infective endocarditis, lung abscess, osteomyelitis, ophthalmitis.
- Viral infections: hepatitis B, hepatitis C, HIV infection.
- Neurological complications: transverse myelitis, nerve trauma.
- Physical disability: malnutrition.

Social

Alienation from family, loss of employment, loss of assets, criminal activity (theft, burglary, prostitution, drug trafficking).

Management

Management is complex because it includes not only the medical management of physical dependence and withdrawal but also of the individual complex social and emotional factors. The issue of HIV prevention also has to be addressed. Patients should be referred to a treatment clinic and then a shared care approach can be used. The treatments include 'cold turkey' with pharmacological support, acupuncture, megadoses of vitamin C, methadone substitution and drug-free community education programs.

Methadone maintenance programs which include counselling techniques are widely used for heroin dependence.

The natural history of the opiate dependence indicates that many patients do grow through their period of dependence and, irrespective of treatments provided, a high percentage become rehabilitated by their mid thirties.

Cannabis (marijuana)

Cannabis is a drug that comes from a plant called *Cannabis sativa* or the Indian hemp plant. It contains a chemical called tetrahydrocannabinol, which makes people get 'high'. It is commonly called marijuana, grass, pot, dope, hash or hashish. Other slang terms are Acapulco Gold, ganga, herb, J, jay, hay, joint, reefer, weed, locoweed, smoke, tea, stick, Mary Jane and Panama Red. Marijuana comes from the leaves, while hashish is the concentrated form of the resinous substances from the head of the female plant and can be very strong (it comes as a resin or oil). The drug is usually smoked as a leaf (marijuana) or a powder (hashish), or hashish oil is added to a cigarette and then smoked. The effects of taking cannabis depend on how much is taken, how it is taken, how often, whether it is used with other drugs and on the particular person. The effects vary from person to person. The effects of a small to moderate amount include:

- feeling of well-being and relaxation
- decreased inhibitions
- woozy, floating feeling
- lethargy and sleepiness

- talkativeness and laughing a lot
- red nose, gritty eyes and dry mouth
- unusual perception of sounds and colour
- nausea and dizziness
- loss of concentration
- looking 'spaced out' or drunk
- lack of co-ordination

The effects of smoking marijuana take up to 20 minutes to appear and usually last 2 to 3 hours, then drowsiness follows. The main problem is habitual use with the development of dependence, although dependence (addiction) is not very common.

Long-term use and addiction

The influence of 'pot' has a severe effect on the personality and drive of the users. They lose their energy, initiative and enterprise. They become bored, inert, apathetic and careless. A serious effect of smoking pot is loss of memory. Some serious problems include:

- crime
- lack of morality—scant respect for others and their property
- respiratory disease (more potent than nicotine for lung disease): causes COAD, laryngitis and rhinitis
- often prelude to taking hard drugs
- becoming psychotic (resembling schizophrenia): the drug appears to unmask an underlying psychosis

Withdrawal

Sudden withdrawal produces insomnia, nausea, myalgia and irritability.

Driving under the influence

Cannabis affects co-ordination and perception, and so it is dangerous to drive a car or ride a motorbike after using it. In an experiment, several people were given 'pot' to smoke and then asked to drive around a test circuit. Most made a mess of their driving, including crashing into posts and retaining walls. It is particularly dangerous when mixed with alcohol. Other activities such as surfing and waterskiing are also dangerous.

Management

The best treatment is prevention. People should either not use it or limit it to experimentation. If it is used, people should be prepared to 'sleep it off' and not drive.

Anabolic steroids

The apparent positive effects of anabolic steroids include gains in muscular strength (in conjunction with diet and exercise) and quicker healing of muscle injuries. However the adverse effects, which are dependent on the dose and duration, are numerous.

Adverse effects in women are:

- masculination—male pattern beard growth
- suppression of ovarian function
- changes in mood and libido
- hair loss

In adult men, adverse effects are:

- feminisation: enlarged breasts, high-pitched voice
- acne
- testicular atrophy and azoospermia
- libido changes
- hair loss

Severe effects with prolonged use include:

- liver function abnormalities including hepatoma
- tumours of kidneys, prostate
- heart disease

In pre-pubescent children there can be premature epiphyseal closure with short stature.

References

1. Kumer PJ, Clark ML. *Clinical medicine* (2nd edition), London: Bailliere Tindall, 1990, 733–740.
2. Holman CDJ. *The quantification of drug-caused morbidity and mortality in Australia*. Commonwealth Department of Community Services and Health, Canberra, 1988.
3. Bittoun R. How to treat nicotine addiction. Aust Dr Weekly, 11 August 1989, I–VIII.
4. Murtagh JE. Alcohol abuse in an Australian community. Aust Fam Physician, 1987; 16:20–25.
5. Jagoda J. *Drug dependence and narcotic abuse: clinical consequences*. Course handbook: Monash University of Community Medicine, 1987, 66–71.
6. Goldman L. *Handbook on alcohol and other drug problems for medical practitioners*. Canberra: Australian Government Printing Service, 1991:35.

Table 16.3 *A street drug dictionary*

Amphetamines or uppers

- Benzedrine: roses, beanies, peaches
- Dexedrine: dexies, speed, hearts
- Methedrine: meth, crystals, white light
- Drinamyl: purple hearts, goof balls

Hallucinogens

LSD: acid, blue cheer, strawberry fields, barrells, sunshine, pentagons, purple haze, peace pills, blue light.

Cannabis (Indian hemp)

1. Hashish (the resin): hash, resin
2. Marijuana (from leaves): pot, tea, grass, hay, weed, locoweed, Mary Jane, rope, bong, jive, Acupulco gold.
   Cigarettes: reefers, sticks, muggles, joints
   Smoking pot: blow a stick, blast a joint, blow, get high, get stoned

Narcotics

Morphine: Morph, Miss Emma

Heroin: H, Big H, Big Harry, GOM (God's own medicine), crap, junk, dynamite (high-grade heroin), lemonade (low-grade heroin)
Injection of dissolved powder: mainlining, blast, smack
Inhalation of powder: sniffing

Cocaine: coke, snow, lady of the streets, nose candy, toot, snort, crack

H & C: speed balls

Miscellaneous

Barbiturates: devils, barbies, goof balls

Mandrax: mandies

17

Anaemia

Anaemia is a label, not a specific diagnosis. Anaemia is defined as a haemoglobin (Hb) below the normal reference level for the age and sex of that individual. It is regarded as a masquerade because the problem can develop surreptitiously and the patient may present with many seemingly undifferentiated symptoms before the anaemia is detected. Once identified, a cause must be found.

Key facts and checkpoints

- In Australia, most people with anaemia will have iron deficiency ranging from up to 5% for children to 20% for menstruating females.[1]
- The remainder will mainly have anaemia of chronic disease.
- The incidence of haemoglobinopathy traits, especially thalassaemia, is increasing in multicultural Western societies.
- If a patient presents with precipitation or aggravation of myocardial ischaemia, heart failure or intermittent claudication, consider the possibility of anaemia.
- The serum ferritin, which is low in iron deficiency anaemia, is probably the best test to monitor iron deficiency anaemia as its level reflects the amount of stored iron.
- Normal reference values for peripheral blood are presented in Table 17.1.

Table 17.1 *Normal reference values for peripheral blood*

	Male	*Female*
Haemoglobin g/dL	13-17.5	11.5-15.5
Red cells × 10^{12}/L	4.5-6	4-5.5
PCV (haematocrit)	40-53	35-47
MCV (fL)	80-95 to 100	
Platelets × 10^9/L	150-400	
White cell count × 10^9/L	4-11	
Neutrophils	2.5-7.5	
Lymphocytes	<4.5	
Monocytes	<0.8	
Eosinophils	<0.45	
Reticulocytes %	0.2-2	
ESR mm/hour	<20	

Reproduced with permission from Dr M. Gribble[2]

Clinical features of anaemia

Patients with anaemia may be asymptomatic. When symptoms develop they are usually non-specific.

Symptoms

- tiredness/fatigue
- muscle weakness
- headache
- lack of concentration
- faintness/dizziness
- dyspnoea on exertion
- palpitations
- angina of effort
- intermittent claudication

Signs

Non-specific signs

- pallor
- tachycardia
- systolic flow murmur

If severe

- ankle oedema
- cardiac failure

Specific signs

- jaundice—haemolytic anaemia
- koilonychia (spoon-shaped nails)—iron deficiency anaemia

History

The history may indicate the nature of the problem:

- iron deficiency: inadequate diet, pregnancy, GIT loss, menorrhagia, NSAID and anticoagulant ingestion
- folate deficiency: inadequate diet especially pregnancy and alcoholism, small bowel disease
- Vitamin B deficiency: previous gastric surgery, ileal disease or surgery, pernicious anaemia, selective diets, e.g. vegetarians, fad
- haemolysis: abrupt onset anaemia with mild jaundice

Classification of anaemia

The various types of anaemia are classified in terms of the red cell size—the mean corpuscular volume (MCV).

- microcytic — MCV ≤ 80 fL
- macrocytic — MCV > 98 fL
- normocytic — MCV 80–98 fL

Note: Upper limit of MCV varies from 95–100 depending on age and laboratory.

Table 17.2 outlines a classification of some of the more common causes encountered in general practice. There can be an interchange of disorders between the above groups, e.g. the anaemia of chronic disorders (chronic infection, inflammation and malignancy) can occasionally be microcytic as well as normocytic; the anaemia of hypothyroidism can be macrocytic in addition to the more likely normocytic; the anaemia of bone marrow disorder or infiltration can also be occasionally macrocytic.

Microcytic anaemia—MCV ⩽ 80 fL

The main causes of microcytic anaemia are iron deficiency and haemoglobulinopathy, particularly thalassaemia.

Iron deficiency anaemia

Iron deficiency is the most common cause of anaemia world-wide. It is the big cause of microcytic anaemia with the main differential diagnosis of microcytic anaemia being a haemoglobinopathy such as thalassaemia.

Key features

- microcytic anaemia
- serum ferritin low (NR: 20–200 g/L)
- serum iron low
- response to iron therapy

Non-haematological effects of chronic iron deficiency

- angular stomatitis
- glossitis
- oesophageal webs
- atrophic gastritis
- malabsorption
- brittle nails and koilonychia

Important causes[1]

Blood loss

- menorrhagia
- gastrointestinal bleeding, e.g. carcinoma, haemorrhoids, peptic ulcer
- frequent blood donations

Increased physiological requirements

- prematurity, infant growth
- adolescent growth
- pregnancy

Malabsorption

- coeliac disease
- postgastrectomy

Dietary

- inadequate intake
- special diets, e.g. fad, vegetarianism

Investigations

Investigations are based on the history and physical examination including the rectal

Table 17.2 *Selected causes and investigations of anaemia (adapted from Anaemia, MIMS Disease Index[1], with permission of MIMS Australia Pty Ltd)*

Causes/ classification	Primary diagnostic feature	Secondary investigations
Microcytic (MCV $<$ 80 fL)		
Iron deficiency	s.Fe ↓; s.ferr ↓	Therapeutic trial of iron; GIT evaluation for blood loss
Haemoglobinopathy e.g. thalassaemia	s.Fe N; s.ferr N or ↑	Haemoglobin investigation
Sideroblastic anaemia (hereditary)	s.Fe N; s.ferr N or ↑	Bone marrow examination
Occasionally microcytic		
Anaemia of chronic disease (sometimes microcytic)	s.Fe ↓; s.ferr N or ↑	Specific for underlying disorder
Macrocytic (MCV $>$ 98 fL)		
a) With megaloblastic changes		
Vitamin B_{12} deficiency	s.B_{12} ↓; rc/Fol N or ↑	IF antibody assay; Schilling test
Folate deficiency	s.B_{12} N; rc.Fol ↓	Usually none
Cytotoxic drugs	Appropriate setting; s.B_{12}N; rc.Fol N	None
b) Without megaloblastic changes		
Liver disease/alcoholism	Appropriate setting; uniform macrocytosis; s.B_{12}N; rc.Fol N	Liver function tests
Myelodysplastic disorders (including sideroblastic anaemia)	Specific peripheral blood findings; s.B_{12}N; rc.Fol N	Bone marrow examination
Normocytic (MCV 80–98 fL)		
Acute blood loss/occult	Isolated anaemia; Retic ↑	Dictated by clinical findings
Anaemia of chronic disease [1]	Appropriate setting; Retic ↓	s.Fe ↓ and s.ferr N or ↑
Haemolysis	Specific red cell changes; Retic ↑	s.Bil and s.LDH ↑; s.hapt ↓; specific tests for cause
Chronic renal disease	Isolated anaemia; Retic ↓	Renal function
Endocrine disorders	Appropriate setting; isolated anaemia; Retic ↓	Specific endocrine investigation

Abbreviations: MCV = mean corpus volume; s.Fe = serum iron; s.ferr = serum ferritin; s.B_{12} = serum vitamin B_{12}; rc.Fol = red cell folate; IF = intrinsic factor; Retic = reticulocyte count; s.Bil =serum bilirubin; s.LDH = serum lactate dehydrogenase; s.hapt = serum haptoglobin; N = normal; ↓ = reduced; ↑ = elevated

examination. If GIT bleeding is suspected the faecal occult blood is not considered very valuable but investigations such as gastroscopy and colonoscopy may be most valuable.

Haemological investigations: typical findings

- microcytic, hypochromic red cells
- anisocytosis (variation in size), poikilocytosis (shape)
- low serum iron
- raised iron-binding capacity
- serum ferritin low (the most useful index)

The state of the iron stores is assessed by considering the serum iron, the serum ferritin and the serum transferrin in combination. Typically, in iron deficiency, the serum iron and ferritin are low and the transferrin high, but the serum iron is also low in all infections—severe, mild and even subclinical—as well as in inflammatory states, malignancy and other chronic conditions. Serum ferritin estimations are spuriously raised in liver disease of all types, chronic inflammatory conditions and malignancy; and transferrin is normally raised in pregnancy. Since each of these estimations can be altered in conditions other than iron deficiency, all three quantities have to be considered together to establish the iron status.[2]

Treatment

- Correct the identified cause.
- Iron preparations
  - — oral iron
  - — parenteral iron is probably best reserved for special circumstances

  Response
  - — anaemia responds after about 2 weeks and is usually corrected after 2 months[1]

- — oral iron is continued for 3 to 6 months to replenish stores
- — monitor progress with regular serum ferritin
- — a serum ferritin > 50 g/L generally indicates adequate stores

Failure of iron therapy

Consider:

- — poor compliance
- — continuing blood loss
- — malabsorption, e.g. severe coeliac disease
- — incorrect diagnosis, e.g. thalassaemia minor, chronic disease
- — bone marrow infiltration

Thalassaemia

This inherited condition is seen mainly (although not exclusively) in people from the Mediterranean basin, the Middle East, North and Central India and South-East Asia including South China. The heterozygous form is usually asymptomatic; patients show little if any anaemia, and the condition is relatively common in people from these areas. The homozygous form is a very severe congenital anaemia needing lifelong transfusional support, but is comparatively rare, even among the populations prone to thalassaemia.[2]

The key to the diagnosis of the heterozygous 'thalassaemia minor' is significant microcytosis quite out of proportion to the normal Hb or slight anaemia, and confirmed by finding a raised Hb A2 on Hb electrophoresis. The importance of recognising the condition lies in distinguishing it from iron deficiency anaemia, for iron does not help thalassaemics and is theoretically contraindicated. Even more importantly it lies in recognising the risk that, if both parents have thalassaemia minor, they run a one in four chance of having a baby with thalassaemia major in every pregnancy, with devastating consequences for both the affected child and the whole family.

Haemoglobin E

This Hb variant is common throughout South-East Asia.[2] It has virtually no clinical effects in either the homozygous or heterozygous forms, but these people have microcytosis which must be distinguished from iron deficiency; moreover, if the Hb E gene is combined with the thalassaemia gene, the child may have a lifelong anaemia almost as severe as thalassaemia major. Both genes are well established in the South-East Asian populations in Australia as well as in their own countries.

Macrocytic anaemia—MCV > 98 fL

Alcohol and liver disease

Each individually, or in combination, leads to macrocytosis with or without anaemia. The importance of this finding lies in its often being the first indication of alcohol abuse, which can so frequently go unnoticed unless there is a firm index of suspicion. Chronic liver disease due to other causes may also be late in producing specific clinical symptoms.

Drug toxicity

Cytotoxic drugs, anticonvulsants in particular, and various others (see Table 17.3) may cause macrocytosis. It is of little clinical significance and does not need correction unless associated with anaemia or other cytopenia.

Table 17.3 *Drugs causing macrocytosis*[2]

Alcohol	
Cytotoxics	Azathiprine Methotrexate 5.fluorouracil
Antibiotics	Co-trimoxazole Pyrimethamine (incl. Fansidar and Maloprim)
Anticonvulsants	Phenytoin Primodone Phenobarbitone
Sedatives	Glutethamide (Doriden)

Myelodysplastic syndromes

These conditions have been recognised under a variety of names, such as 'refractory anaemia' and 'pre-leukaemia', for a long time, but only relatively recently have they been grouped together. They are quite common in the elderly but may be seen in any age group (refer Table 17.2).

These conditions frequently present as a macrocytic anaemia with normal serum B_{12} and red cell folate, and are unresponsive to these or any other haematinics; they are usually associated with progressive intractable neutropenia or thrombocytopenia or both, and progress slowly but relentlessly to be eventually fatal, terminating with infection, haemorrhage or, less often, acute leukaemia.

Vitamin B_{12} deficiency (pernicious anaemia)

Although well recognised, this is a much less common cause of macrocytosis than the foregoing conditions. Usually caused by lack of intrinsic factor due to autoimmune atrophic changes, anaemia does not develop for about three years after total gastrectomy. B_{12} deficiency may also be seen together with other deficiencies in some cases of malabsorption and Crohn's disease.

Vitamin B_{12} is found only in foods of animal origin and consequently very strict vegetarians may eventually develop deficiency. The clinical features are anaemia (macrocytic), weight loss and neurological symptoms especially a polyneuropathy. The serum Vitamin B_{12} is below the normal level.

Replacement therapy[1]

- Vitamin B_{12} (1000 μg) IM injection body stores (3 to 5 mg) are replenished after 10–15 injections given every 2 to 3 days.
- maintenance with 1000 μg injections every second month

Folic acid deficiency

The main cause is poor intake associated with old age, poverty and malnutrition, usually associated with alcoholism. It may be seen in malabsorption and regular medication with antiepileptic drugs such as phenytoin.[3] It is rarely, but very importantly, associated with pregnancy, when the demands of the developing foetus together with the needs of the mother outstrip the dietary intake—the so-called 'pernicious anaemia of pregnancy' which, if not recognised and treated immediately, can still be a fatal condition. Unlike Vitamin B_{12}, folic acid is not stored in the body to any significant degree and requirements have to be satisfied by the daily dietary intake.

Replacement therapy Oral folate 1.5 mg/day, to replenish body stores (5–10 mg) in about 4 weeks.

Normocytic anaemia[2] (anaemias without change in the MCV)

Acute haemorrhage

This is the most common cause of normocytic anaemia and is usually due to haematemesis and/or melaena.

Chronic disease

Chronic inflammation Intercellular iron transport within the marrow is suppressed in inflammation so that, despite normal iron stores, the developing red cells are deprived of iron and erythropoiesis is depressed. If the inflammation is short-lived, the fall in Hb is not noticeable but, if it continues, an anaemia may develop which responds only when the inflammation subsides.

Malignancy Anaemia may develop for the same reasons that apply to chronic inflammation.

Renal failure

This is often associated with anaemia due to failure of haemopoietin secretion and is unresponsive to treatment, other than by alleviating the insufficiency or until haemopoietin becomes available as a therapeutic agent.

Haemolysis

Haemolytic anaemias are relatively infrequent. The more common of the congenital ones are hereditary spherocytosis and deficiences of the red cell enzymes, pyruvate kinase and G6PD, although most cases of G6PD deficiency haemolyse only when the patient takes oxidant drugs like sulphonamides or eats broad beans—'favism'.

Acquired haemolytic anaemias include those of the newborn due to maternal haemolytic blood group antibodies passing back through the placenta to the foetus, and adult anaemias due to drug toxicity or to acquired autoantibodies. About half of the latter are 'idiopathic' and half associated with non-Hodgkin's lymphomas, and the anaemia may be the presenting sign of lymphoma. Some of these antibodies are active only at cool temperatures—cold agglutinin disease; others act at body temperature and are the more potent cause of autoimmune haemolytic anaemia.

Bone marrow replacement

This may be due to foreign tissue such as carcinomatous metastases or fibrous tissue as in myelofibrosis; it may also be due to overgrowth by one or other normal elements of the bone marrow as in chronic myeloid leukaemia, chronic lymphocytic leukaemia and lymphoma as well as by acute leukaemic tissue. A leuko-erythroblastic picture, in which immature red and white cells appear in the peripheral blood, is often seen when the marrow is replaced by foreign tissue.

References

1. Van Der Weyden M. Anaemia. In: MIMS Disease Index, Sydney: IMS Publishing, 1991–2, 34–37.
2. Gribble M. Haematology. CHECK Unit 188. Melbourne: CHECK Programme, 1987, 3–22.
3. Kumer PJ, Clark ML. *Clinical medicine* (2nd edition), London: Bailliere Tindall, 1990, 297–307.

18

Thyroid and other endocrine disorders

—

Thyroid disorders can be a diagnostic trap in family practice and early diagnosis is a real challenge. A family practice of 2500 patients can expect one new case of thyroid disorder each year and 10 'cases' in the practice with a slight preponderance of hyperthyroid patients compared with hypothyroid patients.[1] The diagnosis of an overactive or underactive thyroid can be difficult as the early clinical deviations from normality can be subtle.

The clinical diagnosis of classical Grave's disease is usually obvious with the features of exophthalmos, hyperkinesis and a large goitre but if the eye and neck signs are absent it can be misdiagnosed as an anxiety state. Elderly patients may present with only cardiovascular signs such as atrial fibrillation and tachycardia or with unexplained weight loss.

The hypothyroid patient can be very difficult to diagnose in the early stages especially if the patient is being seen frequently. Hypothyroidism often has a gradual onset with general symptoms such as constipation and lethargy and the diagnosis is usually made late by which time the disorder is quite florid in manifestation.

If suspected, the thyroid function tests, serum free thyroxine (T_4) and thyroid stimulating hormone (TSH), should be requested. Serum tri-iodothyronine (T_3) measurement can be useful in suspected T_3 toxicosis where serum T_4 may be normal.

Other endocrine disorders are relatively uncommon and therefore difficult to diagnose in the early stages of development. Certain symptoms (Table 18.1) alert one to the possibility of an endocrine disorder.

Thyroid disorders

Thyroid function tests

Advances in technology have allowed the biochemical assessment of thyroid function to change dramatically in recent years with the introduction of the serum free thyroxine (T_4) and the monoclonal TSH assays. With the highly sensitive TSH assays it is now possible to distinguish suppressed TSH levels (as in hyperthyroidism) from low but normal levels of TSH in the euthyroid state. However, the new assays are not foolproof and require interpretation in the context of the clinical picture. The serum TSH is the most sensitive index of thyroid function.

Guidelines for ordering thyroid function tests are:

- If hypothyroidism suspected: TSH + T_4
- If hyperthyroidism suspected: TSH + T_3

The relative values are summarised in Table 18.2.

Table 18.1 *Symptoms related to the endocrine system*

Psychogenic changes
- depression
- anxiety
- psychosis

Constitutional symptoms
- tiredness, lethargy
- weakness

Sexual dysfunction
- menstrual dysfunction, e.g. amenorrhoea
- loss of libido
- loss of pubic hair
- hirsutism

Diabetogenic symptoms
- polyuria/polydipsia

Glycaemia fluctuations
- hypoglycaemia
- hyperglycaemia

Weight changes
- weight loss
- weight gain

Cardiac changes
- heart rate disturbances
- myocardial ischaemia

Skeletal changes
- osteoporosis
- bone pain

Muscle changes

Skin changes
- pigmentation
- vitiligo
- coarse dry skin
- striae

Blood pressure fluctuations
- postural hypotension
- hypertension

Gastrointestinal
- anorexia
- nausea
- constipation
- diarrhoea

Tongue enlargement
- hypothyroidism, myxoedema, acromegaly

Hypothyroidism (myxoedema)

Hypothyroidism, which is relatively common, is more prevalent in elderly women (up to 5%).[2] The term 'myxoedema' refers to the accumulation of mucopolysaccharide in subcutaneous tissues. The early changes are subtle and can be misdiagnosed, especially if only a single symptom is dominant.

Patients at risk include:

- previous Grave's disease
- autoimmune disorders, e.g. rheumatoid arthritis
- Down syndrome
- drug treatment: lithium, amiodarone
- previous thyroid surgery
- previous radioactive ablation of the thyroid

Clinical features

The main features are:

- constipation
- cold intolerance
- lethargy
- physical slowing
- mental slowing
- huskiness of voice
- puffiness of face and eyes
- pallor
- loss of hair

Physical examination (Fig. 18.1)

- sinus bradycardia
- delayed reflexes (normal muscular contraction, slow relaxation)
- coarse, dry and brittle hair
- dry, cool skin
- obesity
- goitre

Other diverse presentations of thyroid disorders are given in Table 18.3.

Table 18.2 *Summary of thyroid function tests*

	TSH ***thyroid stimulating hormone***	T_4 ***free thyroxine***	T_3 ***tri-iodothyronine***
Hypothyroidism			
• primary	↑ *	↓ *	N or ↓ (not useful)
• secondary (pituitary dysfunction)	N or ↓	↓	N or ↓
Hyperthyroidism	↓ *	↑	↑ *
Sick euthyroid	N or ↓	N or ↓	N or ↓

Note: Results similar to hyperthyroidism can occur with acute psychiatric illness.

* Main tests

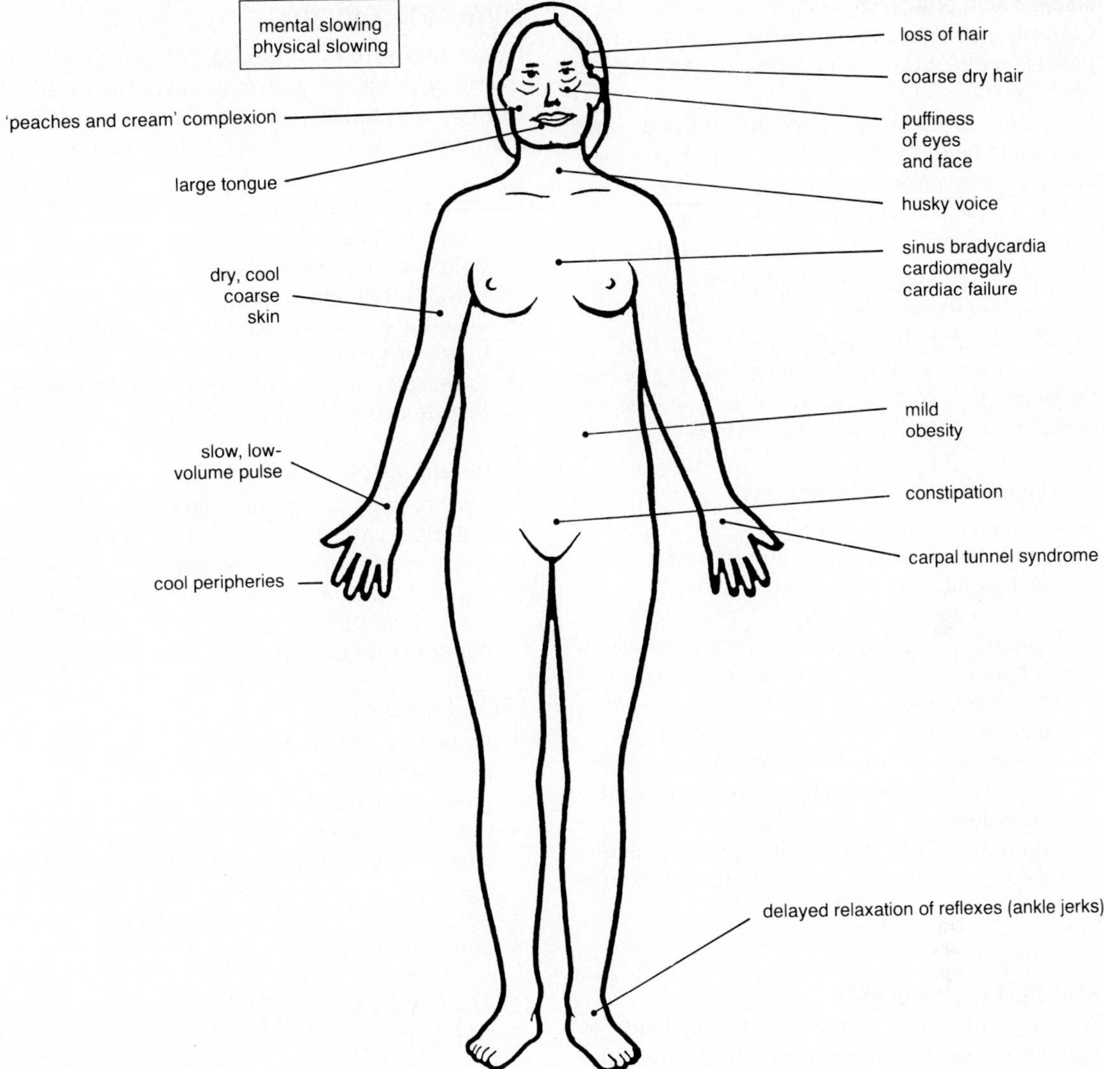

Fig. 18.1 *Clinical features of hypothyroidism*

Hashimoto's disease

Hashimoto's disease, which is an autoimmune thyroiditis, is the commonest cause of bilateral non-thyrotoxic goitre in Australia. Features are:

- bilateral goitre
- classically described as firm and rubbery
- patients may be hypothyroid or euthyroid

Hashimoto's disease commonly presents as postpartum hypothyroidism. The hypothyroidism may resolve in 6–12 months or may be permanent.[3]

Laboratory diagnosis of hypothyroidism

Thyroid function tests (Table 18.2)

T_4—subnormal
TSH—elevated

If T_4 low and TSH low or normal, consider pituitary dysfunction (secondary hypothyroidism) or sick euthyroid syndrome.

Other abnormal tests

- serum cholesterol elevated
- anaemia usually normocytic, may be macrocytic
- ECG: sinus bradycardia, low voltage, flat T waves

Management principles

Confirm the diagnosis; provide appropriate patient education; refer the patient where appropriate.

Exclude co-existing hypoadrenalism and ischaemic heart disease before T_4 replacement.

Thyroid medication

thyroxine 100–150 μg daily (once daily)

Note: Start with low doses (25–50 μg daily) in elderly and ischaemic heart disease. Avoid overdosage.

Monitor T_4 and TSH levels monthly at first. As euthyroidism is achieved, monitoring may be less frequent, e.g. 2–3 months. When stable on optimum dose of T_4, every 2 to 3 years.

Special treatment considerations

- Ischaemic heart disease
  Rapid thyroxine replacement can precipitate myocardial infarction.
- Pregnancy and postpartum
  Continue thyroxine during pregnancy; watch for hypothyroidism (often an increased dose of T_4 is required).
- Elective surgery
  If euthyroid—can stop thyroxine for one week. If subthyroid—defer surgery until euthyroid.
- Myxoedema coma
  Urgent hospitalisation under specialist care. Intensive treatment is required which may involve parenteral T_4 or T_3.

Neonatal hypothyroidism

Misdiagnosing this serious condition leads to failure to thrive, retarded growth and poor school performance. If untreated it leads to permanent intellectual damage ('cretinism'). It is detected by routine heel prick blood testing. Thyroxine replacement should be started by the 14th day.

> *When to refer*[2]
> - Doubt about diagnosis, diagnostic tests or optimum replacement dosage
> - Apparent secondary hypothyroidism, severe illness and associated ischaemic heart disease
> - Concurrent autoimmune disease
> - Hypothyroidism with goitre, postpartum and in the neonate
> - Myxoedema coma

Hyperthyroidism

Hyperthyroidism (thyrotoxicosis) is also relatively common and may affect up to 2% of women, who are affected 4 to 5 times more often than men.

Causes of thyrotoxicosis

- Grave's disease (typical symptoms with a diffuse goitre and eye signs)
- autonomous functioning nodules
- subacute thyroiditis (de Quervain's thyroiditis)—viral origin
- excessive intake of thyroid hormones—thyrotoxicosis factitia

Important notes

- The classic symptoms may be lacking in elderly patients who may have only cardiovascular manifestations, e.g. unexplained heart failure or cardiac arrhythmias.
- Care has to be taken not to dismiss hyperthyroidism as severe anxiety.

Clinical features

- loose bowel motions
- heat intolerance
- sweating of hands
- muscle weakness
- weight loss despite normal or increased appetite
- emotional lability, especially anxiety
- palpitations

Physical examination (Fig. 18.2)

- agitated restless patient
- warm and sweaty hands
- fine tremor
- goitre
- proximal myopathy

Eye signs

- lid retraction (small area of sclera seen above iris)
- lid lag
- exophthalmos
- ophthalmoplegia

Investigations

- T_4 (and T_3) elevated
- TSH suppressed
- radioisotope scan

The isotope scan has a role in diagnosis. It enables a diagnosis of Grave's disease to be made

Table 18.3 *Various diverse presentations of thyroid disorders*[2]

	Hypothyroidism	*Hyperthyroidism*
General	Lethargy Dry skin Husky voice	Weakness Sweaty skin, especially hands
Psychiatric	Depression Dementia Psychosis (myxoedema madness)	Anxiety/irritability Hyperkinesis Psychosis
Musculoskeletal	Myofibrositis Myalgia Joint effusions	Muscle weakness Proximal myopathy
Skin	Dry cool skin Vitiligo	Warm, thin, soft, moist skin Vitiligo Pretibial myxoedema
Cardiovascular	Ischaemia Cardiomegaly Pericardial effusion Bradycardia Hyperlipidaemia	Tachycardia Atrial fibrillation Heart failure Systolic hypertension
Endocrine	Galactorrhoea Goitre Infertility	Goitre Gynaecomastia
Gynaecological	Menstrual irregularity Menorrhagia (mainly) Oligomenorrhea	Oligomenorrhea
Neurological	Neuropathy Nerve entrapment e.g. carpal tunnel Ataxia	Periodic paralysis Tremor
Haematological	Anaemia	-
Emergency	Myxoedema coma Postanaesthetic hypoventilation	Thyroid crisis
Other	Reduced libido	Reduced libido Eye signs Fever (uncommon) Premature grey hair

when the scan shows uniform increased uptake. Increased irregular uptake would suggest a toxic multinodular goitre, while there is poor or no uptake with de Quervain's thyroiditis and thyrotoxicosis factitia.

Management principles

- Establish the precise cause before initiating treatment.
- Educate patients and emphasise possibility of development of recurrent hyperthyroidism or hypothyroidism and need for lifelong monitoring.

Treatment modalities

- radioactive iodine therapy (I_{131})
- thionamide antithyroid drugs
  - — carbimazole
  - — propylthiouracil
- adjunctive drugs
  - — beta-blockers (for symptoms in acute florid phase)
  - — lithium carbonate (rarely used when there is intolerance to thionamides)
  - — Lugol's iodine: mainly used prior to surgery
- surgery
  - — subtotal thyroidectomy

    or
  - — total thyroidectomy

Treatment of Grave's disease

There is no ideal treatment and selection of antithyroid drugs, radioiodine or surgery depends

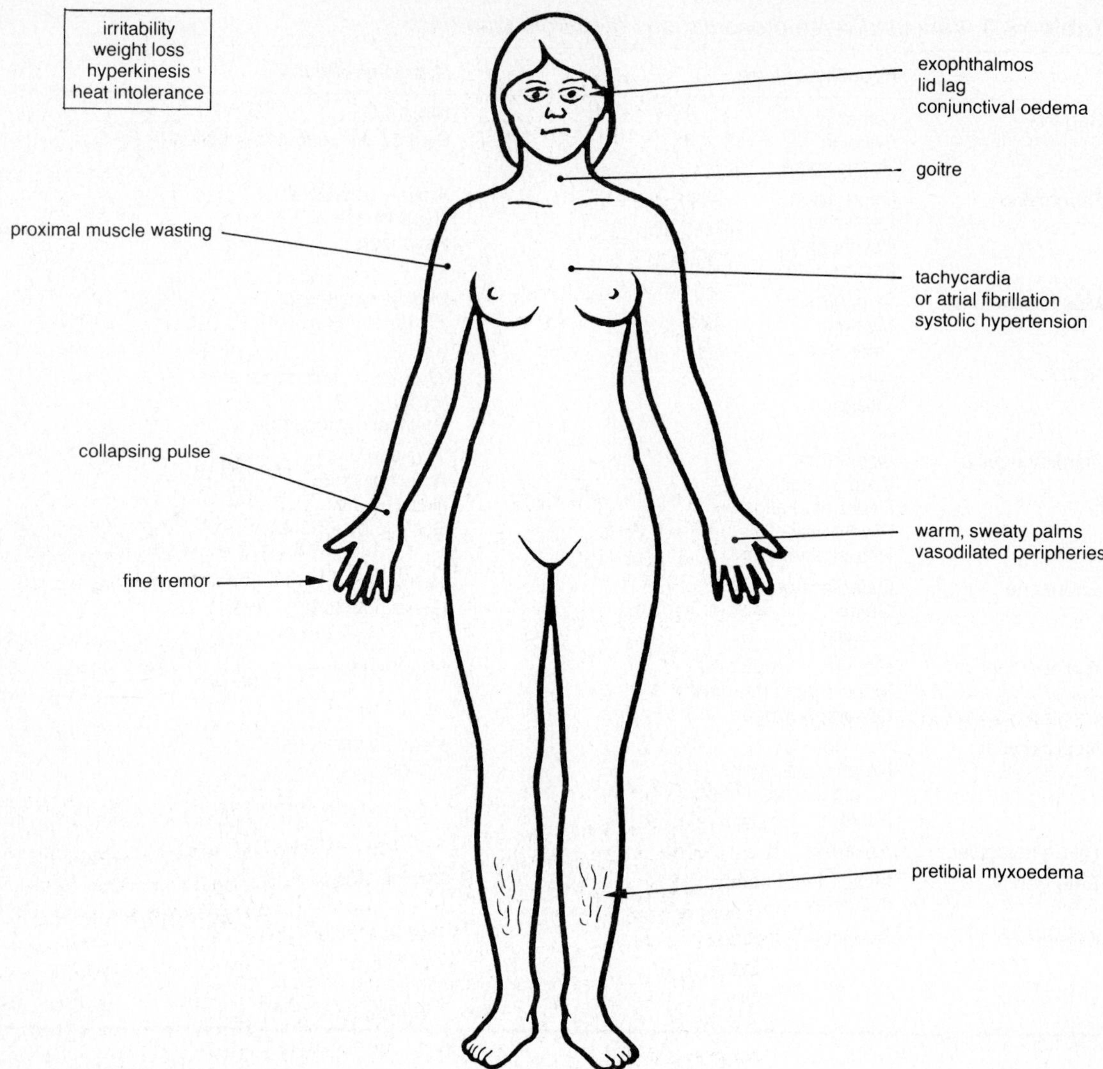

Fig. 18.2 *Clinical features of hyperthyroidism*

on many factors including age, size of goitre, social and economic factors and complications of treatment.

Guidelines[4]

- Younger patients with small goitres and mild case—18 month course antithyroid drugs;
- Older patients with small goitres—as above or radioiodine (when euthyroid);
- Large goitres or moderate to severe cases—antithyroid drugs until euthyroid, then surgery;
- In Australia (as in the USA) I_{131} is being increasingly used.

Treatment of autonomous functioning nodules

Control hyperthyroidism with antithyroid drugs, then surgery or I_{131}. Long-term remissions on antithyroid drugs in a toxic nodular goitre are rare.

Treatment of subacute thyroiditis

Hyperthyroidism is usually transient and follows a surge of thyroxine after a viral-type illness. Symptoms include pain and/or tenderness over the goitre (especially on swallowing) and fever. In the acute phase treatment is based on rest, analgesics and soft foods. Rarely, when pain is severe, corticosteroids may be used. Antithyroid drugs are not indicated but beta-blockers can be used to control symptoms.

Thyroid crisis

Clinical features: marked anxiety, weakness, hyperpyrexia, tachycardia (> 150 per month), heart failure and arrhythmias. Usually precipitated by minor surgery or an infection in an undiagnosed patient.

Requires urgent intensive hospital management with antithyroid drugs; IV saline infusion, IV corticosteroids, anti-heart failure and anti-arrhythmia therapy.

> *When to refer*[4]
> - Doubt about the diagnosis
> - Severe hyperthyroidism, especially if there is co-existing thyrocardiac disease
> - Pregnant patients with hyperthyroidism
> - Progression of exophthalmos

Adrenal cortex disorders

It is worth keeping in mind the uncommon disorders of the adrenal cortex which can also be difficult to diagnose in the early stages, namely:

- chronic adrenal insufficiency (Addison's disease)—deficiency of cortisol and aldosterone
- Cushing's syndrome—cortisol excess
- primary hyperaldosteronism (refer Chap. 103)

Addison's disease

Clinical features

- lethargy/excessive fatigue
- anorexia and nausea
- diarrhoea/abdominal pain
- weight loss
- dizziness/funny turns
  - — hypoglycaemia (rare)
  - — postural hypotension (common)
- hyperpigmentation, especially mucous membranes of mouth and hard palate. If Addison's disease remains undiagnosed, wasting leading to death may occur. Severe dehydration can be a feature.

Diagnosis

- elevated serum potassium, low serum sodium
- low plasma cortisol (fails to respond to synthetic ACTH)

Addisonian crisis

An Addisonian crisis develops because of an inability to increase cortisol in response to stress, which may include intercurrent infection, surgery or trauma.

Clinical features

- nausea and vomiting
- acute abdominal pain
- severe hypotension progressing to shock
- weakness, drowsiness progressing to coma

Urgent management

- establish IV line with IV fluids
- hydrocortisone sodium succinate 200 mg IV
- arrange urgent hospital admission

Cushing's syndrome

The four main causes are:

- Iatrogenic—chronic corticosteroid administration
- Pituitary ACTH excess
- Adrenal tumour
- Ectopic ACTH or corticotrophin releasing hormone (CRH) from non-endocrine tumours, e.g. oat cell carcinoma of lung

The clinical features are caused by the effects of excess cortisol and/or adrenal androgens.

Clinical features

- proximal muscle wasting and weakness
- central obesity, buffalo hump
- Cushing's facies: plethora, moon face, acne
- hirsutism
- abdominal striae
- thin skin, easy bruising
- hypertension
- hyperglycaemia
- menstrual changes, e.g. amenorrhoea
- osteoporosis
- psychiatric changes, especially depression

Diagnosis (apart from iatrogenic cause)

- cortisol excess (plasma or 24 hour urinary cortisol)
- dexamethasone suppression test
- serum ACTH
- radiological localisation
  - — MRI for ACTH-producing pituitary tumours
  - — CAT scanning for adrenal tumours

Other endocrine disorders

Acromegaly

Symptoms suggestive of acromegaly include:

- excessive growth of hands (increased glove size)
- excessive growth of tissues, e.g. nose, lips, face
- excessive growth of feet (increased shoe size)
- increased size of jaw and tongue
- general: weakness, sweating, headaches
- sexual changes including amenorrhoea and loss of libido

Hypopituitarism

This rare disorder should be considered with:

- a history of postpartum haemorrhage
- symptoms of hypothyroidism
- symptoms of adrenal insufficiency
- symptoms suggestive of a pituitary tumour

Primary hyperparathyroidism

Hyperparathyroidism is caused by an excessive secretion of parathyroid hormone and is usually due to a parathyroid adenoma. The classic clinical features of hyperparathyroidism are due to the effects of hypercalcaemia. Rarely, a parathyroid crisis in a misdiagnosed patient may result in death from severe hypercalcaemia.

Clinical features

- renal — polyuria with nocturia (and thirst)
  — renal colic
- musculoskeletal — aching legs, especially shins
  — muscle aching
  — muscle weakness
  — back pain
- gastrointestinal — anorexia, nausea
  — constipation
- psychiatric — depression
  — personality changes

classic mnemonic: bones, moans, stones, abdominal groans

Diagnosis

- serum parathyroid hormone (elevated)

Hypoparathyroidism

Hypoparathyroidism, which is uncommon, causes hypocalcaemia. Causes include congenital deficiency (Di George's syndrome), idiopathic (autoimmune) hypoparathyroidism and postoperative thyroidectomy and parathyroidectomy. The main features are neuromuscular hyper-excitability, tetany and neuropsychiatric manifestations.

Two important signs of hypocalcaemia are Trousseau's sign and Chvostek's sign.

Treatment involves careful adjustments in dosage of calcitriol and calcium to correct hypocalcaemia and avoid hypercalcaemia (the latter may lead to renal impairment).

References

1. Fry J. *Common diseases* (4th edition). Lancaster MTP Press Limited, 1985, 358–361.
2. Stockigt J, Topliss DJ. Hypothyroidism. In: MIMS Disease Index. Sydney:IMS Publishing, 1991–2, 282–284.
3. Yuen R. *Endocrinology 1*. RACGP: CHECK Programme, unit 243,1992, 2–5.
4. Hales I. Thyrotoxicosis. In: MIMS Disease Index. Sydney:IMS Publishing,1991–2, 541–543.

19

Spinal dysfunction

Spinal or vertebral dysfunction can be regarded as a masquerade mainly because the importance of the spine as a source of various pain syndromes has not been emphasised in medical training. Practitioners whose training and treatment are focused almost totally on the spine may swing to the other extreme and some may attribute almost every clinical syndrome to dysfunction of spinal segments. The true picture lies somewhere in between.

The diagnosis is straightforward when the patient is able to give a history of a precipitating event such as lifting, twisting the neck or having a motor vehicle accident and can then localise the pain to the midline of the neck or back. The diagnostic problem arises when the pain is located distally to its source, whether it is radicular (due to pressure on a nerve root) or referred pain. The problem applies particularly to pain in anterior structures of the body.

If a patient has pain anywhere it is possible that it could be spondylogenic and practitioners should always keep this in mind.

The various syndromes caused by spinal dysfunction will be presented in more detail under neck pain, thoracic back pain and lumbar back pain. The important messages in this clinical problem will be vividly illustrated in the case histories that follow.

Cervical spinal dysfunction[1]

The cervical spine is the origin of many confusing clinical problems such as headache, migraine-like headache, arm pain, facial pain, periauricular pain, anterior chest pain and even visual dysfunction and dizziness. If the cervical spine is overlooked as a source of pain (such as in the head, shoulder, arm, upper chest—anterior and posterior—and around the ear or face) the cause of the symptoms will remain masked and mismanagement will follow. The following case histories illustrate such problems.

Case 1

Nellie P, aged 39, a charge nurse, presented with a seven-year history of unilateral headaches. They were migraine-like, associated with neck ache, and they appeared to follow a motor vehicle accident. After four years under the care of a neurologist she spent three years under a psychiatrist having psychotherapy for functional headache. My partner determined that it was referred from the left side of C2–3 and administered one cervical manipulation. The atypical headaches disappeared completely, never to return (to date).

Case 2

Tania B, aged 36, was a regular attender with multiple complaints, especially 'migraine' headaches, which were unusual in that the headaches could last three days or so and occurred at least weekly. We had just completed a D and C for excessive uterine bleeding and were shifting her from the operating table onto the trolley when her head flopped to one side with a huge, resounding 'crack'. We were most concerned about this wrench in her neck but relieved when she woke with no ill effects. When she presented in about three months she said, 'Well, my bleeding hasn't improved much but I can recommend a D and C for migraines. I haven't had one since.'

Case 3

Margaret B, aged 43, an American tourist, presented with an episode of severe vertigo, which she said had bothered her on and off for the past five years since a motor accident. After spells of being well the bouts could be precipitated by actions such as collecting overhead luggage from a plane. She had associated headaches but no nausea or vomiting. She marvelled at the wonderful tests performed at the University of Birmingham (USA): scans, MRI, angiograms and so on, but they all showed zero. She produced Persantin tablets and Stemetil tablets for the treatment of alleged spasm of her cerebral arteries and inner ear inflammation respectively. On examination she had an extremely tender C2–3 level of her neck and it appeared that the problem could be benign positional vertigo associated with cervical dysfunction. Since vertebrobasilar inefficiency tests were negative, I performed mobilisation and a gentle rotational manipulation with resounding effects. Seven months later I received this letter from Goodwater, Alabama:

I have sung your praises to all who will listen. I have not been bothered with inner ear ever since you gave me that adjustment. I arrived at the conclusion that it isn't inner ear in all cases.

Discussion

Dysfunction of the cervical spine can cause many unusual symptoms such as headache and vertigo, a fact that is often not recognised. Despite teaching to the contrary from some lecturers, the cervical spine is a common cause of headache, especially dysfunction of the facet joints at the C1–2 and C2–3 levels. The afferent pathways from these levels share a common pathway in the brain stem as the trigeminal nerve, hence the tendency for pain to be referred to the head and the face (see page 455).

Manipulation of the cervical spine can be a dramatically effective technique, but it should be used with care and never used in the presence of organic disease and vertebrobasilar insufficiency. It should, therefore, be given only by skilled therapists. Two groups at special risk from quadriplegia are those with rheumatoid arthritis of the neck and Down syndrome, because of the instability of the odontoid process.

Thoracic spinal dysfunction

The most common and difficult masquerades related to spinal dysfunction occur with disorders of the thoracic spine (and also the low cervical spine) which can cause vague aches and pains in the chest, including the anterior chest.

Pain in the thoracic spine with referral to various parts of the chest wall and upper abdomen is common in all ages and can closely mimic the symptoms of visceral disease such as angina pectoris and biliary colic. If a non-cardiac cause of chest pain is excluded then the possibility of referral from the thoracic spine should be considered in the differential diagnosis. People of all ages can experience thoracic problems and it is surprisingly common in young people, including children.

Pain of thoracic spinal origin may be referred anywhere to the chest wall, but the commonest sites are the scapular region, the paravertebral region 2–5 cm from midline and, anteriorly, over the costochondral region.

Thoracic pain of lower cervical origin[2]

The clinical association between injury to the lower cervical region and upper thoracic pain is well known, especially with 'whiplash' injuries. It should be noted that the C4 dermatome is in close proximity to the T2 dermatome.

The T2 dermatome appears to represent the cutaneous areas of the lower cervical segments, as the posterior primary rami of C5,6,7,8 and T1 innervate musculature and have no significant cutaneous innervation.

The pain from the lower cervical spine can also refer pain to the anterior chest, and mimic coronary ischaemic pain. The associated autonomic nervous system disturbance can cause considerable confusion in making the diagnosis.

Illustrative case histories[1]

Case 1

Marge T, aged 52, presented with an extraordinary story of modern medical mismanagement. While carrying heavy suitcases in Hong Kong she developed anterior chest pain. She was taken to an emergency department where, despite a normal ECG, she was told she had heart trouble and had to be careful.

Upon returning to Melbourne and while under the care of her son-in-law who was a specialist, she developed episodes of central chest pain with, at times, mid-thoracic back pain. She felt tired and languid. A stress ECG was normal. She was admitted to a teaching hospital for further investigation. Unfortunately, an ultrasound examination was reported to be abnormal (? chronic relapsing pancreatitis). The incompatible clinical history was ignored as she went from investigation to investigation over a period of nine months. The eventual diagnosis was chest pain of unknown cause with anxiety.

Diagnosis and outcome

The anxious and devastated Marge, as a result, first consulted me with classic depression. The history was interesting—the pain invariably followed a lifting or laborious activity such as vacuuming or bed-making. The associated back pain tended to get ignored as the focus was on the retrosternal pain. Examination revealed tenderness at the T5 and T6 levels of her thoracic spine while X-ray showed mild degenerative changes. She had dysfunction of her mid-thoracic spine with referred pain. After three treatments by spinal mobilisation and manipulation, her pain completely subsided, as did her 'stress-related problem', anxiety and depression.

Case 2

Elana W, aged 32, presented as a new patient with epigastric pain brought on by physical activity including lifting her children. A careful history determined associated back pain 'just around my bra strap'. The problematic T7 area of her thoracic spine was appropriately treated.

Elana came in with one of her children some weeks later and said, 'You know, Doctor, that stomach pain I've had for three years has gone. To think that it was thought to be an ulcer and then a hiatus hernia. I've had two barium meals and a tube passed down but they found nothing.'

Case 3

Joan G, aged 41, requested a second opinion about recurrent pains under her right costal margin for 12 months or so. Cholecystectomy did not help at all, but correction of her thoracic spinal problem at T7–T8 completely alleviated the pain.

Case 4

The writer has a personal testimony worth recording. Poliomyelitis affected the back at 8 years of age and then from age 12 to 24 with persistent thoracic back pain that would radiate anterolaterally just below the nipple line, either right or left side. 'You have to learn to live with it, John—it will probably get worse as you get older,' came the reassuring prognostication from my attending neurologist. Other more adventurous doctors proffered diagnoses such as post-polio neuralgia, da Costa's syndrome and Tietze's syndrome. I noted during medical school that if patients were unfortunate enough to get the pain on the left side of the chest it was called 'cardiac neurosis'. However, while attending a football club physiotherapist for an ankle injury, he noted my thoracic deformity and asked if it gave me pain. 'I can fix that.' 'No, you can't.' 'Yes, I can—let me try.' Thumbs and hands deftly worked on the T4 to T6 levels—impressive sound effects with cracking and clicking. To the profound relief and gratitude of this impressionable patient, the 13 years of pain was relieved. It returns occasionally but is likewise alleviated with physical therapy.

Discussion

The medical profession tends to have a blind spot about various pain syndromes in the chest, especially the anterior chest and upper abdomen, caused by the common problem of dysfunction of the thoracic spine. Doctors who gain this insight are amazed at how often they diagnose the cause that previously did not enter their 'programmed' medical minds.

Physical therapy to the spine can be dramatically effective when used appropriately. Unfortunately, many of us associate it with quackery. It is devastating for patients to create doubts in their minds about having a 'heart problem' or an 'anxiety neurosis'. Substituting vague or even dogmatic labels for ignorance is most inappropriate management.

Lumbar spinal dysfunction

The association between lumbar dysfunction and pain syndromes is generally easier to correlate. The pain is usually located in the low back and referred to the buttocks or the backs of the lower limbs. Problems arise with referred pain to the pelvic area, groin and anterior aspects of the leg. Such patients may be diagnosed as suffering from inguinal or obturator hernial and nerve entrapment syndromes.

Typical examples of referral and radicular pain patterns from various segments of the spine are presented in Figure 19.1.

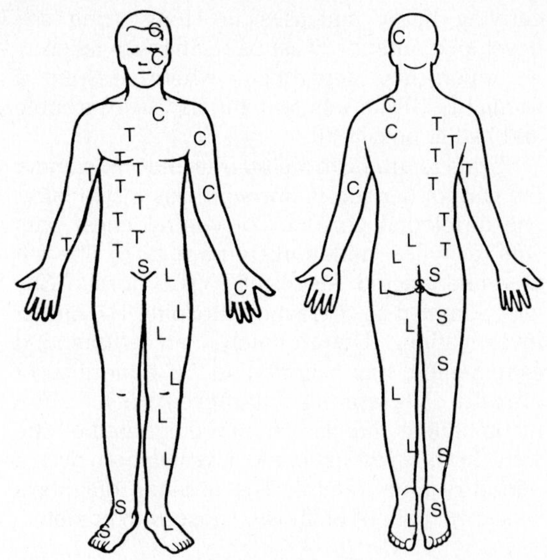

C = cervical; T = thoracic; L = lumbar; S = sacral

Fig. 19.1 *Examples of referred and radicular pain patterns from the spine (one side shown for each segment)*

References

1. Murtagh J. *Cautionary tales.* Sydney:McGraw-Hill,1992, 36–130.
2. Kenna C, Murtagh J. Back pain and spinal manipulation. Sydney: Butterworths,1989, 167–170.

20

Urinary tract infection

Urinary tract infection (UTI) is a common problem affecting all ages and accounts for approximately 1% of all attendances in general practice. It is very common in sexually active women but uncommon in men and children.

Organisms causing UTI in the community are usually sensitive to most of the commonly used antibiotics. The important decision to make is whether to proceed with further investigation of the urinary tract. The morbidity of urinary infections in both children and adults is well known but it is vital to recognise the potential for progressive renal damage, ending in chronic renal failure. The main task in the prevention of chronic pyelonephritis is the early identification of patients with additional factors, such as reflux or obstruction, which could lead to progressive renal damage.

Key facts and checkpoints

- Screening of asymptomatic women has shown that about 5% have bacterial UTI.[1]
- About 1% of neonates and 1–2% of schoolgirls have asymptomatic bacteruria.[2]
- About one-third of women have been estimated to have symptoms suggestive of cystitis at some stage of their life.
- The vast majority of these women have anatomically normal renal tracts, are at no significant risk from the UTI and respond quickly to simple therapy. The prevalence of underlying abnormalities is estimated at around 4%.[3]
- UTIs are largely caused by organisms from the bowel which colonise the perineum and reach the bladder via the urethra. In many young women infections are precipitated by sexual intercourse. Ascending infection accounts for 93% of UTIs.
- Haematogenous infection can occur sometimes, especially with the immunocompromised patient.
- All men and children presenting with a UTI require investigation for an underlying abnormality of the urinary tract.
- In the presence of a normal urinary tract there is no evidence that UTI leads to progressive renal damage.

UTI as a masquerade

Urinary tract infection can be regarded as a masquerade when it presents with a constitutional problem or general symptoms, without symptoms suggestive of a urinary infection such as frequency, dysuria and loin pain. This applies particularly to infants and young children and the elderly but is not uncommon in adult women and in pregnancy. Acute UTI may occasionally present as acute abdominal pain.

In infants and children, presenting non-specific symptoms include:

- fever
- failure to thrive
- vomiting
- abdominal pain
- diarrhoea

In the elderly

- confusion
- behaviour disturbance
- fever of undetermined origin

Classification and clinical syndromes

Sterile pyuria

This is defined as the presence of pus cells but a sterile urine culture.[2] The common causes of sterile pyuria are:

- contamination of poorly collected urine specimens
- urinary infections being treated by antibiotics
- analgesic nephropathy
- staghorn calculi
- bladder tumours
- tuberculosis

Asymptomatic bacteriuria

This is defined as the presence of a significant growth of bacteria in the urine, which has not produced symptoms requiring consultation.[1] On close questioning many patients admit to mild urinary symptoms.

- Common only in sexually active women, the elderly and those with urinary tract abnormalities. UTI can exist without any symptoms.[1]
- These patients are more likely to have a past history of symptomatic UTI or to develop symptoms in the future than subjects with sterile urine.[1]
- During pregnancy, asymptomatic bacteriuria leads to acute clinical UTI in up to 30% of women.

Symptomatic bacteriuria

This is defined as the presence of frequency, dysuria and loin pain alone or in combination, together with a significant growth of organisms on urine culture.[2]

The clinical differentiation between cystitis or lower UTI and renal or upper UTI cannot be made accurately on the basis of symptoms, except in those patients with well defined loin pain and/ or tenderness.

Acute cystitis (dysuria-frequency syndrome)[1]

- Inflammation of the bladder and/or urethra is associated with dysuria (pain or scalding with micturition) and/or urinary frequency.
- In severe cases, haematuria may be present, and the urine may have an offensive smell.
- Constitutional symptoms are minimal or absent.
- Other causes of dysuria and frequency include urethritis, prostatitis and vulvovaginitis, all of which can normally be distinguished clinically.

Acute pyelonephritis[1]

- Acute bacterial infection of the kidney produces loin pain and constitutional upset, with fever, rigor, nausea and sometimes vomiting.
- The symptoms of acute cystitis are often also present.
- The differential diagnosis includes causes of the acute abdomen such as appendicitis, cholecystitis and acute tubal or ovarian diseases. The presence of pyuria and absence of rebound tenderness are helpful in distinction.

The clinical manifestations of UTI are summarised in Figure 20.1.

Uncomplicated urinary tract infection

This is cystitis occurring in the uninstrumented non-pregnant female without structural or neurological abnormalities.

Urethral syndrome

The urethral syndrome (sometimes termed abacterial cystitis) is that where the patient presents with dysuria and frequency but does not show a positive urine culture.[3]

- 30–40% of adult women with urinary symptoms have this syndrome.[3]
- Many actually have bacterial cystitis but a negative culture.
- The organisms may be anaerobic or fastidious in their culture requirements.
- The organisms may include Ureaplasma, Chlamydia and viruses.
- The urine may have antiseptic contamination or residual antibiotic.
- The infection may be undergoing spontaneous resolution at the time of the culture.

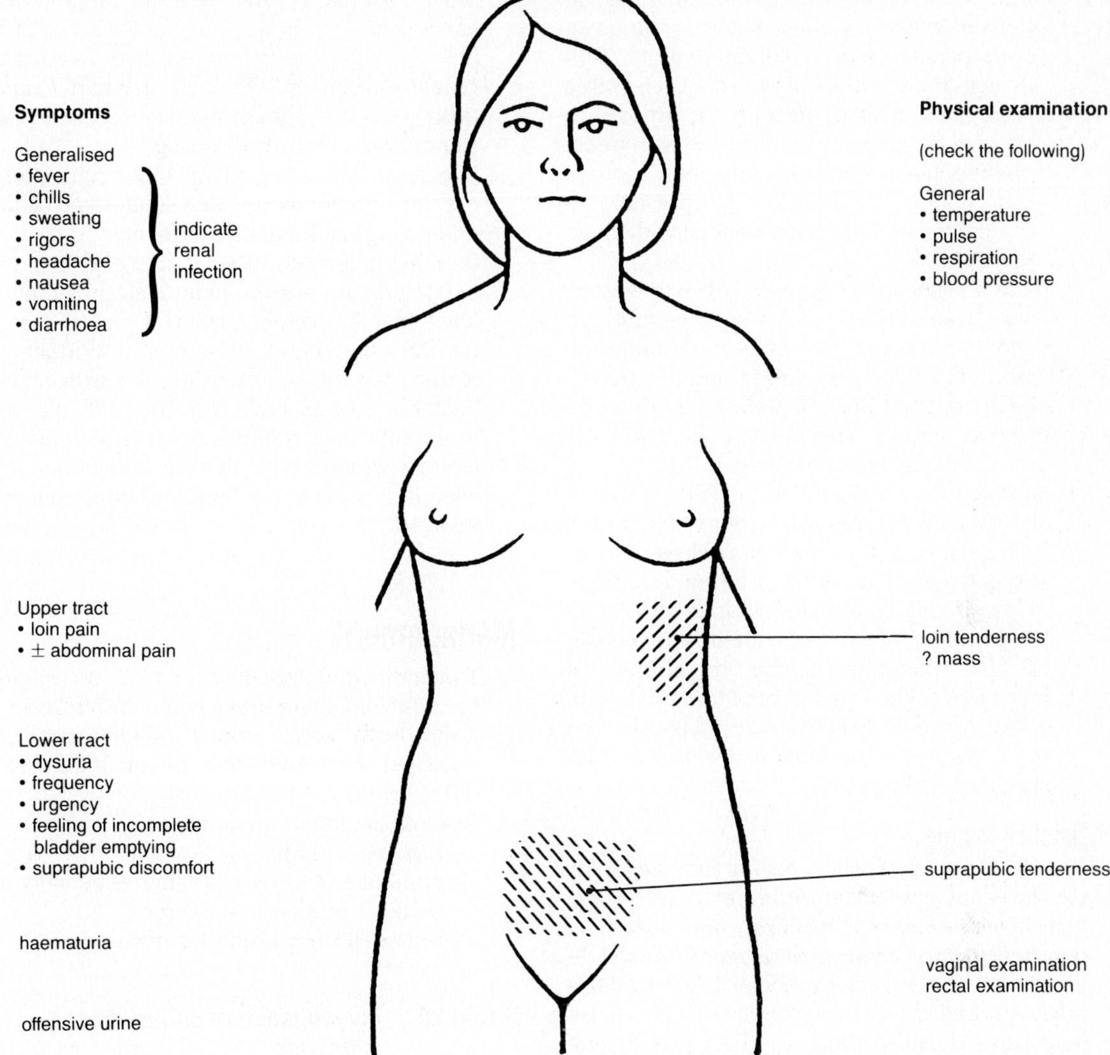

Fig. 20.1 *Clinical manifestations of urinary tract infection*

Interstitial cystitis[3]

This is an uncommon but important cause of the urethral syndrome.

- The classical symptoms are frequency day and night and a dull suprapubic ache relieved briefly by bladder emptying.
- The feature is small haemorrhages on distension of the bladder.

Laboratory diagnosis

The laboratory diagnosis of UTI depends on careful collection, examination and culture of urine.

Collection of urine[1]

It is best to collect the first urine passed in the morning, when it is highly concentrated and any bacteria have been incubated in the bladder overnight. Preferably the urine should be taken to the laboratory immediately, but it can be stored for up to 24 hours at 4°C to prevent bacterial multiplication.

- Midstream specimen of urine (MSU): this is best collected from a full bladder, to allow at least 200 ml of urine to be passed before collection of the MSU. It is important that the urine flow is continuous, and the container is moved in and out of the stream collecting at least 20 ml.

— In women, a tampon should first be inserted and the vulva washed with clean water (to avoid contamination with vaginal and vulval organisms). The labia are then held apart with the fingers to prevent contact with the urinary stream while the specimen is collected.
— In males, the foreskin (if present) is retracted and the glans washed with clean water.

- Catheter specimen of urine (CSU): in women who have difficulty with collecting an uncontaminated MSU (as is commonly the case in the elderly, the infirm and the grossly obese), a short open-ended catheter can be inserted and a specimen collected after 200 ml has flushed the catheter.
- Suprapubic aspirate of urine (SPA): this is an extremely reliable way to detect bacteruria in neonates and in patients where UTI is suspected but cannot be confirmed because of low colony counts or contamination in an MSU. Under local anaesthetic, a needle (lumbar puncture needle in adults) is inserted into the very full bladder about 1 cm above the pubic symphysis. 20 ml is collected by a syringe. Any organisms in an SPA specimen indicate UTI.

Dipstick testing

The reagents in dipstick testing are generally sensitive but have to be interpreted with care. 'Leucocyte esterase dipsticks' are useful in detecting pyuria and give a good guide to infection with a specificity of 94–98% (2–6% false positive) and 74–96% sensitivity (4–26% false negatives).[4] Positive nitrite dipsticks give a useful guide to the presence of bacteria. Unexplained haematuria detected by 'dipstick' analysis needs investigation.

Microscopic examination

The urine is examined under a microscope to detect pyuria (more than ten pus cells (WBCs) per high-powered field) but should be examined in a counting chamber to calculate the number of WBCs/ml of urine. In the counting chamber pyuria is > 8000 WBC/ml in phase contrast microscopy. Pyuria is a very sensitive sign of UTI.

Vaginal squames and debris indicate contamination.

Culture of the urine

The nature and number of organisms present in the urine are the most useful indicators of UTI.[1]

- Most common are enteric organisms. *Escherichia coli* is responsible for about 90% of UTIs with other Gram-negative organisms (Klebsiella sp and Proteus sp) and Gram-positive cocci (*Streptococcus faecalis* and staphylococci) also occurring.
- Infections due to organisms other than *E.coli*, e.g. Pseudomonas sp, are suggestive of an underlying renal tract abnormality.
- If $> 10^5$ colony forming units (cfu) per ml of bacteria are present in an MSU, it is highly likely that the patient has a UTI.
- On the other hand, it is most important to realise that up to 30% of women with acute bacterial cystitis have less than 10^5 cfu/ml in the MSU. For this reason, it is reasonable to treat women with dysuria and frequency even if they have $< 10^5$ cfu/ml of organisms in an MSU.

Management

- The indications for investigation of urinary tract infections are presented in Table 20.1.
- Appropriate antimicrobial therapy can be expected to cure 80–90% of uncomplicated UTIs.
- Optimal treatment includes:
  — high fluid intake
  — complete bladder emptying, especially at bedtime or after intercourse
  — urinary alkalinisation for severe dysuria

Table 20.1 *Investigation of urinary tract infections*

Investigations are indicated in:
- all children
- all males
- all woman with:
  — acute pyelonephritis
  — recurrent infections
  — confirmed sterile pyuria
  — other features of renal disease

Basic investigations include:
- MSU—microscopy and culture (post-treatment)
- Renal function tests: plasma urea and creatinine
- Intravenous urogram (IVU), and/or ultrasound

Special considerations:
- In children: micturating cystogram
- In adult males: consider prostatic infection studies if IVU normal
- In severe pyelonephritis: ultrasound or IVU (urgent) to exclude obstruction
- In pregnant women: ultrasound to exclude obstruction

Acute uncomplicated cystitis

Advice to women (especially if recurrent attacks):

- Keep yourself rested.
- Drink a lot of fluid: 2–3 cups of water at first and then 1 cup every 30 minutes.
- Try to empty your bladder completely each time.
- Gently wash or wipe your bottom from front to back with soft, moist tissues after opening your bowels (for prevention in recurrent attacks).
- Use analgesics such as paracetamol for pain.
- Make the urine alkaline by using sodium citrotartrate (4 g orally 6 hourly) (not if taking nitrofurantoin).

Antimicrobial regimen (for women)

Multiple dose therapy preferred.

Single dose therapy[1,5]

- trimethoprim 600 mg orally

or

- gentamicin 120 mg IM

Multiple dose therapy[5]

use for 5 days in women (trimethoprim—3 days)
use for 10 days in women with known UT abnormality
use for 10 days in men with acute cystitis

- trimethoprim 300 mg (o) daily for 3 days

or

- cephalexin 250 mg (o) 6 hourly

or

- amoxycillin/potassium clavulanate 250/125 mg (o) 8 hourly (preferred agent)

or

- norfloxacin 400 mg (o) 12 hourly (if resistance to above agents proven)

Follow-up: MSU 3 weeks later.

Acute pyelonephritis

Mild cases can be treated with oral therapy alone using double the dosage of drugs recommended for uncomplicated cystitis, except for trimethoprim when the same dosage is recommended. Norfloxacin is used if resistance to these drugs is proven.

For severe infection with suspected septicaemia admit to hospital and treat initially with parenteral antibiotics for 2 to 5 days after taking urine for microscopy and culture and blood for culture.

amoxycillin 1 g IV 6 hourly[5]

plus

gentamicin 120–160 mg IV 12 hourly

Follow with oral therapy for a total of 14 days therapy.

All patients should be investigated for an underlying urinary tract abnormality.

Recurrent or chronic urinary tract infections

Recurrent infections occur as a relapse of a previously treated infection or because of reinfection, often with differing organisms. Persistent (chronic) UTIs indicate that the organism is resistant to the antimicrobial agents employed or that there is an underlying abnormality such as a renal stone or a chronically infected prostate in the male patient. Such infections may be treated with prolonged courses of an appropriate antibiotic or removal of the focus of infection.

In men and children an anatomical abnormality is usual, while recurrent cystitis in women often occurs despite a normal tract. In women, instruction on perineal hygiene, more frequent bladder emptying and postintercourse voiding may assist in the prevention of reinfection.

Treatment of recurrent or chronic UTI[5]

A 10 to 14 day course of

- amoxycillin/potassium clavulanate (250/125 mg) (o) 8 hourly

or

- nitrofurantoin 100 mg (o) 6 hourly

or

- norfloxacin 400 mg (o) 12 hourly (if proven resistance to above agents)

Prophylaxis for recurrent UTI[5]

In some female patients a single dose of a suitable agent after intercourse is adequate but, in more severe cases, courses may be taken for 6 months or on occasions longer.

- nitrofurantoin (macrocrystals) 50–100 mg (o) nocte

or

- trimethoprim 150 mg (o) nocte

or

- norfloxacin 200–400 mg (o) nocte (if proven resistance to others)

Asymptomatic bacteruria

- In neonates and preschool children, treat and investigate for evidence of vesicoureteral reflux.
- In men less than 60 years old, treat and investigate, especially for chronic prostatitis.
- In women, give single dose therapy and investigate only those in whom UTI persists or recurs.
- In pregnant women, treat because of the risk of developing pyelonephritis (up to 40% risk).
- School-age children and elderly men and women (over 60 years) probably do not require treatment if their urinary tracts are normal.
- In patients with long-term indwelling catheters treatment is not usually required or useful.
- Prophylaxis should be given for recurrent asymptomatic bacteruria in pregnant women, in patients with associated renal tract abnormality, in those undergoing genito-urinary instrumentation or surgery or intermittent catheterisation.

Urinary tract infection in children

UTI in infants and very young children is often renal in nature and may be associated with generalised symptoms such as fever, vomiting, diarrhoea and failure to thrive. Symptoms of dysuria and frequency only appear after the age of 2 years when the child is able to indicate the source of the discomfort. In a girl or boy (rare presentation) with symptoms of dysuria and frequency an underlying abnormality is likely to be present with a reported incidence of vesicoureteric reflux as high as 40% and scarred kidneys (reflux nephropathy) in 27%.[3]

Thus the early detection of children with vesicoureteric reflux and control of recurrent renal infection could prevent the development of scars, hypertension and chronic renal failure. Radiological investigation of children with UTIs shows normal kidneys in approximately 66% and reflux in approximately 33%.

Antimicrobial treatment for acute cystitis in children[5]

Treatment should be continued for 7 to 10 days.

- trimethoprim 6 mg/kg (maximum 300 mg) orally, daily (suspension is 50 mg/5 ml)

or

- cephalexin 10 mg/kg (maximum 250 mg) orally 6 hourly

or

- amoxycillin/potassium clavulanate 10/2.5 mg/kg (maximum 250/125 mg) orally 8 hourly

Norfloxacin is contraindicated in children.
Check MSU in three weeks.

Urinary infections in the elderly

The typical settings in which UTIs occur in the elderly are in the frail, those who are immobilised, those with faecal incontinence and inadequate bladder emptying. The presenting symptoms may be atypical, especially with upper UTI where fever of undetermined origin and behaviour disturbances may be a feature. In men obstructive uropathy from prostatism should be excluded by ultrasound.

Uncomplicated infections should be treated the same way as for other age groups but no antimicrobial treatment is recommended for asymptomatic bacteruria.

Urinary infections in pregnancy

UTI in pregnant women requires careful surveillance. Asymptomatic bacteruria should always be excluded during early pregnancy because it tends to develop into a full-blown infection. Acute cystitis is treated for 10 to 14 days with any of the following antimicrobials: cephalexin, amoxycillin/potassium clavulanate or nitrofurantoin (if a beta-lactam antibiotic is contraindicated). The dosages are the same as for other groups. Asymptomatic bacteruria should be treated with a week-long course.

Genitourinary tuberculosis

The genitourinary tract is involved in 3–5% of cases of tuberculosis.[6] The genital and urinary tracts are often involved together as a result of miliary spread.

The commonest presenting complaints are dysuria and frequency which can be severe. Other symptoms include stranguary when the bladder is severely affected, loin pain and haematuria. Routine urine culture shows sterile pyuria.

Diagnosis is made on specific culture for mycobacterium, or biopsy of bladder lesions or the typical X-ray appearance of distorted calyces and medullary calcification. Treatment is with antituberculosis drugs.

Common treatment errors[1]

- Not treating women with dysuria and frequency merely because there are $< 10^5$ cfu/ml in an MSU.
- Overtreating women with acute cystitis and normal urinary tracts. Single-dose therapy is effective in 70–80% of cases, and overtreatment often leads to vaginal candidiasis or antibiotic-induced diarrhoea.
- Using single-dose therapy in patients with known anatomical abnormalities.
- Failing to consider chronic prostatic infection in men with recurrent UTI and a normal IVU.

When to refer

- It is wise to refer all patients with urinary tract abnormalities to a nephrologist or urologist for advice on specific management.
- Refer also if the simple methods outlined above do not control recurrent UTI.
- Males with urinary infections that are not clearly localised to the prostate.
- Patients with impaired renal function.

Practice tips

- Most symptomatic UTIs are acute cystitis occurring in sexually active women with anatomically normal urinary tracts.
- A clinical diagnosis based on experience, plus positive nitrite dipstick test and the finding of pyuria by office microscopy will generally enable immediate curative treatment.
- A three day course of trimethoprim 300 mg daily for 3 days is a suitable first choice for acute uncomplicated cystitis in women.
- Avoid overinvestigation of patients in whom there is a low likelihood of demonstrating structural abnormalities.
- In males the prostate is the most common source of recurrent UTI.
- Urinary tract infection is commonly associated with microscopic haematuria (occasionally macroscopic haematuria).
- Persisting haematuria should be investigated.
- Due to the rising level of *E. coli* resistance, amoxycillin is no longer recommended unless susceptibility to the organism is proven.[5]

References

1. Becker GJ. Urinary tract infection. In: MIMS Disease Index. Sydney: IMS Publishing, 1991–92, 569–572.
2. Heale W. *Renal disease*. CHECK Programme. Melbourne: RACGP: 1987;1–20.
3. Kincaid-Smith P, Larkins R, Whelan G. *Problems in clinical medicine*. Sydney: MacLennan & Petty, 1990, 280–283.
4. Sloane P, Slatt M, Baker R. *Essentials of family medicine*. Baltimore: Williams and Wilkins, 1988, 162–168.
5. Mashford ML. *Antibiotic guidelines*. (8th edition), Melbourne: Victorian Medical Postgraduate Foundation, 1994, 30–35.
6. Bullock N, Sibley G, Whitaker R. *Essential urology*. Edinburgh: Churchill Livingstone, 1989:126–129.

21

Malignant disease

The terms malignancy, cancer and neoplasia are usually used interchangeably. The differences between a malignant tumour and a benign tumour are summarised in Table 21.1.

Table 21.1 *Different characteristics of benign and malignant tumours*

Benign	*Malignant*
Well differentiated	Undifferentiated
Non-invasive	Invasive
Slow growth	Rapid growth
Not anaplastic	Anaplastic
Not metastatic	Metastatic

Malignant disease accounts for 1 in 8 deaths of people under 35 years in Australia and 1 in every 4 (25%) of deaths in those over 45 years.[1] Cancer is the only major cause of death in Australia which is increasing in both sexes. At current rates about one in three males and one in four females will develop a cancer, excluding non-melanoma skin cancers, by the age of 75.[1]

The six most common causes of death from cancer in Australia are cancer of the bowel, lung, breast, prostate, bladder and skin (melanoma).

Neoplasia, especially malignancy of the silent areas, can present as undifferentiated illness and be a real masquerade. The so-called 'silent' malignancies which pose a special problem include carcinoma of the ovary, kidney, caecum and ascending colon, liver (hepatoma) and haematological tissue.

Acute emergency problems which can develop with various malignancies include spinal cord compression, malignant effusions, disseminated intravascular coagulation and hypercalcaemia.

Clinical manifestations

The clinical manifestations of malignancy are usually due to:

- pressure effects of the growth
- infiltration or metastases in various organs, e.g. liver, brain, lungs, bone, blood vessels
- systemic symptoms including paraneoplastic effects

Systemic symptoms

These can be divided into general non-specific effects and paraneoplastic syndromes which are the remote effects caused by the tumour.

Undifferentiated general symptoms

- tiredness/fatigue/weakness
- anorexia and nausea
- weight loss

Paraneoplastic effects

The paraneoplastic effects or syndromes are very important clinically because they may provide an early clue to the presence of a specific type of cancer, in addition to the possible lethal effect of the metabolic or toxic effect, e.g. hyponatraemia. These effects include:

- ectopic hormone production
- skin abnormalities
- metabolic effects
  - fever/sweats
  - weight loss
- haematologic disorders
  - anaemia
  - erythrocytosis
  - coagulation disorder
  - others
- neuropathies and CNS abnormalities
- collagen vascular disorders

A summary of various paraneoplastic syndromes is presented in Table 21.2.

Table 21.2 *Paraneoplastic syndromes and associated tumours: more common examples*

Hormone excess/ syndrome	***Tumour***
Cushing's	Lung, kidney, adrenal, thymoma, pancreas
ACTH	Lung, kidney, thymoma, thyroid
Gonadotrophins	Lung, choriocarcinoma, hepatoma
Other syndromes	
Hypercalcaemia	Lung, breast, kidney, multiple myeloma, prostate, pancreas, adrenal, hepatoma
Fever	Kidney, hepatoma, lymphoma, pancreas, thymoma
Neurologic	Lung, breast, thymoma, Hodgkin's, prostate
Coagulopathy	Lung, breast, hepatoma, prostate, pancreas
Thrombophlebitis	Kidney, pancreas, prostate
Polycythaemia	Kidney, hepatoma
Dermatomyositis	Lung, breast, pancreas

Clinical approach

A history of constitutional symptoms that are often quite undifferentiated (often bizarre) may provide the clue to the possibility of an underlying malignancy. An occupational history may be relevant to the clinical problem (see Table 21.3).

Tumour markers

A tumour marker is an abnormal characteristic which is specific for a particular type of malignancy, e.g. the Philadelphia chromosome for chronic myeloid leukaemia. Other examples include human chorionic gonadotrophin (elevated in trophoblastic tumours and germ cell neoplasms of the testes and ovaries) and the oncofetal antigens—carcino-embryonic antigen (CEA) and alpha fetoprotein (AFP).

CEA and AFP are not specific markers but are elevated in certain tumours and are very useful in monitoring tumour activity.

Tumour markers, some of which are yet unidentified, would appear to have an important role in future diagnosis and management of malignant disease.

Lung cancer

Apart from non-melanoma skin cancer, lung cancer is the most common cancer in Australia both in terms of incidence and death, accounting for at least 20% of cancer deaths.[1] In the United States it accounts for 35% of cancer deaths in men and 21% of deaths in women. Only 10–25% are asymptomatic at the time of diagnosis but lung cancer can cause an extraordinary variety of clinical symptoms and signs with a reputation for several paraneoplastic syndromes.

Table 21.3 *Occupational causes of cancer*

Agent	***Occupation***	***Cancer***
Arsenic	Chemical industry	Lung, skin, liver
Asbestos	Insulation worker	Mesothelioma
Benzene	Glue worker, varnisher	Leukaemia
Soot, coal tar	Chimney sweep	Skin
Radiation	Mining, watch dials	Various
Ultraviolet light	Farmer, sailor	Skin
Vinyl chloride	PVC manufacturing	Liver (angiosarcoma)

The paraneoplastic syndromes include hypercalcaemia, Cushing's syndrome, carcinoid syndrome, dermatomyositis, visual loss progressing to blindness from retinal degeneration, cerebellar degeneration and encephalitis.

The presentation of cough and chest pain renders it less of an 'occult' malignancy than several other types.

Renal tumours

The most important tumours of the kidney are adenocarcinoma (80% of all renal tumours)[2] and nephroblastoma (Wilms' tumour).

Adenocarcinoma

Adenocarcinoma of the kidney has a great diversity of presenting symptoms, including:

- general symptoms of neoplasia
- haematuria (60%)
- loin pain (40%)
- loin mass
- signs of anaemia
- left supraclavicular lymphadenopathy
- varicocele
- hypertension
- symptoms of metastases (to liver, lungs, brain, bones)
  - — respiratory symptoms
  - — neurological symptoms and signs
  - — bone pain
  - — pathological fracture (vertebral collapse)
- urinalysis: 67% positive for blood

The classic triad of symptoms (in 10–15% of patients) is:[2]

- haematuria
- loin pain
- palpable kidney mass

Wilms' tumour

Wilms' tumour is responsible for 10% of all childhood malignancies. Clinical features[2] include:

- peak incidence 2–3 years
- general symptoms of neoplasia
- palpable mass 80%
- abdominal pain 30%
- haematuria 25%

Early diagnosis with nephrectomy and chemotherapy leads to a very favourable prognosis.

Ovarian cancer

Ovarian cancer has the highest mortality rate of all the gynaecological cancers because the majority of patients present in the late stage of the disease. It is usually asymptomatic prior to the development of metastases. Epithelial tumours are the most common of malignant ovarian tumours. They are uncommon under 40 years of age and the average age of diagnosis is 50 years.[3]

The most common presentation is abdominal swelling (mass and/or ascites). Non-specific symptoms which may be present for a long time before diagnosis include abnormal uterine bleeding, weight loss, abdominal discomfort, reduced capacity for food, anorexia, nausea and vomiting.

Carcinoma of caecum and ascending colon

Malignancy in this area is more likely to present with symptoms of anaemia without the patient noting obvious blood in the faeces or alteration of bowel habit.

The leukaemias

The leukaemias are caused by an acquired malignant transformation in the stem cell in the haemopoietic system. Acute leukaemia has a rapidly fatal course if untreated, while chronic leukaemia has a variable chronic course with an inevitable fatal outcome. The main features of each type are as follows.

Acute leukaemia

Symptoms

- general constitutional, e.g. malaise
- symptoms of anaemia
- susceptibility to infection, e.g. sore throat, mouth ulceration, chest infection
- easy bruising and bleeding, e.g. epistaxis, gingival bleeding
- bone pain (notably in children with ALL) and joint pain
- symptoms due to infiltration of tissues with blast cells, e.g. gingival hypertrophy in AML

Signs

- pallor of anaemia
- petechiae, bruising

- gum hypertrophy/gingivitis/stomatitis
- signs of infection
- variable enlargement of liver, spleen and lymph nodes
- bone tenderness, especially sternum and liver

Diagnosis

- FBE and film
  - normochromic/normocytic anaemia
  - pancytopenia with circulatory blast cells
  - platelets: usually reduced
- Bone marrow examination

Chronic myeloid leukaemia

Main clinical features

- a disorder of middle age
- insidious onset
- constitutional symptoms: malaise, weight loss, fever
- symptoms of anaemia
- splenomegaly (very large)
- priapism
- gout
- markedly elevated white cell count (granulocytes)
- marked left shift in myeloid series
- presence of Philadelphia chromosome

Chronic lymphocytic leukaemia

Main clinical features

- a disorder of late middle age and elderly
- insidious onset
- constitutional symptoms: malaise, weight loss, fever
- lymphadenopathy—neck, axilla, groin (80%)
- moderately enlarged spleen and liver (about 50%)
- mild anaemia
- lymphocytosis $> 15 \times 10^9$/L
- 'mature' appearance of lymphocytes

The lymphomas

Lymphomas, which are malignant tumours of lymphoid tissue, are classified as Hodgkin's disease and non-Hodgkin's lymphoma on the basis of histological appearance of the involved lymph tissue.

Hodgkin's disease

Clinical features

- painless (rubbery) lymphadenopathy, especially cervical nodes
- constitutional symptoms, e.g. malaise, weakness, weight loss
- fever and drenching night sweats
- pruritus
- alcohol-induced pain in any enlarged lymph nodes
- possible enlarged spleen and liver

Diagnosis is by lymph node biopsy with histological confirmation.

Non-Hodgkin's lymphomas

Non-Hodgkin's lymphomas are a heterogeneous group of cancers of lymphocytes derived from the malignant clones of B or T cells.

Main clinical features

- painless lymphadenopathy—localised or widespread
- constitutional symptoms possible, especially sweating
- pruritus is uncommon
- extra nodal sites of disease, e.g. skin, GIT
- possible enlarged liver and spleen
- possible nodular infiltration of skin, e.g. mycosis fungoides

Diagnosis is by lymph node biopsy.

Multiple myeloma

Multiple myeloma is regarded as a disease of the elderly, the mean age of presentation being 60 years.[4] The classic presenting triad in an older man is anaemia, back pain and elevated ESR.

Main clinical features

- bone pain, e.g. backache (in more than 80% of patients)
- bone tenderness
- weakness, tiredness
- recurrent infections
- symptoms of anaemia
- bleeding tendency
- replacement of bone marrow by malignant plasma cells

Diagnostic criteria

The presence of:[4]

- paraprotein in serum
- Bence-Jones protein in urine
- bony lytic lesions

Carcinoid syndrome

Hormone secretion by carcinoid cells causes the characteristic carcinoid syndrome long before local growth of metastatic spread of the tumour is apparent.

The syndrome

Classic triad:	skin flushing (especially face), diarrhoea (with abdominal cramps), valvular heart disease
Other features:	wheezing, telangiectasia, hypotension
Sites of tumours:	ileum, stomach, bronchi

Potentially curable malignant tumours

Several tumours are curable by chemotherapy even in the advanced stage. Such tumours are:

Haematological tumours

- some lymphomas
- Hodgkin's disease
- acute lymphatic leukaemia
- acute myeloid leukaemia

Solid tumours

- choriocarcinoma
- testicular carcinoma
- neuroblastoma
- Wilms' tumour
- Burkitts' tumour
- embryonal rhabdomyosarcoma
- small cell lung cancer

Tumours curable by adjuvant chemotherapy

- breast cancer (especially up to stage 2)
- osteogenic cancer
- soft tissue cancer
- colorectal cancer

References

1. Australia's Health 1990. Canberra: Australian Institute of Health, 1990, 57–64.
2. Bullock N, Sibley G, Whitaker Q. *Essential urology*. Edinburgh: Churchill Livingstone, 1989, 202–208.
3. Dalrymple C. Ovarian cancer: a sinister and silent disease. Mod Medicine Australia, July 1992, 26–37.
4. Kumer PJ, Clark ML. *Clinical medicine* (2nd edition), London: Bailliere Tindall, 1990, 349–351.

22

Human immunodeficiency virus infection—could it be HIV?

Human immunodeficiency virus infection (HIV), the cause of the well known acquired immunodeficiency syndrome (AIDS) can rightly be included as one of the clinical masquerades of modern medicine. The infection probably represents the tip of the iceberg as we are still considered to be at the early stages of the HIV epidemic in Western countries. The average incubation period from HIV infection to AIDS was considered to be about 10 years in developed countries but this time has been extended by treatment with zidovudine (azidothymidine—AZT).[1]

Unfortunately the diagnosis is missed too often, resulting in a significant disservice to patients and the community. The benefits of early HIV diagnosis are summarised in Table 22.1.

Table 22.1 *The benefits of early HIV diagnosis*

To individual patients
- Prolongation of the asymptomatic period
- Delayed disease progression
- Prevention of opportunistic infections
- Optimal maintenance of health through patient education and counselling
- Cures are only likely with early intervention

To the cohort of HIV-positive individuals
- Monitoring of advances in treatment
- Increased participation in research and clinical trials
- Development of new services to meet changing patient needs

To the community
- Documentation of changes in epidemiology
- Reduced high-risk activities
- Contact tracing
- Control of HIV transmission

To the doctors
- Time to influence the course of disease
- Time to counsel the patient

Penny R. Could it be HIV? 2. Benefits of early diagnosis of HIV infection. Med J Aust 1993; 158: 35–36 © Copyright 1993, *The Medical Journal of Australia*—reproduced with permission.

Key facts and checkpoints

- HIV is a retrovirus with two known strains which cause a similar spectrum of syndromes: HIV_1 and HIV_2.
- About 50% of patients develop an acute infective illness similar to glandular fever within weeks of acquiring the virus (the HIV seroconversion illness)[2]. The main features are fever, lymphadenopathy, lethargy and possibly sore throat and a generalised rash.

- If these patients have a negative infectious mononucleosis test, perform an HIV antibody which may have to be repeated in four weeks or so if negative.
- Patients invariably recover to enter a long period of good health for five years or more.[1]
- Pneumocystitis pneumonia is the commonest presentation of AIDS.
- Approximately 15–25% of HIV-positive children are infected from HIV-infected mothers.[3]
- Infants born to these mothers may develop the disease within a few months, with 30% affected by the age of 18 months.
- The time for the onset of AIDS in HIV-affected adults varies from one year to several years; the median time is around 10 years.
- In family practice the most common presentation of HIV-related illness is seen in the skin/oral mucosa.[4]
- HIV antibody testing is a two stage process: ELISA test for screening is followed by another method, e.g. Western blot, if ELISA is positive.
- The seroconversion period from acquiring HIV infection to a positive antibody test varies between individuals: this period is known as the 'window period'.
- The level of immune depletion is best measured by the CD_4 positive T lymphocyte (helper T cell) count—the CD_4 cell count. The cut-off points for good health and severe disease appear to be 500/μL and 200/μL respectively.[1]

Occurrence and transmission

HIV can be isolated from blood, tissues, semen, saliva, breast milk, cervical and vaginal secretions and tears of infected persons. HIV is transmitted in semen, blood and vaginal fluids, transplanted organs and breast milk through:

- unprotected sexual intercourse (anal or vaginal) with an infected person
- infected blood entering the body (through blood transfusion or by IV drug users sharing needles/syringes)
- artificial insemination, organ transplantation
- infected mothers (to babies during pregnancy, at birth or in breast milk)

Infection with HIV can occur via the vagina, rectum or open cuts and sores, including any on the lips or in the mouth. Social (non-sexual) contact and insect vectors have not been implicated in transmission.

Clinical manifestations[5]

The classification system devised by the Centers for Disease Control (CDC) in the United States in 1987 for the reporting of HIV infection has been adopted for use in Australia. It comprises four mutually exclusive clinical groups. Persons classified in a particular group should not be reclassified in a preceding group if clinical findings resolve.

Group I—acute illness

At least 50% of patients have an acute illness associated with seroconversion. The illness usually occurs within six weeks of infection and is characterised by fever, night sweats, malaise, severe lethargy, anorexia, nausea, myalgia, arthralgia, headache, photophobia, sore throat, diarrhoea, lymphadenopathy, generalised maculoerythematous rash and thrombocytopaenia. Neurological manifestations including meningoencephalitis and peripheral neuritis are commonly observed. Acute HIV infection should be considered in the differential diagnosis of illnesses resembling glandular fever.

Chronic lethargy, depression and irritability may persist after the acute illness. Non-specific viraemic sequelae such as mucosal ulceration, desquamation, exacerbation of seborrhoea and recurrences of herpes simplex may occur (see Fig. 22.1).

Acute illness may be accompanied by neutropenia, lymphopenia, thrombocytopenia, and mildly elevated ESR with serum transaminases. During recovery a lymphocytosis may occur with appearance of atypical mononuclear cells and an inversion of the CD_4+:CD_8+ ratio due to elevation of CD_8+ cells.

Differential diagnoses are given in Table 22.2.

Table 22.2 *Differential diagnoses of primary HIV infection*

Epstein-Barr mononucleosis
Syphilis: secondary
TORCH organisms • toxoplasmosis • rubella • cytomegalovirus • herpes simplex
Disseminated gonococcal infection
Hepatitis A,B,C,D or E
Influenza
Other virus infections

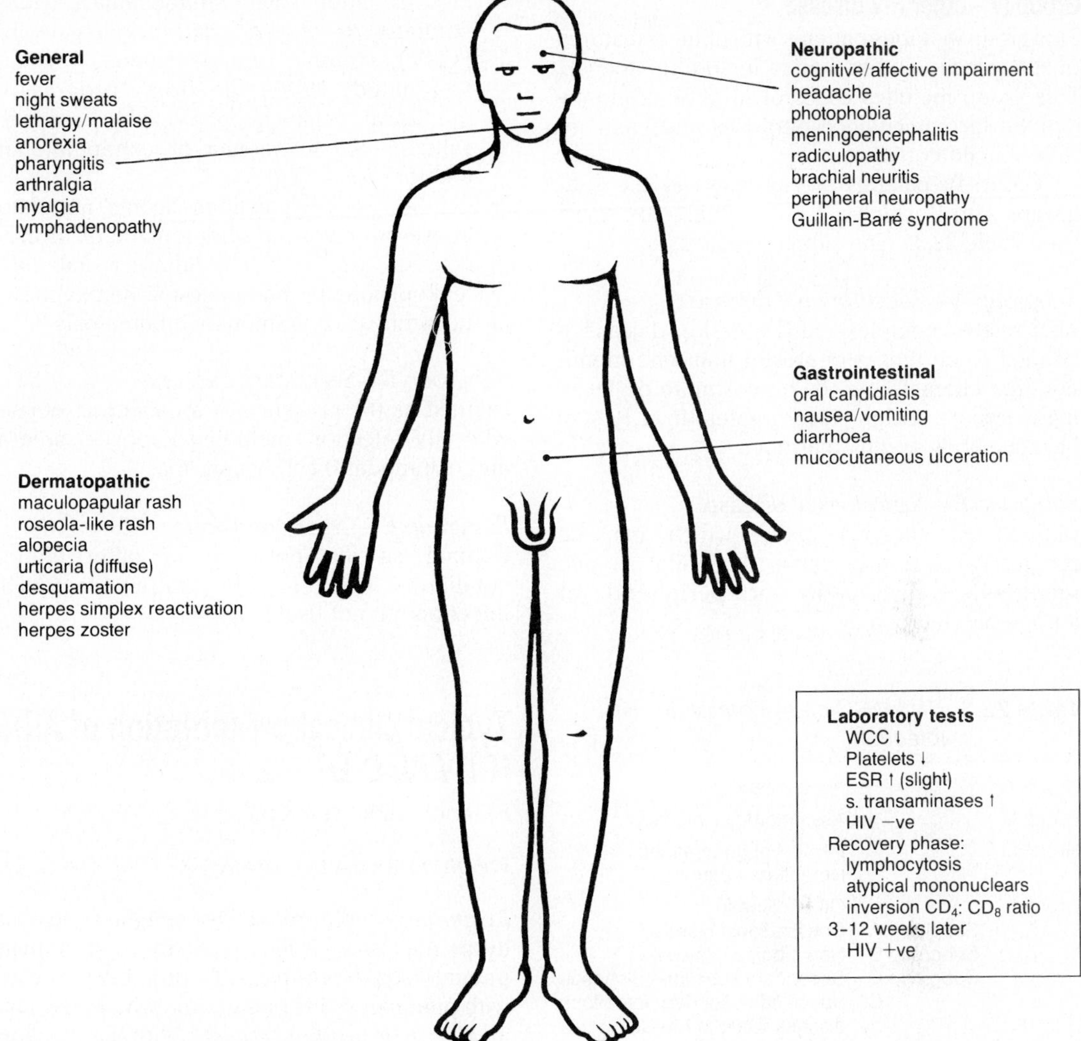

Fig. 22.1 *Possible clinical features of primary HIV infection*

Group II—asymptomatic infection

Whether or not there has been an acute illness, infection is usually followed by a latent period of months or years during which the patient is infectious but asymptomatic. Fifty per cent of patients with HIV infection will develop AIDS within 10 years. Seroconversion usually occurs within three months of infection but occasionally takes longer. Group II patients have a confirmed positive test for HIV antibody and may or may not be immunodeficient.

Group III—persistent generalised lymphadenopathy (PGL)

Patients with PGL alone are classified as Group III. PGL is defined as palpable lymphadenopathy (>1 cm) at two or more extrainguinal sites, persisting for more than three months. The lymph node groups most commonly enlarged are the anterior and posterior cervical and axillary groups. PGL is not a predictor of progression to AIDS.

Group IV—other HIV disease

This group includes patients with clinical features of HIV infection other than or in addition to PGL. This group includes cases of AIDS as originally defined for surveillance purposes and cases of AIDS-related complex.

Group IV patients are assigned to the subgroups A to E which are not mutually exclusive (see Table 22.3). The subgroups are:

Subgroup A—Constitutional disease

AIDS-related complex (ARC) or slim disease—defined as an illness of greater than one month duration characterised by one or more of: fever, night sweats, weight loss greater than 10% of baseline body weight, diarrhoea.

Subgroup B—Neurological disease

Defined as encephalopathy, which can be progressive and may cause dementia, aseptic meningitis, myelopathy or peripheral or autonomic neuropathy.

Table 22.3 *NH&MRC classification for HIV infection*

Group 1		Acute infection
Group II		Asymptomatic infection
Group III		Persistent generalised lymphadenopathy
Group IV		Other disease
	Subgroup A	Constitutional disease
	Subgroup B	Neurological disease
	Subgroup C	Secondary infectious diseases
	C1	Specified secondary infectious disease listed in the CDC surveillance definition for AIDS
	C2	Other specified secondary infectious disease
	Subgroup D	Secondary cancers
	Subgroup E	Other conditions

Subgroup C

Defined as the presence of a disease at least moderately indicative of a defect in cell mediated immunity. These are divided in subgroups:

- C-1 Patients with disease due to one of the organisms listed in the surveillance definition of AIDS, viz. Pneumocystis carinii pneumonia, chronic cryptosporidiosis, toxoplasmosis, extraintestinal strongyloidiasis, isosporiasis, candidiasis (oesophageal, bronchial or pulmonary), cryptococcosis, histoplasmosis, Mycobacterium avium-intracellulare (MAI) complex or *M. Kansasii*, cytomegalovirus (CMV), chronic mucocutaneous or disseminated HSV infection, progressive multifocal leukoencephalopathy, recurrent salmonella bacteraemia or extrapulmonary tuberculosis.
- C-2 Secondary infectious agents not listed above but involving symptomatic or invasive disease, e.g. oral candidiasis, oral hairy leukoplakia, multidermatomal herpes zoster, nocardiosis or pulmonary tuberculosis.

Subgroup D—Secondary cancers

Defined as the presence of a cancer associated with HIV infection, including Kaposi's sarcoma and extranodal B-cell lymphoma.

Subgroup E—Other conditions

Defined as the presence of other clinical conditions which may be attributable to HIV infection but not listed above.

Typical clinical presentation of AIDS (CDV IV, C-D)

Fever of unknown origin

Weight loss (usually severe)

Respiratory: non-productive cough, increasing dyspnoea and fever: due to opportunistic pneumonias. More than 50% of patients present with pneumocystitis pneumonia which may have an abrupt or insidious onset.[6] With the insidious type of onset, examination and chest X-ray are often normal early. Many other agents, e.g. CMV, cryptococcosis and TB, can be responsible. Exclusion of pneumocystitis pneumonia is important as this condition carries a high mortality if untreated.

Gastrointestinal

- chronic diarrhoea (many causes) with weight loss or dehydration
- oral candidiasis
- oral hairy cell leukaemia (frequently mistaken for candidiasis but affects lateral border of tongue)

Neurological

- progressive dementia (HIV encephalopathy)
- ataxia due to myelopathy

- Toxoplasma encephalitis
- cryptococcal meningitis
- peripheral neuropathy
- progressive visual loss (CMV retinitis)
- CNS lymphoma

Skin

- Kaposi's sarcoma (painless red-purple lesions on any part of the body including palms, soles, oral cavity and other parts of the GIT)
- Shingles, especially multidermatomal

Figure 22.2 presents the chronology of HIV-induced disease correlated with time since infection and CD_4 cell levels.

Investigations and diagnosis

The laboratory investigation of AIDS covers three broad areas:

1. Tests for HIV infection:
   e.g. enzyme linked immunosorbent assay (ELISA); Western blot technique (used for confirmation)
2. Tests of immune function:
   measure T-helper cells (with CD_4 markers) as opposed to T-suppressor cells (with CD_8 markers)
   Low CD_4 cells (counts $< 500\ \mu L$) = defective cell mediated immunity.[1,5]
3. Tests for opportunistic infections and other problems:
   e.g. other STDs, EBV, CMV, hepatitis.

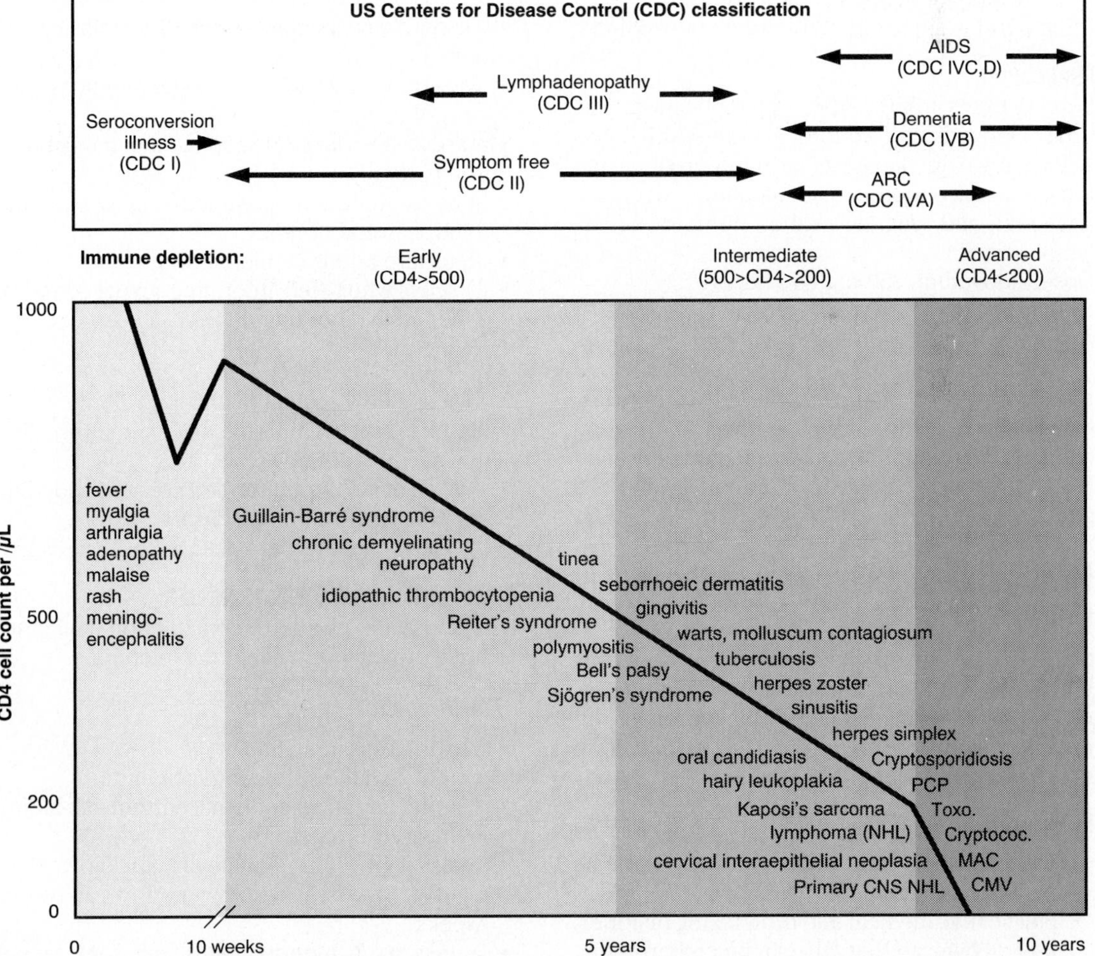

Fig. 22.2 *Chronology of HIV-induced disease correlated with time since infection* STEWARD GJ, 'COULD IT BE HIV?' 1. THE CHALLENGE: CLINICAL DIAGNOSIS OF HIV. *MEDICAL JOURNAL OF AUSTRALIA*, 1993 158: 31–34. c COPYRIGHT 1933 *THE MEDICAL JOURNAL OF AUSTRALIA*. REPRODUCED WITH PERMISSION

Management

Patients with HIV infection require considerable psychosocial support, counselling and regular assessment from a non-judgemental caring practitioner.

The holistic approach to life

There is interesting evidence that the common-sense approach of a positive healthy lifestyle will prolong the asymptomatic stage by boosting the immune system. This includes:

- a very healthy balanced diet: high fruit and vegetable intake, pure fruit juices, high fibre, low fat, high complex carbohydrates
- toxic avoidance: processed foods, caffeine, illicit drugs, alcohol, cigarettes
- relaxation and meditation (reduction of and self-monitoring of stress levels)
- appropriate sleep and exercise
- consider supplementary antioxidants
- support groups and continuing counselling

Medication

Several drugs inhibit HIV viral replication. The drug zidovudine (azidothymidine—AZT) has been shown to decrease mortality, reduce the incidence of opportunistic infections, decrease viraemia and increase the number of T_4 lymphocytes.

Dose: zidovudine 250 mg (o) bd, *or*
200 mg (o) tds

Alternative drugs: didanosine, zalcitabine.

Antimicrobial agents can be used to effectively treat opportunistic infections. Chemotherapy may be effective in treating malignancies such as Kaposi's sarcoma and lymphoma, particularly if immune function is good.

HIV counselling: the role of the family doctor

Many HIV-positive patients have described how the results left them bewildered and devastated, especially with an unexpected positive result. Part of the reason given was the lack of any form of pre-test counselling.

Initial consultation

- Explore the 'hidden component' of the patient's consultation.
- Full sexual, medical and drug-taking histories. It is recognised that this can be embarrassing for both the doctor and the patient, but those experienced in this process advise the following approach:

  Establish a supportive, non-judgemental atmosphere. Encourage disclosure of history and patterns of partners and sexual practices in a gender-neutral situation. Make no assumptions about sexual preferences; they will be indicated by the patient as the history evolves provided you allow this to happen; this will take time.

  Stress the importance of disclosure of prior, known infections with STDs. Assess the patient's risk for an STD.

Pre-test counselling

- Give information on the test (what it tells and does not tell).
- Explain about the false negative and 'window period'.
- Give appropriate information about HIV disease and other STDs.
- Dispel any myths about transmission of infection.
- Give preventive advice on safer practices (sex and IV drugs).
- Assess the possible coping mechanisms of the patient.
- Assess their social support networks and interpersonal bonds.
- Reassure about confidentiality.
- Discuss who to tell: informing sexual contacts.
- Offer tests other than STDs.

Finally

- Discuss how patient 'will cope with the test'.
- Discuss legal requirements (check with state laws).
- Advise of need for informed consent (not only for HIV test but other STDs).
- Make arrangements to discuss the test results.

Test result (about 2 weeks later)

This must be given in consultation (whether positive or negative): avoid the telephone.

The negative test result

- provide reassurance
- emphasise the safe sex information
- counter any suggestion that current risk-taking behaviour is safe
- retest if in high-risk category or known HIV contact or in a 'window period' of twelve weeks
- a test in 3 months helps rule out recent acquisition

The positive test result

Start immediate post-test counselling and education. Emphasise that HIV-positive does not equal AIDS and need not lead to it in the short term.

Interview and full clinical assessment

- Assessment of general health
- Particular assessment of prior psychiatric history and confirm prior STDs and drugs
- Evidence of EBV (glandular fever), hepatitis B, HIV illness (acute seroconversion illness)
- Further counselling and discussion of specific problems
- Assessment of bonds and relationships with regard to support

Examination—to set a base level

- Full examination; skin, CNS—especially fundi, chest, abdomen and genitals; urine and lung function test
- Monitor temperature and weight

Blood tests—to set a base level and check immune status

- Repeat HIV antibody test (to eliminate possibility of error)
- CD_4 cells with FBE and a differential WCC
- G6PD screen for enzyme deficiency
- Serology for syphilis (RPR), hepatitis B, toxoplasmosis, cytomegalovirus
- Test for gonorrhoea and chlamydia, herpes and thrush (if indicated)

Encourage a holistic approach to health maintenance and enhancement. Explore their feelings, anxieties, fears and confidentiality concerns. Reinforce safer practices.

The second post-positive result consultation (2 weeks later)

- Give results of repeat HIV test and base-line tests.
- Explore patient's understanding, feelings, coping abilities and spiritual issues (if appropriate).
- Some of the common questions which patients with HIV infection ask are:
  - Am I going to get sick?
  - How long will I live for?
  - Are there any treatments available?
  - Is there a cure around the corner?
  - What is going to happen to me?
  - Should I tell my friends?
  - Should I tell my family?
  - What are the social and legal issues?

It is worth pre-empting these questions and having ready appropriate answers for that particular patient.

- Give appropriate reassurance: prognosis may be much better, in respect of long remission, than appreciated.
- Discuss support systems.
- Check personal prophylaxis (safer sex and needle-sharing habits).
- Reinforce lifestyle strategies and suggest how patients can help themselves: give case examples.
- Recommend meditation and appropriate literature.
- Provide appropriate referrals (if needed):
  - specialist counsellors
  - self-help and support groups
  - meditation classes
- Advise patients about their legal and ethical responsibilities not to pass on the infection to others.
- Organise contact tracing.
- Address the difficult issue of telling sexual partners.

Continuing maintenance consultations

- Appropriate support, encouragement and counselling
- Frequency—depends on CD_4 cell count (e.g. 3 to 6 monthly)
- Examination
  - General condition, temperature and weight
  - Look for unusual lung infection, diarrhoea, skin lesions, tongue and oropharynx, fevers, wasting and neurological signs
  - Examine for signs of cytomegalovirus retinitis
  - Look for early signs of AIDS-related dementia (SEM test)
- Tests
  - CD_4 cell count and syphilis serology
  - Chest X-ray and induced sputum (if cough, SOB), faeces microculture if diarrhoea persists, Candida mouth swabs and herpes swabs appropriately.
- Treat intercurrent illness (Table 22.4).

Table 22.4 *General practice treatment of HIV-related dermathopathy (after Pohl)[4]*

Dermatoses	Treatment
Common	
Oral candidiasis	miconazole oral gel or amphotericin lozenges or nystatin lozenges
Hairy leukoplakia on tongue	no treatment or acyclovir
Seborrhoic dermatitis, e.g. nasolabial folds, hairy areas	miconazole 2% or ketoconazole 2% hydrocortisone 1% (if very itchy)
Itchy folliculitis	oral antihistamines miconazole +hydrocortisone topical
Less common	
Perianal herpes simplex	Mild: topical acyclovir cream (if available) Betadine or silver nitrate Severe: acyclovir 200 mg 5 times daily
Molluscum contagiosum	needle incision then Betadine or liquid nitrogen
Candidal angular stomatitis	clotrimazole or miconazole cream
Herpes zoster	Mild: menthol in flexible collodion Severe: refer for IV acyclovir
Severe tinea pedis	topical clotrimazole or miconazole ketoconazole 200 mg (o) daily

Contact tracing

Contacts of HIV-positive patients should be traced and offered testing with counselling.[5] Patients with HIV infection must be advised of the risk they pose to seronegative sexual partners. A person who has HIV or is at risk of HIV infection must not make any blood, semen or tissue donation. Because of the probable association between genital ulcerative disease and HIV transmission, the effective management of STDs is part of the general strategy for HIV control.

Prevention of HIV infection

1. Counselling the person at risk re 'safer practices'

No effective vaccine has been developed. Modification of behaviour is the only valid strategy for prevention of HIV infection. Education programs to encourage sexual practices that reduce the exchange of genital secretions (safe sex) may achieve risk reduction for sexually active individuals. Condoms provide a barrier if used properly and consistently but may be too easily damaged to offer reliable protection during anal intercourse. A water-based lubricant such as KY gel or Lubifax should be used: oil-based lubricants such as Vaseline weaken condoms.

Discuss alternative sex practices including touching, cuddling, body to body rubbing and mutual masturbation. Abstinence from anal, vaginal and oral sex is to be encouraged.

Emphasise the importance of being in control with drug taking, IV usage, safe sex practices and the needle exchange program.

2. Health professionals

Care should be exercised whenever blood samples are taken or sharps have been used. Advise safe disposal of sharps and other disposables and appropriate sterilisation of material.

Community education

Educating the community in a non-emotional, responsible way about AIDS should be a priority. While the personal, community and global benefits of effective AIDS education are generally acknowledged, the fear of addressing such a sensitive issue sometimes results in failure to act.[7] AIDS education in schools in particular can be an important strategy. People with HIV infection would be appropriate resource educators and the use of videos would be a most appropriate medium for education.

When to refer

- Most patients with HIV disease need referral to a specialist or clinic which can manage the patient expertly and sympathetically.
- Onset of a life-threatening opportunistic infection.
- The need to initiate zidovudine therapy.
- Serious psychological problems related to HIV-positive status.

References

1. Stewart GJ. The challenge: the clinical diagnosis of HIV. Medical Journal of Australia, 1993, 158:31–34.
2. Boyle MJ, McMurchie M, Tindall B, Cooper D. HIV seroconversion illness. Medical Journal of Australia, 1993, 158:42–44.
3. Kumar P, Clark M. *Clinical medicine* (2nd edition), London: Bailliere Tindall, 1990, 68–73.
4. Pohl M. Managing HIV patients in general practice. Patient Management, June 1989, 49–61.
5. NH&MRC. *Handbook on sexually transmitted diseases.* Canberra: Department of Community Services and Health, 1990, 1–55.
6. Turnidge J. *Sexually transmitted disease.* CHECK Programme, Melbourne: RACGP, 1989, unit 210/211.
7. World Health Organisation report. AIDS prevention through health promotion. Geneva: WHO, 1991, 68–73.

Acknowledgement

Part of this text, including clinical manifestations, prevention, and contact tracing is reproduced from the *Handbook on sexually transmitted diseases*[5]. Commonwealth of Australia copyright, reproduced by permission.

23

Baffling viral and protozoal infections

Almost any infection, especially if subacute or insidious in its onset, can be baffling and can belong to the 'fever of undetermined origin' group of infections. Syphilis and tuberculosis were the great mimics of the past. Now malaria and Epstein-Barr mononucleosis can be regarded as important mimics. Epstein-Barr mononucleosis (syn: infectious mononucleosis, glandular fever) can be a perennial baffler and can be confused with HIV infection in its primary clinical phase. Any of the febrile diseases can be confusing before declaring themselves with classical symptoms such as the jaundice of hepatitis or the rash of dengue fever, or before serological tests become positive.

Viral and protozoal infections which can present as masquerades include:

- HIV infection (especially primary)
- Epstein-Barr mononucleosis (EBM)
- TORCH organisms
  - — toxoplasmosis
  - — rubella
  - — cytomegalovirus (CMV)
  - — herpes simplex virus
- Hepatitis A,B,C,D,E
- Mosquito-borne infections
  - — malaria
  - — dengue fever
  - — yellow fever
  - — Japanese encephalitis
  - — Ross River fever

The TORCH organisms (TORCH being an acronym for toxoplasmosis, rubella, cytomegalovirus and herpes) are well known for their adverse intrauterine effects on the foetus. Three are viral (toxoplasmosis is a protozoa) and the first three of these foetal pathogens are acquired by passage across the placenta. Most of these organisms are noted for being opportunistic infections in immunocompromised patients, especially in HIV stage 4 infection.

The mosquito-borne infections are mainly viral, apart from the protozoa causing malaria, and are of particular significance in travellers returning from endemic areas.

Four similar clinical presentations

The four infections (EMB, primary HIV, CMV and toxoplasmosis) produce almost identical clinical presentations and tend to be diagnosed as glandular fever or pseudoglandular fever. It is important for the first contact practitioner to consider all four possibilities, especially keeping in mind the possibility of HIV infection.

A worthwhile approach is to make a provisional diagnosis based on the clinical variations as presented in Table 23.1.

Screening tests are:

- Full blood count, especially WCC
- Paul Bunnell test (for heterophil antibodies)

Table 23.1 *Clinical features differentiating HIV, EBV, CMV and toxoplasmosis infections (all can present with a similar illness)*

Feature	EBV infection	HIV infection	CMV infection	Toxoplasmosis
Onset	Insidious	Acute	Insidious	Insidious or acute
Fever	A feature Intermittent	A feature	Quotidian (afternoon spikes)	Low grade
Fatigue/malaise	Common	Common, severe	Common	Common
Tonsillar hypertrophy	Common	Mild enlargement	Uncommon	Uncommon
Exudative pharyngitis	Common	Rare	Rare	Occurs
Mucocutaneous ulcers	Rare	Common	Unknown	Unknown
Skin rash	About 5%	Common	About 5%	About 10%
Jaundice	About 8%	Rare	Uncommon	Uncommon
Diarrhoea	Unknown	Occurs	Unknown	Unknown
Cervical lymphadenopathy	Common	Common	Uncommon	Common (a feature)
Hepatomegaly	About 8%	Rare	Common	Occasional
Splenomegaly	About 50%	Rare	About 50%	Up to 30%
Atypical lymphocytes	In 80–90%	In < 50%	Common	Uncommon

- Serological test for cytomegalovirus (specific antibodies)
- Serological test for toxoplasmosis (specific antibodies)
- HIV antibody test (ELISA)

Epstein-Barr mononucleosis

Epstein-Barr mononucleosis (infectious mononucleosis, glandular fever) (EBM) is a febrile illness caused by the herpes (Epstein-Barr) virus. It can mimic diseases such as HIV primary infection, streptococcal tonsillitis, viral hepatitis and acute lymphatic leukaemia. There are three forms: the febrile, the anginose (with sore throat) and the glandular (with lymphadenopathy).

It may occur at any age but usually between 10 and 35 years, commonest in 15–25 year old age group.

The typical clinical features are presented in Table 23.2 and Figure 23.1.

Epidemiology

EB mononucleosis has an annual incidence of 4–5 new cases in a population of 2500.[3] It usually affects people in their late teenage years or early twenties. It is endemic in most countries. Subclinical infection is common in young children. The incubation period is at least one month but data are insufficient to define it accurately.

Table 23.2 *Clinical features of EBM*[1,2]

Symptoms

- slow onset malaise 1–6 weeks
- fever
- headaches, anorexia
- blocked nose—mouth breathing
- nasal quality to voice
- sore throat (85%)
- nausea ± vomiting
- rash—primary 5%
- dyspepsia

Clinical findings

- exudative pharyngitis
- petechiae of palate (not pathognomonic)
- lymphadenopathy, esp. posterior cervical
- rash—maculopapular
- splenomegaly (50%)
- jaundice ± hepatomegaly (5–10%)
- clinical or biochemical evidence of hepatitis

Epstein-Barr virus is excreted in oropharangeal secretions during the illness and for some months (sometimes years) after the clinical infection. EBM has a low infectivity and isolation is not necessary. It is apparently transmitted only by close contact such as kissing and sharing drinking vessels.

Progress of the primary infection is checked partly by specific antibodies (which might prevent cell to cell spread of the virus) and partly by a cellular immune response, involving cytotoxic T cells, which eliminates the infected cells. This response accounts for the clinical picture. The virus is never eliminated from the body.

Second attacks and fatalities do occur and there is a possible association between EBM and lymphoma.[3]

The rash

The rash of EBM is almost always related to antibiotics given for tonsillitis. The primary rash, most often non-specific, pinkish and maculopapular (similar to that of rubella), occurs in about 5% of cases only.

The secondary rash is most often precipitated by one of the penicillins, especially ampicillin or amoxycillin. About 90–100% of patients prescribed ampicillin or amoxycillin will be affected; up to 50% of those given penicillin will develop the rash. It can be extensive and sometimes has a purplish tinge.

The complications of EB mononucleosis are presented in Table 23.3 and the differential diagnoses in Table 23.4.

Laboratory diagnosis

The following confirm the diagnosis of EB mononucleosis.

- white cell count shows absolute lymphocytosis
- blood film shows atypical lymphocytes
- Paul Bunnell test for heterophil antibody is positive (although positivity can be delayed or absent in 10% of cases)

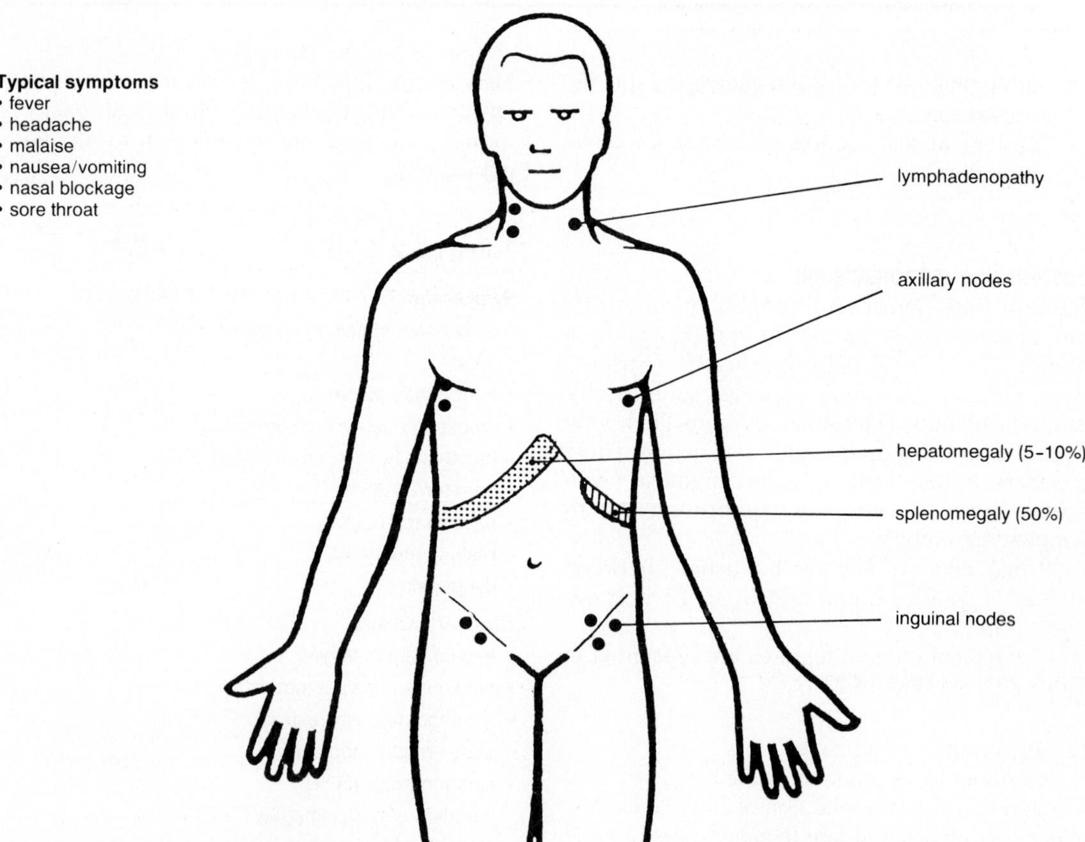

Fig. 23.1 *Clinical features of Epstein-Barr mononucleosis*

Table 23.3 *Complications of EB mononucleosis*[1]

Common

- antibiotic-induced skin rash
- prolonged debility
- hepatitis
- depression

Rare

Cardiac
- myocarditis
- pericarditis

Haematological
- agranulocytosis
- haemolytic anaemia
- thrombocytopenia

Respiratory tract
- upper airway obstruction (lymphoid hypertrophy)

Miscellaneous
- ruptured spleen

Neurological
- cranial nerve palsies, especially facial palsy
- Guillain-Barré syndrome
- meningoencephalitis
- transverse myelitis

Although culture for Epstein-Barr virus and tests for specific virus antibodies are possible, they are not done routinely.

False positives for Paul Bunnell test:

- hepatitis
- Hodgkin's disease
- acute leukaemia

Table 23.4 *Differential diagnoses of EB mononucleosis*[1]

Other agents that cause typical EBM syndrome
- HIV infection (acute initial illness)
- cytomegalovirus
- toxoplasmosis

Exudative tonsillitis resembling EBM
- acute streptococcal pharyngitis
- adenovirus infection
- diphtheria (unlikely in Australia)

Hepatitis A,B,C,D,E

Lymphadenopathy, fever and splenomegaly
- lymphoma
- leukaemia

Complications of EBM without other manifestations
- encephalitis, for example

Others
- drug reaction, e.g. PAS
- influenza

Prognosis

EBM usually runs an uncomplicated course over 6–8 weeks. Major symptoms subside within 2 to 3 weeks. Patients should be advised to take about 4 weeks off work.

Treatment

- supportive measures (no specific treatment)
- rest (the best treatment) during the acute stage, preferably at home and indoors
- aspirin or paracetamol to relieve discomfort
- gargle soluble aspirin or 30% glucose to soothe the throat
- advise against: alcohol, fatty foods, continued activity
- corticosteroids for:
  - — neurological involvement
  - — thrombocytopenia
  - — threatened airway obstruction

Post-EBM malaise

Some young adults remain debilitated and depressed for some months. Lassitude and malaise may extend up to a year or so.

Cytomegalovirus infection

Cytomegalovirus (CMV) has a world-wide distribution and causes infections that are generally asymptomatic. The virus (human herpes virus 5) may be cultured from various sites of healthy individuals. It has its most severe effects in the immunocompromised, especially those with AIDS, and also in recipients of solid organ transplants and bone marrow grafts. 90% of AIDS patients are infected with CMV and 95% have disseminated CMV at autopsy. CMV infection can be an important development following massive blood transfusion, including those given to infants. The incubation period of CMV ranges from 20–60 days and the illness generally lasts about 2 to 6 weeks.[4]

Clinical features

Three important clinical manifestations are described.

1. *Perinatal disease*

Intrauterine infection may cause serious abnormalities in the foetus including CNS involvement (microcephaly, hearing defects, motor disturbances), jaundice, hepato-splenomegaly, haemolytic anaemia and thrombocytopenia. Up to 30% of CMV-affected infants have mental retardation.[5]

2. *Acquired CMV infection*

In healthy adults CMV produces an illness similar to Epstein-Barr mononucleosis with fever, malaise, arthralgia and myalgia, generalised lymphadenopathy and hepatomegaly. However, cervical lymphadenopathy and exudative pharyngitis are rare.

The infection may be spread by blood transfusion and CMV should be suspected on clinical grounds in a patient with a febrile illness resembling EBM following major surgery such as open heart surgery or renal transplantation and where extensive transfusion has been necessary.

The fever often manifests as quotidian intermittent fever spiking to a maximum in the mid-afternoon and falling to normal each day (Fig. 23.2). There is often a relative lymphocytosis with atypical lymphocytes but the heterophil antibody test is negative. Liver function tests are often abnormal. Specific diagnosis can be made by demonstrating rising antibody titres. The virus can be isolated from the urine and blood.

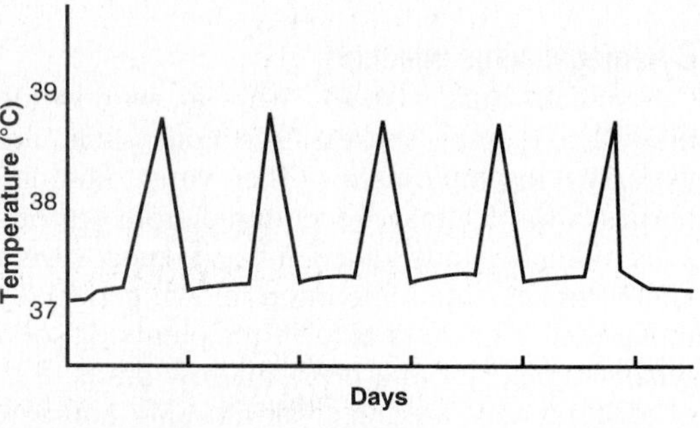

Fig. 23.2 *Cytomegalovirus infection: typical quotidian intermittent fever pattern*

3. *CMV disease in the immunocompromised host*

Disseminated CMV infection occurs in the immune-deficient person, notably HIV infection causing opportunistic severe pneumonia, retinitis (a feature of AIDS), encephalitis and diffuse involvement of the gastrointestinal tract.

Treatment

In the patient with normal immunity no treatment apart from supportive measures is required, as the infection is usually self-limiting. In immunosuppressed patients various antiviral drugs have been used with some benefit.

Toxoplasmosis

Toxoplasmosis, which is caused by *Toxoplasma gondii*, an obligate intracellular protozoon, is world-wide, albeit a rare infection. The definitive host in its life cycle is the cat (or pig or sheep) and the human is an intermediate host. However, clinical toxoplasmosis is very uncommon. Infection in humans usually occurs through eating foodstuffs contaminated by infected cat faeces. Its main clinical importance is an opportunistic infection.

The five major clinical forms of toxoplasmosis are:[6]

1. Asymptomatic lymphadenopathy (the commonest).
2. Lymphadenopathy with a febrile illness, similar to EB mononucleosis.
3. Acute primary infection: a febrile illness similar to acute leukaemia or EB mononucleosis. A rash, myocarditis, pneumonitis, chorioretinitis and hepatosplenomegaly can occur.
4. Neurological abnormalities: includes headache and neck stiffness, sore throat and myalgia.
5. Congenital toxoplasmosis: this is a rare problem but if it occurs it typically causes CNS involvement and has a poor prognosis.

In the immunocompromised, clinical forms 3 and 4 are typical features with meningoencephalitis being a serious development.

Diagnosis

Serological tests which are sensitive and reliable.

Treatment

Patients with a mild illness or with asymptomatic infection require no treatment. Children under 5 years may be treated to avoid the possible occurrence of chorioretinitis. Symptomatic patients are treated with pyrimethamine plus sulphadiazine. Spiramycin is usually used in pregnant patients.

Malaria

Malaria, a protozoal infection, is an important masquerade and mimic. The diagnosis requires a high index of suspicion in a traveller returning from an endemic area (see page 85 for more details).

In humans malaria is caused by four species of plasmodium:

- *P. vivax* and *P. ovale*—tertian malaria
- *P. falciparum*—malignant tertian malaria
- *P. malariae*—quartan malaria

Some clinical features

- an incubation period of 7 to 40 days
- most present within 2 months of returning from malaria area
- can present after 2 or more years
- an acute febrile illness
- can have atypical presentations such as gastrointestinal symptoms (diarrhoea, nausea, vomiting, abdominal pains), dry cough and arthralgia
- typical relapsing patterns may be absent

Special notes

- Beware of treatment-modified infection.
- Early diagnosis is essential as it must be treated within 4 days.

Diagnosis

Diagnosis is with thick and thin smears. Two or three blood samples should be taken each day for 3 to 4 days and found to be negative before a patient is declared malaria-free. The presence of monocytosis is a helpful diagnostic pointer.

Amoebiasis

Amoebiasis can be diagnosed in a sick traveller returning from an endemic area with severe diarrhoea characterised by blood and mucus. Complications include fulminating colitis, amoebomas (a mass of fibrotic granulation tissue) in the bowel and liver abscess.

Amoebic liver abscess

Clinical features

- high swinging fever
- profound malaise and anorexia
- tender hepatomegaly
- effusion or consolidation of base of right chest

There is often no history of dysentery and jaundice is unusual. Diagnosis is by serological tests for amoeba and by imaging (CT scan). Treatment is with metronidazole and by percutaneous CT guided aspiration.

Dengue fever

Also known as 'breakbone fever', dengue is an arthropod-borne viral disease found mainly in Asia and Africa (see page 86). The features are the acute onset of fever, headache, retrobulbar pain, severe backache and aching of muscles and joints. Lymphadenopathy, petechiae on the soft palate and skin rashes may occur.

The diagnosis of dengue is based on clinical suspicion and also viral isolation by tissue culture in sera obtained early in the disease. Severe fatigue and depression (with suicidal risk) is a feature of convalescence. The patients are managed symptomatically and with support and reassurance.

Japanese encephalitis

This viral illness is also acquired overseas, especially in South-East Asia and the Far East. The onset is heralded by severe rigors, fever, headache and malaise. The encephalitic stage is marked by fever, neck rigidity and neurological signs such as altered consciousness and convulsions. Coma can follow. Diagnosis is by specific antibody detection. Treatment is symptomatic.

Yellow fever

This viral illness, acquired in the tropical areas of Africa and South America, can have a variety of presentations. If yellow fever is mild it resembles influenza. However, the typical clinical features are a febrile illness (high fever, headache, flushed face, arthralgia, GIT symptoms, relative bradycardia (Faget's sign)) followed by apparent recovery and then the classical features of fever, deepening jaundice, proteinuria and bleeding from the gums.

Ross River fever

Epidemic polyarthritis or Ross River virus occurs in all states of Australia. It is most prevalent in mosquito-prone areas (especially during the summer) and in tropical and temperate coastal regions and inland riverine areas.[7] Subclinical infection is common with variable clinical manifestations.

Clinical features

- all age groups especially 20–30 years
- incubation period 3–21 days (usually 7–11)

Major symptoms

- polyarthritis (75% of patients), mainly fingers, wrists, feet, ankles and knees
- maculopapular rash—widespread, often 'subtle', mainly trunk and limbs
- myalgia

Other symptoms

- pyrexia (mild)
- headache
- nausea
- fatigue with exercise

Signs (which may be present) include joint swelling (mainly hands and feet), tenosynovitis around the wrists and ankles (poor prognostic sign), the rash and mild lymphadenopathy.

Outcome

In many patients the illness resolves within 2 to 4 weeks and most feel normal within 3 months, but some with a more severe arthritis can enter a chronic phase lasting 18 months or more.

Diagnosis

Diagnosis is by antibody testing of serum. The differential diagnosis includes other viral infections that cause arthritis such as hepatitis B, rubella and dengue and early rheumatoid arthritis and rheumatic fever.

Treatment

Treatment is symptomatic with bed rest and simple analgesics such as aspirin. NSAIDs are used for more severe cases. Oral corticosteroids are effective but should be avoided if possible.

References

1. Nye F. The mononucleoses. Medicine International, 1984, 1:29–34.
2. Mead M, Patterson H. *Tutorials in general practice*. London: Pitman, 1983:3–4.
3. Fry J. *Common diseases*: 85–90.
4. Wilson J et al. *Harrison's principles of internal medicine* (12th edition), New York, 1991, 613–695.
5. Schroeder SA. *Current medical diagnosis and treatment*. Englewood Cliffs: Prentice Hall International, 1990:917–918.
6. Kumar PJ, Clark ML. *Clinical medicine* (2nd edition), London: Bailliere Tindall, 1990:83–84.
7. Whitby M. Ross River fever. In: MIMS Disease Index. Sydney: IMS Publishing, 1992:466–467.

24

Baffling bacterial infections

Bacterial infections can present diagnostic brain-teasers and a high index of suspicion is needed to pinpoint the diagnosis. Many are rarely encountered, thus making diagnosis more difficult yet demanding vigilance and clinical flexibility.

The list includes:

- syphilis
- tuberculosis
- infective endocarditis
- the zoonoses, e.g. brucellosis, Lyme disease
- clostridial infections
  - — tetanus
  - — gas gangrene
  - — puerperal infection
  - — botulism
- hidden suppuration
  - — abscess
  - — osteomyelitis
- mycoplasma infections
  - — atypical pneumonia
- Chlamydia infections
  - — psittacosis
  - — non-specific arthritis
  - — pelvic inflammatory disease
  - — trachoma
  - — atypical pneumonia
- Legionnaire's disease

Chlamydia and rickettsial organisms have been confirmed as being small bacterial organisms.

Syphilis

Although syphilis is uncommon in the general population it is extremely common in certain Aboriginal groups and is frequently acquired from homosexual activity or sexual contacts overseas.[1]

It presents either as a primary lesion or through the chance finding of positive syphilis serology. Family physicians should be alert to the various manifestations of secondary syphilis which can cause difficulties in diagnosis. Congenital syphilis is rare where there is general serological screening of antenatal patients.

Clinical manifestations[2]

Primary syphilis

The primary lesion or chancre usually develops at the point of inoculation after an incubation period averaging 21 days. The chancre is typically firm, painless, punched out and clean. The adjacent lymph nodes are discretely enlarged, firm and non-suppurating. Anorectal changes may occur in homosexual men.

Untreated, early clinical syphilis usually resolves spontaneously within 4 weeks, leading to latent disease which may proceed to late destructive lesions.

Secondary syphilis

The interval between the appearance of the primary chancre and the onset of secondary manifestations varies from 6 to 8 weeks. Constitutional symptoms including fever, headache, malaise and general aches and pains may precede or accompany the signs of secondary syphilis.

The most common feature of the secondary stage of infection is a rash which is present in about 80% of cases. The rash is typically a symmetrical, generalised, coppery red maculopapular eruption on face, palms and soles and is neither itchy nor tender. It can resemble any skin disease except those characterised by vesicles. Other features may be:

- condylomata lata which are broad-based, moist, warty or papular growths occurring in skin folds or creases
- patchy alopecia (scalp, outer third of eyebrow)
- oral, pharyngeal or vulvovaginal ulcers or 'mucous patches' which are round lesions with a greyish-white base edged by a dull red areola which may coalesce to produce a serpingious ulcer—the 'snail-track ulcer'
- lymphadenopathy characterised by firm, enlarged painless nodes typically involving inguinal, suboccipital, posterior cervical, axillary and preauricular groups.

Latent syphilis

Positive serology in a patient without symptoms or signs of disease is referred to as latent syphilis and is the commonest presentation of syphilis in Australia today. Possibly because of the widespread use of antibiotics the infection often proceeds to the latent stage without a recognised primary or secondary stage.

Late syphilis

Tertiary manifestation of syphilis, which is very rare, may be 'benign' with development of gummas (granulomatous lesions) in almost any organ, or more serious with cardiovascular or central nervous system involvement. Benign gummatous disease is rare but cardiovascular disease and neurosyphilis occasionally occur. Careful management and follow-up of patients with early or latent disease is essential to prevent late sequelae.

Late syphilis should be excluded in any patient with aortic incompetence or dilatation of the ascending arch of the aorta. Syphilis should be excluded as the cause of dementia, personality change, multifocal neurological disorders, nerve deafness, pupillary abnormalities, retinal disease or uveitis.

Think of syphilis

Syphilis should not be overlooked as a cause of oral or anorectal lesions. The diagnosis of syphilis depends on a detailed history, careful clinical examination and specific examinations.

Underlying these approaches is the need to think of the possibility of syphilis for concurrent STDs.

Syphilis and HIV infection[2]

HIV and syphilis are commonly associated. In patients with AIDS and syphilis, standard regimens for syphilis are not always curative. Seronegative syphilis has been reported in patients with HIV infection. Lymphadenopathy in a patient with HIV infection may be due to coexisting secondary syphilis.

Diagnostic tests

Dark ground examination[2]

Spirochaetes can be demonstrated by microscopic examination of smears from early lesions using dark ground techniques and provides an immediate diagnosis in symptomatic syphilis. Antibiotics or antiseptics should not be used until satisfactory examination has been completed. Dark ground examination is not suitable for oral lesions. The direct fluorescent antibody techniques (FTA-ABS) can be used on this smear.

Serology

Serological tests provide indirect evidence of infection and the diagnosis of asymptomatic syphilis relies heavily on these tests. The two main types of tests are:

- Reagin tests (VDRL and RPR)—not specific for syphilis but useful for screening
- Treponemal tests (TPHA, FTA-ABS)—specific but useful only for the diagnosis of the first infection

Treatment: refer to Chapter 90.

Tuberculosis

Tuberculosis, caused by *Mycobacterium tuberculosis*, still has a world-wide distribution with a very high prevalence in Asian countries where 60–80% of children below the age of 14 years are affected.[3] This has special implication in Australia where large numbers of Asian migrants are settling.

Tuberculosis can be a mimic of other diseases and a high level of suspicion is necessary to consider the diagnosis especially if there are extrapulmonary manifestations.

Primary infection

The primary infection usually involves the lungs. The focus is usually subpleural in the upper to mid zones and is almost always accompanied by lymph node involvement.

Erythema nodosum may accompany the primary infection. Primary TB is symptomless in most cases although there may be a vague illness associated with a cough. In most people this pulmonary focus heals but leaves some surviving tubercle bacilli, even if it becomes calcified.

Progressive primary tuberculosis

If the immune response is inadequate, progressive primary TB develops, with constitutional and pulmonary symptoms. Rarely haematogenous spread can occur to the lungs ('miliary tuberculosis'), to the pleural space (tuberculosis pleural effusion) or to extrapulmonary sites such as the meninges and bone.

Post-primary or adult type pulmonary TB

Most cases of TB in adults are due to reactivation of disease some years later and not to re-infection. The factors causing this include poor social living conditions with malnutrition, diabetes and other factors lowering natural immunity such as immunosuppressant drugs, corticosteroids, lymphoma and HIV infection (later stage).

Reactivated pulmonary TB

This usually presents with constitutional symptoms of poor health and night sweats and a cough which is initially dry but may become productive and be bloodstained (refer to page 339). Sometimes the infection will be asymptomatic.

Extrapulmonary TB

The main sites of extrapulmonary disease (in order of frequency in Australia) are the lymph nodes (the commonest especially in young adults and children), genitourinary tract (kidney, epididymis, Fallopian tubes), pleura and pericardium, the skeletal system (arthritis and oestomyelitis with cold abscess formation), central nervous system (meningitis and tuberculomas), the eye (choroditis, iridocyclitis), the skin (lupus vulgaris), and the adrenal glands (Addison's disease), gastrointestinal tract (ileocaecal area and peritoneum).

These sites are illustrated in Figure 24.1.

Miliary tuberculosis

This disorder follows diffuse dissemination of tubercle bacilli via the bloodstream and is fatal without treatment. It can occur within three years of the primary infection or much later because of reactivation.

Diagnosis of TB

A high index of suspicion is critical for the diagnosis of TB.

- mantoux test (a guide only)
- chest X-ray
- sputum for stain (acid fast bacilli)
- sputum for culture (takes about 6 weeks but important)
- biopsies on lesions/lymph nodes } may be necessary
- fibre optic bronchoscopy to obtain sputum } may be necessary

Treatment: refer to Chapter 36.

Infective endocarditis

Infective endocarditis can be a difficult problem to diagnose but must be considered in the differential diagnosis of fever especially in patients with a history of cardiac valvular disorders. It is caused by microbial infection of the cardiac valves or endocardium. Previously referred to as bacterial endocarditis, the term *infective endocarditis* is preferred because not all the infecting organisms are bacteria.

It may present as a fulminating or acute infection but more commonly runs an insidious course and is referred to as subacute (bacterial) endocarditis. Its incidence is increasing probably due to the increasing number of elderly people with degenerative valve disease, more invasive procedures, IV drug use and increased cardiac catheterisation.[4]

Predisposing factors

- past history of endocarditis
- rheumatically abnormal valves
- congenitally abnormal valves
- mitral valve prolapse
- calcified aortic valve
- congenital cardiac defects, e.g. VSD, PDA
- prosthetic valves
- IV drug use
- central venous catheters
- temporary pacemaker electrode catheters

Note: Only about 50% of patients with infective endocarditis have previously known heart disease.[4]

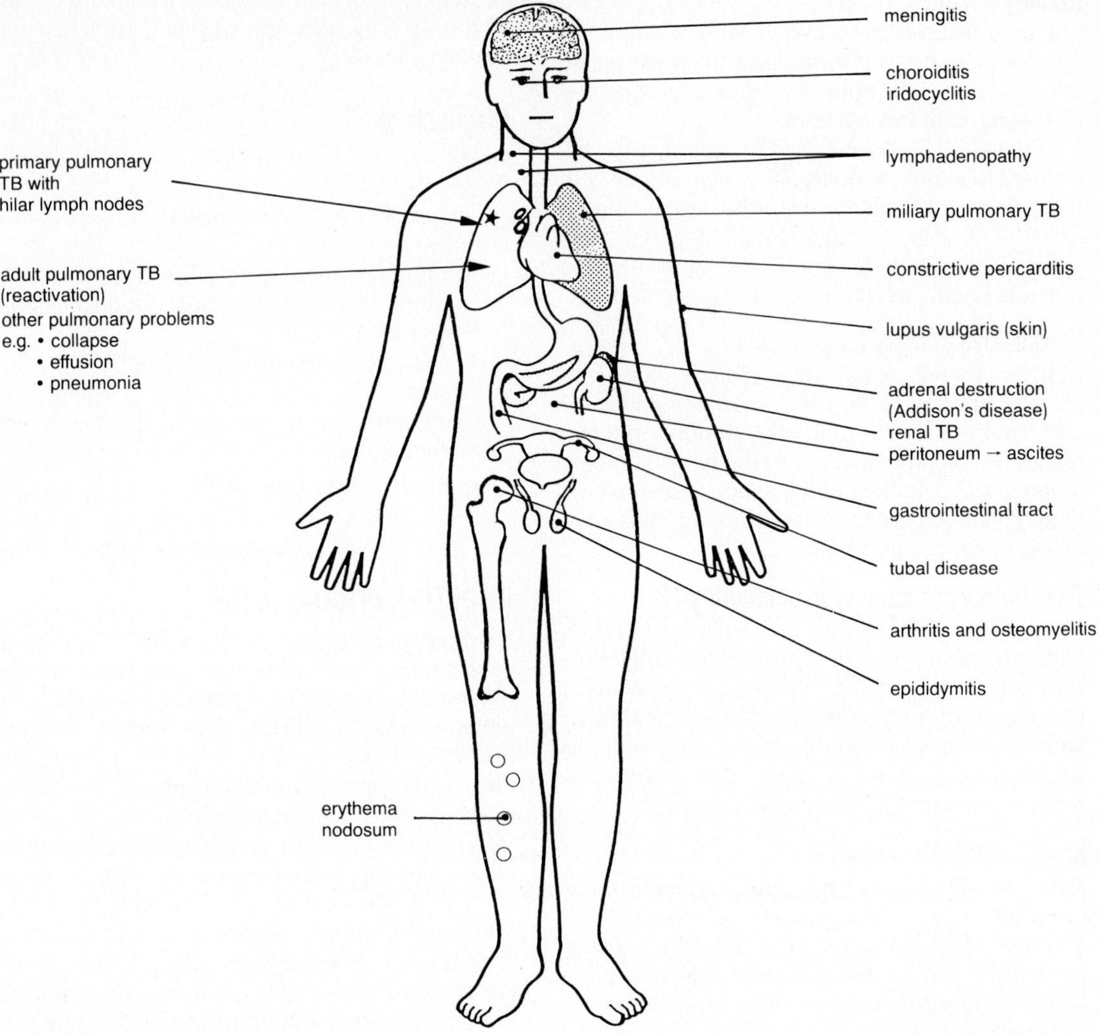

Fig. 24.1 *Pulmonary and extrapulmonary distribution of tuberculosis: the primary infection starts in the lung and then spread can occur throughout the body, especially to lymph nodes*

Responsible organisms

- *Streptococcus viridans* (50% of cases)
- *Streptococcus faecalis*
- *Staphylococcus aureus* (causes 50% of acute form)
- *Candida albicans/Aspergillus* (IV drug users)
- *Staphylococcus epidermidis*
- *Coxiella burnetti (Q fever)*

Presentations

- Acute endocarditis
- Subacute endocarditis
- Prosthetic endocarditis

Infective endocarditis without cardiac murmur is frequently seen in IV drug users who develop infection on the tricuspid valve.

Warning signs for development of endocarditis

- change in character of heart murmur
- development of a new murmur
- unexplained fever and cardiac murmur = infective endocarditis (until proved otherwise)
- a febrile illness developing after instrumentation (e.g. urethral dilatation) or

minor and major surgical procedures, e.g. dental extraction, tonsillectomy, abortion.

- the 'classic tetrad' of clinical features[4]
  - signs of infection
  - signs of heart disease
  - signs of embolism
  - immunological phenomena

There is a significant high mortality and morbidity from infective endocarditis which is often related to a delay in diagnosis.

A golden rule Culture the blood of every patient who has a fever and a heart murmur.

Clinical features

The classic clinical features are summarised in Figure 24.2.

The patients are often elderly, appear pale and ill, with intermittent fever and complain of vague aches and pains. The full clinical presentation takes time to develop. A febrile illness of 1 to 2 weeks duration is a common presentation.

Investigation

This includes:

- full blood count and ESR: ESR ↑, anaemia and leucocytosis

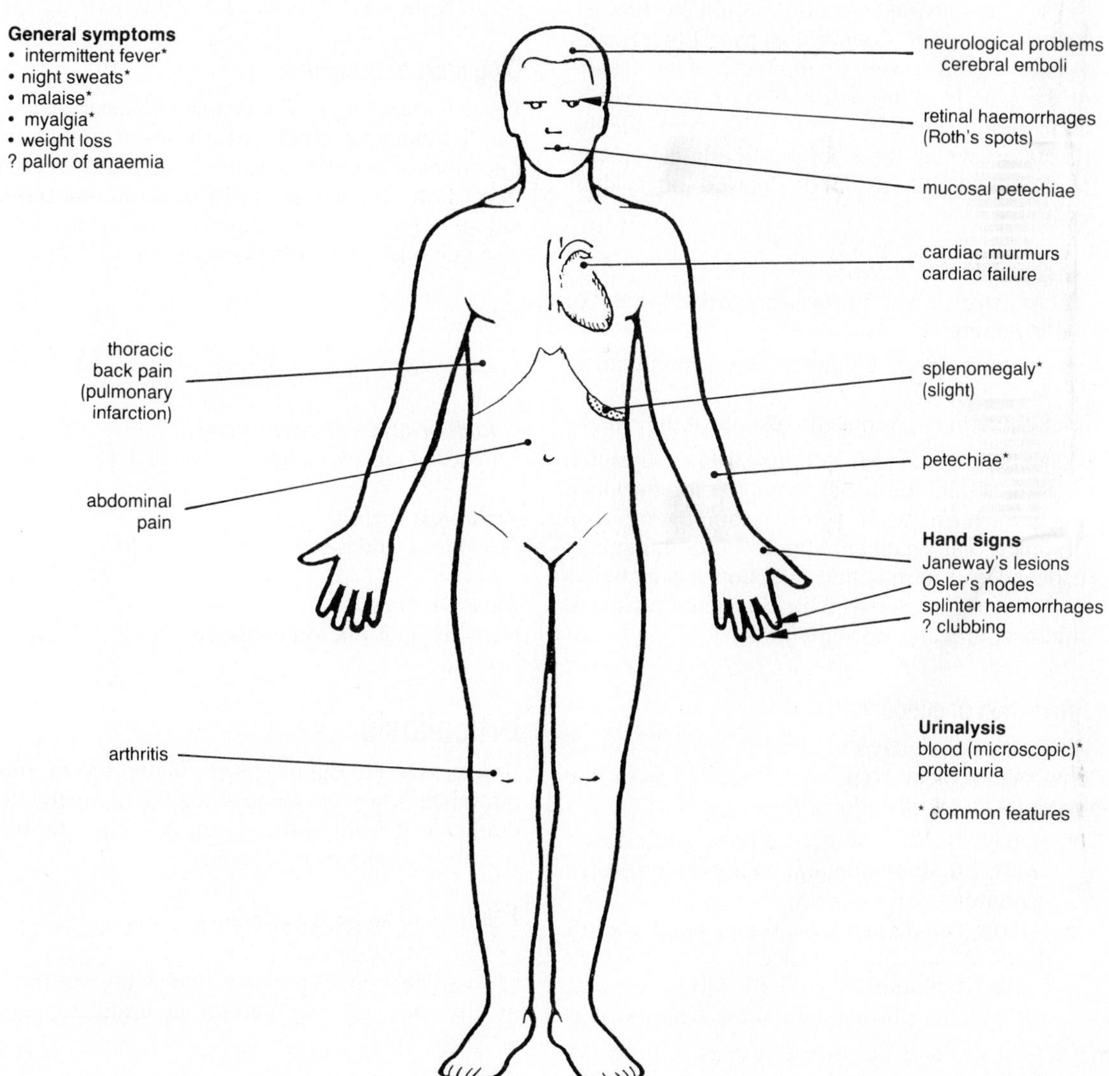

Fig. 24.2 *Infective endocarditis: possible clinical features*

- urine: proteinuria and microscopic haematuria
- blood culture: positive in about 75%[4]
  - at least 6 sets of samples (aerobic and anaerobic culture)
- echocardiography: to visualise vegetations
- chest X-ray
- ECG

Management

The patient should be referred because optimal management requires close co-operation between physician, microbiologist and cardiac surgeon.

Any underlying infection should be treated, e.g. drainage of dental abscess. Bactericidal antibiotics are chosen on the basis of the results of the blood culture and antibiotic sensitivities. Four blood cultures should be sent to the laboratory within the first hour of admission and treatment should seldom be delayed longer than 24 hours.

Antimicrobial treatment[5]

There are two important principles of management:

- treatment must be given intravenously for at least 2 weeks
- treatment is prolonged—usually 4 to 6 weeks

Consultation with an infectious disease physician or clinical microbiologist should be sought. Once cultures have been taken prompt empirical antimicrobial treatment should be commenced, especially in fulminating infection suspected to be endocarditis. Benzylpenicillin, gentamicin and flucloxacillin are recommended.

Prevention of endocarditis

Antibiotic prophylaxis[6]

Low-risk patients (no prosthetic valves or previous attack of endocarditis):

- amoxycillin 3 g (50 mg/kg up to adult dose) orally, 1 hour beforehand (if not on long-term penicillin)
- (amoxy) ampicillin 1 g (50 mg/kg up to adult dose) IV just before procedure commences or IM 30 minutes before; if having a general anaesthetic, followed by 500 mg, 6 hours later.

High-risk patients (prosthetic valves or previous attacks of endocarditis), having dental procedures, oral surgery or upper respiratory tract surgery, GIT or GU surgery:

- (amoxy) ampicillin 1 g IV or IM (as above) with 500 mg, 6 hours later

  plus
- gentamicin 1.5 mg/kg (2.5 mg/kg in children to maximum dose 80 mg) IV (just before) or IM (30 minutes before).

Zoonoses

Zoonoses are those diseases and infections which are naturally transmitted between vertebrate animals and humans (see Table 24.1). There is a long list of diseases which vary from country to country and includes plague, rabies, scrub typhus, Lyme disease and tularaemia.

Diagnosis of zoonoses

Fever and sweats (influenza-like illness)

Any patient with undiagnosed fever should be questioned about exposure to animals, recent travel both in and out of Australia, animal bites, cat scratches, consumption of raw milk, mosquito and tick bites, pets and occupation.

Rash

Consider rickettsial illness such as leptospirosis, Q fever, Lyme disease.

Cough or atypical pneumonia

Consider Q fever, psittacosis, bovine TB.

Arthralgia/arthritis

Consider Lyme disease, Ross River fever.

Meat workers

Consider Q fever, leptospirosis.

Brucellosis

Brucellosis (undulant fever, Malta fever) has diminished in prevalence since the campaign to eradicate it from cattle. Entry is mainly by the mouth or abraded or cut skin.

Features of acute brucellosis

- incubation period 1–3 weeks
- insidious onset: malaise, headache, weakness
- the classic fever pattern is undulant (see page 431).

Possible:

- lymphadenopathy
- hepatomegaly

Table 24.1 *Major zoonoses in Australia*

Zoonosis	***Organism/s***	***Animal host***	***Mode of transmission***	***Main presenting features***
Q fever	*Coxiella burnetti*	Various wild and domestic animals	Inhaled dust Animal contact Unpasteurised milk	Fever, rigors, myalgia, headache, dry cough
Leptospirosis	*Leptospira pomona*	Various domestic animals	Infected urine contaminating cuts or sores	Fever, myalgia, severe headache, macular rash
Brucellosis	*Brucella abortus*	Cattle	Contamination of cuts or sores by animal tissues Unpasteurised milk	Fever (undulant) sweats, myalgia, headache, lymphadenopathy
Lyme disease	*Borrelia burgdorferi*	Marsupials (probable)	Tick bites	Fever, myalgia, arthritis, bachache, doughnut-shaped rash
Psittacosis	*Chlamydia psittaci*	Birds: parrots, pigeons, ducks, etc.	Inhaled dust	Fever, myalgia, headache, dry cough
Bovine tuberculosis	*Mycobacterium bovis*	Cattle	Unpasteurised milk	Fever, sweats, weight loss, cough (as for human pulmonary TB)

- spinal tenderness
- splenomegaly (if severe)

Complications such as epididymo-orchitis, oesteomyelitis and endocarditis can occur. Localised infections in sites such as bones, joints, lungs, CSF, testes and cardiac valves are possible but uncommon.

Symptoms of chronic brucellosis are virtually indistinguishable from the 'chronic fatigue syndrome' and can present with FUO.

Diagnosis

- blood cultures (positive in 50% during acute phase)[6]
- Brucella agglutination test (rising titre)

Treatment

- oral tetracycline with erythromycin or rifampicin
- relapses do occur

Prevention and control

Involves eradication of brucellosis in cattle, care handling infected animals and pasteurisation of milk. No vaccine is currently available for use in humans.

Q fever

Q fever is a zoonosis due to *Coxiella burnetti.* It is the most common abattoir-associated infection in Australia and can also occur in farmers and hunters. Rash is not a major feature but can occur if the infection persists without treatment.

Clinical features

- incubation period 1–3 weeks
- sudden onset fever, rigors and myalgia
- dry cough (may be pneumonia in 20%)[7]
- petechial rash (if persisting infection)

Persistent infection may cause pneumonia or endocarditis so patients with valvular disease are at risk of endocarditis. It is a rare cause of hepatitis. The acute illness may resolve spontaneously. Untreated chronic infection is usually fatal.

Diagnosis

- serodiagnosis by complement fixation tests

Treatment

- tetracycline
- for endocarditis: prolonged course tetracycline and clindamycin

Prevention

The disease can be prevented in abattoir workers by using Q fever vaccine.

Leptospirosis

Leptospirosis follows contamination of abraded or cut skin or mucous membranes with leptospira-infected urine of many animals including pigs, cattle, horses, rats and dogs. In Australia it is almost exclusively an occupational infection of farmers and workers in the meat industry.[7] Early diagnosis is important to prevent passing into the immune phase.

Clinical features

- incubation period 3–20 days (average 10)
- fever, myalgia
- severe headache
- macular rash: conjunctivitis

Some may develop the immune phase (after an asymptomatic period of 1–3 days) with aseptic meningitis or jaundice and nephritis (icterohaemorrhagic fever, Weil's disease) with a significant mortality.

Diagnosis

- high or rising titre of antibodies: can be cultured

Treatment

- penicillin and tetracycline

Lyme disease

Lyme disease (known as Lyme borreliosis) was first described in 1975 and named after the town Lyme in Connecticut (US). It is now widespread in the United States and is now appearing in Europe, Asia and Australia. Very infective, it is caused by a spirochaete, *Borrelia burgdorferi* and transmitted by Ixodes ticks, so that people living and working in the bush are susceptible. It has been reported in deer farmers. Lyme disease presents in three phases.

Stages of Lyme disease

Stage 1

- *Erythema migrans*—a characteristic pathognomonic rash, usually a doughnut-shaped well-defined rash about 6 cm in diameter at the bite site (Fig. 24.3).
- ± a flu-like illness: malaise, fever, myalgia, arthralgia, backache.

Stage 2 (weeks or months later)

- Neurological problems, e.g. limb weakness, muscle pain, aseptic meningitis, painful radiculopathies, cranial nerve palsies, e.g. Bell's palsy.
- Cardiac problems: arrhythmias, myocarditis.

Stage 3

- Arthritis (weeks or months later). In children it can be mistaken for juvenile chronic arthritis. In adults, it usually affects one or two joints, especially the knee joints. A LIMP syndrome (localised intermittent musculoskeletal pain) is described, which is severe pain without significant findings on examination.

Diagnosis

- Clinical pattern especially rash of *erythema migrans*. Serology to demonstrate Lyme antibodies which take about 6 weeks to develop from the onset of the disease.

Treatment

- A typical regime for adults is doxycycline 100 mg bd for 21 days (the earlier the diagnosis the more effective the treatment).

Psittacosis

Most patients are bird fanciers. Psittacosis accounts for 1–5% of hospital admissions for pneumonia. The disease may follow a low-grade course over several months but can have a dramatically acute presentation.

Clinical features

- incubation period 1–2 weeks
- fever, malaise, myalgia
- headache
- cough
- minimal chest signs
- splenomegaly (sometimes)

Mortality can be as high as 20% if untreated.

Diagnosis

- serology—rising antibody

Treatment

- tetracycline or erythromycin

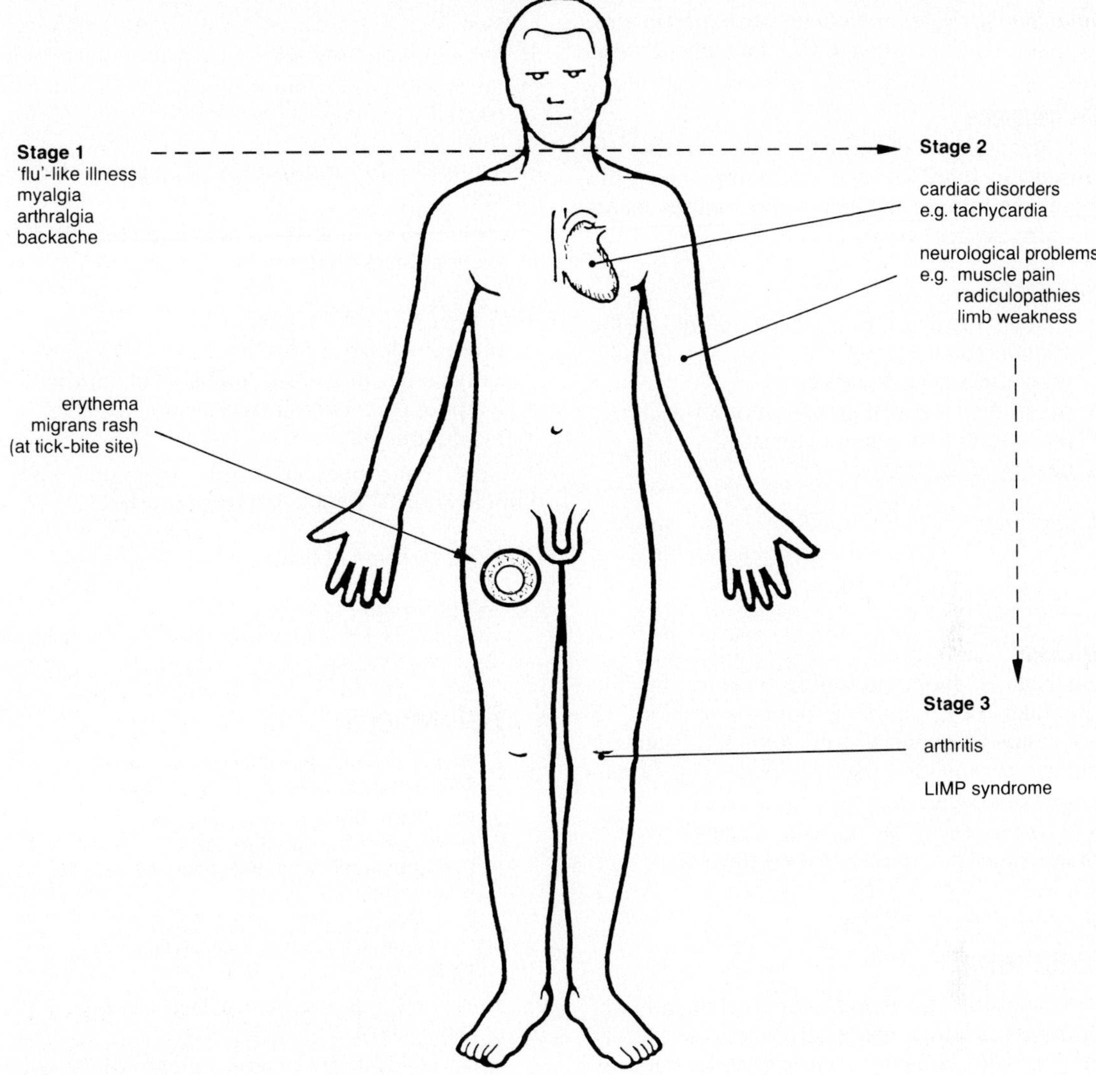

Fig. 24.3 *Lyme disease: clinical features*

Other zoonoses

- mosquito-transmitted infections—Murray Valley encephalitis, Ross River virus
- infections from bites and scratches—cat scratch disease, rat bite fever
- hydatid disease, orf, milker's nodule
- toxoplasmosis

Clostridial diseases

Tetanus

This sometimes misdiagnosed bacterial infection (*Clostridium tetani*) can appear from one day to several months after the injury, which can be forgotten. A total of 10–20% of patients with tetanus have no identifiable wound of entry.[8]

Clinical features

- prodrome: fever, malaise, headache
- trismus (patient cannot close mouth)
- risus sardonicus (a grin-like effect from hypertonic facial muscles)
- opisthothonus (arched trunk with hyperextended neck)
- spasms, precipitated by minimal stimuli

Differential diagnosis: phenothiazine toxicity, strychnine poisoning, rabies.

Management Refer immediately to expert centre. Intubate and ventilate if necessary.

Gas gangrene

Gas gangrene (clostridial myonecrosis) is caused by entry of one of several clostridia organisms into devitalised tissue such as exists following severe trauma to a leg.

Clinical features

- sudden onset of pain and swelling in the contaminated wound
- brownish serous exudate
- gas in the tissue on palpation or X-ray
- prostration and systemic toxicity
- circulatory failure ('shock')

Management Refer immediately to surgical centre. Start benzyl penicillin 2.4 g IV, 4 hourly.

Botulism

Botulism is food poisoning caused by the neurotoxin of *Clostridium botulinum*. From 12 to 36 hours after ingesting the toxin from canned, smoked or vacuum packed food (e.g. home-canned vegetables or meat) visual problems such as diplopia suddenly appear. General muscle paralysis and prostration quickly develop.

Pneumonia

Surprisingly the initial presentation of pneumonia can be misleading, especially when the patient presents with constitutional symptoms such as fever, malaise and headache rather than respiratory symptoms. A cough, although usually present, can be relatively insignificant in the total clinical picture. This problem applies particularly to atypical pneumonia but can occur with bacterial pneumonia especially lobar pneumonia.

The atypical pneumonias

Clinical features

- fever, malaise
- headache
- minimal respiratory symptoms, non-productive cough
- signs of consolidation absent
- chest X-ray (diffuse infiltration) incompatible with chest signs

Causes

Mycoplasma pneumoniae—the commonest:

- adolescents and young adults
- treated with tetracycline

Legionella pneumophilia (Legionnaire's disease):

- related to cooling systems in large buildings
- incubation 2–10 days

Diagnostic criteria include:

- prodromal-like illness
- a dry cough, influenza, confusion or diarrhoea
- lymphopenia with marked leucocytosis
- hyponatraemia

Patients can become very prostrate with complications—treat with erythromycin.

Chlamydia psittaci (psittacosis)

Coxiella burnetti (Q fever)

References

1. Hart G. Syphilis. In: MIMS Disease Index. Sydney: IMS Publishing, 1991–2, 524–527.
2. NH & MRC. *Handbook on sexually transmitted diseases*. Canberra: Department of Community Services and Health, 1990, 23–29.
3. Kumar PJ, Clark ML. *Clinical medicine* (2nd edition), London: Bailliere Tindall, 1990, 41–42.
4. Oakley C. Infective endocarditis. Medicine International, 1986, 21:872–878.
5. Mashford ML. *Antibiotic guidelines* (7th edition), Melbourne: Victorian Postgraduate Medical Foundation, 1992/93:94–95.
6. Kumar PL, Clark ML. *Clinical medicine* (2nd edition). London: Bailliere Tindall, 1990, 30–65.
7. Benn R. Australian zoonoses. Current Therapeutics, July 1990, 31–40.
8. Wilson J et al. *Harrison's principles of internal medicine* (12th edition), New York, 1991, chapter 105 (tetanus).

Acknowledgement

Part of this text, on the clinical manifestations of syphilis, is reproduced from the *Handbook on sexually transmitted diseases*[2]. 'Commonwealth of Australia, copyright reproduced by permission'.

25

Chronic renal failure

Chronic renal failure (CRF) is defined as a severe reduction in nephron mass over an extended period of time resulting in uraemia.[1] It is not common but can present surreptitiously and be a real master of disguise in clinical practice. Asymptomatic CRF may be discovered on routine health screening, as a chance finding in hospitalised or hypertensive patients, or during follow-up of patients with known renal disease.[2]

Key facts and checkpoints

- At least 50 to 60 people per million of the population are treated for end-stage renal failure (ESRF) each year.
- Two-thirds of these are under 60 years of age.
- Approximately one-third have glomerulonephritis, 2–18% analgesic nephropathy, 10% diabetes mellitus, 7% polycystic kidney disease, 6% reflux nephropathy and 4% hypertension. (Table 25.1)[3]
- The commonest cause of nephritis leading to renal failure in Australia is IgA nephropathy.
- In children the incidence of chronic renal failure is quite low (1 to 2 per million of the population).[3]
- Warmer climates, poorer living conditions and certain genetic predispositions are associated with a higher prevalence of renal failure.
- Renal failure should be considered in the diagnosis of patients with:
  - — unexplained anaemia
  - — unexplained poor health
  - — unusually high analgesic intake[3]
- Uraemic symptoms are non-specific and usually are not recognised until the creatinine clearance is less than 20% of normal.
- CRF is characterised by the accumulation of uraemic toxins and a deficiency of renal hormones which cause dysfunction of organs other than kidneys.
- This interaction can cause phosphate retention, secondary hyperparathyroidism and bone disorders such as osteomalacia.

Table 25.1 *Significant causes of chronic renal failure*

Chronic glomerulonephritis
Analgesic nephropathy
Reflux nephropathy
Diabetes mellitus
Polycystic kidneys
Hypertension
Obstructive nephropathy
- bilateral ureteric obstruction
- bladder outflow obstruction
  - — prostatic enlargement
  - — urethral stenosis

Lupus nephritis
Renal artery stenosis
Gout
Amyloidoisis
Hypercalcaemia
Drugs

Important clinical associations

The possibility of CRF should be monitored in patients with:

- diabetes mellitus
- hypertension
- severe gout
- a history of urinary tract abnormality
  e.g. vesico-ureteric reflux
  bladder outflow obstruction

The possibility of CRF should be considered and investigated in patients presenting with:

- unexplained poor health
- hypertension
- anaemia
- pruritus
- hyperparathyroidism
- pericarditis
- urinary tract symptoms or signs
  e.g. proteinuria
  haematuria
  oedema
  nocturia
  loin pain
  prostatic obstruction
- neurological disturbances
  e.g. confusion
  coma
  peripheral neuropathy
  seizures

Patients with CRF may present with features of acute renal failure with the intervention of complicating factors such as:

- drug toxicity
- infection
- fluid imbalance

Urgent treatment of the following conditions, which can lead to rapid renal failure, is essential:

- progressive nephritis
- systemic lupus erythematosus
- vasculitides
  e.g. polyarteritis nodosa
  Wegener's granulomatosis

The clinical approach

History

A hallmark of early stage CRF is a non-specific history and examination and the diagnosis is a very difficult one in the absence of a known past history of renal disease. The diagnosis can only be established by renal function tests. Symptoms from CRF are rare unless the creatinine clearance is less than 20% of normal and only become common when less than 10% of normal.

In patients with chronic renal disease, symptomatic uraemia may be precipitated by prerenal factors such as fluid loss from vomiting or diarrhoea, infection, antibiotic therapy especially tetracyclines, or increasing hypertension.

Symptoms and signs

The symptoms and signs of CRF are summarised in Figure 25.1.

The common early presenting symptoms are generally non-specific and referable to the gastrointestinal tract, presumably due to the formation of ammonia in the upper GIT.

Such symptoms include:

- anorexia
- nausea
- vomiting
- tiredness
- lethargy

If a patient presents with these symptoms and has a sallow appearance due to combination of anaemia and brownish pigmentation, then CRF should be highly suspected.

Physical examination

General inspection of the patient with CRF will usually reveal a sallow complexion with yellow–brown pigmentation in the skin, which is often dry and pruritic. The patient's mental state should be noted. The respiratory and pulse rates are usually rapid because of anaemia and metabolic acidosis. Other findings may include bruising, uraemic foetor, reduced mental status, pericarditis and peripheral neuropathy. The abdomen should be carefully palpated especially in the renal areas. A rectal examination is indicated to detect prostatomegaly or other rectal or pelvic pathology. Ophthalmoscopic examination may show hypertensive or diabetic retinopathy. Urinalysis should test glucose, blood and protein. Proteinuria should be confirmed with a 24 hour urine protein estimation.

Investigations

Renal function tests (most appropriate for the general practitioner):

- plasma urea
- plasma creatinine
- creatinine clearance (more precise)

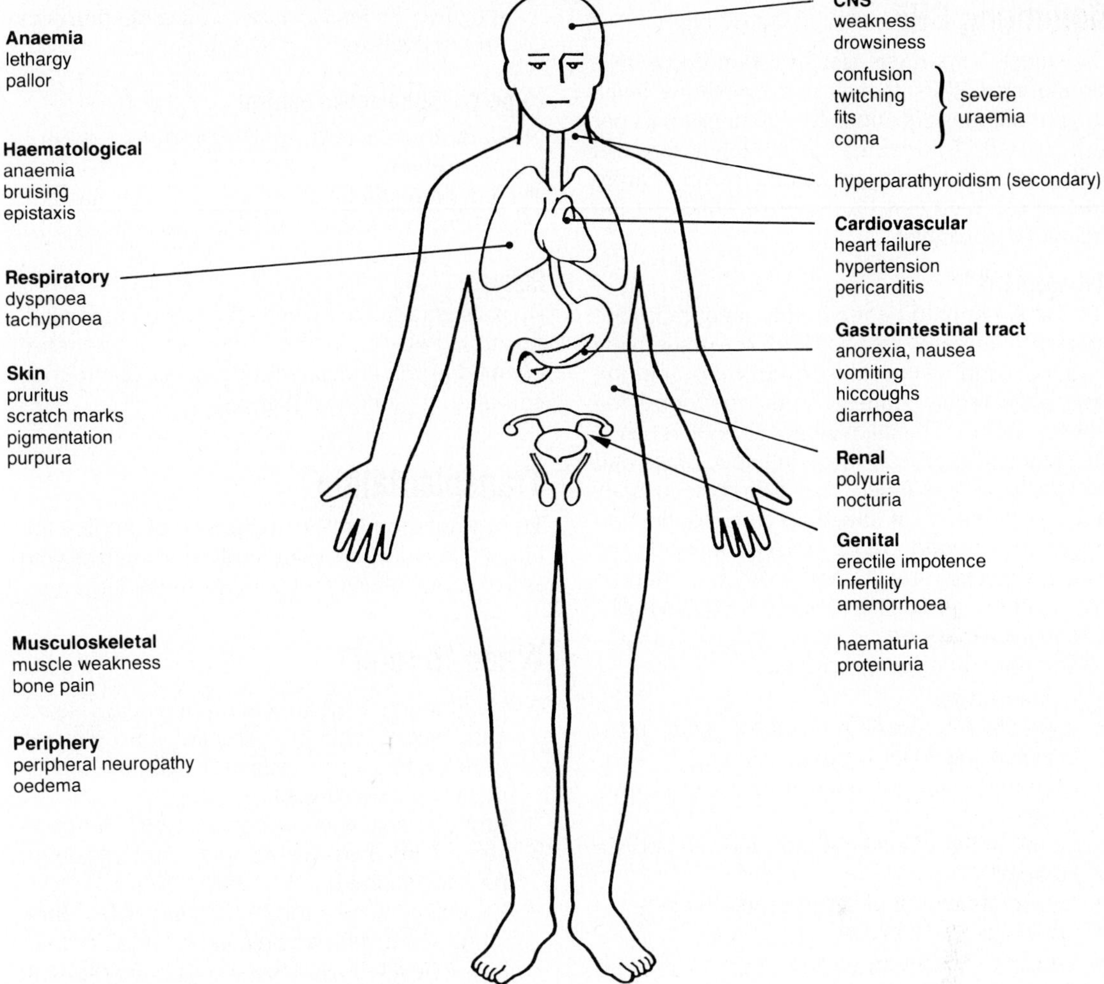

Fig. 25.1 *Clinical features of chronic renal disease*

Plasma electrolytes

- sodium, potassium, chloride, bicarbonate
- calcium and phosphate

Consider:

- magnesium, urate, glucose
- lipids
- prescribed drug level
- cardiac studies
- full blood ? anaemia

Determination of underlying cause

- imaging of urinary tract—ultrasound
- immunological tests
- renal biopsy

Chronic renal failure in children

The incidence of CRF in children is about 2 per million of the total population per year. The commonest causes include chronic glomerulonephritis, obstructive nephropathy and reflux nephropathy. Identification of structural renal abnormalities by obstetric ultrasound and early investigation of urinary tract infections may decrease the incidence of CRF. Dialysis and transplantation are normally considered for children over 2 years of age with end-stage CRF. For children under 2 years there are complex ethical, psychological and technical problems.[4] Nevertheless the prognosis for such treatment is poor.

Monitoring CRF

The most important test in identifying and monitoring CRF is the plasma creatinine level. The normal range is about 40–120 micromols per litre (0.04–0.12 mmol/L) but the laboratory will indicate their appropriate reference level. A more precise estimate can be made by checking the creatinine clearance.

Management

The patient should be referred to an appropriate specialist as early as possible. The underlying disease and any abnormalities causing progressive renal damage must be corrected where possible. The management of CRF is based on the team approach involving specialists and paramedical personnel. The patient is usually faced with years of ongoing care so that an empathic support team based around the patient's general practitioner is very important to the patient who will require considerable psychosocial support.

Optimum treatment includes:

- regular review
- good blood pressure control (the most effective way to slow progression)
- keeping plasma phosphate levels in normal range
- maintaining effective fluid and electrolyte balance
- prompt treatment of intercurrent illness
- judicious use of drugs
- avoiding treatment errors, especially with drugs
  — avoid potassium-sparing diuretics
- other drugs that may cause problems include digoxin, tetracyclines, gentamicin, NSAIDs, nitrofurantoin and ACE inhibitors
- rapid treatment of complications, especially salt and water depletion and acute urinary infection
- low protein diet
- treating anaemia with human recombinant erythropoietin.

Blood pressure control

- no added salt diet (with care)
- drug control: none of the antihypertensive agents are specifically contraindicated but those eliminated mainly by the kidney (e.g. ACE inhibitors, atenolol, sotalol) should be given in lower dosage. ACE inhibitors should not be used in presence of renal artery stenosis; loop diuretics, e.g. frusemide, are effective in larger doses (thiazide diuretics are ineffective).[3]

Hyperphosphataemia control

- balanced nutrition to reduce dietary phosphate
- protein restriction
- calcium carbonate (to bind phosphate)

Dialysis

Dialysis is indicated when all other methods fail. About two-thirds of patients receive haemodialysis and one-third are on continuous ambulatory peritoneal dialysis.

Transplantation

Transplantation is the treatment of choice for failure except where contraindicated such as with active tuberculosis and perhaps the elderly.

When to refer

- Haematuria is an indication of active disease and such patients should be referred immediately for investigation. Oliguria makes this even more urgent.
- Any patient with impaired renal function should be investigated and a management plan formulated.
- Patients with creatinine clearance of less than 20 mL/min (plasma creatinine > 0.05 mmol/L) are best followed in a renal clinic. Diabetic patients warrant specialist referral when the plasma creatinine is at 0.2 mmol/L.[3]

References

1. Tally N, O'Connor S. *Clinical examinations* (2nd edition), Sydney: Maclennan & Petty, 1992, 195–209.
2. Kumar PJ, Clark M. *Clinical medicine* (2nd edition), London: Bailliere Tindall, 1990, 475–478.
3. Dawborn JK. Chronic renal failure. In: MIMS Disease Index. Sydney: IMS Publishing, 1991–2, 451–453.
4. Robinson MJ. *Practical paediatrics* (2nd edition), Melbourne: Churchill Livingstone, 1990, 441–442.
5. Kincaid Smith P, Larkins R, Whelan G. *Problems in clinical medicine*. Sydney: Maclennan & Petty, 1990, 319–324.

26

Connective tissue disorders and the vasculitides

The connective tissue disorders and the vasculitides are groups of diseases that are difficult to classify because their causation is generally unknown. They all cause joint and soft tissue inflammation and multiple other possible manifestations which create diagnostic difficulties.

It is convenient to consider a working classification of joint pain (Table 26.1) which includes apparent joint pain (arthralgia), as some of the inflammatory disorders cause problems in the soft tissues around joints, e.g. giant cell arteritis and hydroxyapatite crystalopathy of the tendons around the shoulder joint.

Vasculitis is, in fact, a condition common to the connective tissue disorders and to the so-called vasculitides.

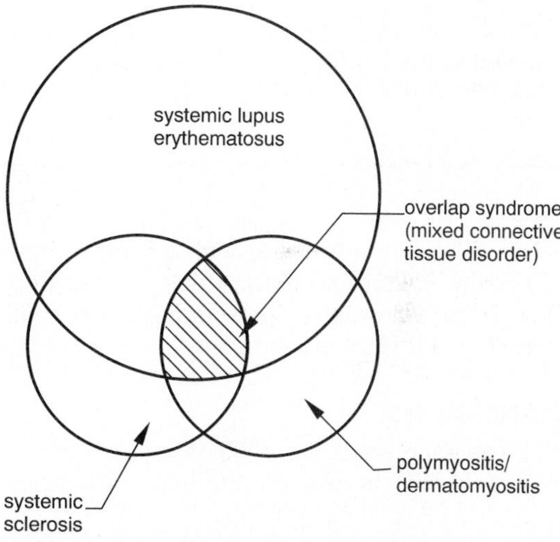

Fig. 26.1 *The connective tissue disorders*

Connective tissue disorders

The connective tissue disorders or diseases comprise three distinct conditions, namely systemic lupus erythematosus, systemic sclerosis and polymyositis/dermatomyositis (Fig. 26.1).[1]

Mixed connective tissue disorder is that disease which includes features of all three disorders and is sometimes referred to as 'overlap' syndrome.

Common features include:

- arthralgia or arthritis
- multisystem involvement
- vasculitis
- immunological abnormalities

Systemic lupus erythematosus

Systemic lupus erythematosus (SLE) is the commonest of the connective tissue disorders.

Table 26.1 *A classification of rheumatological pain (after Dr Stephen Hall)*

Hyperacute (red hot) joints	Crystals	• urate: gout • calcium pyrophosphate • hydroxyapatite
	Pus	e.g. staphylococcal septic arthritis
Inflammation of joints	Symmetrical	e.g. rheumatoid arthritis
	Asymmetrical	e.g. spondylo-arthropathies
Non-inflammatory joint disorder osteoarthritis	Typical	Primary, e.g. in hands
	Atypical	e.g.post-trauma haemochromatosis
Joint and soft tissue inflammation	Connective tissue disorders	• SLE • systemic sclerosis • polymyositis/ dermatomyositis
	Vasculitides	• polyarteritis nodosa • giant cell arteritis • polymyalgia rheumatica
Non-articular (soft tissue) inflammation	Generalised	e.g. fibrositis
	Localised	e.g.plantar fasciitis epicondylitis

It is a multisystem disease with a wide variety of clinical features which are due to vasculitis (Fig. 26.2). Arthritis is the commonest clinical feature of SLE (90% of cases).

Clinical features

- prevalence about 1 in 1000 of population
- mainly affects women in 'high oestrogen' period (90% of cases)
- peak onset between 20 and 40 years
- fever, malaise, tiredness common
- multiple drug allergies
- Raynaud's phenomenon
- butterfly rash (only one-third of patients)
- finger changes—nail-fold hyperaemia, telangiectasia
- vasculitis
- serosal: pleuritis, pericarditis
- renal (uncommon)—glomerulonephritis
- CNS (uncommon)—intractable headache, epileptic seizures, psychoses
- blood: anaemia, leucopenia and thrombocytopenia
- problems with OC and pregnancy
- polymyositis

Investigations

- ESR—elevated in proportion to disease activity
- antinuclear antibodies—positive in 95%
- double stranded DNA antibodies—specific for SLE but present in only 50%
- rheumatoid factor—positive in 50%
- LE test—inefficient and not used

Management

- appropriate explanation, support and reassurance
- drug treatments
  - — mild: NSAIDs
  - — moderate: low-dose antimalarials, e.g. hydroxychloroquine/ chloroquine
  - — severe: corticosteroids immunosuppressive drugs, e.g. azathioprine

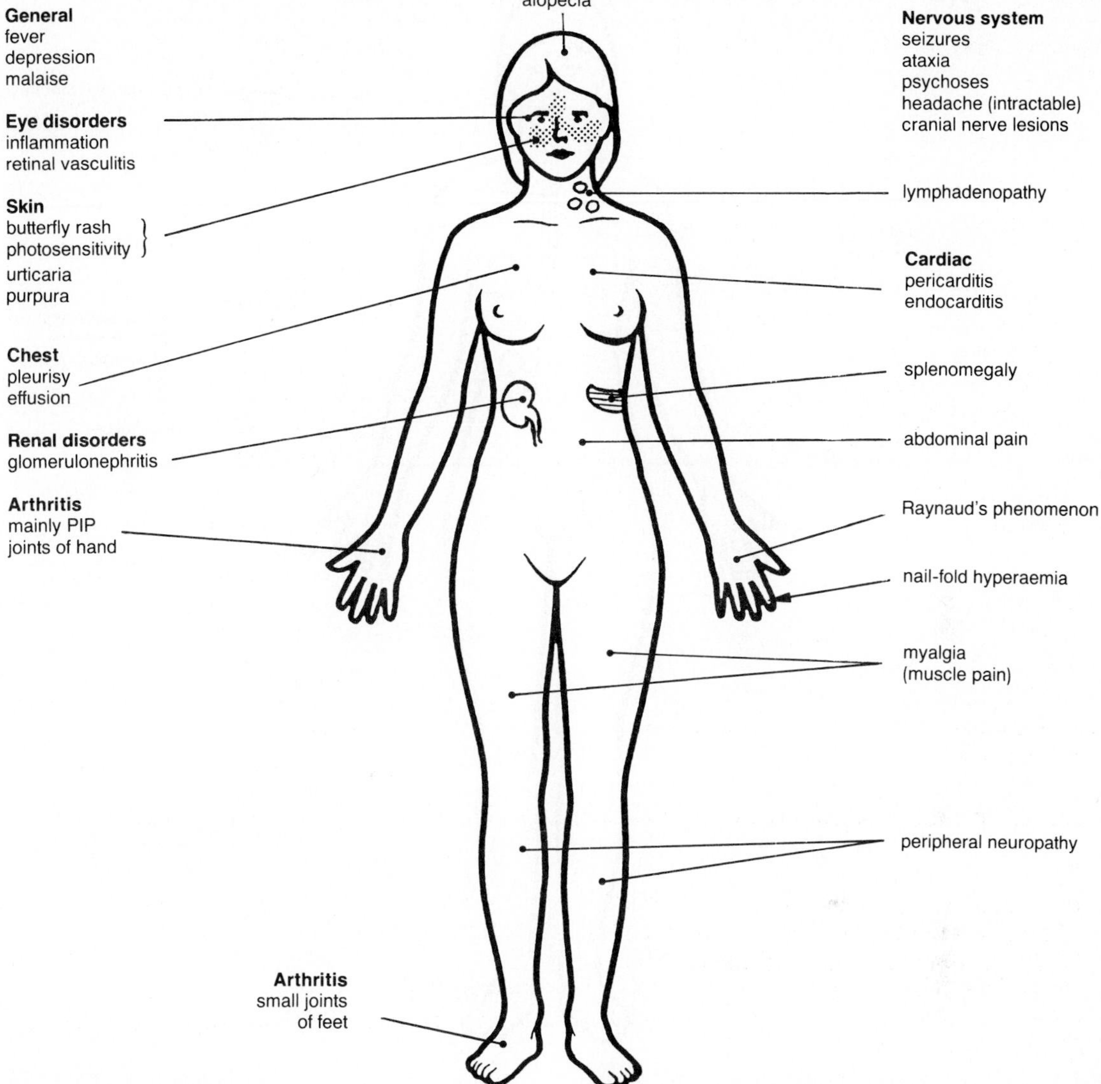

Fig. 26.2 *Clinical features of SLE*

Systemic sclerosis (scleroderma)

It can present as a polyarthritis affecting the fingers of the hand in 25% of patients, especially in the early stages. Soft tissue swelling produces a 'sausage finger' pattern. Systemic sclerosis mainly affects the skin, presenting with Raynaud's phenomenon in over 85% (Fig. 26.3).

Features

- females/males 2:1
- a progressive disease of multiple organs
- Raynaud's phenomenon
- stiffness of fingers and other skin areas
- 'bird-like' facies (mouth puckered)
- dysphagia and diarrhoea (malabsorption)
- respiratory symptoms
- cardiac symptoms: pericarditis, etc.
- look for tight skin on chest (Roman breastplate)

Investigations

- ESR may be raised
- normocytic normochromic anaemia may be present
- antinuclear antibodies—up to 50% positive

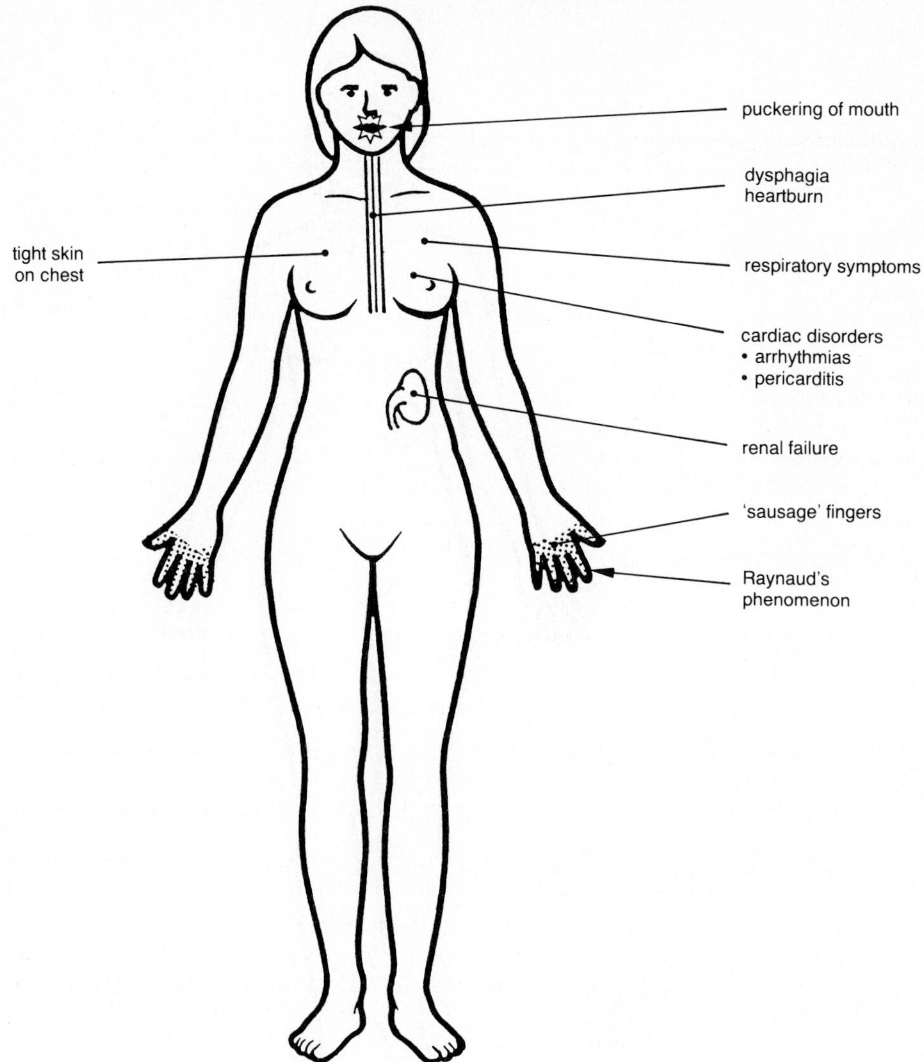

Fig. 26.3 *Clinical features of systemic sclerosis*

- rheumatoid factor—positive in 30%
- hypergammaglobulinaemia—50% positive
- antinuclear and anticentromere ABs—specific

Management

- empathic explanation, patient education
- NSAIDs for pain
- avoid vasospasm (no smoking, beta-blockers, ergotamine)
- treat malabsorption if present.

Polymyositis and dermatomyositis

Polymyositis is an uncommon systemic disorder whose main feature is symmetrical muscle weakness and wasting involving the proximal muscles of the shoulder and pelvic girdles.

Polymyositis + associated rash = dermatomyositis

Clinical features

- any age group
- peak incidence 40–60 years

- female to male ratio 2:1
- muscle weakness and wasting proximal limb muscles
- main complaint is weakness
- muscle pain and tenderness in about 50%
- arthralgia or arthritis in about 50% (resembles distribution of rheumatoid arthritis)
- dysphagia in about 50% due to oesophageal involvement
- Raynaud's phenomenon
- consider associated malignancy: lung and ovary

The rash

The distinctive rash shows features of photosensitivity. There is violet discolouration of the eyelids, forehead and cheeks and possible erythema resembling sunburn and periorbital oedema. There is a characteristic rash on the hands especially the fingers and nail folds. The knees and elbows are commonly involved.

The main features are summarised in Figure 26.4 below.

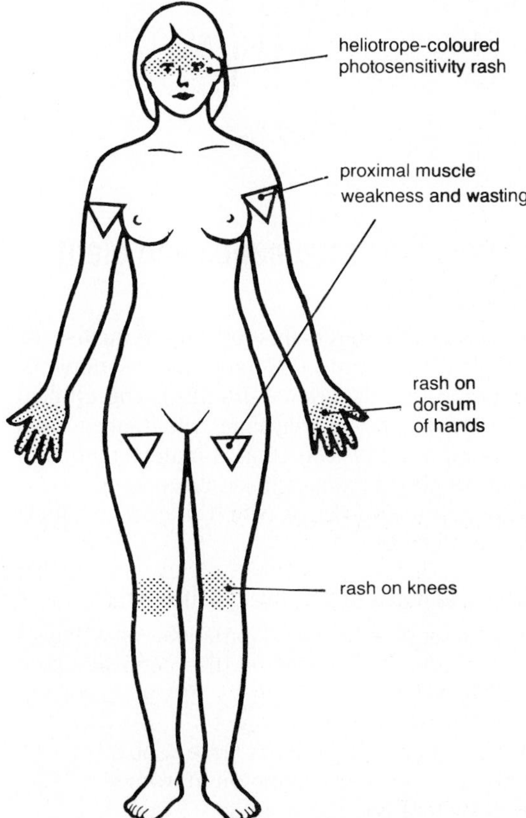

Fig. 26.4 *Clinical features of polymyositis/dermatomyositis*

Diagnosis

- muscle enzyme studies
- biopsies—skin and muscle
- EMG studies—show characteristic pattern

Treatment includes corticosteroids and cytotoxic drugs. Early referral is appropriate.

The vasculitides

The vasculitides or vasculitis syndromes are a heterogeneous group of disorders involving inflammation and necrosis of blood vessels, the clinical effects and classification depending on the size of the vessels involved.

Small vessel vasculitis is the common type encountered in practice. Medium vessel vasculitis includes polyarthritis nodosa and large vessel vasculitis includes giant cell arteritis.

Small vessel vasculitis

This is associated with many important diseases such as rheumatoid arthritis, SLE, bacterial endocarditis, Henoch-Schönlein purpura and hepatitis B. Skin lesions are usually associated with these disorders and the most common presentation is painful, palpable purpura such as occurs with Henoch-Schönlein purpura.

Rarer causes

The major vasculitides are polyarteritis nodosa (PN), polymyalgia rheumatica (PR), and giant cell arteritis (GCA), and Wegener's granulomatosis (WG). Unfortunately, many of these patients die or become terminally ill before the diagnosis is suspected.

Henoch-Schönlein purpura

More details are presented about this disorder on page 296.

Clinical features

- all ages, mainly in children
- rash mainly on buttocks and legs (Fig.26.5)
- can occur on hands, arms and trunk
- arthritis: mainly ankles and knees
- abdominal pain (vasculitis of GIT)
- haematuria (reflects nephritis)

Polyarteritis nodosa

The hallmark of polyarteritis nodosa is necrotising vasculitis of large arteries leading to skin nodules, infarctive ulcers and other serious

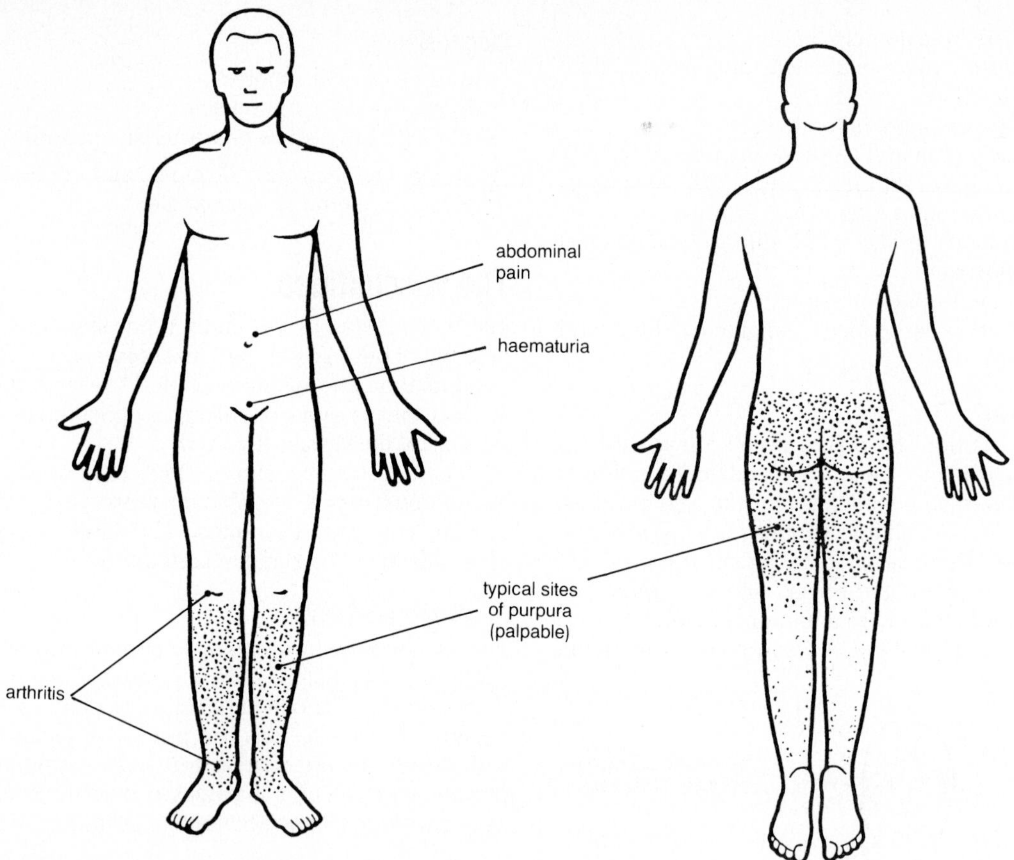

Fig. 26.5 *Henoch-Schönlein purpura: typical distribution*

manifestations (Fig. 26.6). The cause is unknown but associations are found with drug abusers (especially adulterated drugs), B cell lymphomas, other drugs and hepatitis B surface antigen. It should be suspected in any multisystemic disease of obscure aetiology.

Clinical features

- young to middle-aged men
- constitutional symptoms: fever, malaise, myalgia, weight loss
- migratory arthralgia or polyarthritis
- subcutaneous nodules along arterial lines
- livedo reticularis and skin ulcers
- renal impairment and hypertension
- cardiac disorders: arrhythmia, failure, infarction
- diagnosis confirmed by biopsy or angiogram
- ESR raised
- treatment with corticosteroids and immunosuppressants
- death is usually from renal disease

Polymyalgia rheumatica and giant cell arteritis

The basic pathology of this very important disease complex is giant cell arteritis (synonyms: temporal arteritis; cranial arteritis). The clinical syndromes are polymyalgia rheumatica and temporal arteritis. The clinical manifestations of polymyalgia rheumatica invariably precede those of temporal arteritis of which there is about a 20% association.

Clinical features of polymyalgia rheumatica

- pain and stiffness in proximal muscles of shoulder and pelvic girdle, cervical spine (Fig.26.7)
- symmetrical distribution
- typical ages 60-70 years (rare < 50)
- both sexes: more common in women
- early morning stiffness
- may be systemic symptoms: weight loss, malaise, anorexia

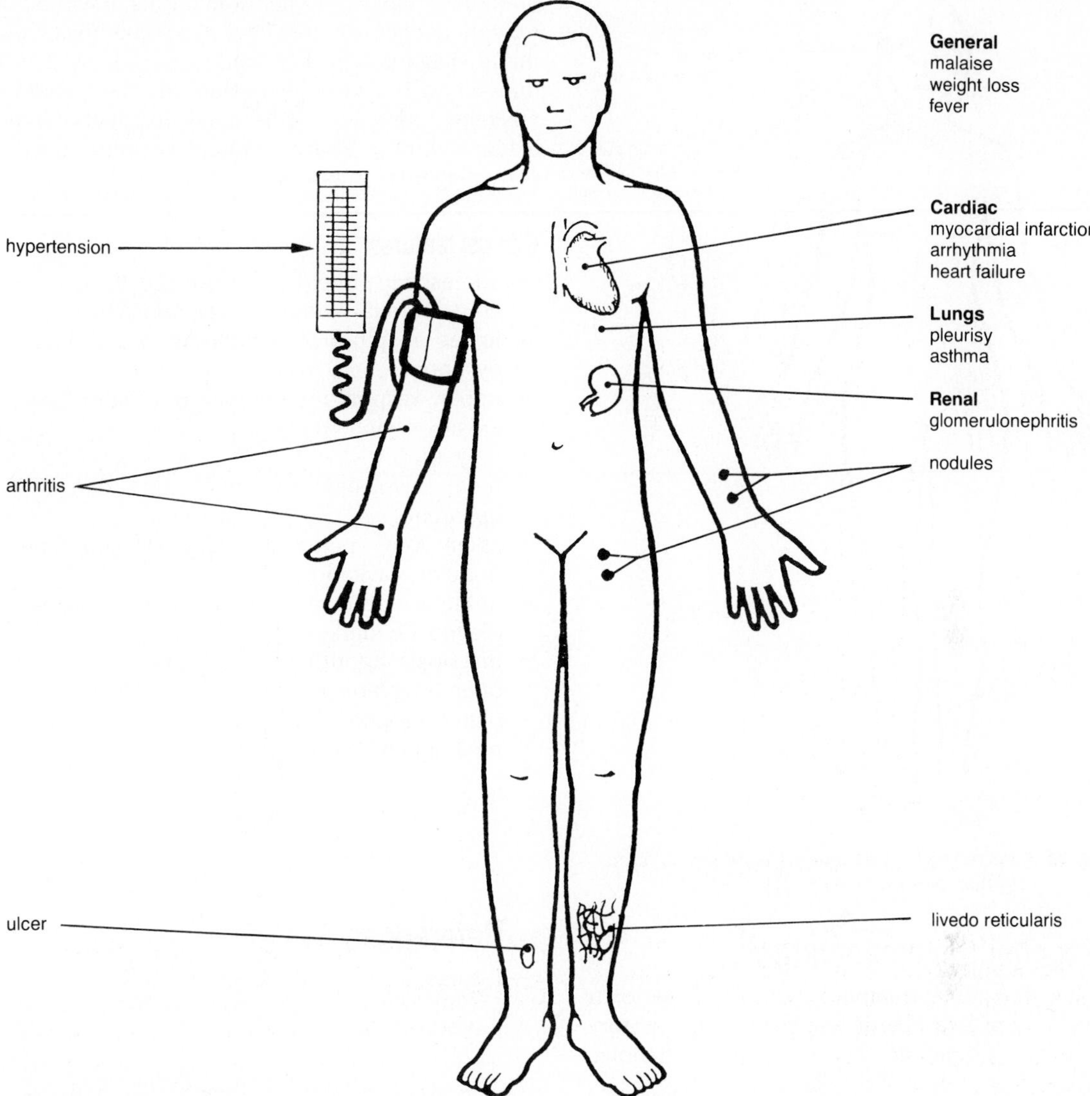

Fig. 26.6 *Clinical features of polyarteritis nodosa*

- painful restriction of movement of shoulders and hips
- signs may be absent later in day

Clinical features of temporal arteritis

- headache—unilateral, throbbing
- temporal tenderness
- loss of pulsation of temporal artery
- jaw claudication
- biopsy of artery (5 cm) is diagnostic

Investigation

- no specific test for polymyalgia rheumatica
- ESR—extremely high, around 100
- mild anaemia (normochromic, normocytic)

Treatment

Prednisolone

- Starting dose
  - — temporal arteritis 60 mg
  - — polymyalgia rheumatica 15 mg
- Taper down gradually to the minimum effective dose (often < 5 mg daily) according to the clinical response and the ESR. Aim for treatment for 2 years: relapses are common.

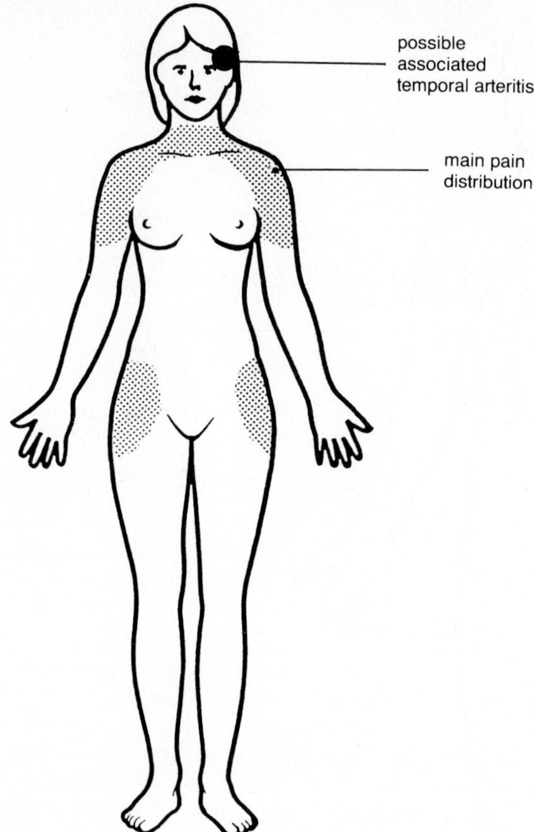

Fig. 26.7 *Polymyalgia rheumatica: typical sites of areas of pain and stiffness*

Wegener's granulomatosis

In this rare granulomatous vasculitis of unknown cause there is a classic triad: upper respiratory tract granuloma, fleeting pulmonary shadows (nodules) and glomerulonephritis. Without treatment it is invariably fatal and sometimes the initial diagnosis is that made at autopsy. It is difficult to diagnose, especially as the patient (usually young to middle aged) presents with a febrile illness and respiratory symptoms, but early diagnosis is essential.

Clinical features

- adolescence to elderly, mean age 40–45
- constitutional symptoms (as for PN)
- lower respiratory symptoms, e.g. cough, dyspnoea
- upper respiratory symptoms: rhinorrhoea, epistaxis, sinus pain
- polyarthritis
- renal involvement—usually not clinically apparent
- chest X-ray points to diagnosis—multiple nodules, cavitations
- antineutrophil antibodies are a useful diagnostic marker (not specific)
- diagnosis confirmed by biopsy, usually an open lung biopsy
- better prognosis with early diagnosis and treatment with cyclophosphamide.

References

1. Kumer PJ, Clark ML. *Clinical medicine* (2nd edition), London: Bailliere Tindall, 1990, 392–399.

27

Neurological dilemmas

In general practice there are many neurological problems that present a diagnostic dilemma with some being true masquerades for the non-neurologist. This applies particularly to various seizure disorders, space-occupying lesions in the cerebrum and the cerebellum, demyelinating disorders, motor neurone disorders and peripheral neuropathies.

The most common pitfall that occurs with neurological disorders is misdiagnosis and the most common reason for misdiagnosis is an inadequate history. Failure to appreciate the neurological meaning of points elicited during the history is another reason for misdiagnosis.

Some very important neurological disorders are presented in this section: Parkinson's disease, which is common and can be easily misdiagnosed especially when the classic 'pill rolling' tremor is absent or mild; multiple sclerosis (MS), because it is difficult to diagnose initially; and acute idiopathic demyelinating polyneuropathy (Guillain-Barré syndrome), because it can be rapidly fatal if misdiagnosed. MS can masquerade as almost anything—'If you don't know what it is, think of MS.'

Another brain teaser for the family doctor is to diagnose accurately the various types of epilepsy. The most commonly misdiagnosed seizure disorders are complex partial seizures or atypical generalised tonic clonic seizures (see Chapter 46).[1] Even more difficult is the differentiation of real seizures from pseudoseizures.

Tremor

Tremor is an important symptom to evaluate correctly. A list of causes is presented in Table 27.1. A common pitfall in patients presenting with tremor is for Parkinson's disease to be diagnosed as benign essential tremor and for benign essential tremor to be diagnosed as Parkinson's disease, but the clinical distinction is not always easy and it must be remembered that as many as 20% will experience both concurrently.

Table 27.1 *Causes of tremor*

- Physiological
- Benign essential (familial) tremor
- Senile
- Anxiety, including hyperventilation
- Hyperthyroidism
- Toxic, e.g. alcohol, liver failure, uraemia
- Drugs, e.g. lithium, narcotic withdrawal
- Parkinson's disease
- Drug-induced Parkinsonism
- Cerebellar disease
- Cerebral tumour (frontal lobe)
- Alzheimer's dementia
- Wilson's disease
- Miscellaneous, e.g. red-nucleus lesion, hypoglycaemia

Tremors can be classified as follows:

Resting tremor—Parkinsonian

The tremor of Parkinson's disease is present at rest. The hand tremor is most marked with the arms supported on the lap and during walking. The characteristic movement is 'pill-rolling' where movement of the fingers at the metacarpophalangeal joints is combined with movements of the thumb. The resting tremor decreases on finger-nose testing but a faster action tremor may supervene. The best way to evoke the tremor is to distract the patient, such as focusing attention on the left hand with a view to 'examining' the right hand.

Action or postural tremor

This fine tremor is noted by examining the patient with the arms outstretched and the fingers apart. The tremor may be rendered more obvious if a sheet of paper is placed over the dorsum of the hands. The tremor is present throughout movement, being accentuated by voluntary contraction.

Causes include:

- essential tremor (also called familial tremor or benign essential tremor)
- senile tremor
- physiological
- anxiety/emotional
- hyperthyroidism
- alcohol
- drugs, e.g. drug withdrawal (e.g. heroin, cocaine, alcohol), dexedrine, lithium, sympathomimetics (bronchodilators), sodium valproate, heavy metals (e.g. mercury)
- phaeochromocytoma

Intention tremor (cerebellar disease)

This coarse oscillating tremor is absent at rest but exacerbated by action and increases as the target is approached. It is tested by 'finger-nose-finger' touching or running the heel down the opposite shin, and past pointing of the nose is a feature. It occurs in cerebellar lobe disease and with lesions of cerebellar connections.

Flapping (metabolic tremor)

A flapping or 'wing-beating' tremor is observed when the arms are extended with hyperextension of the wrists. It involves slow, coarse and jerky movements of flexion and extension at the wrists.

Causes

- Wilson's disease
- hepatic encephalopathy
- uraemia
- respiratory failure
- lesions of the red nucleus of the midbrain

Essential tremor

Essential tremor, which is probably the most common movement disorder, has been variously called benign, familial, senile or juvenile tremor. However, it is not always benign and there is no family history in about half the cases.

Features

- autosomal dominant disorder (variable penetrance)
- often begins in early adult life, even adolescence
- begins with a slight tremor in one hand and spreads to other with time
- may involve head (titubation), chin and tongue and rarely trunk and legs
- interferes with writing (not micrographic), handling cups of tea, spoons, etc.
- tremor most marked when arms held out (postural tremor)
- anxiety exacerbates the tremor
- may affect speech if involves bulbar musculature

Triad of features

- positive family history
- tremor with little disability
- normal gait

Distinguishing essential tremor from Parkinson's disease

This is not always easy as a postural tremor can be present in Parkinson's disease although the hand tremor is most marked at rest with the arms supported on the lap. Parkinsonian tremor is slower at 4–6 Hz while essential tremor is much faster at around 8–13 Hz.

A most useful way to differentiate the two causes is to observe the gait. It is normal in essential tremor but in Parkinson's there may be loss of arm swing and the step is usually shortened.

Management of essential tremor

Most patients do not need treatment and all that is required is an appropriate explanation[1]. If necessary, use propranolol (first choice) or primidone[2]. If the tremor is only intrusive at times of increased emotional stress, intermittent use of benzodiazepines, e.g. lorazepam, 30 minutes before exposure to the stress may be all that is required.

Parkinson's disease

One of the most important clinical aspects of Parkinson's disease, which has a slow and insidious onset, is the ability to make an early diagnosis. Sometimes this can be very difficult especially when the tremor is absent or mild, as occurs with the atherosclerotic degenerative type of Parkinsonism. The lack of any specific abnormality on special investigation leaves the responsibility for a diagnosis based on the history and examination. As a general rule of thumb the diagnosis of Parkinson's disease is restricted to those who respond to levodopa—the rest are termed Parkinsonism.

Key facts and checkpoints

- Parkinson's disease is the most common and disabling chronic neurological disorder.
- The prevalence in Australia is 100–120 per 100 000.[3]
- The mean age of onset is between 58 and 62.[3]
- The incidence rises sharply over 70 years of age.[3]
- The classic triad of Parkinson's disease (Fig. 27.1) is:
  - — tremor
  - — rigidity
  - — bradykinesia (poverty of movement)
- Hemi-parkinsonism can occur; all the signs are confined to one side and thus must be differentiated from hemiplegia. In fact most Parkinson's disease starts unilaterally.
- Always consider drug-induced Parkinsonism. The usual drugs are phenothiazines, butyrophenones and reserpine. Tremor is uncommon but rigidity and bradykinesia may be severe.

Physical signs

- Power, reflexes and sensation usually normal.
- The earliest abnormal physical signs to appear are loss of dexterity of rapid alternating movements and absence of arm swing; in addition to increased tone with distraction.

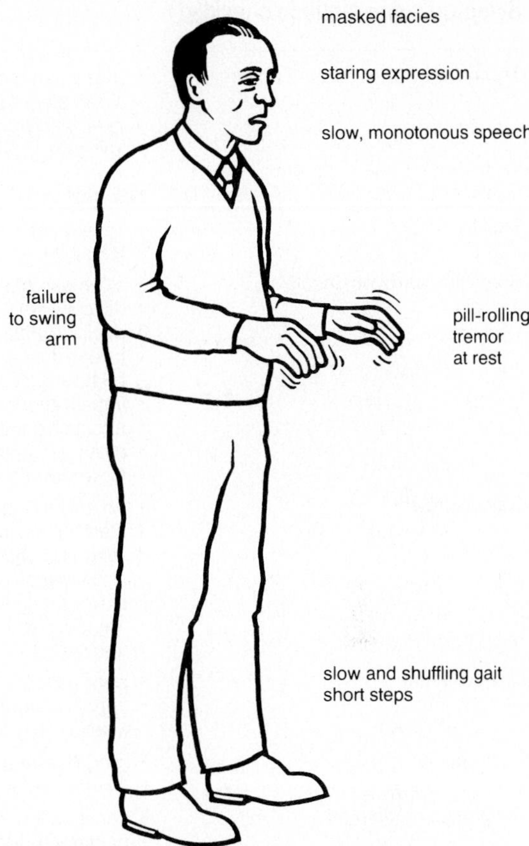

Fig. 27.1 *Basic clinical features of Parkinson's disease*

- Frontal lobe signs such as grasp and glabellar taps (only allow 3 blinks) are more common with Parkinsonism.

Note: There is no laboratory test for Parkinson's—it is a clinical diagnosis. Hypothyroidism and depression, which also cause slowness of movement, may cause confusion with diagnosis.

The Steele-Richardson syndrome (Parkinsonism, dementia and vertical gaze dysfunction) is worth considering.

Principles of management

- Appropriate explanation and education.
- Explain that Parkinson's disease is slowly progressive, is improved but not cured by treatment. It does not usually shorten life.
- Support systems are necessary for advanced Parkinson's disease.
- Walking sticks with appropriate education into their use may be necessary to help

Symptoms and signs (a checklist)

Tremor	• present at rest • slow rate—4 to 6 cycles per second • alternating, especially arms • 'pill-rolling' (severe cases) NB: may be absent or unilateral
Rigidity	• 'cogwheel' • lead pipe
Bradykinesia/hypokinesia	• slowness of initiating a movement • difficulty with fine finger tasks • micrographia (Fig. 27.2) • masked facies • relative lack of blinking • impaired convergence of eyes • excessive salivation (late) • difficulty turning over in bed and rising from a chair • slow monotonous speech/dysarthria
Gait disorder	• no arm swing on one or both sides • start hesitation • slow and shuffling • short steps (petit pas) • slow turning circle • 'freezing' when approaching an obstacle • festination
Disequilibrium	• poor balance • impaired righting reflexes • falls (usually late)
Posture	• progressive forward flexion of trunk • flexion of elbow at affected side
Autonomic symptoms	• constipation (common) • postural hypotension • depression (early)
Psychiatric	• progressive dementia in 30–40% usually after 10 years[3]

prevent falls and constant care is required, so that admission to a nursing home for end-stage disease may be appropriate.

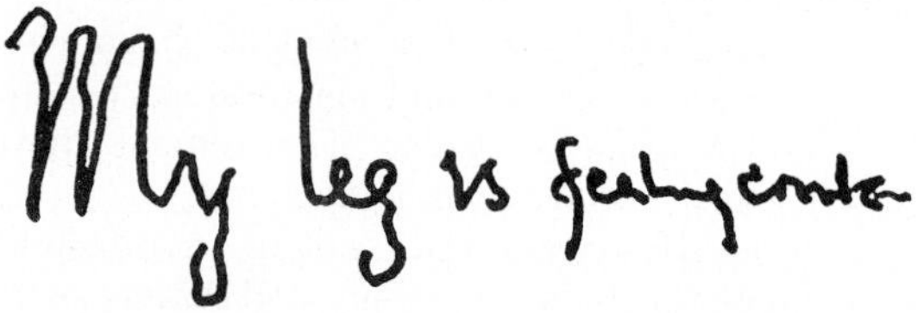

Fig. 27.2 *Micrographia, one of the signs of Parkinson's disease*

Pharmacological management

This should be commenced as soon as symptoms interfere with working capacity or the patient's enjoyment of life. This will only be apparent if the correct questions are asked as the patient may accept impaired enjoyment without appreciating that it is due to Parkinson's disease. The dosage should be tailored so that the patient neither develops side effects nor is on an inadequate dose of medication without significant therapeutic benefit (Table 27.2).

The older drugs such as anticholinergics and amantadine have minimal usage in modern management as levodopa, which basically counters bradykinesia, is the best drug and the baseline of treatment. With the onset of disability (motor disturbances) levodopa in combination with a decarboxylase inhibitor (carbidopa or benserazide) in a 4:1 ratio should be introduced. Levodopa therapy does not significantly improve tremor but improves rigidity, dyskinesia and gait disorder.

Bromocriptine can be used in treatment especially with the levodopa 'on-off' phenomenon (fluctuations throughout the day). Bromocriptine can be used alone or with levodopa—it appears to be most effective when used in combination. The major side effects of bromocriptine are similar to levodopa. Dyskinesia

Table 27.2 *Anti-Parkinson drugs*

Agent	***Main side effects***
Amantadine	• nausea and vomiting • ankle oedema • livedo reticularis
Anticholinergic agents • benzhexol • benztropine • biperiden • orphenadrine • procyclidine	• dryness of mouth • confusion in elderly • contraindicated in glaucoma and prostatism • other anticholinergic effects, e.g. constipation
Bromocriptine	• nausea and vomiting • dizziness, fatique • psychiatric disturbances • pleuropulmonary changes
Levodopa Levodopa + benserazide Levodopa + carbidopa	• nausea and vomiting • involuntary dyskinetic movements • psychiatric disturbances • on-off phenomena • end of dose failure
Selegiline	• dry mouth • nausea • dizziness, fatigue
Apomorphine (SC injection)	• nausea • psychosis • dyskinesia

and nausea are less problematic but severe psychiatric disturbances are more common with bromocriptine. It should therefore be used with caution in patients with a history of confusion or dementia. Selegiline promises to be an effective first-line drug. If there is associated pain, depression or insomnia, the tricyclic agents, e.g. amitryptiline, can be effective.

Treatment strategy

Mild (minimal disability):

- levodopa preparation (low dose)

Moderate (independent but disabled, e.g. writing, movements, gait):

- levodopa preparation
- add if necessary—bromocriptine or selegiline

Severe (disabled, dependant on others):

- levodopa (to maximum tolerated dose) + bromocriptine or selegiline
- consider antidepressants

Long-term problems

After 3–5 years of levodopa treatment side effects may appear in about one half of patients:[3]

- involuntary movements (use lower dose + bromocriptine)
- end of dose failure (reduced duration of effect to 2–3 hours only)
- ‘on-off’ phenomenon (sudden inability to move with recovery in 30–90 minutes)

Contraindicated drugs

- phenothiazines
- butyrophenones
- MAO inhibitors

Surgical treatment

The indication of surgery (stereotactic thalamotomy)[4] is the presence of tremor or rigidity not responding to chemical therapy. The success rate of surgery is at least 80%. It alleviates tremor and rigidity but does not prevent progression of bradykinesia, dysarthria or dementia. This is a very effective treatment which has often been overlooked but should never be forgotten.

When to refer

If the diagnosis is unclear at the time of initial presentation, it is appropriate either to review the patient at a later date or to refer the patient for more neurological assessment.

Once diagnosed or highly suspected it is best to refer to establish the diagnosis and to seek advice on initiation of treatment. Patients and families usually prefer this approach. In the initial years before motor fluctuations develop, management could be performed by the general practitioner according to an overall plan developed in liaison with a neurological colleague. When fluctuations develop and end-stage diseases manifest (e.g. gait disorders) specialist supervision is appropriate.[1]

Practice tips

- Levodopa is the gold standard for therapy.
- Longer-acting levodopa preparations may reduce the 'end of dose' failure effect but remember the possible need for a 'kick start' with short-acting preparations, e.g. first thing in the morning.
- Ensure that a distinction is made between drug-induced involuntary movements and the tremor of Parkinson's disease.
- Keep the dose of levodopa as low as possible to avoid these drug-induced involuntary movements.
- In the elderly with a fractured hip always consider Parkinson's disease (a manifestation of disequilibrium).
- Remember the balance of psychosis and Parkinson's disease in treatment.
- Don't fail to attend to the needs of the family, who often suffer in silence.

Multiple sclerosis

Multiple sclerosis (MS) is the most common cause of progressive neurological disability in the 20–50 year age group[5]. Early diagnosis is difficult because MS is characterised by widespread neurologic lesions that cannot be explained by a specific anatomical lesion and the various symptoms and signs are subject to irregular exacerbations and remissions. The most important issue in diagnosis is the need for a high index of suspicion.

MS is a primary demyelinating disorder with demyelination occurring in plaques throughout the white matter of the brain, brain stem, spinal cord and optic nerves. The clinical features depend on their location.

Clinical features (Fig. 27.3)

- more common in females
- peak age of onset is in the fourth decade
- transient motor and sensory disturbances
- upper motor neurone signs
- symptoms develop over several days
- monosymptomatic initially in about 80%
- multiple symptoms initially in about 20%
- common initial symptoms include:
  - — visual disturbances of optic neuritis
    - blurred vision or loss of vision in one eye (sometimes both)
    - central scotoma with pain on eye movement (looks like unilateral papilloedema)
  - — diplopia (brain stem lesion)
  - — weakness in one or both legs, paraparesis or hemiparesis
  - — sensory impairment in the lower limbs and trunk
    - numbness, paraesthesia
    - band-like sensations
    - clumsiness of limb (loss of position sense)
    - feeling as though walking on cotton wool
  - — vertigo (brain stem lesion)
- subsequent remissions and exacerbations that vary from one individual to another

Neurological examination

The findings depend on the site of the lesion or lesions and include optic atrophy, weakness, hyper-reflexia, extensor plantar responses, nystagmus (two types: cerebellar or ataxia), ataxia, inco-ordination and regional impairment of sensation.

Symptoms causing diagnostic confusion

- bladder disturbances, including retention of urine
- 'useless hand' due to loss of position sense
- facial palsy
- trigeminal neuralgia
- psychiatric symptoms

In established disease common symptoms are fatigue, impotence and bladder disturbances.

Diagnosis

The diagnosis is clinical and depends on the following determinants:

- lesions are invariably UMN
- lesions affect the CNS white matter
- >1 part of CNS involved, although not necessarily at time of presentation

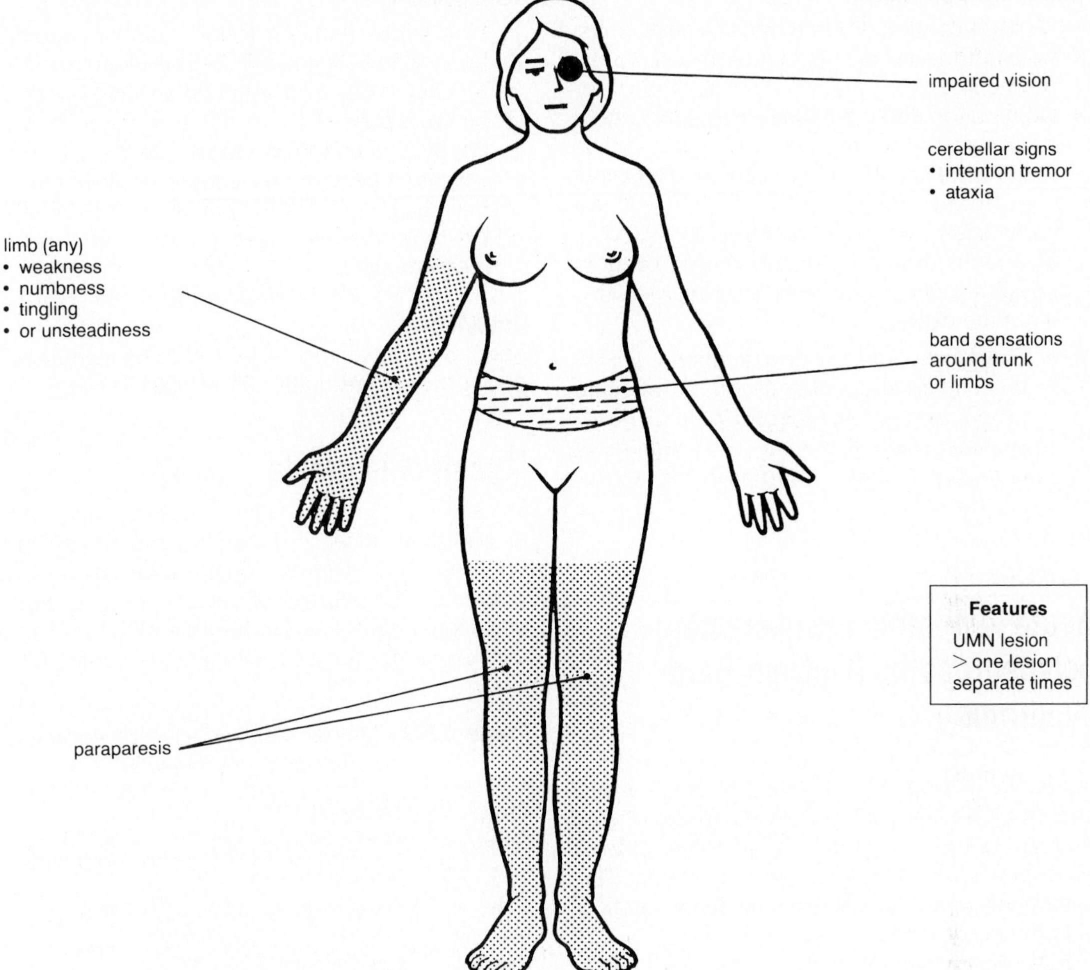

Fig. 27.3 *Basic clinical signs in multiple sclerosis*

- episodes separated in time (it is possible to make a diagnosis with the first episode)

Other neurological diseases such as infections (e.g. encephalitis), malignancies, spinal cord compression, spinocerebellar degeneration and others must be excluded.

Investigations

- Lumbar puncture : oligoclonal IgG detected in CSF in 90% of cases[5]
- Visual evoked potentials : abnormal in about 90% of cases.
- CT scan : rarely demonstrates MS lesions but useful in excluding other pathology
- MRI scan : usually abnormal, demonstrating MS lesions in about 90% of cases[5]

Course and prognosis

- The course is variable and difficult to predict. An early onset (<30) is usually 'benign' while a late onset ($\geqslant 50$) is often 'malignant'.
- MS follows a classical history of relapses and remissions in 80–85% of patients.[6]
- The rate of relapse is about once in two years.
- About 20% have a progressive course from the onset with a progressive spastic paraparesis (applies mainly to late-age onset).
- The average duration of MS is about 30 years from diagnosis to death.[5]
- A benign course occurs in about 40% of patients.
- The likelihood of developing MS after a single episode of optic neuritis is about 60%.

Management principles

- All patients should be referred to a neurologist for confirmation of the diagnosis, which must be accurate.
- Explanation about the disease and its natural history should be given.
- Acute relapses require treatment if causing significant disability. Agents are corticosteroids and corticotrophin (ACTH). Treatment should be introduced as soon as possible and can improve the rate of recovery, if not the degree.

Note: There is no specific drug treatment for MS but certain drugs are useful for specific problems, e.g. baclofen for painful flexor spasms, carbamazepine for trigeminal neuralgia. Beta interferon is under evaluation.

Acute idiopathic demyelinating polyneuropathy (Guillain-Barré syndrome)

Guillain-Barré syndrome is the best known of the peripheral neuropathies that have an acute onset, and it is potentially fatal. Early diagnosis of this serious disease by the family doctor is crucial as respiratory paralysis will lead to death. The underlying pathology is segmental demyelination of peripheral nerves.

Clinical features

- paraesthesiae or pain in the limbs
- weakness in the limbs
- both proximal and distal muscles affected
- facial and bulbar paralysis
- weakness of extraocular muscles (sometimes)
- reflexes depressed or absent
- variable sensory loss

Within 3–4 weeks, the motor neuropathy which is the main feature progresses to a maximum disability, often with complete quadriparesis and respiratory paralysis.[7]

Investigations

- CSF protein is elevated, cells usually normal
- nerve conduction studies abnormal

Management

- Respiratory function (vital capacity) should be measured regularly (2–4 hours at first).
- Tracheostomy and artificial ventilation may be necessary.
- Physiotherapy to prevent foot and wrist drop and other general care should be provided.
- Plasmapheresis is the mainstay of treatment.
- Corticosteroids are not generally recommended.

Outcome

About 80% of patients recover without significant disability. Approximately 5% relapse.[7]

Myasthenia gravis

Myasthenia gravis (MG) is an acquired autoimmune disease. Patients have fluctuating symptoms and variable distribution of muscle weakness. All degrees of severity ranging from occasional mild ptosis to fulminant quadriplegia and respiratory arrest can occur.[8] (See Table 27.3.)

Table 27.3 *Clinical classification of acquired myasthenia gravis (MG)*

Group I	Ocular MG
Group IIA	Mild generalised MG
IIB	Moderate to severe MG
Group III	Acute severe (fulminating) MG with respiratory muscle weakness
Group IV	Late (chronic) severe MG

Clinical features

- painless muscle weakness with exercise
- weakness also precipitated by emotional stress, pregnancy, infection, surgery
- variable distribution of weakness:
  - — ocular • ptosis (60%) and diplopia
    • ocular myasthenia only remains in about 10%
  - — bulbar: weakness of chewing, swallowing, speech, whistling and head lolling
  - — limbs (proximal and distal)
  - — generalised
  - — respiratory: breathlessness, ventilatory failure

Note: The classical MG image is 'the thinker'—the hand used to hold the mouth closed and the head up.

Diagnostic tests

- serum anti-acetylcholine receptor antibodies
- electrophysiological tests if antibody test negative
- CT scan and chest X-ray to detect thymoma

Management principles[8]

- Detect possible presence of thymoma with CT or MR scan of thorax. If present, removal is recommended.
- Thymectomy is recommended early for generalised myasthenia, especially in all younger patients with hyperplasia of the thymus.
- Plasmapheresis : useful for acute crisis or where temporary improvement required or those resistant to treatment.
- Avoid drugs which are relatively contraindicated.
- Pharmacological agents:
  - anticholinesterase drugs, e.g. pyridostigmine, neostigmine or distigmine: should be used only for mild to moderate symptoms
  - corticosteroids: useful for all grades of MG; should be introduced slowly.

Practice tips

- The combination of ocular and facial weakness should alert the family doctor to the possibility of a neuromuscular disorder, especially MG or mytochondrial myopathy.[8] Look for weakness and fatigue.
- Ptosis may develop only after looking upwards for a minute or longer.
- Smiling may have a characteristic snarling quality.

References

1. Iansek R. *Pitfalls in Neurology*. Proceeding of Monash University Medical School Update Course, 1992, 40–44.
2. Morris JGL Essential tremor. In: MIMS Disease Index, Sydney: IMS Publishing, 1991–92, 183–184.
3. Selby G. Parkinson's disease. In: MIMS Disease Index, Sydney: IMS Publishing, 1991-92, 406–410.
4. Selby G. Stereotactic surgery. In: Koller WC ed, *Handbook of Parkinson's disease*. New York: Marcel Dekker Inc., 1987, 421–435.
5. McLeod JR. Multiple sclerosis. In: MIMS Disease Index, Sydney: IMS Publishing, 1991–92, 343–346.
6. Matthews B. Multiple sclerosis. Medicine International 1988, 48, 1961–1967.
7. McLeod J.G. Peripheral neuropathy. Medicine International 1988, 48, 1980–1984.
8. Darveniza P. Myasthenia gravis In: MIMS Disease Index, Sydney: IMS Publishing, 1991-92, 347-349.

PART 3

PROBLEM SOLVING IN GENERAL PRACTICE

28

Abdominal pain

—

Abdominal pain represents one of the top 15 presenting symptoms in primary care[1] and varies from a self-limiting problem to a life-threatening illness requiring immediate surgical intervention. Abdominal pain can be considered to be acute, subacute, chronic or recurrent. It can embrace all specialties including surgery, medicine, gynaecology, geriatrics and psychiatry. For acute abdominal conditions it is important to make a rapid diagnosis in order to reduce morbidity and mortality. Most cases require surgical referral (Table 28.1). Lower abdominal pain in women adds another dimension to the problem and will be presented in a separate chapter.

Table 28.1 *Surgical causes of the acute abdomen*

Process	***Organ involved***	***Disorder***
Inflammation	Bowel	Inflammatory bowel disease
	Appendix	Appendicitis
	Gall bladder	Cholecystitis
	Pancreas	Pancreatitis
	Fallopian tube	Salpingitis
	Colonic diverticulae	Diverticulitis
Perforation	Duodenum	Perforated duodenal ulcer
	Stomach	Perforated gastric ulcer
	Colon (diverticula or carcinoma)	Faecal peritonitis
	Gall bladder	Biliary peritonitis
	Appendix	Appendicitis
Obstruction	Gall bladder	Biliary colic
	Small intestine	Acute small bowel obstruction
	Large bowel	Acute large bowel obstruction
	Ureter	Ureteric colic
	Urethra	Acute urinary retention
	Mesenteric artery occlusion	Intestinal infarction
Haemorrhage	Fallopian tube	Ruptured ectopic pregnancy
	Spleen or liver	Ruptured spleen or liver (haemoperitoneum)
	Ovary	Ruptured ovarian cyst
	Abdominal aorta	Ruptured AAA
Torsion (ischaemia)	Sigmoid colon	Sigmoid volvulus
	Ovary	Torsion ovarian cyst
	Testes	Torsion of testes

Key facts and checkpoints

- The commonest causes of the acute abdomen in two general practice series were: *Series 1* acute appendicitis (31%) and the colics (29%); *Series 2* acute appendicitis (21%), the colics (16%), mesenteric adenitis (16%).[3] The latter study included children.
- As a general rule upper abdominal pain is caused by lesions of the upper GI tract and lower abdominal pain by lesions of the lower GI tract.
- Colicky midline abdominal pain (severe) → vomiting → distension = small bowel obstruction.
- Midline abdominal pain → distension → vomiting = large bowel obstruction.
- If the acute abdomen has a surgical cause, the pain nearly always precedes the vomiting.
- Mesenteric artery occlusion must be considered in an elderly person with arteriosclerotic disease or in patients with atrial fibrillation presenting with severe abdominal pain or following myocardial infarction.

A diagnostic approach

A summary of the separate diagnostic models for acute abdominal pain and chronic abdominal pain are presented in Tables 28.2 and 28.3.

Probability diagnosis

The most common causes of acute abdomen are acute appendicitis, acute gastroenteritis, an irritable bowel syndrome, the various 'colics' and ovulation pain (Mittelschmerz). Mesenteric adenitis is common in children. The various causes of chronic or recurrent abdominal pain are presented in Tables 28.1 and 28.3. A study on chronic abdominal pain[4] showed that the commonest reasons were (approximate percentages): no discoverable causes (50%), minor causes including muscle strains (16%), irritable bowel syndrome (12%), gynaecological causes (8%), peptic ulcers and hiatus hernia (8%).

Serious disorders not to be missed

Most of the causes of the acute abdomen are serious and early diagnosis is mandatory to reduce mortality and morbidity. It is vital not to misdiagnose a ruptured ectopic pregnancy, which causes lower abdominal or suprapubic pain of sudden onset, or the life-threatening vascular causes such as a ruptured or dissecting aortic aneurysm, mesenteric artery occlusion and myocardial infarction (which can present as epigastric pain).

Perforated ulcers and strangulated bowel, such as volvulus of the sigmoid and entrapment of small bowel in a hernial orifice or around adhesions, also demand an early diagnosis.

Table 28.2 *Acute abdominal pain (adults): diagnostic strategy model*

Q. *Probability diagnosis*
A. Acute gastroenteritis
Acute appendicitis
Mittelschmerz
Irritable bowel syndrome

Q. *Serious disorders not to be missed*
A. Cardiovascular
- myocardial infarction
- ruptured AAA
- dissecting aneurysm aorta
- mesenteric artery occlusion

Neoplasia
- large or small bowel obstruction

Severe infections
- acute salpingitis
- peritonitis
- ascending cholangitis
- intra-abdominal abscess

Ectopic pregnancy
Small bowel obstruction
Sigmoid volvulus
Perforated ulcer

Q. *Pitfalls (often missed)*
A. Acute appendicitis
Myofascial tear
Pulmonary causes
- pneumonia
- pulmonary embolism

Faecal impaction (elderly)
Rarities
- porphyria
- lead poisoning
- haemochromatosis
- sickle cell disease
- tabes dorsalis

Q. *Seven masquerades checklist*

A.	
Depression	✓
Diabetes	✓
Drugs	✓
Anaemia	sickle cell
Thyroid disease	—
Spinal dysfunction	✓
UTI	✓

Q. *Is the patient trying to tell me something?*
A. May be very significant.
Consider Munchausen syndrome, sexual dysfunction and abnormal stress.

Table 28.3 *Chronic or recurrent abdominal pain (adult): diagnostic strategy model*

Q. *Probability diagnosis*
A. Irritable bowel syndrome
Mittelschmerz
Peptic ulcer/gastritis

Q. *Serious disorders not to be missed*
A. Cardiovascular
- mesenteric artery ischaemia
- abdominal aortic aneurysm

Neoplasia
- carcinoma bowel/stomach
- carcinoma pancreas
- ovarian tumours

Severe infections
- hepatitis
- recurrent PID

Q. *Pitfalls (often missed)*
A. Food allergies
Lactase deficiency
Constipation
Chronic pancreatitis
Crohn's disease
Endometriosis
Herpes zoster
Diverticulitis
Rarities
- uraemia
- lead poisoning
- Crohn's disease
- porphyria
- sickle cell disease
- Addison's disease

Q. *Seven masquerades checklist*

A.	
Depression	✓
Diabetes	—
Drugs	✓
Anaemia	—
Thyroid disease	—
Spinal dysfunction	✓
UTI	✓

Q. *Is the patient trying to tell me something?*
A. A strong possibility: consider hypochondriasis, anxiety, sexual dysfunction.

There are some important 'red flag' symptoms and signs[1] of abdominal emergencies demanding urgent attention:

- collapsing at toilet (points to intra-abdominal bleeding)
- light-headedness
- progressive intractable vomiting
- progressive abdominal distension
- progressive intensity of pain
- prostration

Signs
- pallor and sweating
- hypotension
- atrial fibrillation or tachycardia
- fever
- rebound tenderness and guarding
- decreased urine output

Dangers of misdiagnosis
- ectopic pregnancy → rapid hypovolaemic shock
- ruptured aortic aneurysm → rapid hypovolaemic shock
- gangrenous appendix → peritonitis/pelvic abscess
- perforated ulcer → peritonitis
- obstructed bowel → gangrene

Pitfalls

A very common pitfall is misdiagnosing acute appendicitis especially in the elderly and in children where the presentation may be atypical. Early appendicitis presents typically with central abdominal pain which shifts to the right iliac fossa (RIF) some 4 to 6 hours later. This causes confusion early on. It can cause diarrhoea with abdominal pain, especially if a pelvic appendix, and can be misdiagnosed as acute gastroenteritis.

Disaccharidase deficiencies such as lactase deficiency are associated with cramping abdominal pain which may be severe. The pain follows some time, maybe hours, after the ingestion of milk and is accompanied by the passage of watery stool. The association with milk may be unrecognised by the patient.

Herpes zoster especially in the elderly patient with unilateral abdominal pain in the dermatomal distribution is a trap. Referred pain from conditions above the diaphragm such as myocardial infarction, pulmonary embolism and pneumonia can be misleading. The rare general medical causes such as diabetes ketoacidosis, acute porphyria, Addison's disease, lead poisoning, tabes dorsalis, sickle cell disease, haemochromatosis and uraemia often create a diagnostic dilemma and should be kept in mind.

Specific pitfalls
- Misdiagnosing a ruptured ectopic pregnancy in the patient on contraception or with a history of normal menstruation or where the brownish vaginal discharge is mistaken for a normal period.
- Failing to examine hernial orifices in a patient with intestinal obstruction.
- Misleading temporary improvement (easing of pain) in perforation of gangrenous appendix or perforated peptic ulcer.

- Overlooking a perforation in the elderly or in patients taking corticosteroids, because of relative lack of pain.
- Overlooking acute mesenteric artery obstruction in an elderly patient with colicky central abdominal pain.
- Attributing abdominal pain, frequency and dysuria to a urinary infection when the cause could be diverticulitis, pelvic appendicitis, salpingitis or a ruptured ectopic pregnancy.

Seven masquerades checklist

Depression, diabetes, drugs, spinal dysfunction and urinary tract infection can all cause abdominal pain although the pain may be more subacute or chronic. Abdominal pain and even tenderness can accompany diabetic ketoacidosis. Drugs that can cause abdominal pain are listed in Table 28.4.

Table 28.4 *Drugs to consider as a cause of abdominal pain*

Alcohol
Antibiotics, e.g. erythromycin
Aspirin
Corticosteroids
Cytotoxic agents
Imipramine
Iron preparations
Nicotine
NSAIDs
Sodium valproate
Phenytoin

Spinal dysfunction of the lower thoracic spine and thoracolumbar junction can cause referred pain to the abdomen (Fig. 28.1). The pain is invariably unilateral, radicular in distribution, and related to activity. It can be confused with intra-abdominal problems such as biliary disease (right-sided), appendicitis and Crohn's disease (right side), diverticular disease (left-sided) and pyelonephritis.

Psychogenic considerations

Psychogenic factors can be most relevant especially in recurrent or chronic abdominal pain where no specific cause can be identified in most cases.[4] Bain and Spaulding found that 40% of presenting adult abdominal pain had non-structural causes with 28% having psychiatric diagnoses and 6% spastic colon. They noted that 'psychological disturbances are often fairly easy to identify if care is taken to obtain the personal history and to assess the patient's personality, but the diagnostic terms used to describe psychological disturbances lack precision'.

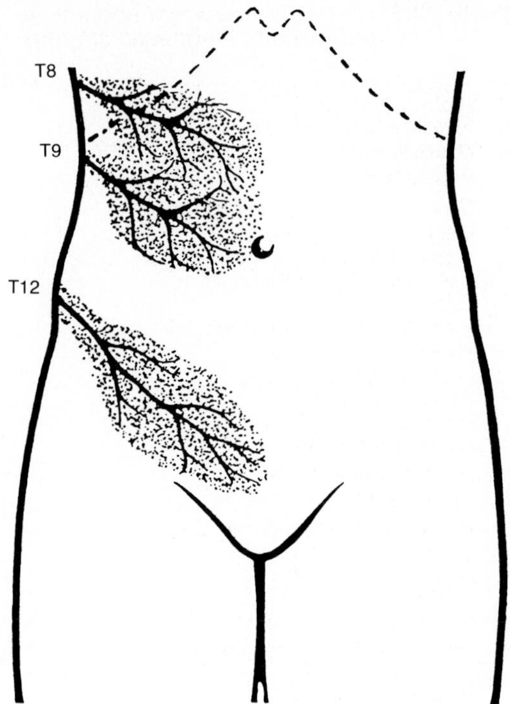

Fig. 28.1 *Referred pain patterns to the anterior abdominal wall from dysfunction of the thoracic spine via anterior cutaneous branches of the nerve roots (right side). Note the possibility of confusion with biliary pain, appendicitis and inguinal disorders*

The clinical approach

History

The urgency of the history will depend on the manner of presentation, whether acute or chronic. Pain has to be analysed according to its quality, quantity, site and radiation, onset, duration and offset, aggravating and relieving factors and associated symptoms and signs.

Special attention has to be paid to:

- anorexia, nausea or vomiting
- micturition
- bowel function
- menstruation
- drug intake

Key questions

Point to where the pain is and where it travels to.
What type of pain is it: is it constant or does it come and go?
How severe would you rate it from 1 to 10?
Have you ever had previous attacks of similar pain?
What else do you notice when you have the pain?
Do you know of anything that will bring on the pain? or relieve it?
What effect does milk, food or antacids have on the pain?
Have you noticed any sweats or chills or burning of urine?
Are your bowels behaving normally? Have you been constipated or had diarrhoea or blood in your motions?
Have you noticed anything different about your urine?
What medications do you take?
How much aspirin do you take?
Are you smoking heavily or taking heroin or cocaine?
How much alcohol do you drink?
How much milk do you drink?
Have you travelled recently?
What is happening with your periods? Is it mid-cycle or are your periods overdue?
Does anyone in your family have bouts of abdominal pain?
Do you have a hernia?
What operations have you had for your abdomen?
Have you had your appendix removed?

Physical examination

A useful checklist for conducting the examination is:

- general appearance
- oral cavity
- vital parameters: temperature, pulse, BP, respiratory rate
- chest: check heart and lungs for upper abdominal pain (especially if absent abdominal signs)
- abdomen: inspection, palpation, percussion and auscultation.

The abdominal examination should be performed with the patient lying flat and the abdomen uncovered from xiphisternum to groin. Consider the following:

- inguinal region (including hernial orifices) and femoral arteries
- rectal examination: mandatory
- vaginal examination (females): for suspected problems of the fallopian tubes, uterus or ovaries
- thoracolumbar spine (if referred spinal pain suspected)
- urine analysis: white cells, red cells, glucose and ketones, porphyrins
- special clinical tests
  - — Murphy's sign (a sign of peritoneal tenderness with acute cholecystitis)
  - — iliopsoas and obturator signs

Guidelines

Palpation: palpate with gentleness—note any guarding or rebound tenderness

- guarding indicates peritonitis
- rebound tenderness indicates peritoneal irritation (bacterial peritonitis, blood). Feel for maximum site which corresponds to focus of the problem.

Patient pain indicator: the finger pointing sign indicates focal peritoneal irritation; the spread palm sign indicates visceral pain.

Atrial fibrillation: consider mesenteric artery obstruction.

Tachycardia: sepsis and volume depletion.

Tachypnoea: sepsis, pneumonia, acidosis.

Pallor and 'shock': acute blood loss.

Physical signs may be reduced in the elderly, grossly obese, severely ill and patients on corticosteroid therapy.

Investigations

The following investigations may be selected:

- haemoglobin—anaemia with chronic blood loss, e.g. peptic ulcer, carcinoma, oesophagitis
- blood film—abnormal red cells with sickle cell disease
- white cell count—leucocytosis with appendicitis (75%),[2] acute pancreatitis, mesenteric adenitis (first day only), cholecystitis (especially with empyema), pyelonephritis
- ESR—raised with carcinoma, Crohn's disease, abscess
- serum amylase—if raised to greater than 5 times normal upper level acute pancreatitis

is most likely; also raised with most intra-abdominal disasters, e.g. ruptured ectopic, perforated peptic ulcers, ruptured empyema of gall bladder, ruptured aortic aneurysm
- pregnancy tests—urine and serum β HCG: for suspected ectopic
- urine:
  - — blood: ureteric colic (stone or blood clot), urinary infection
  - — white cells: urinary infection, appendicitis (bladder irritation)
  - — bile pigments: gall bladder disease
  - — porphobilinogen: porphyria (add Ehrilch's aldehyde reagent)
  - — ketones: diabetic ketoacidosis
  - — air (pneumaturia): fistula, e.g. diverticulitis, other pelvic abscess, pelvic carcinoma
- faecal blood—mesenteric artery occlusion, intussusception ('redcurrent jelly'), carcinoma colon, diverticulitis, Crohn's disease

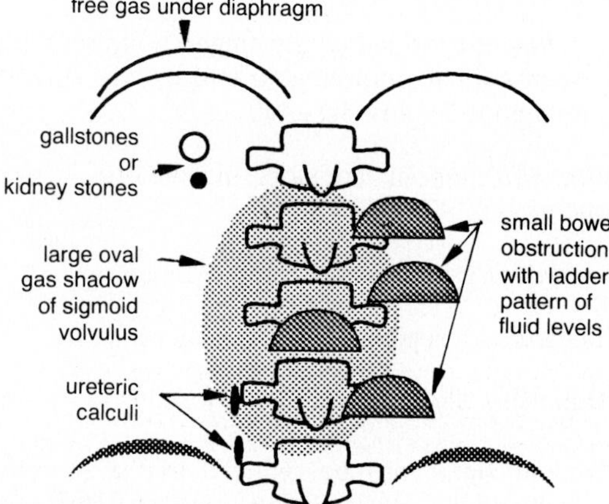

Fig. 28.2 *The acute abdomen: signs to watch for on plain abdominal X-ray*

Radiology

The following tests can be considered, according to the clinical presentation:

- plain X-ray abdomen (erect and supine): look for (Fig. 28.2)
  - — renal/uteric stones—70% opaque[2]
  - — biliary stones—only 10–30% opaque
  - — calcified aortic aneurysm
  - — marked distension sigmoid → sigmoid volvulus
  - — distended bowel with fluid level → bowel obstruction
  - — enlarged caecum with large bowel obstruction
  - — blurred R psoas shadow → appendicitis
  - — a senital loop of gas in LUQ → acute pancreatitis
- chest X-ray: air under diaphragm → perforated ulcer
- ultrasound: look for
  - — gallstones
  - — ectopic pregnancy
  - — pancreatic pseudocyst
  - — aneurysm aorta
  - — hepatic metastases and abdominal tumours
  - — thickened appendix
  - — paracolic collection
- IVP
- barium enema
- HIDA nuclear scan—diagnosis of acute cholecystitis
- CT scan
- ERCP

Other tests:

- ECG
- endoscopy upper GIT
- sigmoidoscopy and colonoscopy

Diagnostic guidelines

General rules

- Upper abdominal pain is caused by lesions of the upper GIT.
- Lower abdominal pain is caused by lesions of the lower GIT or pelvic organs.
- Early severe vomiting indicates a high obstruction of the GIT.
- Acute appendicitis features a characteristic 'march' of symptoms: pain → anorexia → nausea → vomiting

Pain patterns

The pain patterns are presented in Figure 28.3. Colicky pain is a rhythmic pain with regular spasms of recurring pain building to a climax and fading. It is virtually pathognomonic of intestinal obstruction. Ureteric colic is a true colicky abdominal pain, but so-called biliary colic and renal colic are not true colics at all.

Site of pain

Typical pain sites of abdominal pain (general guidelines only) are presented in Figures 28.4 and 28.5. Epigastric pain usually arises from disorders of the embryologic foregut such as the oesophagus, stomach and duodenum,

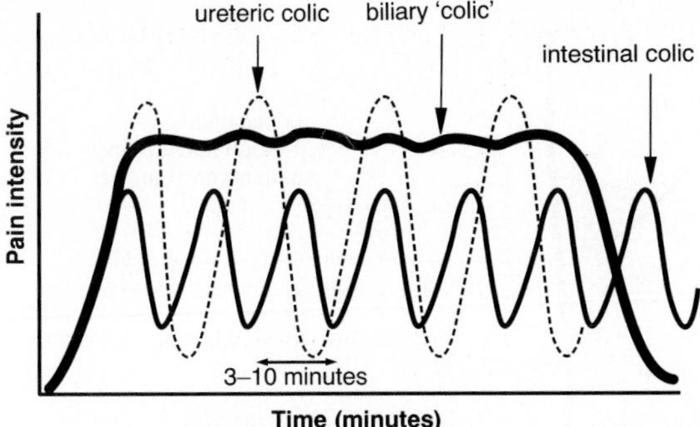

Fig. 28.3 *Characteristic pain patterns for various causes of 'colicky' acute abdominal pain*

hepatobiliary structures, pancreas and spleen. However, as some disorders progress the pain tends to shift from the midline to the right (gall bladder and liver) or left (spleen). Periumbilical pain usually arises from disorders of structures of the embryologic midgut, while structures from the hindgut tend to refer pain to the lower abdomen or suprapubic region.

Abdominal pain in children

Abdominal pain is a common complaint in children, especially recurrent abdominal pain which is one of the most common complaints in childhood. The problem causes considerable anxiety in parents and it is important to differentiate the severe problems demanding surgery from non-surgical problems.

Acute abdominal pain

The causes of abdominal pain can be considered in the diagnostic model category.

1. Common causes/probability diagnosis
   - infantile colic
   - gastroenteritis
   - mesenteric adenitis
2. Serious causes, not to be missed
   - intussusception
   - acute appendicitis
   - bowel obstruction
3. Pitfalls
   - constipation
   - torsion of testes
   - lactose intolerance
   - peptic ulcer
   - infections
     — mumps
     — tonsillitis
     — pneumonia
     — Epstein-Barr mononucleosis
     — urinary tract infection

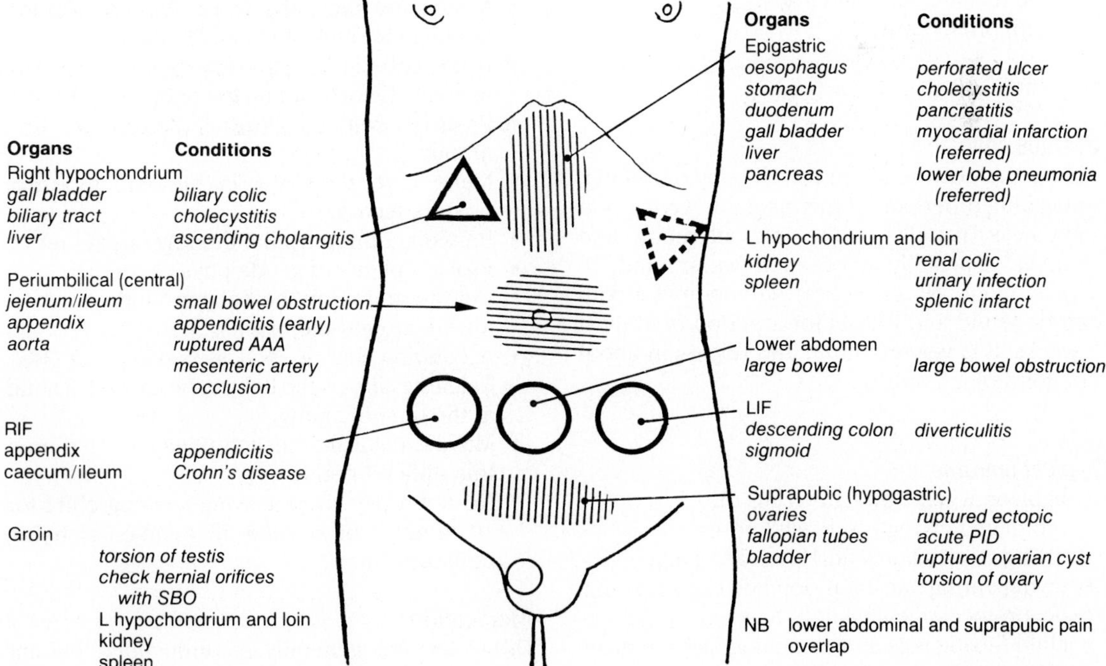

Fig. 28.4 *Typical sites of various causes of acute abdominal pain*

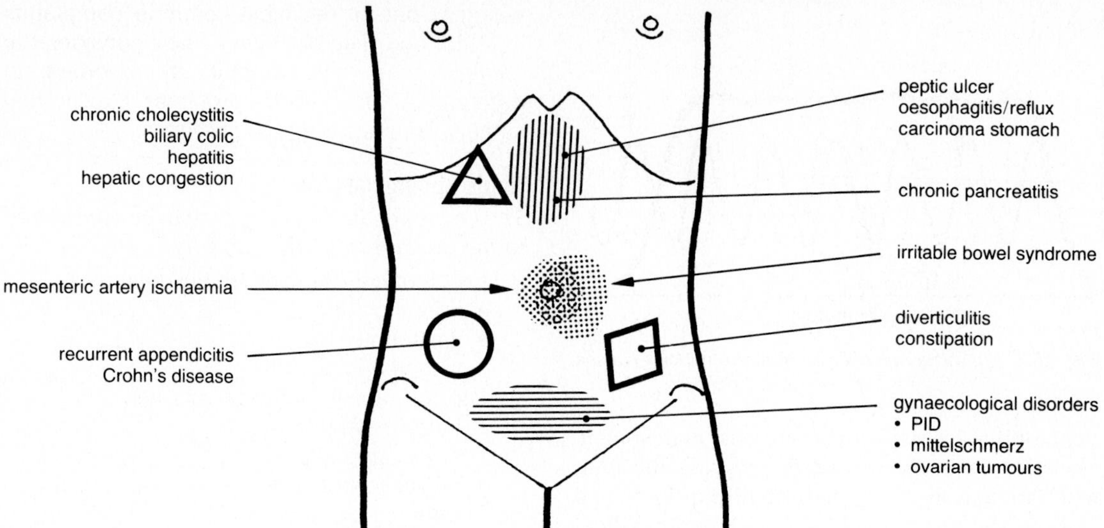

Fig. 28.5 *Typical sites of various causes of chronic or recurrent abdominal pain*

Rarities
- Meckel's diverticulitis
- Henoch-Schönlein purpura
- sickle crisis
- lead poisoning

4. Seven masquerades checklist
   - diabetes mellitus
   - drugs
5. Psychogenic consideration
   - important cause

Infantile colic

This is the occurrence in a well baby of regular, unexplained periods of inconsolable crying and fretfulness, usually in the late afternoon and evening, especially between 2 weeks and 16 weeks of age. No cause for the abdominal pain can be found and it lasts for a period of at least 3 weeks. It is very common and occurs in about one-third of infants.

Typical features

- baby between 2 and 16 weeks old
- prolonged crying—at least 3 hours
- crying worst at around 10 weeks of age
- crying during late afternoon and early evening
- occurrence at least 3 days a week
- child flexing legs and clenching fists because of the 'stomach ache'
- normal physical examination

Management

Reassurance and explanation to the parents. Advice for the parents:

- Use gentleness (such as subdued lighting where the baby is handled, soft music, speaking softly, quiet feeding times).
- Avoid quick movements that may startle the baby.
- Make sure the baby is not hungry—underfeeding can make the baby hungry.
- If the baby is breast-fed, express the watery foremilk before putting the baby to the breast.
- Provide demand feeding (in time and amount).
- Make sure the baby is burped, and give posture feeding.
- Provide comfort from a dummy or pacifier.
- Provide plenty of gentle physical contact.
- Cuddle and carry the baby around (e.g. take a walk around the block).
- A carrying device such as 'snuggly' or 'Meh Tai Sling' allows the baby to be carried around at the time of crying.
- Make sure the mother gets plenty of rest during this difficult period.
- Do not worry about leaving a crying child for 10 minutes or so after 15 minutes of trying consolation.

Medication

Drugs are not generally recommended but for very severe problems some preparations can be very helpful, e.g. simethicone preparations.

Intussusception

Intussusception is the diagnosis that should be foremost in one's mind with a child aged between 5 months and 2 years presenting with sudden onset of severe colicky abdominal pain, coming at intervals of about 15 minutes and lasting 2–3 minutes. Early diagnosis, within 24 hours of the onset, is essential, for after this time there is a significant rise in morbidity and mortality. It is due to telescoping of the segment of bowel into the adjoining distal segment, e.g. ileocaecal segment, resulting in intestinal obstruction.

Typical clinical features (Fig. 28.6)

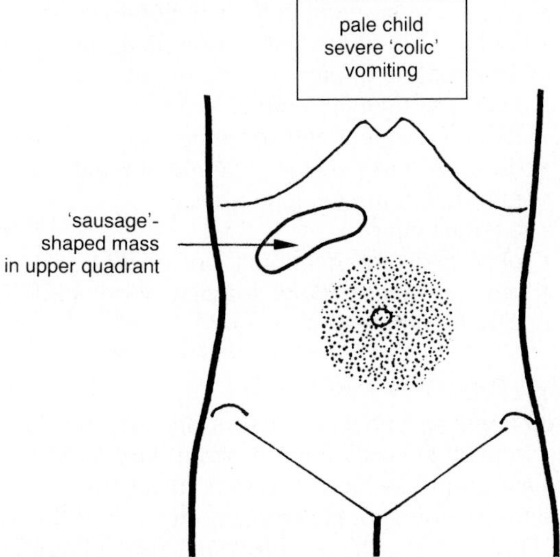

Fig. 28.6 *Typical features with pain distribution of acute intussusception*

- male babies > female
- age 6–12 months
- range: birth to school age, usually 5–24 months
- sudden onset acute pain with shrill cry
- vomiting
- pallor with attacks
- intestinal bleeding: redcurrant jelly (60%)[6]

Physical signs

- pale, anxious and unwell
- sausage-shaped mass in RUQ, especially during attacks (difficult)
- signe de dance, i.e. emptiness in RIF to palpation
- alternating high-pitched active bowel sounds with absent sounds
- rectal examination: ± blood

Diagnosis

- barium enema

Treatment

- hydrostatic reduction by barium enema under radiological control or hydrostatic reduction with oxygen
- surgical intervention may be necessary

Differential diagnosis

- Acute gastroenteritis: can be difficult in those cases where there is some loose stool with intussusception and with blood and mucus without much watery stool in gastroenteritis. However, usually, attacks of pain are of shorter duration, there is loose watery stool, fever and no abdominal mass. If doubtful refer as possible intussusception.
- Impacted faeces can lead to spasms of colicky abdominal pain; usually an older child with a history of constipation.
- Other causes of intestinal obstruction, e.g. irreducible inguinal hernia, volvulus, intra-abdominal band.

Drugs

In any child complaining of acute abdominal pain, enquiry should be made into drug ingestion. A common cause of colicky abdominal pain in children is cigarette smoking (nicotine); consider other drugs such as marijuana, cocaine and heroin.

Acute appendicitis in children

This may occur at any age, being more common in children of school age and in adolescence and uncommon under 3 years of age. Special problems of early diagnosis occur with the very young (less than 3 years) and in mentally retarded children, many of whom present with peritonitis.

Vomiting occurs in at least 80% of children with appendicitis and diarrhoea in about 20%. The temperature is usually only slightly elevated but in about 5% of cases it is in excess of 39°C.[1]

In children the physical examination, especially eliciting abdominal including rebound tenderness, and the rectal examination demand considerable tact, patience and gentleness.

A serious point of confusion can occur between pelvic appendicitis, causing diarrhoea and vomiting, and acute gastroenteritis. A particularly severe case of apparent gastroenteritis, especially if persistent, should be regarded as pelvic appendicitis until proved otherwise.

Mesenteric adenitis

This presents a difficult problem in differential diagnosis with acute appendicitis because the history can be very similar. At times the distinction may be almost impossible. In general, with mesenteric adenitis localisation of pain and tenderness is not as definite, rigidity is less of a feature, the temperature is higher and anorexia, nausea and vomiting are also lesser features. The illness lasts about five days followed by a rapid recovery. Comparisons between the two are presented in Table 28.5 but if in any doubt it is advisable to consider the problem as acute appendicitis and perhaps proceed to laparotomy.

Mesenteric adenitis can sometimes present an anaesthetic risk and patients are usually quite ill in the immediate postoperative period.

Recurrent abdominal pain

Recurrent abdominal pain (RAP) occurs in 10% of school-aged children. In only 5–10% of children will an organic cause be found so that in most the cause remains obscure.[8]

Organic causes

An organic cause, however, must be considered and excluded. Organic disease is more likely if:

- the pain is other than periumbilical
- the pain radiates rather than remains localised
- the pain wakens the child from sleep
- the pain is accompanied by vomiting
- the child is not completely well between attacks
- there is associated weight loss
- there is failure to thrive

Possible causes

- childhood migraine equivalent (pain with extreme pallor)
- lactose intolerance (symptoms related to milk ingestion)
- intestinal parasites (may disturb child about 60 minutes after falling asleep)

Investigations

- stool microscopy and culture
- urine analysis
- full blood count and ESR

Non-organic RAP

Typical clinical features:

- acute and frequent colicky abdominal pain
- localised to or just above umbilicus
- no radiation of pain
- lasts less than 60 minutes
- nausea frequent and vomiting rare
- diurnal (never wakes the child at night)
- minimal umbilical tenderness
- anxious child
- obsessive or perfectionist personality
- one or both parents intense about child's health and progress

Psychogenic factors

Although psychogenic factors are very relevant in individual cases there is scant hard evidence to support the widely held hypothesis[8] that such factors account for the vast majority of RAP. Some children will have obvious psychological problems or even be school avoidant, a common factor being family disruption.

Table 28.5 *Comparison of the features of acute appendicitis and mesenteric adenitis in children (guidelines only)*

	Acute appendicitis	**Mesenteric adenitis**
Typical child	older	younger
Site of onset of pain	midline shifting to right	RIF can be midline
Preceding respiratory illness	uncommon	invariable: URTI or tonsillitis
Anorexia, nausea, vomiting	++	±
Colour	usually pale	flushed: malar flush
Temperature	N or ↑	↑↑ → ↑↑↑
Abdominal palpation	tender in RIF guarding ± rigidity	tender in RIF minimal guarding usually no rigidity
Rectal examination	invariably tender	often tender but lesser degree
Psoas and obturator tests	usually positive	usually negative

Managment options

- Give explanation, reassurance and support.
- Reassurance can only be given following a careful examination and thoughtfully chosen investigations.
- Emphasise that the disorder is common, and usually traverses childhood without ill effects.
- Identify any life stresses and provide insight therapy.
- Enquire about family structures and function and school performance.
- Discourage identification with the sick role.
- Refer for psychological assessment and counselling if necessary.

Abdominal pain in the elderly

The elderly can suffer from a wide spectrum of disorders. Ischaemic events, emboli, cancer (in particular) and diverticulae of the colon are more common in old age; duodenal ulcer is less so. Those causes of abdominal pain that occur with more frequency include:

- vascular catastrophies
  - — ruptured abdominal aortic aneurysm
  - — mesenteric artery occlusion
- perforated peptic ulcer
- biliary disorders: bilary pain and acute cholecystitis
- diverticulitis
- sigmoid volvulus
- strangulated hernia
- intestinal obstruction
- carcinoma, especially of the colon
- herpes zoster, causing unilateral root pain
- constipation and faecal impaction

Problems arise with management because the pain threshold is raised (colic in particular is less severe) and there is an attenuated response to infection so that fever and leucocytosis can be absent. Non-specific signs such as confusion, anorexia and tachycardia might be the only systemic evidence of infection.

Specific causes of acute abdominal pain

Abdominal aortic aneurysm (AAA)

AAAs may be asymptomatic until they rupture or may present with abdominal discomfort and a pulsatile mass noted by the patient. There tends to be a family history and thus screening is appropriate in such families. Ultrasound screening is advisable in first-degree relatives over 50 years.

The risk of rupture is related to the diameter of the AAA and the rate of increase in diameter. The normal diameter of the abdominal aorta, which is palpated just above the umbilicus, is 10–30 mm, being 20 mm on average in the adult; an aneurysm is greater than 30 mm in diameter. Greater than 50 mm is significantly enlarged and is chosen as the arbitrary reference point to operate because of the exponential rise in risk of rupture with an increasing diameter. The patency of a dacron graft after five years is approximately 95% (Fig. 28.7).

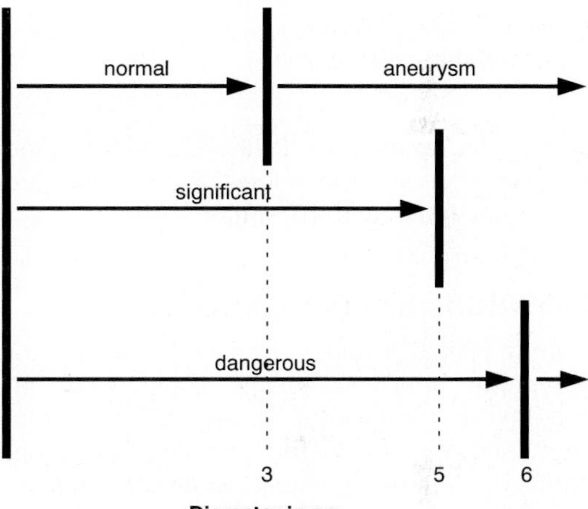

Fig. 28.7 *Guidelines for normal and abnormal widths of the abdominal aorta in adults (to exact scale)*

Investigations

- ultrasound (good for screening)
- CT scan (clearer imaging)
- MRI scan (best definition)

Rupture of aneurysm

This is a real surgical emergency in an elderly person who presents with acute abdominal and perhaps back pain with associated circulatory collapse (Fig. 28.8). The patient often collapses at toilet because they feel the need to defaecate and the resultant Valsalva manoeuvre causes circulatory embarrassment.

The patient should be transferred immediately to a vascular surgical unit which should be notified in advance. Two important emergency measures for the 'shocked' patient are

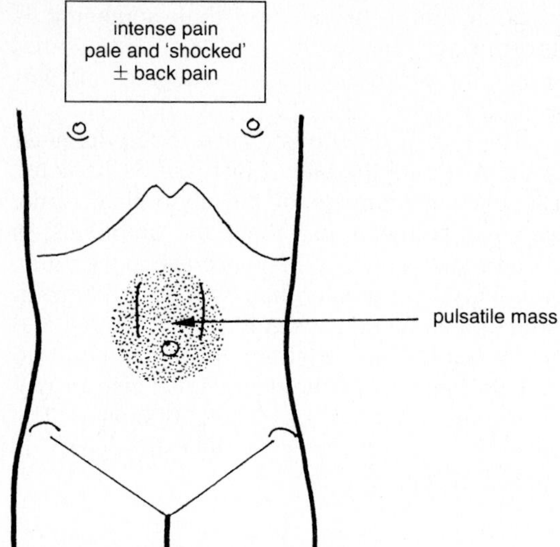

Fig. 28.8 *Typical pain distribution of a ruptured aortic abdominal aneurysm*

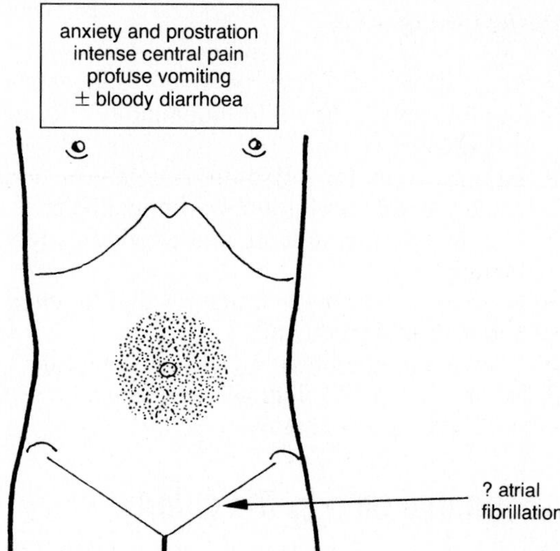

Fig. 28.9 *Typical pain distribution of mesenteric arterial occlusion*

intravenous access for plasma expanding fluid (a central venous line is best if possible) and the application of a MAST suit.

Mesenteric artery occlusion

Acute intestinal ischaemia arises from superior mesenteric artery occlusion either from an embolus or thrombosis in an atherosclerotic artery. Another cause is an embolus from atrial fibrillation. Necrosis of the intestine soon follows if intervention is delayed.

Typical clinical features

- abdominal pain gradually becomes intense (Fig. 28.9)
- profuse vomiting
- watery diarrhoea—blood in one-third of patients(later)

Signs

- localised tenderness, rigidity and rebound over infarcted bowel (later finding)
- absent bowel sounds (later)
- shock develops later
- tachycardia (maybe atrial fibrillation and other signs of atheroma)

X-ray (plain): shows 'thumb printing' due to mucosal oedema on gas-filled bowel. CT scanning may be helpful while mesenteric arteriography is performed if embolus is suspected.

Management

Early surgery may prevent gut necrosis but massive resection of necrosed gut may be required as a life-saving procedure. Early diagnosis (within a few hours) is essential.

Note Mesenteric venous thrombosis can occur but usually in patients with circulatory failure.
Inferior mesenteric artery occlusion is less severe and survival more likely.

Acute retention of urine

Acute retention of urine usually causes severe lower abdominal pain which may not be apparent in a senile or demented person. Apart from the common cause of an enlarged prostate it can also result from bladder neck obstruction by faecal loading or other pelvic masses or anticholinergic drugs. It is often precipitated by extreme cold or an excess of alcohol.

Management

- Perform a rectal examination and empty rectum of any impacted faecal material.
- Catheterise with size 14 Foley catheter to relieve obstruction and drain.
- Have the catheter *in situ* and seek a urological opinion.
- If there is any chance of recovery, e.g. if the problem is drug-induced: withdraw drug, leave catheter in for 48 hours, remove and give trial of prazosin 0.5 mg bd.

Faecal impaction

Faecal impaction is encountered typically in the aged, bedridden, debilitated patient. It may closely resemble malignant obstruction in its clinical presentation.[9] Spurious diarrhoea can occur, which is known as 'faecal incontinence'.

Acute appendicitis

Acute appendicitis is mainly a condition of young adults but affects all ages (although uncommon under 3 years). It is the commonest surgical emergency and special care has to be taken with the very young and the very old. The symptoms can vary because of the different positions of the appendix.

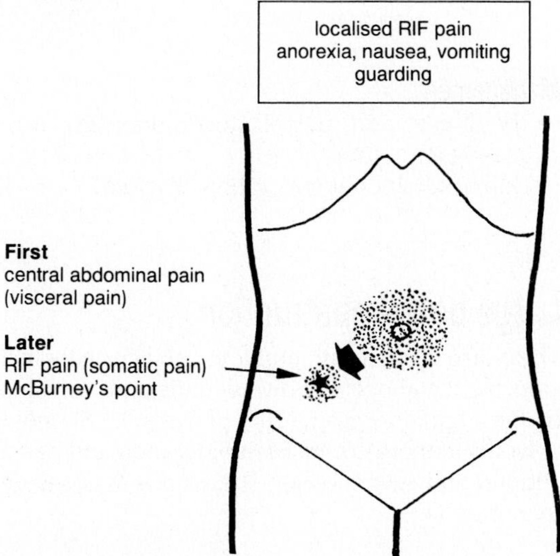

Fig. 28.10 *Typical pain distribution for acute appendicitis*

Typical clinical features (Fig. 28.10)

- maximum incidence 20–30 years
- initial pain is central abdominal (sometimes colicky)
- increasing severity and then continuous
- shifts and localises to RIF within 6 hours
- may be aggravated by walking (causing a limp) or coughing
- sudden anorexia
- nausea and vomiting a few hours after the pain starts

Signs

- patient looks unwell
- flushed at first, then pale
- furred tongue and halitosis
- may be febrile
- tenderness in RIF, usually at McBurney's point
- local rigidity and rebound tenderness
- guarding
- ± superficial hyperaesthesia
- ± psoas sign: pain on resisted flexion of leg or on hip extension (due to irritation of psoas especially with retrocaecal appendix)
- ± obturator sign: pain on flexing patient's right thigh at the hip with the knee bent and then internally rotating the hip (due to irritation of internal obturator muscle)

PR: tenderness to right, especially if pelvic appendix or pelvic peritonitis.

Variations and cautions

- abscess formation → localised mass and tenderness
- retrocaecal appendix: pain and rigidity less and may be no rebound tenderness; loin tenderness; positive psoas test
- pelvic appendix: no abdominal rigidity; urinary frequency; diarrhoea and tenesmus; very tender PR; obturator tests usually positive
- elderly patients: pain often minimal and eventually manifests as peritonitis; can simulate intestinal obstruction
- pregnancy (occurs mainly during second trimester): pain is higher and more lateral; harder to diagnose; peritonitis more common
- perforation more likely in the very young, the aged and the diabetic.

Investigations

Few investigations are of value:

- blood cell count shows a leucocytosis (75%) with a left shift
- plain X-ray: may show local distension, blurred psoas shadow and fluid level in caecum
- ultrasound shows a thickened appendix

Management

Immediate referral for surgical removal.

Small bowel obstruction

The symptoms depend on the level of the obstruction (Table 28.6). The more proximal the obstruction the more severe the pain.

Table 28.6 *Small bowel obstruction: difference between a high and a low obstruction*

	High	*Low*
Frequency of spasms	3–5 minutes	6–10 minutes
Intensity of pain	+ + +	+
Vomiting	early, frequent violent	later less severe
content:	gastric juices then green	feculent (later)
Dehydration and degree of illness	marked	less prominent
Distension	minimal	marked

Main causes

- outside obstruction, e.g. adhesions, strangulation in hernia or pockets of abdominal cavity
- lumen obstructions, e.g. foreign body, trichobezoar, gallstones, intussusception, malignancy

Typical clinical features

- severe colicky epigastric and periumbilical (mainly) pain (Fig. 28.11)
- spasms last about 1 minute
- spasms every 3–10 minutes (according to level)
- vomiting
- absolute constipation (nil after bowel emptied)
- no flatus
- abdominal distension (especially if lower SBO)

Signs

- patient weak and sitting forward in distress
- visible peristalsis, loud borborygmi
- abdomen soft (except with strangulation)
- tender when distended
- increased sharp tinkling bowel sounds
- dehydration rapidly follows, especially in children and elderly

PR: empty rectum, may be tender
NB: check all hernial orifices including umbilicus
X-ray: 'stepladder' fluid levels in 3–4 hours (erect film)

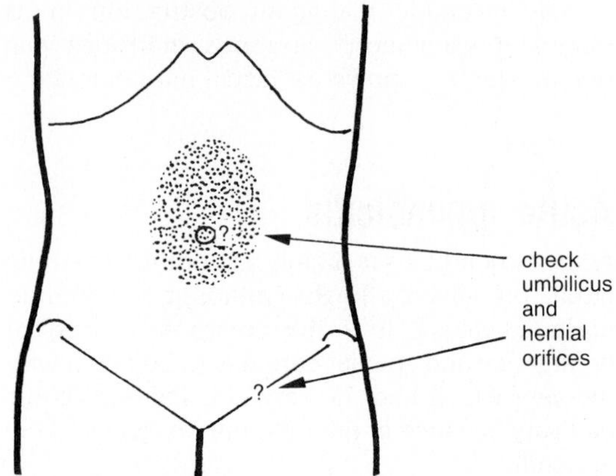

Fig. 28.11 *Typical pain distribution for small bowel obstruction*

Management

- IV fluids and bowel decompression with nasogastric tube
- laparotomy (not for Crohn's disease)

Large bowel obstruction

The cause is often carcinoma, especially on the left side, but it can occur in diverticulitis or in volvulus of the sigmoid colon (10% of cases).[9] Sigmoid volvulus is more common in older men and has a sudden and severe onset. The pain is less severe than in SBO.

Typical clinical features

- sudden onset colicky pain (even with carcinoma)
- each spasm lasts less than 1 minute
- usually hypogastric midline pain (Fig. 28.12)
- vomiting may be absent (or late)
- constipation, no flatus

Signs

- increased bowel sounds, especially during pain
- distension early and marked
- local tenderness and rigidity

PR: empty rectum; may be rectosigmoid carcinoma or blood. Check for faecal impaction.

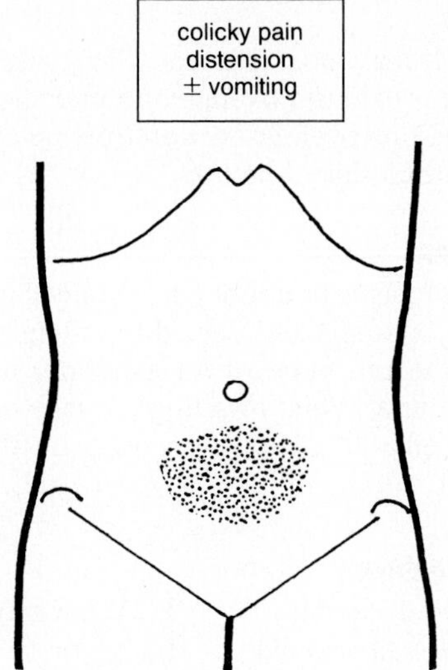

Fig. 28.12 *Typical pain distribution for large bowel obstruction*

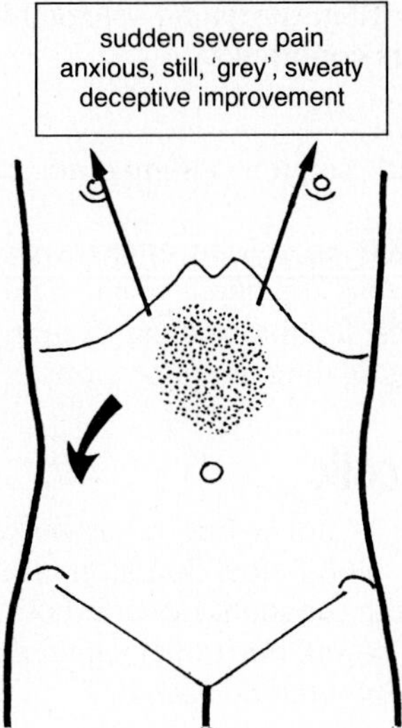

Fig. 28.13 *Typical features of perforated peptic ulcer*

X-ray: Distension of large bowel with separation of haustral markings, especially caecal distension.
Sigmoid volvulus shows a distended loop.

Management

Surgical referral.

Perforated peptic ulcer

Perforation of a peptic ulcer can cause acute abdominal pain both with and without a prior history of peptic ulcer. It is an acute surgical emergency requiring immediate diagnosis. Consider a history of drugs, especially NSAIDs and H_2 antagonists. Perforated ulcers may follow a heavy meal. There is usually no back pain.

The maximal incidence is 45–55 years, most common in males, and a perforated duodenal ulcer is more common than a gastric ulcer.

Consider the clinical syndrome in 3 stages:

1. prostration
2. reaction (after 2–6 hours)—symptoms improve
3. peritonitis (after 6–12 hours)

Typical clinical features (Fig. 28.13)

- sudden onset severe epigastric pain
- continuous pain but lessens for a few hours
- epigastric pain at first, then generalised to whole abdomen
- pain may radiate to one or both shoulders (uncommon) or right lower quadrant
- nausea and vomiting (delayed)
- hiccough is a common late symptom

Signs

- patient lies quietly (pain aggravated by movement and coughing)
- pale, sweating or ashen at first
- board-like rigidity
- guarding
- maximum signs at point of perforation
- no abdominal distension
- contraction of abdomen (forms a 'shelf' over lower chest)
- bowel sounds reduced (silent abdomen)
- shifting dullness may be present
- pulse, temperature and BP usually normal at first
- tachycardia (later) and shock later (3–4 hours)
- breathing is shallow and inhibited by pain

PR: pelvic tenderness
X-ray: chest X-ray may show free air under diaphragm (in 75%)—need to sit upright for prior 15 minutes.

Special problems

- Beware of easing of pain as peritoneal fluid accumulates.
- Elderly patients may have minimal pain.
- Painless perforation can occur with steroids.

- Avoid giving morphine or pethidine until diagnosis confirmed.

Management

- drip and suction (immediate nasogastric tube)
- immediate laparotomy after resuscitation
- conservative treatment may be possible, e.g. later presentation and gastrografin swallow indicates sealing of perforation

Ureteric colic

Renal colic is not a true colic but a constant pain due to blood clots or a stone lodged at the pelvic-ureteric junction; ureteric colic, however, presents as severe true colicky pain due to stone movement and ureteric spasm.

Typical clinical features

- maximum incidence 30–50 years (M > F)
- intense colicky pain
- begins in loin and radiates around the flank to the groin, thigh, testicle, or labia (Fig. 28.14)
- usually lasts < 8 hours
- ± vomiting

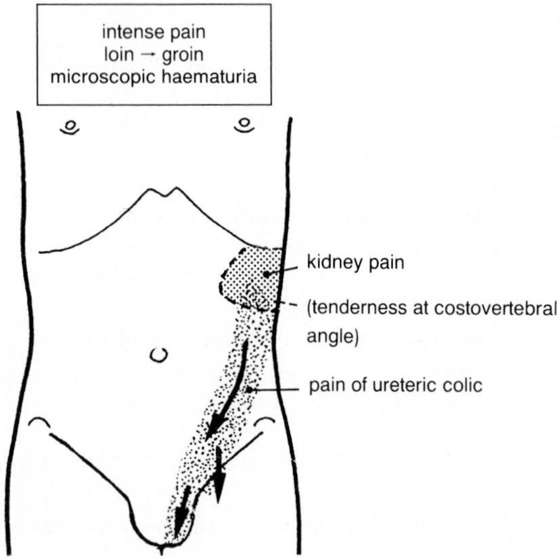

Fig. 28.14 *Ureteric colic: typical radiation of pain in left ureteric colic*

Signs

- patient restless: may be writhing in pain
- pale, cold and clammy
- tenderness at costovertebral angle
- ± abdominal and back muscle spasm
- smoky urine due to haematuria

Diagnosis

- plain X-ray: most stones (75%) are radio-opaque (calcium oxalate and phosphate)
- intravenous pyelogram: confirms opacity and indicates kidney function

Management

If the diagnosis is in doubt (especially if narcotic addiction is suspected) get the patient to pass urine in the presence of an examiner and test for haematuria. While awaiting passage of urine, an indomethacin suppository may be tried for pain relief.

Routine treatment

- Pethidine 100 mg (average size adult) and metoclopramide 10 mg } IM injection or IV titration 50 mg (preferable)
- Liberal fluids and exercise.
- Most cases settle and the patient can go home when pain relief is obtained and an intravenous pyelogram (IVP) arranged for the next day.
- Further pain can be alleviated by indomethacin suppositories but should be limited to 2 a day.

Outcome and follow-up

- The calculus is likely to pass spontaneously if < 5 mm (90% < 4 mm pass spontaneously[10]).
- If > 5 mm intervention will usually be required by lithotripsy or surgery.
- If the patient passes the calculus, he/she should retrieve it and present it for analysis.
- A repeat IVP may be necessary if there is evidence of obstruction for more than 3 weeks.
- The cause of the 'stone' should be considered. Search for causes such as hyperparathyroidism or hypercalcaemia.
- Fever with ureteric colic indicates an obstructed infected kidney.

Biliary pain

Abdominal pain can be produced by contraction of the biliary tree upon an obstructing stone or inspissated bile. Although the sterotyped patient is female, forty, fat, fair and fertile it can occur from adolescence to old age and in both sexes.

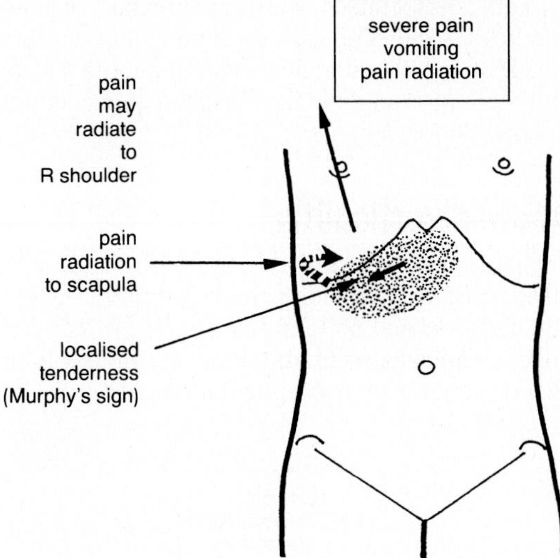

Fig. 28.15 *Typical site of pain of biliary colic and acute cholecystitis*

Typical clinical features (Fig. 28.15)

- acute onset severe pain
- constant pain (not colicky)
- lasts 20 minutes to 6 hours
- maximal RUQ or epigastrium
- may radiate to tip of right shoulder or scapula
- painful episode builds to a crescendo for about 20 minutes; may recede or last for hours
- some relief by assuming flexed posture
- nausea and vomiting with considerable retching
- often a history of biliary pain (may be mild) or jaundice

Signs

- patient anxious and restless, usually in a flexed position or rolling in agony
- localised tenderness (Murphy's sign) over fundus of gall bladder (on transpyloric plane)
- slight rigidity

Diagnosis

- abdominal ultrasound/HIDA
- intravenous cholangiography if previous cholecystectomy
- LFTs may show elevated bilirubin and alkaline phosphatase

Management

- gallstone dissolution or lithotripsy
- cholecystectomy (main procedure)

Acute cholecystitis

Cholecystitis is associated with gallstones in over 90% of cases[11] and there is usually a past history of biliary pain. It occurs when a calculus becomes impacted in the cystic duct and inflammation develops. It is very common in the elderly. The acute attack is often precipitated by a large or fatty meal.

Typical clinical features

- steady severe pain and tenderness
- localised to right hypochondrium or epigastrium
- nausea and vomiting (bile) in about 75%
- aggravated by deep inspiration

Signs

- patient tends to lie still
- localised tenderness over gall bladder (positive Murphy's sign)
- muscle guarding
- rebound tenderness
- palpable gall bladder (approximately 15%)
- jaundice (approximately 15%)

Diagnosis

- ultrasound: gallstones but not specific for cholecystitis
- HIDA scan: demonstrates obstructed cystic duct—the usual cause

Treatment

- rest in bed
- IV fluids
- nil orally
- analgesics
- antibiotics
- cholecystectomy

Acute pancreatitis

With acute pancreatitis there may be a past history of previous attacks or a past history of alcoholism (35%) or gallstone disease (40–50%).

Typical clinical features (Fig. 28.16)

- sudden onset of severe epigastric pain
- pain may radiate to back
- nausea and vomiting
- sweating and weakness

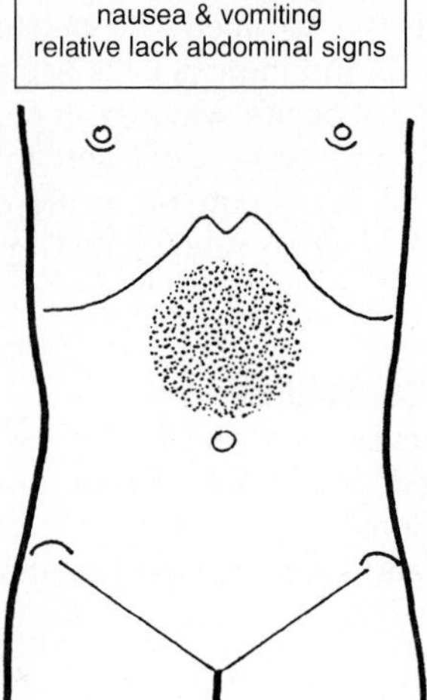

severe pain
nausea & vomiting
relative lack abdominal signs

Fig. 28.16 *Typical pain distribution of acute pancreatitis*

Signs

- patient is weak, pale, sweating and anxious
- tender in epigastrium
- lack of guarding, rigidity or rebound
- reduced bowel sounds (may be absent if ileus)
- ± abdominal distension
- fever, tachycardia

Diagnosis

- WCC—leucocytosis
- serum amylase (usually 5-fold increase)
- plain X-ray, may be senital loop
- CT scan
- ultrasound better for detecting cysts

Management

- Arrange admission to hospital.
- Basic treatment is bed rest, nil orally, nasogastric suction (if vomiting), IV fluids and analgesics (pethidine, not morphine).

Chronic pancreatitis

In contrast to acute pancreatitis the pain of chronic pancreatitis is milder but more persistent. The patient with this problem is often labelled as 'gastritis', 'ulcer' or 'neurotic' because of the indeterminate nature of the pain. Malabsorption and diabetes may result from pancreatitis and weight loss and steatorrhoea become prominent features.

Pain associated with carcinoma of the pancreas is indistinguishable from that of chronic pancreatitis but generally tends to be more severe and more prominent in the back. Use paracetamol or codeine for pain.

Acute diverticulitis

The patient with acute diverticulitis is usually over 40 years of age, with longstanding grumbling left-sided abdominal pain and constipation, but can have irregular bowel habit. It occurs in less than 10% of patients with diverticular disease.[2]

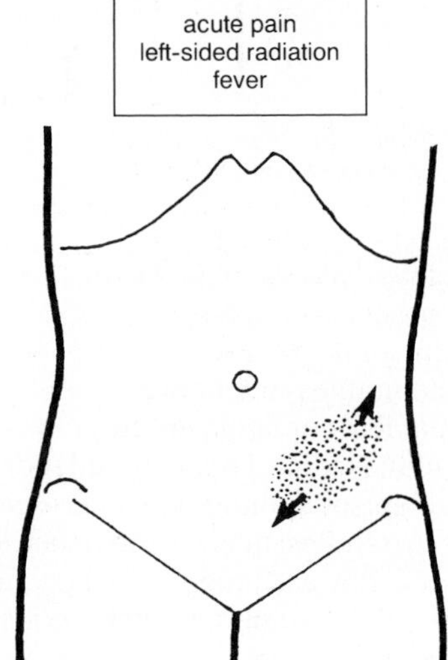

Fig. 28.17 *Typical pain distribution of acute diverticulitis*

Typical clinical features (Fig. 28.17)

- acute onset of pain in the left iliac fossa
- pain increased with walking and change of position
- usually associated with constipation

Signs

- tenderness, guarding and rigidity in LIF
- fever
- may be inflammatory mass in LIF

Investigations

- leucocytosis
- elevated ESR
- pus and blood in stools
- abdominal ultrasound/CT scan

Complications

- bleeding (can be profuse, especially in elderly)
- perforation (high mortality)
- abscess
- peritonitis
- fistula (bladder, vagina, small bowel)
- intestinal obstruction

Treatment

- antibiotics
- surgery for complications

When to refer

- all cases of acute abdominal pain where urgent surgical intervention is required. Special urgency and early diagnosis is important with:
  - — ruptured ectopic pregnancy
  - — ruptured abdominal aortic aneurysm
  - — mesenteric artery occlusion
  - — ruptured viscus
  - — perforated peptic ulcer
  - — strangulated bowel
  - — intussusception
- all cases where the diagnosis is not apparent
- all cases where surgery is necessary
- medical causes such as diabetic ketoacidosis and porphyria

Practice tips

- Special caution is required at the extremes of age when the symptoms and signs do not often reflect the seriousness of the underlying pathology.
- If an elderly patient presents with intense acute abdominal pain, inadequately relieved by strong parenteral injections, likely causes include mesenteric artery occlusion, acute pancreatitis and ruptured or dissecting aortic aneurysm.
- When an inflamed appendix ruptures the abdominal pain improves for a significant period of time.
- A false sense of security can also occur with a perforated ulcer.
- Pus cells and red cells may be present in the urine with appendicitis when a pelvic appendix involves the bladder and a retrocaecal appendix involves the ureter.
- Consider diabetic ketoacidosis in a patient with abdominal pain, tenderness and rigidity and deep sighing respiration.

References

1. Sloane PD, Slatt LM, Baker RM. *Essentials of family medicine*. Baltimore: Williams and Wilkins, 1988, 135–141.
2. Sandler G, Fry J. Acute abdominal pain. In: *Early clinical diagnosis*. Lancaster: MTP Press, 1986, 137–176.
3. Murtagh J. *The anatomy of a rural practice*. Melbourne: Monash University Monograph, 1980:34.
4. Sandler G, Fry J. Chronic abdominal pain. In: *Early clinical diagnosis*. Lancaster: MTP Press, 1986, 177–186.
5. Bain ST, Spaulding WB. The importance of coding presenting symptoms. Canadian Med Ass Journal, 1967; 97(16):953–959.
6. Hodgkin K. *Towards earlier diagnosis* (5th edition), Edinburgh: Churchill Livingstone, 1985, 483–486.
7. Robinson MJ. *Practical paediatrics* (2nd edition), Melbourne: Churchill Livingstone, 1990:526–531.
8. Feekery C. The Australian Paediatric Review, 1991; 5:1–2.
9. Hunt P, Marshall V. *Clinical problems in general surgery*. Sydney: Butterworths, 1991, 193–243.
10. Farrell T. Emergency call. Aust Fam Physician, 1988; 17:467.
11. Schroeder SA et al. *Current medical diagnosis and treatment*. East Norwalk: Appleton and Lange, 1990, 450.

29

Arthritis

Rheumatic disorders are common in old age: much of rheumatology is geriatric and much of geriatrics is rheumatology.

Dr Frank Dudley Hart[1] 1983

The clinical evaluation of the patient presenting with the complaint of arthralgia (painful joints) or arthritis (inflammation of the joints) can be a difficult and challenging exercise because it can be a presentation of many systemic disorders, some of which are rare. Important considerations are sex, age, the pattern of joint involvement (monoarticular or polyarticular), immediate and more remote history, family history and drug use—all of which may provide important diagnostic clues.

Key facts and checkpoints

- In a UK National Morbidity Survey rheumatic disease comprised just over 7% of all morbidity presenting to the family doctor.[2]
- The commonest cause was osteoarthritis, which affects 5–10% of the population.
- The same study indicated an episode rate for arthritis/arthralgia of 38.6 per 1000 population.
- The population incidence of rheumatoid arthritis is 2–3%.
- There should be no systemic manifestations with osteoarthritis.
- One quarter of disability in elderly people is due to severe joint disease.
- Systemic diseases that may predispose to or present with an arthropathy include the connective tissue disorders; diabetes mellitus; a bleeding disorder; previous tuberculosis; the spondyloarthropathies such as psoriasis; SBE; hepatitis B; rheumatic fever; the various vasculitic or arteritic syndromes (the vasculitides) such as Wegener's granulomatosis; HIV infection; carcinoma of the lung; haemochromatosis; sarcoidosis; hyperparathyroidism; Paget's disease.
- The pain of inflammatory disease is worse at rest, e.g. on waking in the morning, and improved by activity.
- Gout and septic arthritis have a recognised cause and cure.
- Acute gout is almost exclusive to males: it is usually only seen in postmenopausal women or those on thiazide diuretics.

A diagnostic approach

A summary of the safety diagnostic model is presented in Table 29.1.

Probability diagnosis

The probability diagnoses for the patient presenting with arthritis are:

- osteoarthritis (mono or polyarthritis)
- viral arthritis (if acute and polyarthritis)

Osteoarthritis is very common in general practice. It may be primary, which is usually symmetrical, and can affect many joints. This clinical pattern

Table 29.1 *Arthralgia: diagnostic strategy model*

Q. Probability diagnosis
A. Osteoarthritis
Viral polyarthritis

Q. Serious disorders not to be missed
A. Rheumatoid arthritis
Connective tissue disorders
- SLE
- systemic sclerosis
- dermatomyositis

Neoplasia
- carcinoma bronchus
- leukaemia

HIV arthropathy
Severe infections
- rheumatic fever
- endocarditis
- tuberculosis
- brucellosis
- pyogenic arthritis
  - gonoccocus
  - staphylococcus

Q. Pitfalls (often missed)
A. Fibromyalgia syndrome
Polymyalgia rheumatica
Crystal deposition
- gout
- pyrophosphate (pseudogout)

Haemarthrosis
Dengue fever
Lyme disease

Rarities
Other vasculitides
Haemochromatosis
Sarcoidosis
Hyperparathyroidism
Familial Mediterranean fever

Q. Seven masquerades checklist

A.	
Depression	✓
Diabetes	✓
Drugs	✓
Anaemia	—
Thyroid disease	✓
Spinal dysfunction	the spondyloarthropathies
UTI	—

Q. Is the patient trying to tell me something?
Always a consideration with pain.
Psychogenic factors aggravate chronic arthritic conditions

is different to secondary osteoarthritis, which follows injury and other wear and tear causes.

Viral polyarthritis is more common than realised. It presents usually as a symmetric inflammation, mainly of the hands and feet, and is usually mild. It tends to terminate quickly and spontaneously without permanent damage to joints. It is caused by many viruses, including those causing influenza, mumps, rubella, varicella, hepatitis A and B, infectious mononucleosis, cytomegalovirus, parvovirus and Australian epidemic polyarthritis due to Ross River virus.

Serious disorders not to be missed

These include rheumatoid arthritis, which can start as a monoarthritis; pyogenic arthritis, including gonococcus, staphylococcus and streptococcus infections; tuberculosis, rheumatic fever and bacterial endocarditis.

It is important to be forever watchful for rheumatic fever. It presents typically as a migratory polyarthritis involving large joints sequentially, one becoming hot, red, swollen and very painful as the other subsides. It rarely lasts more than five days in any one joint.

A flitting polyarthritis can also occur with endocarditis in addition to a systemic upset and a cardiac murmur. Gonococcal infection may present in a single joint or as flitting polyarthritis, often accompanied by a rash. Brucellosis can cause arthritis and sacroiliitis and can be confused with the spondyloarthropathies.

HIV infection is becoming a great mimicker. It can present as a chronic oligoarticular asymmetrical arthritis.[3] It can also present as a rash very similar to psoriasis.

With the large influx of migrants from South-East Asia the possibility of tuberculosis presenting as arthritis should be kept in mind.

Connective tissue disorders may be involved. They include systemic lupus erythematosis, progressive systemic sclerosis (scleroderma), and dermatomyositis. It is most inappropriate to settle with a general diagnosis such as 'rheumatism' or 'arthritis' and where doubtful it is important to find the specific entity causing the problem.

In respect to malignant disease, arthralgia is associated with acute leukaemia, lymphoma and neuroblastoma in children and with carcinoma of the bronchus which may cause hypertrophic osteoarthopathy especially of the wrist and ankle (not a true arthritis but simulates it). Occasionally polyarthritis may be the first feature of an occult neoplasm. Monoarticular metastatic disease may involve the knee (usually from lung or breast).

Pitfalls

There are several pitfalls, most of which are rare. A common pitfall is gout. This applies particularly to older women taking diuretics, whose osteoarthritic joints, especially of the hand, can be affected. The condition is often referred to as nodular gout and does not usually present as acute arthritis.

Fibromyalgia syndrome is a real puzzle (see page 289) as it can mimic the connective tissue disorders in its early presentation—typically a woman in the third or fourth decade.

Another 'trap' is haemarthrosis in a patient with a bleeding disorder.

Infective causes that may be overlooked are dengue fever, especially in travellers returning from a tropical or subtropical area, and Lyme disease, which is now surfacing in many countries, especially where ticks are found.

There are many rare causes of arthritis. Sarcoidosis causes two forms: an acute benign form, usually in the ankles and knees, and a chronic form with longstanding sarcoidosis which involves joints (large or small) adjacent to underlying bone disease.

Then there are the uncommon vasculitides, which can cause confusion in diagnosis. This group includes polyarteritis nodosa, hypersensitive vasculitis, polymyalgia rheumatica/giant cell arteritis, Wegener's granulomatosis, Henoch-Schönlein purpura and Behcet's syndrome.

Haemochromatoses can present with a degenerative arthropathy that characteristically affects the second or third metacarpophalangeal joints.[3]

Other rare causes of arthritis are erythema nodosum, serum sickness and Sjögren's syndrome.

General pitfalls

- not searching beyond RA when an RA pattern polyarthritis may be part of another systemic disease
- failing to search for some cause of arthritis other than osteoarthritis in a patient, especially an elderly patient, i.e. underdiagnosing; an important example of this is polymyalgia rheumatica
- failing to consider the various drug interactions between NSAIDs, 'over the counter' medications and other drugs used by the elderly
- underdiagnosing and misdiagnosing through lack of appreciation of the many causes of arthritis, especially those presenting as part of a systemic disease

Seven masquerades checklist

- Depression—unlikely but complaints of arthralgia are possible.
- Diabetes—occasionally causes an arthropathy.
- Drugs—yes, a major consideration.
- Anaemia—no.
- Thyroid disease—possible.
- Urinary infection—no.
- Spinal dysfunction—only with the spondyloarthropathies.

Drug-induced arthritis is the main feature of this important group of disorders. It usually affects the hands and is generally symmetrical. Drugs that cause arthritis are listed in Table 29.2.

Table 29.2 *Drug-induced arthralgia*

Commonest drugs inducing arthralgia
Note Usually affects the hands and is symmetrical
Drugs inducing Lupus syndrome
• hydralazine
• procaineamide
• anticonvulsants, e.g. phenytoin
• chlorpromazine
• isoniazid
• methyldopa
Others
• cotrimoxazole
• amoxycillin
• mianserin
• carbimazole
• nitrofurantoin
• antihypertensives

Note Diuretics, especially frusemide and thiazides, can precipitate gout.

Intravenous drug abuse may be associated with septic arthritis, hepatitis B and C, HIV-associated arthropathy, SBE with arthritis and serum sickness reactions.

Hyperthyroidism can uncommonly cause acropathy (clubbing and swelling of the fingers) and may present as pseudogout, while hypothyroidism can present with an arthropathy or cause proximal muscle pain, stiffness and weakness. Diabetes mellitus may cause an arthropathy which can be painless or mild to moderately painful.

The spondyloarthropathies may be a causative factor. They often present with an acute monoarthritis particularly in teenagers some time before causing sacroiliitis and spondylitis.

Psychogenic considerations

Although 'arthralgia' is an uncommon complaint in psychoneurotic disorders, any pain syndrome can be a significant manifestation. The usual cause of arthralgia is inflammation in the joint, that is arthritis, but a functional cause is encountered from time to time.

Furthermore some patients who are unfortunate enough to acquire arthritis, especially the more serious disorders, certainly develop ongoing emotional and psychological problems which appear to aggravate their total problem.

So-called 'growing pains' of the lower limb are common in children and the physical examination and investigations are normal. Parents need to be reassured that it is a benign condition while recognising that emotional factors may be quite significant. As Apley pointed out, 'physical growth is not painful, but emotional growth can hurt like hell'.[4]

The clinical approach

A priority is to determine whether or not the arthritis is caused by a primary rheumatic disorder or whether it is part of an underlying systemic disorder.

History

Very careful enquiry about the exact onset of the arthritis is important. This includes whether it was acute or insidious, confined to specific joints or flitting as in rheumatic fever and sometimes in infective endocarditis. Is it a true polyarthritis or monoarthritis? Symmetrical or asymmetrical? It is also important to differentiate between arthralgia (pains in or around the joints) and arthritis (inflammation of the joints). Not all arthralgia is arthritis.

A family history is important because a positive family history is associated with conditions such as rheumatoid arthritis (rarely), ankylosing spondylitis, connective tissue disorders (rarely), psoriasis, gout, pseudogout and haemophilia.[5]

A very hot, red, swollen joint suggests either infection or crystal arthritis.

Key questions

I want you to carefully point out exactly where you feel the pain.
Does the pain move from joint to joint or stay in the same joint?
Are you aware of anything that brought on the pain?
Does the pain disturb you at night?
Do your joints feel very sore or stiff when you wake up in the morning?
What effect does exercise or activity have on the pain or stiffness?
Have you had an injury in the past to your painful joint(s)?
Do you get pain over both your shoulders and upper arms?
Have you got a skin rash? Is it new?
Have you had a fever, sweats or chills?
Do you get very tired, weak or out of sorts?
Have you noticed any change in the colour of your urine?
Have you had a sore throat?
Have you had sinus trouble?
Have you had acute pain in your big toe or in other joints before?
Do you have a history of psoriasis?
Do you have a history of rheumatic fever?
Do you have pain in your neck or lower back or in other joints?
Have you had any diarrhoea?
Have you had a discharge from your penis?
Have you had any problems with your eyes?
What drugs are you taking? Are you taking fluid tablets (diuretics)?
How much alcohol would you drink a day?
Have you been visiting the country or exposed to ticks or been to a deer farm?
Have you travelled overseas recently?
Have you been at risk of getting a sexually transmitted disease?
Have you been drinking untreated milk recently?

Physical examination

A systematic examination of the affected joint or joints should be performed, looking for signs of inflammation, deformity, swelling and limitation of movement. Tenderness and warmth indicates inflammatory activity. Erythema indicates gouty arthritis or other crystalopathy, rheumatic fever or septic arthritis.

Joint swelling:

acute (1–4 hours) with intense pain = blood, infection or crystals, e.g. gout
subacute (1–2 days) and soft = fluid (synovial effusion)
chronic and bony = osteoarthritis
chronic and soft/boggy = synovial proliferation

A coarse crepitus suggests osteoarthritis. Each joint should be examined specifically. Inspection should note the presence of lumps or bumps such as Heberden's nodes on the osteoarthritic DIP joints of the hands, Bouchard's nodes on the osteoarthritic PIP joints of the hands, rheumatoid nodules which are the only pathognomonic finding of RA and gouty tophi. Signs that may be of diagnostic help are presented in Figure 29.1.

The specific inflamed joint or joints may give an indication of the disease process. Typical joints affected by various arthropathies are illustrated in Figure 29.2.

Investigations

Table 29.3 lists the many investigations that are used to reach a diagnosis.[6] Clinical acumen permits a judicious selection of specific tests rather than ordering an expensive battery.

It is important to keep in mind the many specific serological tests to detect infective causes of arthralgia. These include Australian epidemic polyarthritis, Lyme disease, rubella, brucella, hepatitis B, gonococcus, mycoplasma, HIV tests.

Plain X-ray is invaluable, although in some conditions radiological changes may only be

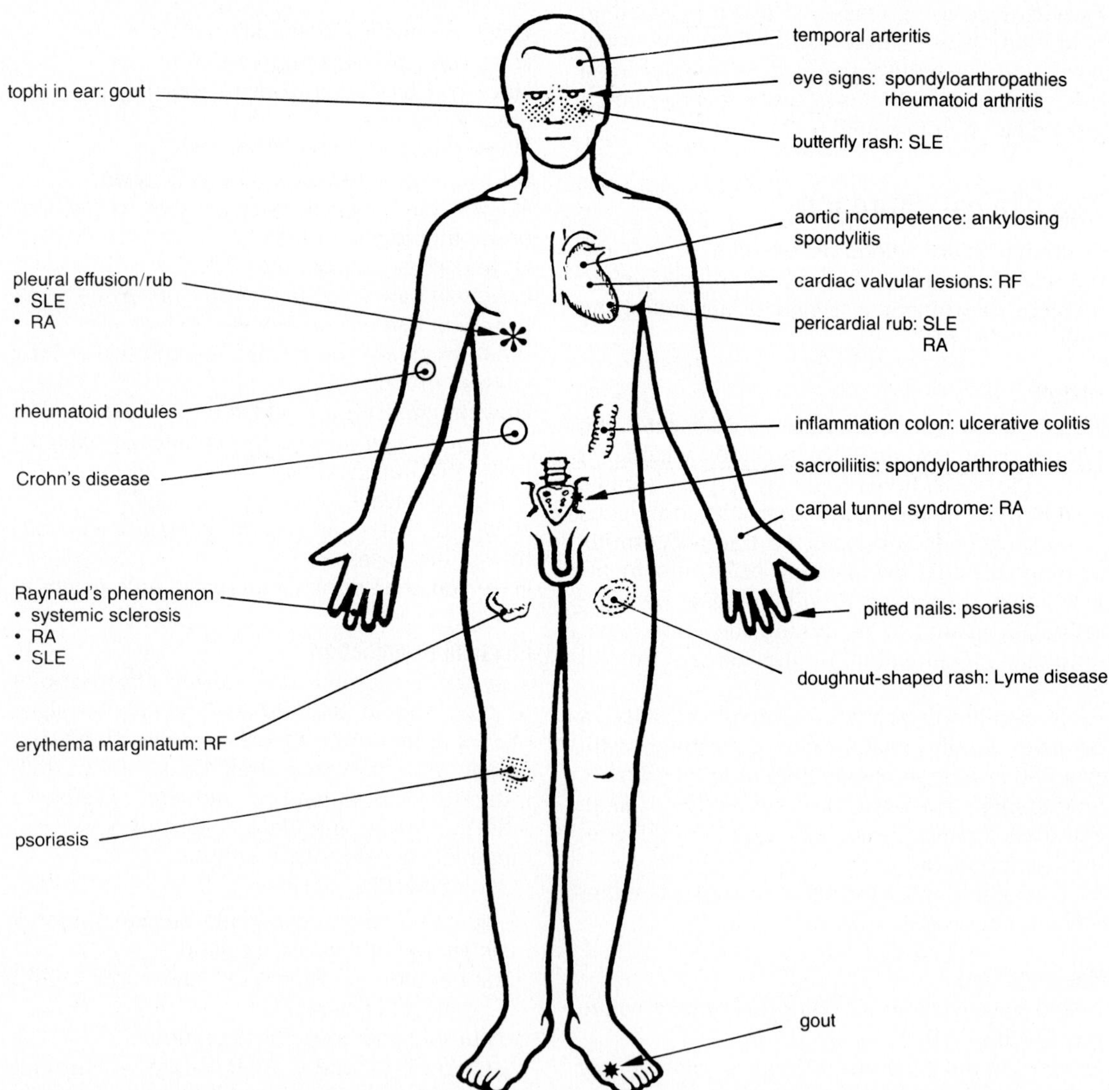

Fig. 29.1 *Physical examination: possible findings to consider in diagnosis*

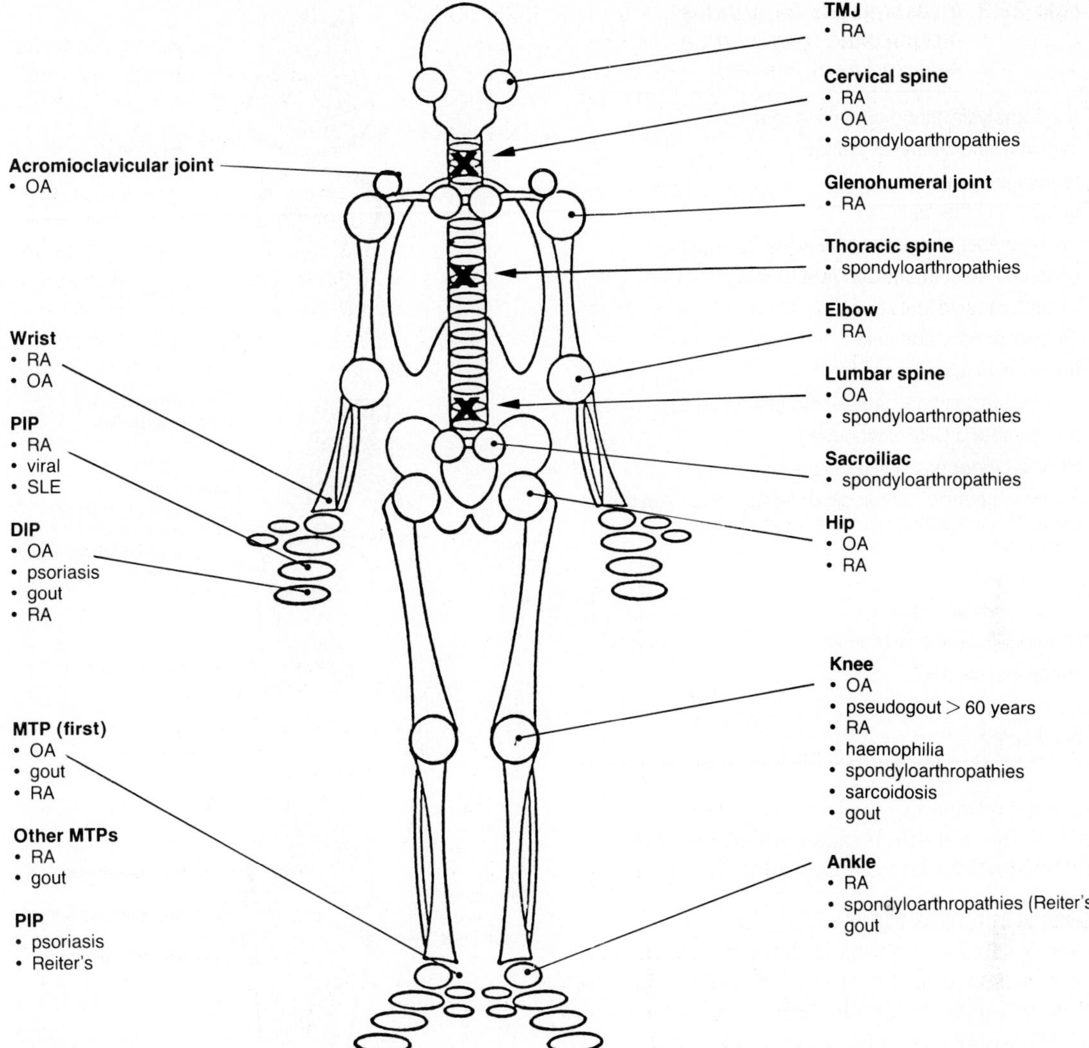

Fig. 29.2 *Joints typically affected by various arthropathies*

apparent when the disease is well established. Typical X-ray changes for common conditions are presented in Figure 29.3. Arthrography has limited value in the diagnosis of polyarthritis but is very useful for specific joints such as the shoulder and the knee. Ultrasound examination for joints such as the shoulder and the hip can be very useful.

The various immunological tests for diagnosis of the connective tissue disorders are outlined with the description of each condition. Such screening tests include:

- rheumatoid factor
- antinuclear antibodies
- double stranded DNA antibodies

The LE cell test has been superseded by the antinuclear and ds DNA antibody tests.

Arthritis in children

Arthralgia (joint pain) is a common problem in childhood and, although arthritis is rare, the complaint demands considerable respect because of the many serious problems causing it. Arthritis may be part of an infectious disease such as rheumatic fever, rubella, mumps, cytomegalovirus infection, erythema infectiosum (human parvovirus), influenza or other viral infection, and is occasionally encountered with Henoch-Schönlein purpura. It is worth noting that

Table 29.3 *Investigations for arthritis (appropriate tests can be selected from this list)*

- urine analysis: blood, protein, sugar
- synovial fluid: analysis, culture
- radiology—plain X-ray
- blood and other cultures
- haemoglobin and differential white cell count
- erythrocyte sedimentation rate (ESR)
- serum uric acid, creatinine
- 24 hour urinary uric acid
- rheumatoid factor
- antinuclear antibody (screening test for SLE)
- double strand DNA antibodies
- HLA B_{27} (poor predictive value)
- various specific serological tests, e.g. Australian epidemic polyarthritis, rubella, Lyme disease, hepatitis B
- HIV serology
- antistreptolysin O titre
- streptococcal anti DNAse B
- streptococcal AHT
- arthroscopy and biopsy
- bone scan

underlying bone tumours can be present as joint pain if the tumour is adjacent to the joint. A checklist of causes is presented in Table 29.4.

Juvenile chronic arthritis

Juvenile chronic arthritis is defined as a chronic arthritis persisting for at least 3 months in one or more joints in a child less than 16 years of age.[4] It is rare, affecting only about one in 1000 children, but produces profound medical and psychosocial problems.

The commonest types of juvenile chronic arthritis are oligoarthritis (about 50%) and polyarthritis (about 40%). Systemic onset arthritis, previously known as Still's disease, accounts for about 10% of cases. It is usually seen in children under the age of 5 but can occur throughout childhood. The children present with a high remittent fever and coppery red rash, plus other features including lymphadenopathy, splenomegaly and pericarditis. Arthritis is not an initial feature but develops ultimately, usually involving the small joints of the hands, wrists, knees, ankles and metatarsophalangeal joints.

These children should be referred once the problem is suspected or recognised.

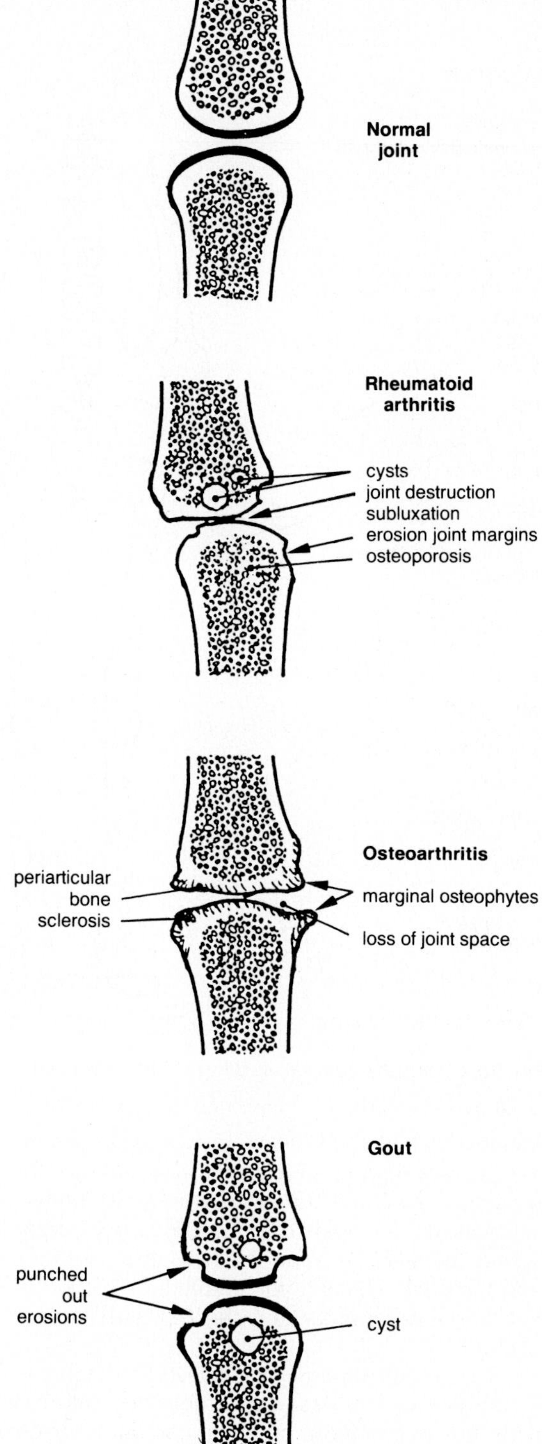

Fig. 29.3 *X-rays for common arthritic conditions: typical changes*

Table 29.4 *Arthritis in children: causes to consider*

Infections
- Rheumatic fever
- Septic arthritis
- Meningococcaemia
- Osteomyelitis
- Reactive arthritis (post-infectious)
- Tuberculosis
- Viral infections, e.g. rubella, HIV

Inflammation—chronic arthritis
- Juvenile chronic arthritis
  - oligoarthritis
  - polyarticular (juvenile rheumatoid arthritis)
  - systemic disease (Still's disease)
  - juvenile ankylosing spondylitis
- Psoriatic arthritis
- Inflammatory bowel arthritis

Haematological disorders
- Thalassaemia
- Sickle cell disease
- Haemophilia

Neoplasms
- Leukaemia
- Lymphoma
- Neuroblastoma

Orthopaedic conditions
- Perthe's disorder
- Slipped upper femoral epiphyses
- Chondromalacia

Others
- Henoch-Schönlein disorder
- Scurvy
- Traumatic arthritis
- Osteochondritis
- Psychogenic rheumatism
- Malignant tumour
  - bone
  - cartilage
  - synovium

Rheumatic fever

Rheumatic fever typically occurs in children and young adults, the first attack usually occurring between 5 and 15 years of age.

Arthritis in perspective

Five per cent of all children complain of recurrent lower limb pain which often awakens them from their sleep. There may be emotional factors involved and parents need appropriate reassurance. A careful history and physical examination are essential and perhaps simple basic investigations may be appropriate. As Rudge[4] points out, we have to be vigilant against underdiagnosis, misdiagnosis and overdiagnosis.

Arthritis in the elderly

Osteoarthritis is very common with advancing age and for this reason care has to be taken not to simply attribute other causes of arthritis to osteoarthritis. Other musculoskeletal conditions that become more prevalent with increasing age are:

- polymyalgia rheumatica
- Paget's disease of bone
- avascular necrosis
- gout
- pseudogout (pyrophosphate arthropathy)
- malignancy, e.g. bronchogenic carcinoma

Pseudogout

This crystal deposition arthropathy (chondocalcinosis) is noted by its occurrence in people over 60 years. It usually affects the knee joint but can involve other joints.

Rheumatoid arthritis

Although it usually begins between the ages of 30 and 40 it can occur in elderly patients, when it often begins suddenly and dramatically. This is called 'explosive' RA and fortunately tends to respond to small doses of prednisolone and has a good prognosis.[7]

Rheumatic fever

Rheumatic fever (RF) is an inflammatory disorder that typically occurs in children and young adults following a group A streptococcus pyogenes infection. It is common in developing countries but uncommon in first world countries.

Clinical features

- young person 5–15 (can be older)
- acute onset fever, joint pains, malaise
- flitting arthralgia mainly in leg (knees, ankles) and elbows and wrists of the arm
- one joint settles as the other is affected

However, the symptoms depend on the organs affected and arthritis may be absent.

Diagnosis

Based on 2 or more major criteria
or
1 major + 2 or more minor criteria

in the presence of supporting evidence of preceding streptococcal infection.

Major criteria

- carditis
- polyarthritis
- chorea
- subcutaneous nodules
- erythema marginatum

Minor criteria

- fever
- previous RF or rheumatic heart disease
- arthralgia
- raised ESR/C-reactive protein
- ECG—prolonged PR intervals

Investigations

A selective combination of:

- throat swab
- ESR
- streptococcal ASOT
- streptococcal anti DNAse B
- streptococcal AHT
- C-reactive protein

Treatment

- rest in bed
- penicillin
- high-dose aspirin
- corticosteroids for carditis
- prophylactic long-term penicillin

Osteoarthritis

Osteoarthritis (OA) is the most common type of arthritis, occurring in about 10% of the adult population and in 50% of those aged over 60.[8] It is a degenerative disease of cartilage and may be primary or secondary to causes such as trauma and mechanical problems, septic arthritis, crystalopathy or previous inflammatory disorders, or structural disorders such as SUFE and Perthe's disorder.

The arthritis

Primary OA is usually symmetrical and can affect many joints. Unlike other inflammatory disease the pain is worse on initiating movement and loading the joint, and eased by rest. OA is usually associated with pronounced stiffness, especially after activity, in contrast to RA.

Joints involved

In primary osteoarthritis all the synovial joints may be involved, but the main ones are:

- first carpometacarpal (CMC) joint of thumb
- first metatarsophalangeal (MTP) joint of great toe
- distal interphalangeal (DIP) joints of hands

Other joints that are affected significantly are the proximal interphalangeal joints, the knees, hips, acromioclavicular joints and joints of the spine, especially the facet joints of the cervical (C5-6, C6-7) and lumbar regions (L3-4, L4-5, L5-S1) (Fig. 29.4).

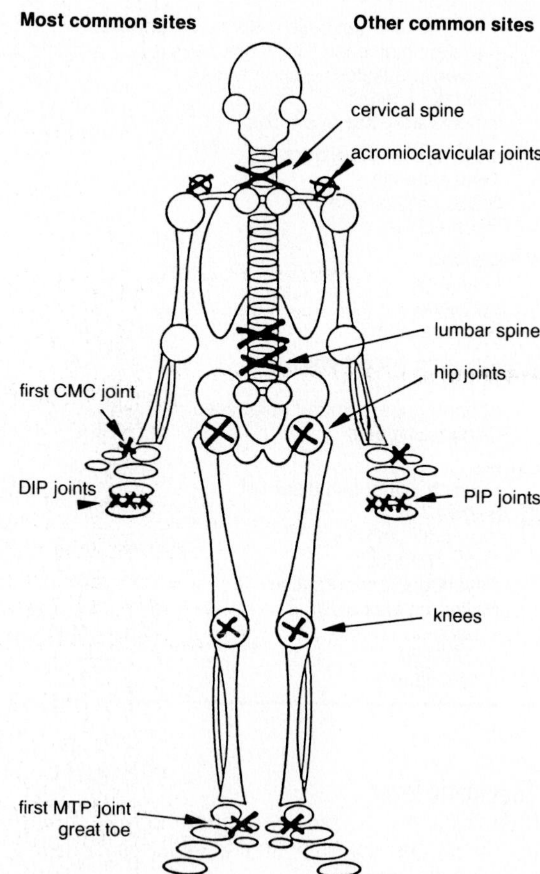

Fig. 29.4 *Osteoarthritis: typical joint distribution*

Clinical features

- pain: worse by the end of the day
  aggravated by use
  relieved by rest
  worse in cold and damp
- variable morning stiffness
- variable disability

Signs

- hard and bony swelling
- crepitus
- signs of inflammation (mild)
- restricted movements
- joint deformity

Note There should be no systemic manifestations.

Crystal arthropathy can complicate OA, especially in the fingers of people on diuretics, e.g. nodular gout.

Diagnosis

The diagnosis is clinical and radiological but the degree of changes on X-ray do not always parallel levels of symptoms.[8]

X-ray findings

- joint space narrowing with sclerosis of subchondral bone
- formation of osteophytes on the joint margins or in ligamentous attachments
- cystic areas in the subchondral bone
- altered shape of bone ends

Principles of management

- Explanation and reassurance including patient education handouts.
- Control of pain and maintenance of function with appropriate drugs.
- Judicious activity, exercise and physical therapy.
- Consideration of factors lowering the coping threshold, e.g. stress, depression, anxiety, overactivity.
- Referral for surgical intervention for debilitating and intractable pain or disability. Examples include OA of hip, knee, shoulder, first CMC joint of thumb, and first MTP joint where surgery is now very successful. Osteotomies still have a limited place for a varus or valgus deformity of the knee.

Optimal treatment

- *Explanation*: patient education and reassurance that arthritis is not the crippling disease perceived by most patients.
- *Rest*: during an active bout of inflammatory activity only; prolonged bed rest contraindicated.
- *Exercise*: a graduated exercise program is essential to maintain joint function. Aim for a good balance of relative rest with sensible exercise. It is necessary to stop or modify any exercise or activity that increases the pain.
- *Heat*: recommended is a hot-water bottle, warm bath or electric blanket to soothe pain and stiffness. Advise against getting too cold.
- *Diet*: if overweight it is important to reduce weight to ideal level; otherwise no specific diet has been proven to cause or improve OA. Some people claim that their arthritis is improved by having a nutritious balanced diet consisting of fish, rice and vegetables and avoiding meat, dairy produce, alcohol, pepper and spices.
- *Correction of predisposing factors and aids*: apart from weight reduction the following may help:
  - — walking stick
  - — heel raise for leg length disparity
  - — back brace
  - — elastic or hinged joint support, e.g. knee
- *Physiotherapy*: referral should be made for specific purposes such as:
  - — correct posture and/or leg length disparity
  - — supervision of a hydrotherapy program
  - — heat therapy and advice on simple home heat measures
  - — teaching and supervision of isometric strengthening
  - — exercises, e.g. for the neck, back, quadriceps muscle.
- *Occupational therapy*: refer for advice on aids in the home, more efficient performance of daily living activities, protection of joints, and on the wide range of inexpensive equipment and tools.
- *Simple analgesics* (regularly for pain): paracetamol/acetaminophen (avoid codeine or dextropropoxyphene preparations and aspirin if recent history of dyspepsia or peptic ulceration).
- *NSAIDs and aspirin* are the first-line drugs for more persistent pain or where there is evidence of inflammation, such as pain worse with resting and nocturnal pain. The risk *v* benefit equation always has to be weighed carefully. As a rule, NSAIDs should be avoided if possible.

  Significant risks of NSAIDs:
  - — gastric erosion with bleeding
  - — gastric ulceration
  - — depression of renal function
  - — hepatotoxicity

Note Change to a suppository form will not necessarily render upper GI tract safe from irritation.

- *Intrarticular corticosteroids*: as a rule IA corticosteroids are not recommended but occasionally can be very effective for an inflammatory episode of distressing pain and disability on a background of tolerant pain, e.g. a flare-up in an osteoarthritic knee.
- *Contraindicated drugs* for OA include the immunosuppressive and disease-modifying drugs such as oral corticosteroids, gold, antimalarials and cytotoxic agents.

Rheumatoid arthritis

RA is the commonest chronic inflammatory polyarthritis and affects about 3% of the population. The disease can vary from a mild to a most severe debilitating expression. About 10–20% of patients have a relentless progression and require more aggressive drug therapy.

The arthritis

RA generally presents with the insidious onset of pain and stiffness of the small joints of the hands and feet. The pain is persistent rather than fleeting and mainly affects the fingers where symmetrical involvement of the PIP joints produces spindling while the metacarpophalangeal joints develop diffuse thickening as does the wrist. In 25% of cases RA presents as arthritis of a single joint such as the knee[7], a situation leading to confusion with Lyme disease or a spondyloarthropathy.

Joints involved (Fig. 29.5)

- hands: MCP and PIP joints, DIP joints (30%)
- wrist and elbows
- feet: MTP joints, tarsal joints (not IP joints), ankle
- knees (common) and hip (delayed—up to 50%)
- shoulder (glenohumeral) joints
- temporomandibular joints
- cervical spine

Clinical features

- insidious onset but can begin acutely (explosive RA)
- any age 10–70 years—peak 30–50
- women:men ratio 3:1

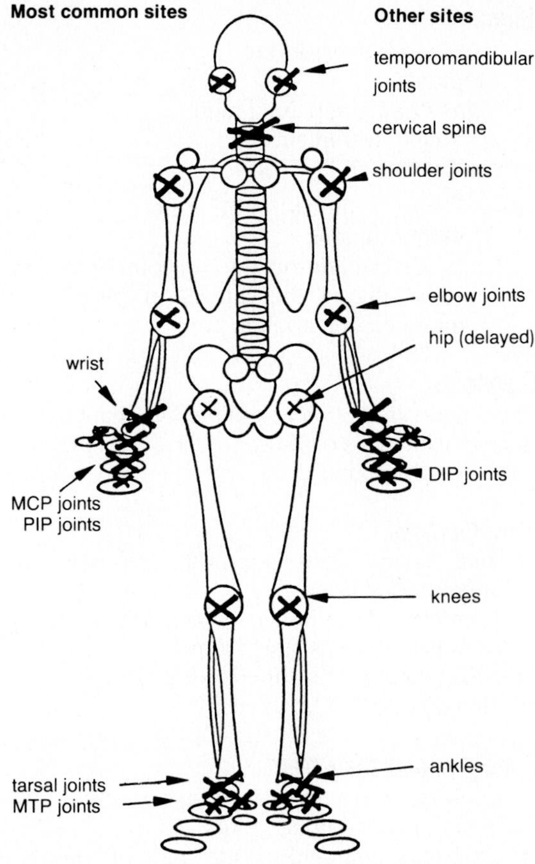

Fig. 29.5 *Rheumatoid arthritis: typical joint distribution*

- joint pain—worse on waking, nocturnal pain, disturbed sleep
  —relieved with activity
- morning stiffness—can last hours
- rest stiffness, e.g. after sitting
- general: malaise, weakness, weight loss, fatigue
- disability according to involvement

Signs

- soft swelling (effusion and synovial swelling)
- warmth
- tenderness on pressure or movement
- limitation of movement
- muscle wasting
- later stages: deformity, subluxation, instability or ankylosing

The various possible extra-articular manifestations are summarised in Figure 29.6.

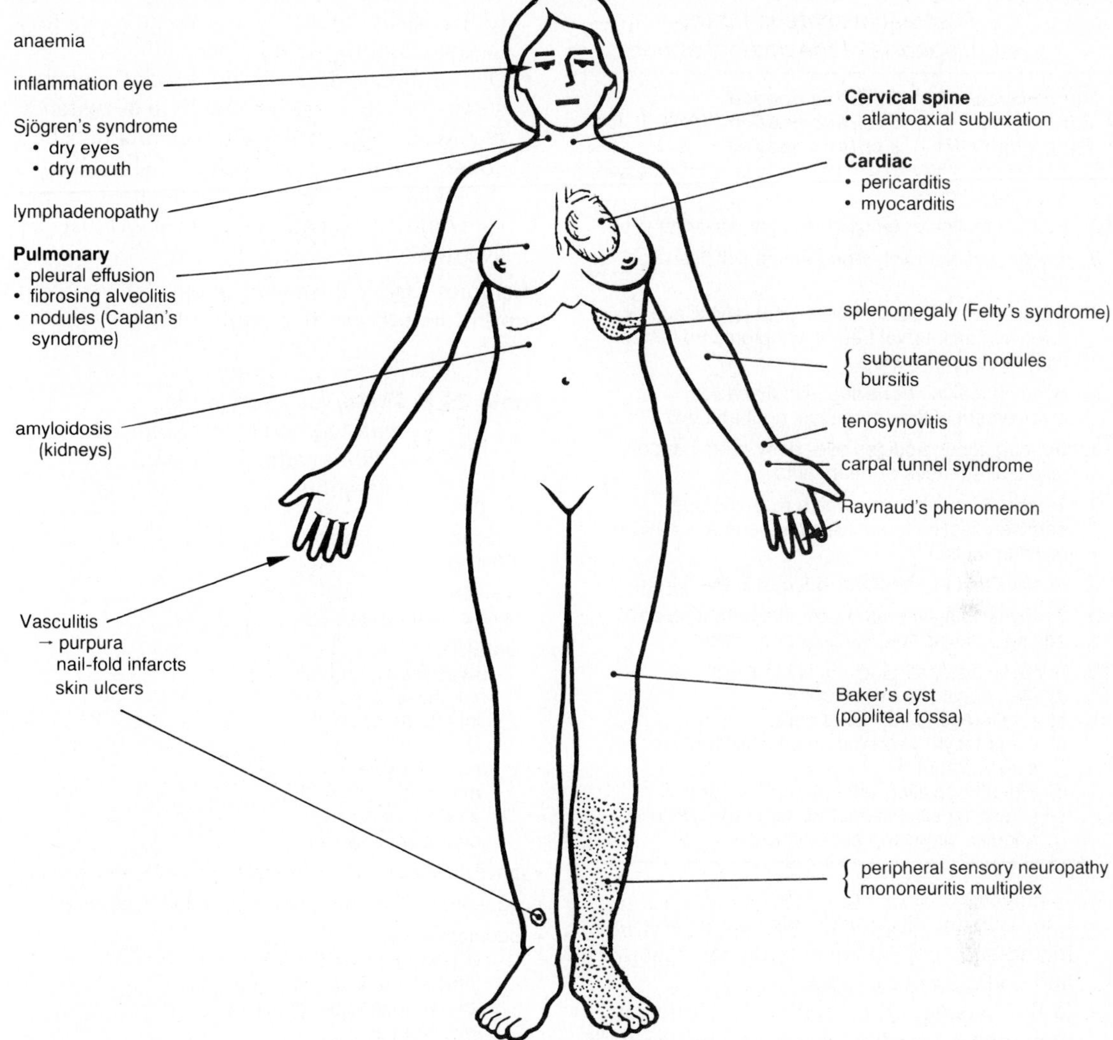

Fig. 29.6 *Rheumatoid arthritis: significant non-articular clinical manifestations*

Investigations

- ESR usually raised according to active disease
- anaemia (normochromic and normocytic) may be present
- rheumatoid factor—positive in about 80–85%
- antinuclear antibodies—positive in 30%
- X-ray changes:
  - — erosion of joint margin: 'mouse-bitten' appearance
  - — loss of joint space (may be destruction)
  - — juxta-articular osteoporosis
  - — cysts
  - — advanced: subluxation or ankylosing

Criteria for the diagnosis of rheumatoid arthritis are presented in Table 29.5.

Management principles[9]

- Give patient education support and appropriate reassurance. The diagnosis generally has distressful implications so the patient and family require careful explanation and support. It should be pointed out that the majority of patients have little or no long-term problems. Even in mild cases, continuing care and medical supervision is important.

Table 29.5 *American Rheumatism Association: criteria for the diagnosis of rheumatoid arthritis*

- ***For classical RA*** ***7 criteria needed***
- ***For definite RA*** ***5 criteria needed***
- ***For probable RA*** ***3 criteria needed***

1. Morning stiffness
2. Pain on motion or tenderness in at least one joint
3. Swelling of one joint, representing soft tissue or fluid
4. Swelling of at least one other joint (soft tissue or fluid) with an interval free of symptoms no longer than three (3) months
5. Symmetrical joint swelling (simultaneous involvement of the same joint, right and left)
6. Subcutaneous nodules over bony prominences, extensor surfaces or near joints
7. Typical X-ray changes which must include demineralisation in periarticular bone as an index of inflammation.
8. Positive test for rheumatoid factor in the serum
9. Synovial fluid—a poor mucin clot formation on adding synovial fluid to dilute acetic acid
10. Synovial histopathology consistent with RA:
    a) Marked villous hypertrophy
    b) Proliferation of synovial cells
    c) Lymphocyte plus plasma cell infiltration in subsynovium
    d) Fibrin deposition within or upon microvilli
    e) Characteristic histopathology of rheumatoid nodules biopsied from any site

- Use a team approach where appropriate, including a consultant referral for diagnosis and collaborative support.
- Fully assess the patient's functional impairment and impact on home life, work and social activity. Involve the family in decision making.
- Make judicious use of pharmaceutical agents. For serious cases consultant collaboration is essential.
- Review the patient regularly, continually assessing progress and drug tolerance.

Specific advice

- Rest and splinting: this is necessary where practical for any acute flare-up of arthritis.
- Exercise: it is important to have regular exercise especially walking and swimming. Hydrotherapy in heated pools.
- Referral to physiotherapists and occupational therapists for expertise in exercise supervision, physical therapy and advice regarding coping in the home and work is important.
- Joint movement: each affected joint should be put daily through a full range of motion to keep it mobile and reduce stiffness.
- Diet: although there is no special diet that seems to cause or cure RA there is evidence that avoiding animal fats (dairy products and some meats) and using fish oils is beneficial.[10] A nourishing well-balanced diet is common sense and obesity must be avoided.

Therapies used in the management of rheumatoid arthritis are presented in Table 29.6.[10]

Table 29.6 *Therapies used in the management of rheumatoid arthritis (after Reilly and Littlejohn)*

- education (rest, literature, weight loss, joint protection advice)
- NSAIDs
- simple analgesics
- DMARDs*:
  - hydroxychloroquine
  - sulphasalazine
  - injectable gold
  - D-penicillamine
  - methotrexate
  - oral gold
  - azathioprine
  - cyclophosphamide
- physical therapy (hydrotherapy, isometric exercises)
- occupational therapy (splints, aids and appliances)
- corticosteroids:
  - oral prednisolone
  - intra-articular
  - intravenous (steroid 'pulses')
  - intramuscular
- orthopaedic surgery:
  (synovectomy, joint replacement, arthrodesis, plastic hand surgery)
- chiropody, footwear, insoles

*DMARDs = disease-modifying antirheumatic drugs

Pharmaceutical agents

First line: simple analgesics, e.g.
paracetamol
aspirin
NSAIDs

Second line: Disease-modifying agents
e.g. hydroxychloroquine
gold compounds (IM or orally)
D-penicillamine
sulphasalazine

Third line: corticosteroids
immunosuppressive agents
e.g. methotrexate
azathioprine
cyclophosphamide

Connective tissue disorders

The three connective tissue disorders have the common feature of arthritis or arthralgia. Refer to Chapter 26.

Systemic lupus erythematosus (SLE)

Arthritis is the commonest clinical feature of SLE (over 90%).[7] It is a symmetrical polyarthritis involving mainly small and medium joints, especially the proximal interphalangeal and carpal joints of the hand. It is usually non-erosive and non-deforming, although deformities of fingers and thumbs can occur due to laxity of ligaments, tendons and capsules causing joint instability.

The initial presentation is similar to rheumatoid arthritis. The fibromyalgia syndrome can cause confusion although it has a distribution confined mainly to the trunk, especially the back.

Investigations

- ESR—elevated in proportion to disease activity
- antinuclear antibodies—positive in 95%
- double-stranded DNA antibodies—specific for SLE but present in only 50%
- rheumatoid factor—positive in 50%
- LE test—inefficient and not used

Drug treatment

Mild—NSAIDs/aspirin
Moderate—low-dose antimalarials, e.g. hydroxychloroquine or chloroquine
Moderate to severe—corticosteroids; immunosuppressive drugs, e.g. azathioprine

Systemic sclerosis

It can present as a polyarthritis affecting the fingers of the hand in 25% of patients, especially in the early stages. Soft tissue swelling produces a 'sausage finger' pattern. Systemic sclerosis mainly affects the skin, presenting with Raynaud's phenomenon in over 85%.

Investigations

- ESR may be raised
- normocytic normochronic anaemia may be present
- antinuclear antibodies—up to 50% positive
- rheumatoid factor—positive in 30%
- hypergammaglobulinaemia—50% positive
- antinucleolar and anticentromere ABs—specific

Polymyositis and dermatomyositis

Arthralgia and arthritis occur in about 50% of patients and may be the presenting feature before the major feature of muscle weakness and wasting of the proximal muscles of the shoulder and pelvic girdles appear. The small joints of the hand are usually affected and it may resemble rheumatoid arthritis.

Crystal arthritis

Arthritis, which can be acute, chronic or asymptomatic, is caused by a variety of crystal deposits in joints. The three main types of crystal arthritis are monosodium urate (gout), calcium pyrophosphate dihidrate (CPPD) and calcium phosphate (usually hydroxyapatite).[11] Refer to Table 29.7.

Table 29.7 *Crystal-induced disease*

Crystals	*Associated disease/syndrome*	*Typical joints or region affected*
Monosodium urate	Acute gout Tophaceous gout Asymptomatic Chronic gouty arthritis	Metatarsophalangeal joint of big toe Also: other foot joints ankle knee and patellar bursa wrist fingers
Calcium pyrophosphate dihidrate (CPPD)	Acute pseudogout Destructive arthropathy (like RA) Asymptomatic (most common)	Knee, wrist In older people > 60 years M = F
Basic calcium phosphate	Acute calcific periarthritis Destructive arthropathy Acute arthritis	Shoulder (supraspinatus)

Gout (monosodium urate crystal disease)

Gout is an abnormality of uric acid metabolism resulting in hyperuricaemia and urate crystal deposition. Urate crystals deposit in:

- joints—acute gouty arthritis
- soft tissue—tophi and tenosynovitis
- urinary tract—urate stones

Four typical stages of gout are recognised:

Stage 1	asymptomatic hyperuricaemia
Stage 2	acute gouty arthritis
Stage 3	intercritical gout (intervals between attacks)
Stage 4	chronic tophaceous gout and chronic gouty arthritis

Asymptomatic hyperuricaemia

- 10 times more common than gout[7]
- elevated serum uric acid
- absence of clinical manifestations
- usually does not warrant treatment

Typical clinical features of gout

- mainly a disease of men
- onset earlier in men (40–50) than women (60+)[5]
  acute attack
  —excruciating pain in great toe
  —early hours of morning
- skin over joint—red, shiny, swollen and hot
- exquisitely tender to touch
- may be precipitated by
  —alcohol excess, e.g. binge drinking
  —surgical operation
  —starvation
  —drugs, e.g. frusemide, thiazide diuretics
- relief with colchicine, NSAIDs, corticosteroids
- can subside spontaneously (3 to 10 days) without treatment

The arthritis (Fig. 29.7)

Monoarthritis in 90% of attacks:

- MTP joint great toe—75%
- other joints—usually lower limbs
  —other toes
  —ankles
  —knees

Polyarticular onset uncommon but may occur in DIP joints of fingers. No synovial joint is immune.

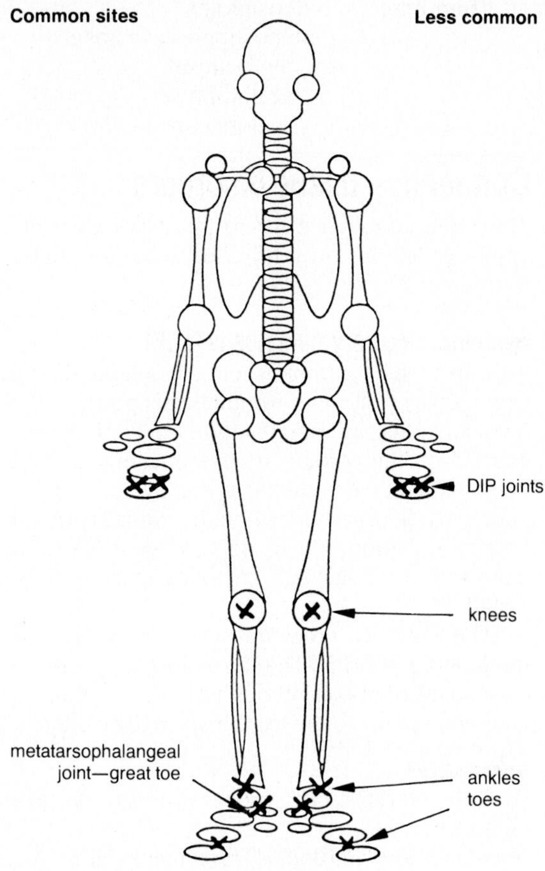

Fig. 29.7 *Gout: possible joint distribution*

Other features

- prone to recurrence
- tophi in ears, elbows, big toes, fingers, Achilles tendon (take many years)
- can cause patellar bursitis

Nodular gout

Develops in elderly women with renal impairment on diuretic therapy who develop pain and tophaceous deposits around osteoarthritic interphalangeal (especially DIP) joints of fingers.[12]

Diagnosis

- elevated serum uric acid (up to 30% can be within normal limits with a true acute attack)[11]
- synovial fluid aspirate → typical uric acid crystals using compensated polarised microscopy. This should be tried first as it is the only real diagnostic feature.
- X-ray: punched out erosions at joint margins

Management

The acute attack:

- NSAIDs, e.g. indomethacin 100 mg (o) statim, 75 mg 2 hours later, then 50 mg (o) tds for 24–48 hours.
- corticosteroids: intra-articular following aspiration and culture (gout and sepsis can occur together); a digital anaesthetic block is advisable. An oral course can be used.
- corticotrophin (ACTH) IM in difficult cases
- colchicine (only if NSAIDs not tolerated)

NB Avoid aspirin.

Long-term therapy

When acute attack subsides preventive measures include:

- weight reduction
- a normal, well-balanced diet
- avoidance of purine-rich food, e.g. organ meats (liver, brain, kidneys, sweetbread), tinned fish (sardines, anchovies, herrings) and game
- reduced intake of alcohol
- good fluid intake, e.g. water
- avoidance of drugs such as diuretics (thiazine, frusemide) and salicylates
- wearing comfortable shoes

Drug prophylaxis

Allopurinol (a xanthine oxidase inhibitor) is the drug of choice.
Dose: 300 mg daily
Indications:

- frequent acute attacks
- tophi or chronic gouty arthritis
- renal stones

Method

- Commence 4 weeks after last acute attack.
- Start with 100 mg daily and increase by 100 mg daily after each month.
- Add colchicine 0.5 mg bd for 6 months (to avoid precipitation of gout).

The spondyloarthropathies

The spondyloarthropathies are a group of disorders with common characteristics affecting the spondyles (vertebrae) of the spine. It is appropriate to regard them as synonymous with the seronegative spondyloarthropathies in distinction to rheumatoid arthritis which is seropositive and affects the cervical spine only. Apart from back pain this group tends to present with oligoarthropathy in younger patients.

Features[13]

- sacroiliitis with or without spondylitis
- enthesopathy, especially plantar fasciitis, Achilles tendinitis, costochondritis
- arthritis, especially larger lower limb joints
- extra-articular features, e.g. iritis, mucocutaneous lesions
- absent rheumatoid factor
- increased prevalence HLA-B_{27} antigen
- familial predisposition

The group of disorders

1. Ankylosing spondylitis
2. Reiter's syndrome/reactive arthritis
3. Inflammatory bowel disease (enteropathic arthritis)
4. Psoriatic arthritis
5. Juvenile chronic arthritis
6. Unclassified spondyloarthritis—partial features only

Ankylosing spondylitis

This usually presents with inflammatory back pain (sacroiliac joints and spine) and stiffness in young adults and 20% present with peripheral joint involvement before the onset of back pain. It usually affects the girdle joints (hips and shoulders), knees or ankles. At some stage over 35% have joints other than the spine affected.

Key clinical features

- insidious onset of discomfort
- age less than 40 years
- persistence for > 3 months
- associated morning stiffness
- improvement with exercise or NSAIDs

Reactive arthritis (Reiter's syndrome)

This is a form of reactive arthropathy in which non-septic arthritis and often sacroiliitis develop after an acute infection with specific venereal or dysenteric organisms.

Reiter's syndrome = NSU + conjunctivitis ± iritis + arthritis

Reactive arthritis = similar syndrome without occular or mucocutaneous lesions

The arthritis tends to affect the larger peripheral joints especially the ankle (talocrural) and knees but the fingers and toes can be affected in a patchy polyarthritic fashion. Mucocutaneous lesions including keratoderma blennorrhagia and circinate balanitis may occur, although the majority develop peripheral arthritis only (see Fig. 29.8).

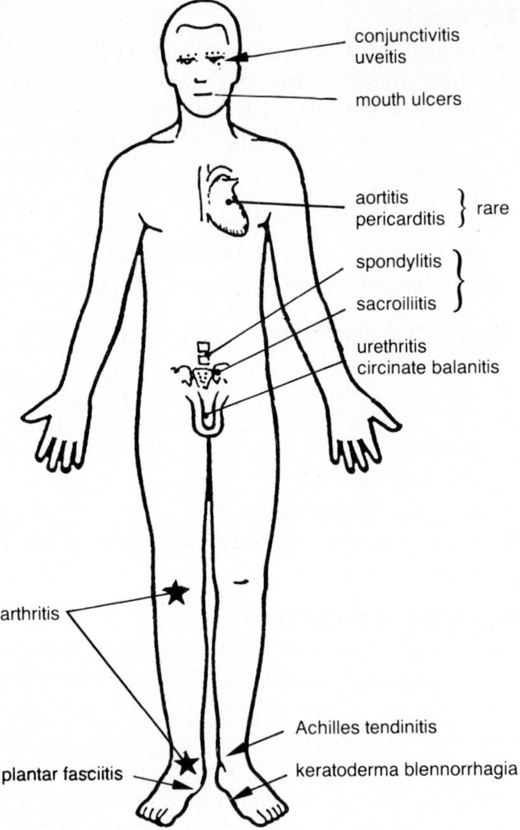

Fig. 29.8 *Possible clinical features of Reiter's disease*

Enteropathic arthritis

Inflammatory bowel disease (ulcerative colitis, Crohn's disease and Whipple's disease) may rarely be associated with peripheral arthritis and sacroiliitis.

Psoriatic arthritis

Like Reiter's syndrome, this can develop a condition indistinguishable from ankylosing spondylitis. It is therefore important to look beyond the skin condition of psoriasis, for about 5% will develop psoriatic arthropathy. It can have several manifestations:

1. mainly DIP joints
2. identical RA pattern but RA factor negative
3. identical ankylosing spondylosis pattern with sacroiliitis and spondylitis
4. monoarthritis, especially knees
5. severe deformity or 'mutilans' arthritis

Unclassified spondyloarthritis

Patients in this category seem to be the most frequently encountered in family practice. They clearly have a spondyloarthropathy but fail to meet the criteria for any one of the individual entities within the group. A typical patient is a young male in his third decade with a painful knee or other joint, unilateral (or bilateral) back pain with one of the entheseal problems, e.g. plantar fasciitis.

Management principles

- Identify the most active elements of the disease and treat accordingly.
- Provide patient and family education with appropriate reassurance: this is vital; stress that, although the disease is non-curable, treatment is effective and long-term prognosis generally good.
- Provide regular assessment and support.
- Give genetic counselling: e.g. in ankylosing spondylitis the risk to offspring is significant.
- Give advice regarding work, especially with posture.
- Refer for physiotherapy for exercises, postural exercises and hydrotherapy.
- Consider referral for occupational therapy.
- Pharmacological agents:
  —NSAIDs, e.g. indomethacin 75–200 mg daily to control pain, stiffness and synovitis
  —sulphasalazine (if NSAIDs ineffective)
  —intra-articular corticosteroids for severe monoarthritis and intralesional corticosteroids for enthesopathy.

Cautions

- Careful monitoring is required with NSAIDs and sulphasalazine.
- Systemic corticosteroids are not indicated.
- Immunosuppressants may be needed for severe intractable problems with psoriasis and reactive arthritis.
- These conditions should be managed in collaboration with a consultant.

Lyme disease

Lyme disease (known as Lyme borreliosis) was first described in 1975 and named after the town of Lyme in Connecticut. It has spread to almost all the states of the United States and is appearing in Europe and Asia at an increasing rate. Very infective, it is caused by a spirochete, *Borrelia burgdorferi*, and transmitted by *Ixodes* ticks, in particular the deer tick.

Diagnostic serology should be considered for patients with a history of tick bites, typical rash (a doughnut-shaped red rash about 6 cm in diameter) at the bite site, heart disorders (especially arrhythmias), unusual joint arthralgia or central nervous system disease. CNS disease includes muscle weakness of the limbs, muscular pain or evidence of meningitis. In children Lyme disease can be mistaken for juvenile chronic arthritis.

The arthralgia

The typical picture is that months (even years) after the tick bite up to 60% of patients will develop joint and periarticular pain (without objective findings), specific arthritis, mainly of the large joints such as the knee, and/or chronic synovitis.[14]

Treatment

Treatment is with penicillin, tetracycline or cephalosporins. If antibiotics are given early in the acute illness it tends to terminate abruptly.

The vasculitides

The vasculitides or vasculitis syndromes are a heterogeneous group of disorders involving inflammation and necrosis of blood vessels, the clinical effects and classification depending on the size of the vessels involved.

More common causes

These are the small vessel vasculitis effects associated with many important diseases such as rheumatoid arthritis, SLE, infective endocarditis, Henoch-Schönlein purpura and hepatitis B. Skin lesions and arthritis are usually associated with these disorders.

Rarer causes

The major vasculitides are polyarteritis nodosa, giant cell arteritis, polymyalgia rheumatica and Wegener's granulomatosis. Arthritis or limb girdle pain can be a component of the clinical presentation. The vasculitides are presented in more detail in Chapter 26.

When to refer

- Consider referring most severe true inflammatory disorders for diagnosis and initiation of treatment, e.g. rheumatoid arthritis, spondyloarthropathy, connective tissue disorders and suspicion of a vasculitide.
- Osteoarthritis
  - — generalised joint pain
  - — associated systemic symptoms
  - — deteriorating joint function
  - — intractable pain (especially at rest)
  - — if surgical procedure is contemplated[8]
- Rheumatoid arthritis
  - — persistent inflammation of a joint or joints
  - — patient ill and corticosteroids contemplated
  - — if a surgical procedure is contemplated
- Spondyloarthropathies
  - — initial referral for confirmation of diagnosis and initiation of treatment
  - — disease unresponsive to conventional treatment
  - — sudden deterioration in symptoms, especially pain
  - — onset of uveitis or other ocular complications
  - — adverse drug reactions
- Undiagnosed arthritis in presence of constitutional symptoms
- Suspicion of a suppurative or serious infective condition, e.g. septic arthritis, endocarditis, brucellosis
- Children with evidence of juvenile arthritis, e.g. Still's disease.

Practice tips

- Morning stiffness and pain, improving with exercise = rheumatoid arthritis.
- Flitting polyarthritis and fever = rheumatic fever; ? endocarditis; ? SLE.
- Polyarthritis (usually PIPs) and rash = viral arthritis or drug reaction.
- If rheumatoid arthritis involves the neck, beware of atlantoaxial subluxation and spinal cord compression.
- If the patient is young—think of SLE.
- If a patient returns from overseas with arthralgia, think of drug reactions, hepatitis, Lyme disease, but if the pain is intense consider dengue fever.
- Consider the possibility of Lyme disease in people with a fever, rash and arthritis who have been exposed to tick bites in rural areas.
- If a patient presents with Raynaud's phenomenon and arthritis, especially of the hands, consider foremost RA, SLE, and systemic sclerosis.
- Consider the possibility of septic arthritis in RA patients on corticosteroids.
- Most viral infections can cause polyarthritis,

which is invariably self-limiting and non-destructive. Treat simply with aspirin or NSAIDs.

- Consider HIV arthropathy and hepatitis B in young people with a history of intravenous drug abuse.
- Avoid the temptation to apply on doubtful grounds a broad label such as arthritis or rheumatoid, or a precise diagnosis such as rheumatoid arthritis, and introduce drugs.[15] Table 29.8 presents the diagnostic guidelines.[16]

Table 29.8 *Diagnostic guidelines for arthritis*

Disorder	***Sex ratio***	***Typical age***	***Typical common joints involved***	***Associated features***
Osteoarthritis (generalised—primary)	FM 6:1	> 50	DIP > PIP fingers base thumb (1st CMC) 1st MTP joint cervical and lumbar spines hips and knees	Pain worse in evenings, relieved by rest
Rheumatoid arthritis	FM 3:1	30–50	PIP, MCP hands wrist base of toes (MTP joints) symmetrical	Any joint: worse at rest, better with activity. Morning stiffness Constitutional symptoms Carpal tunnel syndrome Many other general effects
SLE	FM 9:1	15–35	symmetrical and variable small joints fingers often slight	Constitutional symptoms Fever Adverse drug reactions Any other system affected Rash (80%) Pleuritic symptoms (67%) Raynaud's
Systemic sclerosis	FM 3:1	20–50	symmetrical polyarthritis fingers	Raynaud's (90%) other skin changes Dysphagia
Viral arthropathies (excluding HIV)	M = F	Children	transient usually PIP joints fingers	Rash, fever
Ankylosing spondylitis	FM 3:1	18–30	sacroiliacs vertebral column esp. lumbar costovertebral also knees, hips or ankles	• Iridocyclitis • Chest dysfunction • Enthesopathy, e.g. plantar fasciitis
Psoriatic arthritis	M = F	any age	DIP joints—fingers and toes, sacroiliacs	Psoriasis rash (pre-existing) Pitted nails, 'sausage digits'
Enteropathic arthritis	M = F	any age	lower extremity: knees, feet, ankles, hips: sacroiliacs	Ulcerative colitis Crohn's disease
Reactive arthritis: Genitourinary eg. Reiter's Post-dysentery e.g. Salmonella	MF 20:1 M = F	15–30	as above	Preceding dysentery or urethritis entheseal problems
Gout	MF 20:1	M 40–50 F > 60	big toe (MTP joint): any other possible esp. lower limb DIP—osteoarthritis	Tophi Raised s. uric acid Urate crystals in joints Diuretics in elderly
Pseudogout	M = F	> 60 esp > 70	knee	Chondrocalcinosis Pyrophosphate crystals in joint
Polymyalgia rheumatica	FM 3:1	> 60	morning stiffness and pain in girdles esp. shoulder Joints normal or osteoarthritic	ESR ↑↑↑

References

1. Hart FD. *Practical problems in rheumatology*. London: Dunitz, 1985, 77.
2. Cormack J, Marinker M, Morrel D. *Practice: A handbook of primary health care*. London: Kluwer-Harrop Handbooks, 1980; 3.61:1–12.
3. Lassere M, McGuigan L. Systemic disease presenting as arthritis—a diagnostic approach. Aust Fam Physician, 1991; 20:1683–1714.
4. Rudge S. Joint pain in children: assessing the serious causes. Mod Med of Australia, May 1990:113–121.
5. Sandler G, Fry J. *Early clinical diagnosis*. Lancaster: MTP Press, 1986.
6. Nash PT, Webb J. Polyarticular and monoarticular arthritis. A diagnostic approach. Aust Fam Physician, 1986; 15:1265–1275.
7. Kumer PJ, Clarke ML. *Clinical medicine* (2nd edition), London: Baillere Tindall, 1990:382.
8. Muirden K. Osteoarthritis. In: MIMS Disease Index. Sydney: IMS Publishing, 1991–2:348–382.
9. Brooks P. Rheumatoid arthritis. In: MIMS Disease Index. Sydney: IMS Publishing, 1991–2:457–461.
10. Reilly P, Littlejohn G. Current treatment concepts in arthritis. Aust Fam Physician, 1989; 18:1499–1509.
11. Hall S. Crystal arthritis: a clinician's view. Aust Fam Physician, 1991, 20:1717–1724.
12. MacFarlane DG, Dieppe PA. Diuretic induced gout in elderly women. Br J Rheumatol, 1985; 24:155–159.
13. Creamer P. Edmonds J. Spondyloarthropathies. In: MIMS Disease Index. Sydney: IMS Publishing, 1991–2:509–512.
14. Schroder SA et al. *Current medical diagnosis and treatment*. East Norwalk: Appleton and Lange, 1990, 977–978.
15. Kincaid-Smith P, Larkins R, Whelan G, eds. *Problems in clinical medicine*. Sydney: MacLennan and Petty, 1989, 391.
16. Hart FD. Early clinical diagnosis of 12 forms of arthritis. Mod Med Australia, March 1989, 34–40.

30

Anorectal disorders

Anorectal problems are common in family practice and tend to cause anxiety in the patient that is often related to the fear of cancer. This fear may be well founded for many instances of rectal bleeding and lumps. It is important to keep in mind the association between haemorrhoids and carcinoma of the large bowel.

Anorectal problems include:

- pain
- lumps
- discharge
- bleeding
- pruritus

Common anorectal conditions are illustrated in Figure 30.1.

Anorectal pain

The patient may complain that defecation is painful or almost impossible because of anorectal pain.

Summary of causes

Pain without swelling:

- anal fissure
- anal herpes
- ulcerative proctitis
- proctalgia fugax
- solitary rectal ulcer

Painful swelling:

- perianal haematoma
- strangulated internal haemorrhoids
- abscess—perianal
  —ischiorectal

Anal fissure

Anal fissures cause pain on defecation and usually develop after a period of constipation (may be brief period) and tenesmus. Sometimes the pain can be excruciating, persisting for hours and radiating down the back of both legs. Anal fissures, especially if chronic, can cause minor anorectal bleeding (bright blood) noted as spotting on the toilet paper.

Examination

On inspection the anal fissure is usually seen in the anal margin, situated in the midline posteriorly (6 o'clock). The fissure appears as an elliptical ulcer involving the lower third of the anus from the dentate line to the anal verge.[1]

Digital examination and sigmoidoscopy are difficult because of painful anal sphincter spasm.

If there are multiple fissures Crohn's disease should be suspected. These fissures look different, being indurated, oedematous and bluish in colour.

In chronic anal fissures a senital pile is common and in longstanding cases a subcutaneous fistula is seen at the anal margin, with fibrosis and anal stenosis.[1]

Treatment

A trial of a high residue diet and avoidance of constipation may lead to resolution. Four finger anal dilatation (for 4 minutes) under general anaesthetic can be successful. This is usually followed by a brief period of incontinence.

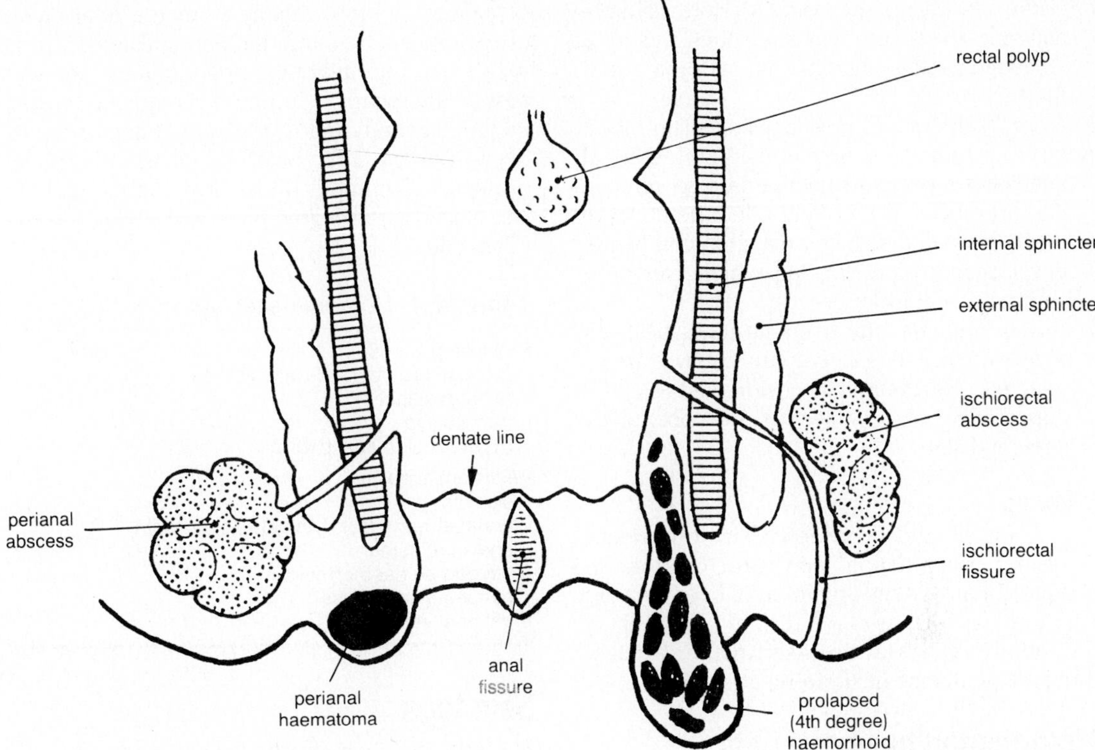

Fig. 30.1 *Common anorectal conditions*

Lateral sphincterotomy is indicated in patients with a recurrent fissure and a chronic fissure with a degree of fibrosis and anal stenosis. This surgical procedure is very effective.

Proctalgia fugax

Main features:

- fleeting rectal pain
- varies from mild discomfort to severe spasm
- lasts 3–30 minutes
- often wakes patient at night
- a functional bowel disorder
- affects adults, usually professional males

Management

- explanation and reassurance
- salbutamol inhaler (2 puffs statim) worth a trial

Solitary rectal ulcer syndrome

These ulcers occur in young adults; they can present with pain but usually present as the sensation of a rectal lump causing obstructed defecation and bleeding with mucus. The ulcer, which is usually seen on sigmoidoscopy about 10 cm from the anal margin on the anterior rectal wall, can resemble carcinoma. Management is difficult and a chronic course is common. Treatment includes a high residue diet and the avoidance of constipation.

Perianal haematoma

A perianal haematoma is a purple tender swelling at the anal margin caused by rupture of an external haemorrhoidal vein following straining at toilet or some other effort involving a Valsalva manoeuvre. The degree of pain varies from a minor discomfort to severe pain. It has been described as the 'five day, painful, self-curing pile'.

Management

Surgical intervention is recommended, especially in the presence of severe discomfort. The treatment depends on the time of presentation after the appearance of the haematoma.

1. *Within 24 hours of onset* Perform simple aspiration without local anaesthetic using a 19 gauge needle while the haematoma is still fluid.
2. *From 24 hours to 5 days of onset* The blood has clotted and a simple incision under local anaesthetic over the haematoma to remove the thrombosis is recommended. Removal of the haematoma reduces the chances of the development of a skin tag which can be a source of anal irritation.
3. *Day 6 onwards* The haematoma is best left alone unless it is very painful or (rarely) infected. Resolution is evidenced by the appearance of wrinkles in the previously stretched skin.

Follow-up

The patient should be reviewed in four weeks for rectal examination and proctoscopy, to examine for any underlying internal haemorrhoid that may predispose to further recurrence. Prevention includes an increased intake of dietary fibre and avoidance of straining at stool.

Strangulated haemorrhoids

A marked oedematous circumferential swelling will appear if all the haemorrhoids are involved. If only one haemorrhoid is strangulated proctoscopy will help to distinguish it from a perianal haematoma. Initial treatment is with rest and ice packs and then haemorrhoidectomy at the earliest possible time.

Perianal abscess

Clinical features

- severe, constant, throbbing pain
- fever and toxicity
- hot, red, tender swelling adjacent to anal margin
- non-fluctuant swelling

Careful examination is essential to make the diagnosis. Look for evidence of a fistula.

Treatment

Drainage via a cruciate incision over the point of maximal induration.

Anorectal lumps

Anorectal lumps are relatively common and patients are often concerned because of the fear of cancer. A lump arising from the anal canal or rectum, such as internal haemorrhoids, tends to appear intermittently upon defecation, and reduce afterwards.[1] Common prolapsing lesions include second- and third-degree haemorrhoids, hypertrophied anal papilla, polyps and rectal prolapse. Common presenting lumps include skin tags, fourth-degree piles and perianal warts (Table 30.1).

Table 30.1 *Common anal lumps*

Prolapsing lumps
- 2nd and 3rd degree haemorrhoids
- rectal prolapse
- rectal polyp
- hypertrophied anal papilla

Persistent lumps
- skin tag
- perianal warts (condylomata accuminata)
- anal carcinoma
- 4th degree haemorrhoids
- perianal haematoma
- perianal abscess

Skin tags

The skin tag is usually the legacy of an untreated perianal haematoma. It may require excision for aesthetic reasons, for hygiene or because it is a source of pruritus ani or irritation.

Method of excision

A simple elliptical excision at the base of the skin is made under local anaesthetic. Suturing of the defect is usually not necessary.

Perianal warts

It is important to distinguish the common viral warts from the condylomata lata of secondary syphilis. Local therapy includes the application of podophyllin every two or three days by the practitioner.

Internal haemorrhoids

Haemorrhoids or piles are common and tend to develop between the ages of 20 and 50. About one out of two westerners suffer from them by the time they are 50.[3] Internal haemorrhoids are a complex of dilated arteries, branches of the superior haemorrhoidal artery and veins of the internal haemorrhoidal venous plexus (Fig. 30.2). The commonest cause is chronic constipation related to a lack of dietary fibre.

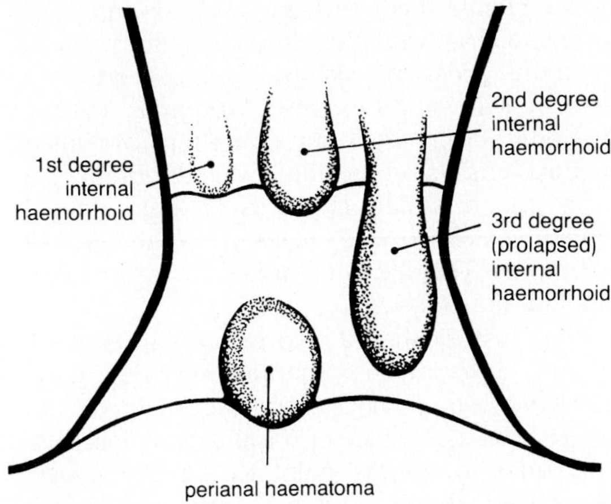

Fig. 30.2 *Classification of haemorrhoids*

Anatomically there are three classical sites, namely 3, 7 and 11 o'clock (Fig. 30.3).

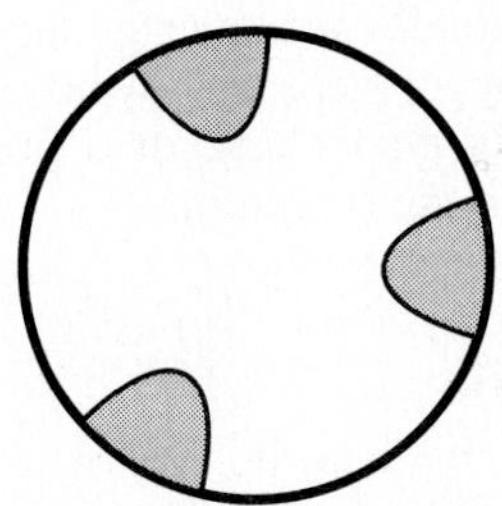

Fig. 30.3 *Three sites of primary haemorrhoids, looking into the anus from below*

Clinical stages and pathology[3]

Stage 1 1st degree internal haemorrhoids: three bulges form above the dentate line. Bright bleeding is common.

Stage 2 2nd degree internal haemorrhoids: the bulges increase in size and slide downwards so that the patient is aware of lumps when straining at stool, but they disappear upon relaxing. Bleeding is a feature.

Stage 3 3rd degree internal haemorrhoids: the pile continues to enlarge and slide downwards, requiring manual replacement to alleviate discomfort. Bleeding is also a feature.

Stage 4 4th degree internal haemorrhoids: prolapse has occurred and replacement of the prolapsed pile into the anal canal is impossible.

Symptoms

Bleeding is the main, and in many people, the only symptom. The word 'haemorrhoid' means flow of blood. Other symptoms include prolapse, mucoid discharge, irritation/itching, incomplete bowel evacuation and pain.

Treatment

The treatment of haemorrhoids is based on four procedures: namely, injection, rubber band ligation, cryotherapy and sphincterotomy. Surgery is generally reserved for large strangulated piles. The best treatment however is prevention, and softish bulky faeces that pass easily prevent haemorrhoids. People should be advised to have a diet with adequate fibre by eating plenty of fresh fruit, vegetables, whole grain cereals or bran. They should complete their bowel action within a few minutes and avoid using laxatives.

Anal discharge

Anal discharge refers to the involuntary escape of fluid from or near the anus. The causes may be considered as follows.[2]

Continent

- anal fistula
- pilonidal sinus
- sexually transmitted diseases
  - — anal warts
  - — gonococcal ulcers
  - — genital herpes
- solitary rectal ulcer syndrome
- carcinoma of anal margin

Incontinent

- minor incontinence—weakness of internal sphincter
- severe incontinence—weakness of levator ani and puborectalis

Partial continence

- faecal impaction
- rectal prolapse

Rectal bleeding

Patients present with any degree of bleeding from a smear on the toilet tissue to severe haemorrhage. Various causes are presented in Figure 30.4.

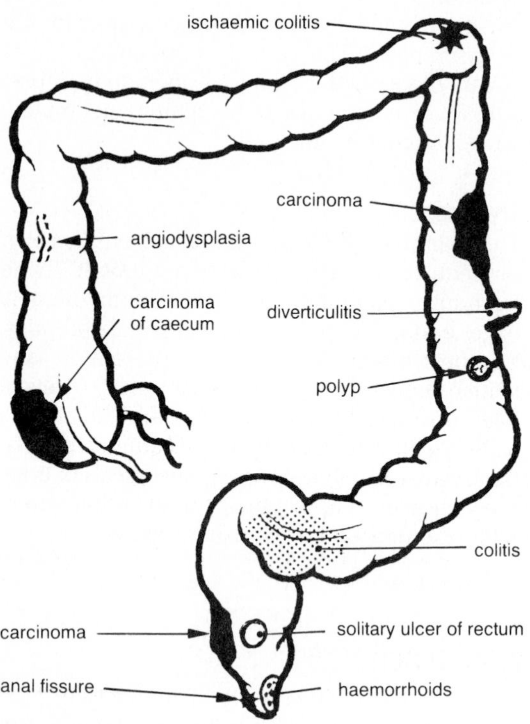

Fig. 30.4 *Various causes of rectal bleeding*

Local causes of bleeding include excoriated skin, anal fissure, a burst perianal haematoma and anal carcinoma. A characteristic pattern of bright bleeding is found with haemorrhoids. It is usually small non-prolapsing haemorrhoids that bleed.

The nature of the blood (e.g. bright red, dark red or black) and the nature of the bleeding (e.g. smear, streaked on stool, mixed with stool, massive) gives an indication of the source of the bleeding (Table 30.2). Black tarry (melaena) stool indicates bleeding from the upper gastrointestinal tract and is rare distal to the lower ileum.

Frequent passage of blood and mucus indicates a rectal tumour or proctitis, whereas more proximal tumours or extensive colitis present different patterns.

Substantial haemorrhage, which is rare, can be caused by diverticular disease, angiodysplasia or more proximal lesions such as Meckel's diverticulum and even duodenal ulcers. Angiodysplasias are 5 mm collections of dilated mucosal capillaries and thick-walled submucosal veins, found usually in the ascending colon of elderly patients who have no other bowel symptoms. The site is identified by technetium-labelled red cell scan.

The history should also include an analysis of any associated symptoms such as pain, diarrhoea or constipation, presence of lumps and a sensation of urgency or unsatisfied defecation. The latter symptoms point to a rectal cause. Associated change of bowel habit suggests a diagnosis of carcinoma of the rectum or left colon. Bleeding from right colon cancer is often occult, presenting as anaemia.

The examination includes a general assessment, anal inspection, digital rectal examination and proctosigmoidoscopy. Even if there is an anal lesion, proximal bleeding must be excluded in all cases by sigmoidoscopy[2] and by colonoscopy if there are any bowel symptoms or no obvious anal cause or a doubt about a lesion causing the symptoms.

Pruritus ani

Pruritus ani, which is itching of the anus, can be a distressing symptom that is worse at night, during hot weather and during exercise. It is seen typically in adult males with considerable inner drive, often at times of stress and in hot weather when sweating is excessive. In children, threadworm infestation should be suspected. It may be part of general itching, such as with a skin disease, or localised whereby various anorectal disorders have to be excluded.

Physical signs

The skin changes can vary from minimal signs to marked pathology which can show linear ulceration, maceration or lichenification. Superficial skin changes can be moist and macerated or dry and scaly. Full anorectal examination is necessary.

Causes and aggravating factors

Psychological factors:

- stress and anxiety
- fear of cancer

Table 30.2 *Presentation and causes of rectal bleeding*[3]

Presentation	Causes
Bright red blood in toilet separate from faeces	Internal haemorrhoids
Bright red blood on toilet paper	Internal haemorrhoids Fissure Anal carcinoma Pruritus Anal warts and condylomata
Blood and mucus on underwear	3rd degree haemorrhoids 4th degree haemorrhoids Prolapsed rectum Mucosal prolapse Prolapsed mucosal polyp
Blood on underwear (no mucus)	Ulcerated perianal haematoma Anal carcinoma
Blood and mucus mixed with faeces	Colorectal carcinoma Proctitis Colitis, ulcerative colitis Large mucosal polyp
Blood mixed with faeces (no mucus)	Small colorectal polyps Small colorectal carcinoma
Melaena (black tarry stools)	Gastrointestinal bleeding with long transit time to the anus
Torrential haemorrhage (rare)	Diverticular disease Angiodysplasia
Large volumes of mucus in faeces (little blood)	Villous papilloma of rectum Villous papilloma of colon
Blood in faeces with menstruation (rare)	Rectal endometriosis

Source: Orlay, G. *Office Proctology*, p. 11. © Copyright 1987 George Orlay—reproduced with permission.

Generalised systemic or skin disorders:

- eczema
- diabetes mellitus
- candidiasis
- antibiotic treatment
- worms: pinworm, threadworm
- diarrhoea causing excoriation

Local anorectal conditions:

- piles
- fissures
- warts

Zealous hygiene

Contact dermatitis:

- dyed or perfumed toilet tissue, soap, powder
- clothing

Excessive sweating:

- e.g. tight pantyhose in summer

Diagnostic approach

- urinalysis (? diabetes)
- anorectal examination
- scrapings and microscopy to detect organisms
- stool examination for intestinal parasites

Rules of treatment: patient education

1. *Scratching* Stop—it's taboo! If you scratch at night, wear light cotton gloves to bed.
2. *Bathing* Avoid hot water. Excessive showering and scrubbing is also bad for this condition. Use a cream such as bland aqueous cream for cleaning rather than soap.
3. *Drying* Keep the area as dry and cool as possible. After washing, dry gently and thoroughly with a soft towel or soft tissue: do not rub. Warm air from a hair drier is very useful.
4. *Bowel movements* Keep bowels regular and smooth by eating plenty of high-fibre foods such as bran, fresh carrots and apples. Some doctors claim that your bowel actions should be so smooth and complete that toilet paper should hardly be necessary.
5. *Toilet* Clean gently after bowel movements. Soft paper tissue (avoid pastel tints) may be used, then clean with tufts of cotton wool with aqueous cream or bland soap and water. The best way is to use cotton wool in warm water.
6. *Soaps and powder* Do not use perfumed soaps and talcum powder, including baby powder.

7. *Clothing* Wear loose clothing and underwear. In men, boxer shorts should be used in preference to jockey shorts. Cottons should be used. Let the air circulate in the area. At times a skirt but no underpants (in women) is desirable. Avoid pantyhose if possible.
8. *Topical creams* Do not use ointments unless your doctor has prescribed them. If a cream has to be used, simple creams may be the most soothing (e.g. toilet lanoline).

Topical treatment

- Treat the cause (if known).
- Avoid local anaesthetics, antiseptics.
- Advise aqueous cream to wash anus (instead of soap).
- Most effective preparations:

  hydrocortisone 1% cream

  or

  hydrocortisone 1% cream with clioquinol 3%

  (especially if dermatosis suspected)

Practice tips for pruritus ani

- Most cases of uncomplicated pruritus ani resolve with simple measures including explanation and reassurance.
- Otherwise prescribe hydrocortisone/ clioquinol cream.
- Lifestyle stress and anxiety underlies most cases.
- In obese patients with intertrigo and excessive sweating strap the buttocks apart with adhesive tape.

References

1. Hunt P, Marshall V. *Clinical problems in general surgery*. Sydney: Butterworths, 1991, 311.
2. Ryan P. *A very short textbook of surgery* (2nd edition), Canberra: Dennis and Ryan, 1990, 37–42.
3. Orlay G. *Office proctology*. Sydney: Australasian Medical Publishing Company, 1987, 11–52.

31

Low back pain

—

Low back pain accounts for at least 5% of general practice presentations. The most common cause is minor soft tissue injury, but patients with this do not usually seek medical help because the problem settles within a few days.

Most back pain in patients presenting to general practitioners is due to dysfunction of elements of the mobile segment, namely the facet joint, the intervertebral joint (with its disc) and the ligamentous and muscular attachments. This problem, often referred to as mechanical pain or traumatic joint derangement, will be described as vertebral dysfunction—a general term which, while covering radicular and non-radicular pain, includes dysfunction of the joints of the spine.

Key facts and checkpoints

- Back pain accounts for at least 5% of all presenting problems in general practice in Australia and 6.5% in Britain.[1]
- In the United States it is the commonest cause of limitation of activity under the age of 45.[2]
- Approximately 85% of the population will experience back pain at some stage of their life, while 70% of the world's population will have at least one disabling episode of low back pain in their lives.[2]
- At least 50% of these people will recover within two weeks and 75% within one month, but recurrences are frequent and have been reported in 40–70% of patients.
- The most common age groups are the 30s, 40s and 50s, the average age being 45 years.
- The most common cause of back pain is a minor strain to muscles and/or ligaments, but people suffering from this type of back pain usually do not seek medical treatment as most of these soft tissue problems resolve rapidly.
- The main cause of back pain presenting to the doctor is dysfunction of the intervertebral joints of the spine due to injury, also referred to as mechanical back pain (at least 70%).
- The causes of this dysfunction are disorders of the facet joints and internal disruption of the intervertebral disc, the exact balance being uncertain.
- The second most common cause of back pain is spondylosis (synonymous with osteoarthritis and degenerative back disease). It accounts for about 10% of cases of low back pain.
- L5 and S1 nerve root lesions represent most of the cases of sciatica presenting in general practice. They tend to present separately but can occur together with a massive disc protrusion.
- An intervertebral disc prolapse has been proven in only 6–8% of cases of back pain.[2]

Causes of low back pain

To develop a comprehensive diagnostic approach, the practitioner should have a clear understanding of the possible causes of low back and leg pain and of the relative frequency of their clinical presentations. The major causes of low back pain in several hundred patients presenting to the author's general practice are summarised in Table 31.1.

Table 31.1 *Major causes of low back ± leg pain presenting in the author's general practice*

Patients	%
Vertebral dysfunction	71.8
Lumbar spondylosis	10.1
Depression	3.0
Urinary tract infection	2.2
Spondylolisthesis	2.0
Spondyloarthropathies	1.9
Musculoligamentous strains/tears	1.2
Malignant disease	0.8
Arterial occlusive disease	0.6
Other	6.4
	100.0

Relevant causes are illustrated in Figure 31.1.

Anatomical and pathophysiological concepts

Recent studies have focused on the importance of disruption of the intervertebral disc in the cause of back pain. A very plausible theory has been advanced by Maigne[3] who proposes the existence, in the involved mobile segment, of a minor intervertebral derangement (MID). He defines it as 'isolated pain in one intervertebral segment, of a mild character, and due to minor mechanical cause'.

It is independent of radiological and anatomical disturbances of the segment. The most common clinical situation occurs where a vertebral level is found to be painful and yet to have a normal static and radiological appearance.

The MID always involves one of the two apophyseal joints in the mobile segment, thus initiating nociceptive activity in the posterior primary dermatome and myotome. The overlying skin is tender to pinching and rolling, while the muscles are painful to palpation and feel cord-like.

Maigne points out that the functional ability of the mobile segment depends intimately upon the condition of the intervertebral disc. Thus, if the disc is injured, other elements of the segment will be affected. Even a minimal disc lesion can produce apophyseal joint dysfunction which is a reflex cause of protective muscle spasm and pain in the corresponding segment, with loss of function (Figure 31.2).

A diagnostic approach

A summary of the safety diagnostic model is presented in Table 31.2.

Table 31.2 *Low back pain: diagnostic strategy model*

Q. *Probability diagnosis*
A. Vertebral dysfunction esp. facet joint and disc
Spondylosis (degenerative OA)

Q. *Serious disorders not to be missed*
A. Cardiovascular
- ruptured aortic aneurysm
- retroperitoneal haemorrhage (anticoagulants)

Neoplasia
- myeloma
- metastases

Severe infections
- osteomyelitis
- discitis
- tuberculosis
- pelvic abscess/PID

Cauda equina compression

Q. *Pitfalls (often missed)*
A. Spondyloarthropathies
- ankylosing spondylitis
- Reiter's disease
- psoriasis
- bowel inflammation

Sacroiliac dysfunction
Spondylolisthesis
Claudication
- vascular
- neurogenic

Prostatitis
Endometriosis

Q. *Seven masquerades checklist*

A.	
Depression	✓
Diabetes	—
Drugs	—
Anaemia	—
Thyroid disease	—
Spinal dysfunction	✓
UTI	✓

Q. *Is this patient trying to tell me something?*
A. Quite likely. Consider lifestyle, stress, work problems, malingering, conversion reaction

Note Associated buttock and leg pain included.

Probability diagnosis

The commonest cause of low back pain is vertebral dysfunction which then has to be further analysed.

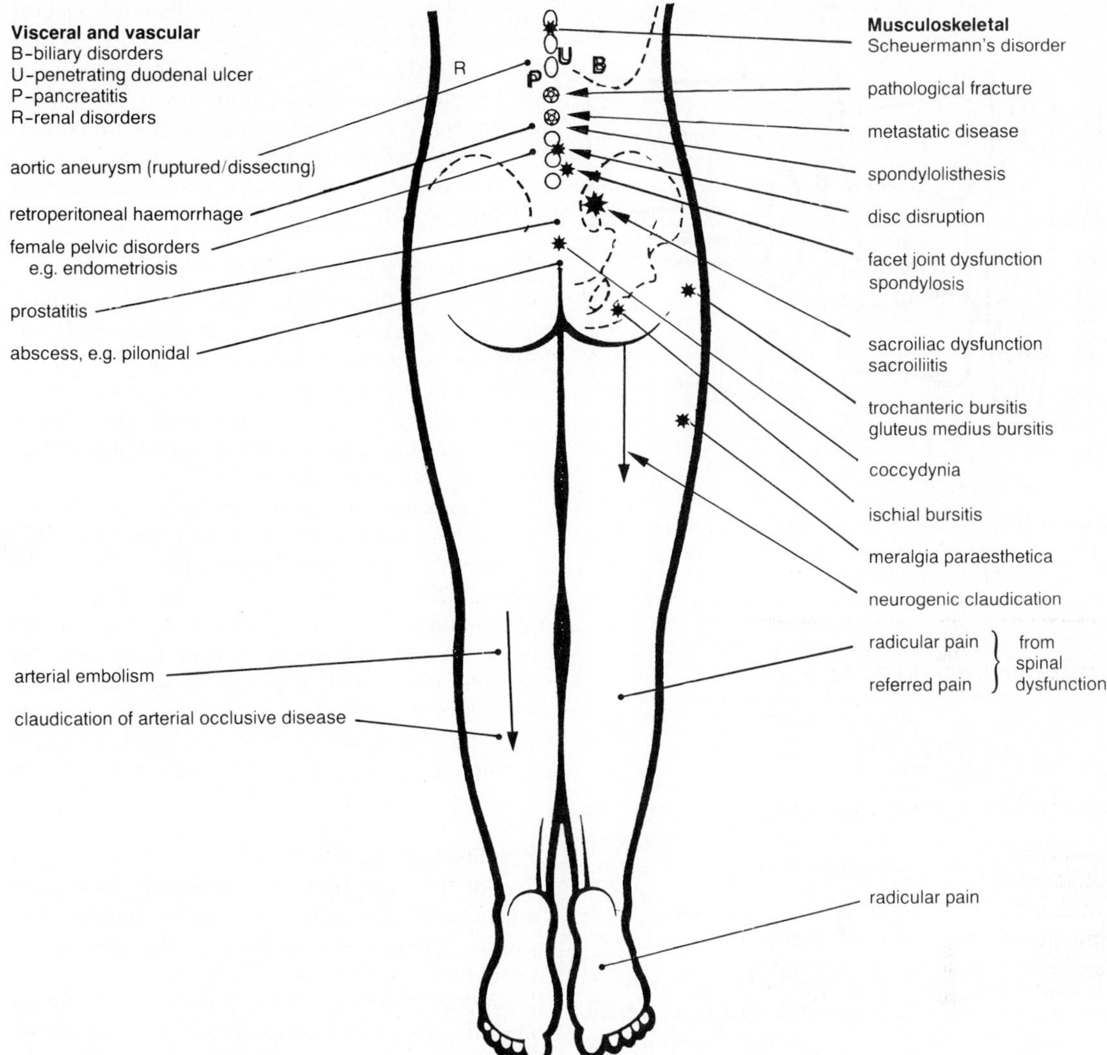

Fig. 31.1 *Relevant causes of back pain with associated buttock and leg pain*

Muscle or ligamentous tears or similar soft tissue injuries are uncommon causes of back pain alone: they are generally associated with severe spinal disruption and severe trauma such as that following a motor vehicle accident.

In the lumbar spine most problems originate from either the apophyseal joints or the intervertebral discogenic joint, or from both simultaneously. The disc can cause pain, either intrinsically from internal disruption or extrinsically by pressure on adjacent pain-sensitive structures, leading to radicular pain (if the nerve root is involved) or non-radicular pain.

Degenerative changes in the lumbar spine (lumbar spondylosis) are commonly encountered in the older age group. This problem, and one of its complications, spinal canal stenosis, is steadily increasing along with the ageing population.

Serious disorders not to be missed

It is important to consider malignant disease, especially in an older person. It is also essential to consider infection such as acute osteomyelitis and tuberculosis which is often encountered in recent immigrants, especially those from Asia. These conditions are considered in more detail under thoracic back pain. For pain or anaesthesia of sudden onset, especially when accompanied by neurological changes in the legs, consider

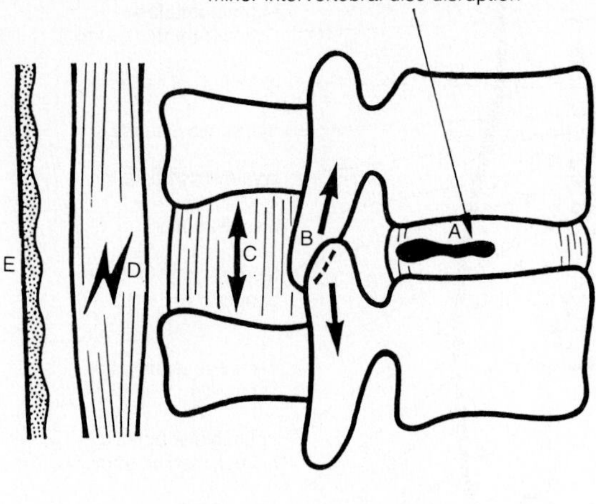

Fig. 31.2 *Reflex activity from a MID in the intervertebral motion segment. Apart from the local effect caused by the disruption of the disc (A), interference can occur in the facet joint (B) and interspinous ligament (C) leading possibly to muscle spasm (D) and skin changes (E) via the posterior rami*
REPRODUCED FROM C.KENNA AND J.MURTAGH *BACK PAIN AND SPINAL MANIPULATION*, BUTTERWORTHS, SYDNEY, 1989, WITH PERMISSION

cauda equina compression due to a massive disc prolapse and also retroperitoneal haemorrhage. It is important to ask patients if they are taking anticoagulants.

Pitfalls

The inflammatory disorders must be kept in mind, especially the spondyloarthropathies which include psoriatic arthropathy, ankylosing spondylitis, Reiter's disease, inflammatory bowel disorders such as ulcerative colitis and Crohn's disease, and reactive arthritis. The spondyloarthropathies are more common than appreciated and must be considered in the younger person presenting with features of inflammatory back pain, i.e. pain at rest, relieved by activity. The old trap of confusing claudication in the buttocks and legs, due to a high arterial obstruction, with sciatica must be avoided.

General pitfalls

- Being unaware of the characteristic symptoms of inflammation and thus misdiagnosing one of the spondyloarthropathies.
- Overlooking the early development of malignant disease or osteomyelitis. If suspected, and an X-ray is normal, a radionuclide scan should detect the problem.
- Failing to realise that mechanical dysfunction and osteoarthritis can develop simultaneously, producing a combined pattern.
- Overlooking anticoagulants as a cause of a severe bleed around the nerve roots and corticosteroids leading to osteoporosis.
- Not recognising back pain as a presenting feature of the drug addict.

Seven masquerades checklist

Of these conditions, depression and urinary tract infection have to be seriously considered. For the young woman with upper lumbar pain, especially if she is pregnant, the possibility of a urinary tract infection must be considered. These patients may not have urinary symptoms such as dysuria and frequency.

Depressive illness has to be considered in any patient with a chronic pain complaint. This common psychiatric disorder can continue to aggravate or maintain the pain even though the provoking problem has disappeared. This is more likely to occur in people who have become anxious about their problem or who are under excessive stress. Many doctors treat such patients with a therapeutic trial of antidepressant medication, for example, amitriptyline or doxepin.

Psychogenic considerations

The patient may be unduly stressed, not coping with life or malingering. It may be necessary to probe beneath the surface of the presenting problem.

A patient with low back pain following lifting at work poses a problem that causes considerable anguish to doctors, especially when the pain becomes chronic and complex. Chronic pain may be the last straw for patients who have been struggling to cope with personal problems; their fragile equilibrium is upset by the back pain. Many patients who have been dismissed as malingerers turn out to have a genuine problem. The importance of a caring, competent practitioner with an insight into all facets of his or her patient's suffering, organic and functional, becomes obvious. The tests for non-organic back pain are very useful in this context.

Nature of the pain

The nature of the pain may reveal its likely origin. Establish where the pain is worst—whether it is central (proximal) or peripheral. The following are general characteristics and guides to diagnosis:

- aching throbbing pain = inflammation, e.g. spondylitis
- deep aching diffuse pain = referred pain, e.g. dysmenorrhoea
- superficial steady diffuse pain = local pain, e.g. muscular strain
- boring deep pain = bone disease, e.g. neoplasia, Paget's disease
- intense sharp or stabbing (superimposed on a dull ache) = radicular pain, e.g. sciatica

A comparison of the significant features of the two most common types of pain—mechanical and inflammatory—is presented in Table 31.3.

The clinical approach

History

Analysing the history invariably guides the clinician to the diagnosis. The pain patterns have to be carefully evaluated and it is helpful to map the diurnal variations of pain to facilitate the diagnosis (Fig. 31.3).

It is especially important to note the intensity of the pain and its relation to rest and activity. In particular, ask whether the pain is present during the night, whether it wakes the patient, is present on rising or is associated with stiffness.

Continuous pain present day and night is suggestive of neoplasia or infection. Pain on waking also suggests inflammation or depressive illness. Pain provoked by activity and relieved by rest suggests mechanical dysfunction while pain worse at rest and relieved by moderate activity is typical of inflammation. In some patients the co-existence of mechanical and inflammatory causes complicates the pattern.

Pain aggravated by standing or walking that is relieved by sitting is suggestive of spondylolisthesis. Pain aggravated by sitting (usually) and improved with standing indicates a discogenic problem.

Pain of the calf that travels proximally with walking indicates vascular claudication; pain in the buttock that descends with walking indicates neurogenic claudication. This latter problem is encountered more frequently in older people who have a tendency to spinal canal stenosis associated with spondylosis.

Key questions

What is your general health like?
Describe the nature of your back pain.
Was your pain brought on by an injury?
Is it worse when you wake in the morning or later in the day?
How do you sleep during the night?
What effect does rest have on the pain?
What effect does activity have on the pain?
Is the pain worse when sitting or standing?
What effect does coughing or sneezing or straining at the toilet have?
What happens to the pain in your back or leg if you go for a long walk?
Do you have a history of psoriasis, diarrhoea, penile discharge, eye trouble or severe pain in your joints?
Do you have any urinary symptoms?
What medication are you taking? Are you on anticoagulants?
Are you under any extra stress at work or home?
Do you feel tense or depressed or irritable?

Physical examination

The basic objectives of the physical examination are to reproduce the patient's symptoms, detect

Table 31.3 *Comparison of the patterns of pain for inflammatory and mechanical causes of low back pain*[4]

Feature	***Inflammation***	***Mechanical***
History	Insidious onset	Precipitating injury/previous episodes
Nature	Aching, throbbing	Deep dull ache, sharp if root compression
Stiffness	Severe, prolonged Morning stiffness	Moderate, transient
Effect of rest	Exacerbates	Relieves
Effect of activity	Relieves	Exacerbates
Radiation	More localised, bilateral or alternating	Tends to be diffuse, unilateral
Intensity	Night, early morning	End of day, following activity

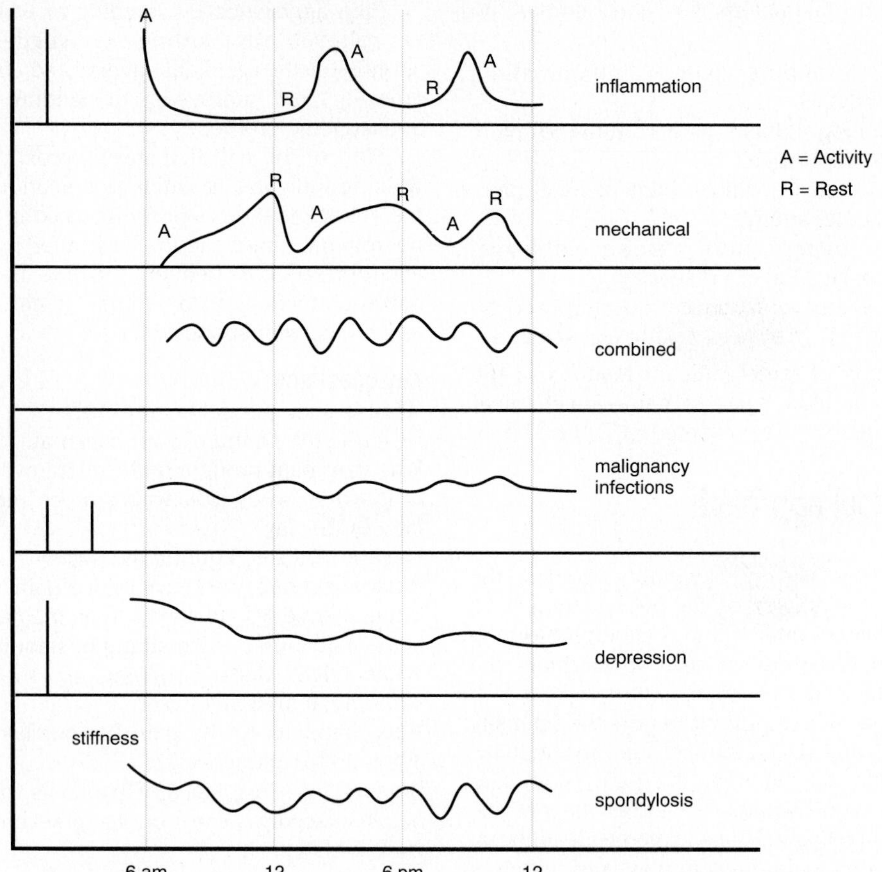

Fig. 31.3 *Typical daily patterns of pain for conditions causing back pain. Note conditions that can wake patients from sleep and also the combined mechanical and inflammatory patterns*

the level of the lesion and determine the cause (if possible) by provocation of the affected joints or tissues. This is done using the time-honoured method of joint examination—look, feel, move and test function. The patient should be stripped to a minimum of clothing so that careful examination of the back can be made. A neurological examination of the lower limb should be performed if symptoms extend below the buttocks.

A useful screening test for a disc lesion and dural tethering is the slump test.[4]

The main components of the physical examination are:

1. Inspection
2. Active movements
   - forward flexion
   - extension
   - lateral flexion (R & L)

   } to reproduce the patient's symptoms
3. Provocative tests
4. Palpation (to detect level of pain)
5. Neurological testing of lower limbs (if appropriate)
6. Testing of related joints (hip, sacroiliac)
7. Assessment of pelvis and lower limbs for any deformity, e.g. leg shortening
8. General medical examination including rectal examination

Important landmarks

The surface anatomy of the lumbar region is the basis for determining the vertebral level. Key anatomical landmarks include the iliac crest, spinous processes, the sacrum and the posterior superior iliac spines (PSIS).

- The tops of the iliac crest lie at the level of the L4–L5 interspace (or the L4 spinous process).
- The PSISs lie opposite S2 (Fig. 31.4).

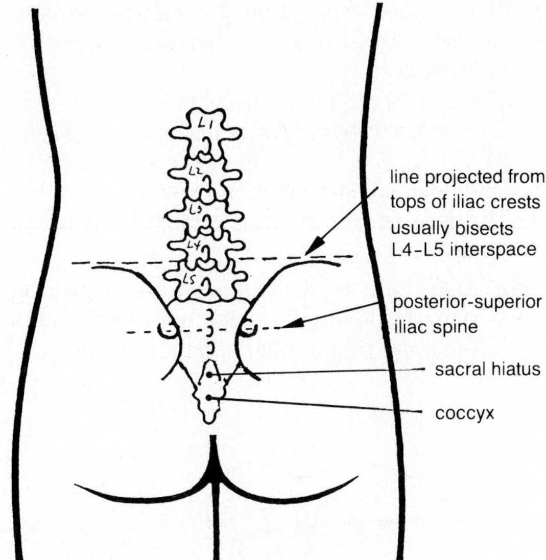

Fig. 31.4 *Surface anatomy and important landmarks of the lumbosacral spine*

Inspection

Inspection begins from the moment the patient is sighted in the waiting room. A patient who is noted to be standing is likely to have a significant disc lesion. Considerable information can be obtained from the manner in which the patient arises from a chair, moves to the consulting room, removes the shoes and clothes, gets onto the examination couch and moves when unaware of being watched.

The spine must be adequately exposed and inspected in good light. Patients should undress to their underpants; women may retain their brassiere and it is proper to provide them with a gown that opens down the back. Note the general contour and symmetry of the back and legs, including the buttock folds, and look for muscle wasting. Note the lumbar lordosis and any abnormalities such as lateral deviation. If lateral deviation (scoliosis) is present it is usually away from the painful side.

Note the presence of midline moles, tufts of hair or haemangioma that might indicate an underlying congenital anomaly such as spina bifida occulta.

Movements of the lumbar spine

There are three main movements of the lumbar spine. As there is minimal rotation, which mainly occurs at the thoracic spine, rotation is not so important. The movements that should be tested, and their normal ranges are as follows:

- extension (20°–30°) (Fig. 31.5a)
- lateral flexion, left and right (30°) (Fig. 31.5b)
- flexion (75°–90°: average 80°) (Fig. 31.5a)

Measurement of the angle of movement can be made by using a line drawn between the sacrum and large prominence of the C7 spinous process.

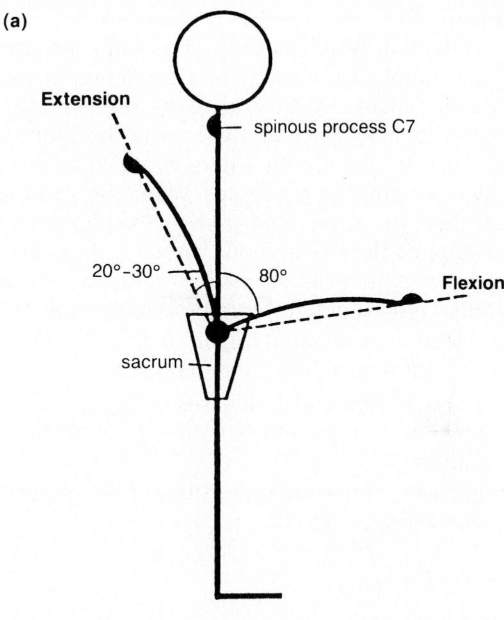

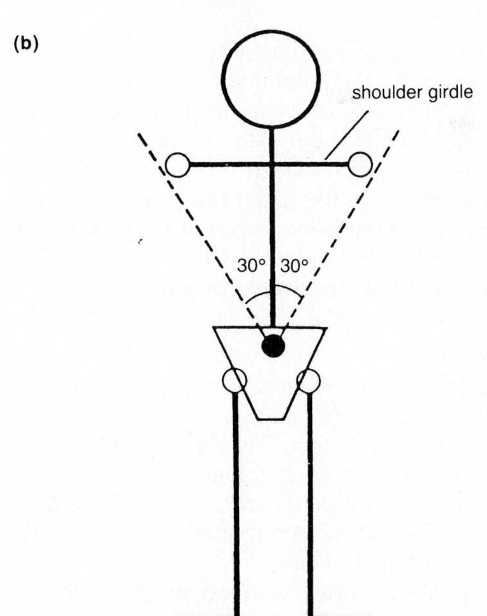

Fig. 31.5 **(a)** *Degrees of movement of the lumbar spine: flexion and extension;* **(b)** *degree of lateral flexion of the lumbar spine* REPRODUCED FROM C.KENNA AND J.MURTAGH *BACK PAIN AND SPINAL MANIPULATION*, BUTTERWORTHS, SYDNEY, 1989, WITH PERMISSION

Palpation

Have the patient relaxed, lying prone, with the head to one side and the arms by the sides. The levels of the spinous processes are identified by standing behind the patient and using your hands to identify L4 and L5 in relation to the top of the iliac crests. Mark the important reference points.

Palpation, which is performed with the tips of the thumbs opposed, can commence at the spinous process of L1 and then systematically proceed distally to L5 and then over the sacrum and coccyx. Include the interspinous spaces as well as the spinous processes. When the thumbs (or other part of the hand such as the pisiforms) are applied to the spinous processes, a firm pressure is transmitted to the vertebrae by a rocking movement for three or four 'springs'. Significant reproduction of pain is noted.

Palpation occurs at three main sites:

- centrally (spinous processes to coccyx)
- unilateral—right and left sides (1.5 cm from midline)
- transverse pressure to the sides of the spinous processes (R and L)

Provocation tests

Quadrant test

This test compresses the spinal joints, especially facet joints, on the painful side and can be used if active movements fail to reproduce the patient's pain. Stand behind the patient, place a hand on each shoulder and extend the lumbar spine to its limit. Ensuring the patient does not bend the knees, extend the spine to its limit, then laterally flex to the painful side, then rotate to that side and apply some downwards pressure.

Slump test

The slump test is an excellent provocation test for lumbosacral pain and more sensitive than the straight leg raising test. It is a screening test for a disc lesion and dural tethering. It should be performed on patients who have low back pain with pain extending into the leg, and especially for posterior thigh pain.

A positive result is reproduction of the patient's pain, and may appear at an early stage of the test (when it is ceased).

Method

1. The patient sits on the couch in a relaxed manner.
2. The patient then slumps forward (without excessive trunk flexion), then places the chin on the chest.
3. The unaffected leg is straightened.
4. The affected leg only is then straightened (Fig. 31.6).
5. Both legs are straightened together.
6. The foot of the affected straightened leg is dorsiflexed.

Note: Take care to distinguish from hamstring pain. Deflexing the neck relieves the pain of spinal origin, not hamstring pain.

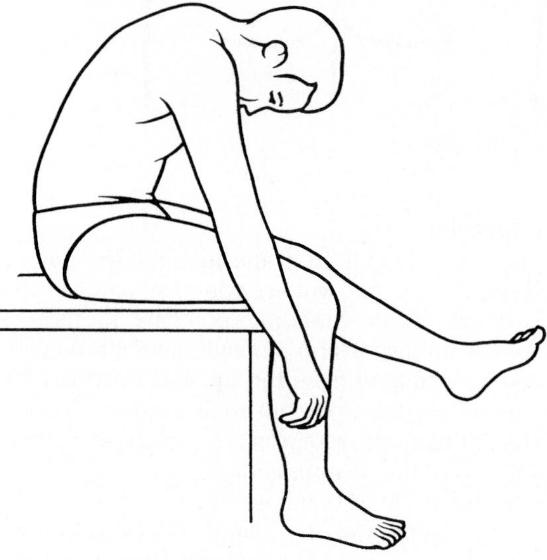

Fig. 31.6 *The slump test: one of the stages*

Significance of the slump test

- It is positive if the back or leg pain is reproduced.
- If positive, it suggests disc disruption.
- If negative, it may indicate lack of serious disc pathology.
- If positive, one should approach manual therapy with caution.

Neurological examination

A neurological examination is performed only when the patient's symptoms, such as pain, paraesthesia, anaesthesia and weakness, extend into the leg.

The importance of the neurological examination is to ensure that there is no compression of the spinal nerves from a prolapsed disc or from a tumour. This is normally tested by examining those functions that the respective spinal nerves serve, namely skin sensation, muscle power and reflex activity.

The examination is not daunting but can be performed quickly and efficiently in two to three minutes by a methodical technique that improves with continued use. The neurological examination consists of:

1. Quick tests
   — walking on heels (L5)
   — walking on toes (S1)
2. Dural stretch tests
   — slump test
   — straight leg raising (SLR)
3. Specific nerve root tests (L4,L5,S1)
   — sensation
   — power
   — reflexes

Main nerve roots (see Fig. 31.7)

L3:
- femoral stretch test (prone, flex knee, extend hip)
- motor—extension of knee
- sensation—anterior thigh
- reflex—knee jerk (L3, L4)

L4:
- motor—resisted inversion foot
- sensation—inner border of foot to great toe
- reflex—knee jerk

L5:
- motor—walking on heels
  —resisted extension great toe
- sensation—middle three toes (dorsum)
- reflex—nil

S1:
- motor—walking on toes
  —resisted eversion foot
- sensation—little toe, most of sole
- reflex—ankle jerk

Other examination

The method of examining the sacroiliac and hip joints is outlined in Chapter 55.

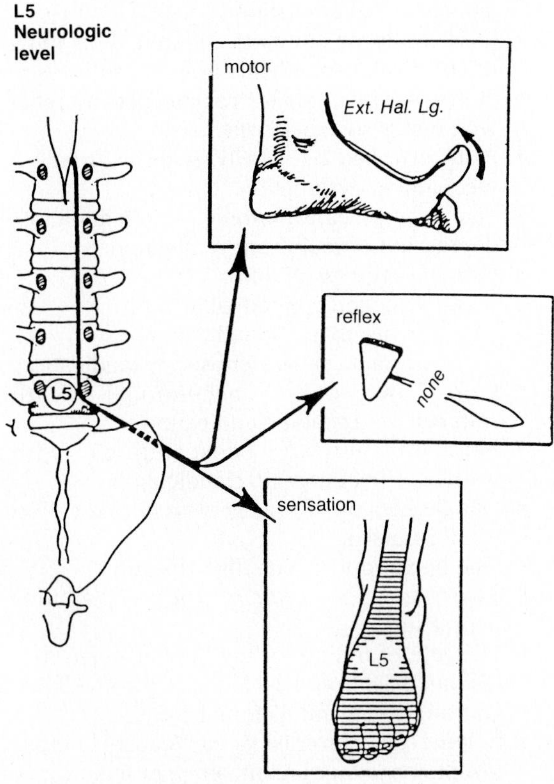

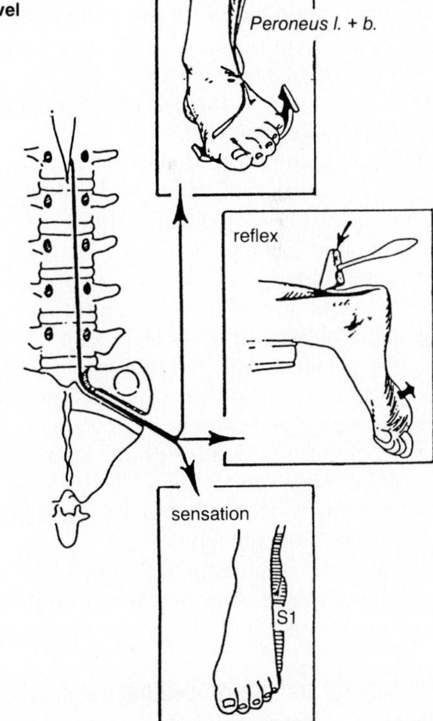

Fig. 31.7 *The main motor, sensory and reflex features of the nerve roots L5 and S1* REPRODUCED FROM S.HOPPENFELD *PHYSICAL EXAMINATION OF THE SPINE AND EXTREMITIES*, APPLETON AND LANGE, NORWALK, CT, USA, 1976, WITH PERMISSION

Investigations

Investigations for back pain can be classified into three broad groups: front-line screening tests; specific disease investigations; and procedural and pre-procedural tests.

Screening tests

These are most important for the patient presenting with chronic back pain when serious disease such as malignancy, osteoporosis, infection or spondyloarthropathy must be excluded. The screening tests for chronic pain are:

- plain X-ray
- urine examination (office dipstick)
- erythrocyte sedimentation rate (ESR)
- serum alkaline phosphatase
- prostatic specific antigen (in males > 50)

Specific disease investigation

Such tests include:

- peripheral arterial studies
- HLA-B_{27} antigen test for ankylosing spondylitis and Reiter's disease
- rheumatoid factor for rheumatoid arthritis
- serum electrophoresis for multiple myeloma
- brucella agglutination test
- blood culture for pyogenic infection and bacterial endocarditis
- bone scanning to demonstrate inflammatory or neoplastic disease and infections (e.g. osteomyelitis) before changes are apparent on plain X-ray
- tuberculosis studies
- X-rays of shoulder and hip joint
- electromyographic (EMG) studies to screen leg pain and differentiate neurological diseases from nerve compression syndromes
- radioisotope scanning
- technetium pyrophosphate scan of SIJ for ankylosing spondylitis
- selective anaesthetic block of facet joint under image intensification
- selective anaesthetic block of medial branches of posterior primary rami and other nerve roots

Procedural and pre-procedural diagnostic tests

These tests should be kept in reserve for chronic disorders, especially mechanical disorders, that remain undiagnosed and unabated, and where surgical intervention is planned for a disc prolapse requiring removal.

Depending on availability and merit, such tests include:

- computerised tomography (CT scan)
- myelography or radiculography
- discography
- magnetic resonance imaging (MRI)

Summary of diagnostic guidelines for spinal pain

- Continuous pain (day and night) = neoplasia, especially malignancy or infection.
- The big primary malignancy is multiple myeloma.
- The big three metastases are from lung, breast and prostate.
- The other three metastases are from thyroid, kidney/adrenal and melanoma.
- Pain with standing/walking (relief with sitting) = spondylolisthesis.
- Pain (and stiffness) at rest, relief with activity = inflammation.
- In a young person with inflammation think of ankylosing spondylitis or Reiter's disease.
- Stiffness at rest, pain with or after activity, relief with rest = osteoarthritis.
- Pain provoked by activity, relief with rest = mechanical dysfunction.
- Pain in bed at early morning = inflammation, depression or malignancy/infection.
- Pain in periphery of limb
  = discogenic → radicular
  or vascular → claudication
  or spinal canal stenosis → claudication.
- Pain in calf (ascending) with walking = vascular claudication.
- Pain in buttock (descending) with walking = neurogenic claudication.
- One disc lesion = one nerve root (exception is L5–S1 disc).
- One nerve root = one disc (usually).
- Two or more nerve roots—consider neoplasm.
- The rule of thumb for the lumbar nerve root lesions is L3 from L2–L3 disc, L4 from L3–L4, L5 from L4–L5 and S1 from L5–S1.
- A large disc protrusion can cause bladder symptoms, either incontinence or retention.
- A retroperitoneal bleed from anticoagulation therapy can give intense nerve root symptoms and signs.

Back pain in children

The common mechanical disorders of the intervertebral joints can cause back pain in children, which must always be taken seriously. Like abdominal pain and leg pain, it can be related to psychogenic factors, so this possibility should be considered by diplomatically evaluating problems at home, at school or with sport.

Especially in children under the age of ten, it is very important to exclude organic disease. Infections such as osteomyelitis and tuberculosis are rare possibilities, and 'discitis' has to be considered. This painful condition can be idiopathic, but can also be caused by the spread of infection from a vertebral body. It has characteristic radiological changes.

Tumours causing back pain include the benign osteoid osteoma and the malignant osteogenic sarcoma. Osteoid osteoma is a very small tumour with a radiolucent nucleus that is sharply demarcated from the surrounding area of sclerotic bone. Although more common in the long bones of the leg, it can occur in the spine.

In older children and adolescents the organic causes of back pain are more likely to be inflammatory, congenital or from developmental anomalies and trauma.

A prolapsed intervertebral disc, which can occur (uncommonly) in adolescents, can be very unusual in its presentation. There is often marked spasm, with a stiff spine and lateral deviation which may be out of proportion to the relatively lower degree of pain.

Spondylolisthesis can occur in older children, usually due to a slip of L5 or S1, because the articular facets are congenitally absent or because of a stress fracture in the parsinter-articularis. It is necessary to request standing lateral and oblique X-rays.

Back pain in the elderly

Traumatic spinal dysfunction is still the most common cause of back pain in the elderly and may represent a recurrence of earlier dysfunction. It is amazing how commonly disc prolapse and facet joint injury can present in the aged. However, degenerative joint disease is very common and, if advanced, can present as spinal stenosis with claudication and nerve root irritation due to narrowed intervertebral foraminae.

Special problems to consider are malignant disease, degenerative spondylolisthesis, vertebral pathological fractures and occlusive vascular disease.

Acute back and leg pain due to vertebral dysfunction

Mechanical disruption of the vertebral segment or segments is the outstanding cause to consider while the main serious clinical syndromes are secondary to disruption with or without prolapse of the intervertebral disc, usually L4–L5 or L5–S1.

Table 31.4 presents the general clinical features and diagnosis in acute back pain (fractures excluded) following vertebral dysfunction: the symptoms and signs can occur singly or in combination.

Fortunately, syndromes A and B are extremely rare but, if encountered, urgent referral to a surgeon is mandatory. Clinical features of the cauda equina syndrome are presented in Figure 31.8. Syndrome B can follow a bleed in patients taking anticoagulant therapy or be caused by a disc sequestration after inappropriate spinal manipulation.

Vertebral dysfunction with non-radicular pain

This outstanding common cause of low back pain is considered to be due mainly to dysfunction of the pain-sensitive facet joint. The precise pathophysiology is difficult to pinpoint but invariably is dysfunction of one of the spinal joints, most likely a facet joint of the MID as proposed by Maigne.

Typical profile[4]

Age:	Any age—late teens to old age, usually 30–60
History of injury:	Yes, lifting or twisting
Site and radiation:	Unilateral lumbar (may be central) Refers over sacrum, SIJ areas, buttocks
Type of pain:	Deep aching pain, episodic
Aggravation:	Activity, lifting, gardening, housework (vacuuming, making beds, etc.)
Relief:	Rest, warmth

Table 31.4 *Clinical features and diagnosis of vertebral dysfunction leading to low back and leg pain*[4]

Clinical features	*Frequency*	*Diagnosis*
Syndrome A (surgical emergency)	very rare	Spinal cord (UMN) or cauda equina (LMN) compression
Saddle anaesthesia (around anus, scrotum or vagina) Distal anaesthesia Evidence of UMN or LMN lesion Loss of sphincter control or urinary retention Weakness of legs peripherally		
Syndrome B (probable surgical emergency)	uncommon	Large disc protrusion, paralysing nerve root
Anaesthesia or paraesthesia of the leg Foot drop Motor weakness Absence of reflexes		
Syndrome C	common	Posterolateral disc protrusion on nerve root or disc disruption
Distal pain with or without paraesthesia Sciatica Positive dural stretch tests		
Syndrome D	very common	Disc disruption or facet dysfunction
Lumbar pain (unilateral, central or bilateral)		

Associations:	May be stiffness, usually good health
Physical examination (significant):	Localised tenderness—unilateral or central L4,L5 or S1 levels. May be restricted flexion, extension, lateral flexion
Diagnosis confirmation:	Investigation usually normal *Note*: diagnosis made clinically

Management

- complete rest for 2 to 3 days (for acute pain), otherwise activity directed by degree of pain
- back education program
- analgesics
- exercise program and swimming (as tolerated)
- physical therapy—mobilisation, manipulation (for persistent problems)

Radiculopathy

Radicular pain, caused by nerve root compression from a disc protrusion (most common cause) or tumour or a narrowed intervertebral foramina, typically produces pain in the leg related to the dermatome and myotome innervated by that nerve root. Leg pain may occur alone without back pain and vary considerably in intensity.

Typical profile of radicular pain (discogenic)

Age:	Any age, usually middle-aged
History of injury:	Yes, lifting or twisting Can be spontaneous
Site and radiation:	Unilateral low back, distal radiation along dermatome, tends to have a 'distal' emphasis
Type of pain:	Deep aching or stabbing pain (episodic) develops soon after rising in morning Has a 'travelling' nature
Aggravation:	Activity, lifting, intercourse, sitting, bending, car travel, coughing, sneezing, straining
Relief:	Rest, lying, standing
Associations:	Distal paraesthesia ± numbness, stiffness

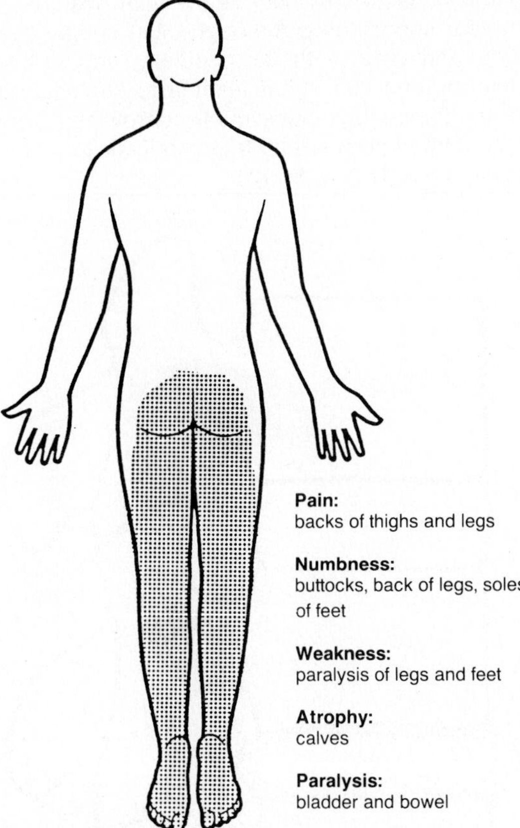

Fig. 31.8 *Cauda equina syndrome due to massive prolapsed intervertebral disc*

Physical examination (significant):	Guarded and restricted movement Loss of lumbar lordosis Lateral deviation (scoliosis) Restricted flexion, extension, lateral flexion
typically unilateral	SLR and slump test positive ± specific muscle/myotomal weakness ± reduced distal sensation ± reduced ankle jerk (S1)
Diagnostic confirmation (for special reasons):	CT scan, discogram, radiculogram, MRI or myelogram

The two nerve roots that account for most of these problems are L5 and S1. Most settle with time (6 to 12 weeks). The management is outlined under sciatica (Chapter 56).

Spondylolisthesis

About 5% of the population have spondylolisthesis but not all are symptomatic. The pain is caused by extreme stretching of the interspinous ligaments or of the nerve roots. The onset of back pain in many of these patients is due to concurrent disc degeneration rather than a mechanical problem.

Typical profile[4]

Age:	Any age; young adult if congenital, older person (over 50) if degenerative
History of injury:	May precipitate problem
Site and radiation:	Low lumbar Radiates bilaterally or unilaterally into buttocks, hip, thighs and feet
Type of pain:	Dull ache, episodic depending on activity
Onset:	Onset usually mid-morning after standing
Aggravation:	Prolonged standing, walking, exercise
Relief:	Sitting down, lying down
Associations:	Paraesthesia in legs Stiffness after exercise May be associated discogenic lesion
Physical examination (significant):	Stiff waddling gait Increased lumbar lordosis Flexed knee stance Tender prominent SP of 'slipped' vertebrae Limited flexion Hamstring tightness or spasm
Diagnosis confirmation:	Lateral X-ray (standing) (Fig. 31.9)

Management

It is amazing how this instability problem can be alleviated with excellent relief of symptoms by getting patients to follow a strict flexion exercise program for at least three months. The objective is for patients to 'splint' their own spine by strengthening abdominal and spinal muscles.

Extension of the spine should be avoided, especially hyperextension. Gravity traction might help. Recourse to lumbar corsets or surgery (for spinal fusion) should be resisted although appropriate in a few severe intractable cases.

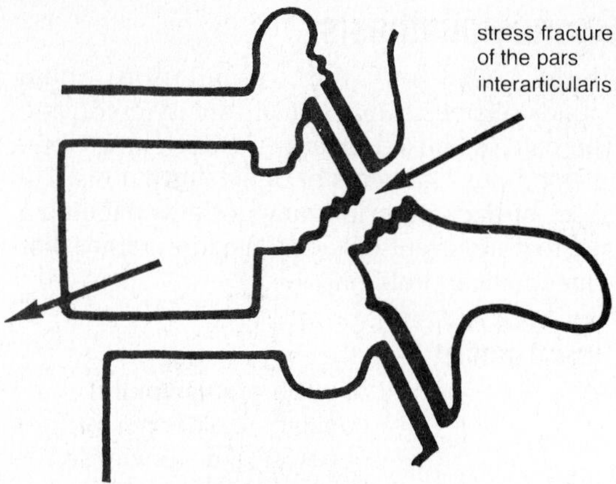

Fig. 31.9 *Spondylolisthesis: illustrating a forward shift of one vertebra on another*

Lumbar spondylosis

Lumbar spondylosis, also known as degenerative osteoarthritis or osteoarthrosis, is a common problem of wear and tear that may follow vertebral dysfunction, especially following severe disc disruption and degeneration.

Typical profile[4]

Age:	Over 50 years More common with increasing age
History of injury:	Heavy manual work, trauma to spine, e.g. motor vehicle accident
Site and radiation:	Low back pain May radiate to buttocks
Type of pain:	Dull nagging ache (often constant) Acute episodes on chronic background
Aggravation:	Heavy activity, bending Limited tolerance of standing and sitting
Relief:	Resting by lying straight, gentle exercise, hydrotherapy
Associations:	Stiffness, especially in mornings Stiffness with immobility Generally good health
Physical examination	All movements restricted
Diagnosis confirmation:	X-ray

Stiffness of the low back is the main feature of lumbar spondylosis. Although most people live with and cope with the problem, progressive deterioration can occur leading to subluxation of the facet joints. Subsequent narrowing of the spinal and intervertebral foramen leads to spinal canal stenosis (Fig. 31.10).

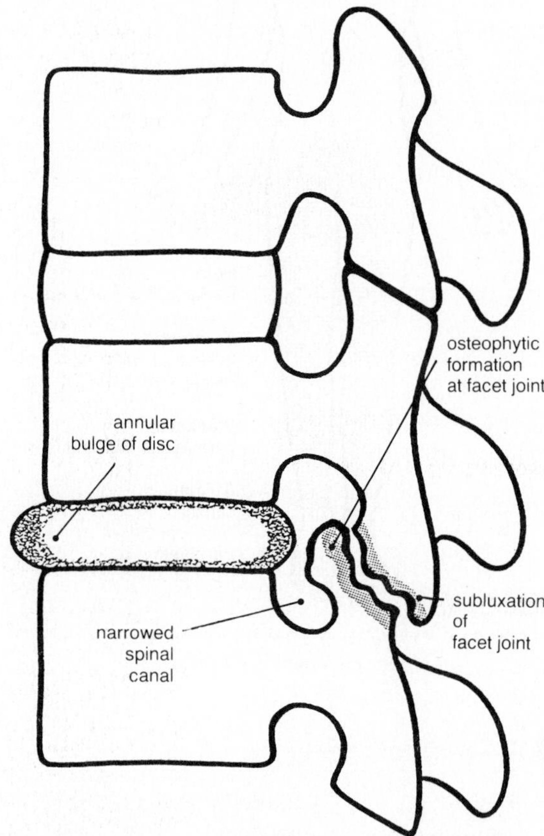

Fig. 31.10 *Lumbar spondylosis with degeneration of the disc and facet joint, leading to narrowing of the spinal canal and intervertebral foramen*

Management

- basic analgesics (depending on patient response and tolerance)
- non-steroidal anti-inflammatory drugs (judicious use)
- appropriate balance between light activity and rest
- exercise program and hydrotherapy (if available)
- regular mobilisation therapy may help
- consider trials of electrotherapy such as TENS and acupuncture

The spondyloarthropathies

The seronegative spondyloarthropathies are a group of disorders characterised by involvement of the sacroiliac joints with an ascending spondylitis and extraspinal manifestations such as oligoarthritis and enthesopathies (Figs. 31.11a, b, c) (refer Chapter 29). The pain and stiffness which are the characteristic findings of spinal involvement are typical of inflammatory disease; namely, worse in the morning, may occur at night and improves rather than worsens with exercise.

The main disorders in this group are ankylosing spondylitis, psoriatic arthritis, Reiter's disease, reactive spondyloarthropathies and the inflammatory bowel disorders. Hence the importance of searching for a history of psoriasis, diarrhoea, urethral discharge, eye disorders and episodes of arthritis in other joints. The following profile for ankylosing spondylitis serves as a typical clinical presentation of back pain for this group.

Typical profile of ankylosing spondylitis[4]

Age and sex:	Young men 15–30 (rare onset after 40)
History of injury:	None, unless coincidental Has a slow insidious onset
Site and radiation:	Low back, may radiate to both buttocks or posterior thigh (rare below knees) Can alternate sides
Type of pain:	Aching, throbbing pain of inflammation Commonly episodic
Aggravation:	Often worse at night (can wake patient), turning over in bed and rising in the morning
Relief:	Activity including exercise Patient may walk around during night for relief
Associations:	Back stiffness, especially in morning Pain and stiffness in thoracic or cervical spine Pain and stiffness in thoracic cage Peripheral joint pain (up to 50% of cases) Iritis (up to 25% of cases)

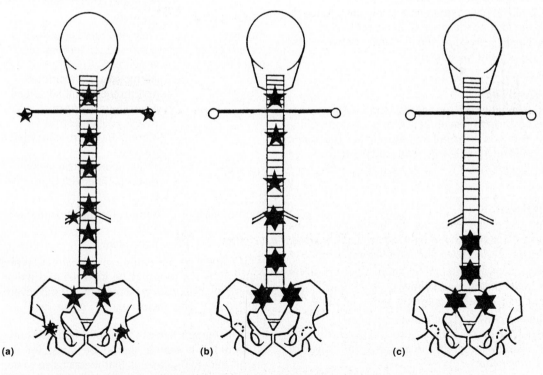

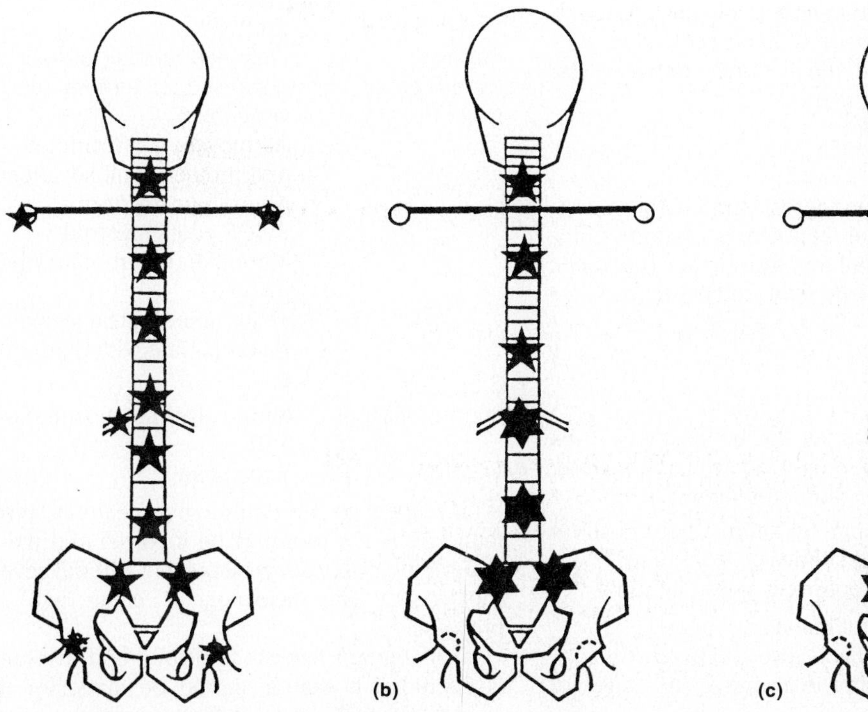

Fig. 31.11 **(a)** *Ankylosing spondylitis and psoriasis: main target areas on vertebral column and girdle joints*
(b) *Crohn's disease and ulcerative colitis: main target areas of enteropathies*
(c) *Reiter's disease: main target areas*

Physical examination (significant):	Absent lumbar lordosis Lateral flexion limited first, then flexion and extension Positive sacroiliac joint stress tests Positive Schober's test
Diagnosis confirmation:	X-ray of pelvis (sacroiliitis) Bone scans and CT scans ESR usually elevated $HLA\text{-}B_{27}$ antigen positive in over 90% of cases

Schober's test

This test is a useful objective means of measuring the mobility of the lumbar spine and is useful to detect the spondyloarthropathies in younger patients.

Modified method

- Stand the patient erect and mark the spine in line with the dimples of Venus (the posterior superior iliac spines).
- Place another mark 10 cm above the first and a third mark 5 cm below the first mark.
- Ask the patient to bend forward, as if to touch the toes, to the point of maximal flexion.
- Finally, measure the distance between the upper and lower marks.

Interpretation

- Normal is > 5 cm increase in length.
- Less than 5 cm represents hypomobility, common in the inflammatory spinal disorders, severe spondylosis and intervertebral disc disorders.

Treatment

The earlier the treatment the better the outlook for the patient; the prognosis is usually good. The basic objectives of treatment are:

- prevention of spinal fusion in a poor position
- relief of pain and stiffness
- maintenance of optimum spinal mobility

The basic methods of management are:

- advice on good back care and posture
- exercise programs to improve the range of movement
- drug therapy, especially tolerated NSAIDs
- sulphasalazine—a useful second-line agent if the disease progresses despite NSAIDs

Malignant disease

It is important to identify malignant disease and other space-occupying lesions as early as possible because of the prognosis and the effect of a delayed diagnosis on treatment.

Typical profile[4]

Age:	Usually over 50, but the older the patient the greater the risk
History of injury:	Usually insidious onset
Site and radiation:	Localised pain anywhere in lumbar spine Radiates into buttocks or legs (if nerve root involved)
Type of pain:	Boring deep ache, can be referred or radicular, unrelenting continuous pain, getting worse
Aggravation:	Movement Specific activities such as lifting, gardening
Relief:	Usually none No response to treatment
Associations:	Malaise, fatigue, weight loss Muscular weakness Night pain
Physical examination (significant):	Flattened lumbar lordosis Localised tenderness over vertebrae All movements restricted and protective (if advanced) Neurologically normal unless roots involved More than one root may be involved Major neurological signs incompatible with pain level
Diagnosis confirmation:	X-ray Serum alkaline phosphatase ESR Bone scan

With respect to the neurological features, more than one nerve root may be involved and major neurological signs may be present without severe root pain. The neurological signs will be progressive.

If malignant disease is proved and myeloma is excluded a search should be made for the six primary malignancies that metastasise to the spine (Fig. 31.12). If the bone is sclerotic consider prostatic secondaries, some breast secondomas or Paget's disease.

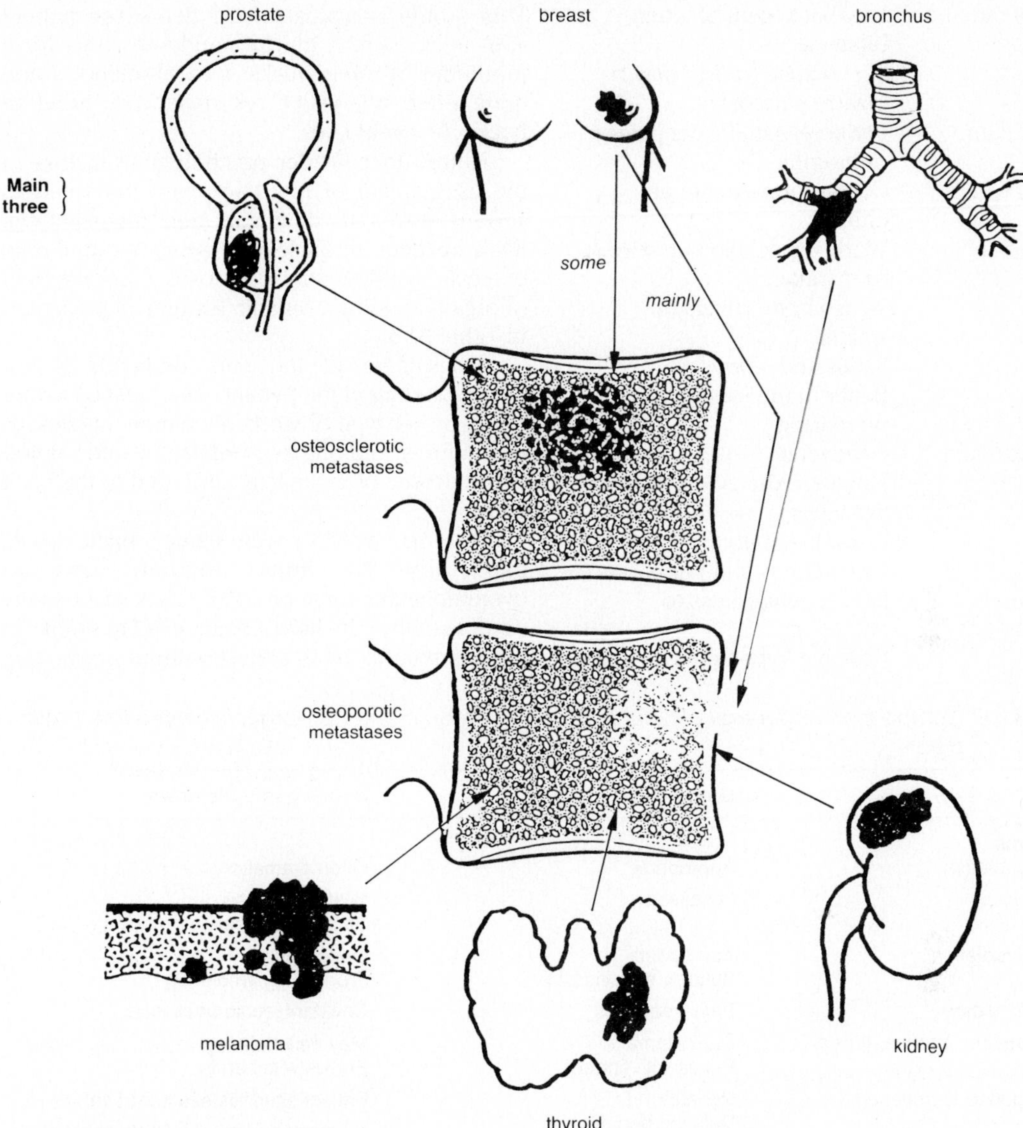

Fig. 31.12 *Important primary malignancies metastasing to the spine. Note the difference between sclerotic and osteoporotic metastases; multiple myeloma also causes osteoporotic lesions*

Non-organic back pain

Like headache, back pain is a symptom of an underlying functional, organic or psychological disorder.[4] Preoccupation with organic causation of symptoms may lead to serious errors in the assessment of patients with back pain. Any vulnerable aching area of the body is subject to aggravation by emotional factors.

Depressed patients are generally less demonstrative than patients with extreme anxiety and conversion disorders and malingerers, and it is easier to overlook the non-organic basis for their problem.

Typical profile[4]

Age:	Any age, typical 30–50
History of injury:	Yes—usually remote in the past; often motor vehicle accident

Site and radiation:	Low back, central, often bilateral May radiate to leg (may be bizarre pattern)
Type of pain:	Variable, usually deep ache or burning Continuous—acute or chronic
Aggravation:	Work, especially housework, or manual Worse in mornings on waking Stress and worry
Relief:	Better in the evenings and on retiring
Associations:	Headache Fatigue, exhaustion, tiredness Insomnia, inability to cope Other aches and pains
Physical examination:	Diffuse tenderness to palpation Possible hyperactive reflexes

This profile is typical of the depressed patient with back pain. A trial of antidepressants for a minimum of three weeks is recommended and quite often a positive response with relief of backache eventuates.

Failure to consider psychological factors in the assessment of low back pain may lead to serious errors in diagnosis and management. Each instance of back pain poses a stimulating exercise in differential diagnosis. A comparison of organic and non-organic features is presented in Table 31.5.

Assessment of the pain demands a full understanding of the patient. One must be aware of his or her type of work, recreation, successes and failures; and one must relate this information to the degree of incapacity attributed to the back pain.

Patients with psychogenic back pain, especially the very anxious, tend to overemphasise their problem. They are usually demonstrative, the hands being used to point out various painful areas almost without prompting.

Table 31.5 *Comparison of general clinical features of organic and non-organic based low back pain*[4]

	Organic disorders	***Non-organic disorders***
Symptoms		
Presentation	Appropriate	Often dramatic
Pain	Localised	Bilateral/diffuse Sacrococcygeal
Pain radiation	Appropriate Buttock, specific sites	Inappropriate Front of leg/whole leg
Time pattern	Pain-free times	Constant, acute or chronic
Paraesthesia/anaesthesia	Dermatomal Points with finger	May be whole leg Shows with hands
Response to treatment	Variable Delayed benefit	Patient often refuses treatment Initial improvement (often dramatic) then deterioration (usually within 24 hours)
Signs		
Observation	Appropriate Guarded	Overreactive under scrutiny Inconsistent
Tenderness	Localised to appropriate level	Often inappropriate level Withdraws from probing finger
Spatial tenderness (Magnuson)	Consistent	Inconsistent
Active movements	Specific movements affected	Often all movements affected
Axial loading test	No back pain (usually)	Back pain
SLR 'distraction' test	Consistent	Inconsistent
Sensation	Dermatomal	Non-anatomical 'sock' or 'stocking'
Motor	Appropriate myotome	Muscle groups, e.g. leg 'collapses'
Reflexes	Appropriate May be depressed	Brisk hyperactive

There is diffuse tenderness even to the slightest touch and the physical disability is out of proportion to the alleged symptoms. The pain distribution is often atypical of any dermatome and the reflexes are almost always hyperactive. It must be remembered that patients with psychogenic back pain—for example, depression and conversion disorders—do certainly experience back pain and do not fall for the traps set for the malingerer.

Tests for non-organic back pain

Several tests are useful in differentiating between organic and non-organic back pain (e.g. that caused by depression or complained of by a known malingerer).

Magnuson's method (the 'migratory pointing' test)

1. Request the patient to point to the painful sites.
2. Palpate these areas of tenderness on two occasions separated by an interval of several minutes, and compare the sites.

Between the two tests divert the patient's attention from his or her back by another examination.

Leg raising

Perform the usual straight leg raising test. The patient might manage a limited elevation, for example 30°. Keep the degree in mind. Ask the patient to sit up and swing the leg over the end of the couch. Distract attention with another test or some question, then attempt to lift the straight leg to the same level achieved on the first occasion. If it is possible, then the patient's response is inconsistent.

Burn's 'kneeling on a stool' test

1. Ask the patient to kneel on a low stool, lean over and try to touch the floor.
2. The person with non-organic back pain will usually refuse on the grounds that it would cause great pain or that he or she might overbalance in the attempt.

Patients with even a severely herniated disc usually manage the task to some degree.

The axial loading test

1. Place your hands over the patient's head and press firmly downward (Fig. 31.13).
2. This will cause no discomfort to (most) patients with organic back pain.

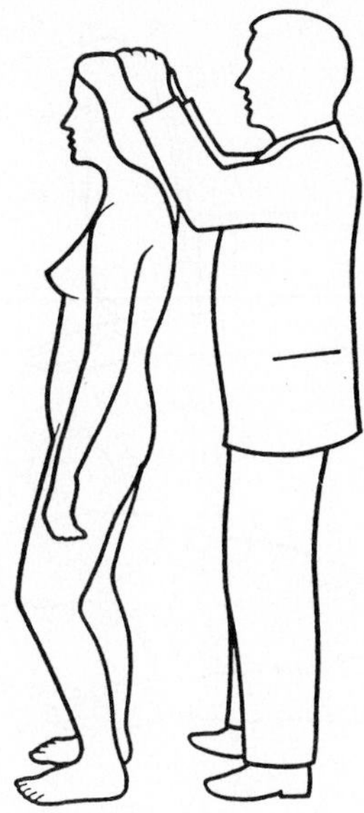

Fig. 31.13 *The axial loading test*

Treatment options for back pain

General aspects of management

Relative rest

For acutely painful back problems two to three days strict rest lying on a firm surface is optimal treatment.[6] Resting for longer than three days does not produce any significant healing.

Patient education

Appropriate educational material leads to a clear insight into the causes of and aggravation of the back disorder plus coping strategies.

Exercises

An early graduated exercise program as soon as the attack phase settles has been shown to promote healing and prevent relapses.[7] All forms of exercise (extension, flexion and isometric) appear to be equally effective with extension exercises being favoured for a discogenic problem and flexion exercises for most dysfunctional problems (See Figs 31.14a, b). Swimming is an excellent exercise for back disorders.

Pharmacological agents

Basic analgesics

Analgesics such as aspirin and codeine plus acetaminophen (paracetamol) should be used for pain relief.

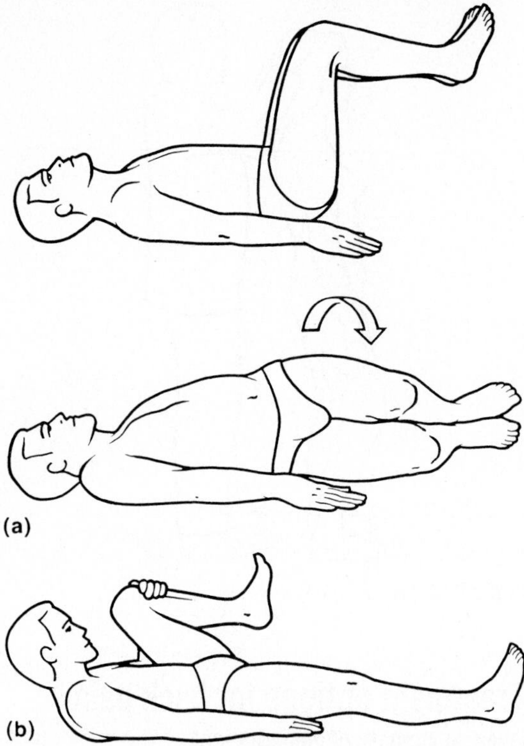

Fig. 31.14 *Examples of exercises for low back pain:* **(a)** *rotation exercise;* **(b)** *flexion exercise*

NSAIDs

Useful where there is clinical evidence of inflammation, especially with the spondyloarthropathies, severe spondylosis and in acute radicular pain, to counter the irritation on the nerve root. NSAIDs should not be used for mechanical dysfunction.

Antiepileptic drugs

These have been helpful in controlling acute radicular pain subject to repetitive bursts of lightning-like pains. Examples include carbamazepine and clonazepam.

Antidepressants

These have been used with success in the treatment of chronic back pain (especially without demonstrable pathology) and in patients with depression and associated back pain.

Injection techniques

Trigger point injection: may be effective for relatively isolated points using 5–8 ml of local anaesthetic.

Chymopapain: this enzyme has been advocated for the treatment of acute nuclear herniation which is still intact. The indications are similar for surgical discectomy. However, its use is controversial.

Facet joint injection: corticosteroid injection under radio image intensification is widely used in some clinics. The procedure is delicate and expertise is required. Some good results are obtained.

Epidural injections: injections of local anaesthetic with or without corticosteroids are used especially for nerve root pain. The author favours the caudal (trans-sacral) epidural injection for persistent sciatica using 15 ml of half-strength local anaesthetic only, e.g. 0.25% bupivacaine (Fig. 31.15).

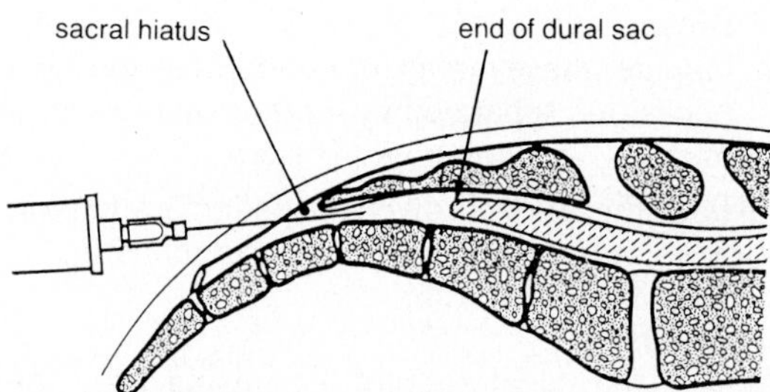

Fig. 31.15 *Caudal epidural injection: the needle should lie free in the space and be well clear of the dural sac*

Physical therapy

Active exercises are the best form of physical therapy (Fig. 31.14a, b).

Spinal mobilisation is a gentle, repetitive, rhythmic movement within the range of movement of the joint. It is safe and quite effective (Fig. 31.16).

Spinal manipulation is a high velocity thrust at the end range of the joint. It is generally more effective and produces a faster response but requires accurate diagnosis and greater skill. It is extremely effective for uncomplicated persistent dysfunctional low back pain (without radicular pain) and, together with exercises, is the treatment of choice (Fig. 31.17).

Other treatments

The following treatments have a significant role in the management of back pain:

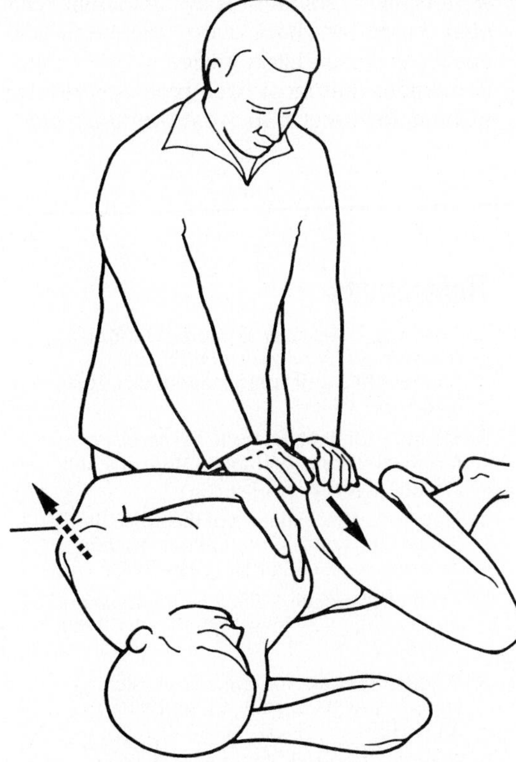

Fig. 31.16 *Lumbar spinal mobilisation (for left-sided pain): illustration of the effective forces involved* REPRODUCED FROM C.KENNA AND J.MURTAGH *BACK PAIN AND SPINAL MANIPULATION*, BUTTERWORTHS, SYDNEY, 1989, WITH PERMISSION

- hydrotherapy
- traction
- transcutaneous electrical nerve stimulation (TENS)
- facet joint injection
- posterior nerve root (medial branch) blocks with or without denervation (by cryotherapy or radiofrequency)
- deep friction massage (in conjunction with mobilisation and manipulation)
- acupuncture
- pain clinic (if unresponsive to initial treatments)
- biofeedback
- gravitational methods (home therapy)

Prevention of further back pain

Patients should be informed that an ongoing back care program should give them an excellent outlook. Prevention includes:

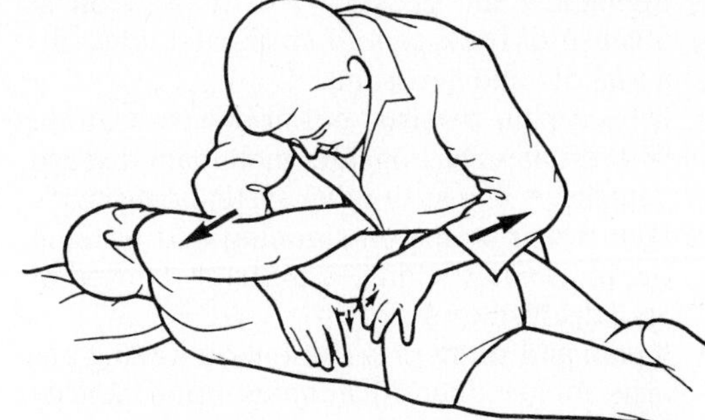

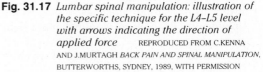

Fig. 31.17 *Lumbar spinal manipulation: illustration of the specific technique for the L4–L5 level with arrows indicating the direction of applied force* REPRODUCED FROM C.KENNA AND J.MURTAGH *BACK PAIN AND SPINAL MANIPULATION*, BUTTERWORTHS, SYDNEY, 1989, WITH PERMISSION

- education about back care, including a good layman's reference
- golden rules to live by: how to lift, sit, bend, play sport and so on
- an exercise program: a tailor-made program for the patient
- posture and movement training, e.g.
  —the Alexander technique[8]
  —the Feldenkrais technique[9]

When to refer

Urgent referral

- myelopathy, especially acute cauda equina compression syndrome
- severe radiculopathy with neurologic deficit
- spinal fractures

Other referrals

- neoplasia or infection
- undiagnosed back pain
- Paget's disease
- continuing pain of 3 months duration without a clearly definable cause

Practice tips

- Back pain which is related to posture, aggravated by movement and sitting, and relieved by lying down is due to vertebral dysfunction, especially a disc disruption.
- The pain from most disc lesions is generally relieved by rest.
- Plain X-rays are of limited use, especially in younger patients, and may appear normal in disc prolapse.

- Remember the possibility of depression as a cause of back pain; if suspected, consider a trial of antidepressants.
- If back pain persists, possibly worse during bed rest at night, consider malignant disease, depressive illness or other systemic diseases.
- Pain that is worse on standing and walking, but relieved by sitting, is probably caused by spondylolisthesis.
- If pain and stiffness is present on waking and lasts longer than 30 minutes upon activity, consider inflammation.
- Avoid using strong analgesics (especially opioids) in any chronic non-malignant pain state.
- Bilateral back pain is more typical of systemic diseases, while unilateral pain typifies mechanical causes.
- Back pain at rest and morning stiffness in a young person demand careful investigation: consider inflammation such as ankylosing spondylitis and Reiter's disease.
- A disc lesion of L5–S1 can involve both L5 and S1 roots. However, combined L5 and S1 root lesions should still be regarded with suspicion, e.g. consider malignancy.
- A large central disc protrusion can cause bladder symptoms, either incontinence or retention.
- Low back pain of very sudden onset with localised spasm and protective lateral deviation may indicate a facet joint syndrome.
- The T12–L1 and L1–L2 discs are the groin pain discs.
- The L4–L5 disc is the back pain disc.
- The L5-S1 disc is the leg pain disc.
- Severe limitation of SLR (especially to less than 30°) indicates lumbar disc prolapse.
- A preventive program for dysfunctional back pain based on back care awareness and exercises is mandatory advice.
- Remember that most back problems resolve within a few weeks, so avoid overtreatment.

References

1. Cormack J, Marinker M, Morrell D. *Practice: a handbook of primary health care.* London: Kluwer-Harrap Handbooks, 1980; 3.68:1–10.
2. Sloane P, Slatt M, Baker R. *Essentials of family medicine.* Baltimore: Williams and Wilkins, 1988, 228–235.
3. Maigne R. Manipulation of the spine. In: JV Basmajian, (ed). *Manipulation, traction and massage.* Paris RML. 1986, 71–96.
4. Kenna C, Murtagh J. *Back pain and spinal manipulation.* Sydney: Butterworths, 1989, 70–164.
5. Waddell G et al. Non-organic physical signs in low back pain. Spine, 1980; 5:117–125.
6. Deyo RA, Diehl AK, Rosenthal M. How many days of bed rest for acute low back pain? A randomised clinical trial. N Eng J Med, 1986; 315:1064–70.
7. Kendall PH, Jenkins SM. Exercises for backache: a double blind controlled study. Physiotherapy, 1968; 54:154–157.
8. Hodgkinson L. *The Alexander technique.* London: Piatkus, 1988, 1–97.
9. Feldenkrais M. *Awareness through movement.* New York: Harper and Row, 1972.

32

Thoracic back pain

Thoracic (dorsal) back pain is common in people of all ages including children and adolescents. Dysfunction of the joints of the thoracic spine, with its unique costovertebral joints, which are an important source of back pain, is very commonly encountered in medical practice, especially in people whose lifestyle creates stresses and strains through poor posture and heavy lifting. Muscular and ligamentous strains may be common, but rarely come to light in practice because they are self-limiting and not severe.

This dysfunction can cause referred pain to various parts of the chest wall and can mimic the symptoms of various visceral diseases such as angina, biliary colic and oesophageal spasm. In similar fashion, heart and gall bladder pain can mimic back pain.

Key facts and checkpoints

- The commonest site of pain in the spine is the costovertebral articulations especially the costotransverse articulation (Fig. 32.1).
- Pain of thoracic spinal origin may be referred anywhere to the chest wall, but the commonest sites are the scapular region, the paravertebral region 2–5 cm from midline, and anteriorly, over the costochondral region.
- Thoracic (also known as dorsal) pain is more common in patients with abnormalities such as kyphosis and Scheuermann's disorder.
- Trauma to the chest wall (including falls on the chest such as those experienced in body contact sport) commonly lead to disorders of the thoracic spine.
- Patients recovering from open heart surgery, when a longitudinal sternal incision is made and the chest wall is stretched out, commonly experience thoracic back pain.
- Unlike the lumbar spine the joints are quite superficial and it is relatively easy to find the affected (painful) segment.
- The intervertebral disc prolapse is very uncommon in the thoracic spine.

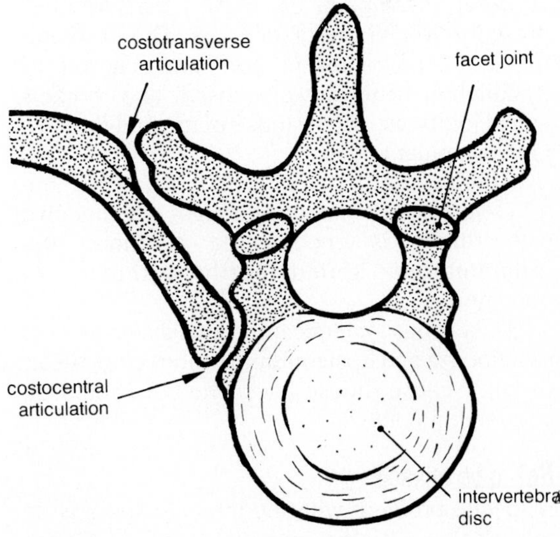

Fig. 32.1 *The functional unit of the thoracic spine*

- The older patient presenting with chest pain should be regarded as having a cardiac cause until proved otherwise.
- If the chest pain is non-cardiac, then the possibility of referral from the thoracic spine should be considered.
- The thoracic spine is the commonest site in the vertebral column for metastatic disease.
- Scheuermann's disorder, which affects the lower thoracic spine in adolescents, is often associated with kyphosis and recurrent thoracic back pain. Always inspect the thoracic spine of the younger patient for kyphosis and scoliosis.
- The most useful movements to detect hypomobile lesions and painful levels in the thoracic spine are lateral flexion and rotation. The application of overpressure at the active end range is useful to detect the painful segment.
- Palpation is the most important component of the physical examination.

A diagnostic approach

A summary of the safety diagnostic model is presented in Table 32.1.

Probability diagnosis

The commonest cause of thoracic back pain is musculoskeletal, due usually to musculoligamentous strains caused by poor posture. However, these pains are usually transitory and present rarely to the practitioner. The problems that commonly present are those caused by dysfunction of the lower cervical and thoracic spinal joints, especially those of the mid-thoracic (interscapular) area.

Arthritic conditions of the thoracic spine are not relatively common although degenerative osteoarthritis is encountered at times; the inflammatory spondyloarthropathies are uncommon.

The various systemic infectious diseases such as influenza and Epstein-Barr mononucleosis can certainly cause diffuse backache but should be assessed in context.

Not to be missed

A special problem with the thoracic spine is its relationship with the many thoracic and upper abdominal structures which can refer pain to the back. These structures are listed in Table 32.2 but, in particular, myocardial infarction and dissecting aneurysm must be considered.

Table 32.1 *Thoracic back pain: diagnostic strategy model*

Q. Probability diagnosis
A. musculoligamentous strains (mainly postural)
vertebral dysfunction

Q. Serious disorders not to be missed
A. Cardiovascular
- myocardial infarction
- dissecting aneurysm
- pulmonary infarction

Neoplasia
- myeloma
- lung (with infiltration)
- metastatic disease

Severe infections
- pleurisy
- infectious endocarditis
- osteomyelitis

Pneumothorax
Osteoporosis

Q. Pitfalls (often missed)
A. angina
gastrointestinal disorders
- oesophageal dysfunction
- peptic ulcer (penetrating)
- hepatobiliary
- pancreatic

herpes zoster
spondyloarthropathies
fibromyalgia syndrome
polymyalgia rheumatica
chronic infection
- tuberculosis
- brucellosis

Q. Seven masquerades checklist

A.	
Depression	✓
Diabetes	—
Drugs	—
Anaemia	—
Thyroid disease	—
Spinal dysfunction	✓✓
UTI	✓

Q. Is this patient trying to tell me something?
A. Yes, quite possible with many cases of back pain.

Cardiopulmonary problems

The acute onset of pain can have sinister implications in the thoracic spine where various life-threatening cardiopulmonary and vascular events have to be kept in mind. The pulmonary causes of acute pain include spontaneous pneumothorax, pleurisy and pulmonary infarction. Thoracic back pain may be associated with infective endocarditis due to embolic phenomena. The ubiquitous myocardial

Table 32.2 *Non-musculoskeletal causes of thoracic back pain*

Heart	• myocardial infarction • angina • pericarditis
Great vessels	• dissecting aneurysm • pulmonary embolism (rare) • pulmonary infarction • pneumothorax • pneumonia/pleurisy
Oesophagus	• oesophageal rupture • oesophageal spasm • oesophagitis
Subdiaphragmatic disorders of	• gall bladder • stomach } including • duodenum } ulcers • pancreas • subphrenic collection
Miscellaneous infections	• herpes zoster • Bornholm's disease • infective endocarditis
Psychogenic	

infarction or acute coronary occlusion may, uncommonly, cause interscapular back pain, while the very painful dissecting or ruptured aortic aneurysm may cause back pain with hypotension.

Osteoporosis

Osteoporosis, especially in elderly women, must always be considered in such people presenting with acute pain, which can be caused by a pathological fracture. The association with pain following inappropriate physical therapy such as spinal manipulation should also be considered.

Acute infections

Infective conditions that can involve the spine include osteomyelitis, tuberculosis, brucellosis, syphilis and salmonella infections. Such conditions should be suspected in young patients (osteomyelitis), farm workers (brucellosis) and migrants from South-East Asia and Third World countries (tuberculosis). The presence of poor general health and fever necessitates investigations for these infections.

Neoplasia

Fortunately, tumours of the spine are uncommon. Nevertheless, they occur frequently enough for the full-time practitioner in back disorders to encounter some each year, especially metastatic disease.

The three common primary malignancies that metastasise to the spine are those originating in the lung, breast and the prostate (all paired structures). The less common primaries to consider are the thyroid, the kidney and adrenals and malignant melanoma.

Reticuloses such as Hodgkin's disease can involve the spine. Primary malignancies that arise in the vertebrae include multiple myeloma and sarcoma.

Benign tumours to consider are often neurological in origin. An interesting tumour is the osteoid osteoma, which is aggravated by consuming alcohol and relieved by aspirin.

The tumours of the spine are summarised in Table 32.3.

Table 32.3 *Significant tumours affecting the thoracic and lumbar spine[1] (after Kenna and Murtagh)*

	Benign	**Malignant**
of bone	• osteoid osteoma • haemangioma • ostoblastoma • aneurysmal bone cyst • eosinophilic granuloma	Primary • multiple myeloma • lymphomas, e.g. Hodgkin's • sarcoma
spinal	Extradural • lipoma • neuroma • fibroma Intradural • neuroma • ependymoma • chordoma • meningioma	Secondary • breast • lung • prostate • adrenals/kidney • thyroid • melanoma Direct spread • stomach • large bowel • pancreas • uterus/cervix/ovary

The symptoms and signs that should alert the clinician to malignant disease are:

- back pain occurring in an older person
- unrelenting back pain, unrelieved by rest (this includes night pain)
- rapidly increasing back pain
- constitutional symptoms, e.g. weight loss, fever, malaise
- a history of treatment for cancer, e.g. excision of skin melanoma

A common trap for the thoracic spine is carcinoma of the lung such as mesothelioma which can invade parietal pleura or structures adjacent to the vertebral column.

Pitfalls

Pitfalls include ischaemic heart disease presenting with interscapular pain, herpes zoster at the pre-eruption stage and the various gastrointestinal disorders. Two commonly misdiagnosed problems are a penetrating duodenal ulcer presenting with lower thoracic pain and oesophageal spasm which can cause thoracic back pain.

Inflammatory rheumatological problems are not common in the thoracic spine but occasionally a spondyloarthropathy such as ankylosing spondylitis manifests here, although it follows some time after the onset of sacroiliitis.

Seven masquerades checklist

Spinal dysfunction is the outstanding cause in this checklist, but urinary infection may occasionally cause lower thoracic pain. Depression always warrants consideration in any pain syndrome, especially back pain. It can certainly cause exaggeration of pre-existing pain from vertebral dysfunction or some other chronic problem.

Psychogenic considerations

Psychogenic or non-organic causes of back pain can present a complex dilemma in diagnosis and management. The causes may be apparent from the incongruous behaviour and personality of the patient, but often the diagnosis is reached by a process of exclusion. There is obviously some functional overlay to everyone with acute or chronic pain, hence the importance of appropriate reassurance to these patients that their problem invariably subsides with time and that they do not have cancer.

Anatomical and clinical features

The functional unit of the thoracic spine is illustrated in Figure 32.1. It appears that pain from the thoracic spine originates mainly from the apophyseal joints and rib articulations. Any one thoracic vertebra has ten separate articulations, so the potential for dysfunction and the difficulty in clinically pinpointing the precise joint at a particular level are apparent.

The costovertebral joints are synovial joints unique to the thoracic spine and have two articulations—costotransverse and costocentral. Together with the apophyseal joints, they are capable of presenting with well-localised pain close to the midline or as referred pain, often quite distal to the spine, with the major symptoms not appearing to have any relationship to the thoracic spine.

Generalised referral patterns are presented in Figure 32.2, while the dermatome pattern is outlined in Figure 32.3.

The pain pattern acts as a guide only because there is considerable dermatomal overlap within the individual and variation from one person to another. It has been demonstrated that up to five nerve roots may contribute to the innervation of any one point in the anterior segments of the trunk dermatomes, a fact emphasised by the clinical distribution of herpes zoster.

Lower cervical referred pain

Disorders of the lower cervical segments can cause referred pain in the upper thoracic area, as evidenced clinically by pain in this region following a 'whiplash' injury. The C4 dermatome is in close proximity to the T2 dermatome which appears to represent the cutaneous areas of the lower cervical segments, as the posterior primary rami of C5, 6, 7, 8 and T1 innervate musculature and have no significant cutaneous innervation.

The pain from the lower cervical spine can also refer pain to the anterior chest, and mimic coronary ischaemic pain. The associated autonomic nervous system disturbance can cause considerable confusion in making the diagnosis.

Upper thoracic pain[1]

Dysfunction of the joints of the upper thoracic spine usually gives rise to localised pain and stiffness posteriorly but also can cause distal symptoms, probably via the autonomic nervous system.

A specific syndrome called the T4 syndrome[2] has been shown to cause vague pain in the upper limbs and diffuse, vague head and posterior neck pain.

However, most of the pain, stiffness and discomfort arises from dysfunction of the upper and middle thoracic segments with patients

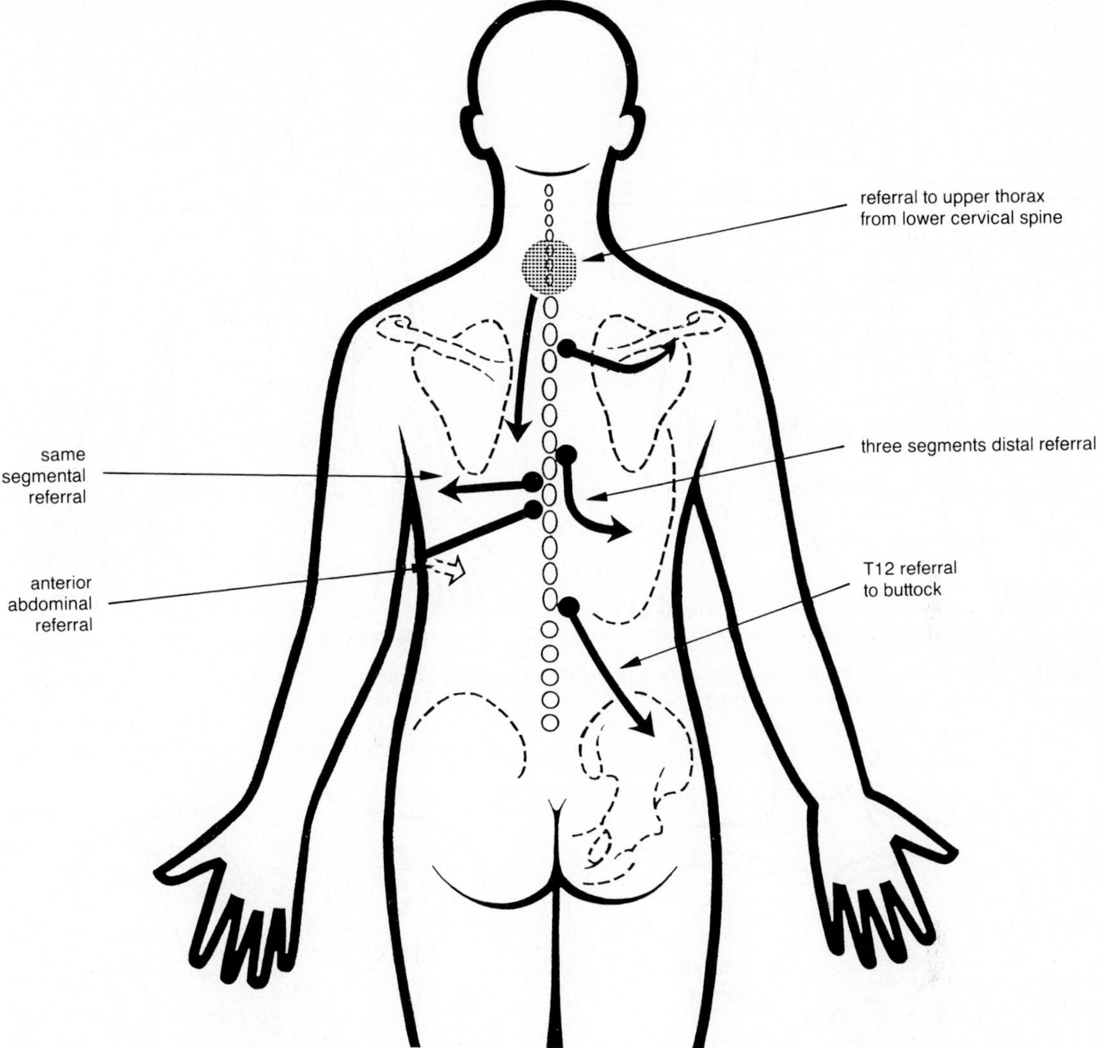

Fig. 32.2 *Examples of referral patterns for the thoracic spine*

presenting with the complaint of pain between 'my shoulder blades'.

Costovertebral joint dysfunction[1]

The unique feature of the thoracic spine is the costovertebral joint. Dysfunction of this joint commonly causes localised pain approximately 3–4 cm from the midline where the rib articulates with the transverse process and the vertebral body. In addition it is frequently responsible for referred pain ranging from the midline, posterior to the lateral chest wall, and even anterior chest pain. When the symptoms radiate laterally, the diagnosis is confirmed only when movement of the rib provokes pain at the costovertebral joint. This examination will simultaneously reproduce the referred pain.

Figure 32.4 presents the pattern of referred pain from these joints and highlights the capacity of the thoracic spine to refer pain centrally to the anterior chest and upper abdomen. Confusion arises for the clinician when the patient's history focuses on the anterior chest pain and fails to mention the presence of posterior pain, should it be present. The shaded areas on Figure 32.4 represent those areas where the patient experiences pain following the injection of hypertonic saline into the posterior elements of the spine.

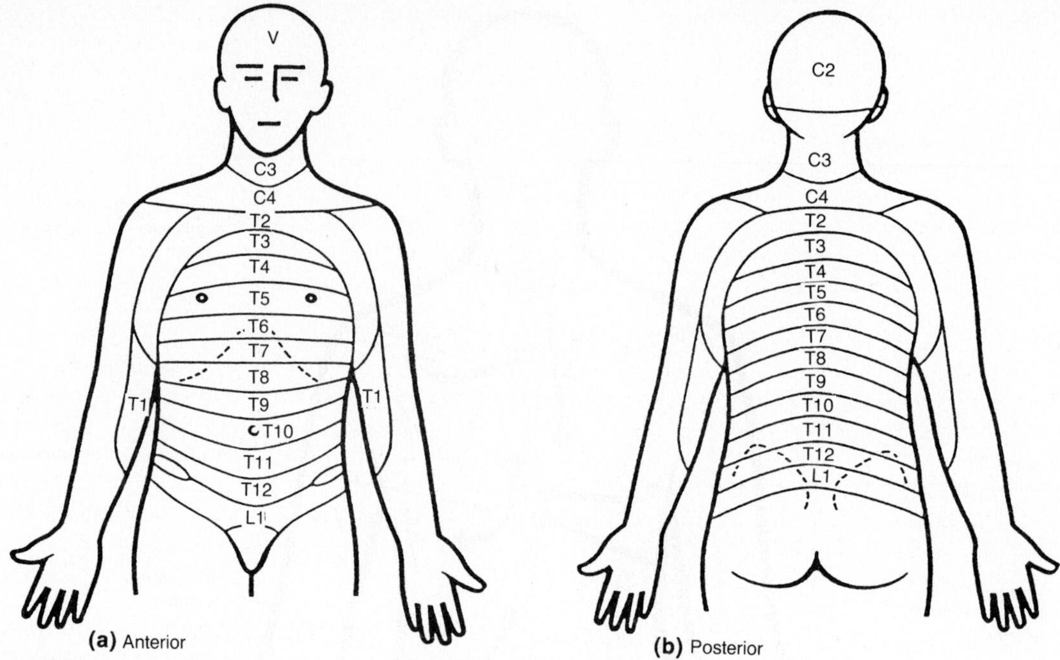

Fig. 32.3 *Dermatomes for the thoracic nerve roots, indicating possible referral areas* REPRODUCED FROM C.KENNA AND J.MURTAGH *BACK PAIN AND SPINAL MANIPULATION*, BUTTERWORTHS, SYDNEY, 1989, WITH PERMISSION

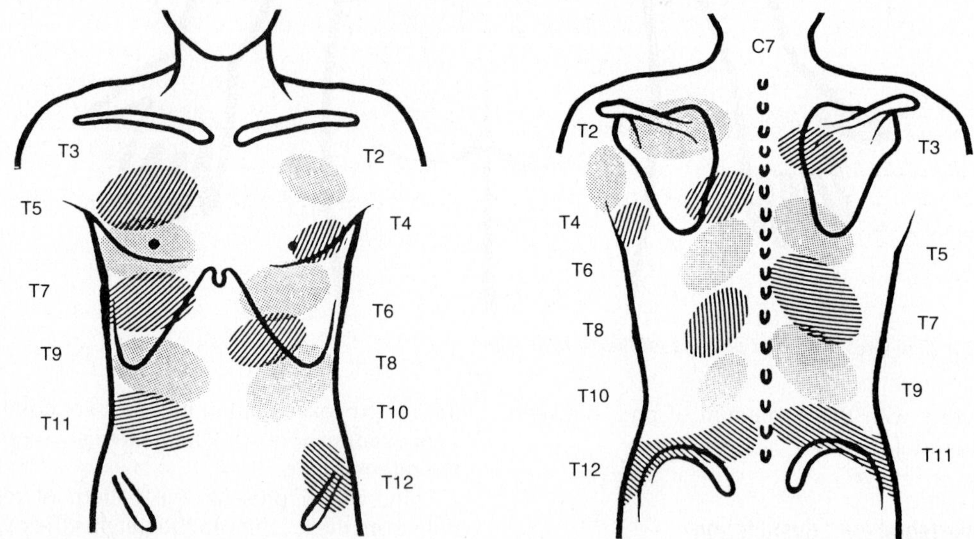

Fig. 32.4 *Kellegren's (1939) pain referral patterns after stimulation of deep joints of the thoracic spine*

The clinical approach

History

The history of a patient presenting with thoracic back pain should include a routine pain analysis, which usually provides important clues for the diagnosis. The age, sex and occupation of the patient are relevant. Pain in the thoracic area is very common in people who sit bent over for long periods, especially working at desks. Students, secretaries and stenographers are therefore at risk, as are nursing mothers, who have to lift their babies.

People who are kyphotic or scoliotic or who have 'hunchbacks' secondary to disease such as tuberculosis and poliomyelitis also suffer from recurrent pain in this area.

Older people are more likely to present with a neoplastic problem in the thoracic spine and with osteoporosis. Senile osteoporosis is usually a trap because it is symptomless until the intervention of a compression fracture. Symptoms following such a fracture can persist for three months.

Pain that is present day and night indicates a sinister cause.

Features of the history that give an indication that the pain is arising from dysfunction of the thoracic spine include:

- Aggravation and relief of pain on trunk rotation: the patient's pain may be increased by rotating (twisting) towards the side of the pain but eased by rotating in the opposite direction.
- Aggravation of pain by coughing, sneezing or deep inspiration: this can produce a sharp catching pain which, if severe, tends to implicate the costovertebral joint.
- Relief of pain by firm pressure: patients may state that their back pain is eased by firm pressure such as leaning against the corner of a wall.

It is very important to be able to differentiate between chest pain due to vertebral dysfunction and that caused by myocardial ischaemia.

Key questions

Can you recall injuring your back, such as by lifting something heavy?
Did you have a fall onto your chest or back?
Is the pain present during the night?
Do you have low back pain or neck pain?
Does the pain come on after walking or any strenuous effort?
Does the pain come on after eating or soon after going to bed at night?
Have you noticed a fever or sweating at any time, especially at night?
Have you noticed a rash near where you have the pain?
What drugs are you taking? Do you take drugs for arthritis or pain? Cortisone?
What happens when you take a deep breath, cough or sneeze?

Physical examination

The examination of the thoracic spine is straightforward with the emphasis on palpation of the spine—central and laterally. This achieves the basic objective of reproducing the patient's symptoms and finding the level of pain. The 'look, feel, move, X-ray' clinical approach is most appropriate for the thoracic spine.

Inspection

Careful inspection is important since it may be possible to observe at a glance why the patient has thoracic pain. Note the symmetry, any scars, skin creases and deformities, 'flat spots' in the spine, the nature of the scapulae or evidence of muscle spasm. Look for kyphosis and scoliosis.

Kyphosis may be generalised, with the back having a smooth uniform contour, or localised where it is due to a collapsed vertebra such as occurs in an older person with osteoporosis. Generalised kyphosis is common in the elderly, especially those with degenerative spinal disease. In the young it may reflect the important Scheuermann's disorder.

The younger person in particular should be screened for scoliosis, which becomes more prominent on forward flexion (Fig. 32.5). Look for any asymmetry of the chest wall, inequality of the scapulae and differences in the levels of the shoulders. A useful sign of scoliosis is unequal shoulder levels and apparent 'winging' of scapula. When viewed anteriorly a difference in the levels of the nipples indicates the presence of scoliosis, or other problems causing one shoulder to drop. Inspection should therefore take place with posterior, lateral (side) and anterior views.

Palpation

The best position is to have the patient prone on the examination table with the thoracic spine preferably in slight flexion. This is achieved by lowering the top of the table.

Test passive extension of each joint with firm pressure from the pad of the thumbs or the bony hand (either the pisiform prominence or the lateral border of the fifth metacarpal). Spring up and down with a few firm oscillations, keeping the elbows straight, but being well above the patient. Ask the patient if the pressure reproduces the pain.

Apart from asking the patient 'Is that the pain?' note:

- the distribution of pain and its change with movement
- the range of movement
- the type of resistance in the joint
- any muscle spasm

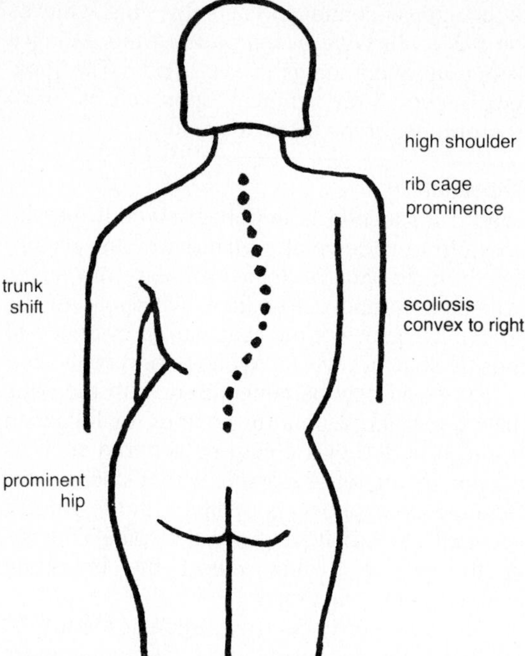

Fig. 32.5 *Screening for idiopathic adolescent scoliosis: configuration of the thoracic spine on forward flexion*

Palpation must follow a set plan in order to reproduce the patient's pain. The sequence is as follows:

1. Central—over spinous processes
2. Unilateral—over apophyseal joints (2–3 cm from midline)
3. Transverse—on side of spinous processes
4. Unilateral—costotransverse junctions (4–5 cm from midline)
5. Unilateral—over ribs (spring over posterior rib curve with ulnar border of hand, along axis of rib)

Movements

There are four main movements of the thoracic spine to assess, the most important of which is rotation, as this is the movement that so frequently reproduces the patient's pain where it is facetal joint or costovertebral in origin.

The movements of the thoracic spine and their normal ranges are:

Extension	30°
Lateral flexion L and R	30°
Flexion	90°
Rotation L and R	60°

Ask the patient to sit on the table with hands placed behind the neck and then perform the movements. Check these four active movements noting any hypomobility, the range of movement, reproduction of symptoms and function and muscle spasm.

Passive movement, superimposed on active movements, is needed to stress the joints and reproduce pain if it has not been elicited by normal active movement. A passive 'overpressure' can be applied at the end range of each movement, especially with rotation. This is a sensitive method to stress the joint and reproduce the patient's pain. Record the patient's direction of movement, degree of restriction and presence of pain on the DOM diagram (Fig. 10.1).

Investigations

The main investigation is an X-ray which may exclude the basic abnormalities and diseases such as osteoporosis and malignancy. If serious diseases such as malignancy or infection are suspected, and the plain X-ray is normal, a radionuclide bone scan may detect these disorders.

Other investigations to consider are:

- full blood examination and ESR
- serum alkaline phosphatase
- serum electrophoresis for multiple myeloma
- Bence-Jones protein analysis
- brucella agglutination test
- blood culture for pyogenic infection and bacterial endocarditis
- tuberculosis studies
- HLA B_{27} antigen for spondyloarthropathies
- ECG or ECG stress tests (suspected angina)
- gastroscopy or barium studies (peptic ulcer)

Thoracic back pain in children

The most common cause is 'postural backache' also known as 'TV backache' which is usually found in adolescent schoolgirls and is a diagnosis of exclusion.

Important, although rare, problems in children include infections (tuberculosis, discitis and osteomyelitis) and tumours such as osteoid osteoma and malignant osteogenic sarcoma.

Dysfunction of the joints of the thoracic spine in children and particularly in adolescents is very common and often related to trauma such as a heavy fall in sporting activities or falling from a height, e.g. off a horse. Fractures, of course, have to be excluded.

Inflammatory disorders to consider are juvenile ankylosing spondylitis and spinal osteochondritis (Scheuermann's disorder), which may affect adolescent males in the lower thoracic spine (around T9) and thoracolumbar spine. The latter condition may be asymptomatic, but can be associated with back pain, especially as the patient grows older. It is the commonest cause of kyphosis.

It is important to screen adolescent children for idiopathic scoliosis, which may be without associated backache.

Scheuermann's disorder

Typical features

- age 11–17
- males > females
- lower thoracic spine
- thoracic pain or asymptomatic
- increasing thoracic kyphosis over 1–2 months
- wedging of the vertebrae
- pain in the wedge especially on bending
- short hamstrings
- cannot touch toes
- diagnosis confirmed by X-ray

Treatment

- explanation and support
- extension exercises, avoid forward flexion
- postural correction
- avoidance of sports involving lifting and bending
- consider bracing or surgery if serious deformity

Idiopathic adolescent scoliosis

A degree of scoliosis is detectable in 5% of the adolescent population.[3] The vast majority of curves, occurring equally in boys and girls, are mild and of no consequence. Eighty-five per cent of significant curves in adolescent scoliosis occur in girls.[4] Such curves appear during the peripubertal period usually coinciding with the growth spurt. The screening test (usually in 12–14 year olds) is to note the contour of the back on forward flexion (Fig. 32.6).

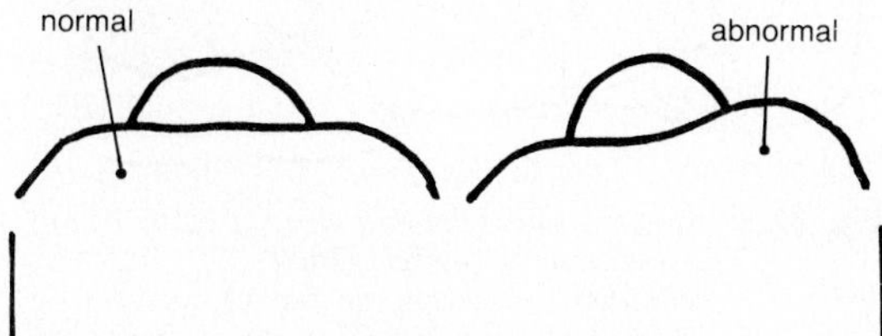

Fig. 32.6 *Screening for idiopathic adolescent scoliosis: testing asymmetry by forward flexion*

Investigation

A single erect PA spinal X-ray is sufficient[5]; the Cobb angle (Fig. 32.7) is the usual measurement yardstick.

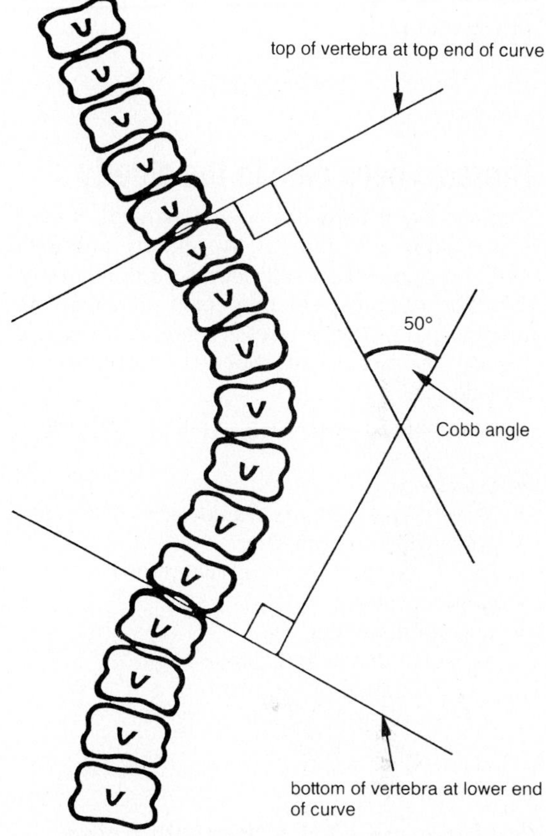

Fig. 32.7 *Scoliosis: the Cobb method of curve measurement*

Management

Aims:
- preserve good appearance—level shoulders and no trunk shift
- prevent increasing curve in adult life: less than 45°
- *not* to produce a straight spine on X-ray

Methods:
- Braces: Milwaukee brace
Total contact brace
To be worn for 20–22 hours each day until skeletal maturity is reached.
- Surgical correction: depends on curve and skeletal maturity

Guidelines for treatment:

still growing: $< 20^\circ$ observe (repeat examination + X-ray)
$20–30^\circ$ observe, brace if progressive
$30–45^\circ$ brace
$\geq 45–50^\circ$ operate

growth complete:
$< 45^\circ$ leave alone
$> 45^\circ$ operate

Thoracic back pain in the elderly

Thoracic back pain due to mechanical causes is not such a feature in the elderly although vertebral dysfunction still occurs quite regularly. However, when the elderly person presents with thoracic pain, a very careful search for organic disease is necessary. Special problems to consider are:

- malignant disease, e.g. multiple myeloma, lung, prostate
- osteoporosis
- vertebral pathological fractures
- polymyalgia rheumatica
- Paget's disease (may be asymptomatic)
- herpes zoster
- visceral disorders, e.g.
  - — ischaemic heart disease
  - — penetrating peptic ulcer
  - — oesophageal disorders
  - — biliary disorders

Dysfunction of the thoracic spine

This is the outstanding cause of pain presenting to the practitioner, is relatively easy to diagnose and usually responds dramatically to a simple spinal manipulation treatment.

Typical profile[1]

Age:	Any age, especially between 20 and 40
History of injury:	Sometimes slow or sudden onset
Site and radiation:	Spinal and paraspinal—e.g. interscapular, arms, lateral chest, anterior chest, substernal, iliac crest
Type of pain:	Dull, aching, occasionally sharp, severity related to activity, site and posture
Aggravation:	Deep inspiration, postural movement of thorax, slumping or bending, walking upstairs, activities (e.g. lifting children, making beds), beds too hard or soft, sleeping or sitting for long periods
Association:	Chronic poor posture
Diagnosis confirmation:	Examination of spine, therapeutic response to manipulation

Management

- explanation and reassurance
- analgesics for a painful episode
- spinal mobilisation or manipulation
- exercise program
- preventive program

Spinal mobilisation and manipulation

Spinal mobilisation is helpful but the more forceful manipulative therapy produces better and quicker results. There are many techniques that can be employed, the choice depending on which part of the back is affected.[1] The sternal thrust (Nelson hold) technique is widely used for upper thoracic segments and the crossed pisiform technique (patient prone) or posteroanterior indirect thrust (patient supine [Fig. 32.8]) which is the most effective for mid-thoracic spine.

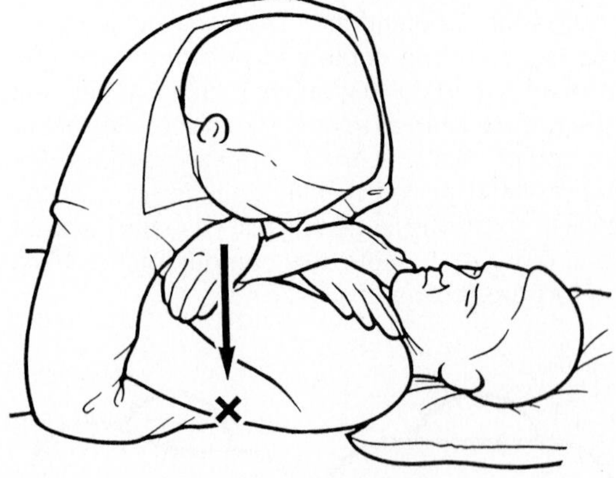

Fig. 32.8 *Manipulation of the mid-thoracic spine by the posteroanterior indirect thrust technique* REPRODUCED FROM C.KENNA AND J.MURTAGH *BACK PAIN AND SPINAL MANIPULATION*, BUTTERWORTHS, SYDNEY, 1989, WITH PERMISSION

Preventive exercise program

A key to helping these patients who are prone to recurrences is to prescribe an exercise program for their thoracic spine.[1,6]

Thoracic disc protrusion

Fortunately, a disc protrusion in the thoracic spine is uncommon. This reduced incidence is related to the firm splintage action of the rib cage. Most disc protrusions occur below T9, with the commonest site, as expected, being T11–T12.

The common presentation is back pain and radicular pain which follows the appropriate dermatome.

However, disc lesions in the thoracic spine are prone to produce spinal cord compression manifesting as sensory loss, bladder incontinence and signs of upper motor neurone lesion. The disc is relatively inaccessible to surgical intervention, but over the past decade there has been a significant improvement in the surgical treatment of thoracic disc protrusions, due to the transthoracic lateral approach.

Muscle injury

Muscular injuries such as tearing are uncommon in the chest wall. The strong paravertebral muscles do not appear to be a cause of chest pain, but strains of intercostal muscles, the serratus anterior and the musculotendinous origins of the abdominal muscles can cause pain. Injuries to these muscles can be provoked by attacks of violent sneezing or coughing or overstrain, for example, lifting a heavy suitcase down from an overhead luggage rack.

Fibromyalgia, fibrositis and myofascial trigger points

Fibromyalgia is relatively uncommon but when encountered presents an enormous management problem. It is not to be confused with so-called fibrositis or tender trigger points.

Fibrositis is not a diagnosis but a symptom indicating a localised area of tenderness or pain in the soft tissues, especially of the upper thoracic spine. It is probably almost always secondary to upper thoracic or lower cervical spinal dysfunction.

Myofascial trigger points

As described by Travell[7] a trigger point is characterised by:

- circumscribed local tenderness
- localised twitching with stimulation of juxtaposed muscle
- pain referred elsewhere when subjected to pressure

Trigger spots also tend to correspond to the acupuncture points for pain relief.

Treatment

Local injection is relatively easy and may give excellent results. Identify the maximal point of pain and inject 5–8 ml of local anaesthetic, e.g. lignocaine/lidocaine 1% into the painful point (Fig. 32.9). Post-injection massage or exercises should be performed.

Don't: use large volumes of LA; use corticosteroids; cause bleeding

Do: use a moderate amount of LA (only)

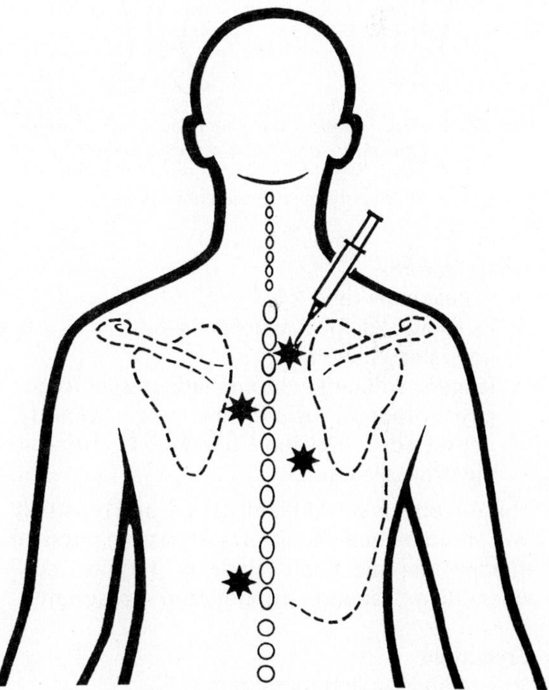

Fig. 32.9 *Injection for myofascial trigger points*

Fibromyalgia syndrome[8]

The main diagnostic features are:

1. a history of widespread pain (neck to low back)
2. pain in 11 of 18 tender points on digital palpation

These points must be painful, not tender. Smythe and Moldofsky have recommended 14 of these points on a map as a guide for management[9] (see Fig. 32.10).

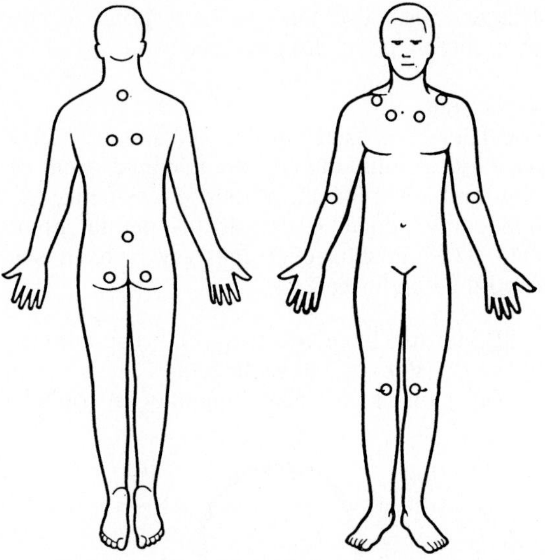

Fig. 32.10 *Fibromyalgia syndrome: typical tender points (the tender point map represents the 14 points recommended for use as a standard for diagnostic or therapeutic studies)*

Other features

- female:male ratio 4:1
- usual age 29–37: diagnosis 44–53
- poor sleep pattern
- fatigue (similar to chronic fatigue syndrome)
- psychological disorders, e.g. anxiety, depression, tension headache, irritable digestive system.

This disorder is very difficult to treat and is usually unresponsive in the long term to passive physical therapy or injections. Patients require considerable explanation, support and reassurance.

Treatment

- explanation and reassurance
- attention to sleep disorders, stress factors and physical factors
- rehabilitation exercise program, e.g. walking, swimming or cycling

Medication

- antidepressants (of proven value)—amitriptyline or prothiaden

  or
- clonazepam (Rivotril) 0.5 mg bd

Serious pitfalls

The following points regarding serious vertebral organic disease are worth repeating in more detail.

Metastatic disease[10]

Secondary deposits in the thoracolumbar spine may be the first presenting symptoms of malignant disease. Any patient of any age presenting with progressive severe night pain of the back should be regarded as having a tumour and investigated with a technetium bone scan as part of the primary investigations.

Secondary deposits in the spine can lead to rapid onset paralysis due to spinal cord infarction. Many such metastases can be controlled in the early stages with radiotherapy.

Multiple myeloma

Osteoporotic vertebral body collapse should be diagnosed only when multiple myeloma has been excluded. Investigations should include an ESR, Bence-Jones protein analysis, and immunoglobulin electrophoresis.

Early treatment of multiple myeloma can hold this disease in remission for many years and prevent crippling vertebral fractures.

Infective discitis and vertebral osteomyelitis

Severe back pain in an unwell patient with fluctuating temperature (fever) should be considered as infective until proved otherwise. Investigations should include blood cultures, serial X-rays and nuclear bone scanning. Biphasic bone scans using technetium with either indium or gallium scanning for white cell collections usually clinch this diagnosis.

Strict bed rest with high-dose antibiotic therapy is usually curative. If left untreated, vertebral end plate and disc space collapse is common and extremely disabling.

When to refer

- persistent pain or dysfunction—refer to a physical therapist
- evidence or suspicion of a sinister cause, e.g. neoplasia, infective discitis/osteomyelitis in a child
- suspicion of cardiac or gastrointestinal referred (persistent) pain
- significant idiopathic adolescent scoliosis or kyphosis, e.g. Scheuermann's disorder

Practice tips

- Feelings of anaesthesia or paraesthesia associated with thoracic spinal dysfunction are rare.
- Thoracic back pain is frequently associated with cervical lesions.
- Upper thoracic pain and stiffness is common after 'whiplash'.
- The T4 syndrome of upper to mid thoracic pain with radiation (and associated paraesthesia) to the arms is well documented.
- Symptoms due to a fractured vertebra usually last three months and to a fractured rib six weeks.
- The pain of myocardial ischaemia, from either angina or myocardial infarction, can cause referred pain to the interscapular region of the thoracic spine.
- Beware of the old trap of herpes zoster in the thoracic spine, especially in the older person.
- Consider multiple myeloma as a cause of an osteoporotic collapsed vertebra.
- Examine movements with the patient sitting on the couch and hands clasped behind the neck.
- Spinal disease of special significance in the thoracic spine includes osteoporosis and neoplasia, while disc lesions, inflammatory diseases and degenerative diseases (spondylosis) are encountered less frequently than with the cervical and lumbar spines.
- It is imperative to differentiate between spinal and cardiac causes of chest pain: either cause is likely to mimic the other. A working rule is to consider the cause as cardiac until the examination and investigations establish the true cause.
- Always X-ray the thoracic spine following trauma, especially after motor vehicle accidents, as wedge compression fractures (typically between T4 and T8) are often overlooked.

References

1. Kenna C, Murtagh J. *Back pain and spinal manipulation*. Sydney: Butterworths, 1989:165–174.
2. McGuckin N. The T4 syndrome. In: GD Grieve, *Modern manual therapy of the vertebral column*. London: Churchill Livingstone, 1986, 370–6.
3. Stephens J. Idiopathic adolescent scoliosis. Aust Fam Physician, 1984; 13:180–184.
4. Kane WJ, Moe JH. A scoliosis prevalence survey in Minnesota. Clin Orthop 1970; 69:216–218.
5. Anonymous *The Easter Seal Guide to Children's Orthopaedics*. Toronto: The Easter Seal Society, 1982, 64–67.
6. Murtagh J. *Patient education*. Sydney: McGraw-Hill, 1992.
7. Travell J, Rinzler SH. The myofascial genesis of pain. Postgrad Med, 1952; 11:425–34.
8. Reilly P, Littlejohn G. Current thinking on fibromyalgia syndrome. Aust Fam Physician, 1990; 19:1505–1576.
9. Smythe HA, Moldofsky H. Two contributions to understanding of the 'fibrositis' syndrome. Bull Rheum Dis, 1977; 28:928–931.
10. Young D, Murtagh J. Pitfalls in orthopaedics. Aust Fam Physician, 1989; 18:653–654.

33

Bruising and bleeding

Many patients present with the complaint that they bruise easily but only a minority turn out to have an underlying blood disorder. Purpura is bleeding into the skin or mucous membranes, appearing as multiple small haemorrhages which do not blanch on pressure. Smaller purpuric lesions that are 2 mm or less in diameter (pinhead size) are termed petechiae while larger purpuric lesions are called ecchymoses (Fig. 33.1).

Bruises are large areas of bleeding which are a result of subcutaneous bleeding. If bruising is abnormal and out of proportion to the offending trauma then a disturbance of coagulation is suggested.

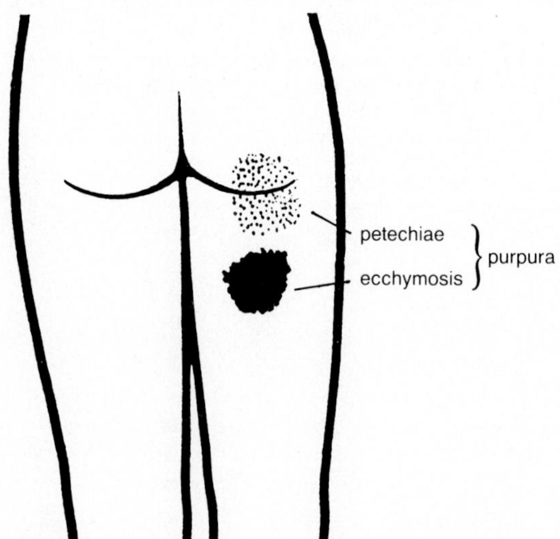

Fig. 33.1 *Purpuric rash (petechiae and ecchymoses)*

Differential diagnosis: 'Palpable purpura' due to an underlying systemic vasculitis is an important differential problem. The petechiae are raised so finger palpation is important. The cause is an underlying vasculitis affecting small vessels, e.g. polyarteritis nodosa.

The decision to investigate is difficult because decisions have to be made about which patients warrant investigation and whether the haemostatic defect is due to local or systemic pathology.[1] The ability to identify a bleeding disorder is important because of implications for surgery, pregnancy, medication and genetic counselling.

Key facts and checkpoints

- Purpura = petechiae + ecchymoses.
- Abnormal bleeding is basically the result of disorders of (1) the platelet, (2) the coagulation mechanism, or (3) the blood vessel.
- There is no substitute for a good history in the assessment of patients with bleeding disorders.
- An assessment of the personal and family histories is the first step in the identification of a bleeding disorder.
- When a patient complains of 'bruising easily' it is important to exclude thrombocytopenia due to bone marrow disease and clotting factor deficiencies such as haemophilia.

- In general, bleeding secondary to platelet defects is spontaneous, associated with a petechial rash and occurs immediately after trauma or a cut wound.[1]
- Laboratory assessment should be guided by the clinical impression.
- Bleeding caused by coagulation factor deficiency is usually traumatic and delayed, e.g. haemorrhage occurring 24 hours after a dental extraction in a haemophiliac.
- The routine screening tests for the investigation of patients with bleeding disorders can be normal despite the presence of a severe haemorrhagic state.

Causes of clinical disorders

The three major mechanisms of systemic bleeding disorders are:

1. Coagulation deficiencies (reduction or inhibition of circulatory coagulation factors)
2. Platelet abnormalities: of platelet number or function
3. Vascular defects: of vascular endothelium

A list of differential diagnoses of systemic bleeding disorders is presented in Table 33.1.[1]

The clinical approach

Differentiation of coagulation factor deficiencies and platelet disorders as the cause of a bleeding problem can usually be determined by a careful evaluation of the history and physical examination.

History

Factors that suggest the presence of a systemic bleeding defect include:

- spontaneous haemorrhage
- severe or recurrent haemorrhagic episodes
- bleeding from multiple sites
- bleeding out of proportion to the degree of trauma

If a bleeding diathesis is suspected it is essential to determine whether local pathology is contributing to the blood loss, e.g. postoperative bleeding, postpartum bleeding, gastrointestinal haemorrhage.

Diagnostic tips

- Platelet abnormalities present as early bleeding following trauma.
- Coagulation factor deficiencies present with delayed bleeding after initial haemostasis is achieved by normal platelets.
- A normal response to previous coagulation stresses, e.g. dental extraction, circumcision, pregnancy, indicates an acquired problem.
- If acquired, look for evidence of drugs, malignancy and liver disease.
- A diagnostic strategy is outlined in Table 33.2.

Table 33.1 *Differential diagnoses of systemic bleeding disorders (after Jane and Salem[1])*

Vascular disorders

a) Inherited
- hereditary haemorrhagic telangiectasia
- Marfan's syndrome

b) Acquired
- purpura simplex
- senile purpura
- Henoch-Schönlein purpura
- steroid purpura
- scurvy

Coagulation factor deficiency or inhibitor

a) Inherited
- haemophilia A
- haemophilia B
- von Willebrand's disease

b) Acquired
- disseminated intravascular coagulation
- liver disease
- vitamin K deficiency
- oral anticoagulant therapy or overdosage

Thrombocytopenia

a) Inherited
- Fanconi syndrome
- amegakaryocytic thrombocytopenia

b) Acquired
- immune thrombocytopenic purpura
- drug-induced thrombocytopenia
- disseminated intravascular coagulation
- bone marrow replacement or failure
- thrombotic thrombocytopenic purpura
- post-transfusion purpura
- splenic pooling
- burns
- systemic infection
- HIV infection

Functional platelet disorders

a) Inherited
- Glanzmann's thrombasthenia
- Bernard-Soulier syndrome
- storage pool deficiency

b) Acquired
- drug-induced
- uraemia
- myeloproliferative disorders
- dysproteinaemias

Adapted from Bleeding disorders, MIMS Disease Index 1991-92 with permission of MIMS Australia Pty Ltd

Table 33.2 *Purpura: diagnostic strategy model*

Q. Probability diagnosis
A. Simple purpura (easy bruising syndrome)
Senile purpura
Corticosteroid-induced purpura
Anaphylactoid purpura (Henoch-Schönlein)

Q. Serious disorders not to be missed
A. Malignant disease
- leukaemia
- myeloma

Aplastic anaemia
Myelofibrosis
Severe infections
- septicaemia
- meningococcal infection
- measles
- typhoid

Disseminated intravascular coagulation
Thrombocytopenic purpura

Q. Pitfalls (often missed)
A. Haemophilia A,B
von Willebrand's disease
Connective tissue disorders, e.g. SLE, RA
Post-transfusion purpura
Trauma, e.g. domestic violence

Rare
- hereditary telangiectasia (Osler-Weber-Rendu syndrome)
- Ehlers-Danlos syndrome
- scurvy
- Fanconi syndrome

Q. The masquerades
A. Drugs
- chloramphenicol
- corticosteroids
- sulphonamides
- quinine/quinidine
- thiazide diuretics
- NSAIDs

Anaemia
- aplastic anaemia

Q. Psychogenic factors
A. Factitial purpura

Family history

A positive family history can be a positive pointer to the diagnosis:

- sex-linked recessive pattern
  —haemophilia A or B
- autosomal dominant pattern
  —von Willebrand's disease
  —dysfibrinogenaemias
- autosomal recessive pattern
  —deficiency coagulation factors V, VII and X

Enquire whether the patient has noticed blood in the urine or stools and whether menorrhagia is present in women. A checklist for a bleeding history is presented in Table 33.3. The actual size and frequency of the bruises should be recorded where possible and if none are present at the time of the consultation the patient should return if any bruises reappear.

Table 33.3 *Checklist for a bleeding history*

Skin bruising
Epistaxis
Injury
Domestic violence
Menorrhagia
Haemarthrosis
Tooth extraction
Tonsillectomy
Other operations
Childbirth
Haematuria
Rectal bleeding
Drugs
Family history

Key questions

How long has the problem been apparent to you?
Do you remember any bumps or falls that might have caused the bruising?
What sort of injuries cause you to bruise easily?
Have you noticed bleeding from other areas such as your nose or gums?
Has anyone in your family had a history of bruising or bleeding?
What is your general health like?
Any tiredness, weight loss, fever or night sweats?
Did you notice a viral illness or sore throat beforehand?
How much alcohol do you drink?
What happened in the past when you had a tooth extracted?
Do you get widespread itchiness of your skin?
Have you ever had painful swelling in your joints?

Medication record

It is mandatory to obtain a complete drug history. Examples of drugs and their responses are:

- vascular purpura
  — prednisolone
- thrombocytopenia
  — chloramphenicol
  — cytotoxic drugs
  — gold

- heparin
- phenylbutazone
- sulphonamides
- quinine, quinidine
- thiazide diuretics

• functional platelet abnormalities
  - aspirin
  - NSAIDs

• coagulation factor deficiency
  - warfarin

Physical examination

Careful examination of the skin is important. Note the nature of the bleeding and the distribution of any rash, which is characteristic in Henoch-Schölein purpura. Senile purpura in the elderly is usually seen over the dorsum of the hands, extensor surface of the forearms and the shins.

Note the lips and oral mucosa for evidence of hereditary telangiectasia. Gum hypertrophy occurs in monocytic leukaemia. Search for evidence of malignancy such as sternal tenderness, lymphadenopathy and splenomegaly. Examine the ocular fundi for evidence of retinal haemorrhages. Urinalysis, searching for blood (microscopic or macroscopic), is important.

Investigations

The initial choice of investigations depends upon the bleeding pattern.

If coagulation defect suspected:

- prothrombin time (PT)
- activated partial thromboplastin time (APTT)

If platelet pathology suspected:

- platelet count
- skin bleeding time

The full blood examination and blood film is useful in pinpointing the aetiology. Platelet morphology gives a diagnostic guide to inherited platelet disorders. Other sophisticated tests can be advised by the consulting haematologist. One of considerable value is the bone marrow examination which is useful to exclude the secondary causes of thrombocytopenia such as leukaemia, other marrow infiltrations and aplastic anaemia.

A summary of appropriate tests is presented in Table 33.4 and of blood changes for some coagulation factor deficiencies in Table 33.5.

Table 33.4 *Laboratory investigation checklist for the easy bruiser*

Full blood count
Platelet count
Prothrombin time
Activated partial thromboplastin time
Skin bleeding time

Abnormal bleeding in children

Abnormal bleeding in children is not uncommon and once again the clinical history, particularly the past and family history, provides the most valuable information. It is important to keep non-accidental injury such as child abuse in mind in the child presenting with 'easy bruising'. However, it is appropriate to exclude a bleeding disorder, especially a platelet disorder.

Coagulation disorders, including haemophilia and von Willebrand's disease, are usually suspected on clinical grounds because of widespread bruising or because of prolonged bleeding following procedures such as circumcision and tonsillectomy.

A common condition is haemorrhagic disease of the newborn, which is a self-limiting disease usually presenting on the second or third day of life because of a deficiency of coagulation factors dependent on vitamin K. The routine use of prophylactic vitamin K in the newborn infant has virtually eliminated this problem.

Idiopathic (immune) thrombocytopenic purpura (ITP) is the commonest of the primary platelet disorders in children. Both acute and chronic forms have an immunological basis. The diagnosis is based on the peripheral blood film and platelet count. The platelet count is

Table 33.5 *Blood changes for specific coagulation factor disorders*

	Haemophilia A	*von Willebrand's disease*	*Vitamin K deficiency*
PT	Normal	Normal	↑
APTT	↑	↑	↑
Bleeding time	Normal	↑	Normal

commonly below 50 000/mm^3 (50 × 10^9/L). Spontaneous remission within 4 to 6 weeks occurs with acute ITP in childhood.[2]

The commonest vascular defects in childhood are:

1. anaphylactoid (Henoch-Schönlein) purpura
2. infective states
3. nutritional deficiency (usually inadequate dietary vitamin C)

Anaphylactoid (Henoch-Schönlein) purpura

This is diagnosed clinically by the characteristic distribution of the rash over the buttocks and backs of the legs. It may be accompanied by joint swelling, abdominal pain and rarely melaena and glomerulonephritis.

The bleeding time, coagulation time and platelet counts are normal. The prognosis is generally excellent. No specific therapy is available but corticosteroids may be helpful.[2]

Infective states

The purpura associated with severe infections such as meningococcaemia and other septicaemias is due primarily to a severe angiitis. Disseminated intravascular coagulation usually follows.[2]

Abnormal bleeding in the elderly

The outstanding causes are senile purpura and purpura due to steroids.[3] The cause in both instances is atrophy of the vascular supporting tissue.

Vascular disorders

The features are:

- easy bruising and bleeding into skin
- ± mucous membrane bleeding
- investigations normal

Simple purpura (easy bruising syndrome)

This is a benign disorder occurring in otherwise healthy women usually in their twenties or thirties. The feature is bruising on the arms, leg and trunk with minor trauma. The patient may complain of heavy periods. Major challenges to the haemostatic mechanism such as dental extraction, childbirth and surgery have not been complicated by excessive blood loss.

Factitial purpura

Unexplained bruising or bleeding may represent self-inflicted abuse or abuse by others. In self-inflicted abuse the bruising is commonly on the legs or areas within easy reach of the patient.

Platelet disorders

The features are:

- petechiae ± ecchymoses
- bleeding from mucous membranes
- platelet counts <50 000/mm^3 (50 × 10^9/L)

Immune thrombocytopenic purpura

Essential features:

- easy bruising
- epistaxis and menorrhagia common
- no systemic illness
- splenomegaly is rare
- isolated thrombocytopenia
- other blood cells normal
- otherwise normal physical examination
- normal bone marrow with normal or increased megakaryocytes

The two distinct types caused by immune destruction of platelets are:

- acute ITP: usually in children, often post-viral
- chronic ITP: autoimmune disorder, usually in adult women; all cases should be referred to a specialist unit

Chronic ITP rarely undergoes spontaneous remission and may require treatment with prednisolone. Some require splenectomy but this operation is avoided where possible, especially in young children, because of the subsequent risk of severe infection, particularly with *Streptococcus pneumoniae*.[3]

Coagulation disorders

The features are:

- ecchymoses
- haemarthrosis and muscle haematomas
- usually traumatic and delayed

The inherited disorders such as haemophilia A and B are uncommon and involve deficiency of one factor only. The acquired disorders such as disseminated intravascular coagulation (DIC) occur more commonly and invariably affect several anticoagulation factors (Table 33.6).

Table 33.6 *International nomenclature of clotting factors*

Factor	Common synonyms
I	Fibrinogen*
II	Prothrombin*
III	Thromboplastin*
IV	Calcium*
V*	Proaccelerin
VI	No longer used
VII*	Proconversion
VIII	Antihaemophilic factor Antihaemophilic globulin
IX*	Christmas factor, plasma thromboplastin component
X*	Stuart-Prower factor
XI*	Plasma thromboplastin antecedent
XII	Hageman factor, contact factor
XIII	Fibrin stabilising factor

Common terminology in use indicated by *

Management principles[1]

- Make the correct diagnosis.
- Stop or avoid drugs affecting the haemostatic system.
- Control bleeding episodes with appropriate drugs, blood products and local measures such as simple compression or topical haemostatic agents.
- Refer patients with identified defects to a consultant haematologist or haemophilia centre.
- Supervise advanced planning in patients seeking pregnancy, surgery or dental extraction.

When to refer[1]

- Management of haemorrhage not amenable to simple measures such as local therapy with simple compression and other measures.
- Planning for elective surgery or pregnancy.

Practice tips

- A careful history and physical examination will usually pinpoint the cause of the bleeding disorder.
- Drug therapy can lead to unmasking of pre-existing haemostatic disorders, e.g. platelet dysfunction induced by aspirin may cause spontaneous bleeding in patients with underlying von Willebrand's disease.
- Think of DIC in any acutely ill patient with abnormal bleeding from sites such as the mouth, nose, venepuncture or with widespread ecchymoses. The clinical situations are numerous, e.g. septicaemia, obstetric emergencies, disseminated malignant disease, falciparum malaria, snake bites.

References

1. Jane S, Salem H. Bleeding disorders. In: MIMS Disease Index. Sydney: IMS Publishing, 1991–2, 77–79.
2. Robinson MJ. *Practical paediatrics* (2nd edition), Melbourne: Churchill Livingstone, 1990, 349–356.
3. Kumer PJ, Clark ML. *Clinical medicine* (2nd edition), London: Bailliere Tindall, 1990, 335–344.

34

Chest pain

—

The presenting problem of chest pain is common yet very threatening to both patient and doctor because the underlying cause in many instances is potentially lethal, especially with chest pain of sudden onset. The causes of acute chest pain are summarised and presented in Figure 34.1.

Checkpoints and golden rules

- Chest pain represents myocardial infarction until proved otherwise.
- Immediate life-threatening causes of spontaneous chest pain are (1) myocardial infarction, (2) pulmonary embolism, (3) dissecting aneurysm of the aorta, and (4) tension pneumothorax.
- The main differential diagnoses of myocardial infarction include angina, dissecting aneurysm, pericarditis, oesophageal reflux and spasm and hyperventilation with anxiety.
- The history remains the most important clinical factor in the diagnosis of ischaemic heart disease. With angina a vital clue is the reproducibility of the symptom.

A diagnostic approach

The safety diagnostic model (Table 34.1) can be used to analyse chest pain according to the five self-posed questions.

Probability diagnosis

The commonest causes encountered in general practice are musculoskeletal or chest wall pain and psychogenic disorders. The former is a very important yet often overlooked cause and

Table 34.1 *Chest pain: diagnostic strategy model*

Q. Probability diagnosis
A. Musculoskeletal (chest wall)
Psychogenic
Angina

Q. Serious disorders not to be missed
A. Cardiovascular
- myocardial infarction
- dissecting aneurysm
- pulmonary embolism

Neoplasia
- carcinoma lung
- tumours of spinal cord and meningitis

Severe infections
- pneumonia-pleurisy
- mediastinitis
- pericarditis

Pneumothorax

Q. Pitfalls (often missed)
A. Mitral valve prolapse
Oesophageal spasm
Gastro-oesophageal reflux
Herpes zoster
Fractured rib, e.g. cough fracture
Spinal dysfunction

Rarities
- Bornholm disease (pleurodynia)
- cocaine inhalation

Q. Seven masquerades checklist

A.		
Depression	✓	possible
Diabetes	—	
Drugs	—	
Anaemia	✓	indirect
Thyroid disease	—	
Spinal dysfunction	✓	
UTI	—	

Q. Is the patient trying to tell me something?
A. Consider functional causes, especially anxiety with hyperventilation

NB Chest pain is myocardial ischaemia until proved otherwise.

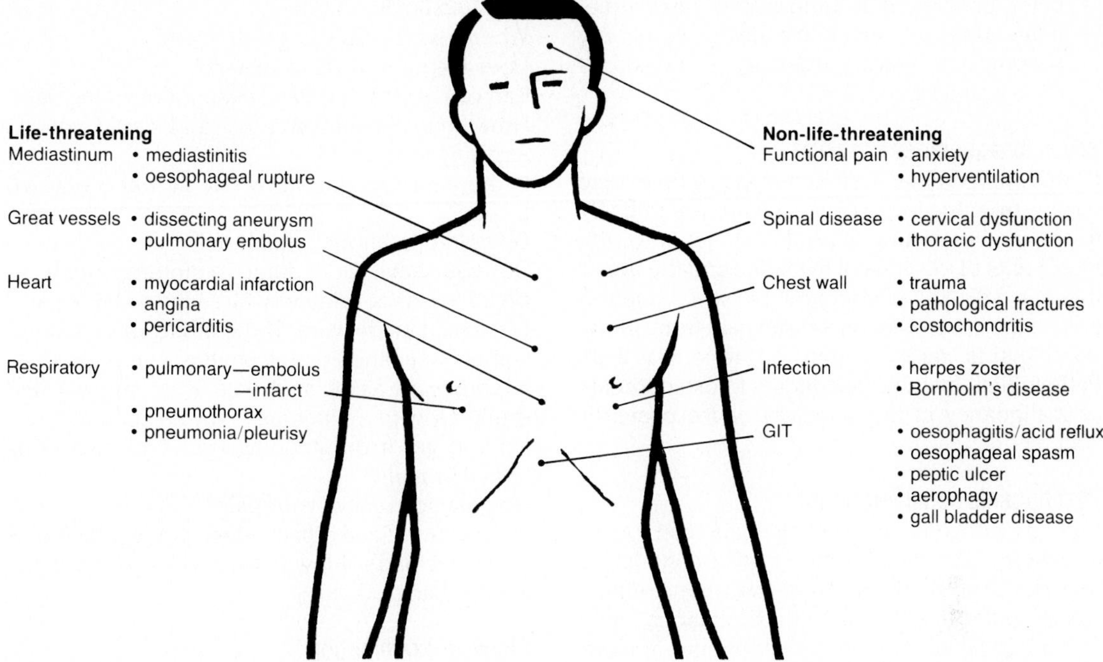

Fig. 34.1 *Causes of acute chest pain*

sometimes inappropriately referred to as fibrositis or neuralgia. Causes include costochondritis, muscular strains, dysfunction of the sternocostal joints and dysfunction of the lower cervical spine or upper thoracic spine which can cause referred pain to various areas of the chest wall. Angina is common and must always be considered. If angina-like pain lasts longer than 15 minutes myocardial infarction must be excluded.

Serious disorders not to be missed

The usual triad of malignancy, myocardial ischaemia and severe infections (Table 34.1) must be considered. In addition other cardiovascular catastrophes such as a dissecting aortic aneurysm and pulmonary embolus must be excluded, albeit uncommon, especially in those at risk. Spontaneous pneumothorax should also be considered especially in a young male of slight build. Malignancies of the lung are relatively common and may present as pain when the previously asymptomatic tumour invades nerves or the spine.

The severe infections that cause chest pain include pneumonia/pleurisy, pericarditis and mediastinitis.

Pitfalls

Unfortunately, myocardial infarction and angina are often missed. Referred pain from spinal dysfunction, especially if referred anteriorly, is commonly overlooked. Other pitfalls include a cough fracture of a rib, herpes zoster (prior to the eruption) and gastrointestinal disorders, including oesophageal spasm, reflux and cholecystitis. Oesophageal problems may be clinically indistinguishable from angina. Mitral valve prolapse can cause chest pain although the mechanism is unclear: think of it in an unwell female prone to palpitations and chest pain. The pain tends to be sharp, fleeting, non-exertional and located near the cardiac apex.

General pitfalls include:

- not being 'coronary aware' in patients presenting with chest pain;
- referred pain from spinal disorders, especially of the lower cervical spine—one of the great pitfalls in medical practice;
- labelling chest pain as psychological in an anxious patient presenting with acute chest pain;
- assuming that pain radiating down the inside of the left arm is always cardiac in origin;

- being unaware that up to 20% of myocardial infarctions are silent, especially in elderly patients, and that pulmonary embolism is often painless.

Seven masquerades checklist

Of this group spinal dysfunction is possible. Disc lesions from the lower cervical spine are unlikely to cause chest wall pain, but dysfunction of the facet joints of this area of the spine and the upper thoracic spine is a common cause of referred pain to the chest wall. Nerve root pain from spinal problems is rarely found in the chest wall. Pathological fractures secondary to osteoporosis or malignancy in the vertebrae cause posterior wall pain.

Psychogenic considerations

With psychogenic causes the pain can occur anywhere in the chest, and tends to be continuous and sharp or stabbing rather than constricting. Associated symptoms include palpitations, deep breathing, fatigue, tremor, agitation and anxiety. Abnormal stress, tension, anxiety or depression may precipitate the pain, which often lasts hours or days.

The clinical approach

History

A meticulous history of the behaviour of the pain is the key to diagnosis. The pain should be analysed into its usual characteristics: site and radiation, quality, intensity, duration, onset and offset, precipitating and relieving factors, and associated symptoms. Association with serious medical problems such as diabetes, Marfan's syndrome, anaemia and systemic lupus erythematosus should be kept in mind. The ability to take a detailed history will obviously be limited with severe acute pain.

Associated symptoms

- Syncope: consider myocardial infarction, pulmonary embolus and dissecting aneurysm.
- Pain on inspiration: consider pleurisy, pericarditis, pneumothorax and musculoskeletal (chest wall pain).
- Thoracic back pain: consider spinal dysfunction, myocardial infarction, angina, dissecting aneurysm, pericarditis and gastrointestinal disorders such as a peptic ulcer, cholecystitis and oesophageal spasm.

Key questions

Where exactly do you get the pain?
Does the pain travel anywhere?
Can you give me a careful description of the pain?
How long did the pain last and could you do anything to relieve it?
Is the pain brought on by exertion and relieved by rest?
Do cold conditions bring it on?
Do you have any other symptoms such as breathlessness, faintness, sweating or back pain?
Is the pain made worse by breathing or coughing?
Is there any blood in any sputum you bring up?
Is your pain associated with what you eat and drink? Or with a bitter taste in your mouth?
Do you get it on stooping over and after lying in bed at night?
Do antacids relieve your pain?
Have you noticed a rash where you get the pain?
Have you had a blow to your chest or an injury to your back?

Physical examination

The examination should focus on the following areas:

- general appearance: evidence of atherosclerosis (senile arcus, thickened vessels), pale and sweating (myocardial infarction, dissecting aneurysm or pulmonary embolus), hemiparesis (? dissecting aneurysm);
- pulses—radial and femoral: check for nature of pulse and absence of femoral pulses;
- blood pressure;
- temperature;
- palpation of chest wall, lower cervical spine and thoracic spine: look for evidence of localised tenderness, pathological fracture, spinal dysfunction, herpes zoster;
- palpation of legs: check for evidence of deep venous thrombosis;
- examination of chest: check for evidence of pneumothorax;
- Auscultation of chest
  - — reduced breath sounds and vocal fremitus → pneumothorax
  - — friction rub → pericarditis or pleurisy
  - — basal crackles → cardiac failure
  - — apical systole murmur → mitral valve prolapse
  - — aortic diastolic murmur → proximal dissection

  In the presence of a myocardial infarction, the examination may be normal but the patient, apart from being cold, clammy or

shocked, may have muffled heart sounds, a gallop rhythm, a systolic murmur. With a dissecting aneurysm the patient may also appear cold, clammy and shocked, but may show absent femoral pulses, hemiparesis and a diastolic murmur of aortic regurgitation.
- upper abdominal palpation: check for tenderness suggestive of gall bladder disease or peptic ulceration.

Possible findings on examination of a patient with chest pain are presented in Figure 34.2.[1]

Investigations

The following investigations to aid diagnosis are available, although the majority are sophisticated and confined to hospitals with high technology imaging departments. The fundamental tests that are readily available to the GP—ECG, chest X-ray and cardiac enzymes—should help confirm the diagnosis in most instances.

Electrocardiogram (ECG)

This may be diagnostic for angina and myocardial infarction although it is important to bear in mind that it may be normal with both, including the early minutes to hours of an acute infarction.

It can be helpful to differentiate between myocardial infarction, pulmonary embolism and pericarditis (Fig. 34.3). The ECG in pulmonary embolism may show right axis deviation. Pericarditis is characterised by low voltages and saddle-shaped ST segment elevation.

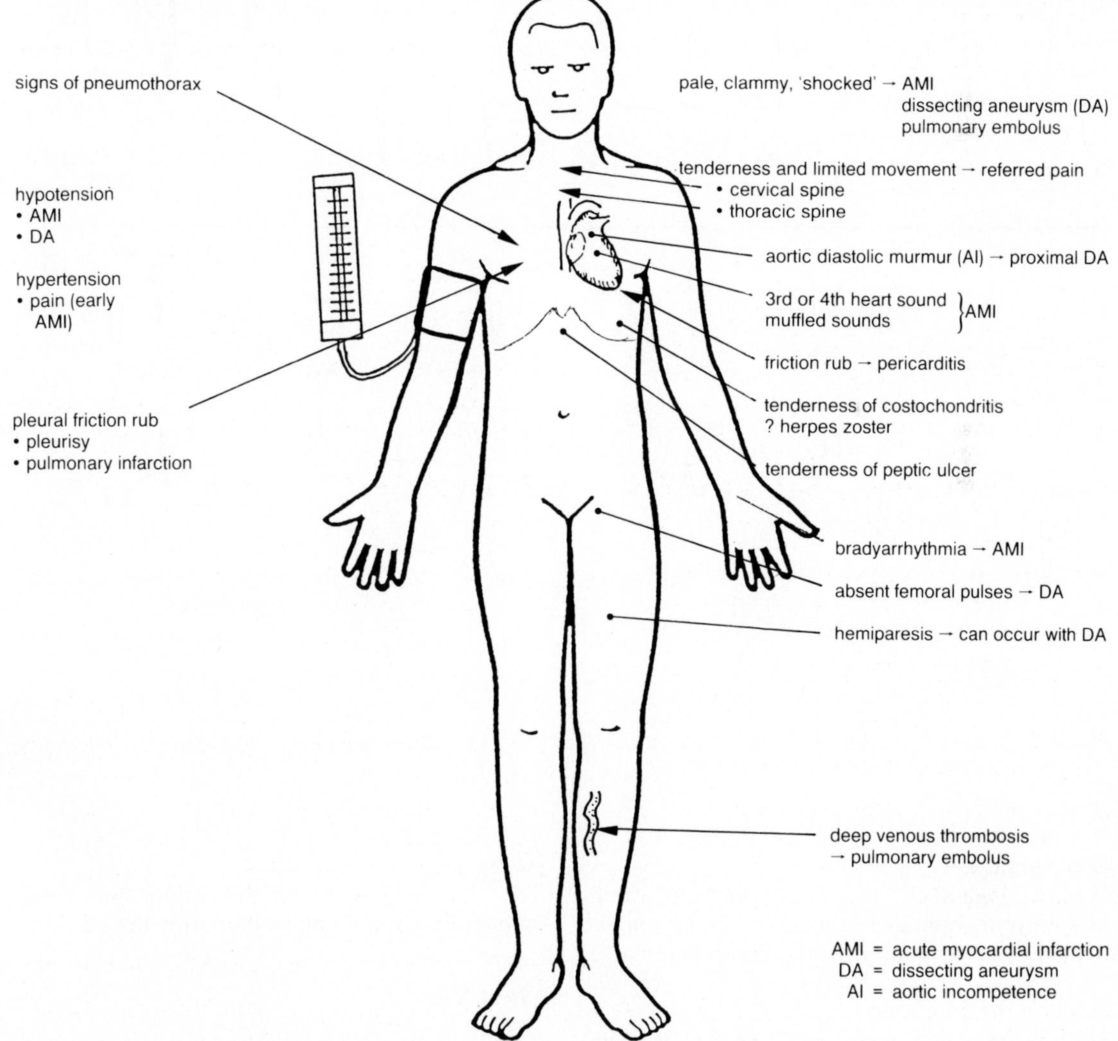

Fig. 34.2 *Possible examination findings in a patient with chest pain*

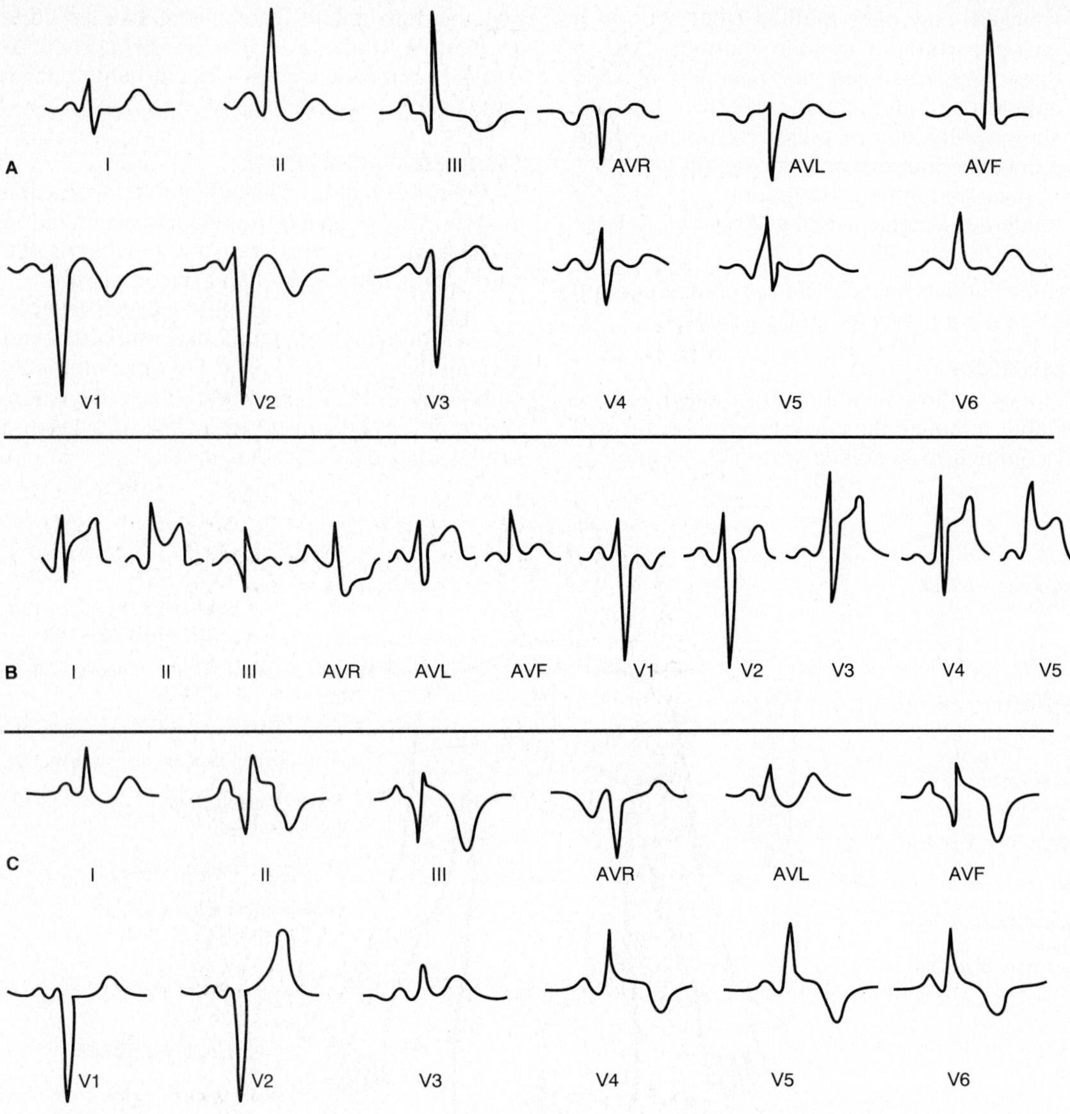

Fig. 34.3 *Typical ECG pattern for specific causes of acute chest pain:* **(a)** *acute pulmonary embolism;* **(b)** *acute pericarditis;* **(c)** *acute inferior myocardial infarction*

Exercise ECG

Physical stress such as the motor-driven treadmill or a bicycle ergometer is used to elicit changes in the ECG to diagnose myocardial ischaemia.

Exercise thallium scan

This radionuclide myocardial perfusion scan using thallium can compliment the exercise ECG.

Ambulatory Holter monitor

This monitor is especially useful for silent ischaemia, variant angina and arrhythmias.

Chest X-ray

Haemoglobin and blood film

Serum enzymes

Damaged necrosed myocardial tissue releases cellular enzymes, three of which are commonly assayed:

- creatinine kinase (CK) and creatinine kinase–myocardial bound fraction (CK–MB)
- aspartate aminotransferase (AST)
- lactic dehydrogenase (LDH)

Echocardiography

This can be used in the early stages of myocardial infarction to detect abnormalities in heart wall motion, when ECGs and enzymes are not diagnostic.

Isotope scanning

1. Technetium 99 m pyrophosphate studies:
   A. myocardium: to diagnose posterolateral myocardial infarction in the presence of bundle branch block:
   B. pulmonary: to diagnose pulmonary embolism.
2. Gated blood pool nuclear scan (radionuclide ventriculography). This scan tests left ventricular function at rest and exercise in patients with myocardial ischaemia.

Angiography (arteriography)

Angiography should be selective:

1. coronary—to evaluate coronary arteries
2. aortic—to diagnose dissecting aneurysm
3. pulmonary—to diagnose pulmonary thromboembolism

Oesophageal studies

- endoscopy
- barium enema
- oesophageal manometry
- radionuclide transit studies

Spine—X-ray

- cervical spine
- thoracic spine

Site, radiation and features of chest pain syndromes

Myocardial infarction and angina

The typical retrosternal distribution is shown in Figure 34.4. Retrosternal pain or pain situated across the chest anteriorly should be regarded as cardiac until proved otherwise.

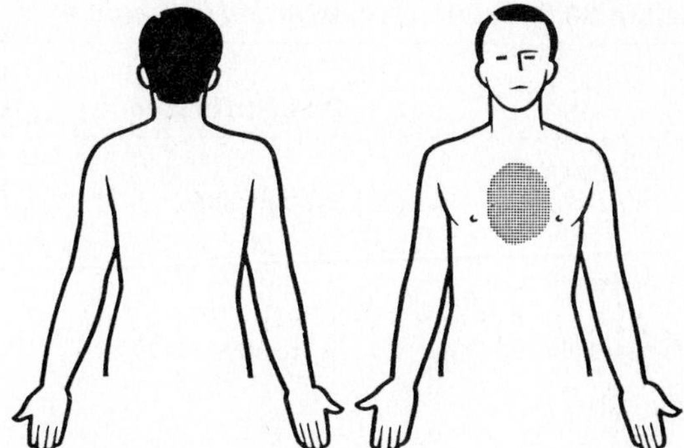

Fig. 34.4 *Pain of myocardial ischaemia: typical site*

The wide variation of sites of pain, e.g. jaw, neck, inside of arms, epigastrium and interscapular, should always be kept in mind (Fig. 34.5). Pain is referred into the left arm twenty times more commonly than into the right arm.

The quality of the pain is usually typical. The patient often uses the clenched fist sign to illustrate a sense of constriction.

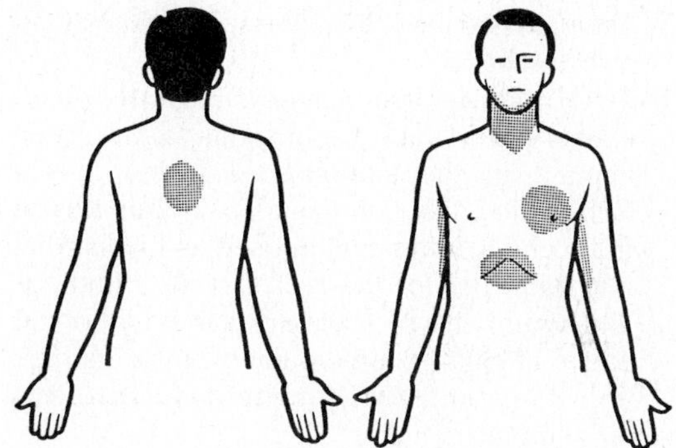

Fig. 34.5 *Pain of myocardial ischaemia: other sites*

The radiation of pain will assist in differentiating ischaemic pain from that caused by pericarditis. Enquiry about precipitating and relieving factors will enable a differentiation to be made between ischaemic pain and the almost identical pain caused by reference from the spine.

If a retrosternal pain almost identical with that of myocardial ischaemia is precipitated not by exertion but by bending, lifting, straining or lying down, oesophageal reflux and spasm is a possible diagnosis. This is frequently confused with ischaemic heart disease and can cause radiation into the left arm.

The main types of myocardial ischaemia are summarised in Table 34.2.

Table 34.2 *Types of myocardial ischaemia*

	Duration of pain	***Precipitating factors or characteristic setting***	***Other features***
Angina pectoris			
Stable	3–10 minutes	Physical or emotional stress	Relieved by rest and glyceryl trinitrate
Unstable	5–15 minutes	Not defined; rest or effort	Slow relief from glyceryl trinitrate
Myocardial infarction	$>$ 15–20 minutes	Any time	May be nausea, vomiting, hypotension, arrhythmia Not relieved by glyceryl trinitrate

1. Myocardial infarction: ischaemic pain lasting longer than 15 to 20 minutes is usually infarction. The pain is typically heavy and crushing and can vary from mild to intense. Occasionally the attack is painless, typically in diabetics. Pallor, sweating and vomiting may accompany the attack.
2. Angina: the pain tends to last a few minutes only (average 3–5 minutes) and is relieved by rest and glyceryl trinitrate (nitroglycerine). The pain may be precipitated by an arrhythmia.
3. Acute coronary insufficiency: this term, which appears to include variant angina, has been applied to the situation in which severe ischaemic chest pain lasts 15–20 minutes or more and would be diagnosed as myocardial infarction but for the fact that ECG findings and serum enzymes are normal. It can occur when angina is precipitated by a cardiac arrhythmia and lasts for the duration of the arrhythmia.

Dissecting aneurysm

The pain, which is usually sudden, severe and midline, has a tearing sensation and is usually situated retrosternally and between the scapulae (Fig. 34.6). It radiates to the abdomen, flank and legs. An important diagnostic feature is the inequality in the pulses, e.g. carotid, radial and femoral. There may also be occlusion of the coronary or renal arteries with appropriate symptoms and signs. Hemiplegia, aortic incompetence or cardiac tamponade can occur.

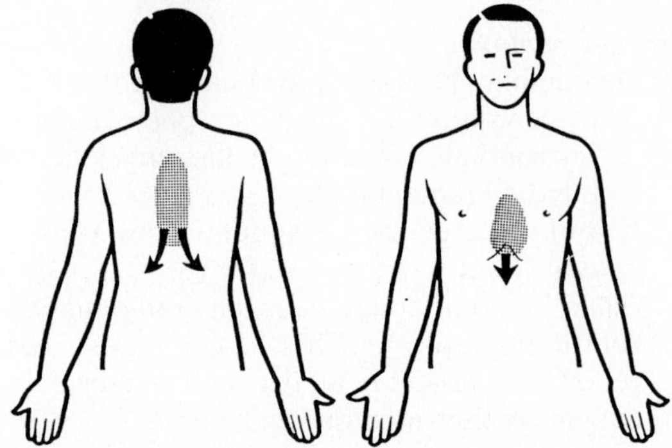

Fig. 34.6 *Pain of dissecting aneurysm*

Pulmonary embolism

This has a dramatic onset following occlusion of the pulmonary artery or a major branch, especially if more than 50% of the cross-sectional area of the pulmonary trunk is occluded.

The diagnosis can present clinical difficulties, especially when dyspnoea is present without pain. Embolism usually presents with retrosternal chest pain (Fig. 34.7) and may be associated with syncope and breathlessness. In addition, hypotension, acute right heart failure or cardiac arrest occurs with a massive embolus. The physical examination can be deceptively normal. Pulmonary infarction is generally less dramatic than embolism and it is usually accompanied by pleuritic chest pain and haemoptysis. It complicates embolism in about 10% of patients.

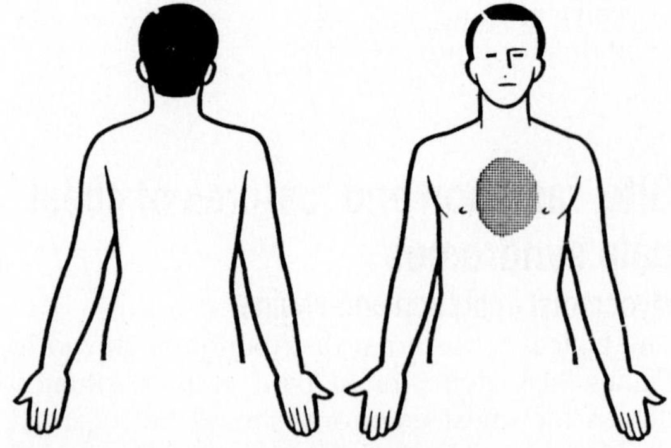

Fig. 34.7 *Pain of pulmonary embolism*

Acute pericarditis

Pericarditis causes three distinct types of pain:

1. pleuritic (the commonest) aggravated by cough and deep inspiration, sometimes brought on by swallowing;
2. steady, crushing, retrosternal pain that mimics myocardial infarction;
3. pain synchronous with the heartbeat and felt over the praecordium and left shoulder.

Occasionally two and rarely all three types of pain may be present simultaneously (Fig. 34.8).

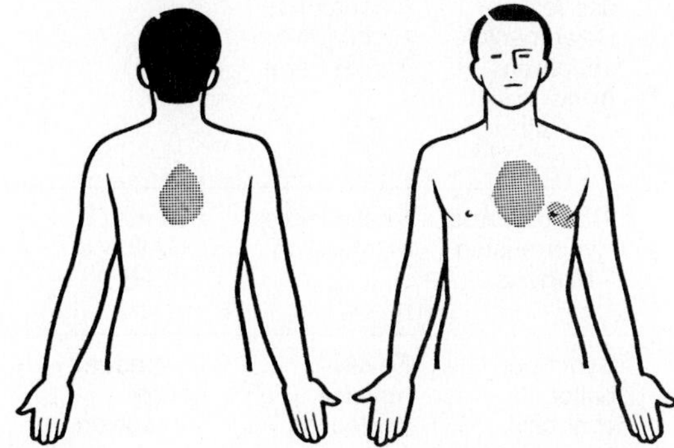

Fig. 34.8 *Pain of pericarditis*

Spontaneous pneumothorax

The acute onset of pleuritic pain and dyspnoea in a patient with a history of asthma or emphysema is the hallmark of a pneumothorax. It often occurs in young slender males without a history of lung disorders. The pain varies from mild to severe and can be felt anywhere in the chest, being sometimes retrosternal. Typical pain distribution is shown in Fig. 34.9.

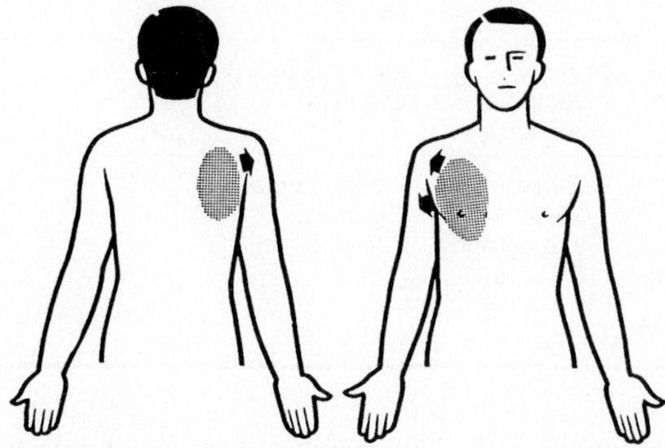

Fig. 34.9 *Pain of pneumothorax (right side)*

If a tension pneumothorax becomes painful and dyspnoea becomes rapidly more intense, urgent decompression of air is essential. A comparison of the serious causes of acute chest pain is summarised in Table 34.3.

Oesophageal pain

Gastro-oesophageal reflux can cause oesophagitis characterised by a burning epigastric or retrosternal pain that may radiate to the jaw. The pain is aggravated or precipitated by lying flat or bending over, especially after meals, and is more frequent at night. The pain is worse if oesophageal spasm is present. Oesophageal motor disorders including spasm may occur in isolation. The pain may radiate to the back (Fig. 34.10). It may be precipitated by eating, especially hot or cold food and drink, and may be relieved by eating or by glyceryl trinitrate (nitroglycerine) and other nitrates. Features differentiating angina-like oesophageal pain and cardiac pain are presented in Table 34.4.[2] Gastrointestinal causes of chest pain are summarised in Table 34.5.[1]

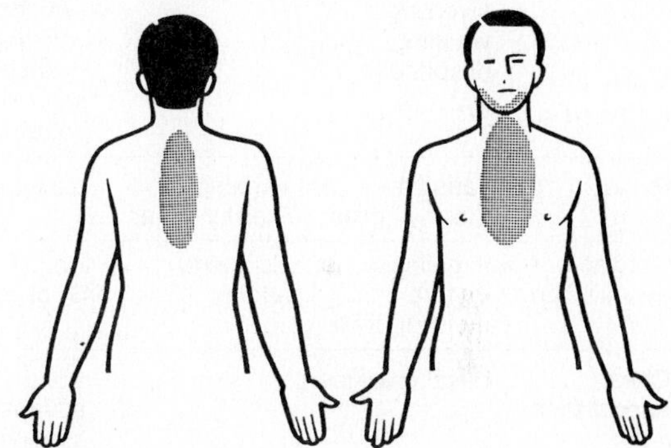

Fig. 34.10 *Oesophageal pain*

Spinal pain

The commonest cause of pain of spinal origin is vertebral dysfunction of the lower cervical or upper dorsal region. The spinal problem may be a disc prolapse (relatively common in the lower cervical spine, but rare in the upper thoracic spine) or dysfunction of the facet joints or costovertebral joints causing referred pain. This referred pain can be present anywhere in the chest wall including anterior chest, which causes confusion with cardiac pain (Fig. 34.11). The pain is dull and aching. It may be aggravated by exertion, certain body movements or deep inspiration. The old trap for unilateral nerve root pain is herpes zoster.

Table 34.3 *A comparison of the serious causes of acute chest pain*

	Myocardial infarction	**Angina**	**Pulmonary embolus**	**Dissecting aneurysm**	**Pericarditis**	**Pneumothorax**
Pain intensity	+ → ++++	+	+ → +++	+++++	+ → +++	+ → +++
Pain quality	Heavy Crushing Vice-like Burning	Heavy Aching Tightness Burning	Dull Heavy	Tearing Searing	Heavy Aching ± sharp	Tightness Sharp Stabbing
Pain site	Deep retrosternal	Deep retrosternal	Retrosternal	Anterior chest	Sternal surface	Lateral chest
Pain radiation	Throat/lower jaw Left arm (often) Right arm (uncommon) Back (uncommon)	As for infarction	Lateral chest (pleuritic)	Front to back of chest Down back to abdomen Arms	Left arm (uncommon) Right arm (rare) Throat (rare)	Lateral chest
History	Family, risk factors	Family, risk factors	Phlebitis Calf pain Immobility Surgery	Atherosclerosis Hypertension ? Marfans	Viral infection M.Infarction	Asthma COAD Old TB
Associated symptoms	Pallor, nausea, sweating, vomiting, dyspnoea, syncope	Strangling in throat	Dyspnoea, syncope, sweating, vomiting, cyanosis, agitation, ?haemoptysis	Syncope, pallor, cyanosis, Neurological • hemiparesis • paraplegia	Fever, malaise ± pleuritic pain	Dyspnoea, cough, ? cyanosis
Pulse	variable ? arrhythmias	variable ? arrhythmias	tachycardia	unequal some ?absent	weak if effusion	tachycardia
Cardiac auscultation	± gallop rhythm murmur of MI	S_3 during attack	↓ pulmonary S_2 S_3 or S_4	± murmur of AI	± pericardial friction rub	
Chest auscultation	basal crackles		± adventitious sounds			hyperresonant ↓ breath sounds ↑ percussion
Chest X-ray			± localised oligaemia or infarction	widening of mediastinum	↑ cardiac silhouette if effusion	diagnostic—expiration film
ECG	Q waves ST elevation T inversion	normal or ST depression	normal or R heart strain S_1,Q_3,T_3	may show myocardial infarction	elevated S-T segments	
Special definitive diagnostic tests	• serum enzymes CK, CKMB, AST, LDH • cardiac scanning	• stress ECG • coronary angiography	• lung scanning • pulmonary angiography	• ultrasound • aortic angiography • CT scan	• echocardiography (if effusion)	

Psychogenic pain

Psychogenic chest pain can occur anywhere in the chest, but often it is located in the left submammary region, usually without radiation (Fig. 34.12). It tends to be continuous and sharp or stabbing. It may mimic angina but tends to last for hours or days. It is usually aggravated by tiredness or emotional tension and may be associated with shortness of breath, fatigue and palpitations.

Table 34.4 *Features differentiating angina-like, oesophageal pain and cardiac pain*[2]

	Favour oesophageal	***Favour cardiac***	***Non-discriminating***
Precipitating factors	Meals, posture	Consistently with exercise	Emotion
Relieving factors	Antacids		Rest, nitrates
Radiation	Epigastrium	Arm	Back
Associated symptoms	Heartburn, regurgitation, dysphagia	Dyspnoea	Sweating

Table 34.5 *A comparison of gastrointestinal causes of chest pain*

	Acid reflux	***Oesophageal spasm***	***Peptic ulcer***	***Gall bladder disease***
Site	epigastric	deep retrosternal	deep retrosternal	right hypochondrium
Radiation	retrosternal throat	back	to back (DU)	below right scapula tip right shoulder
Quality	burning	constricting	gnawing	deep ache
Precipitation	heavy meals wine/coffee lying bending	eating hot/cold food and drinks	eating GU-30 mins DU-2-3 hrs	fatty food
Relief	standing antacids	antispasmodics nitroglycerine	antacids	
Associated symptoms	water brash	dysphagia	dyspepsia	flatulence dyspepsia

GU—gastric ulcer
DU—duodenal ulcer

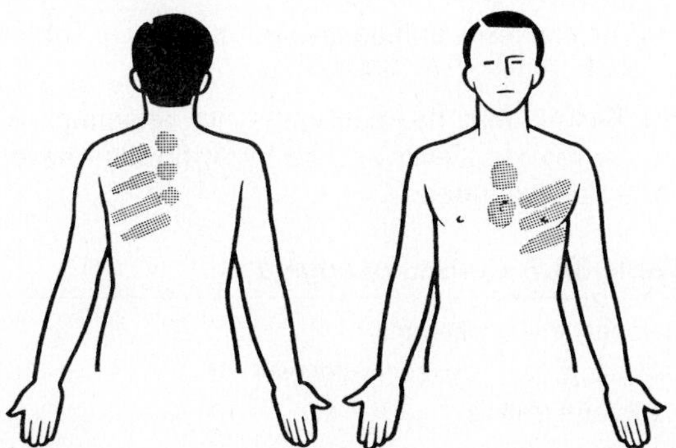

Fig. 34.11 *Possible pain sites for thoracic spinal dysfunction (left side)*

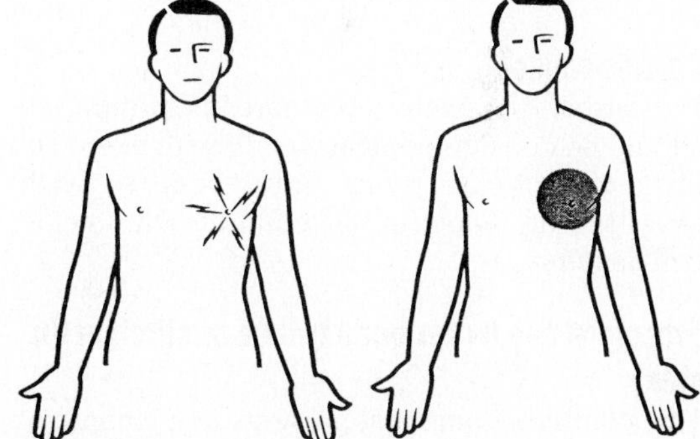

Fig. 34.12 *Typical sites of psychogenic pain*

Chest pain in children

Chest pain in children is rarely the result of serious pathology but is an important complaint especially in adolescents. A United States study has shown that the mean age for childhood chest pain is 11.9 years.[3,4] Most cases are of unknown aetiology (probably psychogenic), while common causes include musculoskeletal disorders, cough-induced pain, costochondritis, psychogenic disturbance (includes hyperventilation) and asthma. See Table 34.6.

Chest pain in children less than 12 years old is more likely to have a cardiorespiratory cause such as cough, asthma, pneumonia or heart disease, while chest pain in adolescents is more likely to be associated with a psychogenic disturbance.

Table 34.6 *Common causes of chest pain in children (adapted from Selbst[3])*

idiopathic	21%
musculoskeletal	16%
cough	10%
costochondritis	9%
psychogenic	9%
asthma	7%
trauma	5%
pneumonia	4%
GIT problems	4%
cardiovascular	4%

Causes of musculoskeletal pain include strains to pectoral, shoulder or back muscles after excessive exercise, and minor trauma from sports such as football or wrestling.

Breast problems can present as chest pain.

Costochondritis

This causes mild to moderate anterior chest wall pain that may radiate to the chest, back or abdomen. It is usually unilateral, sharp in nature and exaggerated by breathing, physical activity or a specific position. It may be preceded by exercise or an URTI and can persist for several months. It is diagnosed by eliciting tenderness at the chondrosternal junction of the affected ribs and needs to be differentiated from Tietze's syndrome where there is a tender, fusiform swelling at the chondrosternal junction.

Cardiac causes

Myocardial ischaemia is very rare in children but should be considered in any child with exercise-induced chest pain, adolescents with longstanding diabetes and children with sickle cell anaemia.

Precordial catch (Texidor's twinge or stitch in the side)

This common complaint presents as a unilateral low chest pain that lasts a few seconds or minutes, typically with exercise such as long-distance running. The pain is relieved by straightening up and taking very slow deep breaths followed by shallow breaths.

Chest pain in the elderly

Chest pain is a very important symptom in the elderly as the life-threatening cardiovascular conditions—myocardial infarction and angina, dissecting aneurysm and ruptured aorta—are an increasing manifestation with age. In a community survey in Glasgow 20% of men and 12% of women over 65 were found to have ischaemic heart disease.[5] The elderly patient presenting with chest pain is most likely to have angina or myocardial infarction. Other important disorders to consider are herpes zoster, cough fracture of the rib, malignancy, pleurisy, pulmonary embolus and gastro-oesophageal reflux.

Angina pectoris

Main features

- There is a 2–3% incidence between 25 and 64 years.[6]
- The history is the basis of diagnosis.
- Angina is an oppressive discomfort rather than a pain.
- It is mainly retrosternal: radiates to arms, jaw, throat, back.
- It may be associated with shortness of breath.
- It occurs during exercise, emotion, after meals or in cold.
- It is relieved within a few minutes with rest.
- Physical examination is usually not helpful, except during an attack.
- Mitral valve prolapse, oesophageal spasm and dissecting aneurysm are important differential diagnoses.
- The causes of angina are summarised in Table 34.7.

NB Ensure that the patient is not anaemic or thyrotoxic. Fever and tachycardia also have to be excluded.

Table 34.7 *Causes of angina*

Coronary artery atheroma
Valvular lesions, e.g. aortic stenosis
Rapid arrhythmias
Anaemia
Rarities
• trauma
• collagen disease

Variants of angina

1. *Stable angina* Pain occurs with exertion and is usually predictable.
2. *Unstable angina* (also referred to as crescendo angina, pre-infarct angina and acute coronary insufficiency) It is increasing angina (severity and duration) over a short

period of time, precipitated by less effort and may come on at rest, especially at night. It may eventually lead to complete infarction, often with relief of symptoms.
3. *Nocturnal angina* Pain occurs during the night. It is related to unstable angina.
4. *Decubitus angina* The pain occurs when lying flat and is relieved by sitting up.
5. *Variant angina or Pinzmetal angina or spasm angina*[7] The pain occurs at rest and without apparent cause. It is associated with typical transient ECG changes of ST elevation (as compared with the classical changes of ST depression during effort angina). It can lead to infarction and cause arrhythmias. It is caused by coronary artery spasm.

Aids to diagnosis

ECG may be normal or show ischaemia or evidence of earlier infarction. During an attack it may be normal or show well-marked depression of the ST segment, symmetrical T-wave inversion (Fig. 34.13) or tall upright T waves.

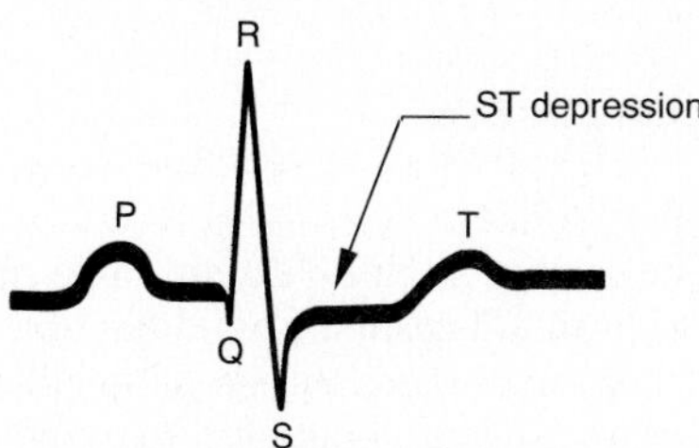

Fig. 34.13 *Typical ECG pattern for angina pectoris: this tracing is usually observed during an attack. Note: there is no specific ECG of angina; the most that can be said is that an ECG is consistent with angina*

Exercise ECG is positive in about 75% of patients with severe coronary artery disease and should be performed if the diagnosis is in doubt, for prognostic reasons or to aid in timing of additional investigations, e.g. coronary angiography. A normal stress test does not rule out coronary artery disease.

Exercise thallium 201 scan: this very expensive test is helpful in some difficult circumstances such as in the presence of LBBB, old infarction and WPW syndrome (when exercise test of little use) and with mitral valve prolapse which gives high false positive tests. It helps determine the presence and extent of reversible myocardial ischaemia.

Ambulatory Holter monitoring may be useful in some patients.

Gated blood pool nuclear scan: this test assesses regional wall motion abnormalities with exercise. The ejection fraction is a reliable index of ventricular function and thus aids assessment of patients for coronary artery bypass surgery.

Coronary angiography: this test accurately outlines the extent and severity of coronary artery disease. It is usually used to determine the precise coronary artery anatomy prior to surgery.

The relationship between the degree of angina and coronary artery disease is not clear cut. Some people with severe angina have normal coronary arteries.

Indications for coronary angiography are presented in Table 34.8.

Table 34.8 *Indications for coronary angiography*

Strong positive exercise stress test
Suspected left main CAD
Unstable or variant angina
Angina resistant to medical treatment
Suspected but not otherwise proven angina
Angina or myocardial infarction in young person < 50
Angina after myocardial infarction
Patients over 30 with aortic and mitral valve disease being considered for valve surgery

Management of angina

Prevention

This is especially important for those with a positive family history and an unsatisfactory lifestyle. Modification of risk factors:

- no smoking
- weight reduction
- optimal low-fat diet
- control of hypertension
- control of diabetes

General advice for the angina patient

- Reassure patient angina has a reasonably good prognosis
  —30% survival more than 10 years[8]
  —spontaneous remission can occur.
- Attend to any risk factors.
- If inactive, take on an activity such as walking for 20 minutes a day.
- Regular exercise to the threshold of angina.

- If tense and stressed, cultivate a more relaxed attitude to life—consider a stress management/relaxation course.
- Avoid precipitating factors.
- Don't excessively restrict lifestyle.

Medical treatment

The acute attack[9]

- glyceryl trinitrate (nitroglycerine) 600 μg tab or 300 μg (½ tab) sublingually (SL)

Alternatives

- isosorbide dinitrate 5mg SL every 5 min (to maximum of 3)

or

- glyceryl trinitrate SL spray: 1-2 sprays to maximum of 3 in 15 minutes

or

- nifedipine 5 mg capsule (suck or chew) if intolerant of nitrates

Tips about glyceryl trinitrate tablets

- Warn patient about headache and other side effects.
- Sit down to take the tablet.
- Take ½ (initially) or 1 tablet every 5 minutes.
- Maximum of 3 tablets in 15 minutes.
- Must be fresh.
- Discard the bottle opened for 3 months or after 2 days if carried on the person.
- Keep out of light and heat.
- If pain relieved quickly, spit out residual tablet.
- Advise that if no relief after 3 tablets get medical advice.

Mild stable angina (angina that is predictable, precipitated by more stressful activities and relieved rapidly):

- aspirin 150 mg (o) daily
- glyceryl trinitrate (SL or spray) prn
- consider a beta-blocker or transdermal nitrate

Moderate stable angina (regular predictable attacks precipitated by moderate exertion):

add
- beta-blocker
- glyceryl dinitrate (transdermal: ointment or patches) 10 mg daily (use for 12 hr only)

  or
- isosorbide nitrate 10 mg (o) tds

  or
- isosorbide mononitrate 60 mg daily
- consider calcium antagonist therapy as an alternative to a beta-blocker

Persistent angina (persistent and more severe):

add
- calcium antagonist

  nifedipine 20 mg (o) bd or tds (1st choice)

  or

  verapamil 40–160 mg (o) bd or tds

  or

  diltiazem 30–90 mg (o) qid

  or

  amlodipine 2.5–10 mg (o) once daily

However Consider hospitalisation for stabilisation and further evaluation. The objectives are to optimise therapy, give IV trinitrate if necessary and consider coronary angiography with a view to a corrective procedure.

Rules of practice

- In IHD, use of nifedipine may require a beta-blocker.
- For variant angina (spasm) use nitrates and calcium antagonist (avoid beta-blockers).
- If it is necessary to use a beta-blocker with perhexiline or verapamil, extreme caution is necessary.
- Tolerance to nitrate use is a problem, so 24-hr coverage with long-acting preparations is not recommended.

Coronary angioplasty

The current technique is dilating coronary atheromatous obstructions by inflating a balloon against the obstruction (Fig. 34.14). Other methods (which may supplant the balloon) include arthrectomy with laser devices or maintaining patency with intracoronary stent devices.

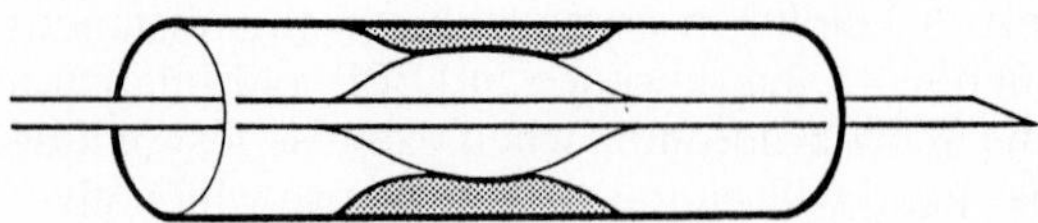

Fig. 34.14 *Percutaneous transluminal angioplasty with an inflatable balloon*

Two complications of the balloon inflation angioplasty are acute coronary occlusion (2–4%) and restenosis which occurs in 30% in the first 6 months after angioplasty.[8]

Coronary artery surgery

The main surgical techniques in current use are coronary artery bypass grafting (CABG) using either a vein (usually the saphenous) (Fig. 34.15) or internal mammary arterial implantation (Fig. 34.16) or both and endarterectomy.

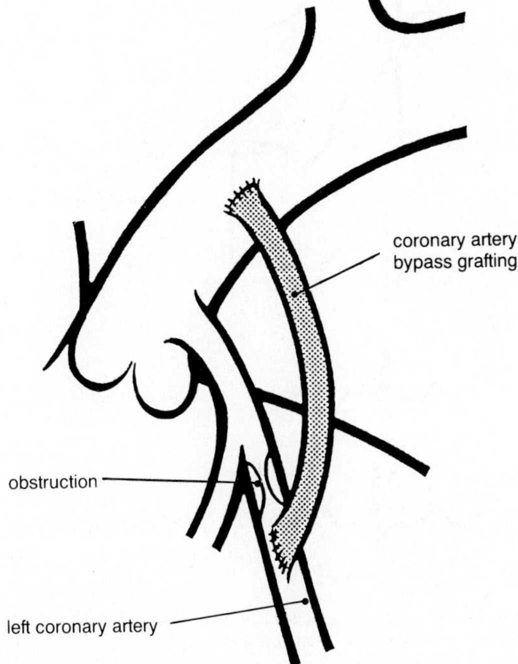

Fig. 34.15 *Coronary artery bypass grafting to relieve coronary obstruction*

Symptomatic patients with significant left main coronary obstruction should undergo bypass surgery and those with two or three vessel obstruction and good ventricular function are often considered for angioplasty or surgery. A significant improvement in the quantity and quality of life can be expected.

Myocardial infarction

Clinical guidelines

- variable pain; may be mistaken for indigestion
- similar to angina but more oppressive

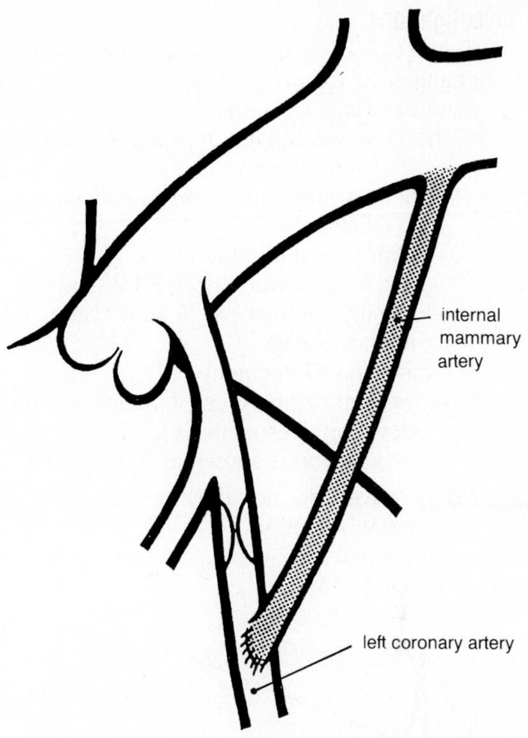

Fig. 34.16 *Internal mammary arterial transplantation to relieve coronary obstruction*

- so severe, patient may fear imminent death—'angor animi'
- about 20% have no pain
- 'silent infarcts' in diabetics, hypertensives and elderly
- 60% of those who die do so before reaching hospital, within two hours of the onset of symptoms
- hospital mortality is 8–10%[10]

Aetiology

- thrombosis with occlusion
- haemorrhage under a plaque
- coronary artery spasm

Physical signs

These may be:

- no abnormal signs
- pale/grey, clammy, dyspnoeic
- restless and apprehensive
- variable BP ↑ with pain
  ↓ heart pump failure
- variable pulse: watch for bradyarrhythmias
- mild cardiac failure: 3rd or 4th heart sound, basal crackles

Investigations

1. *The ECG* is valuable with characteristic changes in a full thickness infarction. The features (Fig. 34.17) are:
   - The Q wave: broad (> 1 mm) and deep > 25% length R wave
     — occurs normally in leads AVR and V_1; III (sometimes)
     — abnormal if in other leads
     — occurs also with LBBB, WPW and VT
     — usually permanent feature after full thickness AMI
   - T wave and ST segment
     — transient changes (inversion and elevation respectively). The typical progression is shown in Figure 34.18.

   NB Q waves do not develop in subendocardial infarction.
   A normal ECG, especially early, does not exclude AMI.

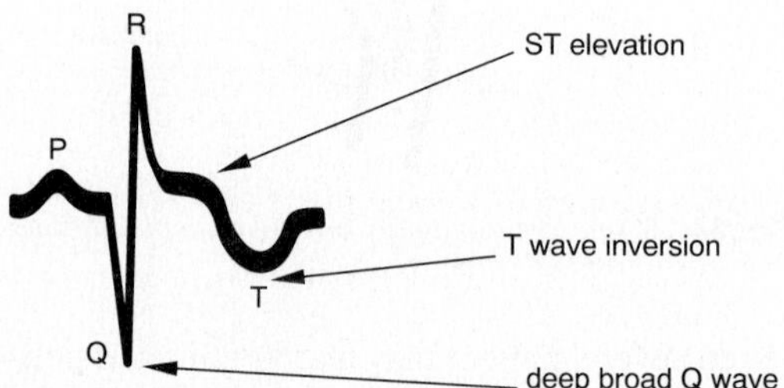

Fig. 34.17 *Typical ECG features of myocardial infarction, illustrating a Q wave, ST elevation and T wave inversion*

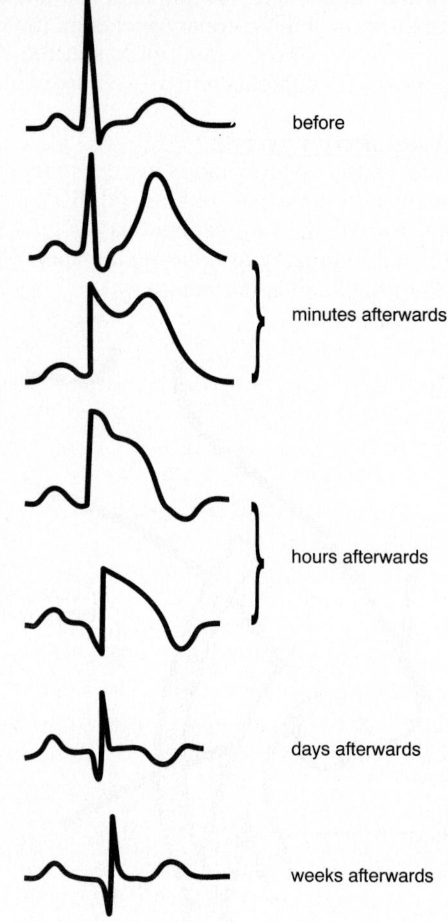

Fig. 34.18 *Typical evolution of ECG changes with myocardial infarction*

2. *Cardiac enzymes* The typical enzyme patterns are presented in Figure 34.19. As a rule large infarcts tend to produce high serum enzyme levels. The elevated enzymes can help time the infarct:
   - Creatinine kinase (CK)
     — After delay of 6–8 hours from the onset of pain it peaks at 20–24 hours and usually returns to normal by 48 hours.
     — An early peak (<15 hours) indicates coronary reperfusion and thus the success of coronary thrombolysis (if used).
     — CK-MB: myocardial necrosis is present if > 15% of total CK. Unlike CK, is not affected by intramuscular injections.
   - Aspartate transferase (AST): formerly SGOT
     — Slower to peak in the plasma (24–48 hours) and persists longer than CK.
     — May fall to normal by 72 hours.

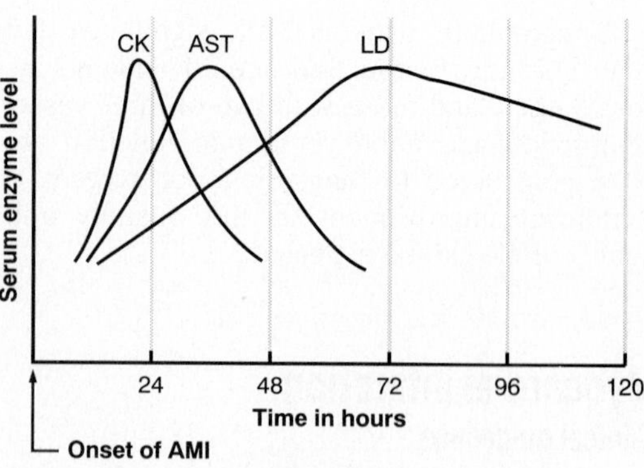

Fig. 34.19 *Typical cardiac enzyme patterns following myocardial infarction*

- Lactic dehydrogenase (LD)
  - — Peaks at 3–4 days and remains elevated for 7–14 days.
  - — Useful if the patient presents late for CK and AST levels.

3. *Technetium pyrophosphate scanning*
   - Performed from 24 hours to 14 days after onset.
   - Scans for 'hot spots' especially when a posterolateral AMI is suspected and ECG is unhelpful because of pre-existing LBBB.
4. *Echocardiography* is used to assist diagnosis when other tests are not diagnostic.

   NB The clinical diagnosis may be the most reliable and the ECG and enzymes may be negative.

Management of myocardial infarction

General principles:[10]

- Aim for immediate attendance if suspected.
- Call a mobile coronary care unit, especially if severe.
- Optimal treatment is in a modern coronary care unit (if possible) with continuous ECG monitoring (first 48 hours), a peripheral IV line and intranasal oxygen.
- Pay careful attention to relief of pain and apprehension.
- Establish a caring empathy with the patient.
- Consider all patients for thrombolytic therapy, e.g. streptokinase (the sooner the better).
- Give aspirin as early as possible (if no contraindications).
- Prescribe a beta-blocker drug early (if no contraindications).
- Prevent possible sudden death in early stages from ventricular fibrillation by monitoring and availability of a defibrillator.

First-line management, e.g. outside hospital

- oxygen 2–4 L/minute
- secure an IV line
- glyceryl trinitrate (nitroglycerine)
  300 mg (½ tab) SL
  (beware of bradycardia—correct with atropine)
- aspirin 300 mg
- morphine 5 mg IV statim bolus: 1 mg/min until pain relief (up to 15 mg)
  ± metoclopramide 10 mg IV (as antiemetic)
  (If feasible it is preferable to give IV morphine 1 mg/min until relief of pain: this titration is easier in hospital.)

Hospital management

- As for first-line management.
- Take blood for cardiac enzymes, urea and electrolytes.
- Consider streptokinase:
  - — 1 500 000 units IV infusion over 30–60 minutes
  - — (aim for 30 minutes and if problems such as hypotension occur slow down the infusion)

  Rules for streptokinase infusion:
  - — must have ECG evidence of AMI
  - — ideal if evidence of transmural infarct
  - — need informed consent
  - — the earlier given, the lower the mortality
  - — give within 3–4 hours of onset AMI (max. 6 hrs)
  - — monitor for hypotension, allergy and arrhythmias
  - — local bleeding a problem but usually minor and controlled by local pressure
  - — contraindications
    - active bleeding
    - recent CVA/TIA
    - poorly controlled hypertension
    - history of bleeding peptic ulcer
    - recent arterial (e.g. femoral) puncture
    - recent CPR
  - — do not use 3 days to 12 months after prior use; instead use recombinant tissue plasminogen activator (rt-PA)

  Note Streptokinase and rt-PA are of similar efficiency but rt-PA is much more expensive (about 10 times).

- Full heparinisation for 24–36 hours (after streptokinase), especially for large anterior transmural infarction with risk of embolisation, supplemented by warfarin.
- Beta-blocker (if no contraindications) as soon as possible:

  atenolol 2-10 mg IV or 25 mg (o) statim → 25-50 mg (o) mane

  or

  metoprolol 5-10 mg IV or 25 mg (o) statim → 50 mg (o) bd
- Treat complications as necessary.
- Consider glyceryl trinitrate IV infusion if pain recurs.
- Consider early introduction of ACE inhibitors.
- Treat hypokalaemia.
- Consider magnesium sulphate (after thrombolysis).
- Consider frusemide.

Home or small hospital (no CCU) care

The admission to coronary care units has helped improve the survival of AMI patients, especially with complications. However, management outside CCUs could be considered for:

- older stable patient, e.g. >70 years
- the AMI suffered >24 hours previously
- no evidence of complications: hypotension or arrhythmias

Ongoing management

- education and counselling
- bed rest 24–48 hours
- check serum potassium and magnesium
- early mobilisation to full activity over 7–12 days
- light diet
- sedation
- beta-blocker (o): atenolol or metoprolol
- warfarin where indicated (certainly if evidence of thrombus with echocardiography)
- consider ACE inhibitors for cardiac failure

On discharge

- rehabilitation program
- continued education and counselling
- no smoking
- reduce weight
- regular exercise, especially walking
- exercise test (to be considered)
- continue beta-blockers for 2 years
- consider ACE inhibitors
- aspirin 100–150 mg daily (at least 4 weeks)
- warfarin where indicated (at least 3 months)

Special management issues

Indications for coronary angiography

- development of angina
- strongly positive exercise test

Management of the extensive infarction

- ACE inhibitors (even if no CCF)
- radionuclide studies (to assess left ventricular function)
- beta-blockers (proven value in severe infarction) if no contraindications or LV dysfunction
- anticoagulation

Treating and recognising complications of AMI

Acute left ventricular failure

- signs: basal crackles
  extra (3rd or 4th) heart sounds
  X-ray changes
- treatment (according to severity): oxygen
  diuretic, e.g. frusemide
  glyceryl trinitrate; IV, SL, O or topical
  ACE inhibitors

Cardiogenic shock (a major hospital management procedure)

- dobutamine

Pericarditis occurs in first few days after AMI (usually anterior AMI), with onset of sharp pain.

- signs: pericardial friction rub
- treatment: anti-inflammatory medication
  e.g. aspirin 600 mg (o) 4 hourly
  or
  indomethacin 25 mg (o) 4 hourly (or by suppository)
  or
  corticosteroids (keep in reserve)

NB Avoid anticoagulants.

Post-AMI syndrome (Dressler's syndrome) occurs weeks or months later, usually around 6 weeks.

- Features: pericarditis
  fever
  pericardial effusion (an autoimmune response)
- Treatment: as for pericarditis

Left ventricular aneurysm a late complication.

- Clinical: cardiac failure
- Features: arrhythmias
  embolisation
- Signs: double ventricular impulse
  4th heart sound
  visible bulge on X-ray
- Diagnosis: 2D electrocardiography
- Treatment: antiarrhythmic drugs
  anticoagulants
  medication for cardiac failure
  possible aneurysmectomy

Ventricular septal rupture and mitral valve papillary rupture

- Presents with severe cardiac failure and a loud pansystolic murmur. Both have a poor prognosis and early surgical intervention may be appropriate.

Management of other serious causes of chest pain

Dissecting aneurysm

- Early definitive diagnosis is necessary: best achieved by transoesophageal echocardiography.
- 50% of patients are hypertensive, so need pharmacological control of hypertension with IV nitroprusside.
- Emergency surgery needed for many, especially for type A (ascending aorta involved).

Note Has an increased risk during pregnancy.

Pulmonary embolus

Needs supportive medical care and anticoagulation:

- Heparin IV: 5000 U as immediate bolus
  continuous infusion 30 000 U over 24 hours
  or
  heparin 12 500 U (sc) bd

  Note The dose of heparin should then be adjusted daily to maintain the APTT between 1.5-2 times control.
- Continue heparin 5–10 days.
- Warfarin (o) after 3 to 4 days then continue heparin for 3 days after INR at desired level.

  Note: Streptokinase either IV or into the pulmonary artery can be used.
  Surgical embolectomy is rarely necessary but needed if very extensive.

Ruptured oesophagus

Refer for early thorocotomy and repair of the defect, usually a longitudinal repair in the supra-diaphragmatic lower oesophagus—with mediastinal and pleural drainage.[12]

Pneumothorax

- Most episodes resolve spontaneously without drainage (at least 20% lung collapse).
- Drainage of the pleural space indicated for a large pneumothorax >30% pleural area, with persistent dyspnoea.
- For recurrent attacks, excision of cysts or pleurodesis may be necessary.

Methods

1. *Simple aspiration without underwater drainage*
   Under strict sepsis insert a 16 gauge polyethylene IV catheter into the second intercostal space in the mid-clavicular line on the affected side (under local anaesthetic). Then aspirate air into a 20 ml syringe to confirm entry into the pleural space, remove the stilette, connect the catheter via a flexible extension tube to a three-way tap and a 50 ml syringe. Aspirate and expel air via the three-way tap until resistance indicates lung re-expansion. Obtain a follow-up X-ray. Repeat aspiration may be necessary, but most patients do not require inpatient admission.
2. *Standard intercostal catheter insertion with connection to an underwater seal drainage*

Acute tension pneumothorax

For urgent cases insert a 12–16 gauge needle into the pleural space through the second intercostal space on the affected side. Replace with a formal intercostal catheter connected to underwater seal drainage.

Treatment of oesophageal disorders

Gastro-oesophageal reflux

- Achieve normal weight if overweight.
- Avoid coffee, alcohol and spicy foods.
- Avoid large meals and overeating (keep to small meals).
- Antacids or alginate compounds, e.g. Gaviscon, Mylanta plus.
  If persistent:
  acid suppression
  H_2 blockers, e.g. cimetidine, ranitidine
  or
  proton pump inhibitors, e.g. omeprazole

Oesophageal spasm

long-acting nitrates, e.g. isosorbide nitrate 10 mg tds
or

calcium channel blockers, e.g
nifedipine (SL) 10 mg tds

NB Attend to lifestyle and dietary factors, as for reflux.

Oral anticoagulation

Many patients with cardiovascular problems are now being discharged from hospital on oral anticoagulants (warfarin) or aspirin (150–300 mg daily). A greater responsibility rests with the patient's GP for careful monitoring of this anticoagulation lest bleeding, including intracerebral haemorrhage, occurs. For all practical purposes the only orally active anticoagulant is warfarin. Indications and contraindications are presented in Table 34.9.

Table 34.9 *Warfarin anticoagulation*

Indications
Prosthetic cardiac valves
Deep venous thrombosis
Deep venous thrombois, pulmonary thromboembolism
Atrial fibrillation (selected cases)
Transient ischaemic attacks
Severe peripheral vascular disease
Perioperatively in lower limb orthopaedic surgery (low dose)
Postcoronary bypass surgery
Contraindications
Active bleeding
Recent surgery
History of intracranial haemorrhage
Uncontrolled hypertension
Liver disease with impaired synthetic function—based on international normalised ratio (INR)
Pregnancy

Warfarin

Actions[11]

- antagonises vitamin K
- depresses factors V11, IX and X (half-life of 30–40 hours)
- achieves full anticoagulation effect after 3–4 days
- prothrombin time (INR ratio) of 2 times normal control indicates therapeutic effect
- duration of effect is 2–3 days
- antidote is vitamin K

Initiation of warfarin treatment

An estimate of the patient's final steady dose is made. The patient is commenced on this dose and the INR monitored daily and the dose altered accordingly. The INR should be measured before treatment is initiated to establish a baseline. **NB** The early phase of warfarin therapy is a hypercoagulable state and in general full anticoagulation with heparin must be maintained until the INR falls into the therapeutic range. The initial dose is influenced by factors such as the patient's age and weight, the presence of intercurrent illness and any medications.

Typical loading dosage

Day 1: 10 mg
Day 2: 10 mg
Day 3: 5 mg

NB Avoid dose >30 mg over 3 days.

Maintenance dose

Most patients can be stabilised on doses ranging from 2 to 10 mg a day according to the INR. The acceptable therapeutic range of the INR for most conditions is 2–3.5. Elderly patients with atrial fibrillation can be maintained at the lower end of the range (2–2.5) while patients with prosthetic cardiac valves are usually kept at the upper end of the range.

INR measurement schedule

daily for 1 week
↓
2 times weekly for 2 weeks
↓
weekly for 4 weeks
↓
monthly

Overdosage of warfarin

Signs of warfarin overdosage include:

- unexpected bleeding after minor trauma
- epistaxis
- spontaneous bruising
- unusually heavy menstrual bleeding
- gastrointestinal bleeding

Management of overdosage

1. Urgent measurement of INR.
2. If the only evidence of overdosage is a small increase of the INR above the therapeutic range, cessation of warfarin for 1 to 2 days followed by a continuation at a lower dose is appropriate.

3. If bleeding is minor, transient action as in point 2 is still appropriate.
4. If bleeding is persistent, severe or involves closed body cavities (such as pericardium, intracranial, fascial compartment), urgent admission to hospital is essential. The anticoagulation may need to be reversed by administering oral or parenteral vitamin K. Infusion of fresh frozen plasma may also be necessary.

Drug interactions

There are so many potential interactions between warfarin and other drugs that the following general principles should be applied:

1. Maintain the simplest possible drug regimens. Avoid polypharmacy.
2. Aspirin is contraindicated while the patient is on warfarin because of the combined antiplatelet and anticoagulation effects. The risk of gastrointestinal bleeding is also increased. Other non-steroidal anti-inflammatory drugs should also be avoided (Table 34.10).
3. If the patient's drug regimen must be altered during warfarin therapy then the INR should be followed closely until stable.

Practice tips

- The INR result reflects the warfarin dose administered 48–72 hours earlier.
- Advise and encourage patients to keep a record in an 'anticoagulant diary' of drug dosage and INR results.

Advice to the patient

- Keep to a consistent diet.
- Do not take aspirin or liquid paraffin.
- Always mention that you take warfarin to any doctor or dentist treating you.
- Remember to take tablets strictly as directed and have your blood tests.
- Report signs of bleeding, e.g. black motions, blood in urine, easy bruising, unusual nose bleeds, heavy periods.

Table 34.10 *Some important drug interactions with warfarin*

Effects on warfarin activity	***Drug***
↑ Increased	allopurinol
	amiodarone
	antibiotics (broad spectrum)
	aspirin—salicylates (high doses)
	chloral hydrate
	cimetidine
	clofibrate
	gemfibrozil
	metronidazole
	NSAIDs
	quinidine/quinine
	sulphonamides
	tamoxifen
	thyroxine
↓ Decreased	antacids
	antihistamines
	barbiturates
	carbamazepine
	cholestyramine (reduced absorption)
	haloperidol
	oestrogen/oral contraceptives
	phenytoin
	rifampicin
Increased or decreased	alcohol
	chloral hydrate
	diuretics
	ranitidine

Musculoskeletal causes of chest wall pain

There are many musculoskeletal causes, most of which can be eliminated by the history and physical examination. Some of the causes listed in Table 34.11 are very uncommon and often part of a general disorder such as ankylosing spondylitis. Muscular tears or strains of the chest wall are quite common. A differential diagnosis is a fractured rib including a cough fracture.

Musculoskeletal chest pain is typically aggravated or provoked by movements such as stretching, deep inspiration, sneezing and coughing. The pain tends to be sharp and stabbing in quality but can have a constant aching quality.

Costochondritis is a common cause of anterior pain which is generally well localised to the costochondral junction and may also be a component of an inflammatory disorder such as one of the spondyloarthropathies.

Management is generally conservative with analgesics, gentle massage with analgesic creams and NSAIDs if there is an inflammatory component. Other measures that can help for very painful chest wall problems are localised injections of local anaesthetic with or without corticosteroids (with care not to penetrate the

Table 34.11 *Causes/origins of chest wall pain (front and back)*

Musculoskeletal causes	
Injury to thoracic spine → dysfunction	
Vertebral fracture • trauma • pathological —osteoporosis —metastatic disease —multiple myeloma	
Intercostal muscle strains/tears	
Rib disorders • fractures • slipping rib	
Costochondritis	
Tietze's syndrome	
Fibromyalgia	
Non-musculoskeletal causes	
Heart	• myocardial infarction • angina • pericarditis
Great vessels	• dissecting aneurysm • pulmonary embolism
Pulmonary	• pulmonary embolus/infarction • pneumothorax • pneumonia/pleurisy
Oesophagus	• oesophageal rupture • oesophageal spasm/reflux • oesophagitis • aerophagy
Subdiaphragmatic disorder of	• gall bladder • stomach } including • duodenum } ulcers • pancreas • subphrenic collection
Miscellaneous infections	• herpes zoster • Bornholm's disease • infective endocarditis

parietal pleura) and a modified support (especially for rib injuries) in the form of a special elasticised rib belt (called a universal rib belt) that gives excellent support and symptom relief while permitting adequate lung expansion.

Posterior chest (thoracic back) pain

Disorders of the musculoskeletal system represent the most common cause of thoracic (dorsal) back pain, especially dysfunction of the joints of the thoracic spine. Refer to Chapter 32 for more detail. Probably the commonest cause is costovertebral dysfunction caused by overstress of rib articulations with vertebrae (the costovertebral joints). This fact is clearly demonstrated with the midline thoracic back pain following cardiac surgery when these joints are compressed during sternotomy and splaying of the chest walls.

The back pain may be associated with simultaneous referred anterior chest pain or abdominal pain (Fig. 32.4).

Acute thoracic back pain

Although posterior pain is invariably caused by vertebral dysfunction, there are several other important causes including serious bone disease (leading to compression fractures) and life-threatening visceral and vascular causes. Refer to Tables 32.2 and 32.3.

Note Intervertebral disc protrusions are rare in the thoracic spine.
Rarely, a penetrating peptic ulcer can present with mid to lower thoracic back pain.

Management

Management has to be according to the cause. The most appropriate treatment for thoracic spine dysfunction (in the absence of organic disease such as osteoporosis and inflammation and if the patient is not on anticoagulants) is physical therapy: mobilisation or manipulation, as described in Chapter 32.

When to refer

- obvious or suspected myocardial infarction especially with extensive infarction
- transfer to major centre with complications of AMI
  — rupture of septum or papillary muscle
  — aneurysm
  — refractory arrhythmias
  — cardiogenic shock
- patients with persistent postinfarction angina
- angina
  — patient with angina not responding to drug treatment
  — patient with unstable angina
  — angina lasting for longer than 15 minutes (unresponsive to sublingual nitrate) needs urgent hospital admission

- suspected or proven pulmonary embolus or dissecting aneurysm or other serious life-threatening problem (after initial first-line measures, e.g. decompression of tension pneumothorax)
- suspected oesophageal or other gastro-intestinal disorder, e.g. duodenal ulcer, for endoscopy or appropriate gastroenterological evaluation

Practice tips

- All sudden acute chest pain is cardiac (and potentially fatal) until proven otherwise.
- A careful history is the basis of the diagnosis.
- Mitral valve prolapse is often an undiagnosed cause of chest pain: keep it in mind especially if pain is recurrent and intermittent (proved by echocardiography).
- Calcium antagonists can cause peripheral oedema so be careful not to attribute this to heart failure.
- The pain of oesophageal spasm can be very severe and mimic myocardial infarction.
- Oesophageal spasm responds to glyceryl trinitrate: do not confuse with angina.
- Intervertebral disc protrusions are a very rare cause of severe sudden thoracic pain (T2–T9).
- Infective endocarditis can cause pleuritic posterior chest pain.
- Family doctors need to monitor carefully patients who are on anticoagulants. The INR ratio, which needs to be kept between 2 and 3, should be tested at least monthly.
- The sudden onset of dyspnoea without chest pain can occur frequently with (painless) myocardial infarction and pulmonary embolism.
- If a patient recovering from an AMI suddenly develops shortness of breath, consider ventricular septal rupture, mitral valve papillary rupture (with mitral regurgitation), pulmonary embolus and other serious complications.

References

1. Sandler G, Fry J. *Early clinical diagnosis.* Lancaster: MTP Press, 1986, 5–24.
2. Lambert J. Chest pain. From *Oesophageal disorders* in Proceedings of Monash University Faculty of Medicine 4th Annual Postgraduate Medical Refresher Course, 1991.
3. Selbst S. Chest pain in children. Amer Fam Physician, January 1990, 179–186.
4. Selbst S, Ruddy R, Clark B et al. Paediatric chest pain: a prospective study. Paediatrics, 1988; 82:319–23.
5. Kennedy RD, Andrews GR, Mitchell JRA. Ischaemic heart disease in the elderly. Br Heart J 1977; 39:1121–1127.
6. Caspari P. Angina pectoris. In: MIMS Disease Index. Sydney: IMS Publishing, 1991–2:43–46.
7. Kincaid-Smith P, Larkins R, Whelan G. *Problems in clinical medicine.* Sydney: MacLennan and Petty, 1990:10–11.
8. Kumar P, Clark M. *Clinical medicine.* London: Bailliere Tindall, 1990:569–582.
9. Moulds RFW. *Cardiovascular drug guidelines.* Victorian Medical Postgraduate Melbourne Foundation, 1991:13–45.
10. Thompson P. Myocardial infarction. In: MIMS Disease Index. Sydney: IMS Publishing, 1991–2:353–356.
11. Coughlin PB, Salem H. Management and prevention of venous thromboembolism. Aust Fam Physician, 1990; 19:1249–1256.
12. Hunt P, Marshall V. *Clinical problems in general surgery.* Sydney: Butterworths, 1991:87–88.

35

Constipation

—

Definition

Constipation is the difficult passage of small hard stools. It has also been defined as infrequent bowel actions or a feeling of unsatisfied emptying of the bowel. However, the emphasis is on the consistency of the stool rather than on the frequency of defecation; for example, a person passing a hard stool with difficulty once or twice a day is regarded as constipated, but the person who passes a soft stool comfortably every two or three days is not constipated. Various causes of chronic constipation are summarised in Figure 35.1

Key facts and checkpoints

- A UK study[1] showed that the diagnostic range is 12 per 1000 patients per year.
- The survey showed 10% of adults and 6% of children reported constipation in the preceding 2 weeks.
- Up to 20% of British adults take regular laxatives.[2]
- Constipation from infancy may be due to Hirschsprung's disease.
- Diet is the single most important factor in preventing constipation.
- Beware of the recent onset of constipation in the middle aged and the elderly.
- Bleeding suggests carcinoma, haemorrhoids, diverticular disease and inflammatory bowel disease.
- Unusually shaped stools (small pellets or ribbon-like) suggest the irritable bowel syndrome.
- Always examine the abdomen and rectum.
- Plain abdominal X-rays are generally not useful in the diagnosis of chronic constipation.
- The flexible sigmoidoscopy is far superior to the rigid sigmoidoscope in investigation of the lower bowel.

A diagnostic approach

Using the safe diagnostic strategy model (Table 35.1) the five self-posed questions can be answered as follows.

Probability diagnosis

The commonest is 'idiopathic' constipation where there is no structural or systemic disease. This is also referred to as 'functional' constipation.

Probably the most frequent single factor causing constipation in western society is deficiency in dietary fibre including fruit, green leafy vegetables and wholemeal products. The amount of fibre in our diet is directly related to stool weight and to colonic transit time. The average colonic transit time in the large bowel for westerners is 60 hours; for a rural African on a very high fibre diet it is 30 hours. Constipation is also a common problem in pregnancy.

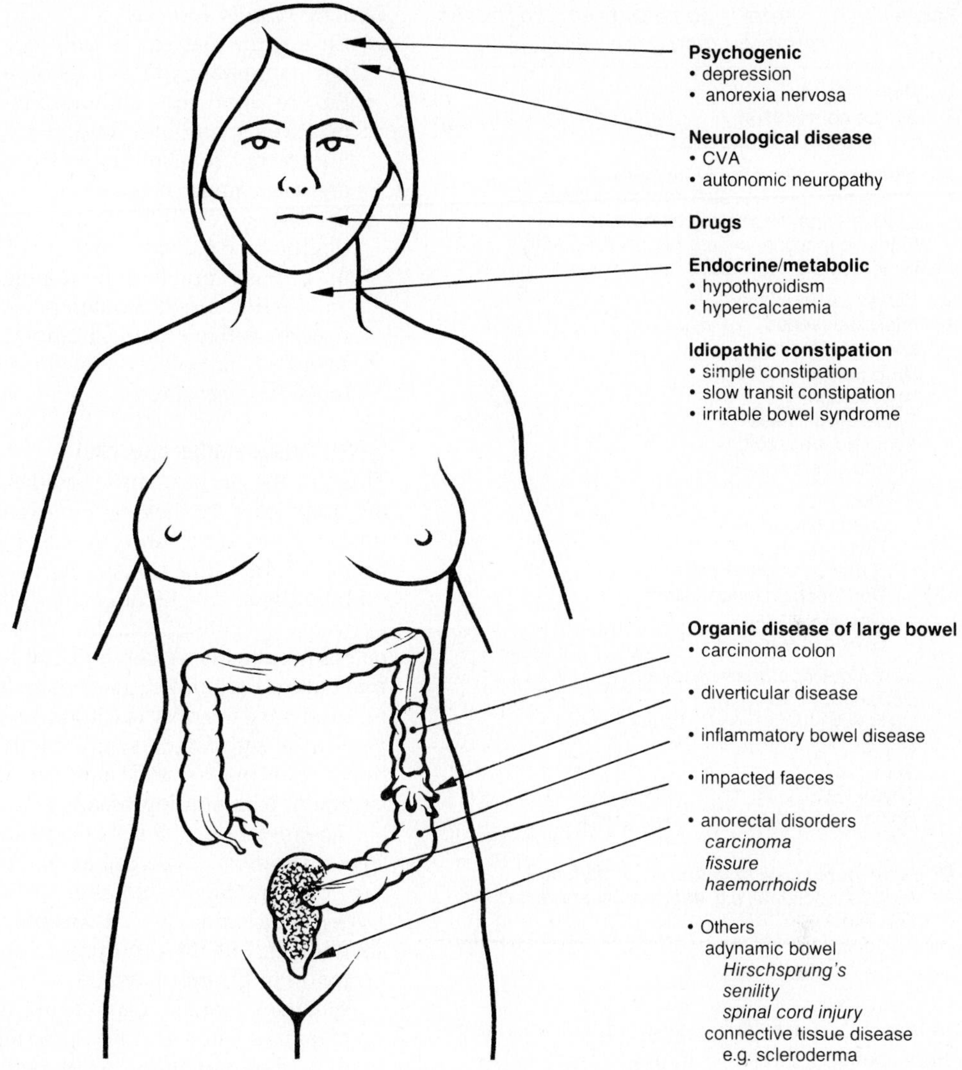

Fig. 35.1 *Causes of chronic constipation*

Serious disorders not to be missed

Neoplasia

It is obvious that colonic or anorectal neoplasms must not be missed in a patient, especially middle-aged or elderly, presenting with constipation or other change in bowel habit. Most cases present with either complete or incomplete bowel obstruction.

Extrinsic malignancy such as lymphoma or carcinoma of the ovary, compressing or invading the rectum, also have to be considered. Carcinoma of the large bowel is most prevalent in our society and appropriate screening examinations, including rectal examination, sigmoidoscopy and colonoscopy, must be considered where appropriate.

Megacolon

In children it is important to detect the presence of megacolon, for example, megacolon secondary to Hirschsprung's disease. Symptoms dating from birth suggest Hirschsprung's disease, which occasionally may present for the first time in adult life.[3]

Neurological disorders

Constipation, often with faecal impaction, is a common accompaniment to paraplegia, multiple

Table 35.1 *Chronic constipation: diagnostic strategy model*

Q.	*Probability diagnosis*	
A.	Simple constipation: low fibre diet and bad habit	
Q.	*Serious disorders not to be missed*	
A.	Intrinsic neoplasia: colon, rectum or anus, especially carcinoma of colon Extrinsic malignancy, e.g. lymphoma, ovary Hirschsprung's (children)	
Q.	*Pitfalls (often missed)*	
A.	Impacted faeces Local anal lesions Drug/purgative abuse Hypokalaemia Depressive illness Acquired megacolon Diverticular disease	
	Rarities Lead poisoning Hypercalcaemia Hyperparathyroidism Dolichocolon (large colon) Chaga's disease Systemic sclerosis	
Q.	*Seven masquerades checklist*	
A.	Depression	✓
	Diabetes	rarely
	Drugs	✓
	Anaemia	—
	Thyroid	✓ hypo
	Spinal dysfunction	severe only
	UTI	—
Q.	*Is the patient trying to tell me something?*	
A.	May be functional, e.g. depression, anorexia nervosa.	

sclerosis, cerebral palsy and autonomic neuropathy.

Pitfalls

The pitfalls can be summarised as follows:

- impacted faeces
- depressive illness
- purgative abuse
- local anal lesions
- drugs

Although patients with impacted faeces usually present with spurious diarrhoea, it is a form of idiopathic constipation and is very commonly encountered in general practice, especially in bedridden elderly people.

Anal pain or stenosis, such as fissure-in-ano, thrombosed haemorrhoids, perianal haematoma, or ischiorectal abscess, leads to constipation when the patient is hesitant to defecate.

General pitfalls and tips

- Ensure the patient is truly constipated, not having unreal expectations of regularity.
- Ensure that the anthraquinone group of laxatives, including, 'Ford pills', is never used long-term because they cause melanosis coli and associated megacolon.
- Be very wary of alternating constipation and diarrhoea, e.g. carcinoma of colon.
- In a busy practice be careful not to let 'familiarity breed contempt', e.g. onset of hyperparathyroidism, carcinoma.
- Avoid relying solely on the rectal examination to exclude carcinoma.

Seven masquerades checklist

Three of the primary masquerades (Table 35.1) are important causes of constipation, namely drugs, depression and hypothyroidism. Many drugs (Table 35.2) may be associated with constipation, especially codeine and its derivatives, antidepressants, aluminium and calcium antacids. A careful drug history is thus mandatory. Fortunately the constipation is usually relieved once the drug is withdrawn. Constipation can be a significant symptom in all types of depressive illness and may be aggravated by treatment with antidepressants.

The metabolic causes of constipation include hypothyroidism, hypercalcaemia and porphyria. We occasionally encounter the patient with hypercalcaemia, for example, hyperparathyroidism, but thyroid dysfunction is relatively common in general practice.

Diabetes rarely can be associated with constipation when an autonomic neuropathy can lead to alternating bouts of constipation and diarrhoea.

Psychogenic considerations

Constipation may be a manifestation of an underlying functional problem and psychiatric disorder such as depression, anorexia nervosa, schizophrenia or drug abuse. Drug abuse must always be considered, keeping in mind that narcotics and laxatives present with rebound constipation. More commonly, it may reflect the inactive lifestyle of the patient and provide a good opportunity for appropriate counselling.

The clinical approach

History

It is important to ask patients to define exactly what they mean by constipation. Some people

Table 35.2 *Drugs associated with constipation*

Analgesics (inhibitors of prostaglandin synthesis)
Antacids (containing calcium carbonate or aluminium hydroxide)
Anticholinergic agents
Antidiarrhoeal agents
Antihistamines (H_1 blockers)*
Antiparkinsonian drugs*
Barbiturates
Barium sulphate
Benzodiazepines
Clonidine
Cytotoxic drugs
Diuretics that cause hypokalaemia
Ganglionic blocking agents
Heavy metal (especially lead)
Iron supplements
Laxatives (chronic use)
Monoamine oxidase inhibitors
Muscle relaxants
Opiate analgesics
Phenothiazines*
Polystyrene resins
Tricyclic antidepressants*
Verapamil

* denotes anticholinergic effect

believe that just as the earth rotates on its axis once a day, so should their bowels open daily to ensure good health. As always, a careful history is appropriate, including stool consistency, frequency, ease of evacuation, pain on defecation and the presence of blood or mucus. A dietary history is very relevant in the context of constipation.

Key questions

How often do you go to the toilet?
What are your bowel motions like?
Are they bulky, hard, like rabbit pellets or soft?
Is there pain on opening your bowels?
Have you noticed any blood?
Have you noticed any lumps?
Do you have any soiling on your underwear?
How do you feel in yourself?

Physical examination

The important aspects are abdominal palpation and rectal examination. Palpation may reveal the craggy mass of a neoplasm, faecal retention (especially in the thin patient) or a tender spastic colon. The perianal region should be examined for localised disease. The patient should be asked to bear down to demonstrate perianal descent, haemorrhoids or mucosal prolapse.[3] Perianal sensation and the anal reflex should be tested. Digital rectal examination is mandatory, and may reveal a rectal tumour and faecal impaction, as well as testing for rectal size and tone. If there is a history from infancy, a normal or narrow rectum suggests congenital megacolon (Hirschsprung's disease) but, if dilated, acquired megacolon.

General signs that may be significant in the diagnosis of constipation are summarised in Figure 35.2.

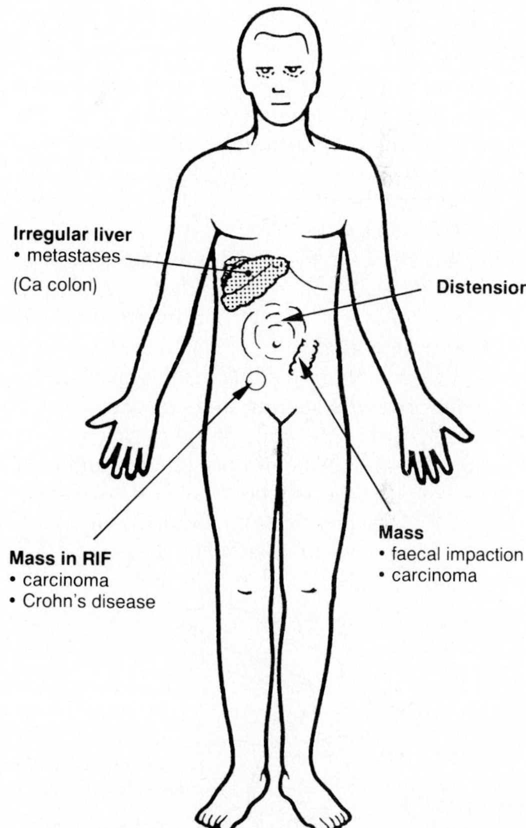

Fig. 35.2 *Possible significant abdominal signs in the patient with constipation*

The rectal examination

The most important first step is to *do* the examination.

Method

- Explain to the patient what will happen.

- After inspection with the patient in the left lateral position and with knees drawn up, a lubricated gloved index finger is placed over the anus.
- Ask the patient to concentrate on slow deep breathing.
- With gentle backwards pressure the finger is then inserted slowly into the anal canal and then into the rectum (it helps patient comfort if they push down or squeeze to accommodate the finger).
- The finger will reach to about 7–8 cm with gentle thrusting into the perineum.
- Gently withdraw the finger and examine the whole circumference of the rectum by sweeping the finger from posterior on both sides.

Points to note:

- any pain, e.g. fissure, proctitis, excoriation from diarrhoea (a rectal examination will not be possible in the presence of a fissure)
- induration from a chronic fissure or fistula in the anal canal
- the sphincter tone
- the nature of the faeces (? impaction)
- the rectal wall
  - — carcinoma is usually indurated, elevated and ulcerated
  - — a villous adenoma has a soft velvety feel
- posteriorly—the sacrum and coccyx
- laterally—the side walls of the pelvis
- anteriorly — cervix and pouch of Douglas in the female
  - — prostate and rectovesical pouch in the male (Fig. 35.3)

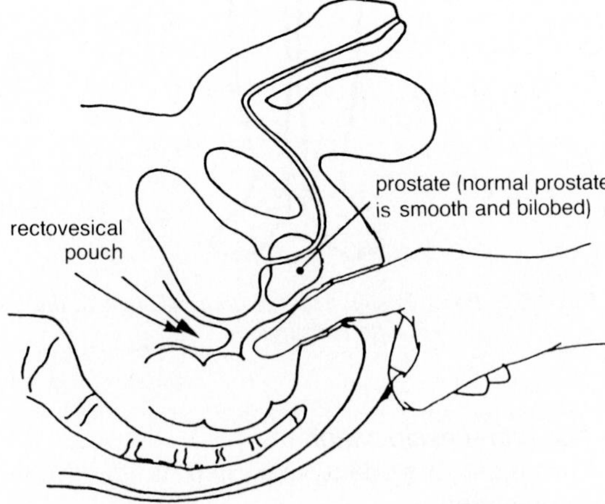

Fig. 35.3 *Rectal examination in the male: the normal prostate is bilobed with a central sulcus*

The prostate

- It feels larger if the patient has a full bladder.
- The normal prostate is a firm smooth rubbery bilobed structure (with a central sulcus) about 3 cm in diameter.
- A craggy hard mass suggests carcinoma.
- An enlarged smooth mass suggests benign hypertrophy.
- A tender, nodular or boggy mass suggests prostatitis.

A common pitfall: in the female the cervix or a vaginal tampon can be mistaken for a mobile extrarectal tumour (Fig. 35.4).

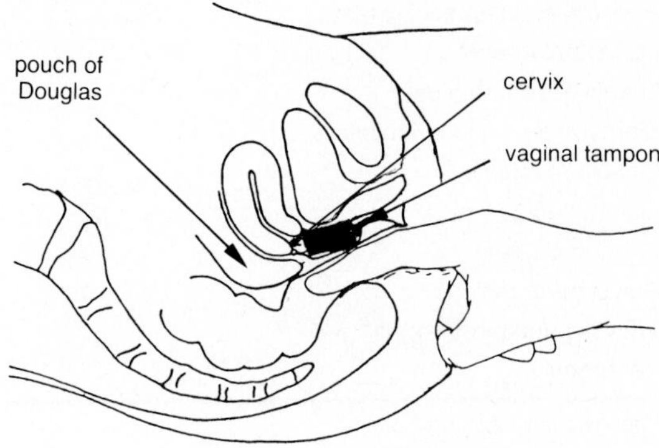

Fig. 35.4 *Rectal examination in the female: the cervix or a vaginal tampon may be mistaken for a rectal mass*

Endoscopy

Sigmoidoscopy—in particular, flexible sigmoidoscopy with examination of the rectosigmoid—is important in excluding local disease; search for abnormalities such as blood, mucus or neoplasia. The insufflation of air sometimes reproduces the pain of the irritable bowel syndrome.

It is worth noting that 60% of polyps and cancers will occur in the first[5] 60 cm of the bowel and diverticular disease should be evident with the flexible sigmoidoscope.

The presence of melanosis coli is an important sign—it may give a pointer to the duration of the constipation and the consequent chronic intake (perhaps denied) of anthraquinone laxatives.

Investigations

These can be summarised as follows.

Haematological
- haemoglobin
- erythrocyte sedimentation rate

Stools for occult blood

Biochemistry (where suspected)
- thyroid function tests
- serum calcium
- serum potassium
- carcinoembrogenic antigen (a tumour marker)

Radiological
- double contrast barium enema (especially for primary colonic disease, e.g. megacolon)
- bowel transit studies, using radio-opaque shapes taken orally and checking progresses by abdominal X-ray or stool collection

Physiological tests
- anal manometry—test anal tone
- rectal sensation and compliance, using an inflatable rectal balloon
- dynamic proctography, to determine disorders of defecation
- rectal biopsy, to determine aganglionia

Endoscopy

Constipation in children

Constipation is quite common in children and often related to diet. Most children develop normal bowel control by 4 years of age (excluding any physical abnormality). It is important to differentiate between encopresis and constipation.

Encopresis is the inappropriate passage of normal stool, which usually indicates a psychological disorder or stress.

Constipation is difficulty or delay in passing the stool with incomplete emptying of the rectum. This can present as *soiling*, due to faecal retention with overflow of liquid faeces.

Other important conditions

Hirschsprung's disease
- consider if delay in passing first meconium stool and subsequent constipation

Anal fissure in infants
- consider if stool hard and associated with pain or bleeding

Principles of treatment of functional constipation

- Encourage relaxed child–parent interaction with toilet training, e.g. appropriate encouragement; 'after breakfast habit' training.
- Introduce psychotherapy or behaviour modification program, especially where 'fear of the toilet' exists.
- Establish an empty bowel: remove any impacted faeces with microenemas, e.g. Microlax, and even disimpaction under anaesthesia if necessary.
- Advice for parents of children over 18 months:
  - drink ample fluids each day, e.g: several glasses of water, unsweetened fruit juice or milk.
  - get regular exercise, e.g. walking, running, outside games or sport.
  - provide high-fibre foods, e.g. high-fibre cereals, wholegrain bread, brown rice, wholemeal pasta, fresh fruit with skins left on where possible, dried fruits such as sultanas, apricots or prunes, fresh vegetables.
- Use a pharmaceutical preparation as a last resort to achieve regularity:

  first line: bulk-producing agent, e.g. Normacol plus

  second line: osmotic laxative, e.g. lactulose:
  1–5 years: 5 ml bd
  6–12 years: 10 ml bd
  > 12 years: 15 ml bd

Constipation in the elderly

Constipation is a common problem in the elderly with a tendency for idiopathic constipation to increase with age. In addition the chances of organic disease increase with age, especially colorectal carcinoma, so this problem requires attention in the older patient. Faecal impaction is a special problem in the aged confined largely to bed. Constipation is often associated with Parkinson's disease.

Practice tip on treatment

A suitable method of doing a rectal examination on a home visit (in the absence of gloves in the doctor's bag) is to apply moist soap around the finger and caked under the nail (in case of breakage) then plastic wrap and finally petroleum jelly (e.g. Vaseline).

Before resorting to a good old-fashioned '3H' enema (hot water, high and a hell of a lot), use a sorbitol compound, e.g. Microlax 5 ml enema. It can be carried in the doctor's bag, is very easy to insert and most effective.

Manual disimpaction

However, if manual disimpaction should be necessary, the unpleasant procedure can be rendered virtually odourless if the products are 'milked' or scooped directly into a container of water. A large plastic cover helps restrict the permeation of the smell.

Discomfort and embarrassment are reduced by this method and by adequate premedication (e.g. IV midazolam and IV fentanyl) if large faecoliths are present.

Idiopathic constipation

It is best to classify idiopathic constipation into three subgroups:[3]

1. simple constipation
2. slow transit constipation
3. normal transit constipation (irritable bowel syndrome)

Of these, the commonest is simple constipation, which is essentially related to a faulty diet and bad habit. Avery-Jones[4], who defined the disorder, describes it as being due to one or more of the following causes:

- faulty diet
- neglect of the call to stool
- unfavourable living and working conditions
- lack of exercise
- travel

Dyschezia, or lazy bowel, is the term used to describe a rectum that has become unresponsive to faecal content and this usually follows repeated ignoring of calls to defecate.

Slow transit constipation occurs primarily in women with an apparently normal colon, despite a high-fibre intake and lack of the other causes described by Avery-Jones. Many are young, with a history dating from early childhood or, more commonly, adolescence. Constipation may follow childbirth, uncomplicated abdominal surgery or a period of severe dieting. However, in the majority no precipitating cause is evident.

Management

Most patients have simple constipation and require reassurance and education once an organic cause has been excluded.

Basic advice to the patient

- Adequate exercise, especially walking, is important.
- Develop good habit: answer the call to defecate as soon as possible. Develop the 'after breakfast habit'. Allow time for a good relaxed breakfast and then sit on the toilet.
- Avoid laxatives and codeine compounds (tablets or mixture).
- Take plenty of fluids, especially water and fruit juices.
- Eat an optimal bulk diet. Eat foods that provide bulk and roughage such as vegetables and salads, cereals (especially bran), fresh and dried fruits, and wholemeal bread. Enough fibre should be taken to convert stools that sink to stools that float.[3]

  Examples of food with good bulk properties are presented in Table 35.3.[6] Fruit has good fibre, especially in the skin, and some have natural laxatives (e.g. prunes, figs, rhubarb, apricots).
- If the diet is insufficient, unprocessed bran, e.g. 15–30 g (1–2 tablespoons) a day spread onto fruit or cereal for breakfast, may be necessary.

Table 35.3 *Foods with bulk-forming properties (from least to most)*

Potato
Banana
Cauliflower
Peas
Cabbage
Lettuce
Apple
Carrot
Bran

Pharmaceutical preparations

Some patients may not tolerate unprocessed bran but tolerate pharmaceutical preparations better (Table 35.4). An appropriate choice would be one of the hydrophilic bulk-forming agents such as ispaghula or psyllium.

Table 35.4 *Therapeutic agents to treat constipation (with examples)*

Hydrophilic bulk-forming agents
psyllium mucilloid (Agiofibe, Metamucil)
sterculia (Granocol, Normacol)
ispaghula (Agiolax, Fybogel)
methylcellulose (Cellulone)
wheat bran

Stimulant (irritant) laxatives
phenolphthalein (Laxettes)
danthron
senna (Senokot)
cascara
castor oil
bisacodyl (Durolax)

Osmotic laxatives
magnesium sulphate (Epsom salts)
magnesium hydroxide (Milk of Magnesia)
lactulose
mannitol

Stool-softening agents
liquid paraffin (Agarol)
dioctyl sodium sulphosuccinate (Coloxyl)
glycerine suppositories
sorbital/sodium compounds (Microlax)

Colorectal cancer

Clinical features

- commonest GIT malignancy
- second most common cause of death from cancer in Western society
- generally men over 50 years
- mortality rate about 60%
- has a good prognosis if diagnosed early
- two-thirds in descending colon and rectum

Predisposing factors

- ulcerative colitis (longstanding)
- familial polyposis coli
- colonic adenomata

Lifetime risk

- general population 1 in 25
- family history (first-degree relative) 1 in 3
- familial polyposis coli 100% by age 40–50

Symptoms

- blood in the stools
- mucus
- recent change in bowel habits (constipation more common than diarrhoea)
- bowel leakage when flatus passed
- unsatisfactory defecation (the mass is interpreted as faeces)
- abdominal pain (colicky) or discomfort (if obstructing)
- rectal discomfort
- symptoms of anaemia

Various forms of presentation of large bowel cancers are shown in Figure 35.5.

Investigations

- faecal and occult blood (limited value)
- sigmoidoscopy, especially flexible sigmoidoscopy
- barium enema (accurate as a double contrast study) but may miss tumours
- colonoscopy: essential if suspicion on clinical grounds remains and barium enema normal (more useful if rectal bleeding)
- ultrasonograph and CT scanning not useful in primary diagnosis; valuable in detecting spread especially hepatic metastases

Screening

Current faecal occult blood testing is not recommended. Colonoscopy is recommended for those at risk and, in addition, flexible sigmoidoscopy and rectal biopsy for those with ulcerative colitis.

Management

Early surgical excision is the treatment, with the method depending on the site and extent of the carcinoma. Duke's classification gives a guide to prognosis (Table 35.5).

Table 35.5 *Modified Duke's classification of colorectal cancer*

Stage	Pathologic description	Approx. 5 year survival %
A	Cancer limited to mucosa and submucosa	>90
B	Cancer extends into muscularis or serosa	70–80
C	Cancer involves regional lymph nodes	30
D	Distant metastases, e.g. liver	5

Megacolon

Hirschsprung's disease (aganglionosis)

Features

- congenital
- constipation from infancy

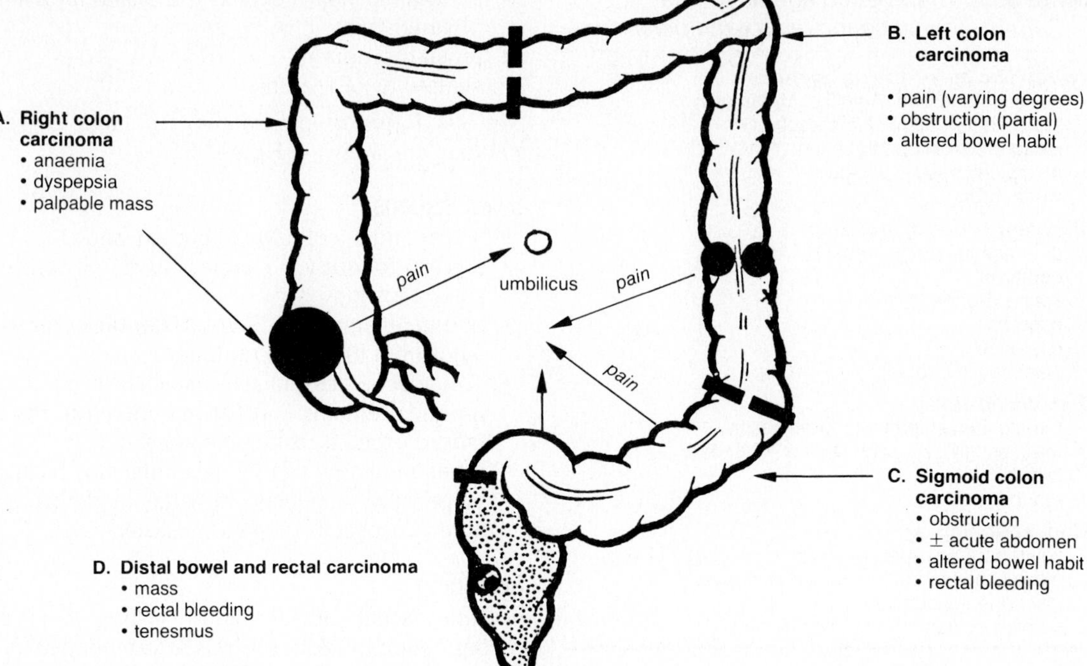

Fig. 35.5 *Various forms of presentation of large bowel carcinoma*

- abdominal distension from infancy
- possible anorexia and vomiting
- male:female 8:1
- rectal examination—narrow or normal rectum
- abdominal X-ray/barium enema—distended colon full of faeces to narrow rectum
- diagnosis confirmed by full thickness biopsy shows absence of ganglion cells
- absent rectoanal reflex on anal manometry

Treatment

Resect narrow segment after preliminary colostomy.

Acquired megacolon

Features

- in older children and adults
- mainly due to bad habit
- can be caused by
  - — chronic laxative abuse
  - — milder form of Hirschsprung's disease
  - — Chaga's disease (Latin America)[2]
  - — hypothyroidism (cretinism)
  - — systemic sclerosis
- marked abdominal distension
- rectal examination—dilated loaded rectum, lax sphincter
- abdominal X-ray/barium enema—distended colon full of faeces but no narrowed segment

Treatment

Re-education of bowel habit.

When to refer

- Patients with constipation or change in bowel habit of recent onset without obvious cause need further investigation.
- Patients with chronic symptoms which do not respond to simple measures.

Practice tips

- The objectives of treatment should be to exclude organic disease and then reassure and re-educate the patient about normal bowel function.
- Discourage long-term use of laxatives, suppositories and microenemas.
- The laxatives to discourage should include anthraquinone derivatives, bisacodyl, phenolphthalein, magnesium salts, castor oil and mineral oils.

- Bleeding with constipation indicates associated organic illness—exclude carcinoma of the bowel. Bright red blood usually means haemorrhoids.
- Beware of hypokalaemia causing constipation in the elderly patient on diuretic treatment.
- If carcinoma can be felt on rectal examination an abdominal perineal procedure with colostomy usually follows; if not, an anterior resection is generally the rule.

An appropriate management plan for the patient presenting with constipation is that given by Barnes[3] as in Table 35.6.

References

1. Cormack JJC. *Practice: a handbook of primary medical care*. London: Kluwer-Harrap, 1980; 3(47):1–2.
2. Sandler G, Fry J. *Early clinical diagnosis*. Lancaster: MTP Press, 1986, 209.
3. Barnes PRH. Assessment and management of constipation. What's new in gastroenterology? Gastroenterological Society of Australia 1989; 34:1–4.
4. Avery-Jones F, Godding FW. *Management of constipation*. Oxford: Blackwell Scientific Publications, 1972, 16.
5. Bolin T. Constipation. In: MIMS Disease Index. Sydney: IMS Publishing, 1991–2, 117-119.
6. Sali A. Preventive initiatives in medicine and surgery. Aust Fam Physician 1985; 14:1314.
7. Khot A, Polmear A. *Practical general practice*. Oxford: Butterworths Heinemann, 1991, 57–58.
8. Wilson JD et al. *Harrison's principles of internal medicine* (12th edition), New York: McGraw-Hill, 1991, 1292.

Table 35.6 *Management plan for constipation[3] (after Barnes)*

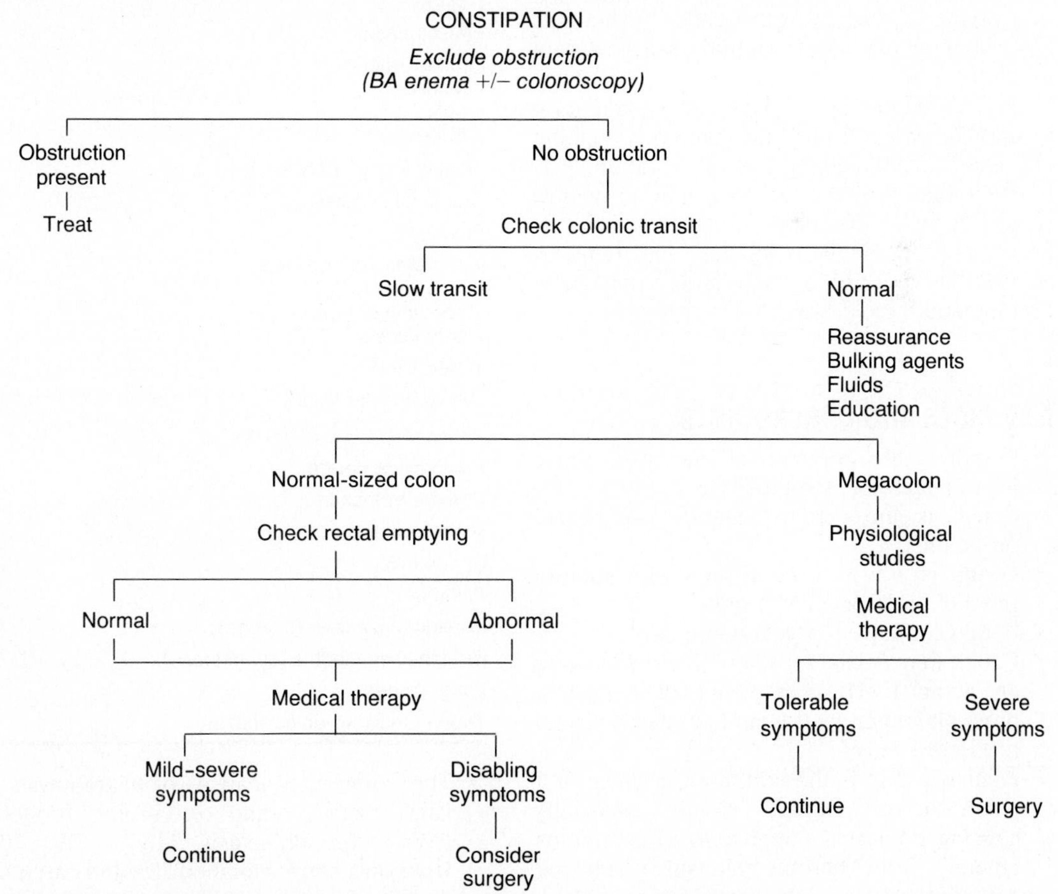

36

Cough

Cough is one of the five most common symptoms presenting in family practice. There is a wide range of causes (Table 36.1) with the great majority being minor and self-limiting, although the possibility of serious causes such as bronchogenic carcinoma should always be kept in mind.

It is a feature of smokers, who often have a morning cough with little sputum. Coughing can also be initiated by pleural irritation. It is a reflex that provides an essential protective service. It serves to remove substances that may have been accidentally inhaled and removes excess secretions or exudates that may accumulate in the airway.

Table 36.1 *Common causes of cough*

Non-productive (dry cough)

Upper respiratory tract infection
- viral
- mycoplasma

Inhaled irritants
- smoke
- dust
- fumes

Inhaled foreign body

Bronchial neoplasm

Pleurisy

Interstitial lung disorders
- fibrosing alveolitis
- pneumoconiosis
- sarcoidosis

Tuberculosis

Left ventricular failure

Whooping cough (pertussis)

Productive cough

Chronic bronchitis

Bronchiectasis

Pneumonia

Asthma

Foreign body (later response)

Bronchial carcinoma (dry or loose)

Lung abscess

Tuberculosis (when cavitating)

Key facts and checkpoints

- Cough is the commonest manifestation of lower respiratory tract disease.
- Cough is the cardinal feature of chronic bronchitis.
- Cough is a feature of asthma with sputum production, especially at night.
- Cough can have a psychogenic basis.
- Cough may persist for many weeks following an acute URTI as a result of persisting bronchial inflammation and increased airway responsiveness.[1]
- Postnasal drip is the commonest cause of a persistent or chronic cough, especially causing nocturnal cough due to secretions (mainly from chronic sinusitis) tracking down the larynx and trachea during sleep.
- The commonest causes of haemoptysis are URTI (24%), acute or chronic bronchitis (17%), bronchiectasis (13%), TB (10%). Unknown causes totalled 22% and carcinoma 4% (figures from a UK study).[2]

A diagnostic approach

A summary of the safety diagnostic model is presented in Table 36.2.

Table 36.2 *Cough: diagnostic strategy model*

Q. Probability diagnosis
A. Upper respiratory infection
Postnasal drip
Acute bronchitis
Chronic bronchitis

Q. Serious disorders not to be missed
A. Cardiovascular
- left ventricular failure

Neoplasia
- carcinoma of lung

Severe infections
- tuberculosis
- pneumonia
- influenza
- lung abscess
- HIV infection

Asthma
Cystic fibrosis
Foreign body

Q. Pitfalls (often missed)
A. Gastro-oesophageal reflux
Smoking (children)
Bronchiectasis
Whooping cough
Interstitial lung disorders
Sarcoidosis

Q. Seven masquerades checklist

A.	
Depression	—
Diabetes	—
Drugs	✓
Anaemia	—
Thyroid disease	—
Spinal dysfunction	—
UTI	—

Q. Is the patient trying to tell me something?
A. Anxiety and habit

Probability diagnosis

The most common cause of cough is an acute respiratory infection, whether an upper respiratory infection (URTI) or acute bronchitis.[3] Persistent coughing with an URTI is usually due to the development of sinusitis with a postnasal drip.

Chronic bronchitis is also a common cause of cough.

Serious disorders not to be missed

Bronchial carcinoma must not be overlooked. A worsening cough is the commonest presenting problem. A bovine cough is suggestive of carcinoma: the explosive nature of a normal cough is lost when laryngeal paralysis is present, usually resulting from bronchial carcinoma infiltrating the left recurrent laryngeal nerve.

Chronic cough may be the first presentation of *Pneumocystis carinii* pneumonia in an HIV-infected patient. Careful but tactful questioning of the patient in relation to IV drug use, sexual practice and previous blood transfusions is important. Important causes of a chronic cough are summarised in Table 36.3.

The possibility of a foreign body should always be kept in mind, especially in children, and severe infections such as tuberculosis and pulmonary abscess must not be misdiagnosed.

It is also important not to overlook asthma in which a nocturnal cough, without wheezing, is a feature in children.

Table 36.3 *Causes of chronic cough (after Cooke)*

Condition	*Percentage*
Main causes	
chronic postnasal drip	29
asthma	25
asthma + postnasal drip	18
chronic bronchitis	12
gastro-oesophageal reflux	10
Other causes	
bronchiectasis	
bronchial carcinoma	
laryngeal carcinoma	
interstitial pulmonary fibrosis	
cardiac (left ventricular failure)	
tuberculosis	
inhaled foreign body	
COAD	
whooping cough	
cystic fibrosis	
psychogenic	

Pitfalls

Causes that tend to be overlooked, especially in the presence of a normal X-ray, are gastro-oesophageal reflux, postnasal drip and asthma. Gastro-oesophageal reflux is more common as a cause of reflex coughing, especially at night, than appreciated. Whooping cough, especially immunisation-modified, can be difficult to diagnose particularly if the characteristic whoop is absent.

General pitfalls

- Attributing cough due to bronchial carcinoma in a smoker to 'smoker's cough'.
- Overlooking TB, especially in the elderly, by equating symptoms to old age, bronchitis or even smoking.
- Overlooking the fact that bronchial carcinoma can develop in a patient with other pulmonary conditions such as chronic bronchitis.
- Being slow to order a chest X-ray.

Seven masquerades checklist

The applicable masquerade is drugs, many of which can produce a wide variety of disorders of the respiratory tract that cause a cough. Pulmonary infiltration with fibrosis may result from some cytotoxic drugs, especially bleomycin. Over 20 different drugs are known to produce an SLE-like syndrome, sometimes complicated by pulmonary infiltrates and fibrosis. Cough can be a feature of some of the ACE inhibitors.

Psychogenic considerations

A cough can occur for psychosocial reasons. Coughing is under cerebral control and a slight cough before commencing a speech is normal and presumably assists in clearing mucus from around the vocal cords.[4] This can readily become a nervous habit or mannerism.

The clinical approach

History

The nature of the cough may provide important diagnostic clues but it is the associated symptoms, such as the nature of the sputum, breathlessness, wheezing and constitutional symptoms, that provide the most helpful diagnostic value. A history of smoking habits, past and present, is essential and an occupational and hobby history requires investigation. Significant occupations (past or present) include mining (pneumoconiosis), aircraft manufacturing (asbestosis and mesothelioma), farming ('farmer's lung'—allergic pneumonitis from mouldy hay) and bird handling ('bird fancier's lung'—allergic alveolitis or psittacosis from pigeons or budgerigars). A past history of recurrent lung infections from childhood is suggestive of cystic fibrosis and bronchiectasis; a history of hay fever and eczema suggests asthma, while a family history involves asthma, cystic fibrosis, emphysema (α_1-antitrypsin deficiency) and tuberculosis.

Key questions[5]

How would you describe the cough?
How long has the cough been present?
Do you cough up sputum?
Describe the sputum, especially its colour.
Is there any blood in the sputum?
How much sputum do you produce—a teaspoonful, an eggcupful or more?
Is there a burning sensation in your throat or chest when you cough?
Have you noticed any other symptoms?
What about chest pain or fever, shivers or sweats?
Do you have a wheeze?
Have you had previous attacks of wheezing or hay fever?
Is there a history of asthma in your family?
Have you lost weight?
Has anyone in the family had tuberculosis or a persistent cough?
How much do you smoke?
Are you exposed to any smoke or fumes?
Tell me about your work.
Where have you worked in the past?
Is there a chance you have been exposed to asbestos?
Do you keep birds at home?
Do you have any birds nesting outside your bedroom?
Is there a possibility of a foreign body such as a peanut 'having gone down the wrong way'?
Have you had an operation recently or been confined to bed?
Have you noticed any swelling of your legs?

Physical examination

Physical examination includes a general examination with a search for features such as enlarged cervical or axillary glands which may indicate bronchial carcinoma, as would Horner's syndrome (dilated pupil, ptosis). A careful examination of the lungs and cardiovascular system is also appropriate. Careful inspection of the sputum forms an important part of the physical examination of the lungs. This should include its colour and consistency, presence of particulate matter and a 24 hour sputum watch.

Investigations

This applies particularly to patients with haemoptysis. Investigations include:

- haemoglobin, blood film and white cell count
- sputum cytology and culture
- ESR (elevated with bacterial infection, bronchiectasis, TB, lung abscess and bronchial carcinoma)

- respiratory function tests
- radiology
  - plain chest X-ray (shows many problems)
  - tomography
    - helps more precise localisation of lesion
    - may show cavitation
  - bronchography
    - shows bronchiectasis (a very unpleasant procedure)
  - CT scanning (more sensitive than plain X-ray)
  - ventilation/perfusion isotope scan
    - for pulmonary infarction
- skin tests
- lung biopsy
- bronchoscopy (best at time of haemoptysis)

A schemata for the investigation of chronic cough is presented in Figure 36.1.[6]

Diagnostic characteristics

There are important characteristics of cough that may point to the causation. Table 36.1 compares typical causes of dry and productive cough.

Character of the cough

brassy → • tracheitis and bronchitis (major bronchi)
• extrinsic pressure on trachea

barking → laryngeal disorders, e.g. laryngitis

croupy (with stridor) → laryngeal disorders, e.g. laryngitis, croup

bovine (no power) → vocal cord paralysis (left recurrent laryngeal nerve)

weak cough → indicates bronchial carcinoma

paroxysmal with whoops → whooping cough

painful → • tracheitis
• left ventricular failure

Timing

nocturnal cough → • asthma
• left ventricular failure
• postnasal drip
• chronic bronchitis
• whooping cough

waking cough → • bronchiectasis
• chronic bronchitis
• gastro-oesophageal reflux

Associations

changing posture → • bronchiectasis
• lung abscess

meals → • hiatus hernia (possible)
• oesophageal diverticulum
• tracheo-oesophageal fistula

wheezing → • asthma

breathlessness → • asthma
• left ventricular failure
• chronic obstructive airways disease

Sputum

A healthy non-smoking individual produces approximately 100–150 ml of mucus a day. This normal bronchial secretion is swept up the airways towards the trachea by the mucociliary clearance mechanism and is usually swallowed. The removal from the trachea is assisted also by occasional coughing although this is carried out almost subconsciously.[4]

Excess mucus is expectorated as sputum. The commonest cause of excess mucus production is cigarette smoking. Mucoid sputum is clear and white.

Character of sputum

clear white (mucoid) → normal or uninfected bronchitis

yellow or green (purulent) → due to cellular material (neutrophils or eosinophil granulocytes)
• ± infection (not necessarily bacterial infection)
• asthma due to eosinophils
• bronchiectasis (copious quantities)

rusty → lobar pneumonia (*Strep. pneumoniae*): due to blood

thick and sticky → asthma

profuse, watery → alveolar cell carcinoma

thin, clear mucoid → viral infection

redcurrent jelly → bronchial carcinoma

profuse and offensive → • bronchiectasis
• lung abscess

thick plugs (cast-like) → • allergic bronchopulmonary aspergillus
• bronchial carcinoma

pink frothy sputum → • pulmonary oedema

Haemoptysis

Blood-stained sputum (haemoptysis), which varies from small flecks of blood to massive bleeding, requires thorough investigation. Often

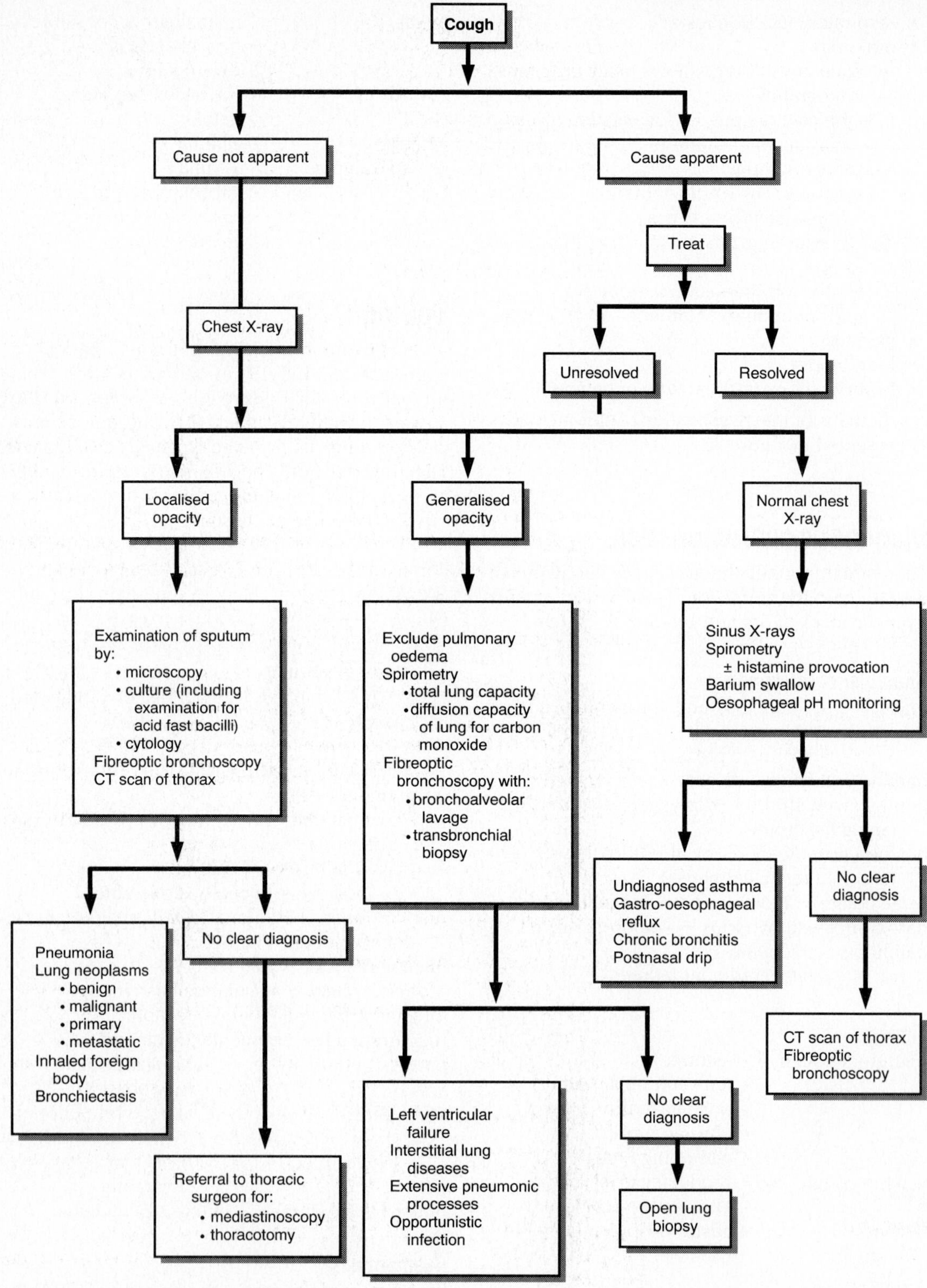

Fig. 36.1 *A recommended schematica for investigation of chronic cough* REPRODUCED FROM T.J.WILLIAMS AND G.BOWES *MOD MED AUSTRALIA*, JUNE 1992, WITH PERMISSION

the diagnosis can be made by chest X-ray. Causes are presented in Table 36.4. Haemoptysis must be distinguished from blood-stained saliva caused by nasopharyngeal bleeding or sinusitis and also from haematemesis.[4]

Table 36.4 *Causes of haemoptysis (blood-stained sputum)*

Acute infection	• URTI • acute bronchitis	} commonest cause[1]
Chronic bronchitis		
Bronchiectasis		
Lobar pneumonia (rusty sputum)		
Tuberculosis		
Neoplasic	• bronchogenic carcinoma • metastatic carcinoma	
Pulmonary infarction		
Foreign body		
Cardiac	• left ventricular failure • mitral stenosis	
Unknown		
Rarer causes		
Idiopathic pulmonary haemosiderosis		
Goodpasture's syndrome		
Blood disorders including anticoagulants		
Trauma		
Iatrogenic, e.g. endotracheal tubes		

NB Haemoptysis must be distinguished from blood-stained saliva caused by nasopharyngeal bleeding or sinusitis.[4] Copious haemoptysis is due to bronchiectasis or tuberculosis.

Productive cough

- chronic bronchitis — mucoid or purulent — rarely exceeds 250ml per day[4]
- bronchiectasis — purulent sputum — up to 500 ml/day
- asthma — mucoid or purulent — tenacious sputum
- lung abscess — purulent and foul-smelling
- foreign body — can follow impaction

Cough in children

Cough in children is a very common symptom, but troublesome persistent cough is a great cause of anxiety among parents and probably the commonest symptom for which the family doctor is consulted. Age-related causes of chronic cough (present at least four weeks) are presented in Table 36.5.

Table 36.5 *Chronic cough in children: age-related causes to consider[8] (after Selecki and Helman)*

Early months of life
- milk inhalation/reflux
- asthma

Toddler/preschool child
- asthma
- bronchitis
- whooping cough
- cystic fibrosis
- croup
- foreign body inhalation
- tuberculosis
- bronchiectasis

Early school years
- asthma
- bronchitis
- mycoplasma pneumonia

Adolescence
- asthma
- psychogenic
- smoking

Common causes are:

- asthma
- acute URTIs
- allergic rhinitis

Disorders not to be missed are:

- asthma
- cystic fibrosis
- inhaled foreign body
- tracheo-oesophageal fistula

Several clinicians describe the catarrhal child syndrome as the commonest cause of cough.[3] This refers to children who develop a postnasal drip following acute respiratory infection and allergic rhinitis.

Psychogenic causes

Habit cough can occur in children, especially those with a history of school phobia. The cough does not occur during sleep and remains unchanged with exertion or infection.

Croup (Laryngotracheobronchitis)

Clinical features:

- characteristic barking cough with stridor
- children 9 months to 3 years
- usually 11 pm to 2 am
- occurs in small local epidemics

Management (refer Chapter 111).

Cough in the elderly

Important causes of cough to consider in the elderly include chronic bronchitis, carcinoma of the lung, bronchiectasis and left ventricular failure in addition to the acute upper and lower respiratory infections to which they are prone. It is important to be surveillant for bronchial carcinoma in an older person presenting with cough, bearing in mind that the incidence rises with age.

Common respiratory infections

Respiratory infections, especially those of the upper respiratory tract, are usually regarded as trivial, but they account for an estimated one-fifth of all time lost from work and three-fifths of time lost from school and are thus of great importance to the community. The majority of respiratory infections are viral in origin and antibiotics are therefore not indicated.

Upper respiratory tract infections (URTIs) are those involving the nasal airways to the larynx, while lower respiratory tract infections (LRTIs) affect the trachea downwards.

Combined URTI and LRTI include influenza, measles, whooping cough and laryngotracheobronchitis.

The common cold (acute coryza)

This highly infectious URTI, which is often mistakenly referred to as 'the flu', produces a mild systemic upset and prominent nasal symptoms (Fig. 36.2).

Typical clinical features

- malaise and tiredness
- sore, runny nose
- sneezing
- sore throat
- slight fever

Other possible symptoms:

- headache
- hoarseness
- cough

The watery nasal discharge becomes thick and purulent in about 24 hours and persists for up to a week. Secondary bacterial infection is uncommon.

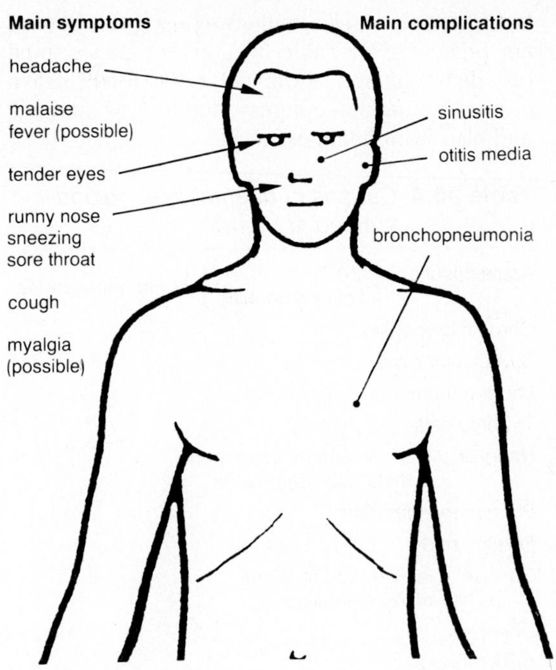

Fig. 36.2 *The main symptoms and complications of the common cold*

Management

Advice to the patient includes:

- rest: adequate sleep and rest
- analgesics: paracetamol (acetaminophen) or aspirin (maximum 8 tablets a day in adults)
- steam inhalations (as per Fig. 44.3) for a blocked nose
- cough mixture for a dry cough
- gargling aspirin in water or lemon juice for a sore throat
- vitamin C powder or tablets, e.g. 2 g daily, may aid recovery

Influenza

Influenza causes a relatively debilitating illness and should not be confused with the common cold. The differences are presented in Table 36.6. The incubation period is usually 1–3 days and the illness commences abruptly with a fever, headache, shivering and generalised muscle aching (Fig. 36.3).

Typical clinical features

Initial:

- fever, shivering
- headache
- generalised muscle aching, especially limbs

Table 36.6 *Common cold and influenza compared*

	Common cold	*Influenza*
Incubation period	12 hours to 5 days	1-3 days
Fever	±	++
Cough	(later)	+
Sore throat	++	±
Rhinitis sneezing rhinorrhoea	+	−
Muscle aches	−	+
Toxaemia	−	±
Causes	rhinoviruses parainfluenza influenza B,C corona virus respiratory syncytial virus	influenza A influenza B

Followed by:

- sore throat
- dry cough (can last several weeks)
- rhinorrhoea
- depression (a common sequela)

Complications

- secondary bacterial infection
- pneumonia due to *Staphylococcus aureus* (mortality up to 20%)[1]
- encephalomyelitis (rare)

Management

Advice to the patient includes:

- rest in bed until the fever subsides
- analgesics: aspirin is effective or codeine and aspirin (or paracetamol), especially if a dry cough
- fluids: maintain high fluid intake

Prophylaxis

Influenza vaccination offers some protection for up to 70% of the population for about 12 months.[1]

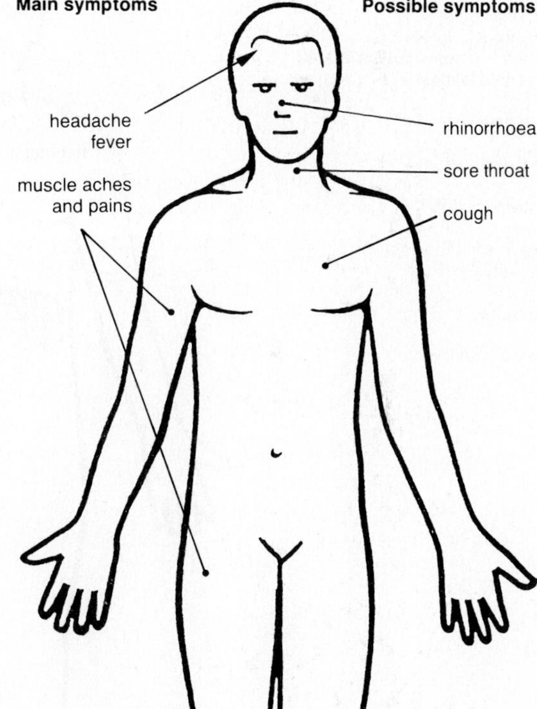

Fig. 36.3 *The main features of influenza*

Bronchial carcinoma

Lung cancer accounts for 35% of cancer deaths in men and 21% of cancer deaths in women (rapidly rising) in the United States, with cigarette smoking being the most common cause of lung cancer in both sexes.[7]

Clinical features

- most present between 50 and 70 years
- only 10–25% asymptomatic at time of diagnosis[7]
- if symptomatic—usually advanced and not resectable

Local symptoms

- cough (42%)
- chest pain (22%)
- wheezing (15%)
- haemoptysis (7%)
- dyspnoea (5%)

General
- anorexia, malaise
- weight loss

Others
- hoarseness
- symptoms from metastases

The possible physical findings are summarised in Figure 36.4.

Investigations
- chest X-ray
- computerised tomography
- fibreoptic bronchoscopy

Bronchiectasis

Bronchiectasis is dilatation of the bronchi when their walls become inflamed, thickened and irreversibly damaged, usually following obstruction followed by infection. Predisposing causes include whooping cough, measles, tuberculosis, inhaled foreign body (e.g. peanuts in children), bronchial carcinoma, cystic fibrosis and congenital ciliary dysfunction (Kartagener's syndrome). The left lower lobe and lingula are the commonest sites for localised disease.

Clinical features
- chronic cough—worse on waking

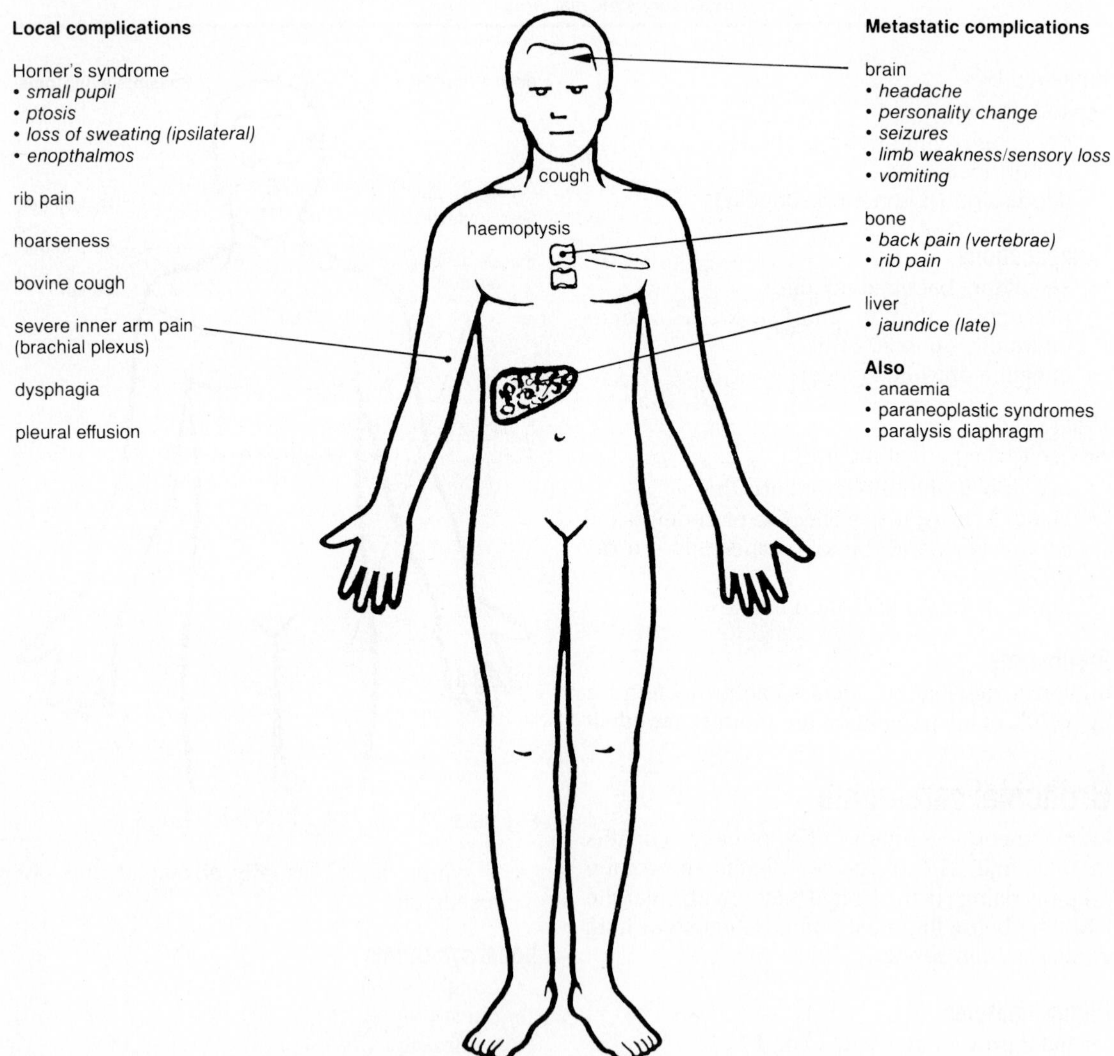

Fig. 36.4 *Possible physical findings of bronchial carcinoma*

- mild cases: yellow or green sputum only after infection
- advanced—profuse purulent offensive sputum
  —persistent halitosis
  —recurrent febrile episodes
  —malaise, weight loss
- episodes of pneumonia
- sputum production related to posture
- haemoptysis (blood-stained sputum or massive) possible

Physical examination

- clubbing
- coarse crackles over infected areas (usually lung base)
- other respiratory signs in Table 41.5

Investigations

- chest X-ray (normal or bronchial changes)
- sputum examination—for resistant pathogens
  —to exclude TB
- main pathogens: *Staphylococcus aureus, Pseudomonas aeruginosa, Haemophilus influenzae*
- CT scan: can show bronchial wall thickening
- bronchograms: very unpleasant and used only if diagnosis in doubt or possible localised disease amenable to surgery (rare)

Management

- explanation and preventive advice
- postural drainage, e.g. lie over side of bed with head and thorax down for 10–20 minutes 3 times a day
- antibiotics according to organism—it is important to eradicate infection to halt the progress of the disease
- bronchodilators if evidence of bronchospasm

Tuberculosis

Pulmonary tuberculosis may be symptomless and detected by mass X-ray screening.[3]

Typical clinical features

Respiratory symptoms

- cough
- sputum: initially mucoid, later purulent
- haemoptysis
- dyspnoea (especially with complications)
- pleuritic pain

General (usually insidious)

- anorexia
- fatigue
- weight loss
- fever (low grade)
- night sweats

Physical examination

- may be no respiratory signs or signs of fibrosis, consolidation or cavitation (amphoric breathing)
- finger clubbing

Investigations

- chest X-ray
- micro and culture sputum (for tubercle bacilli)
- ESR
- tuberculin test (misleading if previous BCG vaccination)

Management

Tuberculosis is a notifiable disease and must be reported to state (and local) health departments. Hospitalisation for the initial therapy of pulmonary TB is not necessary in most patients. Monthly follow-up is recommended including sputum smear and culture. Multiple drug therapy is initiated primarily to guard against the existence and/or emergence of resistant organisms. Standard initial therapy consists of rifampicin + isoniazid + pyrazinamide daily for at least 2 months, followed by rifampicin + isoniazid for 4 months if the organism is susceptible to these drugs.[9] If isoniazid resistance is suspected, ethambutol or streptomycin (with care) is added.

Symptomatic treatment of cough

Symptomatic treatment of cough should be reserved for patients who have acute self-limiting causes of cough, especially an acute viral infection. There are many cough mixtures available and the major constituents of these mixtures are shown in Table 36.7.[6] The recommended mixture should be tailored to the patient's individual requirements. These mixtures should be used only in the short term.

When to refer

- Patients in whom bronchoscopy is necessary to exclude bronchial carcinoma.

Table 36.7 *Cough mixtures: major constituents (after Williams and Bowes[6])*

Cough suppressants	Decongestants
Opiate	*Sympathomimetic*
Codeine	Ephedrine
Dihydrocodeine	Pseudoephedrine
Hydrocodone	Phenylephrine
Pholcodine	Phenylpropanolamine
Ethylmorphine	Methoxyphenamine
Normethadone	*Antihistamine*
Other	Promethazine
Carbetapentane	Pheniramine
Dextromethorphan	Chlorpheniramine
Expectorants/mucolytics	Diphenhydramine
Senega	Dexchlorpheniramine
Ammonia	Brompheniramine
Guaiphensin	Mebhydrolin
Bromhexine	Triprolidine
Analgesics/antipyretics	*Anticholinergic*
Paracetamol (acetaminophen)	Atropine
Salicylates (e.g. aspirin)	Isopropamide

- Persistent hoarseness in a patient who requires expert laryngeal examination.
- Evidence of pulmonary tuberculosis.

Practice tips

- Unexplained cough over the age of 50 is bronchial carcinoma until proved otherwise (especially if there is a history of smoking).
- Bronchoscopy is essential to exclude adequately a suspicion of bronchial carcinoma when the chest X-ray is normal.
- Bright red haemoptysis in a young person may be the initial symptom of pulmonary tuberculosis.
- Avoid settling for a diagnosis of bronchitis as an explanation of haemoptysis until bronchial carcinoma has been excluded.
- Coughing may be so severe that it terminates in vomiting or loss of consciousness (post-tussive syncope).
- Large haemoptyses are usually due to bronchiectasis or tuberculosis.
- The presence of white cells in the sputum renders it yellow or green (purulent) but does not necessarily imply infection.

References

1. Kumar PJ, Clarke ML. *Clinical medicine* (2nd edition). London: Bailliere Tindall, 1990, 637–638.
2. Walsh TD. *Symptom control*. Oxford: Blackwell Scientific Publications, 1989; 81:81–88 and 235–239.
3. Sandler G, Fry J. *Early clinical diagnosis*. Lancaster: MTP Press, 1986, 233–257.
4. Kincaid-Smith P, Larkins R, Whelan G. *Problems in clinical medicine*. Sydney: MacLennan & Petty, 1990, 105–108.
5. Davis A, Bolin T, Ham J. *Symptom analysis and physical diagnosis* (2nd edition). Sydney: Pergamon Press, 1990, 56–60.
6. Williams TJ, Bowes G. Cough as a symptom in adult life. Mod Med Australia, June 1992, 84–92.
7. Schroeder SA et al. *Current medical diagnosis and treatment*. East Norwalk: Appleton and Lange, 1990, 179–180.
8. Selecki Y, Helman A. Chronic cough in children. Australian Dr Weekly, 18 Sept. 1989.
9. Mashford ML et al. *Antibiotic guidelines*. Melbourne: Victorian Medical Postgraduate Foundation, 1992–93, 30–32.

37

Deafness and hearing loss

Deafness is defined as impairment of hearing, regardless of its severity.[1] It is a major community health problem requiring a high index of suspicion for diagnosis, especially in children. Deafness may be conductive, sensorineural or a combination of both (mixed).

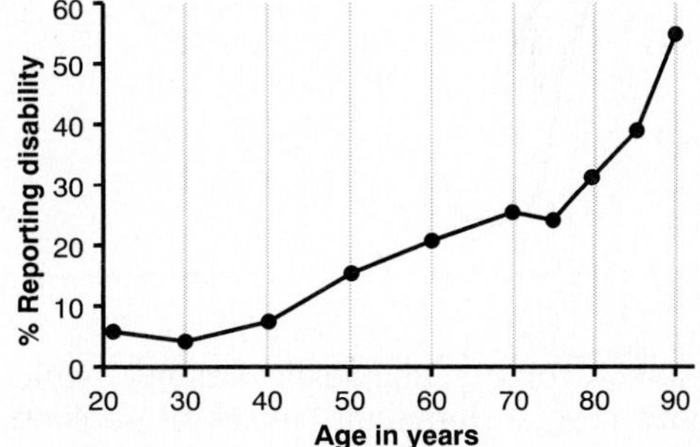

Fig. 37.1 *Prevalence of hearing problems with increasing age*

Key facts and checkpoints

- Deafness occurs at all ages but is more common in the elderly (Fig. 37.1).
- The threshold of normal hearing is from 0 to 20 decibels (dB), about the loudness of a soft whisper.
- One in seven of the adult population suffers from some degree of significant hearing impairment (over 20 dB in the better hearing ear).[2]
- Degrees of hearing impairment[2,3]
  mild = loss of 20 dB (soft spoken voice)
  moderate = loss of 40 dB (normal spoken voice)
  severe = loss of 60 dB (loud spoken voice)
  profound = loss of over 60 dB (shout)
- More women than men have a hearing loss.
- People who have worked in high noise levels (> 85 dB) are more than twice as likely to be deaf.
- There is a related incidence of tinnitus with deafness.

A diagnostic approach

It is useful to consider the causes of deafness in terms of pathophysiology (conductive or sensorineural hearing loss) and anatomical sites (Fig. 37.2).

Conductive hearing loss is caused by an abnormality in the pathway conducting sound waves from the outer ear to the inner ear,[1] as far as the footplate of the stapes.

Sensorineural hearing loss is a defect central to the oval window involving the cochlear (sensor), cochlear nerve (neural) or, more rarely, in central neural pathways.[1]

Congenital deafness is an important consideration in children, while presbyacusis is very common in the aged. The commonest acquired causes of deafness are impacted cerumen (wax), serous otitis media and otitis externa. Noise-induced deafness is also a common problem.

It is important not to misdiagnose an acoustic neuroma which can present as acute deafness, although slow progressive loss is more typical.

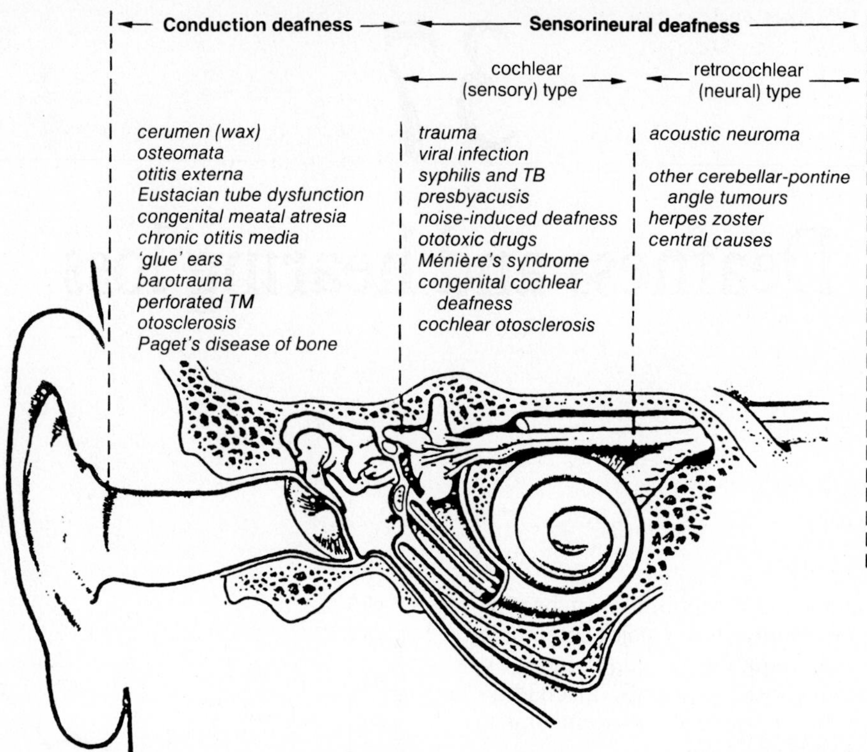

Fig. 37.2 *Causes of deafness according to anatomical site*

A summary of the diagnostic strategy, which includes several important causes of deafness, is presented in Table 37.1 and a checklist of ototoxic drugs in Table 37.2.

The clinical approach

History

The history should include an account of the onset and progression of any deafness, noise exposure, drug history, and a history of swimming or diving, air travel, head injury and family history. A recent or past episode of a generalised infection would be relevant and the presence of associated aural symptoms such as ear pain, discharge, tinnitus and vertigo. Vertigo may be a symptom of Ménière's disease, multiple sclerosis, acoustic neuroma or syphilis.

Several important clues can be obtained from the history. The often sudden onset of hearing loss in an ear following swimming or showering is suggestive of wax, which swells to block the ear canal completely.

Patients with conductive loss may hear better in noisy conditions (paracusis) because we raise our voices when there is background noise. Conversely, people with sensorineural deafness (SND) usually have more difficulty hearing in noise as voices become unintelligible.

Examination

Inspect the facial structures, skull and ears. The ears are inspected with an otoscope to visualise the external meatus and the tympanic membrane (TM) and the presence of obstructions such as wax, inflammation or osteomata. The examination requires a clean external auditory canal. Gentle suction is useful for cleaning pus debris. Syringing is reserved for wax in people with an intact TM and a known healthy middle ear.

It is an advantage to have a pneumatic attachment to test drum mobility. Reduction of TM mobility is an important sign in secretory otitis media.

There are several simple hearing tests. The distance at which a ticking watch can be heard can be used but the advent of the digital watch has affected this traditional method.

The hair-rubbing method

In children and in adults with a reasonable amount of hair grab several hairs close to the

Table 37.1 *Deafness and hearing loss: diagnostic strategy model*

Q. *Probability diagnosis*
A. Impacted cerumen
Serous otitis media
Otitis externa
Congenital (children)
Presbyacusis

Q. *Serious disorders not to be missed*
A. Neoplasia
- acoustic neuroma
- temporal lobe tumours (bilateral)
- otic tumours

Severe infections
- generalised infections, e.g. mumps
- syphilis

Perforated tympanic membrane
Cholesteatoma
Perilymphatic fistula (post-stapedectomy)

Q. *Pitfalls (often missed)*
A. Foreign body
Temporal bone fracture
Otosclerosis
Barotrauma
Noise-induced deafness

Rarities
Paget's disease of bone
Multiple sclerosis
Osteogenesis imperfecta

Q. *Seven masquerades checklist*

A.		
	Depression	—
	Diabetes	✓
	Drugs	✓
	Anaemia	—
	Thyroid disease	✓ hypo
	Spinal dysfunction	—
	UTI	—

Q. *Is this patient trying to tell me something?*
A. Unlikely.

Table 37.2 *Known ototoxic drugs*

Alcohol

Aminoglycosides
- gentamycin
- kanamycin
- neomycin
- streptomycin
- tobramycin

Diuretics
- ethacrynic acid
- frusemide

Chemotherapeutic agents

Quinine and related drugs

Salicylates

external auditory canal between the thumb and index finger. Rub the hairs lightly together to produce a relatively high-pitched 'crackling' sound (Fig. 37.3). If this sound cannot be heard, a moderate hearing loss is likely (usually about 40 dB or greater). Like the whisper test, this test is a rough guide only.

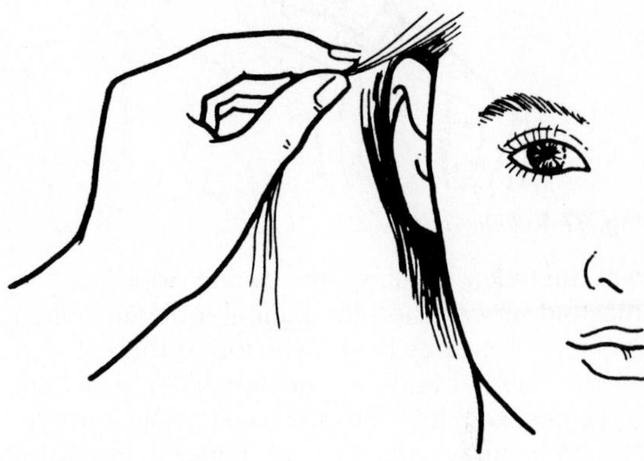

Fig. 37.3 *The simple hair-rubbing method of testing possible deafness*

Tuning fork tests

If deafness is present, its type (conduction or sensorineural) should be determined by tuning fork testing. The most suitable tuning fork for preliminary testing is the C_2 (512 cps) fork. The fork is best activated by striking it firmly on the bent elbow.

1. *Weber test*

The vibrating tuning fork is applied firmly to the mid-point of the skull or to the central forehead or to the teeth.

This test is of value only if the deafness is unilateral or bilateral and unequal (Fig. 37.4). Normally the sound is heard equally in both ears in the centre of the forehead. With sensorineural deafness the sound is transmitted to the normal ear, while with conduction deafness it is heard better in the abnormal ear.

2. *Rinné test*

The tuning fork is held:

- outside the ear (tests air conduction) and
- firmly against the mastoid bone (tests bone conduction).

It therefore compares air and bone conduction in the same ear (Fig. 37.5). A variation of the

Fig. 37.4 *Weber test*

test includes placing the tuning fork on the mastoid process and the patient indicates when it can no longer be heard. The fork is then placed at the external auditory meatus and the patient indicates whether the sound is now audible. Normally air conduction is better than bone conduction and the sound will again be heard.

Fig. 37.5 *Rinné test*

A comparison of the interpretation of these tests is summarised in Table 37.3.

Audiometric assessment

Audiometric assessment has two basic parts:

1. Puretone audiometry
2. Impedance tympanometry

Puretone audiometry

Puretone audiometry is a graph of frequency expressed in Hertz versus loudness expressed in decibels. The tone is presented either through the ear canal—a test of the conduction and the cochlear function of the ear—or through the bone—a test of cochlear function.

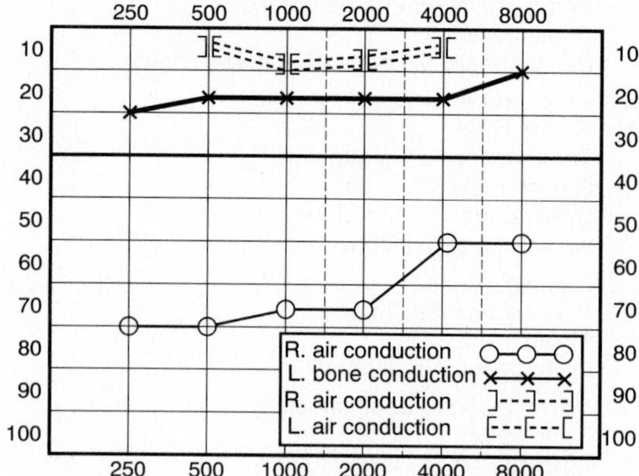

Fig. 37.6 *Puretone audiogram for severe conductive deafness in right ear*

Figures 37.6 and 37.7 are typical examples of puretone audiograms.

The difference between the two is a measure of conductance. If the two ears have different thresholds, a white noise masking sound is applied to the better ear to prevent it hearing sound presented to the test ear. The normal speech range occurs between 0–20 decibels across the frequency spectrum.

Table 37.3 *A comparison of the Rinné and Weber tests*

State of the hearing	***Rinné test***	***Weber test***
Normal	Positive: A.C.>B.C.	Equal in both ears
Conduction deafness	Negative: B.C.>A.C.	Louder in the deaf ear
Very severe conduction deafness	Negative: B.C.>A.C. May hear B.C. only	Louder in the deaf ear
Sensorineural deafness	Positive: A.C.>B.C.	Louder in the better ear
Very severe sensorineural deafness	'False' negative (without masking)	Louder in the better ear

A.C. = air conduction; B.C. = bone conduction

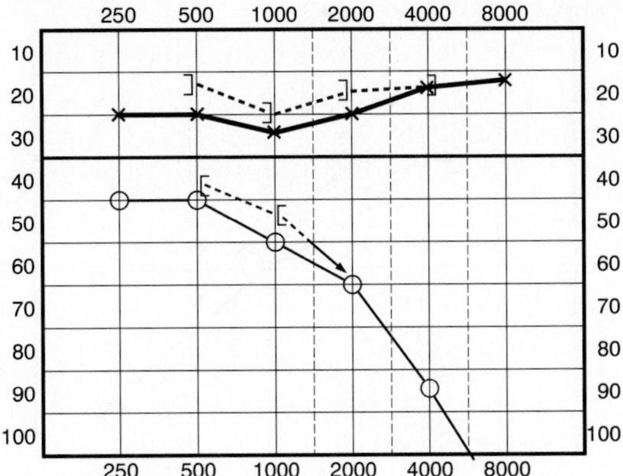

Fig. 37.7 *Puretone audiogram for unilateral (right) sensorineural deafness. Suspect a viral or congenital origin in children; check adults for acoustic neuroma*

Tympanometry

Tympanometry measures the mobility of the tympanic membrane, the dynamics of the ossicular chain and the middle ear air cushion. The test consists of a sound applied at the external auditory meatus otherwise sealed by the soft probe tip.

Deafness in children

Deafness in childhood is relatively common and often goes unrecognised. One to two of every 1000 newborn infants suffer from sensorineural deafness.[1] Congenital deafness may be due to inherited defects, to prenatal factors such as maternal intrauterine infection or drug ingestion during pregnancy, or to perinatal factors such as birth trauma, and haemolytic disease of the newborn.

Deafness may be associated with Down syndrome and Waardenburg's syndrome. Waardenburg's syndrome, which is dominantly inherited, is diagnosed in a patient with a white forelock of hair and different coloured eyes.

Acquired deafness accounts for approximately half of all childhood cases. Purulent otitis media and secretory otitis media are common causes of temporary conductive deafness. However, 1 in 10 children will have persistent middle ear effusions and mild to moderate hearing loss in the 15–40 decibel range.[4] Permanent deafness in the first few years of life may be due to virus infections such as mumps, meningitis, ototoxic antibiotics and several other causes.

Screening[1]

The aim of screening should be to recognise every deaf child by the age of 8 months to 1 year—before the vital time for learning speech is wasted. High-risk groups should be identified and screened, for example a family history of deafness, maternal problems of pregnancy, perinatal problems, cerebral palsy and those with delayed or faulty speech. The guidelines for early signs of normal hearing are presented in Table 37.4.

Table 37.4 *Early signs of normal hearing*

Age	Typical response
1 month	Should notice sudden constant sounds (e.g. car motor, vacuum cleaner) by pausing and listening.
3 months	Should respond to loud noise, e.g. will stop crying when hands are clapped.
4 months	Should turn head to look for source of sound such as mother speaking behind the child.
7 months	Should turn instantly to voices or even to quiet noises made across the room.
10 months	Should listen out for familiar everyday sounds.
12 months	Should show some response to familiar words and commands, including his or her name.

Optimal screening times:

- 8 to 9 months
- school entry

Early signs of hearing loss

A high index of suspicion is essential in detecting hearing loss in children and any parental concern should be taken seriously. The presentation of hearing loss will depend on whether it is bilateral or unilateral, its severity and age of onset.

Typical presentations include:

- malformation of skull, ears or face
- failure to respond in an expected way to sounds, especially one's voice
- preference for or response only to loud sounds
- no response to normal conversation or to television
- speech abnormality or delay
- absence of 'babbling' by 12 months
- no single words or comprehension of simple words by 18 months
- learning problems at school

- disobedience
- other behavioural problems
- inability to detect sound direction (unilateral loss)
- inability to follow simple commands or less than 20 spoken words by 2 years

Screening methods

Hearing can be tested at any age. No child is too young to be tested and this includes the newborn. Informal office assessments, such as whispering in the child's ear or rattling car keys, are totally inadequate for excluding deafness and may be potentially harmful if they lead to false reassurance.

Pneumatic otoscopy is essential to exclude middle ear effusions.

Puretone audiometry is unreliable in children under four years of age so special techniques such as tympanometry are required. Tympanometry assesses TM compliance and is highly sensitive and specific for detecting middle ear pathology in children beyond early infancy.

Auditory brain stem response testing is used to evaluate children (particularly young infants) for whom information on behavioural hearing tests is either unobtainable or unreliable.[4]

Management

Children with middle ear pathology and hearing loss should be referred to a specialist. All children with SNHL (even those with profound deafness), as well as children with conductive losses not correctable by surgery, benefit from amplification. All children need referral to a specialist centre skilled in educational and language remediation.

Deafness in the elderly

The prevalence of hearing loss increases exponentially with age. The commonest reason for bilateral progressive SND is presbyacusis which is the high frequency hearing loss of advancing age (Fig. 37.8). There appears to be a genetic predisposition to presbyacusis. It is usually accompanied by tinnitus.

Deafness is associated with various types of mental illness in the aged including anxiety, depression, paranoid delusions, agitation and confusion because of sensory deprivation. The possibility of deafness should be kept in mind when assessing these problems.

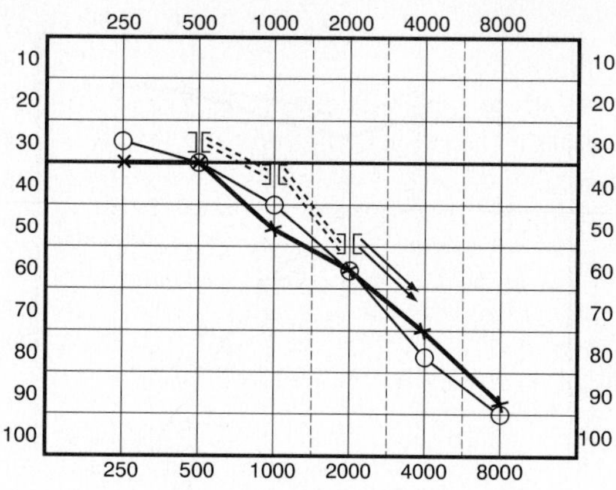

Fig. 37.8 *Presbyacusis: bilateral high frequency sensorineural deafness*

Sudden deafness

Sudden deafness refers to sudden sensorineural hearing loss of greater than 30–35 dB with an onset period of between 12 hours and 3 days.[5] It specially excludes gradual progressive causes of sensorineural deafness such as cumulative noise trauma or presbyacusis and also excludes causes of sudden deafness which may be related to pathology in the external auditory canal, TM or middle ear.

The main causes are given in Table 37.5.

Table 37.5 *Causes of sudden deafness*

Trauma
- head injury
- diving
- flying
- acoustic blast

Postoperative
- previous stapedectomy

Viral infections, e.g. mumps, measles, herpes zoster

Ototoxic drugs, e.g. aminoglycosides

Cerebellopontine angle tumours, e.g. acoustic neuroma

Vascular disease
- polycythaemia
- diabetes

Ménière's syndrome

Cochlear otosclerosis

In several instances, despite a careful clinical examination and investigation, an explanation for sudden SND cannot be found. The cause of deafness in these cases is thought to be either vascular obstruction of the end artery system or viral cochleitis.[5]

Patients with sudden SND require immediate referral. It is a difficult problem both in diagnosis and management. Early diagnosis and a high index of suspicion are fundamental.[5] Two important conditions that deserve special reference are perilymphatic fistula, which occurs after stapedectomy, and an acoustic neuroma presumably causing compression of the internal auditory artery by the tumour in the internal auditory meatus.

Otosclerosis

Features

- a progressive disease
- develops in the 20s and 30s
- family history (autosomal dominant)
- female preponderance
- affects the footplate of the stapes
- conductive hearing loss
- SND may be present
- impedance audiometry shows characteristic features (Fig. 37.9)

Management

- stapedectomy (approximately 90% effective)

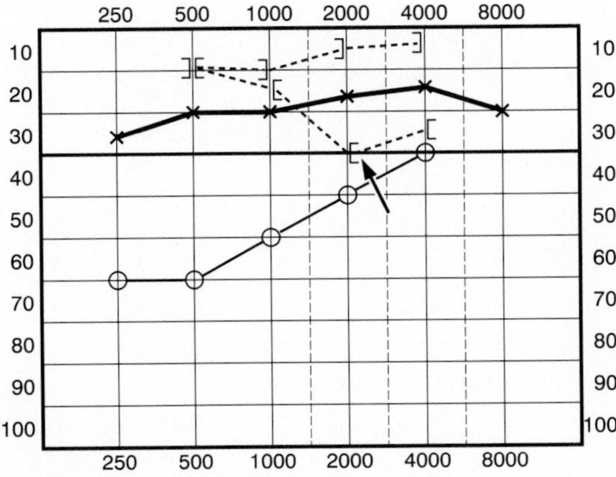

Fig. 37.9 *Otosclerosis: the conductive loss is commonly associated with a mild sensorineural loss at 2000 cycles per second (Carhardt's notch)*

Noise-induced hearing loss

Features

- onset of tinnitus after work in excessive noise
- speech seems muffled soon after work
- temporary loss initially but becomes permanent if noise exposure continues
- high-frequency loss on audiogram

Sounds exceeding 85 dB are potentially injurious to the cochlea, especially with prolonged exposures. Common sources of injurious noise are industrial machinery, weapons and loud music.

Hearing aids

Hearing aids are most useful in conductive deafness. This is due to the relative lack of distortion, making amplification simple. In SND the dual problem of recruitment and the hearing loss for higher frequencies may make hearing aids less satisfactory. Modern aids selectively amplify higher frequencies and 'cut out' excessive volume peaks which would cause discomfort. A trial of such aids should be made by a reliable hearing aid consultant following full medical assessment.

Advice for families

Relatives and close friends need considerable advice about coping with deaf members. They should be told that the deaf person may hear in a quiet room but not in a crowd, and advised of the range of aids and services available and the importance of proper maintenance of any hearing aids (especially with aged people).

Do

- Face the light when speaking to them.
- Speak directly to them.
- Speak clearly and naturally.
- Speak at a uniform pitch: avoid lowering your voice during or at the end of a sentence.
- Speak within 2 metres.
- Be tolerant and relaxed.
- Be patient with mistakes.
- Write key words on a paper pad when necessary.

Don't

- Speak with your back to them.
- Mumble your words.
- Use exaggerated lip movements.
- Shout.
- Put your hand or fingers over your mouth when talking.
- Repeat one word over and over.

When to refer

- Sudden deafness.
- Any child with suspected deafness, including poor speech and learning problems, should be referred to an audiology centre.
- Any child with middle ear pathology and hearing loss should be referred to a specialist.
- Unexplained deafness.

Practice tips

- A mother who believes her child may be deaf is rarely wrong in this suspicion.
- Suspect deafness in an infant with delayed development and children with speech defects or behavioural problems.
- Audiological assessment should be performed on children born to mothers with evidence of intrauterine infection by any of the TORCH organisms (toxoplasmosis, rubella, cytomegalovirus and herpes virus).
- No child is too young for audiological assessment. Informal office tests are inadequate for excluding hearing loss.
- Sounds tend to be softer in a conductive hearing loss and distorted with sensorineural loss.
- People with conductive deafness tend to speak softly, hear better in a noisy environment, hear well on the telephone and have good speech discrimination.
- People with SND tend to speak loudly, hear poorly in a noisy environment, have poor speech discrimination and hear poorly on the telephone.

References

1. Ludman H. *ABC of ear, nose and throat.* London: British Medical Association, 1989, 10–22.
2. Stephens S. Hearing problems. Medical Observer, 14 September, 1990, 51–52.
3. Schroeder SA et al. *Current medical diagnosis and treatment.* East Norwalk: Appleton and Lange, 1990, 124–131.
4. Jarman R. Hearing impairment. In: *Australian Paediatric Review*, 1991, 4;2.
5. Pohl DV. Sudden deafness. Modern Medicine Australia, June 1990, 72–78.

38

Diarrhoea

Diarrhoea is defined as the frequent passage of loose or watery stools.

Essential features are:

- an increase in frequency of bowel action
- an increase in softness, fluidity or volume of stools

Acute self-limiting diarrhoea, which is very common and frequently not seen by the medical practitioner, is usually infective and resolves within days. The causes of diarrhoea are numerous, thus making a detailed history and examination very important in leading to the diagnosis. Important causes are presented in Figure 38.1.

Key facts and checkpoints

- The characteristics of the stool provide a useful guide to the site of the bowel disorder.
- Disease of the upper GIT tends to produce diarrhoea stools that are copious, watery or fatty, pale yellow or green.
- Colonic disease tends to produce stools that are small, of variable consistency, brown and may contain blood or mucus.
- Acute gastroenteritis should be regarded as a diagnosis of exclusion.
- Chronic diarrhoea is more likely to be due to protozoal infection (amoebiasis, giardiasis or cryptosporodium) than bacillary dysentery.
- A history of travel, especially to countries at risk of endemic bowel infections, is essential.
- Certain antibiotics can cause an overgrowth of *Clostridium difficile*, which produces pseudomembranous colitis.
- Coeliac disease, although a cause of failure to thrive in children, can present at any age.
- In disorders of the colon the patient experiences frequency and urgency but passes only small amounts of faeces.

A diagnostic approach

A summary of the safety diagnostic model is presented in Table 38.1.

Probability diagnosis

Acute diarrhoea

Common causes are:

- gastroenteritis
  - — bacterial
    - salmonella sp
    - *Campylobacter jejuni*
    - *Staphylococcus aureus* (food poisoning)
    - *Clostridium perfringens*
    - enteropathic *E.coli*
  - — viral
    - rotavirus (50% of children hospital admissions[1])
- dietary indiscretions, e.g. binge eating
- antibiotic reactions

Chronic diarrhoea

Irritable bowel syndrome was the commonest cause of chronic diarrhoea in a UK study.[2]

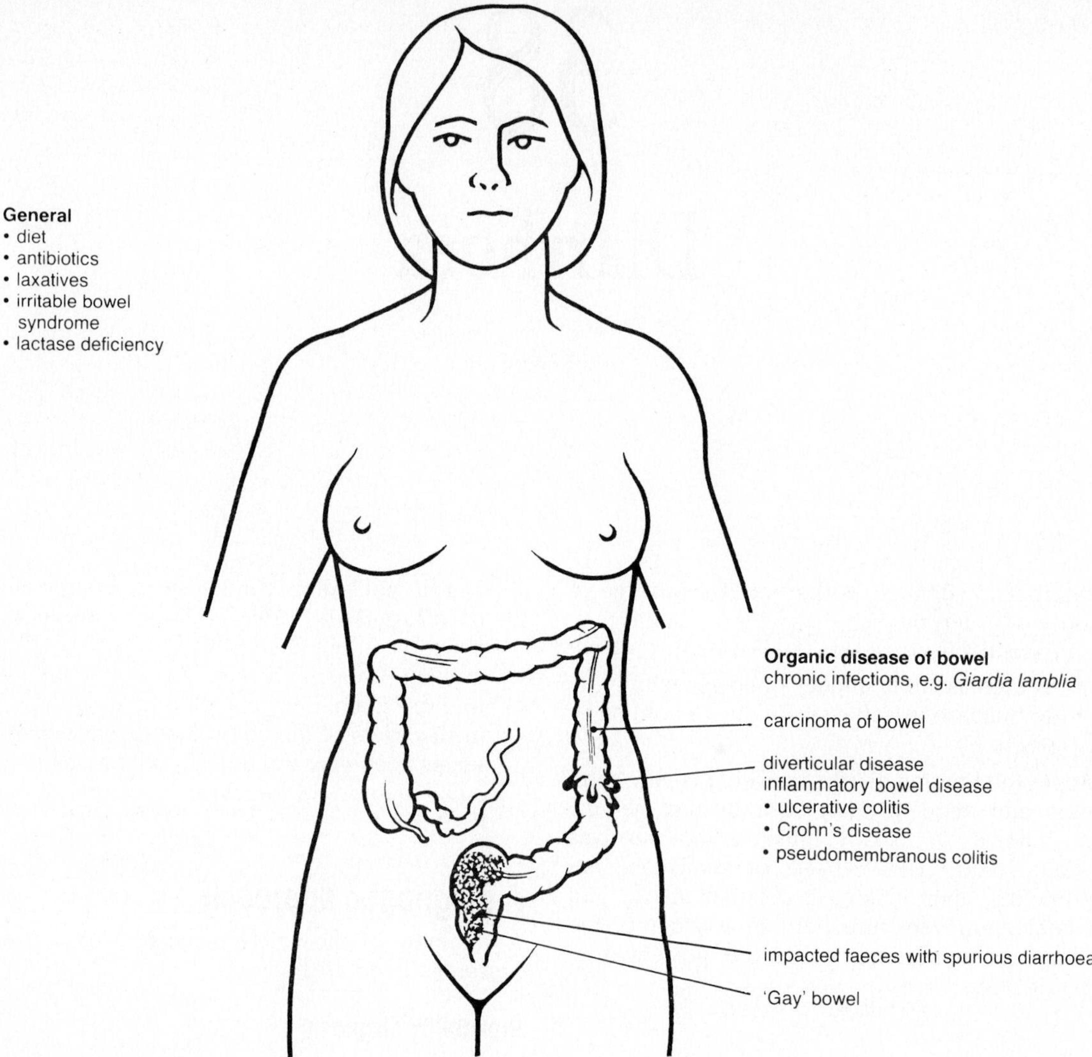

Fig. 38.1 *Important causes of chronic diarrhoea*

Drug reactions are also important. These include ingestion of laxatives, osmotic agents such as lactose and sorbitol in chewing gum, alcohol, antibiotics, thyroxine and others.

Acute gastroenteritis which persists into a chronic phase is relatively common, especially in travellers returning from overseas. Important considerations are *Giardia lamblia, Clostridium difficile, Yersinia, Entamoeba histolytica* and HIV infection.

Serious disorders not to be missed

Colorectal carcinoma must be considered with persistent diarrhoea, especially if of insidious onset.

AIDS due to symptomatic HIV infection needs consideration, especially in those at risk. The serious infectious disorders that can affect international travellers such as cholera, typhoid, paratyphoid and amoebiasis should also be kept in mind.

In children coeliac disease and fibrocystic disease can present as chronic diarrhoea while intussusception, although not causing true diarrhoea, can present as loose redcurrent jelly-like stools and should not be misdiagnosed (as gastroenteritis). Appendicitis must also be considered in the onset of acute diarrhoea and vomiting.

Table 38.1 *Diarrhoea: diagnostic strategy model*

Q. Probability diagnosis
A. *Acute*
- Gastroenteritis
- Dietary indiscretion
- Antibiotic reaction

Chronic
- Irritable bowel syndrome
- Drug reactions, e.g. laxatives
- Chronic infections

Q. Serious disorders not to be missed
A. Neoplasia
- Carcinoma of bowel

HIV infection (AIDS)
Infections
- Cholera
- Typhoid/paratyphoid
- Amoebiasis
- Malaria

Inflammatory bowel disease
- Crohn's/ulcerative colitis
- Pseudomembranous colitis

Intussusception
Pelvic appendicitis/pelvic abscess

Q. The pitfalls
A. Faecal impaction with spurious diarrhoea
Lactase deficiency
Giardia lamblia infection
Malabsorption states, e.g coeliac disease
Vitamin C and other oral drugs
Radiotherapy
Diverticulitis
Post GIT surgery
'Gay bowel'
Ischaemic colitis (elderly)

Rarities
- Addison's disease
- Carcinoid tumours
- Short bowel syndrome
- Amyloidosis
- Toxic shock

Q. Seven masquerades checklist

A.	
Depression	—
Diabetes	✓
Drugs	✓
Anaemia	—
Thyroid disease	✓ hyper
Spinal dysfunction	—
UTI	—

Q. Is the patient trying to tell me something?
A. Yes, diarrhoea may be a manifestation of anxiety state or irritable bowel syndrome.

Pitfalls

There are many traps in evaluating the patient with diarrhoea including drug ingestion, especially vitamin C (sodium ascorbate powder) which causes diarrhoea. Faecal impaction with spurious diarrhoea is an age-old pitfall, as is lactase deficiency which may go undiagnosed for many years. In recent times infection with *Giardia lamblia* may smoulder on for months with watery offensive stools before diagnosis.

General pitfalls

- Not considering acute appendicitis in acute diarrhoea—can be retrocaecal or pelvic appendicitis.
- Missing faecal impaction with spurious diarrhoea.
- Failing to perform a rectal examination.
- Failing to consider acute ischaemic colitis in an elderly patient with the acute onset of bloody diarrhoea stools (following sudden abdominal pain in preceding 24 hours).

Seven masquerades checklist

The significant masquerades include diabetes, when an autonomic neuropathy may cause alternating bouts of constipation and diarrhoea, thyrotoxicosis and drugs. Drugs that can cause diarrhoea are summarised in Table 38.2.

Table 38.2 *Drugs that can cause diarrhoea*

Alcohol, esp. chronic abuse
Antibiotics, esp. penicillin derivatives
Cardiac agents, e.g. digoxin, quinidine
Chenodeoxycholic acid
Colchicine
Heavy metals
Laxatives
Magnesium containing antacids
Metformin
Prostaglandins
Theophylline
Thyroxine

Pseudomembranous colitis (antibiotic-associated diarrhoea)

This colitis can be caused by the use of any antibiotic, especially clindamycin, lincomycin, ampicillin and the cephalosporins (an exception is vancomycin). It is usually due to an overgrowth of *Clostridium difficile* which produces a toxin that causes specific inflammatory lesions, sometimes with a pseudomembrane. It may occur, uncommonly, without antibiotic usage.

Features

- profuse watery diarrhoea
- abdominal cramping and tenesmus, maybe fever
- within 2 days of taking antibiotic (can start up to 4 to 6 weeks after usage)
- persists 2 weeks (up to 6) after ceasing antibiotic

Diagnosed by characteristic lesions on sigmoidoscopy and a tissue culture assay for *C. difficile* toxin.

Treatment

- cease antibiotic
- choice 1: metronidazole 400 mg (o) tds for 7–10 days

or

- choice 2: vancomycin 125 mg (o) qid for 10 days

Psychogenic considerations

Anxiety and stress can cause looseness of the bowel. The irritable bowel syndrome, which is a very common condition, may reflect underlying psychological factors and most patients find that the symptoms are exacerbated by stress. Look for evidence of depression.

In children chronic diarrhoea can occur with the so-called 'maternal deprivation syndrome', characterised by growth and developmental retardation due to adverse psychosocial factors.

The clinical approach

History

As always, the history is the key to the diagnosis. First establish what the patient means by the term 'diarrhoea', his or her normal pattern and how the presenting problem varies from normal.

It is important to analyse the nature of the stools, the frequency of diarrhoea, associated symptoms including abdominal pain and constitutional symptoms such as fever. Food intake in the past 72 hours and recent travel abroad may give a clue to acute gastroenteritis or food poisoning. The difference between food poisoning and infective gastroenteritis is presented in Table 38.3. A summary of non-microbial food poisoning is presented in Table 38.4.

A drug history is relevant and a family history of diarrhoea which may be significant for coeliac disease, Crohn's disease and cystic fibrosis.

Patients at risk from HIV infection should be discretely evaluated.

Table 38.3 *Comparison of acute diarrhoea due to bacterial food poisoning and infective gastroenteritis*

	Food poisoning	***Infective gastroenteritis***
Responsible organisms	**Toxins from:** *Staphylococcus aureus* *Clostidrium perfringens* *Salmonella* sp *Aeromonas hydrophilia* *Bacillus cereus*	 viral bacterial *Campylobacter jejuni* *E.coli* Shigella sp
Incubation period (onset from contact)	short—within 24 hours average—12 hours *S.aureus*—2-4 hours	3-5 days
Diarrhoea	watery	bloody diarrhoea
Other features	abdominal cramps dehydration headache	abdominal cramps (milder)
Typical foods	chicken meat seafood rice custards and cream (*S.aureus*)	milk water chicken

Table 38.4 *Non-microbial food poisoning*

Food (specific types)	***Toxin***	***Onset***	***Features (symptoms)***
Mushrooms **Toadstools**	muscarine	minutes to hours	N,V,D,P multiple CNS symptoms
Immature or sprouting potatoes	solanine	within hours	N,V,D,P throat constriction
Fish	ichthysarcotoxin	10–60 minutes (occasionally longer)	N,V,D,P circumoral tingling CNS symptoms collapse
Mussels	mytilotoxism	5–30 minutes	N,V,P CNS: paralysis
Grain, esp. rye	ergot fungus	minutes to 24 hours	N,V,P circulatory and CNS
Fava beans (favism)	enzyme deficiency	rapid	V,D acute haemolysis

N=nausea
V=vomiting
D=diarrhoea
P=abdominal pain

Key questions

Acute diarrhoea

Where did you eat in the 24 hours before the diarrhoea started?
What food did you eat during this time?
Did you have chicken or seafood recently?
Did any other people get the same problem?
Have you travelled overseas recently? Where?
Have you noticed any blood or mucus in your motions?
Have you had any previous attacks?

Chronic diarrhoea

Have you noticed any blood or mucus in the motion?
Have you travelled overseas recently? Where?
Do you have pain and is it relieved by opening your bowels or passing wind?
Does anyone else in your family have diarrhoea?
Have you had any operations on your abdomen recently?
What medications are you taking?
Are you taking antibiotics?
Do you take vitamin C for your health?
Do you take laxatives?
How much alcohol do you drink?
How much milk do you drink?
What about thick shakes, ice-cream and yoghurt?
Do you get clammy, shaky or have you lost weight?
Have you had trouble with pain in your joints, back pain, eye trouble or mouth ulceration?
Do you have trouble flushing your motions down the toilet?
Do you get diarrhoea during the night?
Are you under a lot of stress?

Significance of symptoms

Abdominal pain

Central colicky abdominal pain indicates involvement of the small bowel, while lower abdominal pain points to the large bowel.

Nature of the stools

If small volume consider inflammation or carcinoma of colon, and if large volume consider laxative abuse and malabsorption.

If there is profuse bright red bleeding consider diverticulitis or carcinoma of colon, and if small amounts with mucus or mucopus consider inflammatory bowel disease. The presence of blood in the stools excludes functional bowel disease. Diarrhoea at night suggests organic disease. In steatorrhoea the stools are distinctively pale, greasy, offensive, floating and difficult to flush. It is exacerbated by fatty foods.

The consistency of the stool as an aid to diagnosis[2,3] is summarised in Table 38.5 and the characteristics that distinguish between small and large bowel diarrhoea[1] are presented in Table 38.6.

Table 38.5 *Stool consistency as an aid to diagnosis*

Consistency	***Probable cause***
liquid and uniform	small bowel disease, e.g. gastroenteritis
loose with bits of faeces	colonic disease
watery, offensive, bubbly	*Giardia lamblia* infection
liquid or semiformed, mucous ± blood	*Entamoeba histolytica*
bulky, pale, offensive	malabsorption
pellets or ribbons	irritable bowel syndrome

Table 38.6 *Distinction between small and large bowel diarrhoea*

	Small bowel	***Large bowel***
Volume	Large	Small
Pain	Central	Lower
Borborygmi	++	−
Undigested food	+	−
Steatorrhoea	+/−	−
Blood	−	+
Mucus	−	+
Urgency	−	+
Tenesmus	−	+

Physical examination

The extent of the examination depends on the nature of the presenting problem. If it is acute, profuse and associated with vomiting, especially in a child, the examination needs to be general to assess the effects of fluid, electrolyte and nutritional loss. An infant's life is in danger from severe gastroenteritis and this assessment is a priority. The general nutritional and electrolyte assessment is also relevant in chronic diarrhoea with malabsorption and this includes looking for evidence of muscle weakness (e.g. hypokalaemia, hypomagnesaemia, tetany [hypocalcaemia], bruising [vitamin K loss]).

The examination should also focus on the abdomen (systematic palpation), the rectum and the skin. Possible helpful signs are included in Figure 38.2.

The stool

In all cases the stool should be examined. Note the presence of blood or mucus or steatorrhoea.

Investigations

The following list includes a range of tests that may be required. Appropriate tests should be judiciously selected and in some instances, such as acute self-limiting diarrhoea, no investigations are necessary.

- Stool tests
  - — microscopy for parasites and red and white cells (warm specimen for amoebiasis)
  - — cultures: may need special requests for Campylobacter sp, *Cl. difficile* and toxin, Yersinia sp, Cryptosporidium sp, Aeromonas sp (stools must be collected fresh on three occasions)
- Blood tests
  - — haemoglobin; MCV; WCC; ESR; iron; ferritin; folate; vitamin B_{12}; calcium; electrolytes; thyroid function; HIV tests
- Haemagglutination tests for amoebiasis
- *Cl. difficile* tissue culture assay
- Malabsorption studies
- Endoscopy
  - — proctosigmoidoscopy
  - — flexible sigmoidoscopy/colonoscopy (with biopsy)
- Radiology
  - — plain X-ray abdomen—of limited value
  - — barium enema, especially double contrast

Note: HIV patients should be investigated in specialist centres.

Malabsorption

It is important to distinguish the steatorrhoea of various malabsorption syndromes from diarrhoea. Important causes are presented in Table 38.7.

The common causes are coeliac disease, chronic pancreatitis and postgastrectomy.

Table 38.7 *Important causes of malabsorption*

Primary mucosal disease
- gluten-sensitive enteropathy (coeliac disease)
- tropical sprue
- lactose intolerance (lactase deficiency)
- Crohn's disease (regional enteritis)
- parasite infections, e.g. *Giardia lamblia*
- Lymphoma

Maldigestion states
Lumenal abnormalities
- postsurgery, e.g. gastrectomy, ileal resection
- systemic sclerosis

Pancreatic disease
- chronic pancreatitis
- cystic fibrosis
- pancreatic tumours, e.g. Zollinger-Ellison

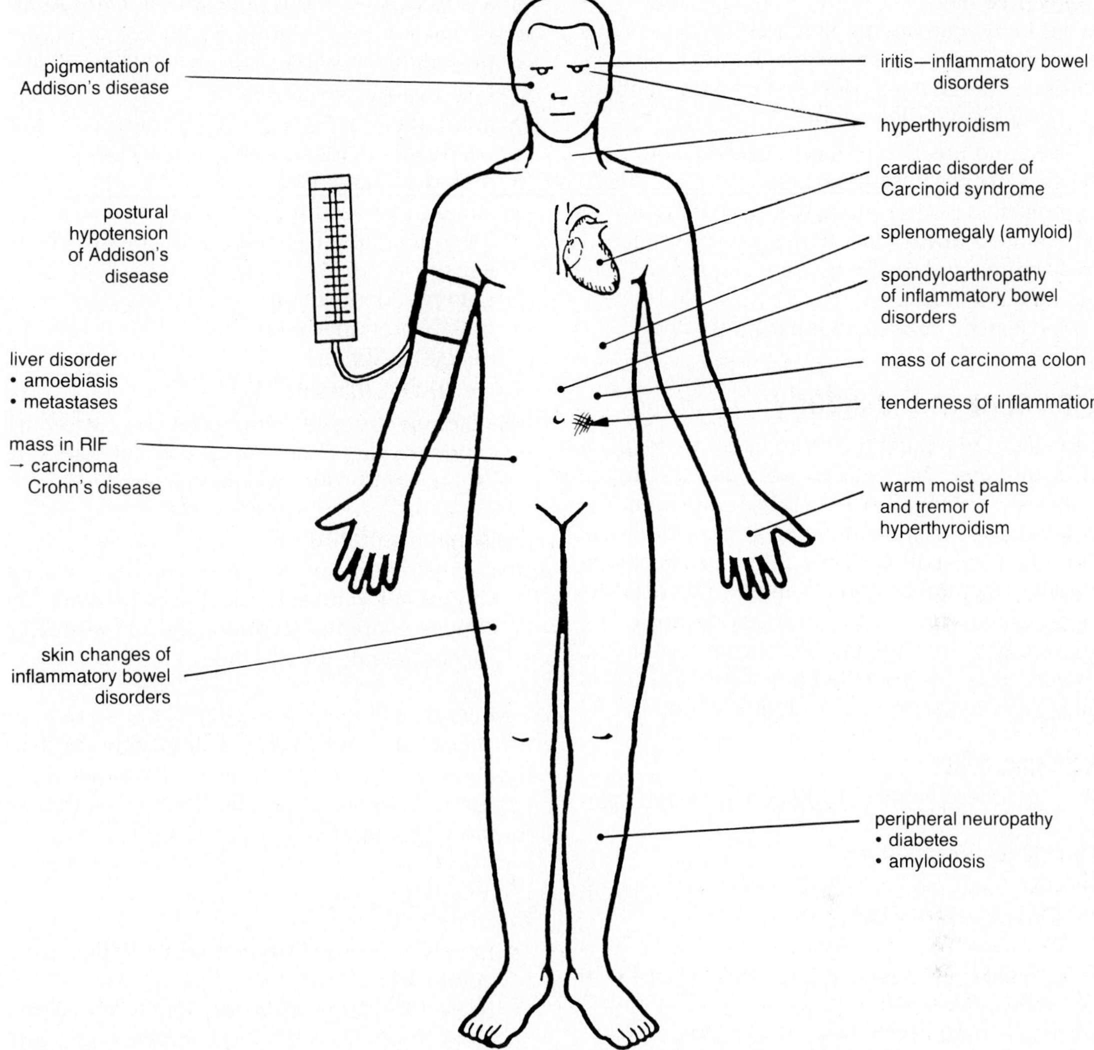

Fig. 38.2 *Possible significant signs in the patient with diarrhoea*

Clinical features:

- bulky, pale, offensive, frothy, greasy stools
- stools difficult to flush down toilet
- weight loss
- failure to thrive (in infants)
- increased faecal fat
- signs of multiple vitamin deficiencies, e.g. A,D,E,K
- sore tongue (glossitis)
- hypochromic or megaloblastic anaemia (possible)

Refer for specific investigations, e.g. FBE, barium studies, small bowel biopsy, faecal fat (>21 g/ 3 days).

Coeliac disease

Synonyms: coeliac sprue, gluten-sensitive enteropathy

NB: can appear at *any* age; refer to coeliac disease in children (page 358).

Diagnosis

- elevated faecal fat
- characteristic small bowel biopsy

Management

- diet control: high complex carbohydrate and protein, low fat, gluten-free (no wheat, barley, rye and oats)
- treat specific vitamin deficiencies

Gluten-free diet

Avoid foods containing gluten either as obvious component, e.g. flour, bread, oatmeal, or as a hidden ingredient, e.g. dessert mix, stock cube.[4]

Forbidden foods include:

- standard bread, pasta, crispbreads, flour
- standard biscuits and cakes
- breakfast cereals made with wheat or oats
- oatmeal, wheat bran, barley/barley water
- 'battered' or bread-crumbed fish, etc.
- meat and fruit pies
- most stock cubes and gravy mixes

Diarrhoea in the elderly

The older the patient the more likely a late onset of symptoms that reflect serious underlying organic disease, especially malignancy. Colorectal cancer needs special consideration. The older the patient, especially the bedridden elderly patient, the more likely the presentation of faecal impaction with spurious diarrhoea. The possibility of drug interactions, including digoxin, should also be considered. Ischaemic colitis must be considered in an elderly patient.

Ischaemic colitis

Due to atheromatous occlusion of mesenteric vessels.

Clinical features include:

- sharp abdominal pain in an elderly patient with bloody diarrhoea

or

- periumbilical pain and diarrhoea about 15–30 minutes after eating
- maybe loud bruits over central abdomen
- other evidence of generalised atherosclerosis
- barium enema shows 'thumb printing' sign due to submucosal oedema
- the definitive test is aortography and selective angiography of mesenteric vessels
- most episodes resolve—may be followed by a stricture

Diarrhoea in children

The commonest cause of diarrhoea in children is acute infective gastroenteritis, but there are certain conditions that develop in childhood and infancy and require special attention. The presentation of small amounts of redcurrent jelly stool with intussusception should also be kept in mind. Of the many causes only a few are commonly seen. The two commonest causes are infective gastroenteritis and antibiotic-induced diarrhoea.

Important causes of diarrhoea in children are:

- infective gastroenteritis
- antibiotics
- overfeeding (loose stools in newborn)
- dietary indiscretions
- sugar (carbohydrate) intolerance
- food allergies, e.g. milk, soya bean, wheat, eggs
- maternal deprivation
- malabsorption states
  - — cystic fibrosis
  - — coeliac disease

NB Exclude surgical emergencies, e.g. acute appendicitis, infections, e.g. pneumonia, septicaemia, otitis media < 5 years.

Acute gastroenteritis

NB Dehydration from gastroenteritis is an important cause of death, particularly in obese infants (especially if vomiting accompanies the diarrhoea).

Definition

An illness of acute onset, of less than 10 days duration associated with fever, diarrhoea and/or vomiting, where there is no other evident cause for the symptoms.[5]

Features

Causes

- mainly rotavirus (developed countries) and adenovirus
- bacterial: *Campylobacter jejuni* and *E.coli* (two commonest), *Salmonella sp* and *Shigella sp*
- protozoal: *Giardia lamblia*, *Entamoeba histolytica*, *Cryptosporidium*
- food poisoning—staphylococcal toxin

Differential diagnoses include septicaemia, urinary tract infection, intussusception, appendicitis, pelvic abscess, partial bowel obstruction, diabetes mellitus and antibiotic reaction[3] (see Table 38.8).

NB Exclude acute appendicitis and intussusception in the very young.

Symptoms

- anorexia, nausea, poor feeding, vomiting, fever, diarrhoea (fever and vomiting may be absent)
- fluid stools (often watery) 10–20 per day

- crying—due to pain, hunger, thirst or nausea
- bleeding—uncommon (usually bacterial)
- anal soreness

Viral indication: large volume, watery
Bacterial indication: small motions, blood, mucus, abdominal pain and tenesmus
Dehydration must be assessed (see Table 38.9).

Complications
- febrile convulsions
- sugar (lactose) intolerance (common)

Table 38.8 *Differential diagnosis of acute diarrhoea and vomiting in children*

Bowel infection
- viruses
- bacteria
- protozoal
- food poisoning—staphylococcal toxin

Systemic infection

Abdominal disorders
- appendicitis
- pelvic abscess
- intussusception
- Hirschsprung's disease

Antibiotic reaction

Diabetes mellitus

Management

Management is based on the assessment and correction of fluid and electrolyte loss.[5,6] Since dehydration is usually isotonic with equivalent loss of fluid and electrolytes, serum electrolytes will be normal.

Note The most accurate way to monitor dehydration is to weigh the child, preferably without clothes, on the same scale each time.

Avoid:
- Drugs: antidiarrhoeals, antiemetics and antibiotics
- Lemonade: osmotic load too high: can use if diluted 1 part to 4 parts water

To treat or not to treat at home:
- Treat at home—if family can cope, vomiting is not a problem and no dehydration.
- Admit to hospital—if dehydration or persisting vomiting or family cannot cope.

Advice to parents (for mild to moderate diarrhoea)

General rules

- Give small amounts of fluids often.
- Start solids after 24 hours.
- Continue breast-feeding.

or

Start bottle feeding after 24 hours.

Day 1

Give fluids, a little at a time and often (e.g. 50 ml every 15 minutes if vomiting a lot). A good method

Table 38.9 *Assessment of hydration*

	Mild	*Moderate*	*Severe*
Body weight loss	5%	6–9%	≥ 10%
Symptoms/general observations	thirsty alert restless	thirsty restless lethargic irritable	*Infants*: drowsy, limp, cold, sweaty, cyanotic limbs, comatose *Older*: apprehensive, cold and sweaty, cyanotic limbs
Signs	normal	dry mucous membranes, absent tears	rapid feeble pulse, hypotensive, sunken eyes and fontanelles, very dry mucous membranes
Pinched skin test	normal	retracts slowly (1–2 seconds)	retracts very slowly > 2 seconds
Urine output	normal	decreased	nil
Treatment	*Oral rehydration* • small amounts of fluids often • continue breastfeeding • solids after 24 hours • provide maintenance fluid and loss	*Oral rehydration* consider nasogastric tube for steady fluid infusion or IV infusion	Urgent IV infusion: isotonic fluid

is to give 200 ml (about 1 cup) of fluid every time a watery stool is passed or a big vomit occurs.

The ideal fluid is Gastrolyte. Other suitable oral rehydration preparations are WHO recommended solutions 'Electrolade' and 'Glucolyte'.

Alternatives are:

- lemonade (not low-calorie) 1 part to 4 parts water
- sucrose (table sugar) 1 teaspoon to 120 ml water
- glucose 1 teaspoon to 120 ml water
- cordials (not low-calorie) 1 part to 6 parts water

Warning: Do *not* use straight lemonade or mix up Gastrolyte with lemonade or fluids other than water.

Days 2 and 3

Reintroduce your baby's milk or formula diluted to half strength (i.e. mix equal quantities of milk or formula and water).

Do not worry that your child is not eating food. Solids can be commenced after 24 hours. Start with bread, plain biscuits, jelly, stewed apple, rice, porridge or non-fat potato chips. Avoid fatty foods, fried foods, raw vegetables and fruit, and wholegrain bread.

Day 4

Increase milk to normal strength and gradually reintroduce the usual diet.

Breast-feeding If your baby is not vomiting, continue breast-feeding but offer extra fluids (preferably Gastrolyte) between feeds. If vomiting is a problem, express breast milk for the time being while you follow the oral fluid program.

Chronic diarrhoea in children

Sugar intolerance

Synonyms: carbohydrate intolerance, lactose intolerance.
The commonest offending sugar is lactose.
Diarrhoea often follows acute gastroenteritis when milk is reintroduced into the diet. Stools may be watery, frothy, smell like vinegar and tend to excoriate the buttocks. They contain sugar.

A simple test

- Line the napkin with thin plastic and collect fluid stool.
- Mix 5 drops of liquid stool with 10 drops of water and add a Clinitest tablet (detects lactose and glucose but not sucrose).
- A positive result indicates sugar intolerance.

Treatment

- Remove the offending sugar from the diet.
- Use milk preparations in which the lactose has been split to glucose and galactose by enzymes, or use soya protein.

Milk allergy

Not as common as lactose intolerance. Diarrhoea is related to taking a cow's milk formula and relieved when it is withdrawn.

Inflammatory bowel disorder

These disorders, which include Crohn's disease and ulcerative colitis, can occur in childhood. A high index of suspicion is necessary to make an early diagnosis. Approximately 5% of cases of chronic ulcerative colitis have their onset in childhood.[5]

Chronic enteric infection

Responsible organisms include *Salmonella sp, Campylobacter, Yersinia, Giardia lamblia* and *Entamoeba histolytica*. With persistent diarrhoea it is important to obtain microscopy of faeces and aerobic and anaerobic stool cultures. *Giardia lamblia* infestation is not an uncommon finding and may be associated with malabsorption, especially of carbohydrate and fat. Giardiasis can mimic coeliac disease.

Coeliac disease

Clinical features in childhood:

- usually presents at 9–18 months, but any age
- previously thriving infant
- anorexia, lethargy, irritability
- failure to thrive
- malabsorption: abdominal distension
- offensive frequent stools

Diagnosis: duodenal biopsy
Treatment: remove gluten from diet

Cystic fibrosis

Cystic fibrosis is the commonest of all inherited disorders (1 per 2500 live births). Clinical features include:

- family history
- presents in infancy
- meconium ileus in the neonate
- recurrent chest infections (cough and wheeze)

- failure to thrive
- malabsorption

Diagnosis: can be diagnosed antenatally (in utero)
neonatal screening—immunoreactive trypsin

Treatment: pancreatic enzyme replacement for malabsorption
attention to respiratory problems

Acute gastroenteritis in adults

Features

- Invariably a self-limiting problem (1–3 days)
- Abdominal cramps
- Possible constitutional symptoms, e.g. fever, malaise, nausea, vomiting
- Other meal sharers affected → food poisoning
- Consider dehydration, especially in the elderly
- Consider possibility of enteric fever

Traveller's diarrhoea

The symptoms are usually as above but very severe diarrhoea, especially if associated with blood or mucus, may be a feature of a more serious bowel infection such as amoebiasis. Possible causes of diarrhoeal illness are presented in Table 11.1. Most traveller's diarrhoea is caused by an *Escherichia coli* which produces a watery diarrhoea within 14 days of arrival in a foreign country.

Persistent traveller's diarrhoea

Any traveller with persistent diarrhoea after visiting less developed countries, especially India and China, may have a protozoal infection such as amoebiasis or giardiasis.

If there is a fever and blood or mucus in the stools, suspect amoebiasis. Giardiasis is characterised by abdominal cramps, flatulence and bubbly foul-smelling diarrhoea.

Principles of treatment

Acute diarrhoea

- maintenance of hydration
- antiemetic injection (for severe vomiting)
  prochlorperazine IM, statim
  or
  metoclopramide IV, statim
- antidiarrhoeal preparations
  (avoid if possible: loperamide preferred)
  diphenoxylate with atropine (Lomotil) 2 tabs statim then 1–2 (o) 8 hourly
  or
  loperamide 2 mg caps (Imodium) 2 caps statim then 1 after each unformed stool (max: 8 caps/day)

General advice to patient

Rest

Your bowel needs a rest and so do you. It is best to reduce your normal activities until the diarrhoea has stopped.

Diet

It is vital that you starve but drink small amounts of clear fluids such as water, tea, lemonade and yeast extract (e.g. Marmite) until the diarrhoea settles. Then eat low-fat foods such as stewed apples, rice (boiled in water), soups, poultry, boiled potatoes, mashed vegetables, dry toast or bread, biscuits, most canned fruits, jam, honey, jelly, dried skim milk or condensed milk (reconstituted with water).

Avoid alcohol, coffee, strong tea, fatty foods, fried foods, spicy foods, raw vegetables, raw fruit (especially with hard skins), Chinese food, wholegrain cereals and cigarette smoking.

On the third day introduce dairy produce such as a small amount of milk in tea or coffee and a little butter or margarine on toast. Add also lean meat and fish (either grilled or steamed).

Antimicrobial drugs[7]

It is advisable not to use these except where the following specific organisms are identified. The drugs should be selected initially from the list below or modified according to the results of culture and sensitivity tests.[7] Adult doses are shown.

Pseudomembranous colitis See page 351.

Shigella dysentery (moderate to severe)

co-trimoxazole (double strength) 1 tab (o) 12 hourly for 7–10 days
or
norfloxacin 400 mg (o) 12 hourly for 7–10 days

Campylobacter jejuni (if prolonged)

norfloxacin 400 mg (o) 12 hourly for 7 days
or
erythromycin 500 mg (o) qid for 7 days (preferable)

Giardiasis

tinidazole 2 g (o), single dose
or
metronidazole 400 mg (o) tds for 7 days

Amoebiasis (intestinal)

metronidazole 600–800 mg (o) tds for 6–10 days

then

diloxanide furoate 500 mg (o) tds for 10 days

Specialist advice should be sought.

Special enteric infections

Typhoid/paratyphoid fever

- ciprofloxacin 500 mg (o) 21 hourly for 12 days

  If ciprofloxacin is contraindicated (e.g. in children) or not tolerated, then use:
- chloramphenicol 500–750 mg (o) 6 hourly for 14 days

  or
- co-trimoxazole (DS) 1 tablet (o) 12 hourly for 14 days

  or
- amoxycillin 1 g (o) 6 hourly for 14 days

If severe: administer same drug and dosage IV for first 4–5 days.

Cholera

Antibiotic therapy reduces the volume and duration of diarrhoea

doxycycline 100 mg (o) 12 hourly for 4 days

or

co-trimoxazole (DS) 1 tablet (o) 12 hourly for 4 days

Inflammatory bowel disease

Inflammatory bowel disease should be considered when a young person presents with:

- bloody diarrhoea and mucus
- colonic pain and fever
- extra-abdominal manifestations such as arthralgia, low back pain, (spondyloarthropathy), eye problems (iridocyclitis), liver disease and skin lesions (pyoderma granulosum, erythema nodosum)

Two important diseases are ulcerative colitis and Crohn's disease which have equal sex incidence and can occur at any age, but onset peaks between 20 and 40 years.

Ulcerative colitis

Features

- mainly a disease of 'Western' societies
- mainly in young adults (15–40) years
- high-risk factors—family history, previous attacks, low-fibre diet
- recurrent attacks of loose stools
- blood, or blood or pus, in mucus
- abdominal pain slight or absent
- fever, malaise and weight loss uncommon
- begins in rectum (continues proximally)—affects only the colon
- an increased risk of carcinoma after 7–10 years

Main symptom

- bloody diarrhoea

Diagnosis

- proctosigmoidoscopy: a granular red proctitis with contact bleeding
- barium enema: characteristic changes

Prognosis

- 5% mortality in an acute attack
- recurrent attacks common
- 75% ten year survival rate

Crohn's disease

Synonyms: regional enteritis, granulomatous colitis

Features

- recurrent diarrhoea in a young person (20–40 years)
- blood and mucus in stools (less than ulcerative colitis)
- colicky abdominal pain (small bowel colic)
- right iliac fossa pain (confused with appendicitis)
- constitutional symptoms, e.g. fever, weight loss, malaise
- signs include perianal disorders, e.g. anal fissure, fistula, ischiorectal abscess
- skip areas in bowel: ½ ileocolic, ¼ confined to small bowel, ¼ confined to colon

Main symptom

- colicky abdominal pain

Diagnosis

- sigmoidoscopy: 'cobblestone' appearance (patchy mucosal oedema)
- colonoscopy: useful to differentiate from ulcerative colitis (UC)

Prognosis

Less favourable than UC with both medical and surgical treatment.

Management principles for both diseases

- Treat under consultant supervision.
- Treatment of acute attacks depends on severity of the attack and the extent of the disease:
  - — mild attacks: manage out of hospital
  - — severe attacks: hospital, to attend to fluid and electrolyte balance.
- Role of diet controversial: consider a high-fibre diet.
- Pharmaceutical agents (the following can be considered):

  5-aminosalicylic acid derivatives (mainly UC)
  - — sulfasalazine (mainstay)
  - — olsalazine; mesalazine

  corticosteroids— oral
  - — parenteral
  - — topical (rectal foam, suppositories or enemas)

  immunosuppressive drugs, e.g. azathioprine
- Surgical treatment: reserve for complications.

Alternating diarrhoea and constipation

Alternating diarrhoea and constipation are well known symptoms of incomplete bowel obstruction (carcinoma of colon and diverticular disease) and irritable bowel syndrome.

Irritable bowel syndrome (IBS)

Clinical features

- typically in younger women (21–40)
- any age or sex can be affected
- may follow attack of gastroenteritis/traveller's diarrhoea
- cramping abdominal pain (central or iliac fossa) (Fig. 38.3)
- pain usually relieved by passing flatus or by defecation
- variable bowel habit (constipation more common)
- diarrhoea usually worse in morning—several loose, explosive bowel actions with urgency
- often precipitated by eating
- faeces sometimes like small, hard pellets or ribbon-like
- anorexia and nausea (sometimes)
- bloating, abdominal distension, ↑ borborygmi
- tiredness common

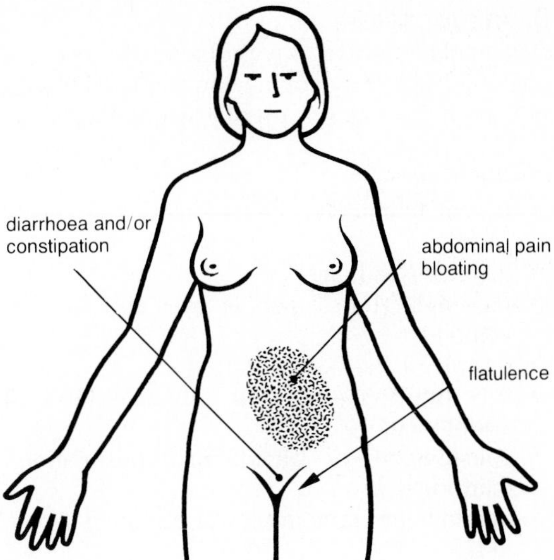

Fig. 38.3 *Classic symptoms of irritable bowel syndrome*

IBS is a diagnosis of exclusion. A thorough physical examination and sigmoidoscopy is necessary. Insufflation of air at sigmoidoscopy may reproduce the abdominal pain of IBS.

Possible related causes

Bowel infection, food irritation (e.g. spicy foods), lactose (milk) intolerance, low-fibre diet, laxative overusage, use of antibiotics and codeine-containing analgesics.

Management

The patient must be reassured and educated with advice that the problem will not cause malignancy or inflammatory bowel disease and will not shorten life expectancy.

Self-help advice to the patient

Anyone with irritable bowel should try to work on the things that make the symptoms worse. If you recognise stresses and strains in your life, try to develop a more relaxed lifestyle. You may have to be less of a perfectionist in your approach to life.

Try to avoid any foods that you can identify causing the problem. You may have to cut out smoking and alcohol and avoid laxatives and codeine (in painkillers). A high-fibre diet may be the answer to your problem. This can be achieved by adding two teaspoonfuls of unprocessed bran to your diet each day.

Diverticular disease

Diverticular disease is a problem of the colon (90% in descending colon) and is related to lack of fibre in the diet. It is usually symptomless.

Clinical features

- typical in middle aged or elderly—over 40 years
- increases with age
- present in 1 in 3 people over 60 (Western world)
- diverticulosis—symptomless
- diverticulitis—infected diverticula and symptomatic
- constipation or alternating constipation/ diarrhoea
- intermittent cramping lower abdominal pain in LIF
- tenderness in LIF
- rectal bleeding—may be profuse (± faeces)
- may present as acute abdomen or subacute obstruction
- usually settles in 2–3 days

Complications (of diverticulitis)

- abscess
- perforation
- peritonitis
- obstruction
- fistula—bladder, vagina

Investigations

- WBC and ESR—to determine inflammation
- sigmoidoscopy
- barium enema

Management

It usually responds to a high-fibre diet.

Advice to the patient

The gradual introduction of fibre with plenty of fluids (especially water) will improve any symptoms you may have and reduce the risk of complications. Your diet should include:

1. cereals, such as bran, shredded wheat, muesli or porridge
2. wholemeal and multigrain breads
3. fresh or stewed fruits and vegetables

Bran can be added to your cereal or stewed fruit starting with one tablespoon and gradually increasing to three tablespoons a day. Fibre can make you feel uncomfortable for the first few weeks, but the bowel soon settles to your improved diet.

When to refer

Children with diarrhoea

- infant under three months
- moderate to severe dehydration
- diagnosis of diarrhoea and vomiting in doubt, e.g. blood in vomitus or stool, bile-stained vomiting, high fever or toxaemia, abdominal signs suggestive of appendicitis or obstruction
- failure to improve or deterioration
- a pre-existing chronic illness

Adults

- patient with chronic or bloody diarrhoea
- any problem requiring colonoscopic investigation
- patients with anaemia
- patients with weight loss, abdominal mass or suspicion of neoplasia
- patients with anal fistulae
- patients not responding to treatment for Giardiasis
- infection with *Entamoeba histolytica*
- long-term asymptomatic carrier of typhoid or paratyphoid fever
- patient with persistent undiagnosed nocturnal diarrhoea
- patients with 'irritable bowel syndrome' with a significant change in symptoms
- patients with inflammatory bowel disorders with severe exacerbations, possibly requiring immunosuppressive therapy and with complications
- patients with ulcerative colitis of more than seven years duration (screening by colonoscopy for carcinoma)

Practice tips

- Oral antidiarrhoeal drugs contraindicated in children; besides being ineffective they may prolong intestinal recovery.
- Antiemetics can readily provoke dystonic reactions in children, especially if young and dehydrated.
- Acute diarrhoea is invariably self-limiting (lasts 2–5 days). If it lasts longer than 7 days investigate with culture and microscopy of the stools.
- If diarrhoea associated with episodes of facial flushing or wheezing, consider carcoid syndrome.
- Recurrent pain in the right hypochondrium is usually a feature of the irritable bowel syndrome (not gall bladder disease).

- Recurrent pain in the right iliac fossa is more likely to be irritable bowel syndrome than appendicitis.
- Beware of false correlations or premature conclusions, e.g. attributing the finding of diverticular disease on barium meal to the cause of the symptoms.
- Undercooked chicken is a common source of enteropathic bacterial infection.
- Consider alcohol abuse if a patient's diarrhoea resolves spontaneously on hospital admission.

References

1. Selby W. Diarrhoea—differential diagnosis. Aust Fam Physician, 1990; 19:1683–1689.
2. Sandler G, Fry J. *Early clinical diagnosis.* Lancaster: MTP Press, 1986, 25–30.
3. Borody TJ. Diarrhoea (acute and chronic). In: MIMS Disease Index. Sydney: IMS Publishing, 1991–2, 151–152.
4. Kumer PJ, Clarke ML. *Clinical medicine* (2nd edition). London: Balliere Tindall, 1990, 1054.
5. Barnes G. The child with diarrhoea. In: MJ, Robinson. *Practical paediatrics.* Melbourne: Churchill Livingstone, 1990:505–508.
6. Oberklaid F. Management of gastroenteritis in children. In: *The Australian paediatric review*, Melbourne: Royal Children's Hospital, 1990:1–2.
7. Mashford ML. *Antibiotic guidelines* (7th edition). Melbourne: Victorian Medical Postgraduate Foundation, 1993, 54–56.
8. Schmidt G. Irritable bowel syndrome. In: MIMS Disease Index. Sydney: IMS Publishing, 1991–2, 298–300.

39

Dizziness

When patients complain of 'dizziness', they can be using this term to describe many different phenomena, and hence a careful history is required to unravel the problem. Other patients may use different terms to explain the same sensation, for example, 'giddiness', 'swimming in the head', 'my brain spinning', 'whirling' and 'swinging'.

'Dizzy' comes from an old English word, *dysig*, meaning foolish or stupid. Strictly speaking, it means unsteadiness or lightheadedness—without movement or motion or spatial disorientation.

'Vertigo', on the other hand, comes from the Latin word for turning. The modern medical definition of vertigo is 'a sudden sense of movement'[1]. It should describe an hallucination of rotation of self or the surroundings in a horizontal or vertical direction.

The term 'dizziness', however, is generally used collectively to describe all types of equilibrium disorders and, for convenience, can be classified as shown in Figure 39.1.

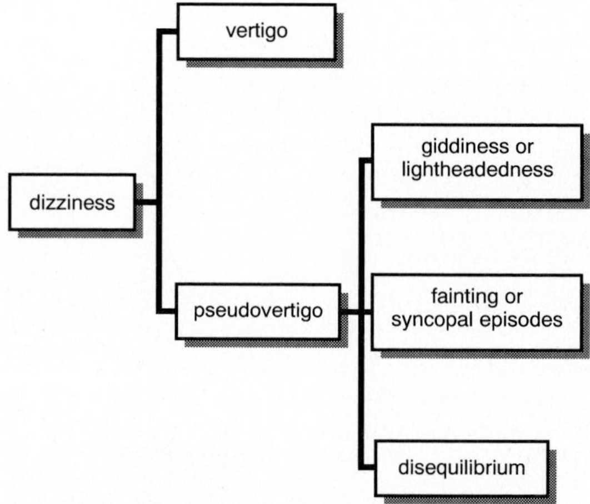

Fig. 39.1 *Classification of dizziness*

Key facts and checkpoints

- Approximately one-third of the population will have suffered from significant dizziness by age 65 and about a half by age 80.[2]
- The commonest causes in family practice are postural hypotension and hyperventilation.
- The ability to examine and interpret the sign of nystagmus accurately is important in the diagnostic process.
- A drug history is very important, including prescribed drugs and others such as alcohol, cocaine, marijuana and illicit drugs.
- Ménière's syndrome is overdiagnosed. It has the classical triad: vertigo–tinnitus–deafness (sensorineural).
- Vertebrobasilar insufficiency is also overdiagnosed as a cause of vertigo. It often causes dizziness and sometimes vertigo but rarely in isolation.

Defined terminology

Vertigo

Vertigo is an episodic sudden sensation of circular motion of the body or of its surroundings.

Other terms used by the patient to describe this symptom include 'everything spins', 'my head spins', 'the room spins', 'whirling', 'reeling', 'swaying', 'pitching' and 'rocking'.

Vertigo is characteristically precipitated by standing or turning the head or by movement. Patients have to walk carefully and may become nervous about descending stairs or crossing the road and usually seek support. Therefore the vertiginous patient is usually very frightened and tends to remain immobile during an attack.

They may feel as though they are being impelled by some outside force that tends to pull them to one side, especially while walking.

True vertigo is a symptom of disturbed function involving the vestibular system or its central connections. It invariably has an organic cause. Important causes are presented in Table 39.1, while Figure 39.2 illustrates central neurological centres that can cause vertigo.

Nystagmus is often seen with vertigo and, since 80–85% of causes are due to an ear problem, tinnitus and hearing disorders are also associated. In acute cases there is usually a reflex autonomic discharge producing sweating, pallor, nausea and vomiting.

Table 39.1 *Causes of vertigo*

1. Peripheral disorders

Labyrinth
- labyrinthitis
- Ménière's syndrome
- benign recurrent vertigo
- drugs
- trauma

8th nerve
- vestibular neuronitis
- acoustic neuroma
- drugs

2. Central disorders

Brain stem
- vertebrobasilar insufficiency
- infarction

Cerebellum
- degeneration
- tumours

Giddiness

Giddiness is a sensation of uncertainty or ill-defined lightheadedness. Other terms used by patients include 'a swimming sensation', 'walking on air' and 'ground going beneath me'. It usually

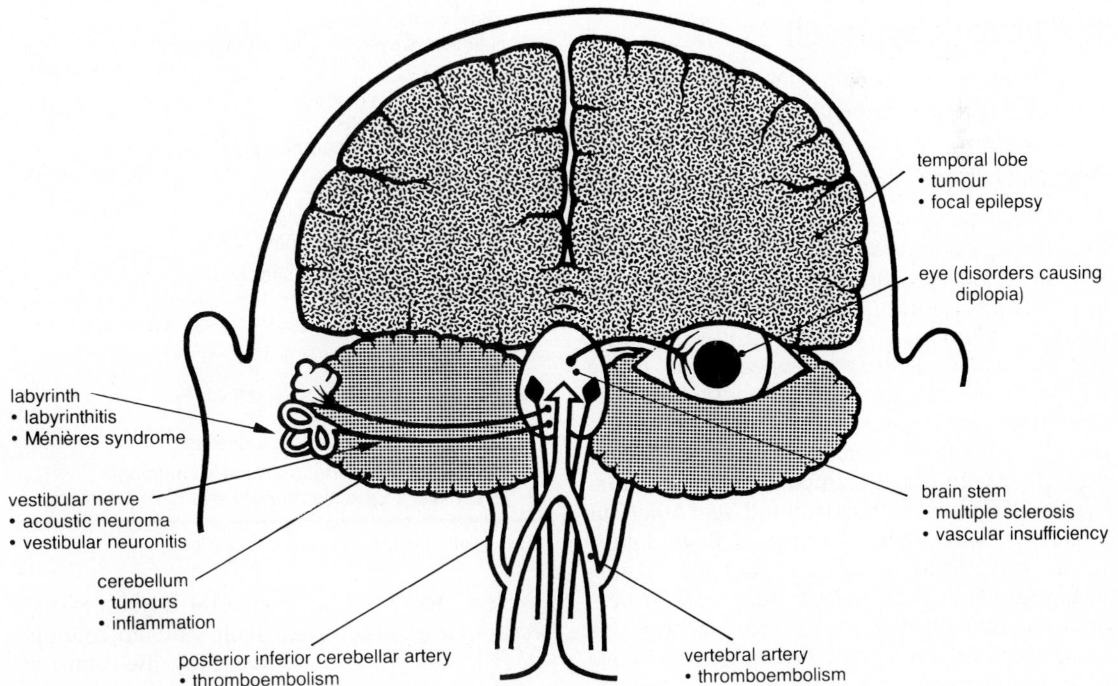

Fig. 39.2 *Diagrammatic illustration of central centres that can cause vertigo*

contains no elements of rotation, impulsion, tinnitus, deafness, nausea or vomiting.

The patient with giddiness, although fearful of falling or swooning, can nonetheless walk without difficulty if forced to do so.

Giddiness is a typical psychoneurotic symptom.

Syncopal episodes

Syncope may present as a variety of dizziness or lightheadedness in which there is a sensation of impending fainting or loss of consciousness. Common causes are cardiogenic disorders and postural hypotension, which are usually drug-induced.

Disequilibrium

Disequilibrium implies a condition in which there is a loss of balance or instability while walking, without any associated sensations of spinning. Other terms used to describe this include 'unsteadiness on feet', 'the staggers', 'swaying feeling' and 'dizzy in the feet'.

Disequilibrium is usually of neurogenic origin.

A diagnostic approach

A summary of the safety diagnostic model is presented in Table 39.2.

Probability diagnosis

In medical school we gain the wrong impression that the common causes of dizziness or vertigo are the relatively uncommon causes such as Ménière's syndrome, aortic stenosis, Stokes-Adams attacks, cerebellar disorders, vertebrobasilar disease and hypertension. In the real world of medicine one is impressed by how often dizziness is caused by relatively common benign conditions such as hyperventilation associated with anxiety, simple syncope, postural hypotension due to drugs and old age, inner ear infections, wax in the ears, post head injury, motion sickness and alcohol intoxication. In most instances making the correct diagnosis (which, as ever, is based on a careful history) is straightforward, but finding the underlying cause of true vertigo can be very difficult.

The common causes of vertigo seen in general practice are benign positional vertigo (so often related to cervical vertebral dysfunction), vestibular neuronitis and acute viral labyrinthitis.

Viral labyrinthitis is basically the same as vestibular neuronitis, except that the whole of the inner ear is involved so that deafness and tinnitus arise simultaneously with severe vertigo.

Table 39.2 *Dizziness/vertigo: diagnostic strategy model*

Q. *Probability diagnosis*
A. Anxiety-hyperventilation (G)
Postural hypotension (G/S)
Simple faint—vasovagal (S)
Ear infection—acute labyrinthitis (V)
Vestibular neuronitis (V)
Benign positional vertigo (V)
Motion sickness (V)
Post head injury (V/G)

Q. *Serious disorders not to be missed*
A. Neoplasia
- acoustic neuroma
- posterior fossa tumour
- other brain tumours 1° or 2°

Intracerebral infection, e.g. abscess
Cardiovascular
Cardiac
- arrhythmias
- myocardial infarction
- aortic stenosis

Cerebrovascular
- vertebrobasilar insufficiency
- brain stem infarct

Multiple sclerosis

Q. *Pitfalls (often missed)*
A. Ear wax—otosclerosis
Arrhythmias
Hyperventilation
Alcohol and other drugs
Cough or micturition syncope
Vertiginous migraine
Parkinson's disease
Ménière's syndrome (overdiagnosed)

Rarities
Addison's disease
Neurosyphilis
Autonomic neuropathy
Hypertension
Subclavian steal
Perilymphatic fistula
Shy-Dragar syndrome

Q. *Seven masquerades checklist*

A.	
Depression	✓
Diabetes	✓
Drugs	✓
Anaemia	✓
Thyroid disease	possible
Spinal dysfunction	✓
UTI	possible

Q. *Is the patient trying to tell me something?*
A. Very likely. Consider anxiety and/or depression.

G = giddiness; S = syncope; V = vertigo

Serious disorders not to be missed

Neoplasia

The important serious disorders to keep in mind are space-occupying tumours, such as acoustic neuroma; medulloblastoma and other tumours (especially posterior fossa tumours) capable of causing vertigo; intracerebral infections and cardiovascular abnormalities.

It is important to bear in mind that the commonest brain tumour is a metastatic deposit from carcinoma of the lung.[3]

Cardiac disorders

Cardiac disorders that must be excluded for giddiness or syncope are the various arrhythmias, such as Stokes-Adams attacks caused by complete heart block, aortic stenosis and myocardial infarction.

Cerebrovascular

The outstanding cerebrovascular causes of severe vertigo are vertebrobasilar insufficiency and brain stem infarction. Vertigo is the commonest symptom of transient cerebral ischaemic attacks in the vertebrobasilar distribution.[1]

Severe vertigo, often in association with hiccups and dysphagia, is a feature of the variety of brain stem infarctions known as the lateral medullary syndrome.

Neurological causes

Important neurological causes of dizziness are multiple sclerosis and complex partial seizures.

The lesions of multiple sclerosis may occur in the brain stem or cerebellum. Young patients who present with a sudden onset of vertigo with 'jiggly' vision but without auditory symptoms should be considered as having multiple sclerosis. Five per cent of cases of multiple sclerosis present with vertigo.

Pitfalls

A list of conditions causing dizziness that may be misdiagnosed is presented in Table 39.2. Wax in the ear certainly causes dizziness, though its mechanism of action is controversial. Cough and micturition syncope do occur, although they are uncommon.

Ménière's syndrome is a pitfall in the sense that it tends to be overdiagnosed.

Seven masquerades checklist

Of these conditions drugs and vertebral dysfunction (of the cervical spine) stand out as important causes. Depression demands attention because of the possible association of anxiety and hyperventilation.

Diabetes mellitus has an association through the possible mechanisms of hypoglycaemia from therapy or from an autonomic neuropathy.

Drugs

Drugs usually affect the vestibular nerve rather than the labyrinth. Drugs that cause dizziness are presented in Table 39.3.

Table 39.3 *Drugs that can cause dizziness*

Alcohol
Aspirin and salicylates
Antibiotics: streptomycin, gentamycin, kanamycin, tetracyclines
Anticonvulsants: phenytoin
Antidepressants
Antihypertensives
Antihistamines
Cocaine
Quinine-quinidine
Tranquillisers: phenothiazines, phenobarbitone, benzodiazepines
Diuretics in large doses: intravenous frusemide, ethacrynic acid
Glyceryl trinitrate

Cervical spine dysfunction

It is not uncommon to observe vertigo in patients with cervical spondylosis or post cervical spinal injury. It has been postulated[4] that this may be caused by the generation of abnormal impulses from proprioceptors in the upper cervical spine, or by osteophytes compressing the vertebral arteries in the vertebral canal. Some instances of benign positional vertigo are associated with disorders of the cervical spine.

Psychogenic considerations

This may be an important aspect to consider in the patient presenting with dizziness, especially if the complaint is giddiness or lightheadedness. An underlying anxiety may be the commonest cause of this symptom in family practice and clinical investigation of hyperventilation may confirm the diagnosis. The possibility of depression must also be kept in mind.[5] Many of these patients harbour the fear that they may be suffering from a serious disorder, such as a brain tumour or multiple sclerosis, or face an impending stroke or insanity. Appropriate reassurance to the contrary is often positively therapeutic for that patient.

The clinical approach

The essentials of the diagnostic approach include careful attention to the history and physical examination and judicious selection of specific office tests and special investigations.

History

It is important to get patients to explain the precise nature of the symptoms, even asking their opinion as the cause of their dizziness.

The following questions should be addressed:

- Is it vertigo or pseudovertigo?
- Symptom pattern:
  - — paroxysmal or continuous?
  - — effect of position and change of posture?
- Any aural symptoms?
  - — tinnitus?
  - — deafness?
- Any visual symptoms?
- Any neurological symptoms?
- Any nausea or vomiting?
- Any symptoms of psychoneurosis?
- Any recent colds?
- Any recent head injury (even trivial)?
- Any drugs being taken?
  - — alcohol?
  - — marijuana?
  - — hypotensives?
  - — psychotropics?
  - — other drugs?

Physical examination

A full general examination is appropriate with particular attention being paid to the cardiovascular and central nervous systems and the auditory and vestibular mechanisms.

Examination guidelines are:

1. ear disease
   - auroscopic examination: wax? drum?
   - hearing tests
   - Weber and Rinné tests
2. the eyes
   - visual acuity
   - test movements for nystagmus
3. cardiovascular system
   - evidence of atherosclerosis
   - blood pressure: supine, standing, sitting
   - cardiac arrhythmias
4. cranial nerves
   - 2nd, 3rd, 4th, 6th and 7th
   - corneal response for 5th
   - 8th—auditory nerve
5. the cerebellum or its connections
   - gait
   - co-ordination
   - reflexes
   - Romberg test
   - finger nose test: ? past pointing
6. the neck, including cervical spine
7. general search for evidence of:
   - anaemia
   - polycythemia
   - alcohol dependence

Special office tests for dizziness

- Ask the patient to perform any manoeuvre that may provoke the symptom.
- Head positional testing to induce vertigo and nystagmus (Fig. 39.3).
- Blood pressure measurements in three positions.
- Forced hyperventilation (20 to 25 breaths per minute) for 2 minutes.
- Palpation of carotid arteries and carotid sinus (with care).

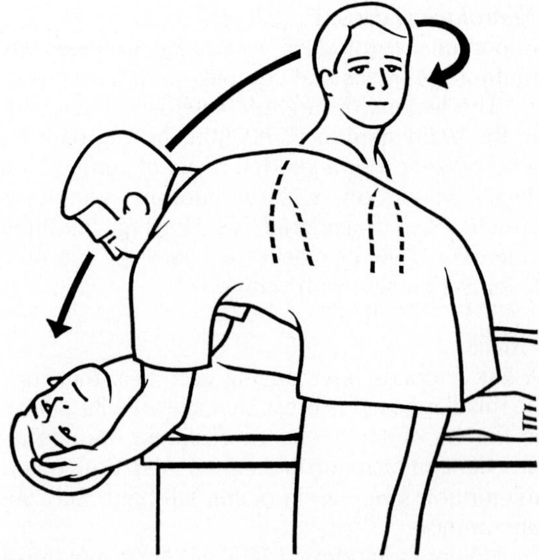

Fig. 39.3 *Positional testing for benign positional vertigo (head taken rapidly from sitting position to hanging position with head turned to right: one of the three positions)*

Investigations

Appropriate laboratory tests should be selected from Table 39.4.

Table 39.4 *Investigations*

Haemoglobin
Blood glucose
ECG: ? Holter monitor
Audiometry
Brainstem evoked audiometry
Caloric test
Visual evoked potentials (MS)
Electrocochleography
Electro-oculography (electronystagmography)
Rotational tests
Radiology
- chest X-ray (? bronchial carcinoma)
- cervical spine X-ray
- CT scan
- MRI (the choice to locate acoustic neuroma or other tumour—may detect MS)

Diagnostic guidelines

- A sudden attack of vertigo in a young person following a recent URTI is suggestive of vestibular neuronitis.
- Dizziness is a common symptom in menopausal women and is often associated with other features of vasomotor instability.
- Phenytoin therapy can cause cerebellar dysfunction.
- Postural and exercise hypotension are relatively common in the older atherosclerotic patient.
- Acute otitis media does not cause vertigo but chronic otitis media can, particularly if the patient develops a cholesteotoma which then erodes into the internal ear causing a perilymph fistula.

Dizziness in children

Dizziness is not a common symptom in children. Vertigo can have sinister causes and requires referral because of the possibility of tumours such as a medulloblastoma. A study by Eviatar and Eviatar[6] of vertigo in children found that the commonest cause was a seizure focus particularly affecting the temporal lobe. Other causes included psychosomatic vertigo, migraine and vestibular neuronitis.

Apart from the above causes it is important to consider:

- infection, e.g. meningitis, meningoencephalitis, cerebral abscess
- trauma, especially to the temporal area
- middle ear infection
- labyrinthitis, e.g. mumps, measles, influenza
- benign paroxysmal vertigo (short-lived attacks of vertigo in young children between 1 and 4 years of age: tends to precede adulthood migraine)[7]
- hyperventilation
- drugs—prescribed
- illicit drugs, e.g. cocaine, marijuana
- cardiac arrhythmias
- alcohol toxicity

A common trap is the acute affect of alcohol in curious children who can present with the sudden onset of dizziness.

Dizziness in the elderly

Dizziness is a relatively common complaint of the elderly. Common causes include postural hypotension related mainly to drugs prescribed for hypertension or other cardiovascular problems. Cerebrovascular disease, especially in the areas of the brain stem, is also relevant in this age group. True vertigo can be produced simply by an accumulation of wax in the external auditory meatus, being more frequent than generally appreciated.

Middle ear disease is also sometimes the cause of vertigo in an older person but disease of the auditory nerve, inner ear, cerebellum, brain stem and cervical spine are common underlying factors.

Malignancy, primary and secondary, is a possibility in the elderly. The possibility of cardiac arrhythmias as a cause of syncopal symptoms increases with age.

Vestibular neuronitis

This is considered to be a viral infection of the vestibular nerve that causes a prolonged attack of vertigo that can last for several days and be severe enough to require admission to hospital. It is analagous to a viral infection of the 7th nerve causing Bell's palsy. The attack is similar to Ménière's syndrome except that there is no hearing disturbance. Characteristic features are:

- single attack of vertigo without tinnitus or deafness
- usually preceding upper respiratory tract infection
- mainly in young adults
- abrupt onset with vertigo, nausea and vomiting
- may take 6 weeks or so to subside
- examination shows nystagmus—rapid component away from side of lesion (no hearing loss)
- caloric stimulation confirms impaired vestibular function

Note Acute labyrinthitis has a similar pattern. It is the diagnosis if hearing loss if present.

Treatment

The following drugs can be used:

meclozine (Ancolan) 50 mg tds

or

dimenhydrinate (Dramamine) 50 mg 6 hourly

or

prochlorperazine (Stemetil) 12.5 mg IM (if severe)

An alternative is diazepam (which decreases brainstem response to vestibular stimuli)[2], 5–10 mg IM for the acute attack then 5 mg(o) tds.

Benign positional vertigo

This is a common type of vertigo that is induced by changing head position—particularly tilting the head backwards, changing from a recumbent to a sitting position or turning to the affected side. Characteristic features:

- affects all ages
- recurs periodically for several days
- each attack is brief, usually a minute, and subsides rapidly
- attacks not accompanied by vomiting, tinnitus or deafness
- cause is unknown; may be related to cervical spondylosis or mechanical dysfunction of the cervical spine
- diagnosis confirmed by head position testing (From a sitting position the patient's head is rapidly taken to a head-hanging position 30° below the level of the couch—do three times, with the head (1) straight, (2) rotated to the right, (3) rotated to the left. Hold on for 30 seconds and observe the patient carefully for vertigo and nystagmus. There is a latent period of a few seconds before the onset of the symptoms (Fig. 39.3).)
- tests of hearing and vestibular function normal

Management

- appropriate explanation and reassurance
- avoidance measures: the patient quickly begins to move in a certain way and avoids attacks of vertigo

Ménière's syndrome

- Commonest in 30–50 age group
- Characterised by paroxysmal attacks of:
  - — vertigo
  - — tinnitus
  - — nausea and vomiting
  - — sweating and pallor
  - — deafness (progressive)
- Abrupt onset—patient may fall
- Attacks last 30 minutes to several hours
- Variable interval between attacks (twice a month to twice a year)
- Nystagmus observed only during an attack (often to side opposite affected inner ear)
- Examination
  - — sensorineural deafness
  - — caloric test—impaired vestibular function
  - — audiometry
    - sensorineural deafness
    - loudness recruitment
  - — special tests
- Characteristic changes in electrocochleography

Treatment

- explanation and advice about stress management
- avoid coffee and smoking
- low salt diet
- sodium depleting diuretic (regular estimation serum Na and K)
- oral urea: 20–30 g in orange juice (when warning of an attack)
- consider surgical management
- diazepam 2.5–5 mg IV then 5 mg 8 hourly for severe vertigo

When to refer

- Vertigo of uncertain diagnosis, especially in children.
- Possibility of tumour, or bacterial infection.

- Persistent Ménière's syndrome, not responding to conservative medical management.
- Evidence of vertebrobasilar insufficiency.

Practice tips

- A careful drug history often pinpoints the diagnosis.
- Always consider cardiac arrhythmias as a cause of acute dizziness.
- Consider phenytoin therapy as a cause of dizziness in an epileptic patient.
- If an intracerebral metastatic lesion is suspected, consider the possibility of carcinoma of the lung as the primary source.
- Three important office investigations to perform in the evaluation are blood pressure measurement (lying, sitting and standing), hyperventilation and head positional testing.

References

1. Kincaid-Smith P, Larkins R, Whelan G. *Problems in clinical medicine*. Sydney: MacLennan and Petty, 1989, 165.
2. Sloane PD, Slatt LM, Baker RM. *Essentials of family medicine*. Baltimore: Williams and Wilkins, 1988.
3. Sandler G, Fry J. *Early clinical diagnosis*. Lancaster: MTP Press, 1986, 361–382.
4. Lance JW. *A physiological approach to clinical neurology*. London: Butterworths, 1970, 162–179.
5. Ell J. The dizzy patient. Mod Med, 1991; 34:26–32.
6. Eviatar L, Eviatar A. Vertigo in children. Differential diagnosis and treatment. Paediatrics, 1977; 59:833–837.
7. Tunnessen WW Jr. *Signs and symptoms in paediatrics*. Philadelphia: Lippincott, 1988, 591–594.

40

Dyspepsia (indigestion)

Half the patients who get you up in the middle of the night and think they are dying are suffering from wind!

Advice to a younger doctor, from Francis Young (1884–1954)

Dyspepsia or indigestion is a difficult, sometimes vague, symptom to define or evaluate and requires very careful questioning to clarify the exact nature of the complaint.

Definitions

Dyspepsia is a discomfort related to eating. It is a symptom complex which includes one or more of the following symptoms during or after the ingestion of food.[1]

- nausea
- heartburn/regurgitation
- upper abdominal discomfort
- lower chest discomfort
- acidity
- epigastric fullness or unease
- abdominal distension
- flatulence

The discomfort can sometimes amount to pain. Diagnoses to consider in dyspeptic patients are summarised in Table 40.1.[1]

Heartburn is a central retrosternal or epigastric burning sensation that spreads upwards to the throat.

Flatulence is excessive wind. It includes belching, abdominal bloating or passing excessive flatus.[2]

Table 40.1 *Diagnoses to consider in dyspeptic patients*

Gastrointestinal disorders
Functional (non-ulcer) dyspepsia
Oesophageal reflux/hiatus hernia
Oesophageal motility disorders, e.g. spasm
Peptic ulcer
Upper GIT malignancies e.g. oesophagus, stomach, pancreas
Hepatobiliary disease e.g. hepatitis biliary dyskinesia cholelithiasis
Pancreatitis
Upper GIT inflammation gastritis giardiasis Crohn's disease
Irritable bowel syndrome
Non-gastrointestinal disorders
Myocardial ischaemia Drug reaction Alcohol effect Anxiety/stress Depression

Excessive belching

- usually functional
- organic disease uncommon
- due to air swallowing (aerophagy)

- common in anxious people who gulp food and drink
- associated hypersalivation

Key facts and checkpoints

- Dyspepsia or indigestion is a common complaint; 80% of the population[1] will have experienced it at some time.
- The oesophagus more commonly causes central chest discomfort than ischaemic heart disease.
- Consider heartburn as ischaemic heart disease until proved otherwise.
- The presence of oesophagitis is suggested by pain on swallowing hot or cold liquids (odynophagia).
- All reflux is not due to hiatus hernia.
- Many patients with hiatus hernia do not experience heartburn.
- All patients with dysphagia must be investigated to rule out malignancy.
- 10% of people in the community develop peptic ulcer disease.
- The major feature of peptic ulcer disease is epigastric pain.
- The pain of duodenal ulcer classically occurs at night.
- At any time 10–20% of chronic NSAIDs users have peptic ulceration (greater than non-users).[3]
- NSAIDs mainly cause gastric ulcers (gastric antrum and prepyloric region) with duodenum affected to a lesser extent.
- Dyspeptic symptoms correlate poorly with NSAID-associated ulcer.

Table 40.2 *Dyspepsia: diagnostic strategy model*

Q. *Probability diagnosis*
A. Irritable upper GIT (functional dyspepsia)
Gastro-oesophageal reflux
Oesophageal motility disorder (? spasm)

Q. *Serious disorders not to be missed*
A. Neoplasia
- carcinoma: stomach, pancreas

Cardiovascular
- ischaemic heart disease
- congestive cardiac failure

Pancreatitis
Peptic ulcer

Q. *Pitfalls (often missed)*
A. Myocardial ischaemia
Food allergy, e.g. lactose intolerance
Pregnancy (early)
Biliary motility disorder
Other gall bladder disease
Post vagotomy
Duodenitis
Rarities
Hyperparathyroidism
Mesenteric ischaemia
Zollinger-Ellison syndrome
Renal failure

Q. *Seven masquerades checklist*

A.		
	Depression	✓
	Diabetes	rarely
	Drugs	✓
	Anaemia	-
	Thyroid disease	-
	Spinal dysfunction	-
	UTI	-

Q. *Is this patient trying to tell me somthing?*
A. Anxiety and stress common associations of which patients are often unaware. Consider irritable bowel syndrome.

A diagnostic approach

A summary of the safety diagnostic model is presented in Table 40.2.

Probability diagnosis

The commonest cause of dyspepsia is an irritable upper gastrointestinal tract where the patient complains of discomfort after eating and no specific organic cause can be demonstrated. It parallels the irritable bowel syndrome of the lower gastrointestinal tract.

Alcohol is an important cause, both in the occasional drinker who has wine, especially red wine, with a large evening meal and in the problem drinker with alcoholic gastritis.

Oesophageal reflux and motility disorders are also common causes. They classically produce 'heartburn' which may result from the reflux of gastric contents into the lower end of the oesophagus or from gastric distension. It is not necessarily due to excessive gastric acidity as the same symptom often occurs in achlorhydria.

Serious disorders not to be missed

It is important not to overlook ischaemic heart disease, either angina or myocardial infarction, especially if the pain appears to have an epigastric focus. Patients often rationalise that their cardiac pain is 'heartburn' or indigestion.

Carcinoma of the upper gastrointestinal tract should be excluded.

Pitfalls

Perhaps the commonest mistake is to attribute the discomfort of myocardial ischaemia to a disorder of the GIT. A sense of fullness or pressure in the epigastrium can certainly accompany ischaemia.

General pitfalls

- Reflux oesophagitis and peptic ulcer can mimic ischaemic heart disease.
- Overlooking gastric carcinoma as a cause of dyspepsia.
- Failing to stress that weight reduction to ideal level will generally alleviate gastro-oesophageal reflux.

Seven masquerades checklist

The two most relevant masquerades are depression and drug reactions. Dyspepsia is a relatively common feature of depression and anxiety, while there are many drugs that cause dyspepsia. A list of such important drugs appears in Table 40.3. Diabetic autonomic neuropathy can cause dyspepsia by causing gastric outlet obstruction with subsequent delayed emptying.

Table 40.3 *Drugs that may cause dyspepsia*

Alcohol
Anticholinergics
Aspirin
Calcium channel blockers
Corticosteroids
Digitalis
Lipid-lowering agents
Narcotics
Nicotine
NSAIDs
Potassium supplements (slow release)
Theophylline
Tricyclic antidepressants
Tetracycline

Psychogenic considerations

Factors such as depression, anxiety and stress can play a very important part in this common problem. Ironically, patients may have no insight that they are anxious, under stress or hyperactive. This may be more obvious to the observer. Feelings of fear or guilt may be a component of this complex. There is an inseparable relationship between the mind and the gastrointestinal tract.

The clinical approach

History

It is worthwhile spending some time clarifying the exact nature of the presenting complaint: what the patient means by 'indigestion' or 'heartburn'.[4] The relationship of the symptom to eating is very important, and whether it occurs after each meal or after specific meals.

In particular, care should be taken to consider and perhaps exclude ischaemic heart disease.

Key questions

How would you describe the discomfort?
Can you show me exactly where it is and where it radiates?
What makes your discomfort worse?
What relieves your discomfort?
What effect do food, milk and antacids have?
What effect do coffee, onions or garlic have?
What effect does a big meal have?
What about drinking alcohol? Wine?
What effect does exercise have?
Do fried or fatty foods make it worse?
Do hot spicy foods affect it?
Does the problem come on at night soon after you go to bed?
Does it wake you up at night?
Does bending over, e.g. gardening, make it worse?
Do you have periods of freedom from the problem?
Are you under a lot of stress or have a lot of worry?
Do you go flat out all day?
Do you rush your meals?
Do you chew your food properly?
What drugs or medicines do you take?
How much alcohol do you have? Do you smoke?
Have you noticed anything else when you have the problem?
Do you get constipated or have diarrhoea?
Have you lost weight recently?
Do you feel the discomfort between your shoulder blades, or in your shoulders or throat?

Symptoms analysis

Site and radiation

The site and radiation of pain or discomfort can provide a lead to the diagnosis.[5] Refer to Figure 34.10. If it is felt in the interscapular area consider oesophageal spasm, gall bladder disease or a duodenal ulcer. Retrosternal discomfort indicates oesophageal disorders or angina, while epigastric discomfort suggests disorders of the biliary system, stomach and duodenum.

Character of the pain

There tends to be considerable overlap in the character of the pain from the various disorders but some general characteristics apply.

- burning pain → gastro-oesophageal (G-O) reflux
- constricting pain → ischaemic heart disease or oesophageal spasm
- deep gnawing pain → peptic ulcer
- heavy ache or 'killing' pain → psychogenic pain

Aggravating and relieving factors

Examples of these factors include:

- eating food may aggravate a gastric ulcer but relieve a duodenal ulcer
- eating fried or fatty foods will aggravate biliary disease, functional dyspepsia and oesophageal disorders
- bending will aggravate G-O reflux
- alcohol may aggravate G-O reflux, oesophagitis, gastritis, peptic ulcer, pancreatitis

Associated symptoms

Relevant examples:

- difficulty in swallowing → oesophageal disorders
- 'lump or constricting in throat' → psychogenic
- acid regurgitation → G-O reflux; oesophagitis
- anorexia, weight loss → carcinoma of the stomach
- water brash → G-O, hiatus hernia, peptic ulcer
- symptoms of anaemia → chronic oesophagitis or gastritis, peptic ulcer, carcinoma (stomach, colon)
- flatulence, belching, abnormal bowel habits → irritable bowel syndrome
- diarrhoea 30 minutes after meal → mesenteric ischaemia

Physical examination

The physical examination does not often provide the key to the diagnosis but it is important to perform very careful palpation and inspection. Look for evidence of clinical anaemia and jaundice. Diffuse mild abdominal tenderness and a pulsatable abdominal aorta are common findings but do not necessarily discriminate between organic and functional problems. Specific epigastric tenderness suggests peptic ulceration while tenderness over the gall bladder area (Murphy's sign) indicates gall bladder disease. An epigastric mass indicates carcinoma of the stomach.

Investigations

Investigations tend to be unrewarding in most instances of dyspepsia and could be postponed if the history is suggestive of a functional cause and the symptoms are not severe.[1] A trial of treatment such as changing adverse lifestyle factors, dietary modification and antacids could be the initial approach. Age is important in determining the extent of investigations, which are more relevant in those over 40 years.

Investigations will certainly be required for persisting symptoms, or for more severe and debilitating symptoms. Use them discreetly without engendering anxiety in the patient: 'the doctor is obviously searching for something serious'. These include:

- Haemoglobin and film: serum iron
- ESR
- Stool occult blood
- Liver function tests
- Exercise ECG
- Abdominal ultrasound
  - — a safe and reassuring technique
  - — gives information about liver, biliary tree, pancreas, kidneys, retroperitoneal lymph nodes. It is the superior investigation for gallstone disease.
- CT scan
  - — no great advantage over ultrasound
  - — reserved where ultrasound suggests pathology but undefined
- HIDA scan: excludes an obstructed cystic duct
- Barium swallow and meal
  - — better than endoscopy for motility problems
- Endoscopy
  - — superior to barium studies in investigation of the upper GIT
- ERCP in presence of jaundice (provides diagnosis in 85% of jaundiced patients)
- Manometric (oesophageal motility) studies
- Tumour markers:
  - — Carcinoembryonic antigen—for carcinoma of bowel
  - — Alphafetoprotein—for hepatoma

Dyspepsia in the elderly

An organic disorder is more likely in the older patient in whom it is important to consider carcinoma of the stomach. Symptoms such as anorexia, vomiting and weight loss point to such a problem.

Other conditions causing dyspepsia which are more prevalent in this age group are:

- constipation
- mesenteric artery ischaemia
- congestive cardiac failure

Dyspepsia in children

Dyspepsia is an uncommon problem in children but can be caused by drugs, oesophageal disorders and gastro-oesophageal reflux in particular.[6]

Gastro-oesophageal reflux

Regurgitation of feeds because of gastro-oesophageal reflux is a common physiological event in newborn infants. A mild degree of reflux is normal in babies, especially after they burp; this condition is called *posseting.*

Symptoms

Milk will flow freely from the mouth soon after feeding, even after the baby has been put down for a sleep. Sometimes the flow will be forceful and may even be out of the nose.

Despite this vomiting or regurgitation, the babies are usually comfortable and thrive. Some infants will cry, presumably because of heartburn.[6]

In a small number the reflux may be severe enough to cause serious problems such as oesophagitis with haematemesis or anaemia, stricture formation, failure to thrive, apnoea and aspiration.

Prognosis

Reflux gradually improves with time and usually ceases soon after solids are introduced into the diet. Most cases clear up completely by the age of 9 or 10 months, when the baby is sitting. Severe cases tend to persist until 18 months of age.

Investigations

These are not necessary in most cases but in those with persistent problems or complications referral to a paediatrician is recommended. The specialist investigations include barium meal with cine scanning, oesophageal pH monitoring or oesophagoscopy and biopsy.

Management

Appropriate reassurance with parental education is important. It should be pointed out that changes in feeding practice and positioning will control most reflux.

The infant should be placed prone at 30° after meals: sitting at 60° may increase intra-abdominal pressure and make the reflux worse.[6] The old bucket method, in which the child is placed in a bucket, is not necessary. Suspending the child in one of the new suspended swings for periods of 30–60 minutes after feeds will help.

Smaller, more frequent feeds and thickening agents are appropriate.

Thickening of feeds

Giving the baby thicker feeds usually helps those with more severe reflux. The old-fashioned remedy of using cornflour blended in bottles is still useful.

Bottle-fed babies (powdered milk formula)

Carobel: Add slightly less than 1 full scoop per bottle.

Gaviscon: Mix slightly less than ½ teaspoon of Infant Gaviscon Powder with 120 ml of formula in the bottle.

Cornflour: Mix 1 teaspoon with each 120 ml of formula. Check with your doctor or nurse for the proper method.

Breast-fed babies

Carobel: Add slightly less than 1 full scoop to 20 ml cool boiled water or 20 ml expressed breast milk and give just before the feed.

Gaviscon: Mix slightly less than ½ teaspoon of Infant Gaviscon Powder with 20 ml cool boiled water or expressed breast milk and give just after the feed.

For persistent or complicated reflux, including oesophagitis, specialist-monitored treatment will include the use of antacids, pH_2 receptor blocking agents or prokinetic agents.

Heartburn

Heartburn (pyrosis), which is a more definite type of dyspepsia, is a central retrosternal burning sensation which can radiate from the epigastrium to the throat.[7]

It must be distinguished from ischaemic heart disease and the different features to aid this distinction are presented in Table 34.4.

Features

- burning and retrosternal
- rising in the chest
- associated reflux
- aggravating factors
  - heavy meal
  - swallowing hot and cold liquids
  - stooping
  - lying flat
  - lifting or straining
- water brash is a symptom of G-O reflux
- more likely to occur at rest than on exertion
- reflux can cause cough or wheeze at night (? throat irritation from gastric contents due to reflux)

Causes and associations

- G-O reflux
- oesophagitis
- hiatus hernia
- medications, e.g. NSAIDs, aspirin (Table 40.3)
- peptic ulcer
- scleroderma
- pregnancy
- obesity
- smoking and alcohol
- coffee and other caffeine products

NB The lower oesophageal sphincter is a zone of high pressure at the gastro-oesophageal junction. Any dysfunction which affects clearance of oesophageal contents including refluxed gastric contents causes discomfort or predisposes to oesophagitis. Smoking, alcohol, coffee and chocolate all affect this pressure by lowering it.

Differential diagnosis

- ischaemic heart disease
- pericarditis
- oesophageal motility disorders
- musculoskeletal pain, e.g. cervical spine dysfunction
- subdiaphragmatic
  - biliary disorders
  - peptic ulcer

Special forms of oesophagitis

- Barrett's oesophagus
  - lower oesophagus lined with gastric mucosa (at least 3 cm)
  - prone to ulceration
  - premalignant condition
- Scleroderma oesophagitis

Management of heartburn

Applies particularly for G-O reflux and hiatus hernia.

Stage 1

If the patient has heartburn without any sinister symptoms such as dysphagia and weight loss or clinical evidence of anaemia, it is appropriate to direct therapy to lifestyle changes and antacid therapy.[8]

Lifestyle advice to patient (if applicable)

- Patient education about problem with appropriate reassurance.
- If overweight—weight reduction (this alone may abolish heartburn).
- Reduction or cessation of smoking.
- Reduction or cessation of alcohol intake.
- Reduction of coffee, tea and chocolate.
- Avoid coffee and alcohol late at night.
- Avoid onions and garlic (bring on reflux).
- Leave at least 3 hours between the evening meal and retiring.
- Avoid a heavy evening meal, have the main meal at midday.
- Avoid fatty foods such as pastries.
- Avoid tight belts or corsets.
- Avoid spicy foods and tomato products.
- Take medication with ample water and in an upright position.
- Avoid lying down immediately after meals.
- Drugs to avoid: anticholinergics, theophylline, calcium channel blockers, doxycycline.

Antacids

Antacids	(10–20 ml)	–on demand –1½-2 hours before meals
	(20–30 ml)	–at bedtime

Appropriate effective antacid: combination alginate/antacid mixture, e.g. Gaviscon liquid, Mylanta Plus liquid.

Note: Liquid antacids are more effective than tablets, although the latter may help. Antacids in common use and important side effects are summarised in Tables 40.4 and 40.5.

Elevation of bed head

If reflux occurs in bed, sleep with head of bed elevated 10–20 cm with wooden blocks. Poor compliance is a problem, especially with the effect on the patient's partner.

Note: At least 50% of patients will respond to stage 1 therapy.

Table 40.4 *Antacids in common use*

Antacids	
Water soluble	Calcium carbonate Sodium — bicarbonate — citrotartrate
Note Excess is prone to cause alkalosis—apathy, mental changes, stupor, renal dysfunction, tetany	
Water insoluble	Aluminium — hydroxide — glycinate — phosphate Magnesium — alginate — carbonate — hydroxide — trisilicate
Combination antacids	
Antacid + alginic acid + oxethazine + simethicone	

Table 40.5 *Side effects of common antacids*

Aluminium hydroxide	— constipation
Magnesium trisilicate	— diarrhoea
Sodium bicarbonate	— alkalosis — milk alkali syndrome
Calcium carbonate	— alkalosis — constipation — milk alkali syndrome — hypercalcaemia

Stage 2

If no relief after several weeks, the following guidelines may be appropriate.

Investigations

These will be selected from:

- endoscopy (investigation of first choice)
- barium meal: good for detecting hiatus hernia and some motility problems, e.g. diffuse spasm, achalasia
- oesophageal motility studies: to evaluate undiagnosed chest pain and dysphagia
- acid perfusion (Bernstein) test: introduces 0.1% HCI into distal oesophagus via a nasogastric tube—reproduces symptoms if due to oesophagitis
- oesophageal pH monitoring: overnight or ambulatory 24 hour monitoring to determine the severity and duration of acid reflux into the oesophagus

Stage 2 therapy

Step 1 *Reduce acid secretion* (select from)

H_2 receptor antagonists (oral use)

cimetidine 400 mg bd pc for 8 weeks

or

ranitidine 150 mg bd pc for 8 weeks

or

famotidine 40 mg nocte

or

nizatadine 150 mg bd

Proton pump blocker (if no response)

omeprozole 20–40 mg mane

(very effective for ulcerative oesophagitis and reflux)

Step 2 *Prokinetic agents* (select from)

—to facilitate gastric emptying

—very useful in reflux

bethanecol 10–25 mg tds or qid

or

domperidone 10 mg tds or qid

or

metoclopramide 10 mg tds

or

cisapride 10 mg tds

NB Long-term use of metoclopramide may cause agitation, confusion or extrapyramidal side effects, e.g. dystonia

Step 3 *Cytoprotective agents*

sucralfate IG qid

Functional (non-ulcer) dyspepsia

Note This condition overlaps with heartburn and in many cases the management is similar. It is also referred to as an irritable upper digestive tract and exhibits many similarities to the irritable bowel syndrome of the lower gastrointestinal tract.

Features

- Discomfort on eating in absence of demonstrable organic disease
- Causative factors include
  —overweight
  —eating too much too rapidly
  —inadequate mastication (? poor dentition)
  —anxiety/stress, which influences motility
  —emotional upsets, especially overeating
  —aerophagy
  —excessive smoking
  —drinking alcohol with meals, especially red wine
  —poorly cooked foods
  —fatty foods, e.g. pastries
  —caffeine, especially hot coffee
  —specific vegetables, e.g. cucumbers, radishes, onions, beans, cabbage
  —constipation

Physiology

- dysfunctional gastric motor activity
- prolonged gastric emptying time, e.g. fats
- distension of stomach, e.g. aerophagy

Management

- Provide appropriate reassurance and support.
- Avoid giving the impression that the symptoms are 'in the mind'.
- Provide psychotherapy where appropriate.
- Give lifestyle advice as for heartburn management.
- Prescribe antacid treatment.
- Avoid H_2 receptor antagonists.
- Use a prokinetic agent if a motility disorder is likely.

Peptic ulcer disease

General features

- common: 10–20% incidence over a lifetime
- point prevalence of ulcer disease: 3–5%
- DU:GU = 4:1
- DUs common in men 3:1
- cumulative mortality of 10%
- risk factors
  —male sex
  —family history
  —smoking (cause and delayed healing)
  —stress
  —common in blood group O
  —NSAIDs 2–4 times increase in GU and ulcer complications
  —*Helicobacter pylori*: if absent, no ulcer, but can be present in those without an ulcer. Now generally assummed to cause DUs.
- unproven risk factors
  —corticosteroids
  —alcohol
  —diet (does reduce recurrence of PU)
- types of ulcers
  —lower oesophageal
  —gastric
  —stomal (post gastric surgery)
  —duodenal

Clinical features

- episodic burning epigastric pain related to meals (1–2 hours after)
- relieved by food or antacids (generally)
- dyspepsia common
- may be 'silent' in elderly on NSAIDs
- physical examination often unhelpful (may be epigastric tenderness but a poor discriminating sign)

Investigations

- endoscopy (investigation of choice)[9]
  92% predictive value
- barium studies
  54% predictive value
- serum gastrin (consider if multiple ulcers)

Complications

- perforation
- bleeding → haematemesis and melaena
- obstruction—pyloric stenosis
- chronic (blood loss) anaemia
- carcinoma (in gastric ulcer)
- oesophageal stenosis

Management

Aims of treatment:

- relieve symptoms
- accelerate ulcer healing
- prevent complications
- minimise risk of relapse

Refer Figure 40.1.

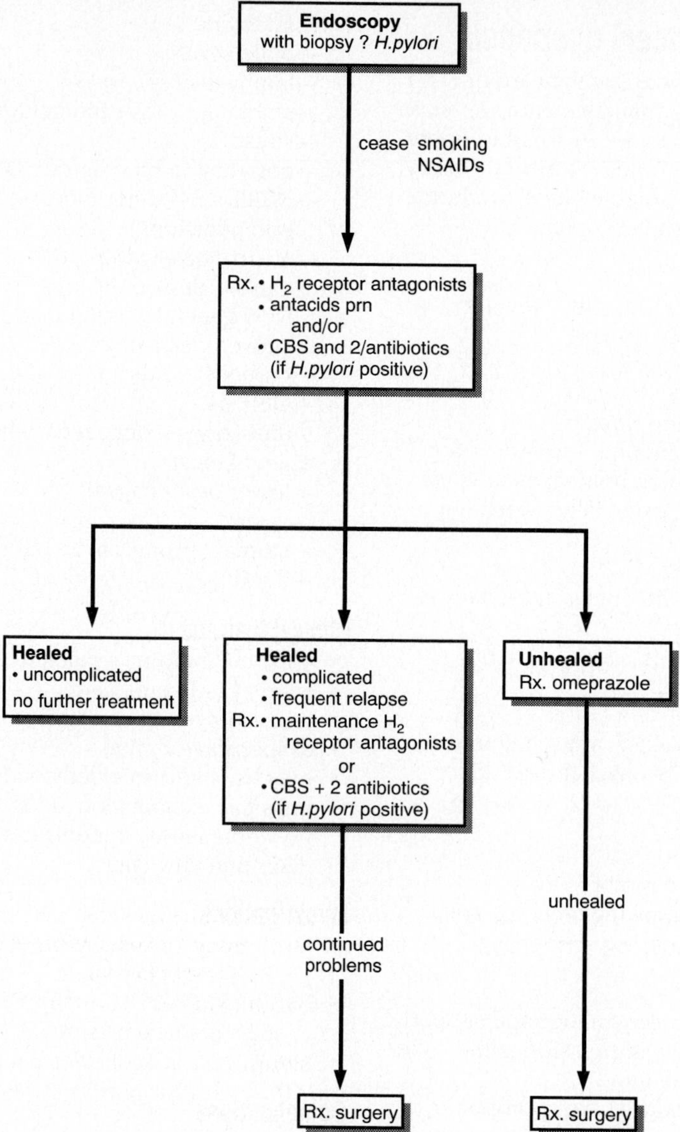

Fig. 40.1 *A recommended schemata for peptic ulcer management*

Stage 1: Treatment

General measures

- stop smoking
- avoid irritant drugs
  —NSAIDs
  —aspirin
- normal diet but avoid foods that upset
- antacids

H_2 receptor antagonists (first-line agent)

8 week oral course of
cimetidine 400 mg bd pc
or 800 mg nocte
or
ranitidine 150 mg bd pc
or
famotidine 40 mg nocte
or
nizatadine 300 mg nocte

Use with caution in:

- elderly
- those on drugs, especially warfarin, anticonvulsants, beta-blockers
- liver disease

Outcome[9,10]

DU: 80% healing rate
prone to spontaneous remissions and relapse
once healed
60% relapse within one year
20% persist but asymptomatic
GU: 50% do not recur
other 50% recurrence within 2 years

Note: Use maintenance or continuous treatment for two or more exacerbations in 12 months.

Stage 2: Pharmacological agents

The following can be used for ulcers not responding to an H_2 receptor antagonist, for frequent relapses or complicated ulcers.

Proton pump blocker

omeprazole 20 mg cap (o) mane for 4–8 weeks

- used for resistant ulcers
- 100% inhibition of acid
- high healing rates

Cytoprotective agents

sucralfate 1 g tab (o) qid, 1 hour ac and nocte

Prostaglandin analogue

misoprostol 800 μg daily (divided doses))

Colloidal bismuth subcitrate (CBS)

bismuth subcitrate (De-Nol)
2 tabs (chewed) bd

- effective for relapsing ulcers
- appears to be effective against *H. pylori*

Helicobacter pylori-induced gastroduodenitis

This organism has been linked with peptic ulcer disease because of mucosal infection. This hypothesis is supported by a very low relapse of DU in subjects eradicated of *H. pylori*.

Treatment

CBS
+
2 antibiotics: tetracycline or amoxycillin
+ metronidazole

Surgical treatment

Indications include:

- failed medical treatment after 1 year
- complications
  —uncontrollable bleeding
  —perforation
  —pyloric stenosis
- suspicion of malignancy in gastric ulcer
- recurrent ulcer after previous surgery

NSAIDs and peptic ulcers

1. Ulcer identified in NSAID user:
   - stop NSAID (if possible)
   - check smoking and alcohol use
   - try alternative anti-inflammatory analgesic
     e.g. paracetamol
     enteric-coated, slow-release aspirin
     corticosteroids I/A or oral
   - H_2 receptor antagonist (full dose)
     or
     misoprostol 800 mg a day (used for GU)

   Note: Healing time doubled if NSAID continued[3]. About 90% heal within 12 weeks. Check healing by endoscopy at 12 weeks.
2. Prevention of ulcers in NSAID user
   Try alternatives (as above). Prophylactic drugs are rarely justified but reasonable in those over 75 years and in those with a past history of peptic ulcer.
   misoprostol (prevents GU recurrence)
   H_2 receptor antagonist (prevents DU, not GU)
   Increased dietary fibre assists DU healing and prevention.

Carcinoma of stomach

Clinical features

- male: female 3:1
- usually asymptomatic early
- consider if upper GIT symptoms in patients >40, especially weight loss
- recent onset dyspepsia in middle age
- dyspepsia unresponsive to treatment
- vague fullness or epigastric distension
- anorexia, nausea, ± vomiting

- dysphagia—a late sign
- onset of anaemia
- changing dyspepsia in gastric ulcer
- changing symptoms in pernicious anaemia

Limited physical findings

- palpable abdominal mass (20%)
- signs (Fig. 40.2) in advanced cases

Investigations

- endoscopy and biopsy is optimal test
- barium meal—false negatives

Treatment

- surgical excision

When to refer

- Infants with persistent gastro-oesophageal reflux not responding to simple measures.
- Failure to respond to stage 1 therapy for heartburn, when endoscopy is required.
- Patients with persistent or recurrent ulcers.
- Any patient with a peptic ulcer complication such as haemorrhage, obstruction or perforation.

Practice tips

- Scleroderma is a rare but important cause of oesophagitis.
- Advise patients never to 'dry swallow' medications.
- Dysphagia always warrants investigation, not observation.
- Beware of attributing anaemia to oesophagitis.
- Epigastric pain aggravated by any food, relieved by acids = chronic gastric ulcer.
- Epigastric pain before meals, relieved by food = chronic duodenal ulcer
- Keep in mind the malignant potential of a gastric ulcer.
- A change in nature of symptoms with a gastric ulcer suggests the possibility of malignant change.

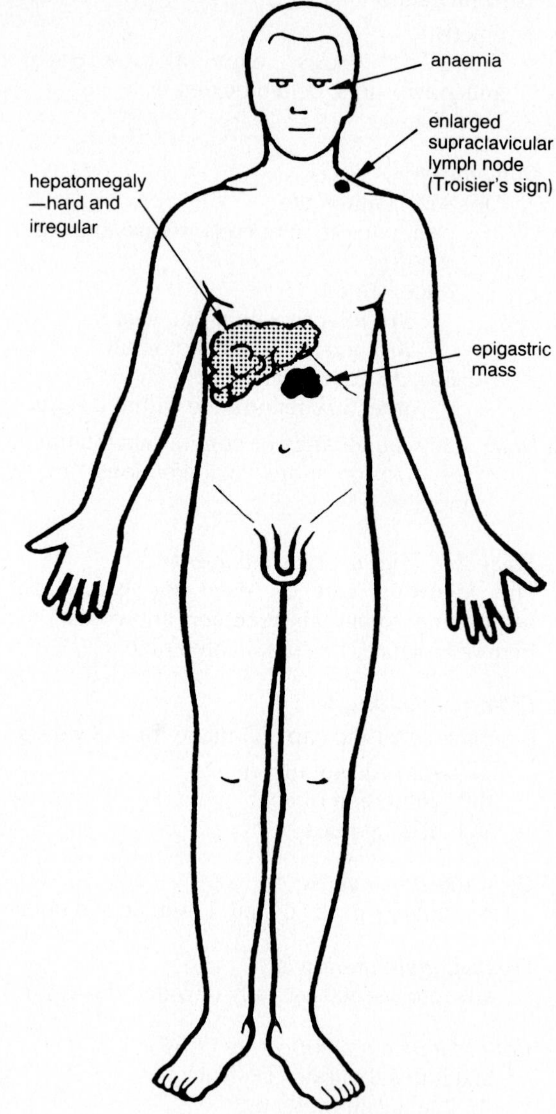

Fig. 40.2 *Late signs of carcinoma of the stomach*

- Avoid the long-term use of water-soluble antacids.
- Investigate the alarm symptoms—dysphagia, bleeding, anaemia, weight loss, waking at night, pain radiating to the back.

References

1. Smallwood R. Dyspepsia. Medical Observer, 27 September, 1991:33–34.
2. Holvey DN. *The Merck manual* (12th edition). Rahway: Merck Sharp & Dohme, 1975, 679–682.
3. Pritchard P. The management of upper gastrointestinal problems in patients taking NSAIDs. Aust Fam Physician, 1991; 20:1739–1741.
4. Kincaid-Smith P, Larkins R, Whelan G. *Problems in clinical medicine*. Sydney: MacLennan and Petty, 1989, 207–212.
5. Sandler G, Fry J. *Early clinical diagnosis*. Lancaster: MTP press, 1986, 99–135.
6. Sewell J. Gastro-oesophageal reflux. The Australian Paediatric Review, 1991, 3:2.
7. Hansky J. Gastro-oesophageal reflux. In: MIMS Disease Index. Sydney: IMS Publishing, 1991–2:195–197.
8. Bolin T et al. *Heartburn*. Sydney: The GUT Foundation booklet, 1988.
9. Korman M, Sievert W. Peptic ulcers. In: MIMS Disease Index. Sydney: IMS Publishing, 1991–2, 413–415.
10. Sandler G. *Common medical problems*. London: ADIS, 1984, 139–176.

41

Dyspnoea

Dyspnoea is the subjective sensation of breathlessness that is excessive for any given level of physical activity. It is a cardinal symptom affecting the cardiopulmonary system and can be very difficult to evaluate. Appropriate breathlessness following activities such as running to catch a bus or climbing several flights of stairs is not abnormal but may be excessive due to obesity or lack of fitness.

Key facts and checkpoints

- Determination of the underlying cause of dyspnoea in a given patient is absolutely essential for effective management.
- The main causes of dyspnoea are lung disease, heart disease, obesity and functional hyperventilation.[1]
- The most common cause of dyspnoea encountered in family practice is airflow obstruction, which is the basic abnormality seen in chronic asthma and chronic obstructive airways disease (COAD).[2]
- Wheezing, which is a continuous musical or whistling noise, is an indication of airflow obstruction.
- Some patients with asthma do not wheeze and some patients who wheeze do not have asthma.
- Other important pulmonary causes include restrictive disease such as fibrosis, collapse and pleural effusion.
- Dyspnoea is not inevitable in lung cancer but occurs in about 60% of cases.[3]

Terminology

It is important to emphasise that dyspnoea or breathlessness is a subjective sensation of the desire for increased respiratory effort and must be considered in relation to the patient's lifestyle and individual tolerance of discomfort. It also depends on the age, physical fitness and physical expectations of the person. Patients may complain of tightness in the chest and this must be differentiated from angina.

The New York Heart Association functional and therapeutic classification applied to dyspnoea:

Grade 1	No breathlessness
Grade 2	Breathlessness on severe exertion
Grade 3	Breathlessness on mild exertion
Grade 4	Breathlessness at rest

Orthopnoea is breathlessness lying down flat.

Paroxysmal nocturnal dyspnoea is inappropriate breathlessness causing waking from sleep.

Tachypnoea is an increased rate of breathing.

Hyperpnoea is an increased level of ventilation, e.g. during exertion.

Hyperventilation is overbreathing.

Difference between heart and lung causes

The distinguishing features between dyspnoea due to heart disease and to lung disease are presented in Table 41.1. The history is a good indication and a useful guideline is that dyspnoea at rest is typical of lung disease, especially asthma, while it tends to be present on effort with heart disease as well as with COAD.

Table 41.1 *Comparison of distinguishing features between dyspnoea due to heart disease and to lung disease (after Sandler[1])*

Lung disease	*Heart disease*
History of respiratory disease	History of hypertension, cardiac ischaemia or valvular heart disease
Slow development	Rapid development
Present at rest	Mainly on exertion
Productive cough common	Cough uncommon, and then 'dry'
Aggravated by respiratory infection	Usually unaffected by respiratory infection

Wheezing

Wheezing is any continuous musical expiratory noise heard with the stethoscope or otherwise. Wheeze includes stridor, which is an inspiratory wheeze.

Common causes of wheezing

Localised:

- partial bronchial obstruction
  e.g.— impacted foreign body
  — impacted mucus plugs
  — extrinsic compression

Generalised:

- asthma
- obstructive bronchitis

'Cardiac asthma' and bronchial asthma

The term 'cardiac asthma' is used to describe a wheezing sensation such as that experienced with paroxysmal nocturnal dyspnoea. Differentiating features are presented in Table 41.2.

A diagnostic approach

A summary of the diagnostic strategy model is presented in Table 41.3.

Probability diagnosis

The common causes of dyspnoea are lung disease, heart disease, obesity, anaemia (tissue hypoxia) and functional hyperventilation. More specifically, bronchial asthma, COAD, acute pulmonary infections and left heart failure (often insidious) are common individual causes.

Serious disorders not to be missed

Severe cardiovascular events such as acute heart failure which may be precipitated by myocardial infarction (may be silent especially in diabetics), a life-threatening arrhythmia, pulmonary embolism, dissecting aneurysm or a cardiomyopathy (such as viral myocarditis) require early diagnosis and corrective action. Recurrent pulmonary embolism may present a diagnostic problem. There may be a history of deep venous thrombosis, pregnancy, malignancy or taking the contraceptive pill.[4]

Severe infections such as lobar pneumonia, tuberculosis and myocarditis must be

Table 41.2 *Comparison of distinguishing features between 'cardiac asthma' and bronchial asthma (after Sandler[1])*

	Cardiac	*Bronchial*
Dyspnoea	Mainly inspiratory	Mainly expiratory
Cough	Follows dyspnoea	Precedes dyspnoea
Sputum	Pink and frothy	Thick and gelantinous
Relief	Standing up (by an open window) Intravenous diuretic/morphine	Coughing up sputum Bronchodilator
Lung signs	Mainly crackles	Mainly wheezes

Table 41.3 *Dyspnoea: diagnostic strategy model*

Q. Probability diagnosis
A. Bronchial asthma
Left heart failure
COAD
Obesity

Q. Serious disorders not to be missed
A. Cardiovascular
- acute heart failure, e.g. AMI
- pulmonary embolism
- dissecting aneurysm
- cardiomyopathy
- pericardial tamponade
- cardiac tamponade

Neoplasia
- bronchial carcinoma

Severe infections
- pneumonia
- acute epiglottitis (children)

Respiratory disorders
- inhaled foreign body
- upper airways obstruction
- pneumothorax
- atelectasis

Neuromuscular disease
- infective polyneuritis
- poliomyelitis

Q. Pitfalls (often missed)
A. Fibrosing alveolitis
Extrinsic allergic alveolitis
Chemical pneumonitis
Metabolic acidosis
Radiotherapy
Renal failure (uraemia)
Multiple small pulmonary emboli

Q. Seven masquerades checklist

A.		
	Depression	✓
	Diabetes	✓
	Drugs	✓
	Anaemia	✓
	Thyroid disease	✓
	Spinal dysfunction	(ankylosing spondylitis)
	UTI	–

Q. Is the patient trying to tell me something?
A. Consider functional hyperventilation (anxiety and panic attacks).

considered. In children acute epiglottitis, croup, pneumonia and bronchitis are serious infections responsible for respiratory distress.

Primary carcinoma is an important consideration especially in dyspnoea of gradual onset. Other malignant conditions to consider are metastases, lymphangitis carcinomatosis, lymphomas and pleural mesothelioma. Pleural effusion may be the mode of presentation of some of these serious disorders.

Pitfalls

Interstitial pulmonary disease can be a diagnostic dilemma because the physical signs and X-ray appearances can be minimal in the early stages despite the presence of significant dyspnoea. Allergic alveolitis, such as that caused by birds (e.g. hypersensitivity to their droppings), can be a pitfall. The diagnosis is easier if a known disease associated with pulmonary infiltration, such as sarcoidosis, is present. Measuring the diffusing capacity will help with diagnosis.

Pericardial tamponade may cause difficulty in diagnosis either with an acute onset, such as malignancy involving pericardium, or insidiously. The patient usually has a weak pulse with pulsus paradoxus, hypotension and a raised jugular venous pressure.

Seven masquerades checklist

Most of the masquerades have to be considered as underlying causes. Depression can be associated with dyspnoea, anaemia is an important cause of dyspnoea, thyrotoxicosis can present with dyspnoea, and diabetic ketoacidosis can cause rapid deep breathing.

Drugs must also be considered, especially as a cause of interstitial pulmonary fibrosis which presents with dyspnoea, cough and fever. Drugs which cause this disorder include several cytotoxic agents (especially bleomycin, cyclophosphamide, methotrexate), amiodarone, sulfasalazine, penicillamine, nitrofurantoin, gold salts and adrenergic nasal sprays.[3] Poisons that may cause hyperventilation are salicylate, methyl alcohol, theophylline overdosage and ethylene glycol. Anaemia must be considered especially in those at risk. Dyspnoea is unlikely to be caused solely by chronic anaemia unless the haemoglobin is less that 8 g/dL.[4] It is more likely to occur if another predisposing cause such as ischaemic heart disease is present.

Psychogenic considerations

Functional dyspnoea or hyperventilation is common. However, it is important to exclude organic causation such as asthma, drugs and thyrotoxicosis before settling with the psychogenic label and to reassure the patient strongly if there is no organic cause. Any uncomfortable sensation in the chest may be interpreted as dyspnoea by anxious patients. Depression, anxiety and panic attacks may be underlying the problem. Characteristic associated features of hyperventilation with anxiety include dizziness, faintness, palpitations, yawning, paraesthesia of the hands and legs, inability to take a deep breath or a sensation of smothering. These patients may exhibit sighing and irregular breathing on examination. In true psychogenic dyspnoea, chest X-rays and pulmonary function tests are normal but symptoms are often reproduced after 15–30 seconds of voluntary hyperventilation. It is important to remember that it may be present in a patient who has organic disease of a mild degree such as asthma.

Table 41.4 *Typical causes of dyspnoea related to time of onset*

Sudden
- lung collapse
- inhaled foreign body
- spontaneous pneumothorax
- pulmonary embolism

Rapid (over a few hours)
- asthma
- diabetic ketoacidosis
- extrinsic allergic alveolitis
- high altitude
- left heart failure (acute pulmonary oedema)
- pericardial tamponade
- poisons

Over days or weeks
- congestive heart failure
- pleural effusion
- carcinoma of the bronchus/trachea

Over months or years
- COAD
- tuberculosis
- fibrosing alveolitis
- pneumoconiosis

Non-respiratory causes
- anaemia
- hyperthyroidism
- obesity

The clinical approach

History

Special attention should be paid to evaluating exactly what the patient means by breathlessness or restriction of breathing. The analysis should then include provoking factors and associated symptoms with a view to differentiating between pulmonary causes such as asthma and COAD. Wheeze is often (but not always) present in asthma and chronic airflow obstruction. Most respiratory causes of dyspnoea also produce cough. The rate of development of dyspnoea gives an indication of the possible cause (Table 41.4).[5] The sudden onset of dyspnoea at rest is suggestive of pulmonary embolism or pneumothorax. Severe dyspnoea developing over one or two hours is most likely due to left heart failure or bronchial asthma. Bronchial asthma is usually easily distinguished from left heart failure by the history of previous attacks, by the absence of chest pain and the absence of cardiac murmurs. 'My breathing feels tight' indicates asthma. A complaint of 'suffocation, or feeling smothered' or 'just not getting enough air' may be a pointer to functional dyspnoea.

The dyspnoea of asthma tends to occur at rest and at night while that with chronic airflow obstruction occurs with exertion.

Examination

The routine findings from inspection, percussion and auscultation will determine whether the underlying lung disease is localised or generalised. The generalised findings for various disorders of the lungs are summarised in Table 41.5. Careful inspection is mandatory. The patient should be stripped to the waist and observed for factors such as cyanosis, clubbing, mental alertness, dyspnoea at rest, use of accessory muscles, rib retraction and any other abnormalities of the chest wall. A coarse tremor or flap of the outstretched hands indicates CO_2 intoxication.[5] To obtain maximum value from auscultation request the patient to open his/her mouth and take deep breaths. Adventitious sounds which are not audible during tidal breathing may then be heard. Wheezes are high-pitched continuous sounds heard either in expiration or inspiration, being more pronounced in expiration.

Crackles are short interrupted sounds heard mainly at the end of inspiration, resembling the crackling sound of hair being rubbed between the fingers near the ear. Fine crackles, previously referred to as crepitations, occur typically in lobar pneumonia and diffuse interstitial fibrosis, and are not cleared by coughing. Medium crackles are typical of congestive cardiac failure and coarse crackles indicate airway mucus and usually clear on coughing.

Investigations

The two most important initial investigations for respiratory disease are chest X-ray and respiratory function tests.

Table 41.5 *Comparison of examination findings for various lung disorders*

	Trachea	***Chest wall movement***	***Percussion note***	***Breath sounds***	***Vocal fremitus***	***Adventitious sounds***
Normal	Midline	Equal expansion	Resonant	Vesicular	Normal	Nil: ± few transient inspiratory basal crackles
Asthma	Midline	Decreased (bilateral)	Resonant	Vesicular—prolonged expiration	Normal or decreased	Expiratory wheezes
Emphysema	Midline	Decreased (bilateral)	Resonant to hyper-resonant	Vesicular—decreased	Decreased	Nil or the crackles and wheezes of chronic bronchitis
Consolidation, e.g. lobar pneumonia	Midline	Decreased on affected side	Dull	Bronchial	Increased	Fine late inspiratory crackles
Collapse: major bronchus	Towards affected side	Decreased (unilateral)	Dull	Absent or decreased	Absent or decreased	Nil
Collapse: peripheral bronchus	Towards affected side	Decreased (unilateral)	Dull	Bronchial	Increased	Coarse crackles
Pleural effusion > 500 ml	Towards opposite side (if massive)	Decreased (unilateral)	Stony dull	Absent or decreased	Absent or decreased	None
Pneumothorax (large)	Towards opposite side (if tension)	Decreased (unilateral)	Hyperresonant	Absent or decreased	Absent or decreased	None
Fibrosis (generalised)	Midline	Decreased (bilateral)	Normal	Vesicular	Increased	Fine crackles
Bronchiectasis	Midline	Slight decrease	Resonant to dull	Bronchial	Normal or decreased	Coarse crackles ± localised wheeze

Respiratory function tests

These relatively simple tests provide considerable information.

Peak expiratory flow rate

The most practical instrument for office use to detect chronic airway obstruction due to asthma or chronic bronchitis is the mini peak flow meter which measures peak expiratory flow rate (PEFR).

The interpretation of the tests, which vary according to sex, age and height, requires charts of predicted normal values. A chart for PEFR in normal adult subjects is presented in Appendix V. The value for a particular patient should be the best of three results.

Spirometry

The measurement of the forced vital capacity (FVC) and the forced expiratory volume in one second (FEV_1) will provide a very useful guide to the type of ventilatory deficit. Both the FVC and the FEV_1 are related to sex, age and height.

The FEV_1 expressed as a percentage of the FVC is an excellent measure of airflow limitation. In normal subjects it is approximately 70%. Figure 41.1 summarises the relative values for these conditions.

Lung volume

Tidal volume and vital capacity can be measured by a simple spirometer but the total lung capacity and the residual volume are measured by the

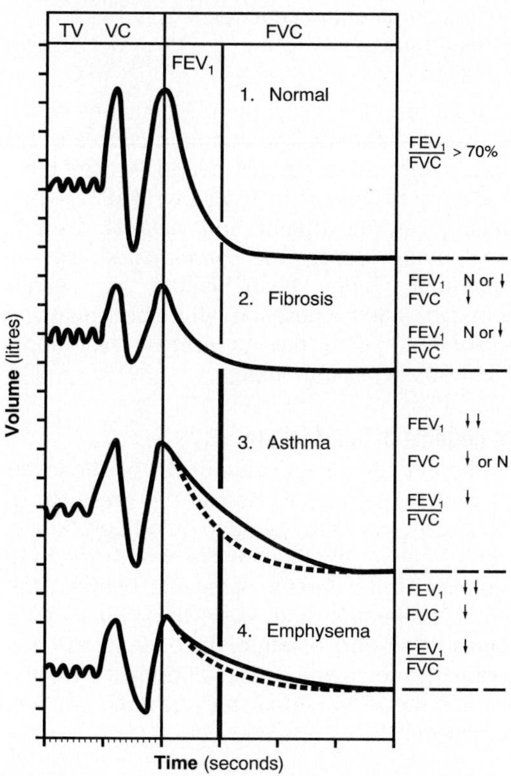

Fig. 41.1 *Spirometry patterns for respiratory disorders*

helium dilution method in a respiratory laboratory.

Gas transfer factor

This test measures the carbon monoxide uptake by a single breath analysis for whole lungs. In normal lungs the transfer factor is a true measure of the diffusing capacity of the lungs for oxygen and depends on the thickness of the alveolar-capillary membrane.[5] Gas transfer is usually reduced in patients with severe degrees of emphysema and fibrosis, anaemia and congestive cardiac failure.

Histamine challenge test

This test indicates the presence of airway or bronchial hyper-reactivity which is a fundamental feature with asthma. The test should not be performed on those with poor lung function and only performed by a respiratory technician under medical supervision. The test is potentially dangerous.

Other investigations (to select from)

- Haemoglobin, red cell indices and PCV
- White blood cell count, e.g. eosinophilia of asthma
- ESR
- Arterial blood gas analysis
- Oximetry: pulse oximeters monitor oxygen saturation
- Cardiological investigations
  - ECG including exercise
  - echocardiography (technically difficult in emphysema)
  - nuclear gated blood pool scan to assess heart function
  - cardiac enzymes
- Other medical imaging
  - high resolution computerised tomography
  - magnetic resonance imaging
  - ventilation and perfusion radionuclide scan (pulmonary embolism)
- Bronchoscopy, especially fiberoptic bronchoscopy
- Thoracocentesis and pleural biopsy
- Bronchoalveolar lavage
- Open lung biopsy

Dyspnoea in children

There are numerous causes of dyspnoea in children but the common causes are asthma and pulmonary infections. The important infections that can be fatal—croup, epiglottitis and myocarditis—must be kept in mind and intensively managed.

Sudden breathlessness or stridor may be due to an inhaled foreign body. Signs of lobar collapse may be present but physical examination may be of little help and a chest X-ray is essential.

Cardiovascular disorders including congenital heart disease can cause dyspnoea. Extra respiratory causes include anaemia, acidosis, aspiration, poisoning and hyperventilation.

Dyspnoea in the elderly

Dyspnoea in the elderly is common and is caused usually by heart failure and COAD. The other associations with ageing such as carcinoma of the lungs, pulmonary fibrosis and drugs are relevant. The classic problem of the aged is acute heart failure which develops typically in the early morning hours. The acute brain syndrome is a common presentation of all these disorders.

Respiratory disease in the elderly

The respiratory system, like most other bodily systems, matures until about the age of 25 years and subsequently slowly loses efficiency due to a variety of factors such as disease, smoking, pollution and ageing. There is a decline in lung function and gas exchange and decreased ventilatory responses to hypoxia and hypercapnia.

Heart failure

Heart failure occurs when the heart is unable to maintain sufficient cardiac output to meet the demands of the body. Dyspnoea is a common early symptom as pulmonary congestion causes hypoxia (increased ventilation) and decreased compliance (increased work). The incidence of congestive cardiac failure (CCF) has been increasing steeply, partly due to the ageing population.

Symptoms

- increasing dyspnoea
  progressing to (in order)
- fatigue, especially exertional fatigue
- paroxysmal nocturnal dyspnoea
- weight change: gain or loss

It is convenient to divide heart failure into left and right heart failure but they rarely occur in isolation and often occur simultaneously. Right failure is invariably secondary to left failure. Furthermore some cardiologists stress the importance of differentiating between systolic and diastolic dysfunction. Both present in the same way clinically and hence referral for cardiac studies to obtain measurement of the left ventricular function. This permits an accurate diagnosis and guide to treatment, and an accurate prognosis.

Signs

It is helpful clinically to differentiate between the signs of right and left heart failure.

Left heart failure

- tachycardia
- low volume pulse
- tachypnoea
- bilateral basal crackles
- gallop rhythm
- pleural effusion
- poor peripheral perfusion

Right heart failure

- elevated venous pressure
- peripheral/ankle oedema
- hepatomegaly
- ascites

Heart failure may cause pleural effusions which are usually bilateral. The common causes of left heart failure are ischaemic heart disease (there is often a history of at least one AMI), hypertension, cardiomyopathy and valvular disease. Many acute cases are precipitated by an arrhythmia. Right heart failure is usually secondary to left ventricular failure but can occur in isolation when due to primary respiratory conditions (cor pulmonale).

The oedema of heart failure

Peripheral oedema appears initially on the lower legs and is 'pitting'. To assess the presence of pitting, which is usually graded on a 4 point scale, press firmly yet gently with the thumb for 5–10 seconds over the dorsum of the feet, behind each medial malleolus and over the shins. With increasing severity of failure the oedema extends proximally to involve the abdomen. In the recumbent position it may only be apparent over the sacrum.[7]

Investigations

Investigations for heart failure include:

- renal function tests
- serum electrolytes
- full blood count
- chest X-ray
- ECG
- serum digoxin (if appropriate)
- echocardiogram
- nuclear gated blood pool scan

Left ventricular function should be measured by echocardiography or nuclear gated blood pool scanning to determine the ejection fraction, which is usually very low in heart failure.[6] Echocardiography also provides objective information on the size and function of the cardiac chambers.

Determining severity of heart failure

The severity of heart failure can be considered from three different perspectives: the severity of the symptoms, the degree of impairment of cardiac function and the severity of the congestive state. The severity of the symptoms or the degree of functional disability is usually described according to the New York Heart Association criteria (Table 41.6). The left ventricular ejection fraction provides an indication of cardiac function.

Table 41.6 *New York Heart Association classification of functional disability in heart failure*

Class I	No limitation; cardiac disease present, but ordinary physical activity. Causes no symptoms such as fatigue, breathlessness or palpitation, or rapid forceful breathing.
Class II	Slight limitation; ordinary activity causes symptoms but patients comfortable at rest.
Class III	Marked limitation; symptoms with less than ordinary physical activity although patients still comfortable at rest.
Class IV	Unable to carry on any activity without symptoms; may have symptoms at rest.

Treatment of heart failure

The treatment of heart failure includes appropriate patient education, determination and treatment of the cause, removal of any precipitating factors, general non-pharmaceutical measures and drug treatment.

Prevention of heart failure

The emphasis on prevention is very important since the onset of heart failure is generally associated with a very poor prognosis. Approximately 50% of patients with severe heart failure die within two years of diagnosis.[8]

The scope for prevention includes the following measures.[9]

- dietary advice, e.g. achievement of ideal weight
- emphasising the dangers of smoking and excessive alcohol
- control of hypertension
- control of other risk factors such as hypercholesterolaemia
- early detection and control of diabetes mellitus
- early intervention in myocardial infarction to preserve myocardial function, e.g. thrombolytic therapy
- secondary prevention after the occurrence of myocardial infarction, e.g. beta-blockers and aspirin
- appropriate timing of surgery or angioplasty for ischaemic or valvular heart disease

Treatment of causes and precipitating factors

Determination of and treatment of the causes has been largely covered in the section on prevention. Precipitating factors that should be treated include:

- arrhythmias, e.g. atrial fibrillation
- electrolyte imbalance, especially hypokalaemia
- anaemia
- myocardial ischaemia, especially myocardial infarction
- dietary factors, e.g. malnutrition, excessive salt or alcohol
- adverse drug reactions, e.g. fluid retention with NSAIDs
- infection, e.g. bronchopneumonia, endocarditis
- thyrotoxicosis
- lack of compliance with therapy

General non-pharmacological management

- reduction in physical activity: rest if symptoms severe; moderate activity when symptoms are absent or mild
- weight reduction, if patient obese
- salt restriction: advise no-added-salt diet (60–100 mmol/day)
- water restriction: water intake should be limited to 1.5L/day or less in patients with advanced heart failure, especially when the serum sodium falls below 130 mmol/day[8]
- fluid aspiration if a pleural effusion or pericardial effusion is present

Drug therapy of heart failure

Any identified underlying factor should be treated. Initial drug therapy should consist of a diuretic. Loop diuretics such as frusemide are preferred for acute episodes although other diuretics may be used for long-term maintenance therapy.

Atrial fibrillation should be treated with digoxin. Vasodilators are widely used for heart failure and ACE inhibitors are currently the most favoured vasodilator.

NB: Monitor and maintain potassium level in all patients.

Initial therapy of heart failure

1. Diuretic[9]
   frusemide 40 mg (o) once or twice daily
   or
   chlorothiazide 500 mg (o) daily
   or
   hydrochlorothiazide 25 mg (o) daily

2. Add ACE inhibitor
Dosage of ACE inhibitor: Commence with ¼ to ½ lowest recommended therapeutic dose and then adjust it for the individual patient by gradually increasing it to the maintenance dose (Table 41.7).

Table 41.7 *ACE inhibitors in common usage*

	Initial daily dose	*Maintenance daily dose*
Captopril	6.25 mg (o) nocte	25 mg (o) tds
Enalapril	2.5 mg (o) nocte	10 mg (o) bd
Lisinopril	2.5 mg (o) nocte	5-20 mg (o) nocte

ACE inhibitors

- Some authorities promote ACE inhibitors as the drugs of first choice because they correct neuroendocrine abnormalities and reduce cardiac load by their vasodilator action.
- In practice the usual initial treatment of heart failure is a diuretic plus an ACE inhibitor. This optimises response and improves diuretic safety.
- The first dose should be given at bedtime to prevent orthostatic hypotension.
- Potassium-sparing diuretics or supplements should not be given with ACE inhibitors because of the danger of hyperkalaemia.
- Renal function and potassium levels should be monitored in all patients.

Heart failure (unresponsive to first-line therapy)

frusemide 40 (o) bd
\+
ACE inhibitor
\+
digoxin (if not already taking it)[9]
0.5–0.75 mg (o) statim
then 0.5 mg (o) 4 hours later
then 0.5 mg the following day
then individualise maintenance
If still uncontrolled consider other vasodilators:
isosorbide nitrate
or
hydralazine

Consider cardiac transplantation for appropriate patients with end-stage heart failure, e.g. patients under 50 with no other major disease.

A flow chart for the basic management of heart failure is presented in Figure 41.2.

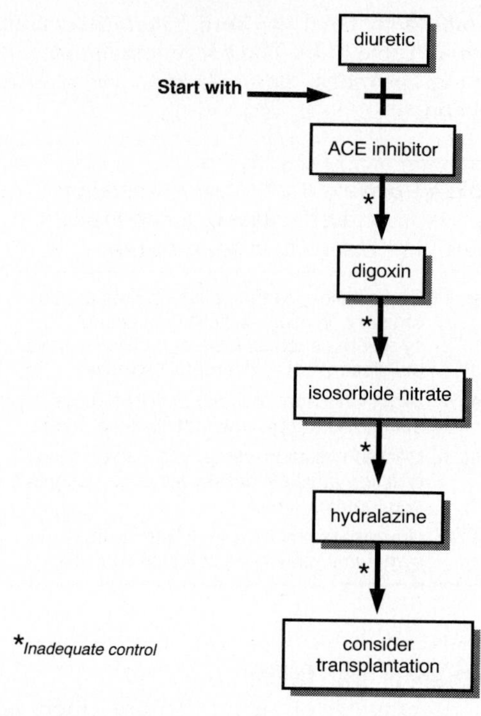

Fig. 41.2 *A management approach for heart failure*

Pitfalls in management

- The most common treatment error is excessive use of diuretics.[5]
- Giving an excessive loading dose of ACE inhibitor.
- Failure to correct remedial causes or precipitating factors.
- Failure to measure left ventricular function.

Acute severe heart failure

For the treatment of acute pulmonary oedema refer to page 983 under emergency care.

Chronic obstructive airways disease

Chronic bronchitis and emphysema should be considered together as both these conditions usually coexist to some degree in each patient. An alternative, and preferable, term—chronic obstructive airway or pulmonary disease (COAD)—is used to cover chronic bronchitis and emphysema with chronic airflow limitation.

Chronic bronchitis is a clinical condition characterised by a productive cough on most days for at least three months of the year for at least two consecutive years in the absence of any other respiratory disease that could be responsible for such excessive sputum production (such as tuberculosis or bronchiectasis).

Emphysema is defined in pathological rather than clinical terms, as permanent dilatation and destruction of lung tissue distal to the terminal bronchioles.

Chronic airflow limitation is a physiological process measured as impairment of forced expiratory flow and is the major cause of dyspnoea in these patients.

Cigarette smoking is undoubtedly the major cause of both chronic bronchitis and emphysema although only 10–15% of smokers develop the diseases.[11]

Factors in causation

- cigarette smoking
- air pollution
- airway infection
- familial factors
- $alpha_1$ antitrypsin deficiency (emphysema)

Clinical features

Symptoms

- onset in 5th or 6th decade
- excessive cough
- sputum production (chronic bronchitis)
- dyspnoea (chronic airflow limitation)
- wheeze (chronic bronchitis)
- susceptibility to colds

Signs

The signs vary according to the nature of the disease and the presence of infection. Signs may be completely absent in the early stages of emphysema and there may be only wheezing with chronic bronchitis and dyspnoea with chronic airflow limitation.

Signs may include:

- tachypnoea
- reduced chest expansion
- hyperinflated lungs
- hyper-resonant percussion
- diminished breath sounds
- 'pink puffer'—always breathless
- 'blue bloater'—oedematous and central cyanosis
- signs of respiratory failure
- signs of cor pulmonale

The diagnosis is usually clinical with a history of increasing dyspnoea and sputum production in a life-time smoker. It is unwise to make a diagnosis of chronic bronchitis and emphysema in the absence of cigarette smoking unless there is a family history suggestive of $alpha_1$ antitrypsin deficiency.[6]

Investigations

Chest X-ray: can be normal (even with advanced disease) but characteristic changes occur late in disease.

Pulmonary function tests:

- peak expiratory flow rate—low with minimal response to bronchodilator
- ratio FEV_1/FVC—reduced with minimal response to bronchodilator
- gas transfer coefficient of CO is low if significant emphysema

Blood gases:

- may be normal
- $Pa\ CO_2 \uparrow$; $PaO_2 \downarrow$ (advanced disease)

ECG: may show evidence of cor pulmonale.

Haemoglobin and PCV may be raised.

Management

Advice to the patient

- If you smoke, you must stop (persuading the patient to stop smoking is the key to management).
- Avoid places with polluted air and other irritants, such as smoke, paint fumes and fine dust.
- Go for walks in clean, fresh air.
- A warm dry climate is preferable to a cold damp place (if prone to infections).
- Get adequate rest.
- Avoid contact with people who have colds and flu.

Physiotherapy

Refer to a physiotherapist for chest physiotherapy, breathing exercises and an aerobic physical exercise program.

Drug therapy

Consider the use of bronchodilators, e.g. inhaled β_2 agonists and ipratropium bromide and corticosteroids, because of associated (often unsuspected) asthma. A carefully monitored trial of these drugs with a peak flow meter is recommended.

Antibiotics: The prompt use of antibiotics for acute episodes of infection is important to help prevent further lung damage. Patients should be instructed to commence antibiotics (a supply should be kept at home) as soon as they develop an infection and notice their sputum turn yellow or green.

The antibiotics of choice are:
amoxycillin 500 mg (o) tds
or
cefaclor 500 mg (o) tds
or
doxycycline 100 mg (o) daily

A sputum micro and culture may help to identify those patients with organisms resistant to antibiotics.

Other treatment

- Annual influenza vaccine
- Consider home oxygen therapy for advanced cases with persistent hypoxia at rest.

Interstitial lung diseases

Interstitial lung diseases comprise a group of disorders that have the common features of inflammation and fibrosis of the interalveolar septum, representing a non-specific reaction of the lung to injury of various causes.[11]

Causes of pulmonary infiltration include:

- sarcoidosis
- fibrosing alveolitis
- extrinsic allergic alveolitis
- lymphangitis carcinomatosis

Common clinical features:

- dyspnoea and dry cough (insidious onset)
- fine inspiratory crackles at lung base
- finger clubbing
- PFTs: restrictive ventilatory deficit
  decrease in gas transfer factor
- characteristic X-ray changes

Sarcoidosis

Sarcoidosis is a multisystemic disorder of unknown aetiology characterised by non-caseating granulomatous inflammation that involves the lung in about 90% of affected patients. A characteristic feature is bilateral hilar lymphadenopathy which is often symptomless and detected on routine CXR. Radiological lung involvement can be associated with or occur independently of hilar lymphadenopathy.

Clinical features:

- may be asymptomatic (one-third)
- onset usually 3rd or 4th decade (but any age)
- bilateral hilar lymphadenopathy (on CXR)
- cough
- fever, malaise, arthralgia
- erythema nodosum
- ocular lesions, e.g. anterior uveitis
- other multiple organ lesions (uncommon)
- overall mortality 2–5%

Erythema nodosum with acute fever, malaise and arthralgia in a young adult female is diagnostic of sarcoidosis.

Diagnosis

Histological evidence from biopsy specimen, usually transbronchial biopsy (essential if an alternative diagnosis, e.g. lymphoma, cannot be excluded) or skin biopsy in cases of erythema nodosum.

Supporting evidence:

- elevated serum ACE
- PFTs: restrictive pattern. Impaired gas transfusion in advanced cases.
- +ve Kveim test (not recommended these days)

Treatment

Sarcoidosis may resolve spontaneously (hilar lymphadenopathy without lung involvement does not require treatment).

Indications for treatment with corticosteroids:

- no spontaneous improvement after 6 months
- symptomatic pulmonary lesions
- eye, CNS and other systems involvement
- hypercalcaemia, hypercalcuria
- erythema nodosum with arthralgia
- persistent cough

Corticosteroid treatment

Prednisolone 30 mg daily for 6 weeks, then reduce to lowest dose which maintains improvement.[6]

Prednisolone 20–30 mg for 2 weeks for erythema nodosum of sarcoidosis.

Fibrosing alveolitis

Cryptogenic fibrosing alveolitis (idiopathic pulmonary fibrosis) is the most common diagnosis among patients presenting with interstitial lung disease.

Patients usually present in the fifth to seventh decade with the clinical features as outlined under interstitial lung diseases. CXR abnormalities are variable but include bilateral diffuse nodular or reticulonodular shadowing favouring the lung bases. Open lung biopsy may be needed for diagnosis and staging. The usual treatment is high doses of oral corticosteroids with or without cyclophosphamide.

Extrinsic allergic alveolitis

This disease is characterised by a widespread diffuse inflammatory reaction in both the small airways of the lung and alveoli, due to the inhalation of allergens which are usually spores of micro-organisms such as *Micropolyspora faeni* in 'farmer's lung' or (more commonly) avian proteins from droppings or feathers in 'bird fancier's lung'. Occupational causes of extrinsic alveolitis have been described by Molina[12] (Table 41.8). Management is based on prevention, namely avoiding exposure to allergens or wearing protective fine mesh masks. Prednisolone can be used (with caution) to control acute symptoms. It should be pointed out that this allergic disease is different to the infection psittacosis.

Table 41.8 *Various causes of extrinsic allergic alveolitis*

Occupation/disease	*Source of antigen*
Farmer's lung	Mouldy hay, grain and straw
Bagassosis	Mouldy sugar cane fibre (bagasse)
Bird fancier's lung	Dropping dust, e.g. pigeons, budgerigars 'bloom' on feathers
Mushroom workers	Mushroom compost
Cheese washer's lung	Moulds or mites on cheese
Wheat weevil lung	Infested wheat flour (insect)
Ventilator pneumonitis	Humidified hot air system Air-conditioning system
Wool pulp worker's disease	Contaminated wood dust
Detergent worker's disease	Proteolytic enzymes
Suberosis	Mouldy cork bark
Rat handler's lung	Rat urine and serum
Malt worker's lung	Mouldy barley
Coffee worker's lung	Coffee dust
Sisal worker's lung	Sisal dust
Sericultural workers	Silkworms
Furrier's lung	Fur dust
Sausage workers	Dust
Prawn workers	Prawn fumes

Occupational pulmonary disease

Various types of acute and chronic pulmonary diseases are related to exposure to noxious substances such as dusts, gases and vapours in the workplace.

Disorders due to chemical agents include:

- obstructive airways disorders, e.g. occupational asthma, acute bronchitis, (chronic) industrial bronchitis, byssinnosis (asthma-like condition due to cotton dust)
- extrinsic allergic alveolitis
- pulmonary fibrosis (pneumoconiosis) due to mineral dust
- lung cancer due to industrial agents such as asbestos, various hydrocarbons
- pleural diseases, usually associated with asbestosis

Pneumoconiosis

The term pneumoconiosis refers to the accumulation of dust in the lungs and the reaction of tissue to its presence, namely chronic fibrosis. The main cause worldwide is inhalation of coal dust, a specific severe variety being progressive massive fibrosis (complicated coal worker's pneumoconiosis) in which the patient suffers severe dyspnoea of effort and cough often productive of black sputum. Table 41.9 summarises the important causes.

Of particular concern are diseases caused by inhalation of fibres of asbestos which is a mixture of silicates of iron, magnesium, cadmium, nickel and aluminium. The diseases include asbestosis, diffuse pleural thickening, pleural plaques, mesothelioma and increased bronchial carcinoma in smokers. It usually takes 20 to 40 years from exposure for mesothelioma to develop while bronchial carcinoma is caused by the synergistic effects of asbestosis and cigarette smoking.

Bronchial carcinoma

Dyspnoea is associated with about 60% of cases of lung cancer.[3] It is not a common early symptom unless bronchial occlusion causes extrinsic collapse. In advanced cancer, whether primary or secondary, direct spread or metastases may cause dyspnoea. Other factors include—pleural effusion, lobar collapse, metastatic infiltration, upper airway obstruction due to SVC obstruction and lymphangitis carcinomatosis. A special problem arises with coexisting chronic bronchitis and emphysema.

Table 41.9 *Selected pneumoconioses*

Fibrotic lung disease	*Agent*	*Typical occupations*
Coal dust		
Coal worker's pneumoconiosis	Coal dust	Coal mining
Metal dust		
Siderosis	Metallic iron or iron oxide	Mining Welding Foundry work
Inorganic dusts		
Silicosis	Silica (silicon dioxide)	Quarrying Rock mining Stone cutting Sandblasting
Silicate dusts		
Asbestosis	Asbestos	Mining Shipbuilding Insulation Power stations Wharf labouring

When to refer

- Patients with acute onset of severe dyspnoea.
- All patients with heart failure resistant to initial therapy or where the diagnosis is in doubt.
- Patients with pulmonary disease of uncertain aetiology, especially those requiring respiratory function tests.
- Those in whom carcinoma of the lung is suspected.

Practice tips

- Remember to order a chest X-ray and pulmonary function tests in all doubtful cases of dyspnoea.
- All heart diseases have dyspnoea as a common early symptom.
- Increasing dyspnoea on exertion may be the earliest symptom of incipient heart failure.
- Several drugs can produce a wide variety of respiratory disorders, particularly pulmonary fibrosis and pulmonary eosinophilia. Amiodarone and cytotoxic drugs, especially bleomycin, are the main causes.
- Dyspnoea in the presence of lung cancer may be caused by many factors such as pleural effusion, lobar collapse, upper airway obstruction and lymphangitis carcinomatosis.
- The abrupt onset of severe dyspnoea suggests pneumothorax or pulmonary embolism.
- If a patient develops a relapse of dyspnoea while on digoxin therapy, consider the real possibility of digoxin toxicity and/or electrolyte abnormalities leading to left heart failure.
- Recurrent attacks of sudden dyspnoea, especially waking the patient at night, are suggestive of asthma or left heart failure.
- Causes of hyperventilation include drugs, asthma, thyrotoxicosis and panic attacks/anxiety.

References

1. Sandler G. *Common medical problems.* London: ADIS Press, 1984, 31–56.
2. Cormack J, Marinker M, Morrell D. *Practice: A handbook of primary health care.* London. Kluwer-Harrap Handbooks, 1980; 3:29.03.
3. Walsh TD. *Symptom control.* Boston: Blackwell Scientific Publications, 1989, 157–164.
4. Beck ER, Francis JL, Souhami RL. *Tutorials in differential diagnosis* (2nd edition). Edinburgh: Churchill Livingstone, 1988, 37.
5. Kelly DT. Cardiac failure. In: MIMS Disease Index. Sydney: IMS Publishing, 1991-2, 103–106.
6. Kumer PJ, Clark ML. *Clinical medicine* (2nd edition). London: Bailliere Tindall, 1990, 637–690.
7. Davis A, Bolin T, Ham J. *Symptom analysis and physical diagnosis* (2nd edition). Sydney: Pergamon Press, 1990, 173.
8. Kumer PJ, Clark ML. *Clinical medicine* (2nd edition). London: Bailliere Tindall, 1990, 562.
9. Moulds RFW. *Cardiovascular drug guidelines.* Melbourne: Victoria Medical Postgraduate Foundation, 1991, 55–61.
10. DiBianco R. An update and practical management approach to the management of heart failure. Aust Fam Physician, 1993.
11. Schroeder SA et al. *Current medical diagnosis and treatment.* East Norwalk: Appleton and Lange, 1990, 162–205.
12. Molina C. Occupational extrinsic allergic alveolitis. In: J Pepys, ed. *Clinics in immunology and allergy.* London: WB Saunders, 1984, 173–190.

42

The painful ear

Pain in the ear (otalgia) is a common symptom in general practice. It affects all ages, but is most prevalent in children, where otitis media is the commonest cause. Ear pain may be caused by disorders of the ear or may arise from other structures, and in many instances the precise diagnosis is difficult to make. Important causes of ear pain are summarised in Table 42.1.[1]

A patient with a painful ear often requests urgent attention, and calls in the middle of the night from anxious parents of a screaming child are commonplace. Infants may present with nothing except malaise, vomiting or screaming attacks.

Table 42.1 *Causes of ear pain*

1. Ear
    - ***External ear***
    - Perichondritis
    - Otitis externa:
        - Candida albicans
        - Aspergillus nigra
        - Pseudomonas pyocyanoea
        - Staphylococcus aureus
    - Furunculosis
    - Trauma
    - Neoplasia
    - Herpes zoster (Ramsay Hunt syndrome)
    - Viral myringitis
    - Wax
    - ***Middle ear***
    - Acute eustachian insufficiency
    - Barotrauma
    - Acute otitis media
    - Chronic otitis media and cholesteatoma
    - Acute mastoiditis
2. Periotic cause
    - Dental disorders
    - Upper cervical spinal dysfunction
    - Temporomandibular joint arthralgia
    - Parotitis
    - Temporal arteritis
    - Lymph node inflammation
    - ***Other referred causes***
    - Pharyngeal disorders
    - Tonsillitis

Key facts and checkpoints

- 77% of patients presenting with earache can be expected to have acute otitis media and 12% otitis externa.[2]
- Approximately 1 of every 25 patients in general practice will present with an earache.
- Two-thirds of children will sustain at least one episode of otitis media by their second birthday; one in seven children will have had more than six episodes by this age.[3]
- Otitis media is unlikely to be present if the tympanic membrane is mobile. Pneumatic otoscopy greatly assists diagnosis since the most valuable sign of otitis media is absent or diminished motility of the tympanic membrane (TM).
- Bullous myringitis, which causes haemorrhagic blistering of the eardrum or external ear canal, is an uncommon cause of severe pain. It is caused by a virus, probably influenza.[4]
- The antibiotic of first choice for acute otitis media (children and adults) is amoxycillin.

A diagnostic approach

Using the safe diagnostic approach model (Table 42.2) the five self-posed questions can be answered as follows.

Table 42.2 *The painful ear: diagnostic strategy model*

Q.	*Probability diagnosis*
A.	Oitis media (viral or bacterial) Otitis externa TMJ arthralgia
Q.	*Serious disorders not to be missed*
A.	Neoplasia of external ear Carcinoma of other sites, e.g. tongue, throat Herpes zoster (Ramsay Hunt syndrome) Acute mastoiditis Cholesteatoma
Q.	*Pitfalls (often missed)*
A.	Foreign bodies in ear Hard ear wax Barotrauma Unerupted wisdom tooth and other dental causes TMJ arthralgia Facial neuralgias Post tonsillectomy • from the wound • from TMJ due to mouth gag
Q.	*Seven masquerades checklist*
A.	Depression ✓ Diabetes — Drugs — Anaemia — Thyroid disease — Urinary infection — Spinal dysfunction ✓
Q.	*Is the patient trying to tell me something?*
A.	Unlikely, but always possible with pain. More likely in children.

Probability diagnosis

The commonest cause of ear pain is acute otitis media. Chronic otitis media and otitis externa are also common. In the tropics, 'tropical ear' due to acute bacterial otitis is a particular problem. TMJ arthralgia, which may be acute or chronic, is also common and must be considered, especially when otitis media and otitis externa are excluded.

Serious disorders not to be missed

As always, it is important not to overlook malignant diseases, especially the obscure ones such as carcinoma of the tongue, palate or tonsils that cause referred pain.

Locally destructive cholesteatoma associated with chronic otitis media must be searched for. It signifies the 'unsafe' ear (Fig. 42.1) that must be distinguished from the so-called 'safe' ear (Fig. 42.2).

Herpes zoster should be considered, especially if it does not erupt on the pinna and is confined to the ear canal (usually the posterior wall), and especially in the older person.

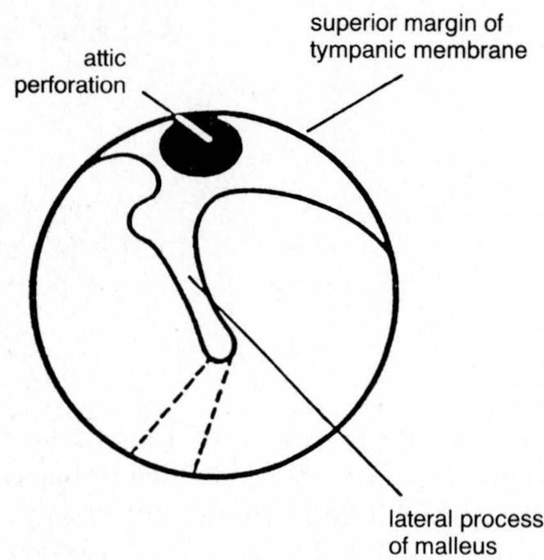

Fig. 42.1 *Infected ear: unsafe perforation*

Fig. 42.2 *Infected ear: safe perforation*

Pitfalls

The medical aphorism 'more things are missed by not looking than by not knowing' applies particularly to the painful ear—good illumination and focusing the auroscope are mandatory. Particular attention should be paid to the external canal—look for hard wax, otitis externa, furuncles and foreign objects such as insects.

It may not be possible to visualise the tympanic membrane, so it is important to clean the canal to permit this (if possible, on the first visit). Otitis media may coexist with otitis externa. Barotrauma should be considered, especially if pain follows air travel or diving.

General pitfalls

- Failing to visualise the tympanic membrane before diagnosis and treatment.
- Not checking out possible referral sites such as the oropharynx and teeth.
- Overlooking common musculoskeletal causes such as TMJ arthralgia and cervical spondylosis.
- Failing to recognise the unsafe ear.

Seven masquerades checklist

Of the conditions in the checklist, depression and dysfunction of the upper cervical spine have to be considered. Depressive illnesses should be considered in any patient complaining of chronic pain.

Disorders of the upper cervical spine are a commonly overlooked cause of periotic pain. Pain from the C2 and C3 levels are referred to the posterior region of the ear.

Psychogenic considerations

Such factors are unlikely, unless the pain causes discomfort in the periotic region, which is likely to be magnified by a depressive state.

The clinical approach

History

In assessing the painful ear the relevant features are:

- site of pain and radiation
- details of the onset of pain
- nature of the pain
- aggravating or relieving factors, especially swimming
- associated features such as deafness, discharge, vertigo, tinnitus and irritation of the external ear

Agonising pain may be caused by perichondritis or furunculosis of the external ear and by the rare problem of herpes zoster (Ramsay Hunt syndrome). Movement of the pinna increases markedly the pain of acute otitis externa and perichondritis, and movement of the jaw usually causes an exacerbation of temporomandibular joint (TMJ) arthralgia or severe otitis externa.

Key questions (especially children)

Where is the pain?
Is it in the ear, behind or below it?
Is it in one ear or both ears?
Have you noticed any other symptoms such as sore throat, fever or vomiting?
Has there been a discharge from the ear?
Have you noticed any deafness?
Are you allergic to penicillin?
Have you been swimming and where?

Physical examination

The patient's general state and behaviour is observed during the history taking. Sudden, jabbing pain may indicate neuralgia or a severe infection. The external ear is carefully inspected and the pinna manipulated to determine any tenderness.

Palpate the face and neck and include the parotid glands, regional lymph nodes and the skin. Inspect the TMJs—tenderness from dysfunction typically lies immediately in front of the external auditory meatus. Palpate the TMJ over the lateral aspect at the joint disc. Ask the patient to open the mouth fully when tenderness is maximal. The TMJ can be palpated posteriorly by inserting the little finger into the external canal.

Inspect both ear canals and tympanic membranes with the auroscope using the largest earpiece that comfortably fits into the canal. Better visualisation of the tympanic membrane (TM) can be achieved by pulling the pinna back in young children and up and back in older children. If herpes zoster involves the facial nerve vesicles may be noted in and around the external auditory meatus (notably the posterior wall).

If the diagnosis is still doubtful look for causes of referred pain; inspect the cervical spine, the nose and postnasal space and the mouth, including the teeth, pharynx and larynx.

Pharyngeal and mandibular causes of periotic pain are summarised in Figures 42.3 and 42.4.

Inspect sites supplied by the nerves V2, IX, X, XI, C1, C2 and C3 to exclude other causes of referred pain.

Investigations

Investigations are seldom necessary. Hearing tests are essential, especially for children. Simple tests such as speech discrimination, hair rubbing and tuning fork tests can be used. Otherwise audiometry can be used. Audiometry combined with tympanometry and physical measurement of the volume of the ear canal can be performed in children, irrespective of age.

Swabs from discharge, especially to determine bacterial causes such as *Staphylococcus aureus* or *Pseudomonas pyocynaea* infection, may be necessary. However swabs are of no value if the TM is intact.

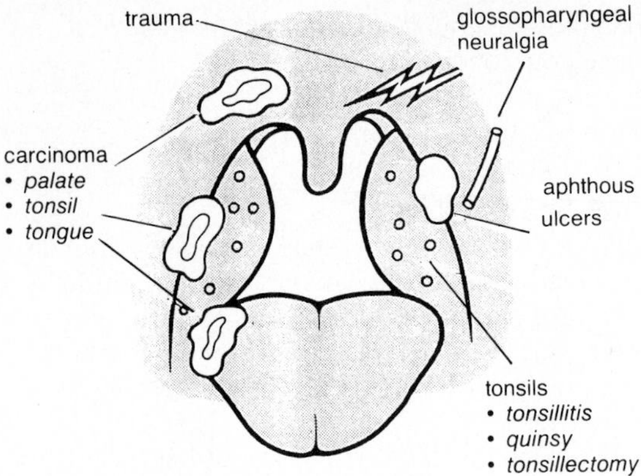

Fig. 42.3 *Pharangeal causes of otalgia* COURTESY OF R. BLACK

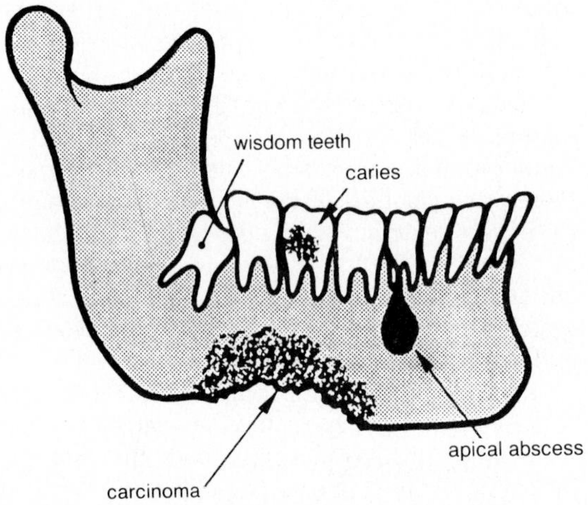

Fig. 42.4 *Mandibular causes of otalgia* COURTESY OF R. BLACK

Radiology and computerised tomography may be indicated for special conditions such as a suspected extraotic malignancy.

Ear pain in children

Important causes of primary otalgia in children include otitis media, otitis externa, external canal furuncle or abscess, chronic eczema with fissuring of the auricle, impacted wax, foreign body, barotrauma, perichondritis, mastoiditis and bullous myringitis. Secondary otalgia includes pharyngeal lesions, dental problems, gingivostomatitis, mumps and postauricular lymphadenopathy. Peritonsillar abscess (quinsy) may cause ear pain.

Foreign bodies

Foreign bodies are frequently inserted into the ear canal. They can usually be syringed out or lifted with thin forceps. Various improvised methods can be used to remove foreign bodies (FB) in co-operative children. These include a probe to roll out FB or a rubber catheter used as a form of suction or otherwise a fine sucker.[6]

Probe method

This requires good vision using a head mirror or head light and a thin probe. The probe is inserted under and just beyond the FB. Lever it in such a way that the tip of the probe 'rolls' the foreign body out of the obstructed passage (Figs 42.5a, b).

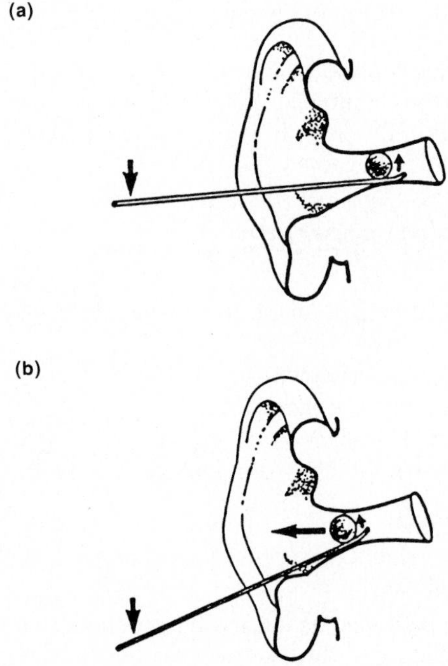

Fig. 42.5 *Probe method of removing a foreign body:* **(a)** *the tip of the probe is lifted by depressing the outer end of the probe;* **(b)** *continued gentle levering 'rolls' the foreign body out*

Rubber catheter suction method

The only equipment required for this relatively simple and painless method is a straight rubber catheter (large type) and perhaps a suction pump. The end of the catheter is cut at right angles, a thin smear of petroleum jelly applied to the rim and this end applied to the FB (Figs 42.6a, b). Suction is applied either orally or by a pump. Gentle pump suction is preferred but it is advisable to pinch closed the suction catheter until close to the FB as the hissing noise may frighten the child.

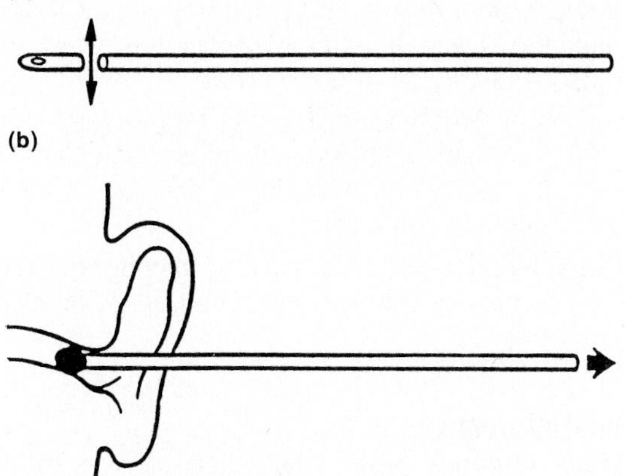

Fig. 42.6 *Extracting the foreign body using a rubber catheter:* **(a)** *catheter cut straight across near its extremity;* **(b)** *application of suction (orally or by pump)*

Insects in the ear

Live insects should be killed by first instilling olive oil, then syringing the ear with warm water (Figs 42.7a, b). Dead flies that have originally been attracted to pus are best removed by suction.

Note: If simple methods such as syringing fail to dislodge the FB it is important to refer for examination and removal under microscopic vision. Syringing should not be performed if there is a possibility of the FB perforating the tympanic membrane (TM).

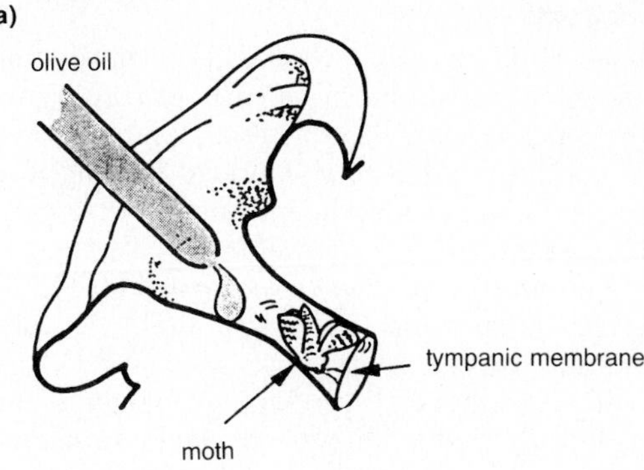

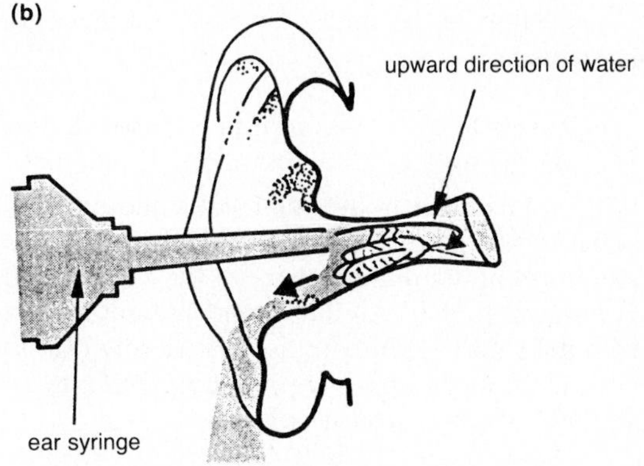

Fig. 42.7 *Insect in the ear:* **(a)** *first aid;* **(b)** *office procedure*

Otitis media in children

Otitis media is very common in children and is the most common reason a child is brought in for medical attention. Persistent middle ear effusions may follow and affect the language and cognitive development of young children.

Features

- Two peaks of incidence: 6–12 months of age and school entry.
- Seasonal incidence coincides with URTIs.
- Bacteria cause two-thirds of cases.[6]
- The two commonest organisms are *Streptococcus pneumoniae* and *Haemophilus influenzae*.
- Fever, irritability, otalgia and otorrhoea may be present.
- The main symptoms in older children are increasing earache and hearing loss.
- Pulling at the ears is a common sign in infants.
- Removal of wax is necessary in about 30% to visualise the TM.

Visualisation of the tympanic membrane

Use the largest ear speculum that will comfortably fit in the child's ear. A good technique to enable the examination of the ears (also nose and throat) in a reluctant child is where the child is held against the parent's chest while the parent's arm embraces the child's arm and trunk.

Note the following features of the TM: translucency, colour, position and motility.

Treatment

Many children with viral URTIs have mild reddening or dullness of the ear-drum and antibiotics are not warranted.[7] In contrast, where the ear-drum is red or yellow and bulging, with loss of anatomical landmarks, antibiotic therapy is indicated.

The antibiotic of choice is amoxycillin 40 mg/kg/day (maximum 1.5 g/day) orally in three divided doses for 10 days.

If B-lactamase producing bacteria are suspected or documented or initial treatment fails, use:

> cefalor 10 mg/kg/day (maximum 750 mg/day) orally in three divided doses for 10 days (cefalor is second choice irrespective of cause)
>
> or
>
> (if resistance to amoxycillin is suspected or proven) amoxycillin/potassium clavulanate

With appropriate treatment most children with acute otitis media are significantly improved within 48 hours. Parents should be encouraged to contact their doctor if no improvement occurs within 72 hours. This problem is usually due to a resistant organism or suppuration. The patient should be re-evaluated at 10 days.

Symptomatic treatment

Rest the patient in a warm room with adequate humidity. Use analgesics such as paracetamol (acetaminophen) in high dosage. Although the use of antihistamines and decongestants has not been verified scientifically, the author has found nasal decongestants (as oxymetazoline nasal drops or sprays) effective in distressed children with an associated URTI. Otherwise avoid antihistamines and decongestants.

Follow-up: adequate follow-up with hearing assessment is mandatory.

Complications

- Middle ear effusion: 70% of children will have an effusion present 2 weeks from the time of diagnosis, 40% at 4 weeks, with 10% having persistent effusions for 3 months or more. If the effusion is still present at 6–8 weeks, a second course of antibiotics should be prescribed.[2] If the effusion persists beyond 3 months refer for an ENT opinion.
- Acute mastoiditis: this is a major complication which presents with pain, swelling and tenderness developing behind the ear associated with a general deterioration in the condition of the child. Such a complication requires immediate referral.[8]
- Chronic otitis media.
- Rare complications include labyrinthitis, petrositis, facial paresis and intracranial abscess.

Recurrent acute otitis media

Prevention of AOM is indicated if it occurs more often than every other month or for three or more episodes in six months.

> Chemoprophylaxis (for about 4 months)
> amoxycillin twice daily (first choice)
> or
> cefalor twice daily

Consider pneumococcus vaccine in children over 18 months of age in combination with the antibiotic.

Viral infections

Most children with viral URTIs have mild reddening or dullness of the ear-drum and antibiotics are not warranted. If painful bullous otitis media is present, either prick the bulla with a sterile needle for pain relief, or instil dehydrating ear drops such as anhydrous glycerol.

Ear pain in the elderly

Causes of otalgia that mainly afflict the elderly include herpes zoster (Ramsay Hunt syndrome), temporomandibular joint arthralgia, temporal arteritis and neoplasia. It is especially important to search for evidence of malignancy.

Acute otitis media

Acute otitis media causes deep-seated ear pain, deafness and often systemic illness. The sequence of symptoms is a blocked ear feeling, pain and fever. Discharge may follow if the TM perforates, with relief of pain and fever.

The commonest organisms are viruses (adenovirus and enterovirus), and the bacteria *Haemophilus influenzae*, *Streptococcus pneumoniae*, *Branhamella* (previously *Neisseria*) *catarrhalis* and *B-haemolytic streptococci*.

The two cardinal features of diagnosis are inflammation and middle ear effusion.

Appearance of the tympanic membrane (all ages)

Translucency: If the middle ear structures are clearly visible through the drum, otitis media is unlikely.

Colour: The normal TM is a shiny pale-grey to brown: a yellow colour is suggestive of an effusion.

Diagnosis

The main diagnostic feature is the redness of the TM. The inflammatory process usually begins in the upper posterior quadrant and spreads peripherally and down the handle of the malleus (Fig. 42.8). The TM will be seen to be reddened and inflamed with engorgement of the vessels particularly along the handle of the malleus. The loss of light reflex follows and anatomical features then become difficult to recognise as the TM becomes oedematous. Bulging of the drum is a late sign. Blisters are often seen on the TM and this is thought to be due to a viral infection in the epidermal layers of the drum.

Treatment of acute otitis media (adults)

- Analgesics to relieve pain
- Adequate rest in a warm room
- Nasal decongestants for nasal congestion
- Antibiotics until resolution of all signs of infection
- Treat associated conditions, e.g. adenoid hypertrophy
- Follow-up: review and test hearing audiometrically

Antibiotic treatment

First choice:

amoxycillin 750 mg (o) bd for 5 days[7]

or

500 mg (o) tds for 5 days

Alternatives:

doxycycline 100 mg (o) bd for 5 days (daily for milder infections)

or

cefaclor 250 mg (o) tds for 5 days

or

(if resistance to amoxycillin is suspected or proven) amoxycillin/potassium clavulanate 500/125 mg (o) tds for 5 days (the most effective antibiotic).

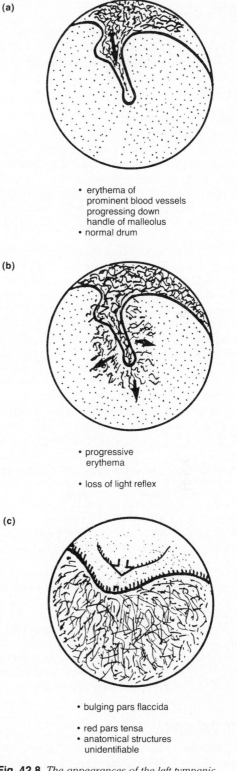

(a)

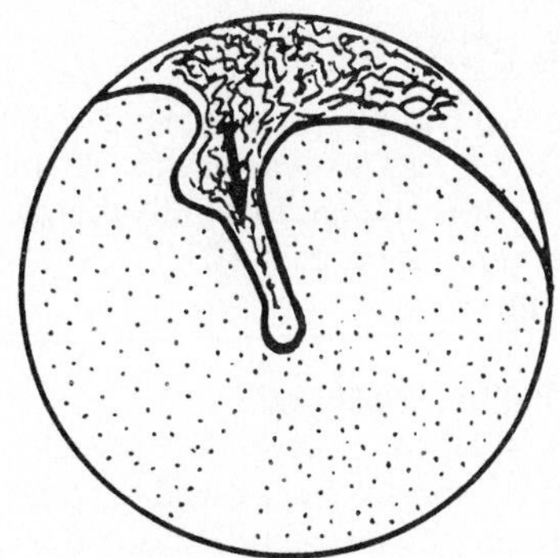

- erythema of prominent blood vessels progressing down handle of malleolus
- normal drum

(b)

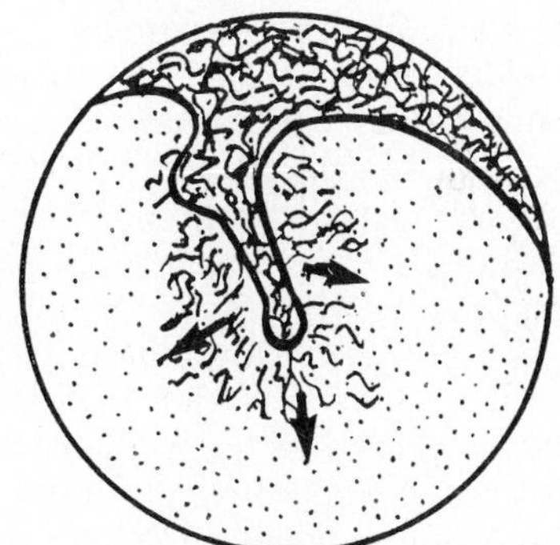

- progressive erythema
- loss of light reflex

(c)

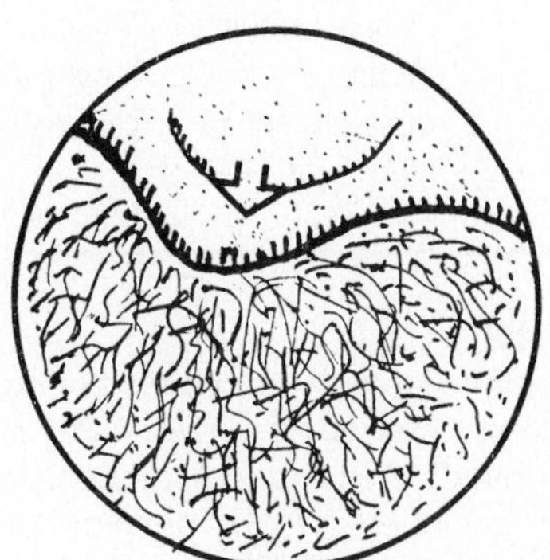

- bulging pars flaccida
- red pars tensa
- anatomical structures unidentifiable

Fig. 42.8 *The appearances of the left tympanic membrane in the progressive development of acute otitis media*

Chronic otitis media

There are two types of chronic suppurative otitis media and they both present with deafness and discharge without pain. The discharge occurs through a perforation in the TM: one is safe, the other unsafe.

Recognising the unsafe ear

Examination of an infected ear should include inspection of the attic region, the small area of drum between the lateral process of the malleus, and the roof of the external auditory canal immediately above it. A perforation here renders the ear 'unsafe' (Fig. 42.1); other perforations, not involving the drum margin (Fig. 42.2), are regarded as 'safe'.

The status of a perforation depends on the presence of accumulated squamous epithelium (termed cholesteatoma) in the middle ear, because this erodes bone. An attic perforation contains such material; safe perforations do not.

Cholesteatoma is visible through the hole as white flakes, unless it is obscured by discharge or a persistent overlying scab. Either type of perforation can lead to chronic infective discharge, the nature of which varies with its origin. Mucus admixture is recognised by its stretch and recoil when this discharge is being cleaned from the external auditory canal. The types of discharge are compared in Table 42.3.

Table 42.3 *Comparison of types of discharge*

	Unsafe	*Safe*
Source	Cholesteatoma	Mucosa
Odour	Foul	Inoffensive
Amount	Usually scant, never profuse	Can be profuse
Nature	Purulent	Mucopurulent

Management

If an attic perforation is recognised or suspected, specialist referral is essential. Cholesteatoma cannot be eradicated by medical means: surgical removal is necessary to prevent a serious infratemporal or intracranial complication.

Otitis externa

Otitis externa (Fig. 42.9), also known as 'swimmer's ear', 'surfer's ear' and 'tropical ear', is common in a country whose climate and coastal living leads to extensive water sport. It is more prevalent in hot humid conditions and therefore in the tropics.

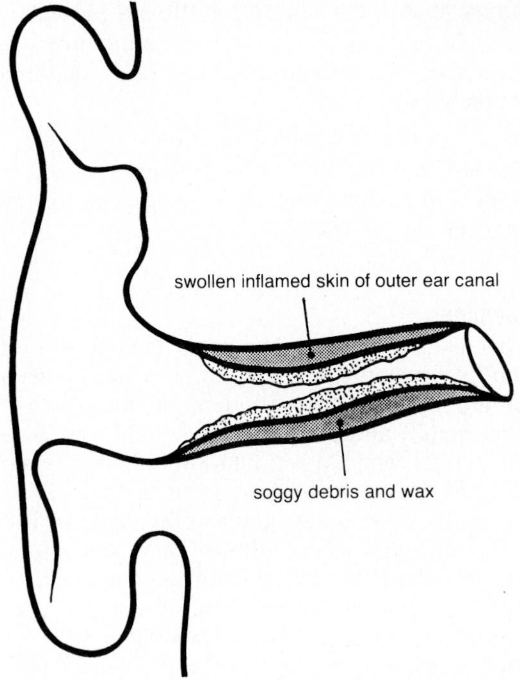

Fig. 42.9 *Otitis externa*

Predisposing factors are allergic skin conditions, ear canal trauma, water penetration (swimming, humidity, showering), water and debris retention (wax, dermatitis, exostoses), foreign bodies and contamination from swimming water.

Common responsible organisms

Bacteria: — *Pseudomonas sp.*
— *Escherichia coli*
— *Staphylococcus aureus*
— *Proteus sp.*
— *Klebsiella sp.*

Fungi: — *Candida albicans*
— *Aspergillus sp.*

Clinical features

- itching at first
- pain (mild to intense)
- fullness in ear canal
- scant discharge
- hearing loss

Signs

- oedema (mild to extensive)
- tenderness on moving auricle or jaw
- erythema
- discharge (offensive if coliform)
- pale cream 'wet blotting paper' debris—*Candida albicans*
- black spores of *Aspergillus niger*
- TM granular or dull red

Obtain culture, especially if resistant *Pseudomonas sp.* suspected, by using small ear swab.

Management

Aural toilet

Meticulous aural toilet by gentle suction and dry mopping with a wisp of cotton wool on a fine broach under good lighting is the keystone of management. This enables topical medication to be applied directly to the skin.

Syringing

This is appropriate in some cases but the canal must be dried meticulously afterwards. For most cases it is not recommended.

Dressings

Dressings are essential in all but the mildest forms. After cleaning and drying, insert 10–20 cm of 4 mm Nufold gauze impregnated with a steroid and antibiotic cream.

For severe otitis externa a wick is important and will reduce the oedema and pain in 12 to 24 hours (Fig. 42.10). The wick can be soaked in an astringent, e.g. aluminium acetate 4% solution or glycerine and 10% ichthamnol. The wick needs replacement daily until the swelling has subsided.

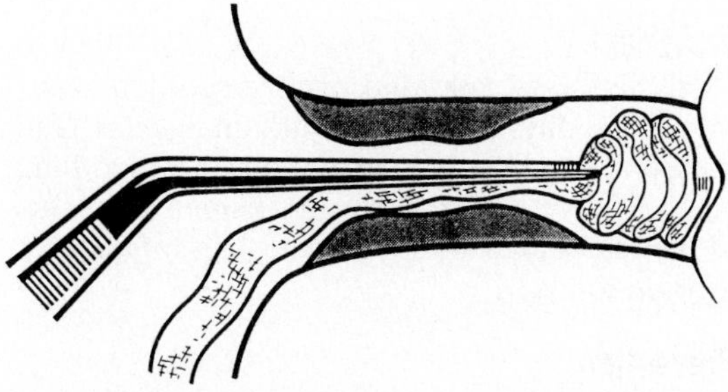

Fig. 42.10 *Insertion of a wick; it is packed gradually by short back-and-forth movements of the forceps* COURTESY OF R. BLACK

Topical antimicrobials

The most effective, especially when the canal is open, is an antibacterial, antifungal and corticosteroid preparation, e.g. Kenacomb or Sofradex drops or ointment.

Other measures

- Strong analgesics are essential.
- Antibiotics have little place in treatment unless a spreading cellulitis has developed.
- Prevent scratching and entry of water.

Practice tip for severe 'tropical ear'

- prednisolone (o) 15 mg statim then 10 mg 8 hourly for 6 doses

followed by

- Merocel ear wick
- topical Kenacomb or Sofradex drops

Prevention

- Keep the ear dry, especially those involved in water sports.
- Protect the ear with various water-proofing methods, e.g.:
  - — cotton wool coated with petroleum jelly
  - — tailor-made ear plugs, e.g. EAR foam plugs
  - — silicone putty or Blu-tack
  - — a bathing cap pulled well forward allows these plugs to stay in situ.
- Avoid poking objects such as hairpins and cotton buds in the ear to clean the canal.
- If water enters, shake it out or use Aquaear drops (spirit drops help dry the canal).

Furunculosis

Furunculosis is a staphylococcal infection of the hair follicle in the outer cartilaginous part of the ear canal. It is usually intensely painful. Fever occurs only when the infection spreads in front of the ear as cellulitis. The pinna is tender on movement—a sign that is not a feature of acute otitis media. The furuncle (boil) may be seen in the external auditory meatus (Fig. 42.11).

Management

- If pointing, it can be incised after a local anaesthetic or freezing spray.
- Warmth, e.g. hot face washer, hot water bottle.
- If fever with cellulitis—flucloxacillin.

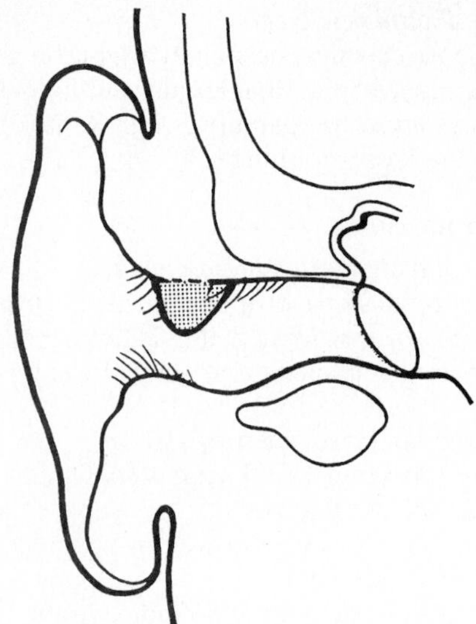

Fig. 42.11 *Furuncle (boil) in hair-bearing area at opening of the ear canal*

Perichondritis

Perichondritis is infection of the cartilage of the ear characterised by severe pain of the pinna which is red, swollen and exquisitely tender. It is rare and follows trauma or surgery to the ear. As the organism is frequently *Pseudomonas pyocyaneus* the appropriate antibiotics must be carefully chosen (e.g. ciprofloxacin).

Infected ear lobe

The cause is most likely a contact allergy to nickel in an ear-ring, complicated by a *Staphylococcus aureus* infection.

Management

- Discard the ear-rings.
- Clean the site to eliminate residual traces of nickel.
- Swab the site then commence antibiotics, e.g. flucloxacillin or erythromycin.
- Instruct the patient to clean the site daily, then apply the appropriate ointment.
- Use a 'noble metal' stud to keep the tract patent.
- Advise the use of only gold, silver or platinum studs in future.

Otic barotrauma

Barotrauma is damage caused by undergoing rapid changes in atmospheric pressure in the presence of an occluded eustachian tube (Fig. 42.12). It affects scuba divers and aircraft travellers. The symptoms include temporary or persisting pain, deafness, vertigo, tinnitus and perhaps discharge.

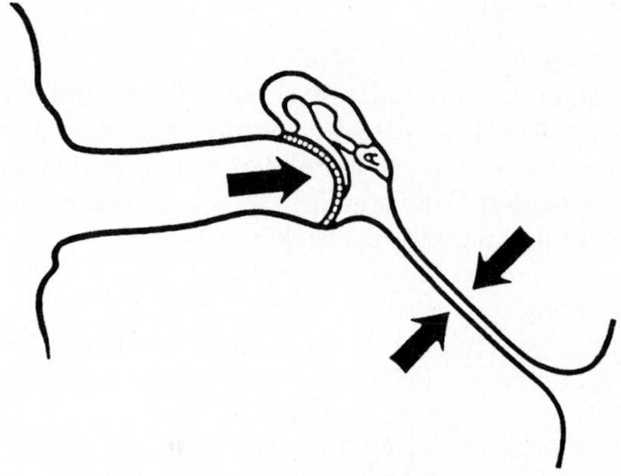

Fig. 42.12 *Mechanism of barotrauma, with blocking of the eustachian tube due to increased pressure at the sites indicated* COURTESY OF R. BLACK

Inspection of the TM may reveal (in order of seriousness): retraction; erythema; haemorrage (due to extravasation of blood into the layers of the TM); fluid or blood in the middle ear; perforation. Perform conductive hearing loss tests with tuning fork.

Treatment

Most cases are mild and resolve spontaneously in a few days, so treat with analgesics and reassurance. Menthol inhalations are soothing and effective. Refer if any persistent problems for consideration of the Politzer bag inflation or myringotomy.

Prevention

Flying: perform repeated Valsalva manoeuvres during descent. Use decongestant drops or sprays before boarding the aircraft, then 2 hours before descent.
Diving: those with nasal problems, otitis media or chronic tubal dysfunction should not dive.

Penetrating injury to tympanic membrane

A penetrating injury to the TM can occur in children and adults from various causes such as pencils and slivers of wood or glass. Bleeding invariably follows and infection is the danger.

Management

- Remove blood clot by suction toilet or gentle dry mopping.
- Ensure no foreign body is present.
- Check hearing.
- Prescribe a course of broad spectrum antibiotics, e.g. co-trimoxazole.
- Prescribe analgesics.
- Instruct patient not to let water enter ear.
- Review in two days and then regularly.
- At review in one month the drum should be virtually healed.
- Check hearing two months after injury.

Complete healing can be expected within eight weeks in 90–95% of such cases.[9]

Temporomandibular joint arthralgia

If rheumatoid arthritis is excluded, a set of special exercises, which may include 'chewing' a piece of soft wood over the molars, invariably solves this problem (Chap. 44). If an obvious dental occlusion is present, referral is necessary.

When to refer

Otitis media

- Incomplete resolution of acute otitis media.
- Persistent middle ear effusion for three months after an attack of acute otitis media.
- Persistent apparent or proved deafness.
- Evidence or suspicion of acute mastoiditis or other severe complications.
- Frequent recurrences, e.g. four attacks a year.
- Presence of craniofacial abnormalities.

Other ear problems

- Attic perforation/cholesteatoma.
- Foreign bodies in ear not removed by simple measures such as syringing.
- No response to treatment after two weeks for otitis externa.
- Suspicion of carcinoma of the ear canal.
- Acute tympanic membrane perforation that has not healed in six weeks.
- Chronic tympanic membrane perforation (involving lower two-thirds of TM).

Practice tips

- The pain of acute otitis media may be masked by fever in babies and young children.
- A red tympanic membrane is not always caused by otitis media. The blood vessels of the drum head may be engorged from crying, sneezing or nose blowing. In crying babies the TM as well as the face may be red.
- In otitis externa, if the ear canal is expanded then cleaned meticulously, most cases will resolve rapidly.
- If an adult presents with ear pain but normal auroscopy examine possible referral sites, namely TMJ, mouth, throat, teeth and cervical spine.
- Antibiotics have no place in the treatment of otic barotrauma.
- It is good medicine to make relief of distressing ear pain a priority. Adequate analgesics must be given. There is a tendency to give too low a dose of paracetamol in children. The installation of nasal drops in infants with a snuffy nose and acute otitis media can indirectly provide amazing relief of pain.
- Spirit ear drops APF are a cheap and simple agent to use for recurrent otitis externa where wetness of the ear canal is a persistent problem.

References

1. Black B. Otalgia. Aust Fam Physician, 1987; 16:292–296.
2. Shires DB, Hennen BK, Rice DI. *Family medicine* (2nd edition). New York: McGraw-Hill, 1987: 86–93.
3. Jarman R. Otitis media. Aust Paed Review, 1991; 4: 1–2.
4. Ludman H. *ABC of ear, nose and throat.* London: British Medical Journal, 1989, 3.
5. Sandler G, Fry J. *Early clinical diagnosis.* Lancaster: MTP Press, 1986, 285–287.
6. Murtagh J. *Practice tips.* Sydney: McGraw-Hill, 1991: 74–77.
7. Mashford L. *Antibiotic guidelines* (7th edition). Victorian Medical Postgraduate Foundation, 1992, 114–115.
8. Robinson MJ. *Practical paediatrics.* Melbourne: Churchill Livingstone, 1990, 607.
9. Kruger R, Black B. Penetrating injury eardrum. Aust Fam Physician, 1986; 15: 735.

43

The red and tender eye

A red eye accounts for at least 80% of patients with eye problems encountered in general practice.[1] An accurate history combined with a thorough examination will permit the diagnosis to be made in most cases without recourse to specialist ophthalmic equipment. A summary of the diagnostic strategy model is presented in Table 43.1.

Key facts and checkpoints

- Acute conjunctivitis accounts for over 25% of all eye complaints seen in general practice.[2]
- A purulent discharge indicates bacterial conjunctivitis.[3]
- A clear or mucous discharge indicates viral or allergic conjunctivitis.
- Viral conjunctivitis can be slow to resolve and may last for weeks.
- Pain and visual loss suggest a serious condition such as glaucoma, uveitis (including acute iritis) or corneal ulceration.
- Beware of the unilateral red eye—think beyond bacterial or allergic conjunctivitis. It is rarely conjunctivitis and may be a corneal ulcer, keratitis, foreign body, trauma, uveitis or acute glaucoma.[4]
- Keratitis (inflammation of the cornea) is one of the most common causes of an uncomfortable red eye. Apart from the well known viral causes (herpes simplex, herpes zoster, adenovirus and measles), it can be caused by fungal infection (usually on a damaged cornea), bacterial infection or inflammatory disease such as ankylosing spondylitis.[5]
- Herpes simplex keratitis (dendritic ulcer) often presents painlessly as the neurotrophic effect grossly diminishes sensation.

Table 43.1 *The red and tender eye: diagnostic strategy model*

Q. *Probability diagnosis*
A. Conjunctivitis
- bacterial
- adenovirus
- allergic

Q. *Serious disorders not to be missed*
A. Acute glaucoma
Uveitis
- acute iritis
- choroiditis

Corneal ulcer
Herpes simplex keratitis
Fungal keratitis
Herpes zoster ophthalmicus
Penetrating injury

Q. *Pitfalls (often missed)*
A. Scleritis/episcleritis
Foreign body
Trauma
Ultraviolet light 'keratitis'

Q. *Seven masquerades checklist*

A.	
Depression	-
Diabetes	-
Drugs	✓ hypersensitivity
Anaemia	-
Thyroid disease	✓ hyperthyroidism
Spinal dysfunction	-
UTI	-

Q. *Is the patient trying to tell me something?*
A. Unlikely.

The clinical approach

The five essentials of the history are:

- history of trauma (especially as indicator of IOFB)
- vision
- the degree and type of discomfort
- presence of discharge
- presence of photophobia

The social and occupational history is also very important. This includes a history of exposure to a 'red eye' at school, work or home; incidents at work such as injury, welding, foreign bodies or chemicals, and genitourinary symptoms.

When examining the unilateral red eye keep the following diagnoses in mind:

- trauma
- foreign body including IOFB
- corneal ulcer
- iritis (uveitis)
- viral conjunctivitis (commonest type)
- acute glaucoma

The manner of onset of the irritation often gives an indication of the cause. Conjunctivitis or uveitis generally has a gradual onset of redness, while a small foreign body will produce a very rapid hyperaemia. Photophobia occurs usually with uveitis and keratitis. It is vital to elicit careful information about visual acuity. The wearing of contact lenses is very important as these are prone to cause infection or the 'overwear syndrome' which resembles an acute ultraviolet burn.

Key questions

Have you noticed blurring of your vision?
Have you been in close contact with others with the same condition?
Have you had a cold or running nose recently?
Do you wear contact lenses?
Can you recall scratching or injuring your eye?
What were you doing at the time you noticed trouble?
Have you been putting any drops, ointments or cosmetics in or around your eye?
Do you suffer from hay fever?
Do you have any problems with your eyelids?
Had your eyes been watering for some time beforehand?
Have you had any other problems?
Have you been exposed to arc welding?

Physical examination

The basic equipment:

- eye testing charts at 18 inches (46 cm) and 10 feet (305 cm)
- multiple pin holes
- torch, e.g. Cobalt blue
- magnifying aid, e.g. binocular loupe
- glass rod or cotton bud to aid eyelid eversion
- fluorescein sterile paper strips
- anaesthetic drops
- Schiotz tonometer
- ophthalmoscope
- Ishihara's colour vision test

The four essentials of the examination are:

- testing and recording vision
- meticulous inspection under magnification
- testing the pupils
- testing ocular tension[4]

Also

- local anaesthetic test
- fluorescein staining
- subtarsal examination

Inspection

A thorough inspection is essential, noting the nature of the inflammatory injection, whether it is localised (episcleritis) or diffuse, viewing the iris for any irregularity, observing the cornea, and searching for foreign bodies, especially under the eyelids, and for any evidence of penetrating injury. No ocular examination is complete until the eyelid is everted and closely inspected. Both eyes must be examined since many patients presenting with conjunctivitis in one eye will have early signs of conjunctivitis in the other. Use fluorescein to help identify corneal ulceration. Local anaesthetic drops instilled prior to the examination of a painful lesion is recommended. The local anaesthetic test is a sensitive measure of a surface problem—if the pain is unrelieved a deeper problem must be suspected.

Palpate for enlarged preauricular lymph nodes, which are characteristic of viral conjunctivitis.

The nature of the injection is important. In conjunctivitis the vessels are clearly delineated and branch from the corners of the eye towards the cornea, since it involves mainly the tarsal plate. Episcleral and scleral vessels are larger than conjunctival vessels and are concentrated towards the cornea (Fig. 43.1). Ciliary injection appears as a red ring around the limbus of the cornea (the ciliary flush) and the individual vessels, which form a parallel arrangement, are not clearly visible. Ciliary injection may indicate a more serious deep-seated inflammatory condition such as anterior uveitis or a deep corneal infection. The presence of fine follicles on the tarsal conjuctivae indicates viral infection while a cobblestone appearance indicates allergic conjunctivitis.

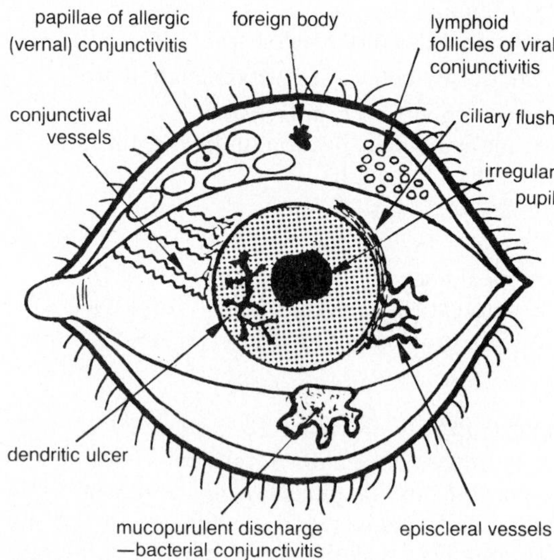

Fig. 43.1 *Physical signs to search for in a patient with a red eye (eyelids everted)*

Note: Slit lamp examination is ideal for the examination of the eye.

Red eye in children

Children can suffer from the various types of conjunctivitis (commonly), uveitis, and trauma. Of particular concern is orbital cellulitis which may present as a unilateral swollen lid and can rapidly lead to blindness if untreated. Bacterial, viral and allergic conjunctivitis are common in all children. Conjunctivitis in infants is a serious disorder because of the immaturity of tissues and defence mechanisms. Serious corneal damage and blindness can result.

Neonatal conjunctivitis (ophthalmia neonatorum)

This is conjunctivitis in an infant less than one month old and is a notifiable disease. Chlamydial and gonococcal infections are uncommon but must be considered if a purulent discharge is found in the first few days of life.[6] In both conditions the parents must be investigated for associated venereal disease and treated accordingly. Chlamydia trachomatis accounts for 50% or more of cases. Its presentation in neonates is acute, usually one to two weeks after delivery, with moderate mucopurulent discharge. It is a systemic disease and may be associated with pneumonia. The diagnosis is confirmed by serological tests on the conjunctival secretions.

Treatment is with oral erythromycin and local sulphacetamide eye drops.

Neisseria gonorrhoeae conjunctivitis, which usually occurs within one to two days of delivery, requires vigorous treatment with intravenous cephalosporins or penicillin and local sulphacetamide drops. The discharge is highly infectious and the organism has the potential for severe corneal infection or septicaemia.[6]

Other common bacterial organisms can cause neonatal conjunctivitis, and herpes simplex virus type II can cause conjunctivitis and/or eyelid vesicles or keratitis.[2]

Trachoma

Trachoma is a chlamydial conjunctivitis that is prevalent in outback areas and in the Aboriginal population. Chlamydia trachomatis is transmitted by human contact and by flies, especially where hygiene is inadequate. It is the most common cause of blindness in the world. Recurrent and untreated disease leads to lid scarring and inturned lashes with corneal ulceration and visual loss. It is important to commence control of the infection in childhood.

Blocked nasolacrimal duct

Delayed development of the nasolacrimal duct occurs in about 6% of infants[6], resulting in blocked lacrimal drainage; the lacrimal sac becomes infected, causing a persistent discharge from one or both eyes. In the majority of infants spontaneous resolution of the problem occurs by the age of six months.

Management

- local antibiotics for infective episodes
- bathing with normal saline
- frequent massage over the lacrimal sac
- referral for probing of the lacrimal passage before 6 months if the discharge is profuse and irritating or between 6 and 12 months if the problem has not self-corrected.

Red eye in the elderly

In an elderly patient there is an increased possibility of acute glaucoma, uveitis and herpes zoster. Acute angle closure glaucoma should be considered in any patient over the age of 50 presenting with an acutely painful red eye.

Eyelid conditions such as blepharitis, trichiasis, entropion and ectropion are more common in the elderly.

Acute conjunctivitis

Acute conjunctivitis is defined as an episode of conjunctival inflammation lasting less than three weeks.[2] The two major causes are infection (either bacterial or viral) and acute allergic or toxic reactions of the conjunctiva (see Table 43.2).

Clinical features

- diffuse hyperaemia of both tarsal or bulbar conjunctivae
- absence of ocular pain; good vision; clear cornea
- infectious conjunctivitis is bilateral (usually) or unilateral (depending on the cause), with a discharge, a gritty or sandy sensation

Bacterial conjunctivitis

Bacterial infection may be primary, secondary to a viral infection or secondary to blepharitis.

History

Purulent discharge with sticking together of eyelashes in the morning is typical. It usually starts in one eye and spreads to the other. There may be a history of contact with a person with similar symptoms. The organisms are usually picked up from contaminated fingers, face cloths or towels.

Examination

There is usually a bilateral mucopurulent discharge with uniform engorgement of all the conjunctival blood vessels and a non-specific papillary response. Fluorescein staining is negative.

Causative organisms

These include:

- *Streptococcus pneumoniae*
- *Haemophilus influenzae*
- *Staphylococcus aureus*
- *Streptococcus pyogenes*
- *Neisseria gonorrhoea* (a hyperacute onset)
- *Pseudomonas aeruginosa*

Diagnosis is usually clinical but a swab should be taken for smear and culture with:[2]

- hyperacute or severe purulent conjunctivitis
- prolonged infection
- neonates

Management

Limit the spread by avoiding close contact with others, use of separate towels and good ocular hygiene.

Mild cases

Mild cases may resolve with saline irrigation of the eyelids and conjunctiva but may last up to 14 days if untreated.[7] An antiseptic eye drop such as propamidine isethionate 0.1% (Brolene) 1–2 drops 6–8 hourly for 5–7 days can be used.

More severe cases

chloramphenicol 0.5% eye drops, 1 to 2 hourly for 2 days,[1] decrease to 4 times a day for another 7 days (maximum 10 days—cases of aplastic anaemia have been reported with long-term use)

Use also chloramphenicol 1% eye ointment each night

or preferably[7]

polymyxin B sulphate 5000 units/ml with either chloramphenicol 0.5% or neomycin 2.5 mg/ml, 1 to 2 drops hourly, decreasing to 6 hourly as the infection improves.

Specific organisms:

Pseudomonas and other coliforms: use topical gentamicin and tobramycin.

Neisseria gonorrhoea: use appropriate systemic antibiotics.

Viral conjunctivitis

The most common cause of this very contagious condition is adenovirus.

History

It is commonly associated with upper respiratory tract infections and is the type of conjunctivitis that occurs in epidemics (pink eye).[1] The conjunctivitis usually has a 2–3 week course; it is initially one-sided but with cross-infection occurring days later in the other eye.

Examination

Usually bilateral with diffuse conjunctival infection and productive of a scant watery discharge. Viral infections typically but not always produce a follicular response in the conjunctivae (tiny, pale lymphoid follicles) and an associated

Table 43.2 *Major causes of a red eye*

	Site of inflammation	*Pain*	*Discharge*	*Vision*	*Photophobia*	*Pupil*	*Cornea*	*Ocular tension*
Bacterial conjunctivitis	Conjunctiva, including lining of lids (usually bilateral)	Irritation—gritty	Purulent, lids stuck in morning	Normal	No	Normal	Normal	Normal
Viral conjunctivitis	Conjunctiva, lining of lids often follicular (uni or bilateral)	Gritty	Watery	Normal	No	Normal	Normal	Normal
Allergic (vernal) conjunctivitis	Conjunctiva, papillary swellings on lid linings (bilateral)	Gritty—itching	Watery	Normal	No	Normal	Normal	Normal
Contact hypersensitivity (dermato-conjunctivitis)	Conjunctiva and eyelids. Oedema	Itching	Watery	Normal—may be blurred	No	Normal	Normal	Normal
Subconjunctival haemorrhage	Beefy red area fading at edge (unilateral)	No	No	Normal	No	Normal	Normal	Normal
Herpes simplex keratitis	Unilateral—circumcorneal. Dendritic ulcer	Yes—gritty	No, reflex lacrimation	Blurred, but variable, depends on site	Yes	Normal	Abnormal	Normal
Corneal ulcer	Unilateral—circumcorneal (exclude foreign body)	Yes	No, reflex lacrimation	Blurred but variable, depends on site	Yes	Normal	Abnormal	Normal
Scleritis/episcleritis	Localised deep redness. Tender area	Yes	No	Normal	No	Normal	Normal	Normal
Acute iritis	Maximum around cornea	Yes—radiates to brow, temple, nose	No, reflex lacrimation	Blurred	Yes	Constricted, may be irregular	Normal	Normal or low
Acute glaucoma	Diffuse but maximum circumcorneal	Yes, severe with nausea and vomiting	No, reflex lacrimation	Haloes around lights	Yes	Dilated Absent light reflex	Hazy	Hard, elevated

preauricular lymph node. Subconjunctival haemorrhages may occur with adenovirus infection. High magnification, ideally a slit lamp, may be necessary to visualise some of the changes, such as small corneal opacities, follicles and keratitis.

Diagnosis is based on clinical grounds and a history of infected contacts. Viral culture and serology can be performed to identify epidemics.

Treatment

- Limit cross-infection by appropriate rules of hygiene and patient education.
- Treatment is symptomatic, e.g. cool compress and topical lubricants (artificial tear preparations).
- Do not pad.
- Watch for secondary bacterial infection.

Primary herpes simplex infection

This viral infection produces a follicular conjunctivitis. About 50% of patients have associated lid or corneal ulcers/vesicles which are diagnostic.[2] Only a minority (less than 15%) develop corneal involvement with the primary infection.

Dendritic ulceration highlighted by fluorescein staining is diagnostic. Antigen detection or culture may allow confirmation.

Treatment of herpes simplex keratitis

- acyclovir 3% ointment, 5 times a day for 14 days or for at least 3 days after healing[7]
- atropine 1% 1 drop, 12 hourly, for the duration of treatment will prevent reflex spasm of the pupil (specialist supervision)
- debridement by a consultant

Allergic conjunctivitis

Allergic conjunctivitis results from a local response to an allergen. It includes:

- vernal (hay fever) conjunctivitis, and
- contact hypersensitivity reactions

Vernal (hay fever) conjunctivitis

This is usually seasonal and related to pollen exposure. There is usually associated rhinitis.

Treatment:

Tailor treatment to the degree of symptoms. Antihistamines may be required but symptomatic measures usually suffice.

- Use sodium cromoglycate 2% drops, 1–2 drops per eye 4 times daily.
- Artificial tear preparations may give adequate symptomatic relief.

Contact hypersensitivity

Common topical allergens and toxins include topical ophthalmic medications, especially antibiotics, contact lens solutions (often the contained preservative) and a wide range of cosmetics, soaps, detergents and chemicals. Clinical features include burning, itching and watering with hyperaemia and oedema of the conjunctiva and eyelids. A skin reaction of the lids usually occurs.

Treatment:

- Withdraw the causative agent.
- Apply normal saline compresses.
- If not responding, refer for possible corticosteroid therapy.

Chlamydial conjunctivitis

Chlamydial conjunctivitis is encountered in three common situations:

- neonatal infection (first 1–2 weeks)
- young patient with associated venereal disease
- isolated Aboriginal people with trachoma

Systemic antibiotic treatment:[7]

Neonates: erythromycin for 3 weeks
Children aged 7 or less: erythromycin for 3 weeks
Adults: doxycycline 100 mg bd for 3 weeks

Subconjunctival haemorrhage

Subconjunctival haemorrhage, which appears spontaneously, is a beefy red localised haemorrhage with a definite posterior margin. If it follows trauma and extends backwards it may indicate an orbital fracture. It is not related to hypertension but it is worthwhile measuring the blood pressure to help reassure the patient.

Management

No local therapy is necessary. The haemorrhage absorbs over two weeks. Patient explanation and reassurance is necessary. If haemorrhages are recurrent a bleeding tendency should be excluded.

Episcleritis and scleritis

Episcleritis and scleritis present as a localised area of inflammation (Figs 43.1 and 43.2). The episclera lies just beneath the conjunctiva and adjacent to the sclera. Both may become inflamed but episcleritis is essentially self-limiting while scleritis (which is rare) is more serious as the eye may perforate.[3]

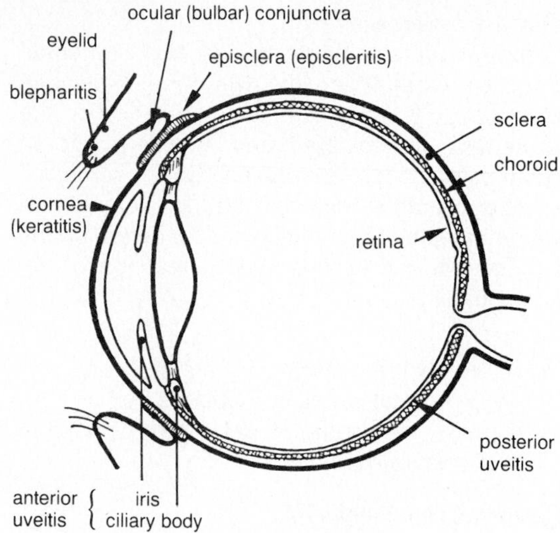

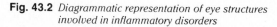

Fig. 43.2 *Diagrammatic representation of eye structures involved in inflammatory disorders*

History

A red and sore eye is the presenting complaint. There is usually no discharge but there may be reflex lacrimation. Scleritis is much more painful than episcleritis.[3]

Examination

With scleritis there is a localised area of inflammation that is tender to touch, and more extensive than with episcleritis. The inflamed vessels are larger than the conjunctival vessels.

Management

An underlying cause such as an autoimmune condition should be identified. Refer the patient, especially for scleritis. Corticosteroids or NSAIDs may be prescribed.

Uveitis

The iris, ciliary body and the choroid form the uveal tract which is the vascular coat of the eyeball.[6]

Anterior uveitis (acute iritis or iridocyclitis) is inflammation of the iris and ciliary body and this is usually referred to as acute iritis (Fig. 43.2). The pupil may become small because of adhesions and the vision is blurred.

Causes include the seronegative arthropathies, e.g. ankylosing spondylitis, sarcoidosis and some infections, e.g. toxoplasmosis and syphilis. The examination findings are summarised in Table 43.2. The affected eye is red with the injection being particularly pronounced over the area covering the inflamed ciliary body (ciliary flush). However, the whole bulbar conjunctivae can be injected. The patient should be referred to a consultant.

Management involves finding the underlying cause. Treatment includes pupil dilatation with atropine drops and topical steroids to suppress inflammation. Systemic corticosteroids may be necessary. The prognosis of anterior uveitis is good if treatment and follow-up are maintained, but recurrence is likely.

Posterior uveitis (choroiditis) may involve the retina and vitreous. Blurred vision and floating opacities in the visual field may be the only symptoms. Pain is not a feature. Referral to detect the causation and for treatment is essential.

Acute glaucoma

Acute glaucoma should always be considered in a patient over 50 years presenting with an acutely painful red eye. Permanent damage will result from misdiagnosis. The attack characteristically strikes in the evening when the pupil becomes semi-dilated.[3]

Features

- patient > 50 years
- pain in one eye
- ± nausea and vomiting
- impaired vision
- haloes around lights
- fixed semi-dilated pupil
- eye feels hard

Management

Urgent ophthalmic referral is essential since emergency treatment is necessary to preserve eyesight. If immediate specialist attention is unavailable, treatment can be initiated with acetazolamide (Diamox) 500 mg IV and pilocarpine 4% drops to constrict the pupil.

Eyelid and lacrimal disorders

There are several inflammatory disorders of the eyelid and lacrimal system that present as a 'red and tender' eye without involving the conjunctiva. Any suspicious lesion should be referred.

Stye

A stye is an acute abscess of a lash follicle or associated glands, caused usually by *Staphylococcus aureus*. The patient complains of a red tender swelling of the lid margin, usually on the medial side.

Management

- Use heat to help it discharge by using direct steam from a thermos (Fig. 43.3) onto the enclosed eye or by hot compresses.
- Perform lash epilation to allow drainage of pus (incise with a D_{11} blade if epilation does not work).
- Use chloramphenicol ointment if the infection is spreading locally.[3]

Fig. 43.3 *Steaming the painful eye: allow steam to rise from a thermos onto the closed eye for 10–15 minutes*

Chalazion (meibomian cyst)

This granuloma of the meibomian gland in the eyelid may become inflamed and present as a tender irritating lump in the lid. Look for evidence of blepharitis.

Management

Conservative treatment may result in resolution. This involves heat either as steam from a thermos or a hot compress (a hand towel soaked in hot water) and the application of chloramphenicol ointment for five days. If the chalazion is very large, persistent, uncomfortable or affecting vision it can be incised and curetted under local anaesthesia. This is best performed through the inner conjunctival surface using a chalazion clamp (blepharostat) (Fig. 43.4).

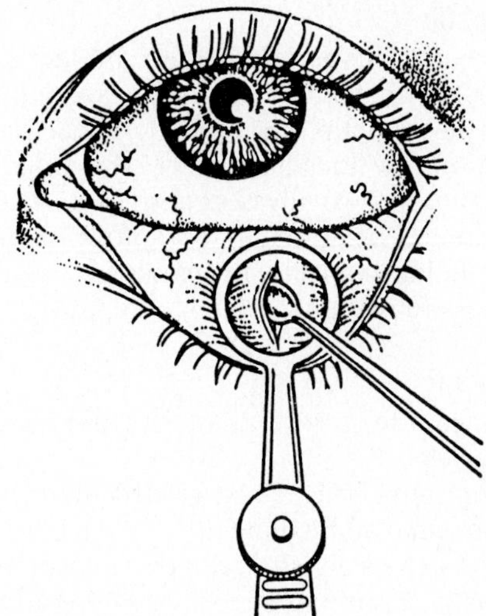

Fig. 43.4 *Excision of a meibomian cyst, using a chalazian clamp and curette*

Blepharitis

This common chronic condition is characterised by inflammation of the lid margins and is commonly associated with secondary ocular effects such as styes, chalazia and conjunctival or corneal ulceration. Blepharitis is frequently associated with seborrhoeic dermatitis (especially) and atopic dermatitis, less so with rosacea.[8] There is a tendency to colonisation of the lid margin with *Staphylococcus aureus.*

Features[8]

- persistent sore eyes or eyelids
- irritation, burning, dryness and 'something in the eye' sensation
- lid or conjunctival swelling and redness
- crusts or scales around the base of the eyelids
- discharge or stickiness, especially in morning
- inflammation and crusting of the lid margins

Management

- Eyelid hygiene is the mainstay of therapy. The crusts and other debris should be gently cleaned with a cotton wool bud dipped in a 1:10 dilution of baby shampoo or a solution of sodium bicarbonate, once or twice daily.
- Treat infection with an antibiotic ointment smeared on the lid margin (this may be necessary for several months) e.g. tetracycline hydrochloride 1% ointment to lid margins 3 to 6 hourly.[7]
- For chronic blepharitis short-term use of a corticosteroid ointment, e.g. hydrocortisone 0.5%, can be very effective.
- Ocular lubricants such as artificial tear preparations may greatly relieve symptoms of keratoconjunctivitis sicca (dry eyes).
- Control scalp seborrhoea with regular medicated shampoos.
- Systemic antibiotics such as flucloxacillin may be required for lid abscess.

Dacryocystitis

Acute dacryocystitis is infection of the lacrimal sac secondary to obstruction of the nasolacrimal duct at the junction of the lacrimal sac. Inflammation is localised over the medial canthus. There is usually a history of a watery eye for months beforehand. The problem may vary from being mild (as in infants) to severe with abscess formation.

Management

- Local heat: steam or a hot moist compress.
- Analgesics.
- Systemic antibiotics (best guided by results of Gram stain and culture).
- Measures to establish drainage are required eventually. Recurrent attacks or symptomatic watering of the eye are indications for surgery such as dacryocystorhinostomy.

Orbital cellulitis

Orbital cellulitis includes two basic types—periorbital (or preseptal) and orbital (or post-septal) cellulitis—and is a potentially blinding and life-threatening condition. It is especially important in children in whom blindness may develop in hours. The patient, often a child, presents with unilateral swollen eyelids that may be red.

Features to look for include:[3]

- an unwell patient
- tenderness over the sinuses
- restriction of eye movements (Fig. 43.5)

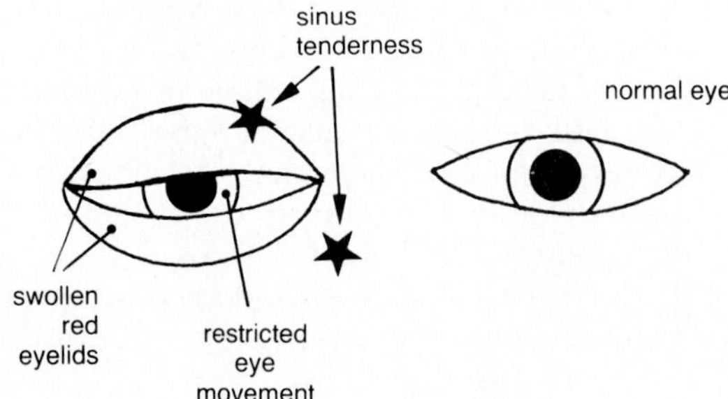

Fig. 43.5 *Important signs in the patient presenting with orbital cellulitis*

Immediate referral for specialist treatment is essential. Consider IV cefotaxime.

Herpes zoster ophthalmicus

Herpes zoster ophthalmicus (shingles) affects the skin supplied by the ophthalmic division of the trigeminal nerve. The eye may be affected if the nasociliary branch is involved. Ocular problems include conjunctivitis, uveitis, keratitis and glaucoma.

Immediate referral is necessary if the eye is red, vision is blurred or the cornea cannot be examined. Apart from general eye hygiene, treatment usually includes oral acyclovir 400 mg, five times daily (provided this is commenced within three days of the rash appearing),[5] and topical acyclovir ointment 4 hourly.

Pinguecula and pterygium

Pinguecula is a yellowish elevated nodular growth on either side of the cornea in the area of the palpebral fissure. It is common in people over 35 years. The growth tends to remain static but can become inflamed—pingueculitis. Usually no treatment is necessary unless they are large, craggy and uncomfortable, when excision is indicated. If irritating, topical astringent drops such as naphazoline compound drops, e.g. Albalon, can give relief.

Pterygium is a fleshy overgrowth of the conjunctiva onto the nasal side of the cornea and usually occurs in adults living in dry, dusty, windy areas. Excision of a pterygium by a specialist is indicated if it is likely to interfere with vision by encroaching on the visual axis, or if it becomes red and uncomfortable or disfiguring.

Flash burns

A common problem usually presenting at night is bilateral painful eyes caused by ultraviolet 'flash burns' to both corneas some 5 to 10 hours previously. The mechanism of injury is ultraviolet rays from a welding machine causing superficial punctuate keratitis. Other sources of UV light such as sunlamps and snow reflection can cause a reaction.

Management

- Local anaesthetic (long-acting) drops: once only application (do not allow the patient to take home more drops).
- Instil homatropine 2% drops statim.

- Analgesics, e.g. codeine plus paracetamol, for 24 hours.
- Broad spectrum antibiotic eye ointment in lower fornix (to prevent infection).
- Firm eye padding for 24 hours, when eyes reviewed (avoid light).

  The eye usually heals completely in 48 hours. If not, check for a foreign body.

  Note: Contact lens 'overwear syndrome' gives the same symptoms.

When to refer

- Uncertainty about the diagnosis.
- Patients with uveitis, acute glaucoma, episcleritis/scleritis or corneal ulceration.
- Deep central corneal and intraocular foreign bodies.
- Prolonged infections, with a poor or absent response to treatment or where therapy may be complicating management.
- Infections or severe allergies with possible ocular complications.
- Sudden swelling of an eyelid in a child with evidence of infection suggestive of orbital cellulitis—this is an emergency.
- Emergency referral is also necessary for hyphaemia, hypopyon, penetrating eye injury, acute glaucoma, severe chemical burn.
- Herpes zoster ophthalmicus: if the external nose is involved then the internal eye may be involved.
- Summary for urgent referral:
  — trauma (significant)
  — corneal ulcer
  — severe conjunctivitis
  — uveitis/acute iritis
  — acute glaucoma
  — orbital cellulitis
  — acute dacryocystitis
  — episcleritis/scleritis
  — herpes zoster ophthalmicus

Note: As a general rule never use corticosteroids or atropine in the eye before referral to an ophthalmologist.

Practice tips

- Avoid long-term use of any medication, especially antibiotics, e.g. chloramphenicol: course for a maximum of 10 days.[2]
- NB: beware of allergy or toxicity to topical medications, especially antibiotics, as a cause of persistent symptoms.
- As a general rule avoid using topical corticosteroids or combined corticosteroid/antibiotic preparations.
- Never use corticosteroids in the presence of a dendritic ulcer.
- To achieve effective results from eye ointment or drops, remove debris such as mucopurulent exudate with bacterial conjunctivitis or blepharitis by using a warm solution of saline (dissolve a teaspoon of kitchen salt in 500 ml of boiled water) to bathe away any discharge from conjunctiva, eyelashes and lids.
- A gritty sensation is common in conjunctivitis but the presence of a foreign body must be excluded.[3]
- Beware of the contact lens 'overwear syndrome' which is treated in a similar way to flash burns.

References

1. McDonnell P. Red eye: an illustrated guide to eight common causes. Modern Medicine of Australia, October 1989, 37–39.
2. Della NG. Acute conjunctivitis. In: MIMS Disease Index. Sydney: IMS Publishing, 1991–2, 113–115.
3. Elkington AR, Khaw PT. *ABC of eyes.* London: British Medical Association, 1990, 6–10.
4. Colvin J. Systemic examination of the red eye. Aust Fam Physician, 1976;5:153–165.
5. Maclean H. Keratitis (viral and fungal). In: MIMS Disease Index. Sydney: IMS Publishing, 1991–2, 301–303.
6. Robinson MJ. *Practical paediatrics* (2nd edition). Melbourne: Churchill Livingstone, 1990, 595–597.
7. Mashford ML. *Antibiotic guidelines* (7th edition). Melbourne: Victorian Medical Postgraduate Foundation, 1992/93.
8. Barras CW. Blepharitis. In: MIMS Disease Index. Sydney: IMS Publishing, 1991–2, 80–82.
9. Colvin J. Painful eye: an emergency call. Aust Fam Physician, 1985; 14:1258

44

Pain in the face

When a patient complains of pain in the face rather than the head the physician has to consider foremost the possibilities of dental disorders, sinus disease, especially of the maxillary sinuses, temporomandibular joint dysfunction, eye disorders, lesions of the oropharynx or posterior third of the tongue, trigeminal neuralgia and chronic paroxysmal hemicrania.

The key to the diagnosis is the clinical examination because even the most sophisticated investigation may provide no additional information.

A basic list of causes of facial pain is presented in Table 44.1.[1] The causes can vary from the simple, such as aphthous ulcers, herpes simplex and dental caries, to serious causes such as carcinoma of the tongue, sinuses and nasopharynx or osteomyelitis of the mandible or maxilla.

Table 44.1 *Diagnoses to consider in orofacial pain*

Positive physical signs

Cervical spinal dysfunction
Dental pathology
Eye disorders
Herpes zoster
Nasopharyngeal carcinoma
Oropharyngeal disorders
- ulceration (aphthous, infective, traumatic, others)
- carcinoma
- gingivitis/stomatitis
- tonsillitis
- erosive lichen planus

Paranasal sinus disorders
Parotid gland
- mumps
- sialectesis
- carcinoma
- pleomorphic adenoma

Temporomandibular joint dysfunction

Absent physical signs

Atypical facial pain
Chronic paroxysmal hemicrania
Depression-associated facial pain
Facial migraine (lower half headache)
Glossopharyngeal neuralgia
Migrainous neuralgia (cluster headache)
Trigeminal neuralgia (tic douloureux)

Key facts and checkpoints

- Dental disorders are the commonest cause of facial pain, accounting for up to 90% of pain in and about the face.[2]
- The most common dental disorders are dental caries and periodontal diseases.
- Trigeminal neuralgia is relatively uncommon with a prevalence of 155 persons per million of the population.[3]
- The mean age of onset of trigeminal neuralgia is 50–52 years.
- There is a similarity in the 'occult' causes of pain in the ear and in the face (refer to Figures 42.3 and 42.4).
- Sinusitis occurs mainly as part of a generalised upper respiratory infection. Swimming is another common predisposing factor.
- Dental root infection must be sought in all cases of maxillary sinusitis.

A diagnostic approach

A summary of the safety diagnostic model is presented in Table 44.2.

Table 44.2 *Pain in the face: diagnostic strategy model*

Q. Probability diagnosis
A. dental pain — caries
— periapical abscess
maxillary sinusitis

Q. Serious disorders not to be missed
A. Cardiovascular
- aneurysm of cavernous sinus
- internal carotid aneurysm
- ischaemia of posterior inferior cerebellar artery

Neoplasia
- carcinoma — mouth
— sinuses
— nasopharynx
— tonsils
— tongue
— larynx
- metastases — orbital
— base of brain
— bone

Severe infections
- periapical abscess → osteomyelitis
- acute sinusitis → spreading infection

Q. Pitfalls
A. Temporomandibular joint dysfunction
Migraine variants
- facial migraine
- chronic paroxysmal hemicrania

Eye disorders—glaucoma, iritis, optic neuritis
Chronic dental neuralgia
Parotid gland—mumps, carcinoma, sialectesis
Glossopharyngeal neuralgia

Q. Seven masquerades checklist

A.		
	Depression	✓
	Diabetes	-
	Drugs	-
	Anaemia	-
	Thyroid disease	-
	Spinal dysfunction	✓
	UTI	-

Q. Is the patient trying to tell me something?
A. Quite probably. Atypical facial pain has underlying psychogenic elements.

Probability diagnosis

The commonest cause of facial pain is dental disorders, especially dental caries. Another common cause is sinusitis, particularly maxillary sinusitis.

Temporomandibular joint (TMJ) dysfunction causing TMJ arthralgia is a very common problem encountered in general practice and it is important to have some simple basic strategies to give the patient.

Serious disorders not to be missed

It is important not to overlook carcinoma of various structures such as the mouth, sinuses, nasopharynx, tonsils, tongue, larynx and parotid gland.

It is important therefore to inspect these areas, especially in the elderly, but lesions in the relatively inaccessible nasopharynx can be easily missed. Nasopharynx carcinoma spreads upwards to the base of the skull early and patients can present with multiple cranial nerve palsies before either pain or bloody nasal discharge.[1]

Tumours may arise in the bones of the orbit, for example, lymphoma or secondary carcinoma, and may cause facial pain and proptosis. Similarly, any space-occupying lesion or malignancy arising from the region of the orbit or base of the brain can cause facial pain by involvement (often destruction) of trigeminal sensory fibres. This will lead to a depressed ipsilateral corneal reflex.

Also aneurysms developing in the cavernous sinus[1] can cause pain via pressure on any of the divisions of the trigeminal nerve, while aneurysms from the internal carotid arising from the origin of the posterior communicating artery can cause pressure on the oculomotor nerve.

Pitfalls

Commonly overlooked causes of facial pain include TMJ arthralgia and dental disorders, especially of the teeth, which are tender to percussion and oral ulceration. Diagnosing the uncommon migraine variants, particularly facial migraine and chronic paroxysmal hemicrania, often presents difficulties including differentiating between the neuralgias. Glossopharyngeal neuralgia, which is rare, causes pain in the back of the throat, around the tonsils and adjacent fauces. The lightning quality of the pain of neuralgia gives the clue to diagnosis.

Common pitfalls

- failing to refer unusual or undiagnosed causes of facial pain
- overlooking infective dental causes which can cause complications
- failing to consider the possibility of malignant disease of 'hidden' structures in the older patient

Seven masquerades checklist

Of these, depression and cervical spinal dysfunction must be considered. The upper cervical spine can cause facial pain from lesions of C2 or C3 via the lesser occipital or greater auricular (Fig. 44.1) nerves which may give pain around the ear. It is important to remember that C2 and C3 share a common pathway with the trigeminal nerve (Chap. 52).

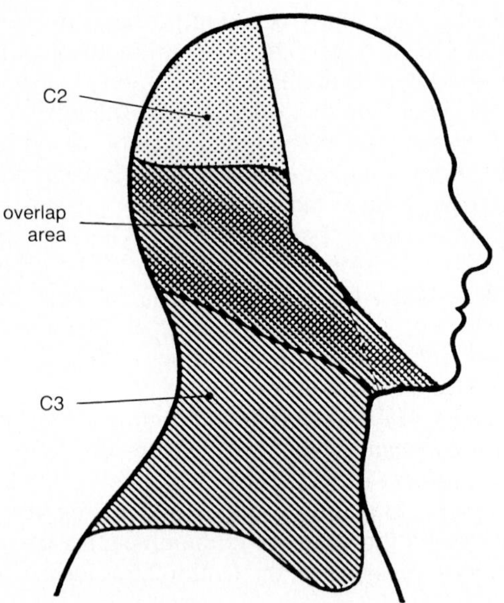

Fig. 44.1 *Dermatomes of C2 and C3, with the overlap area indicated*

Depressive illness can present with a variety of painful syndromes and facial pain is no exception. The features of depression may be apparent and thus antidepressants should be prescribed. Usually the facial pain and the depression subside concomitantly.

Psychogenic considerations

Psychogenic factors have to be considered in every painful condition. They are considered to be high in patients with atypical facial pain.

The clinical approach

History

Diagnosis of nearly all types of facial pain must be based almost entirely on the history. It is often difficult to delineate the exact nature and distribution of the pain. The history should include the typical analysis of pain, especially noting the site and radiation of the pain.

Examination

The patient's general state and behaviour should be noted. Any sudden jabbing pain in the face causing the characteristic 'tic' may indicate neuralgia.

Palpate the face and neck to include the parotid glands, eyes, regional lymph nodes and the skin. Inspect the TMJs and cervical spine. Carefully inspect the nose, mouth, pharynx and postnasal space. In particular inspect the teeth, percussing each tooth if dental disorder is suspected. Bimanual palpation of the floor of the mouth is performed to detect induration or submandibular and submental lymph node enlargement.

The sinuses, especially the maxillary sinuses, should be inspected and a torch light should be placed inside the mouth to test transillumination of the maxillary sinuses. It works best when one symptomatic side can be compared with an asymptomatic side.

Perform a neurological examination on the cranial nerves with special emphasis on the trigeminal, oculomotor and glossopharyngeal nerves.

Investigations

If investigations are being contemplated referral may be appropriate. The association of multiple sclerosis and tumours with neuralgias may have to be investigated. Radiological investigations include plain X-rays such as the paranasal sinuses, CT scans, MRI and orthopantomograms.

Facial pain in children

Apart from trauma, facial pain in children is invariably due to dental problems, rarely migraine variants and occasionally childhood infections such as mumps and gingivostomatitis. A serious problem sometimes seen in children is orbital cellulitis secondary to ethmoiditis.

Facial pain in the elderly

Many of the causes of facial pain have an increased incidence with age, in particular trigeminal neuralgia, herpes zoster, carcinoma, glaucoma, TMJ dysfunction and cervical spondylosis. Glossopharyngeal neuralgia does not seem to have a particular predeliction for the elderly. Xerostomia due to decreased secretions of salivary glands may cause abrasion with minor trauma. It may aggravate the pain of glossitis which is common in the elderly.

Dental disorders

Dental caries, impacted teeth, infected tooth sockets and dental roots can cause pain in the maxillary and mandibular regions. Caries with periapical and apical abscess formation produces pain from infection extending around the apex of the tooth into the alveolar bone. Retention of a fractured root may cause unilateral paroxysmal pain. Impacted third molars (wisdom teeth) may be associated with surrounding soft tissue inflammation, causing pain which may be localised to the mandible or radiate via the auricular temporal nerve to the ear. Candida albicans, which are oral commensals, may colonise dentures causing hyperaemia and painful superficial ulceration of the denture-bearing mucosa.

Features of dental caries

- Pain is usually confined to the affected tooth but may be diffuse.
- Pain is almost always aggravated by thermal changes in the mouth:
  cold — if dental pulp vital
  hot — if dental pulp is necrotic.
- Pain may be felt in more than one tooth.
- Dental pain will not cross the midline.

Treatment of dental pain

- arrange urgent dental consultation
- pain relief[4]
  aspirin 600 mg (o) 4 to 6 hourly
  or
  paracetamol 0.5–1 g (o) 4 to 6 hourly
- if pain severe add
  codeine 30 mg (o) 4 to 6 hourly
- administer penicillin for associated lymphadenopathy or dental abscess formation
  e.g. procaine penicillin 1 g (IM) daily

Pain from paranasal sinuses

Infection of the paranasal sinuses may cause localised pain. Localised tenderness and pain may be apparent with frontal or maxillary sinusitis. Sphenoidal or ethmoidal sinusitis causes a constant pain behind the eye or behind the nose, often accompanied by nasal blockage. Chronic infection of the sinuses may be extremely difficult to detect. The commonest organisms are *Streptococcus pneumoniae* and *Haemophilus influenzae*.

Expanding lesions of the sinuses, such as mucoceles and tumours, cause local swelling and displace the contents of the orbit—upwards for maxillary, laterally for the ethmoids and downwards for the frontal.

Maxillary sinusitis

The maxillary sinus is the one most commonly infected.[5] It is important to determine whether the sinusitis is caused by stasis following an URTI or acute rhinitis or due to dental root infection.

Clinical features of acute sinusitis

- facial pain and tenderness
- toothache
- purulent postnasal drip
- nasal obstruction
- rhinorrhoea
- cough
- fever
- epistaxis

Clinical features of chronic sinusitis

- vague facial pain
- offensive postnasal drip
- nasal obstruction
- toothache
- malaise
- halitosis

Some simple office tests

Diagnosing sinus tenderness[6]

To differentiate sinus tenderness from non-sinus bone tenderness palpation is useful. This is best done by palpating a non-sinus area first and last (Fig. 44.2), systematically exerting pressure over the temporal bones (T), then the frontal (F), ethmoid (E) and maxillary (M) sinuses, and finally zygomas (Z), or vice versa.

Differential tenderness both identifies and localises the main sites of infection (Fig. 44.2).

Diagnosis of unilateral sinusitis

A simple way to assess the presence or absence of fluid in the frontal sinus, and in the maxillary sinus (in particular), is the use of transillumination. It works best when one symptomatic side can be compared with an asymptomatic side.

It is necessary to have the patient in a darkened room and to use a small, narrow-beam torch. For the maxillary sinuses remove dentures (if any). Shine the light inside the mouth, on either side of the hard palate, pointed at the base of the orbit. A dull glow seen below the orbit indicates that the antrum is air-filled. Diminished illumination on the symptomatic side indicates sinusitis.

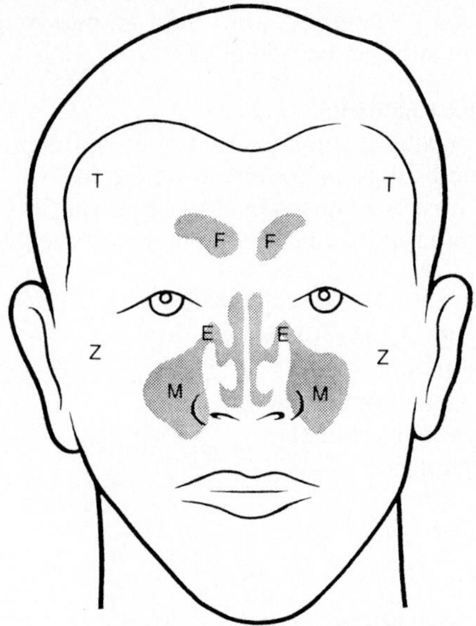

Fig. 44.2 *Diagnosing sinus tenderness: T (temporal) and Z (zygoma) represent no sinus bony tenderness, for purposes of comparison*

Management of maxillary sinusitis

Principles

- exclude dental root infection
- control predisposing factors
- appropriate antibiotic therapy
- establish drainage by stimulation of mucociliary flow and relief of obstruction

Measures

- analgesics
- antibiotics (first choice)

  amoxycillin 750 mg (o) bd for 5 days[7]

  or

  500 mg (o) tds for 5 days

  or

  amoxycillin/potassium clavulanate tds for 5 days (if resistance to amoxycillin is suspected or proven)

  or

  doxycycline 100 mg (o) bd for 5 days
- nasal decongestants (ephedrine-containing nasal drops or sprays)[5] only if congestion
- inhalations (a very important adjunct)

Invasive methods

Surgical drainage may be necessary by atrial lavage or frontal sinus trephine.

Inhalations for sinusitis

The old method of towel over the head and inhalation bowl can be used, but it is better to direct the vapour at the nose. Equipment needed is a container which can be an old disposable bowl, a wide-mouthed bottle or tin, or a plastic container.

For the inhalant, several household over-the-counter preparations are suitable, e.g. friar's balsam (5 ml), Vicks Vapo-rub (one teaspoon), or menthol (5 ml).

The cover can be made from a paper bag (with its base cut out), a cone of paper (Fig. 44.3) or a small cardboard carton (with the corner cut away).

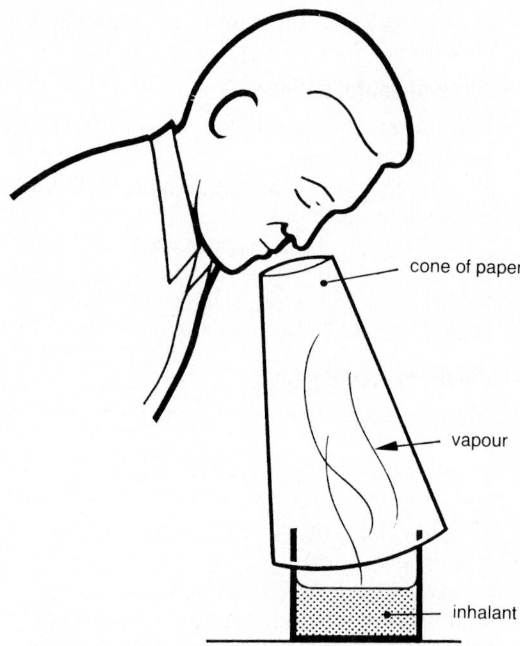

Fig. 44.3 *Method of inhalation for sinusitis*

Method

1. Add 5 ml or one teaspoon of the inhalant to 0.5 L (or 1 pint) of boiled water in the container.
2. Place the paper or carton over the container.
3. Get the patient to apply nose and mouth to the opening and breathe the vapour in deeply and slowly through the nose, and then out slowly through the mouth.
4. This should be performed for 5–10 minutes, three times a day, especially before retiring.

After inhalation, upper airway congestion can be relieved by autoinsufflation.

Temporomandibular joint dysfunction

This condition is due to abnormal movement of the mandible, especially during chewing. The basic cause is dental malocclusion. The pain is felt over the joint and tends to be localised to the region of the ear and mandibular condyle but may radiate forwards to the cheek and even the neck.

Examination of the TMJ

- Check for pain and limitation of mandibular movements, especially on opening the mouth.
- Palpate about the joint bilaterally for tenderness which typically lies immediately in front of the external auditory meatus; palpate the temporalis and masseter muscles.
- Palpate the TMJ over the lateral aspect of the joint disc.
- Ask the patient to open the mouth fully when tenderness is maximal. The TMJ can be palpated posteriorly by inserting the little finger into the external canal.
- Check for crepitus in mandibular movement.

Treatment of TMJ dysfunction

If organic disease such as rheumatoid arthritis and obvious dental malocclusion is excluded, a special set of instructions or exercises can alleviate the annoying problem of TMJ arthralgia in about three weeks.

Method 1 'Chewing' the piece of soft wood

- Obtain a rod of soft wood approximately 15 cm long and 1.5 cm wide. An ideal object is a large carpenter's pencil.
- Instruct the patient to position this at the back of the mouth so that the molars grasp the object with the mandible thrust forward.
- The patient then rhythmically bites on the object with a grinding movement for 2 to 3 minutes at least 3 times a day.

Method 2 The 'six by six' program

This is a specific program recommended by some dental surgeons. The six exercises should be carried out six times on each occasion, six times a day, taking about 1 to 2 minutes.

Instruct the patient as follows:

1. Hold the front one-third of your tongue to the roof of your mouth and take six deep breaths.
2. Hold the tongue to the roof of your mouth and open your mouth six times. Your jaw should not click.
3. Hold your chin with both hands keeping the chin still. Without letting your chin move, push up, down and to each side. Remember, do not let your chin move.
4. Hold both hands behind your neck and pull chin in.
5. Push on upper lip so as to push head straight back.
6. Pull shoulders back as if to touch shoulder blades together.

These exercises should be pain-free. If they hurt, do not push them to the limit until pain eases.

Method 3 The TMJ 'rest' program

This program is reserved for an acutely painful TMJ condition.

- For eating avoid opening your mouth wider than the thickness of your thumb and cut all food into small pieces.
- Do not bite any food with your front teeth—use small bite-size pieces.
- Avoid eating food requiring prolonged chewing, e.g. hard crusts of bread, tough meat, raw vegetables.
- Avoid chewing gum.
- Always try to open your jaw in a hinge or arc motion. Do not protrude your jaw.
- Avoid protruding your jaw, e.g. talking, applying lipstick.
- Avoid clenching your teeth together—keep your lips together and your teeth apart.
- Try to breathe through your nose at all times.
- Do not sleep on your jaw: try to sleep on your back.
- Practise a relaxed lifestyle so that your jaws and face muscles feel relaxed.

Injection into the TMJ

Indications: painful rheumatoid arthritis, osteoarthritis or TMJ dysfunction not responding to conservative measures.

Method

- The patient sits on a chair, facing away from the therapist. The mouth is opened to at least 4 cm.
- The joint line is palpated anterior to the tragus of the ear: this is confirmed by opening and closing of the jaw. A 25 gauge needle is inserted into the depression above the

condyle of the mandible, below the zygomatic arch and one finger-breadth (2 cm) anterior to the tragus. The needle is directed inwards and slightly upwards to lie free within the joint cavity. The 1ml solution containing 0.5 ml of local anaesthetic and 0.5 ml of corticosteroid should flow quite freely.[8]

Inflammatory or ulcerative oropharyngeal lesions

A variety of ulcerative conditions and infections of structures such as gingivae, tongue, tonsils, larynx and pharynx can cause facial pain. Gingivostomatitis, herpes labialis (cold sores) and aphthous ulceration are common examples. Lesions of the posterior third of the tongue, the oropharynx, tonsils and larynx may radiate to the region of the ear via the tympanic branch of the ninth nerve or the auricular branch of the tenth nerve.

Trigeminal neuralgia

Trigeminal neuralgia ('tic douloureux') is a condition of often unknown cause which typically occurs in patients over the age of 50, affecting the second and third divisions of the trigeminal nerve and on the same side of the face.[3] Brief paroxysms of pain, often with associated trigger points, are a feature.

Typical clinical features

Site:	sensory branches of the trigeminal nerve (Fig. 44.4) almost always unilateral
Radiation:	tends to commence in the mandibular division and spreads to the maxillary division and (rarely) to the ophthalmic division
Quality:	excruciating, searing jabs of pain like a burning knife or electric shock
Frequency:	variable and no regular pattern
Duration:	1–2 minutes (up to 15 minutes)
Onset:	spontaneous or trigger point stimulus
Offset:	spontaneous
Precipitating factors:	talking; chewing; touching trigger areas on face, e.g. washing, shaving, eating; cold weather or wind; turning onto pillow
Aggravating factors:	trigger points usually in the upper and lower lip, nasolabial fold or upper eyelid (Fig. 44.5)
Relieving factors:	nil

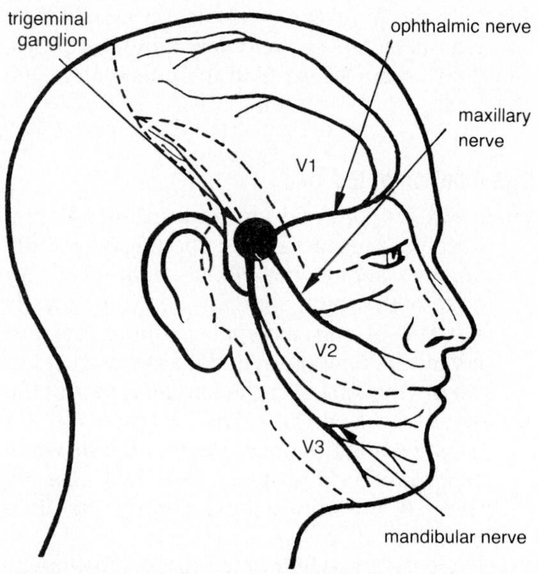

Fig. 44.4 *Typical cutaneous sensory distribution of the trigeminal nerve and its branches*

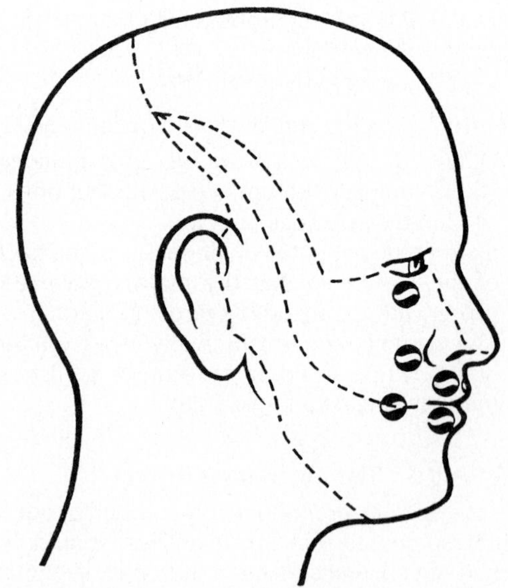

Fig. 44.5 *Trigeminal neuralgia: typical trigger points*

Associated features: rarely occurs at night
spontaneous remissions for months or years

Signs: there are no signs, normal corneal reflex

Causes:
- unknown
- local pressure on the nerve root entry zone by tortuous pulsatile dilated small vessels (probably up to 75%)
- multiple sclerosis
- neurosyphilis
- tumours of the posterior fossa

NB Precise diagnosis is essential.

Treatment

- Patient education, reassurance and empathic support is very important in these patients.
- Medical therapy:
  - — carbamazepine (from onset of the attack to resolution)[4] 100 mg (o) bd initially, gradually increase the dose to avoid drowsiness by 200 mg every four days to 300–600 mg bd (maintenance); testing serum levels is unnecessary
  - — alternative drugs if carbamazepine not tolerated or ineffective (but question the diagnosis if lack of response)
    phenytoin 300–500 mg daily
    clonazepam
    sodium valproate
    baclofen
- surgery:
  - — refer to a neurosurgeon if medication ineffective
  - — possible procedures include:
    - decompression of the trigeminal nerve root, e.g. gel foam packing between the nerve and blood vessels
    - thermocoagulation/radiofrequency neurolysis
    - surgical division of peripheral branches

Glossopharyngeal neuralgia

This is a rare condition with similar clinical features of severe lancinating pains.

Sites: back of throat around tonsillar fossa and adjacent fauces deep in ear.

Triggers: swallowing, coughing, talking.

Treatment: as for trigeminal neuralgia.

Migrainous neuralgia (cluster headache)

As described in Chapter 48 the pain is unilateral and centred around the eye with associated lacrimation and stuffiness of the nose.

Facial migraine (lower half headache)

Migraine may rarely affect the face below the level of the eyes, causing pain in the area of the cheek and upper jaw. It may spread over the nostril and lower jaw. The pain is dull and throbbing and nausea and vomiting are commonly present. The treatment is as for other varieties of migraine.

Chronic paroxysmal hemicrania

In the rare condition of chronic paroxysmal hemicrania there is a unilateral facial pain that can resemble chronic cluster headache but the duration is briefer, about 20 to 30 minutes, and it may recur many times a day even for years. It responds dramatically to indomethacin.[9]

Herpes zoster and postherpetic neuralgia

Herpes zoster may present as hyperaesthesia or a burning sensation in any division of the fifth nerve, especially the ophthalmic division.

Atypical facial pain

This is mainly a diagnosis of exclusion whereby patients, usually middle-aged women, complain of diffuse pain in the cheek (unilateral or bilateral) without demonstrable organic disease. The pain does not usually conform to a specific nerve distribution (although in the maxillary area), varies in intensity and duration and is not lancinating as in trigeminal neuralgia. It is usually described as deep-seated and 'boring', severe, continuous and throbbing in nature. It is a very confusing and difficult problem to treat. These patients tend to show psychoneurotic tendencies but caution is needed in labelling them as functional.

Treatment

dothiepin (Prothiaden) 25–150 mg nocte
or
amitriptyline 50–150 mg nocte

When to refer

- severe trigeminal neuralgia
- unusual facial pain, especially with a suspicion of malignancy
- positive neurological signs, e.g. impaired corneal reflex, impaired sensation in a trigeminal dermatome, slight facial weakness, hearing loss on the side of the neuralgia
- possible need for surgical drainage of sinusitis—indications for surgery include failure of appropriate medical treatment, anatomical deformity, polyps, uncontrolled sinus pain[5]
- dental root infection causing maxillary sinusitis
- other dental disorders

Practice tips

- Malignancy must be excluded in the elderly with facial pain.
- Problems from the molar teeth, especially the third (wisdom), commonly present with periauricular pain without aural disease and pain in the posterior cheek.
- Facial pain never crosses the midline; bilateral pain means bilateral lesions.

References

1. Beck ER, Francis JL, Souhami RL. *Tutorials in differential diagnosis*. Edinburgh: Longman Cheshire, 1987: 161–164.
2. Gerschman JA, Reade PC. Orofacial pain. Aust Fam Physician, 1984;13:14–24.
3. Selby G. Trigeminal neuralgia. In: MIMS Disease Index. Sydney: IMS Publishing, 1991–2: 551–553.
4. Moulds RFW. *Analgesic guidelines*. Melbourne: Victorian Medical Postgraduate Foundation, 1992–3: 69–72.
5. Stevens M. The diagnosis and management of acute and chronic sinusitis. Modern Medicine of Australia, April 1991: 16–26.
6. Bridges-Webb C. Diagnosing sinus tenderness. Practice tip. Aust Fam Physician, 1981;10:742.
7. Moulds RFW. *Antibiotic guidelines*. Melbourne: Victorian Medical Postgraduate Foundation, 1991–2: 114.
8. Corrigan B, Maitland G. *Practical orthopaedic medicine*. Sydney: Butterworths, 1986: 220.
9. Burns R. Pitfalls in headache management. Aust Fam Physician, 1990;19:1825.

45

Fever and chills

Although fever is a sign of disease and usually occurs in response to infection (mainly viral), its presence is recognised to play an important role in the individual's defence against infection. The infecting pathogen triggers hypothalmic receptors, causing the thermostatic mechanisms to be reset to maintain core temperature at a higher level. The elevation in body temperature activates T-cell production, increases the effectiveness of interferons and limits the replication of some common viruses.[1]

Facts and figures

- Fever plays an important physiological role in the defence against infection.
- Normal body temperature (measured orally) is 36–37.3°C (average 36.8°C).
- Normal average values: Mouth 36.8°C; Axilla 36.4°C; Rectum 37.3°C
- Fever (pyrexia): Mouth > 37.3°C; Rectum > 37.7°C
- There can be a normal diurnal variation of 1°C (lowest in early morning and highest in late afternoon).
- Fevers due to infections have an upper limit of 40.5–41.1°C (105–106°F).
- Hyperthermia (temperature above 41.1°C) and hyperpyrexia appear to have no upper limit.
- Infection remains the most important cause of acute fever.[2]
- Symptoms associated with fever include sweats, chills, rigors and headache.
- General causes of fever include infections; malignant disease; mechanical trauma, e.g. crush injury; vascular accidents, e.g. infarction, cerebral haemorrhage; immunogenic diseases, e.g. drug reactions, SLE; acute metabolic disorders, e.g. gout; and haemopoietic disorders, e.g. acute haemolytic anaemia.[2]
- Drugs can cause fever, presumably because of hypersensitivity.[2] Important examples are allopurinol, antihistamines, barbiturates, cephalosporins, cimetidine, methyldopa, penicillins, isoniazid, phenolphthalein (including laxatives), phenytoin, procainamide, salicylates, sulphonamides.
- Infectious diseases at the extremes of age (very young and aged)[2] often present with atypical symptoms and signs. Their condition may deteriorate rapidly.
- Overseas travellers or visitors may have special, even exotic, infections and require special evaluation (refer Chap. 11).
- Immunologically compromised patients, e.g. AIDS patients, pose a special risk for infections including opportunistic infections.
- A febrile illness is characteristic of the acute infection of HIV: at least 50% have an illness like glandular fever. Think of it!

Chills

The abrupt onset of fever with a chill or rigor is a feature of some diseases. Examples include:

- pneumococcal pneumonia
- pyogenic infection with bacteraemia
- lymphoma
- pyelonephritis

Features of a true chill are teeth chattering and bed shaking which is quite different to the chilly sensations that occur in almost all fevers, particularly those in viral infections.

Hyperthermia

Hyperthermia or hyperpyrexia is a temperature greater than 41.1°C (106°F). A more accurate definition is a state when the body's metabolic heat production or environmental heat load exceeds normal heat loss capacity. Hyperthermia may be observed particularly in the tropics, in malaria and heatstroke. It can occur with CNS tumours, infections or haemorrhages because of its effect on the hypothalamus.

Sweats

Sweating is a heat loss mechanism and diffuse sweating which may soak clothing and bedclothing permits rapid release of heat by evaporation. In febrile patients the skin is usually hot and dry—sweating occurs in most when the temperature falls. It is characteristic of only some fevers, e.g. septic infections and rheumatic fever.

Factitious fever

Factitious fever is usually encountered in hospitalised patients attempting to malinger. The situation is usually suspected when:

- a series of high temperatures is recorded to form an atypical pattern of fluctuation
- excessively high temperature (41.1°C) and above
- a recorded high temperature is unaccompanied by warm skin, tachycardia and other signs of fever such as a flushed face and sweating

The patient may have surreptitiously dipped the thermometer in warm water, placed it in contact with a heat source or heated the bulb by friction with bedclothes or even mucous membranes of the mouth.

Neuroleptic malignant syndrome

This is a variant of 'malignant' hyperthermia with muscle rigidity, autonomic dysfunction and altered consciousness due to a rare and potentially lethal reaction to major tranquillisers especially haloperidol, fluphenazine and chlorpromazine.

Measurement of temperature

Temperature can be measured by several methods, including the mercury thermometer, the liquid crystal thermometer and the electronic probe thermometer. The mercury thermometer, however, is probably still the most widely used and effective temperature-measuring instrument.

Basic rules of usage

1. Before use, shake down to 35–36°C.
2. After use:
   — shake down and store in antiseptic
   — do not run under hot water
   — wipe rectal thermometer with alcohol and store separately
3. Recording time is 3 minutes orally and 1–2 minutes rectally.

Oral use

1. Place under the tongue at the junction of the base of the tongue and the floor of the mouth to one side of the frenulum—the 'heat' pocket.
2. Ensure that the mouth is kept shut.
3. Remove dentures.

Note: Unsuitable for children four years and under, especially if irritable.

Rectal use

An excellent and recommended route for babies and young children under the age of four.

Method

1. Lubricate the stub with petroleum or KY jelly.
2. Insert for 2–3 cm (1 inch).
3. Keep the thermometer between the flexed fingers with the hand resting on the buttocks (Fig. 45.1).

Don't:

- dig thermometer in too hard
- hold it too rigidly
- allow the child to move around

Axillary use

Very unreliable, and should be avoided.

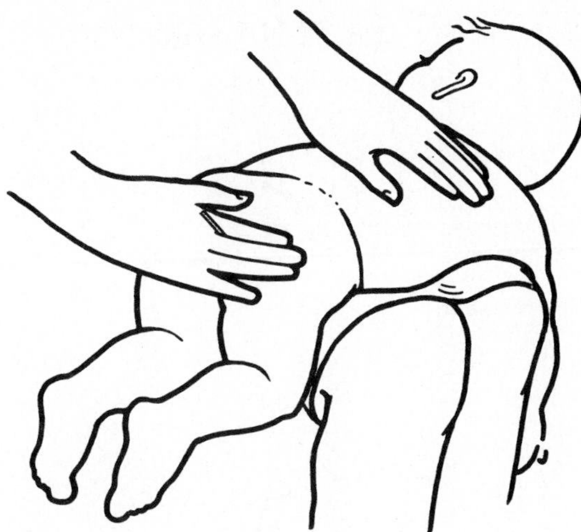

Fig. 45.1 *Rectal temperature measurement in infants*

Groin use

This route is not ideal but is more reliable than the axilla. It closely approximates oral temperature. In infants, the thigh should be flexed against the abdomen.

Vaginal use

Mainly used as an adjunct to the assessment of ovulation during the menstrual cycle. Should be placed deeply in the vagina for five minutes before leaving bed in the morning.

Accidental breakage in the mouth

If children bite off the end of a mercury thermometer there is no need for alarm, as the small amount of mercury is non-toxic and the piece of glass will usually pass in the stool.

The clinical approach

The initial approach is to evaluate the severity of the problem and the nature of the illness. Some infections, particularly bacterial infections, are life-threatening and this requires urgent diagnosis and hospital admission.

According to Yung and Stanley[2] it is helpful to consider fever in three categories: less than 3 days duration; between 4 and 14 days duration and protracted fever (more than 14 days).

Fever of less than 3 days duration

This is very commonly encountered in family practice, often due to a self-limiting viral infection of the respiratory tract. It is important however to be vigilant for other infections, so evidence of an infectious disease, urinary tract infection, pneumonia or other infection should be sought. A routine urine examination, especially in females, is an important screening investigation. The majority of patients can be managed conservatively.

Fever present for 4 to 14 days

If fever persists beyond 4–5 days a less common infection should be suspected since most common viral infections will have resolved by about four days.[2] A checklist of causes is presented in Table 45.1. The careful history is mandatory as outlined for FUO. The basic examination and investigations are along similar lines.

Table 45.1 *Common causes of fever of 4–14 days duration*

Influenza
Sinusitis
Epstein-Barr mononucleosis
Enteroviral infection
Infective endocarditis
Dental infections
Hepatobiliary infections: hepatitis, cholecystitis, empyema of gall bladder
Abscess
Pelvic inflammatory disease
Cytomegalovirus infection
Lyme disease
Travel-acquired infection: typhoid, dengue, hepatitis, malaria, amoebiasis
Zoonosis: brucellosis, Q fever, leptospirosis, psittacosis
Drug fever

Temperature chart

Charting the patterns of fever may be a diagnostic help because some febrile conditions follow a predictable temperature pattern.[4] Examples are presented in Figure 45.2.

Intermittent fever

This is a fever in which the temperature rises for a few hours and then returns to normal (Fig. 45.2a). Malaria is the classic example: in quartan fever, caused by *Plasmodium malariae*, the attacks occur every 72 hours (the term quartan means every 4th day by inclusive counting). This

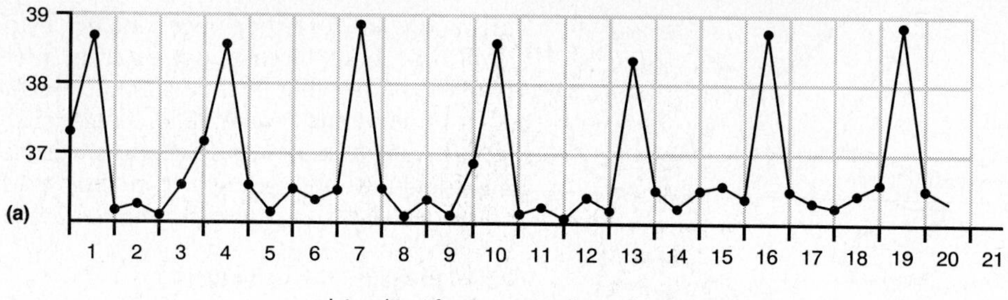

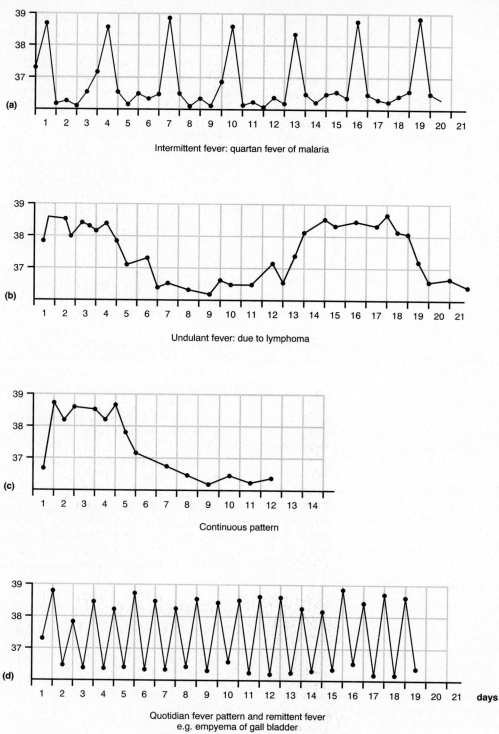

Intermittent fever: quartan fever of malaria

Undulant fever: due to lymphoma

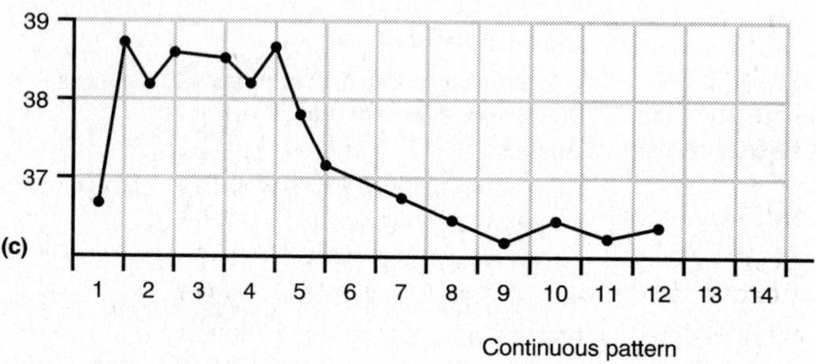

Continuous pattern

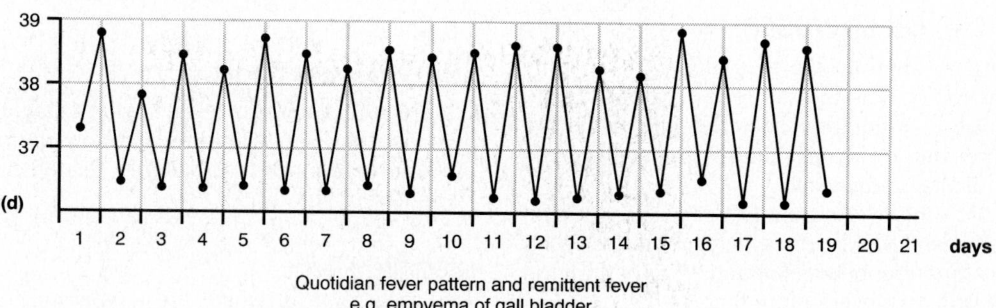

Quotidian fever pattern and remittent fever
e.g. empyema of gall bladder

Fig. 45.2 *Examples of fever patterns from temperature charts* compares with tertian fever from *Plasmodium vivax* in which paroxysms of malaria occur every 48 hours. Other examples are cytomegalovirus, Epstein-Barr mononucleosis and various pyogenic infections, e.g. ascending cholangitis.

Remittent fever

This is a fever in which the temperature returns towards normal for a variable period but is always elevated (Fig. 45.2d). Common examples are collections of pus, e.g. pelvic abscess, wound infection, empyema and carcinoma. It is a common feature of empyema.

Undulant fever

Undulant fever is characterised by bouts of continuous or remittent fever for several days, followed by afebrile remissions lasting a variable number of days. It is commonly a feature of brucellosis infection but is also seen in the lymphomas, especially Hodgkin's lymphoma (Fig. 45.2b).

Continuous fever pattern

This is common with viral infections such as influenza (Fig. 45.2c).

Quotidian fever

In this pattern the fever recurs daily (Fig. 45.2d). Daily fever spikes in the morning are characteristic of pseudomonas infection, e.g. pulmonary superinfection; afternoon spikes are indicative of cytomegalovirus infection; and evening spikes suggest localised collection of pus, e.g. empyema of the gall bladder.

Fever in children

The fever is usually a response to a viral infection. Fever itself is not harmful until it reaches a level of 41.5°.[1] Hyperthermia is uncommon in children. Temperatures above 41°C are usually due to CNS infection or the result of human error, e.g.

- shutting a child in a car on a hot day
- overwrapping a febrile child

Complications include dehydration (usually mild) and febrile convulsions, which occur in 5% of febrile children between six months and five years. Febrile convulsions are triggered by a rapid rise in temperature rather than its absolute level.

Management

- Treatment of low-grade fevers should be discouraged.
- Treatment of high-grade fevers includes:
  - — treatment of the causes of the fever (if appropriate)
  - — adequate fluid intake
  - — paracetamol (acetaminophen) is the preferred antipyretic since aspirin is potentially dangerous in young children. The usual dose of 10–15 mg/kg every 4–6 hours may represent undertreatment. Use 20 mg/kg as a loading dose and then 15 mg/kg maintenance.

Advice to parents

- Dress the child in light clothing (stripping off is unnecessary).
- Do not overheat with too many clothes, rugs or blankets.
- Give frequent small drinks of light fluids, especially water.
- Sponging with cool water and using fans is not effective.

Fever in the elderly

The elderly tend to have a problem with impaired thermoregulation and so they may not develop a fever in response to suppurative infection compared with younger people. This can be misleading in the diagnostic process.

The elderly are more vulnerable to hyperthermia and hypothermia. Heat stroke classically occurs in epidemic form during a heatwave. The syndrome consists of hyperpyrexia, decreased sweating, delirium and coma. The core temperature is usually over 41°C.

Fever of undetermined origin (FUO)

FUO, also referred to as pyrexia of unknown origin (PUO), has the following criteria:

- illness for at least 3 weeks
- fevers > 38°C (100.4°C)
- undiagnosed after 1 week of intensive study

Most cases represent unusual manifestations of common diseases and not rare or exotic diseases. Examples are tuberculosis, bacterial endocarditis, hepatobiliary disease and carcinoma of the lung.[5]

A diagnostic approach

A knowledge of the more common causes of FUO is helpful in planning a diagnostic approach (refer Table 45.2).

Table 45.2 *Common causes of FUO (after Kumar and Clarke)*

Common examples of each group selected
Infection (40%)
Bacteria
• pyogenic abscess, e.g. liver, pelvic
• urinary infection
• biliary infection, e.g. cholangitis
• chronic septicaemia
• infective endocarditis
• Lyme disease
• tuberculosis
• brucellosis
• osteomyelitis
• typhoid/paratyphoid fever
Viral, rickettsial, chlamydia
• Epstein-Barr mononucleosis
• cytomegalovirus
• HIV virus infection (AIDS, ARC)
• Q fever
• psittacosis
Parasitic
• malaria
• toxoplasmosis
• amoebiasis
Malignancy (30%)
Reticuloendothelial
• leukaemia
• lymphomas
Solid (localised) tumours
• kidney
• liver
• pancreas
• stomach
• lung
Disseminated
Immunogenic (20%)
Drugs
Connective tissue diseases/vasculitides
• rheumatic fever
• rheumatoid arthritis
• systemic lupus erythematosus
• polyarthritis nodosa
• giant cell arteritis/polymyalgia
Sarcoidosis
Crohn's disease
Factitious (1-5%)
Remain unknown (5-9%)

History

The history should include consideration of past history, occupation, travel history, sexual history, animal contact, and other relevant factors. Symptoms such as pruritus, a skin rash and fever patterns may provide clues for the diagnosis. The average patient with a difficult FUO needs to have a careful history taken on at least three separate occasions.[3]

Physical examination

A common mistake is the tendency to examine the patient only once and not re-examine. The patient should be examined regularly (as for history taking) as physical signs can develop eventually. Special attention should be paid to the following (Fig. 45.3):

- skin: look for rashes, vesicles and nodules
- the eyes and ocular fundi
- temporal arteries
- sinuses
- teeth and oral cavity: ? dental abscess, other signs
- heart: murmurs, pericardial rubs
- lungs: abnormalities including consolidation, pleuritic rub
- abdomen: enlarged/tender liver, spleen or kidney
- rectal and pelvic examination (note genitalia)
- lymph nodes, especially cervical (supraclavicular)
- blood vessels, especially of the legs ? thrombosis
- urine (analysis)

Investigations

Basic investigations include:

- haemoglobin, red cell indices and blood film
- white cell count
- ESR
- chest X-ray and sinus films
- urine examination (analysis and culture)
- routine blood chemistry
- blood cultures

Further possible investigations:

- stool microscopy and culture
- culture of sputum (if any)
- specific tests for typhoid, E-BM, Q fever, brucellosis, psittacosis, cytomegalovirus, toxoplasmosis, syphilis
- HIV screening
- tests for rheumatic fever
- tuberculin test
- tests for connective tissue disorders, e.g. DNA antibodies, C-reative protein
- upper GIT series with small bowel follow-through

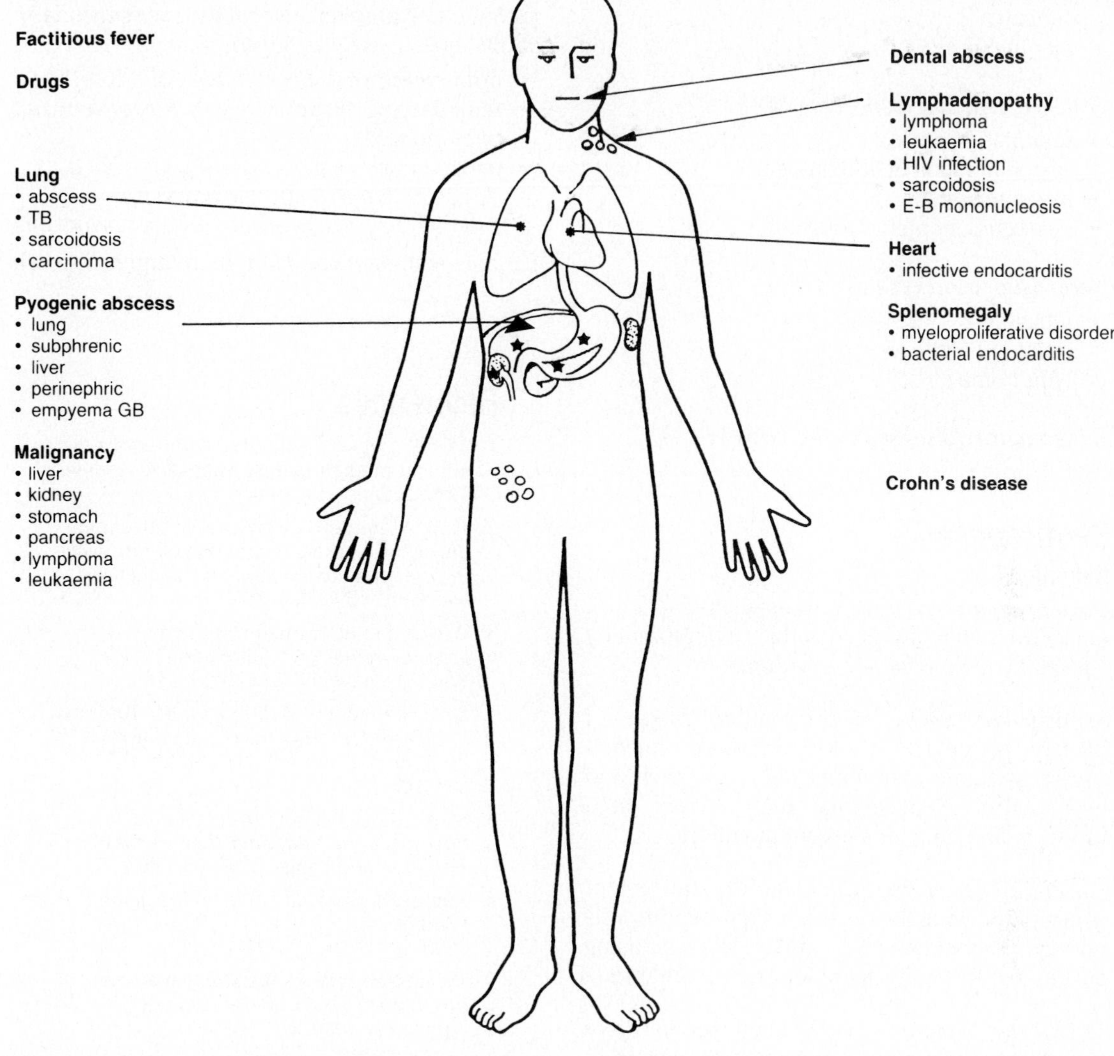

Fig. 45.3 *Sites to consider in FUO (malignancy is indicated by a star)*

- CT and ultrasound scanning
  - for 1° and 2° neoplasia
    - gall bladder functioning
    - occult abscesses
- isotope scanning for specific causes
- aspiration or needle biopsy
- laparoscopy for suspected pelvic infection
- tissue biopsies, e.g. lymph nodes, skin, liver, bone marrow (as indicated)

FUO in children

Fever in children is usually a transient phenomenon and subsides within 4–5 days. At least 70% of all infections are viral. Occasionally a child will present with FUO which may be masked from antibiotic administration. Common causes of prolonged fever in children differ from those in adults. Most cases are not due to unusual or esoteric disorders,[7] the majority representing atypical manifestation of common diseases.

A summary of the common causes (with the most common ranked first) is as follows.[7]

Infectious causes (40%)

- viral syndrome
- urinary tract infection
- pneumonia

- pharyngitis
- sinusitis
- meningitis

Collagen-vascular disorders (15%)

- rheumatic arthritis
- systemic lupus erythematosus
- rheumatic fever
- Henoch-Schönlein syndrome

Neoplastic disorders (7%)

- leukaemia
- reticulum cell sarcoma
- lymphoma

Inflammatory diseases of the bowel (4%)

Septicaemia

Definitions

Bacteraemia refers to the transient presence of bacteria in the blood (usually asymptomatic) caused by local infection or trauma.

Septicaemia refers to the multiplication of bacteria or fungi in the blood, usually causing severe systemic symptoms such as fever and hypotension. Septicaemia has a very high mortality and demands urgent attention.

Pyaemia is a serious manifestation of septicaemia whereby organisms and neutrophils undergo embolisation to many sites, causing abscesses especially in the lungs, liver and brain.

Primary septicaemia refers to septicaemia where the focus of infection is not apparent, while in *secondary septicaemia* a primary focus can be identified. Examples of secondary septicaemia in adults are:

- urinary tract, e.g. *Escherichia coli* (*E.coli*)
- respiratory tract, e.g. *Streptococcus pneumoniae*
- pelvic organs, e.g. *Neisseria gonorrhoea*
- skin, e.g. *Staphylococcus aureus*
- gall bladder, e.g. *E.coli*, *Streptococcus faecalis*

Patients with septicaemia require urgent referral.

References

1. Sewell J. Fever in childhood. Problems in clinical medicine. Aust. Paediatric Review, 1990;2:2.
2. Yung A, Stanley P. Problems in infectious diseases. In: Kincaid Smith et al. *Problems in clinical medicine*. Sydney: MacLennan and Petty, 1990, 326–335.
3. Wilson J et al. *Harrison's principles of internal medicine* (12th edition). New York: McGraw-Hill, 1991, 129–131.
4. Beck ER, Francis JL, Souhami RL. *Tutorials in differential diagnosis* (2nd edition). Edinburgh: Churchill Livingstone, 1987, 205–208.
5. Schroeder SA et al. *Current medical diagnosis and treatment*. East Norwalk: Appleton and Lange, 1990, 891–892.
6. Kumer PJ, Clark ML. *Clinical medicine* (2nd edition). London: Bailliere Tindall, 1990, 9.
7. Tunnessen WW Jr. *Signs and symptoms in paediatrics* (2nd edition). Philadelphia: JB Lippincott, 1988, 3–6.

46

Faints, fits and funny turns

When a patient presents with the complaint of a 'funny turn' it is usually possible to determine that they have one of the more recognisable presenting problems such as fainting, 'blackouts', lightheadedness, weakness, palpitations, vertigo or migraine. However, there are patients who do present with confusing problems that warrant the label of 'funny turn'. The most common problem with funny turns is that of misdiagnosis so a proper and adequate history taking is of great importance.

It is important to remember that seemingly 'funny turns' may be the subjective interpretation of cultural and linguistic communication barriers, especially in an emotional and frustrated patient.[1] Various causes of faints, fits and funny turns are presented in Table 46.1. A useful simple classification is to consider them as:

- snycope
- seizures
- narcolepsy/cataplexy
- labyrinthine

Table 46.1 *Faints, fits and funny turns: checklist of causes (excluding tonic-clonic seizure and stroke)*

Psychogenic/communication problems

Conversion reactions (hysteria)
Culture/language conflicts
Fugue states
Hyperventilation
Malingering
Personality disorders
Phobia/anxiety states
Psychoses/severe depression

Other conditions

Transient ischaemic attacks
Complex partial seizure (temporal lobe epilepsy)
Tonic, clonic or atonic seizures
Primary absence seizure
Migraine variants or equivalents
Cardiovascular disorders
- arrhythmias
- postural hypotension
- aortic stenosis

Vertigo
Drug reaction
Alcohol and other substance abuse
Hypoglycaemia
Anaemia
Amnesic episodes
Metabolic/electrolyte disturbances
Vasovagal/syncope
Carotid sinus sensitivity
Cervical spondylosis
Catoplexy
Narcolepsy
Autonomic failure

Key facts and checkpoints

- The commonest cause of 'funny turns' presenting in general practice is lightheadedness, often related to psychogenic factors such as anxiety, panic and hyperventilation.[2] Patients usually call this 'dizziness'.

- Absence attacks occur with minor forms of epilepsy and with partial seizures such as temporal lobe seizures.
- The psychomotor attack of complex partial seizure presents as a diagnostic difficulty. The most commonly misdiagnosed seizure disorder is that of complex partial seizures or atypical generalised tonic clonic seizures (tonic or clonic or atonic).
- The diagnosis of epilepsy is made on the history (or video EEG), rather than on the standard EEG, although a sleep-deprived EEG is more effective.
- The triad—angina/dyspnoea/blackout or lightheadedness—indicates aortic stenosis.
- Severe cervical spondylosis can cause vertebrobasilar ischaemia by causing pressure on the vertebral arteries which pass through the intervertebral foraminae.

The diagnostic approach

A summary of the diagnostic strategy model is presented in Table 46.2.

Table 46.2 *Faints, fits and funny turns: diagnostic strategy model*

Q. *Probability diagnosis*
A. Anxiety related/hyperventilation
Vasovagal syncope
Postural hypotension

Q. *Serious disorders not to be missed*
A. Cardiovascular
- arrhythmias
- aortic stenosis

Cerebrovascular
- TIAs

Neoplasia
- space-occupying lesions

Severe infections
- infective endocarditis

Hypoglycaemia

Q. *Pitfalls (often missed)*
A. Atypical migraine
Cardiac arrhythmias
Simple partial seizures
Complex partial seizures
Atypical tonic clonic seizures
Drugs/alcohol/marijuana
Electrolyte disturbances, e.g. hypokalaemia
Rarities
- narcolepsy
- atrial myxoma

Q. *Seven masquerades checklist*

A.		
	Depression	✓
	Diabetes	✓ hypoglycaemia
	Drugs	✓
	Anaemia	✓
	Thyroid disease	—
	Spinal dysfunction	✓ cervical spondylosis
	UTI	—

Q. *Is this patient trying to tell me something?*
A. Highly likely. Psychogenic and 'communication' disorders quite significant.

History

The clinical history is of paramount importance in unravelling the problem. A reliable eye witness account of the 'turn' is invaluable, as is the setting or circumstances in which the 'episode' occurred.

It is essential at first to determine exactly what the patient means by 'funny turn'. In the process of questioning it is appropriate to evaluate the mental state and personal and social factors of the patient. It may be appropriate to confront the patient about feelings of depression, anxiety or detachment from reality.

It is important to break up the history into three components. The first is the lead-up to the episode, the second is adequate description of what took place during the episode and, thirdly, the events that took place after the episode.

Apart from the events note the patient's feelings, symptoms, circumstances and provocative factors. Search for possible secondary gain.

Onset

A sudden onset may be due to cardiac causes, especially arrhythmias, which may include the more common supraventricular tachycardias in addition to the less common but more dramatic arrhythmias that may cause unconsciousness. Other causes of a sudden onset include the various epilepsies, vasovagal attacks and TIAs.

Precipitating factors[2]

Enquire about precipitating factors such as emotion, stress, pain, heat, fright, exertion, suddenly standing up, coughing or head movement.

- emotion and stress suggest hyperventilation
- fright, pain → vasovagal attack
- standing up → postural hypotension
- exertion → aortic stenosis
- head movement → cervical spondylosis with vertebrobasilar insufficiency

Associated symptoms[2]

Certain associated symptoms give an indication of the underlying disorder:

- breathing problems and hyperventilation suggest an anxiety state

- tingling in extremities or tightening of the hand → anxiety/hyperventilation
- visual problems → migraine, TIA
- fear or panic → anxiety or complex partial seizure
- hallucinations (taste/smell/visual) → complex partial seizure
- speech problems → TIA/anxiety
- sweating, hunger feelings → hypoglycaemia
- related to food → migraine
- first thing in morning → consider 'hangover'

Drug history
This requires careful analysis and includes alcohol intake and illicit drugs such as marijuana, cocaine and amphetamines. Prescribed drugs that can cause lightheadedness or unconsciousness are listed in Table 46.3.

Sudden cessation of certain drugs such as phenothiazines can also be responsible for 'funny turns'.

Table 46.3 *Typical drugs that may cause lightheadedness or blackouts*

Alcohol
Peripheral vasodilators
• ACE inhibitors
• glyceryl trinitrate
• hydralazine
• prazosin
Anticonvulsants
Antihypertensives
Barbiturates
Benzodiazepines
Phenothiazines
Phenoxybenzamine
Tricyclic antidepressants
OTC anticholinergic compounds

Past history
The past history may give an indication of the cause of the 'turn'. Such conditions include hypertension, migraine, epilepsy, rheumatic heart disease, atherosclerosis, e.g. angina, vascular claudication, alcohol or other substance abuse and psychiatric disorders.

Diary of events
If the diagnosis is elusive it may help to get the patient to keep a diary of circumstances in which events take place, keeping in mind the importance of the time period prior, during and post episode.

The examination

Important focal points of the physical examination include:

- evaluation of the mental state, especially for anxiety
- looking for evidence of anaemia, alcohol abuse and infection
- cerebrovascular examination: carotid arteries, ocular fundi, bruits
- cardiovascular examination: pulses, BP, heart (the BP should be taken lying, sitting and standing)
- the cervical spine

Various manoeuvres
Subject the patient to a number of manoeuvres to try to induce various sensations in order to try to identify the one that affects them. These should include sudden assumption of the erect posture from a squat, spinning the patient and then a sudden stop, head positioning with either ear down (Fig. 39.3), Valsalva manoeuvre, hyperventilation for 60 seconds. Children can spin a showbag 'windmill'. Ask 'which one mimics your complaint?'

Investigations
Depending on the clinical findings investigations can be selected from the following tests:

- Full blood count ? anaemia ? polycythemia
- Blood sugar ? diabetes ? hypoglycaemia
- Urea and electrolytes
- ECG ? ischaemia ? arrhythmia
- 24 hour ambulatory cardiac (Holter) monitor ? arrhythmia
- Radiology/imaging
  - — cervical X-ray
  - — chest X-ray
  - — carotid duplex Doppler scan: ? carotid artery stenosis
  - — CT scan
  - — MRI scan
- Electroencephalogram (EEG) or video EEG EEGs include those recorded with sleep deprivation, hyperventilation or photic stimulation.

Blackouts

The important causes of blackout include the various syncopes that are listed in Table 61.3 and the various forms of epilepsy. The classic tonic clonic seizure is described in Chapter 61 (The unconscious patient) while descriptions of other seizures producing blackouts or funny turns now follow.

Complex partial seizures

In complex partial seizures (previously known as temporal lobe epilepsy) the symptomatology varies considerably from patient to patient and is often a diagnostic problem. It is the commonest type of focal epilepsy and the attacks vary in time from momentary to several minutes.

Possible manifestations[2]

Commonest: slight disturbance of perception and consciousness

Hallucinations
- visual
- taste
- smell
- sounds

Absence attacks or vertigo

Illusions—objects/people shrink or expand

Affective feelings—fear, anxiety, anger

Dyscognitive effects
- déja vu (familiarity)
- jamais vu (unreality)
- waves emanating from epigastrium

Objective signs
- lip-smacking
- swallowing/chewing/sucking
- unresponsive to commands or questions
- pacing around a room

Unreal or detached feelings are common in complex partial seizures. There can be permanent short-term memory loss. The sensation of strange smells or tastes is more common than auditory or visual hallucinations.[1]

Diagnosis

- EEG — diagnostic in 50–60% of cases
  — a repeat EEG will increase rate to 60–80%
- EEG/video telemetry helpful with frequent attacks
- CT or MRI scan—to exclude tumour when diagnosis confirmed

Medication

carbamazepine (1st choice)[4]
or
sodium valproate
or
clonazepam

Atypical tonic clonic seizures

These variants of tonic clonic seizures are more common than realised. Some patients may simply stiffen or drop to the ground while others may have one or two jerks or shakes only.

- stiffen and fall = tonic
- floppy and fall = atonic
- shaking only = clonic

Simple partial seizures

In simple partial seizures there is no loss of consciousness. These include focal seizures which may proceed to a generalised tonic clonic seizure or to motor seizures—Jacksonian epilepsy.

Jacksonian (motor seizure)

Typically, jerking movements begin at the angle of the mouth or in the thumb and index finger and 'march' to involve the rest of the body, e.g. thumb → hand → limb → face ± leg on one side and then on to the contralateral side. A tonic clonic or complex partial seizure may follow.

Medication

carbamazepine (1st choice)[4]
or
phenytoin (2nd choice)
or
sodium valproate

Absence seizure (previously called petit mal)

This type of generalised epilepsy typically affects children from 4 years up to puberty.[2]

- child ceases activity and stares suddenly
- child is motionless
- no warning
- sometimes clonic (jerky) movement of eyelids, face, fingers
- may be lip-smacking or chewing (called complex absence)
- only lasts a few seconds—usually 5–10 seconds
- child then carries on as though nothing happened
- usually several per day (not just one or two)
- may lead to generalised seizures in adulthood

Diagnosis

Best evoked in the consulting room by hyperventilation.

EEG • classic 3–H_2 wave and spike
- may be normal
- always include hyperventilation

Medication

sodium valproate (1st choice)[4]
or
ethosuximide (2nd choice)
or
clonazepam

NB Beware of hepatotoxicity with sodium valproate.

Narcolepsy

Narcolepsy is characterised by brief spells of irresistible sleep during daytime hours, usually at times when the average person simply feels sleepy. Although patients are usually aware of their disorder some may have no insight into the problem and present with the complaint of unusual turns. Narcolepsy can present as 'attacks' in which the patient may crumple and fall without losing consciousness. It can be part of a tetrad syndrome (narcolepsy, cataplexy, hypnogogic hallucinations, sleep paralysis).

Other features:

- onset in teens or twenties
- can have several attacks per day

Diagnosis

- A clinical diagnosis

If doubtful

- EEG monitoring
- sleep laboratory studies—rapid eye movement is a hallmark

Medication

- amphetamines (in slowly increasing doses)
  or
  methylphenidate (Ritalin)
- tricyclic antidepressants, e.g. clomipramine, for associated cataplexy

Amnesic episodes

Amnesic episodes in which people cannot recall events or their own identity can be psychogenic (commonly) or related to an organic problem such as epilepsy or a cerebrovascular disorder. In the latter an unusual disorder—transient global amnesia—can occur.

Cerebrovascular disorders

Cerebrovascular disease is one of the major causes of mortality and morbidity in developed countries and can cause recurrent attacks of ischaemia in the carotid and vertebrobasilar systems (particularly vertebrobasilar insufficiency) which may present as 'funny turns'. In particular, brain stem ischaemia causes 'funny turns' such as impaired consciousness including transient global amnesia, drop attacks and the 'locked in' syndrome.

Stroke

A stroke is a focal neurological deficit lasting longer than 24 hours in a surviving patient, and is caused by a vascular phenomenon.

Interesting facts

- Thromboembolism from vascular disease outside the brain causes 70% of strokes and 90% of TIAs.
- Such sources are atheromatous plaques within the carotid and vertebral systems or cardiac causes, e.g. postmyocardial infarction.

Transient ischaemic attacks

Definitions

Transient ischaemic attack (TIA)

A TIA is a focal neurological deficit lasting less than 24 hours.

Features

- sudden onset
- complete clinical recovery
- average length of time is 5 minutes
- consciousness usually preserved

A comparison of the main clinical features of carotid (anterior circulation) ischaemia and vertebrobasilar (posterior circulation) ischaemia is presented in Figure 46.1.

Some ischaemic syndromes:

- amaurosis fugax
- transient global amnesia
- the 'locked in' syndrome

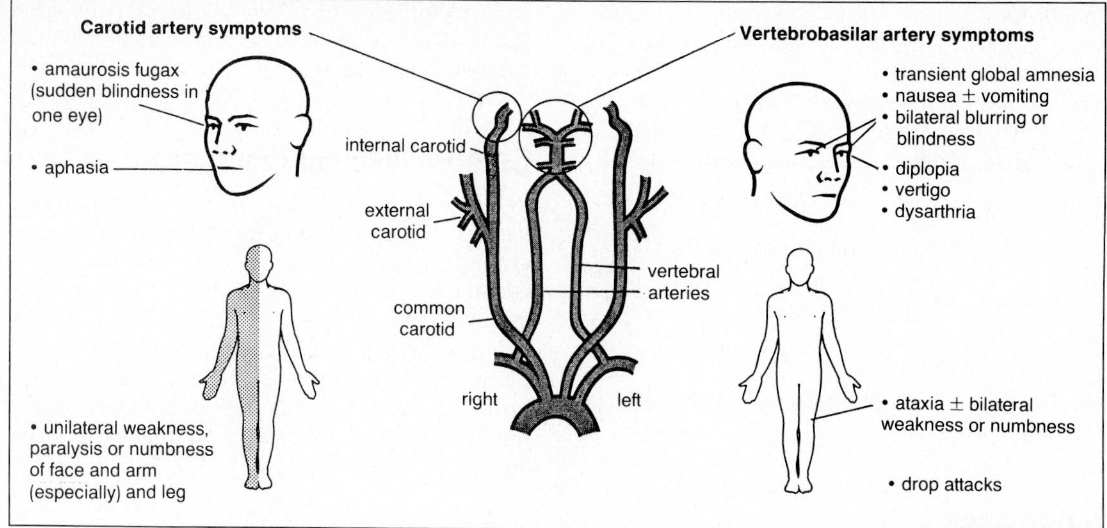

Fig. 46.1 *Cerebral arterial circulation with some important clinical features of carotid and vertebrobasilar ischaemia*
REPRODUCED FROM C. KENNA AND J. MURTAGH *BACK PAIN AND SPINAL MANIPULATION*, BUTTERWORTHS, SYDNEY, 1989, WITH PERMISSION

Amaurosis fugax

This is the sudden transient loss of vision in one eye due to the passage of emboli through the retinal vessels. It is a feature of a TIA in the carotid artery circulation and is often the first clinical evidence of carotid stenosis.[3] Amaurosis fugax may forewarn of the development of hemiparesis or blindness and should be considered a matter for urgent attention and rectification.

Transient global amnesia

This is characterised by amnesia and confusion lasting for hours and tends to suggest vertebrobasilar ischaemia.

The 'locked in' syndrome

In this interesting syndrome, which may be transient or persistent, patients remain conscious and aware of their dilemma but are unable to speak or move the limbs, particularly the arms.

It may be possible to communicate with them with eye responses to commands. The cause is invariably a lesion in the brainstem.

Significance

TIAs have important clinical significance. Studies have shown that five years after a TIA, one out of six patients (without treatment) will have suffered a stroke,[3] the highest risk being in the first six months. A carotid artery TIA has more serious prognostic significance than a vertebrobasilar TIA. Hence referral for investigation is appropriate. Cardiac status should be assessed since there is a strong association with myocardial infarction.

Optimal management of TIAs

- Commence aspirin, e.g. 100 mg daily.
- Aspirin gives about 30% protection from stroke or death after TIA.[5]
- The new antiplatelet agent, ticlopidine, has a proven stroke preventive effect.
- Cease smoking and treat hypertension (if applicable).
- Investigations:
  - — full blood count
  - — blood glucose, creatinine and cholesterol
  - — carotid duplex doppler screening (the investigation of choice)
  - — cardiac function.
- Carotid endarterectomy: although its efficacy is uncertain it does appear to have a place in the management of carotid artery stenosis and the decision depends on the expertise of the unit. There is no evidence that surgery is appropriate for the asymptomatic patient or the symptomatic patient with a stenosis less than 30%, but there is significant benefit for a stenosis greater than 70%.

Indications for carotid duplex doppler studies:

- bruit in neck, because of significant stroke rate
- TIAs

- crescendo TIAs (more frequent and longer-lasting)
- vertebrobasilar insufficiency symptoms
- hemispheric stroke
- prior to major vascular surgery, e.g. CABG

Psychogenic or communication disorders

Psychogenic causes have to be considered. 'Hysterical fugue' is one such manifestation. The problem can be a communication disorder, such as an emotional person trying to communicate a problem in a language foreign to them.

Patients with psychiatric disorders such as schizophrenia or depression may experience feelings of depersonalisation, or unreality, which can be interpreted as a 'turn', or even temporal lobe epilepsy.

Patients who complain of vague and bizarre symptoms such as 'queer feelings in the head', 'swimming sensation', 'unreal feelings' and 'walking on air' are likely to have an anxiety state.

Severe anxiety or panic attacks typically cause lightheadedness which presents as a 'funny turn'. Other somatic symptoms include palpitations, sweating, inability to swallow, headache, breathlessness and manifestations of hyperventilation.

When to refer

- Transient ischaemic attacks, especially if the diagnosis is in doubt.
- Clinical suspicion of or proven cardiac arrhythmias.
- Evidence of aortic stenosis.
- Seizures.
- General uncertainty of the diagnosis.

Pitfalls in management[2]

- The main pitfall associated with seizure disorders and epilepsy is misdiagnosis (not all seizures are generalised tonic clonic in nature).
- Failing to place appropriate emphasis on the history in making the diagnosis.
- Misdiagnosing syncope with some involuntary movements for epilepsy.
- Overlooking cardiac arrhythmias as a cause of funny turns including recurrent dizziness.
- Failing to consider the possibility of aortic stenosis with syncopal attacks.
- Misdiagnosing vertigo and syncope for TIA.
- Mistaking visual or sensory migraine equivalents in young adults for TIA.
- Overlooking drugs (including self-administered drugs) as a cause of lightheadedness.

Practice tips

- A detailed clinical analysis is more important in the first instance than laboratory tests. The key to accurate diagnosis is a very careful history, taking the patient second by second through the attack and events preceding the turn.
- Talk to as many eye witnesses as possible in unravelling the cause.
- For 'undiagnosed turns' ask the patient to keep a diary with an accurate record of the attack including preceding events.
- Remember that migraine is a great mimic and can cause confusion in diagnosis.
- Remember that the EEG can be normal in the confirmed epileptic.
- The more bizarre the description of a 'funny turn', the more likely a functional problem is the cause.

References

1. Kincaid-Smith P, Larkins R, Whelan G. *Problems in clinical medicine*. Sydney: MacLennan & Petty, 1990, 159–164.
2. Sandler G, Fry J. *Early clinical diagnosis*. Lancaster: MTP Press, 1986, 411–430.
3. Kumar PJ, Clark ML. *Clinical Medicine* (2nd edition). London: Bailliere Tindall, 1990, 907–913.
4. Scott AK. 'Management of epilepsy'. In: *Central nervous system*. London: British Medical Association, 1–2.
5. Leicester J. Stroke and transient cerebral ischaemic attacks. In: MIMS Disease Index. Sydney: IMS Publishing, 1991–2, 518–520.

47

Haematemesis and melaena

Acute severe upper gastrointestinal (GI) haemorrhage is an important medical emergency. The dramatic symptom of haematemesis follows bleeding from the oesophagus, stomach and duodenum.

Haematemesis is the vomiting of blood. Melaena is the passage of black tarry stools, with 50 ml or more of blood required to produce melaena stool. Melaena occurs in most patients with upper GI haemorrhage and haematemesis occurs in over 50%.[1]

Key facts and checkpoints

- Chronic peptic ulceration accounts for most cases of upper GI haemorrhage.
- Haematemesis is almost always associated with some degree of blood in the stools, although melaena may not necessarily accompany it especially if bleeding occurs from the oesophagus.
- Black stool caused by oral iron therapy or bismuth-containing antacid tablets can cause confusion.
- Always check for a history of drug intake, especially aspirin and NSAIDs.
- Corticosteroids in conventional therapeutic doses are thought to have no influence on GI haemorrhage.
- The volume of the bleeding is best assessed by its haemodynamic effects rather than relying on the patient's estimation, which tends to be excessive.
- Melaena is generally less life-threatening than haematemesis.
- A sudden loss of 20% or more circulatory blood volume usually produces signs of shock such as tachycardia, hypotension, faintness and sweating. Younger patients can compensate better and tolerate a larger loss prior to the development of shock.[1] A useful guide is that shock in a previously well 70 kg man indicates an acute blood loss of at least 1000–1500 ml.

Causes of upper GI bleeding

The major cause of bleeding is chronic peptic ulceration of the duodenum and stomach, which accounts for approximately half of all cases.[2] The other major cause is acute gastric ulcers and erosions, which account for at least 20% of cases. Aspirin and NSAIDs are responsible for many of these bleeds. Causes are summarised in Table 47.1 and illustrated in Figure 47.1.

Table 47.1 *Causes of upper gastrointestinal bleeding*[3]

1. Duodenal ulcer
2. Gastric erosion
3. Gastric ulcer
4. Reflux oesophagitis
5. Oesophageal varices

Others
- Mallory-Weiss syndrome
- Gastric carcinoma
- Stomal ulcer
- Blood dyscrasias
- Anticoagulant therapy

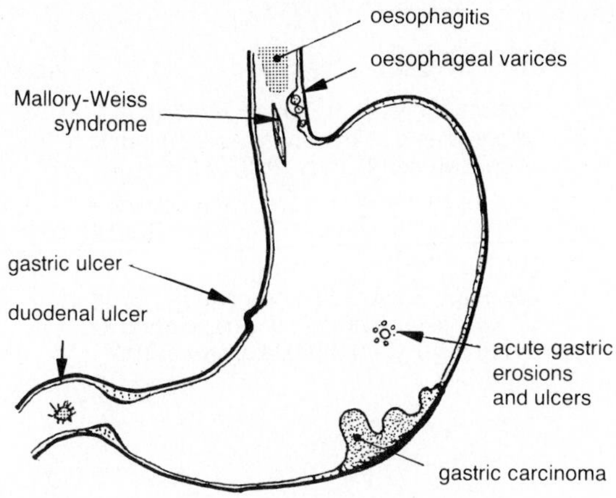

Fig. 47.1 *Important causes of haematemesis and melaena*

Mallory-Weiss syndrome

In this condition a tear occurs at the lower end of the oesophageal mucosa (at the oesophago-gastric junction) because of an episode of severe or protracted vomiting or coughing. Blood appears in the vomitus after a bout of heavy vomiting or dry retching. It is usually seen in alcoholic patients.

Gastro-oesophageal varices

Such varices are caused by portal hypertension which in turn is usually due to cirrhosis of the liver. There is a raised incidence of peptic ulcer in those with liver cirrhosis, especially in biliary and alcohol-induced cirrhosis, so this should be kept in mind as a possible source of bleeding.

The clinical approach

History

It is important to establish the nature of the vomitus and the possibility of bleeding arising from the mouth, nose or pharynx. A coffee grounds vomitus indicates that the blood has been in contact with gastric acid. Oesophageal bleeding tends to lead to vomiting of fresh blood. Questions to help pinpoint the possible aetiology should be asked.

Key questions

What drugs have you been taking?
Have you been taking aspirin or tablets for arthritis or back pain?
How much have you vomited?
What did the vomit look like?
Do you notice black dots like coffee grounds or any blood clots?
Have you had any indigestion, heartburn or stomach pains recently?
Have you opened your bowels and if so what was the colour?
Have you noticed whether your bowel motions were black or unusual in any way?
How much alcohol do you drink?
Have you had any previous operations on your stomach for a peptic ulcer?
Were you vomiting normal vomit before the blood appeared?

Physical examination

The patient's general state, particularly the circulation, should be assessed immediately on presentation. A careful abdominal examination should be performed including a digital rectal examination. As a rule abdominal findings are not remarkable except when a mass, hepatomegaly or splenomegaly is found. Other evidence of liver disease should be sought.

Investigations

Investigations to determine the source of the bleeding should be carried out in a specialist unit. Endoscopy will detect the cause of the bleeding in at least 80% of cases.[2]

The haemoglobin level will not be an appropriate guide to blood loss or the need for transfusion during the early stages, because haemodilution occurs gradually over the 24 hours following a severe bleed. However, a level below 10 g/dL during this period is usually regarded as an indication for transfusion.

Management

The immediate objectives are:

1. restore an effective blood volume (if necessary)
2. establish a diagnosis to allow definitive treatment

All patients with a significant bleed should be admitted to hospital and referred to a specialist unit. Urgent resuscitation is required where there has been a large bleed and there are clinical signs of shock. Such patients require an intravenous line inserted and transfusion with blood cells or fresh frozen plasma (or both) commenced as soon as possible.

In many patients bleeding is insufficient to decompensate the circulatory system and they settle spontaneously. Approximately 85% of patients stop bleeding within 48 hours.[2]

Most patients require no specific therapy after resuscitation. In some instances surgery will be necessary to arrest bleeding but should be avoided if possible in patients with acute gastric erosion.

References

1. Schroeder SA et al *Current medical diagnoses and treatment.* East Norwalk: Appleton and Lange, 1990, 381–382.
2. Kumer PJ, Clark ML. *Clinical medicine* (2nd edition). London: Bailliere Tindall, 1990, 194–196.
3. Beck ER, Francis JL, Souhami RL. *Tutorials in differential diagnosis* (2nd edition). Edinburgh: Churchill Livingstone, 1988, 71–75.

48

Headache

When the head aches, all the body is out of tune.
Cervantes

Headache, one of the cardinal symptoms known to human beings, is a very common complaint in general practice. When a patient presents with 'headache' we need to have a sound diagnostic and management strategy as the problem can be confusing. The key to analysing the symptom of headache is to know and understand the causes, for 'one only sees what they know'.

The patient's manner of presentation can confuse us because many tend to influence us with preconceived ideas that they will verbalise—'I think I need my blood pressure checked' or 'My eyes need testing'—or they may not mention their anxiety about a cerebral tumour or an impending stroke.

Hypertension is such a rare cause of headache that one is tempted to stress the adage 'hypertension does not cause headache', but we do encounter the occasional patient whose headache appears to be caused by hypertension and it is mandatory to measure the blood pressure of patients presenting with headache. Patients expect this routine and reassurance is difficult without the appropriate physical examination.

The diagnosis of serious causes of headache depends on a careful history, a high index of suspicion of the 'different' presentations and the judicious use of CT scanning.

Key facts and checkpoints

- 85% of the population will have experienced headache within one year and 38% of adults will have had a headache within two weeks.[1]
- 40% of children will have experienced one or more headaches by the age of 7 and 75% by the age of 15.[2]
- Migraine affects at least 10% of the adult population and one-quarter of these patients require medical attention for their attacks at some stage.[3]
- 5% of children suffer from migraine by the age of 11 years.[3]
- 70% of sufferers have a positive family history of migraine.
- Migraine and tension headaches are far less common than considered in the past, especially tension headaches.[3]
- Many headaches previously considered to be tension are secondary to disorders of the neck, eyes, teeth, temporomandibular joints or other structures.[3]
- Drug-induced headaches are common and must be considered in the history.
- In children the triad of symptoms—dizziness, headache and vomiting—indicates medulloblastoma of the posterior fossa until proved otherwise.
- A typical triad of symptoms in an adult with a cerebral tumour (advanced) is headache, vomiting and convulsions.

- Bronchial carcinoma is the commonest cause of intracerebral malignancy.

A diagnostic approach

A summary of the safety diagnostic model is presented in Table 48.1.

Table 48.1 *Headache: diagnostic strategy model*

Q. *Probability diagnosis*
A. Acute: respiratory infection
Chronic: tension headache
combination headache

Q. *Serious disorders not to be missed*
A. Cardiovascular
- subarachnoid haemorrhage
- intracerebral haemorrhage
- temporal arteritis

Neoplasia
- cerebral tumour
- pituitary tumour

Severe infections
- meningitis, esp. fungal

Haematoma: extradural/subdural
Glaucoma
Benign intracranial hypertension

Q. *Pitfalls (often missed)*
A. Cervical spondylosis/dysfunction
Dental disorders
Refractive errors of eye
Sinusitis
Ophthalmic herpes zoster (pre-eruption)
Exertional headache
Hypoglycaemia
Post-traumatic headache
Post-spinal procedure, e.g. epidural

Rarities
Paget's disease
Post-sexual intercourse
Cushing's syndrome
Conn's syndrome
Addison's disease
Dysautonomic cephalgia

Q. *Seven masquerades checklist*

A.	
Depression	✓✓
Diabetes	✓
Drugs	✓✓
Anaemia	✓
Thyroid disease	✓
Spinal dysfunction	✓
UTI	✓

Q. *Is the patient trying to tell me something?*
A. Quite likely if there is an underlying psychogenic disorder.

Probability diagnosis

The commonest cause of headache presenting in general practice is respiratory infection.[1] For chronic recurrent headache the author has found that tension and combination headaches are the commonest, with combination (mixed) headache responsible for 21% of these presentations. Combination headaches, typified by relatively constant pain lasting for many days, have a mix of components such as tension, depression, cervical dysfunction, vascular headache and drug dependence. Migraine is not as common in general practice as it is in consultant practice. Tension headache too is far less common than previously promulgated.[3]

Serious disorders not to be missed

For the acute onset of headache it is vital not to miss subarachnoid haemorrhage or meningitis. Intracranial haemorrhage, especially involving cerebellar, intraventricular and frontal lobe areas, needs to be considered. It is worth keeping in mind the special problem of people taking monoamine (MAO) inhibitors who imbibe foodstuffs containing tyramine and other catechol derivatives, for example, cheese, yeast extracts, broad beans, cream, chocolate and alcohol. For chronic headache, space-occupying lesions including subdural haematomas must be considered. Since headaches tend to decrease with age, headaches developing in the elderly should be viewed with suspicion and this includes considering temporal arteritis. Benign intracranial hypertension should be considered, especially in young obese women.

Pitfalls

The list (Table 48.1) contains some controversial causes of headache, although some should be obvious if a careful history is elucidated. These include post-traumatic headache; postprocedural headache, for example, lumbar puncture and spinal anaesthesia; and exertional headache. Sinusitis can be overlooked in the absence of respiratory signs. Refractive errors of the eye, although an uncommon cause of headache, do warrant consideration.

General pitfalls

- Overinvestigating the patient with headache, especially as a substitute for a careful history and examination.
- Failing to appreciate that a combination of factors and cervical dysfunction are common causes of headache.
- Omitting to measure the blood pressure in the patient complaining of headache.

- Rushing in with antibiotics for a patient (especially children) with fever and headache—bacterial meningitis may be masked.
- Attributing the early headache of a space-occupying lesion to tension or hypertension.

Seven masquerades checklist

Of the masquerades, depression and drugs are important causes of headache. Cervical dysfunction is certainly an important cause and tends to be ignored by some doctors. Australian figures are misleading because many of these patients gravitate to alternative health professionals.

A United Kingdom study placed headache from cervical spondylosis on almost equal terms with migraine.[1]

The explanation for referral of pain from disorders of the upper cervical spine to the head and eye is that some afferent fibres from the upper three cervical nerve roots converge on cells in the posterior horn of the spinal cord (which can also be excited by trigeminal afferent fibres) thus conveying to the patient the impression of head pain through this shared pathway (Fig. 48.1).

Significant drug causes are listed in Table 48.2. Anaemia can cause headache, usually if the haemoglobin level falls below 10 g/dL.[4] Hypothyroidism may also cause headache, and in diabetics hypoglycaemia is often responsible.

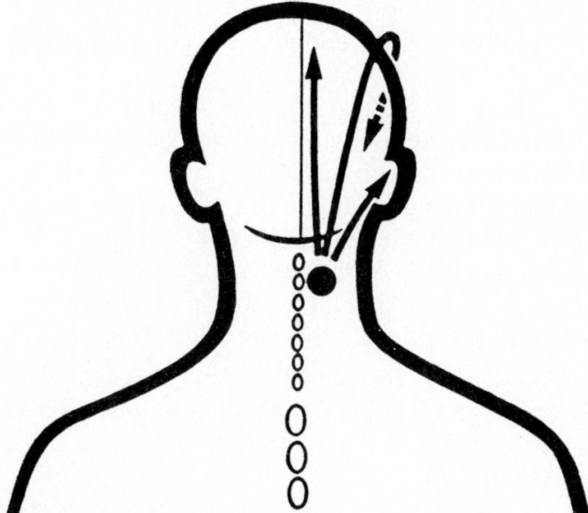

Fig. 48.1 *Typical headache referral patterns for dysfunction of the upper cervical spinal segments*

Psychogenic considerations

Headache, like tiredness, is one of those symptoms that may reflect a 'hidden agenda'. Of course the patient may be depressed (overt or masked) or may have a true anxiety state. The most characteristic feature of psychogenic headache is that the headache is present virtually every minute of the day for weeks or months on end. However, it is common for patients to deny that they are anxious, depressed or unduly stressed. For this reason a detailed history is important to identify lifestyle factors and historical events that can be associated with headache.

Some patients are fearful of their headache lest it represent a cerebral tumour, stroke or hypertension and need appropriate reassurance.

Conversion reactions and other aspects of compensation rewards, especially following an accident, e.g. rear-end collision, may make the symptom of headache difficult to manage. Headache, like backache, is one of the prime symptoms perpetuated or exaggerated for secondary gain.

Severe headaches, especially simulated migraine, are common 'tickets of entry' for drug addicts seeking narcotics from empathic practitioners. Such patients require very skilled management.

Table 48.2 *Drugs that can cause headache*

Alcohol
Analgesics (rebound)
e.g. aspirin
codeine
Antibiotics and antifungals
Antihypertensives
e.g. methyldopa
hydrallazine
reserpine
calcium channel blockers
Caffeine
Corticosteroids
Cyclosporin
Dipyridamole
Ergotamine (rebound)
H_2 antagonists
e.g. cimetidine
ranitidine
MAO inhibitors
Nicotine
Nitrazepam
Nitrous oxide
NSAIDs
e.g. indomethacin
Oral contraceptives
Sympathomimetics
Theophylline
Vasodilators
e.g. calcium channel blockers
nitrates

Diurnal patterns of pain

Plotting the fluctuation of headache during the day provides vital clues to the diagnosis (Fig. 48.2). The patient who wakes up with headache could have vascular headache (migraine), cervical spondylosis, depressive illness, hypertension or a space-occupying lesion. It is usual for migraine to last hours, not days, which is more characteristic of tension headache. The pain of frontal sinusitis follows a typical pattern, namely onset around 9 am, building to a maximum by about 1 pm, then subsiding over the next few hours. In the absence of respiratory symptoms it is likely to be misdiagnosed as tension headache. The pain from combination headache tends to follow a most constant pattern throughout the day and does not usually interrupt sleep.

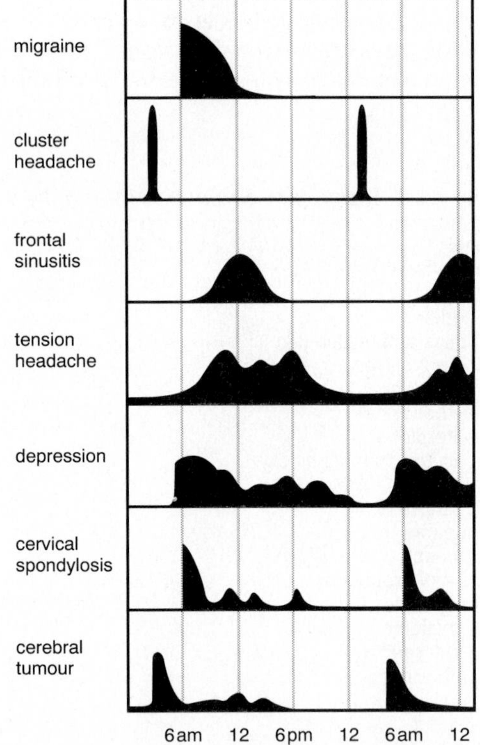

Fig. 48.2 *Typical diurnal patterns of various causes of headache; the relative intensity of pain is plotted on the vertical axis*

The clinical approach

History

A full description of the pain including a pain analysis should be obtained. This includes:

- site
- radiation
- quality
- frequency
- duration
- onset and offset
- precipitating factors
- aggravating and relieving factors
- associated symptoms

It is useful to get the patient to plot on a prepared grid the relative intensity of the pain and the times of day (and night) that the pain is present.

Key questions[5]

Describe your headaches.
How often do you get them?
Point to exactly where in the head you get them.
Do you have any pain in the back of your head or neck?
What time of the day do you get the pain?
Do you notice any other symptoms when you have the headache?
Do you feel nauseated and do you vomit?
Do you experience any unusual sensations in your eyes, such as flashing lights?
Do you get dizzy, weak or have any strange sensations?
Does light hurt your eyes?
Do you get any blurred vision?
Do you notice watering or redness of one or both of your eyes?
Do you get pain or tenderness on combing your hair?
Are you under a lot of stress or tension?
Does your nose run when you get the headache?
What tablets do you take?
Do you get a high temperature, sweats or shivers?
Have you had a heavy cold recently?
Have you ever had trouble with your sinuses?
Have you had a knock on your head recently?
What do you think causes the headaches?

Differences between the clinical features of migraine and tension headache are presented in Table 48.3.

Physical examination

For the physical examination it is appropriate to use the basic tools of trade, namely the thermometer, sphygmomanometer, pen torch, and diagnostic set, including the ophthalmoscope and the stethoscope. Inspect the head, temporal arteries and eyes. Areas to palpate include the temporal arteries, the facial and neck muscles, the cervical spine and sinuses, the teeth and

Table 48.3 *A comparison of typical clinical features of migraine and tension headache*

	Migraine	***Tension headache***
Family history	✓	
Onset before 20	✓	
Prodromata	✓	
Bilateral		✓
Unilateral	✓	
Throbbing	✓	
Constant		✓
Less than 1 per week	✓	
Continuous daily		✓
Lasts less than 24 hrs	✓	
Vomiting	✓	
Aggravated by the pill	✓	
Aggravated by alcohol	✓	
Relieved by alcohol		✓

temporomandibular joints. Search especially for signs of meningeal irritation and papilloedema.

A mental state examination is mandatory and includes looking for altered consciousness or cognition and assessment of mood, anxiety–tension–depression, and any mental changes. Neurological examination includes assessment of visual fields and acuity, reactions of the pupils and eye movements in addition to sensation and motor power in the face and limbs.

Special signs

Upper cervical pain sign: palpate over the C2 and C3 areas of the cervical spine especially two finger-breadths out from the spinous process of C2. If this is very tender and even provokes the headache it indicates headache of cervical origin.

Ewing's sign for frontal sinusitis: press your finger gently upwards and inwards against the orbital roof medial to the supraorbital nerve. Pain on pressure is a positive finding and indicates frontal sinusitis.

The invisible pillow sign: the patient lies on the examination table with head on a pillow. The examiner then supports the head with his or her hands as the pillow is removed. The patient is instructed to relax the neck muscles and the examiner removes the supporting hands. A positive test indicating tension from contracting neck muscles is when the patient's head does not readily change position.

Investigations

Investigations can be selected from:

- Haemoglobin: ? anaemia
- WCC: leucocytosis with bacterial infection
- ESR: ? temporal arteritis
- Radiography
  - — chest X-ray, if suspected intracerebral malignancy
  - — skull X-ray, if suspected brain tumour, Paget's disease, deposits in skull
  - — sinus X-ray, if suspected sinusitis
  - — CT scan
    - detection of brain tumour (most effective)
    - cerebrovascular accidents (valuable)
    - subarachnoid haemorrhage
  - — radioisotope scan (technetium-99) to localise specific tumours and haematoma
  - — magnetic resonance imaging: very effective for intracerebral pathology but expensive; produces better definition of intracerebral structures than CT scanning but not as sensitive for detecting bleeding
  - — lumbar puncture
    - diagnosis of meningitis
    - suspected SAH (only if CT scan normal)

  Note Dangerous if raised intracranial pressure.

Headache in children

Respiratory infections and febrile illnesses are a common cause of headache in children but there are other causes that reflect the common causes in adults. Many childhood headaches are isolated but are chronic in a significant number. Migraine is relatively common before adolescence, while tension or muscle contraction headache is more common after adolescence.

Young children rarely experience sinus headache and this should not really be considered until the sinuses develop, around 5 years for the frontal sinuses.

From 1% of 7 year olds to 5% or more of 15 year old children suffer from migraine, with girls developing it at a higher rate[2] with increasing age. There is a strong family history. As a rule the prognosis is good as the majority will have no migraines in the long term. The type is mainly common migraine with symptoms such as malaise or nausea: classic migraine with the typical aura is not a feature of childhood migraine. The rather dramatic migraines, such as vertebrobasilar migraine, is frequent in adolescent girls and hemiplegia occurs in infants and children, especially with their first migraine attack.[7] Vomiting is not necessarily an associated symptom in children.

The possibility of cerebral space-occupying lesions requires due consideration especially if the headaches are progressive. These are present typically in the morning and associated with symptoms such as vomiting, dizziness, diplopia, ataxia, personality changes and deterioration of school performance. Symptoms that indicate a cerebral tumour or other serious problem are outlined in Table 48.4.

Neonates and children aged 6–12 months are at the greatest risk from meningitis and it is important to keep this in mind.

Table 48.4 *Pointers to serious causes of headache in children (after Wright[2])*

Headache features
Persistent
Present first thing in morning
Wakes child at night
No past history
No family history
Associated poor health
Associated neurological symptoms
Unilateral localisation

Management of the non-serious causes of headache includes reassurance (especially of parents), discouragement of excessive emphasis on the symptom and simple medications such as paracetamol for the younger child and aspirin for the adolescent.

Headaches in the elderly

The recent onset of headache in the elderly has to be treated with caution because it could herald a serious problem such as a space-occupying lesion (e.g. neoplasm, subdural haematoma), temporal arteritis, trigeminal neuralgia or vertebrobasilar insufficiency. Cervical spondylosis is age-related and may be an important factor in the ageing patient. Age-related headaches are summarised in Table 48.5.

Table 48.5 *Age-related causes of headache*

Children	Intercurrent infections Psychogenic Migraine Meningitis Post-traumatic
Adults including middle age	Migraine Cluster headache Tension Cervical dysfunction Subarachnoid haemorrhage Combination
Elderly	Cervical dysfunction Cerebral tumour Temporal arteritis Neuralgias Paget's disease Glaucoma Cervical spondylosis Subdural haemorrhage

Late-life migraine can be mistaken for cerebrovascular disease especially in the presence of preceding neurological symptoms. It is the sequence of the visual and sensory symptoms with the spread from face to tongue to hand over some minutes, with clearing in one area as it appears, that helps distinguish migraine from transient ischaemic attacks (TIAs). Although some patients experience headache with TIAs it is not a distinguishing feature. Vomiting is suggestive of migraine rather than cerebrovascular disease.[7]

Tension headache

Tension or muscle contraction headaches are typically a symmetrical tightness. They tend to last for hours and recur each day. They are often associated with cervical dysfunction and stress or tension, although the patient usually does not realise the headaches are associated with tension until it is pointed out.

Typical clinical features

Site:	frontal, over forehead and temples (Fig. 48.3)
Radiation:	occiput

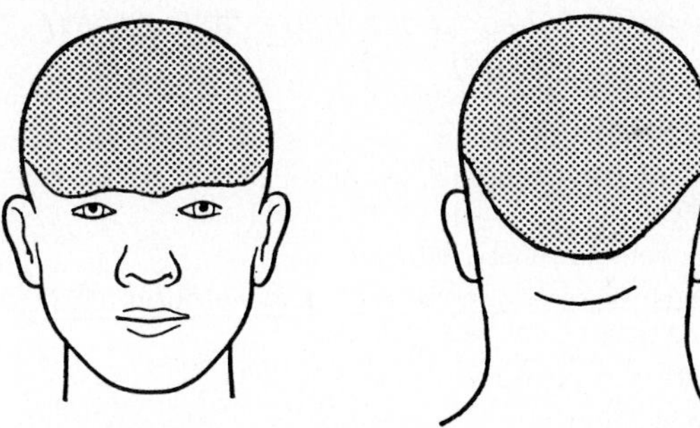

Fig. 48.3 *Typical distribution of pain in tension headache*

Quality:	dull ache, like a 'tight pressure feeling', 'heavy weight on top of head', 'tight band around head'. May be tightness or vice-like feeling rather than pain.
Frequency:	almost daily
Duration:	hours
Onset:	after rising, gets worse during day
Aggravating factors:	stress, overwork with skipping meals
Relieving factors:	alcohol
Associated features:	lightheadedness, fatigue neck ache or stiffness (occiput to shoulders) perfectionist personality anxiety/depression
Physical examination:	muscle tension, e.g. frowning scalp often tender to touch 'invisible pillow' sign may be positive

Management

- Careful patient education: explain that the scalp muscles get tight like the calf muscles when climbing up stairs.
- Counselling and relevant advice, e.g.
  - — Learn to relax your mind and body.
  - — During an attack, relax by lying down in a hot bath and practise meditation.
  - — Be less of a perfectionist: do not be a slave to the clock.
  - — Don't bottle things up, stop feeling guilty, approve of yourself, express yourself and your anger.
- Advise stress reduction, relaxation therapy and yoga or meditation classes.
- Medication—mild analgesics such as aspirin or paracetamol. Avoid tranquillisers and antidepressants if possible but consider these drugs if symptoms warrant medication, e.g. amitriptyline 50–75 mg (o) nocte. Diazepam appears to be very effective in middle-aged men; it is prone to cause depression in women.

Special notes:

- The general aim is to direct patients to modify their lifestyle and avoid tranquillisers and analgesics.
- Beware of depression.
- Consider mobilisation of the neck followed by exercises if evidence of cervical dysfunction.
- Recommend a meditation program.

Migraine

Migraine, or the 'sick headache', is derived from the Greek word meaning 'pain involving half the head'. It affects at least 1 person in 10, is more common in females and peaks between 20 and 50 years. There are various types of migraine (Table 48.6) with classic migraine (headache, vomiting and aura) and common migraine (without the aura) being the best known.

Table 48.6 *Types of vascular headache (after Day[8])*

Common migraine
Classic migraine
Complicated migraine
Unusual forms of migraine • hemiplegic • basilar • retinal • migrainous stupor • ophthalmoplegic • migraine equivalents • status migranosus
Cluster headache
Chronic paroxysmal hemicrania
Lower half headache
Benign exertional-sex headache
Miscellaneous, e.g. icepick pains, ice-cream headache

Typical clinical features of classic migraine

Site:	temporofrontal region (unilateral) (Fig. 48.4)
Radiation:	retro-orbital and occipital
Quality:	intense and throbbing

Frequency:	1 to 2 per month
Duration:	4 to 72 hours (average 6–8 hours)
Onset:	paroxysmal, often wakes with it
Offset:	spontaneous (often after sleep)
Precipitating factors:	tension and stress (commonest); others in Table 48.7
Aggravating factors:	tension, activity
Relieving factors:	sleep, vomiting
Associated factors:	nausea, vomiting irritability aura — visual (scintillation, scotoma, hemianopia, fortification) — sensory (unilateral paraesthesia)
Other pointers:	abdominal pain in childhood family history of migraine, asthma and eczema

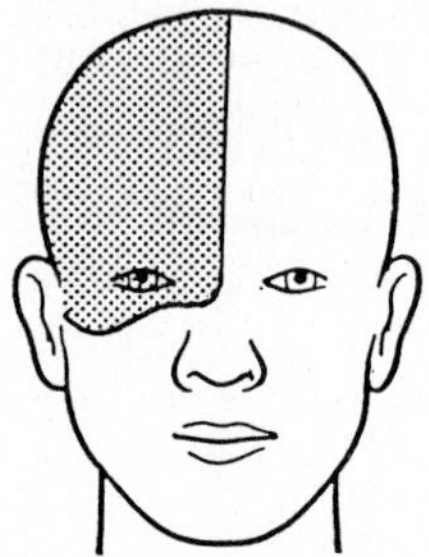
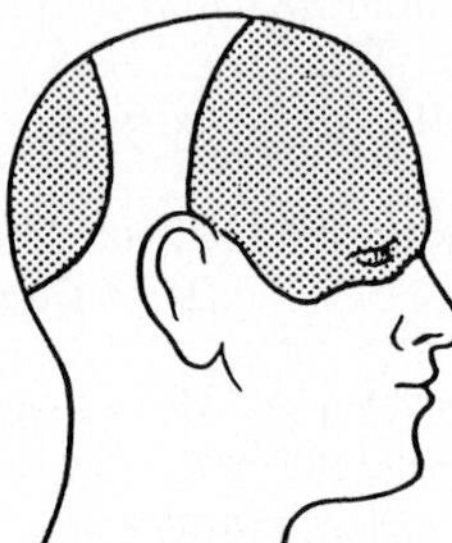

Fig. 48.4 *Typical distribution of pain in migraine (right side)*

Management

Patient education—explanation and reassurance, especially if bizarre visual and neurological symptoms are present. Patients should be reassured about the benign nature of their migraine.

Counselling and advice

- Tailor the advice to the individual patient.
- Avoid known trigger factors, especially tension, fatigue, hunger and constant physical and mental stress.
- Advise keeping a diary of foodstuffs or drinks that can be identified as trigger factors. Consider a low amine diet: eliminate chocolate, cheese, red wine, walnuts, tuna, vegemite, spinach and liver.
- Practise a healthy lifestyle, relaxation programs, meditation techniques and biofeedback training.

Table 48.7 *Migrainous trigger factors (after Day[8])*

Exogenous
Foodstuffs—chocolate, oranges, tomatoes, citrus fruits, cheeses
Alcohol—especially red wine
Drugs—vasodilators, oestrogens, monosodium glutamate, nitrites, indomethacin
Glare or bright light
Emotional stress
Head trauma (often minor) e.g. jarring—'footballer's migraine'
Allergens
Climatic change
Excessive noise
Strong perfume
Endogenous
Tiredness, physical exhaustion, oversleeping
Stress, relaxation after stress: 'weekend migraine'
Exercise
Hormonal changes • puberty • menstruation • climacteric • pregnancy
Hunger
Familial tendency
? Personality factors

Treatment of the acute attack

- Commence treatment at earliest impending sign.
- Mild headaches may require no more than conventional treatment with '2 aspirin (or paracetamol), and a good lie down in a quiet dark room'.[8]
- Rest in a quiet, darkened, cool room.
- Cold packs on the forehead or neck.
- Avoid drinking coffee, tea or orange juice.
- Avoid moving around too much.
- Do not read or watch television.
- For patients who find relief from simply 'sleeping off' an attack, consider prescribing temazepam 10 mg or diazepam 10 mg in addition to the following measures.[3]

Medication (if necessary)

First-line medication

Aspirin + antiemetic:

soluble aspirin 2–3 tablets (o)
and
metoclopramide 10 mg (o)

Alternatives

Choose an ergotamine preparation or the new, effective but expensive sumatriptan.

Ergotamine (helps about 80% of patients)

oral: e.g. ergotamine 1 mg + caffeine 100 mg (Cafergot)
2 tabs at 1st warning then 60 minutes if necessary (maximum 6 per day)
or
suppository: e.g. ergotamine 2 mg + caffeine 100 mg (Cafergot S)
1 suppository at 1st warning then ½ every 60 minutes (maximum 3 per day)
or
medihaler: e.g. 1 inhalation statim then every 5 minutes (maximum 6 per day)
or
IM injection: e.g. dihydroergotamine 1 mg, preceded by metoclopramide 10 mg IM, 20 minutes beforehand.

Sumatriptan (a serotonin antagonist)[9]

100 mg (o) at the time of prodrome, repeat in 2 hours if necessary to maximum dose 300 mg/24 hours
or
6 mg, SC injection, repeat in 1 or more hours to maximum dose 12 mg/24 hours

Sumatriptan is reported to be effective without a sedating effect and has a half-life of 2 hours. Avoid sumatriptan in patients with coronary artery disease, Prinzmetal angina or uncontrolled hypertension.

The severe attack (if other preparations ineffective)

Caution Consider possibility of underlying cerebral vascular malformation, subarachnoid haemorrhage or pethidine addiction.

metoclopramide 10 mg (2ml) IM or IV injection (IV slowly over 2 minutes)
or
lignocaine 1% IV infusion of 1 mg/kg slowly over 90 seconds, e.g. 7 ml in a 70 kg adult.

Note Lignocaine is reportedly successful but awaiting trials. Contraindications include known hypersensitivity to local anaesthetics, bradycardia, patients with pacemakers or on antiarrhythmic medication.

Prophylaxis

Consider prophylactic therapy for frequent attacks that cause disruption to the patient's lifestyle and well-being, a rule of thumb being two or more migraine attacks per month; certainly consider it for weekly attacks and a poor response to therapy for the acute attack. Do not give ergotamine.

The most commonly used drugs include:

- beta-blockers: propranolol, metoprolol, atenolol
- pizotifen
- cyproheptadine (ideal for children)
- tricyclic drugs—amitriptyline
- clonidine
- methysergide (reserve for unresponsive severe migraine)
- calcium channel blockers: nifedipine, verapamil
- NSAIDs: naproxen, indomethacin, ibuprofen
- MAO inhibitors: phenelzine, moclobemide
- sumatriptan

Guidelines

Select the initial drug according to the patient's medical profile.

- if low or normal weight—pizotifen
- if hypertensive—a beta-blocker
- if depressed or anxious—amitriptyline
- if cervical spondylosis—naproxen
- food-sensitive migraine—pizotifen

Commonly prescribed first-line drugs are propanolol or pizotifen[9]

propranolol 40 mg (o) bd or tds (at first) increasing to 240 mg daily (if necessary)
pizotifen 0.5–1 mg (o) nocte (at first) increasing to 3 mg a day (if necessary)

Each drug should be tried for two months before it is judged to be ineffective. Amitriptyline 50 mg nocte can be added to propranolol, pizotifen (beware of weight gain) or methysergide and may convert a relatively poor response to very good control.[3]

Cluster headache

Cluster headache is also known as migrainous neuralgia. It occurs in paroxysmal clusters of unilateral headache which typically occur nightly, usually in the small hours of the morning, although patients may have headaches that occur at other times. A hallmark is the pronounced cyclical nature of the attacks. It occurs typically in males (6:1 ratio).

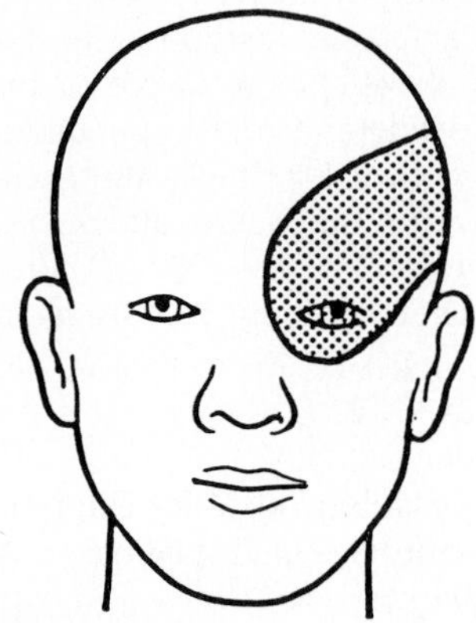

Fig. 48.5 *Typical distribution of pain in cluster headache*

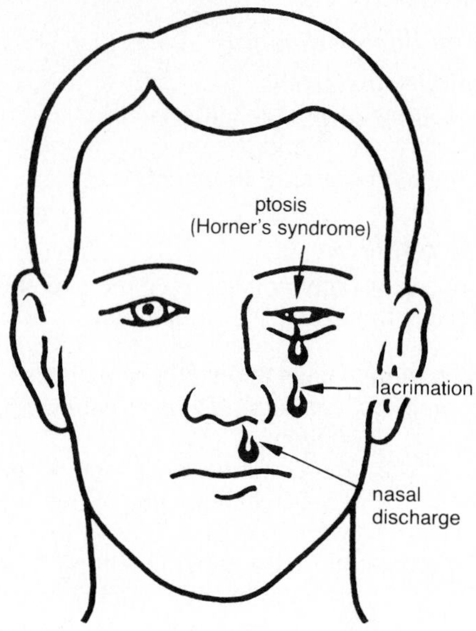

Fig. 48.6 *Features of an attack of cluster headache: ptosis, lacrimation and a discharge from the nostril on the side of pain*

Typical clinical features

Site:	over or about one eye (Fig. 48.5)
Radiation:	frontal and temporal regions
Quality:	severe
Frequency:	1–3 times a day, at regular times like clockwork
Duration:	15 minutes to 2–3 hours (average 30 minutes); the clusters last 4–6 weeks
Onset:	suddenly during night (usually), same time about 2–3 hours after falling asleep
Offset:	spontaneous
Aggravating factors:	alcohol (during cluster)
Relieving factors:	drugs
Associated features:	family history
	rhinorrhoea, ipsilateral nose
	lacrimation
	flushing of forehead and cheek
	redness of ipsilateral eye
	Horner's syndrome (uncommon) (Fig. 48.6)

Management

Acute attack (brief treatment seldom effective):

- avoid alcohol during cluster
- consider 100% oxygen 6 L/min for 15 min (usually good response)
- sumatriptan 6 mg SC injection

  or
- ergotamine, e.g. medihaler or rectally
- consider local anaesthetic—greater occipital nerve block

Prophylaxis (once a cluster starts); consider the following:

- ergotamine (the drug of choice: take at night during a cluster)
- methysergide
- prednisolone 50 mg/day
- lithium carbonate
- propranolol
- pizotifen

Cervical dysfunction/spondylosis

Headache from neck disorders, often referred to as occipital neuralgia, is far more common than realised and is very rewarding to treat by physical therapy, including mobilisation and manipulation and exercises in particular.

Headache can be caused by abnormalities in any structure innervated by the upper three cervical nerves C1, C2, C3 (usually the C1–2, C2–3 facet joints). Pain from cervical structures can be referred retro-orbitally and over one-half of the head (see page 000). The headache is often incorrectly diagnosed as migraine.[10]

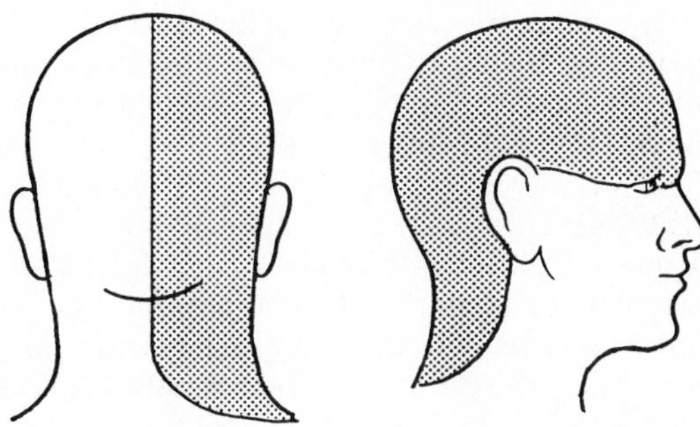

Fig. 48.7 *Typical distribution of pain in cervical dysfunction (right side)*

Typical clinical features

Site:	occipital region (Fig. 48.7)
Radiation:	parietal region (unilateral), vertex of skull, behind an eye
Quality:	nagging dull aching pain of mild to moderate intensity
Frequency:	usually daily
Duration:	1 to 6 hours
Onset:	usually on waking in morning
Offset:	usually settles towards midday
Precipitating factors:	often an accident—MVA or striking head
Aggravating factors:	neck movement, especially reversing car
Relieving factors:	heat or cold compress to neck
Associated features:	paraesthesia posterior half of scalp (uncommon) stiffness and grating in neck
Other pointers:	head can feel very heavy (like a metal ball)
Examination:	tenderness to palpation over C1, C2 or C3 levels of cervical spine, especially on side of headache (if unilateral)

Treatment

- physiotherapy modalities: hydrotherapy, mobilisation, manipulation (from experts) and neck exercises (very important)
- NSAIDs for cervical spondylosis
- for intractable cases consider manipulation under general anaesthesia, injections of corticosteroids around, or surgical section of, the greater occipital nerve.[10]

Combination headache

Combined (also known as mixed) headaches are common and often diagnosed as psychogenic headache or atypical migraine. They have a combination of various degrees of:

- tension and/or depression
- cervical dysfunction
- vasospasm (migraine)
- drugs, e.g. analgesics (rebound)
  alcohol
  nicotine
  caffeine
  NSAIDs

The headache, which has many of the features of tension headache, is usually described as a heavy deep ache 'as though my head is ready to burst'. It tends to be constant, being present throughout every waking moment. It tends to last for days (average 3–7) but can last for weeks or months. It is often related to stress and adverse working conditions and sometimes follows an accident.

Management

An important strategy is to evaluate each possible component of the headache as a stepwise trial by an elimination process:

- drug evaluation and modification
- cervical dysfunction—physical therapy if present
- depression
- tension and stress
- other psychogenic factors, e.g. conversion reaction
- vasospasm

Treatment includes insight therapy, reassurance that the patient does not have a cerebral tumour, and lifestyle modification. The most effective medication is amitriptyline or other antidepressant.

Temporal arteritis

Temporal arteritis (TA) is also known as giant cell arteritis or cranial arteritis. There is usually a persistent unilateral throbbing headache in the temporal region and scalp sensitivity with localised thickening, with or without loss of pulsation of the temporal artery. It is related to polymyalgia rheumatica—20% of sufferers will develop TA.

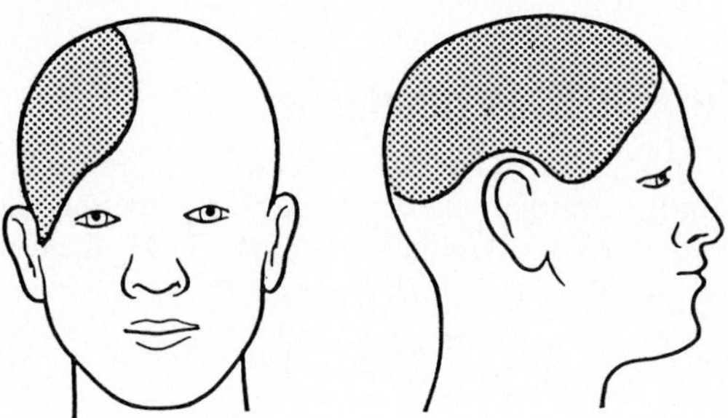

Fig. 48.8 *Typical distribution of pain in temporal arteritis (right side)*

Typical clinical features

Age:	over 50 years (mean age 70 years)
Site:	forehead and temporal region (unilateral) (Fig. 48.8)
Radiation:	down side of head towards occiput
Quality:	severe burning pain
Frequency:	daily, a constant ache
Duration:	usually constant (getting worse)
Onset:	non-specific, tends to be worse in morning
Offset:	nil
Aggravating factors:	stress and anxiety
Relieving factors:	nil
Associated features:	malaise, vague aches and pains in muscles (especially of neck), weight loss
Other pointers:	• intermittent blurred vision • tenderness on brushing hair • jaw claudication on eating • polymyalgia rheumatica • hypertension • abnormal emotional behaviour

Description

Temporal arteritis is a type of collagen disease causing inflammation of extracranial vessels, especially the superficial temporal artery. It usually presents as a unilateral intermittent headache in a person over 50 years.

TA may also involve the intracranial vessels, especially the ophthalmic artery or posterior ciliary arteries, causing optic atrophy and blindness. Vision is impaired in about one-half of patients at some stage. Once the patient goes blind it is usually irreversible.

Diagnosis

Diagnosis is by biopsy and histological examination of the superficial temporal artery. The ESR is usually markedly elevated but may be normal. The biopsy may be normal as TA has a focal nature.

Treatment

TA is very responsive to corticosteroids; start treatment immediately to prevent permanent blindness. Initial medication is prednisolone 60–100 mg orally daily. Dose reduction and progress is monitored by the clinical state and ESR levels.[9] Concomitant use of H_2 receptor antagonists may be appropriate initially. Temporal arteritis may take 1–2 years to resolve.

Frontal sinusitis

The headache of frontal sinusitis can be a diagnostic problem especially in the absence of, or a lapse in time since, an obvious upper respiratory infection or vasomotor rhinitis. Some patients do not have a history of a preceding respiratory infection nor have signs of nasal obstruction or fever. Contrary to popular belief, sinusitis is a relatively uncommon source of headache.

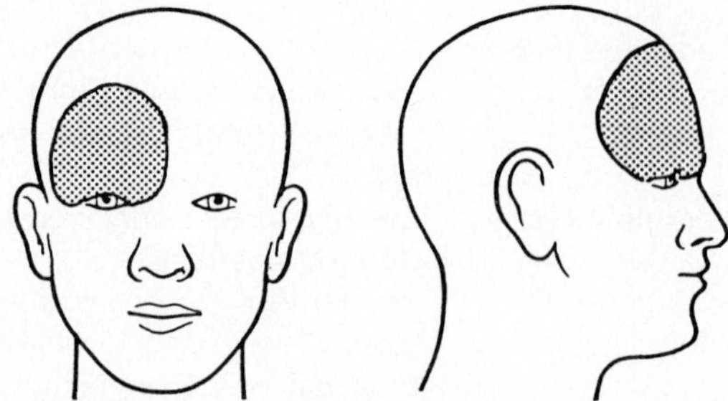

Fig. 48.9 *Typical distribution of pain of frontal sinusitis (right side)*

Typical clinical features

Site:	frontal and retro-orbital (unilateral > bilateral) (Fig. 48.9)
Radiation:	vertex
Quality:	dull and throbbing, moderate severity
Frequency:	daily
Duration:	about 6 to 9 hours
Onset:	develops in morning around 9 am
Offset:	late afternoon around 6 pm
Precipitating factors:	URTI
Aggravating factors:	bending forward
Relieving factors:	drainage from nose
Associated features:	malaise ± fever

Examination

Tenderness over frontal sinus, pain on percussion over the sinus. Ewing's sign may be elicited. Fever and oedema of the upper eyelid may be present.

Management

Principles of treatment:

- drain the sinus conservatively using steam inhalations
- antibiotics: amoxycillin or amoxycillin/clavulanate or doxycycline
- analgesics

Referral

If resolution cannot be accomplished by conservative means then referral to an ENT specialist is advisable. Acute purulent sinusitis can be treacherous if it persists and spreads, causing collections of pus in the extradural or subdural space, cerebral abscess or blood-borne spread of infection.

Complications

- orbital cellulitis
- subdural abscess
- osteomyelitis
- cavernous sinus thrombosis

Symptoms indicating spread of infection:

- increase in fever and chills
- vomiting
- oedema of the eyelids and forehead
- visual disturbances
- dulling of the sensorium
- convulsions

Raised intracranial pressure

Important causes of a space-occupying lesion include a cerebral tumour and subdural haematoma. Sometimes it is not possible to differentiate between a subdural and an extradural haematoma although the latter classically follows an acute injury. Typical features are generalised headache, usually worse in the morning, aggravated by abrupt changes in intracranial pressure and later associated with vomiting and drowsiness. Headache is an uncommon presenting symptom of a cerebral tumour.

Typical clinical features of the headache

Site:	generalised, often occipital
Radiation:	retro-orbital
Quality:	dull, deep steady ache
Frequency:	daily
Duration:	may be hours in morning
Onset:	worse in mornings, usually intermittent, can awaken from sleep
Offset:	later in day (if at all)
Aggravating factors:	coughing, sneezing, straining at toilet
Relieving factors:	analgesics, e.g. aspirin, sitting, standing
Associated features:	vomiting (without preceding nausea) vertigo/dizziness drowsiness confusion (later) neurological signs (depending on side)

Examination

- focal CNS signs
- papilloedema (but may be absent)

Intracerebral tumours

- incidence is 5–10 per 100 000 population
- 2 peaks of incidence: children < 10 years[3]
  35–60 years
- main types of tumour:
  - children
    - medulloblastoma
    - astrocytoma (posterior fossa)
    - ependymoma
    - glioma (brain stem)

— adults
  - cerebral glioma
  - meningioma
  - pituitary adenoma
  - cerebral metastases, e.g. lung

Investigations
CT scan and MRI.

Subarachnoid haemorrhage (SAH)

SAH is a life-threatening event that should not be overlooked at the primary care level. The incidence is 12 per 100 000 population per annum. About 40% of patients die before treatment, while about one-third have a good response to treatment.

Clinical features:

- sudden onset headache (moderate to intense severity)
- occipital location
- localised at first, then generalised
- pain and stiffness of the neck follows
- vomiting and loss of consciousness often follow
- Kernig's sign positive
- neurological deficit may include
  - — hemiplegia (if intracerebral bleed)
  - — third nerve palsy (partial or complete) (Fig. 48.10)

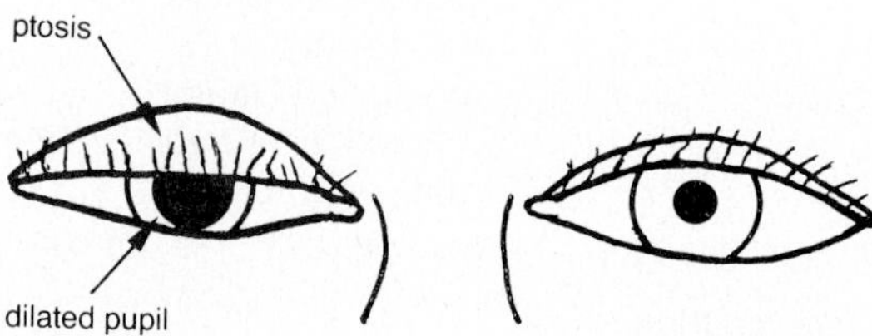

Fig. 48.10 *Third nerve palsy (right side)*

Diagnosis

CT scanning is the investigation of choice. Lumbar puncture is not necessary if the diagnosis can be made by CT, but is used if the CT scan is negative (usually 10–20% of cases). Even blood staining of CSF and xanthochromia is a positive feature on lumbar puncture.

Special notes

- Less severe headaches can cause diagnostic difficulties.
- Consider an angioma rather than an aneurysm as the cause of SAH if previous episodes.

Management

Immediate referral. If there is lingering doubt review the patient within 12 or 24 hours.

Meningitis

The headache of meningitis is usually generalised and radiates to the neck. It is constant and severe and occasionally may begin abruptly. It is aggravated by flexion of the neck. Kernig's sign is positive. Fever and neck stiffness is usually present. Urgent referral to hospital is necessary. If meningitis is suspected or if a child or adult has headache with fever and neck stiffness, antibiotics must not be given until a lumbar puncture has been performed.

Drug rebound headache

Rebound headaches are usually associated with analgesic and ergotamine dependence. The headache is present on waking and typically persists throughout the day but fluctuates in intensity. It is a mild to moderate, dull, bilateral ache with a distribution similar to tension headache. Drug rebound headaches should be suspected in any patient who complains of headache 'all day, every day'. A careful drug history should be taken. Treatment includes gradual withdrawal of the drugs and the substitution of antiemetics and sedatives over about 14 days.

Chronic paroxysmal hemicrania

This is a rare headache syndrome which overlaps with cluster headache and facial pain. The unilateral pain which can be excruciating is located in the area of the temple, forehead, eye and upper face. It can radiate to the ear, neck and shoulder. It differs from cluster headaches in that the patients are invariably female, the paroxysms are short (average 20–30 minutes) and more frequent, with attacks occurring up to 14 times a day. The disorder resembles cluster headaches in nature and distribution and associated autonomic features such as ipsilateral nasal stuffiness or rhinorrhoea, lacrimation, conjunctival injection and ptosis. The aetiology is unknown but the headache responds dramatically to indomethacin (25 mg (o) tds).

Trigeminal neuralgia

The pain of trigeminal neuralgia comes in excruciating paroxysms which last for seconds to minutes only and usually affect the face rather than the head (see page 424). The lightning-like jabs of searing or burning pain usually last 1 to 2 minutes but can last as long as 15 minutes.

Hypertension headache

It tends to occur only in severe hypertension such as malignant hypertension or hypertensive encephalopathy. The headache is typically occipital, throbbing and worse on waking in the morning.

The headache may be psychogenic in origin, developing after the diagnosis of hypertension is disclosed to the patient. However, the occasional patient has genuine headache related to milder hypertension and this serves as an accurate indicator of their blood pressure level.

Benign intracranial hypertension (pseudotumour)

This is a rare but important sinister headache condition which typically occurs in young obese women. Key features are headache, visual blurring and obscurations, nausea, papilloedema. The CT scan is normal but lumbar puncture reveals increased CSF pressure and normal CSF analysis.

It is sometimes linked to drugs including tetracyclines (most common), nitrofurantoin, oral contraceptive pill and vitamin A preparations. The main concern is visual deficits from the high intracranial pressure. Medical treatment includes weight reduction, corticosteroids and diuretics. Surgery, which involves decompression of the optic nerves or lumboperitoneal shunting, is sometimes required for failed medical therapy.

Headaches related to specific activities

Sex headaches

This can manifest as a dull or explosive headache, provoked by sexual arousal and activity especially with orgasm. Some are clearly a form of exertional headache. Sometimes sex headache is mistaken for SAH but if the severe headache coincided with orgasm, was not associated with vomiting or neck stiffness, or settled within hours, SAH is unlikely.

Cough and exertional headache

Some people experience a severe transient pain with factors such as coughing, sneezing, stooping, straining, lifting and various sporting activities. It is usually benign and examination is normal. A CT scan is indicated if there are focal signs or if the symptoms do not settle.

Gravitational headaches

Occipital headache, coming on when standing upright and relieved by lying down, is characteristic of a postlumbar puncture, an epidural block or low pressure headache. It can last for several weeks after the procedure.

'Ice-cream' headache

Frontal or global headache can be provoked by the rapid ingestion of very cold food and drink. It is a form of vascular headache.

When to refer

- Evidence of or suspicion of subarachnoid haemorrhage or intracerebral haematoma.
- Complicated migraine.
- Uncertain diagnosis.
- Positive neurological signs despite typical headaches.
- Headaches increasing in frequency, despite prophylaxis.
- Danger signals with headache:
  - — sudden onset without previous history
  - — recent onset for first time in an older person
  - — recurrent in children
  - — progressive
  - — wakes the patient at night

- — localised pain in definite area or structure, e.g. ear, eye
- — precipitated by raised intracranial pressure, e.g. coughing
- — associated neurological symptoms or signs:
  - convulsions
  - fever
  - confusion
  - impaired consciousness
  - neck stiffness
  - dizziness/vertigo
  - personality change

Practice tips

- A middle-aged or elderly patient presenting with unaccustomed headache has an organic disorder such as temporal arteritis, intracerebral tumour or subdural haematoma until proved otherwise.
- The ESR is an excellent screening test to diagnose temporal arteritis but occasionally can be normal in the presence of active TA.
- If a patient presents twice within 24 hours to the same practice or hospital with headache and vomiting, consider other causes apart from migraine before discharging the patient.[7]
- Treat an unusual or unaccustomed headache with a lot of respect.
- If migraine attacks are severe and unusual (e.g. always on the same side) consider the possibility of cerebral vascular malformation.
- CT scans and MRI have superseded other investigations in the diagnosis of cerebral tumours and intracranial haemorrhage but should be ordered sparingly and judiciously.
- If a headache is occipital in origin or accompanied by neck pain, consider the likely possibility of cervical dysfunction and refer to the appropriate therapist once the diagnosis is established.
- For recurrent migraine sufferers emphasise the importance of trigger factor avoidance and of taking aspirin and metoclopramide medication at the earliest warning of an attack.
- A severe headache of sudden onset is subarachnoid haemorrhage until proved otherwise.
- SAH is overlooked sometimes, mainly because it is not considered in the differential diagnosis. Suspect with very severe and protracted headache, drowsiness and neck stiffness.
- A 'stranger' presenting with a severe migraine attack may well be a pethidine addict. Your regular migraine patient may also be a narcotic addict. Avoid giving narcotic analgesics to your migraine patients—establish a conservative drug regimen backed by patient education and empathy.
- Prophylactic ergotamine medication commonly causes a dull, constant, steady headache.
- If women with migraine demand the oral contraceptive, use a low-dose oestrogen preparation and monitor progress.
- The use of narcotics for migraine treatment (such as pethidine and codeine) is to be avoided whenever possible—the frequent use of ergotamine, analgesics or narcotics can transform episodic migraine into chronic daily headache.

References

1. Cormack J, Marinker M, Morrell D. The patient complaining of headache. In: *Practice*. London: Kluwer Medical, 3.12.
2. Wright M. Recurrent headaches in children. In: The Australian Paediatric Review, 1991; 1(6):1–2.
3. Anthony M. Migraine and tension headache. In: MIMS Disease Index. Sydney: IMS Publishing, 1991–2, 335–338.
4. Sandler G, Fry J. *Early clinical diagnosis*. Lancaster: MTP Press, 1986, 297–325.
5. Davis A, Bolin T, Ham J. *Symptom analysis and physical diagnosis*. Sydney: Pergamon, 1990.
6. Lance JW. *Mechanism and management of headache* (3rd edition). London: Butterworths, 1978, 109–112.
7. Burns R. Pitfalls in headache management. Aust Fam Physician, 1990; 19:1821–1826.
8. Day TJ. Migraine and other vascular headaches. Aust Fam Physician, 1990; 19:1797–1804.
9. Moulds RFW et al. *Analgesic guidelines* (2nd edition). Melbourne: Victorian Medical Postgraduate Foundation, 1992–3:63–65.
10. Anthony M. The treatment of migraine—old methods, new ideas. Aust Fam Physician, 1993; 22:1401–1405.

49

Jaundice

Jaundice is a yellow discolouration of the skin and mucosal surfaces caused by the accumulation of excessive bilirubin.[1] It is a cardinal symptom of hepatobiliary disease and haemolysis. Important common causes include gallstones, hepatitis A, hepatitis B, hepatitis C, drugs, alcohol and Gilbert's disease. The commonest clinical encounter with jaundice, especially physiological jaundice, is in the newborn. As for all patients, the history and examination are paramount, but investigations are essential to clinch the diagnosis of jaundice.

Table 49.1 *Abbreviations used in this chapter*

Hepatitis A virus	HAV
Hepatitis A antibody	anti-HAV
Immunoglobulin M	IgM
Immunoglobulin G	IgG
Hepatitis B virus	HBV
Hepatitis B surface antigen	HBsAg
Hepatitis B surface antibody	anti-HBs
Hepatitis B core antibody	anti-HBc
Hepatitis Be antigen	HBeAg
Hepatitis C virus	HCV
Hepatitis C virus antibody	anti-HCV
Hepatitis D (Delta) virus	HDV
Hepatitis E virus	HEV

The three major categories of jaundice are (Fig. 49.1):

- obstructive
  - — extrahepatic
  - — intrahepatic
- hepatocellular
- haemolysis

Key facts and checkpoints

- Jaundice is defined as a serum bilirubin exceeding 17 μmol/L.[2]
- Clinical jaundice manifests only when the bilirubin exceeds 50 μmol/L.[1]
- However, jaundice is difficult to detect visually below 85 μmol/L if lighting is poor.
- It can be distinguished from yellow skin due to hypercarotenaemia (due to dietary excess of carrots, pumpkin, mangoes or pawpaw) and hypothyroidism by involving the sclera.
- The most common causes of jaundice recorded in a general practice population are (in order) viral hepatitis, gallstones, carcinoma of pancreas, cirrhosis, pancreatitis and drugs.[3]
- Always take a full travel, drug and hepatitis contact history in any patient presenting with jaundice.
- A fatty liver (steatosis) can not only occur with alcohol excess but also with obesity, diabetes and starvation. There is no liver damage and thus no jaundice.

A diagnostic approach

A summary of the diagnostic safety model is presented in Table 49.2.

Probability diagnosis

The answer depends on the age and social grouping of the patient, especially if the patient

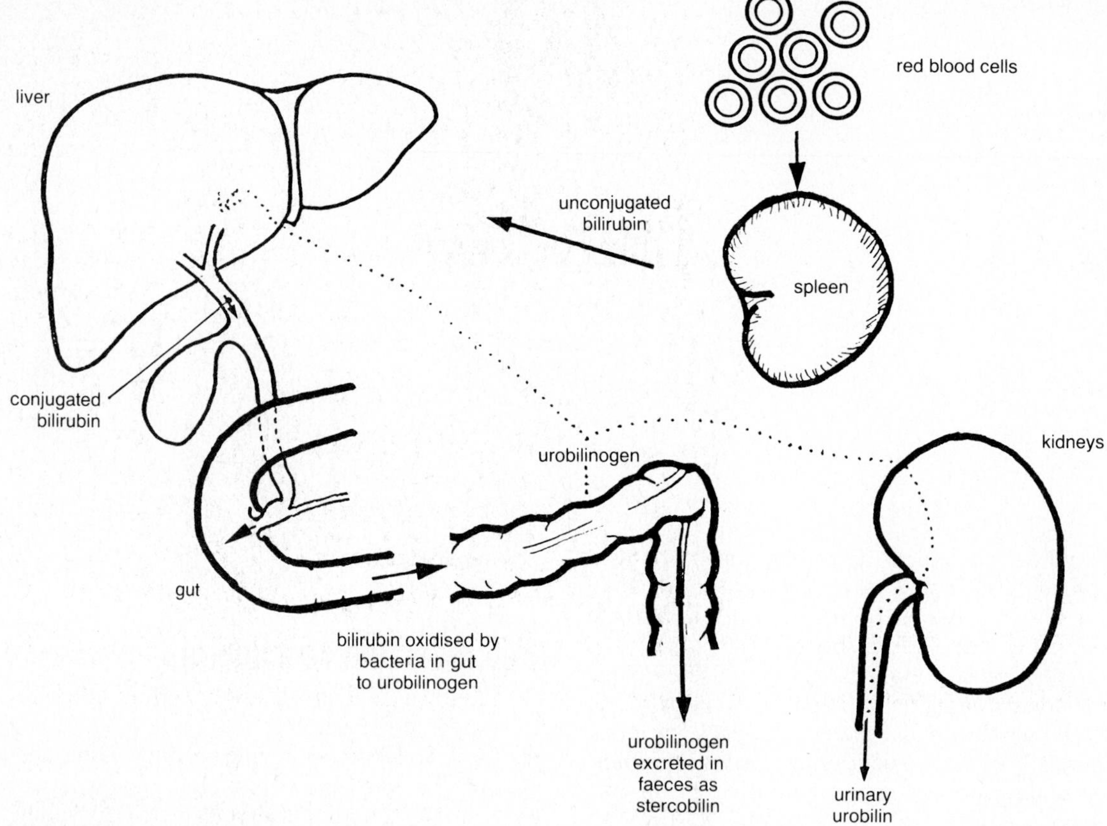

Fig. 49.1 *The jaundice pathway*

indulges in risk-taking behaviour or has travelled overseas.

Viral hepatitis A,B or C accounts for the majority of cases of jaundice.

In the middle-aged and elderly group, a common cause is obstruction from gallstones or cancer. It is common for older people to have painless obstructive jaundice; bear in mind that the chances of malignancy increase with age.

Alcoholic liver disease is common and may present as chronic alcoholic cirrhosis with liver failure or as acute alcoholic hepatitis. It is worth emphasising that such patients can make a dramatic recovery when they cease drinking alcohol.

In family practice we encounter many cases of drug-induced jaundice, especially in the elderly. These drugs are outlined later in the chapter, under the 'seven masquerades'.

Serious disorders not to be missed

Malignancy must always be suspected, especially in the elderly patient and those with a history of chronic active hepatitis, e.g. post hepatitis B infection. The former is more likely to have carcinoma of the head of the pancreas and the latter, hepatocellular carcinoma (hepatoma).

Metastatic carcinoma must be kept in mind, especially in those with a history of surgery, such as large bowel cancer, melanoma and stomach cancer.

Hepatic failure can be associated with severe systemic infection, e.g. septicaemia and pneumonia, and after surgery in critically ill patients. A patient who has the classic Charcot's triad of upper abdominal pain, fever (and chills) and jaundice should be regarded as having ascending cholangitis until proved otherwise. Wilson's disease, although rare, must be considered in all young patients with acute hepatitis. A history of neurological symptoms, such as a tremor or a clumsy gait, and a family history is important. If Wilson's disease is suspected the patient should have an ocular slit lamp examination, serum ceruloplasmin levels (low in 95% of patients) and a liver biopsy. Early diagnosis and treatment mean a better prognosis.

Table 49.2 *Jaundice (adults): diagnostic strategy model*

Q.	*Probability diagnosis*
A.	Hepatitis A,B,C Gallstones Alcoholic hepatitis/cirrhosis
Q.	*Serious disorders not to be missed*
A.	Malignancy • pancreas • biliary tract • hepatocellular (hepatoma) • metastases Severe infections • septicaemia • ascending cholangitis • fulminant hepatitis *Rarities* • Wilson's disease • Reye's disease • acute fatty liver of pregnancy
Q.	*Pitfalls (often missed)*
A.	Gallstones Gilbert's disease Cardiac failure Primary biliary cirrhosis Chronic active hepatitis Haemochromatosis
Q.	*Seven masquerades checklist*
A.	Depression —
	Diabetes —
	Drugs ✓
	Anaemia ✓
	Thyroid disease —
	Spinal dysfunction —
	UTI —
Q.	*Is this patient trying to tell me something?*
A.	Not usually applicable.

Reye's syndrome is a rare and severe complication of influenza and some other viral diseases, especially in children when given aspirin. There is rapid development of hepatic failure and encephalopathy.

Pitfalls

Gallstones, especially in the absence of upper abdominal pain, can be overlooked, so this possibility should be kept in mind in the elderly.

Gilbert's disease is worth considering, especially as it is the commonest form of unconjugated hyperbilirubinaemia. It affects at least 3% of the population. Like the more severe but rarer Crigler-Najjar syndrome there is a deficiency of glucuronyl transferase. In Gilbert's disease the serum bilirubin, which may rise to 50 μmol/L but seldom higher,[2] tends to fluctuate and to rise during intercurrent infections, such as influenza and in episodes of fasting. All other liver function tests are normal, as is liver serology, but a history of intermittent mild jaundice, a family history or vague right upper quadrant pain may be useful pointers. Patients diagnosed by the author appeared to have a consistently coloured skin resembling a 'suntan' despite living in a cool climate. Gilbert's disease is benign with an excellent prognosis and no treatment is required.

Cardiac failure can present as jaundice with widespread tenderness under the right costal margin. It can be insidious in onset or manifest with gross acute failure. It can be confused with acute cholecystitis. The biochemical abnormalities seen are very variable. Usually there is a moderate rise in bilirubin and alkaline phosphatase and sometimes, in acute failure, a marked elevation of transaminase may occur, suggesting some hepatocellular necrosis.

There are many other pitfalls for a family doctor, who may encounter the conditions very rarely, if at all. Such disorders include:

- inherited conjugated hyperbilirubinaemias (Dubin-Johnson and Rotor syndromes) caused by faulty excretion by liver cells
- haemochromatosis (associated pigmentation and diabetes)
- chronic active hepatitis
- primary biliary cirrhosis
- sclerosing cholangitis (associated with ulcerative colitis)

General pitfalls

- Excluding jaundice by examining the sclera in artificial light.
- Not realising that the sclera in elderly patients often have an icteric appearance (without jaundice).
- Omitting to take a careful history including illicit drugs.
- A liver biopsy is essential in all patients with chronic hepatitis.

Seven masquerades checklist

Of this group the haemolytic anaemias and drugs have to be considered.

Drug-related jaundice

Drug-induced jaundice is common and many drugs are implicated. The patterns of drug-related liver damage include cholestasis, necrosis ('hepatitis'), granulomas, chronic active hepatitis, cirrhosis, hepatocellular tumours and veno-occlusive disease.[4] Some drugs, such as methyldopa, can initiate haemolysis.

The important drugs to consider are presented in Table 49.3.

Table 49.3 *Drugs that can cause jaundice*

Haemolysis
- methyldopa
- phenylhydralazine

Hepatocellular damage

dose-dependent
- paracetamol (can cause acute hepatic necrosis)
- salicylates
- tetracycline

dose-independent

• anaesthetics	e.g. halothane
• antidepressants	e.g. MAO inhibitors
• anticonvulsants	e.g. phenytoin sodium valproate
• antibiotics	e.g. penicillins sulphonamides
• antimalarials	e.g. Fansidar
• antituberculosis	e.g. isoniazid
• anti-inflammatories	e.g. NSAIDs (various)
• carbon tetrachloride	
• cardiovascular	e.g. amiodarone methyldopa perhexilene

Cholestasis
- antithyroid drugs
- chlorpromazine
- erythromycin estolate
- penicillins
- gold salts
- oral contraceptives/oestrogens
- synthetic anabolic steroids, e.g. methyl testosterone
- hyperglycaemic drugs, e.g. chlorpropamide

Others
- allopurinol
- cimetidine (aggravated by alcohol)
- cytotoxics, e.g. methotrexate
- etretinate
- hydralazine
- nitrofurantoin
- vitamin A (mega dosage)

Haemolysis

The patient may present with the symptoms of underlying anaemia and jaundice with no noticeable change in the appearance of the urine and stool. The degree of haemolysis may vary from the lemon yellow tinge of pernicious anaemia in an elderly patient to a severe haemolytic crisis precipitated by drugs or broad beans (favism) in a patient with an inherited red cell deficiency of glucose-6-phosphate dehydrogenase. More common causes include the hereditary haemolytic anaemias, such as congenital spherocytosis and thalassaemia major. Acquired causes include incompatible blood transfusions, malignancies, such as lymphoma, severe sepsis and some drugs.

Splenomegaly occurs in most patients with haemolytic anaemia, and decreased red cell survival can be measured.

Psychogenic considerations

This is not really applicable for an organic problem like jaundice. Nevertheless, the cause may be related to factors in the patient's lifestyle such as homosexuality, sexual promiscuity or intravenous drug abuse and the patient may be reluctant to offer this information. Discreet, concerned probing will be necessary.

The clinical approach

History

The history should include questioning about the following:

- any episodes of jaundice
- change in colour of faeces and urine
- anorexia, sore throat, weight loss, pruritus
- abdominal pain
- residence and members of household
- contact with patients with hepatitis or jaundice
- recent overseas travel
- exposure to blood or blood products
- needlestick injuries or exposure to needles, such as acupuncture, tattooing and intravenous drugs
- dietary history: shellfish, drinking water
- sexual history: evidence of promiscuity
- drug history, including alcohol
- recent medical history, including surgery
- family history: family contacts who have had jaundice, haemolytic disease, and other genetic liver diseases
- ethnic history: liable to haemolytic disease, contact with hepatitis B
- occupational history: exposure to hazards

Significance of various symptoms

pain in the right hypochondrium
- gallstones
- acute hepatitis (a constant ache)
- cholecystitis

anorexia, dark urine, fever
- viral hepatitis probable
- alcoholic liver disease possible
- drug-induced hepatitis possible

pruritus
- cholestasis probable
- possible with all liver diseases

The examination

The abdominal examination is very important. The liver should be palpated carefully for enlargement, consistency and tenderness under the right costal margin. Search for enlargement of the gall bladder and the spleen. The gall bladder lies in the transypyloric line. A palpable gall bladder indicates extrahepatic biliary obstruction, and splenomegaly may indicate haemolytic anaemia, portal hypertension or viral hepatitis. Test for ascites.

Skin excoriation may indicate pruritus, which is associated with cholestatic jaundice. Look for evidence of chronic liver disease, such as palmar erythema, easy bruising, spider naevi and muscle wasting, and testicular atrophy and gynaecomastia. Test for hepatic flap (asterixis) and fetor, which indicate liver failure. Search for lymphadenopathy which may be indicative of malignancy.

A summary of the possible findings is presented in Figure 49.2.

Investigations

The main investigations are the standard liver function tests and viral serology for the infective causes, particularly hepatitis B virus.

A summary of the general findings for liver function tests is shown in Table 49.4. Consideration should be given to ordering fractionalisation of bilirubin to determine whether it is conjugated or unconjugated (important in diagnosis of Gilbert's disease).

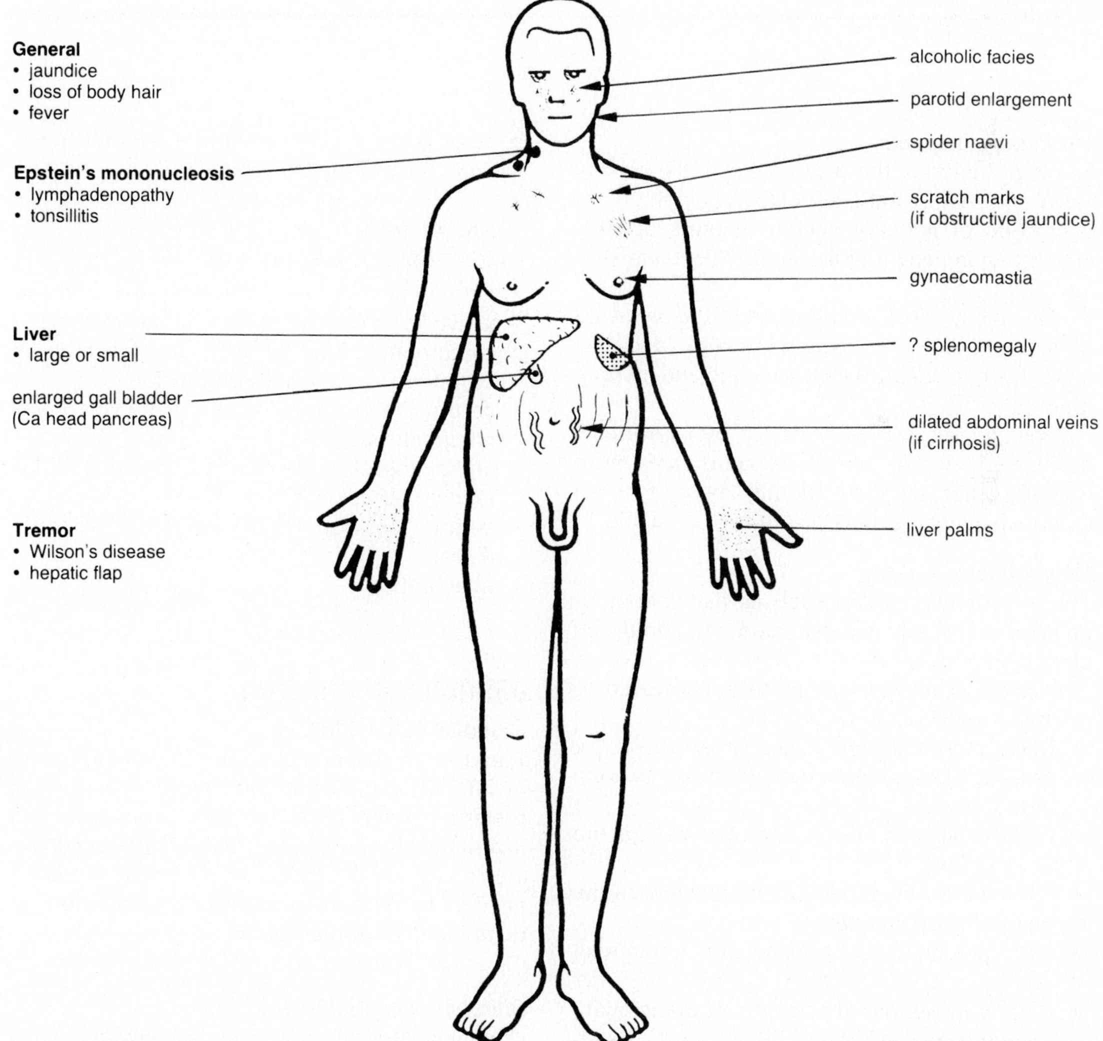

Fig. 49.2 *Possible findings on examining the jaundiced patient*

Table 49.4 *Characteristic liver function tests for selected types of liver disease*

Liver function tests (serological)	*Hepatocellular hepatitis*	*Haemolytic jaundice*	*Obstruction*	*Gilbert's disease*	*Liver metastases /abscess*	*Alcoholic liver disease*
Bilirubin	↑ to ↑↑↑	↑ unconjugated	↑ to ↑↑↑	↑ up to 50 unconjugated	↑ to N	↑ to N
Alkaline phosphatase	↑ <2N	N	↑↑↑ >2N	N	↑↑ to ↑↑↑	↑
Aspartate transferase	↑↑↑ >5N	N	N or ↑	N	↑	↑
Gamma glutamyl transferase	↑↑	N	↑↑	N	↑	↑↑↑
Albumin	N or ↓	N	N	N	N to ↓	N to ↓↓
Globulin	N or ↑	N	N	N	N	N to ↑

N: is within normal limits

Markers for hepatitis

Serology includes the test for hepatitis B virus (HBV) surface antigen (HBsAg) which is diagnostic of infection. Other markers of HBV are HBeAg antigen and the antibodies (anti-HBs and anti-HBe).

Hepatitis A virus is diagnosed by the presence of IgM antibody for recent infection and IgG antibody that indicates past infection and lifelong immunity.

Specific serological tests for the previously designated non-A, non-B hepatitis are more complex, but tests to identify two of these causative agents (C and D) are now available.

Hepatobiliary imaging

Tests to identify causes such as malignancy or gallstones are now sophisticated and should be chosen with care.

- X-ray: a plain abdominal X-ray shows up to 10% of gallstones
- Ultrasound: the most useful investigation for detecting gallstones and dilatation of the common bile duct
- HIDA scintiscan: useful in diagnosis of acute cholecystitis
- CT scan: for diagnosis of enlargement of the head of the pancreas
- PTC: percutaneous transhepatic cholangiography
- ERCP:endoscopic retrograde cholangiopancreatography; PTC and ERCP (best) determine the cause of the obstruction
- Liver isotopic scan: useful for liver cirrhosis, especially of the left lobe

Specific tests

Some specific tests include:

- autoantibodies for autoimmune chronic active hepatitis and primary biliary cirrhosis
- carcinoembryonic antigen to detect liver secondaries, especially colorectal
- serum iron and ferratin—elevated in haemochromatosis
- alphafetoprotein—elevated in hepatocellular carcinoma
- serum ceruloplasmin—low in Wilson's disease
- liver biopsy

Jaundice in children

Jaundice in the infant

Jaundice in the newborn is clinically apparent in 50% of term babies and more than 80% of preterm.[5] Icterus is therefore common and invariably physiologically benign. However, there are many other causes and investigation is needed to determine whether the bilirubin is conjugated or unconjugated.

Bilirubin encephalopathy

Unconjugated bilirubin can be regarded as a neurological poison. With increasing serum levels an encephalopathy (which may be transient) can develop, but if persistent can lead to the irreversible brain damage known as kernicterus. The level of bilirubin causing kernicterus is totally unpredictable, but a guideline as a cause for concern in babies with Rh disease is a serum unconjugated bilirubin of 340 μmol/L (20 mg/dL).

Physiological jaundice

This mild form of jaundice which is very common in infants is really a diagnosis of exclusion. In a term infant the serum bilirubin rises quickly after birth to reach a maximum by day 3–5, then declines rapidly over the next 2–3 days before fading more slowly for the next 1–2 weeks. Management includes phototherapy.

Pathological jaundice

There are many causes of pathological jaundice, including:

- haemolysis, e.g. blood grouping incompatibilities
- polycythemia, e.g. intrauterine growth retardation
- inherited conjugation defects, e.g. uridyl diphosphate glucuronyl transferase deficiency
- breast milk jaundice
- drugs
- sepsis
- hypothyroidism
- biliary atresia

Such cases require referral for evaluation and management.

Jaundice in older children

Viral infection is the commonest cause of jaundice in the older child, especially hepatitis A and hepatitis B. It is uncommon for viral hepatitis to become chronic in childhood.

Jaundice in the elderly

If an elderly person presents with jaundice the usual causes and investigations have to be considered. Obstructive jaundice is the commonest form of jaundice in the elderly and may be caused by gallstones blocking the common bile duct (may be painless) and carcinoma of the head of the pancreas, the biliary tract itself, the stomach or multiple secondaries for other sites. While it is not uncommon for a gallstone to produce marked obstructive jaundice and yet be painless, it is appropriate to adhere to the old adage that painless obstructive jaundice is due to neoplasm—particularly if the gall bladder is palpable (Courvoisier's law).

Alcoholic liver disease, although most frequently affecting patients between 40 and 60 years, can present for the first time over age 60 years. The commonest cause of hepatocellular jaundice in the elderly is probably alcoholic cirrhosis; hepatitis A is still relatively uncommon in old persons.

Drugs do not cause jaundice in the elderly as frequently as they once did, particularly as phenothiazines, especially chlorpromazine, are not prescribed as often as previously. However, drugs should be considered as a potential cause and a careful check of the drug history is important.

Infective causes of jaundice

A generation ago hepatitis A (infectious hepatitis or yellow jaundice) was the commonest recognised form of viral hepatitis, presenting usually with an abrupt onset of fever, anorexia, nausea and vomiting. It usually occurred in epidemics and hence was common in overcrowded institutions and camps. Now hepatitis B and C are very commonly reported types of viral hepatitis with an onset that is more insidious and with a longer incubation period. Symptoms include malaise, anorexia, nausea and polyarthritis.

The various forms of hepatitis are summarised in Table 49.5. All forms of hepatitis are common in developing countries and travellers are at risk of contracting these diseases: hepatitis A and E from faeco-oral transmission; and hepatitis B,C and D from intravenous drugs and bodily fluids (from sexual transmission, in particular, for hepatitis B).

In hepatitis A liver damage is directly due to the virus, but in hepatitis B it is due to an immunologic reaction to the virus.

Other infections that can present with jaundice as part of a systemic disease are malaria, Epstein-Barr mononucleosis, cytomegalovirus, Q fever, toxoplasmosis, leptospirosis and, rarely, measles, varicella, yellow fever, rubella, herpes simplex, dengue fever, Lassa fever and Marberg and Ebola virus.

Table 49.5 *Characteristic profiles of viral hepatitis A–E*

Characteristic	*Hepatitis A*	*Hepatitis B*	*Hepatitis C*	*Hepatitis D*	*Hepatitis E*
Pseudonyms	Infectious hepatitis	Serum hepatitis	Parenterally transmitted non A, non B	Delta hepatitis	Enterically transmitted non A, non B
Agent (virus)	27nm RNA	42nm DNA	50nm RNA	35nm RNA	30 nm RNA
Transmission	Faecal-oral	Blood and other body fluids	Blood ? other body fluids	Blood and other body fluids	Faecal-oral
Incubation period	15–45 days	40–180 days	14–180 days	30–50 days	15–45 days
Severity of acute illness	Mild to moderate Often subclinical —no jaundice	Mild to severe Jaundice common Arthralgia and rash common	Mild to moderate Often subclinical	Moderate to severe High mortality Usually jaundice	Mild to moderate Often subclinical
Chronic liver disease	No	Yes 5–10%	Yes 20–50%	Yes Potentially worst	No
Mortality	0.1–0.2%	1–3%	1–2%	Variable	Variable High (10–20%) in pregnant women
Carrier state	No	Yes	Yes	Yes	Uncertain
Risk in travellers	Yes, applies to all A–E: East and South-East Asia, Asian subcontinent, e.g. India, South Pacific Islands, e.g. Fiji, sub-Saharan Africa, Mexico, USSR, other developing countries. A and E with poor sanitation; B, C, D also with IV drug use; B, D, sexual contact.				
Antigens	HA Ag	HBsAg, HBcAg, HBeAg	HC Ag	HD Ag	?
Serology	IgM anti-HAV diagnosis	HBsAg diagnosis anti-HBs } exposure immunity	anti-HCV (antibody)	HBsAg +ve HDsAg +ve anti-HDV (antibody)	Being developed
Immuno-prophylaxis	Normal Ig	HB Ig	? Ig effective	None	None
Vaccine	Hepatitis A vaccine	Hepatitis B vaccine	None	Hepatitis B vaccine	None

Hepatitis A

Hepatitis A is the commonest type of viral hepatitis and causes 20–40% of clinically apparent hepatitis, although it is becoming relatively less prevalent in first world countries. It is enterically transmitted and arises from the ingestion of contaminated food such as shellfish or water. There is no carrier state and it does not cause chronic liver disease. Hepatitis A most often causes a subclinical or self-limited clinical illness.

Clinical features

Preicteric (prodromal) phase:

- anorexia, nausea, ± vomiting
- malaise
- headache
- distaste for cigarettes in smokers
- mild fever
- ± diarrhoea
- ± upper abdominal discomfort

Icteric phase (many patients do not develop jaundice):

- dark urine
- pale stools
- hepatomegaly
- splenomegaly (palpable in 10%)

Recovery usually in 3–6 weeks.

Fulminant hepatitis with liver coma and death may occur but is rare.

Investigations

Liver function tests and viral markers confirm the diagnosis. The antibodies to HAV are IgM which indicates active infection and IgG antibodies which means, immunity and which is common in the general population. Ultrasound is useful to exclude bile duct obstruction, especially in an older patient.

Outcome and treatment

Hepatitis A has an excellent prognosis with most patients making a complete recovery, and patients should be reassured. The mortality is less than 0.5%. Admission to hospital is not usually necessary. There is no specific treatment so management is as follows.

- Appropriate reassurance and patient education.
- Rest as appropriate.
- Fat-free diet.
- Avoid alcohol, smoking and hepatotoxic drugs (until recovery).
- Advice on hygiene at home to prevent spread to close contacts and family members.
- Wash hands carefully after using the toilet and disinfect them with antiseptic.
- Do not handle food for others with your fingers.
- Do not share cutlery and crockery during meals.
- Do not use tea towels to dry dishes.

Prevention

Simple health measures such as good sanitation, effective garbage disposal and hand washing are probably responsible for the major decrease in the disease. Immune serum globulin (0.03–0.06 ml/kg IM) confers satisfactory passive immunity for close contacts (within 2 weeks of contact) and for travellers to endemic areas for up to 3 months. An active vaccine consisting of a 3-dose primary course is now available.

Hepatitis B

Hepatitis B has protean clinical manifestations. Transmission is by blood-spread, sexual transmission, perinatal spread or by close prolonged family contact. Infection may be subclinical or self-limited acute hepatitis. Fulminant hepatitis is rare. Five per cent of subjects go on to become chronic carriers of the virus. Most are 'healthy carriers' but some may develop chronic active hepatitis, cirrhosis and hepatoma. The serology of hepatitis B involves antibody responses to the four main antigens of the virus (core, DNA polymerise, protein X and surface antigens). Passive and active vaccines are available, and should be used freely in groups at risk including babies of infected mothers. High-risk groups are presented in Table 49.6. The clinical features are the same as those found in hepatitis A infection but may be more severe.[6] A serum sickness-like immunological syndrome may be seen with transient rashes, e.g. urticaria or a maculopapular rash, and polyarthritis affecting small joints in up to 25% of cases in the prodromal period.

Table 49.6 *Higher risk groups for contracting hepatitis B (vaccination advisable)*

Babies born to hepatitis B positive (carrier) mothers
Sexual partners of hepatitis B carriers (especially acute HBV)
Household contacts of hepatitis B carriers
Intravenous drug users
Recipients of blood or blood products (prior to testing)
Male homosexuals
Renal dialysis patients
Sex industry workers
Health care workers
Garbage collectors
Institutionalised mentally retarded patients
Prisoners
Travellers to endemic areas

Investigations

The main viral investigation for HBV is HBsAg (surface antigen) which is searched for routinely. If detected, a full viral profile is then formed.

HBsAg may disappear or persist. Its presence indicates a current or chronic infection as well as a carrier state (Fig. 49.3).

Outcome and treatment

The possible course of events is shown in Figure 49.4. The majority of patients recover completely with the outcome depending on several factors including the virulence of the virus and the immune state and age of the patient. Some will develop chronic hepatitis, some will develop a fulminant course and others will become asymptomatic carriers and present a health risk to others.

There is no specific treatment and appropriate reassurance and patient education is necessary. Treatment of chronic hepatitis B infection is with

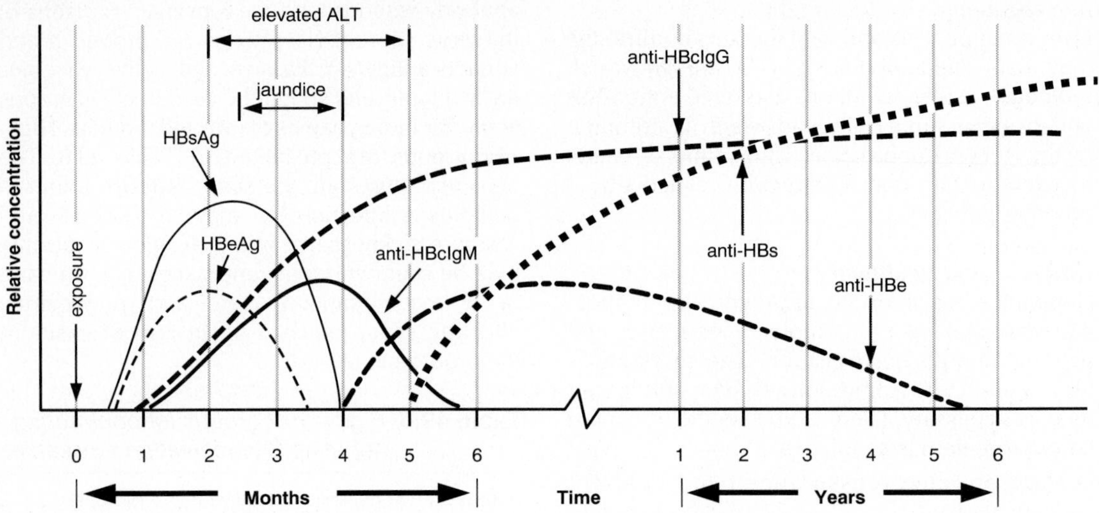

Fig. 49.3 *Time course of clinical events and serological changes following infection with hepatitis B*

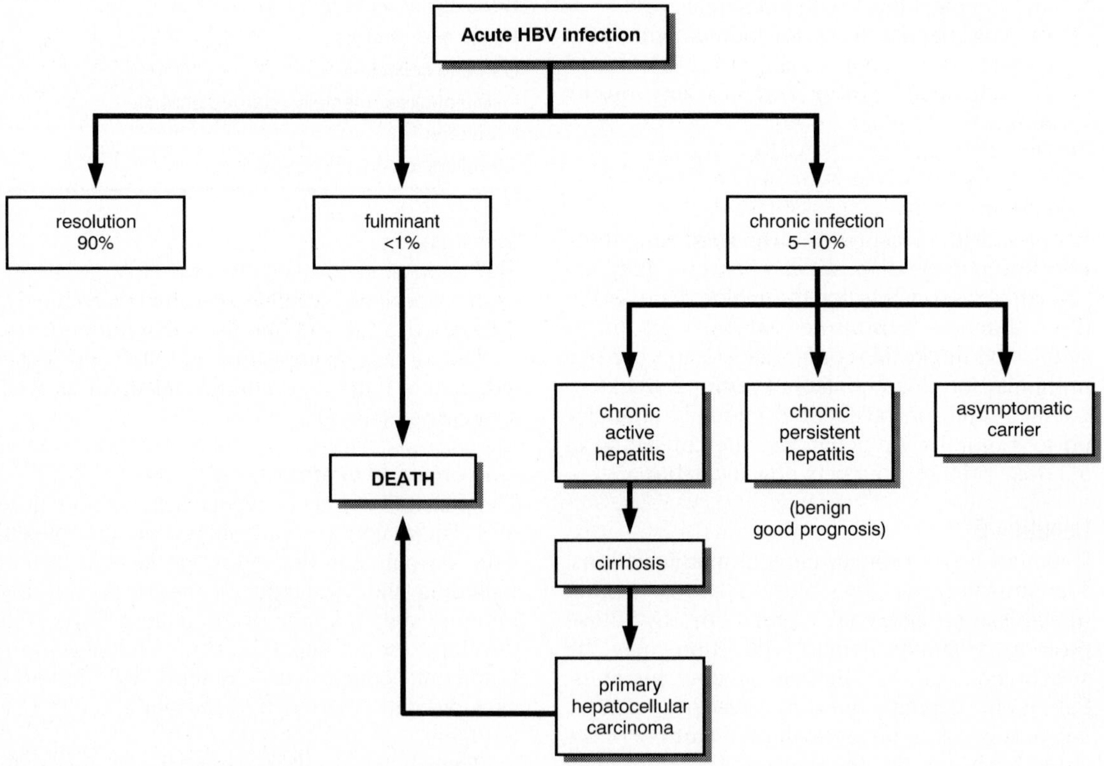

Acute HBV infection

resolution
90%

fulminant
<1%

chronic infection
5–10%

chronic
active
hepatitis

chronic
persistent
hepatitis

(benign
good prognosis)

asymptomatic
carrier

DEATH

cirrhosis

primary
hepatocellular
carcinoma

Fig. 49.4 *Natural history of hepatitis B infection*

the immunomodulatory and antiviral agent interferon alpha. This is expensive but achieves permanent remission in 25% of patients, and temporary remission in a further 25%.[6] Liver transplantation has been performed, but is often followed by recurrence of hepatitis B in the grafted liver.

Prevention
Active immunisation through hepatitis B vaccination has been a major breakthrough in the management of this serious illness. There is a course of three injections. If there is a negative antibody response after 3 months, revaccinate with a double dose. If the response is positive, consider a test in 5 years with a view to a booster injection.

For non-immune patients at risk, e.g. after a needlestick injury, hepatitis B immunoglobin (HBIG), which contains a high level of HBV surface antibody, is appropriate.

Prenatal screening of pregnant women and appropriate use of HBIG and HB vaccine is useful in preventing perinatal vertical transmission of HBV.

Hepatitis C

Hepatitis C virus is responsible for at least 90% of cases of post-transfusion non A, non B patients. It is primarily contracted from intravenous drug use or tattooing. It does not seem to be spread very readily by sexual contact although there is a small risk during heterosexual and homosexual intercourse. It is also not readily spread perinatally.

Hepatitis C infection may be self-limiting, but more commonly (in 50% of cases) causes a slow, relentless progression to chronic hepatitis, cirrhosis (20%) and also hepatoma.

Diagnosis
Presence of HCV antibody.

There is no vaccine yet available. Treatment of chronic hepatitis C infection is also with interferon.

Those at increased risk of having hepatitis C

- blood transfusion recipients (prior to HCV testing)
- intravenous drug users (past or present)
- male homosexuals who have practised unsafe sex
- renal dialysis patients
- sex industry workers
- those with abnormal LFTs with no obvious cause
- tattooed people

Prevention of transmission of hepatitis C virus
Advice to those who are positive for HCV:

- Do not donate blood.
- Do not share needles.
- Advise health care workers, including your dentist.
- Do not share intimate equipment such as toothbrushes, razors, nail files and nail scissors.
- Wipe up blood spills in the home with household bleach.
- Cover up cuts or wounds with an adequate dressing.
- Dispose of bloodstained tissues, sanitary napkins and other dressings safely.
- Use safe sex practices such as condoms.

Hepatitis D

Hepatitis D is a small defective virus which lacks a surface coat. This is provided by hepatitis B virus, and so hepatitis D infection occurs only in patients with concomitant hepatitis B.

It is usually spread parenterally and if chronic is usually associated with progressive disease with a poor prognosis. Treatment with interferon has a poor success rate. Antibodies to the delta virus, both anti-HDV and anti-HDV IgM (indicating a recent infection) as well as HDV Ag can be measured.[7]

Hepatitis E

Hepatitis E is an enterically transmitted virus which occurs in outbreaks in certain countries with a poor water supply such as some Asian subcontinent countries. Epidemiologically, HEV behaves like HAV with well-documented waterborne epidemics in areas of poor sanitation. There is a high case fatality rate (up to 20%) in pregnant females.

Cholestatic jaundice

Cholestasis refers to the syndrome of biliary obstructive jaundice whereby there is obstruction to the flow of bile from the hepatocyte to the duodenum thus causing bilirubin to accumulate in the blood. It is classified into two main groups:

- intrahepatic cholestasis—at the hepatocyte or intrahepatic biliary tree level

- extrahepatic cholestasis—obstruction in the large bile ducts

The significant causes are listed in Table 49.7.

Table 49.7 *Significant causes of cholestasis in adults*

Intrahepatic
- viral hepatitis
- alcoholic hepatitis/cirrhosis
- drugs
- primary biliary cirrhosis

Extrahepatic
- common bile duct gallstones
- cancer of pancreas
- cancer of bile ducts
- other cancer: primary or secondary spread
- cholangitis
- pancreatitis
- postsurgical biliary stricture or oedema

Symptoms

- jaundice (greenish tinge)
- dark urine and pale stools
- pruritus—worse on palms and soles
- pain varies from nil to severe

Gallstones and jaundice

Gallstones can be found in the following (Fig. 49.5):

- gall bladder (asymptomatic up to 75%)—the majority remain here
- neck of gall bladder } biliary 'colic' or
- cystic duct } acute cholecystitis
- common bile duct: may cause severe biliary 'colic', cholestatic jaundice or cholangitis

Acute cholecystitis is accompanied by mild jaundice in 20% of cases, due to accompanying common duct stones.[7]

Common bile duct stones may be asymptomatic or may present with any one or all of the triad of abdominal pain, jaundice and fever. The jaundice varies, depending on the amount of obstruction. The liver is moderately enlarged if the obstruction lasts for more than a few hours.

The investigations of choice for cholestatic jaundice are ultrasound and ERCP.

Acute cholangitis

This is due to bacterial infection of the bile ducts secondary to abnormalities of the bile duct, especially gallstones in the common duct. Other causes are neoplasms and biliary strictures.

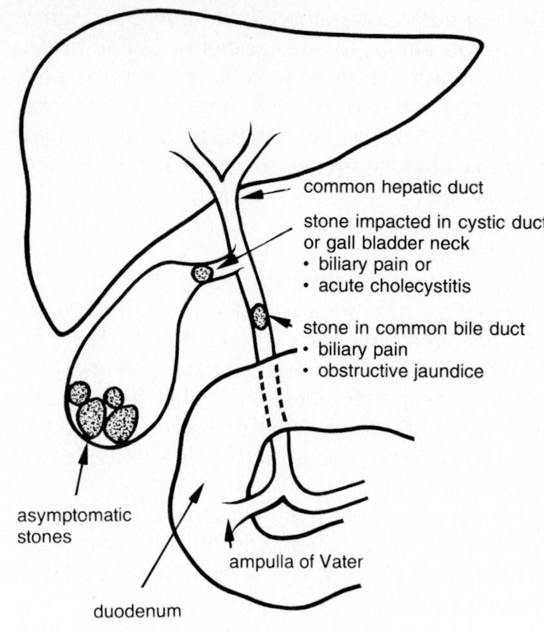

Fig. 49.5 *Clinical presentation of gallstones*

The triad (present in 70%) for acute cholangitis is:

Fever (often with rigor) + *upper abdominal pain* + *jaundice*

Older patients can present with circulatory collapse and Gram-negative septicaemia. Urgent referral is necessary.

Carcinoma of head of the pancreas

Pancreatic carcinoma is the fourth commonest cause of cancer death in the UK and USA.[7]

Typical clinical features

- M > F
- mainly > 60 years of age
- obstructive jaundice
- pain (over 75%)—epigastric and back
- enlarged gall bladder (50–75%)

Possible features

- weight loss, malaise, diarrhoea
- migratory thrombophlebitis
- palpable hard, fixed mass
- metastases, e.g. left supraclavicular gland of Virchow
- occult blood in stool
- glycosuria

Diagnosis
- scanning by ultrasound or CT scan may show mass
- ERCP

Prognosis
Very poor: 5 year survival 1–2%.

Cirrhosis of the liver
Cirrhosis is accompanied by jaundice as a late and serious manifestation with the exception of primary biliary cirrhosis where jaundice appears before advanced liver failure. The development of jaundice usually indicates that there is minimal hepatic reserve and is therefore found in conjunction with other signs of liver failure (Fig. 49.6).

Causes
Common:
- alcohol excess
- chronic active hepatitis (esp. HBV, HCV)

Others:
- primary biliary cirrhosis
- haemochromatosis
- Wilson's disease
- drugs, e.g. methotrexate
- cryptogenic (no cause found)

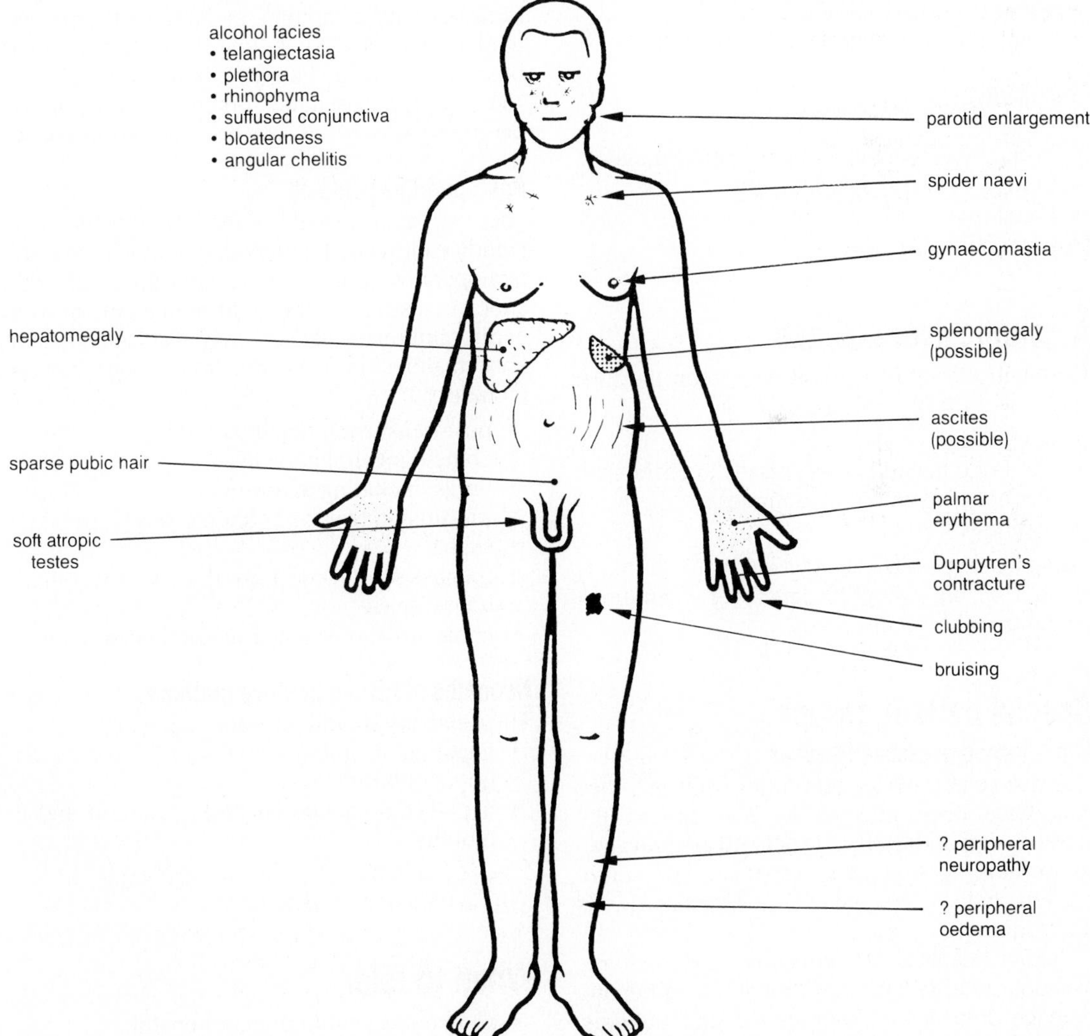

Fig. 49.6 *Possible features of chronic alcoholic liver disease*

Clinical features

- anorexia, nausea, ± vomiting
- swelling of legs
- abdominal distension
- bleeding tendency
- drowsiness, confusion or coma (if liver failure)

Signs

- spider naevi (distribution of superior vena cava)
- palmar erythema of hands
- peripheral oedema and ascites
- jaundice (obstructive or hepatocellular)
- enlarged tender liver (small liver in long-term cirrhosis)
- ascites
- gynaecomastia
- ± splenomegaly (portal hypertension)

Complications

- ascites
- portal hypertension and GIT haemorrhage
- portosystemic encephalopathy
- hepatoma
- renal failure

Alcoholic liver disease

The main effects of alcohol excess on the liver are:

- fatty liver
- alcoholic hepatitis (progresses to cirrhosis if alcohol consumption continues)
- alcoholic cirrhosis

If diagnosed, patients are advised to stop drinking alcohol for life except for fatty liver when small amounts can be drunk later.

Special patient groups

The returned overseas traveller

The overseas traveller presenting with jaundice may have been infected by any one of the viruses—hepatitis A, B, C, D or E. All are prevalent in developing countries, especially in south-eastern and eastern Asia, some Pacific islands and Africa.

Other causes to consider are malaria, ascending cholangitis and drug-induced hepatic damage due to, for example, the antimalarials, including mefloquine (Larium) and Fansidar.

The pregnant patient

Specific types of jaundice related to pregnancy are rare. Viral hepatitis accounts for 40% of all cases of jaundice during pregnancy. Cholestasis of pregnancy is due to an oestrogen sensitivity. The symptoms are mild and the condition clears up rapidly after delivery, but it often recurs if the patient is prescribed oral contraceptives.[8]

Severe pre-eclampsia, eclampsia and hyperemesis gravidarum may cause hepatic damage and failure but the most dramatic condition is acute fatty liver of pregnancy, which is now very rare. It is a serious condition of unknown aetiology and may follow the administration of hepatotoxic agents, especially in the more debilitated patient, usually in the third trimester. Acute fatty liver presents in the last trimester with symptoms of fulminant hepatitis, namely jaundice, vomiting, abdominal pain, possibly coma.[7] It has a high mortality (about 75%) and necessitates urgent termination of pregnancy which may save both mother and baby.

Postoperative jaundice

There are many possible causes of postoperative jaundice either in the immediate or the long-term postoperative phase. Hypoxia associated with shock in a severely ill patient or in a patient with cardiopulmonary disease may lead to transient abnormalities in liver function. Other causes include:

- post-transfusion hepatitis
- coincident viral hepatitis
- drugs, including anaesthetics
- transfusion overload (haemolysis)
- sepsis
- unmasked chronic liver disease and biliary tract disease
- cholestasis: post major abdominal surgery

Neonates of HBeAg positive mothers

The neonates should have the following:

- hepatitis B immunoglobulin IM within 24 hours of birth
- hepatitis B vaccine at birth, 1 month and 6 months

This is not 100% effective because some infants can be infected *in utero*.

When to refer

- all patients with fulminant hepatitis
- all patients with chronic liver disease

- painless obstructive jaundice
- evidence of malignancy
- symptomatic gallstones
- patients with cirrhosis
- acute fatty liver of pregnancy (very urgent)
- suspected rare conditions, e.g. Wilson's disease

Practice tips

- All drugs should be suspected as potential hepatotoxins.
- With hepatitis A the presence of IgM antibodies reflects recent infection, and IgG antibody indicates past infection and lifelong immunity.
- There is no chronic carrier state of hepatitis A and E.
- All patients with jaundice should be tested for hepatitis B surface antigen (HBsAg).
- Hepatitis B infection is usually benign and short-lived, but it can be fatal if chronic hepatitis develops, which may lead later to cirrhosis and hepatocellular carcinoma.
- Up to 5–10% of patients with hepatitis B will become chronic carriers (especially drug addicts and homosexuals).
- Such carriers are identified by persistent titres of HBsAg and possibly HBeAg, the latter indicating the presence of the whole virus and active replication and high infectivity.
- A raised gamma glutamyl transferase accompanied by a raised MCV is a good screening test for alcohol abuse.
- A systolic murmer may be heard over the liver in alcoholic hepatitis and hepatoma.
- A distaste for smoking (with jaundice) suggests acute viral hepatitis.

References

1. Kincaid-Smith R, Larkins R, Whelan G. *Problems in clinical medicine*. Sydney: McLennan and Petty, 1989, 251.
2. Coffman D, Chalstrey J, Smith-Laing G. *Gastrointestinal disorders*. Edinburgh: Churchill Livingstone, 1986, 106.
3. Sandler G. Fry J. *Early clinical diagnosis*. Lancaster: MTP Press, 1986, 468–490.
4. Taggart G. Viral hepatitis. Sigma Clinical Review, 1988, no 17:15.
5. Robinson MJ. *Practical paediatrics*. Melbourne: Churchill Livingstone, 1990, 192.
6. Watson KR. *Viral hepatitis*. Abstract in Monash University 4th annual postgraduate medical refresher course notes. Melbourne 1991.
7. Kumer PJ, Clarke ML. *Clinical medicine* (2nd edition). London: Bailliere Tindall, 1990, 237–292.
8. Beischer NA, MacKay EV. *Obstetrics and the newborn*. Sydney: Saunders, 1986, 307–308.

50

The painful knee

The human knee is a joint and not a source of entertainment.

Percy Hammond 1912 (review of a play)

The knee joint is the largest synovial joint in the body. Its small area of contact of the bone ends at any one time makes it dependent on ligaments for its stability. Although this allows a much increased range of movement it does increase the susceptibility to injury, particularly from sporting activities. Finding the cause of a knee problem is one of the really difficult and challenging features of practice. It is useful to remember that peripheral pain receptors respond to a variety of stimuli. These include inflammation due either to inflammatory disease or chemical irritation such as crystal synovitis, traction pain, e.g. trapped meniscus stretching the capsule, tension on the synovium capsule, e.g. effusion or haemarthrosis, and impact loading of the subcondral bone.

Key facts and checkpoints

- Disorders of the knee account for about one presentation per fifty patients per year.[1]
- The commoner presenting symptoms in order of frequency are pain, stiffness, swelling, clicking and locking.[1]
- The age of presentation of a painful knee has varied significance as many conditions are age-related.
- Excessive strains across the knee, such as a valgus-producing force, are more likely to cause ligament injuries while twisting injuries, tend to cause meniscal tears.
- A ruptured anterior cruciate ligament (ACL) is the most commonly missed injury of the knee.[2]
- A rapid onset of painful knee swelling (minutes to 1–4 hours) after injury indicates blood in the joint—*haemarthrosis*.
- Swelling over 1–2 days after injury indicates synovial fluid—*traumatic synovitis*.
- Any necessary surgery to torn ligaments should be performed during the ten days following the injury. The tissues are unstable from 2–12 weeks post injury.[3]
- Acute spontaneous inflammation of the knee may be part of a systemic condition such as rheumatoid arthritis, rheumatic fever, gout, pseudogout (chondrocalcinosis), a spondyloarthropathy (psoriasis, ankylosing spondylitis, Reiter's disease, bowel inflammation), Lyme disease and sarcoidosis.
- Consider Osgood-Schlatter disorder in the prepubertal child (especially a boy aged 10–14) presenting with knee pain.
- Disorders of the lumbosacral spine (especially L3 to S1 nerve root problems) and of the hip joint (L3 innervation) refer pain to the region of the knee joint.

The knee and referred pain—key knowledge

Pain from the knee joint

Disorders of the knee joint give rise to pain felt accurately at the knee, often at some particular part of the joint, and invariably in the anterior aspect, very seldom in the posterior part of the knee. An impacted loose body complicating osteoarthritis and a radial tear of the lateral meniscus[4] are the exceptional disorders liable to refer pain proximally and distally in the limb, but the problems obviously originate from the knee.

Pain referred to the knee

Referred pain to the knee or the surrounding region is a time-honoured trap in medicine. The two classic problems are disorders of the hip joint and lumbosacral spine.

- The hip joint is mainly innervated by L3, hence pain is referred from the groin down the front and medial aspects of the thigh to the knee (Fig. 50.1). Sometimes the pain can be experienced on the anteromedial aspect of the knee only. It is not uncommon that children with a slipped upper femoral epiphysis present with a limp and knee pain.

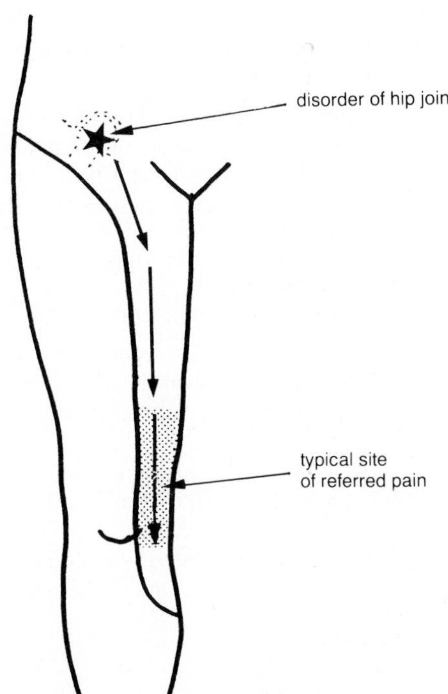

Fig. 50.1 *Possible area of referred pain from disorders of the hip joint*

- Knee pain can be referred from the lumbosacral spine. Patients with disc lesions may notice that sitting, coughing or straining hurts the knee, whereas walking does not.

L3 nerve root pressure from an L2–L3 disc prolapse (uncommon) and L4 nerve root pain will cause anteromedial knee pain; L5 reference from an L4–L5 disc prolapse can cause anterolateral knee pain, while S1 reference from an L5–S1 prolapse can cause pain at the back of the knee (Fig. 56.1).

A diagnostic approach

A summary of the safety diagnostic model is presented in Table 50.1.

Table 50.1 *The painful knee: diagnostic strategy model*

Q. *Probability diagnosis*
A. Ligament strains and sprains
± traumatic synovitis
Osteoarthritis
Patellofemoral syndrome
Prepatellar bursitis

Q. *Serious disorders not to be missed*
A. Acute cruciate ligament tear
Vascular disorders
- deep venous thrombosis
- superficial thrombophlebitis

Neoplasia
- primary in bone
- metastases

Severe infections
- septic arthritis
- tuberculosis

Rheumatoid arthritis
Juvenile chronic arthritis
Rheumatic fever

Q. *Pitfalls (often missed)*
A. Referred pain: back or hip
Foreign bodies
Intra-articular loose bodies
Osteochondritis dissecans
Osteochondrosis
Osgood-Schlatter disorder
Meniscal tears
Fractures around knee
Pseudogout (chondrocalcinosis)
Gout → patellar bursitis

Rarities
Sarcoidosis
Paget's disease
Spondyloarthropathy
Ruptured popliteal cyst

Q. *Seven masquerades checklist*

A.		
	Depression	✓
	Diabetes	✓
	Drugs	(indirect)
	Anaemia	—
	Thyroid disease	—
	Spinal dysfunction	✓
	UTI	—

Q. *Is this patient trying to tell me something?*
A. Psychogenic factors relevant, especially with possible injury compensation.

Probability diagnosis

A UK study[1] has highlighted the fact that the commonest cause of knee pain is simple ligamentous strains and bruises due to overstress of the knee or other minor trauma. Traumatic synovitis may accompany some of these injuries. Some of these so-called strains may include a variety of recently described syndromes such as the synovial plica syndrome, patellar tendinitis and infrapatellar fat-pad inflammation (Fig. 50.2).

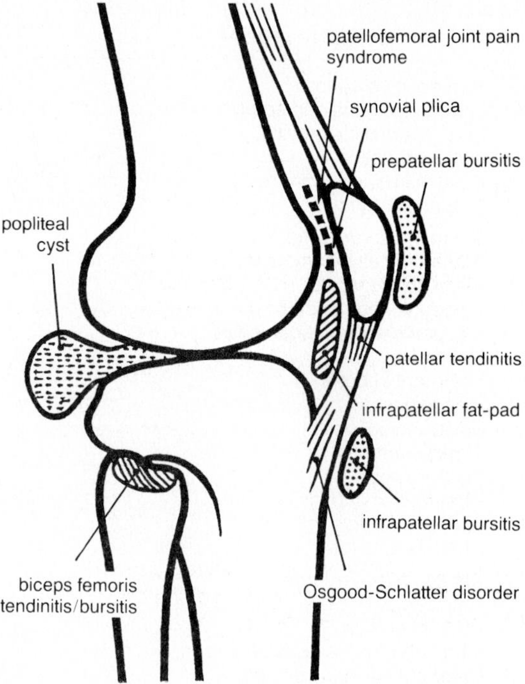

Fig. 50.2 *Lateral view of knee showing typical sites of various causes of knee pain*

Low-grade trauma of repeated overuse such as frequent kneeling may cause prepatellar bursitis known variously as 'housemaid's knee' or 'carpet layer's knee'. Infrapatellar bursitis is referred to as 'clergyman's knee'.

Osteoarthritis of the knee, especially in the elderly, is a very common problem. It may arise spontaneously or be secondary to previous trauma with associated internal derangement and instability.

The most common overuse problem of the knee is the patellofemoral joint pain syndrome (often previously referred to as chondromalacia patellae).

Serious disorders not to be missed

Neoplasia in the bones around the knee is relatively uncommon but still needs consideration. The commonest neoplasias are secondaries from the breast and lung. Uncommon examples include osteoid osteoma, osteosarcoma and Ewing's disease. Septic arthritis and infected bursitis are prone to occur in the knee joint, especially following contaminated lacerations and abrasions. Septic arthritis from blood-borne infection can either be of the primary type in children, where the infection is either staphylococcal or due to *Haemophilus influenzae*, or it is gonococcal arthritis in adults. Rheumatic fever should be kept in mind with a fleeting polyarthritis that involves the knees and then affects other joints.

Inflammatory disorders such as spondyloarthropathies, sarcoidosis, chondrocalcinosis (a crystal arthropathy due to calcium pyrophosphate dihydrate in the elderly), gout and juvenile chronic arthritis have to be considered in the differential diagnosis.

Pitfalls

There are a myriad pitfalls in knee joint disorders, often arising from ignorance, because there are a myriad problems that are difficult to diagnose. Fortunately many of these problems can be diagnosed by X-ray. A particular trap is a foreign body such as a broken needle acquired by kneeling on carpet.

The presence of a spontaneous effusion demands careful attention because it could represent osteochondritis dissecans (more common in the young) or osteonecrosis of the femoral condyle (a necrotic problem in the elderly) and perhaps a subsequent loose body in the joint.

A ruptured Baker's cyst will cause severe pain behind the knee and can be confused with deep venous thrombosis. It is important to bear in mind complications of varicose veins which can cause pain or discomfort around the knee joint.

General pitfalls

- Overlooking referred pain from the hip or low back as a cause of knee pain.
- Failing to realise that meniscal tears can develop due to degeneration of the menisci with only minimal trauma.
- Failing to X-ray the knee joint and order special views to detect specific problems such as a fractured patella or osteochondritis dissecans.

Seven masquerades checklist

Of these, spinal dysfunction is the prime association. Diabetes may cause pain through a complicating neuropathy and drugs such as diuretics may cause gout in the elderly.

Psychogenic considerations

Patients, young and old, may complain of knee pain, imaginary or exaggerated, to gain attention especially if compensation for an injury is involved. This requires discreet clinical acumen to help patients work through this problem.

The clinical approach

History

The history is the key to diagnosis. If any injury is involved careful description of the nature of the injury is necessary. A special problem relates to the elderly who can sustain knee injuries after a 'drop attack', but attention can easily be diverted away from the knee with preoccupation with the cerebral pattern.

It is relevant to define whether the pain is acute or chronic, dull or sharp, and continuous or recurring. Determine its severity and position and keep in mind age-related causes.

Key questions

Related to an injury

- Can you explain in detail how the injury happened?
- Did you land awkwardly after a leap in the air?
- Did you get a direct blow? From what direction?
- Did your leg twist during the injury?
- Did you feel a 'pop' or hear a 'snap'?
- Did your knee feel wobbly or unsteady?
- Did the knee feel as if the bones separated momentarily?
- How soon after the injury did the pain develop?
- How soon after the injury did you notice swelling?
- Have you had previous injury or surgery to the knee?
- Were you able to walk after the injury or did you have to be carried off the ground or court?

No history of injury

- Does the pain come on after walking, jogging or other activity?
- How much kneeling do you do? Scrubbing floors, cleaning carpets?
- Could there be needles or pins in the carpet?
- Does your knee lock or catch?
- Does swelling develop in the knee?
- Does it 'grate' when it moves?
- Does the pain come on at rest and is there morning stiffness?

Significance of symptoms

Swelling after injury

The sudden onset of painful swelling (usually within 60 minutes) is typical of haemarthrosis. Bleeding occurs from vascular structures such as torn ligaments, torn synovium or fractured bones, while injuries localised to avascular structures such as menisci do not usually bleed. About 75% of cases are due to anterior cruciate ligament tears.[5] If a minor injury causes acute haemarthrosis suspect a bleeding diathesis. The causes of haemarthrosis are listed in Table 50.2. Swelling of intermediate rate of onset, stiffness and pain in the order of hours, e.g. 6–24 hours, is typical of an effusion of synovial fluid. Causes include meniscal tears and milder ligamentous injuries. Swelling gradually developing over days and confined to the anterior knee is typical of bursitis such as 'housemaid's knee'.

Table 50.2 *Causes of haemarthrosis*

Torn cruciate ligaments, esp. ACL
Capsular tears with collateral ligament tears
Peripheral meniscal tears
Dislocation or subluxation of patella
Osteochondral fractures
Bleeding disorders, e.g. haemophilia

Recurrent or chronic swelling

This indicates intra-articular pathology and includes:

- patellofemoral pain syndrome
- osteochondritis dissecans
- degenerative joint disease
- arthritides

Locking

Locking usually means a sudden inability to extend the knee fully (occurs at 10–45°, average 30°) but ability to flex fully.[6]

Causes

True locking:

- torn meniscus (bucket handle)
- loose body, e.g. bony fragment from osteochondritis dissecans
- torn anterior cruciate ligament (remnant)
- avulsed anterior tibial spine
- dislocated patella
- synovial osteochondromatosis

Pseudo-locking:

- first or second degree medial ligament tear
- strain of ACL
- gross effusion
- pain and spasm of hamstrings

Catching

'Catching' of the knee implies that the patient feels that something is 'getting in the way of joint movement' but not locking. Causes include any of the conditions that cause locking, but a subluxing patella and loose bodies in particular must be considered.

Causes of loose bodies

- osteochondritis dissecans (usually lateral side of medial femoral condyle)
- retropatellar fragment, e.g. from dislocation of patella
- dislodged osteophyte
- osteochondral fracture—post injury

Clicking

Clicking may be due to an abnormality such as patellofemoral maltracking or subluxation, a loose intra-articular body or a torn meniscus, but can occur in normal joints when people climb stairs or squat.

Physical examination

The provisional diagnosis may be evident from a combination of the history and simple inspection of the joint but the process of testing palpation, movements (active and passive) and specific structures of the knee joint helps to pinpoint the disorder.

Inspection

Inspect the knee with the patient walking, standing erect and lying supine. Get the patient to squat to help localise the precise point of pain. Get the patient to sit on the couch with legs hanging over the side and note any abnormality of the patella. Note any deformities, swelling or muscle wasting.

The common knee deformities are genu valgum 'knock knees' (Fig. 50.3a), genu recurvatum 'back knee' (Fig. 50.3b) and genu varum 'bowed legs' (Fig. 50.3c). A useful way of remembering the terminology is to recall that the 'l' in valgus stands for 'l' in lateral.[7] In the normal knee the tibia has a slight valgus angulation in reference to the femur, the angulation being more pronounced in women.

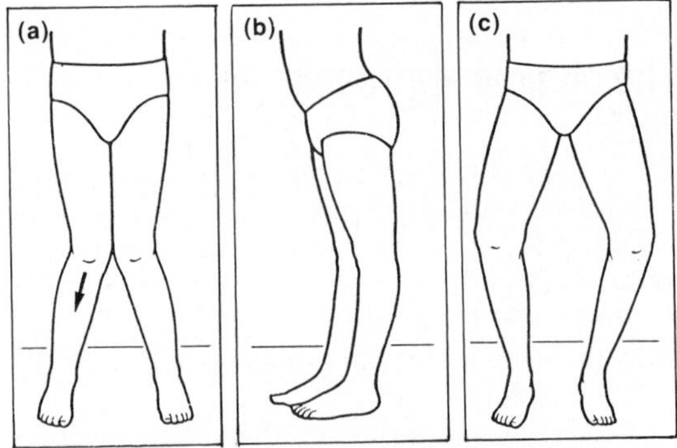

Fig. 50.3 *Knee deformities:* **(a)** *genu valgum ('knock knees'): tibia deviates laterally from knee;* **(b)** *genu recurvatum ('back knee');* **(c)** *genu varum ('bowed legs')*

Palpation

Palpate the knee generally concentrating on the patella, patella tendon, joint lines, tibial tubercle, bursae and popliteal fossa.

Palpate for presence of any fluid; warmth; swelling; synovial thickening; crepitus; clicking and tenderness. Feel for a popliteal (Baker's) cyst in the popliteal fossa. Draw the fingers upwards over the suprapatellar pouch: synovial thickening, a hallmark of chronic arthritis, is most marked just above the patella—it feels warm, boggy, rubbery and has no fluid thrill.

Flex the knees to 45° and check for a pseudocyst, especially of the lateral meniscus (Fig. 50.4).

Fluid effusion

The bulge sign: compress the suprapatellar pouch and evacuate any fluid out of the medial side of the joint. The test is positive when the lateral side of the joint is then stroked and the fluid is displaced across the joint, creating a visible bulge or filling of the medial depression

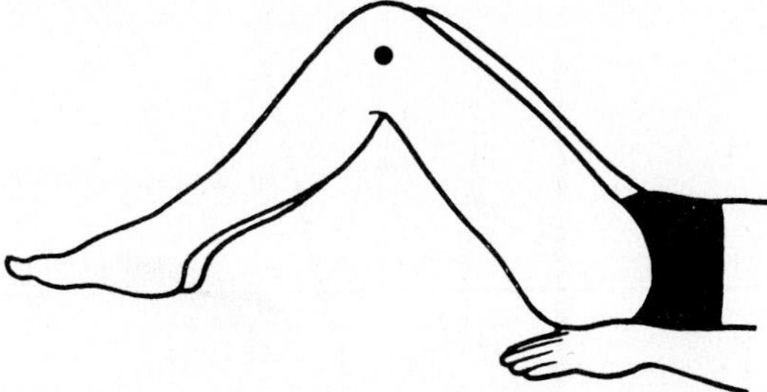

Fig. 50.4 *Pseudocyst of the lateral meniscus: flex the knees to 45° to force lump (if present) to appear*

(Fig. 50.5). The test will be negative if the effusion is gross and tense, in which case the *patellar tap test* (Fig. 50.6) is used by sharply tapping the lower pole of the patella against the femur with the index finger. A positive tap is when the patella can be felt to tap against the femur and then float free.

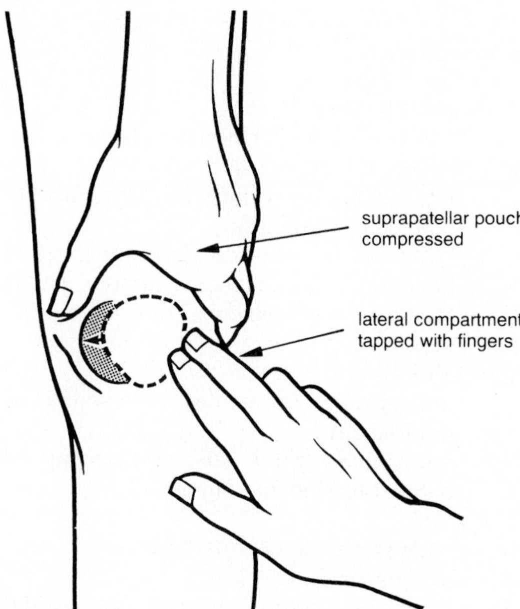

Fig. 50.5 *The bulge sign with a knee effusion: fluid bulges into the medial compartment*

Movements

Extension: normal is 0–5°. The loss of extension is best measured by lifting the heel off the couch with the knee held down. In the normal knee the heel will lift 2.5–4 cm off the couch, that is, into hyperextension.

Flexion (supine or prone): normal to 135°. The normal knee flexes heel to the buttock but in locking due to medial meniscus tears there is a gap of 5 or more centimetres between the heel and buttock.

Rotation: normal 5–10°. Test at 90° with patient sitting over the edge of the couch; rotate the feet with the hand steadying the knee.

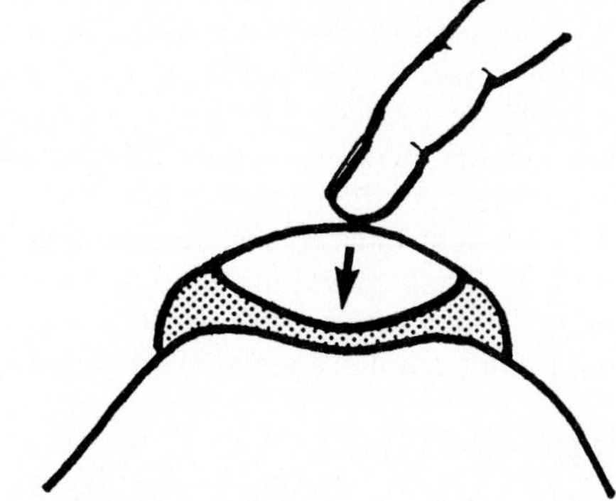

Fig. 50.6 *The patellar tap test*

Note Normally, no abduction, adduction or rotation of the tibia on the femur is possible with the leg fully extended.

Ligament stability tests

Collateral ligaments: adduction (varus) and abduction (valgus) stresses of tibia on femur are applied in full extension and then at 30° flexion with the leg over the side of the couch. With ligament strains there is localised pain when stressed. With a complete (third degree) tear the joint will open out. This endpoint feel should be carefully noted: firmness indicates stability, 'mushiness' indicates damage (Figs. 50.7a, b).

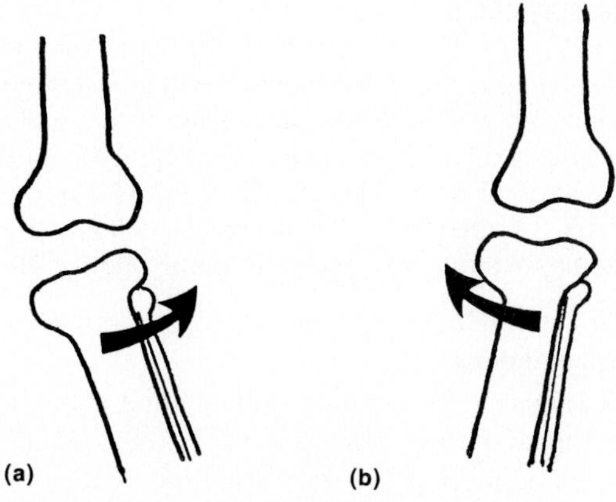

Fig. 50.7 *Medial and lateral ligament instability:* **(a)** *medial instability of knee joint;* **(b)** *lateral instability of knee joint*

Cruciate ligaments: stability of the ACL can be tested by the anterior draw test with the knee flexed to 90° or at 15° (the Lachman test, which is more sensitive). An aberrant positive anterior draw test occurs in the presence of posterior cruciate ligament insufficiency in which the knee is actually brought back to the normal position from a drop back position, thus giving the appearance of a positive anterior draw sign. In that situation a Lachman's test will be negative.

Specific provocation tests

The simplest menisci function tests are those outlined in Table 50.4.

- *McMurray's test* The patient lies on the couch and the flexed knee is rotated in varying degrees of abduction as it is straightened into extension. A hand over the affected knee feels for 'clunking' or tenderness.
- *Apley grind/distraction test*: The patient lies prone, the knee is flexed to 90° and then rotated under a compression force. Reproduction of painful symptoms may indicate meniscal tear. Then repeat rotation under distraction—tests ligament damage.

Patella apprehension test At 15–20° flexion attempt to push the patella laterally and note the patient's reaction.

Patellar tendinitis Palpate patellar tendon (refer Fig. 50.16).

Patellofemoral pain test (refer Fig. 50.15).

Examine the lumbosacral spine and the hip joint of the affected side.

Measurements

Quadriceps: for suspected quadriceps wasting, measure the circumference of the thighs at equal points above the tibial tuberosity. It is helpful to assess quadriceps function by feeling the tone.

Static Q angle (Fig. 50.8): if the Q angle is > 15° in men and 19° in women there is a predisposition to patellofemoral pain and instability.[8]

Investigations

Investigation for the diagnosis of knee pain can be selected from:

- Blood tests
  - RA factor tests
  - ESR
  - blood culture (suspected septic arthritis)

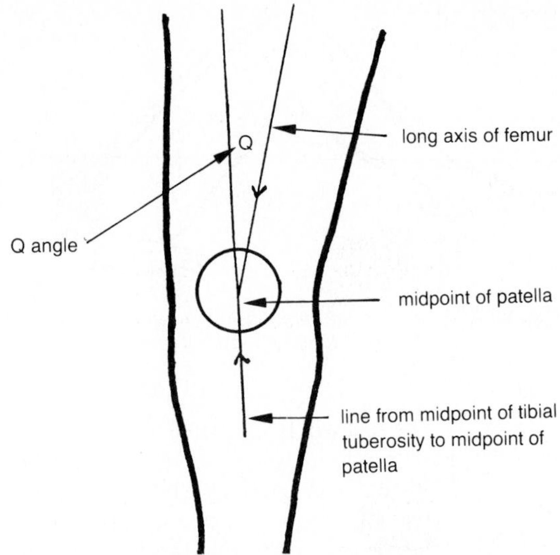

Fig. 50.8 *The Q angle of the knee gives a measure of patellar alignment*

- Radiology
  - plain X-ray
  - special views
    - intercondylar (osteochondritis dissecans, loose bodies)
    - tangential (or skyline view for suspected patella pathology)
    - oblique (to define condyles and patella)
  - bone scan: for suspected tumour, stress fracture, osteonecrosis, osteochondritis dissecans
  - MRI
  - arthrography (generally superseded by arthroscopy)
  - ultrasound: good for assessment of patellar tendon and bursae.
- Special
  - examination under anaesthesia
  - arthroscopy
  - knee aspiration: culture or crystal examination

Knee pain in children

Children may present with unique conditions that are usually related to growth, including epiphyseal problems. Their tendency towards muscle tightness, especially in the growth spurt, predisposes them to overuse injuries such as patellar tendinitis and patellofemoral pain syndrome.

First decade

A painful knee during the first decade of life (0–10 years) in non-athletes is an uncommon presenting symptom, but suppurative infection and juvenile chronic arthritis have to be considered.

Genu valgum or varum is a common presentation but usually not a source of discomfort for the child. However, genu valgum, which is often seen around 4–6 years, may predispose to abnormal biomechanical stresses which contribute to overuse-type injuries if the child is involved in sport.

Second decade

Pain in the knee presents most frequently in this decade and is most often due to the patellofemoral syndrome[9] which is related to the retropatellar and peripatellar regions and usually anterior to the knee. It occurs in the late teenage years of both sexes.

An important problem is subluxation of the patella, typically found in teenage girls. It is caused by maltracking of the patellofemoral mechanism without complete dislocation of the patella (Fig. 50.9). On examination the patella is usually in a high and lateral position. Surgery may be required if symptoms persist.

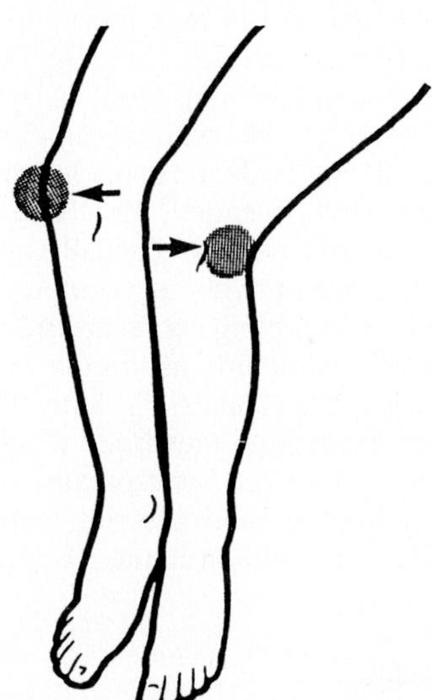

Fig. 50.9 *Lateral subluxation of the patella*

Osgood-Schlatter disorder (OSD) is common in prepubertal adolescent boys but can occur in those aged between 10 and 16 years.

Other conditions found typically in this age group include:

- slipped upper femoral epiphysis—usually in middle teenage years after a growth spurt
- anserinus ('goose foot') bursitis
- osteochondritis dissecans

Age-related causes of the painful knee are presented in Table 50.3.[9]

Table 50.3 *Age-related causes of painful knee*

First decade (0-10 years)
Infection
Juvenile chronic arthritis
Second decade (10-20 years)
Patellofemoral syndrome
Subluxation/dislocation of patella
Slipped femoral epiphysis (referred)
'Hamstrung' knee
Osteochondritis dissecans
Osgood-Schlatter disorder
Anserinus tendinitis
Third decade (20-30 years)
Bursitis
Mechanical disorders
Fourth and fifth decades (30-50 years)
Cleavage tear of medial meniscus
Radial tear of lateral meniscus
Sixth decade and older (50 years and over)
Osteoarthritis
Osteonecrosis
Paget's disease (femur, tibia or patella)
Anserinus bursitis
Chondrocalcinosis and gout
Osteoarthritis of hip (referred pain)

The little athlete

Children competing in sporting activities, especially running and jumping, are prone to overuse injuries such as the patellofemoral pain syndrome, traumatic synovitis of the knee joint and OSD. Haemarthrosis can occur with injuries, sometimes due to a synovial tear without major joint disruption. If knee pain persists, especially in the presence of an effusion, X-rays should be performed to exclude ostochondritis of the femoral condyle.[10]

Osgood-Schlatter disorder

OSD results from repetitive traction stresses at the insertion of the patellar tendon into the tibial tubercle, which is vulnerable to repeated traction in early adolescence.

Clinical features

- commonest ages 10–14
- boys: girls—3:1
- bilateral in about one-third of cases
- common in sports involving running, kicking and jumping
- localised pain in region of tibial tubercle during and after activity
- aggravated by kneeling down and going up and down stairs
- development of lump in area
- localised swelling and tenderness at affected tubercle
- pain reproduced by attempts to straighten flexed knee against resistance

X-ray to confirm diagnosis (widening of the apophysis and possible fragmentation of bone) and exclude tumour or fracture.

Management

This is conservative as it is a self-limiting condition (6–18 months: average 12 months).

- If acute, use ice packs and analgesics.
- Main approach is to abstain from or modify active sports.
- Localised treatments such as electrotherapy are unnecessary.
- Corticosteroid injections should be avoided.[11]
- Plaster cast immobilisation should also be avoided.
- Surgery may be used (rarely) if an irritating ossicle persists[12] after ossification.

Prevention

Promote awareness and early recognition of OSD.

Program of stretching exercises for quadriceps mechanism in children in sport.

Osteochondritis dissecans

This commonly occurs in adolescent boys whereby a segment of articular cartilage of the femoral condyle (85%) undergoes necrosis and may eventually separate to form an intra-articular loose body (Fig. 50.10). It then usually presents as pain, effusion and locking.

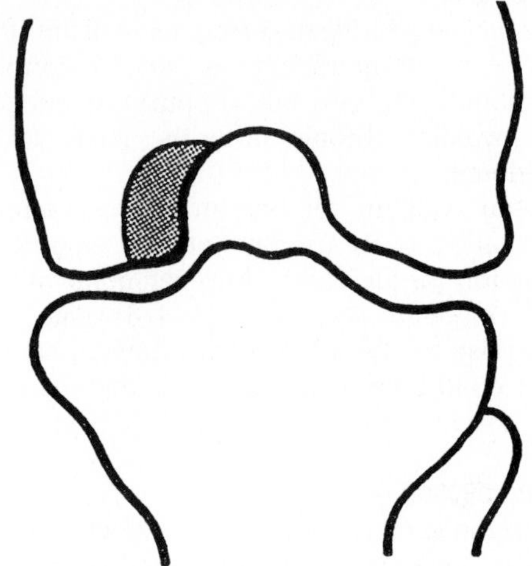

Fig. 50.10 *Osteochondritis dissecans: on X-ray, sclerosis of the lateral aspect of the medial condyle*

Knee pain in the elderly

Rheumatic disorders are very common and responsible for considerable pain or discomfort, disability and loss of independence in the elderly.

Osteoarthritis is also very common and excellent results are now being obtained with total knee replacement in those severely affected.

The elderly are particularly prone to crystal-associated joint diseases including monosodium urate (gout), calcium pyrophosphate dihydrate (CPPD)(pseudogout) and hydroxyapatite (acute calcific periarthritis).

Chondrocalcinosis of knee (pseudogout)

The main target of CPPD is the knee where it causes chondrocalcinosis. Unlike gout, chondrocalcinosis of the knee is typically a disease of the elderly with about 50% of the population having evidence of involvement of the knee by the ninth decade.[13] Most cases remain asymptomatic but patients (usually aged 60 or older) can present with an acutely hot, red, swollen joint resembling septic arthritis.

Investigations include aspiration of the knee to search for CPPD crystals and X-ray. If positive, consider an associated metabolic disorder such as haemochromatosis, hyperparathyroidism or diabetes mellitus. Acute episodes respond well to NSAIDs or intra-articular corticosteroid injection.

Osteonecrosis

Osteonecrosis is more common after the age of 60; it can occur in either the femoral (more commonly) or tibial condyles. The sudden onset of pain in the knee, with a normal joint X-ray, is diagnostic of osteonecrosis. It can take three months for the necrotic area to show radiologically although a bone scan may be positive at an early stage (Fig. 50.11). Surgery in the form of subchondral drilling may be required for persistent pain in the early stages.

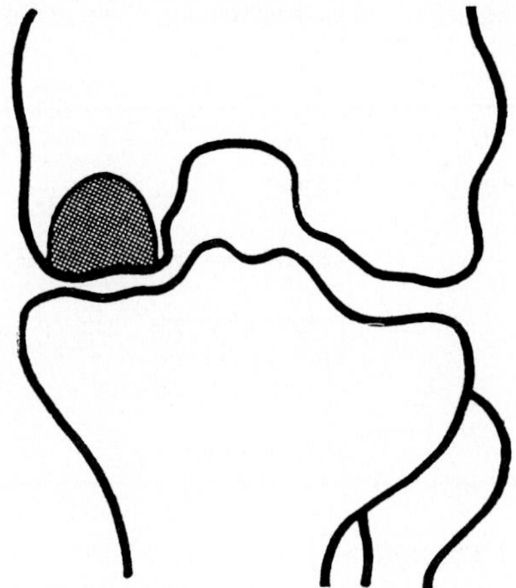

Fig. 50.11 *Osteonecrosis: necrosis in the medial femoral condyle can take three months to show radiologically*

Acute injuries

Meniscal tears

Medial and lateral meniscal tears are usually caused by abduction and adduction forces causing the meniscus to be compressed between the tibial and femoral condyles and then subjected to a twisting force.

The medial meniscus is three times more likely to be torn than the lateral. These injuries are common in contact sports and are often associated with ligamentous injuries. Suspect these injuries when there is a history of injury with a twisting movement with the foot firmly fixed on the ground.

However, pain in the knee can present in the patient aged 30–50 years as the menisci degenerate, with resultant cleavage tears from the posterior horn of the medial meniscus and 'parrot beak' tears of the mid-section of the lateral meniscus. These problems cause pain because these particular deformities create tension on the joint capsule and stretch the nerve ends.

Clinical features

- general symptoms[8]
  - — joint line pain (49%)
  - — locking (17%)
  - — swelling (14%)
- parrot beak tear of lateral meniscus:
  - — pain in the lateral joint line
  - — pain radiating up and down the thigh
  - — pain worse with activity
  - — a palpable and visible lump when the knee is examined at 45°

  Arthroscopic partial meniscectomy offers relief.
- cleavage tear of medial meniscus
  - — pain in medial joint line
  - — pain aggravated by slight twisting of the joint
  - — pain provoked by patient lying on the side and pulling the knees together
  - — pain worse with activity

  Arthroscopic meniscectomy is appropriate treatment.

A diagnostic memoire

Table 50.4 is a useful aid in the diagnosis of these injuries. There is a similarity in the clinical signs between the opposite menisci, but the localisation of pain in the medial or lateral joint lines helps to differentiate between the medial and lateral menisci.

Note The diagnosis of a meniscal injury is made if three or more of the five examination findings ('signs' in Table 50.4) are present.

Ligament injuries

Tears of varying degrees may occur in the

- anterior cruciate ligament
- posterior cruciate ligament
- medial collateral ligament
- lateral collateral ligament

Anterior cruciate ligament (ACL) rupture

This is a very serious and disabling injury which may result in chronic instability. Chronic instability can result in degenerative joint changes if not dealt with adequately. Early diagnosis is essential but there is a high misdiagnosis rate. Sites of ACL rupture are shown in Figure 50.12.

Mechanisms

- internal tibial rotation on a flexed knee (commonest)
- valgus force, e.g. a rugby tackle
- usually a clinical triad with this severe injury
  - — ACL tear
  - — medial collateral ligament tear
  - — medial meniscus disruption

Table 50.4 *Typical symptoms and signs of meniscal injuries*

	Medial meniscus tear	***Lateral meniscus tear***
Mechanism	• Abduction (valgus) force • External rotation of lower leg on femur	• Adduction (varus) force • Internal rotation of leg of femur
Symptoms		
1. Knee pain during and after activity	Medial side of knee	Lateral side of knee
2. Locking	yes	yes
3. Effusion	+ or −	+ or −
Signs		
1. Localised tenderness over joint line (with bucket handle tear)	Medial joint line	Lateral joint line (may be cyst)
2. Pain on hyperextension of knee	Medial joint line	Lateral joint line
3. Pain on hyperflexion of knee joint	Medial joint line	Lateral joint line
4. Pain on rotation of lower leg (knee at 90°)	On external rotation	On internal rotation
5. Weakened or atrophied quadriceps	May be present	May be present

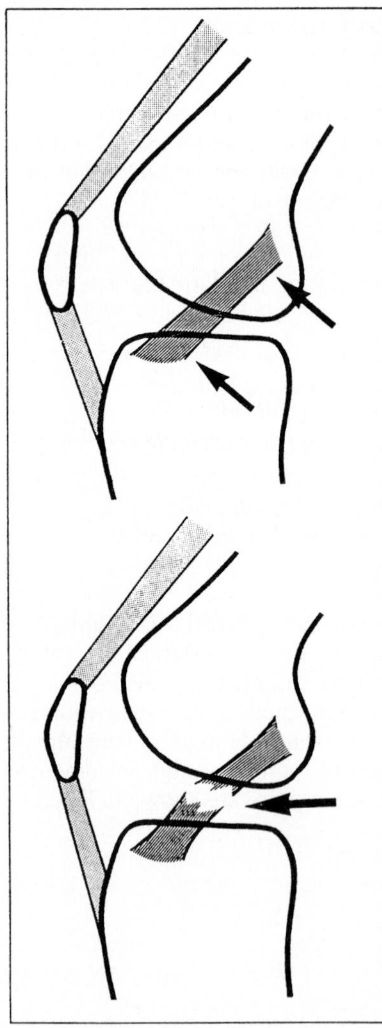

Fig. 50.12 *Sites of rupture of the anterior cruciate ligament*

Clinical features

- onset of severe pain after a sporting injury such as landing from a jump or a forced valgus rotational strain of the knee when another player falls across the abducted leg
- immediate effusion of blood, usually within 30 minutes
- common sports: contact sports, e.g. rugby, football and soccer, basketball, volleyball, skiing
- differential diagnosis is a subluxed or dislocated patella
- subsequent history of pain and 'giving way' of the knee

Examination

- gross effusion
- diffuse joint line tenderness
- joint may be locked due to effusion, anterior cruciate tag or associated meniscal (usually medial) tear
- ligament tests
  - — anterior draw: negative or positive
  - — pivot shift test: positive (only if instability)
  - — Lachman test: lacking an endpoint

Note It may be necessary to examine the knee under anaesthesia, with or without arthroscopy, to assess the extent of injury.

The Lachman test

This test is emphasised because it is a sensitive and reliable test for the integrity of the ACL. It is an anterior draw test with the knee at 15° of flexion. At 90° of flexion, the draw may be negative but the anterior cruciate torn.

Method

1. The examiner should be positioned on the same side of the examination couch as the knee to be tested.
2. The knee is held at 15° of flexion by placing a hand under the distal thigh and lifting the knee into 15° of flexion.
3. The patient is asked to relax, allowing the knee to 'fall back' into the steadying hand and roll slightly into external rotation.
4. The anterior draw is performed with the second hand grasping the proximal tibia from the medial side (Fig. 50.13) while the thigh is held steady by the other hand. The examiner's knee can be used to steady the thigh.

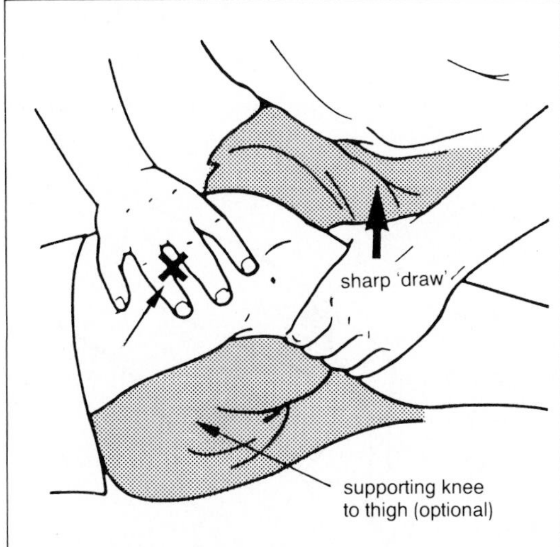

Fig. 50.13 *The Lachman test*

5. The feel of the endpoint of the draw is carefully noted. Normally there is an obvious jar felt as the anterior cruciate tightens. In an anterior cruciate deficient knee there is excess movement and no firm endpoint. The amount of draw is compared with the opposite knee. Movement greater than 5 mm is usually considered abnormal.

Note Functional instability due to anterior cruciate deficiency is best elicited with the pivot shift test. This is more difficult to perform than the Lachman test.

Management

The management depends on the finding by the surgeon. Surgical repair is reserved for severe tears and instability, especially in the elite athlete. For patients with insubstantial tearing of the ACL (mild to moderate laxity) and in those with less need for rotational stability it is possible to adopt a non-surgical regimen based on knee joint immobilisation and protection for six weeks and an intensive exercise program.

Posterior cruciate ligament rupture

Mechanisms

- direct blow to the anterior tibia in flexed knee
- severe hyperextension injury

Clinical features

- posterior (popliteal) pain, radiating to calf
- usually no or minimal swelling
- minimal disability apart from limitation of running or jumping
- pain running downhill
- recurvatum
- posterior sag or draw

Management

- usually managed conservatively with immobilisation and protection for six weeks
- graduated weight bearing and exercises

Medial collateral ligament rupture

Mechanisms

- direct valgus force to knee (lateral side knee), e.g. rugby tackle from side
- external tibial rotation, e.g. two soccer players kicking ball simultaneously

Clinical features

These depend on the degree of tear (1st, 2nd or 3rd degree):

- pain on medial knee
- aggravated by twisting
- localised swelling over medial aspect
- pseudo-locking—hamstring strain
- ± effusion
- no end point on valgus stress testing (3rd degree) (Fig. 50.7a)

Note Check lateral meniscus if MCL tear. Pellegrini-Steida disease—calcification in haematoma at upper (femoral) origin of MCL may follow.

Management

If an isolated injury, this common injury responds to conservative treatment with early limited motion bracing to prevent opening of the medial joint line. Six weeks of limited motion brace at

20–70° followed by knee rehabilitation usually returns the athlete to full sporting activity within 12 weeks.

Note The same principles of diagnosis and management apply to the less common rupture of the lateral collateral ligament which is caused by a direct varus force to the medial side of the knee.

Overuse syndromes

The knee is very prone to overuse disorders. The pain develops gradually without swelling, is aggravated by activity and relieved with rest. It can usually be traced back to a change in the sportsperson's training schedule, footwear, technique or related factors. It may be related also to biomechanical abnormalities ranging from hip disorders to feet disorders.

Overuse injuries include:

- patellofemoral pain syndrome ('joggers' knee' 'runner's knee')
- patellar tendinitis ('Jumpers knee')
- synovial plica syndrome
- infrapatellar fat-pad inflammation
- anserinus bursitis/tendinitis
- biceps femoris tendinitis
- semimembranosus bursitis/tendinitis
- quadriceps tendinitis/rupture
- popliteus tendinitis
- iliotibial band friction syndrome ('runner's knee')
- the hamstrung knee

It is amazing how often palpation identifies localised areas of inflammation (tendinitis or bursitis) around the knee, especially from overuse in athletes and in the obese elderly (Figs 50.14a, b).

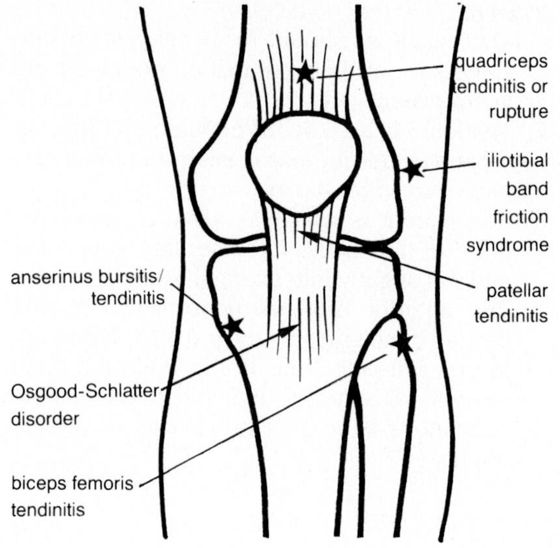

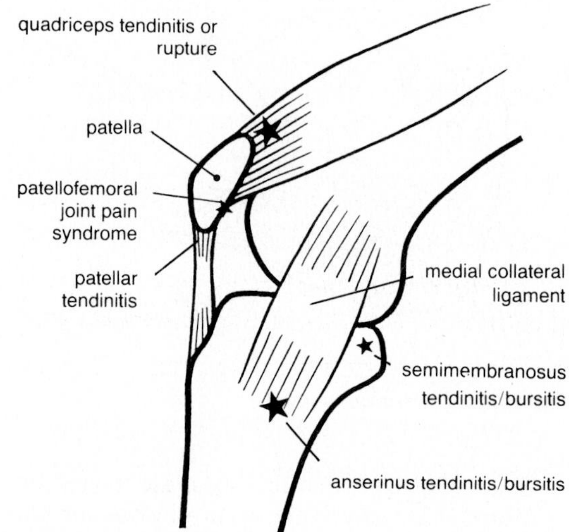

Fig. 50.14 *Typical painful areas around the knee for overuse syndromes:* **(a)** *anterior aspect;* **(b)** *medial aspect*

Patellofemoral pain syndrome

This syndrome, also known as chondromalacia patellae and referred to as 'jogger's knee', 'runner's knee' or 'cyclist's knee', is the most common overuse injury of the knee. There is usually no specific history of trauma. It may be related to biomechanical abnormalities and abnormal position and tracking of the patella, e.g. patella alta.

Clinical features

- pain behind patella or deep in knee
- pain aggravated during activities that require flexion of knee under loading
  - — climbing stairs
  - — walking down slopes or stairs
  - — squatting
  - — prolonged sitting
- the 'movie' sign: using aisle seat to stretch knee
- crepitus around patella may be present

Signs of chondromalacia patellae

Patellofemoral crepitation during knee flexion and extension is often palpable, and pain may be reproduced by compression of the patella onto the femur as it is pushed from side to side with the knee straight or flexed (Perkin's test).

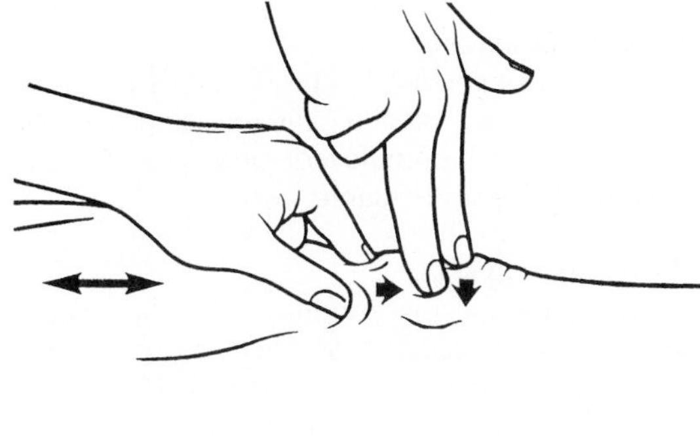

Fig. 50.15 *Special sign of the patellofemoral pain syndrome*

Method for special sign (Fig. 50.15)

- Have the patient supine with the knee extended.
- Grasp the superior pole of the patella and displace it inferiorly.
- Maintain this position and apply patellofemoral compression.
- Ask the patient to contract the quadriceps (a good idea is to get the patient to practise quadriceps contraction before applying the test).
- A positive sign is reproduction of the pain under the patella and hesitancy in contracting the muscle.

Treatment

- Correct any underlying biomechanical abnormalities by use of orthotics and correct footwear.
- Give reassurance and supportive therapy.
- Employ quadriceps exercises.

Patellar tendinitis ('jumper's knee')

'Jumper's knee', or patellar tendinitis (Fig. 50.2), is a common disorder of athletes involved in repetitive jumping sports, such as high jumping, basketball, netball, volleyball and soccer.

Clinical features

- gradual onset of anterior pain
- pain localised to below knee
- pain eased by rest, returns with activity

The diagnosis is often missed because of the difficulty of localising signs. The condition is best diagnosed by eliciting localised tenderness at the inferior pole of the patella with the patella tilted. There may be localised swelling.

Method

- Lay the patient supine in a relaxed manner with the head on a pillow, arms by the side and quadriceps relaxed (a must).
- The knee should be fully extended.
- Tilt the patella by exerting pressure over its superior pole. This lifts the inferior pole.
- Now palpate the surface under the inferior pole. This allows palpation of the deeper fibres of the patellar tendon (Fig. 50.16).
- Compare with the normal side.
- Very sharp pain is usually produced in the patient with patellar tendinitis.

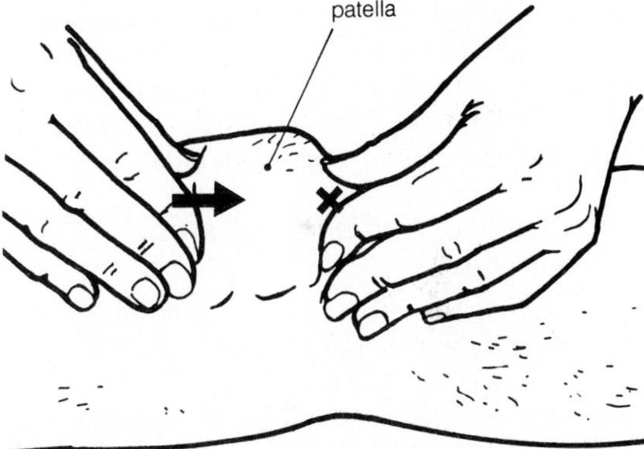

Fig. 50.16 *Patellar tendinitis: method of palpation*

Management

Early conservative treatment including rest from the offending stresses is effective. This includes adequate warm-up and warm-down. The use of NSAIDs and corticosteroid injections is disappointing. Chronic cases invariably require surgery.

Anserinus tendinitis/bursitis

Localised tenderness is found over the medial tibial condyle where the tendons of sartorius, gracilis and semitendinosus insert into the bone.

It is a common cause of knee pain in the middle aged or elderly, especially the overweight woman. Pain is aggravated by resisted knee flexion.

Semimembranous tendinitis/bursitis

This inflamed area is sited either at the tendon insertion or in the bursa between the tendon and the medial head of gastrocnemius. It is an uncommon problem.

Biceps femoris tendinitis/bursitis

The tendon and/or the bursa which lies between the tendon insertion and the fibular collateral ligament at the head of the fibula may become inflamed due to overuse. It is usually encountered in sprinters.

Popliteus tendinitis

Tenosynovitis of the popliteus tendon may cause localised pain in the posterior or the posterolateral aspect of the knee. Tenderness to palpation is elicited with the knee flexed to 90°.

Iliotibial tract tendinitis

Inflammation develops over the lateral aspect of the knee where the iliotibial band passes over the lateral femoral condyle. The problem, which is caused by friction of the iliotibial band on the bone, is common in long-distance runners, especially running up and down hills.

Treatment of tendinitis and bursitis (small area)

Generally (apart from patellar tendinitis), the treatment is an injection of local anaesthetic and long-acting corticosteroids into and deep to the localised area of tenderness. In addition it is important to restrict the offending activity with relative rest and refer for physiotherapy for stretching exercises. Attention to biomechanical factors and footwear is important.

If conservative methods fail for iliotibial tract tendinitis, surgical excision of the affected fibres may cure the problem.

Prepatellar bursitis

Repetitive low-grade direct trauma such as frequent kneeling can cause inflammation with swelling of the bursa which lies between the anterior surface of the patella and the skin. 'Housemaid's knee', or 'carpet layer's knee', can be difficult to treat if rest from the trauma does not allow it to subside. If persistent drain the fluid with a 23 g needle and then introduce 0.5–1 ml of long-acting corticosteroid. The presence of a bursa 'mouse', which is a pedunculated fibrous tumour arising from the bursa wall, and persistent bursitis, usually means that surgical intervention is required.

Acute bursitis may also be caused by acute infection, or one of the inflammatory arthropathies, e.g. gout, Reiter's disease .

Infrapatellar bursitis

'Clergyman's knee' is also produced by the same mechanisms as patellar bursitis and can be involved with inflammatory disorders or infection. Treatment is also the same.

The hamstrung knee

Cross describes this condition in young active sports people (second decade)[9] as one which causes bilateral knee pain and possibly a limp. It is caused by a failure to warm up properly and stretch the hamstring muscles, which become tender and tight during the growth spurt. A six week program of straight leg raising and hamstring stretching will alleviate the pain completely.

Synovial plica syndrome

This syndrome results from a synovial fold (an embryological remnant) being caught between the patella and the femur during walking or running. It causes an acute 'catching' knee pain of the medial patellofemoral joint (Fig. 50.2) and sometimes a small effusion. It generally settles without treatment.

Infrapatellar fat-pad inflammation

Acute compression of the fat-pad, which extends across the lower patella deep to the patellar tendon and into the knee joint (Fig. 50.2), during a jump or other similar trauma, produces local pain and tenderness similar to the sensation of kneeling on a drawing pin.[14]

The pain usually settles without therapy over a period of days or weeks. There is localised tenderness and it can be confused with patellar tendinitis.

Arthritic conditions

Osteoarthritis

Osteoarthritis is a very common problem of the knee joint. Symptoms usually appear in middle life or later. It is more common in women, in the obese, those with knee deformities, e.g. genu varum, and with previous trauma, especially meniscal tears. The degenerative changes may involve either the lateral or medial tibiofemoral compartment, the patellofemoral joint or any combination of these sites.

Clinical features

- slowly increasing joint pain and stiffness
- aggravated by activities such as prolonged walking, standing or squatting
- descending stairs is usually more painful than ascending stairs (suggestive of patello-femoral OA)
- pain may occur after rest, especially prolonged flexion
- minimal effusion and variable crepitus
- restricted flexion but usually full extension
- often quadriceps wasting and tender over medial joint line
- diagnosis confirmed by X-ray (weight-bearing view)

Management

- relative rest
- weight loss
- analgesics and/or judicious use of NSAIDs
- walking aids and other supports
- physiotherapy, e.g. hydrotherapy, quadriceps exercises, mobilisation and stretching techniques
- intra-articular injections of corticosteroids are generally not recommended but a single injection for severe pain can be very effective
- surgery: indicated for severe pain and stiffness; includes arthroscopic debridement and washout, osteotomy, arthrodesis and total joint replacement (Fig. 50.17).

Rheumatoid arthritis

The knee is frequently affected by RA although it rarely presents as monoarticular knee pain. RA shows the typical features of inflammation—pain and stiffness that is worse after resting. Morning stiffness is a feature.

Note The spondyloarthropathies have a similar clinical pattern to RA.

Synovectomy is a useful option with persistent boggy thickening of synovial membrane but without destruction of the articular cartilage.[2]

Septic arthritis

Tends to be more common in the knee than other joints. Septic (pyogenic) arthritis should be suspected when the patient complains of intense joint pain, malaise and fever. In the presence of acute pyogenic infection the joint is held rigidly. The differential diagnosis includes gout and pseudogout (chondrocalcinosis).

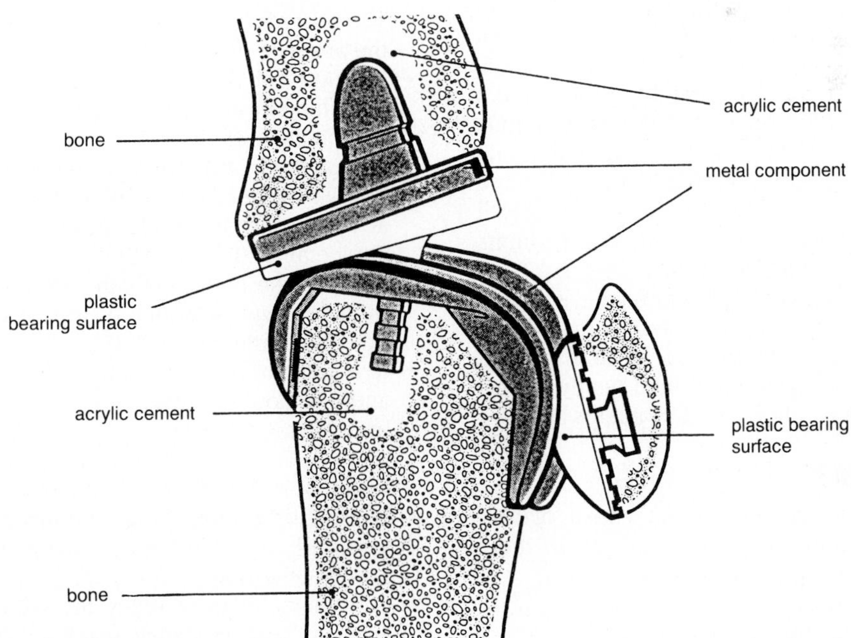

Fig. 50.17 *Total joint replacement of knee*

Principles of management

Most painful knee conditions are not serious and, providing a firm diagnosis is made and internal knee disruption or other serious illness discounted, a simple management plan as outlined leads to steady relief. For more serious injuries the primary goal is to minimise the adverse consequences of forced inactivity.

- First aid: RICE.
- Lose weight if overweight.
- Adequate support for ligament sprains, e.g. supportive elastic tubular (tubigrip) bandage or a firm elastic bandage over Velband.
- Simple analgesics, e.g. paracetamol (acetaminophen).
- Judicious use of NSAIDs and corticosteroid injections.
- Physiotherapy to achieve strength and stability.
- Attend to biomechanical abnormalities, inappropriate footwear and athletic techniques.
- Orthotics and braces to suit the individual patient.
- Specialised exercise techniques, e.g. the McConnell technique.[2]
- Quadriceps exercises: these simple exercises are amazingly effective.

Quadriceps exercises (examples)

- Instruct the patient to tighten the muscles in front of the thighs (as though about to lift the leg at the hip and bend the foot back but keeping the leg straight). The patient should hold the hand over the lower quads to ensure it is felt to tighten. This tightening and relaxing exercise should be performed at least 6 times every 2 hours or so until it becomes a habit. It can be done sitting, standing or lying (Fig. 50.18).
- Sitting on a chair the patient places a weight of 2–5 kg around the ankle (e.g. a plastic bag with sand or coins in a sock) and lifts the leg to the horizontal and then gently lowers it (avoid in patellofemoral problems).

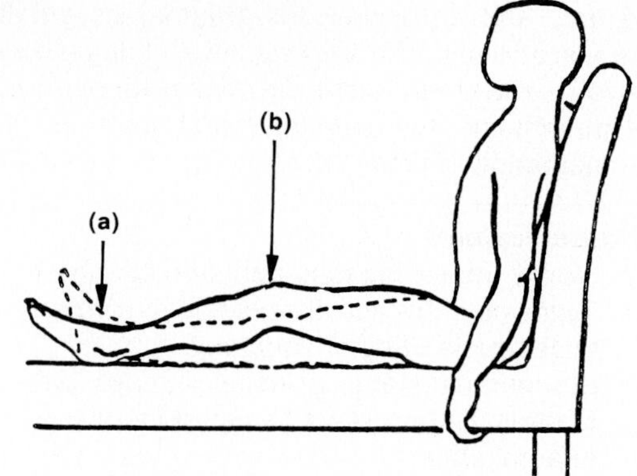

Fig. 50.18 *A quadriceps exercise: with outstretched legs the quadriceps muscle is slowly and deliberately tightened by straightening the knee to position* **(a)** *from the relaxed position* **(b)**

When to refer

- Early referral is required for knees 'at risk' following acute injuries where one or more of the following are present:
  - — locked knee
  - — haemarthrosis
  - — instability
- Clinical evidence of a torn cruciate ligament, third degree tear of the collateral ligaments or torn meniscus.
- Undiagnosed acute or chronic knee pain.
- Recurrent subluxation or dislocation of the patella.
- Suspected septic arthritis.
- Presence of troublesome intra-articular loose body.

Practice tips

- The absence of an effusion does not rule out the absence of severe knee injury.
- Examine the hip and lumbosacral spine if examination of the knee is normal but knee pain is the complaint.
- Always think of an osteoid osteoma in a young boy with severe bone pain in a leg (especially at night) that responds nicely to aspirin or paracetamol or other NSAID.
- Tears of the meniscus can occur, especially in middle age, without a history of significant preceding trauma.
- If a patient presents with a history of an audible 'pop' or 'crack' in the knee with an immediate effusion (in association with trauma) he or she has an anterior cruciate ligament tear until proved otherwise.
- Haemarthrosis following an injury should be regarded as an anterior cruciate tear until proved otherwise.
- The 'movie' sign whereby the patient seeks an aisle seat to stretch the knee is usually due to patellofemoral pain syndrome.

- The 'bed' sign when pain is experienced when the knees touch while in bed is suggestive of a medial meniscal cleavage tear.
- A positive squat test (medial pain on full squatting) indicates a tear of the posterior horn of the medial meniscus.
- Joint aspiration should not be performed on the young athlete with an acute knee injury.
- Reserve intra-articular corticosteroid injections for inflammatory conditions such as rheumatoid arthritis or a crystal arthropathy: regular injections for osteoarthritis are to be avoided. Do not give the injections when the inflammation is acute and diffuse or in the early stages of injury.
- Many inflammatory conditions around the knee joint, such as bursitis or tendinitis, respond to a local injection of local anaesthetic and corticosteroid but avoid giving injections into the tendon, especially the patellar tendon.

References

1. Knox JDE. Knee problems. In: *Practice*. London: Kluwer-Harrap Handbooks, 1980; 3.66:01–05.
2. Selecki Y, Helman T. How to treat knee pain. Australian Dr Weekly.
3. McLean I. Assessment of the acute knee injury. Aust Fam Physician, 1984; 13:575–580.
4. Cyriax J. *Textbook of orthopaedic medicine Volume 1* (6th edition). London:Bailliere Tindall, 1976, 594.
5. Noyes FR. Arthroscopy in acute traumatic haemarthrosis of the knee. J Bone and Joint Surgery, 1980:624–687.
6. Corrigan B, Maitland GD. *Practical orthopaedic medicine*. Sydney: Butterworths, 1986, 126–161.
7. Hoppenfeld S. *Physical examination of the spine and extremities*. Englewood Cliffs: Prentice-Hall, 1976, 172–173.
8. Cross MJ, Crichton KJ. *Clinical examination of the injured knee*. London: Harper and Row, 1987, 21–46.
9. Cross MJ. The painful knee. Aust Fam Physician, 1984; 13:166–168.
10. Larkins P. The little athlete. Aust Fam Physician, 1991; 20:973–978.
11. Rostrom PKM, Calver RF. Subcutaneous atrophy following methyl prednisolone injection in Osgood-Schlatter epiphysitis. J Bone and Joint Surgery, 1979; 61A:627–628.
12. Mital MA, Matza RA, Cohen J. The so-called unresolved Osgood-Schlatter's lesion. J Bone and Joint Surgery, 1980; 62A:732–739.
13. Wilkins E et al Osteoarthritis and articular chondrocalcinosis in the elderly. Ann Rheum Dis, 1983; 42(3):280–284.
14. Fricker P. Anterior knee pain. Aust Fam Physician, 1988; 17:1055–1056.

51

The disturbed patient

The disturbed and confused patient is a complex management problem in general practice. The cause may be a single one or a combination of several abnormal mental states (see Table 51.1)[1]. The cause may be an organic mental disorder which may be a long-term insidious problem such as dementia or an acute disorder (delirium), often dramatic in onset. On the other hand the cause of the disturbance may be a psychiatric disorder such as panic disorder, mania, major depression or schizophrenia.

The manifestations of the disturbance are many and include perceptual changes and hallucinations, disorientation, changes in consciousness, changes in mood from abnormally elevated to gross depression, agitation and disturbed thinking including delusions.

Table 51.1 *A general classification of psychiatric disorders*[1]

Organic mental disorders
Acute organic brain syndrome (delirium)
Chronic organic brain syndrome (dementia)
Psychoactive and substance use disorders
Toxic states
Drug dependency
Withdrawal states
Schizophrenic disorders
Mood disorders
Major depression
Bipolar (manic depressive) disorder
Adjustment disorders with depressed mood
Dysthymia
Anxiety disorders
Generalised anxiety disorder
Panic disorder
Obsessive-compulsive disorder
Phobic disorders
Post-traumatic stress disorder
Disorders specific to children
Other disorders
Postpartum psychiatric illness
Eating disorders

Key facts and checkpoints

- Depression affects 15% of people over 65 and can mimic or complicate any other illness including delirium and dementia.[1]
- Elderly patients with depression are at a high risk of suicide.
- Always search vigorously for the cause or causes of delirium.
- Seeing patients in their home is the best way to evaluate their problem and support systems: it allows opportunities for a history from close contacts and for checking medication, alcohol intake and other factors.
- The diagnosis of dementia can be overlooked: a Scottish study showed that 80% of demented patients were not diagnosed by their GP.[2]
- Patients with a chronic brain syndrome (dementia) are at special risk of an acute brain syndrome (delirium) in the presence of infections and many prescribed drugs.[1]

- Consider prescribed and illicit substances, including the severe anticholinergic delirium syndrome.
- The key feature of dementia is impaired memory.
- The two key features of delirium are disorganised thought and attention.

Definitions

Delirium (also termed 'toxic confusional state') is a relatively acute disorder in which impaired consciousness is associated with abnormalities of perception or mood.

Confusion is disorientation in time, place and person. It may be accompanied by a disturbed conscious state (Table 61.1).

Dementia is an acquired, chronic and gradually progressive deterioration of memory, intellect and personality. Presenile dementia or early onset dementia is dementia under 65 years of age. Senile dementia refers to older patients (usually over 80 years).

Alzheimer's disease is a term used for both senile and presenile dementia which has characteristic pathological degenerative changes in the brain.

Cognition refers to the mental functions of perception, thinking and memory. It is the process of 'knowing'.

Hallucinations are disorders of perception quite divorced from reality. Features:

- mostly auditory or visual
- a false perception—not a distortion
- perceived as normal perceptions
- independent of the person's will

Illusions are false interpretations of sensory stimuli such as mistaking people or familiar things.

Delusions are abnormal, illogical or false beliefs which are held with absolute conviction despite evidence to the contrary.

A diagnostic approach

A summary of the diagnostic strategy model for the disturbed or confused patient is presented in Table 51.2.

Table 51.2 *The disturbed mind: diagnostic strategy model*

Q. *Probability diagnosis*
A. The 4 D's
- dementia
- delirium (look for cause)
- depression
- drugs — toxicity
  — withdrawal

Q. *Serious disorders not to be missed*
A. Cardiovascular
- CVAs
- cardiac failure
- arrhythmia
- myocardial ischaemia/AMI

Neoplasia
- cerebral
- carcinoma, e.g. lung

Severe infections
- septicaemia
- HIV infection
- infective endocarditis

Hypoglycaemia
Bipolar disorder/mania
Schizophrenia states
Anxiety/panic
Subdural haematoma

Q. *Pitfalls (often missed)*
A. Illicit drug withdrawal
Fluid and electrolyte disturbances
Faecal impaction (elderly)
Urinary retention (elderly)
Hypoxia
Pain syndromes (elderly)

Rarities
- hypocalcaemia
- renal failure
- hepatic failure

Q. *Seven masquerades checklist*

A.	
Depression	✓✓
Diabetes	✓✓
Drugs	✓✓
Anaemia	✓✓
Thyroid disease	✓✓
Spinal dysfunction	✓ (severe pain in elderly)
UTI	✓

Q. *Is the patient trying to tell me something?*
A. Consider anxiety, depression, emotional deprivation or upset, change in environment, serious personal loss.

Probability diagnosis

The diagnosis depends on the age and presentation of the patient. In a teenager the probable causes of acute confusion or irrational behaviour include drug toxicity or withdrawal, schizophrenia, severe depression or a behavioural disorder.

It is the elderly who commonly present with confusion. The questions that must be asked are:

- Is the problem one of the 4D's—dementia, delirium, depression, drugs or something else?
- If delirium is the problem, what is the cause?

Depression affects 15% of people over 65, and can mimic other causes of confusion and behavioural disturbance.

Significant prescribed drugs include hypnotics, sedatives, oral hypoglycaemics, antihypertensives, digoxin, antihistamines, anticholinergic drugs and antipsychotics.

Serious disorders not to be missed

There are many serious underlying disorders that must be considered, especially with delirium (Table 51.3). Cerebral organic lesions including space-occupying lesions (e.g. cerebral tumour, subdural haematoma), severe infection (systemic or intracerebral) and carcinoma at any site, especially lung, breast, lymphoma or bowel, must be ruled out.

The sudden onset of delirium may suggest angina, myocardial infarction or a cerebrovascular accident. Twenty per cent of patients with delirium also have underlying heart failure.[3]

Pitfalls

There are many pitfalls, especially with drug toxicity or withdrawal from the so-called illicit drugs. In the elderly in particular fluid and electrolyte disturbances such as dehydration, hypokalaemia, hyponatraemia and hypocalcaemia

Table 51.3 *Important causes of delirium (typical examples of each group)*

Cause	Examples
Drug intoxication and drug sensitivity	anticholinergics antidepressants sedatives alcohol, opiates, etc.
Withdrawal from substances of abuse and prescribed drugs	alcohol opiates amphetamines cannabis sedatives and anxiolytics
Infections	
specific	urinary tract lower respiratory, e.g. pneumonia otitis media cellulitis
intracranial	meningitis encephalitis
systemic	infective endocarditis septicaemia HIV virus other viral infections malaria
Metabolic disturbances	uraemia, hepatic failure electrolyte disturbances dehydration
Endocrine disturbances	diabetes ketosis, hypoglycaemia hypothyroidism
Nutritional and vitamin deficits	Wernicke's encephalopathy
Hypoxia	respiratory failure, cardiac failure, anaemia
Vascular	CVA
Head injury and other intracranial problems	
Seizures	complex partial seizures
'Subtle' causes	pain, e.g. herpes zoster emotional upset environmental change perioperative faecal impaction urinary retention

can cause delirium. Bowel disturbances such as faecal impaction or constipation can cause delirium and incontinence of both faeces and urine.

Seven masquerades checklist

All the following disorders can cause disturbed or confused behaviour, particularly in the elderly:

- depression: a very important cause of 'pseudodementia'
- drugs: toxicity or withdrawal (see Table 51.4)
- diabetes: especially hypoglycaemia which can occur with NIDDM
- anaemia: often from self-neglect or chronic blood loss
- thyroid disorders: both hyperthyroidism and hypothyroidism can present with disturbed behaviour; 'myxoedemic madness' may be precipitated by atropine compounds
- urinary tract infection: causes or contributes to 20% of cases of hallucinations or illusions[2]
- spinal dysfunction: with its many severe pain syndromes, such as sciatica, can be a significant factor

Table 51.4 *Prescribed drugs that can cause delirium*

Anticholinergic
- antiparkinsonian, e.g. benztropine
- tricyclic antidepressants

Tranquillisers and hypnotics
- major tranquillisers
  e.g. chlorpromazine
- minor tranquillisers
  e.g. diazepam
- hypnotics

Anticonvulsants

Antihistamines 1 and 2

Corticosteroids

Cardiac drugs
- digoxin
- diuretics
- beta-blockers

Psychogenic factors

Apart from the primary psychiatric disorders of anxiety, depression, mania and schizophrenia, relatively simple and subtle social problems such as loneliness, boredom, a domestic upset, financial problem or similar issue can trigger a confusional state.

The clinical approach

History

Developing rapport with the disturbed or confused patient is essential and can be helped by a warm handshake or a reassuring pat on the shoulder. The basis of the history is a careful account from relatives or witnesses about the patient's behaviour.

When communicating with the patient, speak slowly and simply (avoid shouting), face them and maintain eye contact. Important features are the past history, recent psychosocial history including recent bereavement, family upsets and changes in environment. Search for evidence of depression and note any organic symptoms such as cough, constipation and so on.

Mental status examination

The most practical bedside screening test of mental function is the Mental Status Questionnaire of Kahn[4] which includes ten simple questions.

1. What is the name of this place?
2. What city are you in now?
3. What year is it?
4. What month is it?
5. What is the date today?
6. What year were you born?
7. When is your birthday?
8. How old are you?
9. Who is the prime minister/president?
10. Who was the prime minister/president before him?

(Interpretation: normal 9–10; mildly impaired 8–9; confused/demented 7 or less.)

If the patient has appropriate mental function ask questions related to possible depressive illness, e.g.

- Do you feel hopeful about your future?
- Do you have good things to look forward to?
- Do you think life is worth living?
- Have you ever thought of taking your life?

Physical examination

The patient's general demeanour, dress and physical characteristics should be noted at all times. Assess the patient's ability to hear, see, speak, reason, obey commands, stand and walk. Any problems related to the special senses can cause confusion.

Look for features of alcohol abuse, Parkinson's disease and hypothyroidism.

Examine the neurological system and keep in mind the possibility of a subdural haematoma which may have followed a forgotten fall.

Don't omit the rectal examination to exclude faecal impaction, melaena, cancer and prostatomegaly (in males) and also check the bladder for evidence of chronic retention.

Investigations

Investigations to consider for delirious or demented patients (unknown cause):

- urinalysis and microscopy
- cultures of blood and urine
- total and differential blood count; ESR
- blood glucose
- urea and creatinine and electrolytes
- calcium and phosphate
- thyroid function tests
- liver function tests
- serum B_{12} and folate levels
- ECG
- chest X-ray
- cerebral CT scan
- syphilis serology

Management of the acutely disturbed patient

Delirious or psychotic patients can be paranoid and respond defensively to the world around them. This behaviour can include aggressive and violent behaviour resulting in danger to themselves, their friends and family and to their medical attendants.

Dangerousness should be assessed from features such as the patient's past history (especially previous dangerous behaviour), age and sex, recent stress, victim behaviour, muscle bulk, presence of weapons, degree of overactivity and the manner of handling of the present distress by others. The patient may be in a state of acute panic and trying to flee a situation or in an agitated psychotic state prepared to confront the situation. It should be emphasised that most violent individuals are not mentally ill.

Most cases require an injection (the ideal intravenous administration can be extremely difficult and hazardous) which is often interpreted as a physical attack. It may not be possible to diagnose the cause of the problem before giving the injection.

Approach to management

- React calmly.
- Try to control the disturbed patient gently.
- Ensure the safety of all staff and that heroics are not attempted in dangerous circumstances.
- An adequate number of staff to accompany the doctor is essential—six is ideal (one for immobilisation of each limb, one for the head and one to assist with drugs).[1]

Principles of sedative administration[1]

- Use safest possible route of administration whenever possible, i.e. oral in preference to parenteral. Intravenous administration has the lowest margin of safety.
- Parenteral administration should be restricted to severely disturbed patients.
- Closely monitor vital signs during and after sedative administration.
- Avoid intramuscular diazepam because of poor absorption.
- Avoid intravenous midazolam (Hypnovel) because of the risk of respiratory depression.
- Avoid benzodiazepines in patients with respiratory insufficiency. Haloperidol is an alternative.
- Patients have died from cardiopulmonary arrest after repeated sedative administration (especially benzodiazepines) so intensive monitoring is essential.

Monitor the following adverse effects:

- respiratory depression
- hypotension
- dystonic reactions, including choking

Treatment options[1]

- diazepam 10–20 mg (o) as single dose (if patient co-operates); repeat every 2–6 hours (up to 120 mg daily) depending on response
- if intramuscular benzodiazepines required
  midazolam (Hypnovel) 2.5–5 mg IM as single dose
- if intravenous benzodiazepines required
  diazepam 5–20 mg IV (slow injection over several minutes) as single dose

Alternatives

- droperidol (Droleptan) 5–10 mg IM

  or
- haloperidol 5–10 mg IM

(These injections can be repeated in 15–30 minutes if required. Droperidol is similar to haloperidol but more sedating. Keep in mind the rare but potentially fatal laryngeal dystonia with high doses of haloperidol.)

or

- chlorpromazine 50–100 mg (o) by tablet or syrup; repeat in 15–30 minutes if required

(Syrup may be preferred as it is less likely to be hidden in the mouth.)

Postdisturbance evaluation

Determine the likely cause, such as:

- acute organic brain syndrome
  e.g. toxic causes
  infection
- alcohol or drugs (illicit or prescribed)
  — intoxication
  — withdrawal
- manic illness
- severe depression
- schizophrenic syndrome
- severe panic

Acute organic brain syndrome (delirium)

The many labels of acute organic brain syndrome include:

- delirium
- acute confusional state
- toxic confusional state
- confusional episode
- acute brain syndrome

Main features (refer Table 51.5)

- clouding of conscious state
- disorientation
- impaired attention
- impaired memory

Table 51.5 *DSM-III (R) criteria for delirium*

Diagnosis of delirium requires evidence of:

A. Clouding of consciousness

B Two or more of
  1. perceptual disturbance
  2. incoherent speech
  3. disturbance of sleep
  4. increased or decreased psychomotor activity

C Disorientation or memory impairment

D Clinical features appearing over a short period

E Evidence of a cause

Other clinical features[1]

- The patients are usually elderly.
- Anxiety and agitation can be severe but in hypoactive deliria (usually due to metabolic disturbance) the conscious state can vary from drowsiness to coma.
- Psychotic symptoms can occur.
- Delusions are usually fleeting.
- The disturbance is usually worse at night and may be aggravated by sedation.
- Visual hallucinations are a feature of alcohol withdrawal.
- Attacks on bystanders may result (uncommon).

Always seek a cause.[1] A list of causes is presented in Table 51.3. The most important causes are:

- infections (usually in urinary tract, lungs or ear, or systemic in young or elderly)
- prescribed drugs

Anticholinergic delirium

Consider this cause (from drugs with anticholinergic properties or illicit substances). Features include hyperactivity, marked thought disorder, vivid visual hallucinations and very disturbed behaviour.

Differential diagnosis of delirium

In the earlier stages it may mimic the various psychiatric disorders including anxiety, depression, various hallucinatory states, particularly agitated schizophrenia (rarely), extreme manic states and complex partial seizures.

Investigations

Investigations are those listed under clinical approach (page 498).

Treatment

Principles:

- Acute delirium is a medical emergency.
- Establish normal hydration, electrolyte, balance and nutrition.
- Attend to helpful environmental factors, e.g. calm atmosphere, a night-light, orientation clues, presence of friends and relatives.

Medication

Medication[1] may not be needed but will be in the presence of anxiety, aggression or psychotic symptoms.

For anxiety and agitation

- diazepam 5–10 mg (o) as a single dose

For psychotic behaviour, add

- haloperidol 1.5–10 mg (o) according to response

For severe symptoms, when parenteral medication required

- haloperidol 5–10 mg (IM) as single dose

or

- droperidol 5–10 mg (IM) as single dose

For anticholinergic delirium

- tacrine hydrochloride 15–30 mg with caution by slow IV injection (an antidote)

Note Benzodiazepines should be avoided in patients with respiratory insufficiency. Consider necessity for pain relief.

Dementia (chronic organic brain syndrome)

Dementia is an important diagnosis to consider in the elderly patient. The DSM-III (R) criteria for dementia are presented in Table 7.1 and elaborated in more detail in Chapter 7.

The main feature of dementia is impairment of memory, especially recent memory, when the person cannot remember what has happened a few hours (or even moments) earlier but may clearly remember the events of the past.

The more serious behavioural changes encountered with dementia tend to occur in the advanced stages. However, these disturbances may be precipitated by illness such as infections, emotional upset and drugs. These serious disturbances include:

- uninhibited behaviour
- hallucinations (generally uncommon)
- paranoid delusions

If a stable patient becomes acutely disturbed, delirium should be suspected.

Presenile dementia—Alzheimer's type

The main features are:

- onset in late 50s and early 60s
- insidious onset
- early loss of short-term memory
- progressive decline in intellect
- death in 5–10 years
- more common in Down syndrome

Differential diagnosis of dementia

There are two approaches to the differential diagnosis, including consideration of the classic causes of disturbed behaviour as summarised in the mnemonic in Table 51.6[5] and those more everyday subtle causes presented in Table 7.2, under an approach to the elderly patient.

Table 51.6 *Differential diagnosis of dementias (after McLean[5])*

D	delirium drugs (*see* toxic)
E	emotional disorder = depression endocrine = thyroid
M	memory = benign forgetfulness
E	elective = anxiety disorders/neuroses
N	neurological - CVA - head trauma
T	toxic - drugs/medication - metabolic disease
I	intellect—low or retarded
A	amnesic disorders—Korsakov's
S	schizophrenia (chronic)

However, the foremost differential diagnosis should be 'pseudodementia' caused by severe depression.

A simple comparison between schizophrenia and dementia is shown in Table 51.7.

A vigorous search for a possible cause of dementia is warranted since there are a significant number of reversible causes. In particular it is important to exclude the psychiatric conditions that may mimic dementia.

Treatment (see page 50)

To control psychotic symptoms or disturbed behaviour

haloperidol 1.5–10 mg (o) daily

To control symptoms of anxiety and agitation

oxazepam 15 mg (o) 1 to 4 times daily

Schizophrenia and associated disorders

The term schizophrenia (Bleuler 1911) refers to a group of severe psychiatric illnesses characterised by severe disturbances of emotion, language, perception, thought processes, volition and motor activity. The causes of schizophrenia disorders are unknown.

Main abnormal clinical features include:[6]

- disorders of thinking
  — poverty of thinking
  — disordered form of thought: 'woolly'

Table 51.7 *Comparison of schizophrenia and dementia*

	Dementia	*Schizophrenia*
Onset	middle aged or elderly	young
Memory	always impaired	usually unaffected
Delusions	rare	frequent
Hallucinations	uncommon	frequent
Thought broadcasting	never	frequent

- — disordered content, e.g. delusional
- — impaired communication
- disorders of emotion
  - — blunted affect
  - — inappropriate affect
- disorders of perception
  - — auditory hallucinations
  - — (visual and somatic hallucinations may occur)
- disorders of volition
  - — apathy
  - — lack of motivation
  - — social withdrawal
  - — social and personality deterioration
- disorders of motor activity
  - — slow or unusual movements

Other features include:

- bizarre behaviour
- subject to tension, anxiety or depression
- deterioration in work and study performance
- peak incidence 15–25 years[6]—smaller peak at 40 years
- lifetime prevalence 1 in 100
- equal sex incidence
- high risk of suicide

Differential diagnosis

Organic factors need to be excluded, especially drugs:

- amphetamines
- hallucinogens, e.g. LSD
- marijuana

A comparison of delirium, dementia and functional psychosis is presented in Table 51.8.[7]

Management

Drug treatment is only a part of the total management. Explanation and appropriate reassurance to the family with patient and family supportive care is obviously essential. A team approach is necessary to cope with the disorder, which usually has a devastating effect on the family.

Acute phase

- hospitalisation usually necessary
- drug treatment for the psychosis[1]

Table 51.8 *Comparison of the clinical features of delirium, dementia and acute functional psychoses[7]*

Feature	*Delirium*	*Dementia*	*Acute psychosis*
Onset	Rapid	Slow—insidious	Rapid
Duration	Hours to weeks	Months to years	Depends on response to treatment
Course over 24 hours	Fluctuates—worse at night	Minimal variation	Minimal variation
Consciousness	Reduced	Alert	Alert
Perception	Misperceptions common, especially visual	Misperceptions rare	May be misperceptions
Hallucinations	Common, visual (usually) or auditory	Uncommon	Common, mainly auditory
Attention	Distractable	Normal to impaired	Variable—may be impaired
Speech	Variable, may be incoherent	Difficulty finding correct words	Variable: normal, rapid or slow
Organic illness or drug toxicity	One or both present	Often absent	Usually absent

1. When oral medication possible and sedation desirable
   chlorpromazine 100–200 mg (o) 3 to 4 times daily
   or
   thioridazine 100–200 mg (o) 3 to 4 times daily
   (average dose about 400–600 mg daily)
2. When oral medication possible but sedation less necessary
   haloperidol 5–10 mg (o) bd
   or
   trifluoperazine 5–10 mg (o) bd
   (average dose 20 mg daily)
3. When parenteral medication required
   haloperidol 5–10 mg IV or IM, initially, up to 20mg in 24 hours, depending on the response
   add
   benztropine 1–2 mg (o) bd (to avoid dystonic reaction)
   If dystonic reaction
   benztropine 1–2 mg IV or IM
   If very agitated, use
   diazepam 10–20 mg (o) or 5–10 mg IV

Chronic phase of schizophrenia

Long-term antipsychotic medication recommended to prevent relapse.

Examples of oral medication regimens:[1]

trifluoperazine 10–30 mg (o) nocte

or

haloperidol 3–20 mg (o) nocte

or

thioridazine 100–400 mg (o) nocte

- Aim for lowest possible dose to maintain control.
- Chlorpromazine is not recommended for long-term use because of photosensitivity reactions.

Use depot preparations if compliance is a problem:

fluphenazine decanoate 25–75 mg IM, every 2–4 weeks

or

haloperidol decanoate 50–300 mg IM, every 4 weeks

Tips with depot preparations:

- May take 2–4 months to produce a stable response so oral supplements may be necessary.
- Not as effective as oral therapy.
- Give as deep IM injection with 21 gauge needle in buttock.
- Use lowest possible dose to avoid tardive dyskinesia.
- Reassess at least every 3 months.
- Closely monitor patient for movement disorders.

A drug of the future

Risperidone: a dopamine and serotonin antagonist.

Movement disorders from antipsychotic medication[1]

Acute dystonias

- usually bizarre muscle spasms affect face, neck, tongue and trunk
- oculogyric crises, opisthotonos and laryngeal spasm

Rx: benztropine 1–2 mg IV or IM

Akathisia

- subjective motor restlessness of feet and legs
- generally later onset in course of treatment

Rx: reduce dosage until akathisia less troublesome or substitute thioridazine
can use diazepam or benztropine as short-term measure

Parkinsonian

- seen relatively early in treatment
- the akinesia can be confused with drug-induced depression

Rx: use lower dose or substitute a phenothiazine in low dosage
alternatively, use benztropine or benzhexol

Tardive dyskinesia

Tardive dyskinesia is a syndrome of abnormal involuntary movements of the face, mouth, tongue, trunk and limbs. This is a major problem with use of long-term antipsychotic drugs and may occur months or years (usually) after starting treatment.

Differential diagnosis:

- spontaneous orofacial dyskinesia
- senile dyskinesia
- ill-fitting dentures
- neurological disorders causing tremor and chorea

There is no specific treatment for tardive dyskinesia. The risks and benefits of continuing therapy have to be weighed.

Note Because of the inability to manage tardive dyskinesia, prevention in the form of using the lowest possible dosage of antipsychotic medication is essential. This involves regular review and adjustment if necessary.

Neuroleptic (antipsychotic) malignant syndrome
This is a potentially fatal adverse effect that can develop at any time.

Syndrome: high temperature, muscle rigidity, altered consciousness. Milder variants can occur.

Treatment:

- discontinue medication
- ensure adequate hydration with IV fluids
- if life-threatening
  bromocriptine 2.5 mg (o) bd, gradually increasing to 5 mg (o) tds
  and
  dantrolene 50 mg (IV) every 12 hours for up to 7 doses
- consultant referral

Bipolar disorder

The mood disorders are divided into depressive disorders and bipolar disorders. The swing in moods in bipolar disorders (manic depressive disorders) is illustrated in Figure 51.1. The symptoms of mania may appear abruptly.

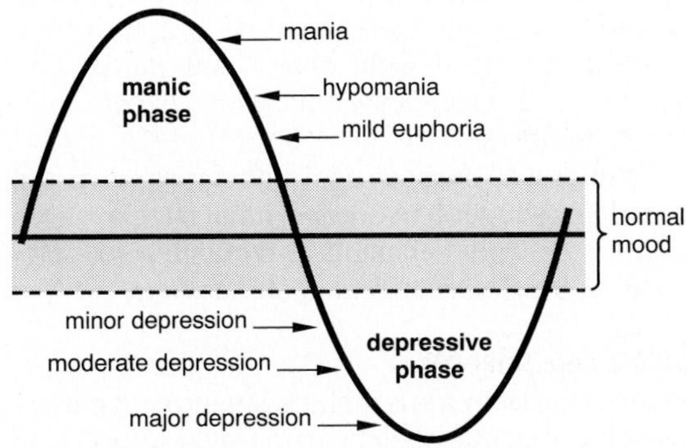

Fig. 51.1 *Bipolar disorder (manic depression): possible mood swings*

The main clinical features of mania are:

- elevated, expansive or irritable mood
- accelerated speech
- agitation
- racing thoughts or flights of ideas
- increased activity
- reduced sleep

Other features include:

- grandiose ideas, sometimes paranoid
- reckless behaviour, overspending
- impaired judgement
- increased sexual drive and activity
- poor insight into the problem

Note The peak onset is in early adult life. There is a strong hereditary basis.

Hypomania is the term used to describe the symptoms of mania that are less severe and of shorter duration.

Management of acute mania

Hospitalisation

- for protection of patient and family
- usually involuntary admission necessary

Drugs of choice[1]

1. co-operative patient
   lithium carbonate 750–1000 mg (o) daily[1]
   - this is the initial dose
   - give in 2 to 3 divided doses
   - can increase by increments of 250–500 mg per day
   - monitor by plasma levels
   - therapeutic plasma level 0.8–1.4 mmol/L
   - required daily dosage usually 1000–2500 mg
   - elderly patients may require reduced dosage
2. unco-operative patients and manic behaviour problematic
   haloperidol 10–20 mg (o) as single dose
   - can be repeated up to 40 mg daily, depending on response
   - use minimum possible dose to achieve control
   - there is a risk of tardive dyskinesia

   If parenteral antipsychotic drug required
   haloperidol 5–10 mg IM or IV
   or
   droperidol 5–10 mg IM
   - repeat in 15–30 minutes if necessary
   - change to oral medication as soon as possible

Note Benzodiazepines, e.g. diazepam, can be used with lithium.

If not responding to medication consider ECT.

Maintenance/prophylaxis

- lithium carbonate—continue for 6 months
  if not tolerated or ineffective use
- carbamazepine or sodium valproate

Prophylaxis for recurrent bipolar disorder
(over 90% will have a recurrence at some time)

- use long-term lithium, e.g. 3–5 years
- target plasma level for maintenance usually 0.6–0.8 mmol/L
- if poor response use carbamazepine or sodium valproate
- unwanted side effects of lithium include
  - — a fine tremor
  - — weight gain
  - — gastrointestinal symptoms

Depression

Depression is very common and presents in a great range of severity. In the context of 'the disturbed patient' depression can be confused with dementia or a psychosis, particularly if the following are present:

- psychomotor agitation
- psychomotor retardation
- delusions
- hallucinations

Assessment[1]

The following questions need to be addressed:

- Is the depression primary (i.e. not secondary to another psychiatric condition such as schizophrenia or anxiety disorder)?
- Is it part of a bipolar disorder? Has there been a previous manic or hypomanic episode? If so, a different approach to treatment is required.
- Is the depression caused by another illness or physical factor (e.g. hypothyroidism, cerebrovascular disease or medication)?
- Is the patient psychotic?
- Is the patient a suicide risk?

The treatment of depression is presented in Chapter 14.

Psychoactive substance use disorders

It is important for the general practitioner to be aware of the effects of self-administration of psychoactive substances, especially their toxic or withdrawal effects. They form significant consideration for the differential diagnosis of disturbed patient behaviour.

Alcohol

Toxic and withdrawal effects, including delirium tremens, are outlined in Chapter 98. Abrupt withdrawal can cause symptoms ranging from tremors, agitation and dysphoria (feeling thoroughly miserable) to fully developed delirium tremens. Epileptic seizures may also occur.

Barbiturate dependence

Tolerance and symptoms on withdrawal are the main features. Barbiturate withdrawal is a very serious life-threatening problem and may be encountered in elderly people undergoing longstanding hypnotic withdrawal. Symptoms include anxiety, tremor, extreme irritability, twitching, seizures and delirium.

Management[1]

Undertake withdrawal with medical supervision as an inpatient.

Transfer the patient to phenobarbitone or diazepam.

phenobarbitone 30 mg for each 100 mg of shorter-acting barbiturate

reduce the dose gradually over 10 to 14 days

or

diazepam 20–40 mg orally, daily,

reduce the dose gradually over 10 to 14 days

Benzodiazepine dependence

Withdrawal symptoms in the dependent patient include anxiety, restlessness, irritability, palpitation and muscle aches and pains, but delirium and seizures are uncommon except with very high doses.

Withdrawal is best achieved by supervising a gradual reduction in dosage aided by relaxation techniques and behavioural strategies to help patients cope with insomnia and anxiety.

Opioid dependence[1]

Withdrawal symptoms include anxiety and panic, sweating, musculoskeletal pain ('aching bones'), gooseflesh, diarrhoea and abdominal colic. These peak at 36–72 hours and tend to subside after 10 days.

Management includes methadone withdrawal (short-term withdrawal) or methadone maintenance. Consider risk of acquiring HIV and hepatitis B infection.

Starting dose

methadone 30–40 mg (o) daily (do not exceed 50 mg daily if patient unwell)

Maintenance (if necessary)

methadone 30–80 mg (o) daily

Stimulant substance abuse

The stimulants include amphetamines and their analogues, epedrine, cocaine and certain appetite suppressants.

Stimulant-induced syndrome[1]

- aggressive behaviour
- paranoid behaviour
- irritability
- transient toxic psychosis
- delirium
- schizophrenic-like syndrome

Treatment:

- withdrawal of drugs
- chlorpromazine 200–600 mg (o) daily for short term

Stimulant-withdrawal syndrome[1]

This syndrome should be suspected in people whose occupation involves shift work, interstate transport driving or multiple jobs presenting with the following symptoms:

- drowsiness
- hypersomnia then insomnia
- irritability
- aggressive behaviour
- dysphoria
- urge to resume drugs

Treatment:

- psychological support and encouragement
- desipramine (or similar tricyclic antidepressant)
  75 mg (o) nocte (increasing as necessary)
- bromocriptine 1.25 mg (o) bd has also been used for cocaine withdrawal

Hallucinogen abuse

Hallucinogens in use include lysergic acid (LSD), phencyclidine (Angel dust), diethylamide and many synthetics. Symptoms include psychotic behaviour including severe hallucinations. Withdrawal from these drugs is not usually a problem but 'flashbacks' can occur.

Medication to counter symptoms[1]

haloperidol 2.5–10 mg (o) daily
or
diazepam 10–40 mg (o) daily

Cannabis use and dependence

Users of cannabis are typically detached and apathetic in nature (Chapter 16).

Psychosis may occur, especially in chronic users, and it is believed that the drug appears to unmask an underlying schizophrenia-type psychosis. No specific treatment is used for use or withdrawal.

Psychiatric disorders of childhood and adolescence[1]

The following disturbance problems do occur and must be taken seriously, especially the potential for suicide in the second decade. Many of these disorders are presented in more detail in Chapter 68.

Attention deficit hyperactivity disorder

Clinical features:

- short attention span
- distractability
- overactivity
- impulsiveness
- antisocial behaviour

Depression

Major depression follows the same criteria as for adults. Suicidal ideation has to be considered and taken very seriously if present. Imipramine is probably the drug of choice.

Bipolar disorders

Mania is seldom diagnosed before puberty. Adolescents may present (uncommonly) with symptoms of mania or hypomania.

Schizophrenia and related disorders

Schizophrenia is rare before puberty. The criteria for diagnosis are similar to adults:

- delusion
- thought disorder
- hallucinations
- six months or more of deterioration in functioning

Autism

Aggression and irritability can be a feature, especially during adolescence.

Tourette's syndrome

Behavioural problems can be part of this syndrome, which requires the attention of an experienced consultant.

Obsessive-compulsive disorders

In about one-third of cases the onset is between 5 and 15 years of age.

Violence and dangerousness

Dangerousness has been defined as a 'propensity to cause serious physical injury or lasting psychological harm to others' and, in the context of the mentally abnormal, 'the relative probability of their committing a violent crime'.[8]

Dangerousness is not only related to mental illness and, interestingly, most offenders have no psychiatric diagnosis. It is not an inherited, immutable characteristic of an individual but tends to surface on impulse in a particular context given a whole range of situational factors. Prediction of the risk of violence is not straightforward.

Various groups have been identified as contributing risk factors for violent conduct.[8]

- Schizophrenic psychoses, including
  - older male paranoid schizophrenics
  - younger males prone to act violently and impulsively, presumably due to hallucinatory commands
- Morbid jealousy
  - associated with delusions of infidelity
- Mood disorder
  - violence, usually associated with depression (rarely mania)
  - married women with severe depression (violence against young children)
  - history of suicide attempts in depression
- Episodic discontrol syndrome (similar to intermittent explosive disorder)
- Mental retardation combined with personality disorder and behavioural disturbances
- Alcohol abuse or dependency
- Amphetamine or benzodiazepine abuse or dependency

From a management viewpoint, homicidal threats must be taken very seriously.

Suicide and parasuicide

The haunting issue of suicide and parasuicide is presented in Chapter 14. The disturbed patient is always a suicide risk rather than a homicide risk. The importance of recognising depression with an associated suicide risk in the elderly patient has been emphasised heavily in this chapter.

Facts and figures[9]

- More than 90% of suicides occur without underlying chronic conditions but most people are significantly depressed at the time.
- In Australia suicide is the second most common cause of death between the ages of 11 and 25. Children as young as five years of age have committed suicide.
- Those who talk about suicide may attempt it later.
- About half those committing suicide have seen a doctor within their last month of life.
- Around 80–90% of suicides have given clear or subtle warnings to family, friends or doctors.
- There is no evidence that asking patients about suicidal ideation provokes suicidal acts.
- Doctors in Australia and other Western countries have a high suicide rate.

Suicide risk

Blumenthal's[10] overlapping model lists five groups of risk factors (Fig. 51.2):

1. Psychiatric disorders
   e.g. — affective disorder and alcohol abuse in adults
   — schizophrenia
   — depression and conduct disorder in young people
2. Personality traits
   e.g. — impulsiveness and aggression
3. Environmental and psychosocial factors
   e.g. — poor social supports
   — chronic medical illness, e.g. AIDS
   — significant loss
4. Family history and genetics (both nature and nurture)
   e.g. — emulation of relatives
   — specific ethnic groups in custody
5. Biological factors
   e.g. — possible serotonin deficiency

Parasuicide

Parasuicide is attempted suicide; in many cases patients are drawing attention to themselves as a 'plea for help'. It is important for the GP to take an active role in the support of the patient and family after discharge from hospital, but preferably in conjunction with a psychiatric or counselling service. Arrange frequent

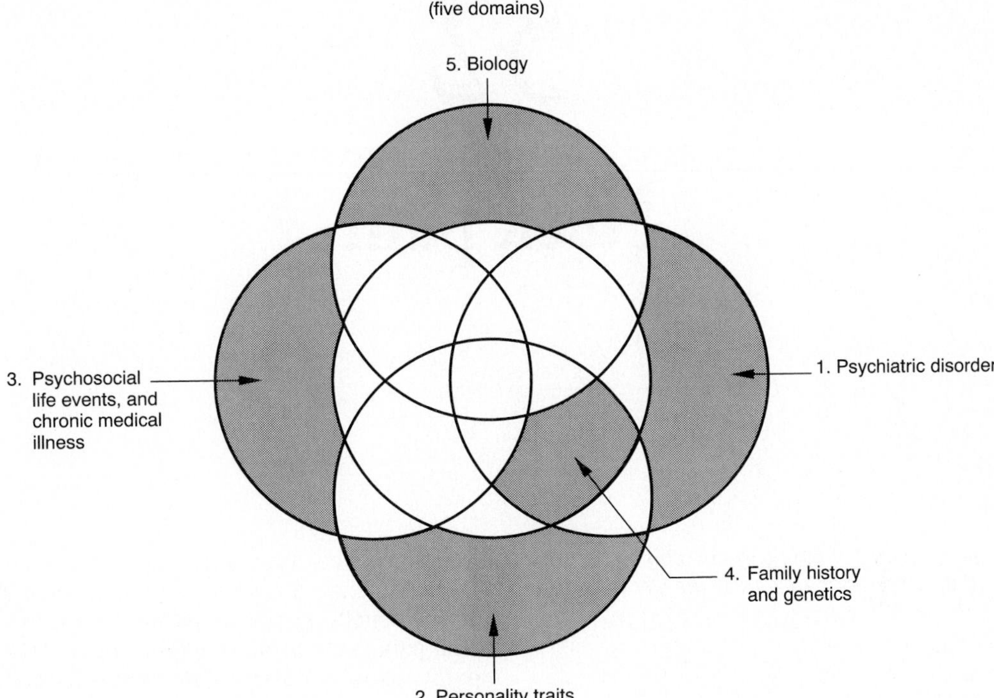

Fig. 51.2 *Overlap model for understanding suicidal behaviour* AFTER BLUMENTHAL AND KUPFER

consultations at first and ensure adequate follow-up, especially for missed appointments.

When to refer[9]

Indications for referral to a psychiatrist:

- severe depression
- high suicide risk
- actual suicide attempt: recent or in past
- suspected psychiatric disorders in the elderly
  ? depression or schizophrenia
  ? depression or dementia
- failure to improve with treatment
- poor family and social supports

References

1. Mashford ML et al *Psychotropic drug guidelines* (2nd edition). Victorian Medical Postgraduate Foundation, 1992-3, 33–67.
2. Biro G. Dementia. Australian Dr Weekly, 16 February 1990, I–VIII.
3. Biro G. Delirium in the elderly. Australian Dr Weekly, 1 December 1989, I–VIII.
4. Kahn RL et al Brief objective measures of the determination of mental status in the aged. American Journal of Psychiatry, 1960; 117:326–329.
5. McLean S. Is it dementia? Aust Fam Physician, 1992; 21:1762–1776.
6. Norman T, Judd F. Schizophrenia. In: MIMS Disease Index. Sydney: IMS Publishing, 1991–2, 472–474.
7. Kumar PJ, Clark ML. *Clinical medicine* (2nd edition). London: Bailliere Tindall, 1990.
8. Beaumont PJV, Hampshire RB. *Textbook of psychiatry*. Melbourne: Blackwell Scientific Publications, 1989, 283–284.
9. Biro G. Suicide. Australian Dr Weekly, 26 April 1991, I–VIII.
10. Blumenthal S. Suicide—a guide to risk factors, assessment and treatment of suicidal patients. Medical Clinics of North America, 1988; 72:937–63.

52

Neck pain

We have all heard of the courtiers who mimicked the wry neck of Alexander the Great.

William Heberden (1710–1801)

Neck pain is a very common symptom in both sexes at all ages and although most pain is experienced in the posterior aspect of the neck, anterior neck pain can occur from causes that overlap between front and back. The main cause of neck pain is a disorder of the cervical spine which usually manifests as neck pain but can refer pain to the head, shoulders and chest. Such pain usually originates from the facet (apophyseal) joints but can arise from other musculoskeletal structures such as the intervertebral discs and the muscles or ligaments (Fig. 52.1). The other major symptom is limited movement or stiffness.

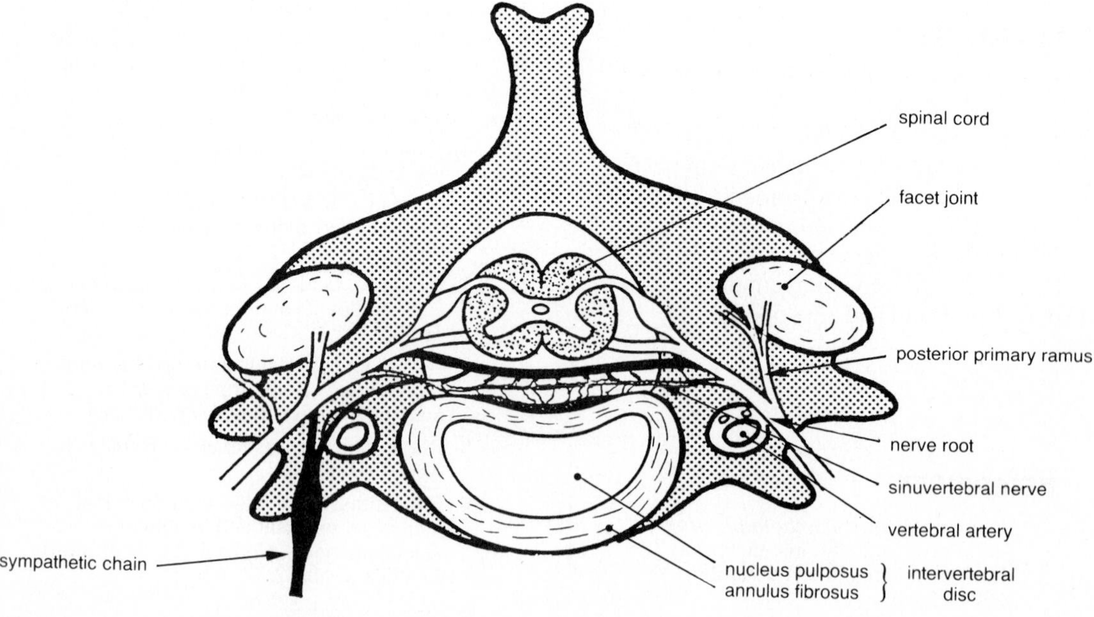

Fig. 52.1 *Transverse section illustrating the functional unit and nervous network of the cervical spine*

General causes of neck pain are presented in Table 52.1.

Key facts and checkpoints

- At any time approximately 10% of the adult population are experiencing[1] an episode of neck pain.
- The commonest cause of neck pain is dysfunction of the facet joints with or without a history of injury.
- Disorders of the intervertebral discs are common, especially in the lower cervical spine, and may cause unilateral pain, paraesthesia or anaesthesia in the arm.
- In a UK study radiological cervical disc degeneration was present in 40% of males and 28% of females[1] between 55 and 64 years.
- Strains, sprains and fractures of the facet joints, especially after a 'whiplash' injury, are difficult to detect and are often overlooked as a cause of persistent neck pain.
- Cervical spondylosis is a disorder of ageing: radiological signs occur in 50% of people over the age of 50 and in 75% over the age of 65.[2]
- In cervical spondylosis, osteophytic projections may produce nerve root and spinal cord compression, resulting in radiculopathy and myelopathy respectively.
- Radiculopathy can be caused by a soft disc protrusion (usually unilateral), a hard calcified lump and osteophytes (may be bilateral).
- Cervical disorders are aggravated by vibration, e.g. riding in a motor vehicle.
- Always determine the C2,C6 and C7 levels by finding the relevant spinous processes (easily palpable landmarks) prior to palpation.
- Palpation of the neck is the cornerstone of cervical management. Palpate gently—the more one presses the less one feels.
- Most episodes of neck pain, including acute torticollis, are transient, lasting from about 2 to 10 days.
- In one study 70% of people with neck pain who sought medical attention had recovered or were recovering within one month.[1]
- Effective management of neck pain is based on the principle that stiff dysfunctional joints are painful and restoration of normal movement may be associated with resolution of pain.

Table 52.1 *Causes of neck pain (a pathological classification)*

Musculoskeletal
Joint dysfunction
- apophyseal
- intervertebral disc

Muscular/ligamentous strains or sprains
Trauma
- 'whiplash'
- fracture
- other disorders

Inflammation
- osteoarthritis*
- rheumatoid arthritis
- ankylosing spondylitis
- psoriasis
- inflammatory bowel disorders
- Reiter's disease/reactive arthritis
- polymyalgia rheumatica
- thyroiditis

Infective
Spinal
- osteomyelitis
- tuberculosis
- herpes zoster

Extraspinal
- cervical adenitis
- poliomyelitis
- tetanus

Extracervical
- meningitis
- febrile states:
  - meningism
  - malaria

Degenerative
- spondylosis*

Neoplasia
- benign
- malignant

Fibromyalgia syndrome

Psychogenic

Referred visceral
- heart
- oesophagus
- carcinoma lung

Referred cranial
- haemorrhage, e.g. subarachnoid
- tumour
- abscess

* Osteoarthritis, or spondylosis, is inflammatory and degenerative

- The optimal treatment for dysfunctional joints (without organic disease or radiculopathy) is active and passive mobilisation, especially as exercises.

A diagnostic approach

A summary of the safety diagnostic model is presented in Table 52.2.

Table 52.2 *Neck pain: diagnostic strategy model*

Q. Probability diagnosis
A. Vertebral dysfunction
Traumatic 'strain' or 'sprain'
Cervical spondylosis

Q. Serious disorders not to be missed
A. Cardiovascular
- angina
- subarachnoid haemorrhage

Neoplasia
- primary
- metastasis
- Pancoast's tumour

Severe infections
- osteomyelitis
- meningitis

Vertebral fractures or dislocation

Q. Pitfalls (often missed)
A. Disc prolapse
Myelopathy
Cervical lymphadenitis
Fibromyalgia syndrome
Outlet compression syndrome, e.g. cervical rib
Polymyalgia rheumatica
Ankylosing spondylitis
Rheumatoid arthritis
Oesophageal foreign bodies and tumours
Paget's disease

Q. Seven masquerades checklist

A.	
Depression	✓
Diabetes	—
Drugs	—
Anaemia	—
Thyroid disease	✓
Spinal dysfunction	✓✓
UTI	—

Q. Is the patient trying to tell me something?
A. Highly probable. Stress and adverse occupational factors relevant.

Probability diagnosis

The main causes of neck pain are vertebral dysfunction, especially of the facet joints, and traumatic strains or sprains affecting the musculoligamentous structures of the neck. The so-called myofascial syndrome is mainly a manifestation of dysfunction of the facet joints. Acute wry neck (torticollis) which is quite common is yet another likely manifestation of apophyseal joint dysfunction. Spondylosis, known also as degenerative osteoarthrosis and osteoarthritis, is also a common cause, especially in the elderly patient.

Intervertebral disc disruption is also a relatively common phenomenon in the cervical spine, especially at the lower levels C5–6and C6–7.[3]

Serious disorders not to be missed

Conditions causing neck pain and stiffness may be a sign of meningitis or of cerebral haemorrhage, particularly subarachnoid haemorrhage, or of a cerebral tumour or retropharyngeal abscess.

Angina and myocardial infarction should be considered in anterior neck pain.

Tumours are relatively rare in the cervical spine but metastases do occur and should be kept in mind, especially with persistent neck pain present day and night.

Metastasis to the spine occurs in 5–10% of patients with systemic cancer, making it the second most common neurological complication of cancer. The cervical spine accounts for some 15% of spinal metastases.[2] The commonest primary tumours are the breast, prostate or lung. Other primaries include the kidney, thyroid and melanoma.

Pitfalls

There are many pitfalls in the clinical assessment of causes of neck pain and many of them are inflammatory.

Rheumatoid arthritis is the prime severe inflammatory arthropathy that involves the neck but the neck can be affected by the seronegative spondyloarthropathies, particularly ankylosing spondylitis, psoriasis and the inflammatory bowel disorders.

While polymyalgia rheumatica affects mainly the shoulder girdle, pain in the lower neck, which is part of the symptom complex, is often overlooked. Diffuse neck pain in myofascial soft tissue with tender trigger areas is part of the uncommon but refractory fibromyalgia syndrome.

General pitfalls

- Failing to appreciate how often the benign problem of facet joint dysfunction occurs in the neck, causing pain and limited movement. This involves failure to appreciate the value of physical therapy, especially exercise programs, in alleviating the problem.
- Failing to adhere to the idiom: one disc—one nerve root. Involvement of more than one nerve root in the upper limb may mean a neoplastic disorder such as metastatic disease, lymphoma in the thoracic outlet and similar serious diseases.

- Missing the insidious onset of myelopathy, especially the spasticity component, caused by rheumatoid arthritis, osteophytic overgrowth or, rarely, a soft disc prolapse.

Seven masquerades checklist

Cervical spinal dysfunction is the obvious outstanding cause. Thyroiditis may cause neck pain, as in the extremely rare cases of acute specific infection in the thyroid (e.g. syphilis, pyogenic infections) which causes severe pain; non-specific thyroiditis (de Quervain's thyroiditis) produces painful swelling with dysphagia. The association between depression and neck pain is well documented.

Psychogenic considerations

The neck is one of the commonest areas for psychological fixation following injury. This may involve perpetuation or exaggeration of pain because of factors such as anxiety and depression, conversion reaction and secondary gain.

The psychological sequelae that can follow a whiplash injury and chronic neck problems such as spondylosis serve as a reminder that the state of the patient's cervical spine can profoundly affect his or her life and that we should always be aware of the whole person. A feeling of depression is a very common sequel to such an injury and these patients demand our dutiful care and understanding.

The clinical approach

History

It is important to analyse the pain into its various components, especially the nature of its onset, its site and radiation and associated features. The diurnal pattern of the pain will provide a lead to the diagnosis (refer to Fig. 31.3: the patterns are similar to low back pain).

Key questions

Point to exactly where in your neck you get the pain.
Do you wake up with pain in the morning?
Does the pain come on when you have to look up for a while?
Do you have trouble reversing your car?
Can you recall an injury to your head or neck such as hitting your head on an overhead bar?
Does your neck grate or get stiff?
Do you get headaches or feel dizzy?
Is the pain present day and night?
Do you get pain or pins and needles or numbness in your arms?
Does the pain come on with activity?
Does the pain wake you at night?
Do you feel pain on both sides of your neck and over your shoulders?
Do your hands or arms feel weak or clumsy?

Physical examination

It is appropriate to follow the traditional rule for examination of any joint or complex of joints: LOOK, FEEL, MOVE, MEASURE, TEST FUNCTION and X-RAY. Careful examination of the cervical spine is essential for the correct diagnosis and for specific treatment at the painful level.

Three objectives of the examination are to:[4]

- reproduce the patient's symptoms
- identify the level of lesion or lesions
- determine the cause (if possible)

A neurological examination is essential if radicular pain is present, or weakness or other upper limb symptoms, including any pain or paraesthesia that extends below the elbow.

Inspection

The patient should be examined sitting on a couch, rather than on a chair. The body should be fully supported with the hands resting on the thighs. The following should be noted:

- willingness to move the head and neck
- level of the shoulders
- any lateral flexion
- contour of the neck from the side

In the patient with torticollis the head is held laterally flexed with, perhaps, slight rotation to one side—usually away from the painful side. Patients suffering from whiplash injury and severe spondylosis tend to hold the neck stiff and the head forward, and tend to turn the trunk rather than rotate the neck.

Palpation

For this vital component of the examination it is essential to know the surface anatomy of the neck so that the affected level can be determined.

Method

The patient lies prone on the examination couch with the forehead resting on the hands (palms up). The neck should be flexed forward and the shoulders relaxed.

1. Central digital palpation
   Systematically palpate the first spinous processes of the cervical vertebrae.
   - C2 (axis) is the first spinous process palpable beneath the occiput
   - C7 is the largest 'fixed' and most prominent process—situated at the base of the neck
   - C6 is also prominent but usually 'disappears' under the palpating finger with extension of the neck
   - the spinous processes of C3, C4 and C5 are difficult to palpate because of cervical lordosis but their level can be estimated (Fig. 52.2).

   Standing at the patient's head, place opposed pulps of the thumbs on the spinous processes (starting at C2) then move down the middle line to C7. Press firmly over each and with arms straight oscillate with moderate firmness three or four times to assess pain, stiffness or muscle spasm.

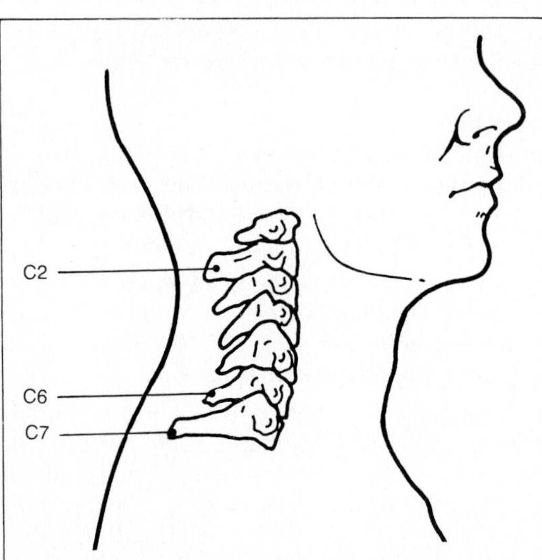

Fig. 52.2 *Relative sizes of spinous processes of the cervical spine*

2. Lateral digital palpation
   The facet joints lie in sequence (called the articular pillar) about 2 to 3 centimetres from the midline. Press with opposed thumbs against this pillar in a systematic manner on either side of the midline (top to base) to determine any painful area.

Palpation should be extended to include the anterior neck, searching for evidence of lymphadenitis, muscle spasm, thyroid disease and other problems.

Movement

Active movements are observed with the patient sitting on the couch. The movements are as follows with normal range indicated.

- flexion—45°
- extension—50°
- lateral flexion (R&L)—45°
- rotation (R&L)—75°

If there is a full range of pain-free movement, apply overpressure slowly at the end range and note any pain.

The range of movements can be plotted on a special grid called a direction of movement diagram (Fig. 52.3). This provides a ready reference for serial assessments.

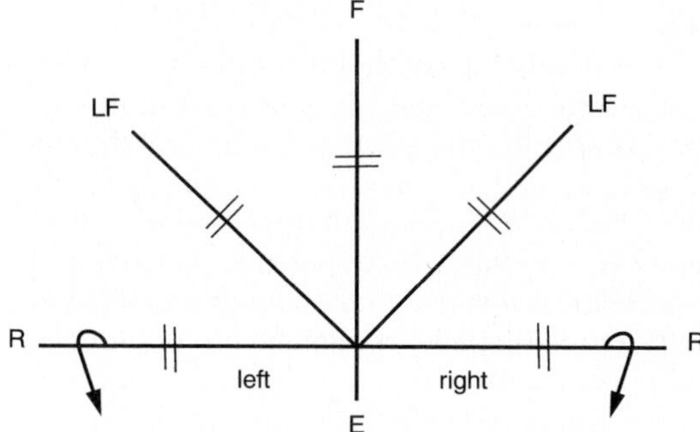

Fig. 52.3 *Direction of movement diagram to record movements of the neck. This record shows restricted and painful movements (indicated by | |) in right lateral flexion and right rotation; the other movements are free*

Neurological examination

A neurological examination for nerve root lesions (C5 to T1) is indicated if the clinical assessment identifies the presence of neurological symptoms and signs such as pain, paraesthesia or anaesthesia in the arm. Nerve root pressure is indicated by:

- pain and paraesthesia along the distribution of the dermatome
- localised sensory loss
- reduced muscular power (weakness or fatigue or both)
- hyporeflexia (reduced amplitude or fatigue or both)

It is necessary to know the sensory distribution for each nerve root and the motor changes. This is summarised in Table 52.3. The dermatomes are illustrated in Figure 52.4.

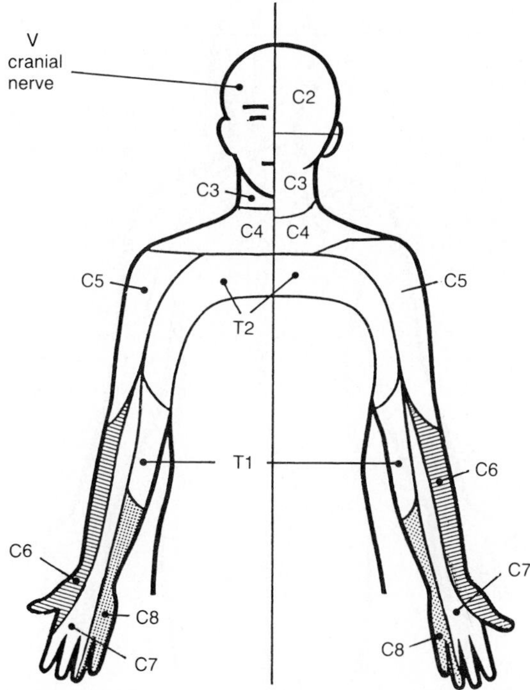

Fig. 52.4 *Dermatomes of the upper limb, head and neck*

Investigations

The investigations are directed to diagnosing the painful condition and determining if suspected or true organic disease is present in the spine. It is inappropriate to perform sophisticated investigations such as CT scans in all patients. Scanning should be reserved where surgery is contemplated and serious disease is suspected but not confirmed by plain X-ray.

Investigations include:

- haemoglobin, film and WCC
- ESR
- rheumatoid arthritis factor
- $HLAB_{27}$ antigen
- radiology
  - — plain X-ray
  - — plain CT scan
  - — CT scan and myelogram (if cervical disc surgery contemplated)
  - — radionuclide bone scan
  - — MRI

Neck pain in children

In children and adolescents neck pain, often with stiffness, may be a manifestation of infection or inflammation of cervical lymph nodes, usually secondary to an infected throat—for example, tonsillitis or pharyngitis. However, it is vital to consider the possibility of meningitis. Sometimes a high fever associated with a systemic infection or pneumonia can cause meningism. In the presence of fever the rare possibility of poliomyelitis should be kept in mind. In both children and adults the presence of cerebral pathology such as haemorrhage, abscess or tumour are uncommon possibilities.[5] Acute torticollis is quite common in this age group and the neck may be involved in chronic juvenile arthritis.

Neck pain in the elderly

In adults the outstanding causes are dysfunction of the joints and spondylosis, with the acute febrile causes encountered in children being rare. However, cerebral and meningeal disorders may cause pain and stiffness in the neck.[5]

Table 52.3 *Cervical nerve root syndromes*

Nerve root	*Sensory change*	*Muscle power*	*Power loss*	*Reflex*
C5	Outer arm	Deltoid	Abduction arm	Biceps jerk
C6	Outer forearm/thumb/ index finger	Biceps	Elbow flexion Extension wrist	Biceps + brachioradialis
C7	Hand/middle and ring fingers	Triceps	Elbow extension	Triceps
C8	Inner forearm /little finger	Long flexors finger, long extensors thumb	Grip	
T1	Inner arm	Interossei	Finger spread	

Rheumatoid arthritis is the prime severe inflammatory arthropathy that involves the neck, but the neck can be affected by the spondyloarthropathies, e.g. ankylosing spondylitis. The painful acute wry neck can affect all ages and is considered to be caused mainly by acute disorders of the apophyseal joints rather than disc prolapse. However, disc lesions do occur and can cause referred pain or radicular pain. In the elderly radicular pain can be caused also by impingement of the nerve root in the intervertebral foramen which has become narrowed from the degenerative changes of longstanding spondylosis.

Problems with a higher probability with increasing age include:

- cervical spondylosis with radiculopathy or myelopathy
- atlantoaxial subluxation complicating rheumatoid arthritis
- polymyalgia rheumatica
- metastatic cancer
- Pancoast's tumour of the lung
- angina and myocardial infarction
- pharyngeal and retropharyngeal infection and tumour

Clinical problems of cervical spinal origin

Pain originating from disorders of the cervical spine is usually, although not always, experienced in the neck. The patient may experience headache, or pain around the ear, face, arm, shoulder, upper anterior or posterior chest.[6]

Possible symptoms:

- neck pain
- neck stiffness
- headache
- 'migraine'-like headache
- facial pain
- arm pain (referred or radicular)
- myelopathy (sensory and motor changes in arms and legs)
- ipsilateral sensory changes of scalp
- ear pain (periauricular)
- scapular pain
- anterior chest pain
- torticollis
- dizziness/vertigo
- visual dysfunction

Figure 52.5 indicates typical directions of referred pain from the cervical spine. Pain in the arm (brachialgia) is common and tends to cover the shoulder and upper arm as indicated.

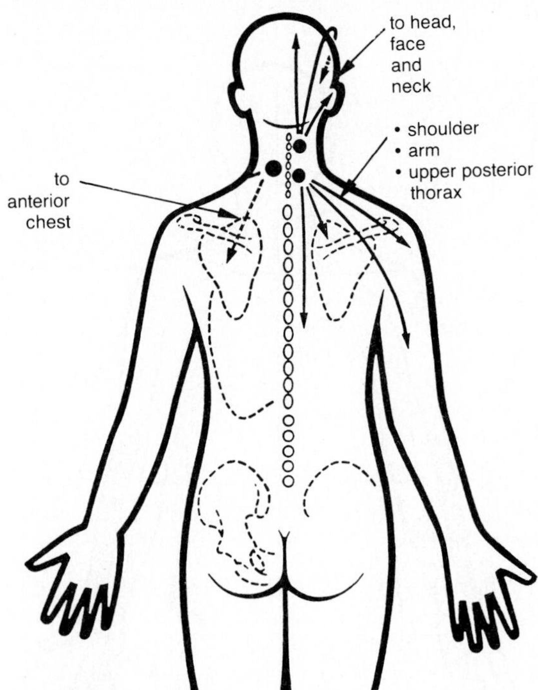

Fig. 52.5 *Possible directions of referred pain from the cervical spine*

Cervical dysfunction

Dysfunction of the 35 intervertebral joints that comprise the cervical spine complex is responsible for most cases of neck pain. The problem can occur at all ages and appears to be caused by disorder (including malalignment) of the many facet joints which are pain-sensitive. Dysfunction of these joints, which may also be secondary to intervertebral disc disruption, initiates a reflex response of adjacent muscle spasm and myofascial tenderness. Dysfunction can follow obvious trauma such as a blow to the head or a sharp jerk to the neck, but can be caused by repeated trivial trauma or activity such as painting a ceiling or gentle wrestling. People often wake up with severe neck pain and blame it on a 'chill' from a draught on the neck during the night. This is incorrect because it is usually caused by an unusual twist on the flexed neck for a long period during sleep.

Typical clinical features:

- typical age range 12–50 years
- dull ache (may be sharp) in neck
- may radiate to occiput, ear, face and temporal area (upper cervical)
- may radiate to shoulder region, especially suprascapular area (lower cervical)
- rarely refers pain below the level of the shoulder
- pain aggravated by activity, improved with rest
- various degrees of stiffness
- neck tends to lock with specific movements, usually rotation
- localised unilateral tenderness over affected joints
- variable restriction of movement but may be normal
- X-rays usually normal

Management

- Provide appropriate reassurance, information and support.
- Advice to the patient about rules of living include:

  Do

  — Keep your neck upright in a vertical position for reading, typing and so on.
  — Keep a good posture—keep the chin tucked in.
  — Sleep on a low firm pillow or a special conforming pillow.
  — Sleep with your painful side on the pillow.
  — Use heat and massage: massage your neck firmly three times a day using an analgesic ointment.

  Don't

  — Look up in a strained position for long periods.
  — Twist your head often towards the painful side, e.g. when reversing a car.
  — Lift or tug with your neck bent forwards.
  — Work, read or study with your neck bent for long periods.
  — Become too dependent on 'collars'.
  — Sleep on too many pillows.
- Monitor the patient's progress without overtreatment.
- Use basic analgesics, e.g. paracetamol.
- Prescribe an exercise program as early as possible.
- Refer to an appropriate therapist for cervical mobilisation. Mobilisation combined with exercises is very effective treatment. Occasionally, manipulation may help with a stubborn 'locked' neck but should be left to an expert.

Chronic pain

Additional treatment modalities to consider include:

- a course of antidepressants
- transcutaneous nerve stimulation (TENS) especially when drugs are not tolerated
- hydrotherapy
- acupuncture
- corticosteroid facet injections (ideally under image intensification)
- facet joint denervation

Cervical spondylosis

Cervical spondylosis following disc degeneration and apophyseal joint degeneration is far more common than lumbar spondylosis and mainly involves the C5–6 and C6–7 segments. The consequence is narrowing of the intervertebral foramen with the nerve roots of C6 and C7 being at risk of compression.

Cervical spondylosis is generally a chronic problem but it may be asymptomatic. In some patients the pain may lessen with age, while stiffness increases.

The main clinical features are as follows:

- dull, aching suboccipital neck pain (Fig. 52.6)
- stiffness
- worse in morning on arising and lifting head
- improves with gentle activity and warmth, e.g. warm showers
- deteriorates with heavy activity, e.g. working under car, painting ceiling
- usually unilateral pain—may be bilateral
- pain may be referred to head, arms and scapulae
- may wake patient at night with paraesthesia in arms
- C6 nerve root most commonly involved
- acute attacks on chronic background
- aggravated by flexion (reading) and extension
- associated vertigo or unsteadiness
- restricted tender movements, especially rotation/lateral flexion
- joints tender to palpation
- X-ray changes invariable

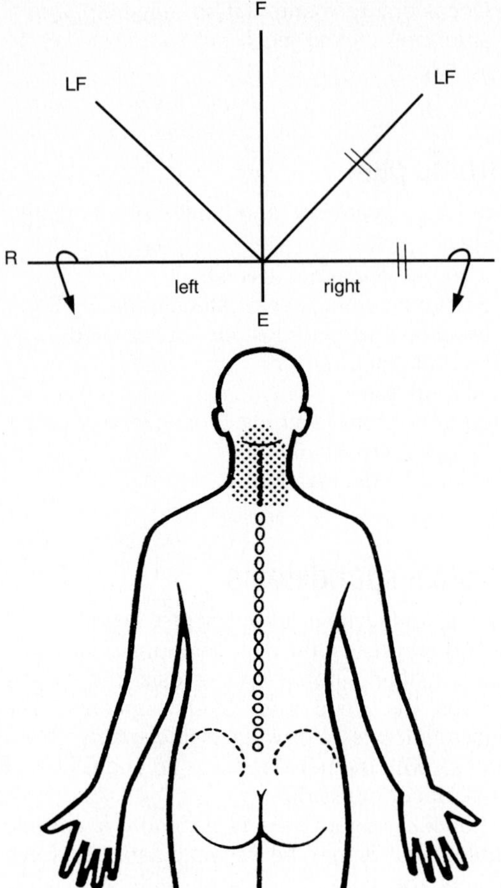

Fig. 52.6 *Cervical spondylosis: typical pain distribution with DOM diagram indicating painful and restricted movements*

Treatment

- provide appropriate reassurance, information and support
- referral for physiotherapy, including warm hydrotherapy
- regular mild analgesics, e.g. paracetamol
- NSAIDs: a trial for three weeks then review
- gentle mobilising exercises as early as possible
- passive mobilising techniques
- outline general rules to live by, including advice regarding sleeping and pillows, and day-to-day activities

Complications

- radiculopathy (unilateral or bilateral)
- myelopathy—pressure on spinal cord

Acute torticollis

Torticollis (acute wry neck) means a lateral deformity of the neck and is usually a transient self-limiting acutely painful disorder with associated muscle spasm of variable intensity.

The typical features include:

- age of patient between 12 and 30 years
- patient usually awakes with the problem
- pain usually confined to neck but may radiate
- deformity of lateral flexion and slight flexion/rotation
- deformity usually away from the painful side
- loss of extension
- mid-cervical spine (C2–C3, C3–C4, C4–C5)
- any segment between C2 and C7 can cause torticollis
- usually no neurological symptoms or signs

The exact cause of this condition is uncertain, but both an acute disc lesion and apophyseal joint lesion are implicated, with the latter the more likely cause. Management by mobilisation and muscle energy therapy is very effective.

Muscle energy therapy

This amazingly effective therapy relies on the basic physiological principle that the contracting and stretching of muscles leads to automatic relaxation of agonist and antagonist muscles.[4] Lateral flexion or rotation or a combination of movements can be used but treatment in rotation is preferred. The direction of contraction can be away from the painful side (preferred) or towards the painful side, whichever is most comfortable for the patient.

Method

1. Explain the method to the patient, with reassurance that it is not painful.
2. Rotate the patient's head passively and gently towards the painful side to the limit of pain (the motion barrier).
3. Place your hand against the head on the side opposite the painful one. The other (free) hand can be used to steady the painful level—usually C3–C4.
4. Request the patient to push the head (in rotation) as firmly as possible against the resistance of your hand. The patient should therefore be producing a strong isometric contraction of the neck in rotation away from the painful side (Fig. 52.7a). Your counterforce (towards the painful side) should be firm and moderate (never forceful)

and should not 'break' through the patient's resistance.

5. After 5–10 seconds (average 7 seconds) ask the patient to relax; then passively stretch the neck gently towards the patient's painful side (Fig. 52.7b).
6. The patient will now be able to turn the head a little further towards the painful side.
7. This sequence is repeated at the new improved motion barrier. Repeat 3 to 5 times until the full range of movement returns.
8. Ask the patient to return the following day for treatment although the neck may be almost normal.

The patient can be taught self-treatment at home using this method.

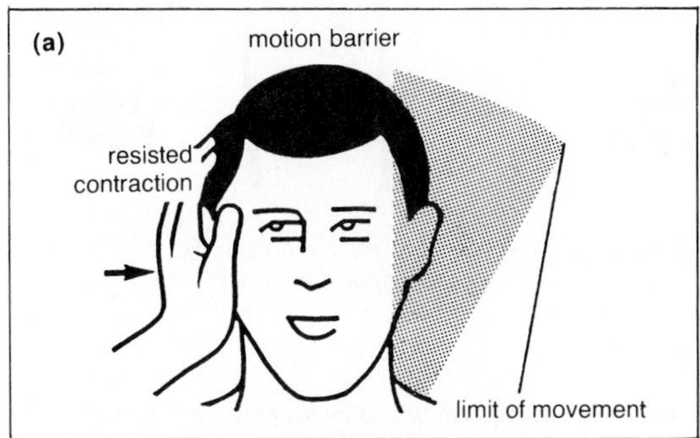

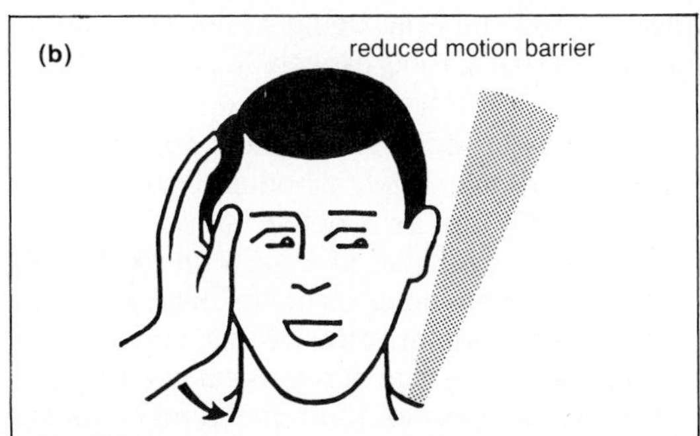

Fig. 52.7 *Muscle energy therapy for acute torticollis:* **(a)** *isometric contraction phase for problem on the left side;* **(b)** *relaxation phase towards the affected (left) side*

Whiplash syndrome

Patients with the whiplash syndrome present typically with varying degrees of pain-related loss of mobility of the cervical spine, headache and emotional disturbance in the form of anxiety and depression. The problem can vary from mild temporary disability to a severe and protracted course.

The injury occurs as a consequence of hyperextension of the neck followed by recoil hyperflexion, typically following a rear-end collision between motor vehicles. There is reversal of sequence of these movements in a head-on collision. In addition to hyperextension, there is prolongation or anterior stretching plus longitudinal extension of the neck.[4]

Whiplash causes injury to soft tissue structures including muscle, nerve roots, the cervical sympathetic chain, ligaments, apophyseal joints and their synovial capsules and intervertebral discs. Damage to the apophyseal joints appears to be severe, with possible microfractures (not detectable on plain X-ray) and long-term dysfunction.

Pain and stiffness of the neck are the most common symptoms. The pain is usually experienced in the neck and upper shoulders but may radiate to the suboccipital region, the interscapular region and down the arms. The stiffness felt initially in the anterior neck muscles shifts to the posterior neck.

Headache is a common and disabling symptom that may persist for many months. It is typically occipital but can be referred to the temporal region and the eyes.

Nerve root pain can be caused by a traction injury of the cervical nerve roots or by inflammatory changes or direct pressure subsequent to herniation of a disc.

Paraesthesia of the ulnar border of the hand, nausea and dizziness are all relatively common symptoms.

Delayed symptoms are common. A patient may feel no pain until 24 (sometimes up to 96) hours later; most experience symptoms within six hours. Complications of whiplash are summarised in Table 52.4.

Table 52.4 *Complications of whiplash*

Referred pain (headache, arm pain)
Visual problems
Vertigo
Dysphagia
Depression
Compensation neurosis
Disc rupture increasing to nerve root pain
Osteoarthritis becomes symptomatic

Management principles

The objective of treatment is to obtain a full pain-free range of free movement of the neck by attending to both the physical and the psychological components of the problem. Other objectives include an early return to work and discouragement of unnecessary and excessive reliance on cervical collars and legal action.

Treatment

- Establish an appropriate empathy and instil patient confidence with a positive professional approach. Discourage multiple therapists.
- Provide appropriate reassurance and patient education.
- Compare the problem with a sprained ankle which is a similar injury.
- Inform that an emotional reaction of anger, frustration and temporary depression is common (lasts about 2 weeks).
- X-ray.
- Rest.
- Cervical collar (limit to 2 days).
- Analgesics, e.g. paracetamol (avoid narcotics).
- NSAIDs for 2 weeks.
- Tranquillisers, mild—up to 2 weeks.
- Physiotherapy referral.
- Neck exercises (as early as possible).
- Heat and massage; 'spray and stretch'.
- Passive mobilisation (not manipulation).

Cervical disc disruption

Disruption of a cervical disc can result in several different syndromes.

1. Referred pain over a widespread area due to pressure on adjacent dura mater

   Note A disc disruption is capable of referring pain over such a diffuse area (Fig. 52.8) that the patient is sometimes diagnosed as functional, e.g. hysterical.
2. Nerve root or radicular pain (radiculopathy). The pain follows the dermatomal distribution of the nerve root in the arm.
3. Spinal cord compression (myelopathy).

Radiculopathy

Apart from protrusion from an intervertebral disc, nerve root pressure causing arm pain can be caused by osteophytes associated with cervical spondylosis. The pain follows neurological patterns down the arm, being easier to localise with lower cervical roots especially C6, C7 and C8.

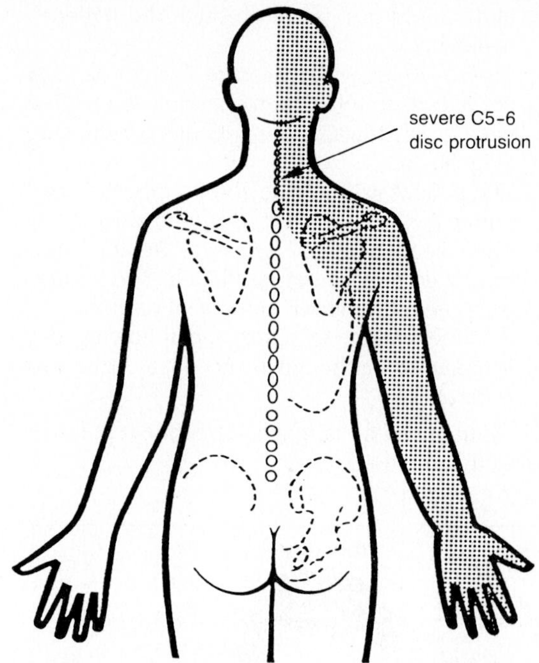

Fig. 52.8 *Zone of possible referred pain distribution caused by a cervical disc lesion on the right side*

Note 1. The cervical roots exit above their respective vertebral bodies. For example, the C6 root exits between C5 and C6 so that a prolapse of C5–C6 intervertebral disc or spondylosis of the C5-C6 junction affects primarily the C6 root (Fig. 52.9).
2. One disc—one nerve root is the rule.
3. Spondylosis and tumours tend to cause bilateral pain, i.e. more than one nerve root.

Clinical presentation

- a sharp aching pain in the neck, radiating down one or both arms
- onset of pain may be abrupt, often precipitated by a sudden neck movement on awakening
- stiffness of neck with limitation of movement
- nocturnal pain, waking patient during night
- pain localised to upper trapezius and possible muscle spasm

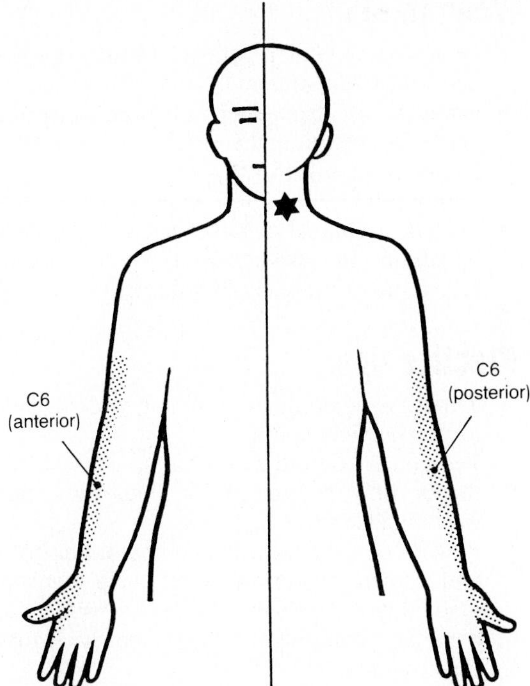

Fig. 52.9 *Typical C6 nerve root (radicular) pain*

Investigations

- plain X-ray (A–P, lateral E and F, oblique views to visualise foramina;) good for diagnosis, not for surgery
- plain CT scan
- CT scan and myelogram—excellent visualisation of structures but invasive
- MRI—excellent but expensive, sometimes difficult to distinguish soft disc from osteophytes

Treatment

Many patients respond to conservative treatment, especially from a disc prolapse:

- bed rest
- soft cervical collar
- analgesics
- tranquillisers, especially at night
- traction
- careful mobilisation (manipulation is contraindicated)

Myelopathy

Clinical features:

- older patients, typically men > 50
- insidious onset: symptoms over 1–2 years
- numbness and tingling in fingers
- leg stiffness
- numb clumsy hands, especially with a high cervical lesion
- signs of UMN: spastic weakness, increased tone and hyper-reflexia (arms > legs)
- neurological deficit which predicts the level with reasonable accuracy
- bowel and bladder function usually spared

Note LMN signs occur at the level of the lesion and UMN signs and sensory changes below this level.

Causes

- cervical spondylosis
- atlantoaxial subluxation
  - rheumatoid arthritis
  - Down syndrome
- primary spinal cord tumours, e.g. meningiomas
- metastasis to cervical spine → epidural spinal cord compression

Investigations

- CT scan with myelogram (most accurate)

Central cord syndrome[7]

This rather bizarre condition occurs classically in a patient with a degenerative cervical spine following a hyperextension injury which causes osteophytes to compress the cord anteriorly and posteriorly simultaneously.

The maximum damage occurs in the central part of the cord leading to sensory and motor changes in the upper limbs with relative sparing of the lower limbs due to the arrangements of the long tracts in the cord.

Fortunately, the prognosis is good with most patients achieving a good neurological recovery.

Anterior cord syndrome

The anterior cord syndrome occurs with hyperflexion injuries which produce 'tear drop' fractures of the vertebral bodies or extrusion of disc material. The syndrome can also be produced by comminuted vertebral body fractures.

It is characterised by complete motor loss and the loss of pain and temperature discrimination below the level of the injury, but deep touch, position and vibration sensation remain intact.

Because it is probably associated with obstruction of the anterior spinal artery, early surgical intervention to relieve pressure on the front of the cord may enhance recovery. Otherwise the prognosis for recovery is poor.

Down syndrome

One of the more sinister problems with trisomy 21 syndrome is hypoplasia of the odontoid process, leading to C1–2 subluxation and dislocation. If unrecognised in the early stages, sudden death can occur in these children. If suspected, flexion-extension lateral views of the cervical spine will highlight the developing instability and the need for early specialist opinion.

Rheumatoid arthritis

Involvement of the cervical spine is usually a late manifestation of RA. It is important to be aware of the potentially lethal problem of C1–2 instability due to erosion of the major odontoid ligaments in the rheumatoid patient. These patients are especially vulnerable to disasters when under general anaesthesia and when involved in motor vehicle accidents. Early cervical fusion can prevent tragedies, especially with inappropriate procedures such as cervical manipulation. It is imperative to X-ray the cervical spine of all patients with severe RA before major surgery to search for C1–2 instability.

Treatment of spondylotic myelopathy

Conservative (may help up to 50%):[1]

- soft cervical collar
- physiotherapy for muscle weakness
- analgesics and/or NSAIDs

Surgery is indicated when the myelopathy interferes with daily activities. One procedure is the 'Cloward' method which is anterior decompression with discectomy and fusion.

When to refer

- Persisting radicular pain in an arm despite conservative treatment.
- Evidence of involvement of more than one nerve root lesion in the arm.
- Evidence of myelopathy such as weakness, numbness or clumsiness of the upper limbs.
- Evidence, clinical or radiological, of cervical instability in post-accident victims, Down syndrome or rheumatoid arthritis.

Practice tips

- 'One disc—one nerve root' is a working rule for the cervical spine.
- The patient should sit on the couch with the thighs fully supported for inspection and movements of the neck.
- Beware of patients with rheumatoid arthritis and Down syndrome who have cervical instability. Physical treatments such as cervical manipulation may easily cause quadriplegia.
- All acutely painful conditions of the cervical spine following trauma should be investigated with a careful neurological examination of the limbs, sphincter tone and reflexes. Plain film radiology is mandatory.
- In conscious patients, flexion and extension lateral cervical spinal plain films are useful for diagnosing instability of spinal segements with or without associated spinal fractures.
- The so-called 'whiplash' syndrome is a diagnosis of exclusion of spinal fractures or severe ligamentous disruption causing instability, and even then, for medicolegal and psychological reasons, would best be termed a 'soft tissue injury of the cervical spine'.
- Most 'soft tissue cervical spine injuries' heal within three months with conservative treatment. If severe pain persists, follow-up investigations may be required.
- Dysfunction of the cervical spine is an underestimated cause of headache.
- Always consider dysfunction of the cervical spine as a possible cause of shoulder pain.
- Strains and fractures of the apophyseal joints, especially after a whiplash injury, are difficult to detect, and are often overlooked causes of neck and referred pain.

References

1. Cohen ML. Neck pain. Modern Medicine of Australia, November 1989, 44–53.
2. Payne R. Neck pain in the elderly: a management review. Modern Medicine of Australia, July 1988, 56–67.
3. Bogduk N. Neck pain. Aust Fam Physician, 1984; 13:26–29.
4. Kenna C, Murtagh J. *Back pain and spinal manipulation*. Sydney: Butterworths, 1989:212–281.
5. Hart FD. *Practical problems in rheumatology*. London: Dunitz, 1985, 10–14.
6. Sloane PD, Slatt LM, Baker RM. *Essentials of family medicine*. Baltimore: Williams and Wilkins, 1988:236–240.
7. Young D, Murtagh J. Pitfalls in orthopaedics. Aust Fam Physician, 1989; 18:645–646.

53

Shoulder pain

The painful shoulder is a relatively common and sometimes complex problem encountered in general practice. The diagnostic approach involves determining whether the disorder causing the pain arises from within the shoulder structures or from other sources such as the cervical spine (Fig. 53.1), the acromioclavicular joint or diseased viscera, especially heart, lungs and subdiaphragmatic structures.[1]

Key facts and checkpoints

- Virtually all shoulder structures are innervated by the fifth cervical vertebra (C5) nerve root. Pain present in the distribution of C5 can arise from:
  - — cervical spine
  - — upper roots of brachial plexus
  - — glenohumeral joint
  - — rotator cuff tendons, especially supraspinatus
  - — biceps tendon
  - — soft tissue, e.g. polymyalgia rheumatica
  - — viscera, especially those innervated by the phrenic nerve (C3, 4, 5)
- The visceral diseases causing a painful shoulder include cardiac disorders such as angina and pericarditis; lung diseases, especially Pancoast's tumour; mediastinal disorders; and diaphragmatic irritation, as from intra-abdominal bleeding or a subphrenic abscess.

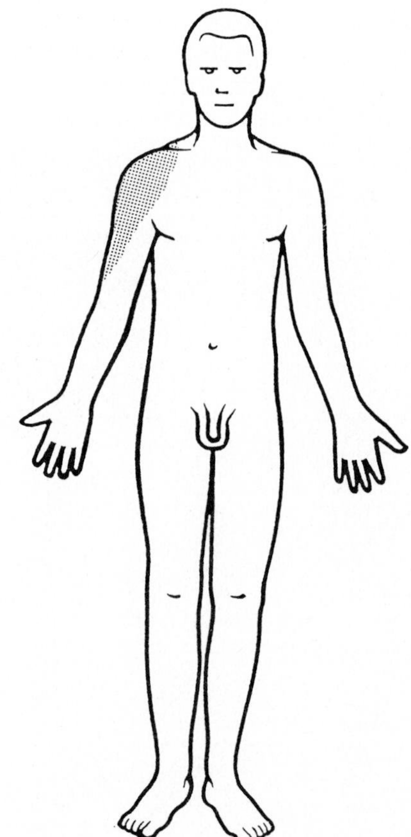

Fig. 53.1 *Typical pain zone arising from disorders of the shoulder joint and the lower cervical spine (C5 level)*

- A careful history should generally indicate whether the neck or the shoulder is responsible for the patient's pain.
- By the age of 50 about 25% of people have some wear and tear of the rotator cuff, making it more injury-prone.[2]
- Disorders of the rotator cuff are common, especially supraspinatus tendinitis. The most effective tests to diagnose these problems are the resisted movement tests.[3]
- Injections of local anaesthetic and long-acting corticosteroid produce excellent results for inflammatory disorders around the shoulder joint, especially for supraspinatus tendinitis.

Functional anatomy of the shoulder

A working knowledge of the anatomical features of the shoulder is essential for the understanding of the various disorders causing pain or dysfunction of the shoulder. Apart from the acromioclavicular (AC) joint there are two most significant functional joints—the glenohumeral (the primary joint) and the subacromial complex (the secondary joint) (Fig. 53.2). The glenohumeral joint is a ball and socket joint enveloped by a loose capsule. It is prone to injury from traumatic forces and develops osteoarthritis more often than appreciated. Two other relevant functional joints are the scapulothoracic and stenoclavicular joints.

The clinically important subacromial space lies above the glenohumeral joint between the head of the humerus and an arch formed by the bony acromion, the thick coracoacromial ligament and the coracoid process. This relatively tight compartment houses the subacromial bursa and the rotator cuff, particularly the vulnerable supraspinatus tendon.[4] Excessive friction and pinching in this space renders these structures prone to injury.

There is a critical zone of relative ischaemia that appears to affect the rotator cuff about 1cm medial to the attachment of the supraspinatus

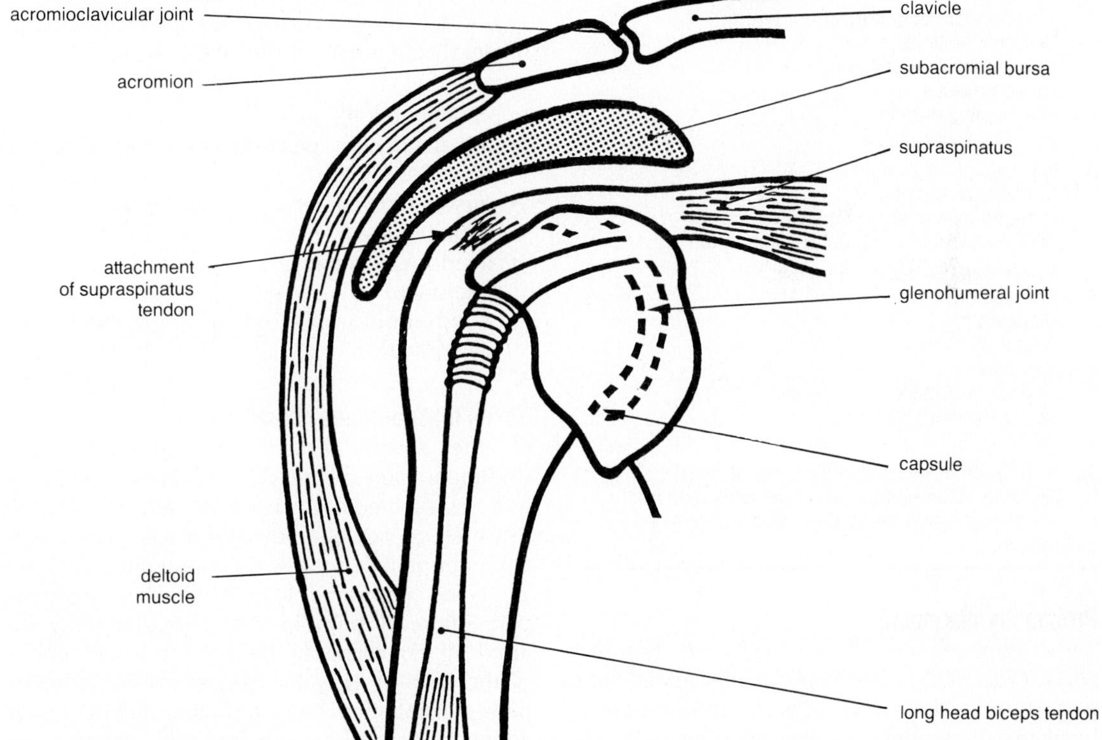

Fig. 53.2 *The basic anatomical structures of the shoulder joint*

tendon[5] and this area is compromised during adduction and abduction of the arm due to pressure on the rotator cuff tendons from the head of the humerus.

Such factors are largely responsible for the many rotator cuff syndromes, bicipital tendinitis, subacromial bursitis and lesions of supraspinatus tendon.

A diagnostic approach

A summary of the safety diagnostic model is presented in Table 53.1.

Table 53.1 *Shoulder pain: diagnostic strategy model*

Q. *Probability diagnosis*
A. Cervical spine dysfunction
Supraspinatus tendinitis

Q. *Serious disorders not to be missed*
A. Cardiovascular
- angina
- myocardial infarction

Neoplasia
- Pancoast's tumour
- primary or secondary in humerus

Severe infections
- septic arthritis (children)
- osteomyelitis

Rheumatoid arthritis

Q. *Pitfalls (often missed)*
A. Polymyalgia rheumatica
Cervical dysfunction
Osteoarthritis of acromioclavicular joint
Winged scapula—muscular fatigue pain

Q. *Seven masquerades checklist*
A.

Depression	✓
Diabetes	✓
Drugs	✓
Anaemia	—
Thyroid dysfunction	rarely
Spinal dysfunction	✓
UTI	—

Q. *Is the patient trying to tell me something?*
A. Shoulder is prone to psychological fixation for secondary gains, depression and conversion reaction.

Probability diagnosis

The commonest causes of pain in the shoulder zone (Fig. 53.1) are cervical disorders and periarthritis, i.e. soft tissue inflammation involving the tendons around the glenohumeral joint. The outstanding common disorders of the shoulder joint are the various disorders of the tendons comprising the rotator cuff and biceps tendon. Of these, supraspinatus tendon disorders, which include tendinitis, calcific degeneration and tearing, are the commonest. It is obvious that the supraspinatus tendon is subjected to considerable friction and wear and tear.

Serious disorders not to be missed

As usual it is important to exclude any malignancy or septic infection, be it septic arthritis or osteomyelitis. Carcinoma of the lung (Pancoast's syndrome) should be kept in mind. For pain in the region of the left shoulder the possibility of myocardial ischaemia (MI) has to be considered. Referred pain to the right shoulder from MI is rare, occurring about once for every 20 episodes of left shoulder referral.

With an acute onset of painful capsulitis the possibility of rheumatoid arthritis (or even gout) is worth considering.

Pitfalls

The shoulder is notorious for diagnostic traps, especially for referred pain from visceral structures, but polymyalgia rheumatica is the real pitfall. A good rule is to consider it foremost in any older person (over 60) presenting with bilateral shoulder girdle pain worse in the morning.

Specific pitfalls include:

- misdiagnosing posterior dislocation of the shoulder joint
- misdiagnosing recurrent subluxation of the shoulder joint
- overlooking an avascular humeral head (post fracture)
- misdiagnosing rotator cuff tear or degeneration

Seven masquerades checklist

Of the seven primary masquerades spinal dysfunction and depression are those most likely to be associated with shoulder pain. The degree to which cervical spondylosis is associated with shoulder pain is not always appreciated.

It is important to realise that patients' perception of pain in the 'shoulder' may be amazing. For example, pain in the lower border of the scapula may be referred to as shoulder pain. Diabetics have a higher incidence of adhesive capsulitis. Drugs are relevant as cortiocosteroids can cause avascular necrosis of the humeral head and anabolic steroids (weightlifters) can cause osteolysis of the AC joint.

Psychogenic considerations

The shoulder is closely connected with psychological factors. Cyriax emphasises this fact with the interesting comment that 'the outstretched arm is a symbol of pleasure and welcome. The arm held into the side is a symbol of rejection. Hence, those who feel withdrawn from the world or view it with disgust readily develop an inability to abduct the arm'.[6]

The clinical approach

History

In analysing the pain pattern it is appropriate to keep the various causes of shoulder pain in mind (Table 53.2). Many of these conditions, such as rheumatoid arthritis, osteoarthritis and gout, are uncommon.

A careful history should generally indicate whether the neck or the shoulder (or both) is responsible for the patient's pain. However, once the shoulder joint is implicated as the source of pain the history is often unrewarding, and the diagnosis is dependent on the physical examination.

Key questions

Did you have any injury, even very minor, before your pain started?

Does the pain keep you awake at night?

Do you have pain or stiffness in your neck?

Do you have pain or restriction when clipping or handling your bra or touching your shoulder blades? (indicates painful internal rotation and a problem of capsular restriction or a disorder of the acromioclavicular joint)

Do you have trouble combing or attending to your hair? (indicates problematic external rotation and also a disorder of the capsule, e.g. adhesive capsulitis)

Do you get the pain on walking or with some stressful activity?

Is the pain worse when you wake in the morning? (indicates inflammation)

Do you have aching in both your shoulders or around your hips?

Do you get pain associated with sporting activity, including weight training, or with housework, dressing or other activities?

Physical examination

The diagnosis is based on systematic examination of the cervical spine followed by examination of the shoulder joint. For details of examination of the cervical spine, refer to Chapter 52.

Table 53.2 *Causes of shoulder pain (excluding trauma, fractures and dislocations*

Cervical
- dysfunction
- spondylosis

Cervical radiculopathy

Polymyalgia rheumatica (bilateral)

Acromioclavicular joint
- dysfunction
- osteoarthritis

Shoulder complex

Subacromial bursitis

Glenohumeral joint
- traumatic adhesive capsulitis
- rheumatoid inflammation
  - — rheumatoid arthritis
  - — ankylosing spondylitis
  - — psoriatic arthropathy
- osteoarthritis

Rotator cuff disorders
- supraspinatus lesions
- infraspinatus tendinitis
- subscapularis tendinitis

Bicipital tendinitis

Winged scapula—muscular fatigue pain

Malignant disease
- primary or secondary in humerus
- Pancoast (ref. lung)

Referred pain

Cardiac
- ischaemic heart disease
- pericarditis

Lung

Mediastinum, including oesophagus

Diaphragmatic irritation

Herpes zoster

Examination of the shoulder

For the examination of the shoulder it is important to understand the functional anatomy of all important tendons.

The tendon disorders are diagnosed by pain on resisted movement (Table 53.3). A knowledge of the anatomical attachments of the rotator cuff tendons to the head of the humerus (Fig. 53.3) provides an understanding of the shoulder movements powered by these muscles.

With tendon disorders (rotator cuff tendons or biceps) there is painful restriction of movement in one direction, but with capsulitis and subacromial bursitis there is usually restriction in all directions.

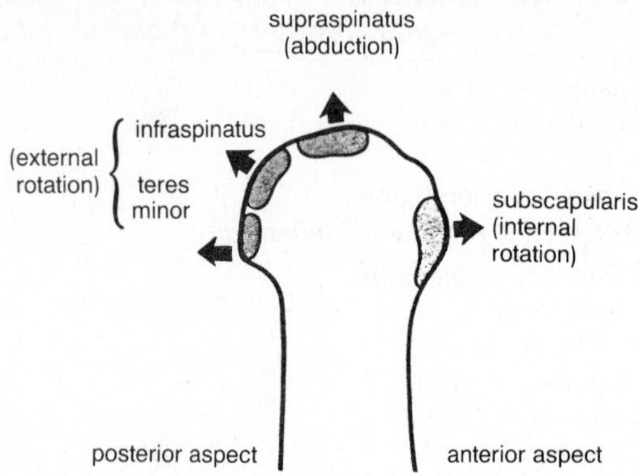

Fig. 53.3 *The attachments of the rotator cuff tendons to the head of the humerus* REPRODUCED FROM C. KENNA AND J. MURTAGH *BACK PAIN AND SPINAL MANIPULATION*, BUTTERWORTHS, SYDNEY, 1989, WITH PERMISSION

Table 53.3 *Tendon disorders: determining resisted movements*

Painful resisted movement at shoulder	***Affected tendon***
1. Abduction	Supraspinatus
2. Internal rotation	Subscapularis * Teres minor
3. External rotation	Infraspinatus * Biceps
4. Adduction	Pectoralis major * Latissimus dorsi

* lesser role

Inspection

Observe the shape and contour of the shoulder joints and compare both sides. Note the posture and the position of the neck and scapulae. The position of the scapulae provides considerable clinical information. Note any deformity, swelling or muscle wasting.

Palpation

Stand behind the patient and palpate significant structures such as the acromioclavicular (AC) joint, the subacromial space, the supraspinatus tendon and the long head of biceps. The subacromial bursa is one area where it is possible to localise tenderness with inflammation. Feel also over the supraspinatus and infraspinatus muscles for muscle spasm and trigger points.

Movements

The movements of the shoulder joint are complex and involve the scapulothoracic joint as well as the glenohumeral joint, with each joint accounting for about half the total range. Significant signs of a painful capsular pattern can be gained by determining the movements of flexion, abduction, external rotation and internal rotation.

For each movement, note:

- the range of movement
- any pain reproduction
- any trick movement by the patient
- scapulothoracic rotation

Movements should be tested bilaterally and simultaneously wherever possible.

1. Active movements

Flexion (anterior elevation) 180°
Extension (posterior elevation) 45°
With the palm facing medially the patient moves the arm upwards through 180° to a vertical position above the head and then backwards through this plane.

Abduction—180°
Adduction— 80° (from neutral position)
Abduction is only possible if the arm is fully externally rotated. It is a key combined glenohumeral and scapulothoracic movement which should reach 180° and these components should be differentiated if the movement is limited. This is done by fixing the scapula with one hand holding the scapula at its inferior angle and noting the degree of movement of each component (initial glenohumeral range 85–100°). Look for the presence of a painful arc, which occurs usually between 60° and 120° of abduction (Fig. 53.4). The commonest cause is supraspinatus tendinitis. Other causes include infraspinatus tendinitis and subacromial bursitis (milder degree).

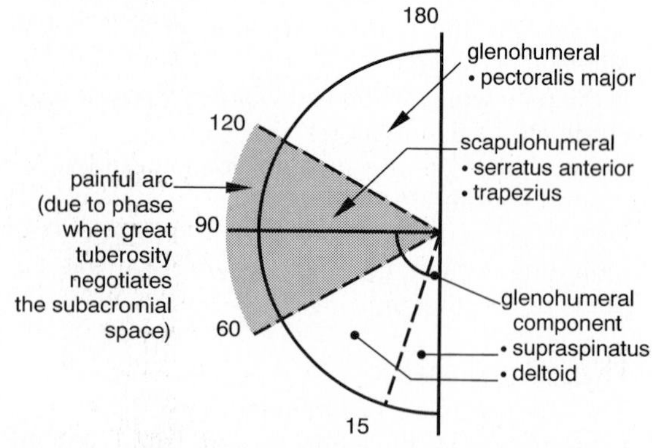

Fig. 53.4 *The painful arc syndrome*

Internal rotation—90°
External rotation—90°
These movements are tested with the arm by the side and the elbow flexed to 90° with palm facing medially. The hand is carried outwards to test external rotation and inwards towards the abdomen for internal rotation.

2. Resisted movements

Resisted movements (isometric contractions of a muscle) are important ways of testing capsulitis and for pinpointing tenderness of muscle insertions around the shoulder joint and no examination of the shoulder is complete without them (see Table 53.3).

Abduction (supraspinatus test) With the arm abducted to no more than 15° the patient pushes the elbow away from the side while the examiner's hands resist and prevent the movement, holding for five seconds. Compare both sides and note any reproduction of the patient's pain.

A better and more specific test for supraspinatus is testing resisted elevation in the 'emptying the can' position (90° of abduction, 30° horizontal flexion and full internal rotation).

Internal rotation (subscapularis test) The examiner stands behind the patient and grasps the palmar surface of the patient's wrists (with the arm by the side and elbow at 90°). The patient attempts to move the forearm internally (medially) against resistance.

External rotation (infraspinatus test) With the examiner and patient adopting a similar position to that for internal rotation, the examiner grasps the dorsal surface of the forearm near the wrist and asks the patient to press outwards, using the forearm as a lever to produce external rotation. This test is also positive for a C5 nerve root lesion.

3. Special tests

Supraspinatus/infraspinatus rapid differentiation test A quick test that helps to differentiate between a lesion of either of these tendons causing a painful arc syndrome is the 'thumbs up/thumbs down' abduction test. To test supraspinatus, perform abduction with thumbs pointing upwards, then with the thumbs pointing downwards to test infraspinatus.

Long head of biceps test The best test is opposed forward elevation of the arm with the elbow straight. A positive test is reproduction of pain in the bicipital groove.

The brachial plexus tension test This test devised by Elvey[7] tests the nerve roots and sheaths of the brachial plexus without implicating the cervical spine and the glenohumeral joint. The upper cervical roots of the plexus are sometimes injured in accidents so this test is an effective differentiation test.

Impingement test for supraspinatus lesions Refer to page 529.

Investigations

Appropriate investigations for shoulder pain include:

- ESR (especially for polymyalgia rheumatica)
- rheumatoid factor
- serum uric acid (acute pain)
- ECG
- radiology
  - X-ray of a specific part of the shoulder, e.g. AC joint, axillary view of glenohumeral joint (best view to show osteoarthritis)
  - X-ray of cervical spine and chest (if relevant)
  - radionuclide bone scan
  - shoot through axillary views (posterior dislocation)
  - ultrasound: modern techniques make this the ideal test to assess shoulder pain due to rotator cuff lesions, especially if surgery is contemplated.
  - arthrogram of shoulder (beware of false negatives)
  - CT scan (limited use)
  - MRI

Shoulder tip pain

Pain at the shoulder tip may be caused by local musculoskeletal trauma or inflammation or can be referred. Referred causes include:

- peptic ulceration
- diaphragmatic irritation
- ruptured viscus, e.g. perforated ulcer
- intraperitoneal bleeding, e.g. ruptured spleen
- pneumothorax
- myocardial infarction

Shoulder pain in children

Shoulder pain in children is not a common presenting problem but the following require consideration:

- septic arthritis/osteomyelitis
- swimmer's shoulder

Swimmer's shoulder

Although it occurs in adults, shoulder pain is the most common complaint in swimmers in the teenage years (over 12 years of age). American studies of college and national competition swimmers showed 40–60% had suffered significant pain.[8]

The problem, which is considered to be associated with abnormal scapular positioning and cervicothoracic dysfunction, occurs in the supraspinatus tendon where an avascular zone is compressed by the greater tuberosity when the arm is adducted and relieved when abducted. Swimmers' shoulders are forced through thousands of revolutions each day so the susceptible area tends to impinge on the coracoacromial arch, leading to the impingement syndrome which can progress with continued stress and age.[9]

Symptoms

Stage 1: pain only after activity
Stage 2: pain at beginning only, then after activity
Stage 3: pain during and after activity, affects performance

Management

- early recognition important
- discuss training program with coach
- consider alteration of technique
- application ICE after each swim
- NSAIDs
- avoid corticosteroid injections
- physiotherapy for scapular stabilisation and cervicothoracic mobilisation

Shoulder pain in the elderly

As a rule most of the shoulder problems increase with age. Special features in the elderly are:

- polymyalgia rheumatica (increased incidence with age)
- supraspinatus tears and persistent 'tendinitis'
- other rotator cuff disorders
- stiff shoulder due to adhesive capsulitis
- osteoarthritis of acromioclavicular and glenohumeral joints
- cervical dysfunction with referred pain
- the avascular humeral head

The avascular humeral head

The humeral head may become avascular after major proximal humeral fractures. With experience, it is usually possible to predict the fractures at special risk. Early humeral head replacement with a prosthesis can lead to excellent pain relief and to a return of good function. Once the head has collapsed, there is secondary capsular contracture. Prosthetic replacement of the head is then rarely associated with an adequate return of joint movement. Thus early referral of comminuted proximal humeral fractures for an expert opinion in all age groups is good practice. Early replacement can improve the functional outcome.[10]

Supraspinatus tendinitis

Supraspinatus tendinitis is the commonest inflammatory problem encountered around the shoulder joint and can vary in intensity from mild to extremely severe. The severe cases usually involve calcification (calcific periarthritis) of the tendon and spread to the subacromial bursa.

Typical pain profile

Site:	the shoulder and outer border of arm; maximal over deltoid insertion
Radiation:	to elbow
Quality:	throbbing pain, can be severe
Frequency:	constant, day and night
Duration:	constant
Onset:	straining the shoulder (e.g. dog on leash, working under car, fall onto outstretched arm)
Offset:	nil
Aggravation:	heat, putting on shirt, toilet activity, lying on shoulder
Relief:	analgesics only
Associated features:	trigger point over supraspinatus origin
Examination (typical features):	• painful resisted abduction • painful arc • painful resisted external rotation • positive impingement test • positive 'emptying the can' sign

The impingement test

This is an effective test for supraspinatus lesions as it forces impingement of the greater tuberosity under the acromion.

Method

- The patient places the arms in the position of semiflexion (90° of forward flexion) and internal rotation with the forearms in full pronation.
- You then test resisted flexion by pushing down as the patient pushes up against this movement (Fig. 53.5).
- If pain is reproduced, this is called a positive 'impingement sign' and is a very sensitive test for the upper components of the rotator cuff, especially supraspinatus.

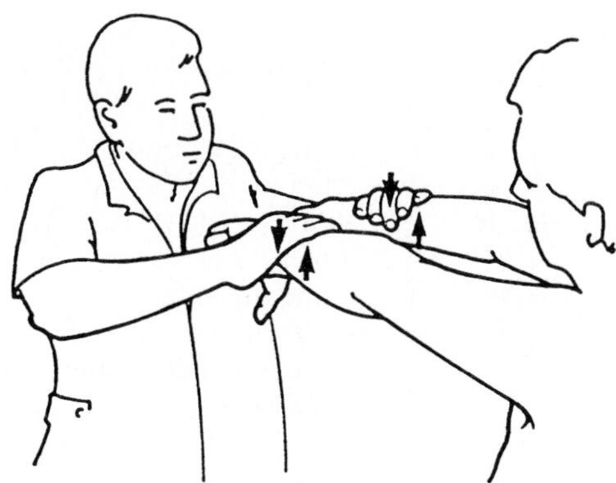

Fig. 53.5 *The impingement test: resisted flexion in semiflexion, internal rotation and pronation*

The 'emptying the can' resistance test

This effective test is described on page 527.

Treatment of supraspinatus tendinitis

- rest during the acute phase
- analgesics
- peritendon injection

Injection technique

The ideal injection is a specific injection onto the tendon rather than general infiltration into the subacromial space. As a rule the therapeutic result is quite dramatic after one or two days of initial discomfort (often severe). The tendon can be readily palpated as a tender cord anterolaterally as it emerges from beneath the acromion to attach to the greater tuberosity of the humerus. This identification is assisted by depressing the shoulder via a downward pull on the arm and then externally and internally rotating the humerus. This manoeuvre allows the examiner to locate the tendon readily.

Method

- Identify and mark the tendon.
- Place the patient's arm behind the back, with the back of the hand touching the far waistline. This locates the arm in the desired internal rotation and forces the humeral head anteriorly.
- Insert a 23-gauge 32 mm needle under the acromion along the line of the tendon, and inject around the tendon just under the acromion (Fig. 53.6). If the gritty resistance of the tendon is encountered, slightly withdraw the needle to ensure that it lies in the tendon sheath.
- The recommended injection is 1 ml of a soluble or long-acting corticosteroid with 5 ml of 1% lignocaine.

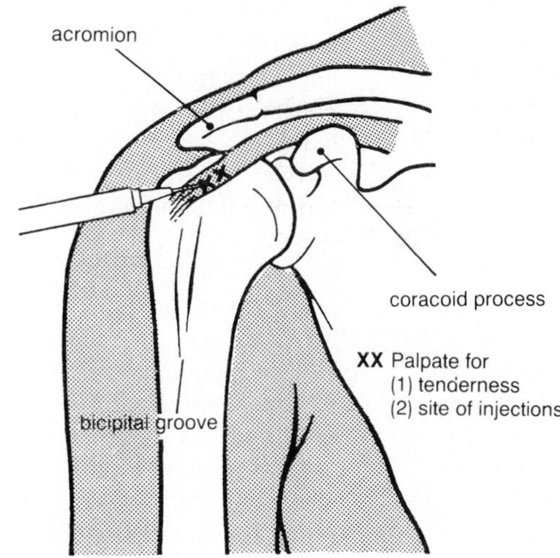

Fig. 53.6 *Injection placement for supraspinatus tendinitis*

Persistent supraspinatus tendinitis

There are three factors to consider with this problem:

1. A very tight subacromial space: refer for subacromial decompression by division of the thickened coracoacromial ligament. Even in

younger patients this procedure (with or without acromioplasty) may be indicated for those with pain persisting beyond 12 months.
2. Rotator cuff tear or degeneration: in middle-aged and elderly patients persisting tendinitis is usually due to rotator cuff tear and degeneration, an underdiagnosed condition. Excellent clinical and functional results can be achieved if surgery is performed when the tear is small.
3. Calcification of the tendon: this problem usually settles but occasionally surgical intervention is necessary.

Subacromial bursitis

Subacromial (subdeltoid) bursitis is the more severe association of the frozen shoulder and may require hospital admission for pain control. It is the only inflammatory disorder around the shoulder joint where localised tenderness is a reliable sign.

Typical pain profile

Site:	outer shoulder, outer arm
Radiation:	to outer elbow and upper forearm
Quality:	intense pain
Frequency:	constant
Duration:	constant
Onset:	either spontaneous or following unaccustomed work
Offset:	nil
Aggravation:	heat, brushing hair, most activities
Relief:	very strong analgesics only
Examination (typical features):	• 'frozen' shoulder • difficult to undress and dress • marked tenderness below acromion over deltoid • all active movements limited and painful

Management

- strong analgesics, e.g. paracetamol and codeine
- large local injection of 5–8 ml of LA into and around the bursa, followed immediately by 1ml of corticosteroid (long-acting) into the focus of the lesion.

Traumatic adhesive capsulitis

Adhesive capsulitis or traumatic arthritis is an acute inflammation affecting the glenohumeral joint associated with trauma which can be trivial or substantial. The differential diagnoses are monoarticular rheumatoid arthritis, a crystal arthropathy such as gout, and septic arthritis.

Typical pain profile

Site:	around the shoulder and outer border of arm
Radiation:	to elbow
Quality:	deep throbbing pain
Frequency:	constant, day and night
Duration:	constant
Onset:	following minor fall onto shoulder, e.g. against wall; wakes the patient from sleep
Offset:	nil
Aggravation:	activity, dressing, combing hair, heat
Relief:	analgesics only (partial relief)
Associated features:	stiffness of arm, may be frozen
Examination (typical features):	• 'frozen' shoulder • all active and passive movements painful and restricted • resisted movements pain-free

Treatment

This problem can persist for at least 12 months so an intra-articular injection of corticosteroid is recommended. Once the acute episode subsides active exercises are important to restore function. Fifty per cent of people with adhesive capsulitis do not regain normal movement.

Persistent restriction of motion is a good reason for referral.

Bicipital tendinitis

Bicipital tendinitis is a tenosynovitis of the long head of biceps. Important signs include pain on restricted flexion of the elbow joint and on resisted supination. A painful arc may be present when the intrascapular part is affected. Hence it is often confused with one of the rotator cuff lesions. Sometimes it is possible to elicit local tenderness along the course of the tendon in the bicipital groove. Most active shoulder movements, especially external rotation, bring on the pain.

Bicipital tendinitis is not a common problem. It usually follows chronic repetitive strains in young to middle-aged adults, e.g. home decorating, tennis, swimming freestyle, cricket and baseball pitching. Two complications are complete rupture and subluxation of the tendon out of its groove.

Typical pain profile

Site:	in front of shoulder
Radiation:	outside and middle of upper arm to just below elbow
Quality:	dull pain, sharp with certain movements
Frequency:	daily, after activity
Duration:	hours
Onset:	can follow activity such as painting and wallpapering
Offset:	rest
Aggravating factors:	tennis, swimming, housework
Relief:	rest
Examination (typical features):	• tender external rotation • painful resisted flexion of elbow • painful resisted supination of elbow • positive Yergason's test • may be painful arc • tender along tendon in bicipital groove
Diagnosis:	detecting abnormal tenderness over tendon in bicipital groove when the arm is externally rotated

Injection method

- The patient sits with arm hanging by the side and palm facing forwards.
- Find and mark the site of maximal tenderness. This is usually in the bicipital groove and more proximal than expected.
- Insert a 23-gauge needle at the proximal end of the bicipital groove above the tender area.
- Slide the needle down the groove to reach the tender area (Fig. 53.7).
- Inject 1 ml of long-acting corticosteroid and 2 ml of LA around this site.

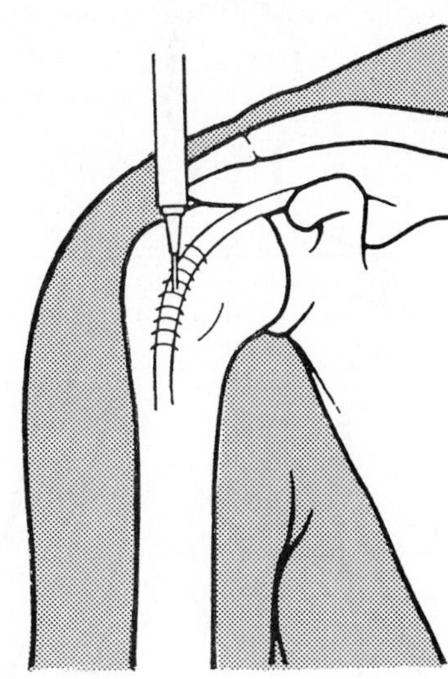

Fig. 53.7 *Injection placement for bicipital tendinitis*

Polymyalgia rheumatica

It is very important not to misdiagnose polymyalgia rheumatica in the older person presenting with bilateral pain and stiffness in the shoulder girdle. It may or may not be associated with hip girdle pain. Polymyalgia rheumatica sometimes follows an influenza-like illness. The patients seem to complain bitterly about their pain and seem flat and miserable. In the presence of a normal physical examination they are sometimes misdiagnosed as 'rheumatics' or 'fibrositis'.

Typical pain profile

Site:	shoulders and upper arms (Fig. 53.8)
Radiation:	towards lower neck
Quality:	a deep intense ache
Frequency:	daily
Duration:	constant but easier in afternoon and evening
Onset:	wakes with pain at greatest intensity
Offset:	nil
Aggravating factors:	staying in bed, inactivity
Relieving factors:	activity (slight relief)
Associated features:	severe morning stiffness 'in muscles' malaise ± weight loss, depression

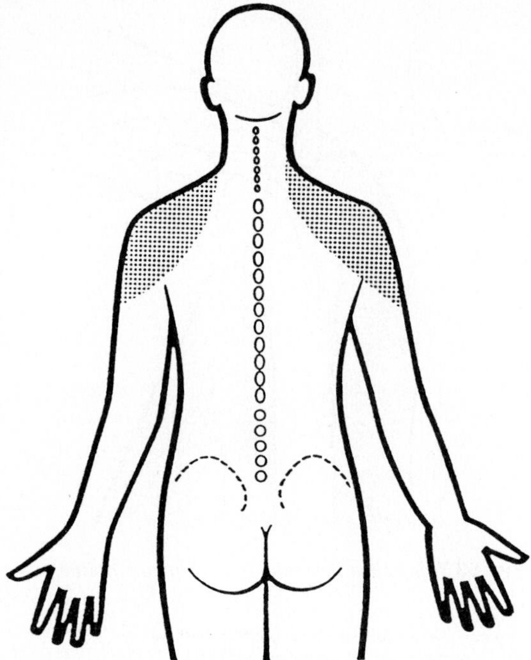

Fig. 53.8 *Polymyalgia rheumatica: typical area of pain around the shoulder girdle*

Diagnosis:	greatly elevated ESR (can be normal)
Treatment:	corticosteroids give dramatic relief but long-term management can be problematic; regular review and support is essential

Posterior dislocation of the shoulder

This is a rare form of shoulder instability which is often misdiagnosed. On first inspection there may not be an obvious abnormality of the shoulder contour. Consider this condition if there is a history of electric shock or a tonic-clonic convulsion. The major clinical sign is painful restriction of external rotation, which is usually completely blocked. Routine shoulder X-rays following trauma should always include the 'axillary shoot through' view and then the diagnosis becomes obvious. Early diagnosis and management can prevent a poor outcome and perhaps litigation.[10]

Recurrent subluxation

Recurrent anterior or inferior subluxations, or both, are probably more common than recurrent dislocations, yet frequently are not diagnosed. Patients complaining of attacks of sudden weakness and even a 'dead arm feeling' lasting for a few minutes with overhead activities of the arm should be investigated for this condition.

The disorder is usually apparent on careful stress testing of the shoulder. Air-contrast computerised tomography (CT) arthrography is considered the best investigation. Surgery is usually curative while conservative treatment often fails for younger patients.

Acromioclavicular osteoarthritis

This condition is usually traumatic or degenerative and is relatively common in builders and sports people, especially rowers. It is treated with rest and support. Intra-articular injections of corticosteroids can be used for resistant or severe cases.

When to refer

- Persisting night pain with shoulder joint stiffness.
- Persisting supraspinatus tendinitis. Consider possibility of rotator cuff tear or degeneration, especially in the elderly.
- Persisting restriction of movement, e.g. restricted cross-body flexion (indicates capsular constriction).
- Persisting supraspinatus tendinitis or other rotator cuff problem, because decompression of the subacromial space with division of the coracoacromial ligament $\pm$ acromioplasty gives excellent results.
- Confirmed or suspected posterior dislocation of the shoulder—the most commonly missed major joint dislocation.
- Confirmed or suspected recurrent subluxation or avascular humeral head.
- Children with shoulder joint instability.
- Swimmer's shoulder refractory to changes in technique and training schedule.
- Severe osteoarthritis of the glenohumeral joint (which usually follows major trauma) for consideration of prosthetic replacement.
- Severe osteoarthritis of acromioclavicular joint.

Practice tips

- Consider dysfunction of the cervical spine, especially C4–C5 and C5–C6 levels, as a cause of shoulder pain.

- Tendinitis and bursitis are very refractory to treatment and tend to last for several months. One well-placed injection of local anaesthetic and corticosteroid may give rapid and lasting relief.
- Test for supraspinatus disorders (including swimmer's shoulder) with the impingement tests, including the 'emptying the can' test.
- Modern ultrasound is the investigation of choice for painful disorders of the rotator cuff, especially to investigate tears in tendons.
- An elderly person presenting with bilateral shoulder girdle pain has polymyalgia rheumatica until proved otherwise. Relief from corticosteroids is dramatic. Although bilateral it may start as unilateral discomfort.
- Dysfunction of the cervical spine can coexist with dysfunction of the shoulder joints.

References

1. Corrigan B. Painful shoulder. Patient Management 1978; 2:23.
2. Sloane PD, Slatt LM, Baker RM. *Essentials of family medicine*. Baltimore: Williams & Wilkins, 1988, 242.
3. Cormack J, Marinker M, Morrell D. *Practice: a handbook of primary health care*. London: Kluwer-Harrap, 1980; 3.62:1–4.
4. Kenna C, Murtagh J. *Back pain and spinal manipulation*. Sydney: Butterworths, 1989, 283–294.
5. Rathburn JB, Macnab I. The microvascular pattern of the rotator cuff. J Bone and Joint Surg, 1970; 52B:540.
6. Cyriax J. *Textbook of orthopaedic medicine Vol. 1* (6th edition). London: Bailliere Tindall, 1976, 202.
7. Elvey R. The investigation of arm pain. In: GP Grieve. *Modern manual therapy of the vertebral column*. London: Churchill Livingstone, 1986:530–5.
8. Dominguez RH. Shoulder pain in swimmers. The Physician and Sportsmedicine, 1980; 8:36.
9. McLean ID. Swimmers' injuries. Aust Fam Physician, 1984; 13:499–500.
10. Young D, Murtagh J. Pitfalls in orthopaedics. Aust Fam Physician, 1989; 18:645–648.

54

Pain in the arm and hand

Pain in the arm and hand is a common problem in general practice, tending to affect the middle aged and elderly in particular.

Overview of causes of a painful arm and hand

Like pain in the shoulder, pain originating from the cervical spine and shoulder disorders can extend down the arm. While pain from disorders of the shoulder joint (because of its C5 innervation) does not usually extend below the elbow, radiculopathies originating in the cervical spine can transmit to distal parts of the arm (Fig. 52.4).

Important causes are illustrated in Figure 54.1. Myocardial ischaemia must be considered, especially for pain experienced down the inner left arm.

Soft tissue disorders of the elbow are extremely common, especially tennis elbow. Two types of tennis elbow are identifiable: 'backhand' tennis elbow, or lateral epicondylitis, and 'forehand' tennis elbow, or medial epicondylitis, which is known also as golfer's or pitcher's elbow.

Other significant elbow disorders include inflammatory disorders of the elbow joint such as rheumatoid arthritis, osteoarthritis and olecranon bursitis, which may follow recurrent trauma, gout, rheumatoid arthritis or infection.

Another important group of disorders are the various regional pain syndromes around the wrists, including the common de Quervain's

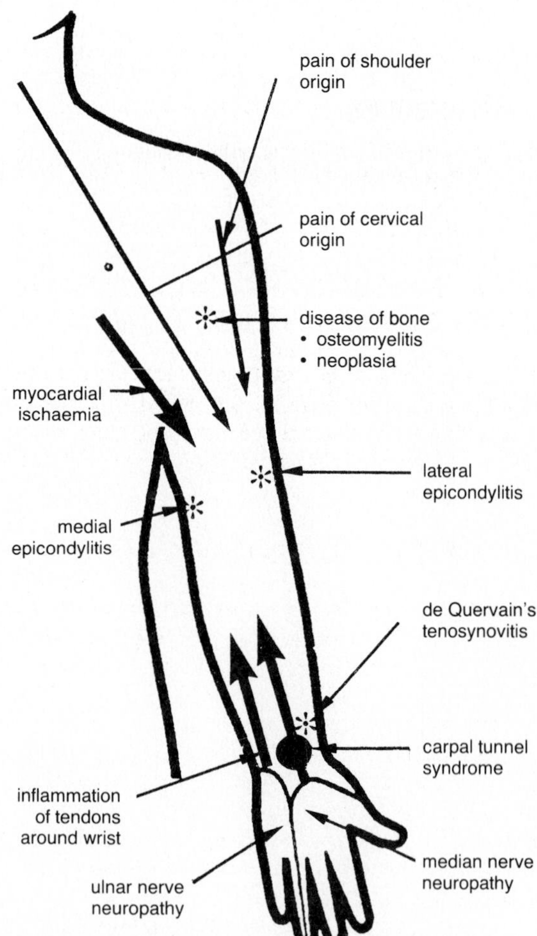

Fig. 54.1 *Important causes of arm pain (excluding trauma and arthritis)*

tenosynovitis (affecting the tendons of extensor pollicis brevis and abductor pollicis longus) and to a lesser extent the extensor tendons to the fingers. Pain from these overuse syndromes can be referred in a retrograde manner into the forearm.

A fascinating and poorly understood syndrome is that related to dysfunction of the upper four vertebral segments of the thoracic spine, which can cause referred pain in the arm that does not correspond to the dermatomes. This syndrome is often confused with the more common regional pain disorders such as tenosynovitis and tennis elbow.

The various causes of the painful arm can be considered with the diagnostic model (Table 54.1).

Table 54.1 *Pain in the arm and hand: diagnostic strategy model*

Q. *Probability diagnosis*
A. Dysfunction of cervical spine (lower)
Disorders of the shoulder
Medial or lateral epicondylitis
Overuse tendinitis of the wrist
Carpal tunnel syndrome
Osteoarthritis of thumb and DIP joints

Q. *Serious disorders not to be missed*
A. Cardiovascular
- angina (referred)
- myocardial infarction

Neoplasia
- Pancoast's tumour
- bone tumours (rare)

Severe infections
- septic arthritis (shoulder/elbow)
- osteomyelitis
- infections of tendon sheath and fascial spaces of hand

Q. *Pitfalls (often missed)*
A. Entrapment neuropathies
e.g. median nerve, ulnar nerve
Pulled elbow—children
Foreign body, e.g. elbow

Rarities
Polymyalgia rheumatica (for arm pain)
Reflex sympathetic dystrophy
Thoracic outlet syndrome
Arm claudication (left arm)
Kienbock's disease

Q. *Seven masquerades checklist*

A.	
Depression	✓
Diabetes	✓
Drugs	—
Anaemia	—
Thyroid disease	—
Spinal dysfunction	✓
UTI	—

Q. *Is the patient trying to tell me something?*
A. Highly likely, especially with so-called RSI syndromes.

A diagnostic approach

Probability diagnosis

The commonest causes of arm pain are referred pain and radiculopathies caused by disorders of the cervical spine, the tennis elbows (lateral and, to a lesser extent, medial epicondylitis), carpal tunnel syndrome and regional pain syndromes caused by inflammation of the tendons around the wrist and thumb.

Disorders of the shoulder, particularly supraspinatus tendinitis, should be considered if the pain is present in the C5 dermatome distribution. Pain in the hand is commonly caused by osteoarthritis of the carpometacarpal joint of the thumb and the distal interphalangeal (DIP) joints and also by the carpal tunnel syndrome.

Serious disorders not to be missed

Like any other presenting problem it is vital not to overlook malignant disease or severe infection. In the case of the arm, possible malignant disease includes tumours in bones, lymphoma involving axillary glands and Pancoast's syndrome.

Neoplastic tumours of the hand are uncommon and usually benign. Benign tumours include giant cell tumour of the tendon sheath, pigmented villonodular synovitis, neurilemmoma and neurofibroma. Malignant tumours are exceptionally rare but can include synovioma and rhabdomyosarcoma.

In addition, myocardial ischaemia, especially infarction in the case of pain of sudden onset, should be considered for left arm pain.

Sepsis can involve joints, the olecranon bursa and the deeper compartments of the hand, the latter leading to serious sequelae if not rapidly diagnosed and treated.

Pitfalls

Such conditions may include entrapment syndromes for peripheral nerves. If in doubt the patient should be referred for electromyography. Variations of peripheral nerve entrapments include the pronator syndrome (compression of the median nerve by the pronator teres or a fibrous band near the origin of the deep flexor muscles) and ulnar nerve entrapment at the elbow in the cubital fossa and, rarely, in Gryon's canal in the wrist.

Lesions of the nerve roots comprising the brachial plexus can also cause arm pain, especially in the C5 and C6 distribution. These can be detected by the brachial plexus tension tests.

Rarer causes of arm pain

These include polymyalgia rheumatica, although the pain typically involves the shoulder girdle, reflex sympathetic dystrophy (Sudek's atrophy) and the thoracic outlet syndromes.

The thoracic outlet syndromes include problems arising from compression or intermittent obstruction of the neurovascular bundle supplying the upper extremity, for example, cervical rib syndrome, costoclavicular syndrome, scalenus anterior and medius syndrome, 'effort thrombosis' of axillary and subclavian veins and the subclavian steal syndrome.

The commonest cause of the thoracic outlet syndrome is sagging musculature related to ageing, obesity, and heavy breasts and arms, aptly described by Swift and Nichols as 'the droopy shoulder syndrome'[1].

Cervical ribs are relatively common and may, or may not, contribute to the thoracic outlet syndrome. Often the cause is a functional change in the thoracic outlet due to the 'droopy shoulder syndrome' with no significant anatomical fault.[2]

Arm claudication is also rare. It can occur with arterial obstruction due to occlusion of the proximal left subclavian artery or the innominate artery. Exercise of the arm may be associated with central nervous system symptoms as well as claudication.

Seven masquerades checklist

Of the seven primary masquerades, spinal dysfunction and depression are those most likely to be associated with arm pain. Nerve root pain arising from entrapment in intervertebral foramina of the cervical spine or from a disc prolapse frequently leads to pain and/or paraesthesia in the arm.

Although diabetic neuropathy primarily manifests in the lower limbs it may be associated with neuropathies in the hands, including erythermalgia (redness and burning related to heat). Hypothyroidism may cause a carpal tunnel syndrome.

Psychogenic considerations

The hand can be regarded as a highly emotive 'organ' that is frequently used to give outward expression to inner feelings. These can range from grossly disturbed psychiatric behaviour, manifested as a hysterical conversion disorder by a non-functioning hand, to occupational neuroses such as repetition strain injury (RSI) and malingering.[3] Experienced occupational physicians and surgeons[3] find the hand and arm a source of functional disability most often as a result of industrial injury. Of great concern are the various so-called RSI disorders, which in some people may be a means of work avoidance or a 'ticket' for compensation or both.

The clinical approach

History

The painful arm represents a real diagnostic challenge so the history is very relevant.

It is common for arm pain to cause sleep disturbances and three causes are cervical disorders, carpal tunnel syndrome and the thoracic outlet syndrome. The working rule is:

- thoracic outlet syndrome—patients cannot fall asleep
- carpal tunnel syndrome—patients wake in the middle of the night
- cervical spondylosis—wakes the patient with pain and stiffness that persists well into the day[4]

The history should include an analysis of the pain and a history of trauma, particularly unaccustomed activity. In children evidence should be obtained about the nature of any injury, especially pulling the child up by the arms or a fall on an outstretched hand which can cause potentially serious fractures around the elbow.

Physical examination

As part of the physical examination of the painful arm it may be necessary to examine a variety of joints including the cervical spine (Chapter 52), shoulder (Chapter 53), elbow, wrist and the various joints of the hand. The arms should be inspected as a whole and it is very important to have both arms free of clothing and compare both sides.

Elbow joint

Inspection (from anterior, lateral and posterior aspects) Hold in an anatomical position to measure the carrying angle of forearm—elbow fully extended, forearm supinated (palm facing forwards) normal 5–15° (greater in females). Note any swellings:

- olecranon bursitis (bursa over olecranon)
- nodules
  - RA (subcutaneous border ulna)
  - gout
  - SLE (rare) and rheumatic fever (very rare)
  - granulomas, e.g. sarcoid

Palpation Perform with patient supine and elbow held in approximately 70° flexion. Palpate bony landmarks and soft tissue. Note especially any tenderness over lateral epicondyle (tennis elbow) and medial epicondyle (golfer's elbow).

Movement (test active and passive) Hinge joint:

- extension—flexion (0° to 150°)
  - the arc for daily living is 30–130°
  - limitation of extension is an early sign of synovitis
- pronation–supination (rotation)
  - occurs at radiohumeral joint
  - test in two positions:
    1. 90° flexion (held to side of body)
    2. at full extension
  - supination 85° plus
  - pronation 75° plus

Resisted movements

- painful resisted flexion at wrist = medial epicondylitis
- painful resisted extension at wrist = lateral epicondylitis

Wrist joint

Follow the usual rules: LOOK, FEEL, MOVE, TEST FUNCTION, MEASURE and X-RAY. Note swellings or deformities, including the anatomical snuff box and distal end of radius. Feel for heat, tenderness and swelling, especially over the radial aspect of the wrist.

Movements With elbow fixed at 90° and held into the waist:

1. Compare dorsiflexion and palmar flexion on both sides (normal range 80–90°).
2. Compare ulnar deviation (normal to 45°) and radial deviation (30°).
3. Compare pronation and supination (normal to 90° for both).

Neurological examination
Test sensation, motor power and reflexes where indicated.

Summary of tests for motor power:

C5—test resisted movement deltoid
C6—test resisted movement biceps
C7—test resisted movement triceps
C8—test resisted EPL and FDL
T1—test resisted interossei

Investigations

Pain in the arm and hand can be difficult to diagnose but the rule to follow is: 'If in doubt, X-ray and compare both sides'. This applies particularly to elbow injuries in children. The presence of a foreign body in the hand or arm also requires consideration.

Investigations to consider include:

- blood film and WCC
- ESR
- ECG
- X-rays
  - cervical spine
  - upper thoracic spine
  - elbow/forearm/shoulder
  - wrist and hand
  - ultrasound
  - arthrograms (shoulder, elbow, wrist)
  - CT scanning
  - technetium bone scan
- nerve conduction studies
- electromyography

NB Modern sophisticated ultrasound examination is becoming a vital diagnostic modality for soft tissue disorders.

Arm pain in children

The main concerns with children are the effects of trauma, especially around the elbow. Considerable awareness of potential problems and skilful management is required with children's elbow fractures. Foreign bodies in the arm also have to be considered.

Pulled elbow

This typically occurs in children under 8 years of age, usually at 2–5 years, when an adult applies sudden traction to the child's extended and pronated arm: the head of the radius can be pulled distally through the annular radioulnar ligament (Fig. 54.2a).[5]

Symptoms and signs

- The crying child refuses to use the arm.
- The arm is limp by the side or supported in the child's lap.
- The elbow is flexed slightly (any flexion will be strenuously resisted).
- The forearm is pronated or held in mid-position (Fig. 54.2b).
- The arm is tender around the elbow (without bruising or deformity).

Note An X-ray is not necessary.

Treatment method

1. Gain the child's confidence.
2. The child stands facing the doctor with the parent holding the non-affected arm.
3. Place one hand around the child's elbow to give support, pressing the thumb over the head of the radius.
4. With the other hand, firmly and smoothly flex the elbow and suddenly and firmly twist the forearm into full supination (Fig. 54.2c). A faint click (which will be painful) will be heard. After a few minutes the child will settle and resume full pain-free movement. Warn parents that recurrences are possible up to 6 years.

Note Spontaneous resolution can occur eventually.

Fractures and avulsion injuries around the elbow joint, which are a major problem in children, are discussed in more detail in Chapter 106.[6]

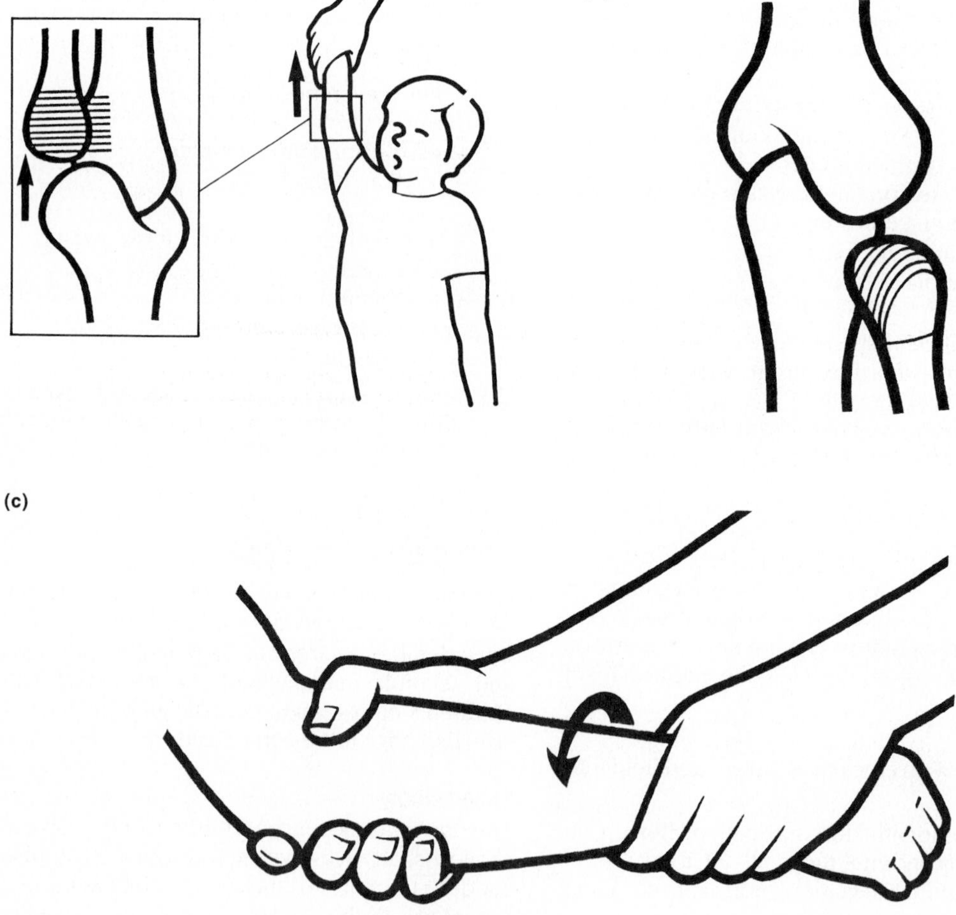

Fig. 54.2 *Pulled elbow:* **(a)** *mechanism of injury;* **(b)** *annular ligament displaced over head of radius;* **(c)** *reduction by supination*

Arm pain in the elderly

Elderly patients are more likely to be affected by problems such as referred pain, radiculopathy or myelopathy from cervical spondylosis, tumours, polymyalgia rheumatica, entrapment neuropathies such as carpal tunnel syndrome and ulnar nerve entrapment. The latter can be related to trauma such as Colle's fractures. In addition the elderly are more prone to suffer from the thoracic outlet syndrome as previously described under 'Pitfalls'. Osteoarthritis of the hand and tenosynovitis, such as trigger thumb or finger, are more common with advancing age.

Tennis elbow

Tennis elbow is caused by overuse or overload of the muscles of the forearm, especially in the middle aged. Two types are identifiable: 'backhand' tennis elbow, or lateral epicondylitis, and 'forehand' tennis elbow, or medial epicondylitis, which is known also as golfer's, or pitcher's elbow. 'Backhand' tennis elbow, which will be termed lateral tennis elbow, is the common classic variety. It is caused by excessive strain on the extensor muscles of the forearm resulting from wrist extension.

Lateral tennis elbow (lateral epicondylitis)

The patient who presents with this common and refractory problem is usually middle-aged (between 40 and 60 years of age) and only about one in 20 plays tennis. It is common in golfers, carpenters, bricklayers, squash players, violinists and housewives.

The disorder is obviously an overuse sporting or occupational injury, being common in those who are relatively unfit or those commencing an unaccustomed activity. Tennis elbow is an overload injury following mainly minor and often unrecognised trauma (microtrauma), involving the extensor muscles of the forearm. It may be provoked by any exercise that involves repeated and forcible extension movements of the wrist, such as playing tennis, using a screwdriver, wringing wet clothes, carrying buckets or picking up bricks.

Symptoms

Tennis elbow usually has a gradual onset but occasionally it can be sudden. At the moment the tear occurs the patient feels nothing. Several days after this event, an ache in the forearm is noticed when movements involve extension of the wrist. The ache gets worse and a tennis player is unable to play. The typical clinical profile is presented in Table 54.2.

Table 54.2 *Lateral tennis elbow: typical clinical profile*

Age:	40–60
Occupation:	carpenter, bricklayer, housewife, gardener, dentist, violinist
Sport:	tennis, squash
Symptoms:	• pain at outer elbow, referred down back of forearm • rest pain and night pain (severe cases) • pain in the elbow during hand movements, e.g. turning on taps, turning door handles, picking up objects with grasping action, carrying buckets, pouring tea, shaking hands
Signs:	• no visible swelling • localised tenderness over lateral epicondyle, anteriorly • pain on passive stretching wrist • pain on resisted extension wrist • normal elbow movement
Course:	6 to 24 months
Management:	Basic • rest from offending activity • RICE and oral NSAIDs if acute • exercises—stretching and strengthening Additional (if refractory) • corticosteroid/LA injection (maximum two) • manipulation • surgery

RICE: rest, ice, compression, elevation
LA: local anaesthetic

Signs

On examination the elbow looks normal and flexion and extension is painless.

There are three important positive physical signs:

1. localised tenderness to palpation over the anterior aspect of the lateral epicondyle
2. pain on passive stretching at the wrist with the elbow held in extension and the forearm prone (Fig. 54.3)
3. pain on resisted extension of the wrist with the elbow held in extension and the forearm prone (Fig. 54.4)

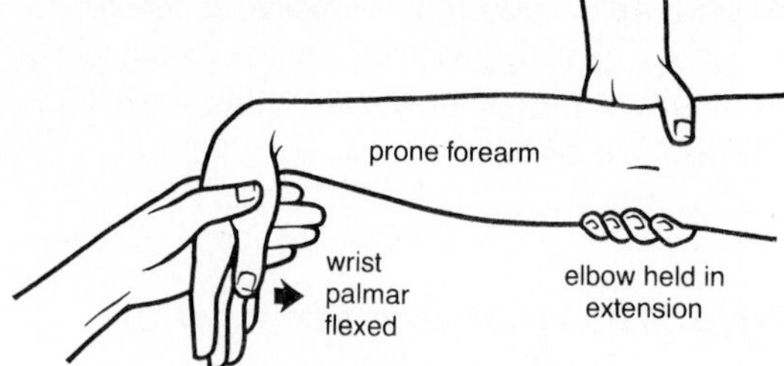

Fig. 54.3 *Lateral tennis elbow test: reproducing pain on passive stretching at the wrist*

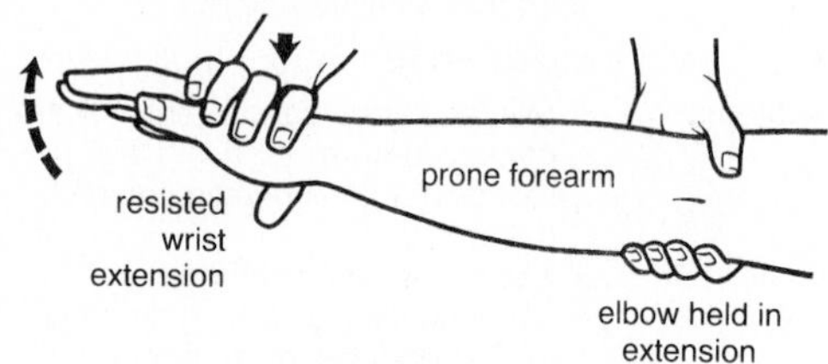

Fig. 54.4 *Lateral tennis elbow test: reproducing pain on resisted extension of the wrist*

Management

Although there are a myriad of treatments the cornerstones of therapy are rest from the offending activity and exercises to strengthen the extensors of the wrist.

Exercises

Stretching and strengthening exercises for the forearm muscles represent the best management for tennis elbow. Three options are presented.

1. *The wringing exercise* Chronic tennis elbow can be cured by a simple wringing exercise using a small hand towel.[7]

Method

- Roll up the hand towel.
- With the arm extended, grasp the towel with the affected side placed in neutral.
- Then exert maximum wring pressure:
  — first flexing the wrist for 10 seconds
  — then extending the wrist for 10 seconds

  This is an isometric 'hold' contraction.

This exercise should be performed only twice a day, initially for 10 seconds in each direction. After each week increase the time by 5 seconds in each twisting direction until 60 seconds is reached (week 11). This level is maintained indefinitely.

Note Despite severe initial pain, the patient must persist, using as much force as possible. Review at six weeks to check progress and method.

2. *'Weights' exercise* The muscles are strengthened by the use of hand-held weights or dumbbells. A suitable starting weight is 0.5 kg, building up gradually (increasing by 0.5 kg) to 5 kg, depending on the patient.

Method

- To perform this exercise the patient sits in a chair beside a table.
- The arm is rested on the table so that the wrist extends over the edge.
- The weight is grasped with the palm facing downwards (Fig. 54.5).
- The weight is slowly raised and lowered by flexing and extending the wrist.
- The flexion/extension wrist movement is repeated 10 times, with a rest for 1 minute, and the program repeated twice.

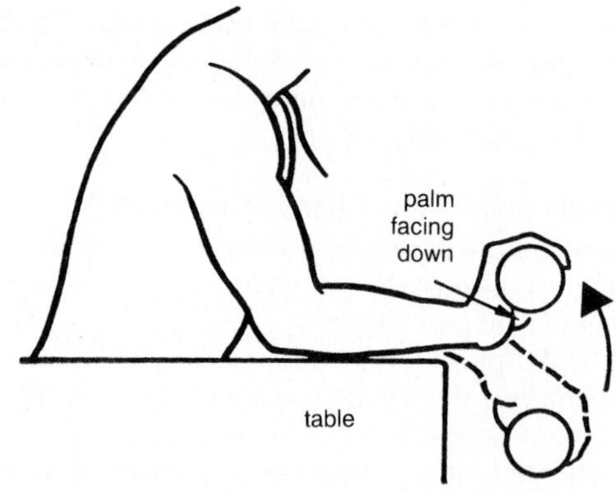

Fig. 54.5 *Lateral tennis elbow: the dumbbell exercise with the palm facing down*

3. *The pronating exercise* A suitable stretching exercise is to rhythmically rotate the hand and wrist inwards with the elbow extended and the forearm pronated (Fig. 54.6). Another proven exercise program is that outlined by Nirschl[9] and this can be provided by referral to a physiotherapist familiar with the program.

Injection therapy

The injection of 1 ml of corticosteroid and 1 ml of local anaesthetic should be reserved for more severe cases when pain occurs on most activities, and not used initially for those patients with only intermittent pain. The key to a successful injection

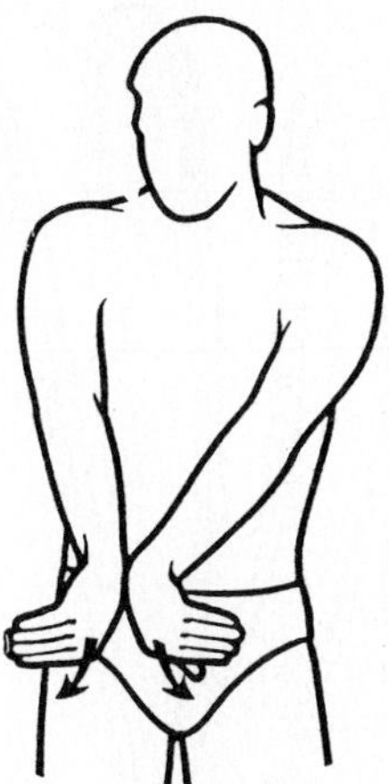

Fig. 54.6 *Tennis elbow stretching exercise: the hand and wrist are rhythmically rotated inwards until the painful point is reached*

is to have the tender lesions pinpointed precisely. The point of maximal tenderness is usually on or just distal to the lateral epicondyle.

Method

- The patient sits with the elbow resting on a table, flexed to a right angle and fully supinated.
- Using an anterior approach, palpate the tender area and mark it with a pen.
- With the thumb (of the non-dominant hand) over the patient's lateral epicondyle to stretch the skin and the fingers spread out around the elbow to steady it, insert the needle (25 or 23 gauge) vertically downwards to touch the periosteum of the tender point (Fig. 54.7).
- After introducing about 0.5 ml of the mixed solution, partly withdraw the needle and reinsert it to ensure that the tender area is covered both deeply and superficially.

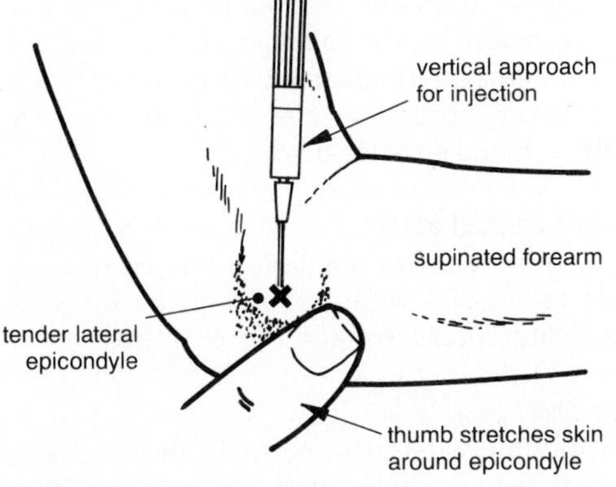

Fig. 54.7 *Lateral tennis elbow: injection technique*

Postinjection:

- Ask patient to 'work it in' during the next few hours with repeated extensions of the elbow joint and pronation of the wrist.
- Warn the patient that the area will be very painful for the next 24 hours and recommend moderately strong analgesics.
- Repeat the injection in 2–4 weeks unless all the symptoms have been abolished.
- A maximum of two injections only is recommended.

Surgery

Severe and refractory cases can be referred for surgery but this is rarely indicated. It appears to have about a 70% success rate. The usual procedure is stripping of the common extensor origin combined with debridement of any granulation tissue.[3]

Medial tennis elbow (medial epicondylitis)

In 'forehand' tennis elbow, or golfer's elbow, the lesion is the common flexor tendon at the medial epicondyle. The pain is felt on the inner side of the elbow and does not radiate far. The main signs are localised tenderness to palpation and pain or resisted flexion of the wrist.

In tennis players it is caused by stroking the ball with a bent forearm action or using a lot of top spin, rather than stroking the ball with the arm extended.

The treatment is similar to that for lateral epicondylitis except that in a dumbbell exercise program that palm must face upwards.

A similar injection method is used to that for lateral epicondylitis. The elbow is flexed and supinated with full external rotation of the shoulder of the affected arm. The anterior approach is used, and the tender area of the medial epicondyle injected as for lateral epicondylitis.

After-care and prevention

Tennis should be resumed gradually. Players recovering from tennis elbow should start quietly with a warm-up period and obtain advice on style, including smooth stroke play. During a game they should avoid elbow bending and 'wristy' shots. A change to a good quality racket (wooden or graphite frame) with a medium-sized head and suitable grip size may be appropriate.[9] The patient should be advised not to use a tightly strung, heavy racket or heavy tennis balls. It is worthwhile to advise the use of a non-stretch band or brace situated about 7.5 centimetres (3 inches) below the elbow.

Olecranon bursitis

Olecranon bursitis presents as a swelling localised to the bursa (which has a synovial membrane) over the olecranon process. The condition may be caused by trauma, arthritic conditions (rheumatoid arthritis and gout) or infection.

Traumatic bursitis may be caused by a direct injury to the elbow or by chronic friction and pressure as occurs in miners (beat elbow), truck drivers or carpet layers. Acute olecranon bursitis with redness and warmth can occur in rheumatoid arthritis, gout, pseudogout, haemorrhage and infection (sepsis).[10] Septic bursitis must be considered where the problem is acute or subacute in onset and hence aspiration of the bursa contents with appropriate laboratory examination is necessary (smear, gram stain, culture and crystal examination). Treatment depends on the cause.

Simple aspiration/injection technique

Chronic recurrent traumatic olecranon bursitis with a synovial effusion may require surgery but most cases can resolve with partial aspiration of the fluid and then injection of corticosteroid through the same needle.

Carpal tunnel syndrome

Patients with carpal tunnel syndrome (CTS) complain of 'pins and needles' affecting the pulps of the thumb, index, middle and half of the ring finger (Fig. 54.8). They usually notice these symptoms after, rather than during, rapid use of the hands. They may also complain of pain, which may even radiate proximally as far as the shoulder, from the volar aspect of the wrist. Causes or associations of carpal tunnel syndrome are presented in Table 54.3.

The pathognomonic symptom

Patients complain of awakening from their sleep at night with 'pins and needles' affecting the fingers. They get out of bed, shake their hands, the 'pins and needles' subside and they return to sleep. In severe cases, the patient may awaken two or three times a night and go through the same routine.

Work-related CTS

CTS is seen in many work situations requiring rapid finger and wrist motion under load such as meat workers and process workers. A type of flexor tenosynovitis develops and thus nerve compression in the tight tunnel. It is advisable to arrange confirmatory investigations by nerve conduction studies and electromyography for this work-induced overuse disorder.

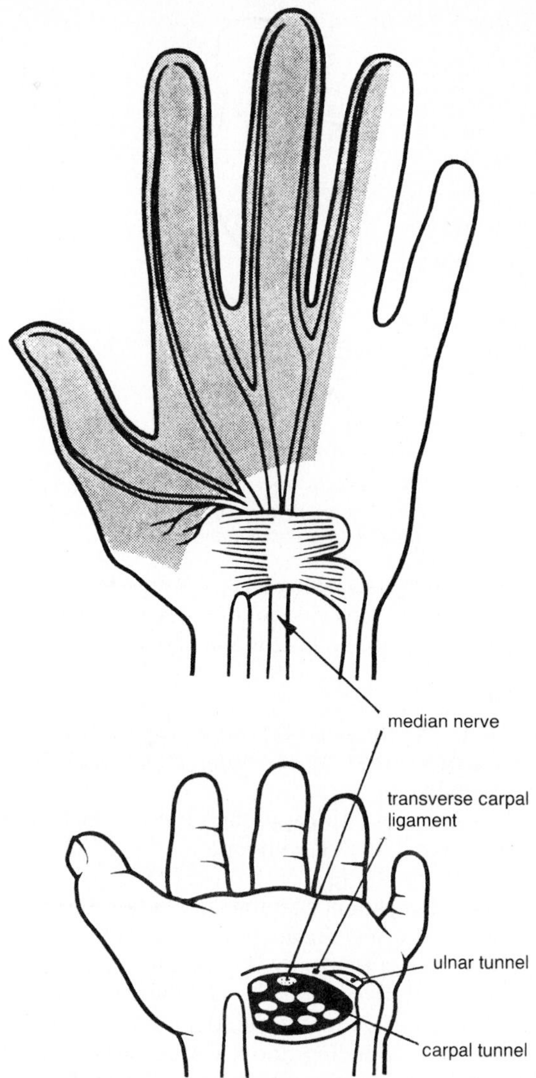

Fig. 54.8 *Carpal tunnel syndrome (median nerve compression syndrome)*

Simple clinical tests

In the physical examination a couple of simple tests can assist with confirming the diagnosis. These are Tinel's test and Phalen's test.

The Tinel test

- Hold the wrist in a neutral or flexed position and tap over the median nerve at the flexor

Table 54.3 *Carpal tunnel syndrome: causes or associations*

Idiopathic
Trauma
Fibrosis
Granulomatous disorders (TB, etc.)
Rheumatoid arthritis
Acromegaly
Amyloidosis
Pregnancy
Premenstrual oedema
Hypothyroidism
Paget's disease
Diabetes mellitus
Tophaceous gout

surface of the wrist. This should be over the retinaculum just lateral to the palmaris longus tendon (if present) and the tendons of flexor digitorium superficialis (Fig. 54.9).

- A positive Tinel's sign produces a tingling sensation (usually without pain) in the distribution of the median nerve.

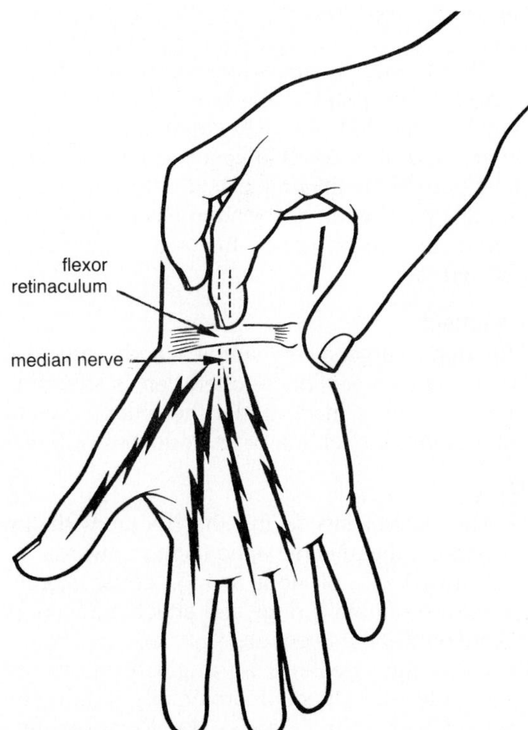

Fig. 54.9 *Carpal tunnel syndrome: Tinel sign*

The Phalen test

- The patient approximates the dorsum of both hands, one to the other, with wrists maximally flexed and fingers pointing downwards (Fig. 54.10).
- This position is held for 60 seconds.
- A positive test reproduces tingling and numbness along the distribution of the median nerve.

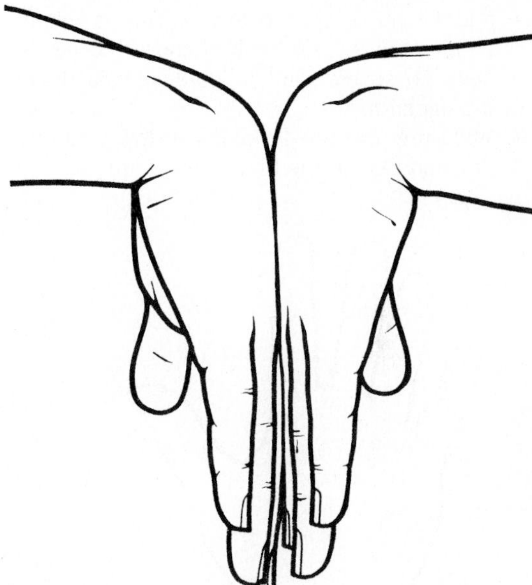

Fig. 54.10 *Carpal tunnel syndrome: Phalen's sign*

Treatment

The treatment is determined by the severity. For mild cases simple rest and splinting (particularly at night) is sufficient. Carpal tunnel corticosteroid infiltration is frequently of diagnostic as well as therapeutic value. Surgical release is necessary for patients with sensory or motor deficits and those with recalcitrant CTS.

Injection into the carpal tunnel

Injections may relieve symptoms permanently or, more commonly, temporarily. The injections may be repeated. Do *not* use local anaesthetic in the injection.

Method

- The patient sits by the side of the doctor with the hand palm upwards, the wrist slightly extended.
- Identify the palmaris longus tendon and ulnar artery.

- Insert the needle (23G) at a point about 2.5–3 cm proximal to the main transverse crease of the wrist and between the palmaris longus tendon and the artery (Fig. 54.11). Take care to avoid the superficial veins.
- Advance the needle distally, parallel to the tendons and nerve at about 5° to the horizontal. It should pass under the transverse carpal ligament (flexor retinaculum) and come to lie in the carpal tunnel.
- Inject 1 ml of corticosteroid. This is usually painless and runs freely. Ensure the patient feels no severe pain or paraesthesia during the injection.
- Withdraw the needle and ask the patient to flex and extend the fingers for 2 minutes.

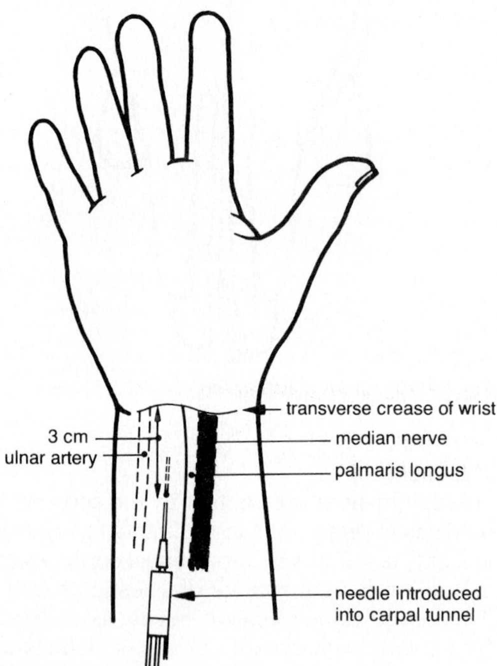

Fig. 54.11 *Injection technique for carpal tunnel syndrome*

Trigger finger/thumb

In the fingers the common work-induced condition is stenosing flexor tenosynovitis, also known as trigger thumb and finger. It is caused by the same mechanism as de Quervain's stenosing tenosynovitis. In middle age these tendons, which are rapidly and constantly being flexed and extended, can undergo attrition wear and tear and fibrillate and fragment; this causes swelling, oedema and painful inflammation and the formation of a nodule on the tendon that triggers back and forth across the thick, sharp edge of the 'pulley' (of the fibrosseous tunnel in the finger) (Fig. 54.12).

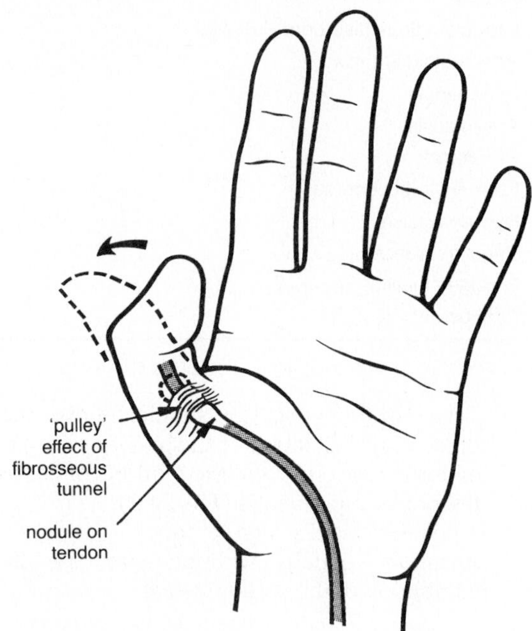

Fig. 54.12 *Trigger thumb*

These patients may present with a finger locked in the palm of the hand; the finger can only be extended passively (manually) with the other hand. It is easily diagnosed by triggering. If the pulp of the finger is placed over the 'pulley' crepitus can be felt and tenderness elicited. The thumb and fourth (ring) finger are commonly affected.

Treatment

Although surgery is simple and effective, treatment by injection is often very successful. The injection is made under the tendon sheath and not into the tendon or its nodular swelling.

Method

- The patient sits facing the doctor with the palm of the affected hand facing upwards.
- Draw 1 ml of long-acting corticosteroid solution into a syringe and attach a 25 gauge needle for the injection.
- Insert the needle at an angle distal to the nodule and direct it proximally within the tendon sheath (Fig. 54.13). This requires tension on the skin with free fingers.

- By palpating the tendon sheath, you can (usually) feel when the fluid has entered the tendon sheath.
- Inject 0.5–1 ml of the solution, withdraw the needle and ask the patient to exercise the fingers for 1 minute.

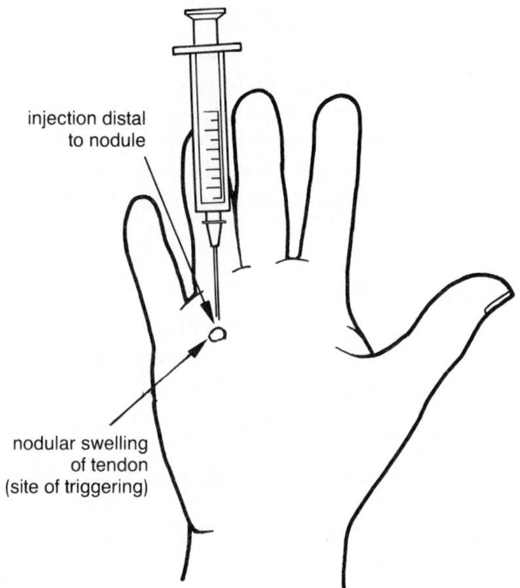

Fig. 54.13 *Injection site for trigger finger*

Postinjection

Improvement usually occurs after 48 hours and may be permanent. The injection can be repeated after three weeks if the triggering is not completely relieved. If triggering recurs, surgery is indicated. This involves division of the thickened tendon sheath only.

De Quervain's tenosynovitis (washerwoman's sprain)

At the wrist a not uncommon work-induced condition is de Quervain's stenosing tenosynovitis of the first dorsal extensor compartment tendons (extensor pollicus brevis and abductor pollicis longus) which pass along the radial border of the wrist to the base of the thumb. It is usually seen when the patient is required to engage in rapid, repetitious movements of the thumb and the wrist, especially for the first time, and thus is common in assembly line workers, such as staple gun operators.

Clinical features

- typical age 40–50
- pain at and proximal to wrist on radial border
- pain during pinch grasping
- pain on thumb and wrist movement
- dull ache or severe pain (acute flare-up)
- can be disabling with inability to use hand, e.g. writing

Triad of diagnostic signs

- tenderness to palpation over and just proximal to radial styloid
- firm tender localised swelling in area of radial styloid (may be mistaken for exostosis)
- positive Finklestein's sign (the pathognomonic test)

Finklestein's test

- The patient folds the thumb into the palm with the fingers of the involved hand folded over the thumb, thus making a fist.
- Rotate the wrist in an ulnar direction to stretch the involved tendons as you stabilise the forearm with the other hand (Fig. 54.14).
- A positive test is indicated by reproduction of or increased pain.

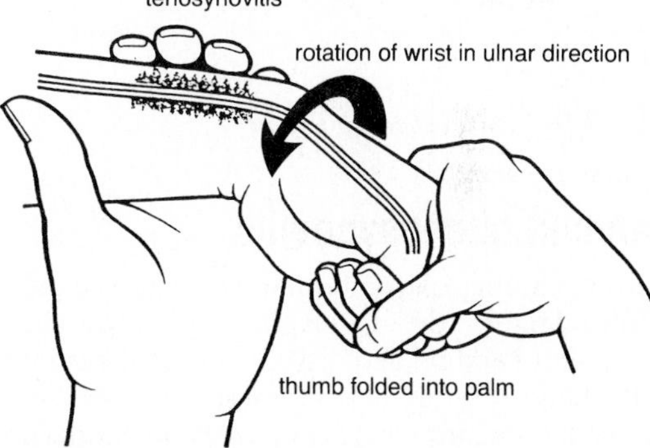

Fig. 54.14 *Finkelstein's test*

Treatment

- Resting and avoidance of the causative stresses and strains on the thumb abductors.
- A custom-made splint that involves the thumb and immobilises the wrist.
- Local long-acting corticosteroid injection can relieve and may even cure the problem but care should be taken to inject the suspension within the tendon sheath rather than into the tendon.
- Surgical release is required for chronic cases.

Method of tendon sheath injection

- Identify and mark the most tender site of the tendon and the line of the tendon. Identify and avoid the radial artery.
- Thoroughly cleanse the skin with an antiseptic such as providone iodine 10% solution.
- Insert the tip of the needle (23G) about 1 cm distal to the point of maximal tenderness (Fig. 54.15).
- Advance the needle almost parallel to the skin along the line of the tendon.
- Inject about 0.5 ml of the corticosteroid suspension within the tendon sheath. If the needle is in the sheath very little resistance to the plunger should be felt, and the injection causes the tendon sheath to billow out.

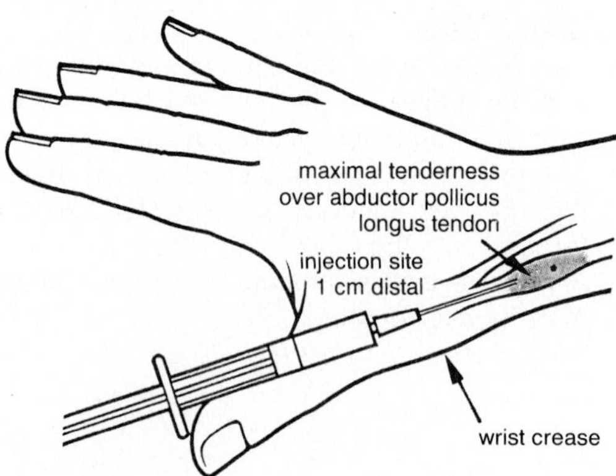

Fig. 54.15 *Tendon sheath injection*

Tendinitis/tenosynovitis

After excluding carpal tunnel syndrome, trigger thumb/finger, de Quervain's tenosynovitis, rheumatoid and related disease, tendinitis is rare in the hand.[11] Tendinitis may rarely occur in other extensor compartments of the wrist and hand with unusual repetitive stressful actions such as power drills jamming, and in conveyer quality control where an object is picked up with the forearm prone, supinating to examine it and pronating to replace it.

Treatment is rest from the provoking activity, splintage and tendon sheath injection with long-acting corticosteroid in a manner similar to that described for de Quervain's tenosynovitis.

Neurovascular disorders of the hand

Painful vascular disorders, which are more likely to occur in women in cold weather, include Raynaud's phenomenon, erythermalgia, chilblains and acute blue fingers syndrome. Acrocyanosis is not a painful condition.

Raynaud's phenomenon and disease

The basic feature of Raynaud's phenomenon, which is a vasospastic disorder, is sequential discolouration of the digits from pallor to cyanosis to rubor upon exposure to cold and other factors (a useful mnemonic is WBR, namely white → blue → red). The rubor is a reactive hyperaemia when fingers become red and tender. It is possible to get loss of tissue pulp at the ends of the fingers and subsequent necrotic ulcers.

Causes

- Raynaud's disease (idiopathic)
- Occupational trauma (vibrating machinery)
- Connective tissue disorders
  - rheumatoid arthritis
  - SLE
  - systemic sclerosis, CREST
  - polyarteritis nodosa
- Arterial disease
  - Buerger's disease
- Haematological disorders
  - polycythaemia
  - cold agglutinin disease
  - leukaemia
- Drugs
  - beta-blockers
  - ergotamine

Investigations

Exclude underlying causes with appropriate tests.

Treatment

- total body protection from cold
- gloves and thick woollen socks
- avoid smoking
- vasodilators, e.g. reserpine (o) 0.25–5 mg/day during cold weather
- topical glyceryl trinitrate ointment
- consider sympathectomy

Erythermalgia

This condition is characterised by erythema (redness), a burning sensation and swelling of the hands (and feet) after exposure to heat and exercise. It may be primary or secondary to a disease such as diabetes, haematological[10] disorders and connective tissue disease. Treatment of primary erythermalgia includes trials of aspirin, phenoxybenzamine (Dibenyline), methysergide or sympathectomy.

Acute blue fingers in women syndrome

This unusual syndrome involves the sudden onset of pain and cyanosis of the ventral aspect of the digit initially, then the entire digit. It lasts for two or three days and the attacks recur one or more times per year. No abnormalities are found on physical or laboratory examination.

Chilblains (perniosis)

Refer Chapter 111.

Reflex sympathetic dystrophy

Sudek's atrophy is a form of reflex sympathetic dystrophy in which the patient presents with severe pain, swelling and disability of the hand. It may occur spontaneously or, more usually, follows trauma which may even be trivial. It can occur after a Colle's fracture, especially with prolonged immobilisation.

Clinical features

- throbbing burning pain, worse at night
- paraesthesia
- initial: red, swollen hand; warm, dry skin
- later: cold, cyanosed and mottled, moist skin, shiny and stiff fingers
  wasting of small muscles
- X-rays—patchy decalcification of bone (diagnostic)

The problem eventually settles but may take years. Patients need considerable support, encouragement, basic pain relief, mobility in preference to rest and perhaps referral to a pain clinic.

Kienbock's disease

Kienbock's disease is avascular necrosis of the carpal lunate bone (Fig. 54.16) which may fragment and collapse, eventually leading to osteoarthritis of the wrist.

It presents usually in young adults over the age of 15 as insidious, progressive wrist pain and stiffness that limits grip strength and hand function. Males are affected more often than females and the right hand more than the left indicating the relationship to trauma.

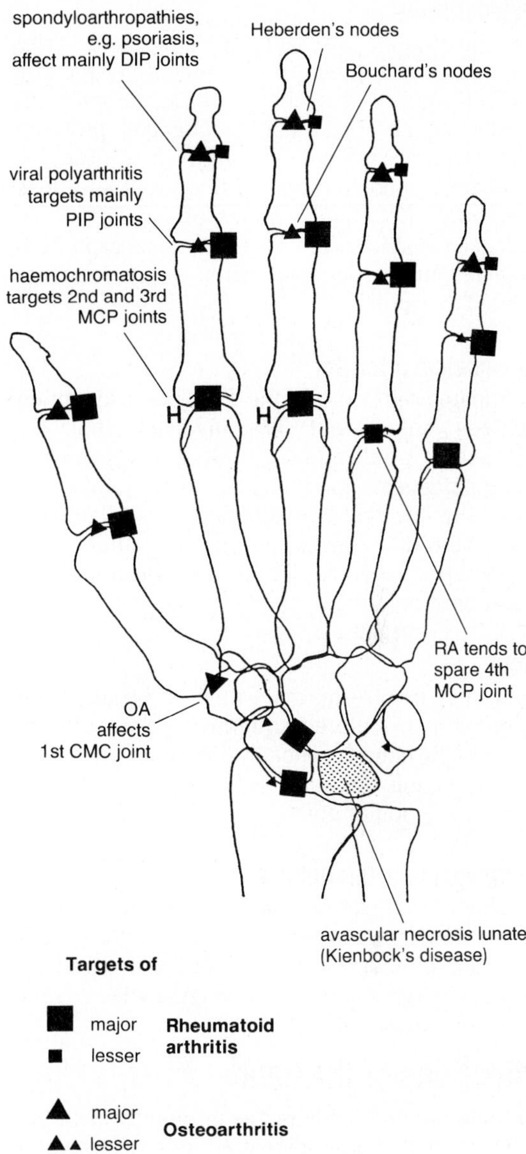

Fig. 54.16 *Typical sites of arthritic conditions and osteochondritis in the hand*

Arthritic conditions of the wrist and hand

Arthritis of the hand is an inappropriate diagnosis and specificity is required to highlight the various joints that are the targets of the specific arthritides which include osteoarthritis, rheumatoid arthritis, spondyloarthropathies, gout, haemochromatosis, and connective tissue disorders. Typical target areas in the hand are shown in Figure 54.16.

Osteoarthritis

Osteoarthritis commonly involves the interphalangeal joints of the fingers (especially the DIP joints)[12] and the carpometacarpal joint of the thumb. Degenerative changes produce bony swellings around the margins of the joints—Hebeden's nodes of the DIP joints and less commonly Bouchard's nodes of the PIP joints. A patchy distribution occurs in metacarpophalangeal, intercarpal and wrist joints, usually related to trauma.

Rheumatoid arthritis

In rheumatoid arthritis the DIP joints are often spared (only about 30% involved) but the metacarpophalangeal and proximal interphalangeal joints and wrist joints are generally affected symmetrically and bilaterally. Rheumatoid arthritis tends to affect the metacarpophalangeal joints of the fourth finger less commonly.

Gout

Gout may involve normal joints of the hand but is encountered more frequently in osteoarthritic joints of the hand (especially DIP joints) in elderly people taking diuretics. This clinical feature is known as nodular gout.

Seronegative arthropathies

A similar appearance to rheumatoid arthritis occurs except that with psoriatic arthritis the terminal joints are often involved with swelling, giving the appearance of 'sausage digits'.

Infections of the hand

Although not encountered as frequently as in the past, serious suppurative infections of the deep fascial spaces of the hand and tendon sheath can still occur, especially with penetrating injuries and web space infection.

Infections of the hand include:

- Infected wounds with superficial cellulitis or lymphangitis (*Streptococcus pyogenes*)
- Subcutaneous tissues
  — nail bed (paronychia)
  — pulp (whitlow, e.g. herpes simplex)
- Erysipeloid—this is a specific infection in one finger of fishermen or meat handlers, caused by *Erysipelothrix insidiosa*. There is a purplish erythema that gradually extends over days. It is rapidly cured by penicillin.
- Tendon sheath infection (suppurative tenosynovitis)—this is a dangerous and painful infection which can cause synovial adhesions with severe residual finger stiffness. The affected finger is hot and swollen and looks like a sausage.
- Deep palmar fascial space infection—infection from an infected tendon sheath or web space may spread to one of the two deep palmar spaces: the medial (midpalmer space) or lateral (thenar) space.

Management of serious infection

- Early appropriate antibiotic treatment for infection and early surgical referral where necessary.
- Antibiotics (adult doses)[13]

  Streptococcus pyogenes (cellulitis, lymphangitis)

  procaine penicillin 1 g IM daily
  or
  phenoxymethyl penicillin 500 mg (o) 6 hourly

  Staphylococcus aureus infection (suspected or proved)

  flucloxacillin 500 mg–1 g (o) 6 hourly
  or
  cephalexin 500 mg (o) 6 hourly
  or
  erythromycin 500 mg (o) 12 hourly

When to refer

- Disabling osteoarthritis of carpometacarpal joint for possible surgical repair.
- Myelopathy (motor weakness) and persistent radiculotherapy (nerve root pain and sensory changes) in the arm.
- Unresolving nerve entrapment problems such as median and ulnar nerves.
- Elbow injuries in children with proven or possible supracondylar fracture or avulsion epicondylar fractures.
- Evidence or suspicion of suppurative infection of the tendon sheaths or deep palmar fascial spaces.
- Septic arthritis and osteomyelitis.
- Reflex sympathetic dystrophy.
- Other conditions not responding to conservative measures.

Practice tips

- With elbow injuries in children, X-ray both elbows and compare one side with the other; this helps to determine whether there is displacement of fragments or a disturbance in the normal anatomy of the elbow.
- Tendinitis and other entheseal problems of the arm are common, tend to take 1–2 years to resolve spontaneously, yet resolve rapidly with rest, an exercise program or corticosteroid injections. Surgical relief is effective for refractory cases.
- The so-called thoracic outlet syndrome is probably most often caused by 'the droopy shoulder syndrome' rather than by a cervical rib.
- Consider corticosteroid injections for the carpal tunnel syndrome and stenosing tenosynovitis (de Quervain's and trigger finger or thumb). They are very effective and often curative.
- The site of arthritis in the hand provides a reasonable guide as to the cause.
- Always keep reflex sympathetic dystrophy in mind for persistent burning pain in the hand following injury—trivial or severe.

References

1. Swift TR, Nichols FT. The droopy shoulder syndrome. Neurol, 1984, 34:212–215.
2. Bertelsen S. Neurovascular compression syndromes of the neck and shoulder. Acta Chir Scand, 1969; 135:137–148.
3. Ireland D. The hand (part two). Aust Fam Physician, 1986; 15:1502–1513.
4. Dan NG. Entrapment syndromes. Med J Aust, 1976; 1:528–531.
5. Corrigan B, Maitland GP. *Practical orthopaedic medicine*. Sydney: Butterworths, 1986, 75–77.
6. Young D, Murtagh J. Pitfalls in orthopaedics. Aust Fam Physician, 1989; 18:645–653.
7. White ADN. Practice tip. A simple cure for chronic tennis elbow. Aust Fam Physician, 1987; 16:953.
8. Oakes B, Fuller P, Kenihan M, Sandor S. *Sports injuries*. Melbourne: Pitman, 1985:51–55.
9. Brinbaum AJ. Tennis elbow: Don't worry, it can be avoided and it can be cured. Tennis, 1978; April:96–103.
10. Sheon R, Moskowitz R, Goldberg V. Soft tissue rheumatic pain. Philadelphia: Lea and Febiger, 1987, 105–140.
11. Ireland D. The hand (part one). Aust Fam Physician, 1986; 15:1162–1171.
12. Corrigan B, Maitland G. *Practical orthopaedic medicine*. Sydney: Butterworths, 1986:97–100.
13. Mashford ML. *Antibiotic guidelines* (7th edition). Melbourne: Victorian Medical Postgraduate Foundation: 1992–3, 122–124.

55

Hip and buttock pain

Pain in the hip, buttock, groin and upper thigh tend to be interrelated. Patients often present complaining of pain in the hip yet are referring to pain in the buttock or lower back. Most pain in the buttock has a lumbosacral origin. Pain originating from disorders of the lumbosacral spine (commonly) and the knee (uncommonly) can be referred to the hip region, while pain from the hip joint (L3 innervation) may be referred commonly to the thigh and the knee. Disorders of the abdomen and retroperitoneal region may cause hip and groin pain sometimes mediated by irritation of the psoas muscle.

Key facts and checkpoints

- Hip troubles have a significant age relationship (Fig. 55.1).
- Children can suffer from a variety of serious disorders of the hip, e.g. congenital dislocation (CDH), Perthes' disorder, tuberculosis, septic arthritis and slipped upper femoral epiphysis (SUFE), all of which demand early recognition and management.
- SUFE typically presents in the obese adolescent (10–15 years) with knee pain and a slight limp.

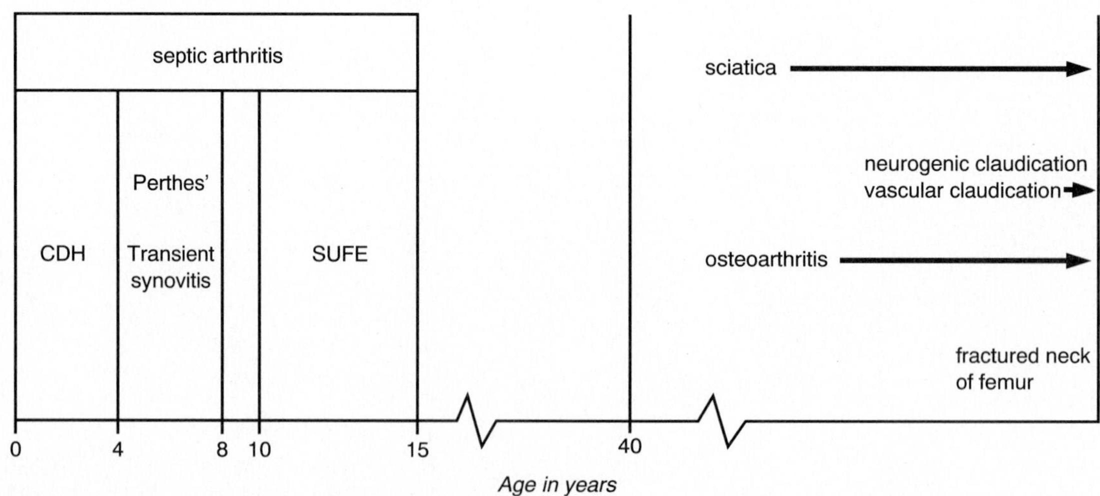

Fig. 55.1 *Typical ages of presentation of hip disorders*

- Every newborn infant should be tested for CDH, which is the most graphic orthopaedic disability that can be prevented.
- Limp has an inseparable relationship with painful hip and buttock conditions, especially those of the hip.
- The spine is the most likely cause of pain in the buttock in adults.
- Disorders of the hip joint commonly refer pain to the knee.
- Disorders of the knee joint can (but rarely do) refer pain to the hip joint.
- If a woman, especially one with many children, presents with bilateral buttock or hip pain, consider dysfunction of the sacroiliac joints as the cause.

A diagnostic approach

A summary of the diagnostic model is presented in Table 55.1.

Probability diagnosis

The commonest cause of hip and buttock pain presenting in general practice is referred pain from the lumbosacral spine and the sacroiliac joints.[1] The pain is invariably referred to the outer buttock and posterior hip area (Fig. 55.2). The origin of the pain can be the facet joints of the lumbar spine, intervertebral disc disruption or, less commonly, the sacroiliac joints. Much of this pain is inappropriately referred to as 'lumbago', 'fibrositis' and 'rheumatism'.

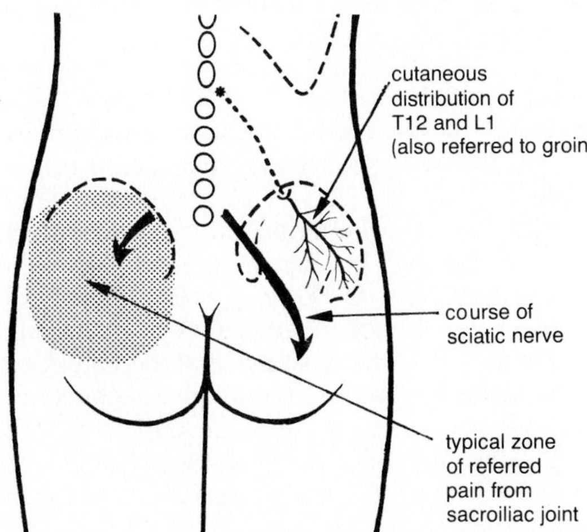

Fig. 55.2 *Referral patterns of pain from the lumbosacral spine and the sacroiliac joints*

Table 55.1 *Hip and buttock pain: diagnostic strategy model*

Q. *Probability diagnosis*
A. Traumatic muscular strains
Referred pain from spine
Osteoarthritis of hip

Q. *Serious disorders not to be missed*
A. Cardiovascular
- buttock claudication

Neoplasia
- metastatic carcinoma

Septic infections
- septic arthritis
- osteomyelitis
- tuberculosis
- pelvic and abdominal infections
  - — pelvic abscess
  - — PID

Childhood disorders
- CDH
- Perthes' disease
- slipped femoral epiphysis
- synovitis (irritable hip)
- juvenile chronic arthritis

Q. *Pitfalls (often missed)*
A. Polymyalgia rheumatica
Fractures • stress fractures femoral neck
• subcapital fractures
• sacrum
Sacroiliac joint disorders
Inguinal or femoral hernia
Gluteus medius tendinitis
Trochanteric bursitis
Neurogenic claudication
Chilblains

Rarities
Paget's disease
Nerve entrapments • sciatica 'hip pocket nerve'
• obturator
• lateral cutaneous nerve thigh

Q. *Seven masquerades checklist*
A.

Depression	✓
Diabetes	—
Drugs	—
Anaemia	—
Thyroid disease	—
Spinal dysfunction	✓
UTI	—

Q. *Is this patient trying to tell me something else?*
A. Non-organic pain may be present. Patient with arthritis fearful of being crippled.

Trauma and overuse injuries from sporting activities are also common causes of muscular and ligamentous[2] strains around the buttock and hip.

The hip joint is a common target of osteoarthritis. This usually presents after 50 years but can present earlier if the hip has been affected by another condition.

Serious disorders not to be missed

The major triad of serious disorders—cardiovascular, neoplasia and severe infections—are applicable to this area albeit limited in extent.

Aortoiliac occlusion

Ischaemic muscle pain including buttock claudication secondary to aortoiliac arterial occlusion is sometimes confused with musculoskeletal pain. An audible bruit over the vessels following exercise is one clue to diagnosis.

Neoplasia

Primary tumours including myeloma and lymphosarcoma can arise rarely in the upper femur and pelvis (especially the ilium). However, these areas are relatively common targets for metastases especially from the prostate and breast.

Infection

Some very important, at times 'occult', infections can develop in and around the hip joint.

Osteomyelitis is prone to develop in the metaphysis of the upper end of the femur and must be considered in the child with intense pain, a severe limp and fever. Tuberculosis may also present in children (usually under 10 years) with a presentation similar to Perthes' disease.

Transient synovitis or 'irritable hip' is the most common cause of hip pain and limp in childhood.

Inflammation of the side wall of the pelvis as in a deep pelvic abscess (e.g. from appendicitis), pelvic inflammatory disease (PID) including pyosalpinx, or an ischiorectal abscess can cause deep hip pain and a limp. This pain may be related to irritation of the obturator nerve.

Retroperitoneal haematoma can cause referred pain and femoral nerve palsy.

Childhood disorders that must not be missed include:

- congenital dislocation of the hip and acetabular dysplasia
- Perthes' disorder
- slipped upper femoral epiphysis (SUFE)
- stress fractures of the femoral neck

Inflammatory disorders of the hip joint that should be kept in mind include:

- rheumatoid arthritis
- juvenile chronic arthritis (JCA)
- rheumatic fever (a flitting polyarthritis)
- spondyloarthropathy

Pitfalls

There are many pitfalls associated with hip and buttock pain and these include the various childhood problems. Fractures can be a pitfall, especially subcapital fractures.

Sacroiliac joint disorders are often missed whether it be the inflammation of sacroiliitis or mechanical dysfunction of the joint.

Inflammatory conditions around the hip girdle are common and so often misdiagnosed. These include the common gluteus medius tendinitis and trochanteric bursitis.

Polymyalgia rheumatica commonly causes shoulder girdle pain in the elderly but pain around the hip girdle can accompany this important problem.

Chilblains around the upper thighs occur in cold climates and are often known as 'jodhpur' chilblains because they tend to occur during horse riding in very cold weather.

Nerve entrapment syndromes require consideration. Meralgia paraesthetica is a nerve entrapment causing pain and paraesthesia over the lateral aspect of the hip (Fig. 56.3).

An interesting modern phenomenon is the so-called 'hip pocket nerve' syndrome. If a man presents with 'sciatica', especially confined to the buttock and upper posterior thigh (without local back pain), consider the possibility of pressure on the sciatic nerve from a wallet in the hip pocket. This problem is occasionally encountered in people sitting for long periods in cars (e.g. taxi drivers). It appears to be related to the increased presence of plastic credit cards in wallets (Fig. 55.3).

Paget's disease can involve the upper end of the femur and the pelvis.

General pitfalls

- Failure to test the hips of neonates carefully and follow up congenital dislocation of the hip.
- Misdiagnosis of arthritis and other disorders of the hip joint because of referred pain.
- Overlooking a SUFE or a stress fracture of the femoral neck in teenage boys, especially athletes. If an X-ray shows that the epiphysis is fusing or has fused, arrange a technetium bone scan. Stress fractures are associated with a significant incidence of avascular necrosis.

Seven masquerades checklist

The one outstanding masquerade is spinal dysfunction, which is the most likely cause of

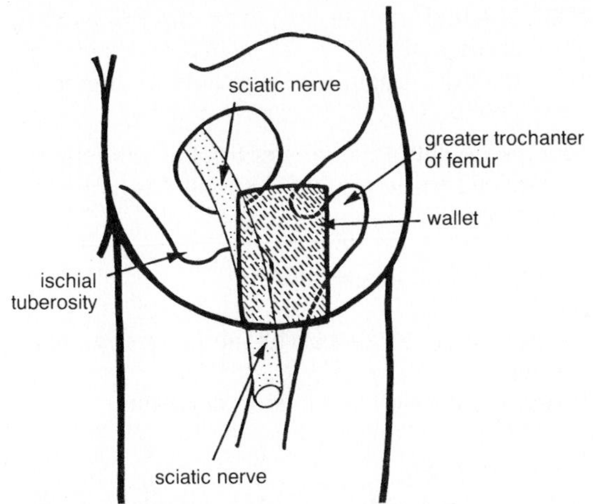

Fig. 55.3 *'Hip pocket nerve' syndrome: location and relations of sciatic nerve in the buttock*

pain in the buttock. Many dermatomes meet at the buttock and theoretically pain in the buttock can result from any lesion situated in a tissue derived from L1, L2, L3, S2, S3, S4.[1] Symptoms from L3 can spread from the outer buttock to the front of the thigh and down the leg, over the medial aspect of the knee to the calf. Such a distribution is common to an L3 nerve root lesion and arthritis of the hip.

Furthermore, dysfunction of the facet joints and sacroiliac joints can refer pain to the buttock. The relatively common L1 lesion due to dysfunction at the T12–L1 spinal level can lead to referred pain over the outer upper quadrant of the buttock (Fig. 55.2) and also to the groin (Fig. 56.1).

Psychogenic considerations

Cyriax[1] claims that the hip shares with the back and the shoulder 'an enhanced liability to fixation' for psychological reasons. This problem is often related to work compensation factors and overpowering stresses at home. A common finding in psychoneurotic patients complaining of buttock and thigh pain is 90° limitation of flexion at the hip joint. The importance of testing passive movements of the hip joint is obvious, for often such limitation of flexion is combined with a full range of rotation. In arthritis of the hip joint internal rotation is invariably affected first.

Such patients often walk into the office with a marked limp and leaning on a thick stick. It requires great skill to evaluate and manage them tactfully and successfully.

On the other hand, patients with genuine osteoarthritis fear being crippled and ending in a wheelchair. They require considerable education and reassurance.

The clinical approach

History

Pain associated with hip joint pathology is usually described as a deep aching pain, aggravated by movement[2] and felt in the groin and anteromedial aspect of the upper thigh, sometimes exclusively around the knee (Fig. 50.1). A limp is a frequent association.

An obstetric history in a woman may be relevant for sacroiliac pain.

Key questions

Can you tell me how the pain started?
Could you describe the pain?
Point to where the pain is exactly.
Does the pain come on after walking for a while and stops as soon as you rest?
Is there any stiffness, especially first thing in the morning?
Do you get any backache?
Do your movements feel free?
Do you have a limp?
Do you have a similar ache around the shoulders?
Have you had an injury such as a fall?
Have you lost any weight recently?

Physical examination

Follow the traditional methods of examination of any joint: *Look, feel, move, measure, test function, look elsewhere, X-ray.* The patient should strip down to the pants to allow maximum exposure.

Inspection

Ask the patient to point exactly to the area of greatest discomfort. Careful observation of the patient, especially walking, provides useful diagnostic information. If walking with a limp, the leg adducted and foot somewhat externally rotated, osteoarthritis of the hip joint is the likely diagnosis.

If called to a patient who has suffered an injury such as a fall or vehicle accident, note the position of the leg. If shortened and externally rotated (Fig. 55.4a), a fractured neck of femur is the provisional diagnosis; if internally rotated, suspect a posterior dislocation of the hip (Fig. 55.4b). With anterior dislocation of the hip, the hip is externally rotated.

Get the patient to lie supine on the couch with ASISs of the pelvis placed squarely and note the shape and position of the limbs.

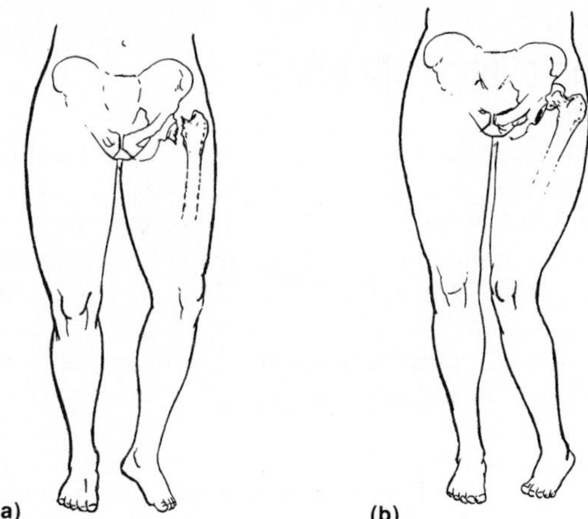

Fig. 55.4 **(a)** *General configuration of the legs for a fractured neck of femur;* **(b)** *general configuration for a posterior dislocated hip*

Palpation

Feel one to two finger-breadths below the midpoint of the inguinal ligament for joint tenderness. Check for trochanteric bursitis, gluteus medius tendinitis and other soft tissue problems.

Movements

Passive movements with *patient supine* (normal range is indicated):

- Flexion (compare both sides) 140°
- External rotation (knee and hip extended in adults) 45–50°
- Internal rotation (knee and hip extended in adults) 45°
- Abduction (stand on same side—steady pelvis) 45°
- Adduction (should see the patella of the opposite leg) 25°

In children it is most important to measure rotation and abduction/ adduction with the knee and hip flexed to detect early Perthes' or SUFE.

Patient prone:

- Extension (one hand held over SIJ) 25°

Note Osteoarthritis of the hip affects IR, extension and abduction first.

Measurements

- true leg length (ASIS to medial malleolus)
- apparent leg length (umbilicus to medial malleolus)

Note unequal true leg length = hip disease on shorter side
unequal apparent leg length = tilting of pelvis

Feel the height of the greater trochanters relative to the ASIS to determine if shortening is in the hip or below.

Test function and special tests

Gait:
Trendelenburg test—tests hip abductors (gluteus medius)
Thomas test—for fixed flexion deformity

Look elsewhere

Examine lumbosacral spine, sacroiliac joints, groin and knee. Consider hernias and possibility of PID.

Investigations

These can be selected from:

- Serological tests
  - RA factor
  - ESR
- X-ray
  - plain X-ray
  - frog views (in children)
  - bone scan
  - ultrasound
  - CT scan
- Needle aspiration of joint

Role of ultrasound Ultrasound diagnosis is now sensitive in children (and adults) in detecting fluid in the hip joint and can diagnose septic arthritis and also localise the site of an osteomyelitic abscess around a swollen joint. It can accurately assess the neonatal hip joint and confirm the position of the femoral head.

Hip pain in children

Hip disorders have an important place in childhood and may present with a limp when the child is walking. These important disorders include:

- congenital dislocation of the hip (CDH)
- congenital subluxation of hip and acetabular dysplasia
- transient synovitis
- Perthes' disorder (pseudocoxalgia or coxa plana)
- septic arthritis
- slipped upper femoral epiphysis (adolescent coxa vara)

- pathological fractures through bone cyst

The important features of hip pain in children are summarised in Table 55.2.

Congenital dislocation of the hip

In CDH the underdeveloped femoral head dislocates posteriorly and superiorly. CDH is described as dislocatable (1 in 80 hips at birth, which stabilise in a few days) and frankly dislocated (1 in 800 hips).[3]

Clinical features

- females: males = 6:1
- bilateral in one-third
- tight adductors and short leg evident
- diagnosed early by Ortolani and Barlow tests (abnormal thud or clunk on abduction); test usually negative after 2 months
- ultrasound excellent (especially up to 3–4 months) and probably more sensitive than clinical examination
- X-ray usually normal

Note 1. When diagnosed and treated from birth it is possible to produce a normal joint after a few months in an abduction splint.

2. Every baby should be examined for CDH during the first day of life and before discharge from hospital or after care.[3] The Ortolani and Barlow tests remain important means of detecting the congenitally unstable or dislocated hip, but ultrasound is becoming more important and is recommended for high-risk babies, e.g. breech, family history CDH.

Screening examination

Carry out the examination on a large firm bench with the baby stripped. Relaxation is essential; give baby a bottle if necessary. Be gentle and have warm hands.

With the legs extended any asymmetry of the legs or skin creases is noted.

- Hold the leg in the hand with knee flexed—thumb over groin (lesser trochanter) and middle finger over greater trochanter (Fig. 55.5).
- Flex hips to about 90°, abduct to 45° (note any clunk).
- Gently rock the femur backwards and forwards on the pelvis by pressing forward with the middle finger and backwards with the thumb.

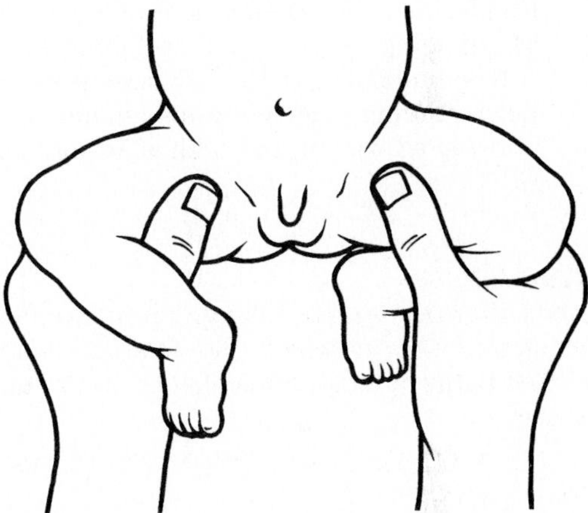

Fig. 55.5 *Examination of the infant for CDH: demonstrating Ortolani's sign on left side*

Table 55.2 *Comparison of important causes of hip pain in children*

	CDH	Transient synovitis	Perthes'	SUFE	Septic arthritis
Age	0–4	4–8	4–8	10–15	Any
Limp	+	+	+	+	Won't walk
Pain	–	+	+	+	+++
Limited movement	Abduction	All, especially abduction and IR	Abduction and IR	All, especially IR	All
Plain X-ray	Normal or dislocation. No diagnostic value in neonatal period (use ultrasound)	Normal	Subchondral fracture. Dense head. Pebble stone epiphysis	AP may be normal. Frog view shows slip.	Normal Use ultrasound

Note any jerk or clunk. If the femoral head displaces, there is dislocation. Plain X-ray has little or no place in the diagnosis of CDH in the neonatal period.[4] Early referral for treatment is essential. If not detected early the femoral head stays out of the acetabulum and after the age of one year the child may present with delay in walking or a limp. The diagnosis is then detected by X-ray.

Treatment (guidelines)

- CDH must be referred to a specialist[3]
- 0–6 months—Pavlik harness
- 8–18 months—reduction (closed or open) and cast
- 18 months—open reduction and osteotomy

Note Despite early treatment some hip conditions progress to acetabulum dysplasia (underdevelopment of the 'roof' of the hip joint) and to premature osteoarthritis. Thus a follow-up X-ray of the pelvis during teenage years should be considered for anyone with a history of CDH.

Perthes' disorder

Perthes' disorder is one of the group of juvenile osteochondroses in which the femoral head becomes partly or totally avascular, i.e. avascular necrosis.

Clinical features

- males: females = 4:1
- usual age 4–8 (rarely 2–18)
- sometimes bilateral
- presents as a limp and aching
- 'irritable' hip early
- limited movement in abduction and IR

X-ray Joint space appears increased and femoral head too lateral: typical changes of sclerosis, deformity and collapse of the femoral capital epiphysis may be delayed.

Management

- urgent referral
- aim is to keep femoral head from becoming flat
- choice of treatment dependent on consultant

If untreated, the femoral head usually becomes flat over some months, leading to eventual osteoarthritis. Some untreated Perthes' heal and have a normal X-ray.

Transient synovitis

This common condition is also known as 'irritable hip' or observation hip[5] and is the consequence of a self-limiting synovial inflammation.

Clinical features

- child aged 4–8
- sudden onset of hip pain and a limp
- child can usually walk (some may not)
- may be history of trauma
- painful limitation of movements especially abduction and IR
- blood tests and X-rays normal (may be soft tissue swelling); ESR may be mildly elevated
- ultrasound shows fluid in the joint

Differential diagnosis: septic arthritis, JCA, Perthes' disease

Outcome: settles to normal within 7 days, without sequelae.

Treatment is bed rest and analgesics. Follow-up X-ray in 4 to 6 months to exclude Perthes' disease. Aspiration under GA may be needed to exclude septic arthritis.

Slipped upper femoral epiphysis (SUFE)

A most distressing aspect of the displaced upper epiphysis of the femoral head is the significant number of patients who develop avascular necrosis despite expert treatment. Therefore diagnosis of the condition before major slipping is important. This necessitates early consultation with the teenager experiencing hip or knee discomfort and then accurate interpretation of X-rays.

Clinical features

- adolescent 10–15 years, often obese
- most common in the oversized and undersexed (e.g. the heavy pre-pubertal boy)
- bilateral in 20%
- limp and irritability of hip on movement
- knee pain
- hip rotating into external rotation on flexion and often lies in external rotation
- most movements restricted, especially IR

Any adolescent with a limp or knee pain should have X-rays (AP and frog view) of both hips (Fig. 55.6). Otherwise this important condition will be overlooked.

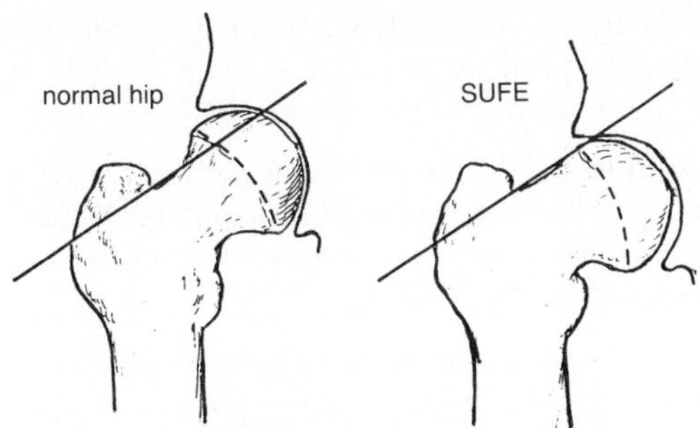

Fig. 55.6 *Appearance of a slipped upper femoral epiphysis. Note that, in the normal state, a line drawn along the superior surface of the femoral neck passes through the femoral head, but passes above it with SUFE*

Management

- Cease weight bearing and refer urgently.
- If acute slip, gentle reduction via traction is better than manipulation in preventing later avascular necrosis.
- Once reduced, pinning is performed.

Septic arthritis

Septic arthritis of the hip should be suspected in all children with acutely painful or irritable hip problems. These patients may not be obviously sick on presentation. A negative needle aspiration does not exclude septic arthritis. If sepsis is suspected it is better to proceed to an arthrotomy if clinically indicated.

The irritable hip syndrome should be diagnosed only after negative investigations, including plain films and ultrasound, full blood examination, ESR and bone scan. Needle aspiration has to be considered but irritable hip is often diagnosed without it, by observing in hospital in traction. If a deterioration or elevated temperature develops, needle aspiration with or without arthrotomy is indicated.

The little athlete

The most common problem in the little athlete is pain or discomfort in the region of the iliac crest or anterior or superior iliac spines, usually associated with traction apophysitis or with acute avulsion fractures.[6] There is localised tenderness with pain on stretching and athletes should rest until they can compete without discomfort.

If there are persistent signs, pain in the knee, hip irritability or restricted range of motion, X-rays should be ordered to exclude serious problems such as SUFE or Perthes' disorder.

Hip and buttock pain in the elderly

The following conditions are highly significant in the elderly:

- osteoarthritis of the hip
- aortoiliac arterial occlusion → vascular claudication
- spinal dysfunction with nerve root or referred pain
- degenerative spondylosis of lumbosacral spine → neurogenic claudication
- polymyalgia rheumatica
- trochanteric bursitis
- fractured neck of femur
- secondary tumours

Subcapital fractures

The impacted subcapital fractured femoral neck can often permit weight bearing by an elderly patient. No obvious deformity of the leg is present. Radiographs are therefore essential for the investigation of all painful hips in the elderly. Patients often give a story of two falls—the first[7] very painful, the second with the hip just 'giving way' as the femoral head fell off.

The displaced subcapital fracture has at least a 40% incidence of avascular necrosis and usually requires prosthetic replacement in patients over 70 years. Bone scans or tomograms are useful if the plain X-rays are equivocal.

Osteoarthritis of the hip

Osteoarthritis of the hip is the most common form of hip disease. It can be caused by primary osteoarthritis, which is related to an intrinsic disorder of articular cartilage, or to secondary osteoarthritis. Predisposing factors to the latter include previous trauma, CDH, acetabular dysplasia, SUFE and past inflammatory arthritis.

Clinical features

- equal sex incidence
- usually after age 50, increases with age
- may be bilateral: starts in one, other follows
- insidious onset
- at first pain worse with activity, relieved by rest then nocturnal pain and pain after resting
- stiffness, especially after rising
- characteristic deformity
- stiffness, deformity and limp may dominate (pain mild)

Physical examination

- abnormal gait
- usually gluteal and quadriceps wasting
- first hip movements lost are IR and extension
- hip held in flexion and ER (at first)
- eventually all movements affected
- order of movement loss is IR, E, abduction, adduction, F, ER

Treatment

- careful explanation: patients fear OA of hip
- weight loss if overweight
- relative rest
- complete RIB for acute pain
- analgesics and NSAIDs (judicious use)
- aids and supports, e.g. walking stick
- physical therapy, including isometric exercises
- hydrotherapy is very useful

Surgery

This is an excellent option for those with severe pain or disability unresponsive to conservative measures. Total hip replacement is the treatment of choice in older patients but a femoral[8] osteotomy may be considered in younger patients in selected cases. The development of cementless total hip replacement has allowed surgery in more patients in their twenties and thirties.

Sacroiliac pain

Pain arising from sacroiliac joint disorders is normally experienced as a dull ache in the buttock but can be referred to the groin or posterior aspect of the thigh. It may mimic pain from the lumbosacral spine or the hip joint. The pain may be unilateral or bilateral.

There are no accompanying neurological symptoms such as paraesthesia or numbness but it is common for more severe cases to cause a heavy aching feeling in the upper thigh.

Causes of sacroiliac joint disorders

- inflammatory (the spondyloarthropathies)
- infections, e.g. TB, *Staphyloccus aureus* (rare)
- osteitis condensans ilii
- degenerative changes
- mechanical disorders
- post-traumatic, after sacroiliac disruption or fracture

Examination of the sacroiliac joints

The SIJs are difficult to palpate and examine but there are several tests that provoke the SIJs.

Direct pressure With the patient lying prone a rhythmic springing force is applied directly to the upper and lower sacrum respectively.

Winged compression test With the patient lying supine and with arms crossed, 'separate' the iliac crests with a downwards and outwards pressure. This compresses the SIJs.

Lateral compression test With hands placed on the iliac crests, thumbs on the ASISs and heels of hand on the rim of the pelvis, compress the pelvis. This distracts the SIJs.

Patrick or Fabere test This method can provoke the hip as well as the SIJ. The patient lies supine on the table and the foot of the involved side and extremity is placed on the opposite knee (the hip joint is now flexed, externally rotated and abducted). The knee and opposite ASIS are pressed downwards simultaneously (Fig. 55.7). If low back or buttock pain is reproduced the cause is likely to be a disorder of the SIJ.

Fig. 55.7 *The Patrick (Fabere) test for right-sided hip or sacroiliac joint lesions, illustrating directions of pressure from the examiner*

Unequal sacral 'rise' test Squat behind the standing patient and place hands on top of the iliac crests and thumbs on the posterior superior iliac spines. Ask the patient to bend slowly forwards and touch the floor. If one side moves higher relative to the other a problem may exist in the SIJs, e.g. a hypomobile lesion in the painful side if that side's PSIS moves higher.

Mechanical disorders of the SIJ

These problems are more common than appreciated and can be caused by hypomobile or hypermobile problems.

Hypomobile SIJ disorders are usually encountered in young people after some traumatic event, especially women following childbirth (notably multiple or difficult childbirth), and in those with structural problems, e.g. shortened leg. Pain tends to follow rotational stresses of the SIJ, e.g. tennis, dancing. Excellent results are obtained by passive mobilisation or manipulation, such as the non-specific rotation technique with the patient lying supine as described in *Practice Tips* by the author.[9]

Hypermobile SIJ disorders are sometimes seen in athletes with instability of the symphysis pubis, in women after childbirth and in those with a history of severe trauma to the pelvis, e.g. MVAs, horse riders with foot caught in the stirrups after a fall. The patient presents typically with severe aching pain in the lower back, buttocks or upper thigh. Such problems are difficult to treat and manual therapy usually exacerbates the symptoms. Treatment consists of relative rest, analgesics and a sacroiliac supportive belt.

Gluteus medius tendinitis and trochanteric bursitis

Pain around the lateral aspect of the hip is a common disorder, and is usually seen as lateral hip pain radiating down the lateral aspect of the thigh in older people engaged in walking exercises, tennis and similar activities. It is analogous in a way to the shoulder girdle, where supraspinatus tendinitis and subacromial bursitis are common wear-and-tear injuries.

The two common causes are tendinitis of the gluteus medius tendon, where it inserts into the lateral surface of the greater trochanter of the femur, and bursitis of one or both of the trochanteric bursae. Distinction between these two conditions is difficult, and it is possible that, as with the shoulder, they are related. The pain of bursitis tends to occur at night; that of tendinitis occurs with such activity as long walks and gardening.

Treatment

Treatment for both conditions is similar.

1. Determine the points of maximal tenderness over the trochanteric region and mark them. (For tendinitis, this point is immediately above the superior aspect of the greater trochanter—see Fig. 55.8).
2. Inject aliquots of a mixture of 1 ml of long-acting corticosteroid with 5–7 ml of LA into the tender area, which usually occupies an area similar to that of a standard marble.

The injection may be very effective. Follow-up management includes sleeping with a small pillow under the involved buttock and stretching the gluteal muscles with knee–chest exercises. One or two repeat injections over 6 or 12 months may be required. Surgical intervention is rarely necessary.

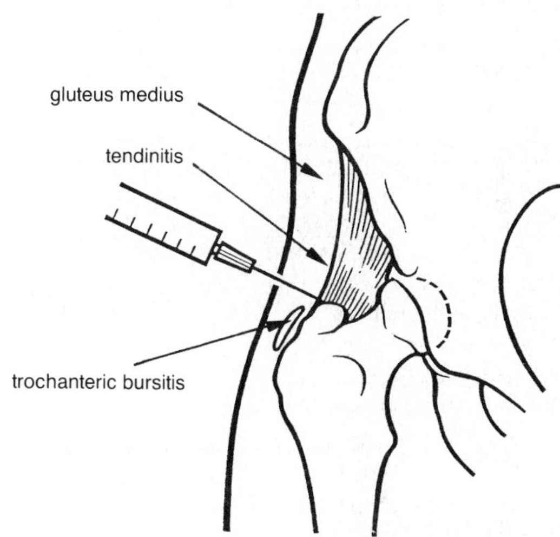

Fig. 55.8 *Injection technique for gluteus medius tendinitis (into area of maximal tenderness)*

Snapping or clicking hip

Some patients complain of a clunking, clicking or snapping hip. This represents a painless, but annoying problem.

Causes

- a taut iliotibial band (tendon or tensor fascia femoris) slipping backwards and forwards over the prominence of the greater trochanter

or

- the iliopsoas tendon snapping across the iliopectineal eminence
- the gluteus maximus sliding across the greater trochanter
- joint laxity

Treatment

The two basics of treatment are:

- explanation and reassurance
- exercises to stretch the iliotibial band[10]

Exercises

1. The patient lies on the 'normal' side and flexes the affected hip, with the leg straight and a weight around the ankle (Fig. 55.9), to a degree that produces a stretching sensation along the lateral aspect of the thigh.
2. This iliotibial stretch should be performed for 1–2 minutes, twice daily.

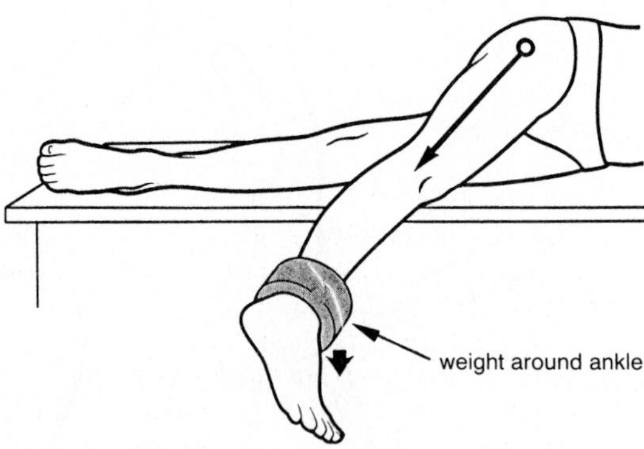

Fig. 55.9 *Treatment for the clicking hip*

When to refer

- Clinical evidence or suspicion of severe childhood disorders: CDH, Perthes' disorder, septic arthritis, slipped upper femoral epiphysis or osteomyelitis.
- Undiagnosed pain, especially night pain.
- Any fractures or suspicion of fractures such as impacted subcapital fracture or stress fracture of the femoral neck.
- Patients with true claudication in buttock whether it is vascular from aortoiliac occlusion or neurogenic from spinal canal stenosis.
- Patients with disabling osteoarthritis of the hip not responding to conservative measures. Excellent results are obtained from surgery to the hip.
- Any mass or lump.

Practice tips

- Training on a plastic CDH model should be essential for all neonatal practitioners in order to master the manoeuvres for examining the neonatal hip.
- True hip pain is usually groin pain or is referred to the medial aspect of the knee.[10]
- The name of the Fabere test is an acronym for Flexion, Abduction, External Rotation and Extension of the hip.
- Night pain adds up to inflammation, bursitis or tumour.
- The hip joint can be the target of infections such as *Staphyloccocus aureus* or tuberculosis or inflammatory disorders such as rheumatoid and the spondyloarthropathies, but these are rare numerically compared with osteoarthritis.

References

1. Cyriax J. *Textbook of orthopaedic medicine Vol 1* (6th edition). London: Balliere Tindall; 1976:568–594.
2. Cormack J, Marinker M, Morell D. Hip problems. In: *Practice*. London: Kluwer-Harrap Handbooks, 1980; 3.65:1–6.
3. Anonymous. *The Eastern Seal guide to children's orthopaedics*. Toronto: Eastern Seal Society, 1982.
4. Robinson M.J. *Practical paediatrics*. Melbourne: Churchill Livingstone, 1990, 72–74.
5. Corrigan B, Maitland G. *Practical orthopaedic medicine*. Sydney: Butterworths, 1986, 103–124.
6. Larkins PA. The little athlete. Aust Fam Physician, 1991; 20: 973–978.
7. Young D, Murtagh J. Pitfalls in orthopaedics. Aust Fam Physician, 1989; 18:654–655.
8. Corrigan B., Maitland G. *Practical orthopaedic medicine*. Sydney: Butterworths, 1986, 324–331.
9. Murtagh J. *Practice tips*. Sydney: McGraw-Hill, 1991: 106.
10. Sheon RP, Moskowitz RW, Goldberg VM. *Soft tissue rheumatic pain* (2nd edition). Philadelphia: Lea and Febiger, 1987:211–212.

56

Pain in the leg

Pain in the leg has many causes, varying from a simple cramp to an arterial occlusion. Overuse of the legs in the athlete can lead to a multiplicity of painful leg syndromes, ranging from simple sprains of soft tissue to compartment syndromes. A major cause of leg pain lies in the source of the nervous network to the lower limb, namely the lumbar and sacral nerve roots of the spine. It is important to recognise radicular pain, especially from L5 and S1 nerve roots, and also the patterns of referred pain such as from apophyseal (facet) joints and sacroiliac joints.

Illustrative case histories

Mrs PJ, aged 38, housewife

This previously well person was walking briskly when she felt intense pain in the area of the lateral aspect of her left calf. It persisted and she visited a casualty department where a diagnosis of a torn lateral head of gastrocnemius was made. The pain then spread to the outer area of the ankle and to the outer foot which started to feel numb.

On review the diagnosis was changed to a sural nerve lesion. Two days later she was found to have persistent severe pain in the leg and anaesthesia corresponding to S1. She had no back pain. Examination showed there was no ankle jerk, and loss of eversion of the left foot.

Diagnosis and outcome: progressive S1 nerve palsy due to an L5–S1 disc prolapse. The disc was removed six days after the onset of pain.

Mr LR, aged 67, farmer

A middle-of-the-night home visit was made to this upset non-English-speaking man because of the sudden onset of severe pain in his right leg. A provisional diagnosis of arterial occlusion was made over the phone but the problem was in fact a simple nocturnal cramp. Smiles of relief and embarrassment all round.

Mrs CM, aged 63, librarian

This obese patient complained of a dull ache in the middle of her thigh for two months. Examination was normal. She was reassured but an X-ray ordered if the pain persisted. A house call two weeks later found the patient lying on the kitchen floor with a fractured femur.

Diagnosis and outcome: pathological fracture due to a single metastasis from a breast primary (removed nine years previously).

These case histories illustrate some of the difficulties experienced by patients and doctors with diagnosing leg pain.

Key facts and checkpoints

- Always consider the lumbosacral spine, the sacroiliac joints and hip joints as important causes of leg pain.
- Hip joint disorders may refer pain around the knee only (without hip pain).
- Nerve root lesions may cause pain in the lower leg and foot only (without back pain).

- Nerve entrapment is suggested by a radiating burning pain, prominent at night and worse at rest.
- Older people may present with claudication in the leg from spinal canal stenosis or arterial obstruction or both.
- Think of the hip pocket wallet as a cause of sciatica from the buttocks down.
- Acute arterial occlusion to the lower limb requires relief within four hours (absolute limit of six hours).
- The commonest site of acute occlusion is the common femoral artery.
- Varicose veins can cause aching pain in the leg.

A diagnostic approach

A summary of the safety diagnostic model is presented in Table 56.1.

Probability diagnosis

Many of the causes, such as foot problems, ankle injuries and muscle tears (e.g. hamstrings and quadriceps), are obvious and common. There is a wide range of disorders related to overuse syndromes in athletes.

A very common cause of acute severe leg pain is cramp in the calf musculature, the significance of which escapes some patients as judged by middle-of-the-night calls.

One of the commonest causes is nerve root pain, invariably single, especially affecting the L5 and S1 nerve roots. Tests of their function and of the lumbosacral spine for evidence of disc disruption or other spinal dysfunction will be necessary. Should multiple nerve roots be involved other causes such as compression from a tumour should be considered. Remember that a spontaneous retroperitoneal haemorrhage in a patient on anticoagulant therapy can cause nerve root pain and present as intense acute leg pain. The nerve root sensory distribution is presented in Figure 56.1

Other important causes of referred thigh pain include ischiogluteal bursitis (weaver's bottom) and gluteus medius tendinitis or trochanteric bursitis.

Serious disorders not to be missed

Neoplasia

Malignant disease, although uncommon, should be considered, especially if the patient has a history of one of the primary tumours such as breast, lung or kidney. Such tumours can metastasise to the femur. Consider also osteogenic sarcoma and multiple myeloma, which is usually seen in the upper half of the femur. The possibility of an osteoid osteoma should be considered with pain in a bone relieved by aspirin.

Table 56.1 *Pain in the leg: diagnostic strategy model*

Q. *Probability diagnosis*
A. Cramps
Nerve root 'sciatica'
Muscular injury, e.g. hamstring
Osteoarthritis (hip, knee)
Overuse injury, e.g. Achilles tendinitis

Q. *Serious disorders not to be missed*
A. Vascular
- Arterial occlusion (embolism)
- Thrombosis popliteal aneurysm
- Deep venous thrombosis

Neoplasia
- Primary, e.g. myeloma
- Metastases, e.g. breast to femur

Infection
- Osteomyelitis
- Septic arthritis
- Erysipelas
- Lymphangitis
- Gas gangrene

Q. *Pitfalls (often missed)*
A. Osteoarthritis hip
Osgood-Schlatter's disease
Spinal canal stenosis
Herpes zoster (early)
Nerve entrapment
'Hip pocket nerve'
Iatrogenic: injection into nerve
Sacroiliac disorders
Gluteus medius tendinitis
Sympathetic dystrophy (causalgia)

Rarities
- Osteoid osteoma
- Polymyalgia rheumatica (isolated)
- Paget's disease
- Popliteal artery entrapment
- Tabes dorsalis
- Ruptured Baker's cyst

Q. *Seven masquerades checklist*

A.		
	Depression	✓
	Diabetes	✓
	Drugs	✓ (indirect)
	Anaemia	✓ (indirect)
	Thyroid disease	—
	Spinal dysfunction	✓✓
	UTI	—

Q. *Is this patient trying to tell me something else?*
A. Quite possible. Common with work-related injuries.

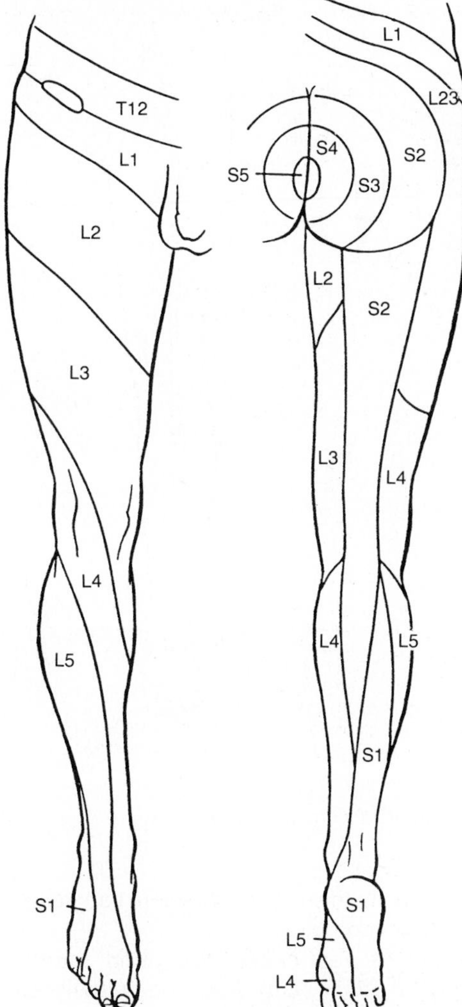

Fig. 56.1 *Dermatomes of the lower limb, representing approximate cutaneous distribution of the nerve roots*

Infections

Severe infections are not so common, but septic arthritis and osteomyelitis warrant consideration. Superficial infections such as erysipelas and lymphangitis occur occasionally.

Vascular problems

Acute severe ischaemia can be due to thrombosis or embolism of the arteries of the lower limb. Such occlusions cause severe pain in the limb and associated signs of severe ischaemia, especially of the lower leg and foot.

Chronic ischaemia due to arterial occlusion can manifest as intermittent claudication or rest pain in the foot due to small vessel disease.[1]

Various pain syndromes are presented in Figure 56.2. It is important to differentiate vascular claudication from neurogenic claudication (Table 56.2).

Venous disorders

The role of uncomplicated varicose veins as a cause of leg pain is controversial. Nevertheless, varicose veins can certainly cause a dull aching 'heaviness' and cramping, and can lead to painful ulceration.

Superficial thrombophlebitis is usually obvious, but it is vital not to overlook deep venous thrombosis. These more serious conditions of the veins can cause pain in the thigh or calf.

Pitfalls

There are many traps and pitfalls in the painful leg. Herpes zoster at the pre-eruption phase is an old trap and more so when the patient develops only a few vesicles in obscure parts of the limbs.

In future we can expect to encounter more cases of spinal canal stenosis (secondary to the degenerative changes) in the elderly. The early diagnosis can be difficult, and buttock pain on walking has to be distinguished from vascular claudication due to a high arterial obstruction.

The many disorders of the sacroiliac joint and hip region can be traps, especially the poorly diagnosed yet common gluteus medius tendinitis. Another more recent phenomenon is the 'hip pocket nerve syndrome', where a heavy wallet crammed with credit cards can cause pressure on the sciatic nerve.

One of the biggest traps, however, is when hip disorders, particularly osteoarthritis, present as leg pain, especially on the medial aspect of the knee.

Nerve entrapments (Fig. 56.3) are an interesting cause of leg pain, although not as common as in the upper limb. Some entrapments to consider include:

- lateral cutaneous nerve of thigh, known as meralgia paraesthetica
- common peroneal nerve
- posterior tibial nerve at ankle (the 'tarsal tunnel' syndrome)
- obturator nerve, in obturator canal
- femoral nerve (in inguinal region or pelvis)

Then there are the rare causes. One overlooked problem is sympathetic dystrophy, which may follow even minor trauma to the limb. This 'causalgia' syndrome manifests as burning or

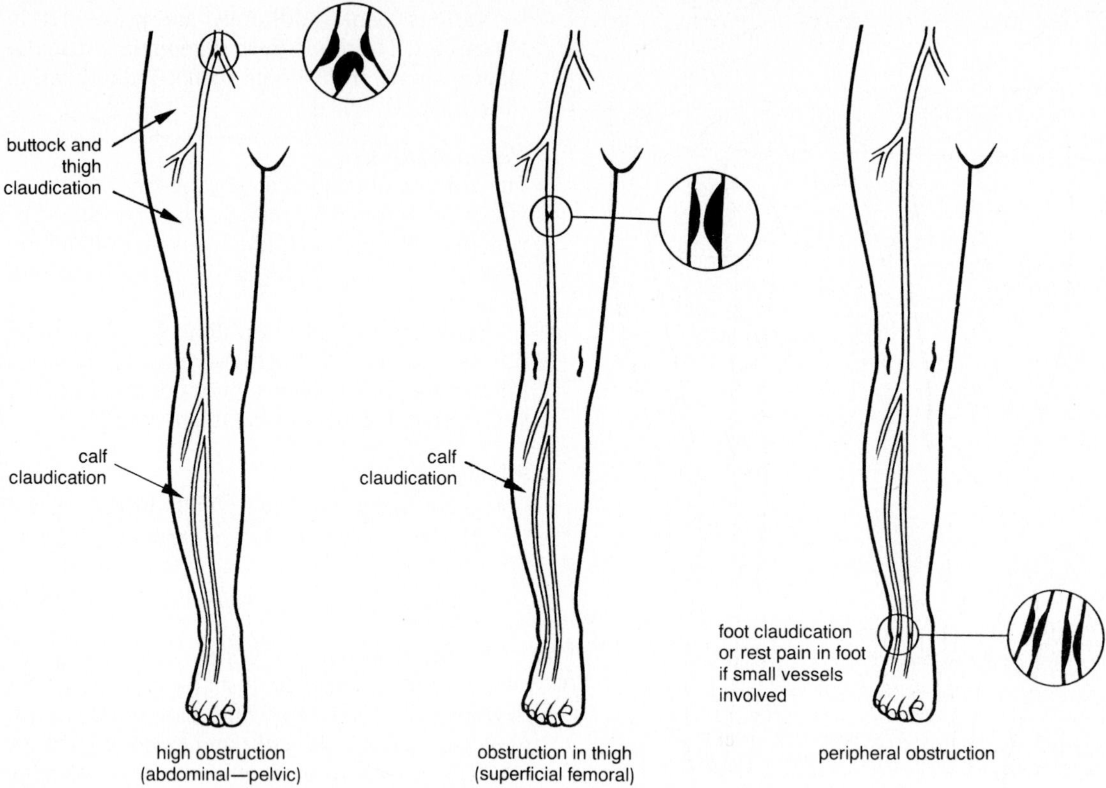

Fig. 56.2 *Arterial occlusion and related symptoms according to the level of obstruction*

aching pain with vasomotor instability in the limbs. The essential feature is the disparity between the intensity of the pain and the severity of the inciting injury.

General pitfalls

- overlooking beta-blockers and anaemia as a precipitating factor for vascular claudication
- overlooking hip disorders as a cause of knee pain
- mistaking occlusive arterial disease for sciatica
- confusing nerve root syndromes with entrapment syndromes

Seven masquerades checklist

The outstanding cause of leg pain in this group is spinal dysfunction. Apart from nerve root pressure due to a disc disruption or foraminal entrapment, pain can be referred from the apophyseal (facet joints). Such pain can be referred as far as the mid calf (Fig. 56.4).

The other checklist conditions—depression, diabetes, drugs and anaemia—can be associated with pain in the leg. Depression can reinforce any painful complex.

Diabetes can cause discomfort through a peripheral neuropathy that can initially cause localised pain before anaesthesia predominates. Drugs such as beta-blockers, and anaemia, can precipitate or aggravate intermittent claudication in a patient with a compromised circulation.

Psychogenic considerations

Pain in the lower leg can be a frequent complaint (maybe a magnified one) of the patient with non-organic pain, such as the malingerer, the conversion reaction patient (hysteria) and the depressed. Sometimes sympathetic dystrophy (reflex or post-traumatic) is incorrectly diagnosed as functional.

The clinical approach

Careful attention to basic detail in the history and examination can point the way of the clinical diagnosis.

Table 56.2 *Clinical features of neurogenic and vascular claudication*

	Neurogenic claudication	***Vascular claudication***
Cause	Spinal canal stenosis	Aortoiliac arterial occlusive disease
Age	Over 50 Long history of backache	Over 50
Pain site and radiation	Proximal location, initially lumbar, buttocks and legs Radiates distally	Distal location Buttocks, thighs and calves (especially) Radiates proximally
Type of pain	Weakness, burning, numbing or tingling (not cramping)	Cramping, aching, squeezing
Onset	Walking (uphill and downhill) Distance walked varies Prolonged standing	Walking a set distance each time, especially uphill
Relief	Lying down Flexing spine, e.g. squat position May take 20-30 minutes	Standing still—fast relief Slow walking decreases severity
Associations	Bowel and bladder symptoms	Impotence Rarely, paraesthesia or weakness
Physical examination		
Peripheral pulses	Present	Present (usually) Reduced or absent in some, especially after exercise
Lumbar extension	Aggravates	No change
Neurological	Saddle distribution Ankle jerk may be reduced after exercise	*Note*: abdominal bruits after exercise
Diagnosis confirmation	Radiological studies	Duplex ultrasound Ankle brachial index Arteriography

History

In the history it is important to consider several distinctive aspects, outlined by the following questions.

- Is the pain of acute or chronic onset?
- If acute, did it follow trauma or activity?
  - — If not, consider a vascular cause: vein or artery; occlusion or rupture.
- Is the pain 'mechanical' (related to movement)?
  - — If it is unaltered by movement of the leg or a change in posture, it must arise from a soft tissue lesion, not from bone or joints.
- Is the pain postural?
  - — Analyse the postural elements that make it better or worse.
  - — If worse on sitting, consider a spinal cause (discogenic) or ischial bursitis.
  - — If worse on standing, consider a spinal cause (instability) or a local problem related to weight bearing (varicose veins).
  - — If worse lying down, consider vascular origin such as small vessel peripheral vascular disease.
  - — Pain unaffected by posture is activity-related.
- Is the pain related to walking?
  - — *No*: determine the offending activity, e.g. joint movement with arthritis.
  - — *Yes*: if immediate onset, consider local cause at site of pain, e.g. stress fracture. If delayed, consider vascular claudication or neurogenic claudication.
- Is the site of pain the same as the site of trauma?
  - — If not, the pain in the leg is referred. Important considerations include lesions in the spine, abdomen or hip and entrapment neuropathy.
- Is the pain arising from the bone?
  - — If so, the patient will point to the specific site and indicate a 'deep' bone pain (consider tumour, fracture or, rarely, infection)

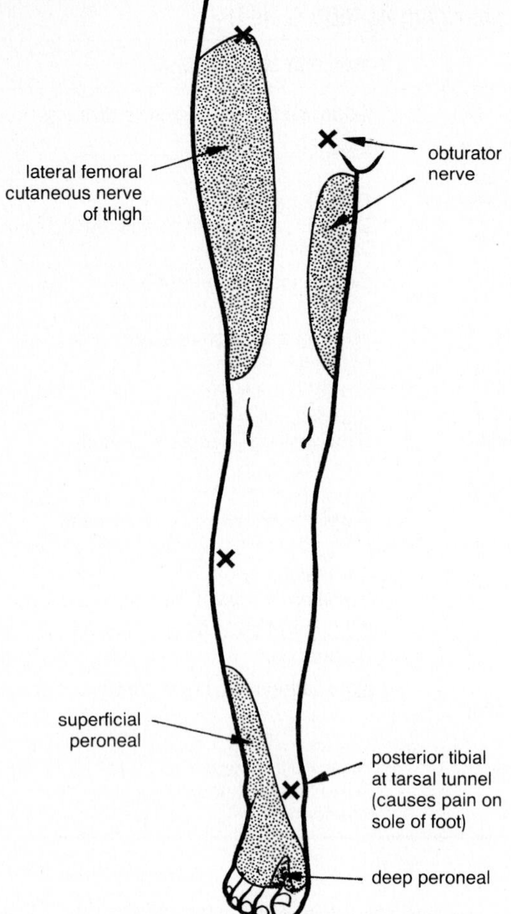

Fig. 56.3 *Distribution of pain in the leg from entrapment of specific nerves; the sites of entrapment are indicated by an* **X**

compared with the more superficial muscular or fascial pain.

- Is the pain arising from the joint?
  - — If so, the clinical examination will determine whether it arises from the joint or juxtaposed tissue.

Physical examination

The first step is to watch the patient walk and assess the nature of any limp.

Note the posture of the back and examine the lumbar spine. Have both legs well exposed for the inspection.

Inspect the patient's stance and note any asymmetry and other abnormalities such as swellings, bruising, discolouration, or ulcers and rashes. Note the size and symmetry of the legs and the venous pattern. Look for evidence of ischaemic changes, especially of the foot.

Palpate for local causes of pain and if no cause is evident examine the spine, blood vessels (arteries and veins) and bone. Areas to palpate specifically are the ischial tuberosity, trochanteric area, hamstrings and tendon insertions. Palpate the superficial lymph nodes. Note the temperature of the feet and legs. Perform a vascular examination including the peripheral pulses and the state of the veins if appropriate.

If evidence of PVD, remember to auscultate the abdomen, adductor hiatus, and iliac, femoral and popliteal vessels.

A neurological examination may be appropriate, particularly to test nerve root lesions or entrapment neuropathies.

Examination of the joints, especially the hip and sacroiliac joints, is very important.

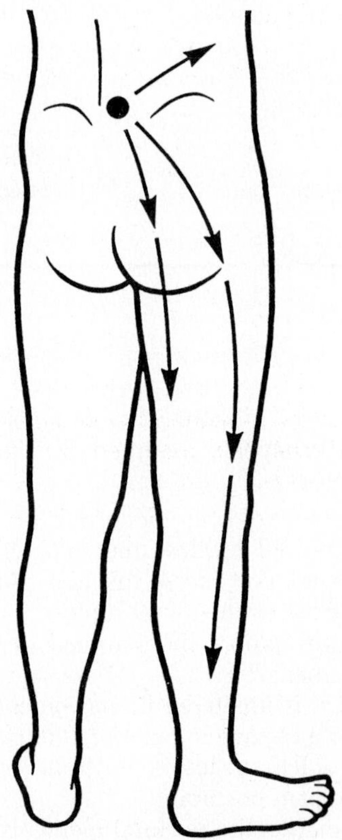

Fig. 56.4 *Possible referred pain patterns from dysfunction of an apophyseal joint, illustrating pain radiation patterns from stimulation by injection of the right L4–L5 apophyseal joint (after Brugger 1962)* REPRODUCED FROM C.KENNA AND J.MURTAGH *BACK PAIN AND SPINAL MANIPULATION*, BUTTERWORTHS, SYDNEY, 1989, WITH PERMISSION

Investigations

A checklist of investigations that may be necessary to make the diagnosis is as follows:

- Full blood examination and ESR
- X-rays: — leg, especially knee, hip
  - — plain X-ray of lumbosacral spine
  - — CT scan of lumbosacral spine
  - — MRI scan of lumbosacral spine
  - — bone scan
- Electromyography
- Vascular — arteriography
  - — duplex ultrasound scan
  - — ankle brachial index
  - — venous pool radionuclide scan
  - — contrast venography
  - — air plethysmograph (varicose veins)

Leg pain in children

Aches and pains in the legs are a common complaint in children. The most common cause is soreness and muscular strains due to trauma or unaccustomed exercise.

It is important to consider child abuse, especially if bruising is noted on the backs of the legs.

Growing pains

So-called 'growing pains', or idiopathic leg pain, is thought to be responsible for up to 20 per cent of leg pain in children.[2] Such a diagnosis is vague and often made when a specific cause is excluded. It is usually not due to 'growth' but related to excessive exercise or trauma from sport and recreation and probably emotional factors.

The pains are typically intermittent and symmetrical and deep in the legs, usually in the anterior thighs or calves. Although they may occur at any time of the day or night, typically they occur at night, usually when the child has settled in bed. The pains usually last for 30 to 60 minutes and tend to respond to attention such as massage with an analgesic balm or simple analgesics.

Serious problems

It is important to exclude fractures (hence the value of X-rays if in doubt), malignancy (such as osteogenic sarcoma, Ewing's tumour or infiltration from leukaemia or lymphoma), osteoid osteoma, osteomyelitis, scurvy and berri-berri (rare disorders in developed countries) and congenital disorders such as sickle cell disease, Gaucher's disease and Ehlers-Danlos syndrome.

Leg pain in the elderly

The older the patient the more likely it is that arterial disease with intermittent claudication and neurogenic claudication due to spinal canal stenosis will develop. Other important problems of the elderly include degenerative joint disease such as osteoarthritis of the hips and knees, muscle cramps, herpes zoster, Paget's disease, polymyalgia rheumatica (affecting the upper thighs) and sciatica.

Spinal causes of leg pain

Problems originating from the spine are an important, yet at times complex, cause of pain in the leg.

Important causes are:

- nerve root (radicular) pain from direct pressure
- referred pain from:
  - — disc pressure on tissues in front of the spinal cord
  - — apophyseal joints
  - — sacroiliac joints
- spinal canal stenosis causing claudication

Various pain patterns are presented in Figures 56.1 and 56.4.

Nerve root pain

Nerve root pain from a prolapsed disc is a common cause of leg pain. A knowledge of the dermatomes of the lower limb (Fig. 56.1) provides a pointer to the involved nerve root, which is usually L5 or S1 or both. The L5 root is invariably caused by an L4–L5 disc prolapse and the S1 root by a L5–S1 disc prolapse. The nerve root syndromes are summarised in Table 56.3.

A summary of the physical examination findings for the most commonly involved nerve roots is presented in Figure 56.5.

Sciatica

Sciatica is defined as pain in the distribution of the sciatic nerve or its branches (L4, L5, S1, S2, S3) that is caused by nerve pressure or irritation. Most problems are due to entrapment neuropathy of a nerve root, either in the spinal canal (as outlined above) or the intervertebral foramen.

It should be noted that back pain may be absent and peripheral symptoms only will be present.

Table 56.3 *Nerve root syndromes*

Nerve root	***Pain distribution***	***Sensory loss***	***Motor weakness changes***	***Reflex***
L3	Front of thigh, inner aspect of thigh, knee and leg	Anterior aspect of thigh	Extension of knee	Knee jerk
L4	Anterior thigh to front of knee	Lower outer aspect of thigh and knee, inner great toe	Flexion, adduction of knee, inversion of foot	Knee jerk
L5	Lateral aspect of leg, dorsum of foot and great toe	Dorsum of foot, great toe, 2nd and 3rd toes, anterolateral aspect of lower leg	Dorsiflexion of great toe	Tibialis posterior (clinically impractical)
S1	Buttock to back of thigh and leg, lateral aspect of ankle and foot	Lateral aspect of ankle, foot (4th and 5th toes)	Plantar flexion of ankle and toes, eversion of foot	Ankle jerk

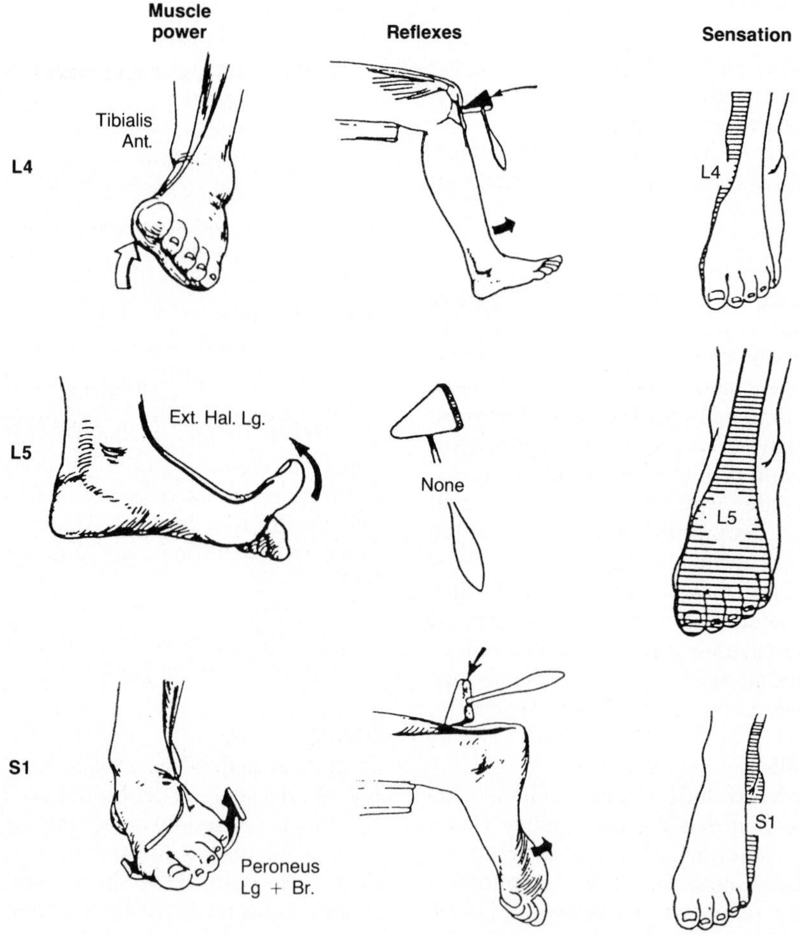

Fig. 56.5 *Comparison of neurological findings of the neurologic levels L4, L5 and S1* REPRODUCED FROM S.HOPPENFELD *PHYSICAL EXAMINATION OF THE SPINE AND EXTREMITIES*, APPLETON AND LANGE, NORWALK, CT, USA, WITH PERMISSION

Treatment of sciatica

Acute sciatica A protracted course can be anticipated, in the order of 12 weeks. The patient should be reassured that spontaneous recovery can be expected. A trial of conservative treatment would be recommended thus:

- back care education
- relative bed rest (2–3 days is optimal)—a firm base is ideal
- analgesics (avoid narcotic analgesics)
- NSAIDs (2–3 weeks is recommended)
- basic exercise program, including swimming
- traction can help, even intermittent manual

Referral to a therapist of your choice, e.g. physiotherapist, might be advisable. Conventional spinal manipulation is usually contraindicated for radicular sciatica. If the patient is not responding or the circumstances demand more active treatment, an epidural anaesthetic injection is appropriate. Surgical intervention is rarely necessary.

Chronic sciatica If a trial of NSAIDs, rest and physiotherapy have not brought significant relief, an epidural anaesthetic (lumbar or caudal) using half-strength local anaesthetic only (e.g. 0.25% bupivacine HCl) is advisable.

Referred pain

Referred pain in the leg can arise from disorders of the sacroiliac joints or from spondylogenic disorders. It is typically dull, heavy and diffuse. The patient uses the hand to describe its distribution compared with the use of fingers to point to radicular pain.

Spondylogenic pain

Non-radicular or spondylogenic pain is that which originates from any of the components of the vertebrae (spondyles) including joints, the intervertebral disc, ligaments and muscle attachments. An important example is distal referred pain from disorders of the apophyseal joints, where the pain can be referred to any part of the limb as far as the calf and ankle but most commonly to the gluteal region and proximal thigh (Fig. 56.4).

Another source of referred pain is that caused by compression of a bulging disc against the posterior longitudinal ligament and dura. The pain is typically dull, deep and poorly localised. The dura has no specific dermatomal localisation so the pain is usually experienced in the low back, sacroiliac area and buttocks. Less commonly it can be referred to the coccyx, groin and both legs to the calves. It is not referred to the ankle or the foot.

Sacroiliac dysfunction

This causes typically a dull ache in the buttock but it can be referred to the iliac fossa, groin or posterior aspects of the thighs. It rarely radiates to or below the knee. It may be caused by inflammation (sacroiliitis) or mechanical dysfunction. The latter must be considered in a postpartum woman presenting with severe aching pain present in both buttocks and thighs.

Nerve entrapment syndromes

Entrapment neuropathy can result from direct axonal compression or secondary to vascular problems but the main common factor is a nerve passing through a narrow rigid compartment where movement or stretching of that nerve occurs under pressure.

Clinical features of nerve entrapment:

- pain at rest (often worse at night)
- variable effect with activity
- sharp, burning pain
- radiating and retrograde pain
- clearly demarcated distribution of pain
- paraesthesia may be present
- tenderness over nerve
- may be positive Tinel's sign

Meralgia paraesthetica

This is the commonest lower limb entrapment and is due to the lateral femoral cutaneous nerve of the thigh being trapped under the lateral end of the inguinal ligament, 1 cm medial to the anterior superior iliac spine.[3]

The nerve is a sensory nerve from L2 and L3. It occurs mostly in middle-aged people, due mainly to thickening of the fibrous tunnel beneath the inguinal ligament, and is associated with obesity, pregnancy, ascites or local trauma such as belts, trusses, corsets. Its entrapment causes a burning pain with associated numbness and tingling (Fig. 56.3).

The distribution of pain is confined to a localised area of the lateral thigh and does not cross the midline of the thigh.

Differential diagnosis

- L2 or L3 nerve root pain (L2 causes buttock pain also)
- femoral neuropathy (extends medial to midline)

Treatment options

- injection of corticosteroid medial to the ASIS, under the inguinal ligament
- surgical release (neurolysis) if refractory

Note Meralgia paraesthetica often resolves spontaneously.

Peroneal nerve entrapment

The common peroneal (lateral popliteal) nerve can be entrapped where it winds around the neck of the fibula or as it divides and passes through the origin of the peroneus longus muscle 2.5 cm below the neck of the fibula. It is usually injured, however, by trauma or pressure at the neck of the fibula.

Symptoms and signs:

- pain in the lateral shin area and dorsum of the foot
- sensory symptoms in the same area
- weakness of eversion and dorsiflexion of the foot (described by patients as 'a weak ankle')

Differential diagnosis

L5 nerve root (similar symptoms)

Treatment:

- shoe wedging or other orthotics to maintain eversion
- neurolysis is the most effective treatment

Tarsal tunnel syndrome

This is an entrapment neuropathy of the posterior tibial nerve in the tarsal tunnel beneath the flexor retinaculum on the medial side of the ankle (Fig. 56.6a). The condition is due to dislocation or fracture around the ankle or tenosynovitis of tendons in the tunnel from injury, rheumatoid arthritis, and other inflammations.

Symptoms and signs

- a burning or tingling pain in the toes and sole of the foot, occasionally the heel
- retrograde radiation to calf, perhaps as high as the buttock
- numbness is a late symptom
- discomfort often in bed at night and worse after standing
- removal of shoe may give relief
- sensory nerve loss variable, may be no loss
- Tinel test (finger or reflex hammer tap over nerve below and behind medial malleolus) may be positive
- tourniquet applied above ankle may reproduce symptoms

The diagnosis is confirmed by electrodiagnosis.

Treatment

- relief of abnormal foot posture with orthotics
- corticosteroid injection
- decompression surgery if other measures fail

Injection for tarsal tunnel syndrome

Using a 23 gauge 32 mm needle, a mixture of triamcinolone 10 mg/ml or 40 mg methylprednisolone in 1% xylocaine or procaine is injected into the tunnel either from above or below the flexor retinaculum. The sites of injection are shown in Figure 56.6b; care is required not to inject the nerve.

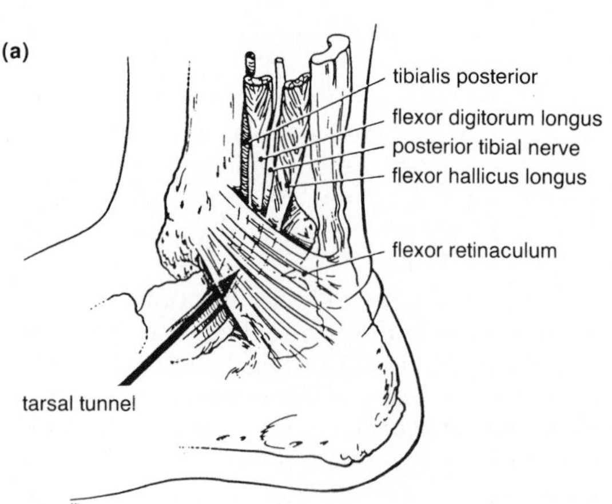

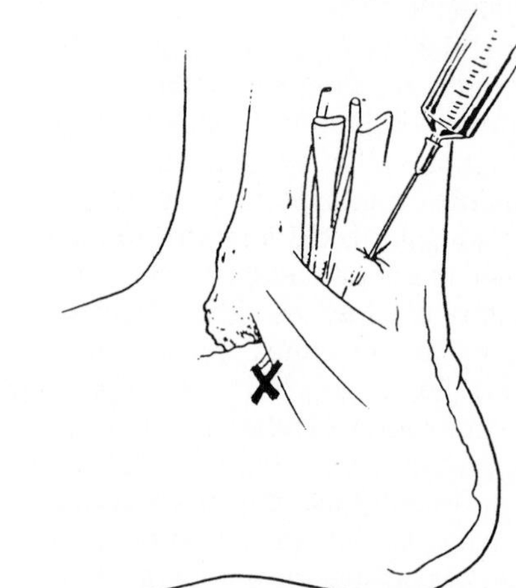

Fig. 56.6 **(a)** *Anatomy of the tarsal tunnel syndrome;* **(b)** *showing injection sites*

Vascular causes of leg pain

Occlusive arterial disease

Risk factors for peripheral vascular disease (for development and deterioration):

- smoking
- diabetes mellitus
- hypertension
- hypercholesterolaemia
- family history
- atrial fibrillation (embolism)

Precipitating factors for insufficiency:

- beta-blocking drugs
- anaemia

Acute lower limb ischaemia

Sudden occlusion is a dramatic event which requires immediate diagnosis and management to save the limb.

Causes:

- embolism—peripheral arteries
- thrombosis — major artery
  — popliteal aneurysm
- traumatic contusion, e.g. postarterial puncture

The symptoms and signs of acute embolism and thrombosis are similar, although thrombosis of an area of atherosclerosis is often preceded by symptoms of chronic disease, e.g. claudication. The commonest sites of acute occlusion are the superficial femoral artery and the common femoral artery (Fig. 56.7).

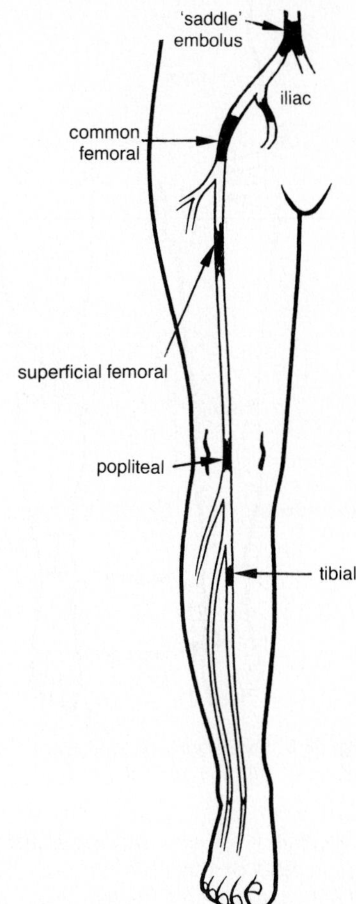

Fig. 56.7 *Common sites of acute arterial occlusion*

Signs and symptoms—the 6 P's

- Pain
- Pallor
- Paraesthesia or numbness
- Pulselessness
- Paralysis
- 'Perishing' cold

The pain is usually sudden and severe and any improvement may be misleading. Sensory changes initially affect light touch, not pinprick. Paralysis (paresis or weakness) and muscle compartment pain or tenderness is a most important and ominous sign.

Other signs include mottling of the legs, collapsed superficial veins, and no capillary return.

NB Look for evidence of atrial fibrillation.

Examination of arterial circulation

This applies to chronic ischaemia and also to acute ischaemia.

Skin and trophic changes

Note colour changes, hair distribution and wasting. Note the temperature of the legs and feet with the backs of your fingers.

Palpation of pulses

It is important to assess four pulses carefully (Fig. 56.8). Note that the popliteal and posterior tibial pulses are difficult to feel, especially in obese subjects.

Femoral artery Palpate deeply just below the inguinal ligament, midway between the anterior superior iliac spine and the symphysis pubis. If absent or diminished, palpate over abdomen for aortic aneurysm.

Popliteal artery Flex the leg to relax the hamstrings. Place fingertips of both hands to meet in the midline. Press them deeply into the

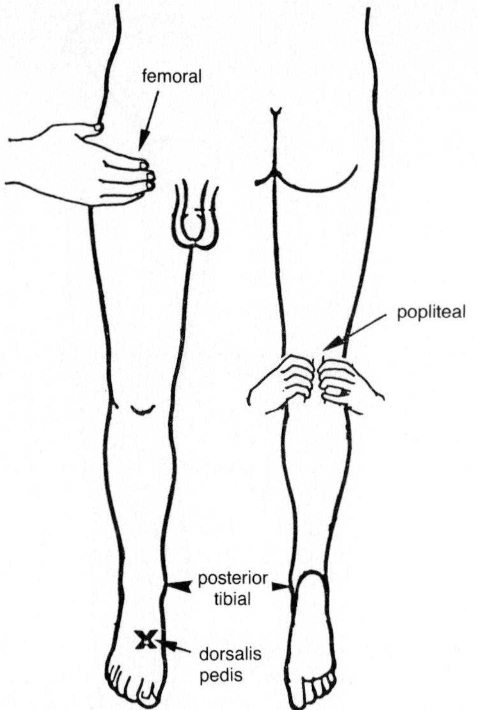

Fig. 56.8 *Sites of palpation of peripheral pulses in the leg*

popliteal fossa to compress artery against the upper end of the tibia, i.e. just below the level of the knee crease. Check for a popliteal aneurysm (very prominent popliteal pulsation).

Posterior tibial artery Palpate, with curved fingers, just behind and below the tip of the medial malleolus of the ankle.

Dorsalis pedis artery Feel at the proximal end of the first metatarsal space just lateral to the extensor tendon of the big toe.

Oedema

Look for evidence of oedema: pitting oedema is tested by pressing firmly with your thumb for at least 5 seconds over the dorsum of each foot, behind each medial malleolus and over the shins.

Postural colour changes (Buerger's test)

Raise both legs to about 60° for about 1 minute, when maximal pallor of the feet will develop. Then get the patient to sit up on the couch and hang both legs down.[4] Note, comparing both feet, the time required for return of pinkness to the skin (normally less than 10 seconds) and filling of the veins of the feet and ankles (normally about 15 seconds). Look for any unusual rubor (dusky redness) which takes a minute or more in the dependent foot. A positive Buerger's test is pallor on elevation–rubor on dependency.

Auscultation for bruits after exercise

Listen over abdomen and femoral area for bruits.

Note Neurological examination (motor, sensory, reflexes) is normal unless there is associated diabetic peripheral neuropathy.

Management of acute ischaemia

Golden rules Occlusion is usually reversible if treated within 4 hours, i.e. limb salvage. It is often irreversible if treated after 6 hours, i.e. limb amputation.

Treatment

- Intravenous heparin (immediately) 5000U
- Emergency embolectomy (ideally within 4 hours)
  - — under general or local anaesthesia
  - — through an arteriotomy at or below site of embolus
  - — embolus extracted with Fogarty balloon or catheter

or

- Arterial bypass if acute thrombosis in chronically diseased artery
- Amputation (early) if irreversible ischaemic changes

Chronic lower limb ischaemia

Chronic ischaemia caused by gradual arterial occlusion can manifest as intermittent claudication or rest pain in the foot.

Intermittent claudication is a pain or tightness in the muscle on exercise (Latin *claudicare*, to limp), relieved by rest. Rest pain is a constant severe burning-type pain or discomfort in the forefoot at rest, typically occurring at night when the blood flow slows down.

The main features are compared in Table 56.4.

Intermittent claudication

The level of obstruction determines which muscle belly is affected (Figs 56.2 and 56.7).

Proximal obstruction, e.g. aortoiliac

- pain in the buttock, thigh and calf, especially when walking up hills and stairs
- persistent fatigue over whole lower limb
- impotence is possible (Leriche syndrome)

Table 56.4 *Comparison between intermittent claudication and ischaemic rest pain*

	Intermittent claudication	*Ischaemic rest pain*
Quality of pain	Tightness/cramping	Constant ache
Timing of pain (typical)	Daytime; walking, other exercise	Night-time: rest
Tissue affected	Muscle	Skin
Site	Calf > thigh > buttock	Forefoot, toes, heels
Aggravation	Walking, exercise	Recumbent, walking
Relief	Rest	Hanging foot out of bed; dependency
Associations	Beta-blockers Anaemia	Night cramps Swelling of feet

Obstruction in the thigh

- superficial femoral (the commonest) causes pain in the calf, e.g. 200–500 metres, depending on collateral circulation
- profunda femoris → claudication about 100 metres
- multiple segment involvement → claudication 40–50 metres

Causes:

- atherosclerosis (mainly men over 50, smokers)
- embolisation (with recovery)
- Buerger's disease: affects small arteries, causes rest pain and cyanosis (claudication uncommon)
- popliteal entrapment syndrome (< 40 years of age)

Management of occlusive vascular disease

Prevention (for those at risk)

- Smoking is *the* risk factor and must be stopped.
- Other risk factors must be attended to and weight reduction to ideal weight is important.
- Exercise is excellent, especially walking.

Diagnostic plan

- Check if patient is taking beta-blockers.
- General tests: blood examination, random blood sugar, urine examination, ECG.
- Measure blood flow by duplex ultrasound examination or ankle brachial index.
- Arteriography performed *only* if surgery contemplated.

Treatment

- General measures (if applicable): control obesity, diabetes, hypertension, hyperlipidaemia, cardiac failure.
- Achieve ideal weight.
- Absolutely no smoking.
- Exercise: daily graduated exercise to the level of pain. About 50% will improve with walking so advise as much walking as possible.
- Try to keep legs warm and dry.
- Maintain optimal foot care (podiatry).
- Drug therapy: aspirin 150 mg daily.

Note Vasodilators and sympathectomy are of little value.
About one-third progress, while the rest regress or don't change.[5]

When to refer to a vascular surgeon

- 'Unstable' claudication of recent onset; deteriorating
- Severe claudication—unable to maintain lifestyle
- Rest pain
- 'Tissue loss' in feet, e.g. heel cracks, ulcers on or between toes, dry gangrenous patches, infection

Surgery Reconstructive vascular surgery is indicated for progressive obstruction, intolerable claudication and obstruction above the inguinal ligament.

- endarterectomy—for localised iliac stenosis
- bypass graft (iliac or femoral artery to popliteal or anterior or posterior tibial arteries)

Percutaneous transluminal dilation: this angioplasty is performed with a special intra-arterial balloon catheter for localised limited occlusions. An alternative to the balloon is laser angioplasty.

Venous disorders

Varicose veins

Varicose veins are dilated, tortuous and lengthened superficial veins in the lower extremity. They may be classified as primary or secondary.

1. *Primary varicose veins* are veins dilated because of incompetence of the valves in the superficial veins or in the communicating or perforating veins between the deep and superficial systems (Fig. 56.9). The cause is unknown but there are several predisposing factors (Table 56.5), the most important being family history, female sex (5:1), pregnancy and multiparity.

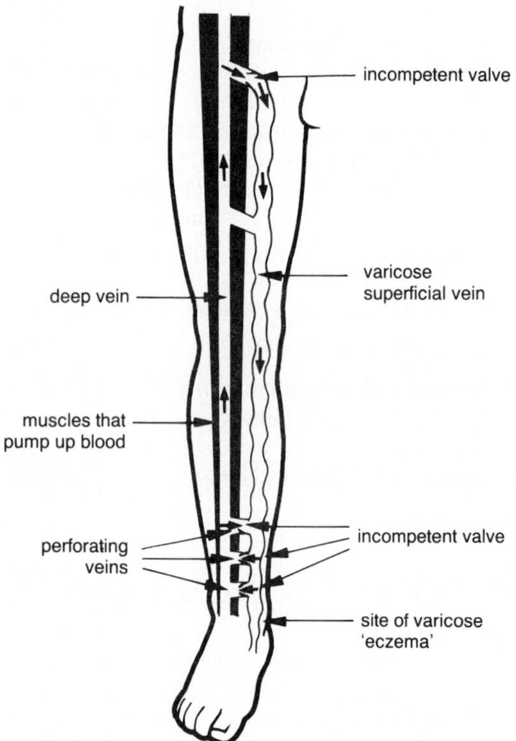

Fig. 56.9 *The common sites of varicose veins*

2. *Secondary varicose veins* have a known cause and are the result of extrinsic compression of the veins by a pelvic or intra-abdominal tumour (e.g. ovarian carcinoma, retroperitoneal fibrosis) or deep vein thrombosis.

Symptoms

Varicose veins may be symptomless, the main complaint being their unsightly appearance. Symptoms include swelling, fatigue, heaviness in the limb, an aching discomfort and itching.

Table 56.5 *Risk factors for varicose veins*

Female sex
Family history
Pregnancy
Multiparity
Age
Occupation
Diet (low-fibre)

Varicose veins and pain

They may be painless even if large and tortuous. Pain is a feature where there are incompetent perforating veins running from the posterior tibial vein to the surface through the soleus muscle.

Severe cases lead to the lower leg venous hypertension syndrome[6] characterised by pain worse after standing, cramps in the leg at night, irritation and pigmentation of the skin, swelling of the ankles and loss of skin features such as hair.

A careful history will usually determine if the aching is truly due to varicose veins and not to transient or cyclical oedema which is a common condition in women.[7]

The complications of varicose veins are summarised in Table 56.6.

Table 56.6 *Complications of varicose veins*

Superficial thrombophlebitis
Skin 'eczema' (10%)
Skin ulceration (20%)
Bleeding
Calcification
Marjolin's ulcer (squamous cell carcinoma)

Examination

The following tests will help determine the site or sites of the incompetent valves.

Venous groin cough impulse This helps determine long saphenous vein incompetence.

Place the fingers over the line of the vein immediately below the fossa ovalis (4 cm below and 4 cm lateral to the pubic tubercle[8]). Ask the patient to cough—an impulse or thrill will be felt expanding and travelling down the long saphenous vein. A marked dilated long saphenous vein in the fossa ovalis (saphena varix) will confirm incompetence. It disappears when the patient lies down.

Trendelenburg test In this test for long saphenous vein competence the patient lies down and the leg is elevated to 45° to empty the veins (Fig. 56.10a). Apply a tourniquet with sufficient pressure to prevent reflux over the upper thigh just below the fossa ovalis. (Alternatively, this opening can be occluded by firm finger pressure, as originally described by Trendelenburg.)

The patient then stands. The long saphenous system will remain collapsed if there are no incompetent veins below the level of the fossa ovalis. When the pressure is released the vein will fill rapidly if the valve at the saphenofemoral junction is incompetent (Fig. 56.10b). This is a positive Trendelenburg test.

Note A doubly positive Trendelenburg test is when the veins fill rapidly before the pressure is released and then with a 'rush' when released. This indicates coexisting incompetent perforators and long saphenous vein.

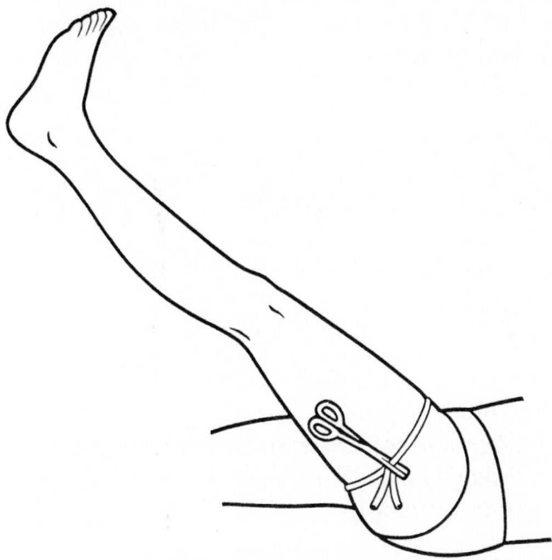

Fig. 56.10a *Trendelenberg test: the leg is elevated to 45° to empty the veins and a tourniquet applied*

Short saphenous vein incompetence test A similar test to the Trendelenburg test is performed with the pressure (tourniquet or finger) being applied over the short saphenous vein just below the popliteal fossa (Fig. 56.11).

Incompetent perforating vein test Accurate clinical tests to identify incompetence in the three common sites of perforating veins on the medial

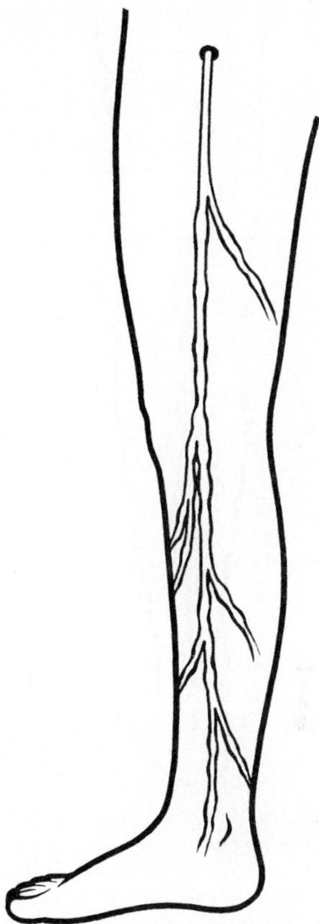

Fig. 56.10b *Trendelenberg test: test for competence of long saphenous venous system (medial aspect of knee)*

aspect of the leg, posterior to the medial border of the tibia, are difficult to perform. The general appearance of the leg and palpation of the sites give some indication of incompetence here.

Note Modern Doppler ultrasound studies over these sites and air plethysmography will accurately localise sites of incompetence.

Management of varicose veins

Prevention:

- Maintain ideal weight.
- Eat a high-fibre diet.
- Rest and wear supportive stockings if at risk (pregnancy, a standing occupation).

Treatment:

- Keep off legs as much as possible.
- Sit with legs on a footstool.
- Use supportive stockings or tights (apply in morning before standing out of bed).
- Avoid scratching itching skin over veins.

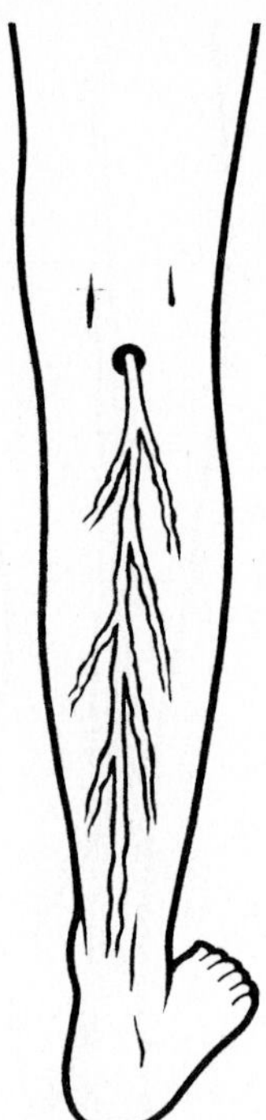

Fig. 56.11 *Testing for competence of the short saphenous vein*

Compression sclerotherapy:

- Use a small volume of sclerosant, e.g. 5% ethanolamine oleate; STD.
- Ideal for smaller isolated veins.

Surgical ligation and stripping:

- The best treatment when a clear association exists between symptoms and obvious varicose veins, i.e. long saphenous vein incompetence.
- Remove obvious varicosities and ligate perforators.

Superficial thrombophlebitis

- usually occurs in superficial varicose veins
- presents as a tender, reddened subcutaneous cord in leg
- usually localised oedema
- no generalised swelling of the limb or ankle
- requires symptomatic treatment only (see below) unless there is extension above the level of the knee when there is a risk of pulmonary embolism

Treatment

The objective is to prevent propagation of the thrombus by uniform pressure over the vein.

- Cover whole tender cord with a thin foam pad.
- Apply a firm elastic bandage (preferable to crepe) from foot to thigh (well above cord).
- Leave pad and bandage on for 7–10 days.
- Bed rest with leg elevated is recommended.
- Prescribe an NSAID, e.g. indomethacin, for 10 days.

Note

- No anticoagulants are required.
- The traditional glycerin and ichthyol dressings are still useful.
- Consider association between thrombophlebitis and deep-seated carcinoma.
- If the problem is above the knee, ligation of the vein at the saphenofemoral junction may be necessary.

Deep venous thrombosis (DVT)

There is an up to 20% association with pulmonary emboli, of which 30% may be fatal. DVT may be asymptomatic but usually causes tenderness in the calf. One or more of the following features may be present.

Clinical features

- ache or tightness in calf
- acute diffuse leg swelling
- pitting oedema
- tender 'doughy' consistency to palpation
- increased warmth
- pain on extension of foot (Homan's sign)

Differential diagnosis

- Pseudophlebitis from ruptured popliteal (Baker's) cyst. This must be excluded before anticoagulation.

Investigations

- duplex ultrasound
  and/or
- radionuclide scan
- contrast venography if these two accurate tests are negative.

Management

Prevention (cases at risk):

- elastic stockings
- physiotherapy
- pneumatic compression

Treatment

- bed rest with leg elevated
- one-way-stretch elastic bandages (both legs to above knees)
- IV heparin—continuous monitored infusion (at least 10 days); aim for partial thromboplastin time 1.5 to 2 normal
- oral anticoagulant (warfarin) for 3 months
- mobilisation with resolution of pain, tenderness and swelling

Surgery is necessary in extensive and embolising cases.

Management of other painful conditions

Cellulitis and erysipelas

- rest in bed
- elevate limb (in and out of bed)
- aspirin for pain and fever

Streptococcus pyogenes (the common cause):[9]
severe
  benzylpenicillin 1.2 g IV 4 hourly
less severe
  procaine penicillin 1 g IM 12 hourly
    or
  phenoxymethyl penicillin 500 mg (o) 6 hourly
if penicillin sensitive
  cephalothin IV or cephalexin 0.5 mg (o) 6 hourly
    or
  erythromycin 500 mg (o) 12 hourly

Staphylococcus aureus:[9]
severe, may be life-threatening
  flucloxacillin 2 g IV 6 hourly
less severe
  flucloxacillin 500 mg (o) 6 hourly
    or
  cephalexin 500 mg (o) 6 hourly
    or
  erythromycin 500 mg (o) 12 hourly

Nocturnal cramps

- treat cause (if known)
- muscle stretching and relaxation exercises: calf stretching for 3 minutes before retiring[10], then rest in chair with the feet out horizontally to the floor with cushion under tendoachilles for 10 minutes
- massage and heat to affected muscles
- drug treatment
  quinine sulphate 300 mg nocte
    or
  biperiden 2–4 mg nocte

Roller injuries to legs

A patient who has been injured by a wheel passing over a limb, especially a leg, can present a difficult problem. A freely spinning wheel is not so dangerous but serious injuries occur when a non-spinning (braked) wheel passes over a limb and are compounded by the wheel then reversing over it. This leads to a 'degloving' injury due to shearing stress. The limb may look satisfactory initially, but skin necrosis may follow.

- Admit to hospital for observation.
- Fasciotomy with open drainage may be an option.
- Surgical decompression with removal of necrotic fat is often essential.

When to refer

- the sudden onset of pain, pallor, pulselessness, paralysis, paraesthesia and coldness in the leg
- worsening intermittent claudication
- rest pain in foot
- presence of popliteal aneurysm
- superficial thrombophlebitis above knee
- evidence of deep venous thrombosis
- suspicion of gas gangrene in leg
- worsening hip pain
- evidence of disease in bone, e.g. neoplasia, infection, Paget's
- severe sciatica with neurological deficit, e.g. floppy foot, absent reflexes

Practice tips

- Always X-ray the legs (including hips) of a patient complaining of unusual deep leg pain, especially a child.
- Pain which does not fluctuate in intensity with movement, activity or posture has an inflammatory or neoplastic cause.
- Hip disorders such as osteoarthritis and slipped femoral epiphysis can present as pain in the knee (usually medial aspect).
- Consider retroperitoneal haemorrhage as a cause of acute severe nerve root pain, especially in people on anticoagulant therapy.

- Avoidance of amputation with acute lower limb ischaemia depends on early recognition (surgery within 4 hours—too late if over 6 hours).

References

1. House AK. The painful limb: is it intermittent claudication? Modern Medicine Australia, November 1990: 16–26.
2. Tunnessen WW. *Signs and symptoms in paediatrics* (2nd edition). Philadelphia: Lippincott, 1988,483.
3. Hart FD. *Practical problems in rheumatology*. London: Dunitz, 1983, 120.
4. Bates B. *A guide to physical examination and history taking* (5th edition). New York: Lippincott, 1991, 450.
5. Fry J, Berry H. *Surgical problems in clinical practice*. London: Edward Arnold, 1987, 125–134.
6. Ryan P. *A very short textbook of surgery* (2nd edition). Canberra: Dennis and Ryan, 1990, 61.
7. Hunt P, Marshall V. *Clinical problems in general surgery*. Sydney: Butterworths, 1991, 172.
8. Davis A, Bolin T, Ham J. *Symptom analysis and physical diagnosis* (2nd edition). Sydney: Pergamon, 1990, 179.
9. Mashford ML. (Chairman) Victorian Medical Postgraduate Foundation *Antibiotic guidelines* (7th edition). Melbourne, 1990, 38–39.
10. Murtagh JE. *Practice tips*. Sydney: McGraw-Hill, 1991, 179.

57

Pain in the foot and ankle

The victim goes to bed and sleeps in good health. About two o' clock in the morning he is awakened by a severe pain in the great toe; more rarely in the heel, ankle, or instep . . . The part affected cannot bear the weight of the bed clothes nor the jar of a person walking in the room. The night is spent in torture.

Thomas Sydenham (1624–1689)

Pain in the foot (podalgia) and ankle problems are a common occurrence in general practice. Various characteristics of the pain can give an indication of its cause, such as the description of gout by Thomas Sydenham. There are many traumatic causes of podalgia and ankle dysfunction, especially fractures and torn ligaments, but this chapter will focus mainly on common everyday problems that develop spontaneously or through overuse. The main causes of foot pain are presented in Table 57.1.[1]

Key facts and checkpoints

- Foot deformities such as flat feet (pes planus) are often painless.
- Foot strain is probably the commonest cause of podalgia.[2]
- A common deformity of the toes is hallux valgus, with or without bunion formation.
- Osteoarthritis is a common sequel to hallux valgus.
- Osteoarthritis affecting the ankle is relatively rare.
- All the distal joints of the foot may be involved in arthritic disorders.
- Many foot and ankle problems are caused by unsuitable footwear and lack of foot care.
- Ankle sprains are the most common injury in sport, representing about 25% of injuries.
- Severe sprains of the lateral ligaments of the ankle due to an inversion force may be associated with various fractures.
- Bunions and hammer toes are generally best treated by surgery.

A diagnostic approach

A summary of the safety diagnostic model is presented in Table 57.2.

Probability diagnosis

Common causes include osteoarthritis, especially of the first metatarsophalangeal joint, acute or chronic foot strain, plantar fasciitis, plantar skin conditions such as warts, corns and calluses and various toe-nail problems.

Serious disorders not to be missed

The very important serious disorders to consider include:

- vascular disease—affecting small vessels
- diabetic neuropathy
- osteoid osteoma
- rheumatoid arthritis
- reflex sympathetic dystrophy

Table 57.1 *Causes of foot pain (after Johnson)*[1]

General
Arthritis—OA, gout, RA, seronegative spondyloarthropathies.
Diabetes—neuropathy [sensory (Charcot), motor, autonomic, single nerve], sepsis, vasculopathy.
Peripheral neuritis—alcohol, B_{12} deficiency.
Vascular—arteriosclerosis (claudication, gangrene), hemiplegia, Raynaud's, RSD (Sudeck's).
Infections—cellulitis, septic arthritis, TB, actinomyces.
Other: Paget's disease of bone, osteoid osteoma, hypermobility syndrome (including Marfan's).

Ankle and hindfoot
Tendoachilles (bursitis, tendinitis, tear), posterior tibial tendinitis or subluxation, plantar fasciitis, sprain, bruised heel, phlebitis, cellulitis.

Midtarsal
Acute or chronic foot strain, synovitis of subtaloid, tarsal coalition, hypomobilty of transverse tarsal joints, osteochondritis of navicular (Kohler's), dorsal exostosis, peroneus brevis tendinitis, flexor hallucis longus tendinitis.

Forefoot
Bunion, bunionette, Tailor's bunion, intermetatarsal bursitis, traumatic synovitis of MTP, sesamoiditis, march fracture, Freiberg's infraction.

Toes
Hallux valgus, hallux rigidus, varus little toe, mallet toe, clawed toe, corn, wet corn, ingrown toenail, onychogryphosis, subungual exostosis, deep peroneal nerve entrapment, digital nerve entrapment (Morton's neuralgia).

Sole
Callus, plantar wart, epidermoid cyst, foreign body, tarsal tunnel syndrome, Dupuytren's (Ledderhose's) contracture.

OA: osteoarthritis RA: rheumatoid arthritis MTP: metatarsophalangeal

Vascular causes

The main problem is ischaemic pain that occurs only in the foot. The commonest cause is atheroma. Vascular causes include:

- acute arterial obstruction
- chilblains
- atherosclerosis, especially small vessel disease
- functional vasospasm (Raynaud's)—rare

Symptoms:

- claudication (rare in isolation)
- sensory disturbances, especially numbness at rest or on walking
- rest pain—at night, interfering with sleep, precipitated by elevation, relieved by dependency.

For treatment refer to page 573.

Reflex sympathetic dystrophy (RSD)

RSD, also known as Sudeck's atrophy, is characterised by severe pain, swelling and disability of the feet. It is a neurovascular disorder resulting in hyperaemia and osteoporosis that may be a sequela of trauma (often trivial) and prolonged immobilisation. RSD usually lasts two years and recovery to normality usually follows.

The clinical features include sudden onset in middle-aged patients, pain worse at night, stiff joints and skin warm and red. X-rays that show patchy decalcification of bone are diagnostic. Treatment includes reassurance, analgesics, mobility in preference to rest, and physiotherapy.

Osteoid osteoma

Osteoid osteomas are rare but important little 'brain teasers' of benign tumours that typically occur in older children and adolescents. Males are affected twice as often as females. Any bone (except those of the skull) can be affected but the tibia and femur are the main sites. Nocturnal pain is a prominent symptom with pain relief by aspirin being a feature.

Diagnosis is dependent on clinical suspicion and then X-ray which shows a small sclerotic lesion with a radiolucent centre. Treatment is by surgical excision.

Pitfalls

There are many traps in the diagnosis and management of problems presenting with a painful foot. Common problems require consideration—these include gouty arthritis, chilblains, a stress fracture and a foreign body in the foot, especially in children. Nerve entrapment as outlined in the painful leg is uncommon but Morton's neuroma is reasonably common.

Less common disorders include RSD which is often misdiagnosed, the spondyloarthropathies (psoriasis, Reiter's disease, ankylosing spondylitis and the inflammatory bowel

Table 57.2 *The painful foot and ankle: diagnostic strategy model*

Q. Probability diagnosis
A. Acute or chronic foot strain
Sprained ankle
Osteoarthritis, esp. great toe
Plantar fasciitis
Achilles tendinitis
Wart, corn or callus
Ingrowing toe-nail/paronychia

Q. Serious disorders not to be missed
A. Vascular insufficiency
- small vessel disease

Neoplasia
- osteoid osteoma
- osteosarcoma

Severe infections (rare)
- septic arthritis
- actinomycosis
- osteomyelitis

Rheumatoid arthritis
Reflex sympathetic dystrophy
Ruptured Achilles tendon

Q. Pitfalls (often missed)
A. Foreign body (especially children)
Gout
Nerve entrapment
- Morton's neuroma
- tarsal tunnel syndrome
- deep peroneal nerve

Chilblains
Stress fracture, e.g. navicular
Erythema nodosum

Rarities
Spondyloarthropathies
Reflex sympathetic dystrophy
Osteochondritis
- navicular (Köhler's)
- metatarsal head (Freiberg)
- calcaneum (Sever's)

Glomus tumour (under nail)
Paget's disease

Q. Seven masquerades checklist

A.	
Depression	?
Diabetes	✓
Drugs	✓
Anaemia	?
Thyroid disease	—
Spinal dysfunction	✓
UTI	—

Q. Is the patient trying to tell me something?
A. A non-organic cause warrants consideration with any painful condition.

disorders) and osteochondritis of the calcaneus, navicular bone and metatarsal head. If there is an exquisitely tender small purple-red spot beneath a toe-nail, a glomus tumour (a benign hamartoma) is the diagnosis. It is worth noting that most of these conditions are diagnosed by X-rays.

General pitfalls

- Failing to order X-rays of the foot.
- Failing to order X-rays of the ankle following injury.
- Failing to appreciate the potential for painful problems caused by diabetes—neuropathy and small vessel disease.
- Neglecting the fact that most of the arthritides can manifest in joints in the foot, especially the forefoot.
- Regarding the sprained ankle in adults and children as an innocuous injury: associated injuries include chondral fractures to the dome of the talus, impaction fractures around the medial recess of the ankle, avulsion fractures of the lateral malleolus and base of fifth metatarsal.
- Misdiagnosing a stress fracture of the navicular which, like the scaphoid fracture, causes delayed union and non-union. Cast immobilisation for eight weeks initially may prevent the need for surgery.
- Misdiagnosing a complete rupture of the Achilles tendon because the patient can plantar flex the foot.

Seven masquerades checklist

The checklist has four conditions that should be considered, especially diabetes and spinal dysfunction. Diabetes may be responsible for a simple type of atherosclerotic pattern, possibly complicated by infection and ulceration. The neuropathy of diabetes can cause a burning pain with paraesthesia. It has a 'sock'-type pattern as opposed to the dermatome pattern of nerve root pressure arising from the lumbosacral spine. The common S1 pain is experienced on the outer border of the foot, into the fifth toe and on the outer sole and heel of the foot.

Drugs and anaemia could indirectly cause pain through vascular insufficiency. The drugs that could cause vasospasm include beta-blockers and ergotamine. An alcoholic neuropathy also has to be considered.

Psychogenic considerations

Any painful condition can be closely associated with psychogenic disorders, including depression.

The clinical approach

History

This is very important, as always, since various characteristics of the pain can give an indication of its cause. Questions should address the quality of the pain, its distribution, mode of onset, periodicity, relation to weight bearing, and associated features such as swelling or colour change. It is relevant to enquire about pain in other joints such as the hand and spine, including the sacroiliac joints, which might indicate that the foot pain is part of a polyarthritis. A history of diarrhoea, psoriasis, urethritis or iritis may suggest that one of the spondyloarthropathies has to be excluded.

Key questions

The practitioner should address the following questions:

- Does the pain arise from a local condition or is it part of a generalised disease?
- Is there a history of psoriasis, chronic diarrhoea or colitis, urethritis or iritis?
- Is pain also present in other joints, thus indicating the foot pain is part of a polyarthritis, such as rheumatoid arthritis?
- Is the problem related to unsuitable footwear?
- Does the nature of the pain point to the cause?
  - throbbing pain → inflammation
  - burning pain → nerve entrapment, diabetic neuropathy or RSD
  - severe episodic pain → gout
  - pain worse at night → ischaemia (small vessel disease), RSD, cramps or osteoid osteoma
  - pain worse at night, relieved by aspirin → osteoid osteoma
  - pain worse on standing after sitting and getting out of bed → plantar fasciitis

For ankle injuries it is important to ask about the nature of the injury:

- Did the foot twist in (invert) or twist out (evert)?
- Was the foot pointing down or up at the time of injury?
- Point with one finger to where it hurts (the finger-pointing sign)
- What happened immediately after the injury?
- Were you able to walk straight away?
- What happened when you cooled off?

If there has been a fall onto the foot from a height, consider the possibility of a fracture of the calcaneus or talus or disruption of the syndesmosis between the tibia and fibula.

Physical examination

Inspection

Inspect the feet with the patient standing, sitting, walking (in shoes and bare-footed) and lying down (note plantar surfaces). Inspect the footwear (normally a shoe wears first on the outer posterior margin of the heel).

Note

- any gait abnormalities including limping and abnormal toe in or toe out
- deformities, e.g. hammer toes, bunions—medial (hallux valgus) and lateral (Tailor's bunion)—and claw toes
- swellings including callosities
- muscle wasting
- skin changes and signs of ischaemia

Palpation

Systematic palpation is very useful as most structures in the foot are accessible to palpation.

Movements (active and passive)

- plantar flexion (normal—50°) and dorsiflexion (20°) of ankle
- inversion and eversion of hindfoot (mainly subtalar joint)—hold heel and abduct and adduct (Fig. 57.1)
- inversion and eversion of forefoot (midtarsal joint)—hold heel in one hand to fix hindfoot, hold forefoot in the other and abduct and adduct (rotation movement) (Fig. 57.2)
- test other joints individually, e.g. metatarsophalangeal, midtarsal

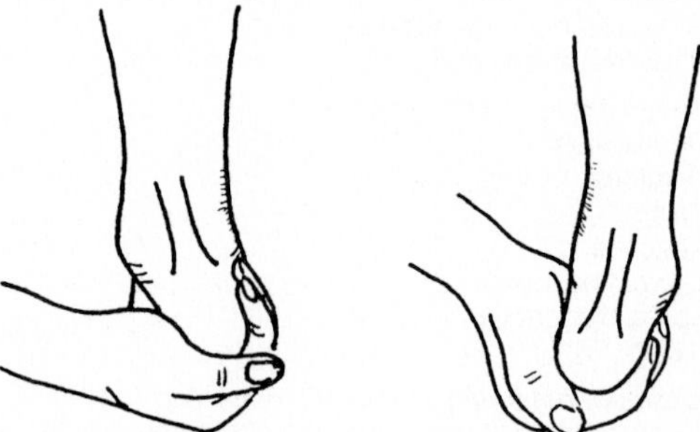

Fig. 57.1 *Testing inversion and eversion of the hindfoot*

Special tests

- Achilles tendon including calf squeeze (Thompson's test) (Fig. 110.11)
- compress metatarsophalangeal joints from above and below

- compress metatarsals mediolaterally between thumb and forefinger
- check circulation—test dorsalis pedis and posterior tibial pulses
- neurological examination including tests for L4, L5 and S1 nerve root function

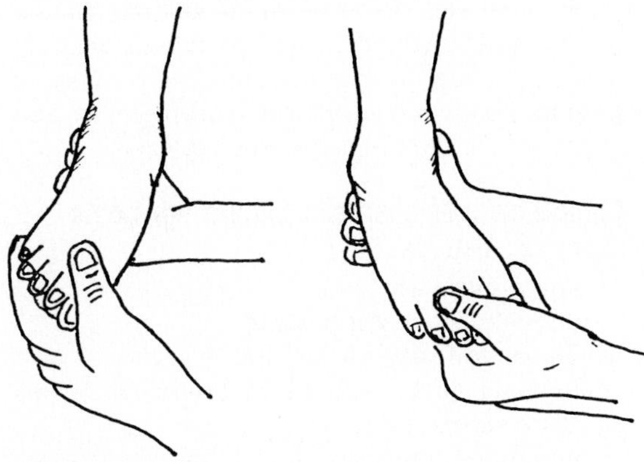

Fig. 57.2 *Testing inversion and eversion of the forefoot*

Investigations

The choice of investigations depends on the clinical features elicited by the history and examination. Select from the following list:

- For systemic diseases
  - blood glucose
  - RA tests
  - ESR
- Serum uric acid
- Radiology
  - X-ray
  - radionuclide scans
  - CT scans
  - ultrasound
- Nerve condition studies

NB High-resolution ultrasound is used to diagnose disorders of the Achilles tendon and to locate foreign bodies such as splinters of wood and glass.

Foot and ankle pain in children

Apart from the common problem of trauma, special problems in children include:

- foreign bodies in the foot
- tumours, e.g. osteoid osteoma, osteosarcoma, Ewing's tumour
- plantar warts
- ingrowing toe-nails
- osteochondritis/aseptic necrosis
- osteochondritis dessicans of talus (in adolescents)
- pitted keratolysis and juvenile plantar dermatosis (adolescents)

Osteochondritis/aseptic necrosis

Three important bones to keep in mind are:

- the calcaneum—Sever's disease
- the navicular—Köhler's disease
- the head of the second metatarsal—Freiberg's disease

Sever's disease is traction osteochondritis while the other disorders are a 'crushing' osteochondritis with avascular necrosis.

Sever's disease of the heel

This is calcaneal apophysitis which presents in a child (usually a boy) aged 8–12 (average of 10 years) with a painful tender heel at the insertion of tendoachilles. It is diagnosed by X-ray. The only treatment is to ensure that the child avoids wearing flat-heeled shoes and wears a slightly raised heel. Strenuous sporting activities should be restricted for 12 weeks.

Köhler's disease of the navicular

This disorder causes a painful limp (usually mild) with some swelling and tenderness around the navicular in a child (usually a boy) aged 3–6 years, although it is seen sometimes in older children. Complete recovery occurs with temporary resting. Sometimes a supportive strapping is helpful.

Freiberg's disease

This problem affects the head of the second metatarsal (rarely the third) which feels tender and swollen on palpation. It is more common in girls aged 12–16 and can present in young adults. The treatment is restriction of activity and protective padding.

Sprained ankle in a child

Children rarely sprain ligaments so it is important to assess apparent strains carefully, including an X-ray.

Skin disorders

Two conditions commonly seen in teenagers are pitted keratolysis and juvenile plantar dermatosis.

Pitted keratolysis

This malodorous condition known as 'stinky feet' or 'sneaker's' feet is related to sweaty feet. Treatment includes keeping the feet dry and using an ointment such as Whitfield's or an imidazole or sodium fusidate to remove the responsible Corynebacterium organism.

Juvenile plantar dermatosis

'Sweaty sock dermatitis' is a painful condition of weight-bearing areas of the feet. The affected skin is red, shiny, smooth and often cracked. It is rare in adults. The treatment is to change to leather or open shoes and to cotton socks. A simple emollient cream gives excellent relief.

The little athlete

The 'little athlete' can suffer a variety of injuries from accidents and overuse. Diffuse heel pain, which is common, is most commonly related to Sever's apophysitis of the calcaneum. Occasionally a juvenile-type plantar fasciitis may occur. Little athletes can develop tendinitis around the ankle, either on the lateral side (peroneals) or medially (tibialis posterior). Occasionally a stress fracture of the metatarsals or other bones can occur.[3] Special attention must be paid to any developmental structural abnormalities and to footwear.

Foot and ankle problems in the elderly

Foot problems are more prevalent in old age. Some are due to a generalised disease such as diabetes or peripheral vascular disease, while others such as bunions, hammer toes, calluses and corns, atrophy of the heel fat-pad and Morton's neuroma increase with ageing. The transverse arch may flatten out and the protective pads under the metatarsals may atrophy, resulting in painful callosities.

Unfortunately many elderly people regard foot problems as a normal process but these problems actually require considerable care and attention, especially in the presence of peripheral vascular disease, diabetes and rheumatoid arthritis. Deformed toe-nails (onychogryphosis) is also common albeit not a painful condition.

Sprained ankle

There are two main ankle ligaments that are subject to heavy inversion or eversion stresses, namely the lateral ligaments and the medial ligaments respectively. Most of the ankle 'sprains' or tears involve the lateral ligaments (up to 90 per cent) while the stronger, tauter medial (deltoid) ligament is less prone to injury. It is important not to misdiagnose a complete rupture of the lateral ligaments.

Most sprains occur when the ankle is plantar flexed and inverted, such as when landing awkwardly after jumping or stepping on uneven ground. It is a very common sporting injury and is presented in more detail in Chapter 110.

Clinical features of sprained lateral ligaments

Common features:

- ankle 'gives way'
- difficulty in weight bearing
- discomfort varies from mild to severe
- bruising (may take 12–24 hours) indicates more severe injury
- may have functional instability: ankle gives way on uneven ground

Physical examination (perform as soon as possible):

- note swelling and bruising
- palpate over bony landmarks and three lateral ligaments (Fig. 110.9)
- test general joint laxity and range of motion
- a common finding is a rounded swelling in front of lateral malleolus (the 'signe de la coquille d'oeuf')
- test stability in A–P plane (anterior draw sign)

Is there an underlying fracture?

For a severe injury the possibility of a fracture—usually of the lateral malleolus or base of fifth metatarsal—must be considered. If the patient is able to walk without much discomfort straight after the injury a fracture is unlikely. However, as a rule, ankle injuries should be X-rayed.

Heel pain

Important causes of heel pain in adults (Fig. 57.3) include:

- Achilles tendon disorders
  - tendinitis/peritendinitis (Chap. 110)
  - bursitis • postcalcaneal • retrocalcaneal
  - tendon tearing (Chap.110) • partial • complete
- bruised heel
- tender heel pad—usually atrophy

- 'pump bumps'
- plantar fasciitis
- calcaneal apophysitis
- peroneal tendon dislocation
- tarsal tunnel syndrome

Ultrasound examination is useful to differentiate the causes of Achilles tendon disorders.

Achilles tendinitis/peritendinitis

The inflammation is a combination of degenerative and inflammatory changes due to overuse and may occur either in the tendon itself or in the surrounding paratendon. The latter is called peritendinitis rather than tenosynovititis because there is no synovial sheath.

Achilles tendon bursitis

Bursitis can occur at two sites:

- posterior and superficial—between skin and tendon
- deep (retrocalcaneal)—between calcaneus and tendon (Fig. 57.3)

The former occurs mainly in young women from shoe friction and is readily palpated. Tenderness from the deep bursitis is elicited by squeezing in front of the tendon with the thumb and index finger: a swelling may be seen bulging on either side of the tendon.

Treatment

- avoid shoe pressure, e.g. wear sandals
- 1–2 cm heel raise inside the shoe
- apply local heat and ultrasound
- NSAIDs
- inject corticosteroid into bursa with a 25 g needle

Plantar fasciitis

This common condition (also known as 'policeman's heel') is characterised by pain on the plantar aspect of the heel, especially on the medial side; it usually occurs about 5 cm from the posterior end of the heel although it can be experienced over a wide area beneath the heel. The pain radiates into the sole.

History

- Pain:
  - — under the heel
  - — first steps out of bed
  - — relieved after walking about
  - — increasing towards the end of the day
  - — worse after sitting
- May be bilateral—usually worse on one side
- Typically over 40 years
- Both sexes
- Sometimes history of injury or overuse
- No constant relationship to footwear

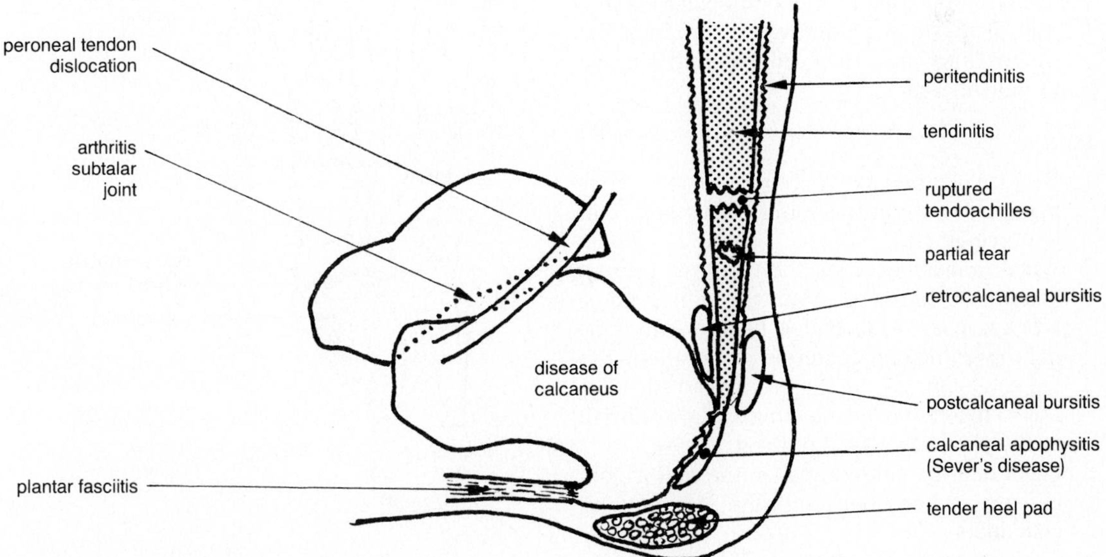

Fig. 57.3 *Important causes of the painful heel*

Signs

- Tenderness:
  - — localised to medial tuberosity
  - — may be more posterior
  - — may be lateral
  - — may be widespread
  - — not altered by tensing fascia (but this action may cause pain)
- Heel pad may bulge or appear atrophic
- Crepitus may be felt
- No abnormality of gait, heel strike, or foot alignment
- Patient often obese

Treatment

Plantar fasciitis tends to heal spontaneously in 12–24 months. It has a variable response to treatment with NSAIDs, injections, ultrasound and insoles. Rest from long walks and from running is important.

Protection

Symptomatic relief is obtained by protecting the heel with an orthotic pad to include the heel and arch of the foot, e.g. Rose insole. Otherwise, a pad made from sponge or sorbo rubber that raises the heel about 1 cm is suitable. A hole corresponding to the tender area should be cut out of the pad to avoid direct contact with the sole.

Injection technique

Plantar fasciitis can be treated by injecting local anaesthetic and long-acting corticosteroid into the site of maximal tenderness in the heel. An alternative is to inject the corticosteroid into the anaesthetised heel.

Method

1. Perform a tibial nerve block. (The area of maximal tenderness should be marked prior to nerve block.)
2. When anaesthesia of the heel is present (about 10 minutes after the tibial nerve block), insert a 23 gauge needle with 1 ml of long-acting corticosteroid perpendicular to the sole of the foot at the premarked site (Fig. 57.4). Insert the needle until a 'give' is felt as the plantar fascia is pierced.
3. Inject half the steroid against the periosteum in the space between the fascia and calcaneus.
4. Reposition the needle to infiltrate into the fascial attachments over a wider area.

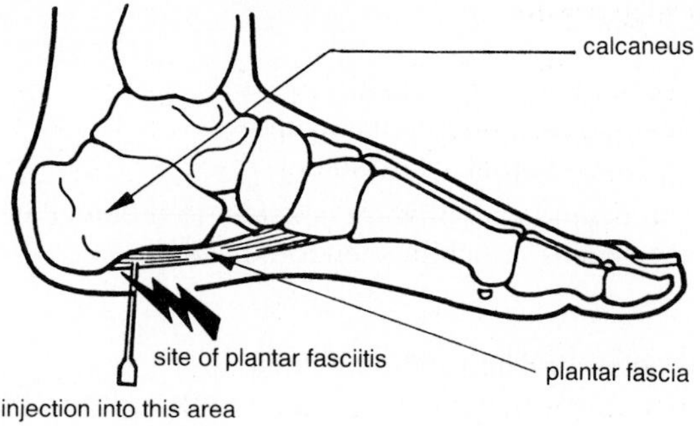

Fig. 57.4 *Injection approach for plantar fasciitis*

Arthritic conditions

Arthritis of the foot or ankle is a rather meaningless diagnosis and specificity is required. Typical sites of arthritic targets are shown in Figure 57.5.

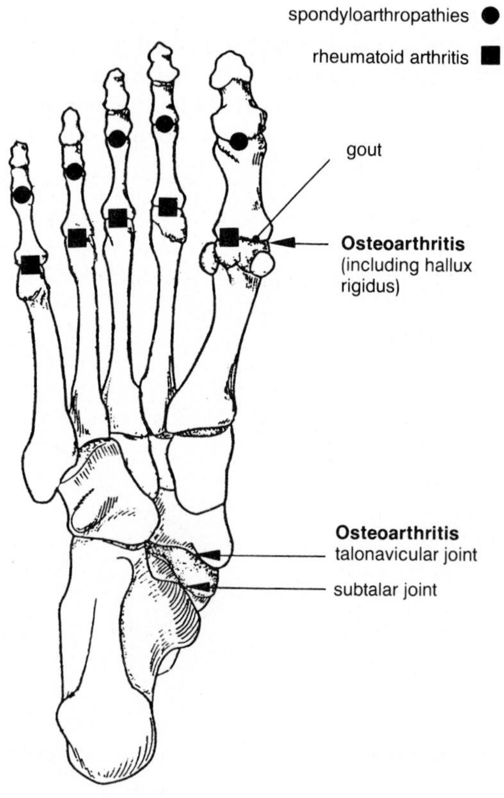

Fig. 57.5 *Typical sites of arthritic causes of podalgia on skeleton of right foot (plantar aspect)*

Osteoarthritis

Osteoarthritis may occur in any of the joints of the foot but it commonly involves the first metatarsophalangeal joint (MTP), leading to hallux rigidus. It can affect the subtalar joint, but the ankle joint proper is usually not affected by osteoarthritis.

Hallux rigidus

Osteoarthritis of the first MTP joint can lead to gradual loss of motion of the toe and considerable discomfort. Roomy protective footwear and relative rest is the basis of treatment, coupled with daily self-mobilisation (stretching toe into plantar flexion morning and night). Other measures include manipulation under general anaesthesia or surgery (arthrodesis or arthroplasty) for severe cases.

Rheumatoid arthritis

Rheumatoid arthritis is typically a symmetrical polyarthritis presenting with pain in the metatarsophalangeal joints. It may also affect the ankle, midtarsal and tarsometatarsal joints. The interphalangeal joints are seldom affected primarily. It causes pain and stiffness under the balls of the feet, especially first thing in the morning.

Gout

Gout typically affects the first MTP and should be considered with the sudden onset of pain, especially in the presence of redness, swelling and tenderness. It can affect any synovial joint and occasionally may be polyarticular. Gout is often dismissed by the patient as a 'sprain'. A history of alcohol consumption or diuretic treatment is relevant.

Spondyloarthropathies

This group of arthritic disorders (Reiter's disease, ankylosing spondylitis, psoriatic arthritis and arthritides associated with chronic bowel disorders) may involve peripheral joints. Other foot involvement includes plantar fasciitis, Achilles tendinitis and sausage-shaped toes due to tenosynovitis, and arthritis of the proximal interphalangeal joints.

Foot strain

Foot strain is probably the commonest cause of podalgia. A foot may be strained by abnormal stress, or by normal stress for which it is not prepared. In foot strain the supporting ligaments become stretched, irritated and inflamed. It is commonly encountered in athletes who are relatively unfit or who have a disorder such as flat feet.

Symptoms and signs:

- aching pain in foot or foot and calf during or after prolonged walking or standing
- initial deep tenderness felt on medial border of plantar fascia (Fig. 57.6)

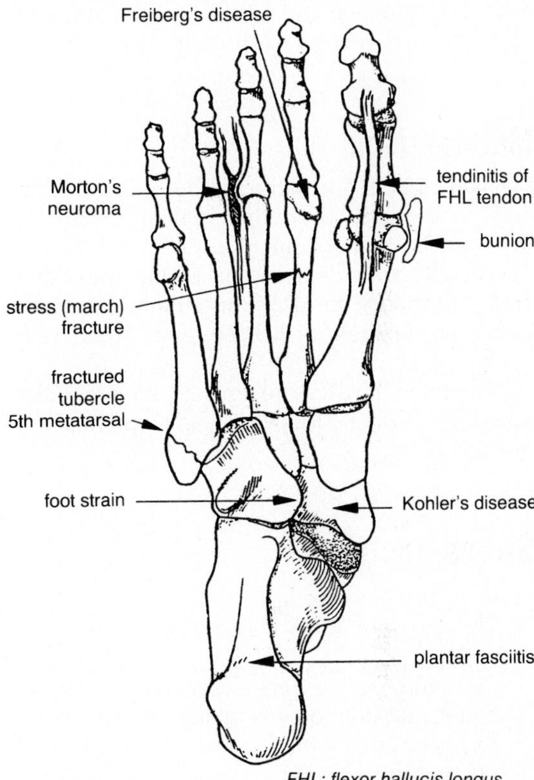

Fig. 57.6 *Typical sites of important causes of podalgia (other than arthritis)—right foot*

Acute foot strain

Acute ligamentous strain, such as occurs to the occasional athlete or to the person taking long unaccustomed walks, is usually self-limiting. It recovers rapidly with rest.

Chronic foot strain

Foot strain will become chronic with repeated excessive stress or with repeated normal stress on a mechanical abnormality. A common consequence is an everted foot leading to flattening of the longitudinal arch on weight bearing. It is important to establish if the symptoms commenced after the patient began wearing a different type of footwear.

Treatment

The treatment is basically the same as that of the adult flat foot. Acute strain is treated with rest and by reducing walking to a minimum. Try the application of cold initially and then heat. The management of chronic strain is based on a exercise program and orthotics, including arch supports, to correct any deformity.

Metatarsalgia

Metatarsalgia is not a disease but refers to pain and tenderness over the plantar heads of metatarsals. Causes include foot deformities (especially with depressions of the transverse arch), arthritis of the MTP joints, trauma, Morton's neuroma, Freiberg's disease and entrapment neuropathy.

Treatment involves treating any known cause, advising proper footwear and perhaps a metatarsal bar.

Stress fractures

Clinical features:

- The aches or pains may be slow in onset or sudden.
- Common in dancers, especially classical ballet, and unfit people taking up exercise.
- Examination often unhelpful: swelling uncommon.[4]
- Routine X-rays often unhelpful.
- A bone scan is the only way to confirm the suspected diagnosis.
- Basis of treatment is absolute rest for six or more weeks with strong supportive footwear.
- A walking plaster is not recommended.

Avulsion fracture of base of fifth metatarsal

Known also as a Jones fracture; it is usually a traumatic fracture but can be a stress fracture and associated with severe ankle sprains.

March fracture of metatarsal

Stress or fatigue fracture of the forefoot usually involves the neck of the second metatarsal (sometimes the third).

Tarsals, especially navicular

Stress fractures of the navicular, which is a disorder of athletes involved with running sports, presents as poorly localised midfoot pain during weight bearing. Examination and plain X-ray are usually normal. It is a recently recognised serious disorder due to the advent of nuclear bone scans and CT scans. A protracted course of treatment can be expected.

Morton's neuroma

Morton's neuroma is probably misdiagnosed more often than any other painful condition of the forefoot. It is not a true neuroma and its aetiology is still uncertain. The diagnosis is made on clinical grounds and special investigations are of no help.

Clinical features

- usually presents in adults <50
- four times more common in women
- bilateral in 15% of cases
- commonest between third and fourth metatarsal heads (Fig. 57.7), then 2–3 (otherwise uncommon)
- severe burning pain between third and fourth toes
- worse on weight bearing on hard surfaces (standing and walking)
- aggravated by wearing tight shoes
- relieved by taking off shoe and squeezing the forefoot
- localised tenderness between metatarsal heads

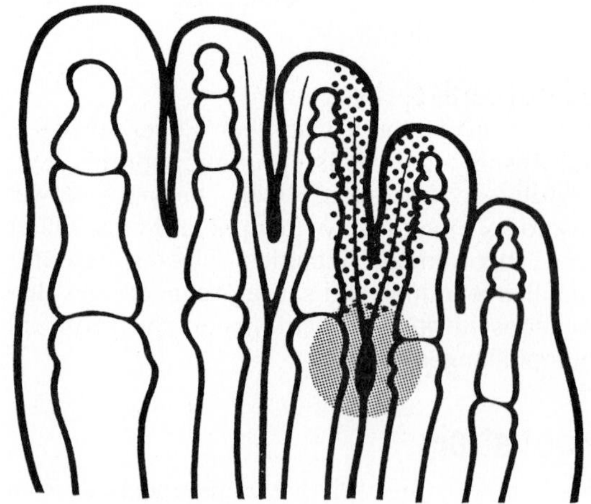

Fig. 57.7 *Morton's neuroma: typical site and pain distribution*

Treatment

Early problems are treated conservatively by wearing loose shoes with a low heel and using a sponge rubber metatarsal pad. An orthosis with a dome under the affected interspace helps to spread the metatarsals and thus takes pressure off the nerve. Most eventually require surgical excision, preferably with a dorsal approach.

Callus, corn and wart

The diagnosis of localised, tender lumps on the sole of the foot can be difficult. The differential diagnosis of callus, corn and wart is aided by an understanding of their morphology and the effect of paring these lumps (Table 57.3).

A callus (Fig. 57.8) is simply a localised area of hyperkeratosis related to some form of pressure and friction. It is very common under the metatarsal heads, especially the second.

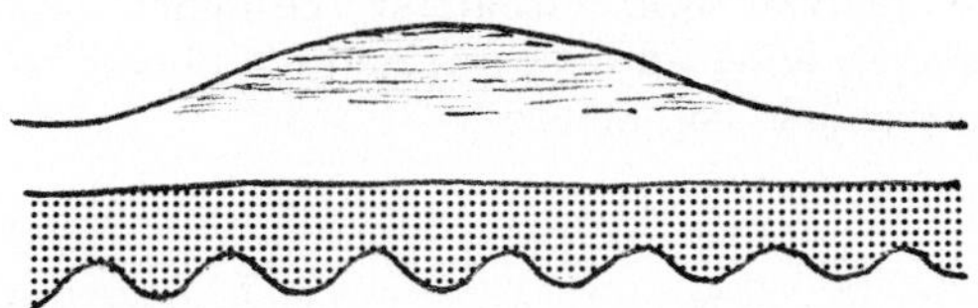

Fig. 57.8 *Callus*

A corn (Fig. 57.9) is a small, localised, conical thickening, which may resemble a plantar wart but which gives a different appearance on paring.

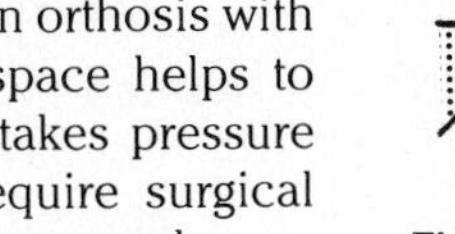

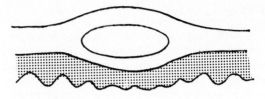

Fig. 57.9 *Corn*

A wart (Fig. 57.10) is more invasive, and paring reveals multiple small, pinpoint bleeding spots.

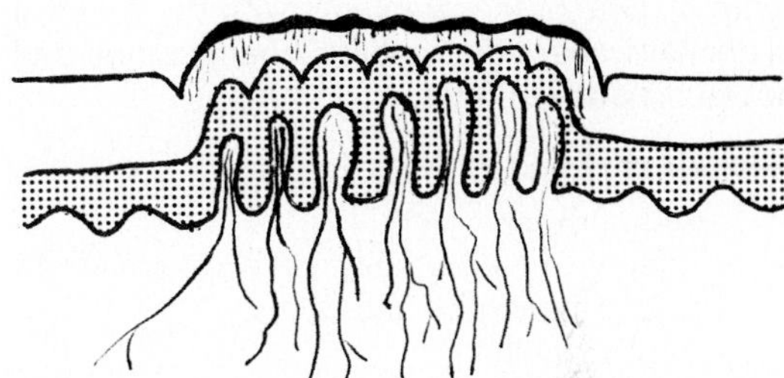

Fig. 57.10 *Plantar wart*

Treatment

Calluses

No treatment is required if asymptomatic. Remove the cause. Proper footwear is essential—wide enough shoes and cushioned pads over ball of foot. Proper paring gives relief, also filing with callus files. If severe, apply daily applications of 10% salicylic acid in soft paraffin with regular paring.

Table 57.3 *Comparison of the main causes of a lump on the sole of the foot*

	Typical site	***Nature***	***Effect of paring***
Callus	where skin is normally thick: beneath heads of metatarsals, heels, inframedial side of great toe	hard, thickened skin	normal skin
Corn	where skin is normally thin: on soles, fifth toe, dorsal projections of hammer toes	white, conical mass of keratin, flattened by pressure	exposes white, avascular corn with concave surface
Wart	anywhere, mainly over metatarsal heads, base of toes and heels; has bleeding points	viral infection, with abrupt change from skin at edge	exposes bleeding points

Corns

Remove cause of friction and use wide shoes to allow the foot to expand to its full width. Soften corn with a few daily applications of 15% salicylic acid in collodion and then pare. For soft corns between the toes (usually last toe-web) keep the toe-webs separated with lamb's wool at all times and dust with a foot powder.

Plantar warts

There are many treatments for this common and at times frustrating problem. A good rule is to avoid scalpel excision, diathermy or electrocautery because of the problem of scarring. One of the problems with the removal of plantar warts is the 'iceberg' configuration and not all may be removed.

Methods of removal

- Liquid nitrogen
  — pare wart (a 21g blade is recommended)
  — apply liquid nitrogen
  — repeat weekly

  Can be painful and results often disappointing.
- Topical chemotherapy
  — pare wart (particularly in children)
  — apply Upton's paste to wart each night and cover
  — review if necessary

  (Upton's paste comprises trichloracetic acid 1 part, salicylic acid 6 parts, glycerin to a stiff paste.)
- Topical chemotherapy and liquid nitrogen
  — pare wart
  — apply paste of 70% salicylic acid in raw linseed oil
  — occlude for 1 week
  — pare on review, then apply liquid nitrogen and review
- Curettage under local anaesthetic
  — pare the wart vigorously to reveal the extent of the wart
  — thoroughly curette the entire wart with a dermal curette
  — hold the foot dependent over kidney dish until bleeding stops (this always stops spontaneously and avoids a bleed later on the way home)
  — apply 50% trichloracetic acid to the base
- Occlusion with topical chemotherapy: a method of using salicylic acid in a paste under a special occlusive dressing is described.

Equipment

— 2.5 cm (width) elastic adhesive tape
— 30% salicylic acid in Lassar's paste of plasticine consistency

Method

— Cut two lengths of adhesive tape, one about 5 cm and the other shorter.
— Fold the shorter length in half, sticky side out (Fig. 57.11a).
— Cut a half-circle at the folded edge to accommodate the wart.
— Press this tape down so that the hole is over the wart.
— Roll a small ball of the paste in the palm of the hand and then press it into the wart.
— Cover the tape, paste and wart with the longer strip of tape (Fig. 57.11b).
— This paste should be reapplied twice daily for 2–3 weeks. The reapplication is achieved by peeling back the longer strip to expose the wart, adding a fresh ball of paste to the wart and then re-covering with the upper tape.

The plantar wart invariably crumbles, and vanishes. If the wart is particularly stubborn, 50% salicylic acid can be used.

(a)

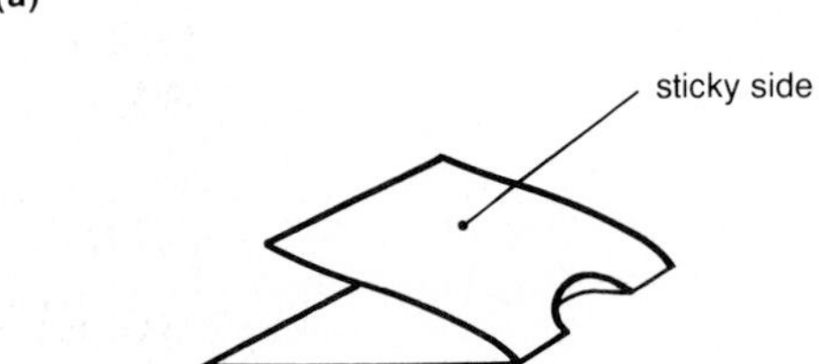

(b)

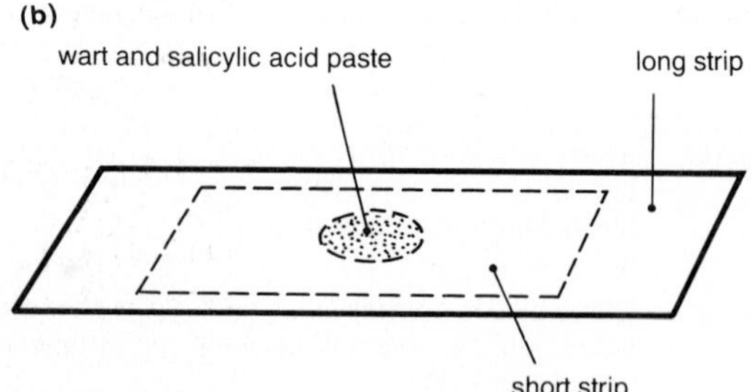

Fig. 57.11 *Treatment of plantar wart:* **(a)** *'window' to fit the wart is cut out of shoulder of elastic adhesive tape;* **(b)** *larger strip covers the wart and shoulder strip*

Ingrown toe-nail (onychocryptosis)

Ingrown toe-nail is a very common condition, especially in adolescent boys. Although not so common in adults, it may follow injury or deformity of the nail bed. It is typically located along the lateral edges of the great toe-nail and represents an imbalance between the soft tissues of the nail fold and the growing nail edge. It is exacerbated by faulty nail trimming, constricting shoes and poor hygiene. A skin breach is followed by infection, then oedema and granulation tissue of the nail fold.[5]

Treatment

Prevention

All patients should be instructed on correct foot and nail care. Foot hygiene includes foot baths, avoiding nylon socks and frequent changes of cotton or wool socks. Cotton wool pledgets can be placed beneath the nail edge to assist separation.

It is important to fashion the toe-nails so that the corners project beyond the skin (Fig. 57.12). The end of the nail (not the corners) should be cut squarely so that the nail can grow out from the nail fold. Then each day, after a shower or bath, use the pads of both thumbs to pull the nail folds as indicted.

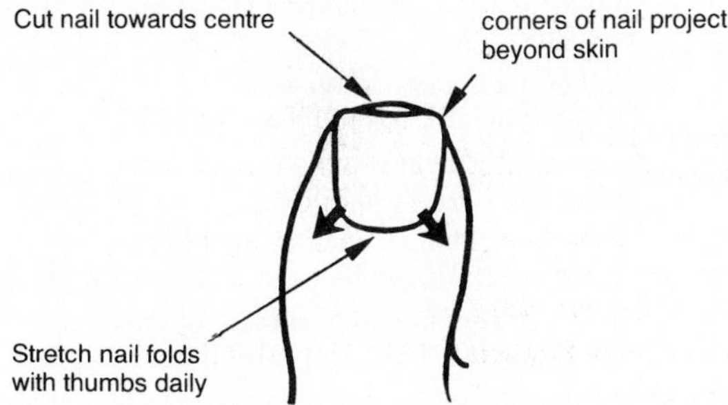

Fig. 57.12 *Method of fashioning toe-nails*

Surgical methods

1. *Excision of ellipse of skin* This 'army method' transposes the skin fold away from the nail. The skin heals, the nail grows normally and the toe retains its normal anatomy.

   Under digital block, an elliptical excision is made such that the skin fold is forced off the nail with a blunt instrument and held there by the wound closure (Fig. 57.13). Any granulation tissue and debris should be removed with a curette.

(a)

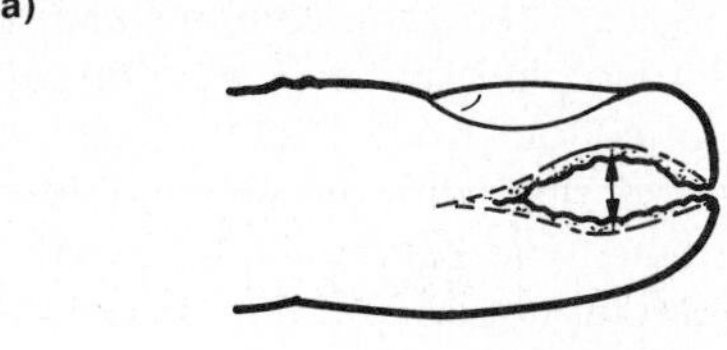

(b)

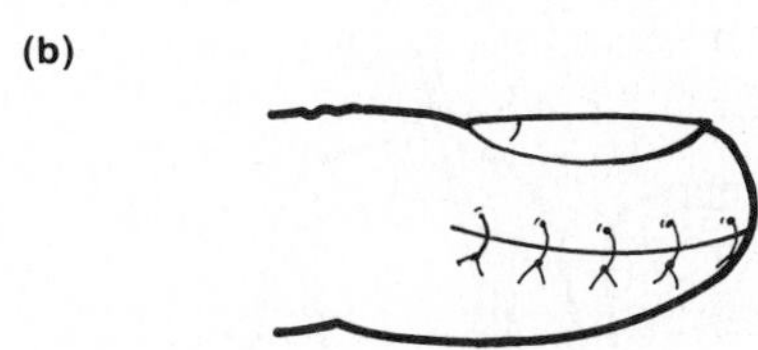

Fig. 57.13 *Treatment of ingrown toe-nail: excision of ellipse of skin*

2. *Electrocautery* This is similar in principle to the preceding method but is simple, quick and very effective with minimal after-pain, especially for severe ingrowing with much granulation tissue. Under digital block the electrocautery needle removes a large wedge of skin and granulation tissue so that the ingrown nail stands free of skin (Fig. 57.14).

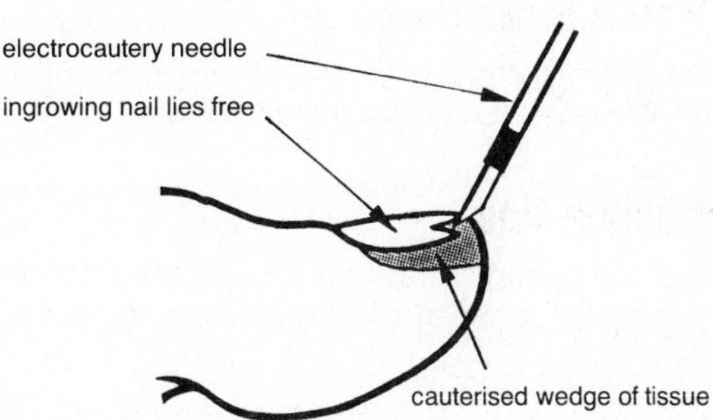

Fig. 57.14 *Treatment of ingrown toe-nail: electrocautery of wedge of tissue*

3. *Wedge of nail excision and phenolisation* This method uses 80% phenol (pure solution) to treat the nail bed following excision with scissors of a wedge for about one quarter of the length (rather than a standard wedge

resection) of the ingrown nail. A cotton wool stick soaked in phenol is introduced deep into the space of the nail bed (Fig. 57.15). Leave the stick in this site for three minutes (by the clock). Then remove and flush this pocket with isotonic saline or alcohol, then dry with a cotton wool stick. Dress with paraffin gauze, then with dry gauze. Redress as appropriate. The success rate is almost 100%. Be careful not to spill the phenol onto the surrounding skin as it is very corrosive.

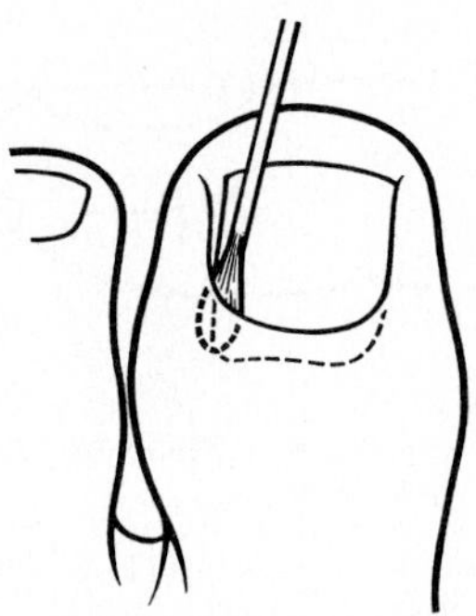

Fig. 57.15 *Phenolisation method*

Paronychia

Initial treatment:

- antiseptic (e.g. Betadine)-soaked dressing
- elevation of nail fold to drain pus
- application of petroleum gauze dressing
- antibiotics if extensive or cellulitis developing

Sometimes the nail requires avulsion to establish free drainage of a periungual abscess.

Practice tips

- Good-quality X-rays are mandatory in all severely sprained ankle injuries.
- If in doubt about the diagnosis of a painful foot—X-ray.
- Children rarely sprain ligaments. All joint injuries causing pain and swelling in children need to be X-rayed.
- Think of the rare problem of a dislocating peroneal tendon if a sharp click and stab of pain is experienced just behind and below the lateral malleolus.
- Paraesthesia of part or whole of the foot may be caused by peripheral neuropathy, tarsal tunnel syndrome, mononeuritis, e.g. diabetes mellitus, rheumatoid arthritis or a nerve root lesion from the lumbosacral spine.
- Avoid giving injections of corticosteroids into the Achilles tendon.
- Avoid invasive procedures such as surgical excision, diathermy or electrocautery for plantar warts. Be aware of the limitations of liquid nitrogen.
- High-resolution ultrasound can help diagnose Achilles tendon disorders.

References

1. Johnson FL. The painful foot: an overview of podalgia. Aust Fam Physician, 1987; 16:1086.
2. Cailliet R. *Foot and ankle pain.* Philadelphia: FA Davis, 1983, 105–115.
3. Larkins PA. The little athlete. Aust Fam Physician, 1991; 20:973–978.
4. Harbison S. Plantar fasciitis. Aust Fam Physician, 1987; 16:113.
5. Quirk R. Stress fractures of the foot. Aust Fam Physician, 1987; 16:1101–1102.

58

Palpitations

Palpitations are an unpleasant awareness of beating of the heart. By definition it does not always imply 'racing' of the heart but any sensation in the chest such as 'pounding', 'flopping', 'skipping', 'jumping', 'thumping' or 'fluttering' of the heart. The problem requires careful attention and reassurance (if appropriate) because heartbeat is regarded as synonymous with life. To the practitioner it may simply represent anxiety or could be a prelude to a cardiac arrest.

Key facts and checkpoints

- The symptom of palpitations is suggestive of cardiac arrhythmia but may have a non-cardiac cause.
- Palpitations not related to emotion, fever or exercise suggest an arrhythmia.
- Perhaps the commonest arrhythmia causing a patient to visit the family doctor is the symptomatic premature ventricular beat (ventricular ectopic).
- The commonest cause of an apparent pause on the ECG is a blocked premature atrial beat (atrial ectopic).
- A 12 lead electrocardiographic diagnosis is mandatory. If the cause is not documented an ambulatory electrographic monitor (e.g. Holter) may be used.
- Consider myocardial ischaemia as a cause of the arrhythmia.
- Consider drugs as a cause, including prescribed drugs and non-prescribed such as alcohol, caffeine and cigarettes.
- Common triggers of paroxysmal supraventricular tachycardia (PSVT) include anxiety and cigarette smoking.
- The commonest mechanism of any arrhythmia is re-entry.
- Get patients to tap out the rate and rhythm of their abnormal beat.

A diagnostic approach

A summary of the safety diagnostic model is presented in Table 58.1, which includes significant causes of palpitations.

Probability diagnosis

If the palpitations are not caused by anxiety or fever, the common causes are sinus tachycardia and premature beats (atrial or ventricular). Sinus tachycardia, which by definition is a rate of 100–160/minute, may be precipitated by emotion, stress, fever or exercise.

Paroxysmal supraventricular tachycardia (PSVT) and atrial fibrillation are also quite common arrhythmias. Some cardiologists claim that the commonest arrhythmia causing a patient to visit the family doctor is the symptomatic ventricular ectopic.[1]

Serious disorders not to be missed

It is vital not to overlook myocardial infarction or other myocardial ischaemia such as unstable angina as a cause of the arrhythmia manifesting as palpitations. About 25% of infarcts are either silent or unrecognised.

Table 58.1 *Palpitations: diagnostic strategy model*

Q. Probability diagnosis
A. Anxiety
Premature beats (ectopics)
Sinus tachycardia

Q. Serious disorders not to be missed
A. Myocardial infarction/angina
Arrhythmias
- ventricular tachycardia
- bradycardia
- sick sinus syndrome
- torsade de pointes

WPW syndrome
Electrolyte disturbances
- hypokalaemia
- hypomagnesaemia

Q. Pitfalls (often missed)
A. Fever/infection
Pregnancy
Menopause
Drugs, e.g. caffeine, cocaine
Mitral valve disease
Aortic incompetence
Hypoxia/hypercapnia

Rarities
Tick bites (T_1-T_5)
Phaeochromocytoma

Q. Seven masquerades checklist

A.	
Depression	✓
Diabetes	indirect
Drugs	✓✓
Anaemia	✓
Thyroid disease	✓
Spinal dysfunction	✓
UTI	possible

Q. Is the patient trying to tell me something?
A. Quite likely. Consider cardiac neurosis, anxiety.

Sinister life-threatening arrhythmias are:
- ventricular tachycardia
- atypical ventricular tachycardia (torsade de pointes)
- sick sinus syndrome
- complete heart block

It is also important not to miss:
- hypokalaemia
- hypomagnesaemia

Pitfalls

There are many pitfalls in the diagnosis and management of arrhythmias, especially in the elderly where symptoms of infection may be masked. Palpitations associated with the menopause can be overlooked. Valvular lesions, usually associated with rheumatic heart disease, such as mitral stenosis, and aortic incompetence may cause palpitations. The rare tumour, phaeochromocytoma, presents with palpitations with the interesting characteristic of postural tachycardia (a change of more than 20 beats/minute). The toxin from tick bites in dermatomes T1–T5 can cause palpitations.

General pitfalls

- Misdiagnosing PSVT as an anxiety state
- Overlooking a cardiac arrhythmia as a cause of syncope or dizziness
- Overlooking atrial fibrillation in the presence of a slow heartbeat
- Overlooking mitral valve prolapse in a patient, especially a middle-aged woman, presenting with unusual chest pains and palpitations (auscultate in standing position to accentuate click(s) ± murmurs)

Seven masquerades checklist

Surprisingly all the masquerades have to be considered, either as direct or indirect causes: depression, especially with anxiety and in the postpartum period; diabetes perhaps as an arrhythmia associated with a silent myocardial infarction or with hypoglycaemia; drugs as a very common cause (Table 58.2); anaemia causing a haemodynamic effect; hyperthyroidism; spinal dysfunction of the upper thoracic vertebrae T1–T5 and urinary tract infection, especially in the elderly.

Table 58.2 *Drugs that cause palpitations*

alcohol
aminophylline
amphetamines
antidepressants
- tricyclics
- MAO inhibitors

caffeine
cocaine
class 1_A and 1_C drugs
digitalis
diuretics
→ K↓, Mg↓
glyceryl trinitrate
sympathomimetics
- in decongestants
- salbutamol
- terbutaline

thyroxine

Paroxysmal supraventricular tachycardia has been described as resulting from injury or dysfunction of the upper thoracic spine (especially T4 and T5) in the absence of organic heart disease.[2] The author has personally encountered several cases of PSVT alleviated by normalising function of the spine.

Psychogenic considerations

Emotional factors can precipitate a tachycardia which in turn can exaggerate the problem in an anxious person. Some people have a cardiac neurosis, often related to identification with a relative or friend. A family history of cardiac disease can engender this particular anxiety. Evidence of anxiety and depression should be sought in patients presenting with palpitations without clinical evidence of cardiovascular disease.

The clinical approach

Careful attention to basic detail in the history and examination can clearly point the way to the clinical diagnosis.

History

Ask the patient to describe the onset and offset of the palpitations, the duration of each episode and any associated features. Then ask the patient to tap out on the desk the rhythm and rate of the heartbeat experienced during the 'attack'. If the patient is unable to do this, tap out the cadence of the various arrhythmias to find a matching beat.

An irregular tapping 'all over the place' suggests atrial fibrillation, while an isolated thump or jump followed by a definite pause on a background or a regular pattern indicates premature beats (ectopics/extrasystoles) usually of ventricular origin. The thump is not the abnormal beat but the huge stroke volume of the beat following the compensatory pause.

Key questions

Do the palpitations start suddenly? How long do they last?
What do you think may bring them on?
Are they related to stress or worry or excitement?
What symptoms do you notice during an attack?
Do you have pain in the chest or breathlessness during the attack?
Do you feel dizzy or faint during the attack?
What medications do you take?
How much coffee, tea or Coke do you drink?
Have you been using nasal decongestants?
Did you eat Chinese food before the attack?
Do you smoke cigarettes, and how many?
Do you take any of the social drugs such as cocaine or marijuana?
Have you ever had rheumatic fever?
Have you lost weight recently or do you sweat a lot?

Chest pain may indicate myocardial ischaemia or aortic stenosis; breathlessness indicates anxiety with hyperventilation, mitral stenosis or cardiac failure; dizziness or syncope suggests severe arrhythmias such as the sick sinus syndrome and complete heart block, aortic stenosis and associated cerebrovascular disease.

Physical examination

The ideal time to examine the patient is while the palpitations are being experienced. Often this is not possible and the physical examination is normal. Measurement of the heart rate may provide a clue to the problem.

As a working guide, a rate estimated to be about 150 beats per minute suggests PSVT, atrial flutter/fibrillation and ventricular tachycardia (Fig. 58.1). A rate less than 150 beats per minute is more likely to be sinus tachycardia which may be associated with exercise, fever, drugs or thyrotoxicosis.[3]

The nature of the pulse, especially the pulse pressure and rhythm, should be carefully evaluated (Fig. 58.2). Look for evidence of fever and infection and features of an anxiety state or depressive illness. Evidence of underlying disease such as anaemia, thyroid disease, alcohol abuse and cardiac disease should be sought. Possible signs in the patient presenting with palpitations are presented in Figure 58.3.[4]

Diagnostic investigations

The number and complexity of investigations should be selected according to the problem and test availability. A checklist would include:

- Blood tests (for underlying disease)
  - — haemoglobin and film
  - — thyroid function tests
  - — serum potassium and magnesium
  - — serum digoxin ? digitalis toxicity
  - — virus antibodies ? myocarditis
- Chest X-ray

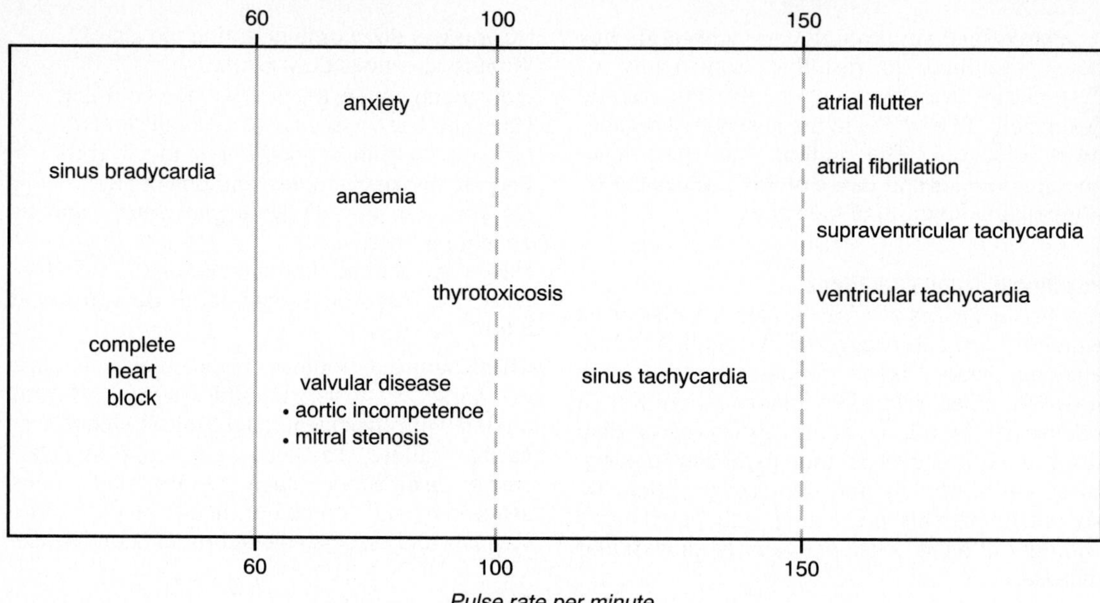

Fig. 58.1 *Heart rate guide to causes of various arrhythmias*

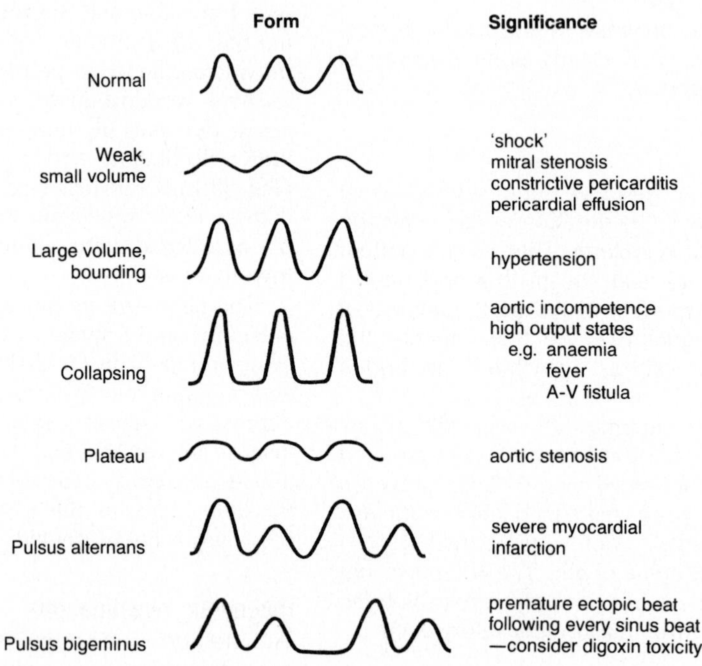

Fig. 58.2 *Various pulse forms*

- Cardiac (ischaemia and function)
  - — ECG (12 lead)
  - — ambulatory 24 hour ECG monitoring
  - — electrocardiography (to look for valvular heart disease and assess left ventricular function)
  - — electrophysiology studies

Palpitations in children

Children may complain of palpitations which may be associated with exercise, fever or anxiety. Various arrhythmias can occur with three requiring special consideration—paroxysmal supraventricular tachycardia, heart block and ventricular arrhythmias.[5]

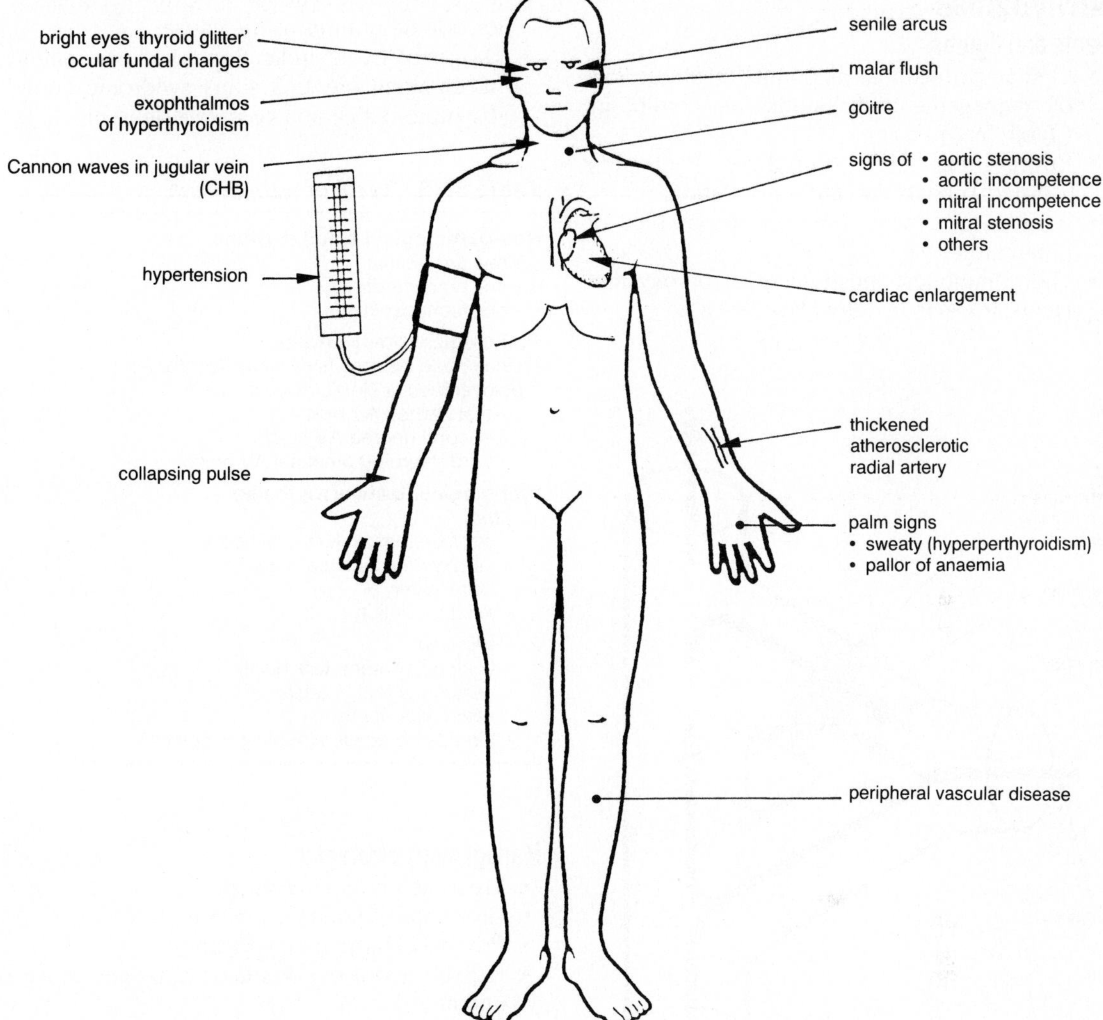

Fig. 58.3 *Signs to consider in a patient with palpitations*

PSVT is characterised by beats at 200–300 per minute, the fastest rates occurring in infants. The cause is often not found but some children have ECG abnormalities compatible with the Wolff-Parkinson-White syndrome. The recommended first-line treatment of PSVT is vagal stimulation via the application of ice packs to the face of the affected infant.

Palpitations in the elderly

The older the patient the more likely the onset of palpitations due to cardiac disease such as myocardial infarction/ischaemia, hypertension, arrhythmias and drugs, especially digoxin. Occasional atrial and ventricular arrhythmias, especially premature beats (ectopics), occur in 40% of old people[6] and treatment is rarely required. Atrial fibrillation occurs in 5–10% of patients over 65 years of age, 30% of whom have no clinical evidence of cardiovascular disease. A rapid ventricular rate with symptoms is the only indication for digoxin in the elderly but beware of the sick sinus syndrome, especially if dizziness or syncope accompanies the fibrillation.

In the elderly thyrotoxicosis may present as sinus tachycardia or atrial fibrillation with only minimal signs—the so-called 'masked thyrotoxicosis'—so it is easy to overlook it. The only clue may be bright eyes ('thyroid glitter') due to conjunctival oedema.

Arrhythmias

Facts and figures

- Cardiac arrhythmias account for about 25% of management decisions in cardiology (Table 58.3).
- Commonest are premature (ectopic) ventricular beats and atrial fibrillation.
- PSVT is next most common—6 per 1000 of population.
- The commonest mechanism of paroxysmal tachycardias is re-entry (Fig. 58.4).

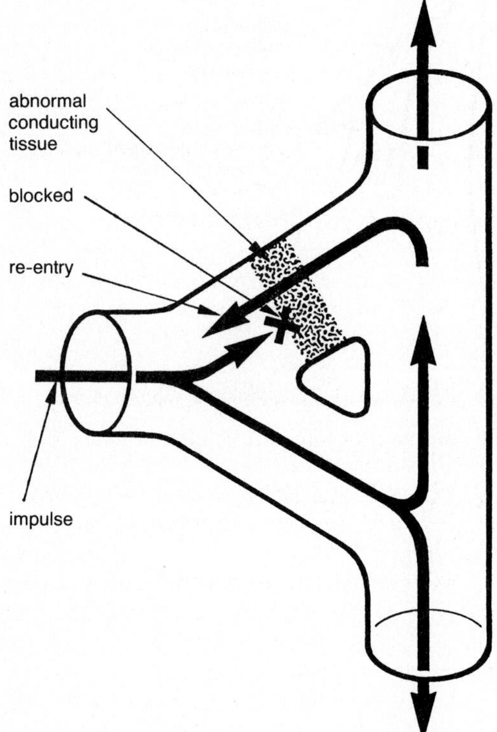

Fig. 58.4 *Diagrammatic mechanism of re-entry tachycardia*

- Electrophysiological studies are the gold standard investigation for tachycardias but are rarely needed for diagnosing most arrhythmias.
- Almost all antiarrhythmic drugs have a proarrhythmic potential, i.e. they may worsen existing arrhythmias or provoke new arrhythmias in some patients (refer Table 58.4).
- Avoid digoxin in cases with an accessory pathway.
- If 'quinidine syncope' occurs, consider torsade de pointes as the cause.
- The two main indications for permanent pacemaking are sick sinus syndrome (only if symptomatic) and complete heart block.

Table 58.3 *Types of arrhythmias*

Non-pathological sinus rhythms
- sinus arrhythmia
- sinus bradycardia
- sinus tachycardia

Pathological bradycardias
- sinus node disease (sick sinus syndrome)
- atrioventricular (AV) block
  - — first degree AV block
  - — second degree AV block
  - — third degree (complete) AV block

Pathological tachyarrhythmias

1. *Atrial*
   - atrial premature (ectopic) beats
   - paroxysmal tachycardia (PSVT)
   - atrial flutter
   - atrial fibrillation
2. *Ventricular*
   - ventricular premature beats
   - ventricular tachycardia
   - ventricular fibrillation
   - torsade de pointes (twisting of points)

Management strategies

- Treat the underlying cause.
- Give appropriate reassurance.
- Provide clear patient education.
- Explain about the problems of fatigue, stress and emotion.
- Advise moderation in consumption of tea, coffee, caffeine-containing soft drinks and alcohol.
- Advise about cessation of smoking and other drugs.

Premature (ectopic) beats

Atrial premature beats

- These are usually asymptomatic.
- Management is based on reassurance.
- Check lifestyle factors such as excess alcohol, caffeine, stress and smoking; avoid precipitating factors.
- Treatment is rarely required and should be avoided if possible.
- At present there is no ideal antiectopic agent.
- They may be a forerunner of other arrhythmias, e.g. PSVT, atrial fibrillation.

Table 58.4 *Electrophysiological classification of common antiarrhythmic drugs (after Vaughan Williams)*

Class	Drug	Usual dosage	Common side effects
1_A	Disopyramide	100-200 mg qid	Blurred vision, dry mouth, urinary problems in males (avoid in men > 50)
	Procainamide	1g qid IV use	Anorexia, nausea, urticaria
	Quinidine	2-3 SR tabs (0.25 g) bd	Diarrhoea, headache, tinnitus
1_B	Lignocaine	IV use	Nausea, dizziness, tremor
	Mexiletine	200 mg tid	Nausea, vomiting, tremor, dizziness
1_C	Flecainide	100 mg bd	Nausea, dizziness, rash
II	Beta-blockers	various	Fatigue, insomnia, nightmares, hypotension, bronchospasm. Avoid in asthmatics
III	Amiodarone	SVT: 200 mg daily VT: 400 mg daily	Rash, pulmonary fibrosis, thyroid, hepatic and CNS effects
	Bretylium	IV use only	Nausea, vomiting, hypotension
	Sotalol	160 mg bd	As for beta-blockers
IV	Verapamil	80 mg tid	Constipation, dizziness, hypotension
	Diltiazem	30-60 mg qid	Hypotension, headache

Note Sotalol is a beta-blocker and thus is a class II and III agent.

- If causing intolerable symptoms, use quinidine bisulphate sustained release tablets 250–750 mg orally, 12 hourly.

Ventricular premature beats

- These are also usually asymptomatic (90%).
- They occur in 20% of people with 'normal' hearts.
- Symptoms are usually noticed at rest in bed at night.
- Check lifestyle factors as for atrial premature beats.
- Drugs which can cause both types of premature beats include digoxin and sympathomimetics.
- Look for evidence of ischaemic heart disease, mitral valve prolapse (especially women), thyrotoxicosis and left ventricular failure.
- They may be a forerunner of other arrhythmias, e.g. ventricular tachycardia.
- If symptomatic but otherwise well with a normal chest X-ray and ECG, reassure the patient.
- Drug therapy:
  - — use beta-blocker if mitral valve prolapse
  - — if intolerable symptoms, use a class I, II or III agent, e.g. disopyramide 100–200 mg qid.

Supraventricular tachycardia

- SVT can be paroxysmal or sustained.
- Rate is 150–220/minute.
- There are at least eight different types of SVT with differing risks and responses to treatment.
- PSVT commonly presents with a sudden onset in otherwise healthy young people.
- Passing copious urine after an attack is characteristic of PSVT.
- Look for predisposing factors such as an accessory pathway and thyrotoxicosis.
- Approximately 60% are due to AV node re-entry and 35% due to accessory pathway tachycardia, e.g. Wolff-Parkinson-White syndrome (WPW).[7]
- Look for evidence of accessory pathways after reversion because accessory pathways can lead to sudden death (avoid digoxin in WPW).
- Consider sick sinus syndrome in a patient with SVT and dizziness.

Management of PSVT

1. Vagal stimulation can be attempted. Carotid sinus massage is the first treatment of choice. Other methods of vagal stimulation include:
   - Valsalva manoeuvre (easiest for patient)

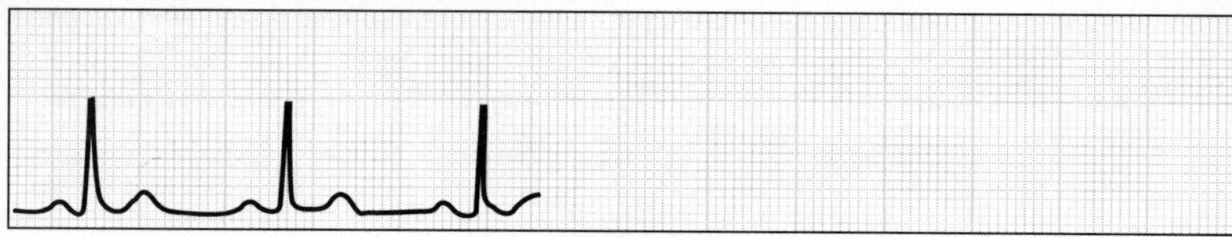

normal sinus rhythm

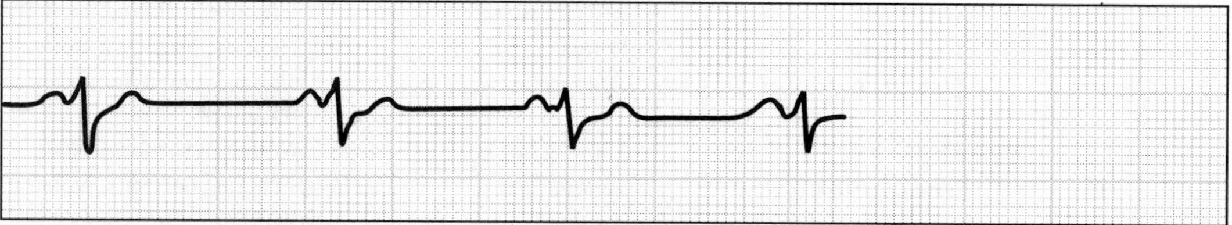

sinus bradycardia and sinus arrhythmia—rate approx. 55 per minute

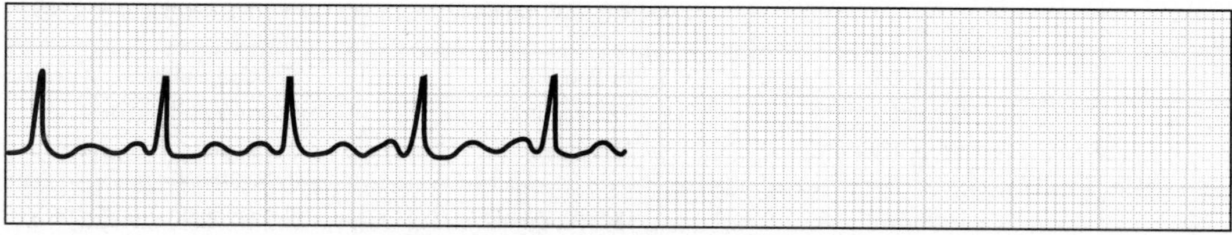

sinus tachycardia—rate approx. 100 per minute

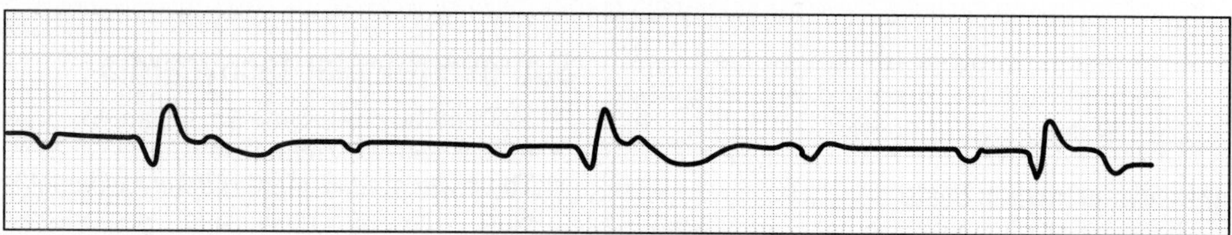

complete heart block

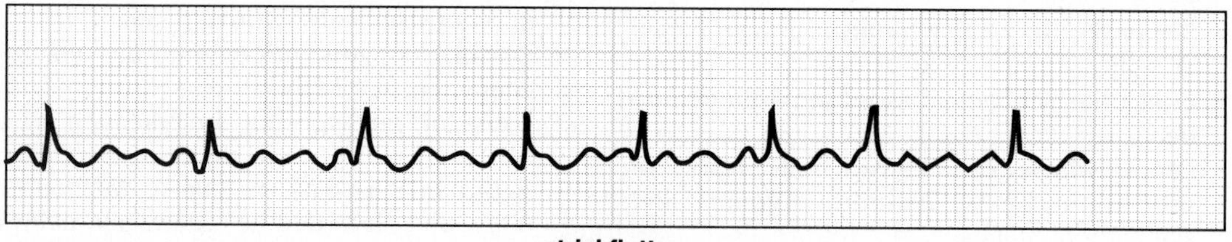

atrial flutter

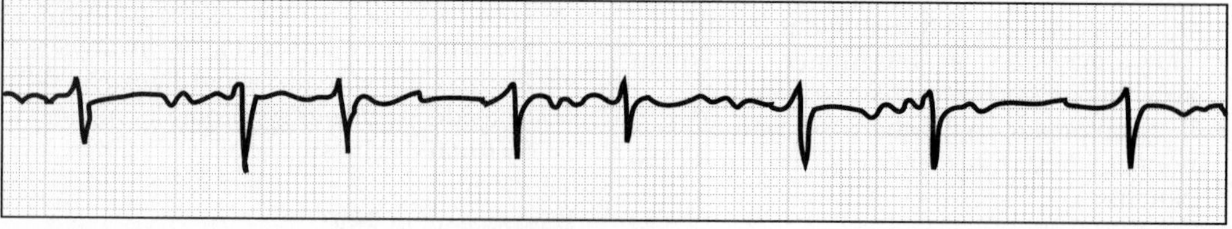

atrial fibrillation

(continues)

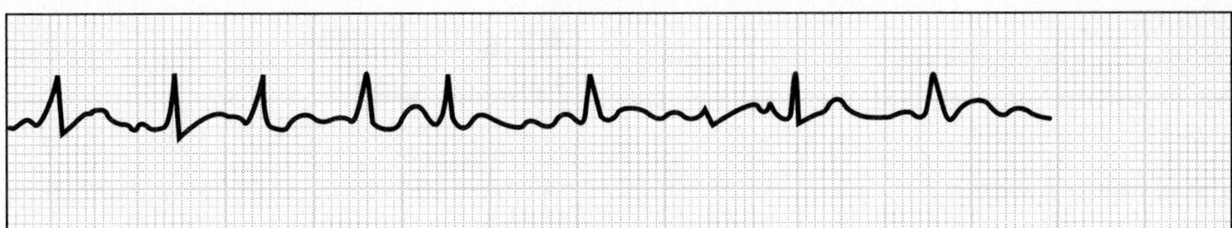

atrial premature beats

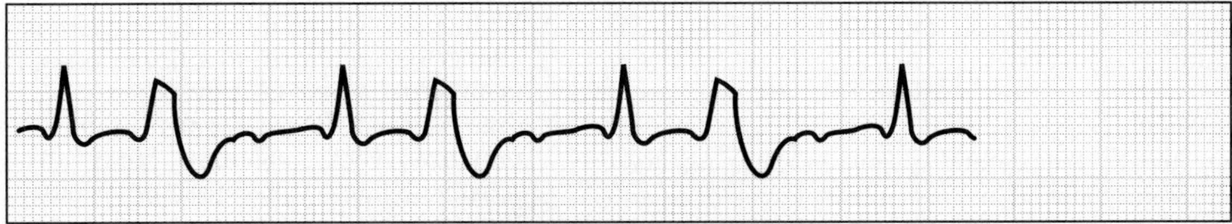

ventricular premature beats

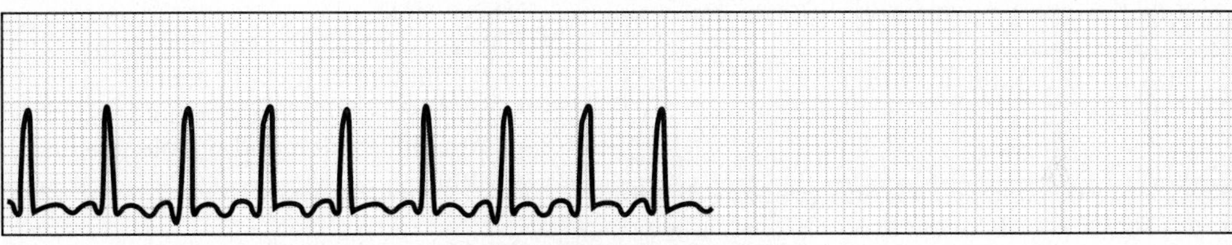

supraventricular tachycardia

ventricular tachycardia

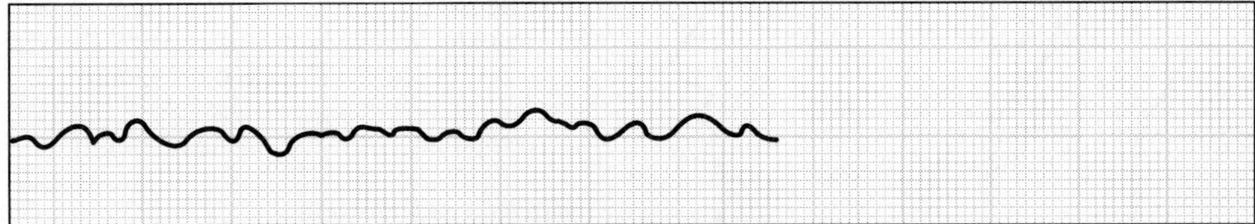

ventricular fibrillation

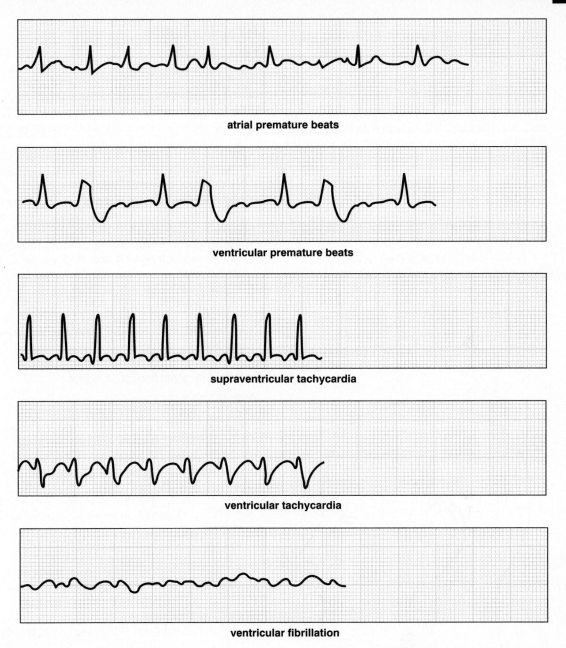

Fig. 58.5 *Tracings of important arrhythmias*

- self-induced vomiting
- ocular pressure (avoid)
- cold (ice) water to face
- immersion of the face in water

2. If vagal stimulation fails, give verapamil IV 1 mg/min up to 10–15 mg.

Precautions

- aim for 10 mg in 10 minutes initially
- only use if narrow QRS and BP > 80
- carefully monitor blood pressure
- **AVOID** verapamil if on beta-blockers

  and

  persistent tachycardia with QRS complexes > 0.14s (indicates ventricular tachycardia)

3. In the rare event of failure of medical treatment, consider DC cardioversion or overdrive pacing.

Prophylaxis
To prevent recurrences use quinidine bisulphate or flecainide or sotalol. If these agents fail, consider amiodarone.

Carotid sinus massage

Carotid sinus massage causes vagal stimulation and its effect on SVT is all or nothing. It has no effect on ventricular tachycardia. It slows the sinus rate and breaks the SVT by blocking AV nodal conduction.

Method

- Locate the carotid pulse in front of the sternomastoid muscle just below the angle of the jaw (Fig. 58.6).
- Ensure that no bruit is present.
- Rub the carotid with a circular motion for 5–10 seconds.
- Rub each carotid in turn if the SVT is not 'broken'.

In general, right carotid pressure tends to slow the sinus rate[8] and left carotid pressure tends to impair AV nodal conduction.

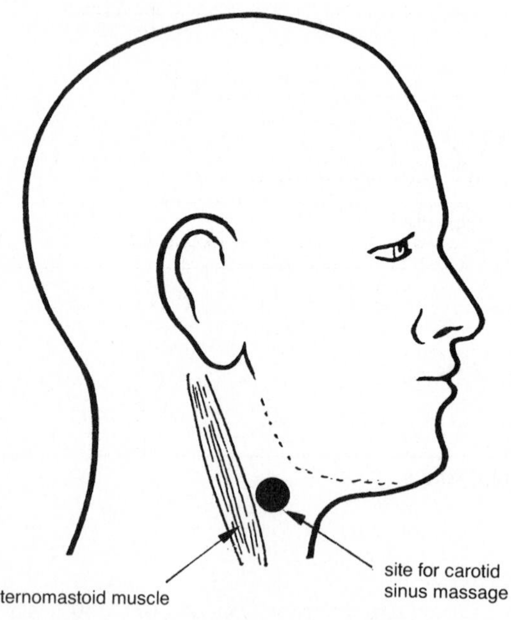

Fig. 58.6 *Carotid sinus massage*

Precautions
In elderly (risk of embolism or bradycardia).

Atrial fibrillation

Facts and figures

- A common problem (9% incidence in the over 70 age group).
- Remember to look for the underlying cause: myocardial ischaemia (15% of cases), mitral valve disease, thyrotoxicosis, hypertension, cardiomyopathy including alcohol.
- With sustained atrial fibrillation there is a 5% chance per annum of embolic episodes. There is a fivefold risk of CVA overall.
- The risk of CVA is greater in those with previous CVA, valvular heart disease, prosthetic mitral valve and cardiac failure.
- For reversion anticoagulate with warfarin for two weeks beforehand and maintain for 2–4 weeks after.
- Digoxin controls the ventricular rate but does not terminate or prevent attacks.
- Quinidine is the classic agent for conversion of atrial fibrillation and maintenance of sinus rhythm.

Treatment for atrial fibrillation/flutter

Medical treatment
For rapid control of ventricular rate:

digoxin	0.5 mg IV then 0.5 mg IV 4 hourly to maximum total dose of 1.5 mg
	or
verapamil	1 mg/min IV up to maximum 15 mg (provided no evidence of heart failure and well maintained BP)

Maintenance:

digoxin	0. 25 mg (o) 0.125 mg (o) in elderly
	or
verapamil	40–160 mg (o) 8 hourly

Medical cardioversion

quinidine bisulphate SR 500 mg (o) 12 hourly

or

flecainide 100 mg bd (if LV function not impaired)

Electrical DC—cardioversion
For failed medical conversion.

The use of warfarin in atrial fibrillation
Warfarin is effective in preventing stroke in patients with lone or non-rheumatic atrial

fibrillation. The decision to use it or an antiplatelet agent, especially in the younger patient, is difficult and should be made in consultation with a cardiologist. If using warfarin, start with a low dose, e.g. 2–4 mg, and maintain a relatively low INR of 1.5–2 with regular checks.

Advances in treatment of arrhythmias

Apart from special rate responsive pacemakers for bradycardia, there are several new modalities of treatment for complex arrhythmias including means of blocking the re-entry phenomenon.

Surgery

Guided by electrophysiologic monitoring, surgeons can dissect a small section of the atrioventricular ring to ensure that all aberrant connections between the atria and the underlying ventricular muscle are severed.

Catheter electrode ablation

Specific abnormal foci in the conducting pathways can be ablated using direct current electrical surgery or radio frequency 'burns' via a catheter electrode. Radio frequency ablation, which will probably supplant surgery as a form of treatment, is indicated for AV junction (HIS bundle) dysfunction, accessory pathways, nodal re-entry tachycardia and ventricular tachycardia.

Automatic implantable cardiac defibrillator (AICD)

This expensive implant is the most effective therapy yet devised for the prevention of sudden cardiac death in patients with documented sustained VT or VF. Operative mortality should be less than 10% after which survival at 1 year is over 90%. These new defibrillators incorporate an antitachycardia pacemaker. Patients can either be paced out of arrhythmia or, if they develop ventricular fibrillation, they can be defibrillated using higher energy.

When to refer

Patients should be referred to a cardiologist[9] when:

- a sustained supraventricular tachycardia is suspected
- a sustained ventricular tachycardia is suspected
- an ECG shows sustained delta waves of WPW syndrome, even if asymptomatic
- syncope or dizziness suggests a cardiovascular cause
- a paroxysmal arrhythmia may be the cause of unexplained cardiovascular symptoms
- anticoagulation has to be considered

Practice tips

- Atrial fibrillation and dizziness (even syncope) is suggestive of the sick sinus syndrome (bradycardia–tachycardia syndrome), which is made worse by digoxin.
- Consider thyrotoxicosis as a cause of atrial fibrillation or sinus tachycardia even if clinical manifestations are not apparent.
- Check for a history of palpitations in a patient complaining of dizziness or syncope (and vice versa). Consider an arrhythmia, especially in the elderly.
- PSVT is rarely caused by organic heart disease in young patients.
- Arrhythmia of sudden onset suggests PSVT, atrial flutter/fibrillation or ventricular tachycardia.
- A normal ECG in sinus rhythm does not exclude an accessory pathway.
- Consider conduction disorders such as the WPW syndrome in PSVT. Avoid digoxin in WPW syndrome.
- Common triggers of premature beats and PSVT are smoking, anxiety and caffeine (especially eight or more cups a day).
- Many antiarrhythmic drugs have pro-arrhythmic potential:
  - — never use digoxin in WPW syndrome and SSS (without pacemaker back-up)
  - — never use digoxin or verapamil for atrial fibrillation in WPW syndrome
  - — beware of quinidine or disopyramide causing torsade de pointes VT
  - — beware of using verapamil with a beta-blocker
  - — beware of giving quinidine without digoxin for atrial flutter
- There is no ideal antiarrhythmic agent for ventricular premature beats.

Table 58.5 presents a summary of the treatment of arrhythmias.

Table 58.5 *Summary of treatment of arrhythmias*

Arrhythmia	*First line*	*Second line*	*Third line*
Sinus tachycardia	Treat cause		
Bradycardias			
Sick sinus syndrome	Permanent pacing		
AV block			
first degree	No treatment		
second degree	No treatment	Pacing if problematic	
third degree			
• acute, e.g. MI	Temporary pacing or Isoprenaline IV		
• chronic	Permanent pacing		
Atrial tachyarrhythmias			
PSVT	Valsalva Carotid sinus massage	Verapamil IV	DC cardioversion Class III drug ? surgery
Atrial fibrillation Atrial flutter	Digoxin or Verapamil	add Quinidine	DC cardioversion
Atrial premature beats	Treat cause Check lifestyle	Quinidine	
Ventricular tachyarrhthmias			
Ventricular premature beats	Treat cause Check lifestyle	Beta-blocker (especially mitral valve prolapse)	Disopyramide
Ventricular tachycardia			
non-sustained	Lignocaine IV	Procainamide	Class III drug
sustained	Lignocaine IV	Class III drug	DC cardioversion
Ventricular fibrillation	DC cardioversion	Bretylium IV DC cardioversion	Lignocaine IV (maintenance) Class III (if recurrent)

References

1. Boxall J. Annual update course for general practitioners. Course abstracts. Melbourne: Monash University, 1991, 16.
2. Lewit K. *Manipulative therapy in rehabilitation of the motor system.* London: Butterworths, 1985, 338–339.
3. Davis A, Bolin T, Ham J. *Symptom analysis and physical diagnosis* (2nd edition). Sydney: Pergamon, 1985.
4. Sandler G, Fry J. *Early clinical diagnosis.* Lancaster: MTP Press, 1986, 327–359.
5. Robinson MJ. *Practical paediatrics.* Melbourne: Churchill Livingstone, 1990, 318–319.
6. Merriman A. *Handbook of international geriatric medicine.* Singapore: PG Publishing, 1989, 99–100.
7. Stafford W. Arrhythmias. Medical Observer: 13 September 1991, 33–34.
8. Kumar P, Clarke M. *Clinical medicine* (2nd edition). London: Bailliere Tindall, 1990, 554.
9. Ross DL. Cardiac arrhythmias. In: MIMS Disease Index. Sydney: IMS Publishing, 1991/92, 101.

59

Sore throat

A sore or painful throat is one of the commonest symptoms encountered in general practice. The most usual cause is viral pharyngitis.

Definitions

pharyngitis = inflammation of pharynx ± tonsils
tonsillitis = inflammation of tonsils only

Key facts and checkpoints

- In the National Morbidity Survey (UK)[1] nine episodes per annum of acute pharyngitis or acute tonsillitis were diagnosed for every 100 patients.
- Sore throats account for about 5% of consultations in general practice per annum.[2]
- In one United Kingdom general practice it was the third most common new presenting symptom—5.4% of presenting problems.
- Although throat infections are common from infancy, children under 4 years of age rarely complain of a sore throat.
- Complaints of a sore throat are prevalent in children between 4 and 8 and in teenagers.
- Sore throats continue to be common up to the age of 45 and then decline significantly.
- The common causes are viral pharyngitis and tonsillitis due to *Streptococcus pyogenes.*
- The sore throat may be the presentation of serious and hidden systemic diseases, such as blood dyscrasias, HIV infection and diabetes (due to moniliasis).
- A very important cause is tonsillitis caused by Epstein-Barr mononucleosis. Treating this cause with penicillin can produce adverse effects.

Presentation

Sore throat may be present as part of a complex of the common upper respiratory infections, such as the common cold and influenza. However, sore throat often presents as a single symptom. The pain is usually continuous and aggravated by swallowing. In those under four years old the presentation of acute pharyngitis or tonsillitis may be confusing as the presenting complaints may be vomiting, abdominal pain and fever rather than sore throat and swallowing difficulty.

It is appropriate to consider sore throat as acute or chronic. Most presentations come as acute problems, the causes of which are listed in Table 59.1.

A diagnostic approach

A summary of the safety diagnostic model is presented in Table 59.2.

Probability diagnosis

At least 50% of sore throats, mainly pharyngitis, will be caused by a virus. The commonest cause of tonsillitis is considered to be Group A beta-haemolytic *Streptococcus pyogenes*[3] (GABHS). A viral infection is supported by the presence of coryza prodromata, hoarseness and nasal stuffiness.

Table 59.1 *Causes of acute sore throat*

BACTERIA
B haemolytic streptococci
Diphtheria (rare)
Gonococcal pharyngitis
Haemophilus influenzae
Quinsy
Staphylococcus aureus (rare)
Syphilis (rare)
Vincent's angina

VIRAL

Severe–moderate soreness

Epstein-Barr mononucleosis
Herpangina
Herpes simplex pharyngitis

Mild–moderate soreness

Adenovirus
Coronavirus
Enterovirus
Influenza virus
Picornavirus
Rhinovirus
Human immunodeficiency virus

OTHER INFECTIONS
Candida albicans, especially in infants
Mycoplasma pneumoniae
Chlamydia pneumoniae

BLOOD DYSCRASIAS
Agranulocytosis
Leukaemia

IRRITANTS
Tobacco smoke
Antiseptic lozenges (oral use)

Serious disorders not to be missed

It is vital to be aware of *Haemophilus influenzae* infection in children, especially between two and four years, when the deadly problem of epiglottitis can develop suddenly. These patients present with a short febrile illness, respiratory difficulty (cough is not a feature) and are unable to swallow.

Apart from acute epiglottitis it is important not to overlook carcinoma of the oropharynx or tongue and the blood dyscrasias including acute leukaemia. The severe infections not to be missed include streptococcal pharyngitis with its complications, including quinsy, diphtheria and HIV infection (including AIDS).

Pitfalls

There are many pitfalls, the classic being to diagnose the exudative tonsillitis of Epstein-Barr mononucleosis as streptococcal tonsillitis and prescribe one of the penicillins, which may precipitate a severe rash. Primary HIV infection can present with a sore throat along with other symptoms. Adenovirus pharyngitis can also mimic streptococcal pharyngitis, especially in young adults.

Traumatic episodes are important but are often not considered, especially in children. They include:

- a foreign body—may cause a sudden onset of throat pain then drooling and dysphagia
- vocal abuse—excessive singing and shouting can cause a sore throat and hoarseness

Table 59.2 *Sore throat: diagnostic strategy model*

Q. *Probability diagnosis*
A. Viral pharyngitis

Q. *Serious disorders not to be missed*
A. Cardiovascular
- angina
- myocardial infarction

Neoplasia
- carcinoma of oropharynx, tongue

Blood dyscrasias, e.g. agranulocytosis
acute leukaemia

Severe infections
- acute epiglottitis (children < 4)
- peritonsillar abscess (Quinsy)
- pharyngeal abscess
- diphtheria (very rare)
- HIV/AIDS

Q. *Pitfalls (often missed)*
A. Foreign body
Epstein-Barr mononucleosis
Monilia
- common in infants
- steroid inhalers

STDs
- gonococcal pharyngitis
- herpes simplex (type II)
- syphilis

Irritants, e.g. cigarette smoke
chemicals
Mouth breathing
Thyroiditis

Rarities
Systemic sclerosis
Sarcoidosis
Malignant granuloma
Tuberculosis

Q. *Seven masquerades checklist*
A.

Depression	✓
Diabetes	✓ (monilia)
Drugs	✓
Anaemia	✓ possible
Thyroid disease	✓ thyroiditis
Spinal dysfunction	—
UTI	—

Q. *Is the patient trying to tell me something?*
A. Unlikely, but the association with depression is significant.

- burns—hot food and drink, acids or alkalis

Various irritants, especially cigarette smoke in the household and smoke inhalation from fires, can cause pharyngeal irritation with sore throat, especially in children.

The mouth and pharynx may become dry and sore from mouth breathing which is often associated with nasal obstruction, e.g. adenoid hypertrophy, allergic rhinitis.

Seven masquerades checklist

Depression may be associated with a sore throat. Diabetes and aplastic anaemia and drugs are indirectly associated through candidiasis, neutropenia and agranulocytosis respectively. The possibility of thyroiditis presenting as a sore throat should be kept in mind.

Making a diagnosis

The issues of making a reliable diagnosis and prescribing antibiotics are rather contentious and at times difficult, a situation not usually appreciated by some academics. The main issue is to determine whether the sore throat has a treatable cause by interpretation of the clinical and epidemiological data.

The appearance of the pharynx and tonsils is not always discriminating. A generalised red throat may be caused by a streptococcal or a viral infection, as may tonsils that are swollen with follicular exudates. On probability, most sore throats are caused by a virus and generally do not show marked inflammatory changes or purulent looking exudates (Fig. 59.1). Such throats should be treated symptomatically.

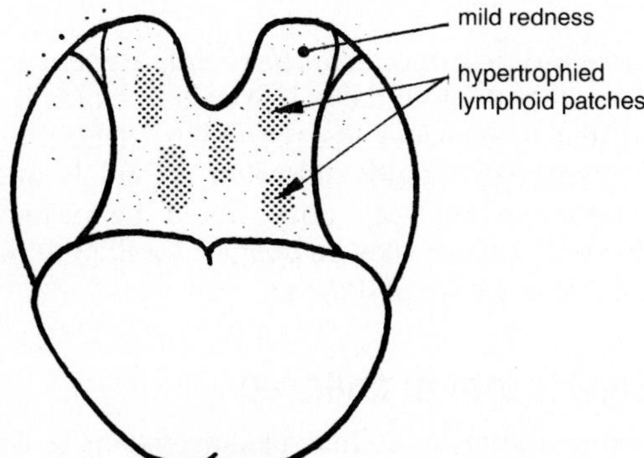

Fig. 59.1 *Viral pharyngitis: the signs may be minimal but mild redness of pharynx and prominent lymphoid patches on the oropharynx are typical*

The clinical approach

History

It is necessary to determine whether the patient has a sore throat, a deep pain in the throat or neck pain. Instruct the patient to point to exactly where the pain is experienced. Enquire about relevant associated symptoms such as metallic taste in mouth, fever, upper respiratory infection, other pain such as ear pain, nasal stuffiness or discharge and cough.

Note whether the patient is an asthmatic and uses a corticosteroid inhaler, or is a smoker, or exposed to environmental irritants. Check the immunisation history, enquiring especially about diptheria.

The history should give a clue to the remote possibility that the painful throat is a manifestation of angina.

Examination

An inspection should note the general appearance of the patient, looking for 'toxicity', the anaemic pallor of leukaemia, the nasal stuffiness of infectious mononucleosis, the characteristic halitosis of a streptococcal throat.

Palpate the neck for soreness and lymphadenopathy, inspect the ears and check the sinus areas.

Then inspect the oral cavity and pharynx. Look for ulcers, abnormal masses and exudates. Note whether the uvula and soft palate, tonsils, fauces or pharynx are swollen, red or covered in exudate. The typical appearances of various conditions causing a sore throat are shown in Figures 59.1 to 59.7, and important causes to exclude in Figure 59.8.

Guidelines

- Small patches of exudate on the palate or other structure indicate *Candida albicans* (oral thrush) (Fig. 59.2).
- A large whitish-yellow membrane virtually covering both tonsils indicates Epstein-Barr mononucleosis (Fig. 59.3).
- A generalised red, swollen appearance with exudate indicates Group A beta-haemolytic streptococcus (GABHS) infection (Figs 59.4 and 59.5).

Investigations

Investigations can be selected from:

- throat swab
- haemoglobin, blood film and white cell count

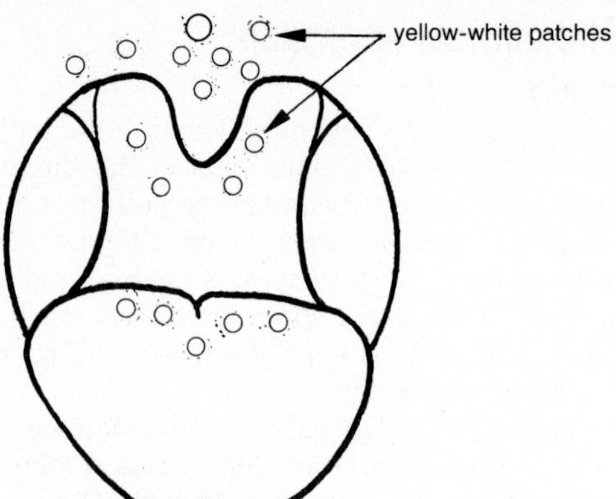

Fig. 59.2 *Oral thrush due to* Candida albicans: *small patches of whitish-yellow exudate on the palate, dorsum of tongue, pharynx and mucosa are typical*

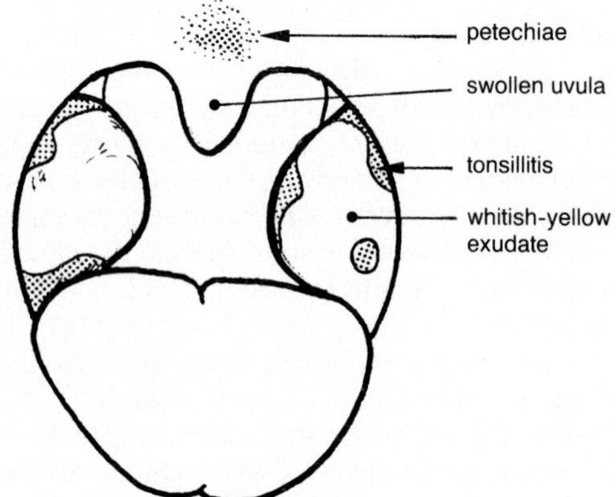

Fig. 59.3 *Epstein-Barr mononucleosis: swollen red tonsils with a whitish-yellow membranous exudate are usually seen; petechiae on the soft palate may be present*

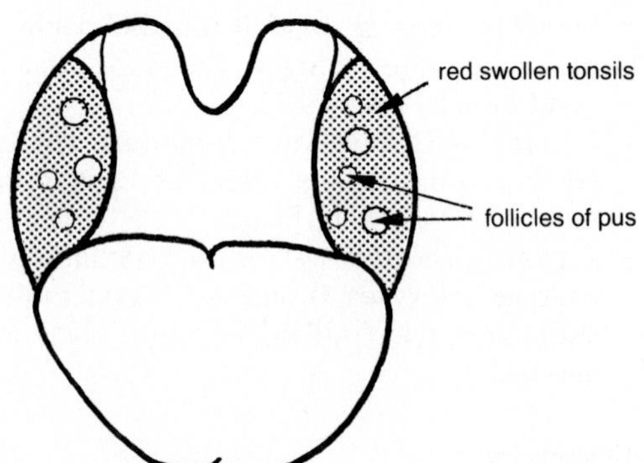

Fig. 59.4 *Follicular tonsillitis due to* Streptococcus pyogenes: *the tonsils are swollen and red with pockets of pus*

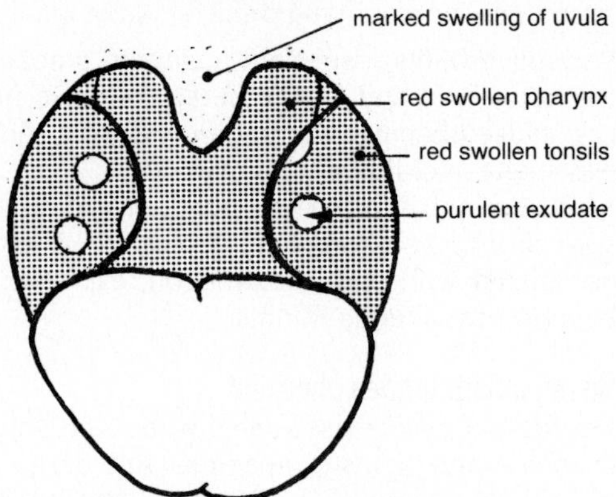

Fig. 59.5 *Streptococcal tonsillopharyngitis: severe inflammation involves both tonsils and pharynx with marked redness, swelling and exudate. Consider herpes simplex and mononucleosis as alternative diagnoses*

- mononucleosis test
- random blood sugar (? diabetes)

To swab or not to swab

Throat swabs are about 90% effective in isolating GABHS from the infected throat. Authorities are divided about management. 'Some recommend that throat cultures be performed for all sore throats and antibiotics given only when GABHS is found. Others regard throat cultures as being unnecessary and recommend therapy based on clinical judgements. Still others recommend throat cultures for selected patients only.[4]

Generally, throat cultures are not necessary except to verify the presence of *Streptococcus pyogenes*, especially in closed institutions such as boarding schools, or if diphtheria is suspected in the non-immunised.

Epstein-Barr mononucleosis (EBM) screening

It is important initially if tonsillar exudate is present to consider the possibility of EBM and if suspected a blood film and a Paul Bunnell heterophile antibody titre should be ordered. However, neither may be positive for EBM during the first few days of illness.[4]

Sore throat in children

A sore throat in a child usually means a viral or, less commonly, bacterial infection of the tonsillopharynx. Other causes to consider are:

- gingivostomatitis, especially primary herpes simplex

- epiglottitis
- laryngotracheobronchitis (croup)
- laryngitis
- oral moniliasis (more a bad taste than pain)
- aphthous ulcers
- foreign bodies
- postnasal drip, e.g. allergic rhinitis
- irritation
  - — low environmental humidity
  - — smoke (e.g. household smoke)

Sore throat in the elderly

Sore throat in the elderly may be caused by a viral infection but otherwise needs to be treated with considerable respect. It is important to exclude pharyngeal carcinoma which can present with the classic triad—pain on swallowing, referred ear pain and hoarseness.

Oropharangeal lesions may occur with herpes zoster but vesicles are usually present on the face.

A metallic taste in the mouth with or without a complaint of a sore throat indicates *Candida albicans* and hence diabetes must be excluded.

Streptococcal tonsillopharyngitis

This infection may involve the pharynx only and vary from mild to severe, it or may involve both tonsils and pharynx. It is uncommon under age 2 or over age 40.[5]

Typical clinical features:

- abrupt onset sore throat
- severe pain
- extreme difficulty in swallowing
- pain on talking
- foul-smelling breath
- constitutional symptoms
  - — fever $\geq$ 38°C
  - — toxicity

Examination

Pharynx very inflamed and oedematous. Tonsils swollen with pockets of yellow exudates on surfaces (Figs 59.4 and 59.5). Very tender enlarged tonsillar lymph nodes.

Treatment

It should be treated with penicillin or an alternative antibiotic (Table 59.3).[6] Antibiotic treatment does not appear to affect the natural history of the illness (i.e. shorten the course or reduce symptoms) nor protect against glomerulonephritis but does protect against rheumatic fever.[5]

Supportive measures include:

- adequate soothing fluids, including icy poles
- analgesia: adults—2 soluble aspirin
  children—paracetamol elixir (not alcohol base)
- rest with adequate fluid intake
- soothing gargles, e.g. soluble aspirin used for analgesia
- advice against overuse of OTC throat lozenges and topical sprays which can sensitise the throat; limited use (3 days) of decongestants for nasal decongestion is helpful

Table 59.3 *Treatment for streptococcal throat (proven or suspected)*[6]

Children
phenoxymethyl penicillin 25 to 50 mg/kg/day (o) in
2 to 3 divided doses for 10 days (to maximum 1 g/day)
or
erythromycin 25 to 50 mg/kg/day (o) in
2 to 3 divided doses for 10 days (to maximum 1 g/day)

Adults
phenoxymethyl penicillin 500 mg (o) 12 hourly for 10 days
(can initiate treatment with one injection of procaine penicillin)
or
erythromycin 500 mg (o) 12 hourly for 10 days

In severe cases:
Procaine penicillin 1-1.5 g IM daily for 3-5 days
plus
Phenoxymethyl penicillin (as above) for 10 days

Note Although symptoms and most evidence will disappear within 1 to 2 days of treatment, a full course of 10 days should be given to provide an optimal chance of eradicating *Streptococcus pyogenes* from the nasopharynx and thus minimising the risk of recurrence or complications such as rheumatic fever.[6]

Quinsy

Quinsy is a peritonsillar abscess characterised by marked swelling of the peritonsillar area with medial displacement of tonsillar tissue (Fig. 59.6). It is usually caused by GABHS or anaerobes, occasionally Haemophilus sp. and *Staphylococcus aureus*. A typical picture of tonsillitis is followed by increasing difficulty in swallowing and trismus.

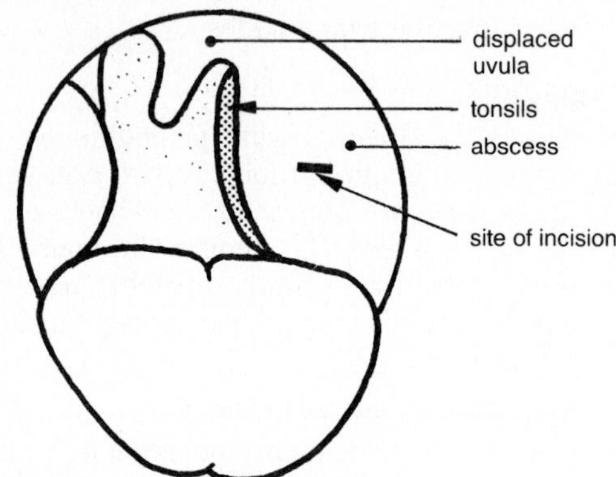

Fig. 59.6 *Peritonsillar abscess (quinsy): a tense red bulging mass is noted and the uvula is displaced from the midline; a site of incision for drainage is indicated*

Treatment

Antibiotics, e.g. procaine penicillin IM or clindamycin plus drainage under local anaesthetic if it is pointing. Oral penicillin treatment is likely to fail. Subsequent tonsillectomy is recommended.

Viral causes of sore throat

Epstein-Barr mononucleosis

The angiose form of EBM is a real trap and must be considered in 15–25 year old patients (peak incidence) with a painful throat which takes about seven days to reach its peak.

Clinical features

- sore throat
- prodromal fever, malaise, lethargy
- anorexia, myalgia
- nasal quality to voice
- skin rash

Examination

- petechiae on palate (not pathognomonic)
- enlarged tonsils with or without yellow exudates (looks but isn't purulent)
- periorbital oedema
- lymphadenopathy, especially posterior cervical
- splenomegaly (50%)
- jaundice, ± hepatomegaly (5–10%)

The rash

- primary rash (5%)
- secondary rash
  - — with ampicillin, amoxycillin (90–100%)
  - — with penicillin (50%)

Diagnosis

- blood film—atypical lymphocytes
- white cell count—absolute lymphocytosis
- heterophil antibodies
- Monospot test

Herpangia

An uncommon infection caused by Coxsackie virus. Presents as small vesicles on soft palate, uvula and anterior fauces. They ulcerate to form small ulcers. The problem is benign and rapidly self-limiting.

Herpes simplex pharyngitis

In adults primary infection is similar to severe streptococcal pharyngitis but ulcers extend beyond the tonsils.

Other viral pharyngitis

Typically the signs are fewer than other causes. The typical case has mild redness without exudate and prominent (sometimes pale) lymphoid patches on the posterior pharynx (Fig. 59.1). Tonsillar lymph nodes are usually not enlarged or tender. This picture is the commonest encountered in general practice.

Diphtheria

The potentially fatal form of this disease almost always occurs in non-immunised people. The clinical presentation may be modified by previous immunisation or by antibiotic treatment.

Typical clinical features

- insidious onset
- mild to moderate fever
- mild sore throat and dysphagia
- patient looks pale and ill
- enlarged tonsils
- pharynx inflamed and oedematous
- membrane (any colour but usually grey-green) can spread beyond tonsils to fauces,

soft palate, lateral pharyngeal wall and downwards to involve larynx (Fig. 59.7)
- enlarged cervical lymph nodes
- soft tissue swelling of neck → 'bull neck' appearance

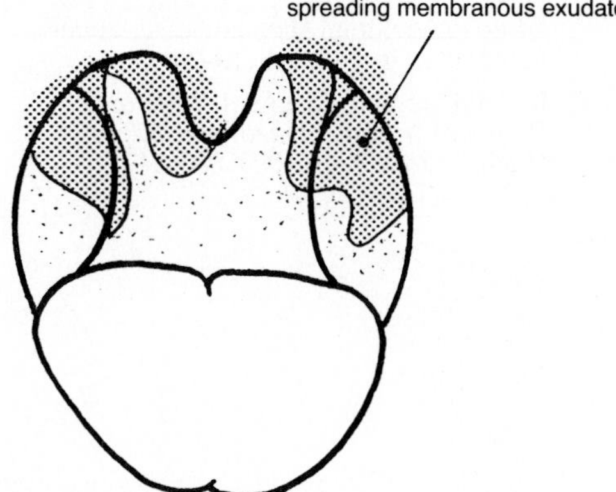

Fig. 59.7 *Diphtheria: tonsils and pharynx are red and swollen; a thick grey-green exudate forms on the tonsils as a spreading membrane*

Management
- Throat swabs
- Antitoxin
- Penicillin or erythromycin 500 mg qid for 10 days
- Isolate patient

Candida pharyngitis

Oral candidiasis typically presents as milky-white growths on the palate, buccal and gingival mucosae, pharynx and dorsum of the tongue (Fig. 59.2). If scraped away a bleeding ulcerated surface remains. A bad (metallic) taste is a feature but the patient may complain of a sore throat and tongue and dysphagia.

Causes or predisposing factors to consider:
- HIV infection
- diabetes mellitus
- broad spectrum antibiotics
- corticosteroids, including inhalers
- dentures
- debility

Management
- Determine underlying cause.
- Nystatin suspension, rinse and swallow qid.

When to refer

- Acute epiglottitis in children (a medical emergency).
- Inaccessible foreign body.
- Abscess: peritonsillar or retropharangeal.
- Recurrent attacks of tonsillitis and adenoid hypertrophy for an opinion about tonsillectomy and/or adenoidectomy.
- Suspicion or evidence of HIV infection or diphtheria.
- Patients not responding to treatment.
- Patients with more generalised disorders that are not yet diagnosed.

Practice tips

- Consider severe tonsillitis with a covering membrane as Epstein-Barr mononucleosis.
- If an adult presents with an intensely painful throat with a heavy exudate and seems toxic, consider primary herpes simplex as well as streptococcal throat.
- Reserve swabs of the throat for verification of a strep throat where it is important to do so, for suspected diphtheria and for suspicion of other serious infections such as tuberculosis.
- Be aware of possible complications such as febrile convulsions in children and abscess formation.
- Do not misdiagnose unusual causes of a sore throat, such as carcinoma (Fig. 59.8).
- The triad: hoarseness, pain on swallowing and referred ear pain = pharyngeal carcinoma.
- The two major considerations in managing the acute sore throat are:
  - Can diphtheria be excluded?
  - Should the patient be treated with an antibiotic?[7]

  Antibiotic treatment is aimed primarily at streptococcal pharyngitis and this is often based on clinical judgement.

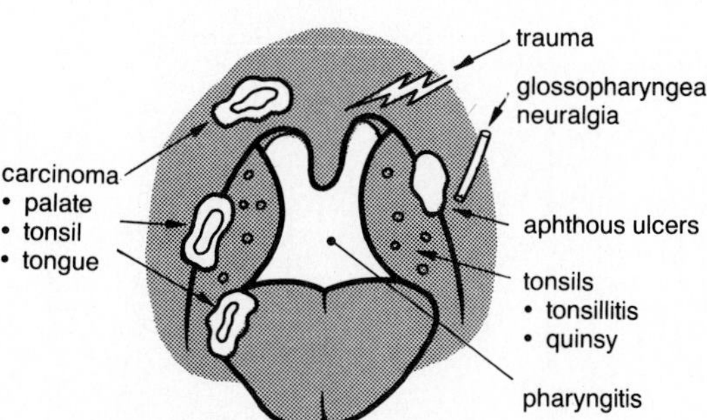

Fig. 59.8 *General causes of a sore throat: note the importance of excluding carcinoma*

References

1. Office of Population Censuses and Surveys. *Morbidity statistics from general practice studies on medical and population subjects. No 26.* London: HSMO, 1974, 33–40.
2. Cormack J, Marinker M, Morrell D. *Practice: a handbook of primary medical care.* London: Kluwer-Harrap, 1980; 3(25):1–7.
3. Fry J. *Common diseases, their nature, incidence and care.* Lancaster: MTP Press, 1987, 74–77.
4. Yung AP, Stanley PA. The patient with the acute sore throat. Curr Ther, 1985; 26:54–55.
5. Shires D, Hennen B, Rice D. *Family medicine* (2nd edition). New York: McGraw-Hill, 1987, 97–103.
6. Mashford ML. *Antibiotic guidelines* (7th edition). Victorian Medical Postgraduate Foundation Inc, 1992–3: 19–20.
7. Kincaid-Smith P, Larkins R, Whelan G. *Problems in clinical medicine.* Sydney: MacLennan & Petty, 1990, 340–347.

60

Tiredness

Tiredness is not a diagnosis but is rather a symptom of illness: it may occur as either a presenting or a supporting symptom. Tiredness is interchangeable with terms such as fatigue, weariness, loss of energy, listlessness and exhaustion. It is a common and difficult presenting symptom. The symptom of tiredness is likely to be 'hidden' behind the request for a tonic or a physical check-up.[1]

Tiredness can be a symptom of a great variety of serious and uncommon diseases including malignant disease. The challenge for the family doctor is to diagnose such disorders quickly without extravagant investigation.

Key facts and checkpoints

- The commonest cause of tiredness is stress and anxiety related to lifestyle.
- The study undertaken by Wadsworth, Butterfield and Blaney[2] showed that the complaint of tiredness or 'feeling very run down all the time' represented about 5% of all complaints presenting to the family doctor.
- Shires and Hennen[3] estimated that about one out of 10 patients in a family practice presents with fatigue as a prime symptom.
- In Jerrett's study[4] no organic cause was found in 62.3% of his patients presenting with lethargy; the constant factors were sleep disturbance and the presence of stress in their lives. Many of them turned out to be suffering from psychological problems or psychiatric illnesses, including depression, anxiety state or bereavement.
- An important cause of daytime tiredness is a sleep disorder such as obstructive sleep apnoea which results in periodic hypoventilation during sleep. It occurs in 2% of the general population in all age groups and in about 10% of middle-aged men.[4] A history of snoring is a pointer to the problem.
- Underlying disorders that need to be considered as possible causes of chronic fatigue are endocrine and metabolic disorders, malignancy, chronic infection, autoimmune disorders, primary psychiatric disorders, neuromuscular disorders, anaemia, drugs and cardiovascular disorders.
- Chronic fatigue syndrome (CFS) is defined as debilitating fatigue, persisting or relapsing over six months, associated with a significant reduction in activity levels of at least 50%, and for which no other cause can be found.

Causes of tiredness

Analysing the symptom and reaching a diagnosis demands considerable skill since tiredness may indicate the first subtle manifestation of a serious physical disease or, more commonly, may represent a patient's inability to deal with the problems of everyday life. Chronic tiredness or fatigue is a feature of the 'high pressure' nature of many people's lifestyles.

Careful consideration must be given to the differentiation of physiological tiredness, which results from excessive physical activity, from psychological tiredness. Furthermore, before diagnosing tiredness as psychological, pathological as well as physical causes must be excluded.

A summary of causes of chronic tiredness is presented in Table 60.1.

Table 60.1 *Causes of chronic tiredness*

Psychogenic/non-organic

Psychiatric disorders
- anxiety
- depression
- other primary disorders
- bereavement

Lifestyle factors
- workaholic tendencies and 'burn out'
- lack of exercise
- mental stress and emotional demands
- exposure to irritants, e.g. carbon monoxide, 'lead' fumes
- inappropriate diet
- obesity

Organic

Congestive cardiac failure
Anaemia
Malignancy
HIV/AIDS
Subacute to chronic infection, e.g. hepatitis, malaria, Lyme disease
Endocrine
- thyroid (hyper- and hypo-)
- adrenal (Cushing's disease, Addison's disease)
- hyperparathyroidism
- diabetes mellitus

Nutritional deficiency
Renal failure
Liver disorders—chronic liver failure, chronic active hepatitis
Respiratory conditions, e.g. chronic bronchitis
Neuromuscular, e.g. MS, myasthenia gravis, Parkinson's disease
Metabolic, e.g. hypokalaemia, hypomagnesaemia
Drug toxicity, addiction or side effects (see Table 60.3)
Autoimmune disorders
Fibromyalgia
Chronic fatigue syndrome
Sleep-related disorders
Postinfectious fatigue syndrome, e.g. influenza, mononucleosis

A diagnostic approach

A summary of the safety diagnostic model is presented in Table 60.2.

Table 60.2 *Tiredness: diagnostic strategy model*

Q. *Probability diagnosis*
A. Stress and anxiety
Depression
Viral/postviral infection
Sleep-related disorders, e.g. sleep apnoea

Q. *Serious disorders not to be missed*
A. Malignant disease
Cardiac arrhythmia, e.g. sick sinus syndrome
Cardiomyopathy
Anaemia
HIV infection

Q. *Pitfalls (often missed)*
A. 'Masked' depression
Chronic infection, e.g. Lyme disease
Incipient CCF
Fibromyalgia
Drugs: alcohol; prescribed; withdrawal
Menopause syndrome
Pregnancy
Neurological disorders
- Post head injury
- CVA
- Parkinson's disease

Renal failure
Metabolic, e.g. hypokalaemia, hypomagnesaemia
Rarities
Hyperparathyroidism
Addison's disease
Cushing's disease
Narcolepsy
Multiple sclerosis
Autoimmune disorders

Q. *Seven masquerades checklist*
A. Depression ✓
Diabetes ✓
Drugs ✓
Anaemia ✓
Thyroid disease ✓
Spinal dysfunction ✓
UTI ✓

Q. *Is the patient trying to tell me something?*
A. Highly likely.

Probability diagnosis

The most probable diagnoses to consider are:

- tension, stress and anxiety
- depression
- viral or postviral infection
- sleep-related disorders

Research studies have reported that over 50% (and in some cases as many as 80%) of reported cases of fatigue have been of psychological causation.[5] Overwork is a common cause of fatigue and is often obvious to everyone but the patient. The modern approach to sleep-related disorders has revealed several important factors causing excessive tiredness.

Serious disorders not to be missed

Many serious disorders such as anaemia, malignant disease and subacute or chronic infections such as hepatitis, bacterial endocarditis and tuberculosis can be 'hidden' or masked in the initial stages or not readily apparent. Neuromuscular diseases such as myasthenia gravis and multiple sclerosis, connective tissue disorders and HIV infection also have to be excluded.

Pitfalls

The symptom of tiredness is fraught with pitfalls. Common ones include depression and other psychoneurotic disorders, and incipient congestive cardiac failure. Drug intake is a very common pitfall whether it be by self-administration (including alcohol) or iatrogenic.

Tiredness is a feature of pregnancy in many women, so this association is worth keeping in mind, especially in the early stages when a change in menstrual history is not given or a young single woman will attempt to conceal the fact. It is also a presenting symptom of the menopause syndrome which should not be misdiagnosed.

Seven masquerades checklist

All these important problems are capable of being responsible for tiredness, especially depression, diabetes, drugs, anaemia and urinary infection. Thyroid disease could certainly be responsible. Spinal pain can indirectly cause tiredness. Drugs that commonly cause tiredness are listed in Table 60.3. Drug withdrawal, especially for illicit drugs such as amphetamines, marijuana, cocaine and heroin, has to be considered.

Table 60.3 *Drugs that can cause tiredness*

Alcohol
Analgesics
Antibiotics
Anticonvulsants
Antiemetics
Antidepressants
Antihistamines
Antihypertensives
Anxiolytics
Corticosteroids
Ergot alkaloids
Digoxin
Hormones, e.g. oral contraceptives
Hypnotics
Nicotine
NSAIDs
Vitamins A and D (early toxic symptoms)

NB Most drugs have a considerable capacity to cause tiredness.

Psychogenic considerations

Tiredness is a symptom that may represent a 'ticket of entry': a plea for help in a stressed, anxious or depressed patient. Any of the primary psychiatric disorders can present as tiredness.

The clinical approach

In routine history taking, it is mandatory that questions be asked about the following if the information is not volunteered by the patient.

- Sleep pattern (it is not uncommon for patients to say they sleep well and yet on questioning it is found they have initial insomnia, or middle insomnia, or both, with or without early morning waking). It is most relevant to talk to any sleeping partners to obtain a history of sleep disturbance.
- Weight fluctuations.
- Energy—performance—ability to cope.
- Sexual activity.
- Suicidal ideas.
- Self-medication—over-the-counter preparations, e.g. bromides, stimulants, analgesics, alcohol, cigarettes, other drugs. This is particularly important in the drug addiction-prone group: doctors, chemists, nurses, workers in the liquor industry, truck drivers.
- Fears (including phobic symptoms, hypochondriasis).
- Precipitating factors (present in over 50% of patients with depressive illness):
  - — postpartum
  - — postoperative
  - — associated with chronic physical illness
  - — bereavement
  - — pain—chronic pain conditions
  - — retirement
  - — medication
  - — post trauma, e.g. motor vehicle accident
  - — postviral infections, especially hepatitis, infectious mononucleosis, influenza.
- Work history—determine if the patient is a workaholic.
- Dietary history—determine pattern, including fad diets or skipped meals.
- Menstrual history and symptoms related to the menopause syndrome.
- Self-question: 'Is this patient depressed?'

Physical examination

A routine physical examination is important, followed by a more detailed specific examination relevant to the individual patient. In particular, it is important to ascertain the presence of hepatosplenomegaly and lymphadenopathy. In general the physical examination is unrewarding. In the chronic fatigue syndrome the relevant abnormal findings are muscle tenderness, mild pharyngitis and tender slightly enlarged cervical lymph nodes. When an alternative underlying medical illness is responsible for the tiredness there will usually be evidence for this on physical examination, e.g. positive Babinski reflex in multiple sclerosis, postural hypotension in Addison's disease, right ventricular lift with an ASD.

Investigations

Investigations should be selected judiciously from the following (tests that most patients should have when the examination is completely normal are marked *):

- Haemoglobin, blood count and film*
- ESR*
- ECG and Holter monitor
- Thyroid function tests
- Liver function tests*
- Urea/renal function tests*
- Serum electrolytes (including calcium and magnesium)*
- Blood sugar*
- Plasma cortisol
- Serum iron and ferritin
- Micro and culture of urine*
- Tests for autoimmune disorders
  - — antinuclear antibodies
  - — rheumatoid factor
- HIV screening
- Chest X-ray and spirometry
- Chronic infection screening (consider): hepatitis A, B, C, D, E, cytomegalovirus, EBM, Ross River virus, Lyme disease, brucellosis, Q fever, tuberculosis, malaria, infective endocarditis, toxoplasmosis
- Primary neuromuscular disorders
  - — muscle enzyme assay
  - — electromyography
- Tissue markers for malignancy
- Referral to a sleep disorder laboratory for sleep apnoea studies

The diagnosis of CFS can only be made when the minimum investigations (listed *) have been shown to be normal or to demonstrate minor abnormalities in liver function or blood film (atypical lymphocytes).

Tiredness in children

Tiredness in children is caused by a range of predictable conditions such as physiological factors (excessive exercise, lack of sleep, poor diet), infections, allergies including asthma, drugs, depression and various illnesses in general.

Overweight children are likely to fatigue more rapidly than children of normal weight.[6] Any bacterial, viral or other infection may be associated with tiredness, with Epstein-Barr mononucleosis being very significant in adolescents. Chronic Epstein-Barr virus infection causing recurrent episodes of fever, pharyngitis, malaise and adenopathy can occur, especially in teenagers, who present with chronic exhaustion which is frequently mistaken for malignancy.[6]

Tiredness is a presenting feature of depression in adolescents, a serious problem that often goes unrecognised. Tonsillar–adenoidal hypertrophy may be large enough to compromise air exchange, particularly during sleep. Snoring may be a feature plus tiredness and lethargy in the waking state.

Tiredness in the elderly

Elderly people tend to tire more quickly and recover more slowly and incompletely than younger ones. Sleep in older people generally is shorter in duration and of lesser depth, and they feel less refreshed and sometimes irritable on awakening.

Fatigue may be present as a result of emotional frustration. Whenever the prospect of gratification is small, a person tends to tire quickly and to remain so until something stimulating appears. Since the prospects for gratifying experience wane with the years, easy fatigability or tiredness is common in this age group.

Bereavement

Although a bereavement reaction is common and a normal human response that occurs at all ages, it is more frequently encountered in the elderly, with the loss of a spouse or a child (young or middle-aged!). Fatigue that occurs during the initial mourning period is striking and might represent a protective mechanism against intense emotional stress. With time, usually around 6 to 12 months, a compensated stage is reached, fatigue gradually abates, and the patient resumes normal activities as the conflicts of grief are gradually resolved. Freud pointed out the complexities of mourning as the bereaved person slowly adjusts to the loss of the loved person. In others various symptoms persist as an 'abnormal grief reaction' including persistence of fatigue. Some factors which may lead to this include:

- unexpected death
- high dependence upon the dead person
- guilt feelings, especially in a love/hate relationship

Studies in general practice have shown that widows see their family doctors for psychiatric symptoms at three times the usual rate in the first six months after bereavement. The consultation rate for non-psychiatric symptoms also increases, by almost 50%.

Role of the family doctor

Following bereavement it is important to watch for evidence of depression, drug dependency, especially on alcohol, and suicidal tendencies. In cases of expected death, management should, if possible, start before the bereavement. Supportive care and ongoing counselling are very important.

Sleep-related disorders

Disorders of sleep are a common and significant contribution to community illness and death. For example, it is now known that untreated moderate to severe obstructive sleep apnoea has an 11–13% five year mortality and a 37% eight-year mortality, mainly from cardiovascular and motor vehicle accident related deaths.[7,8]

A classification of sleep disorders is presented in Table 60.4.[7]

Table 60.4 *Classification of sleep disorders*[7]

Disorders of initiating or maintaining sleep
e.g. nocturnal myoclonus
sleep apnoea syndromes
Disorders of excessive somnolence
e.g. sleep apnoea syndromes
narcolepsy
hypothyroidism
Disorders of sleep/wake cycle
e.g. jet lag
shift work
Dysfunctions associated with sleep
e.g. night terrors
sleepwalking

Many conditions may disturb breathing during the night (Fig. 60.1). Nocturnal dyspnoea may result from cardiac causes (mitral stenosis, ischaemic cardiomyopathy, cardiac arrhythmias, fluid overload or retention) which usually present with orthopnoea, pulmonary crepitations and peripheral oedema. Asthma is another common cause of nocturnal dyspnoea, cough (with or without wheeze) occurring classically between 2 am and 5 am. Gastro-oesophageal reflux with or without aspiration may disturb respiration at night, but it usually presents with daytime or postural reflux. All these conditions can usually be differentiated from sleep apnoea clinically or with further investigation.

The sleep apnoea syndromes are a common group of disorders that result in periodic hypoventilation during sleep. They occur in about 2% of the general population in all age groups, and about 10% of middle-aged men.

Sleep apnoea

The term 'sleep apnoea' is used to describe cyclical brief interruptions of ventilation, each cycle lasting 15–90 seconds and resulting in hypoxaemia, hypercapnia and respiratory acidosis, terminating in an arousal from sleep (often not recognised by the patient). The interruption is then followed by the resumption of normal ventilation, a return to sleep, and further interruption of ventilation.

Sleep apnoea is broadly classified into obstructive and central types.

Obstructive sleep apnoea (OSA) is the commonest type and involves an intermittent narrowing or occlusion of the pharyngeal area of the upper airway. The effects include snoring and hypopnoea, sometimes apnoea.

Predisposing causes include:

- diminished airway size, e.g. macroglossia, obesity, tonsillar-adenoidal hypertrophy
- upper airway muscle hypotonia, e.g. alcohol, hypnotics, neurological disorders
- nasal obstruction

Central sleep apnoea is less common and is due mainly to neurological conditions such as brain stem disorders leading to reduced ventilatory drive, and neuromuscular disorders such as motor neurone disease.

Clinical effects of sleep apnoea syndromes[7]

Important clinical presentations include:

- excessive daytime sleepiness and tiredness

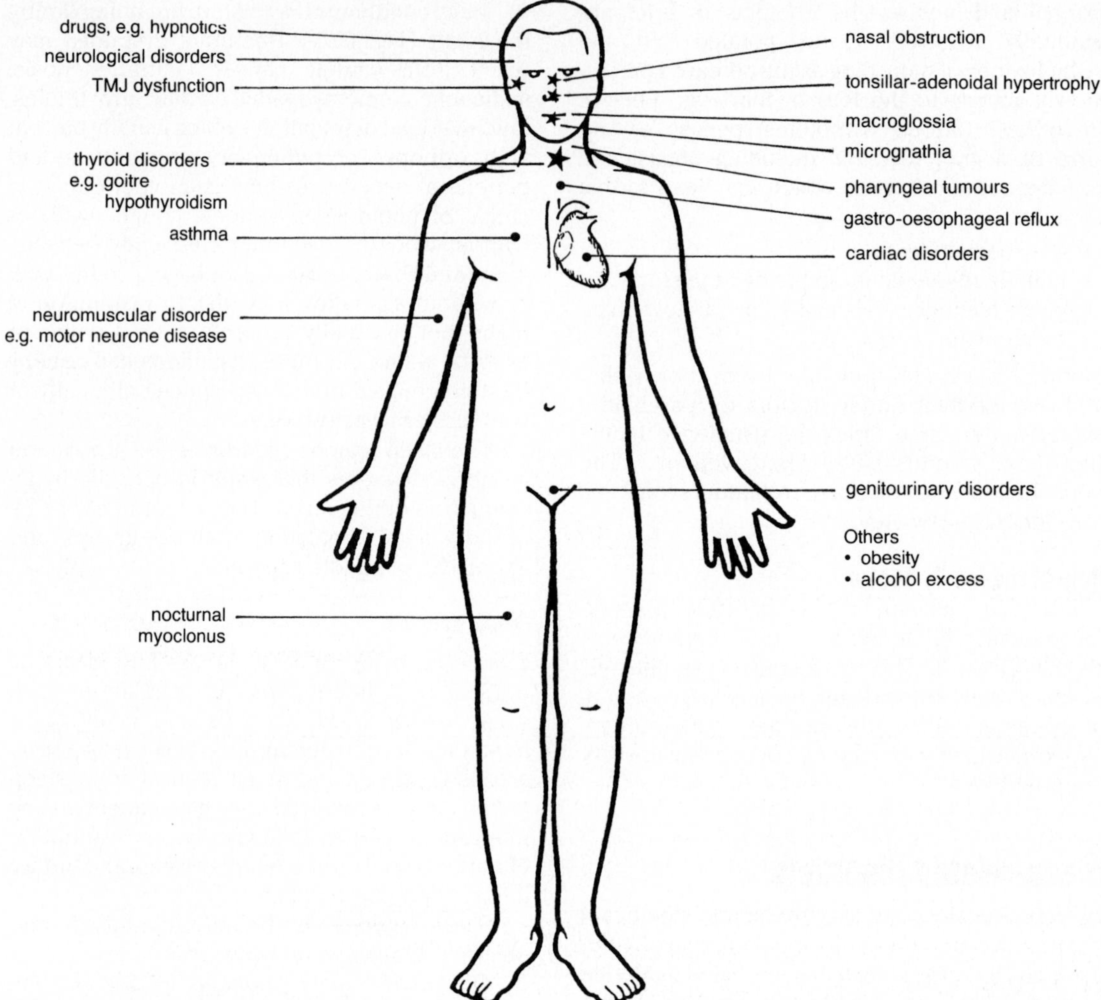

Fig. 60.1 *Significant causes of sleep disturbance*

- nocturnal problems, e.g. loud snoring, thrashing, 'seizures', choking, pain reactions
- morning headache
- subtle neuropsychiatric disturbance—learning difficulties, loss of concentration, personality change, depression
- sexual dysfunction

Causes of excessive daytime sleepiness are presented in Table 60.5. In OSA sleepiness results from repeated arousals during sleep and the effects of hypoxaemia and hypercapnia on the brain. Physical examination may reveal few or no signs.

Referral to a comprehensive sleep disorder centre is appropriate if this disorder is suspected.

Table 60.5 *Causes of excessive somnolence*

Sleep apnoea syndromes
Narcolepsy
Endocrine, e.g. hypothyroidism
Drug induced
Purposeful sleep deprivation
Nocturnal myoclonus
Bereavement
Idiopathic

Narcolepsy

Narcolepsy is a condition where periods of irresistible sleep occur in inappropriate circumstances and consists of a tetrad of symptoms:

- Sudden brief sleep attacks (15–20 minutes).
- Cataplexy—a hidden loss of muscle tone in the lower limbs that may cause the person to slump to the floor, unable to move. These attacks are usually triggered by sudden surprise or emotional upset.
- Sleep paralysis—a frightening feeling of inability to move while drowsy (between sleep and waking).
- Hypnagogic (terrifying) hallucinations on falling asleep.

Narcolepsy usually begins in early adult life and tends to improve at about 30 years of age. Treatment includes methylphenidate (Ritalin) or amphetamines or small doses of tricylic antidepressants (for cataplexy).

Burnout

Patients sometimes claim that they feel 'burn-out'. Burnout can mean many things and include a whole constellation of psychogenic symptoms such as exhaustion, boredom and cynicism, paranoia, detachment, heightened irritability and impatience, depression and psychosomatic complaints such as headache and tiredness. Ellard[9] defines burnout as the syndrome which arises when a person who has a strong neurotic need to succeed in a particular task becomes confronted with the impossibility of success in that task. This seems a realistic explanation, but the important factor is to clarify the nature of the problem with care and determine whether the patient has a psychoneurotic disorder, such as hypomania, anxiety state or depression, or a personality disorder or simply unrealistic goals.

Chronic fatigue syndrome

This complex syndrome, which causes profound and persistent tiredness, is also referred to as myalgic encephalomyelitis, chronic neuromuscular viral syndrome,[10] postviral syndrome, chronic Epstein-Barr viral syndrome, viral fatigue state, epidemic neuromyasthenia, neurasthenia, Icelandic disease, Royal Free disease and Tapanic disease. Chronic fatigue syndrome (CFS) is not to be confused with the tiredness and depression that follow a viral infection such as infectious mononucleosis, hepatitis or influenza. These postviral tiredness states are certainly common but resolve within six months or so.

Typical features of CFS:[11]

- extreme exhaustion (with minimal physical effort)
- headache or a vague 'fuzzy' feeling in the head
- aching in the muscles and legs
- poor concentration and memory
- hypersomnia or other sleep disturbance
- waking feeling tired
- emotional lability
- depressive-type illness
- arthralgia
- sore throat
- subjective feeling of fever (with a normal temperature)
- tender swollen lymph glands

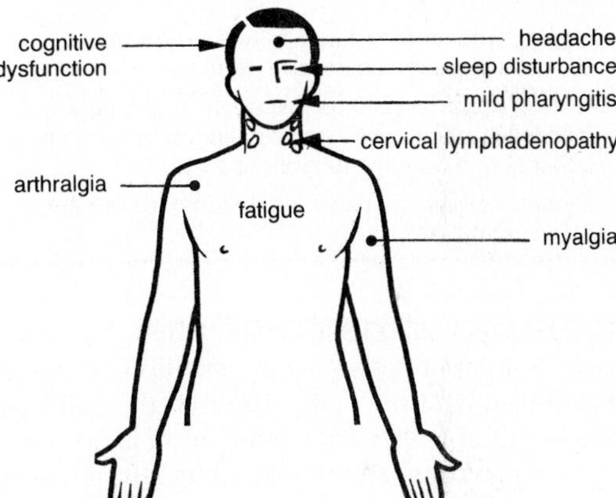

Fig. 60.2 *Chronic fatigue syndrome: characteristic symptoms*

Epidemiologically it has been related to Coxsackie B virus infections.[11] The responsible organism is referred to as a slow virus infection by some authorities.[10]

In approximately two-thirds of patients the illness follows a clearly defined viral illness. However, no single virus has been consistently associated with the development of the syndrome which is known to develop following a wide range of viral and non-viral infective illness. Immune system dysfunction with chronic overproduction of cytokines (e.g. interferon) is a possible pathogenetic mechanism.

Every family doctor probably has patients with this disorder and the syndrome has been observed in isolated endemics from time to time.

There is no doubt that the syndrome is real in these patients. One of the major problems confronting clinicians is that there is no diagnostic test for this illness, so it remains a clinical diagnosis backed up by normal baseline investigations.

Diagnostic criteria for CFS have been published[12] (Table 60.6), which emphasise the positive clinical features of the syndrome and the chronicity of symptoms (greater than six months), in addition to the need for careful exclusion of alternative diagnoses by history, physical examination and laboratory investigation.

Table 60.6 *Criteria for the diagnosis of chronic fatigue syndrome*

1. Chronic severe persisting or relapsing fatigue for 6 months or more.
2. Neuropsychiatric dysfunction with impairment of concentration and short-term memory.
3. Normal physical findings (except mild pharyngitis, mild fever, generalised muscle tenderness, minor cervical or axillary lymphadenopathy).
4. Other diseases are excluded that may cause the above symptoms.

Physical examination and investigation

Apart from mild pharyngeal infection, cervical lymphadenopathy or localised muscle tenderness, the physical examination is normal.

Investigations should be directed towards excluding possible diagnoses for that patient, such as chronic infection, autoimmune disorders, endocrine and metabolic disorders, primary neuromuscular disorders, malignancy and primary psychiatric disorders. The latter is the most difficult of the differential diagnoses and psychiatric referral will often need to be considered.

Management

Patients who have CFS are really suffering and unhappy people, similar to those with fibromyalgia. They require considerable understanding and support. Symptoms last approximately 2½ years.

Management strategies include:[13]

- CFS recognition—explain that the illness is real but the cause unknown and tests are likely to be normal.
- Explanation and reassurance that the illness is usually self-limiting with no permanent complications; and that a slow steady improvement can be anticipated with most CSF patients returning to normal health.
- Provide continued psychological support.
- Review for diagnostic reappraisal (examine at least every 4 months).
- Avoid telling patients they are depressed.
- Treat symptomatically—pain relief, consider NSAIDs.
- Refer to counselling and support groups.
- Provide a realistic, regular, graduated exercise program.
- Reduce relevant stress factors (map a realistic living program).
- Psychiatric referral if appropriate.
- Ask the patient to keep a diary of exercise/stress and symptom severity, in particular.
- Avoid long-distance travel, which is poorly tolerated.

Cognitive therapy appears to help some patients, as do relaxation therapy, meditation, stress management and psychotherapy, where indicated.

The emphasis should be placed on caring, rather than curing, until a scientific solution is found.

Medication options

Consider:

- low-dose tricylic antidepressants (trial if depression significant).
- NSAIDs with or without low-dose tricyclics when necessary.
- domperidone for nausea.

Fibromyalgia

The fibromyalgia syndrome (see Chap. 32) bears a clinical resemblance to CFS. Musculoskeletal pain is more prominent although tiredness (fatigue) and sleep disturbance are features. According to Schwenk[14], fibromyalgia affects 5% of the American population with a peak age of 35 (range 20–60) and the F:M sex ratio 10:1. The management is similar to CFS but the prognosis less optimistic.

References

1. Marinker M, Watter CAH. The patient complaining of tiredness. In: *Practice*. Cormack J, Marinker M, Morrell D, eds. London: Kluwer Medical, 1982, Section 3.1.

2. Wadsworth ME, Butterfield WJ, Blaney R. *Health and sickness: the choice of treatment*. London: Tavistock, 1971, 89–115.

3. Shires DB, Hennen BK. *Family medicine*. New York: McGraw-Hill, 1980, 129–137.

4. Jerrett WA. Lethargy in general practice. Practitioner, 1981; 225:731–737.

5. French MA. The clinical significance of tiredness. Can Med Assoc J, 1960; 82:665–671.

6. Tennessen WW. *Signs and symptoms in paediatrics*. Philadelphia: Lippincott, 1988, 37–40.

7. Pierce R, Naughton M. Sleep-related breathing disorders: recent advances. Aust Fam Physician, 1992; 21:397–405.

8. Partinen M, Guilleminault C. Daytime sleepiness and vascular morbidity: a seven year follow-up in obstructive sleep apnoea patients. Chest, 1990, 97:27–32.

9. Ellard J. A note on burnout. Mod Med Australia, 1987 (January), 32–35.

10. Simpson G. Persistent neuromuscular viral syndrome. Aust Fam Physician, 1987; 16:978–981.

11. Blaiklock DA. The chronically tired patient. Patient Management, 1986; 10 (July): 89–96.

12. Holmes G et al. Chronic fatigue syndrome: a working class definition. Ann Intern Med, 1988; 108: 387–389.

13. Wakefield D, Lloyd A, Hickie I. The chronic fatigue syndrome. Mod Med Australia, July 1990, 16–22.

14 Schwenk TL. Fibromyalgia and chronic fatigue syndrome: solving diagnostic and therapeutic dilemmas. Modern Medicine (USA), 1992; 60:50–60.

61

The unconscious patient

The state of arousal is determined by the function of the central reticular formation which extends from the brain stem to the thalamus. Coma occurs when this centre is damaged by a metabolic abnormality or by an invasive lesion which compresses this centre. Coma is also caused by damage to the cerebral cortex.[1]

The various levels of consciousness are summarised in Table 61.1; the levels vary from consciousness, which means awareness of oneself and the surroundings in a state of wakefulness[2], to coma which is a state of unrousable unresponsiveness. Rather than using these broad terms in clinical practice it is preferable to describe the actual state of the patient in a sentence.

Key facts and checkpoints

- Always consider hypoglycaemia in any unconscious patient, especially of unknown background.
- If a patient is unconscious and cyanosed consider upper airway obstruction until proved otherwise.

Table 61.1 *The five conscious levels*

		State	*Clinical features*	*Simplified classification*
↑	1	Consciousness	Aware and wakeful	Awake
	2	Clouded consciousness	Reduced awareness and wakefulness 'Alcohol effect' Confusion Drowsiness	Confused
Degree of consciousness	3	Stupor	Unconscious Deep sleep-like state Arousal with vigorous stimuli	Responds to shake and shout
↓	4	Semicomatose	Unconscious (deeper) Responds only to painful stimuli (sternal rubbing with knuckles) without arousing	Responds to pain
	5	Coma	Deeply unconscious Unrousable and unresponsive	Unresponsive coma

- The commonest causes of unconsciousness encountered in general practice are syncope, concussion and cerebrovascular accidents. The main causes are presented in Table 61.2.
- Do not allow the person who accompanies the unconscious patient to leave until all relevant details have been obtained.
- Record the degree of coma as a base line to determine improvement or deterioration.

Table 61.2 *Main causes of loss of consciousness*

Episodic causes—blackouts
- Epilepsy
- Syncope
- Drop attacks
- Cardiac arrhythmias, e.g. Stokes-Adams attacks
- Vertebrobasilar insufficiency
- Psychogenic disorders, including hyperventilation
- Breath holding (children)

Coma
(COMA provides a useful mnemonic for four major groups[1] of causes of unconsciousness)

C = CO_2 narcosis: respiratory failure

O = Overdose of drugs
- alcohol
- tranquillisers and antidepressants
- carbon monoxide
- analgesics
- others

M = Metabolic
- diabetes
  - — hypoglycaemia
  - — ketoacidosis
- hypothyroidism
- hepatic failure
- renal failure (uraemia)
- others

A = Apoplexy

Supratentorial
- intracerebral haemorrhage
- haematoma: subdural or extradural
- head injury
- cerebral tumour
- cerebral abscess

Infratentorial (posterior fossa)
- pressure from above
- cerebellar tumour
- brainstem infarct/haemorrhage
- Wernicke's encephalopathy

Meningismus (neck stiffness)
- subarachnoid haemorrhage
- meningitis

Other
- encephalitis
- overwhelming infection

Urgent attention

The initial contact with the unconscious patient is invariably sudden and dramatic and demands immediate action which should take only seconds to minutes. The primary objective is to keep the patient alive until the cause is determined and possible remedial action taken.[2]

Examination	***Action***
Is the patient breathing? Note chest wall movement	If not, clear airway and ventilate
Check pulse and pupils	Perform cardiopulmonary resuscitation if necessary
Is there evidence of trauma?	Consider extradural haematoma
Is the patient hypoglycaemic? Evidence of diabetes (discs, etc)	Consider glucometer estimation of blood sugar
Are vital functions present yet immediate correctable causes eliminated?	Place in coma position

History

A history can be obtained from relatives, friends, witnesses, ambulance officers or others. The setting in which the patient is found is important. Evidence of discs or cards identifying an illness such as diabetes or epilepsy should be searched for. Is there a known history of hypertension, heart disease, respiratory disease or psychiatric illness?

Questions to be considered[3]

- Is the patient diabetic?
  Does the patient have insulin injections?
  Has the patient had an infection?
  Has the patient been eating properly?
- Is drug overdose possible?
  Has the patient been depressed? Has the patient had recent stress or personal 'mishaps'?
  Has the patient been on any medications?
- Is epilepsy possible?
  Was twitching in the limbs observed?
  Did the patient pass urine or faeces?
- Is head injury possible?
  Has the patient been in a recent accident?
  Has the patient complained of headache?
- Has a stroke or subarachnoid haemorrhage occurred?
  Has the patient a history of hypertension?

Did the patient complain of a severe headache?
Has the patient complained of weakness of the limbs?

Examination

General features requiring assessment:

- Breathing pattern:
  Cheyne-Stokes respiration (periodic respiration) = cerebral dysfunction
  Ataxic respiration: shallow irregular respiration = brain stem lesion
  Kussmaul respiration: deep rapid hyperventilation = metabolic acidosis
- Breath: characteristic odours may be a feature of alcohol, diabetes, uraemia and hepatic coma.
- Level of consciousness: degree of coma (Table 61.1); the Glasgow coma scale (Table 61.3) is frequently used as a guide to the conscious state.
- Skin features: look for evidence of injection sites (drug addicts, diabetics) and snake bite marks, colour (cyanosis, purpura, jaundice, rashes, hyperpigmentation) and texture.
- Circulation.
- Temperature: consider infection such as meningitis and hyperpyrexia if raised and hypothermia, e.g. hypothyroidism, if low.
- Hydration: dehydration may signify conditions such as a high fever with infections, uraemia, hyperglycaemic coma.

Examination of the head and neck[2,3]

The following should be considered:

- facial asymmetry
- the skull and neck: palpation for evidence of trauma and neck rigidity
- eyes, pupils and ocular fundi
- tongue
- nostrils and ears
- auscultation of the skull

Examination of the limbs

Consider:

- injection marks (drug addicts, diabetics)
- tone of the limbs by lifting and dropping, e.g. flaccid limbs with early hemiplegia
- reaction of limbs to painful stimuli
- reflexes: tendon reflexes and plantar response

General examination of the body

This should include assessment of the pulses and blood pressure.

Table 61.3 *Glasgow coma scale*

	Score
Eye opening (E)	
• Spontaneous opening	4
• To verbal command	3
• To pain	2
• No response	1
Motor response (M)	
• Obeys verbal command	6
Response to painful stimuli	
• Localises pain	5
• Withdraws from pain stimuli	4
• Abnormal flexion	3
• Extensor response	2
• No response	1
Verbal response (V)	
• Orientated and converses	5
• Disoriented and converses	4
• Inappropriate words	3
• Incomprehensible sounds	2
• No response	1
Coma score = E + M + V	
Minimum 3	
Maximum 15	

Urine examination

Catheterisation of the bladder may be necessary to obtain urine. Check the urine for protein, sugar and ketones.

Diagnosing the hysterical 'unconscious' patient

One of the most puzzling problems in emergency medicine is how to diagnose the unconscious patient caused by a conversion reaction (hysteria). These patients really experience their symptoms (as opposed to the pretending patient) and resist most normal stimuli, including painful stimuli.

Method

- Hold the patient's eye or eyes open with your fingers and note the reaction to light.
- Now hold a mirror over the eye and watch closely for pupillary reaction. The pupil should constrict with accommodation from the patient looking at his or her own image.

Investigations

Appropriate investigations depend on the clinical assessment. The following represents a checklist.

- Blood tests
  — All patients: blood sugar
  urea and electrolytes

— Selected patients: full blood examination
blood gases
liver function tests
blood alcohol
serum cortisol
thyroid function tests

- Urine tests
  — A urine specimen is obtained by catheterisation.
  — Test for glucose and albumin.
  — Keep the specimen for drug screening.
- Stomach contents: aspiration of stomach contents for analysis.
- Radiology: CT scan is the investigation of choice (if available). If unavailable, X-ray of the skull may be helpful.
- Cerebrospinal fluid: lumbar puncture, necessary with neck stiffness, has risks in the comatose patient. A preliminary CT scan is necessary to search for coning of the cerebellum. If clear, the lumbar puncture should be safe and will help to diagnose subarachnoid haemorrhage and meningitis.
- Electroencephalograph
- ECG

Blackouts—episodic loss of consciousness

Episodic or transient loss of consciousness is a common problem. The important causes of blackout are presented in Table 61.2. The history is important to determine whether the patient is describing a true blackout or episodes of dizziness, weakness or some other sensation.

The clinical features of various types of blackouts are summarised in Table 61.4.

Epilepsy

Epilepsy is the commonest cause of blackouts. Most patients have sudden loss of consciousness without warning.

The typical features of a tonic-clonic convulsion are (in order):

- initial rigid tonic phase (up to 60 seconds)
- convulsion (clonic phase) (seconds to minutes)
- mild coma or drowsiness (15 minutes to several hours)

Table 61.4 *Clinical features of blackouts*

Cause	*Precipitants*	*Subjective onset*	*Observation*	*Recovery*
Vasovagal syncope	posture stress haemorrhage micturition	warning of 'faint', 'distant' 'clammy, sweaty'	very pale sweating	gradual feels 'terrible' fatigue nausea
Respiratory syncope	cough weight-lifting trumpet playing	warning (feels faint)	pale	rapid
Carotid sinus syncope	carotid pressure e.g. tight collar + turning neck postendarterectomy	warning (feels faint)	pale	rapid
Cardiac syncope	various	may be palpitations	pale	rapid may be flushing
Migrainous syncope	foods stress sleep deprivation	scotomas	pale	nausea and vomiting throbbing headache
Autonomic syncope	postural change	warning (feels faint)	pale	rapid
Epilepsy	stress sleep deprivation alchohol withdrawal infection menstruation drug non-compliance	aura with complex partial seizures (CPS)	automatism e.g. fidgeting, lip smacking with CPS	slow confused

Associated features:

- cyanosis, then heavy 'snoring' breathing
- eyes rolling 'back into head'
- ± tongue biting
- ± incontinence of urine or faeces

It should be noted that sphincter incontinence is not firmly diagnostic of epilepsy. In less severe episodes the patient may fall without observable twitching of the limbs.[4]

In atonic epilepsy, which occurs in those with tonic-clonic epilepsy, the patient falls to the ground and is unconscious for only a brief period.

Syncope

In syncope there is loss of consciousness but with warning symptoms and rapid return of alertness following a brief period of unconsciousness (seconds to three minutes).

Relevant features:

- occurs with standing or, less commonly, sitting
- warning feelings of dizziness, faintness or true vertigo
- nausea, hot and cold skin sensations
- fading hearing or blurred vision
- sliding to ground (rather than heavy full-length fall)
- rapid return of consciousness
- pallor and sweating
- often trigger factors, e.g. emotional upset, pain

The patient invariably remembers the onset of fainting. Most syncope is of the benign vasomotor type and tends to occur in young people, especially when standing still.

Other forms of syncope

Micturition syncope
This uncommon event may occur after micturition in older men, especially during the night when they leave a warm bed and stand to void. The cause appears to be peripheral vasodilation associated with reduction of venous return from straining.

Cough syncope
Severe coughing can result in obstruction of venous return with subsequent blackout. This is also the mechanism of blackouts with breath-holding attacks.

Carotid sinus syncope
This problem is caused by pressure on a hypersensitive carotid sinus, for example, in some elderly patients who lose consciousness when their neck is touched.

Effort syncope
Syncope on exertion is due to obstructive cardiac disorders such as aortic stenosis and hypertrophic obstructive cardiomyopathy.

Choking

Sudden collapse can follow choking. Examples include the so-called 'cafe coronary' or 'barbecue coronary' when the patient, while eating meat, suddenly becomes cyanosed, is speechless and grasps the throat. This is caused by inhaling a large bolus of meat which obstructs the larynx. To avoid death immediate relief of obstruction is necessary. An emergency treatment is the Heimlich manoeuvre whereby the patient is grasped from behind around the abdomen and a forceful squeeze applied to try to eject the food. If this fails, the foreign body may have to be manually removed from the throat.

Drop attacks

Drop attacks are episodes of 'blackouts' in which people suddenly fall to the ground and then immediately pick themselves up. They involve sudden attacks of weakness in the legs and, although there is some doubt about whether loss of consciousness has occurred, most patients cannot remember the process of falling. Drop attacks occur typically in middle-aged women and are considered to be brain stem disturbances producing sudden changes in tone in the lower limbs. Other causes of drop attacks include vertebrobasilar insufficiency, Parkinson's disease and epilepsy.[4]

Cardiac arrhythmias

Stokes-Adams attacks and cardiac syncope are manifestations of recurrent episodes of loss of consciousness, especially in the elderly, caused by cardiac arrhythmias. These arrhythmias include complete heart block, sick sinus syndrome and ventricular tachycardia. The blackout is sudden with the patient falling straight to the ground without warning and without convulsive movements. The patient goes pale at first and then flushed.

Twenty-four-hour ambulatory cardiac monitoring may be necessary to confirm the diagnosis.

Patients with aortic stenosis are prone to have exercise-induced blackouts.

Vertebrobasilar insufficiency

Loss of consciousness can occur rarely with vertebrobasilar insufficiency (VBI). Typical preceding symptoms of VBI include dyspnoea, vertigo, vomiting, hemisensory loss, ataxia and transient global amnesia.

Hypoglycaemia

Hypoglycaemia can be difficult to recognise but must be considered as it can vary from a feeling of malaise and lightheadedness to loss of consciousness, sometimes with a convulsion. There are usually preliminary symptoms of hunger, sweating, shaking or altered behaviour. Hypoglycaemic attacks are usually related to diabetes and can occur with oral hypoglycaemics as well as insulin.

Psychogenic factors

Psychogenic factors leading to blackouts represent a diagnostic dilemma, especially if occurring in patients with tonic-clonic epilepsy. If the attacks are witnessed by the practitioner then the possibility of functional origin can be determined.

Hysterical blackouts or fits are not uncommon and have to be differentiated from hyperventilation. It is unusual for hyperventilation to cause unconsciousness but it is possible to get clouding of consciousness, especially if the patient is administered oxygen.

Initial management of the unconscious patient

The first principle of management of a person found unconscious is to keep the patient alive by maintaining the airway and the circulation. The basic management essentials are summarised in Table 61.5.

Table 61.5 *Basic management essentials*

Keep patient alive (maintain airway and circulation)
Get history from witnesses
Examine patient
Give IV dextrose
Take blood (for investigations)
CT scan (if diagnosis doubtful)

References

1. Talley N, O'Connor S. *Clinical examination* (2nd edition). Sydney: MacLennan & Petty, 1992, 392–395.
2. Kumer PJ, Clark ML. *Clinical medicine* (2nd edition). London: Bailliere Tindall, 1990, 1.
3. Davis A, Bolin T, Ham J. *Symptom analysis and physical diagnosis* (2nd edition). Sydney: Pergamon Press, 1990, 276–279.
4. Kincaid-Smith P, Larkins R, Whelan G. *Problems in clinical medicine*. Sydney: MacLennan & Petty, 1990, 156–175.

62

Urinary disorders

Disturbances of micturition are a common problem in general practice with an annual incidence of about 20 per thousand patients at risk.[1] Such disturbances include dysuria, frequency of micturition, difficulty or inability to initiate micturition, stress incontinence and haematuria. These symptoms are three times as common in women as in men.[1] The combination of dysuria and frequency is the most common of the symptoms with an incidence of about 14 per thousand patients and a female to male ratio of 5 to 1.[1]

In children and the elderly the patient may complain of urinary incontinence unassociated with stress. However, with the exception of enuresis, disturbances of micturition are uncommon in children.

Dysuria and frequency

Dysuria, or painful micturition, which is characterised mainly by urethral and suprapubic discomfort, indicates mucosal inflammation of the lower genitourinary tract, i.e. the urethra, bladder or prostate. The passage of urine across inflamed mucosa causes pain. Frequency can vary from being negligible to extreme. Sometimes haematuria and systemic symptoms can accompany dysuria and frequency.

A summary of the diagnostic strategy model for dysuria is presented in Table 62.1.

Key facts and checkpoints[1,2]

- Strangury = difficult and painful micturition with associated spasm.
- Tenesmus = painful ineffective straining to pass urine.
- Inflammation usually results in frequent passage of small amounts of urine and a sense of urgency.
- Urethritis usually causes pain at the onset of micturition.
- Cystitis usually causes pain at the end of micturition.
- Suprapubic discomfort is a feature of bladder infection (cystitis).
- Vesicocolonic fistulas (e.g. prostatic cancer) cause severe dysuria, pneumaturia and foul-smelling urine.
- Dysuria and frequency are most common in women aged 15 to 44 years.
- They are four times more common in sexually active women.
- Vaginitis is an important cause and must be considered.
- Dysuria and discomfort is a common feature of postmenopausal syndrome, due to atrophic urethritis. The urethra and lower bladder are oestrogen-dependent.

Is it really a urinary tract infection?

Although urinary tract infections account for the majority of cases of dysuria in women it must be remembered that vaginitis and post-menopausal atrophic vaginitis can cause dysuria (Fig. 62.1). Vaginitis is the most common cause of dysuria in the adolescent age group and is a relatively common cause of dysuria in family practice, estimated at around 15%. Post-menopausal oestrogen deficiency is estimated at

5–10%.[3] In the latter it is worthwhile prescribing oestrogen, either topically or systemically. Acute bacterial cystitis accounts for about 40% of causes of dysuria.

The dysuria associated with vaginitis may be described as burning 'on the outside' with the discomfort usually felt at the beginning or end of micturition. If vaginitis is suspected, a pelvic examination should be carried out to inspect the genitalia and obtain swabs.[3]

The clinical approach

History

It is important to determine whether dysuria is really genitourinary in origin and not attributable to functional disorders such as psychosexual problems. Disturbances of micturition are uncommon in the young male and if present suggest venereal infection.

Table 62.1 *Dysuria: diagnostic strategy model*

Q. Probability diagnosis
A. Urinary infection, esp. cystitis (female)
Urethritis
Urethral syndrome (female)
Vaginitis

Q. Serious disorders not to be missed
A. Neoplasia
• bladder
• prostate
• urethra
Severe infections
• gonorrhoea
• NSU
• genital herpes
Reiter's disease
Calculi, e.g. bladder

Q. Pitfalls (often missed)
A. Menopause syndrome
Prostatitis
Foreign bodies in LUT
Acidic urine
Acute fever
Interstitial cystitis
Urethral caruncle/diverticuli
Vaginal prolapse
Obstruction
• benign prostatic hyperplasia
• urethral stricture
• phimosis
• meatal stenosis

Q. Seven masquerades checklist

A.	
Depression	✓
Diabetes	✓
Drugs	✓
Anaemia	—
Thyroid disease	—
Spinal dysfunction	—
UTI	✓

Q. Is this patient trying to tell me something?
A. Consider psychosexual problems; anxiety and hypochondriasis.

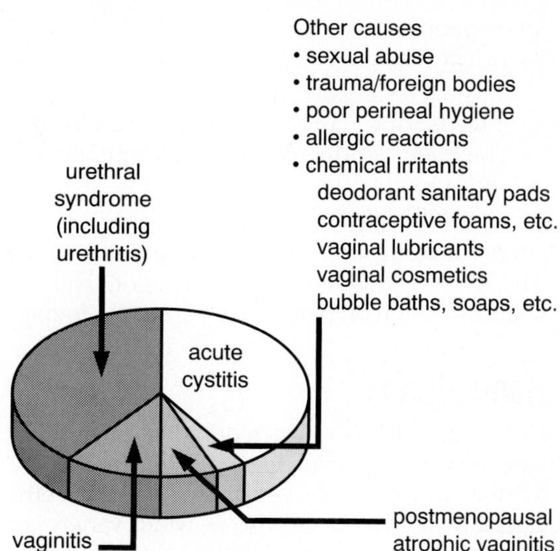

Fig. 62.1 *Relative causes of dysuria in women*

Key questions

Could you describe the discomfort?
What colour is your urine?
Does it have a particular odour?
Have you noticed a discharge?
If so, could it be sexually acquired?
Do you find intercourse painful or uncomfortable (women)?
Have you any fever, sweats or chills?

Examination

The general inspection and examination should include measurement of the basic parameters of pulse, temperature and blood pressure. The possibility of underlying renal disease, especially in the presence of an obstructive component, should be kept in mind.

Abdominal palpation is important with a focus on the loins and suprapubic areas. The possibility of sexually transmitted diseases should also be considered and vaginal examination of the female and rectal and genital examination in the male may be appropriate. In the menopausal female a dry atrophic urethral opening, a ureteral caruncle or urethral prolapse may give the clue to this important and neglected cause of dysuria.

Investigations

Basic investigations include:

- dipstick testing of urine
- microscopy and culture (midstream specimen of urine or suprapubic puncture), and possibly urethral swabs for sexually transmitted diseases

Further investigations depend on initial findings and referral for detailed investigation will be necessary if the primary cause cannot be found.

Haematuria

Haematuria is the presence of blood in the urine and can vary from frank bleeding (macroscopic) to the microscopic detection of red cells. Haematuria can occur in a wide variety of disorders but a careful history and examination can often lead to the source of the bleeding and help with the selection of investigations.

Key facts and checkpoints

- Macroscopic haematuria is the presence of blood visible to the naked eye. It is always abnormal except in menstruating women.
- Small amounts of blood (1 ml/1000 ml urine) can produce macroscopic haematuria.
- Microscopic haematuria is the presence of blood in the urine that can only be detected by microscopic or chemical methods.
- Microscopic haematuria includes the presence of red blood cells (RBC) > 8000 ml of urine (phase contrast microscopy) or > 2000 per ml of urine (light microscopy) representing the occasional RBC on microscopic examination.
- Joggers and athletes engaged in very vigorous exercise can develop transient microscopic haematuria.
- Common sources of macroscopic haematuria are the bladder, urethra, prostate and kidney.[4]
- Macroscopic haematuria occurs in 70% of people with bladder cancer and 40% with kidney cancer.[4]
- Common urological cancers that cause haematuria are the bladder (70%), kidney (17%), renal pelvis or ureter (7%) and prostate (5%).
- It is important to exclude renal damage, so patients should have blood pressure, urinary protein and plasma creatinine measured as a base line.
- All patients presenting with macroscopic haematuria or recurrent microscopic haematuria require both radiological investigation of the upper urinary system and visualisation of the lower urinary system to detect or exclude pathology.
- The key radiological investigation is the intravenous urogram (pyelogram), unless there is a history of iodine allergy, severe asthma or other contraindications, when ultrasound is the next choice.

The clinical approach

History

In many patients the underlying disorder may be suspected from a detailed enquiry about associated urinary symptoms. The presence of blood can be verified rapidly by microscopy so that red discolouration due to haemolysis or red food dye can be discounted.

The time relationship of bleeding is useful because, as a general rule, haematuria occurring in the first part of the stream suggests a urethral or prostatic lesion, while terminal haematuria suggests bleeding from the bladder. Uniform haematuria has no localising features.

The possibility of sexually acquired urethritis should be kept in mind. It is most unusual for haematuria to cause anaemia unless it is massive. Massive haematuria is a feature of radiation cystitis.

Painful haematuria is suggestive of infection, calculi or renal infarction, while painless haematuria is commonly associated with infection, trauma, tumours or polycystic kidneys. Loin pain can occur as a manifestation of nephritis and may be a feature of bleeding in carcinoma of the kidney or polycystic kidney.

A drug history is relevant, especially with anticoagulants and cyclophosphamide. A diet history should also be considered.

It is worth noting that large prostatic veins, secondary to prostatic enlargement located at the bladder neck, may rupture when a man strains to urinate.

A summary of the diagnostic strategy model for haematuria is presented in Table 62.2.

Key questions

Have you had an injury such as a blow to the loin, pelvis or genital area?

Have you noticed whether the redness is at the start or end of your stream or throughout the stream?

Have you noticed any bleeding elsewhere such as bruising of the skin or nose bleed?

Table 62.2 *Haematuria: diagnostic strategy model*

Q. Probability diagnosis
A. Infection[7]
- cystitis/urethrotrigonitis (female)
- urethritis (male)
- prostatitis (male)

Calculi-renal, ureteric, bladder

Q. Serious disorders not to be missed
A. Cardiovascular
- renal infarction
- renal vein thrombosis
- prostatic varices

Neoplasia
- renal tumour
- urothelial: bladder, renal pelvis, ureter
- carcinoma prostate

Severe infections
- infective endocarditis
- renal tuberculosis
- glomerulonephritis
- Blackwater fever

Renal papillary necrosis
Other renal disease

Q. Pitfalls (often missed)
A. Urethral prolapse/caruncle
Pseudohaematuria, e.g. beetroot, porphyria
Benign prostatic hyperplasia
Trauma: blunt or penetrating
Foreign bodies
Bleeding disorders
Exercise
Radiation cystitis

Rarities
- hydronephrosis
- Henoch-Schönlein purpura
- bilharzia
- polycystic kidneys
- renal cysts
- endometriosis (bladder)
- systemic vasculitides

Q. Seven masquerades checklist

A.		
	Depression	—
	Diabetes	—
	Drugs	✓ cytotoxics anticoagulants
	Anaemia	—
	Thyroid disease	—
	Spinal dysfunction	—
	UTI	✓

Q. Is this patient trying to tell me something?
A. Consider artifactual haematuria.

Have you experienced any pain in the loin or abdomen?
Have you noticed any burning or frequency of your urine?
Have you had any problems with the flow of your urine?
Have you been having large amounts of beetroot, red lollies or berries in your diet?
Could your problem have been sexually acquired?
Have you been overseas recently?
What is your general health like?
Have you been aware of any other symptoms?
Do you engage in strenuous sports such as jogging?
Have you had any kidney problems in the past?

Physical examination (Fig. 62.2)

The general examination should include looking for signs of a bleeding tendency and anaemia, and recording the parameters of temperature, blood pressure and the pulse. The heart should be assessed to exclude infective endocarditis with emboli to the kidney, and the chest should be examined for a possible pleural effusion associated with perinephric or renal infections.

The abdomen should be examined for evidence of a palpable enlarged kidney or spleen. The different clinical findings for an enlarged left kidney and spleen are shown in Table 62.3. Renal enlargement may be due to renal tumour, hydronephrosis, or polycystic disease. Splenomegaly suggests the possibility of a bleeding disorder.

The suprapubic region should be examined for evidence of bladder tenderness or enlargement. In men the prostate should be examined rectally to detect benign or malignant enlargement or tenderness from prostatitis.

In women a vaginal examination should be performed to search for possible pelvic masses. The urethral meatus should be inspected to exclude a urethral caruncle or urethral prolapse.

Investigations

It is important to identify the cause, especially if a possible sequel is impaired kidney function.

- Urinalysis by dipstick testing, e.g. 'Hemastix' and its derivatives (affected by Vitamin C intake).
- Urine microscopy
  - — formed RBCs in true haematuria
  - — red cell casts indicate glomerular bleeding
  - — deformed (dysmorphic) red cells indicate glomerular bleeding
- Urinary culture: early culture is important because of the common association with infection and consideration of early treatment with antibiotics. If tuberculosis is suspected, three early morning urines should be cultured for tubercle bacilli.
- Urinary cytology: this test, performed on a

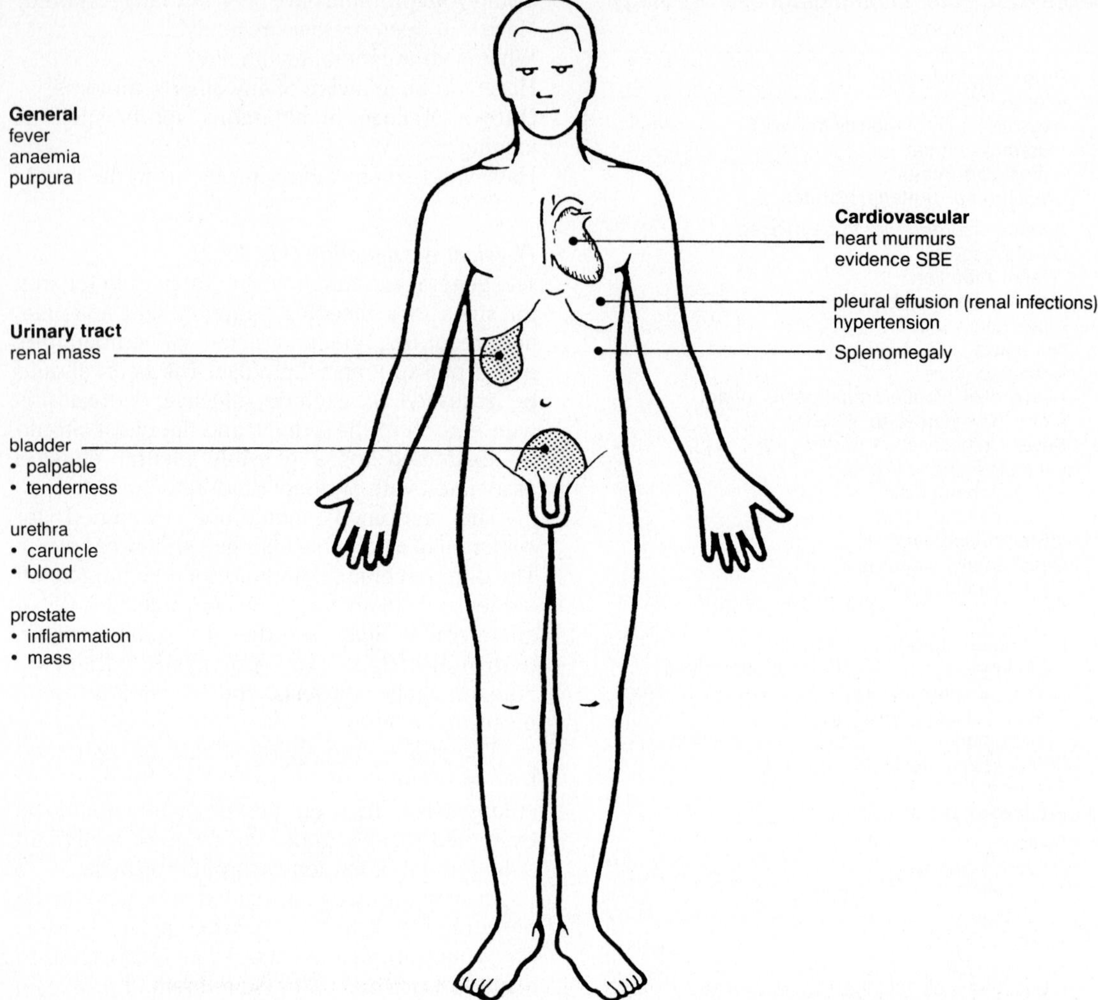

Fig. 62.2 *Features to consider in the physical examination of the patient with haematuria*

Table 62.3 *Differences between spleen and left kidney on abdominal examination*

	Spleen	***Left kidney***
Palpable upper border	Impalpable	Palpable
Movement with inspiration	Inferomedial	Inferior
Notch	Yes	No
Ballotable	No	Yes
Percussion	Dull	Resonant (usually)
Friction rub	Possible	Not possible

urine sample, may be useful to detect malignancies of the bladder and lower tract but is usually negative with carcinoma of the kidney.

Blood tests: appropriate screening tests include a full blood count, ESR and basic renal function tests (urea and creatinine). If glomerulonephritis is suspected, anti-streptolysin O titres and serum complement levels should be measured.

- Radiological techniques: available tests include
  - intravenous urography (intravenous pyelogram)—the key investigation
  - ultrasound (less sensitive at detecting lower UT abnormalities)
  - CT scanning
  - renal angiography
  - retrograde pyelography
- Direct imaging techniques: these include urethroscopy, cystoscopy and ureteroscopy. In all patients, regardless of the IVU findings, cystoscopy is advisable.
  Renal biopsy: indicated if glomerular disease is suspected, especially in the presence of dysmorphic red cells on microscopic examination.

Pseudohaematuria

Pseudohaematuria is red urine caused by pigments other than red blood cells that simply stain the culture red.

Causes include:

- anthrocyanins in food, e.g. beetroot, berries
- red-coloured confectionary
- porphyrins
- free haemoglobin, e.g. haemoglobinuria
- myoglobin (red-black colour)
- drugs, e.g. pyridium, phenolphthalein (alkaline urine)

Exercise haematuria

Exercise or sports haematuria is the passage of a significant number of red cells in the urine during or immediately after heavy exercise. It has been recorded in a wide variety of athletes, including swimmers and rowers. Dipstick testing is usually positive in these athletes. Despite the theory that it is largely caused by the posterior wall of the bladder impacting repetitively on the base of the bladder during running, there are other possible factors and glomerular disease must be excluded in the athlete with regular haematuria, especially if dysmorphic red cells are found on microscopy.

Artifactual haematuria

Macroscopic haematuria is a common presenting ploy of people with Munchausen's syndrome and pethidine addicts simulating renal colic. If suspected it is wise to get these people to pass urine in the presence of an appropriate witness before examining the urine.

Enuresis

Nocturnal enuresis

Nocturnal enuresis refers to the involuntary passage of urine during sleep in the absence of any identified physical abnormality in children (or adults) at a time when control of urine should be reasonably expected (usually the age of 5).

What is normal?

Bed-wetting at night is common in children up to the age of 5. About 50% of 3 year olds wet their beds, as do 20% of 4 year olds and 15% of 5 year olds. It is considered a problem if regular bed-wetting occurs in children 6 years and older, although many boys do not become dry until 8 years. About 2% of 14 year olds are affected.[4] Bed-wetting after a long period of good toilet training with dryness is called secondary enuresis.

Aetiology

There is usually no obvious cause, and most of the children are normal in every respect but seem to have a delay in development of bladder control. Others may have a small bladder capacity or a sensitive bladder. It tends to be more common in boys and seems to run in families. The cause of secondary enuresis can be psychological; it commonly occurs during a period of stress or anxiety, such as separation from a parent or the arrival of a new baby.

Underlying disorders to be excluded

- urinary tract infection
- diabetes mellitus
- diabetes insipidus
- neurogenic bladder
- urinary tract abnormality

After the age of 5, investigations including an intravenous urogram or ultrasound are necessary to exclude urinary tract abnormalities.

Advice for parents on managing the child

If no cause is found, reassure the child that there is nothing wrong, and that it is a common problem that will eventually go away. There are some important ways of helping the child to adjust to the problem.

- Do not scold or punish the child.
- Praise the child often, when appropriate.
- Do not stop the child drinking after the evening meal.

- Do not wake the child at night to visit the toilet.
- Use a night-light to help the child who wakes.
- Some parents use a nappy to keep the bed dry, but try using special absorbent pads beneath the bottom sheet rather than a nappy.
- Make sure the child has a shower or bath before going to kindergarten or school.

Treatment

Many methods have been tried, but the bed-wetting alarm system is generally regarded to be the most effective. If the child has emotional problems, counselling or hypnotherapy may be desirable. Tricyclic antidepressants can be used and may be effective in some children, but they do not always achieve a long-term cure and have limitations. There is no evidence that night waking or evening fluid restriction are effective.

The bed alarm There are various types of alarms: some use pads in the pyjama pants and under the bottom sheet, but recently developed alarms use a small bakelite chip, which is attached to the child's briefs by a safety pin. A lead connects to the buzzer outside the bed, which makes a loud noise when urine is passed. The child wakes, switches off the buzzer and visits the toilet. This method works especially well in older children.

Tricyclic antidepressants The most widely used drug is imipramine in doses of 1–2.5 mg/kg as a single night-time dose.[5]

The persistent problem For the 1–2% of patients whose bed-wetting persists beyond adolescence, a formal urodynamic assessment is advisable. Many of these patients also have daytime symptoms.

Secondary enuresis

Secondary enuresis can develop at any age and should always be fully investigated. It is often caused by urinary infection, especially in the elderly, and may be associated with some neurological disorders and chronic retention of urine associated with prostatic enlargement. Treatment is directed at the cause, which may be a psychologically traumatic event.

Proteinuria

Proteinuria is an important and common sign of renal disease. The protein can originate from the glomeruli, the tubules or the lower urinary tract. Healthy people, however, do excrete some protein in the urine which can vary from day to day and hour to hour; hence the value of collecting it over 24 hours. While proteinuria can be benign, it always requires further investigation. Important causes of proteinuria are presented in Table 62.4.

Table 62.4 *Important causes of proteinuria*

Transient
- Contamination from vaginal secretions
- Urinary tract infection
- Pre-eclampsia

(require exclusion and follow-up)

Renal disease
- Glomerulonephritis
- Nephrotic syndrome
- Congenital tubular disease
  e.g. polycystic kidney
  renal dysplasia
- Acute tubular damage
- Renal papilliary necrosis
  e.g. analgesic nephropathy
  diabetic papillary necrosis
- Overflow proteinuria
  e.g. multiple myeloma
- Systemic diseases affecting the glomeruli
  e.g. diabetes mellitus
  hypertension
  systemic lupus erythematosus
  malignancy
  drugs, e.g. penicillamine, gold salts
  amyloid
  vasculitides

No renal disease
- Orthostatic proteinuria
- Exercise
- Fever
- Postoperative
- Heart failure

Key facts and checkpoints[6]

- The amount of protein in the urine is normally less than 100 mg/24 hours.
- Greater than 150 mg protein/24 hours is abnormal in adults.
- Greater than 300 mg/24 hours is abnormal for children and adults.
- Proteinuria $>$1 g/24 hours indicates a serious underlying disorder.
- If accompanied by dysmorphic haematuria or red cell casts, this tends to confirm glomerular origin.
- Routine dipstick testing will only detect levels greater than 0.3 g/L and thus has limitations.
- In diabetics, microalbuminuria is predictive of nephropathy and an indication for early blood pressure treatment.

If proteinuria is confirmed on repeated dipstick testing it should be measured more accurately by measuring daily protein excretion with a 24 hour urine. High values require referral for investigation. Possible contamination from vaginal secretions and from a low urinary tract infection need to be excluded.

Orthostatic proteinuria

Orthostatic proteinuria is the presence of significant proteinuria after people have been standing but is absent from specimens obtained following recumbency for several hours, such as an early morning specimen.

It occurs in 5–10% of people, especially during their adolescent years. In the majority it is of no significance and eventually disappears without the development of significant renal disease. However, in a small number the proteinuria can foreshadow serious renal disease.

Diabetic microalbuminuria

The presence of protein in the urine is a sensitive marker of diabetic nephropathy, so regular screening for microalbuminuria in diabetics is regarded as an important predictor of nephropathy and other possible complications of diabetes. Dipstick testing for microalbuminuria is now available but more accurate measurement can be performed with radioimmunoassay techniques.

References

1. Cormack J, Marinker M, Morrell D. *Practice. A handbook of primary medical care.* London: Kluwer-Harrap Handbooks, 1980; 3.51:1–10.
2. Kincaid Smith P, Larkins R, Whelan G. *Problems in clinical medicine.* Sydney: MacLennan & Petty, 1990, 105–108.
3. Sloane PD, Slatt PD, Baker RM. *Essentials of family medicine.* Baltimore: Williams & Wilkins, 1988, 169–174.
4. Walsh D. *Symptom control.* Boston: Blackwell Scientific Publications, 1989, 229–233.
5. Robinson MJ. *Practical paediatrics* (2nd edition). Melbourne: Churchill Livingstone, 1990, 547.
6. George C. How to treat haematuria and proteinuria. Australian Dr Weekly, 15 March 1991, I–VIII.
7. Brown R. *Urology.* RACGP: CHECK Programme, unit 226, 1990, 11–12.

63

Visual failure

The commonest cause of visual dysfunction is a simple refractive error. However, there are many causes of visual failure including the emergency of sudden blindness, a problem that requires a sound management strategy. Apart from migraine, virtually all cases of sudden loss of vision require urgent treatment.

The 'white' eye or uninflamed eye presents a different clinical problem from the red or inflamed eye.[1] The 'white' eye is painless and usually presents with visual symptoms and it is in the 'white' eye that the majority of blinding conditions occur.

Criteria for blindness and driving

This varies from country to country. The World Health Organisation (WHO) defines blindness as 'best visual acuity less than 3/60', while in Australia eligibility for the blind pension is 'bilateral corrected visual acuity less than 6/60 or significant visual field loss'; e.g. a patient can have 6/6 vision but severely restricted fields caused by chronic open-angle glaucoma. The minimum standard for driving is 6/12.

Key facts and checkpoints

- The commonest cause of blindness in the world is trachoma.
- In western countries the commonest causes are senile cataract, glaucoma, age-related macular degeneration, trauma and the retinopathy of diabetes mellitus.[2]
- The commonest causes of sudden visual loss are transient occlusion of the retinal artery (amaurosis fugax) and migraine.[3]
- 'Flashing lights' are caused by traction on the retina and have a serious connotation: the commonest cause is vitreoretinal traction which is a classic symptom of retinal detachment.
- The presence of floaters or 'blobs' in the visual fields indicates pigment in the vitreous: causes include vitreous haemorrhage and vitreous detachment.
- Posterior vitreous detachment is the commonest cause of the acute onset of floaters, especially with advancing age.
- Retinal detachment has a tendency to occur in short-sighted (myopic) people.
- Rare causes of visual failure include sarcoidosis and polyarteritis nodosa.
- Suspect a macular abnormality where objects look smaller or straight lines are bent or distorted.

The clinical approach

History

The history should carefully define the onset, progress, duration, offset and the extent of visual loss. An accurate history is important because a longstanding visual defect may only just have been noticed by the patient, especially if it is unilateral. Two questions need to be answered.

- Is the loss unilateral or bilateral?
- Is the onset acute or gradual and progressive?

The distinction between central and peripheral visual loss is useful. Central visual loss presents as impairment of visual acuity and implies defective retinal image formation (through refractive error or opacity in the ocular media) or macular or optic nerve dysfunction. Peripheral field loss is more subtle, especially when the onset is gradual, and implies extramacular retinal disease or a defect in the visual pathway.

It is important to differentiate the central field loss of macular degeneration from the hemianopia of a CVA.

A drug history is very important (Table 63.1). Treatment for tuberculosis with ethambutol or treatment with quinine/chloroquine has to be considered as these drugs are oculotoxic. The family history is relevant for diabetics, migraine, Leber's hereditary optic atrophy, amaurotic familial idiocy and retinitis pigmentosa.

Questions directed to specific symptoms

- presence of floaters → indicates haemorrhage, posterior vitreous detachment, choroiditis
- flashing lights → traction on retina ? retinal detachment, posterior vitreous detachment
- coloured haloes around lights → glaucoma, cataract
- zigzag lines → migraine
- vision worse at night or in dim light → retinitis pigmentosa, hysteria, syphilitic retinitis
- headache → temporal arteritis, migraine, benign intracranial hypertension
- central scotomata → macular disease, optic neuritis
- pain on moving eye → retrobulbar neuritis
- distortion, micropsia (smaller), macropsia (larger) → macular degeneration
- visual field loss:
  - — central loss—macular disorder
  - — total loss—arterial occlusion

It is worth noting that if a patient repeatedly knocks into people and objects on a particular side (including traffic accidents), a bitemporal or homonymous hemianopia should be suspected.

Diseases/disorders to exclude or consider

- diabetes mellitus
- giant cell (temporal) arteritis
- hypopituitarism (pituitary adenoma)

Table 63.1 *Visual disorders associated with drugs*

Disorder	***Drug***
Corneal opacities	Amiodarone Hydroxychloroquine Chlorpromazine Vitamin D Indomethacin Chlorpropamide
Precipitating of acute narrow angle glaucoma	Mydriatic drops Tricyclics Antihistamines
Refractive changes	Thiazides
Lens opacities	Corticosteroids Phenothiazines
Retinopathy	Hydroxychloroquine Chloroquine Thioridazine (other phenothiazines less commonly) Tamoxifen
Papilloedema (secondary to benign intracranial hypertension)	Oral contraceptives Corticosteroids Tetracyclines Nalidixic acid Vitamin A
Optic neuropathy	Ethanol Tobacco Ethambutol Disulfiram

Reprinted from *Central Nervous System: clinical algorithms*, published by the *BMJ*, with permission.

- cerebrovascular ischaemia/carotid artery stenosis (emboli)
- multiple sclerosis
- cardiac disease, e.g. arrhythmias, SBE (emboli)
- anaemia (if severe can cause retinal haemorrhage and exudate)
- Marfan's syndrome (subluxated lenses)

Examination

The same principles of examination should apply as for the red eye. Testing should include:

- visual acuity (Snellen chart)—with pinhole testing
- pupil reactions, to test afferent (sensory) responses to light
- confrontation fields (using a red pin)
- colour vision
- Amsler grid (or graph paper)
- fundus examination with dilated pupil (ophthalmoscope), noting
  — the red reflex
  — appearance of the retina, macula and optic nerve
- tonometry

General examination

General examination should focus on the general features of the patient, the nervous system, endocrine system and cardiovascular system.

Perimetry

Various defects in the visual fields are depicted in Figure 63.1.

Investigations

Depending on the clinical examination the following tests can be selected to confirm the diagnosis:

- Blood tests
  — full blood ? anaemia, lead poisoning, leukaemia
  — ESR ? temporal arteritis
  — blood sugar ? diabetes mellitus

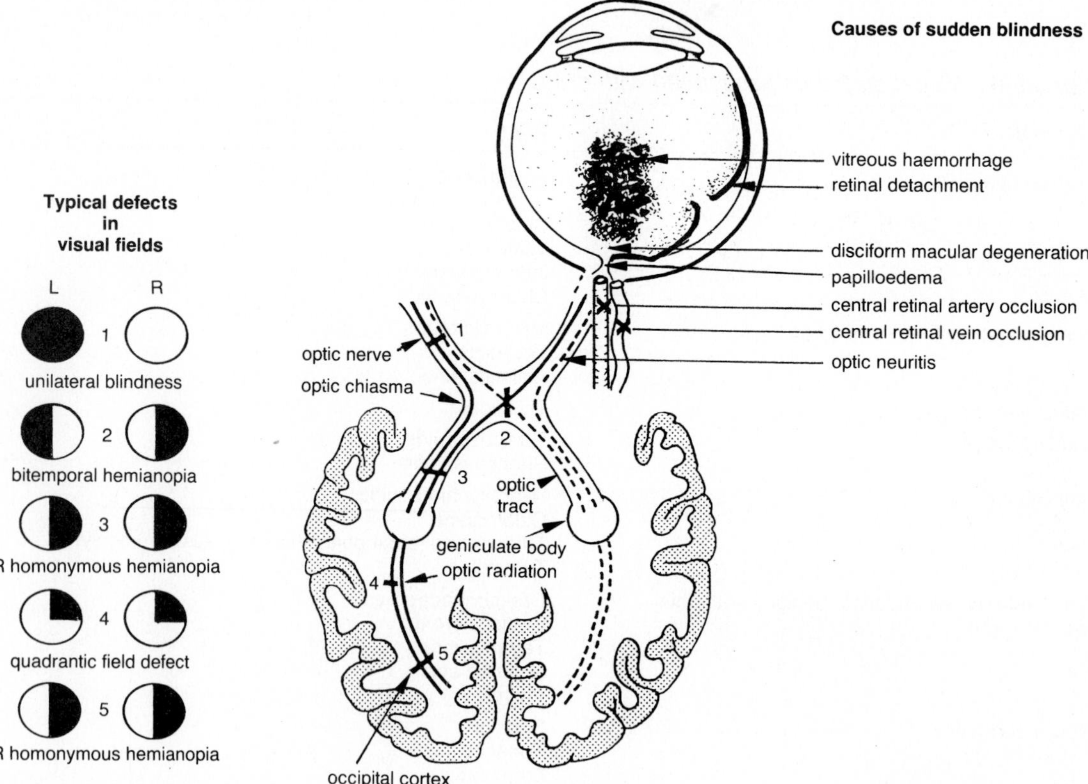

Fig. 63.1 *Diagrammatic representation of important causes of sudden painless loss of vision (right side) and typical defects in the visual fields (left side)*

- Temporal artery biopsy ? temporal arteritis
- CT scan ? CVA, optic nerve lesions, space-occupying lesions
- Formal perimetry and Bjerrum screen
- Fluorescein angiography ? retinal vascular obstruction, diabetic retinopathy
- Visual evoked responses ? demyelinating disorders
- Carotid Doppler ultrasound

Visual failure in children

There are long lists of causes for visual failure or blindness in children. An approximate order of frequency of causes of blindness in children is cortical blindness, optic atrophy, choroidoretinal degeneration, cataracts and retinopathy of prematurity. Almost half the causes of blindness are genetically determined, in contrast to the nutritional and infective causes which predominate in Third World countries.[4]

Some important guidelines in children

Strabismus

- Always refer children with strabismus (squint) when first seen to exclude ocular pathology such as retinoblastoma, congenital cataract and glaucoma, which would require emergency surgery.
- Children with strabismus (even if the ocular examination is normal) need specialist management because the deviating eye will become amblyopic (a lazy eye with reduced vision). The younger the child, the easier it is to treat amblyopia; it may be irreversible if first detected later than school age.

Cataracts

Children with suspected cataracts must be referred immediately; the problem is very serious as the development of vision may be permanently impaired (amblyopia).[2] Cataracts are diagnosed by looking at the red reflex and this should be a routine part of the examination of a young child. Common conditions causing cataracts are genetic disorders and rubella but most are unknown. Rarer conditions such as galactosaemia need to be considered.

Refractive errors

Refractive errors, with the error greater in one eye, can cause amblyopia. Detection of refractive errors is an important objective of screening.

Retinoblastoma

Retinoblastoma, although rare, is the commonest intraocular tumour in childhood. It must be excluded in any child presenting with a white pupil. Such children also have the so-called 'cat's eye reflex'. In 30% of patients the condition is bilateral with an autosomal dominant gene being responsible.

Visual failure in the elderly

Most patients with visual complaints are elderly and their failing vision affects their perception of the environment and their ability to communicate effectively. Typical problems are cataracts, vascular disease, macular degeneration, chronic simple glaucoma and retinal detachment. Retinal detachment and diabetic retinopathy can occur at any age, although they are more likely with increasing age. Macular degeneration in its various forms is the commonest cause of visual deterioration in the elderly. For the elderly with cataracts the decision to operate depends on the patients' vision and their ability to cope. Most patients with a vision of 6/18 or worse in both eyes usually benefit from cataract extraction, but some can cope with this level of vision and rely on a good, well-placed (above and behind) reading light.[5]

Sudden loss of vision in the elderly is suggestive of temporal arteritis or vascular embolism, so this problem should be checked.

Refractive errors

Indistinct or blurred vision is most commonly caused by errors of refraction.

In the normal eye (emmetropia) light rays from infinity are brought to a focus on the retina by the cornea (contributing about two-thirds of the eye's refractive power) and the lens (one-third). Thus the cornea is very important in refraction and abnormalities such as keratoconus may cause severe refractive problems.[5]

The process of accommodation is required for focusing closer objects. This process, which relies on the action of ciliary muscles and lens elasticity, is usually affected by ageing, so that from the age of 45 close work becomes gradually more difficult (presbyopia).[5]

The important clinical feature is that the use of a simple 'pinhole' in a card will usually improve blurred vision or reduced acuity where there is a refractive error only.[1]

Myopia (short-sightedness)

This is usually progressive in the teens. Highly myopic eyes may develop retinal detachment or macular degeneration.

Management

- glasses with a concave lens
- contact lenses
- consider radial keratotomy or excimer laser surgery

Hypermetropia (long-sightedness)

This condition is more susceptible to closed-angle glaucoma. In early childhood it may be associated with convergent strabismus (squint). The spectacle correction alone may straighten the eyes. It is mostly overcome by the accommodative power of the eye, though it may cause reading difficulty. Typically, the long-sighted person needs reading glasses at about 30 years.

Presbyopia

There is a need for near correction with loss of accommodative power of the eye in the 40's.

Astigmatism

This creates the need for a corrective lens more curved in one meridian than another because the cornea does not have even curvature. If uncorrected, this may cause headaches of ocular origin. Conical cornea is one cause of astigmatism.

Pinhole test

The pinhole reduces the size of the blur circle on the retina in the uncorrected eye. A pinhole acts as a universal correcting lens. If visual acuity is not normalised by looking through a card with a 1 mm pinhole, then the defective vision is not solely due to a refractive error. The pinhole test may actually help to improve visual acuity with some cataracts. Further investigation is mandatory.

Cataracts

The term 'cataract' describes any lens opacity. The symptoms depend on the degree and the site of opacity. Cataract causes gradual visual loss with normal direct pupillary light reflex.

The prevalence of cataracts increases with age: 65% at age 50 to 59, and all people aged over 80 have opacities.[4] Significant causes of cataracts are presented in Table 63.2 and causes of progressive visual loss in Table 63.3.

Table 63.2 *Causes of cataracts*

Causes
Advancing age
Diabetes mellitus
Steroids (topical or oral)
Radiation
Trauma
Uveitis
Dystrophia myotonia

Table 63.3 *Progressive bilateral visual loss*

Site	Causes
Globe	Chronic glaucoma Senile cataracts
Retina	Macular degeneration Retinal disease • diabetic retinopathy • retinitis pigmentosa • choroidoretinitis
Optic nerve	Optic neuropathies Optic nerve compression, e.g. aneurysm, glioma Toxic damage to optic nerves
Optic chiasma	Chiasmal compression: pituitary adenoma, craniopharyngioma, etc.
Occipital cortex	Tumours Degenerative conditions

Note Unilateral causes, e.g. cataract, refractive errors, uveitis, glaucoma, progressive optic atrophy and tumours, can affect the second eye.

Typical symptoms:

- reading difficulty
- difficulty in recognising faces
- problems with driving
- difficulty with television viewing
- reduced ability to see in bright light
- may see haloes around lights

Examination

- reduced visual acuity (sometimes improved with pinhole)
- diminished red reflex on ophthalmoscopy
- a change in the appearance of the lens

The red reflex and ophthalmoscopy

The 'red reflex' is a reflection of the fundus when the eye is viewed from a distance of about 60 cm (2 feet) with the ophthalmoscope using a zero lens. This reflex is easier to see if the pupil is dilated. Commencing with the plus 20 lens, reduce the power gradually and, at plus 12, lens opacities will be seen against the red reflex which may be totally obscured by a very dense cataract. The setting up of the ophthalmoscope to examine intraocular structures is illustrated in Figure 63.2.

Management

Advise extraction when the patient cannot cope. Contraindications for extraction include intraocular inflammation and severe diabetic retinopathy. There is no effective medical treatment for established cataracts. The removal of the cataractous lens requires optical correction to restore vision and this is usually performed with an intraocular lens implant. Full visual recovery may take 2–3 months. Complications are uncommon yet many patients may require YAG laser capsulotomy to clear any opacities that may develop behind the lens implant.

Postoperative advice to the patient

- Avoid bending for a few weeks.
- Avoid strenuous exercise.
- The following drops may be prescribed:
  - — steroids (to reduce inflammation)
  - — antibiotics (to avoid infection)
  - — dilators (to prevent adhesions)

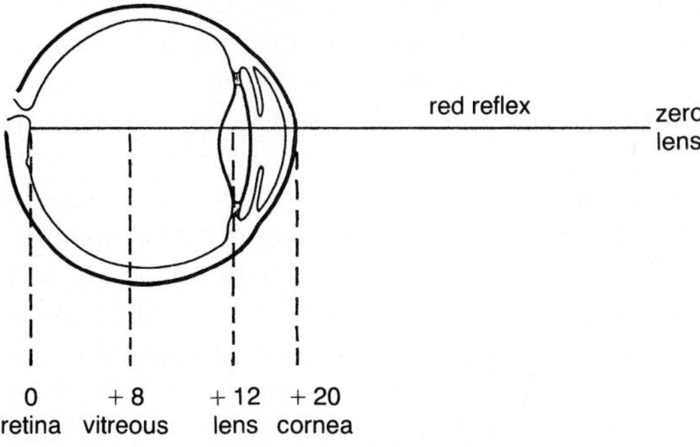

Fig. 63.2 *Settings of the ophthalmoscope used to examine intraocular structures*

Glaucoma

Chronic simple glaucoma is the commonest cause of irreversible blindness in middle age.[1] At a very late stage it presents as difficulty in seeing because of loss of the outer fields of vision due to optic atrophy (Fig. 63.3). Acute glaucoma, on the other hand, has a relatively rapid onset over a few days.

Clinical features of chronic glaucoma

- familial tendency
- no early signs or symptoms
- central vision usually normal
- progressive restriction of visual field

Tonometry

- upper limit of normal is 22 mmHg

Fig. 63.3 *Typical visual field loss for chronic simple glaucoma; a similar pattern occurs with retinitis pigmentosa and hysteria*

Ophthalmoscopy

- optic disc cupping > 30% of total disc area

Screening

- adults 40 years and over: 2–5 yearly (at least 2 yearly over 60)
- start about 30 years, then 2 yearly if family history

Management

- treatment can prevent visual field loss
- medication (for life) usually selected from
  - — timolol drops bd
  - — pilocarpine drops qid
  - — dipivefrine drops bd
  - — acetazolamide (oral diuretics)
- surgery or laser therapy for failed medication

Retinitis pigmentosa

Primary degeneration of the retina is a hereditary condition characterised by a degeneration of rods and cones associated with displacement of melanin-containing cells from the pigment epithelium into the more superficial parts of the retina.

Typical features

- begins as night blindness in childhood
- visual fields become concentrically narrowed (periphery to centre)
- blind by adolescence (sometimes up to middle age)

Ophthalmoscopic examination

- irregular patches of dark pigment, especially at periphery

Trauma

Trauma to the eye may cause only a little discomfort so it is important to keep this in mind.

Intraocular foreign body

A small metal chip may penetrate the eye with minimal pain and the patient may not present with an ocular problem until the history of injury is long forgotten.

If infection does not supervene, presentation may be delayed for months or years until vision deteriorates due to metal degradation. The iris becomes rust-brown. It is important to X-ray the eye if it has been struck by a hammered fragment or if in any doubt at all about the mechanism of the injury.[1]

Chronic uveitis

Pain and redness may be minimal with this chronic inflammation. If untreated, visual loss often develops from secondary glaucoma and cataract. The pupil is bound to the lens by synechiae and is distorted.

HIV infection

AIDS may have serious ocular complications, including Kaposi's sarcoma of the conjunctivae, retinal haemorrhage and vasculitis.[4] Another problem is ocular cytomegalovirus infection which presents as areas of opacification with haemorrhage and exudates.

Sudden loss of vision

It is important to remember that the problem is alarming and distressing to the patient; considerable empathy is needed and care must be taken not to diagnose seemingly inappropriate behaviour as of psychogenic origin.

A comparison of bilateral and unilateral causes of sudden loss of vision is presented in Table 63.4, and the diagnostic strategy model in Table 63.5.

A flow chart for the diagnosis of painless loss of vision is presented in Figure 63.4.

Amaurosis fugax

Amaurosis fugax is transient loss of vision (partial or complete) in one eye due to transient occlusion of a retinal artery. It is painless and lasts less than 60 minutes. It is usually caused by an embolus from an atheromatous carotid artery in the neck. The most common emboli are cholesterol emboli which usually arise from an ulcerated plaque.[7] Other causes include emboli from the heart, temporal arteritis and benign intracranial hypertension. Other symptoms or signs of cerebral ischaemia such as transient hemiparesis may accompany the symptom. The source of the problem should be investigated. The risk of stroke after an episode

Table 63.4 *Causes of sudden loss of vision*[7]

	BILATERAL	*UNILATERAL*	
		Transient	***Permanent***
Vascular causes	Occipital cortex ischaemia Pituitary apoplexy Homonymous hemianopia—vascular	Amaurosis fugax Transient ocular ischaemia Retinal emboli Malignant hypertension	Central retinal artery occlusion Central retinal vein occlusion Vitreous haemorrhage Ischaemic optic neuropathy
Other causes	Bilateral optic neuritis Toxic damage to optic nerve • methanol • ethanol • tobacco • lead Leber's optic atrophy Quinine poisoning of retina Cerebral oedema Occipital lobe trauma Craniopharyngioma Hysteria	Acute angle closure glaucoma Uhthoff's phenomenon Papilloedema Obscurations Posterior vitreous detachment	Optic neuritis Retinal detachment Optic nerve compression Carcinomatous optic neuropathy Intraocular tumour

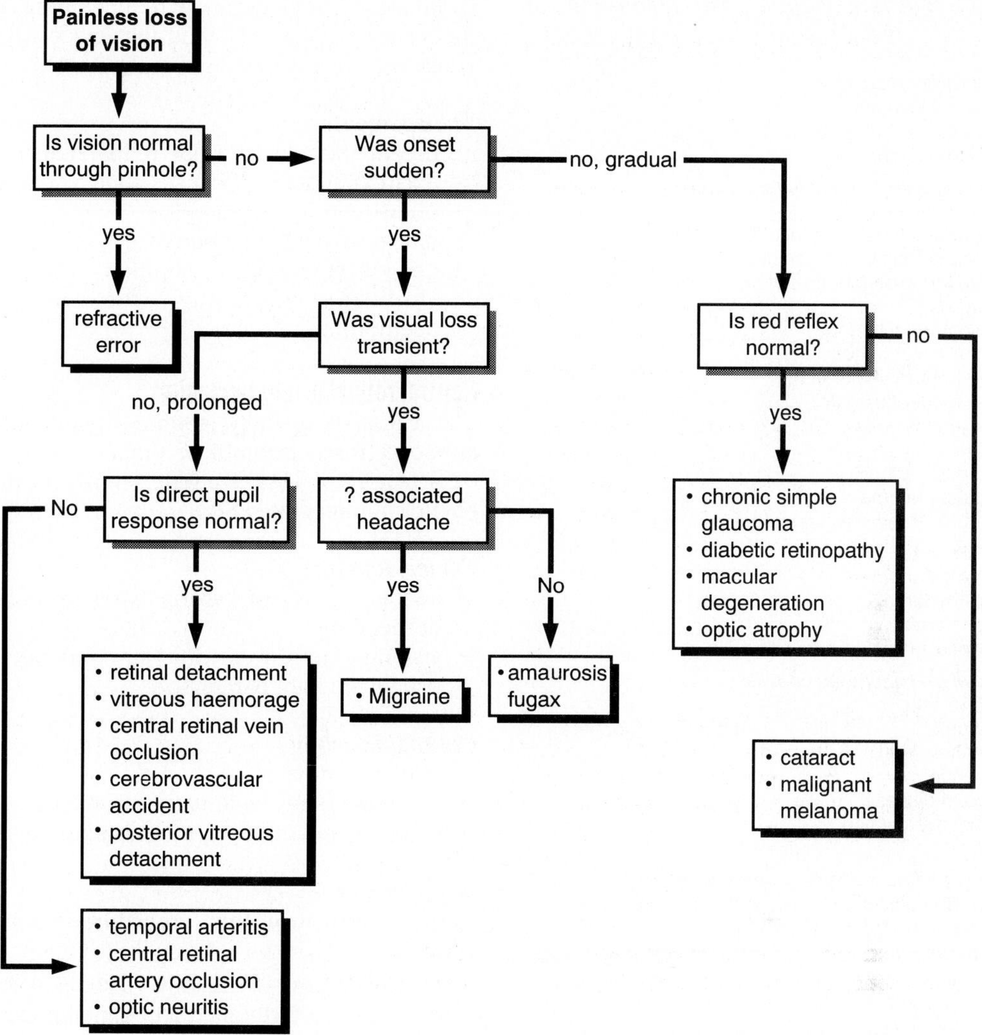

Fig. 63.4 *Diagnosis of painless loss of vision* REPRODUCED WITH PERMISSION DR J.REICH AND DR J.COLVIN

of amaurosis fugax appears to be about 2% per year.[7]

Transient ocular ischaemia

Unilateral loss of vision provoked by activities such as walking, bending or looking upwards is suggestive of ocular ischaemia.[7] It occurs in the presence of severe extracranial vascular disease and may be triggered by postural hypotension and stealing blood from the retinal circulation.

Retinal detachment

Retinal detachment may be caused by trauma, thin retina (myopic people), previous surgery (e.g. cataract operation), choroidal tumours, vitreous degeneration or diabetic retinopathy.

Clinical features

- sudden onset of floaters or flashes or black spots
- blurred vision in one eye becoming worse
- 'a curtain came down over the eye', grey cloud or black spot
- partial or total loss of visual field (total if macula detached)

Ophthalmoscopy may show detached retinal fold as large grey shadow in vitreous cavity.

Table 63.5 *Acute or subacute painless loss of vision: diagnostic strategy model*

Q. *Probability diagnosis*
A. Amaurosis fugax
Migraine
Retinal detachment

Q. *Serious disorders not to be missed*
A. Cardiovascular
- central retinal artery occlusion
- central retinal vein occlusion
- hypertension (complications)

Neoplasia
- intracranial tumour
- intraocular tumour
  - primary melanoma
  - retinoblastoma
  - metastases

AIDS
Temporal arteritis
Acute glaucoma
Benign intracranial hypertension

Q. *Pitfalls (often missed)*
A. Acute glaucoma
Papilloedema
Optic neuritis
Intraocular foreign body

Q. *Seven masquerades checklist*

A.		
	Depression	—
	Diabetes	✓ diabetic retinopathy
	Drugs	✓
	Anaemia	—
	Thyroid disease	✓ hyperthyroidism
	Spinal dysfunction	—
	UTI	—

Q. *Is this patient trying to tell me something?*
A. Consider 'hysterical' blindness, although it is uncommon.

Management

- immediate referral for sealing of retinal tears
- small holes treated with laser or freezing probe
- true detachments usually require surgery

Vitreous haemorrhage

Haemorrhage may occur from spontaneous rupture of vessels, avulsion of vessels during retinal traction or bleeding from abnormal new vessels.[5] Associations include ocular trauma, diabetic retinopathy, tumour and retinal detachment.

Clinical features

- sudden onset of floaters or 'blobs' in vision
- may be sudden loss of vision
- visual acuity depends on the extent of the haemorrhage; if small, visual acuity may be normal

Ophthalmoscopy may show reduced light reflex: there may be clots of blood that move with the vitreous (a black swirling cloud).

Management

- urgent referral to exclude retinal detachment
- exclude underlying causes such as diabetes
- ultrasound helps diagnosis
- may resolve spontaneously
- bed rest encourages resolution
- surgical vitrectomy for persistent haemorrhage

Central retinal artery occlusion

The cause is usually arterial obstruction by atherosclerosis, thrombi or emboli. There may be a history of TIAs. Exclude temporal arteritis (perform immediate ESR).

Clinical features

- sudden loss of vision like a 'curtain descending'
- vision not improved with 1mm pinhole
- usually no light perception

Ophthalmoscopy

- initially normal
- retina becomes oedematous and pale
- classical 'red cherry spot' at macula

Management

If seen early, use this procedure within 30 minutes:

- massage globe digitally through closed eyelids (use rhythmic direct digital pressure)
- rebreathe carbon dioxide (paper bag) or inhale special CO_2 mixture (carbogen)
- intravenous acetazolamide (Diamox) 500 mg
- refer urgently (less than 6 hours)

Prognosis is poor. Significant recovery is unlikely unless treated immediately (within 30 minutes).

Central retinal vein thrombosis

Thrombosis is associated with several possible factors such as hypertension, diabetes, anaemia, glaucoma and hyperlipidaemia.

Clinical features

- sudden loss of central vision (if macula involved)
- vision not improved with 1 mm pinhole

Ophthalmoscopy shows swollen disc and multiple retinal haemorrhages.

Management

No immediate treatment is effective. The cause needs to be found first and treated accordingly. Some cases respond to fibrinolysin treatment. Lasar photocoagulation may be necessary in later stages to prevent thrombotic glaucoma.

Macular degeneration

There are two types: exudative (acute) and pigmentary (slow onset).

- caused by neovascular membranes which develop under the retina of the macular area and leak fluid or bleed
- more common with increasing age (usually over 60) and those with myopia (relatively common)
- may be familial

Clinical features

- sudden fading of central vision
- distortion of vision
- straight lines may seem wavy and objects distorted
- use a grid pattern (Amsler chart): shows distorted lines
- central vision eventually completely lost
- peripheral fields normal

Ophthalmoscopy

- white exudates, haemorrhage in retina
- macula may look normal or raised

Management

Urgent referral for fluorescein angiography and laser photocoagulation where indicated. The chronic pigmentation type has been shown to respond to free-radical treatment with antioxidants such as vitamins A, C or E, zinc and selenium.

Temporal arteritis

With temporal arteritis (giant cell arteritis) there is a risk of sudden and often bilateral occlusion of the short ciliary arteries supplying the optic nerves, with or without central retinal artery involvement.[6]

Clinical features

- usually older person: over 65 years
- sudden loss of central vision in one eye (central scotoma)
- can rapidly become bilateral
- associated temporal headache
- temporal arteries tender, thickened and non-pulsatile
- visual acuity severely impaired
- afferent pupil defect on affected side
- usually elevated ESR > 40

Ophthalmoscopy shows optic disc swollen at first, then atrophic. The disc may appear quite normal.

Management

- other eye must be tested
- immediate corticosteroids (100 mg prednisolone daily for at least one week)
- biopsy temporal artery

Migraine

Migraine may present with symptoms of visual loss. Associated headache and nausea may not be present.

Clinical features

- zigzag lines or lights
- multicoloured flashing lights
- unilateral or bilateral field deficit
- resolution within a few hours

Posterior vitreous detachment

The vitreous body collapses and detaches from the retina. It may lead to retinal detachment.

Clinical features

- sudden onset of floaters
- visual acuity usually normal
- flashing lights indicate traction on the retina

Management

- Refer to an ophthalmologist urgently.
- An associated retinal hole or detachment needs exclusion.

Optic (retrobulbar) neuritis

Causes include multiple sclerosis, neurosyphilis and toxins. Most cases eventually develop multiple sclerosis.

Clinical features

- usually a woman 20–40 years
- loss of vision in one eye over a few days
- retro-ocular discomfort with eye movements
- variable visual acuity
- usually a central field loss (central scotoma)
- afferent pupil defect on affected side

Ophthalmoscopy

- optic disc swollen if 'inflammation' anterior in nerve
- optic atrophy appears later
- disc pallor is an invariable sequel

Management

- Test visual field of other eye.
- Consider magnetic resonance imaging.
- Most patients recover spontaneously but are left with diminished acuity.
- Steroids hasten recovery.

Pitfalls

- Mistaking the coloured haloes of glaucoma for migraine.
- Failing to appreciate the presence of retinal detachment in the presence of minimal visual impairment.
- Omitting to consider temporal arteritis as a cause of sudden visual failure in the elderly.
- Using eye drops to dilate the pupil (for fundal examination) in the presence of glaucoma.

When to refer

- Most problems outlined need urgent referral to an ophthalmologist.
- Acute visual disturbance of unknown cause requires urgent referral.
- Any blurred vision—sudden or gradual, painful or painless—especially if 1 mm pinhole fails to alter visual acuity.
- Refer all suspicious optic discs.

Practice tips

- Tonometry is advised routinely for all people over 40; those over 60 should have tests every two years.
- Any family history of glaucoma requires tonometry at earliest age.
- Sudden loss of vision in the elderly suggests temporal arteritis (check the ESR and temporal arteries). It requires immediate institution of high-dose steroids to prevent blindness in the other eye. A time-scale guide showing the rate of visual loss is presented in Table 63.6.
- Temporal arteritis is an important cause of retinal artery occlusion.
- Suspect field defect due to chiasmal compression if people are misjudging when driving.
- Pupillary reactions are normal in cortical blindness.
- Central retinal artery occlusion may be overcome by early rapid lowering of intraocular pressure.
- Retinal detachment and vitreous haemorrhage may require early surgical repair.
- Keep in mind antioxidant therapy (vitamins and minerals) for chronic macular degeneration.
- Consider multiple sclerosis foremost if there is a past history of transient visual failure, especially with eye pain.
- If the patient has been using a hammer, always X-ray if a fragment of metal has hit the eye but nothing can be seen.

Table 63.6 *Time-scale guide for rate of visual loss*[3,7]

Sudden: less than 1 hour
- amaurosis fugax
- central retinal artery occlusion
- hemianopias from ischaemia (emboli)
- migraine
- vitreous haemorrhage
- acute angle glaucoma
- papilloedema

Within 24 hours
- central retinal vein occlusion
- hysteria

Less than 7 days
- retinal detachment
- optic neuritis
- acute macular problems

Up to several weeks (variable)
- choroiditis
- malignant hypertension

Gradual
- compression of visual pathways
- chronic glaucoma
- cataracts
- diabetic maculopathy
- retinitis pigmentosa
- macular degeneration
- refractive errors

References

1. Colvin J, Reich J. CHECK Programme, Unit 219–220. Melbourne: RACGP, 1990, 1–32.
2. Beck ER, Francis JL, Souhami RL. *Tutorials in differential diagnosis* (2nd edition). Edinburgh: Churchill Livingstone, 1988, 141–144.
3. Enoch B. Painless loss of vision in adults. Update, 5 June 1987, 22–30.
4. Robinson MJ. *Practical paediatrics* (2nd edition). Melbourne: Churchill Livingstone, 1990, 120–122.
5. Elkington AR, Khaw PT. *ABC of eyes.* London: British Medical Association, 1990:20–38.
6. Warne R, Prinsley D. *A manual of geriatric care.* Sydney: Williams and Wilkins, 1988, 191–195.
7. King J. Loss of vision. Modern Medicine Australia, May 1990, 52–61.

64

Weight gain

Obesity is the most common nutrition-related disorder in the western world; as Tunnessen puts it, 'Obesity is the most common form of malnutrition in the United States'.[1] Most overweight adults and children who are obese have exogenous obesity, which tends to imply that 'they ate too much', but the problem is more complex than relative food input. Physical activity, environmental and genetic influences must also be taken into account. There is still a persisting tendency of affected families to blame 'glandular' problems as a cause of obesity.

Key facts and figures

- The cause of exogenous obesity is multifactorial, the end result being increased body fatness (greater than 30% of total body weight in females and greater than 25% in males).[2]
- The onset of obesity can occur at any age.
- Secondary or pathologic causes are rare.
- Less than 1% of obese patients have an identifiable secondary cause of obesity.[3]
- Two conditions causing unexplained weight gain that can be diagnosed by the physical examination are Cushing's syndrome and hypothyroidism.
- After pregnancy, obesity may result from a failure to return to prepartum energy requirements.

A diagnostic approach

A summary of the safety diagnostic model is presented in Table 64.1.

Table 64.1 *Weight gain: diagnostic strategy model*

Q. *Probability diagnosis*
A. Exogenous obesity

Q. *Serious disorders not to be missed*
A. Cardiovascular
- cardiac failure

Hypothalamic disorders
- craniopharyngiomas
- optic gliomas

Liver failure
Nephrotic syndrome

Q. *Pitfalls (often missed)*
A. Pregnancy (early)
Endocrine disorders
- hypothyroidism
- Cushing's syndrome
- insulinoma
- acromegaly
- hypogonadism
- hyperprolactinaemia

Klinefelter's syndrome
Congenital disorders
- Prader-Willi syndrome
- Laurence-Moon-Biedl syndrome

Q. *Seven masquerades checklist*
A.

Depression	✓	
Diabetes	—	
Drugs	✓	
Anaemia	—	
Thyroid disease	✓	hypothyroid
Spinal dysfunction	—	
UTI	—	

Q. *Is the patient trying to tell me something?*
A. Yes: the reasons for obesity should be explored.

Probability diagnosis

The outstanding cause of weight gain in exogenous obesity is excessive calorie intake coupled with lack of exercise. Overweight people often deny overeating but the true situation can be determined by recording actual food intake and energy expenditure, and by interviewing reliable witnesses.

Serious causes not to be missed

It is important not to misdiagnose hypothalamic disorders which may result in hyperphagia and obesity. Injury to the hypothalamus may occur following trauma and encephalitis and with a variety of tumours including craniopharyngiomas, optic gliomas and pituitary neoplasms. Some of these tumours may cause headaches and visual disturbances.

It is important not to overlook major organ failure and renal disorders as a cause of increased body weight, especially cardiac failure, liver failure and the nephrotic syndrome. The associated increase in body water needs to be distinguished from increased body fat.

Pitfalls

Endocrine disorders

The endocrine disorders that cause obesity include Cushing's syndrome, hypothyroidism, insulin-secreting tumours and hypogonadism. They should not represent difficult diagnostic problems.

An insulin-secreting tumour (insulinoma) is a very rare adenoma of the B cells of the islets of Langerhans. The main features are symptoms of hypoglycaemia and obesity.

Congenital disorders

The rare congenital disorders that cause obesity such as Prader-Willi and Laurence-Moon-Biedl syndromes should be easy to recognise in children (see page 650).

Chromosomal abnormalities

An important abnormality to bear in mind is Klinefelter's syndrome (XXY karyotype) which affects one out of every 400–500 males. The boys show excessive growth of long bones and are tall and slim. Without testosterone treatment they become obese as adults.

Some girls with Turner's syndrome (XO karyotype) may be short and overweight.

Seven masquerades checklist

The important masquerades include hypothyroidism and drug ingestion. Hypothyroidism is usually not associated with marked obesity. Drugs which can be an important contributing factor include the tricyclic antidepressants, corticosteroids, pizotifen, thioridazine, and the contraceptive pill. Obesity (overeating) may be a feature of depression, especially in the early stages. Prescribed tricyclic antidepressants may compound the problem.

Psychogenic considerations

An underlying emotional crisis may be the reason for the overweight patient to seek medical advice. It is important to explore diplomatically any hidden agenda and help the patient to resolve any conflict.

The clinical approach

A careful history is very valuable in ascertaining food and beverage intake and perhaps giving patients insight into their calorie intake, since some deny overeating or will underestimate their food intake.[4]

Relevant questions

Do you feel that you have an excessive appetite?
Tell me in detail what you ate yesterday.
Give me an outline of a typical daily meal.
Tell me about snacks, soft drink and alcohol that you have.
What exercise do you get?
Do you have any special problems, such as getting bored, tense and upset or depressed?
What drugs are you taking?

Physical examination

In the physical examination it is very important to measure body weight and height and calculate the BMI, and assess the degree and distribution of body fat and the overall nutritional status. Record the blood pressure and test the urine for sugar. Keep in mind that a standard blood pressure cuff on a large arm may give falsely elevated values. Remember the rare possibilities of Cushing's disease, acromegaly and hypothyroidism. Search for evidence of atherosclerosis and diabetes and for signs of alcohol abuse.

An extensive working up of the CNS is not indicated in obesity without the presence of suspicious symptoms such as visual difficulties.

Investigations

It is essential to perform two measurements:

- weight and height (to calculate BMI)
- waist-hip ratio

Important investigations

- cholesterol/triglycerides
- glucose (fasting)
- liver function tests
- electrolytes and urea

Investigations to consider

- thyroid function tests
- cortisol (if hypertensive)
- testosterone (suspected sleep apnoea)
- ECG and chest X-ray (older than 40)

Anthropometric measurements

Useful measuring instruments include:

- body mass index (BMI): 'healthy' range is between 20 and 25
- waist:hip circumference ratio (W/H ratio): healthy range <0.9
- single skinfold thickness (>25 mm suggests increased body fat)
- upper arm circumference
- 4 skinfold thickness (sum of suprailiac, subscapular, triceps and biceps skinfolds)—for calculation of percentage body fat

Body mass index

The easiest and possibly most accurate assessment of obesity is the BMI (refer Appendix VI):

$$\text{BMI} = \frac{\text{weight (kg)}}{\text{height (M}^2\text{)}}$$

Garrow[5] has produced a simple classification of the BMI associated with the relative degree of risk increase and suggested therapy (Table 64.2).

Weight gain in children

Various studies have found that approximately 10% of prepubertal and 15% of adolescent age groups are obese.[1]

Parents often blame obesity in children on their 'glands', but endocrine or metabolic causes are rare and can be readily differentiated from exogenous obesity by a simple physical examination and an assessment of linear growth. Children with exogenous obesity tend to have an accelerated linear growth whereas children with secondary causes are usually short.

Congenital or inherited disorders associated with obesity

Prader-Willi syndrome

The characteristic features are bizarre eating habits (e.g. binge eating), obesity, hypotonia, hypogonadism, mental retardation, small hands and feet and a characteristic facial appearance (narrow bifrontal diameter, 'almond-shaped' eyes and a 'tented' upper lip). Progressive obesity results from excessive intake in addition to decreased caloric requirements.

Laurence-Moon-Biedl syndrome

The characteristic features are obesity, mental retardation, polydactyly and syndactyly, retinitis pigmentation and hypogonadism.

Beckwirth-Wiedemann syndrome

Characteristics include excessive growth, macrosomia, macroglossia, umbilical hernia and neonatal hypoglycaemia. Children appear obese as they are above the 95th percentile by 18 months of age. Intelligence is usually in the normal range.

Table 64.2 *Classification of obesity (after Garrow 1988)[5]*

BMI	Grading	Suggested therapy
<18	very underweight	diet and counselling
18–20	underweight	diet (and counselling)
20–25	0. healthy weight	
25–30	I. overweight	more exercise diet
30–40	II. obesity	combined program: • behaviour modification • diet • exercise
>40	III. morbid obesity	combined program plus medical therapy

Endocrine disorders

Endocrine disorders in children that can rarely cause obesity include hypothyroidism (often blamed as the cause but seldom is), Cushing's syndrome, insulinomas, hypothalamic lesions, Fröhlich's syndrome (adiposogenital dystrophy) and Stein-Leventhal syndrome in girls.

Managing obesity in children

Childhood obesity usually reflects an underlying problem in the family system. It can be a very difficult emotional problem in adolescents, who develop a poor body image. An important strategy is to meet with family members, determine whether they perceive the child's obesity as a problem and whether they are prepared to solve the problem. The family dynamics will have to be assessed and strategies outlined. This may involve referral for expert counselling. It is worth pointing out that children eat between one-third and two-thirds of their meals at school so schools should be approached to promote special programs for children who need weight reduction.

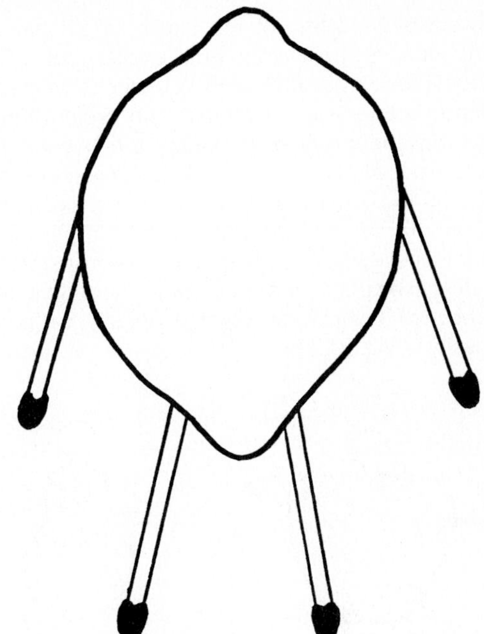

Fig. 64.1 *The traditional 'lemon with matchsticks' configuration of Cushing's syndrome*

Cushing's syndrome

Cushing's syndrome is the term used to describe the chemical features of increased free circulating glucocorticoid. The most common cause is iatrogenic with the prescribing of synthetic corticosteroids. The spontaneous primary forms such as Cushing's disease (pituitary dependent hyperadrenalism) are rare. As the disease progresses the body contour tends to assume the often quoted configuration of a lemon with matchsticks (Fig. 64.1).

Typical clinical features

- change in appearance
- central weight gain (truncal obesity)
- hair growth and acne in females
- muscle weakness
- amenorrhoea/oligomenorrhoea (females)
- thin skin/spontaneous bruising
- polymyalgia/polydypsia (diabetes mellitus)
- insomnia
- depression

Signs

- moon face
- 'buffalo bump'
- purple striae
- large trunk and thin limbs

The patient should be referred for diagnostic evaluation including plasma cortisol and overweight dexamethasone suppression tests.

Untreated Cushing's syndrome has a very poor prognosis, with premature death from myocardial infarction, cardiac failure and infection; hence early diagnosis and referral is essential.

Table 64.3 *Factors predisposing to primary obesity*

Genetic	— familial tendency
Sex	— women more susceptible
Activity	— lack of physical activity
Psychogenic	— emotional deprivation; depression
Social class	— poorer classes
Alcohol	— problem drinking
Smoking	— cessation of smoking
Prescribed drugs	— tricyclic derivatives

Obesity

Obesity and overweight are the most common pathological conditions in our society and are caused by an accumulation of adipose tissue

(Table 64.3). It is not the extra weight *per se* that causes problems but excess fat. The calculation of the BMI gives a better estimate of adiposity and it is convenient and preferable to use this index when assessing the overweight and obese. However, recent data suggest that the distribution of body fat is as important a risk factor as its total amount. Abdominal fat (upper body segment obesity, or 'apple' obesity, is considered a greater health hazard than fat in the thighs and buttocks (lower body segment obesity, or 'pear' obesity) (Fig. 64.2).

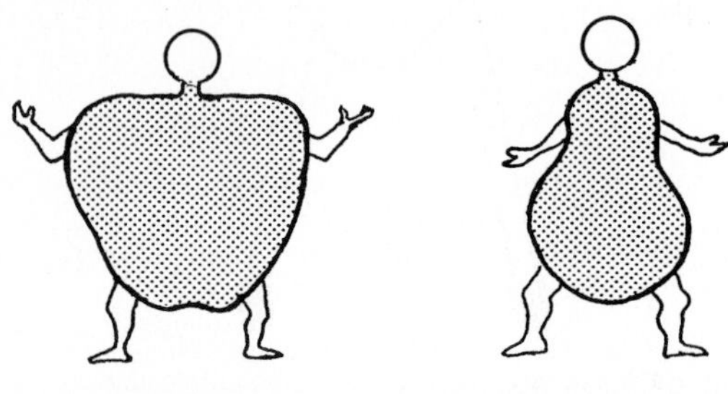

Fig. 64.2 *Comparison of two types of obesity according to distribution of body fat*

Obese patients with high waist–hip ratios (>1.0 in men and >0.9 in women) have a significantly greater risk of diabetes mellitus, stroke, coronary artery disease and early death than equally obese people with lower waist–hip ratios.[3]

In reference to the BMI reference scale it is worth noting that the risks follow a J-shaped curve (Fig. 64.3) and are only slightly increased in the overweight range but increase with obesity so that a BMI of >40 carries a threefold increase in mortality.

The consequences of obesity include:

- cardiovascular
  — increased mortality
  — hypertension
  — varicose veins
- metabolic
  — secondary hyperlipidaemia
  — hyperinsulinaemia
  — infertility
- mechanical
  — osteoarthritis
  — obstructive sleep apnoea
  — spinal dysfunction

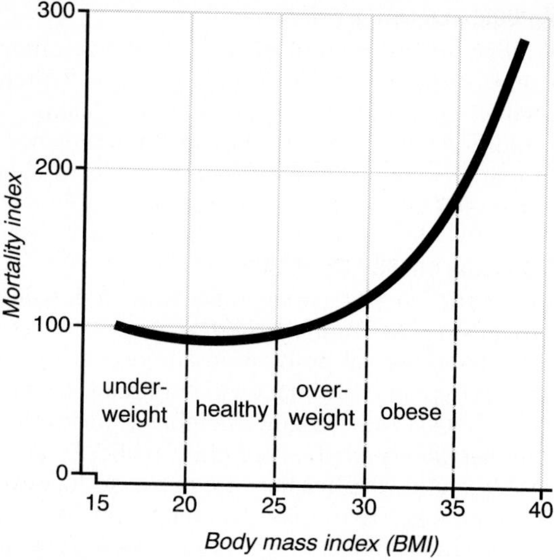

Fig. 64.3 *Body mass index (BMI) reference scale*

Management

Treatment is based around four major interventions, the choice of which depends on the degree of obesity, the associated health problems and the health risk posed.[2]

1. reduction in energy intake
2. change in diet composition
3. increased physical activity
4. behavioural therapy

Pharmacological agents are not used for first-line therapy although they may have a place in management, especially at grade III level of obesity. Surgery is an option for the treatment of morbid obesity.

There is no single effective method for the treatment of obesity, which is a difficult and frustrating problem. A continuing close therapist/patient contact has a better chance of success than any single treatment regimen.

Most successful programs involve a multi-disciplinary approach to weight loss, embracing the four major interventions. Emphasis must be on maintenance of weight loss. Behaviour modification is important and the most valuable strategy is to emphasise planning and record keeping with a continuous weekly diary of menus, exercise and actual behaviour.

Social support is essential for a successful weight loss program. A better result is likely if close family members, especially the chief cook, is involved in the program, preferably striving for the same goals.[3]

A doctor-patient strategy

A close therapeutic supportive relationship with a patient can be effective using the following methods.[6]

1. *Promote realistic goals* Lose weight at the same rate that it was gained, i.e. slowly. For example, 5–10 kg a year. A graph can be used for this purpose with an 'exaggerated' scale on the vertical axis so that small variations appear highly significant and encouraging (Fig. 64.4).
   Promote the equation:
   ENERGY IN = ENERGY OUT + ENERGY STORED
   The only way to reduce the stored energy (fat) is either to reduce energy in (eat less) or increase energy out (exercise).

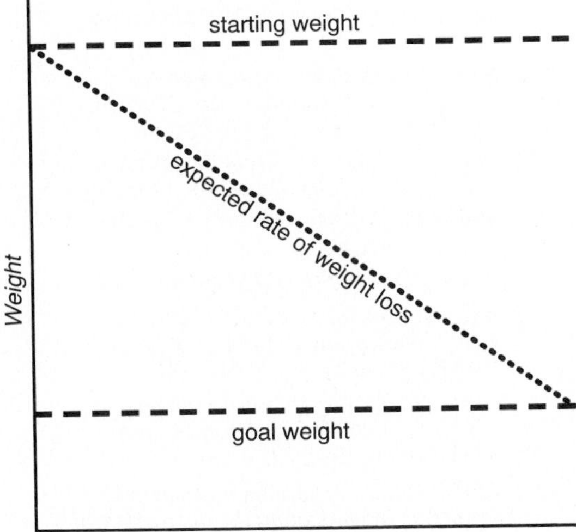

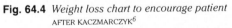

Fig. 64.4 *Weight loss chart to encourage patient*
AFTER KACZMARCZYK[6]

2. *Dietary advice* It is important to be realistic and allow patients to eat their normal foods but advise them about quantity and frequency. Give advice on simple substitutions, e.g. fortified skim milk in place of whole milk, high-fibre wholemeal bread instead of white bread, and fruit and vegetables instead of biscuits and cakes as in-between snacks.[6] A strategy that seems to work effectively is to advise patients, especially those who are overweight (grade I obesity), to eat one-third less than they usually do and discipline themselves not to 'pick' and to avoid second helpings.
3. *Counselling* is simple and common sense. It involves being supportive, interested and encouraging. A list of tips on coping is provided (see following 'a practical plan' for grade II and III obesity) and the patient advised to keep a food, exercise and behaviour diary.
4. *Review* 'Review is the most vital part of the weight loss programme as it stimulates and revitalises motivation and enables assessment of progress'.[6] It should be frequent initially, e.g. fortnightly, and then monthly until the goal weight has been achieved and then three monthly reviews. It is important never to be judgemental or critical if progress is unsatisfactory.

A practical plan

The following patient education sheet to be handed to patients represents useful advice to offer the obese patient.[7]

Physical activity

- A brisk walk for 20–30 minutes each day is the most practical exercise.
- Other activities such as tennis, swimming, golf and cycling are a bonus.

Dietary advice

Breakfast:

- oatmeal (soaked overnight in water); after cooking, add fresh or dried fruit; serve with fat-reduced milk or yoghurt

  or
- muesli (homemade or from a health food store)—medium serve with fat-reduced milk, perhaps add extra fruit (fresh or dried)
- slice of wholemeal toast with a thin scraping of margarine, spread with Vegemite, Marmite or sugar-free marmalade
- fresh orange juice or herbal tea or black tea/coffee

Morning and afternoon tea:

- piece of fruit or vegetable (e.g. carrot or celery)
- freshly squeezed juice or chilled water with fresh lemon

Midday meal:

- salad sandwich with wholemeal or multigrained bread and thin scraping of margarine (for variety use egg, salmon, chicken or cheese fillings)
- drink as for breakfast

Evening meal:
Summer (cold)—lean meat cuts (grilled, hot or cold), poultry (skin removed) or fish; fresh garden salad; slices of fresh fruit
Winter (hot)—lean meat cuts (grilled), poultry (skin removed) or fish; plenty of green, red and yellow vegetables and small potato; fruit for sweets

Weight-losing tips

- Have sensible goals; do not 'crash' diet, but have a 6–12 month plan to achieve your ideal weight.
- Go for natural foods; avoid junk foods.
- Avoid alcohol, sugary soft drinks and high-calorie fruit juices.
- Strict dieting without exercise fails.
- If you are mildly overweight, eat one-third less than you usually do.
- Do not eat biscuits, cakes, buns, etc. between meals (preferably at no time).
- Use high-fibre foods to munch on.
- A small treat once a week may add variety.
- Avoid seconds and do not eat leftovers.
- Eat slowly—spin out your meal.
- Avoid medicines that claim to remove weight.

When to refer

- Patients with grade II or III obesity (BMI > 30) who are resistant to simple weight control measures.[2]
- Patients with associated medical problems such as angina or severe osteoarthritis who require rapid weight reduction.
- Possibility of endocrine cause of obesity.
- Suspicion of congenital or inherited disorder in children.

Practice tips

- Avoid a critical or judgemental attitude to the overweight patient.[8]
- Seek diplomatic independent information from a spouse or parent about food and beverage intake.
- Obtain a chronological history of the patient's weight from infancy onwards and attempt to correlate any significant changes to stressful life events.

References

1. Tunnessen WW jnr. *Signs and symptoms in paediatrics* (2nd edition). Philadelphia: JB Lippincott, 1988, 33–41.
2. Marks S, Walqvist M. Obesity. In: MIMS Disease Index. Sydney: IMS Publishing, 1991–2, 367–370.
3. Schroeder SA et al *Current medical diagnosis and treatment.* East Norwalk: Appleton and Lange, 1990, 874–875.
4. Sloane PD, Slatt PD, Baker RM. *Essentials of family medicine.* Baltimore: Williams and Wilkins, 1988, 200–208.
5. Garrow J. *Treat obesity seriously.* Edinburgh: Churchill Livingstone, 1988.
6. Kaczmarczyk W. The obese patient. In: How I Manage my Difficult Problems. Aust Fam Physician, 1991; 20:417–421.
7. Murtagh JE. Obesity: how to lose weight wisely. In: *Patient Education.* Sydney: McGraw-Hill, 1992, 62.
8. Kincaid-Smith P, Larkins R, Whelan G. *Problems in clinical medicine.* Sydney: MacLennan & Petty, 1990, 105–108.

65

Weight loss

In family practice complaints of loss of weight are more frequent than complaints about being too thin. Of great significance is the problem of recent loss of weight. A very analytical history is required to determine the patient's perception of weight loss. The equivalent problem in children is failure to gain weight or thrive.

Weight loss is an important symptom because it usually implies a serious underlying disorder, either organic or functional. It may or may not be associated with anorexia and thus diminished food intake.

Key facts and checkpoints

- Any loss of more than 5% of normal body weight is significant.
- The most common cause in adults of recent weight loss is stress and anxiety.[1]
- Serious organic diseases to consider are:
  - malignant disease
  - diabetes mellitus
  - chronic infections, e.g. tuberculosis
  - thyrotoxicosis
- The most important variable to consider in evaluating weight loss is appetite. Eating and weight go hand in glove.
- Two conditions commonly associated with weight loss are anaemia and fever; they must be excluded.
- Early detection of eating disorders improves outcome.

A diagnostic approach

A summary of the safety diagnostic model is presented in Table 65.1.

Probability diagnosis

Excluding planned dietary restriction, psychological factors are the most common cause, particularly recent stress and anxiety.[1]

Serious disorders not to be missed

Many of the problems causing weight loss are very serious, especially malignant disease.

Malignant disease

Weight loss may be a manifestation of any malignancy. With carcinoma of the stomach, pancreas and caecum, malignant lymphomas and myeloma, weight loss may be the only symptom. Occult malignancy must be regarded as the most common cause of weight loss in the absence of major symptoms and signs. The mechanisms may be multiple with anorexia and increased metabolism being important factors.

Chronic infections

These are now less common but tuberculosis must be considered, especially in people from less developed countries. Some cases of infective endocarditis may progress only very slowly with general debility, weight loss and fever as major features.[2]

Table 65.1 *Weight loss: diagnostic strategy model (other than deliberate dieting or malnutrition)*

Q. Probability diagnosis
A. Stress and anxiety
Non-coping elderly

Q. Serious disorders not to be missed
A. Congestive cardiac failure
Malignant disease
- stomach
- pancreas
- lung
- myeloma
- caecum
- lymphoma

Chronic infection
- HIV infections (AIDS, ARC)
- tuberculosis
- hidden abscess
- infective endocarditis
- brucellosis
- others

Q. Pitfalls (often missed)
A. Drug dependence, esp. alcohol
Malabsorption states
? intestinal parasites
Other GIT problems
Chronic renal failure
Connective tissue disorders, e.g. SLE

Rarities
Addison's disease
Hypopituitarism

Q. Seven masquerades checklist

A.	
Depression	✓
Diabetes	✓
Drugs	✓
Anaemia	✓
Thyroid disease	✓
Spinal dysfunction	—
UTI	—

Q. Is the patient trying to tell me something?
A. A possiblity. Consider stress, anxiety and depression. Anorexia nervosa and bulimia are special considerations.

Other infections to consider are brucellosis, and protozoal and systemic fungal infection. Infection with HIV virus must be considered, especially in high-risk groups.

Pitfalls

Drug dependency, including alcohol and narcotic drugs, must be considered especially when the problem may result in inappropriate nutrition. Apart from malignant disease there is a whole variety of gastrointestinal disorders that require consideration; these include malabsorption states, gastric ulceration, and intestinal infestations that should be considered especially in people returning from a significant stay in tropical and underdeveloped countries.

Addison's disease can be very difficult to diagnose. Symptoms include excessive fatigue, anorexia, nausea and postural dizziness. Hyperpigmentation is a late sign.

Seven masquerades checklist

Depression and the endocrine disorders, diabetes mellitus and hyperthyroidism, are important causes.

Diabetes

The diabetic who presents with weight loss will be young and insulin-dependent. The initial presentation may be ketoacidosis. The triad of symptoms is *thirst—polyuria—weight loss.*

Hyperthyroidism

This is usually associated with weight loss although in some, such as an elderly male, it may not be obvious. An important clue will be weight loss in the presence of an excellent appetite and this helps to distinguish it from a psychoneurotic disturbance.

Depression

Weight loss is a common feature of depression and is usually proportional to the severity of the disease. In the early stages of depression weight gain may be present but when the classical loss of the four basic drives (appetite, energy, sleep and sex) becomes manifest, weight loss is a feature.

Drugs

Any prescribed drugs causing anorexia can cause weight loss. Important drugs include digoxin, narcotics and cytotoxics.

Psychogenic considerations

Weight loss is a feature of anxiety as well as depression. Some patients with psychotic disturbances, including schizophrenia and mania, may present with weight loss.

Anorexia nervosa is quite common and is almost entirely confined to girls between the ages of 12 and 20. The main differential diagnosis is hypopituitarism, although anorexia nervosa can cause endocrine disturbances through the hypothalamic pituitary axis.

The clinical approach

History

It is important to document the weight loss carefully and evaluate the patient's recordings. The same set of scales should be used. It is also important to determine the food intake. However, in the absence of an independent witness such as a spouse or parent, this can be difficult. Food intake may be diminished with psychogenic disorders and carcinoma but increased or steady with endocrine disorders such as diabetes and hyperthyroidism and with steatorrhoea.

General questions

Exactly how much weight have you lost and over how long?
Have you changed your diet in any way?
Has your appetite changed? Do you feel like eating?
Have your clothes become looser?
What is your general health like?
How do you feel in yourself?
Do you feel uptight (tense), worried or anxious?
Do you get very irritable or tremulous?
Do you feel depressed?
Do you ever force yourself to vomit?
Are you thirsty?
Do you pass a lot of urine?
Do you have excessive sweating?
Do you experience a lot of night sweats?
What are your motions like?
Are they difficult to flush down the toilet?
Do you have a cough or bring up sputum?
Do you get short of breath?
Do you have any abdominal pain?
Are your periods normal (for females)?
What drugs are you taking?
How many cigarettes do you smoke?

Physical examination

A careful general examination is essential with special attention to:

- vital parameters
- the thyroid and signs of hyperthyroidism
- the abdomen (check liver, any masses and tenderness)
- rectal examination (test stool for occult blood)
- reflexes

Investigations

Basic investigations include:

- haemoglobin, red cell indices and film
- white cell count
- ESR
- thyroid function test
- random blood sugar
- chest X-ray
- urine analysis

Others to consider:

- upper GIT (endoscopy or barium meal)
- colonoscopy

Weight loss in children

Weight loss in children can be considered as:

1. Failure to thrive (FTT): the child up to 2 years below 3rd percentile.
2. Weight loss in a child after normal development.

Failure to thrive

The long list of possible causes includes malfunction of any of the organ systems of the body as well as nutritional, environmental, social and psychological factors.

FTT is best determined by sequentially plotting the weight, length and head circumference on growth charts (see growth charts in appendix). The infant with FTT has a decreased growth rate or is losing weight, and may be below the 3rd percentile. The percentile charts mean little without considering the context of the baby's growth, e.g. premature babies, children of small parents.

On an average babies put on 150–200 g a week.[3] A classification of FTT is presented in Table 65.2, divided into organic and non-organic causes. The distinction is not always easy. Psychosocial problems may coexist with organic problems. Feeding problems are common to both.

Non-organic failure to thrive

Non-organic FTT can be caused by emotional deprivation or by poor nutrition from inadequate intake. Emotional deprivation might be anticipated by a knowledge of the mother, her family background, marital relationships, attitude to the pregnancy, delivery and early bonding experience. In her book *The Abused Child* Martin lists factors influencing such bonding.[4]

Factors in the parent

- expectation of the child
- desire for the child
- capacity to give

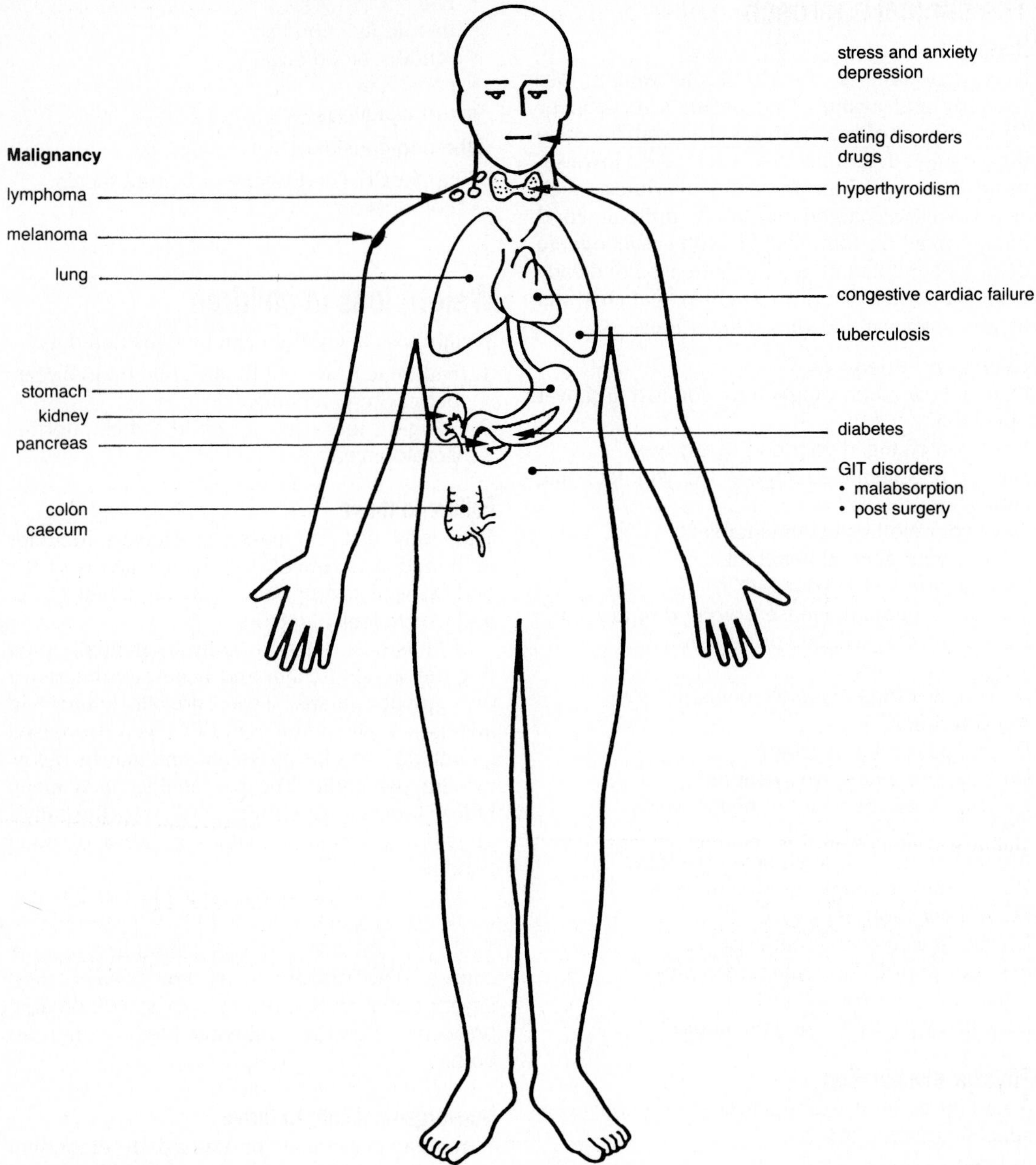

Fig. 65.1 *Weight loss: causes to consider*

- ego-strength to adapt to stress
- ability to accept imperfection
- realistic fantasies of the child

Factors in the child

- absence of defects
- the ability to match the parent's expectations
- good health
- loving behaviour, including smiling, cuddling and thriving

Disturbance of any of these factors may lead to relationship difficulties. The management of FTT due to psychological factors may be complex.[5] At the simplest level the recognition by the mother that she is having difficulty in relating to her baby is essential, and the reassurance that not all babies are as lovable and easy to manage as

Table 65.2 *Failure to thrive: general causes (after Robinson)*

Non-organic causes

1. Inadequate parenting
2. Poor nutrition

Organic causes

1. Failure of intake
   - underfeeding, e.g. nipple disorders
   - congenital abnormalities, e.g. cleft palate
   - dyspnoea, e.g. congenital heart disease
   - neurological lesions, e.g. cerebral birth injuries
   - behavioural factors
2. Abnormal losses
   - vomiting, e.g. pyloric stenosis, galactosaemia
   - stools, e.g. steatorrhoea
   - urine, e.g. renal disease
3. Failure of utilisation
   - chronic infection, e.g. cystic fibrosis
   - metabolic disorders, e.g. phenylketonuria
   - endocrine disorders, e.g. hypothyroidism
   - constitutional, e,g. Down syndrome

portrayed may help. A home visit to evaluate the home environment provides invaluable information. These mothers require considerable caring support and encouragement.

Organic failure to thrive

Any chronic disease will cause FTT. Serious organic diseases include renal failure, hypothyroidism, cystic fibrosis, other causes of malabsorption such as coeliac disease, and various inborn errors of metabolism such as galactosaemia (Table 65.2).

Poor developmental progress may indicate mental retardation. Babies born to mothers who are HIV carriers present with FTT in the first five months, either with or without other signs of disease, such as infections.[3] Another possible cause of growth failure in a baby who has a good intake may be sleep apnoea and this requires investigation.

Examination of the baby

Examine for developmental problems including cerebral palsy, cleft palate, respiratory disorders and abdominal abnormalities.

Investigations

Simple screening tests should be performed if either the history or physical examination suggests organic disease. Tests include routine blood counts, urinalysis and urine culture, Guthrie test for PKU, IVP, thyroid function tests and chromosomal and hormone analysis.

Main causes of FTT (accounts for up to 90%):[6]

- normal variants, and
- nutritional deprivation

Most important considerations

- manner of feeding
- home visit
- environmental factors
- parental problems
- admission to hospital

Rare possibilities

- HIV infection
- sleep apnoea
- hypopituitarism (growth hormone ↓)
- chromosomal abnormalities

Loss of weight in the older child

Acute or chronic infections are the most common causes of weight loss in children beyond infancy.[6] In acute infections the weight loss is transient, and once the infection clears the child generally regains the lost weight. In chronic infections signs may be more difficult to detect; for example, urinary tract infection, pulmonary infection, osteomyelitis, chronic hepatitis. In common with the younger child who fails to thrive, the older may be suffering from malabsorption syndrome, chronic infection of the urinary tract or a rare chromosomal or metabolic disorder.[7] Tuberculosis, diabetes and malignant disease may present as weight loss and it is necessary to exclude organic disease before considering the more common emotional disorders.

Eating disorders in the adolescent

Concerns about body image and dieting are very common among young women in modern society. Among these dieters 5–10% become abnormally preoccupied with dieting and slimness and progress to the eating disorders of anorexia nervosa and bulimia.

The DSM III criteria for diagnosing these disorders, which have serious physical and psychological consequences, are presented in Table 65.3. The differential diagnosis of anorexia nervosa includes most of the problems listed in Table 65.1.

Anorexia nervosa

Anorexia nervosa is a syndrome characterised by the obsessive pursuit of thinness through dieting with extreme weight loss and disturbance of body image.[8]

Table 65.3 *DSM III criteria for diagnosing anorexia nervosa and bulimia*

Anorexia nervosa

1. Refusal to maintain normal body weight
2. Loss of more than 25% of original body weight
3. Disturbance of body image
4. Intense fear of becoming fat
5. No known medical illness leading to weight loss

Bulimia

1. Recurrent episodes of binge eating
2. At least three of the following:
   a. consumption of high-calorie, easily ingested food during binge
   b. termination of binge by abdominal pain, sleep or vomiting
   c. inconspicuous eating during a binge
   d. repeated attempts to lose weight
   e. frequent fluctuations of more than 4.5 kg
3. Awareness of abnormal eating pattern and fear of not being able to stop voluntarily
4. Depressed mood after binge
5. Not due to anorexia or any physical disorder

Typical features

- adolescent and young adult females
- up to 1% incidence among 16 year old schoolgirls[9]
- bimodal age of onset: 13 to 14 and 17 to 18 years[8]
- unknown cause
- severe emaciation
- amenorrhoea
- loss of body fat, dry and scaly skin
- increased lanugo body hair

Bulimia

Bulimia is episodic secretive binge eating followed by self-induced vomiting, fasting or the use of laxatives or diuretics. This binge–purge syndrome is also referred to as bulimarexia. It is more difficult to detect than anorexia nervosa but has a higher incidence.

Typical clinical features

- young females
- begins at later age, usually 17–25 years
- associated psychoneurotic disorders
- fluctuations in body weight
- periods irregular—amenorrhoea rare
- physical complications of frequent vomiting, e.g. dental decay, effects of hypokalaemia

Management of eating disorders

Treatment can be conducted on an outpatient basis but if there are marked trends such as severe weight loss, a family crisis, severe depression and a suicide risk the patient requires hospital admission. There are often problematic family interrelationships which require exploration.

Important goals are:

- establish a good and caring relationship with the patient
- resolve underlying psychological difficulties
- restore weight to a level between ideal and the patient's concept of optimal weight
- provide a balanced diet of at least 3000 calories per day (anorexia nervosa)

Structured behavioural therapy, intensive psychotherapy and family therapy may be tried but supportive care by physicians and allied health staff appears to be the most important feature of therapy.[10] Antidepressants may be helpful for selective patients. It is important to provide ongoing support for both patient and family.

Weight loss in the elderly

General weight loss is a relatively common physiological feature of many elderly people. However, abnormal weight loss is commonly encountered in the socially disadvantaged elderly, especially those who live alone and tend to have a lack of drive and interest in adequate food preparation. Other factors include relative poverty and poor dentition, including ill-fitting and painful false teeth. An important cause that should always be considered is malignant disease.

Congestive cardiac failure, especially secondary to ischaemic heart disease, is a common cause of weight loss. This is due to visceral congestion.

Gastrointestinal causes of weight loss

The following conditions may lead to weight loss:

- poor oral hygiene
- chronic vomiting or diarrhoea, e.g. pyloric stenosis
- gastric ulcer
- carcinoma of the stomach, oesophagus, large bowel
- problem alcohol drinking
- partial or total gastrectomy
- other GIT surgery
- inflammatory bowel disease, e.g. Crohn's disease, ulcerative colitis

- steatorrhoea
- lymphoma of the gut
- parasitic infestation
- cirrhosis of the liver

The mechanisms of weight loss include anorexia, malabsorption, obstruction with vomiting and inflammation.

When to refer

- Any unexplained weight loss, especially if an endocrine cause or malignancy is suspected.
- Weight loss related to a serious psychological illness.
- A serious eating disorder.
- Failure to thrive in a child where a normal variant or simple mismanagement is excluded.

Practice tips

- Ask patients what they really believe is the cause of their weight loss.
- An anxiety state and hyperthyroidism can be difficult to differentiate. Consider the latter and perform thyroid function tests.
- Laboratory tests are rarely needed to establish the diagnosis of an eating disorder. Hormonal levels return to normal following weight gain.
- A high index of suspicion by the family doctor is required to diagnose eating disorders. Think of it in a mid-teen female; weight loss through dieting; wide fluctuation in weight; amenorrhoea and hyperactivity.

References

1. Cormack J, Marinker M, Morrell D. *Practice: A handbook of primary health care*. London: Kluwer-Harrap Handbooks, 1980; 3.42:1–2.
2. Beck ER, Francis JL, Souhami RL. *Tutorials in differential diagnosis* (2nd edition). Edinburgh: Churchill Livingstone, 1988, 117–120.
3. Caswell A, Hutchins P. How to treat failure to thrive. Aust Dr Weekly, 13 April 1990, I–VIII.
4. Martin HP. *The abused child*. Cambridge, Mass: Ballinger, 1976.
5. Cormack J, Marinker M, Morrell D. *Practice: A handbook of primary health care*. London: Kluwer-Harrap Handbooks, 1980; 3.70A:1–8.
6. Tunnessen WW. *Symptoms and signs in paediatrics* (2nd edition). Philadelphia: Lippincott, 1988, 25–28.
7. Robinson MJ. *Practical paediatrics*. Melbourne: Churchill Livingstone, 1990, 140–144.
8. Young D. Eating disorders in the adolescent. Aust Fam Physician, 1988; 17:334–336.
9. Crisp AH, Palmer RL, Kalucy RS. How common is anorexia nervosa? A prevalence study. Br J Psychiatry, 1976; 128, 549–554.
10. Schroeder SA et al. *Current medical diagnosis and treatment*. East Norwalk: Appleton and Lange, 1990, 876-877.

PART 4

CHILD AND ADOLESCENT HEALTH

66

An approach to the child

The diagnostic approach to the child is based on the ability to achieve good lines of communication with both the child and the parent. In the diagnostic approach the relative importance of the various components are clinical history 80%, physical examination 15%, special investigations 5%.[1]

The establishment of rapport can be achieved by showing a genuine interest in the child with strategies such as:

- asking them what they like to be called
- passing a compliment about the child such as a clothing item or a toy or book they are carrying
- taking time to converse with them
- asking them if they would like to be a doctor when they grow up
- asking about their teacher or friends

This process will help set the scene for easier history taking and a sound physical examination.

Children's general behaviour patterns and personality can be classified into broad identifiable categories according to age group. Although there is considerable variation and generalisations can be inappropriate, the following stereotypes are helpful guidelines for parents.

- terrible 2's — mischievous, explorative, dangerous activity, conflicts
- trusting 3's — friendly, amenable to reason, loving
- frustrating 4's — cheeky, inquisitive, hard to reason, no social graces
- fascinating 5's — more co-ordinated and independent
- sociable 6's — enjoys tasks for temporary interests, loves to be wooed
- problematic 7's — tendency to wrongdoing, stubborn, searching for independence
- steady 8's
- noisy and adventurous 9's

History

Obtaining information in the following sequence is recommended:

- presenting problem (focus on this first)
  - allow the parents to elaborate without interruption
  - be a listener and believe the story
- state of health prior to the present complaint
- past history
  - general features
  - pregnancy and neonatal features
  - feeding and diet
  - immunisation
  - toilet training
- family history
  - inherited disorders
  - other

- systems review
  - general features, e.g. fever, energy
  - feeding and elimination
  - hearing
  - vision
- developmental history
  - check list of milestones (Table 66.1)
- social history
- psychological history
  - behavioural problems
  - reaction to other people and situations

Parent-child interaction

It is advisable to observe carefully the parent–child interaction at all times, including in the waiting room. The parent's manner in talking to and handling the child will provide useful clues about possible problems related to the parent's ability to nurture the child adequately.

Physical examination

It is convenient to consider the physical examination for two main groups:[1]

- the infant and child up to the age of 3 years
- the child from 3 years onwards

An important aspect of assessment is to note the development of the child by comparing its growth with standard developmental charts (Appendices I to IV). Developmental milestones are summarised in Table 66.1[2] and the incidence of developmental problems under 5 years in Table 66.2[3]. The examination includes attention to any unusual appearance, which is the beginning of the process of diagnosis of the dysmorphic child.

Table 66.1 *Developmental milestones (m=months) (after Jarman and Oberklaid[2])*

Gross motor	*Expressive language*
Chin up (1 m)	Coos (3 m)
Lifts head (4 m)	Babbles (6 m)
Rolls—prone to supine (4 m)	Da-Da—inappropriate (8 m)
Rolls—supine to prone (5 m)	Da/Ma—appropriate (10 m)
Sits unsupported (8 m)	First word (11 m)
Pulls to stand (9 m)	Two to six words (15 m)
Cruises (10 m)	Two-word phrases (21 m)
Walks alone (13 m)	Speech all understandable (27 m)
Walks up stairs (20 m)	Names one colour (30 m)
Kicks ball forward (24 m)	Uses plurals (36 m)
Walks up stairs—alt. fet (30 m)	Names four colours (42 m)
Rides tricycle (36 m)	Gives first and last names (44 m)
Two-wheeler bike (36 m)	Names two opposites (50 m)
Hops on one foot (60 m)	Strings sentences together (60 m)
Fine motor	***Receptive language***
Unfisting (3 m)	Gesture games (9 m)
Reach and grasp (5 m)	Understands 'no' (9 m)
Transfer (6 m)	Follows one-step command (12 m)
Thumb-finger grasp (9 m)	Points to animal pictures (19 m)
Tower of 2 cubes (16 m)	Points to 6 body parts (20 m)
Handedness (24 m)	Follows two-step command (24 m)
Scribbles (24 m)	
Tower of 4 cubes (26 m)	
Tower of 8 cubes (40 m)	
Social/self help	***Cognitive***
Social smile (6 weeks)	Shows anticipatory excitement (3 m)
Recognises mother (3 m)	Plays with rattle (4 m)
Stranger anxiety (9 m)	Plays peek-a-boo (8 m)
Finger feeds (10 m)	Finds hidden object (9 m)
Uses spoon (15 m)	Pulls string to obtain toy (14 m)
Uses fork (21 m)	Activates mechanical toy (20 m)
Assists with dressing (12 m)	Pretend play (24 m)
Pulls off socks (15 m)	Seeks out other for play (36 m)
Unbuttons (30 m)	
Buttons (48 m)	
Ties shoelaces (60 m)	
Dresses without supervision (60 m)	

Table 66.2 *Incidence of developmental problems under 5 years (after Hutchins)*

More common, less severe	***Less common, more severe***
10–20% behaviour problems	3.0% intellectual handicap (IQ < 70)
10% specific learning deficits	1% intellectual handicap (IQ < 50)
10% conductive hearing loss	0.3% cerebral palsy
10% eye problems, e.g. squint	0.2% neural tube defects
5% isolated speech problems	0.17% severe deafness
3% attention deficit disorder	0.06% blind
1% specific language disorder, e.g. comprehension	0.1% autistic spectrum features 0.05% classical autism

Achieving co-operation of infants

Children, especially if sick and irritable, can be very difficult to examine and may be most unco-operative, particularly if distressed by past experience. However, they can be readily distracted, a characteristic that the family doctor can use effectively to achieve some degree of co-operation for examination, especially for the ears, throat and chest.

Children respond very positively to playing games such as a flashing light, tickling or peek-a-boo, and to any type of noise, particularly animal noises, and good humour from a friendly patient practitioner. Some doctors have strategies such as small animal images on stethoscopes to distract attention.

Distracting children[4]

In the consulting room, a small duck with a rattle inside it can be used for palpating the abdomen of young children. This seems more acceptable to them, as it becomes a game and you obtain the same information as if you had palpated with your hand. When examining the ears of young children sitting on their mother's lap, difficulty is encountered when the child follows the auroscope light and moves its head. A small rabbit or other animal on the desk which, at the press of a button under the desk, will play a drum, distracts the child to the right and enables you to get a good look into the left ear.

Similarly, a clockwork revolving musical toy over the examination couch will distract the child for examination of the ear. It is also a distraction for the general examination of children on the couch, and can become a most useful instrument.

Spatula sketches for children[5]

Many young patients have quickly forgotten any inspection of their throats while observing the preparation of a 'present' in the form of a drawing on the wooden spatula used for the examination.

After the examination they are informed of their special present, and you can then proceed to draw on the unused end of the spatula. The drawings take about 15 seconds. Figure 66.1 illustrates three sketches from one repertoire: a penguin (with optional bow tie), a caterpillar, and a racing car.

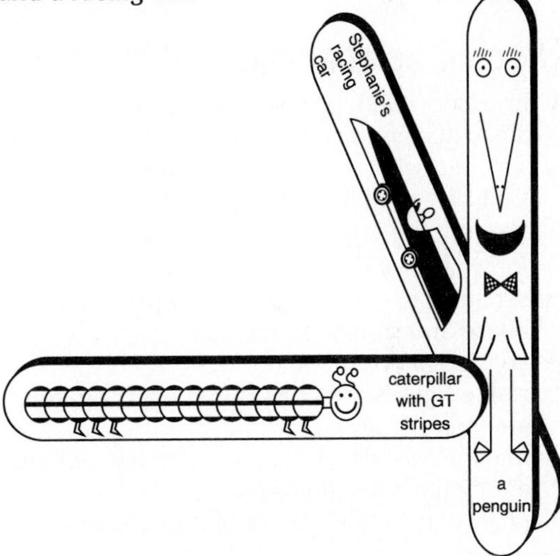

Fig. 66.1 *Spatula sketches for children*

Recognition of serious illness in infancy

It is vital to diagnose serious life-threatening disease in children, especially in early infancy. Certain symptoms and signs which provide a reliable indicator to such a problem are:[6]

- drowsiness
- decreased activity (lies quietly)
- child moves eyes (rather than head) to follow you
- pallor

- whimpers and lies quietly (as opposed to crying lustily)
- reduced feeding (<50% normal intake—over 24 hour period)
- less than four wet nappies in 24 hours
- chest wall retraction

Serious illnesses to consider include:

- haemophilus influenza type B (HiB) infection
  - — acute epiglottitis
  - — meningitis
  - — pneumonia
  - — septicaemia
  - — septic arthritis/osteomyelitis
- meningococcal infection
  - — septicaemia
  - — meningitis
- other forms of meningitis
- acute myocarditis
- asthma/bronchitis
- intussusception

The child as a barometer of the family

A disturbed child is a very common indicator of family disharmony. There is a saying that 'love is to a child what sunlight is to a flower'.

Children need from their parents:[7]

- affection (acceptance for what they are, not for what they might have been)
- security (freedom from fighting parents, child abuse and sibling problems)
- consistent discipline
- stable figures to act as role models (parents are their heroes)
- freedom to develop a personality without emotional entanglements
- play (a need to be active and creative)
- honesty

Parents with their own problems and conflicts will have difficulty meeting the needs of their children. Family tensions, financial problems, marital disharmony, separation and divorce have a major effect on children. Parent frustration may eventuate in child abuse. Depressive illness in a parent can have a profound effect on the child.

The child's reaction to the family disharmony may manifest in three ways (with significant overlap):[7]

- behavioural problems
- psychosomatic symptoms
- school difficulties

The importance of the family doctor

The family doctor is in an important position to detect disharmony in the family through presenting problems that give subtle clues; for example, several uncharacteristic visits from parent and child, inappropriate non-verbal behaviour such as a trembling hand or voice, or somatic symptoms incompatible with physical findings.

It is important to consider the environment of the disturbed child. Search for a possible source of disturbances at home such as parental quarrelling, economic hardship, drug abuse including alcohol, physical or sexual abuse and maternal depression. If detected and addressed, the family dysfunction may be resolved satisfactorily.

Personal health record

Many family practices issue a personal health record to the child's parents as a means of improving health care delivery, including the enhancement of preventive care. The personal health record (PHR), also referred to as the 'parent-held health record' or 'health passport', is distributed in several states and research has shown it to be well received by both health practitioners and parents.[8]

The PHR is a small, loose-leaf booklet with a sturdy plastic cover which can be easily carried around by the parent. The contents can vary from one producer to another but generally it contains:

- records of birth details and newborn examination
- percentile charts for weight gain
- visual check
- hearing check
- developmental check
- immunisation schedules and recordings (Table 66.3)
- progress notes
- advice on accident prevention (Table 66.4)
- other health educational material

The PHR provides a very practical method of promoting communication between various health professionals involved in the child's care and also between the family and their doctor. It promotes the concept of 'self-care' by encouraging a sense of responsibility by parents for the child's health and is also a medium for enhancing preventive care, especially with immunisation, hearing tests and development.[8]

Table 66.3 *Typical page in the personal health record*

IMMUNISATION RECORD—to be completed by doctor/nurse giving immunisation

Age	*Immunisations*	*Date given*	*Batch no.*	*Date next dose*	*Signature/stamp/notes*
2 months	DTP (triple antigen) SABIN (polio) Haemophilus				
4 months	DTP (triple antigen) SABIN (polio) Haemophilus				
6 months	DTP (triple antigen) SABIN (polio) Haemophilus				
12 months	Measles Mumps Rubella				
18 months	DTP (triple antigen) Haemophilus				
Preschool or school (5 years)	CDT (combined diphtheria and tetanus) SABIN (polio)				
12 years	Measles Rubella (girls only) Mumps				
15 years or school leaving	ADT (adult diphtheria and tetanus)				

Boosters of tetanus, toxoid and diphtheria are required every 10 years.
Ask about hepatitis immunisation.

Table 66.4 *Accidents don't have to happen*

Six to eighteen months

- Have cupboards made child-resistant for the storage of medicinals and household chemicals. Pesticides and petroleum products should be locked away in the shed. Don't store in ordinary food and drink containers.
- Fires and radiators should be adequately guarded.
- Cords on electrical food and drink heaters need to be shortened or hooked up out of a toddler's reach. Do not use tablecloths. Put hot food and drinks into the centre of the table. Take care with buckets of hot water.
- Fit dummy plugs in unused power points.
- From 9 kg (20 lb) body weight, baby's car rides should be in an ASA approved child seat.
- Supervise your toddler at all times in or near water. The swimming pool needs to be adequately fenced.
- Keep matches in the child-resistant cupboard in the kitchen. Put scissors, needles and pins well out of reach.
- Have the play yard safely fenced from the street.
- Parents: Walk right round the car before reversing down the drive, or place your child in the car first.
- Do not allow your small child to be unsupervised in the bathroom.
- Never give the child nuts to eat because it cannot chew them properly. Peanuts present a particular hazard because of their shape and hardness. They can cause the child to choke.

References

1. Robinson M.J. Practical paediatrics (2nd edition). Melbourne: Churchill Livingstone, 1990, 61–70
2. Jarman FC, Oberklaid F. The detection of developmental problems in children. Aust Fam Physician, 1992; 21: 1079–1088
3. Hutchins P. The young child with developmental problems. Australian Dr Weekly: How to treat series, 20 July 1990, i–viii.
4. Trollor J. Distracting Children. Aust Fam Physician, 1987; 16: 1372.
5. Malcher G. Spatula sketches for children. Aust Fam Physician, 1990; 19: 1441.
6. Hewson P. Recognition of serious illness in early infancy. The Australian Paediatric Review, 1992, No.2: 6: 1.
7. Connell HM. The child as a barometer of the family. Aust Fam Physician, 1980; 9: 759–763.
8. Jeffs D, Harris M. The personal health record—making it work better for general practitioners. Aust Fam Physician, 1993; 22:1417–1427.

67

Common childhood infectious diseases (including skin eruptions)

Children are subject to a variety of infectious diseases which mainly cause acute skin eruptions. Fortunately many of these diseases, such as scarlet fever, measles and rubella, are being seen less frequently by the family doctor.

Reye syndrome and aspirin

The concern about the ingestion of aspirin for febrile illness in children is the suspected causal relationship between it and Reye syndrome, particularly in children with varicella and influenza infections. However, there is some controversy about the connection. Orlowski and colleagues at the Children's Hospital in Sydney found no association between aspirin use and Reye syndrome from 1973–1985.[1] It is possible that the connection is coincidental or at least confounded with some other factors.

Despite these doubts, aspirin should not be recommended for the treatment of fever in young children in view of our knowledge of the beneficial effects of fever on the immune response and the availability of a safe alternative antipyretic such as paracetamol.

Reye syndrome

Clinical features:

- A rare complication of influenza, chickenpox and other viral diseases, e.g. Coxsackie virus
- Rapid development of:
  - encephalopathy
  - hepatic failure
  - hypoglycaemia

  } seizures and coma
- 30% fatality rate and significant morbidity
- treatment is supportive and directed at cerebral oedema

Varicella (chickenpox)

Varicella, a common and highly infectious disease, affects people mainly during childhood, especially between 2 and 8 years, but no age is exempt. The characteristic crops of small vesicles have a central distribution (face, scalp and trunk). It is caused by the varicella zoster virus, one of the human herpes viruses, which remains latent after infection. Clinical reactivation later in life results in herpes zoster.

Epidemiology

Varicella has a world-wide distribution, causing endemic (occasionally epidemic) disease, with little clear evidence of seasonal incidence in temperate climates. About 75% of people in urban communities have had the infection by 15 years of age and at least 90% by young adulthood.

It is one of the most easily transmitted viruses, probably by airborne spread, usually via a person with chickenpox (occasionally with herpes zoster). Varicella is contagious only while the patient has symptoms and vesicles remain; drying of the vesicles indicates that infectivity has stopped. The scabs are not infectious.

The incubation period is 10–21 days (usually 15–18).

Clinical features

The clinical features of varicella are shown in Table 67.1 and the complications in Table 67.2. Children are not normally very sick but tend to be lethargic and have a mild fever. Adults have an influenza-like illness. The typical distribution is shown in Figure 67.1.

Table 67.1 *Clinical features in varicella*

Onset
- Children: no prodrome
- Adults: prodrome (myalgia, fever, headaches) for 2–3 days

Rash
- Centripetal distribution, including oral mucosa
- Scalp lesions can become infected
- 'Cropping' phenomenon: vesicles, papules, crusting lesions present together
- Pruritic

Degrees of severity
- Number of vesicles can vary from fewer than ten to thousands
- Mild cases can be missed
- More severe in adults, especially the immunocompromised
- Viral pneumonia rare in children, uncommon in adults
- Death rare except in the immunocompromised and neonates with congenital varicella

Table 67.2 *Complications of varicella*

Common
- Bacterial infection of cutaneous lesions (usually staphylococcal or streptococcal); can take form of cellulitis or bullous impetigo
- Can leave pitted scars

Uncommon
- Viral pneumonia
- Thrombocytopenia
- Acute cerebellitis (ataxia, normal mental state)

Rare
- Meningoencephalitis
- Purpura fulminans

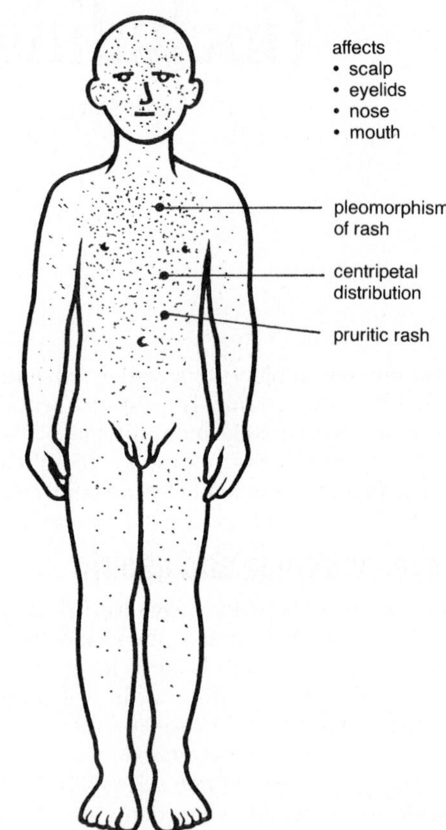

Fig. 67.1 *Chickenpox: typical distribution*

Treatment

Treatment is symptomatic and usually no specific therapy is required. Many people worry about scarring but the lesions invariably heal, leaving normal skin, unless they become infected.

Advice to parents

- The patient should rest until feeling well.
- Give paracetamol for the fever (avoid aspirin).
- Daub calamine or a similar soothing lotion to relieve itching, although the itch is usually not severe.
- Avoid scratching; clean and cut the fingernails of children short. Provide cotton mittens if necessary.
- Keep the diet simple. Drink ample fluids, including orange juice and lemonade.

- Daily bathing is advisable, with the addition of mild antiseptic or sodium bicarbonate if pruritic (half a cup to the bath water). Pat dry with a clean, soft towel; do not rub.

Antihistamines can be prescribed for itching. Acyclovir can be life-saving in the immunocompromised host.

Exclusion from school

Exclusion is recommended until full recovery, usually for seven days. A few remaining scabs are not an indication to continue exclusion. Contacts should not be withdrawn from school.

Prevention

Prevention in contacts who are immunocompromised is possible with zoster immune globulin. An attenuated live virus vaccine is available in some countries.

Measles

Measles (rubeola) is a highly contagious disease caused by an RNA paramyxovirus. It presents as an acute febrile exanthematous illness with characteristic lesions on the buccal mucosa called Koplik's spots (tiny white spots like grains of salt).

The disease is endemic throughout the world and complications are usually respiratory in nature. It is now uncommon in Australia, mainly because of the introduction of an effective vaccine. If an acute exanthematous illness is not accompanied by a dry cough and red eyes, it is unlikely to be measles.

Epidemiology

Measles is transmitted by patient to patient contact through oropharyngeal and nasopharyngeal droplets expelled during coughing and sneezing.

The incubation period is 10–14 days and the patient is infectious for about five days, but especially just before the appearance of the rash. Morbidity and mortality are high in countries with substandard living conditions and poor nutrition.

Immunity appears to be lifelong after infection. Measles, like smallpox, could be eradicated with public health measures.

Clinical features

The clinical presentation can be considered in three stages.

1. *Prodromal stage* This usually lasts three to four days. It is marked by fever, malaise, anorexia, diarrhoea, and 'the three Cs': cough, coryza and conjunctivitis. Sometimes a non-specific rash appears a day before the Koplik's spots (opposite the molars).
2. *Exanthema (rash) stage* Identified by a typically blotchy, bright red maculopapular eruption; this stage lasts four to five days. The rash begins behind the ears and on the first day spreads to the face, the next day to the trunk and later to the limbs. It may become confluent and blanches under pressure. The patient's fever usually subsides within five days of the onset of the rash (Fig. 67.2).

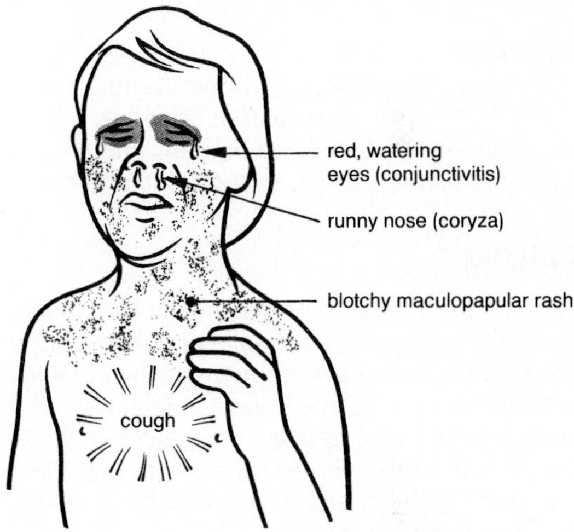

Fig. 67.2 *Measles: typical symptoms. Note the 3C's: cough, coryza, conjunctivitis*

3. *Convalescent stage* The rash fades, leaving a temporary brownish 'staining'. The patient's cough may persist for days, but usually good health and appetite return quickly.

Complications

Respiratory

The patient could develop secondary bacterial otitis media or sinusitis. If pneumonia develops it is more likely to be bacterial superinfection than viral. Laryngotracheobronchitis (croup) is a common complication of measles.

Central nervous system

Encephalitis has an incidence of one in 1500 and although the mortality rate is low there is significant CNS morbidity. Febrile convulsions are another common complication.

Late complications

Two rare complications are bronchiectasis and subacute sclerosing panencephalitis.

Treatment

There is no specific treatment although some symptoms can be relieved, e.g. a linctus for the cough, paracetamol for fever. The patient should rest quietly, avoid bright lights and stay in bed until the fever subsides.

The management of complications is determined by their nature and severity. Children should be kept away from school until they have recovered or for at least seven days from the onset of the rash.

Prevention

Vaccination programs have been most successful. Live attenuated measles virus vaccinations combined with mumps and rubella are recommended at the age of 12–15 months.

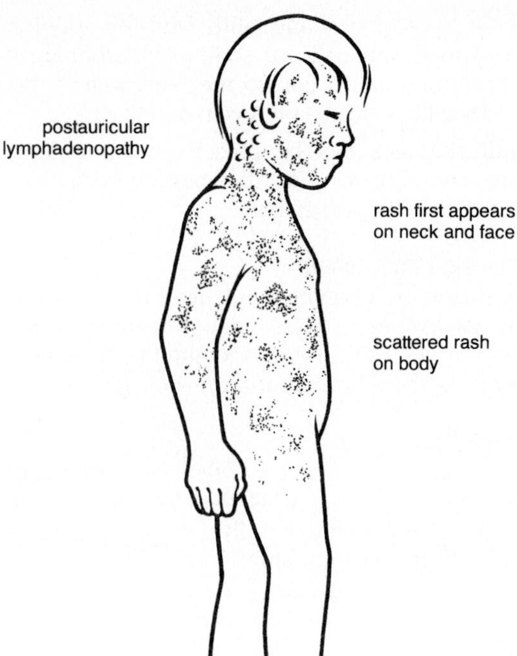

Fig. 67.3 *Rubella: typical symptoms*

Rubella

Rubella (German measles) is a viral exanthema caused by a togavirus. Because of immunisation programs it is seen less frequently now in family practice. It is a minor illness in children and adults, but devastating when transmitted *in utero*. Congenital rubella is still the most important cause of blindness and deafness in the neonate. It is completely preventable.

Epidemiology

Rubella has been reported from virtually every country and is endemic in heavily populated communities. Epidemics occur every six to nine years in non-immunised populations, the disease being spread by droplets from the nose and throat. It is not as communicable as varicella and measles. Intrauterine infection occurs via the placenta.

Approximately one-third of infections are asymptomatic. Infection usually confers lifelong immunity. Infection is proved either by virus culture or by specific serology. Incubation period: 14 to 21 days.

Clinical features

The clinical features of rubella are presented in Table 67.3 and Figure 67.3 and the complications in Table 67.4.

Congenital rubella

Infection of the mother in the first trimester can lead to abortion or stillbirth; foetal malformation such as the classic triad: deafness, blindness (cataract or glaucoma) and congenital heart disease. It can also produce lesions (such as microcephaly), mental retardation, retarded growth, thrombocytopenic purpura (with a 30% mortality rate), jaundice/hepatosplenomegaly and bone abnormalities.

Rubella in pregnancy

Ideally all women of child-bearing age should know their rubella immune status by having serology performed. A history of immunisation is not good enough evidence of immunity. However in Victoria, Australia, almost 95% of women aged 15–40 are immune.

If the immune status is not known, then serology testing should be ordered at the first antenatal visit. Rubella vaccine, while not shown to be embryopathic, should not be given during pregnancy. If maternal rubella antibodies are in adequate titre, there is no risk to the foetus from rubella infection.

Treatment

Treatment is symptomatic, especially as rubella is a mild disease. Patients should rest quietly

Table 67.3 *Clinical features of rubella*

- There is no prodrome
- A generalised, maculopapular rash, sometimes pruritic, may be the only evidence of infection
- Other symptoms are usually mild and short-lived
- There is often a reddened pharynx but sore throats are unusual. An exudate may be seen as well as palatal exanthem
- Fever is usually absent or low-grade
- Other features: headache, myalgia, conjunctivitis and polyarthritis (small joints)
- Lymphadenopathy may be noted; usually postauricular, suboccipital and postcervical
- The patient is infectious for up to 10 days from onset of rash (this aspect is often not appreciated as the patient is asymptomatic by that time)

The rash

- A discrete pale pink maculopapular rash (not confluent as in measles)
- Starts on the face and neck—spreads to the trunk and extremities
- Variable severity: may be absent in subclinical infection
- Exaggerated on skin exposed to sun
- Brief duration—usually fades on the third day
- No staining or desquamation

Table 67.4 *Complications of rubella*

- Encephalitis (one in 5000)
- Polyarthritis, especially in adult women (this complication abates spontaneously)
- Thrombocytopenia with bleeding (one in 3000)
- Congenital rubella

until they feel well and take paracetamol for fever and aching joints.

School exclusion

The child is usually excluded until fully recovered or for at least four days from the onset of the rash.

Viral exanthema (fourth disease)

This mild childhood infection may be caused by a number of viruses, especially the enteroviruses, and produces a rubella-like rash which may be misdiagnosed as rubella. The rash, which is usually non-pruritic and mainly confined to the trunk, does not desquamate and often fades within 48 hours. The child may appear quite well or can have mild constitutional symptoms including diarrhoea.

Erythema infectiosum (fifth disease)

Erythema infectiosum, also known as 'slapped face' syndrome or fifth disease, is a childhood exanthem caused by a parvovirus. It occurs typically in young school-aged children. The bright macular rash erupts on the face first then, after a day or so, a maculopapular rash appears on the limbs.[2] The rash lasts for only a few days but may recur for several weeks.

Clinical features

- mild fever and malaise
- lymphadenopathy (especially cervical)

The rash (Fig. 67.4):

- bright red flushed cheeks with circumoral pallor
- maculopapular rash on limbs (especially) and trunk (sparse)
- reticular appearance on fading

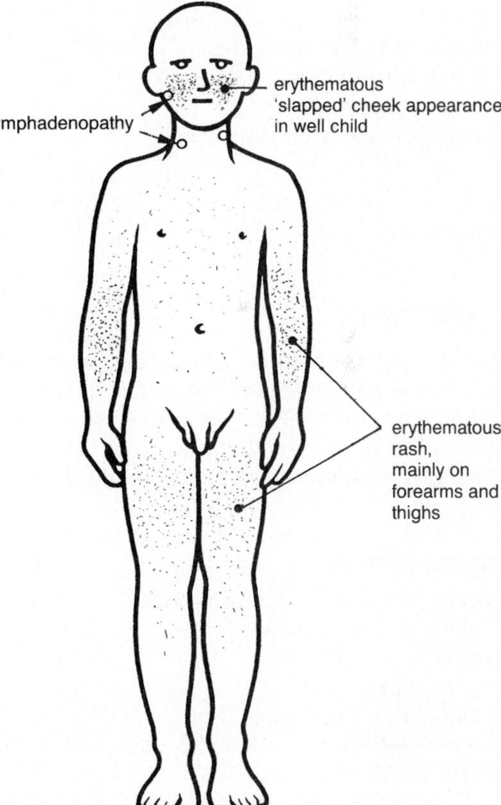

Fig. 67.4 *Erythema infectiosum: typical distribution of rash*

Erythema infectiosum is a mild illness but, if the parvovirus infection occurs during pregnancy, foetal complications including death *in utero* can occur.[3]

Roseola infantum (exanthema subitum or sixth disease)

Roseola infantum is a viral infection of infancy, affecting children at the age of 6–18 months and is rare after this time. Constitutional symptoms are generally mild.

Clinical features

- high fever (up to 40°)
- runny nose
- temperature falls after three days (or so)

then

- red macular or maculopapular rash appears

The rash:

- largely confined to trunk
- usually spares face and limbs
- appears as fever subsides
- disappears within two days
- no desquamation
- mild cervical lymphadenopathy

The infection runs a benign course, although a febrile convulsion can occur. Treatment is symptomatic.

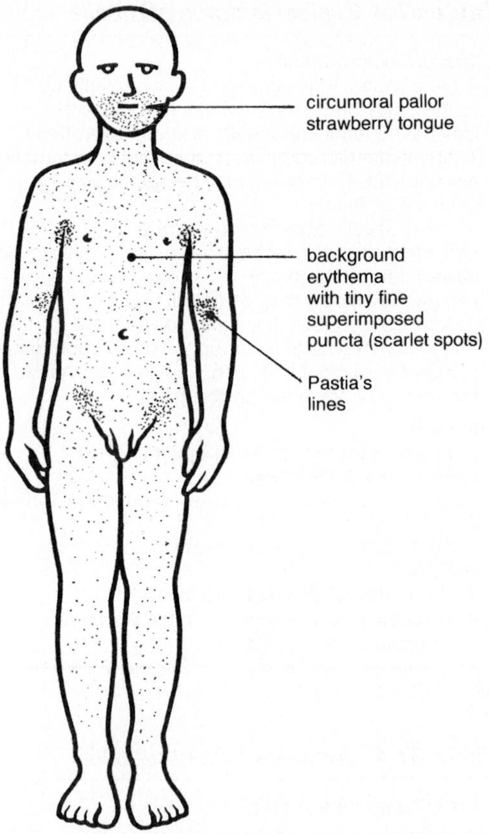

Fig. 67.5 *Scarlet fever: typical presentation of rash*

Scarlet fever

Scarlet fever results when a Group A *Streptococcus pyogenes* organism produces erythrogenic toxin. The prodromal symptoms prior to the acute exanthem is about two days of malaise, sore throat, fever (may be rigors) and vomiting.

Features of the rash

- appears on second day of illness
- first appears on neck
- rapidly generalised
- punctuate and red
- blanches on pressure
- prominent on neck, in axilla, groin, skinfolds (Fig. 67.5)
- absent or sparse on face, palms and soles
- circumoral pallor
- feels like fine sandpaper
- lasts about five days
- fine desquamation

Treatment

Phenoxymethylpenicillin (dose according to age) with rapid resolution of symptoms.

Kawasaki's disease (mucocutaneous lymph node syndrome)

This is an uncommon acute multisystemic disorder in children, characterised by an acute onset of fever of five days or more and accompanied by the following features:

- bilateral conjunctivitis
- maculopapular polymorphous rash
- ± cervical lymphadenopathy
- dryness, redness and cracking of the lips
- erythema of the oral cavity
- erythema of palms and soles with induration and oedema
- desquamation of fingertips (a characteristic)

The disease is generally benign and self-limiting but it is important to make an early diagnosis because early treatment may prevent complications. The major complication is vasculitis, which causes coronary aneurysms in 17–31% of cases, with an overall case fatality rate of 0.5–2.8%[4] due to the aneurysm that usually develops between the second week and the second month of the illness. Early treatment with immunoglobulin and aspirin has been shown to be effective in reducing the prevalence of coronary artery abnormalities. Echocardiography is indicated to detect these aneurysms and determine prognosis.

Mumps (epidemic parotitis)

Mumps is an acute infectious disease caused by a paramyxovirus, with an affinity for the salivary glands and meninges. Although it most often affects children (90% present before adolescence), no one is exempt.[3]

Mumps has a world-wide prevalence. Most adults have antibodies to it, whether or not they have had the clinical infection. Because the antibody crosses the placenta in pregnancy, the infant will be immune for the first 6–9 months of life. One episode of the illness is sufficient to confer permanent immunity.

The patient is most infective during the prodrome, less so by the time the parotid glands are enlarged. Spread of infection is by aerosol droplets from the saliva and nasopharynx and can be rapid in school classrooms and throughout a household.

Mumps in a woman in early pregnancy occasionally causes abortion or foetal abnormalities.

General course and symptoms

The incubation period is two to three weeks.

The patient might be free of symptoms but a high fever, headache and malaise, for 5–7 days (occasionally 2–3 weeks), is usual. Involvement of the salivary glands is common. Dry mouth and discomfort on eating or opening the mouth occur.

Major manifestations

Unilateral or bilateral inflammation of the parotid gland is usual: one parotid gland swells first and in 70% of cases the opposite side swells after one or two days. The submandibular and sublingual glands are less commonly involved. Six per cent of patients will have presternal oedema resembling cellulitis of the neck.

Complications

The complications are summarised in Table 67.5.

Table 67.5 *Complications of mumps*

Common
- Orchitis
- Aseptic meningitis (benign)
- Abdominal pain (transient)

Rare
- Oöphoritis
- Encephalitis
- Arthritis (one or several joints)
- Deafness (usually transient)
- Pancreatitis

Orchitis, usually unilateral, occurs in 25% of postpubertal males, developing 3–4 days after parotitis. Subsequent sterility is rare, even if both testes are affected.

Aseptic meningitis is common but benign.

Many patients suffer transient abdominal pain and vomiting: severe pancreatitis is a rare complication.

Clinical diagnosis

Enlargement of the cervical lymph glands can be mistaken for parotitis but the correct diagnosis is indicated by the anatomy of this area. Lymph nodes are posteroinferior to the ear lobe; the parotid gland is anterior and, when enlarged, obscures the angle of the mandible.

Bacterial (suppurative) parotitis is associated with toxaemia and results in a high leucocyte count. The skin over the parotid gland is tense and shiny and Stensen's duct might discharge pus.

Rare disorders such as Sjögren's syndrome can be misdiagnosed as mumps.

Virological diagnosis

The diagnosis of mumps is usually clinical; virological confirmation is rarely required but the virus can be isolated from the nasopharynx or saliva during the acute illness (and from cerebrospinal fluid in mumps meningitis).

A serological test for antibodies is available.

Management

Treatment is symptomatic. Paracetamol may be prescribed for fever, meningitis and orchitis.

Ample fluid intake and a bland diet is advisable. Bed rest should be taken only according to the symptoms: it does not seem to have an influence on the development of complications.[3]

Children should not return to school until the symptoms subside but contacts need not be excluded.

The patient with orchitis should use supportive underwear. Steroids may be prescribed to relieve severe pain but will have no other effect; nor will they reduce the risk of testicular atrophy.

Prevention

Isolation is generally ineffective. The best protection is immunisation of all children, between 12 and 18 months of age, with live attenuated vaccine combined with measles and rubella.

Epstein-Barr mononucleosis

Although glandular fever is more common in adolescents and young adults, it can occur in young children but is often asymptomatic or atypical. The differential diagnosis includes cytomegalovirus infection and acute lymphatic leukaemia. Diagnosis is confirmed by the Paul-Bunnell test or the Monospot test.

Pertussis

Pertussis (whooping cough) is a respiratory infection caused by *Bordetella pertussis* and occurs world-wide. The incidence of this infectious disease has diminished because of immunisation programs and improvements in standards of living, but the infection is still seen frequently, often modified by partial immunity.

Pertussis is predominantly an illness of infants under two years of age (up to 50% of all cases). Approximately 70% of unimmunised children will eventually develop pertussis, the majority by their fifth birthday.[3] However, no age is exempt. The source of infection is older children or young adults who have relatively mild disease.

The illness is characterised by three stages: catarrhal, paroxysmal and convalescent, with the person being most infectious during the catarrhal stage.

Clinical features

- Incubation period 7–14 days
- Catarrhal stage (7–14 days)
  - — anorexia
  - — rhinorrhoea
  - — conjunctivitis/lacrimation
  - — dry cough
- Paroxysmal stage (about 4 weeks)
  - — paroxysms of severe coughing with inspiratory 'whoop'
  - — vomiting (at end of coughing bout)
  - — coughing mainly at night
  - — lymphocytosis (almost absolute)
- Convalescent stage
  - — coughing (less severe)

Note: Physical findings are minimal or absent.

Diagnosis

The diagnosis is basically a clinical one—virtually no other acute infectious illness in children causes a cough that lasts 4–8 weeks.[3] Confirmed by culture.

Differential diagnosis

Viral pneumonia, acute bronchitis, influenza. Chlamydia respiratory infection can cause a 'pseudopertussis' type of illness in infants.

Complications

These include asphyxia, hypoxia, convulsions and cerebral haemorrhage. Also pulmonary complications, e.g. atelectasis, pneumonia, pneumothorax.

Treatment

Erythromycin estolate may help if given in the catarrahal stage. Cough mixtures are ineffective.[3] Good ventilation is important: avoid dust and smoke, and also emotional excitement and overfeeding during the paroxysmal phase.

Prevention

Active immunisation with pertussis vaccine.

Herpes simplex

Herpes simplex virus infection is common and widespread. Primary HSV infection is basically a disease of childhood, presenting as severe acute gingivostomatitis. However, the infection may be subclinical in children; based on antibody studies approximately 90% of the population acquire herpes simplex infection before the age of four or five years.[5]

The primary infection

Typical clinical features:

- children 1–3 years
- fever and refusal to feed
- ulcers on gums, tongue and palate
- prone to dehydration
- may be lesions on face and conjunctivae
- resolution over 7–10 days

These children are generally very miserable and ill, and some may require hospitalisation for intravenous therapy to correct fluid and electrolyte loss. Otherwise, treatment is symptomatic. Careful nursing and prevention of secondary infection is important. The latter includes gentle mouth toilets.

Serious complications:

- encephalitis can develop in otherwise healthy children
- eczema herpeticum—children with eczema can get widespread herpetic lesions
- disseminated HSV infection in neonates

Herpes zoster

Herpes zoster (shingles) is caused by reactivation of varicella zoster virus (acquired from the primary infection of chickenpox) in the dorsal root ganglion. It occurs at all ages and can occur in children, including infants, who have been exposed to varicella *in utero*.[3]

Recurrences are uncommon except in immunocompromised patients. The diagnosis is a clinical one but can pose difficulties, especially as it is not so common in childhood and may present with only a few vesicles.

Impetigo

Impetigo (school sores) is a contagious superficial bacterial skin infection caused by *Streptococcus pyogenes* or *Staphylococcus aureus* or a combination of these two virulent organisms.

There are two common forms:

1. vesiculopustular with honey-coloured crusts (either *Strep* or *Staph*)
2. bullous type, usually *Staph aureus*

   Ecthyma is a deeper form of impetigo, usually on the legs and other covered areas.

Treatment

If mild with small lesions and a limited area:

- Topical antiseptic cleansing with removal of crusts, using chlorhexadine or povidone-iodine or mupirocin (Bactroban). Topical antibiotics other than mupirocin are not recommended.[6]

If extensive and causing systemic symptoms:[6]

- Flucloxacillin 6.25–12.5 mg/kg up to adult dose (500 mg) (o) 6 hourly for 10 days

  or

- Erythromycin 10–20 mg/kg up to adult dose (500 mg) (o) 12 hourly for 10 days

Boils (furunculosis) and carbuncles (same treatment as impetigo).

Head lice

Head lice is an infestation caused by the louse *Pediculus humanus capitis*. The female louse lays eggs (or 'nits') which are glued to the hairs; they hatch within six days, mature into adults in about ten days and live for about a month. Head lice spread from person to person by direct contact, such as sitting and working very close to one another. They can also spread by the sharing of combs, brushes and headwear, especially within the family. Children are the ones usually affected, but people of all ages and from all walks of life can be infested. It is more common in overcrowded living conditions.

Clinical features

- asymptomatic or itching of scalp
- white spots of nits can be mistaken for dandruff
- unlike dandruff the nits cannot be brushed off
- diagnosis by finding lice or nits

Treatment

- maldison (malathion) 5% (kills both lice and eggs)

  or

- lindane 1%: kills lice but not eggs

Maldison is preferred; lotions are preferable to shampoos.

Method

Apply 20 ml of maldison to the dry hair. Leave 12 hours; wash and comb with a fine-tooth comb. Apply once a week for 2–3 weeks.

Note: The hair does not have to be cut short. All members of the family must be treated whether or not lice or nits can be found. There is no need to treat clothing, pillows or other items. School exclusion should not be necessary after proper treatment. For eyelash involvement apply petrolatum bd for eight days and then pluck off remaining nits.

References

1. Jarman R. A word about aspirin in children. Australian Paediatric Review, 1991;1:6:2.
2. Mansfield F. Erythema infectiosum. Slapped face disease. Aust Fam Physician, 1988;17:737:738.
3. Robinson MJ. *Practical paediatrics* (2nd edition). Melbourne: Churchill Livingstone, 1990, 217–227.
4. Wilson JD et al. *Harrison's principles of internal medicine* (12th edition). New York: McGraw-Hill, 1991, 1462–1463.
5. Schroeder et al. *Current medical diagnosis and treatment.* East Norwalk: Appleton and Lange, 1990, 80.
6. Mashford ML. *Antibiotic guidelines* (7th edition). Melbourne: Victorian Medical Postgraduate Foundation, 1992/3, 121–122.

68

Behaviour disorders in children

—

The prevalence of significant psychiatric disorders in children in western society is at least 12% in the age range 1–14 years, with an increase of 3–4% after puberty.[1] Most of these disorders are behavioural but there is a significant incidence of emotional disorders such as anxiety and depression which tend to be misdiagnosed, as there is a perception that children do not suffer from these psychiatric disorders in the same way as adults.

The author has observed that most of the personality characteristics and behavioural problems of infancy tend to remain throughout childhood and adolescence and form the personality and behavioural disposition of the adult, although many associated problems do not tend to persist into adult life.

Parry, who describes the five phases of childhood development (Table 68.1), emphasises the importance of the first phase of infancy (where the infant is learning to trust the environment) as crucial to overall normal development.

The second phase, in which the child is developing independent skills in the second and third years of life, is also an important phase and needs to be based on a secure and smooth first phase. It is in this toddler stage that many of the behavioural disorders will be discussed.

Table 68.1 *The five phases of childhood development*

1. Infancy	sense of trust
2. Early childhood	sense of autonomy (independence)
3. Preschool	sense of initiative
4. School age	sense of industry
5. Adolescence	sense of identity

Temper tantrums

The tantrum is a feature of the 'terrible twos' toddler whose protestation to frustration is a dramatic reaction of kicking, shouting, screaming, throwing, or banging of the head. Tantrums are more likely to occur if the child is tired or bored. This behaviour may be perpetuated if the tantrums are inadvertently rewarded by the parents to seek peace and avoid conflict.

A careful history is required to gain insight into the family stresses; it also allows parents to ventilate their feelings.

Management

Reassure parents that the tantrums are relatively commonplace and not harmful. Explain the reasons for the tantrums and include the concept that 'temper tantrums need an audience'.

Advice[2]

- Ignore what is ignorable: parents should pretend to ignore the behaviour and leave the child alone without comment, including moving to a different area (but not locking the child in its room).
- Avoid what is avoidable: try to avoid the cause or causes of the tantrums, e.g. visiting the supermarket.
- Distract what is distractable: redirect the child's interest to some other object or activity.

Medication has no place in the management of temper tantrums.

Breath-holding attacks

The age group for the attack is six months to six years (peak 2–3 years). There are two distinct types—one occurring with a tantrum and the other a simple faint in response to pain or fright. The precipitating event can be of a minor emotional or physical nature. In the tantrum situation children will emit a loud cry, then hold their breath. They become pale, then cyanosed. If prolonged it may result in unconsciousness or a fit. The episode lasts 10–60 seconds.

Management

Reassure parents that the attacks are self-limiting and are not associated with epilepsy or mental retardation. Advise parents to maintain discipline and to resist spoiling the child. Try to avoid incidents known to frustrate the child or to precipitate a tantrum.

Conduct disorders

Conduct disorders affect 3–5% of children and represent the largest group of childhood psychiatric disorders.

Clinical features[2]

- antisocial behaviour which is repetitive and persistent
- lack of guilt or remorse for offensive behaviour
- generally poor interpersonal relationships
- manipulative
- tendency to aggressive, destructive, 'criminal' behaviour
- learning problems (about 50%)
- hyperactivity (one-third)

Family and environmental factors[2]

- disrupted childhood care
- socially disadvantaged
- lack of a warm, caring family
- family violence: emotional, physical or sexual abuse
- antisocial peer group exposure

Management

- early intervention and family assistance to help provide a warm, caring family environment
- family therapy to reduce interfamily conflict
- appropriate educational programs to facilitate self-esteem and achievement
- provision of opportunities for interesting, socially positive activities, e.g. sports, recreation, jobs, other skills
- behaviour modification programs

Sleep disorders

Sleep problems in children are very common in late infancy, toddler and early preschool age groups. The majority do not sleep throughout the night until six months of age. Over 50% of toddlers and preschool children resist going to bed.[3] At least 30% of infants and toddlers wake at least once during the night every night. Toddlers begin to have dreams coinciding with language development in the second year of life.[2] The child who wakes during the night needs reassurance, protection and the parent's presence, but it must be given discreetly.

Management

Advice to parents:

- Resist taking the child into bed during the night unless they are happy to encourage this.
- Avoid giving attention to the child in the middle of the night—it encourages attention seeking.
- Return the child to bed promptly and spend only a brief time with it to give reassurance.
- A rigid series of rituals performed before bedtime helps the child to develop a routine. Settling to sleep may be assisted by soft music, a soft toy and a gentle night-light.

Medication has a minimal place in the management of sleep disturbances, although the judicious use of sedative/hypnotic for a short term may break the sleepless cycle. Such drugs include chloral hydrate and trimeprazine (Vallergan).

Poor eating

Some parents may complain that their toddler 'eats nothing'. Apart from taking a careful history about what constitutes 'nothing', it is useful to describe the typical diet for the age group and then match the child's weight on the normal growth chart. The important aspect of management is to point out what is necessary from a nutritional viewpoint as opposed to what is considered normal for the particular culture.

Attention deficit disorder with hyperactivity

This disorder, which is estimated to have a prevalence of about 1%, is three times more common in boys than girls and is usually present from infancy.[1]

Clinical features

- impulsive overactivity
- irritability and moodiness
- poor concentration and school learning problems

The underlying family and environmental factors are similar to those applicable to conduct disorders.

Sibling rivalry

Sibling rivalry is a real concern as a toddler acts out apparent jealousy towards a new baby. The baby needs help from the inappropriate prodding, pinching and smothering attempts. The jealous toddler needs attention from the mother and a fair share of the comforts, cuddling and love that the toddler has been used to having.

It is important that the toddler is encouraged to feel that it is his or her baby too and to have opportunities to experience warmth and smiles from the baby, so that the sense of belonging is engendered.

Stuttering and stammering

This interruption of the orderly flow of speech may be accompanied by blinking and various other tics. It tends to be common in the school years but approximately 80% of sufferers become fluent by adulthood.[4]

Features of stuttering

- more common in boys
- usually begins under six years of age
- no evidence of neurotic or neurological disorder
- causes anxiety and social withdrawal

Management

Although most stutterers improve spontaneously, speech therapy from a caring empathic therapist may be very helpful.

Tics (habit spasm)

Tics are 'sudden, rapid and involuntary movements of circumscribed muscle groups which serve no apparent purpose'.[4] Most are minor, transient facial tics, nose twitching, or vocal tics such as grunts, throat clearing and staccato semi-coughs. Most of these tics resolve spontaneously (usually in less than a year) and reassurance can be given.

Tourette's disorder

Also known as Gilles de la Tourette's syndrome or multiple tic disorder, Tourette's disorder usually first appears in children between the ages of 4 and 15 years and has a prevalence of 1: 10 000.

Clinical features

- more common in boys
- bizarre tics
- echolia (repetition of words)
- coprolalia (compulsive utterances of obscene words)
- familial: dominant gene with variable expression

Treatment: haloperidol or clonidine (if necessary).

Dyslexia

Dyslexia is the condition where a child who has no physical problems and an apparent normal IQ has difficulty in reading and spelling, because the child apparently confuses certain letters whose shape is similar but different in positioning, e.g. b and d, p and q.

Dyslexia usually manifests as a learning problem. The children have faulty interpretation and utilisation of the knowledge they have acquired. Their problem usually responds to special tuition.

Autism

Autism, described first by Kanner in 1943, is a pervasive development disorder commencing early in childhood; it affects at least four children in 10 000, boys four times as commonly as girls. Autism is not due to faulty parenting or birth trauma, but is a biological disorder of the CNS which may have multiple organic aetiologies.

Many autistic children appear physically healthy and well developed although there is an association with a range of other disorders such as Tourette's disorder, tuberous sclerosis, epilepsy (up to 30% onset, usually in adolescence) and rubella encephalopathy. Most have intellectual disability but about 20% function in the normal range.

Autistic children show many disturbed behaviours. The main features are presented in Table 68.2.

Table 68.2 *A guide to the diagnosis of childhood autism (after Tonge[5])*

1. Onset during infancy and early childhood.
2. An impairment of social interactions shown by at least two of the following:
   - lack of awarness of the feelings of others
   - absent or abnormal comfort seeking in response to distress
   - lack of imitation
   - absent or abnormal social play
   - impaired ability to socialise, which may include gaze avoidance
3. Impairment in communication as shown by at least one of the following:
   - lack of babbling, gesture, mime or spoken language
   - absent or abnormal non-verbal communication
   - abnormalities in the form or content of speech
   - poor ability to initiate or sustain conversation
   - abnormal speech production
4. A restricted range of activities, interests and imaginative development, shown in at least one of the following:
   - stereotyped body movements
   - persistent and unusual preoccupations and rituals with objects or activities
   - severe distress over changes in routine or environment
   - an absence of imaginative and symbolic play
5. Behavioural problems:
   - tantrums
   - hyperactivity
   - destructiveness
   - risk-taking activity

The earliest signs of autism in infancy include:[5]

- excessive crying
- no response to cuddling if crying
- failure to mould the body in anticipation of being picked up
- stiffening the body or resisting when being held
- resistance to a change in routine
- appearing to be deaf
- failing to respond or overacting to sensory stimuli
- persistent failure to imitate, such as waving goodbye
- a need for minimal sleep

The diagnosis of autism remains difficult before the age of two years.

Assessment

If a child has delayed and deviant development and autism is suspected, a comprehensive multidisciplinary assessment is necessary. Referral to professionals with experience of autism is essential.

Treatment[6]

Many treatments have been tried and behavioural treatment methods have proved to be the most helpful. Medications are unhelpful for autism *per se* although medications such as tranquillisers, antidepressants and anticonvulsants are helpful for associated disorders.

The best results are achieved by early diagnosis, followed by a firm and consistent home management and early intervention program. Remedial education and speech therapy have an important place in management.

Case histories and 'draw a dream' concept

A useful strategy for communicating with disturbed children and getting to the source of a behaviour problem is to ask them to 'draw a dream'.[7] Professor Tonge believes that the dream is the royal road to the child's mental processes and the family doctor is ideally placed to use this technique. The following case studies concerning insomnia and nightmares illustrate the importance of these symptoms as reflecting a deep emotional problem in the child.

Case study 1[8]

Steven, aged 6, was a bright, happy little boy until he developed an extraordinary and puzzling episode of insomnia which was solved eventually by his teacher.

He presented to our group practice with his bemused mother who claimed that, suddenly, he would not and could not sleep. His parents would be startled at night by the eerie vision of Steven standing silent and motionless beside their bed. When not in his bed at night he would be found hiding under it or in his wardrobe.

His behaviour was normal otherwise, but his teacher reported that his schoolwork had deteriorated and that he was constantly falling asleep at his desk. On direct questioning Steven was shy and evasive, claiming nothing was worrying him. We considered it was a temporary phase of abnormal behaviour and advised conservative measures such as hot beverages, baths and exercises before retiring, but this strategy failed. He was referred to a consultant who also failed to find the cause of the insomnia and advised long midnight jogs.

Eventually Steven's teacher had the bright idea of asking all the children to draw the thing that scared or worried them the most, stipulating that it would be a 'make believe' picture.

Looking at the drawing depicting two robbers stealing his moneybox as he slept (Fig. 68.1), she tactfully confronted Steven, who admitted that his playmate had told him robbers would come one night, steal his moneybox and 'bash' him.

The final chapter of this story saw a happy Steven perched on a bank counter watching his money being counted, deposited in a huge safe and exchanged for a bank book. Steven has slept normally ever since.

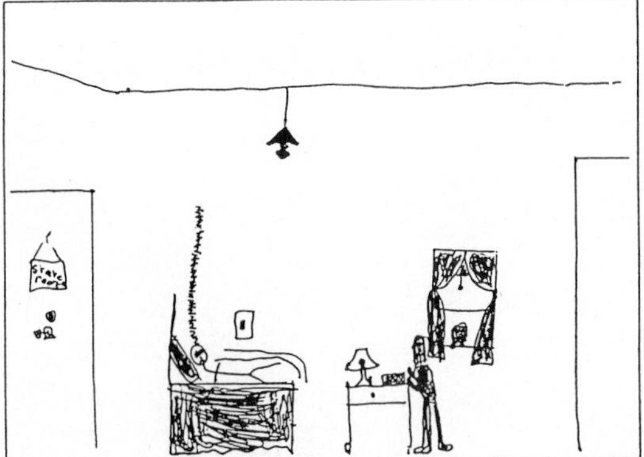

Fig. 68.1 *Steven's drawing*

Case study 2[8]

George, the second child of four children, seemed a normal healthy 3-year-old when his mother presented him for assessment.

For about three months George had been having nightmares, episodes that fractured the entire household. His mother, Mary, was absolutely frustrated by his nocturnal behaviour and said she was 'at her wit's end'. As she excitedly rattled off details of the family dilemma, I noted that she was intense and rather domineering but obviously a very conscientious and dutiful wife and mother.

She explained that George would wake her at night calling out to her because of a monster in his room or outside his window. She had no idea about any causes for this problem and explained that 'our household is very normal—no problems really'. She said George's behaviour was otherwise normal and he was a healthy boy.

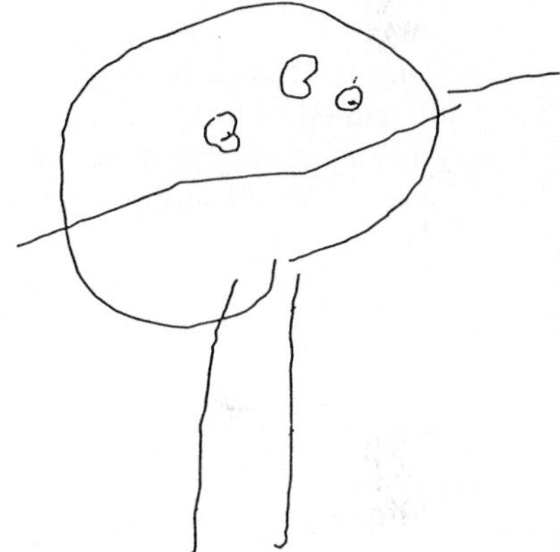

Fig. 68.2 *George's drawing*

Identifying the monster

I then asked George about his problem but could elicit only very scant information. Recalling the immense value of the 'draw a dream' strategy I asked him to draw the monster. George quickly drew the monster as shown in Figure 68.2. I then asked him about the monster and finally confronted him with the question: 'Do you know who or what the monster is?'

'Mum,' replied George, very matter-of-factly.

A shocked Mary looked unbelievingly at George and, for once, seemed stuck for words. Realising the delicacy of the situation, I asked George to tell me what it was about his mother that worried him. He offered the very revealing information: 'I don't think that she loves me. She's always yelling at me.'

Obviously the monster was George's insecurity because George declared how much he did love his mother and was 'scared' of losing her love. With appropriate counselling the outcome was good.

A lesson learned often is that it is important to 'look close to home' for any significant behaviour disorder or other psychological problem. It is important to explore the relationship that is most meaningful to the affected person, e.g. mother–daughter, father–son, student–teacher.

The 'draw a dream' strategy revealed vital information in this case.

When to refer[1]

- When child abuse is known or suspected.
- When an underlying medical problem is present.
- For assessment of associated psychological, family and related factors.
- For failed management, including simple behavioural and family support interventions.

References

1. Tonge B.J. Behavioural, emotional and psychosomatic disorders in children and adolescents. In: MIMS Disease Index. Sydney: IMS Publishing, 1991–1992, 66–68.
2. Parry TS. Behavioural problems in toddlers. Aust Fam Physician, 1986; 15; 1038–1040.
3. Jarman R. Sleep problems. In: Australian Paediatric Review, 1992; Vol. 2, No. 2, 1–2.
4. Robinson MJ. *Practical paediatrics* (2nd edition). Melbourne: Churchill Livingstone, 1990, 543–549.
5. Tonge BJ. Autism. Aust Fam Physician, 1989; 18; 247–250.
6. Curtis J. Autism: Patient Education, 1993; 22:1239.
7. Tonge BJ. 'I'm upset, you're upset and so are my Mum and Dad'. Aust Fam Physician, 1983, 12, 497–9.
8. Murtagh J. *Cautionary tales*. Sydney: McGraw-Hill, 1992, 165–174.

69

Child abuse

The description of the 'battered child syndrome' in 1962 provoked an awareness of a problem facing children which continues to increase in prominence. The possibility of both physical and sexual abuse has to be kept in mind by the family doctor. It may surface in families known to us as respectable and where a good trustful relationship exists between parents and doctor. Another aspect of child abuse is neglect.

The various types of abuse are classified as:

- physical
- neglect
- emotional
- sexual
- potential

Physical abuse occurs most often in the first two years of life, neglect in the first five years and sexual abuse from five years of age[1] (Fig. 69.1). In a Community Services of Victoria study[2] the distribution of child abuse was physical 15%, emotional 48%, sexual 9% and neglect 28%.

In another study[2], the findings were:

- Girls are more likely to be abused than boys.
- Girls are more often assaulted by someone they know.
- Most of the adults who sexually abuse are men (> 90%).
- About 75% of offenders are known to the child.
- Abuse is the misuse of a power situation, e.g. a close relative, coupled with the child's immaturity.

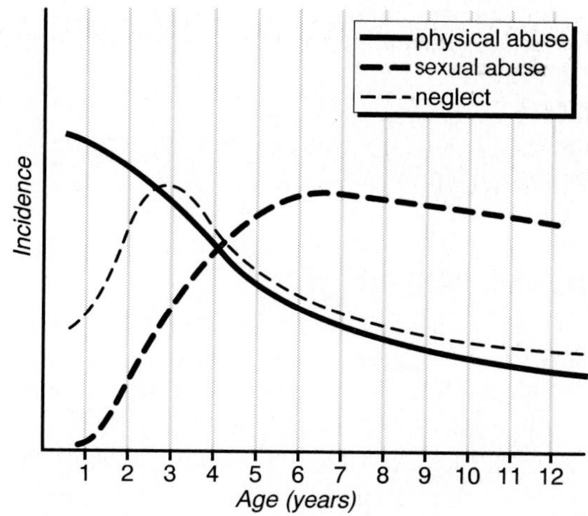

Fig. 69.1 *Typical relative age patterns for child abuse after Bentovin[1]*

Definitions

Child abuse can be defined by the nature of the abusive act or by the result of the abuse. A parent, guardian or other carer can harm a child by a deliberate act or by failure to provide adequate care.

Physical abuse (non-accidental injury)

Physical abuse is defined as 'a child with a characteristic pattern of injuries, the explanation of which is not consistent with the pattern, or where there is definite information through acknowledgment or reasonable suspicion that the injury was inflicted or knowingly not prevented by any person having custody, charge or care of the child'.[1]

Neglect

Neglect is defined as 'the privation of food, drink, medical care, stimulation or affection'.

Emotional abuse

Emotional abuse is the 'systematic destruction of the child's sense of self-esteem and competence, where competence is defined as the ability to act in social contexts'.

Sexual abuse

Sexual abuse in children is defined[3] as 'the involvement of dependent, developmentally immature children and adolescents in sexual activities that they do not fully comprehend, to which they are unable to give informed consent, and which violate the social taboos'.

Incest

Incest is legally defined as 'intercourse between biological family members'.

Abuse: who and why?[2]

The real cause seems to be a combination of several interrelated factors: personal, familial, social/cultural and societal stress. Abused children exist at all levels of society, although the majority of abused children who come to the attention of authorities are from families where there is high mobility, lack of education, loneliness, poverty, unemployment, inadequate housing and social isolation. Sexual abuse, occurring alone, does not follow these patterns and can occur under any socioeconomic circumstances.

Both men and women physically abuse their children. While women are the parents most responsible in cases of neglect and emotional abuse (probably because of a dominant role in child care, social and economic disadvantage and being the only one responsible for the care of children in a single parent arrangement), men are more likely to abuse their children sexually.

The child can be abused at any age (even adolescents can be victims of abuse and neglect). It is important to keep this in mind—*it does happen.*

Underdiagnosing and under-reporting[2]

Although the medical profession remains the foremost focus of child abuse reporting (they are the most likely to encounter injured children and are the most qualified to diagnose abuse), they still contribute only a small percentage of the total reporting to central registries. This could be because there is underdiagnosis of the problem but it could also be because of under-reporting.

Reasons given as to why GPs don't report more cases of child abuse include:

- Concern about drain on time and finances
- Lack of positive feedback about other cases
- Lack of undergraduate education on the topic
- Risk of alienation and stigmatisation to the family
- The feeling by some GPs that they can work on the problem with the family without outside intervention
- Lack of trust or confidence in local officials and agencies
- Uncertainty about *what* to do
- Personal and legal risks, i.e. fear of court, libel suits, irate parents
- Reluctance until absolutely certain of diagnosis

It will always be difficult to take the first step but it is important and it can help, no matter how small that first step is.

Physical abuse

Physical abuse should be suspected, especially in a child aged under three, if certain physical or behavioural indicators in either the child or the parents are present. Bruising, especially fingertip bruising, is the most common sign of the physically abused child.

Physical indicators:[2]

- unexplained injury
- different explanations offered
- injury unlikely to have occurred in manner stated
- unreasonable delays between injury and presentation
- finger-shaped bruises
- multiple bruises/welts of different ages, especially on face or buttocks
- fractures (especially if child $<$ two years old)

- burns, scalds, dislocations, bites, cuts, poisoning
- cigarette butt type burns
- shaking injuries, e.g. retinal damage, torn frenulum
- subdural haematoma
- internal injuries
- episodes of unconsciousness

Behavioural indicators:[2]

- wariness of adult contacts
- inappropriate clothing, e.g. long sleeves on a hot day
- apprehension when other children cry or shout
- behavioural extremes
- fear of parents
- afraid to go home
- child reports injury by parents or gives inappropriate explanation of injury
- excessive compliance
- extreme wariness
- attaches too readily to strangers

Management

The family doctor should diplomatically confront the parent or parents and always act in the best interests of the child. Offer to help the family. An approach would be to say, 'I am very concerned about your child's injuries as they don't add up—these injuries are not usually caused by what I'm told has been the cause. I will therefore seek assistance—it is my legal obligation. My duty is to help you and, especially, your child.'

The stages of management are:[1]

- recognition or disclosure of abuse
- the family separation phase
- working towards rehabilitation
- finding a new family for the child, when rehabilitation fails

Emotional abuse

Physical indicators:

- There are few physical indicators, but emotional abuse can cause delay in physical, emotional and mental development.

Behavioural indicators:

- extremely low self-esteem
- compliant, passive, withdrawn, tearful and/or apathetic behaviour
- aggressive or demanding behaviour
- anxiety
- serious difficulties with peers and/or adult relations
- delayed or distorted speech
- regressive behaviour, e.g. soiling

Neglect

Physical indicators:

- consistent hunger
- failure to thrive, or malnutrition
- poor hygiene
- inappropriate clothing
- consistent lack of supervision
- unattended physical problems or medical needs
- abandonment
- dangerous health or dietary practices

Behavioural indicators:

- stealing food
- extending stays at school
- consistent fatigue, listlessness or falling asleep in class
- alcohol or drug abuse
- child states there is no caregiver
- aggressive or inappropriate behaviour
- isolation from peer group

Sexual abuse

Incest and sexual abuse of children within the family occur more frequently than is acknowledged. One difficulty in recognising sexually abused children is to determine what is appropriate physical contact between adult and child, and what is abusive sexual behaviour.

Sexual abuse presents in three main ways:[4]

- allegations by the child or an adult
- injuries to the genitalia or anus
- suspicious presentations, especially:
  - genital infection
  - recurrent urinary infection
  - unexplained behavioural changes/ psychological disorders

Clinical indicators that may suggest child sexual abuse are presented in Table 69.1.[5,6]

Table 69.1 *Clinical indicators that may suggest child sexual abuse*

- complaint of abuse (rarely invented)
- vaginal discharge
- other STD
- urinary tract infection
- unexplained genital trauma
- unexplained perianal trauma
- overt sexual play
- pregnancy in an adolescent
- deterioration in school work
- family disruption
- indiscriminate attachment
- abnormal sexual behaviour
- poor self-esteem
- psychological disorders
  - — behaviour disturbances
  - — regression in behaviour
  - — sleep disturbances
  - — abnormal fears/reactions to specific places or persons
  - — psychosomatic symptoms
  - — anxiety
  - — lack of trust
  - — overcompliance
  - — aggressive behaviour
- depression
  - — self-destructive behaviour
  - — substance abuse
  - — suicidal tendencies

Examination (abnormal findings uncommon)

- genital trauma
- perforated hymen/lax vagina
- perianal trauma
- vaginal discharge
- look for semen and STDs

Sexual abuse can take many forms, including:

- genital fondling
- digital penetration
- penetration with various objects
- simulated sexual intercourse (anal in boys)
- full sexual penetration
- pornography
- prostitution

Clinical approach

Ideally the child should be assessed by experienced medical officers at the regional sexual assault service, so the temptation for the inexperienced GP to have a quick look should be resisted. For the practitioner having to assess the problem, a complete medical and social history, including a behavioural history, should be obtained prior to examination.

The child's history must be obtained carefully, honestly, patiently and objectively, without leading the child. Use language appropriate to the child and employ aids such as drawings and a model (such as a 'gingerbread man') to help the child illustrate what has happened. The history is more important than the physical findings as there are no abnormal physical findings in 40% of confessed cases.[7]

Physical examination[8]

It is recommended that the physical examination of any child suspected of being sexually abused is performed by a paediatrician or forensic physician experienced in the area of sexual abuse.

It is important to spend time explaining the examination process to the child and the accompanying parent. In prepubescent girls and boys, the examination is limited to visual inspection of the external areas using a good light source. Magnification may be used with a colposcope or magnifying glass, and photographs may be taken for documentation or medicolegal purposes.

Speculum examination is limited to postpubertal girls or used if there is concern about internal injuries (the latter may necessitate general anaesthesia). Rectal examination is usually limited to visualisation.

Three recommended positions are:

1. Supine with legs apart (frog-leg position with soles of feet apposed)
2. Prone knee-chest position (the best position)
3. Lateral decubitus

Always record the findings and note the examination position.

It is useful to remember that examination of urine in female children may show sperm so, if the child is uncharacteristically passing urine at night, get her mother to collect a specimen.

The crisis situation

It is important to realise that the child will be in *crisis*.[5] Children are trapped into the secrecy of sexual abuse, often by a trusted adult, by powerful threats of the consequences of disclosure. They are given the great responsibility of keeping the secret and holding the family together or disclosing the secret and disrupting the family. A crisis occurs when these threats become reality.

Management

It is important to act responsibly in the best interests of the child. When we encounter real or suspected child abuse, immediate action is necessary. The child needs an advocate to act on its behalf and our intervention actions may have to override our relationship with the family.

Some golden rules are:

- Never attempt to solve the problem alone.
- Do not attempt confrontation and counselling in isolation (unless under exceptional circumstances).
- Seek advice from experts (only a phone call away).
- Avoid telling the alleged perpetrator what the child has said.
- Refer to a child sexual assault centre where an experienced team can take the serious responsibility for the problem.

Supporting the child

- Acknowledge the child's fear and perhaps guilt.
- Assure the child it is not his or her fault.
- Tell the child you will help.
- Obtain the child's trust.
- Tell the child it has happened to other children and you have helped them.

Confronting the parents

If certain about the diagnosis the doctor should inform the child's mother and encourage her to notify the protective authority. If abuse is suspected, concerns should be raised that the child may have been sexually abused and that you wonder who the perpetrator could be. Ask who has access to the child, e.g. babysitter, member of a creche or kindergarten, teacher, other males, relatives.

Prevention of child abuse

Prevention of abuse, particularly self-perpetuating abuse, can be helped by creating awareness through media attention, programs in schools and the community in general, and increased knowledge and surveillance by all professionals involved with children. Clear guidelines on reporting and the accessibility of child abuse clinics are important for the strategies to be effective. Teaching children how to protect themselves offers the greatest potential for prevention.[4]

Counselling the secondary victims

Non-offending parents, who are the secondary victims of the abused child, will require help and guidance from their family doctor on how to manage the crisis at home. Parents should be advised to reassure the child of support and safety and to maintain usual routines. The child should be allowed to set the pace, without zealous overattention and pressure from the parents. Siblings should be informed that something has happened but that the child is safe. Ensure that the child will inform if the perpetrator attempts further abuse. Parents need substantial support including alleviation of any guilt.

An unhappy consequence of the crisis is the problem of broken relationships, which may involve the separation of the child from the family. At least one hitherto unsuspecting parent will be devastated if a parent is responsible for the abuse. The sexually abused child needs to be living with a protective parent with the abusive parent living separately.

Support for doctors

The attending doctor also requires support, and sharing the problem with colleagues, mentors and family is recommended. Some helpful guidelines are:

- Carefully record all examination findings (take copious notes).
- Always keep to the facts and be objective.
- Do not become emotionally involved.
- Work with (not for) the authorities.
- Avoid making inappropriate judgements to the authorities; e.g. do not state 'incest was committed', but rather say 'there is evidence (or no evidence) to support penetration of . . .'.
- If called to court, be well prepared; rehearse presentation; be authoritative and keep calm without allowing yourself to be upset by personal affronts.

The main difficulty in diagnosing child abuse is denial that it could be possible.

Practice tips and guidelines

- A child's statement alleging abuse should be accepted as true until proved otherwise.
- Children rarely lie about sexual abuse.
- False allegations, however, are a sign of family disharmony and an indication that the child may need help.
- Do not insist that the child 'has got it wrong', even if you find the actions by the alleged perpetrator unbelievable.
- Do not procrastinate—move swiftly to solve the problem.

- Be supportive to the child by listening, believing, being kind and caring.

When to refer

Unless there are exceptional circumstances, referral to an appropriate child abuse centre where an expert team is available is recommended. If doubtful, relatively urgent referral to a paediatrician is an alternative.

References

1. Bentovin A. Child abuse. Medicine International, 1987, 1851–1857.
2. Lewis D. Child abuse. In: Monash University: Department of Community Medicine. Final year student handbook, 1993, 164–168.
3. Schechter MD, Roberge L. Sexual exploitation. In: Helfer RE, Kempe CH, (eds) *Child abuse and neglect. The family and the community*. Cambridge, Mass: Ballinger, 1976, 127–142.
4. Valman HD. ABC of one to seven. London: British Medical Association, 1988, 112–114.
5. McMichael A. Counselling the victims of child sexual assault. Aust Fam Physician, 1990; 19: 481–489.
6. Steven I, Castell-McGregor S, Francis J, Winefield H. Child sexual abuse. Aust Fam Physician, 1988; 17: 427–433.
7. Irons TG. *Child sexual abuse*. California: Audio Digest, 1993; 41: 2.
8. Murnane M. Child sexual abuse. Aust Fam Physician, 1990; 19: 603–606.

70

Adolescent health

Adolescence is the name given to the psychosocial life stage which starts around the time of puberty. The time of onset and duration varies from one person to another but it commonly occurs between 12 and 18 years. It is a difficult period of considerable physical and mental change in which the young person is trying to cope with an inner conflict of striving for independence while still relying on adult support. There are inevitable clashes with parents, especially during the turbulent years of 13 to 16.

Adolescent patients require special understanding and caring from their doctor. They are often hesitant in approaching adult caregivers but they have a great capacity to appreciate a caring empathic approach. In this setting the family doctor has an excellent opportunity to anticipate their problems, educate them and improve their health.[1]

Adolescent development periods[2]

Early adolescence (puberty: 11–14 years) is dominated by adjustment to the physical and psychosexual changes and by the beginnings of psychological independence from parents. Girls generally advance through this stage more rapidly than boys.

Middle adolescence (the search for independence: 14–17 years) is a time where boys have caught up physically and psychologically with girls, so that peer group sexual attractions and relationships are common preoccupations at this stage. It is a phase of peer group alliances, clothes, music, jargon and food and drink.[2] The average age for first sexual intercourse of both sexes is 16 years. It is a stage where intellectual knowledge and cognitive processes become quite sophisticated. Experimentation and risk-taking behaviour is a feature.

Late adolescence (maturity: 17–19 years) is the stage of reaching maturity and leads to more self-confidence with relationships and successful rapport with parents. Thought is more abstract and reality-based.

Hallmarks of the adolescent

The main hallmarks of the adolescent[1] are:

- self-consciousness
- self-awareness
- self-centredness
- lack of confidence

These basic features lead to anxieties about the body, and so many adolescents focus on their skin, body shape, weight and hair. Concerns about acne, curly hair, round shoulders and obesity are very common.

There are usually special concerns about boy–girl relationships and maybe guilt or frustration about sexual matters. Many adolescents therefore feel a lack of self-worth or have a poor body image. They are very private people, and this must be respected. While there are concerns about their identity, parental conflict, school, their peers and the world around them, there is also an innate separation anxiety.

Needs of the adolescent

Adolescents have basic needs that will allow them the optimal environmental conditions for their development:

- 'room' to move
- privacy and confidentiality
- security (e.g. stable home)
- acceptance by peers
- someone to 'lean on' (e.g. youth leader)
- special 'heroes'
- establishment of an adult sexual role

Rebelliousness

It is quite normal for normal parents and normal teenagers to clash and get into arguments. Adolescents are usually suspicious of and rebellious against convention and authority (parents, teachers, politicians, police and so on). This attitude tends to fade after leaving school (at around 18 years of age).

Common signs are:

- criticising and questioning parents
- putting down family members or even friends
- unusual, maybe outrageous, fashions and hairstyles
- experimenting with drugs such as nicotine and alcohol
- bravado and posturing
- unusual, often stormy, love affairs

Signs of out-of-control behaviour are:[3]

- refusal to attend school
- vandalism and theft
- drug abuse
- sexual promiscuity
- eating disorders: anorexia, bulimia, severe obesity
- depression

Note: Beware of suicide if there are signs of depression.

The clinical approach

Managing behavioural disorders or out-of-control behaviour demands tact and sensitivity on the part of the family doctor. It is important to interview the adolescent separately. The usual comprehensive medical history including psychosocial features is vital, particularly the family interrelationships (Table 70.1). Specifically it is appropriate to enquire about the adolescent's family relationships (parents and siblings), relationships with peers, drug taking, medical problems in the family, and parental abuse (sexual, physical, emotional or neglect).

Table 70.1 *Basic clinical information (after D. Young[3])*

History
- General history
- Drug history
- Psychological
  - — Personality
    - introverted
    - withdrawn
    - anxious
  - — Stress
    - school
    - peers
    - home
  - — Depression
- Parent-adolescent relationship
  - — Overprotectiveness/distant
  - — Separation anxiety
  - — Physical or sexual abuse
- Family interrelationships
  - — Marital conflict
  - — Medical problems
  - — Alcohol abuse

Physical examination

Investigations Keep to bare minimum.

Consider the mnemonic HEADS in the history:[1]

H — home
E — education, employment, economic situation
A — activities, affect, ambition, anxieties
D — drugs, depression
S — sex, stress, suicide, self-esteem

During this process it is necessary to be aware of the fundamental development tasks of adolescence, namely:[3,4]

- establishing identity and self-image
- emancipation from the family and self-reliance
- establishing an appropriate adult sexual role
- developing a personal moral code
- making career and vocational choices
- ego identity and self-esteem

It is necessary to conduct a physical examination and order very basic investigations if only to exclude organic disease and provide the proper basis for effective counselling.

Counselling

Counselling the adolescent involves several important principles and strategies, including:

- seeing the patient alone
- seeing parents and patient together from time to time

- confidentiality and trust
- sensitivity
- engendering the feeling that you are their doctor
- encouraging free talking and then listening carefully
- time and patience
- non-judgemental behaviour
- reassurance
- explanation
- acting as their advocate and friend
- showing genuine respect for their concerns and viewpoint

Intervention strategies on behalf of the adolescent are outlined in Table 70.2.

Table 70.2 *Intervention strategies on behalf of the adolescent (after D. Young[3])*

School
- academic assessment (student services)
- pupil welfare co-ordinator

Family
- simple counselling, e.g. letting go
- family therapy

Adolescent
- direct communication about stress
- be the adolescent's advocate, not the parents'
- psychiatric or psychologist referral

Areas of counselling and anticipation guidance that are most relevant are:

- emotional problems/depression
- significant loss, e.g. breakdown of 'first love'
- sexuality
- contraception
- guilt about masturbation or other concerns

Advice to parents

Wise parenting can be difficult, because one cannot afford to be either overprotective or too distant. A successful relationship depends on good communication, which means continuing to show concern and care but being flexible and giving the adolescent 'space' and time.

Important management tips are:

- Treat adolescents with respect.
- Be non-judgemental.
- Stick to reasonable ground rules of behaviour (e.g. regarding alcohol, driving, language).
- Do not cling to them or show too much concern.
- Listen rather than argue.
- Listen to what they are *not* saying.
- Be flexible and consistent.
- Be available to help when requested.
- Give advice about diet and skin care.
- Talk about sex and give good advice, but only when the right opportunity arises.

Healthy distraction

Most authorities say that the best thing to keep adolescents healthy and adjusted is to be active and interested. Regular participation in sporting activities and other hobbies such as bushwalking, skiing and so on with parents or groups is an excellent way to help them cope with this important stage of their lives.

Depression, parasuicide and suicide

When dealing with adolescents it is important always to be on the lookout for depression and the possibility of suicide, which is the second most common cause of death in this group. Males successfully complete suicide four times more often than females while females attempt suicide 8 to 20 times more often than males.

The features of depression are presented in Chapter 14 but it is worth looking for the following indicators of depression:

- sleep disturbances
- eating disorders
- apathy towards friends, school and family
- sense of worthlessness
- deterioration of school performance
- crying and emotional lability
- psychosomatic symptoms
- preoccupation with death and dying
- suicide attempts (parasuicide)

It is important not to be afraid to enquire about thoughts of suicide as it gives teenagers a chance to unburden themselves; it is not provoking them to contemplate suicide. Parasuicide is a term coined to differentiate suicide attempts from suicide itself. Identification of risk factors as presented in Table 70.3[5] certainly requires positive intervention in the depressed teenager. Such teenagers are especially vulnerable to a precipitating event, which can be unemployment, significant loss such as death, divorce, separation, relationship break-up, anniversary of a loss or some special celebration, additional stress or conflict and poor health.

Depression and suicidal thoughts can respond very well to basic counselling but psychiatric referral is advisable.

Table 70.3 *Risk factors in suicide attempts (after P Birleson[5])*

- Previous threats or attempts at suicide*
- Limited problem-solving and coping strategies
- Unsupportive families with or without marital conflict
- History of separations, psychiatric disorder, alcohol or drug abuse in family
- Family history or culture of suicide attempts
- Family disorganisation and actual neglect or abuse
- Male*
- Major relationship disburbances with social isolation and/or aggression
- Indicators of psychiatric disorders, especially:
  - major depression*
  - school refusal
  - self-injurious behaviour
  - psychosis
  - alcohol/drug abuse
  - personality disorder
- Availability of guns, psychotropic drugs, ropes, etc.*

* These items are the most lethal risk factors.

References

1. Bennett DL. Understanding the adolescent patient. Aust Fam Physician, 1988; 17:345–346.
2. Clarke S. How to treat the adolescent. Aust Dr Weekly, 1991,7 June, i–viii.
3. Young D. The troubled adolescent. Aust Fam Physician, 1991;20:395–397.
4. Abery C. The difficult adolescent. Aust Fam Physician, 1991;20:383–385.
5. Birleson P. Depression and suicide in adolescence. Aust Fam Physician, 1988;17:331–333.

PART 5

WOMEN'S HEALTH

71

Cervical cancer and Pap smears

Carcinoma of the cervix

Carcinoma of the cervix is the most common malignancy in women world-wide; it is the sixth most common in Australia[1] and seventh in the United States of America.[2] The incidence of invasive cervical cancer rises steadily from age 20 to 50 and then remains relatively steady.

The most common form of cervical cancer is squamous cell carcinoma (SCC) 80–85%, with adenocarcinoma representing 12–15%.[2]

A striking epidemiological feature about cervical cancer is that it is a disorder related to sexual activity. It is almost non-existent in virgins but has an increased incidence in women with multiple partners and those who began sexual activity at an early age. Thus epidemiological studies indicate that cervical cancer is a sexually transmitted disease (Table 71.1).

Facts and figures

- Invasive cervical cancer is almost unknown in women under the age of 20, and very rare before age 25.
- There are two small peaks of incidence, in the late 30s and late 60s.[1]
- The lifetime probability of an Australian woman developing cancer is 1 in 90.[3]
- On average, cervical cancer takes at least a decade to develop from a focus of cervical intraepithelial neoplasia.[4]
- SCC of the cervix occurs almost exclusively in women who have had coitus.
- The earlier the age of first intercourse the greater the chance of developing cervical cancer.
- Invasive cervical cancer is a disease for which definite curable premalignant lesions can be

Table 71.1 *Cervical cancer and risk factors*

Age	increased	after 55
Sexuality	increased	• with multiple and or promiscuous sex partners • early age for first intercourse • early age first pregnancy
Viruses	increased	after herpes II or wart virus infection (probable)
Occupation	increased	in prostitutes (decreased in nuns)
Parity	increased	multiparity
Socioeconomic status	increased	with low socioeconomic status

identified using a Papanicolaou's (Pap) smear as a screening test.

- The incidence of cervical cancer has been decreased significantly through the screening procedures of the Pap smear, colposcopy and colposcopically directed cervical biopsy.
- Poor Pap smear technique is a common cause of a false negative result.

Basic pathology

The focus of attention is the transformation zone (Fig. 71.1) where columnar cells lining the endocervical canal undergo metaplasia to squamous cells—in the region of the squamo-columnar junction. It is important clinically to realise that this transformation zone can extend with progressive metaplasia of columnar epithelium and so the squamocolumnar junction may recede into the endocervical canal. This is a feature in postmenopausal women (Fig. 71.2). As squamous cell carcinoma almost always arises in the transformation zone it is vital that cells are taken from it when performing a Pap smear.

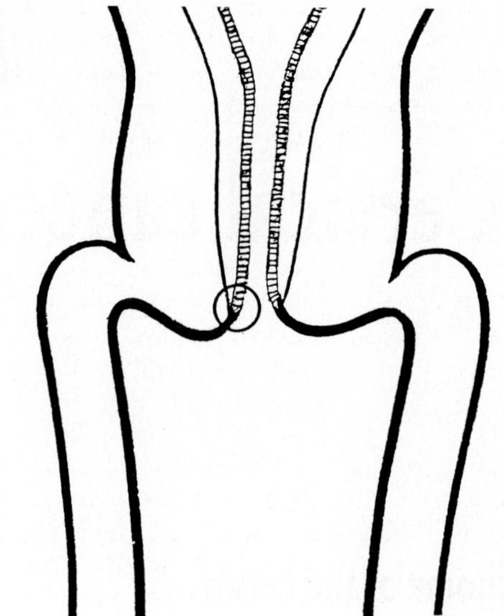

Fig. 71.1 *The transformation zone: it is vital that Pap smears take cells from this zone*

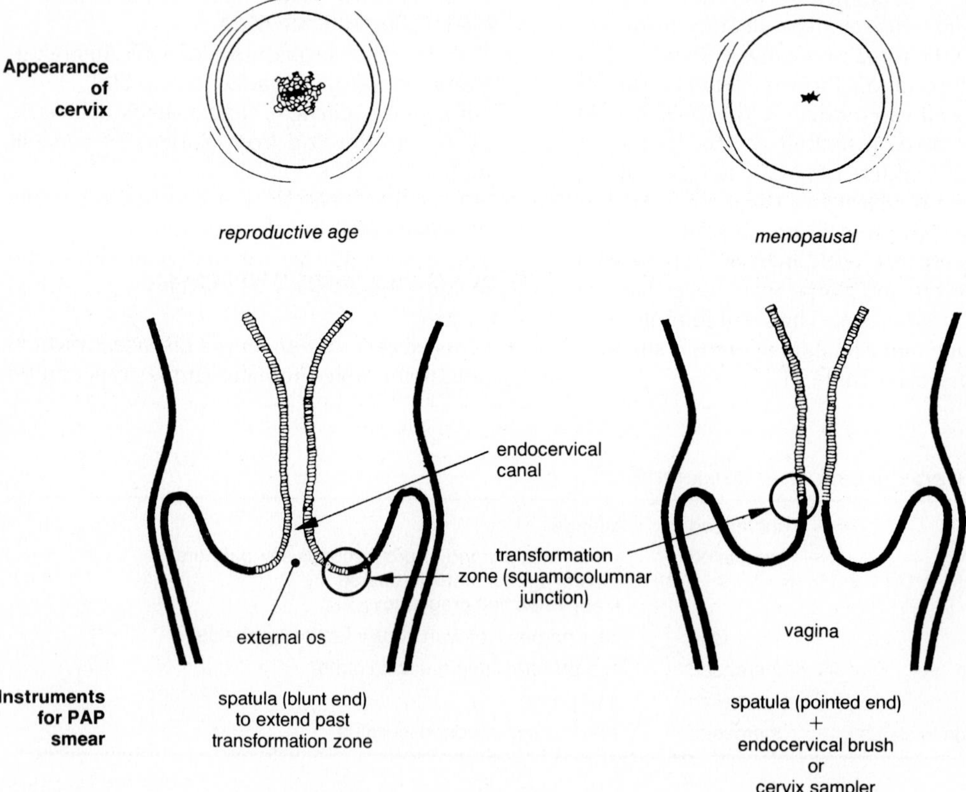

Fig. 71.2 *Changing position of the transformation zone with age, and a selection of sampling instruments according to its position*

Cervical intraepithelial neoplasia (CIN)

Cellular changes can occur in the transformation zone for a variety of reasons, including invasion with human papilloma virus (HPV). One such important change is cervical dysplasia, now known as cervical intraepithelial neoplasia (CIN). CIN has the potential to become invasive cervical cancer.

Staging of CIN:

CIN 1 mild dysplasia (outer third of epithelium involved)
CIN 2 moderate dysplasia (two-thirds of epithelium involved)
CIN 3 severe dysplasia/carcinoma *in situ* (full thickness)

Natural history of CIN

CIN may return to normal, persist or eventually progress to invasive cervical cancer. The reported progression times to the latter range from one to 30 years. On average it takes at least ten years, so it is considered that two-yearly Pap smears are a reasonable safety margin.

Clinical presentation

Many patients with cervical cancer are asymptomatic and when early symptoms do arise they are often dismissed as of little consequence.

Symptoms, if present, may be:

- vaginal bleeding, especially postcoital bleeding
- vaginal discharge
- symptoms of advanced disease, e.g. vaginal urine or flatus, weakness

Screening recommendations

Routine Pap smears:

- Perform every two years for women with no clinical evidence of cervical pathology (some authorities recommend annual smears).
- Perform from beginning of sexual activity up to 70 years.
- Begin Pap smears at 18–20 years or 1–2 years after first sexual intercourse (whichever is later).
- Cease at 70 years in those who have had two normal Pap smears within the last five years.
- Perform a Pap smear on women over 70 years if they request it or if they have never had a smear.
- Ideally, practices should have a reminder or a recall system.

Women who have never engaged in coitus do not need Pap smears. Six-monthly or 12-monthly screening on young asymptomatic women provides only minimal benefit compared with two-year intervals.

Hysterectomy

Smears are needed if the cervix was not completely removed. Vaginal vault smears are needed if there is a history of gynaecological dysplasia or malignancy.

Taking a Pap smear[1]

The importance of a good specimen

The optimal Pap smear contains:

- sufficient mature and metaplastic squamous cells to indicate adequate sampling from the whole of the transformation zone
- sufficient endocervical cells to indicate that the upper limit of the transformation zone was sampled; and to provide a sample for screening of adenocarcinoma and its precursors

Optimal timing of specimens

- The best time is any time after the cessation of the period.
- Avoid smear-taking during menstruation.
- Avoid in the presence of obvious vaginal infection.
- Avoid within 24 hours of use of vaginal creams or pessaries or douching.

Communicating with the pathologist

Good communication with the pathologist is essential. It is important to provide basic details about the reason for the Pap smear and the clinical history on the pathology form sent to the laboratory. Use the opportunity also for breast examination and checking of SBE technique.

The method

1. *Education and explanation*
   Take time to explain the reason for taking the Pap smear, especially if it is the first. Emphasise that it is mainly a preventive measure to detect and treat early cell changes that could develop into cancer. Anatomical models, sample instructions or charts are useful in describing the procedure. Explain that it does not hurt and doesn't take long, that it may be uncomfortable but slow deep breathing will help relaxation and make it

easier. It is preferable to talk to the patient during the examination with appropriate explanation. It is advisable for a male doctor to have a chaperone present.

2. *Equipment*
   Prepare the following equipment:
   - adequate light source
   - speculum (preferably bivalve) warmed under lukewarm water
   - glass slide labelled in pencil with the woman's name and date of birth
   - spray fixative
   - plastic gloves for both hands
   - smear-taking instruments; choose from:
     — Ayres's spatula, wooden or plastic
     — cervix sampler
     — endocervical brush

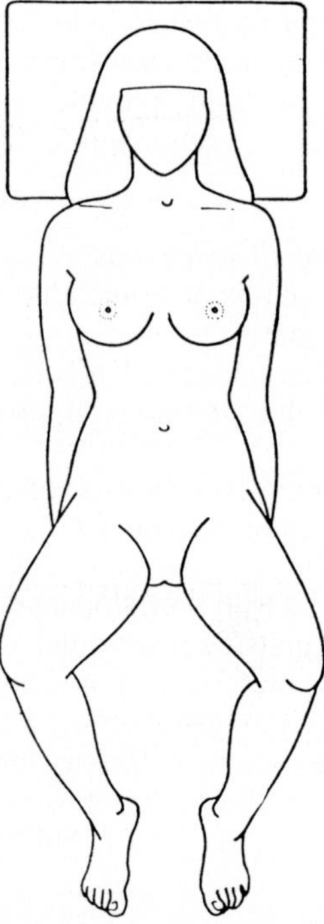

Fig. 71.3 *The supine or dorsal position is the best position for the speculum examination and subsequent bimanual palpation*

3. *Positioning*
   The supine position is usually best (Fig. 71.3). The left lateral position can be used if smears are difficult to obtain, e.g. older women with lax anterior vaginal walls, older women with poor hip mobility and the very embarrassed patient. The Sims exaggerated left lateral position (Fig. 71.4) provides better exposure of the vulva but requires more manipulation of the patient.

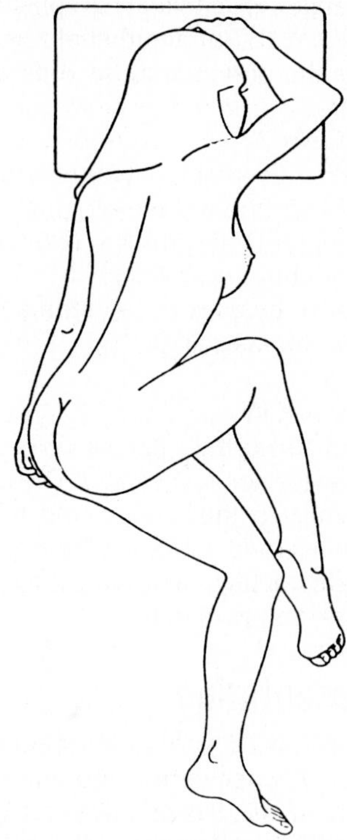

Fig. 71.4 *The Sims exaggerated left lateral position*

4. *Inserting the speculum*[5]
   Avoid using lubricating jelly on the speculum blades. Warming the speculum with water should provide adequate lubrication. Gently spread the labia with a gloved hand and introduce the speculum with the blades vertical or at 45° from the vertical. Gently advance the blades with slow firm pressure towards the rectum as far as possible. Rotate the blades during the process until they are horizontal and exerting gentle pressure against the posterior wall of the vagina.

5. *Visualising the cervix*
   Good lighting and exposure of the cervix is essential. Note any significant features or abnormalities of the cervix. Reassure the woman if the cervix looks normal with a comment such as 'Your tissues look very healthy'.

   A cervical ectropion is normal in most premenopausal women and was formerly incorrectly called an erosion.

6. *Taking the smear*
   Choose the sampling instrument that best suits the shape of the cervix and os. Place the spatula firmly on the os and rotate it through 360°, ensuring that the whole transformation zone is sampled (Fig. 71.5a).

   If the squamous columnar junction is not visible (lying within the endocervical canal), use both spatula and the cytobrush (Fig. 71.5c). Use the spatula first and then the cytobrush (tends to cause bleeding). The cytobrush should be avoided in pregnant women.

   After removing the speculum perform a bimanual pelvic examination.
7. *Preparing the slide*
   Transfer the cervical cell sample on to a glass slide with an even spreading motion (Fig. 71.5b,d). Fix immediately with spray or alcohol (Fig. 71.5e).
8. *Follow-up*
   Discuss mutually suitable arrangements to ensure that the woman obtains the result of the smear whether it is positive or negative. Inform her when her next smear is likely to be due (special cards are available) and arrange to send a reminder note.

   The explanation of the results, especially if there is CIN present (a variety of abnormal smear), should be crystal clear to the patient.

Abnormal cervical cytology

Confirmation of the Pap smear result is by colposcopy and/or by a biopsy and appropriate referral should be arranged.

Inaccurate results can be caused by:[5]

- using dirty glass slides
- using lubricants or doing pelvic examinations before taking the smear
- insufficient material
- endocervical cells not being taken in the smear, i.e. taken from the wrong site
- a thick film with an inadequate spread of material
- air-drying before fixing
- smear not being fixed for long enough or the solution of alcohol being too weak
- the slide not being dry before being placed in the cardboard container (this encourages fungal overgrowth)

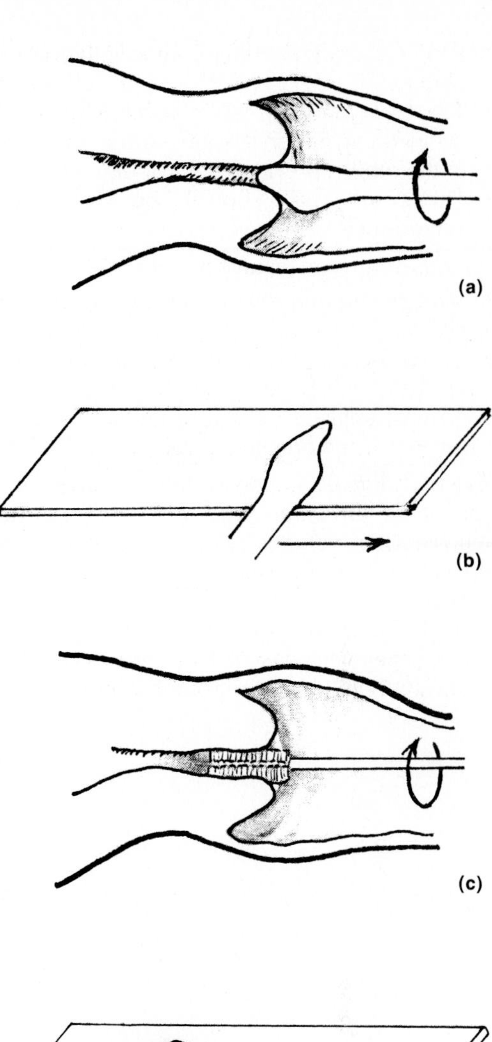

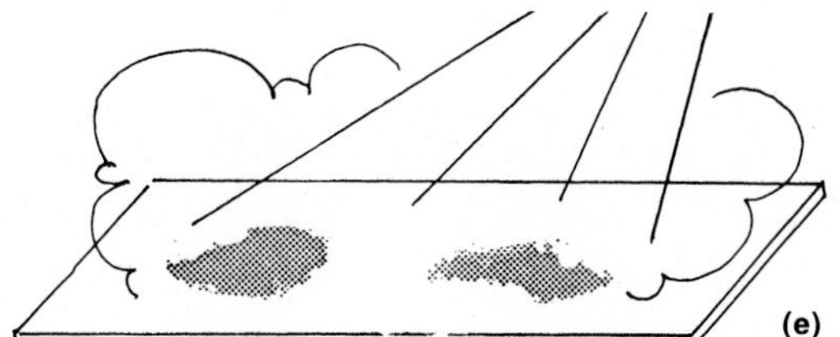

Fig. 71.5 *Method of smear taking and preparing the slide*

Prevention of cervical cancer

'In other words, chastity and fidelity are recommended for those who can, and condoms for those who cannot'.[6] This statement is a succinct recommendation for prevention and includes:

- People should have intercourse with only one partner.
- The male should use a condom on each occasion if either sexual partner is unsure of the other's previous behaviour.
- Those at risk should be counselled accordingly.

Other preventive measures include:

- Women should have Pap smears at least two-yearly.
- Use of beta-carotene has a protective effect against cervical cancer, so 'both sexes would be well advised to ensure regular intake of green leaf and orange vegetables in their diet'.[6]

Advice and reassurance should be given in a diplomatic way that does not produce guilt feelings. This includes reassurance that not all cervical cancer is sexually transmitted, that women with only one partner may develop cervical cancer and that sexual contact with a male partner who has had the wart virus does not always result in cancer of the cervix.[6]

References

1. Screening for the prevention of cervical cancer. Australia: Department of Health, Housing and Community Services, 1991, 1–26.
2. Rakel RE. *Essentials of family practice.* Philadelphia: Saunders, 1993, 130–131.
3. Giles G, Armstrong GK, Smith LR (eds). *Cancer in Australia.* National Cancer Statistics Clearing House. Scientific Publications No. 1, Australasian Association of Cancer Registries and Australian Institute of Health, Melbourne, 1987.
4. Day NE. Screening for cancer of the cervix. J Epi Comm Health, 1989; 43:103–106.
5. Craig S. The smear test. Aust Fam Physician, 1985; 14:1092–1094.
6. Tattersall M. *Preventing cancer.* Sydney: Australian Professorial Publications, 1988, 182–197.

72

Family planning

—

Effective family planning requires a good understanding of the function of the menstrual cycle, whether it is for the purpose of conception or contraception.

The main consultation is the presentation of a young woman for contraceptive advice. It is a very critical visit and provides an excellent opportunity to develop a good rapport with the patient and provide education and counselling about important health concerns, such as health promotion, menses regulation, sexual activity, planned parenthood, fertility and infertility, pregnancy prevention, STD prevention, immunisation and cervical smears.[1]

In counselling and treating patients, especially teenagers, confidentiality is of paramount importance. The issues and contraceptive methods can be confusing so careful education using various charts and other aids is recommended to enhance the therapeutic relationship and facilitate better compliance.[1]

It is worth discussing the patient's attitude to pregnancy, including the fear of pregnancy and the possible reaction to contraceptive failure.

Fertility control

The choice of contraceptive methodology will be determined not only by individual needs, personal preference and resources but also by its safety and incidence of side effects.

It is worth emphasising that the estimated risk of death associated with child-bearing (1 in 10 000 in developed countries) is higher than the risk of death associated with all methods of contraception, with two exceptions: women over 35 years of age who smoke and take the combined oestrogen-progestogen oral contraceptive, and those over 40 years of age taking this type of preparation.[2] In developed countries of the western world the most widely used methods, in order of preference, are combined oral contraceptives (COC), condoms, diaphragms, intrauterine devices, spermicidal agents and rhythm.[2]

A comparison of the efficacy of the various contraceptive methods is presented in Table 72.1.

More than half the pregnancies in the United States are unintended and occur because of non-use of contraception, failure of a specific method or discontinuation of contraception.[1]

For women at risk of acquiring STDs the choice of contraception has to consider methods that protect against both pregnancy and STDs.

Steroidal contraception

Methods of steroidal contraception include:[4]

- combined oral contraceptive pill (COC)
- progestogen-only pill (POP)
- injectables
- postcoital contraception
- implants (Norplant—LNG)
- levonorgestrel-releasing Nova-T
- progestogen-releasing vaginal rings
- oestrogen-progestogen-releasing vaginal rings

Table 72.1 *Effectiveness of contraceptive methods*[3,8]

Method	***Effectiveness (pregnancies per 100 years of use)*** ***Lowest expected (reliable consistent user)***
Natural rhythm methods	20–30
• Billings ovulation (cervical mucus) method	3
Withdrawal (coitus interruptus)	20–25
Spermicides	
• vaginal sponge	10
• diaphragm (with spermicide)	15
• condoms	10–15
Intrauterine devices	3-5
Oral contraceptives	
• combined	1-3
• progestogen only	3
Depomedroxyprogesterone acetate	0.1
Female sterilisation	0.02
Male sterilisation	0.15

Combined oral contraception

Combined oral contraceptives (COC) usually contain a low-dose oestrogen and a moderate dose of progestogen. The main mode of action of COC is inhibition of hypothalamic and pituitary function leading to anovulation.[2]

Which oestrogen to use[4]

Mestranol and ethinyloestradiol (EO) are about equipotent. Mestranol undergoes metabolic conversion to EO in the liver before it exerts its contraceptive effect. EO is therefore the oestrogen of choice.

Which progestogen to use[4]

All progestogens are nor-testosterone derivatives and exhibit a variety of non-progestogenic actions.

The norethisterone (NET) group includes norethisterone acetate, ethynodiol acetate and lynestrenol. The last three progestogens are converted to NET before exerting any contraceptive activity.

Levonorgestrel (LNG) is ten times more potent than NET. It has less effect on the coagulation system than NET and is therefore the preferred progestogen.

Gestogens are the 'third generation' progestogens and include desogestrel, gestodene, norgestimate and cyproterone acetate. These agents are less androgenic than NET and LNG and will be the agents of choice in the future.

Starting the pill: which COC to use[4]

The aim is to provide good cycle control and effective contraception with the least side effects using a pill of the lowest dose. The past menstrual history and contraceptive use of the patient should be documented and taken into account in selecting the appropriate COC. Various COC preparations available in Australia are listed in Table 72.2.[5]

A suitable first choice is a pill containing 30–35 μg of oestrogen: either the triphasic or monophasic pill.

- triphasic pills — Triphasil, Triquilar
- monophasic pills — Nordette, Microgynon 30, Brevinor, Marvelon

Advantages of triphasics

- lowest-dose preparations
- better cycle control
- minimal metabolic effect

Disadvantages[4]

- reduced margin of error in pill taking and therefore a possibly increased failure rate
- increased menstrual blood loss compared to monophasics
- cycle manipulation difficult
- not suitable for bi- or tri-cycle administration

The biphasic pill is useful for women with acne, hirsutism or progestogenic side effects from monophasic COCs.

Table 72.2 *Combined oral contraceptive pill formulations*

Oestrogen	***Dose***	***Progestogen***	***Dose***	***Trade name***
Ethinyloestradiol	30 μg	Levonorgestrel	150 μg	Nordette Microgynon 30
Ethinyloestradiol	30 μg	Desogestrel	150 μg	Marvelon
Ethinyloestradiol	35 μg	Cyproterone acetate	2000 μg	Diane—35 ED
Ethinyloestradiol	35 μg	Norethisterone	500 μg	Brevinor
Ethinyloestradiol	35 μg	Norethisterone	1 mg	Brevinor—1
Ethinyloestradiol	50 μg	Levonorgestrel	125 μg	Nordette 50 Microgynon 50
Ethinyloestradiol	50 μg	Levonorgestrel	250 μg	Nordiol
Mestranol	50 μg	Norethisterone	1 mg	Norinyl—1 OrthoNovum
Ethinyloestradiol	50 μg	Ethynodiol diacetate	500 μg	Ovulen 0.5/50
Ethinyloestradiol	50 μg	Ethynodiol diacetate	1 mg	Ovulen 1/50
1st 11 pills Ethinyloestradiol	50 μg	Levonorgestrel	50 μg	Biphasil Sequilar
2nd 10 pills Ethinyloestradiol	50 μg	Levonorgestrel	125 μg	
1st 6 pills Ethinyloestradiol	30 μg	Levonorgestrel	50 μg	Triphasil Triquilar
2nd 5 pills Ethinyloestradiol	40 μg	Levonorgestrel	75 μg	
3rd 10 pills Ethinyloestradiol	30 μg	Levonorgestrel	125 μg	
1st 7 pills Ethinyloestradiol	35 μg	Norethisterone	500 μg	Synphasic
2nd 9 pills Ethinyloestradiol	35 μg	Norethisterone	1 mg	
3rd 5 pills Ethinyloestradiol	35 μg	Norethisterone	500 μg	

The high-dose monophasic (50 μg EO) should be reserved for the following situations:

- breakthrough bleeding on low dose COCs
- control of menorrhagia
- concomitant use of enzyme-inducing drugs
- low-dose pill failure

Contraindications to COC usage are shown in Table 72.3.

Acne

For women with acne (not on COC), commence with a less androgenic progestogen, e.g. Diane 35 ED, Marvelon.

Efficacy of COCs

Under ideal circumstances the pregnancy rate in women taking COCs is 1–3 per 100 women years

Table 72.3 *Contraindications for use of the COC*[5]

Absolute	***Relative***
• pregnancy (known or suspected) • first 2 weeks postpartum • history of thromboembolic disease • undiagnosed abnormal vaginal bleeding • CVAs • focal migraine • coronary artery disease • steroid-dependent tumours • recent impaired liver function	• > 35 years and smoking • > 40 years • breast-feeding • 4 weeks before surgery • 2 weeks after surgery • gall bladder disease • hypertension • diabetes mellitus • long-term immobilisation • valvular heart disease • hyperlipidaemia

of use, but in practice varies from 2–6 per 100 women years.[2]

Non-contraceptive advantages of COCs

A number of significant beneficial effects arising from the use of COCs have now been documented.

- reduction in most menstrual cycle disorders
- reduction in the incidence of functional ovarian cysts
- 50% reduction in the incidence of PID
- reduced incidence of ovarian and endometrial carcinoma
- benign breast disease reduced
- less sebaceous disorders
- reduced incidence of thyroid disorders

Serious side effects of COCs

The most serious side effects to be considered are the effects of COCs on the circulatory system and the incidence of cancer.

Cardiovascular effects[4]

The following circulatory disorders have been linked with pill usage:

- Venous: deep vein thrombosis; pulmonary embolism; *rarely*: mesenteric, hepatic and renal thrombosis
- Arterial: myocardial infarction; thrombotic stroke; haemorrhagic stroke; *rarely*: retinal and mesenteric thrombosis

The risk of circulatory disease has not been related to duration of use and there is no increased risk in perpetual users.

The oestrogen content of the pill is considered to be the aetiological factor and the problem is increased in women taking high-oestrogen content COCs, but now that the oestrogen content of each pill has been reduced to as low as 30 μg EO, these risks of morbidity and mortality have been reduced.

The progestogen effect on lipid metabolism is not considered significant in the aetiology of circulatory disease. Circulatory diseases have now been recognised as occurring predominantly in certain high-risk groups—the 'at risk female', particularly the smoker over 35 years of age. Other risk groups include those with hyperlipidaemia, diabetes, hypertension, a family history of cardiovascular disease or immobilisation.

Provided low-dose COCs are prescribed in low-risk females it would appear safe to use the COC pill up to 50 years of age.

COCs and cancer

There appears to be no overall increase in the incidence of cancer in women using COCs.

Possible effect (not absolutely proven)

- cervix (take regular smears at yearly intervals)
- breast

Protective effect

- endometrial
- epithelial ovarian

No effect

- melanoma
- chorioncarcinoma
- prolactinomas

Common side effects

The relatively minor side effects listed in Table 72.4 may discourage women from persisting with oral contraception in the absence of appropriate explanation and reassurance. Management of these side effects is listed in the same table. It is useful in practice to have this list available as a ready reference for manipulating the COC if necessary.

Important advice for the patient

- Periods tend to become shorter, regular and lighter.
- No break from the pill is necessary.
- Drugs that interact with the pill include vitamin C, antibiotics, griseofulvin, rifampicin and anticonvulsants (except sodium valproate). Warfarin and oral hypoglycaemics requirements may change for those starting the pill.
- Diarrhoea and vomiting may reduce the effectiveness of the pill.
- Yearly return visits are recommended to update the history and examination and repeat the Pap smear.

The seven-day rule for the missed or late pill (more than 12 hours late):

- Take the forgotten pill as soon as possible, even if it means taking two pills in one day. Take the next pill at the usual time and finish the course.
- If you forget to take it for more than 12 hours after the usual time there is an increased risk of pregnancy so use another contraceptive method (such as condoms) for seven days.

Table 72.4 *Management of common side effects of COC*[6,7]

Symptom change	*Change*	*Examples of pill change*
Acne	Increase oestrogen, reduce progestogen	Triphasil/Triquilar to Biphasil/Sequilar
Amenorrhoea	Increase oestrogen	Nordette/Microgynon 30 to Nordette 50/Microgynon 50
Breakthrough bleeding		
• early to mid cycle	Increase oestrogen	Triphasil/Triquilar to Biphasil/Sequilar
• late cycle	Increase progestogen	Triphasil/Triquilar to Nordette/Microgynon 30
Breast problems		
• fullness/tenderness	Decrease oestrogen	Biphasil/Sequilar to Triphasil/Triquilar
• mastalgia	Decrease progestogen	Nordette/Microgynon 30 to Triphasil/Triquilar
Chloasma	Stop oestrogen Try progestogen-only pill Avoid direct sun (use blockout)	Micronor or Noriday Microlut or Microval
Depression	Decrease or change progestogen	Nordette/Microgynon 30 to Triphasil/Triquilar or Brevinor
Dysmenorrhoea/menorrhagia	Increase progestogen	Triphasil/Triquilar to Nordette/Microgynon
Headache		
• focal migraine	Discontinue pill	
• in pill-free week	Add 10–30 μg ethinyloestradiol daily during pill-free week	
Nausea/vomiting	Decrease or change oestrogen or stop oestrogen	Use Ortho Novum or Norinyl-1 or progestogen-only pill
Weight gain		
• constant	Decrease or change progestogen	Triphasil/Triquilar to Brevinor
• cyclic	Decrease oestrogen	Biphasil/Sequilar to Triphasil/Triquilar

- If these seven days run beyond the last hormone pill in your packet then miss out on the inactive pills (or seven-day gap) and proceed directly to the first hormone pill in your next packet. You may miss a period. (At least seven hormone tablets should be taken.)

Progestogen-only contraceptive pill (POP)

The POP is perhaps an underutilised method of contraception, although it is not as efficacious as the COC.

The two common formulations are:
levonorgestrel 30 μg/day
and
norethisterone 350 μg/day

Providing the mini-pill is taken regularly at the same time each day, the pregnancy rate is 3 per 100 women years.[2] The failure rate decreases with age. There are no serious side effects but compliance is a problem because of cycle irregularity, especially with irregular bleeding. The mini-pill often reduces the cycle length to less than 25 days or alters the regularity of the bleeding phase.

Indications for the POP include age 45 years or more, smokers 45 years or more, contraindications to or intolerance of oestrogens, diabetes mellitus, migraine, chloasma, lactation and well controlled hypertension.

Contraindications include pregnancy, undiagnosed genital tract bleeding, past history of or increased risk of ectopic pregnancy and concomitant use of enzyme-inducing drugs (absolute).

Injectable contraceptives

Medroxyprogesterone acetate ('Depo-Provera') is the only injectable contraceptive available in Australia.

Dose: 150 mg by deep IM injection in first five days of the menstrual cycle. The same dose is given every 12 weeks to maintain contraception.

Failure rate: 1 per 1000 women years.[2]

Side effects include a disrupted menstrual cycle (amenorrhoea rate 70% or irregular or prolonged uterine bleeding), excessive weight gain, breast tenderness, depression and a delay in return of fertility (average six months)[4]. There is no effect on cardiovascular disease or the incidence of cancer.

There are no absolute contraindications.

The main indication for this form of contraception is the desire for a highly effective method when other methods are contraindicated or disliked. Advantages are avoiding the side effects of oestrogen and overcoming compliance problems, e.g. in the mentally handicapped.

Postcoital contraception

Oestrogens in large doses are effective in preventive contraception after mid-cycle exposure to sexual intercourse by making the endometrium unreceptive to the zygote.[2]

Available methods (NB: must be used within 72 hours)

- Use high-oestrogen-containing COC, e.g. 50 μg EO + 250 μg LNG (Nordiol)—two pills initially then repeated 12 hours later

  Nausea is a common side effect and it is common to prescribe an antiemetic. Failure rate 2.6%.[2]
- Danazol 200 mg tablets, e.g. two initially and repeated 12 hours later

  Reduced incidence of nausea—failure rate 4.6%.

Pill failure

Causes of oral contraceptive failure include errors in administration, decreased absorption, missed pills, drug interactions and high doses of vitamin C. It is possible that the use of triphasics may be a factor.

Management options include using a higher-dose pill, improved education and compliance and an alternative method.

Intrauterine contraceptive devices

Intrauterine contraceptive devices (IUCDs) are usually small devices made of an inert material to which may be added a bioactive substance such as copper or a progestogen.[2] IUCDs probably interfere with the implantation of the zygote.

Efficacy: IUCDs give 96–99% protection against pregnancy.[2]

Contraindications for IUCD use.[4]

- Absolute
  - known or suspected pregnancy
  - active PID
  - undiagnosed abnormal genital tract bleeding
  - previous ectopic pregnancy
- Relative
  - menorrhagia
  - dysmenorrhoea
  - uterine cavity distortion
  - very large or very small uterus (> 9.0 or < 5.5 cm)
  - anaemia
  - defective immune system
  - impaired clotting mechanism
  - valvular heart disease
  - acutely anteverted or retroverted uterus
  - increased risk of PID (multiple sex partners)

Problems associated with IUCD usage[2]

Pregnancy/ectopic pregnancy

If pregnancy occurs there is a 40–50% increased risk of abortion and intrauterine sepsis during the second trimester. There is an increased risk of ectopic pregnancy (up to 10 times compared with COC usage) so, if pregnancy occurs, ultrasound examination should be performed to determine the location.

Early removal of the IUCD is essential.

Pelvic inflammatory disease

There is evidence that there is an increased risk of PID in the first thirty days postinsertion. Prophylactic doxycycline reduces this risk.[4] As this risk is related to sexual activity and the number of partners, those at risk of STDs should avoid using IUCDs.

Extrusion, perforation of uterus and translocation

Spontaneous extrusion is greatest during the first month after insertion and the woman is not always aware of this. Perforation of the uterus occurs once in every 1000 insertions and review at six weeks postinsertion is essential. If translocation is proved by X-ray and pelvic ultrasound, removal is mandatory.

Bleeding
Intermenstrual bleeding may follow insertion of an IUCD for two to three months and then disappear. If menstrual loss is excessive the device should be removed.

Pain
Lower abdominal cramp-like pains of uterine origin and backache may occur soon after insertion and persist intermittently for several weeks. Rarely is the pain severe enough to warrant removal of the IUCD.

Checking the IUCD
Women should be taught how to examine themselves vaginally to check if the device remains *in situ* by palpating the strings or threads which protrude from the cervical canal. They should have a medical check two to three months after the device has been fitted and then again after 12 months.

Barrier methods
Barrier methods include condoms, vaginal diaphragms, cervical caps and vaginal vault caps. They are very effective contraceptives with pregnancy rates of five or less per 100 women years.[2]

Condoms are also very effective in preventing the spread of STDs including HIV infection.

Diaphragms have to be individually fitted. After being liberally coated on both sides with a spermicidal cream they are inserted at any convenient time before intercourse and removed after six hours have elapsed since the last act of intercourse.

Spermicides
These are useful adjuncts to barrier methods of contraception. When used alone they have a pregnancy rate of less than 10 per 100 women years. They are available as creams, jellies, foams or pessaries containing nonoxynol 9 or octoxinol.

Natural methods
These methods require high motivation and regular menstrual cycles.

Basal body temperature method
Coitus should only occur after there has been a rise in basal body temperature of 0.2°C for three days (72 hours) above the basal body temperature measurement during the preceding six days, until the onset of the next menstrual period.

Billings ovulation method[8]
This method is based on careful observation of the nature of the mucus so that ovulation can be recognised. Fertile mucus is wet, clear, stringy, increased in amount and feels lubricative. The peak mucus day is the last day with this oestrogenised mucus before the abrupt change to thick tacky mucus associated with the secretion of progesterone. The infertile phase begins on the fourth day after the peak mucus day. Abstinence from intercourse is practised from the first awareness of increased, clearer wet mucus until four days after maximum mucus secretion. If taught correctly and followed as directed, the method is most effective, with a failure rate of only 1–2 (average 3) per 100 women years.[8] There is a failure rate of at least 15 if the rules are not followed properly.

Coitus interruptus
Male withdrawal before ejaculation is still a widely used method of contraception and despite theoretical objections will probably continue to have a definite place in contraceptive practice.

Sterilisation
Vasectomy
With vasectomy it is important to confirm the absence of spermatozoa in the ejaculate two to three months after the operation, before ceasing other contraceptive methods. It takes about 12 to 15 ejaculations to clear all the sperm from the tubes proximal to the surgical division. Vasectomy reversal is successful in up to 80% of patients.[2]

Tubal ligation
Female sterilisation is usually performed by minilaparotomy or laparoscopy at which time clips (Filshie or Hulka) or rings (Falope) are applied to each Fallopian tube. These are potentially reversible methods of contraception with a 50–70% success rate of reversal.[2] There is a subsequent pregnancy rate of 3–4 per 1000 women sterilised.

References

1. Sloane PD, Slatt ML, Baker RM. *Essentials of family medicine*. Baltimore: Williams & Wilkins, 1988, 175–189.
2. Walters W. Fertility control. In: MIMS. Sydney: IMS Publishing, 1991–2, 185–190.
3. Stovall TG. Clinical manual of gynaecology. New York: McGraw-Hill, 1992, 263–266.
4. Waldron K. *Effective family planning*. Proceedings handbook: Monash University Medical School. Update Course for General Practitioners, 1992, 9–15.
5. Benn M. Prescribing oral contraceptives and the medical record. Aust Fam Physician, 1991; 20:1469–1470.
6. Miller C, Murtagh J. Therapeutics for the busy GP: oral contraception. Aust Fam Physician, 1992; 21:1787–1788.
7. Miller C. The combined oral contraceptive: a practical guide. Aust Fam Physician, 1990; 19:897–905.
8. Billings E, Westmore A. *The Billings method*. Melbourne: Anne O'Donovan, 1992, 11–49.

73

Breast pain (mastalgia)

Breast pain, or mastalgia, is a common problem accounting for at least 50% of breast problems presenting in general practice.[1] Many women suffer breast pain so severe that it affects their lifestyles, marriages and sexual relationships, and even prevents them from hugging their children. If no obvious physical cause is found, the problem is all too often dismissed, without appropriate empathy and reassurance, as a normal physiological effect.

A careful, sympathetic clinical approach, however, followed by reassurance after examination, will be sufficient treatment for most patients.

Symptoms

Mastalgia usually presents as a heaviness or discomfort in the breast or as a pricking or stabbing sensation. The pain may radiate down the inner arm when the patient is carrying heavy objects or when the arm is in constant use, as in scrubbing floors.

Key facts and checkpoints

- The typical age span for mastalgia is 30–50 years.
- The peak incidence is 35–45 years.
- There are four common clinical presentations:
  1. diffuse, bilateral cyclical mastalgia
  2. diffuse, bilateral non-cyclical mastalgia
  3. unilateral diffuse non-cyclical mastalgia
  4. localised breast pain.
- The specific type of mastalgia should be identified.
- The commonest type is cyclical mastalgia.
- Premenstrual mastalgia (part of type 1) is common.
- An underlying malignancy should be excluded.
- Less than 10% of breast cancers present with localised pain.
- Only about 1 in 200 women with mastalgia are found to have breast cancer.
- The problems, especially types 2 and 3, are difficult to alleviate.

A diagnostic approach

A summary of the safety diagnostic model is presented in Table 73.1.

Probability diagnosis

In the non-pregnant patient, generalised pain that may be cyclical or non-cyclical is commonest. Typical patterns are illustrated in Figure 73.1.

Cyclical mastalgia is the commonest diffuse breast pain (see page 715). It occurs in the latter half of the menstrual cycle, especially in the premenstrual days, and subsides with the onset of menstruation. It obviously has a hormonal basis, which may be an abnormality in prolactin secretion. The main underlying disorder is benign mammary dysplasia, also referred to as fibroadenosis, chronic mastitis, cystic hyperplasia or fibrocystic breast disease.

Table 73.1 *Mastalgia: diagnostic strategy model*

Q. Probability diagnosis
A. Pregnancy
Cyclical mastalgia
• benign mammary dysplasia

Q. Serious disorders not to be missed
A. Neoplasia
Infection
• mastitis
• abscess
Myocardial ischaemia

Q. Pitfalls (often missed)
A. Pregnancy
Costochondritis
Pectoralis muscle spasm
Referred pain, esp. thoracic spine
Mechanical
• bra problems
• weight change
• trauma

Rarities
Hyperprolactinaemia
Nerve entrapment
Mammary duct ectasia
Sclerosing adenosis
Ankylosing spondylitis

Q. Seven masquerades checklist

A.	
Depression	✓
Diabetes	—
Drugs	✓
Anaemia	—
Thyroid disease	—
Spinal dysfunction	✓
Urinary infection	—

Q. Is this patient trying to tell me something?
A. Yes. Fear of malignancy. Consider psychogenic causes.

Non-cyclical mastalgia is also quite common and the cause is poorly understood. It may be associated with duct ectasia and periductal mastitis (see page 716).

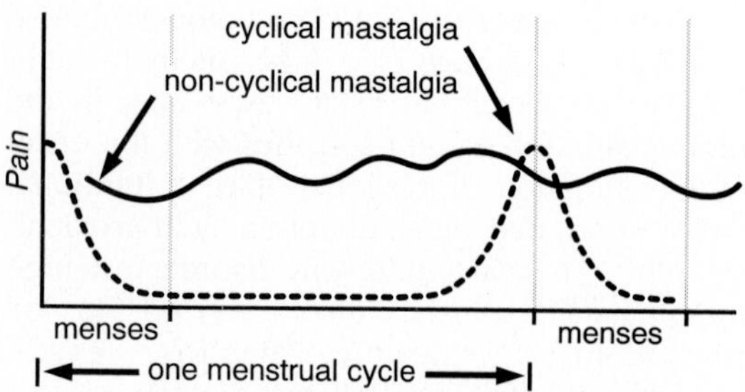

Fig. 73.1 *Pain patterns for cyclical and non-cyclical mastalgia*

Serious disorders not to be missed

The three important serious disorders not to be missed with any painful chest condition—neoplasia, infection and myocardial ischaemia—are applicable for breast pain.

Neoplasia

We must avoid the trap of considering that breast pain is not compatible with malignancy. Mastalgia can be a presenting symptom (although uncommon) of breast cancer. 'Mastitis carcinomatosa', which is a rare florid form of breast cancer found in young women, often during lactation, is red and hot but not invariably painful or tender.[2] Pain may also be a symptom in juvenile fibroadenoma, a soft rapidly growing tumour in adolescents, and in the fibroadenoma of adult women.

Infection

Mastitis is common among nursing mothers. It should be regarded as a serious and urgent problem because a breast abscess can develop quickly. Apart from bacterial infection, infection with *Candida albicans* may occur following the use of antibiotics. Candida infection usually causes severe breast pain, producing a feeling like 'hot cords', especially during and after feeding.

Myocardial ischaemia

A constricting pain under the left breast should be regarded as myocardial ischaemia until proved otherwise.

Pitfalls

These include various causes of apparent mastalgia, such as several musculoskeletal chest wall conditions and referred pain from organs such as the heart, oesophagus, lungs and gall bladder and, in particular, from the upper thoracic spine.

Musculoskeletal conditions include costochondritis, pectoralis muscle strains or spasm, and entrapment of the lateral cutaneous branch of the third intercostal nerve. Ankylosing spondylitis can affect the chest wall under the breasts. Mastalgia may be the first symptom of pregnancy. It should be excluded before commencing drug treatment.

Seven masquerades checklist

Of these, depression, drugs and spinal dysfunction are probable causes. Drugs that can cause breast discomfort include oral contraceptives, hormone replacement therapy and methylxanthine derivatives such as theophylline. Drugs that cause tender gynaecomastia (more applicable to men) include digoxin, cimetidine, spironolactone and marijuana.

Dysfunction of the upper thoracic spine and even the lower cervical spine can refer pain under a breast. If suspected, these areas of the spine should be examined.

Psychogenic considerations

The symptoms may be exaggerated as a result of an underlying psychogenic disorder, but with a symptom such as breast pain most women fear malignancy and need reassurance.

The clinical approach

History

It is important to relate the pain to the menstrual cycle and determine whether the patient is pregnant or not.

Key questions

Could you be pregnant?
Is your period on time or overdue?
Is the pain in both breasts or only one?
Do you have pain before your periods or all the time during your menstrual cycle?
Do you have pain in your back or where your ribs join your chest bone?

Physical examination

The breasts should be systematically palpated to check for soreness or lumps. The underlying chest wall and thoracic spine should also be examined.

Investigations

The following specialised tests could be considered.

Mammography should be considered in older women. It is unreliable in young women. With few exceptions it should not be used under 40 years.

Ultrasound can be complementary to mammography for it is useful to assess a localised mass or tender area. It is inappropriate to evaluate a diffuse area. It is not so useful for the postmenopausal breast which is fatty and looks similar to cancer on ultrasound.

Excision biopsy can be useful for an area of localised pain, especially in the presence of a possible mass.

Mastalgia in children

Breast pain is uncommon in children, including puberty, but it may be a presenting problem in the late teens. Pubertal boys may complain of breast lumps under the nipple (adolescent gynaecomastia) but these are rarely tender and do not require specific treatment.

Mastalgia in the elderly

Breast pain is rare after the menopause but is increasing with increased use of hormone replacement therapy (HRT), where it tends to present as the diffuse bilateral type. If the problem is related to the introduction of HRT, the oestrogen dose should be reduced or an alternative preparation used.

Cyclical mastalgia

The features of cyclical mastalgia are:

- the typical age is 35
- discomfort and sometimes pain are present
- usually bilateral but one breast can dominate
- mainly premenstrual
- breasts diffusely nodular or lumpy
- variable relationship to the pill

It is rare after the menopause.

Management

After excluding a diagnosis of carcinoma and aspirating palpable cysts, various treatments are possible and can be given according to severity.[3]

Mild

- reassurance
- regular review and breast self-examination
- proper brassiere support
- proper low-fat diet, excluding caffeine
- aim at ideal weight
- adjust oral contraception or hormone replacement therapy (if applicable)

Moderate

As for mild, plus options (use one or a combination):

- mefenamic acid 500 mg, three times daily
- vitamin B_1 (thiamine) 100 mg daily, and
- vitamin B_6 (pyridoxine) 100 mg daily
- evening primrose oil 4–6 g daily

If no response

As for mild, plus options (one of the following):

- norethisterone 5 mg daily (for second half of cycle)
- bromocriptine 2.5 mg twice daily
- danazol 200 mg daily

Some of these treatments, particularly vitamin therapy, have not been scientifically tested, but some empirical evidence is convincing. The value of diuretics is not proven, and testosterone or tamoxifen treatment is generally not favoured.

Evening primrose oil contains an essential fatty acid claimed to be lacking in the diet, and replacement allows for the production of prostaglandin E, which counters the effect of oestrogen and prolactin on the breast.

Bromocriptine and danazol have significant side effects but clinical trials have proved their efficacy for this condition.[4,5]

A summary of a treatment strategy for cyclical mastalgia is presented in Table 73.2.

Table 73.2 *Management plan for cyclical mastalgia*

	Progressive stepwise therapy
Step 1	Reassurance Proper brassiere support Diet—exclude caffeine
Step 2	Add Vitamin B_1 100 mg daily Vitamin B_6 100 mg daily
Step 3	Substitute Evening primrose oil 4 g daily
Step 4	Add Danazol 200 mg daily

Non-cyclical mastalgia

The features of non-cyclical mastalgia are:

- the typical age is the early forties
- bilateral and diffuse
- pain present throughout the cycle
- no obvious physical or pathological basis

Typical pain patterns are presented in Figure 73.1.

Management

Non-cyclical mastalgia is very difficult to treat, being less responsive than cyclical mastalgia. It is worth a therapeutic trial.

First-line treatment

- exclude caffeine from diet
- weight reduction if needed
- vitamin B_1 100 mg daily
- vitamin B_6 100 mg daily
- evening primrose oil 4–6 g daily

Second-line treatment

- norethisterone 5 mg daily

Local lesions

Surgical excision may be required for local lesions. If there is no discrete lesion but a tender trigger point (including costochondritis), the injection of local anaesthetic and corticosteroid may relieve the problem.

Costochondritis (Tietze's syndrome)

This is a common cause of referral to a breast pain clinic. The cause is often obscure, but the costochondral junction may become strained in patients with a persistent cough. The pain can appear to be in the breast with intermittent radiation round the chest wall and is initiated or aggravated by deep breathing and coughing.

Features:

- the pain is acute, intermittent or chronic
- the breast is normal to palpation
- palpable swelling about 4 cm from sternal edge due to enlargement of costochondral cartilage
- X-rays are normal
- self-limiting, but may take several months to subside

Treatment: infiltration with local anaesthetic and corticosteroid.

Mastitis

Mastitis is basically cellulitis of the interlobular connective tissue of the breast. Mostly restricted to lactating women, it is associated with a cracked nipple or poor milk drainage. The infecting organism is usually *Staphlococcus aureus* or more rarely *Escherichia coli* or *Candida albicans*. It is a serious problem and requires early treatment. Breast-feeding from the affected side can continue as the infection is confined to interstitial breast tissue and doesn't usually affect the milk supply.

Clinical features:

- a lump and then soreness (at first)
- a red tender area

possibly

- fever, tiredness, muscle aches and pains

Note Candida infection usually causes severe breast pain—a feeling like a hot knife or hot shooting pains, especially during and after feeding. It may occur after a course of antibiotics.

Management

Prevention (in lactation):

- maintain free breast drainage
- attend to breast engorgement and cracked nipples

Treatment

- Antibiotics: resolution without progression to an abscess will usually be prevented by antibiotics

  flucloxacillin 500 mg (o) qid for 10 days

  or

  cephalaxin 500 mg (o) qid for 10 days
- therapeutic ultrasound ($2W/cm^2$ for 6 minutes) daily for 2–3 days
- aspirin or paracetamol for pain

Instructions to patients

- Keep the affected breast well drained.
- Continue breast-feeding: do frequently and start with the sore side.
- Heat the sore breast before feeding, e.g. with hot shower or hot face washer.
- Cool the breast after feeding: use a cold face washer from the freezer.
- Massage any breast lumps gently towards the nipple while feeding.
- Empty the breast well: hand express if necessary.
- Get sufficient rest.
- Keep to a nutritious diet and drink ample fluids.

Breast abscess

If tenderness and redness persist beyond 48 hours and an area of tense induration develops, then a breast abscess has formed. It requires surgical drainage under general anaesthesia or aspiration with a large bore needle under LA every second day until resolution, antibiotics, rest and complete emptying of the breast. Temporary weaning of breast-feeding from the affected side is necessary because of the surgical disruption.

Surgical drainage

Method:

1. Make an incision over the point of maximal tenderness, preferably in a dependent area of the breast. A curvilinear transverse incision which does not continue into breast tissue, following Langer's lines, is optimal (Fig. 73.2a).
2. Use artery forceps to separate breast tissue to reach the pus.
3. Take a swab for culture.
4. Introduce a gloved finger to break down the septa that separate the cavity into loculations (Fig. 73.2b).
5. Insert a corrugated drainage tube into the cavity. Fix it to the skin edge with a single suture (Fig. 73.2c).

(a)

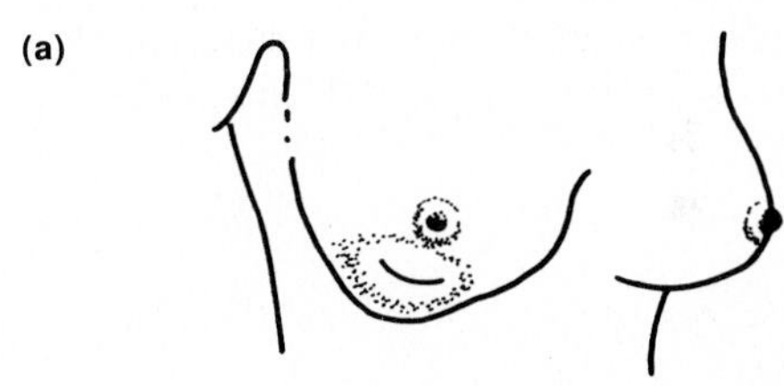

(b)

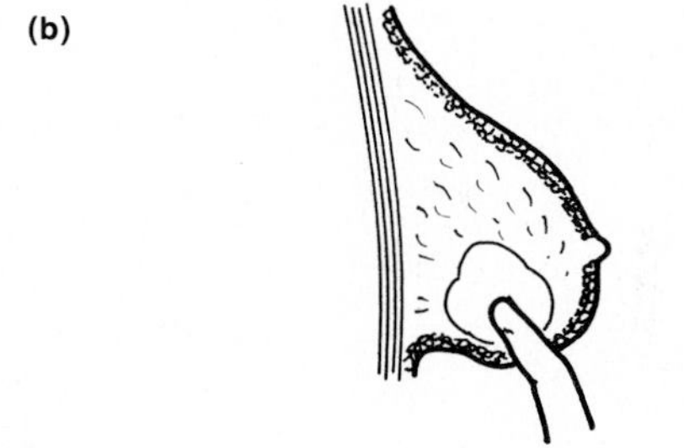

(c)

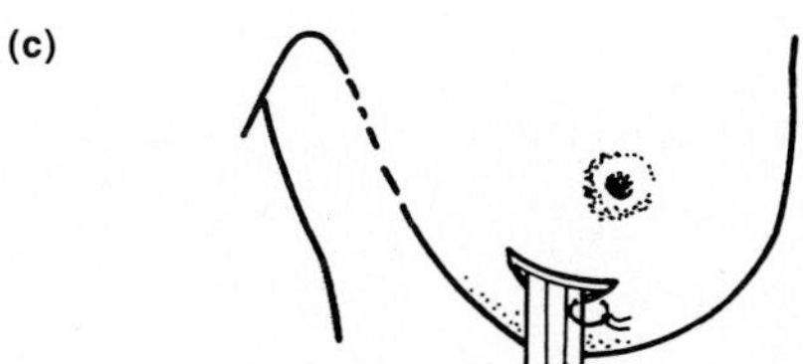

Fig. 73.2 *Surgical drainage of breast abscess:* **(a)** *transverse incision;* **(b)** *exploring abscess cavity;* **(c)** *drainage tube in situ*

Remove the tube two days after the operation. Change the dressings daily until the wound has healed. Continue antibiotics until resolution of the inflammation.

When to refer

- Undiagnosed localised breast pain or lump.

Practice tips

- The basis of management for benign mastalgia is firm reassurance.
- Although breast cancer rarely causes mastalgia, it should be excluded.
- Think of *Candida albicans* if mastitis is very severe with hot shooting pains, especially after antibiotic treatment.
- Look for underlying disorders of the chest wall if examination of the breasts is normal.
- Consider caffeine intake as a cause of benign diffuse mastalgia.
- Mastitis should be treated vigorously—it is a serious condition.
- Fibroadenomas and breast cysts are capable of causing localised pain and tenderness.

References

1. McAvoy PA. Breast problems. In: *Practice.* Cormack J, Marinker M, Morrell D. (eds). London: Kluwer Medical, 1982, Section 3.54.
2. Ryan P. *A very short textbook of surgery* (2nd edition). Canberra: Dennis and Ryan, 1990, 10.
3. Barraclough B. The fibrocystic breast—clinical assessment, diagnosis and treatment. Modern Medicine Aust, 1990; 33(4):16–25.
4. Mansel RE et al. Controlled trial of the antigonadotrophin danazol in painful nodular benign breast disease. Lancet, 1982; 1;928
5. Hinton CP et al. A double blind controlled trial of danazol and bromocriptine in the management of severe cyclical breast pain. British Journal of Clinical Practice, 1986; 40, 326.

74

Lumps in the breast

Breast lumps are common and their discovery by a woman provokes considerable anxiety and emotion (which is often masked during presentation) because to many a 'breast lump' means cancer. Many of the lumps are actually areas of thickening of normal breast tissue. Many other lumps are due to mammary dysplasia with either fibrosis or cyst formation or a combination of the two producing a dominant (discrete) lump.[1] However, a good working rule is to consider any lump in the breast as carcinoma until proved otherwise. See Table 74.1 for causes of breast lumps.

Table 74.1 *Causes of breast lumps*[2]

Common	
• Benign mammary hyperplasia	45%
• Carcinoma	25%
• Cysts	15%
• Fibroadenoma	10%
• Breast abscess/periareolar inflammation	3%
Less common	
• Mammary duct ectasia	
• Duct papilloma	
• Lactation cysts (galactocele)	
• Paget's disease of the nipple	
• Fat necrosis/fibrosis	
• Sarcoma	
• Lipoma	

Key facts and checkpoints

- The commonest lumps are those associated with benign mammary dysplasia (45%).[2] See Table 74.1.
- Benign mammary dysplasia is also a common cause of cysts, especially in the premenopause phase.
- Over 75% of isolated breast lumps prove to be benign but clinical identification of a malignant tumour can only definitely be made following aspiration biopsy or histological examination of the tumour.[3]
- Breast cancer is the most common cancer in females, affecting 1 in 15 women.[3]
- About 25% of all new cancers in women are breast neoplasms.
- A 'dominant' breast lump in an older woman should be regarded as malignant.

The clinical approach

This is based on following a careful history and examination.

History

The history should include a family history of breast disease and the patient's past history, including trauma, previous breast pain, and details about pregnancies (complications of lactation such as mastitis, nipple problems and milk retention).

Key questions[1]

Have you had any previous problems with your breasts?
Have you noticed any breast pain or discomfort?
Do you have any problems such as increased swelling or tenderness before your periods?

Have you noticed lumpiness in your breasts before?
Has the lumpy area been red or hot?
Have you noticed any discharge from your nipple or nipples?
Has there been any change in your nipples?
Did your mother or sisters or any close relatives have any breast problems?

Breast symptoms

- lump
- tenderness or pain
- nipple discharge
- nipple retraction
- periareolar inflammation

Nipple discharge[4]

This may be intermittent from one or both nipples. It can be induced by quadrant compression.

- bloodstained — intraduct papilloma (commonest)
  intraduct carcinoma
  mammary dysplasia
- green-grey — mammary dysplasia
  mammary duct ectasia
- yellow — mammary dysplasia (serous)
  breast abscess (pus)
- milky white (galactorrhoea) — lactation cysts
  lactation
  hyperprolactinaemia
  drugs, e.g. chlorpromazine

Periareolar inflammation

This presents as pain around the areola with reddening of the skin, tenderness and swelling. Causes may be inverted nipple or mammary duct ectasia.

Paget's disease of the nipple

This rare but interesting condition usually occurs in middle-aged and elderly women. It starts as an eczematous-looking dry scabbing red rash of the nipple and then proceeds to ulceration of the nipple and areola. It is always due to an underlying malignancy.

Examination of the breasts

Objectives

- Identify a dominant lump (one that differs from the remainder of the breast tissue).
- Identify a lump that may be malignant.
- Screen the breasts for early development of carcinoma.

Time of examination: ideally, four days after the end of the period.

Method[1]

1. Inspection: sitting—patient seated upright on side of couch in good light, arms by sides, facing the doctor, undressed to waist.
   (i) *Note*
   - Asymmetry of breasts or a visible lump
   - Localised discolouration of the skin
   - Nipples
     — for retraction or ulceration
     — for variations in the level, e.g. elevation on one side
     — for discharge, e.g. bloodstained, clear, yellow
   - Skin attachment or tethering → dimpling of skin (accentuate this sign by asking patient to raise her arms above her head)
   - Appearance of small nodules of growth
   - Visible veins (if unilateral they suggest a cancer)[5]
   - Peau d'orange due to dermal oedema

   (ii) Raise arms above the head (renders variations in nipple level and skin tethering more obvious). Hands are pressed on the hips to contract pectoralis major to note if there is a deep attachment of the lump.
2. Examination of lymph glands in sitting position: patient with hands on hips. Examine axillary and supraclavicular glands from behind and front.

   Note The draining lymphatic nodes are in the axillae, supraclavicular fossae and internal mammary chain.
3. Palpation
   (i) Patient still seated: palpate breast with flat of hand and then palpate the bulk of the breast between both hands.
   (ii) In supine position:
   - patient lies supine on couch with arms above head
   - turn body (slight rotation) towards midline so breasts 'sit' as flat as possible on chest wall

Method

- Use the pulps of the fingers rather than the tips with the hand laid flat on the breast.
- Move the hand in slow circular movements.
- Examine up and down the breast in vertical strips beginning from the axillary tail (Fig. 74.1).
- Systemically cover the six areas of the breast (Fig. 74.2)
  — the four quadrants
  — the axillary tail
  — the region deep to the nipple and areola

4. If a suspicious lump is present, inspect liver, lungs and spine.
5. Inspect the bra. Note possible pressure on breast tissue from underwiring of the bra, usually on the upper outer quadrant.

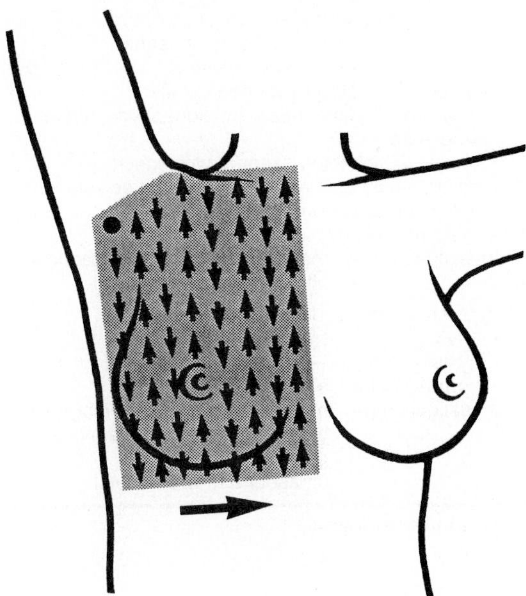

Fig. 74.1 *Systematic examination of the breast*

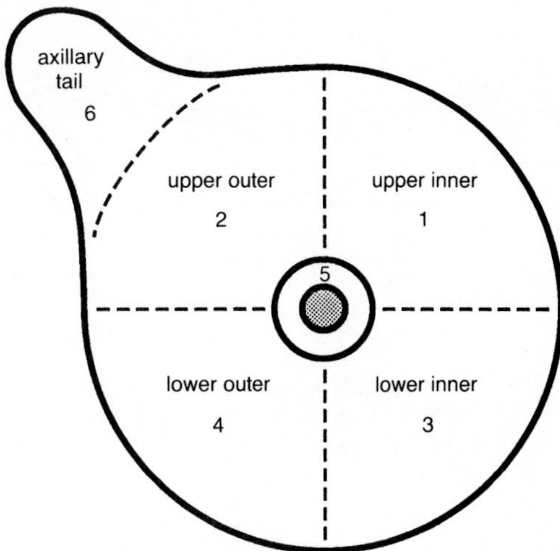

Fig. 74.2 *The six areas of the breast*

Note

- 40–50% of carcinomas occur in the upper outer quadrant[4]
- a hard mass is suspicious of malignancy but cancer can be soft due to fat entrapment
- the inframammary ridge, which is usually found in the heavier breast, is often nodular and firm to hard
- lumpiness (if present) is usually most marked in the upper outer quadrant
- a useful diagrammatic record to record the findings is shown in Figure 74.3
- lumps that are usually benign and require no immediate action are: tiny (< 4 mm) nodules in subcutaneous tissue (usually in the areolar margin); elongated ridges, usually bilateral and in the lower aspects of the breasts; and rounded soft nodules (usually < 6 mm) around the areolar margin.[6]

If a solitary lump is present, assess it for:

- position (breast quadrant and proximity to nipple)
- size and shape
- consistency (firm, hard, cystic, soft)
- tenderness
- mobility and fixation
- attachment to skin or underlying muscle

Investigations

X-ray mammography

Mammography can be used as a screening procedure and as a diagnostic procedure. It is currently the only effective screening tool for breast cancer.[7] Positive signs of malignancy include an irregular infiltrating mass with focal spotty microcalcification.

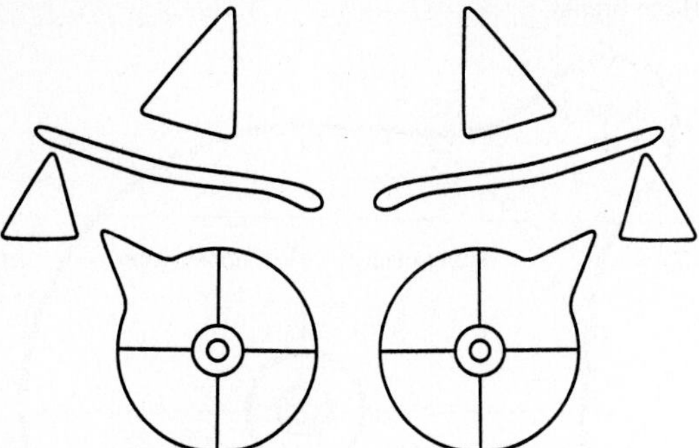

Fig. 74.3 *Diagrammatic scheme for recording the features of breast lumps and any lymphadenopathy (axilla and supraclavicular triangles)*

Screening:

- established benefit for women over 50
- possible benefit for women in their 40's
- follow-up in those with breast cancer, as 6% develop in the opposite breast
- localisation of the lesion for fine needle aspiration

Breast ultrasound

This is mainly used to elucidate an area of breast density and is the best method of defining benign breast disease, especially with cystic changes. It is generally most useful in women less than 30 years old (as compared to X-ray mammography).

Useful for:

- pregnant and lactating breast
- differentiating between fluid-filled cysts and solid mass
- palpable masses at periphery of breast tissue (not screened by mammography)
- for more accurate localisation of lump during fine needle aspiration

Note CT and MRI have limited use. An age-related schemata for likely diagnosis and appropriate investigations is presented in Table 74.2.

Needle aspiration techniques

- cyst aspiration
- fine needle aspiration biopsy: this is a very useful diagnostic test in solid lumps with an accuracy of 90–95% (better than mammography).[4]

Table 74.2 *Age-related schemata for likely diagnoses and appropriate investigations (after Hirst[6])*

1. Very young women—12 to 25
   - inflammed cysts or ducts, usually close to areola
   - fibroadenomata, often giant
   - hormonal thickening, not uncommon
   - malignancy rare

   Investigations — mammography contraindicated
   — ultrasound helpful
2. Young women—26 to 35
   - classical fibroadenomata
   - mammary dysplasia with or without discharge
   - cysts uncommon
   - malignancy uncommon

   Investigations — mammography: breasts often very dense
   — ultrasound often diagnostic
3. Women—36 to 50 (premenopausal)
   - cysts
   - mammary dysplasia, discharges, duct papillomas
   - malignancy common
   - fibroadenomata occur but cannot assume
   - inflammatory processes not uncommon

   Investigations — mammography useful
   — ultrasound useful
4. Women—over 50 (postmenopausal)
   - any new discrete mass—malignant until proven otherwise
   - any new thickening—regard with suspicion
   - inflammatory lesions—probably duct ectasia (follow to resolution)
   - cysts unlikely

   Investigations — mammography usually diagnostic
   — ultrasound may be useful
5. Women—over 50, on hormones
   - any new mass regard with suspicion
   - cysts may occur—usually asymptomatic
   - hormonal change not uncommon

   Investigations — mammography usually diagnostic but breast may become more dense
   — ultrasound may be useful

Reprinted with permission

Tumour markers

Oestrogen receptors are uncommon in normal breasts but are found in two-thirds of breast cancers, although the incidence varies with age. They are good prognostic indicators.

Fine needle aspiration of breast lump[8]

This simple technique is very useful, especially if the lump is a cyst, and will have no adverse effects if the lump is not malignant. If it is, the needle biopsy will help with the preoperative cytological diagnosis.

Method of aspiration and needle biopsy:

1. Use an aqueous skin preparation without local anaesthesia.
2. Use a 23 gauge needle and 5 ml sterile syringe.
3. Identify the mass accurately and fix it by placing three fingers of the non-dominant hand firmly on the three sides of the mass (Fig. 74.4).
4. Introduce the needle directly into the area of the swelling and once in subcutaneous tissue apply gentle suction as the needle is being advanced (Fig. 74.5). If a cyst is involved it can be felt to 'give' suddenly.

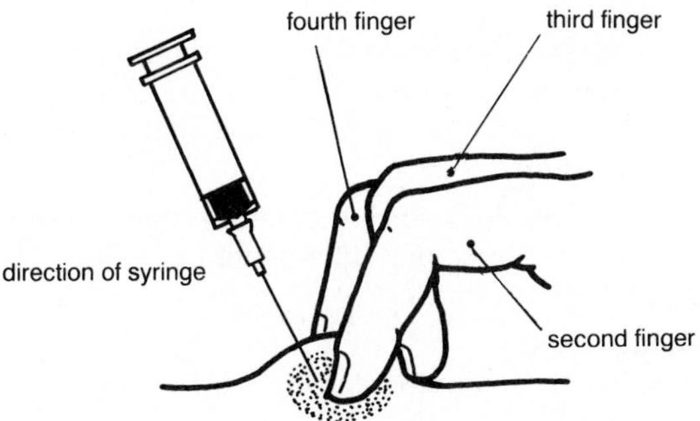

Fig. 74.4 *Aspiration of breast lump: fixation of cyst*

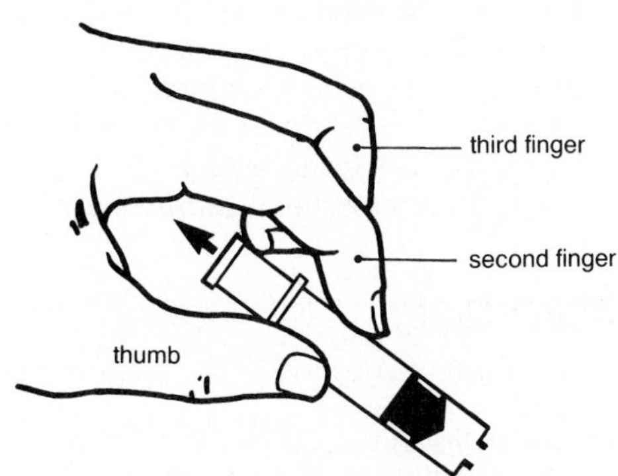

Fig. 74.5 *Aspiration of breast lump: position of the hand—second (index) finger and thumb steady the syringe while the third (middle) finger slides out the plunger to create suction*

5. If fluid is obtained (usually yellowish-green), aspirate as much as possible.
6. If no fluid is obtained, try to get a core of cells from several areas of the lump in the bore of the needle.
7. Make several passes through the lump at different angles, without exit from the skin and maintain suction.
8. Release suction before exit from the skin to keep cells in the needle (not in the syringe).
9. After withdrawal, remove syringe from needle, fill with 2 ml of air, reattach needle and produce a fine spray on one or two prepared slides.
10. Fix to one slide (in Cytofix) and allow one to air dry, and forward to a reputable pathology laboratory to be examined by a skilled cytologist.

Follow-up: the plan for aspiration is outlined in Figure 74.6.

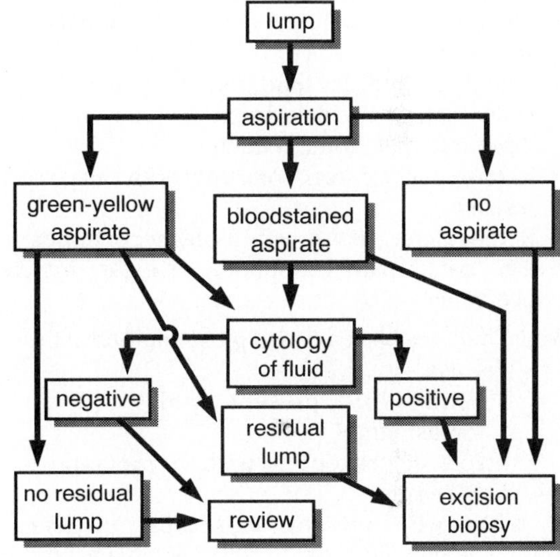

Fig. 74.6 *Scheme for management of a breast lump by fine needle aspiration*

Indications for biopsy or excision of lump:

- The cyst fluid is bloodstained.
- The lump does not disappear completely with aspiration.
- The swelling recurs within one month.

Carcinoma of the breast

Breast carcinoma is uncommon under the age of 30 but it then steadily increases to a maximum at the age of about 60 years.[4] About one-third are premenopausal and two-thirds postmenopausal. About 1 in 10–12 women develop breast cancer. Ninety per cent of breast cancers are invasive duct carcinomas, the remainder being lobular carcinoma, papillary carcinomas, medullary carcinomas and colloid or mucoid carcinomas.[3]

Risk factors include increasing age (> 40 years), Caucasian race, pre-existing benign breast lumps, personal history of breast cancer, family history in a first-degree relative (raises risk about threefold), nulliparity, late menopause (after 53), obesity, childless until after 30 years of age, early menarche.[7]

Clinical features

- The majority of patients with breast cancer present with a lump.
- The lump is usually painless (5% associated with pain).
- Usually the lump is hard and irregular.
- Other symptoms include breast pain, nipple discharge and nipple retraction.
- Rarely cancer can present with Paget's disease.
- Rarely it can present with bony secondaries, e.g. back pain, dyspnoea, weight loss, headache.

Note There are basically two presentations of the disease:
- about 75% present with a local breast lump[3]
- 25% present with metastatic disease

Of those who present with local disease, approximately 50% will develop metastatic disease.

Management

Immediate referral to an expert surgeon on suspicion or proof of breast cancer is essential. The treatment has to be individualised according to the nature of the lump, age of the patient and staging. Accurate staging requires knowledge of whether the draining lymph nodes are involved with the tumour, as this is the single most powerful predictor of subsequent metastases and death. Staging for systemic disease also requires full blood examination and liver function tests (including an alkaline phosphatase). A bone scan may be used as a valuable base line. Size and histological grading of tumour plus nodal status and receptor status are the most important prognostic factors.

Benign mammary dysplasia

Synonyms: fibroadenosis, chronic mastitis, fibrocytic disease, cystic hyperplasia.

Features

- most common in women between 30 and 50
- hormone-related (between menarche and menopause)
- pain and tenderness and swelling
- premenstrual discomfort or pain and increased swelling
- usually settles after the period
- unilateral or bilateral
- nodularity ± a discrete mass
- ache may extend down inner aspect of upper arm
- nipple discharge may occur (various colours, mainly green-grey)
- most cysts are premenopausal (final five years before menopause)

Examination: look for lumpiness in one or both breasts, usually upper outer quadrant.

Management

- Consider mammography if diffuse lumpiness is present in patient > 40.
- Perform needle biopsy if a discrete lump is present and aspirate palpable cysts.
- Reassure patient that there is no cancer.
- Give medication to alleviate mastalgia (see treatment for cyclical mastalgia in Chapter 73).
- Use analgesics as necessary.
- Surgically remove undiagnosed mass lesions.

Breast cyst

- common in 40–50 age group (perimenopausal)
- rare under 30 years
- associated with mammary dysplasia
- tends to regress after the menopause
- pain and tenderness variable
- has a 1 in 1000 incidence of cancer
- usually lined by duct epithelium

Examination: look for a discrete mass, firm, relatively mobile, that is rarely fluctuant.

Diagnosis

- mammography
- ultrasound (X-ray of choice)
- cytology of aspirate

Lactation cysts

- These present postpartum with similar signs to perimenopausal cysts.
- They vary from 1–5 cm in diameter.
- Treat by aspiration: fluid may be clear or milky.

Fibroadenoma

Clinical features

- a discrete lump
- usually in twenties (range: second to sixth decade)
- firm, smooth and mobile (the 'breast mouse')
- usually rounded

Management

Ultrasound and fine needle aspiration with cytology is recommended. It may be left in those in the late teens but as a rule the lump should be removed to be certain of the diagnosis.

Fat necrosis

Fat necrosis is usually the end result of a large bruise or trauma which may be subtle such as protracted breast feeding. The mass that results is often accompanied by skin or nipple retraction and thus closely resembles carcinoma.

The problem of mammary prostheses[6]

Clinical examination is still necessary and fortunately the residual mammary tissue is usually spread over the prosthesis in a thin easily palpable layer. The areas of clinical difficulty lie at the margin of the prosthesis, especially in the upper outer quadrant where most of the breast tissue is displaced. It should be noted that mammography may be of limited value in the presence of prostheses, especially if a fibrous capsule exists around the prosthesis. Ultrasound examination may be helpful.

Mammary duct ectasia

Synonyms: plasma cell mastitis, periductal mastitis.

In this benign condition a whole breast quadrant may be indurated and tender. The lump is usually located near the margin of the areola and is a firm or hard, tender, poorly defined swelling. There may be a toothpaste-like nipple discharge. It is a troublesome condition with a tendency to repeated episodes of periareolar inflammation with recurrent abscesses and fistula formation. Many cases settle but often surgical intervention is necessary to make the diagnosis.

Breast lumps in children

There are several benign conditions that can cause a breast lump in children, although the commonest presentation is a diffuse breast enlargement.

Neonatal enlargement[9]

Newborn babies of either sex can present with breast hyperplasia and secretion of breast milk. This is due to transplacental passage of lactogenic hormones. The swelling usually lasts 7–10 days if left alone. Any attempts to manipulate the breasts to facilitate emptying will prolong the problem.

Premature hyperplasia[9]

The usual presentation is the development of one breast in girls commonly 7–9 years of age but sometimes younger. The feature is a firm discoid lump 1–2 cm in diameter, situated deep to the nipple. The same change may follow in the other breast within 3–12 months. Reassurance and explanation is the management and biopsy must be avoided at all costs.

Subareolar hyperplasia in boys

A discoid subareolar lesion similar to the premature hyperplasia of girls can occur in boys in one or both breasts at about 12–14 years. No specific treatment is necessary, simply explanation and reassurance.

Gynaecomastia

This is not to be confused with pseudogynaecomastia due to fat in obese preadolescents. However, gynaecomastia in thin boys does occur and requires referral for assessment if it cannot be attributed to drugs such as oestrogen. If no cause is found, simple mastectomy may be performed.

Breast lumps in men

Virtually no breast tissue is palpable in normal men and malignancy is rare.

Gynaecomastia

This is a 'true' enlargement of the male breasts, not to be confused with false enlargement of obese men. Gynaecomastia occurs in up to 50% of adolescent boys.[5]

If present in adult men, look for evidence of hypogonodal states such as Klinefelter's syndrome and secondary testicular failure, e.g. orchitis, orchidectomy, traumatic atrophy. Other causes include drugs, e.g. oestrogen, digoxin, marijuana, spironolactone, cimetidine; liver failure; testicular feminisation syndrome; and oestrogen-secreting tumours such as adrenal carcinoma and Leydig cell tumour.

Counselling of patients

'Treat the whole woman, not merely her breasts'.[6] Extreme anxiety is generated by the discovery of a breast lump and it is important that women be encouraged to visit their doctor early, especially as they can learn that there is a nine in ten chance of their lump being benign. It is possible that denial may be a factor or there is a hidden agenda to the consultation. The decision to perform a lumpectomy or a mastectomy should take the patient's feelings into consideration—many do fear that a breast remnant may be a focus for cancer. Longstanding doctor–patient relationships are the ideal basis for coping with the difficulties.

Screening

Screening mammography should be encouraged for women between 50 and 70, and performed at least every 2 years. Technically it is a better diagnostic tool in older women because of the less dense and glandular breast tissue. A management program for women at high risk of breast cancer is presented in Table 74.3. The official recommendation for breast cancer screening in the United States is presented in Table 74.4.

Breast self-examination is a controversial issue and has no proven benefit in reducing morbidity and mortality. It may be helpful, but accurate examination is difficult to teach and it is hard to obtain compliance. The false positive rate is high, especially in those under 40 years.

Table 74.3 *Management program for women at high risk of breast cancer (after Barraclough[7])*

- Monthly breast self-examination
- At least an annual consultation with general practitioner—more frequently if over 40 years of age
- Aspiration of cysts
- Mammography, ultrasound and/or fine needle biopsy to diagnose any localised mass
- Ultrasound alone for further assessment of young, dense breasts
- Regular screening mammography after 50 years of age
- Removal of any undiagnosed mass lesions

Table 74.4 *Official recommendations for breast cancer screening by the American Academy of Family Physicians and the American Cancer Society (1992)*

Age	Investigation	Frequency
20–34	BSE	Monthly
	Clinical breast examination	Every 3 years
35–39	BSE	Monthly
	Clinical breast examination	Every 3 years
	Mammography	Once (baseline)
40–49	BSE	Monthly
	Clinical breast examination	Yearly
	Mammography	Every 2 years
50–59	BSE	Monthly
	Clinical breast examination	Yearly
	Mammography	Yearly
60+	BSE	Monthly
	Clinical breast examination	Yearly
	Mammography	Yearly

When to refer

- Patients with a solitary breast mass.
- Following cyst aspiration:
  — blood in aspirate
  — palpable residual lump
  — recurrence of the cyst
- Patients given antineoplastic drugs, whether for adjuvant therapy or for advanced disease, require skilled supervision.

Lumps that require investigation and referral are presented in Table 74.5.

Table 74.5 *Lumps that require investigation and referral (after Hirst[6])*

A stony hard lump or area, regardless of size, history or position
A new palpable 'anything' in a postmenopausal woman
A persisting painless asymmetrical thickening
An enlarging mass—cyclic or not
A 'slow-to-resolve' or recurrent inflammation
A bloodstained or serous nipple discharge
Skin dimpling, of even a minor degree, or retraction of the nipple
A new thickening or mass in the vicinity of a scar

Practice tips

- Any doubtful breast lump should be removed.
- Fibroadenomas commonly occur in women in their late teens and twenties, benign breast cysts between 35 years and the menopause, and carcinoma is the most common cause of a lump in women over 50 years.[4]
- Never assume a palpable mass is a fibroadenoma in any woman over 30 years of age.[6]
- Gentle palpation is required. Squeezing breast tissue between finger and thumb tends to produce 'pseudolumps'.
- Any eczematous rash appearing on the nipple or areola indicates underlying breast cancer.
- Mammary duct ectasia and fat necrosis can be clinically indistinguishable from carcinoma of the breast.
- The oral contraceptive pill and HRT have been generally shown *not* to alter the risk of breast cancer.
- Never assume that a lump is due to trauma unless you have seen the bruising and can observe the lump decrease in size.[6]
- Never assume a lesion is a cyst—prove it with ultrasound or successful aspiration.[6]
- Never ignore skin dimpling even if no underlying mass is palpable.[6]
- Never ignore a woman's insistence that an area of her breast is different or has changed.[6]

References

1. Davis A, Bolin T, Ham J. *Symptom analysis and physical diagnosis* (2nd edition). Sydney: Pergamon Press, 1990:118.
2. Fry J, Berry HE. *Surgical problems in clinical practice*. London: Edward Arnold, 1987, 57–67.
3. Green M. Breast cancer. In: MIMS Disease Index. Sydney: IMS Publishing, 1991–2, 83–85.
4. Hunt P, Marshall V. *Clinical problems in general surgery*. Sydney: Butterworths, 1991, 63–71.
5. Talley N, O'Connor S. *Clinical examination* (2nd edition). Sydney: Maclennan & Petty, 1992, 300–301.
6. Hirst C. Managing the breast lump. Solving the dilemma—reassurance versus investigation. Aust Fam Physician, 1989; 18:121–126.
7. Barraclough B. The fibrocystic breast—clinical assessment, diagnosis and treatment. Modern Medicine of Australia, April 1990, 16–25.
8. Murtagh J. *Practice tips*. Sydney: McGraw-Hill, 1991, 50–51.
9. Hutson JM, Beasley SW, Woodward AA. *Jones clinical paediatric surgery*. Melbourne: Blackwell Scientific Publications, 1992, 266–267.

75

Abnormal uterine bleeding

Abnormal uterine bleeding is a common problem encountered in general practice. A classification of abnormal uterine bleeding is presented in Table 75.1.

Table 75.1 *Classification of abnormal uterine bleeding*

Abnormal rhythm
- Irregularity of cycle
- Intermenstrual bleeding (metrorrhagia)
- Postcoital bleeding
- Postmenopausal bleeding

Abnormal amount
- Increased amount = menorrhagia
- Decreased amount = hypomenorrhoea

Combination (rhythm and amount)
- Irregular and heavy periods = metromenorrhagia
- Irregular and light periods = oligomenorrhoea

Key facts and checkpoints

- Up to 20% of women in the reproductive age group complain of increased menstrual loss.[1]
- At least 4% of consultations in general practice deal with abnormal uterine bleeding.
- Up to 50% of patients who present with perceived menorrhagia (or excessive blood loss) have a normal blood loss when investigated.[2] Their perception is unreliable.
- The possibility of pregnancy and its complications, such as ectopic pregnancy, abortion (threatened, complete or incomplete), hydatidiform mole or choriocarcinoma should be kept in mind.
- The mean blood loss in a menstrual cycle is 30–40 ml.
- A menstrual record is a useful way to calculate blood loss.
- Blood loss is normally less than 80 ml.
- Menorrhagia is a menstrual loss of more than 120 ml per menstruation.[3]
- Menorrhagia disposes women to iron deficiency anaemia.

Defining what is normal and what is abnormal

This feature is based on a meticulous history, an understanding of the physiology and physiopathology of the menstrual cycle and a clear understanding of what is normal. Most girls reach menarche by the age of 13 (range 10–16).[1] Dysfunctional bleeding is common in the first two or three years after menarche due to many anovulatory cycles resulting in irregular periods, heavy menses and probably dysmenorrhoea.

Once ovulation and regular menstruation are established the cycle usually follows a predictable pattern and any deviation can be considered as abnormal uterine bleeding (see Table 75.2). It is abnormal if the cycle is less than 21 days, the duration of loss is more than eight days, or the volume of loss is such that menstrual pads of adequate absorbency cannot cope with the flow or clots.[3]

Table 75.2 *Normal menstruation in the reproductive age group (after Fung[1])*

	Mean	Range
Length of cycle	26–28 days	21–35 days
Menstrual flow	3–4 days	2–7 days
Normal blood loss	30–40 ml	20–80 ml

Relationship of bleeding to age

Dysfunctional uterine bleeding is more common at the extremes of the reproductive era (Fig. 75.1).[3] The incidence of malignant disease as a cause of bleeding increases with age, being greatest after the age of 45, while endometrial cancer is predicted to be less than 1 in 100 000 in women under the age of 35.[1]

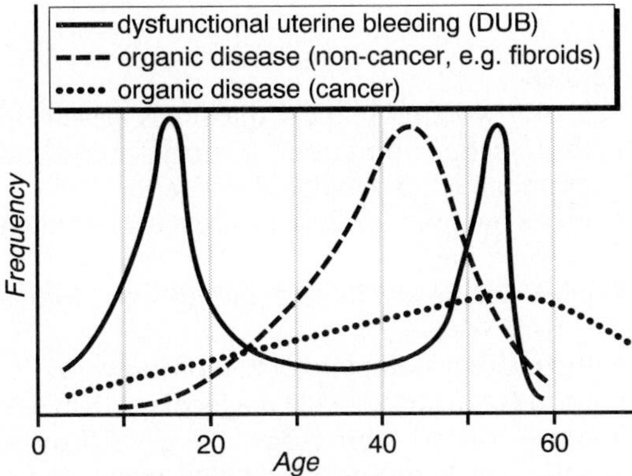

Fig. 75.1 *The relationship between age and various causes of abnormal uterine bleeding* AFTER MACKAY ET AL[3] *DUB is more common in the extremes of the reproductive era, while the incidence of cancer as a cause of bleeding is greatest in the perimenopausal and postmenopausal phases*

Menorrhagia

Menorrhagia, which is excessive blood loss (> 120 ml per period), is essentially caused by hormonal dysfunction (e.g. anovulation), local pathology (e.g. fibroids), or medical disorder (e.g. blood dyscrasia). Heavy bleeding, possibly with clots, is the major symptom of menorrhagia. Dysmenorrhoea may accompany the bleeding and if so endometriosis or pelvic inflammatory disease (PID) should be suspected. With care a 60–80% accuracy can be achieved in clinical assessment.[4] A summary of the diagnostic strategy model is presented in Table 75.3.

By far the most common diagnosis of menorrhagia is dysfunctional uterine bleeding. The most common organic causes are fibromyomatas (fibroids), endometriosis, adenomyosis ('endometriosis' of the myometrium), endometrial polyps and pelvic inflammatory disease.[3]

Table 75.3 *Menorrhagia: diagnostic strategy model*

Q. *Probability diagnosis*
A. Dysfunctional uterine bleeding
Fibroids
Complications of hormone therapy, e.g. pill

Q. *Serious disorders not to be missed*
A. Disorders of pregnancy
- ectopic pregnancy
- abortion or miscarriage

Neoplasia
- cervical cancer
- endometrial cancer
- leukaemia
- benign tumours
  - — polyps, etc.

Severe infections
- pelvic inflammatory disease

Q. *Pitfalls (often missed)*
A. Genital tract trauma
IUCD
Adenomyosis/endometriosis
Pelvic congestion syndrome
SLE

Rare
- endocrine disorders, (e.g. thyroid disease)
- bleeding disorder
- liver disease

Q. *Seven masquerades checklist*

A.		
	Depression	association
	Diabetes	✓
	Drugs	✓
	Anaemia	association
	Thyroid disease	✓ hypothyroidism
	Spinal dysfunction	—
	UTI	—

Q. *Is the patient trying to tell me something?*
A. Consider exaggerated perception. Note association with anxiety and depression.

Clinical approach for menorrhagia

History

Bearing in mind that abnormal uterine bleeding is a subjective complaint, a detailed history is the key initial step in management. The patient's perception of abnormal bleeding may be quite misleading and education about normality is all that is necessary in her management. A meticulous history should include details of the number of tampons or pads used and their degree of saturation. A menstrual calendar (over three or more months) can be a very useful guide. A history of smoking and other psychosocial factors should be checked. For unknown reasons, cigarette smokers are five times more likely to have abnormal menstrual function.[3]

Questions need to be directed to rule out:[1]

- pregnancy or pregnancy complications, e.g. ectopic pregnancy
- complications of the pill
- trauma of the genital tract
- medical disorders, e.g. bleeding disorder
- endocrine disorders
- cancer of the genital tract

Physical examination[1]

A general physical examination should aim at ruling out anaemia, evidence of a bleeding disorder and any other stigmata of relevant medical or endocrine disease.

Specific examinations include:

- speculum examination: ? cervicitis, cervical 'erosion', cervical cancer or polyps
- Pap smear
- bimanual pelvic examination: ? uterine or adnexal tenderness, size and regularity of uterus.

It is prudent to avoid vaginal examination in selected patients, such as a young virgin girl, as the procedure is unhelpful and unnecessarily traumatic.

Investigations

Investigations, especially pelvic scans, should be selected very carefully and only when really indicated. Abnormal pelvic examination findings, persistent symptoms, older patients and other suspicions of disease indicate further investigation to confirm symptoms of menorrhagia and exclude pelvic or systemic pathology.

Consider foremost:

- full blood count (to exclude anaemia and thrombocytopenia)
- iron studies: serum ferritin
- hysteroscopy and endometrial sampling (use directed endometrial biopsy with an instrument such as a Gynoscann, or curettage under general anaesthetic).

Special investigations (only if indicated):

- pregnancy testing
- high-resolution pelvic ultrasound
- laparoscopy where endometriosis, PID or other pelvic pathology is suspected
- serum biochemical screen
- coagulation screen
- thyroid function tests
- tests for SLE: antinuclear antibodies

Dysfunctional uterine bleeding

Dysfunctional uterine bleeding (DUB), which is a diagnosis of exclusion, is defined as 'excessive bleeding, whether heavy, prolonged or frequent, of uterine origin, which is not associated with recognisable pelvic disease, complications of pregnancy or systemic disease'.[4]

Features

- it is a working clinical diagnosis based on the initial detailed history, physical examination and initial investigation
- very common: 10–20% incidence of women at some stage
- peak incidence in late thirties and forties (35–45 years)
- the majority complain of menorrhagia
- up to 40% with the initial diagnosis of DUB will have other pathology (e.g. fibroids, endometrial polyps) if detailed pelvic endoscopic investigations are undertaken

Symptoms

- heavy bleeding: saturated pads, frequent changing, 'accidents', 'flooding', 'clots'
- prolonged bleeding
  - — menstruation > 8 days

    or
  - — heavy bleeding > 4 days
- frequent bleeding—periods occur more than once every 21 days
- pelvic pain and tenderness are not usually prominent features

Management principles[4]

- Establish diagnosis by confirming symptoms and exclude other pathology.

- If no evidence of iron deficiency or anaemia, and significant pathology has been excluded, prospective assessment of the menstrual pattern is indicated using a menstrual calendar.
- Conservative management is usually employed if the uterus is of normal size and there is no evidence of anaemia.
- Drug therapy is indicated if symptoms are persistently troublesome and surgery is contraindicated or not desired by the patient.
- Provide reassurance about the absence of pathology, especially cancer, and give counselling to maximise compliance with treatment.
- Consider surgical management if fertility is no longer important and symptoms cannot be controlled by at least 3–4 months of hormone therapy.

Drug therapy[4]

Treatment regimens are presented in Tables 75.4 and 75.5. First-line treatment is with anti-prostaglandin agents, given throughout the menses. These agents are simple to use, generally very safe and can be used over long periods of time. About 60–80% of patients with ovulatory menorrhagia will respond if compliance is good.[4] Such agents include mefenamic acid, naproxen, ibuprofen and indomethacin. The agent of first choice is usually mefenamic acid.

Table 75.4 *Regimens used in management of menorrhagia*

NSAIDs (prostaglandin inhibitors)
Mefenamic acid 500 mg tds (first sign menses to end of menses)
or
Naproxen 500 mg statim then 250 mg tds

Combined oestrogen-progesterone OC
This is an important first-line therapy.
e.g. 50 μg oestrogen + 1 mg norethisterone, e.g. Norinyl, OrthoNovum

Progestogens (especially for anovulatory patients)
Norethisterone 5-15 mg/day for 14 days
or
Medroxyprogesterone acetate 10-30 mg/day
Give progestogens from day 5-25 (ovulatory patients)

Danazol
Approved for short-term treatment (6 months or less) of severe menorrhagia—dosage 200 mg daily

Hormonal agents include progestogens, combined oestrogen-progestogen oral contraceptives and danazol. Oestrogens can be used but generally are not recommended except in the occasional patient with very heavy bleeding, when intravenous conjugated oestrogens 25 mg can be used (repeated in two hours if no response) and always followed by a 14 day course of oral progestogen. The COC constitutes important first-line therapy in both ovulatory and anovulatory patients, but at least 20% of patients do not respond. It is preferable to use a pill with a higher oestrogen dose, which works better (50 μg rather than 30 μg or 35 μg of oestrogen), and one that contains norethisterone.[1]

Table 75.5 *Typical treatment options for acute and chronic heavy bleeding*

Acute heavy bleeding
- curettage/hysteroscopy
- IV oestrogen (Premarin 20 mg)
  or
  oral high-dose progestogens
  e.g. norethisterone 5-10 mg 2 hourly for 4 doses then 5 mg bd or tds for 14 days[3]

Chronic bleeding
- for anovulatory women
  — cyclical oral progestogens for 14 days
- for ovulatory women
  — cyclical prostaglandin inhibitor
  or
  oral contraceptive
  — oral progestogens (21 days/month)
  — danazol or antifibrinolytic agent

Surgical options

Surgical treatment for menorrhagia is more appropriate if the uterus is enlarged, especially if greater than the size of a 12 week gestation (grapefruit size) or if the patient is anaemic.[1] It is indicated if menorrhagia interferes with lifestyle despite medical (drug) treatment. The surgical options are:

- endometrial resection or electrodiathermy excision—to produce amenorrhoea
- hysterectomy (up to 25% of Australians will have this before age 50); it requires a very carefully planned approach

Cycle irregularity

For practical purposes patients with irregular menstrual cycles can be divided into those under 35 and those over 35 years.

Patients under 35:

- the cause is usually hormonal, rarely organic, but keep malignancy in mind
- management options[1]
  1. explanation and reassurance (if slight irregularity)
  2. COC pill for better cycle control 50 μg oestrogen + 1 mg norethisterone, e.g. Norinyl-1, OrthoNovum
  3. progestogen-only pill (especially anovulatory cycles) norethisterone (Primolut N) 5–15 mg/day from day 5–25 of cycle
  4. combination of 2 and 3.

Patients over 35 should be referred for investigation for organic pathology, usually by endometrial sampling and/or hysteroscopy. If normal the above regimens can be instituted.

Intermenstrual bleeding and postcoital bleeding

These bleeding problems are due to factors such as cervical ectropion (often termed cervical 'erosion'), cervical polyps, the presence of an IUCD and the oral contraceptive pill. Cervical cancer and intrauterine cancer must be ruled out, hence the importance of a Pap smear in all age groups and endometrial sampling, especially in the over 35 age group. Thus intermenstrual bleeding should always be investigated.

Cervical ectropion, which is commonly found in women on the pill and post partum, can be left untreated unless intolerable discharge or moderate postcoital bleeding is present. An IUCD should be removed if causing significant symptoms and the causative pill should be changed to one with a higher oestrogen dose (e.g. from 30 μg oestrogen to 50 μg oestrogen).

Amenorrhoea and oligomenorrhoea

Amenorrhoea is classified as primary or secondary.

Primary amenorrhoea is the failure of the menses to start by 16 years of age.[3] Secondary amenorrhoea is the absence of menses for over six months in a woman who has had established menstruation.

The main approach in the patient with primary amenorrhoea is to differentiate it from delayed puberty. It is important to keep in mind the possibility of an imperforate hymen. A good rule is to note the presence of secondary sex characteristics.[3] If absent it implies that the ovaries are non-functional. Causes of primary amenorrhoea include genital malformations, ovarian disease, pituitary tumours, hypothalamic disease and Turner's syndrome.

In secondary amenorrhoea, consider a physiological cause such as pregnancy, or the menopause, failure of some part of the hypothalamic–pituitary–ovarian–uterine axis, or a metabolic disturbance. Important causes to consider are emotional, psychiatric and constitutional causes such as anorexia nervosa, hyperprolactinaemia, strenuous exercise, weight loss below 75% of ideal, and drugs/hormone therapy, e.g. oral contraceptives.

Oligomenorrhoea is the term for infrequent and usually irregular periods, where the cycles are between six weeks and six months.

Postmenopausal bleeding

Postmenopausal bleeding is vaginal bleeding of any amount occurring six months or more after the menopause.[3] It suggests cervical or uterine body cancer (up to 25%).[3] Other causes include polyps, atrophic vaginitis, endometrial hyperplasia and urethral caruncle. Care has to be taken with women on HRT who have irregular bleeding—they require investigation.

Early referral is usually indicated with a view to a diagnostic procedure. If bleeding recurs despite curettage, hysterectomy should be performed since early cancer of the uterus or ovary may be missed.

When to refer

- Hysterectomy is indicated.
- The patient does not respond to initial therapy.
- There is evidence of underlying disease, e.g. endometriosis, SLE.
- Surgery is indicated.

Practice tips

- Non-menstrual bleeding suggests cancer until proved otherwise: it may be postcoital (cervical cancer); intermenstrual (common with progestogen-only pill); postmenopausal (endometrial cancer).

- Think of a foreign body, especially an IUCD: if it is an IUCD, remove it.
- Hysteroscopy is more effective than the traditional curettage. Studies have shown that usually less than 50% of the uterine cavity is sampled by curettage.[5]

References

1. Fung P. Abnormal uterine bleeding. Modern Medicine of Australia. May 1992, 58–66.
2. Fraser IS, Pearce C, Shearman RP et al. Efficacy of mefenamic acid in patients with a complaint of menorrhagia. Obstet Gynaecol, 1981; 58:543–551.
3. Mackay EV, Beischer NA, Pepperell RJ, Wood C. *Illustrated textbook of gynaecology* (2nd edition). Sydney: WB Saunders, 1992, 77–107.
4. Fraser IS. Dysfunctional uterine bleeding. In: MIMS Disease Index. Sydney: IMS Publishing, 1991–2, 165–167.
5. Wharton B. *Gynaecology*. Melbourne: CHECK programme, RACGP Unit 240; 1992:2–20.

76

Lower abdominal and pelvic pain in women

Pain in the lower abdomen and pelvis is one of the most frequent symptoms experienced by women. The diagnostic approach requires a wide variety of consultative skills, especially when the pain is chronic. The examination of acute abdominal pain has been simplified by the advent of sensitive serum pregnancy tests, ultrasound investigation and the increasing use of laparoscopy. However, an accurate history and examination for all types of pain will generally pinpoint the diagnosis. The ever-present problem of pelvic inflammatory disease (PID), the leading cause of infertility in women, demands an early diagnosis and appropriate management.

Key facts and checkpoints

- A distinction has to be made between acute, chronic and recurrent pain.
- Ectopic pregnancy remains a potentially lethal condition and its diagnosis still requires a high index of suspicion.
- Sudden sharp pain in the pelvis which becomes more generalised indicates rupture of an ectopic pregnancy or an ovarian cyst.
- Recurrent sharp self-limiting pain indicates a ruptured Graafian follicle (mittelschmerz).
- Recurrent pain related to menstruation is typical of dysmenorrhoea or endometriosis.
- A UK study[1] of chronic lower abdominal pain in women showed the causes were adhesions (36%), no diagnosis (19%), endometriosis (14%), constipation (13%), ovarian cysts (11%) and PID (7%). An Australian study found that endometriosis accounted for 30% and adhesions 20%.[2]
- The principal afferent pathways of the pelvic viscera arise from T10,11,12, L1 and S2,3,4. Thus disorders of the bladder, rectum, lower uterus, cervix and upper vagina can refer pain to the low back, buttocks and posterior thigh.[3]

A diagnostic approach

A summary of the safety diagnostic model is presented in Table 76.1.

Probability diagnosis

The commonest causes are primary dysmenorrhoea, the pain of a ruptured Graafian follicle (mittelschmerz) and adhesions. In many instances of pain no diagnosis is made as no pathological cause can be found.

Serious disorders not to be missed

The potentially lethal problem of a ruptured ectopic pregnancy must not be missed, hence the axiom 'be ectopic minded'. Pelvic inflammatory disease (PID) can be overlooked, especially if chronic, and requires early diagnosis and aggressive treatment. Neoplasia must be considered, especially malignancy of pelvic structures including the 'silent' carcinoma of the ovary.

Table 76.1 *Lower abdominal and pelvic pain in women: diagnostic strategy model*

Q. Probability diagnosis
A. Primary dysmenorrhoea
Mittelschmerz
Pelvic/abdominal adhesions

Q. Serious disorders not to be missed
A. Ectopic pregnancy
Neoplasia
- ovary
- uterus
- other pelvic structures

Severe infections
- PID

Acute appendicitis

Q. Pitfalls (often missed)
A. Endometriosis/adenomyosis
Torsion of ovary or pedunculated fibroid
Constipation
Pelvic congestion syndrome
Referred pain (to pelvis)
- appendicitis
- cholecystitis
- diverticulitis
- urinary tract infection

Q. Seven masquerades checklist

A.	
Depression	✓
Diabetes	—
Drugs	✓
Anaemia	—
Thyroid disease	—
Spinal dysfunction	✓
UTI	✓

Q. Is the patient trying to tell me something?
A. Can be very relevant. Consider various problems and sexual dysfunction.

Pitfalls

There are several disorders that are very difficult to diagnose and these include haemorrhage into the ovary or a cyst, torsion of the ovary or pedunculated fibroid. Endometriosis may be missed so it is important to be familiar with its symptoms. Chronic constipation may be a trap. Another relatively common problem is the so-called 'pelvic congestion syndrome' which tends to occur in somewhat neurotic patients and also tends to be a diagnosis of exclusion.

Seven masquerades checklist

Two important conditions to consider are urinary tract infection and spinal dysfunction. Just as disorders of the pelvic organs, such as endometriosis and PID, can refer pain to the low back and buttocks so can disorders of the lumbosacral spine cause referred pain to the lower abdomen and groin.

Psychogenic considerations

These can be extremely relevant. Problems in the patient's social, marital or sexual relationships should be evaluated, especially in the assessment of chronic pain. Many patients with undiagnosed chronic pain exhibit psychoneurotic traits and this renders management very complex. Some appear to have the 'pelvic congestion syndrome' and need to be handled with sensitivity and tact, especially if the help of a psychiatrist or psychologist is sought.

The clinical approach

History

The pain should be linked with the menstrual history, coitus and the possibility of an early pregnancy. For recurrent and chronic pain it is advisable to instruct the patient to keep a diary over two menstrual cycles. The severity of the pain can be assessed as follows:[2]

- does not interfere with daily activity
- results in days off work
- results in confinement to bed

In this way the pain can be classified objectively as mild, moderate or severe.

Risk factors in the past history should be assessed, e.g.

- IUCD (salpingitis, ectopic pregnancy)
- infertility (endometriosis, salpingitis)
- tubal surgery (ectopic)

The typical pain patterns in relation to menstruation are shown in Figure 76.1.

Physical examination

One objective is to correlate any palpable tenderness with the patient's statement of the severity of the pain. Use the traditional abdominal and pelvic examination to identify the site of tenderness and rebound tenderness, and any abdominal or pelvic masses. The pelvis should be examined by speculum (preferably bivalve type) and bimanual palpation.

Proper assessment can be difficult if the patient cannot relax or overreacts, if there is abdominal scarring or obesity, or if extreme tenderness is present. It is therefore important, especially in the younger and apprehensive patient, to conduct a gentle caring vaginal examination with appropriate explanation and reassurance. Explanation of the procedure during vaginal examination, preferably using eye contact with the patient, can help her relax and be more confident in the procedure.

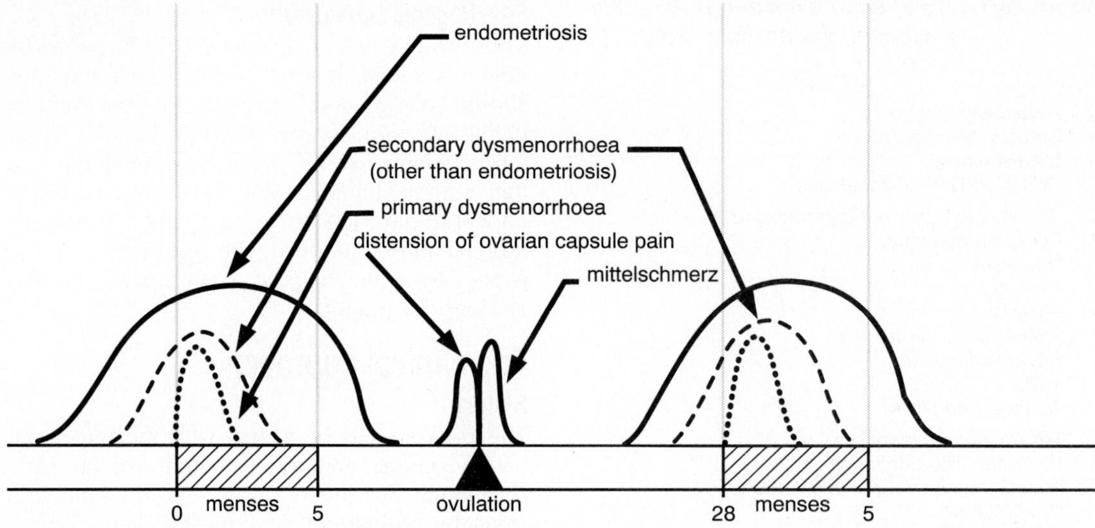

Fig. 76.1 *Typical pain patterns for the menstrual cycle related gynaecological pain*

Investigations

Investigations may be selected from:

- haemoglobin level
- white blood cell count (limited value)
- haematocrit
- ESR
- microbiology (limited value)
  - — urine from micro and culture
  - — endocervical, urethral, cervical and vaginal swabs
- serum β-HCG assay
- urinary HCG tests (can be negative in the presence of an ectopic pregnancy)

Diagnostic imaging

- vaginal ultrasound—to define a gestation sac
- pelvic ultrasound—to differentiate a cystic from a solid pelvic mass

Laparoscopy is indicated if history and examination are suggestive of ectopic pregnancy and ultrasound fails to confirm an intrauteric pregnancy.

Acute pain

The causes of acute pain are summarised in Table 76.2. The patient is usually young (20–30 years old), sexually active and distressed by the pain, and should be considered foremost to have a bleeding ectopic pregnancy. Important differential diagnoses include acute PID, rupture or torsion of an ovarian cyst and acute appendicitis. Cases of acute ruptured ectopics are obviously easier to diagnose in the presence of circulatory collapse.

Table 76.2 *Causes of acute lower abdominal and pelvic pain in women (after Soo Keat Khoo[3])*

Genital

- Acute salpingitis
- Pelvic peritonitis
- Bleeding
- Rupture or torsion of ovarian cyst
- Threatened or incomplete abortion
- Rupture or aborting tubal ectopic pregnancy
- Rupture or bleeding endometrioma

Non-genital

- Acute appendicitis
- Bowel obstruction
- Urinary tract infection (cystitis)
- Ureteric colic (calculus)

Functional

- Primary dysmenorrhoea
- Retrograde menstruation

Chronic pain

The common causes of chronic pain are listed in Table 76.3. Chronic pain is more difficult to diagnose and it is often difficult to differentiate between problems such as endometriosis, PID, an ovarian neoplasm and the irritable bowel syndrome. A comparison of the clinical features of endometriosis and PID is presented in Table 76.4. Furthermore it is difficult to distinguish clinically between endometriosis of the uterus (adenomyosis) and pelvic congestion syndrome. Both conditions are associated with dysmenorrhoea and a tender normal-sized uterus.

Table 76.3 *Causes of chronic lower abdominal and pelvic pain in women*[3]

Genital
- Endometriosis/adenomyosis
- Pelvic inflammatory disease (chronic; adhesions)
- Ovarian neoplasm
- Fibromyomata (rarely)

Non-genital
- Diverticulitis
- Bowel adhesions

Functional
- Pelvic congestion syndrome
- Secondary dysmenorrhoea—IUCD*, polyp
- Irritable bowel, chronic bowel spasm

* intrauterine contraceptive device

In pelvic congestion syndrome the patient is usually one who is para 3 or 4, aged 35–40 years, with a multitude of emotional problems.[3] They often undergo hysterectomy, sometimes without relief of symptoms.

Ectopic pregnancy

Ectopic pregnancy occurs approximately once in every 100 clinically recognised pregnancies. If ruptured it can be a rapid, fatal condition so we have to be ectopic minded. It is the commonest cause of intraperitoneal haemorrhage. There is usually a history of a missed period but a normal menstrual history may be obtained in some instances.

Typical clinical features of a ruptured ectopic pregnancy

- average patient in mid-twenties
- first pregnancy in one-third of patients
- patient at risk
  - — previous ectopic pregnancy
  - — previous PID
  - — previous abdominal or pelvic surgery, especially sterilisation reversal
  - — IUCD use
  - — in-vitro fertilisation/GIFT

Classical triad
amenorrhoea (65–80%)
lower abdominal pain (95+%)
abnormal vaginal bleeding (65–85%)

- prerupture symptoms (many cases)
  - — abnormal pregnancy
  - — cramping pains in one or other iliac fossa
  - — vaginal bleeding

Table 76.4 *Comparison of clinical features of PID and pelvic endometriosis*

Feature	***Chronic PID***	***Endometriosis***
History	acute pelvic infection, e.g. ruptured appendix IUCD usage	dysmenorrhoea infertility dyspareunia pelvic pain
Pelvic pain	++ to +++ (moderate to severe) premenstrual lower abdominal location	++ to +++ (moderate to severe) premenstrual and menstrual acute pain if rupture of endometrioma
Backache	+ mild	++ moderate low sacral pain with menstruation
Secondary dysmenorrhoea	moderate to severe from onset of acute PID decreases with menstruation	moderate to severe gradual onset increases in severity throughout menstruation
Menstruation	irregular and heavy	heavy
Dyspareunia	moderate	often severe
Infertility	+++	++
Urinary symptoms	—	frequency, dysuria and haematuria if bladder wall involved
Bowel symptoms	—	painful defecation if rectal wall involved
Vaginal symptoms	may be chronic purulent discharge or leucorrhoea	—

- rupture
  - — excruciating pain (Fig. 76.2)
  - — circulatory collapse

Note In 10–15% there is no abnormal bleeding.

- pain may radiate to rectum (lavatory sign), vagina or leg
- signs of pregnancy, e.g. enlarged breasts and uterus, usually not present

Examination

- deep tenderness in iliac fossa
- vaginal examination
  - — tenderness on bimanual pelvic examination (pain on moving cervix)
  - — soft cervix
- bleeding (prune juice appearance)
- temperature and pulse usually normal early

Diagnosis

It is possible to diagnose ectopic pregnancy at a very early stage of pregnancy.

- urine pregnancy test (positive in < 50%)
- serum β-HCG assay (invariably positive if a significant amount of viable trophoblastic tissue present)
- vaginal ultrasound can diagnose at 5–6 weeks (empty uterus, tubal sac)
- laparoscopy (the definitive diagnostic procedure)

Management

Treatment may be conservative (based on ultrasound and β-HCG assays); medical, by injecting methotrexate into the ectopic sac; laparoscopic removal; or laparotomy for severe cases. Rupture with blood loss demands urgent surgery.

Ruptured ovarian (Graafian) follicle (mittelschmerz)

When the Graafian follicle ruptures a small amount of blood mixed with follicular fluid is usually released into the pouch of Douglas. This may cause peritonism (mittelschmerz) which is different from the unilateral pain experienced just before ovulation due to distension of the ovarian capsule.

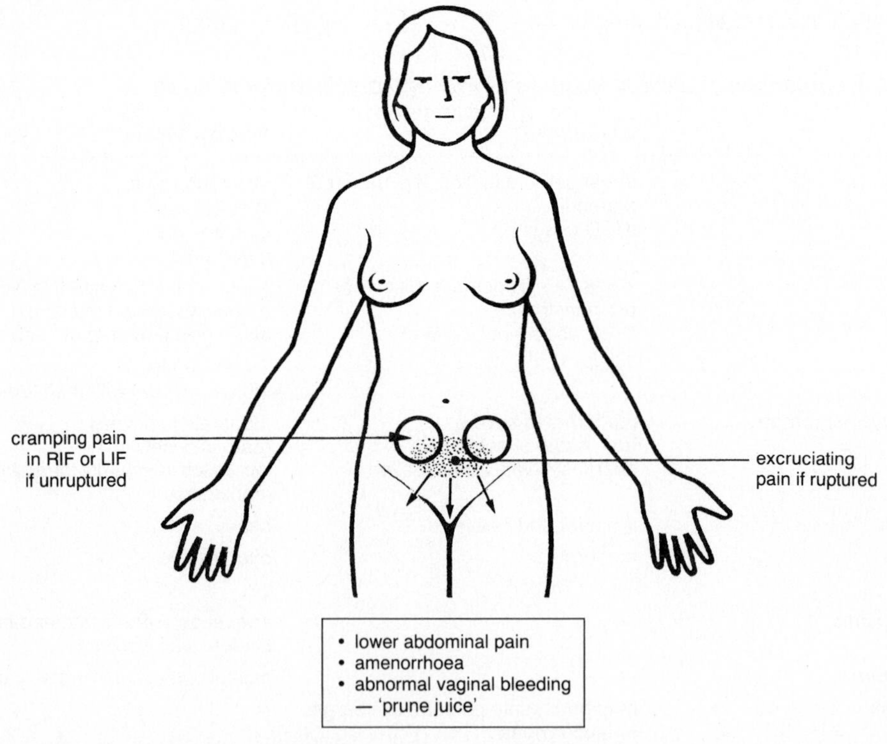

Fig. 76.2 *Clinical features of ectopic pregnancy*

Typical clinical features

- onset of pain in mid cycle
- deep pain in one or other iliac fossa (RIF>LIF)
- often described as a 'horse kick pain'
- pain tends to move centrally (Fig. 76.3)
- heavy feeling in pelvis
- relieved by sitting or supporting lower abdomen
- pain lasts from a few minutes to hours (average five hours)
- patient otherwise well

Note Sometimes it can mimic acute appendicitis.

Management

- explanation and reassurance
- simple analgesics: aspirin or paracetamol (acetaminophen)
- 'hot water bottle' comfort if pain severe

Ovarian tumours

Benign ovarian tumours, particularly ovarian cysts, may be asymptomatic but will cause pain if complicated. They are common in women under 50 years of age. Ovarian cysts are best defined by vaginal ultrasound which can identify whether haemorrhage has occurred inside or outside the cyst.

Ruptured ovarian cyst

The cysts tend to rupture just prior to ovulation or following coitus.

Clinical features

- patient usually 15–25 years
- sudden onset of pain in one or other iliac fossa
- may be nausea and vomiting
- no systemic signs
- pain usually settles within a few hours

Signs

- tenderness and guarding in iliac fossa
- PR: tenderness in rectovaginal pouch

Management

- appropriate explanation and reassurance
- conservative
  — simple cyst < 4 cm
  — internal haemorrhage
  — minimal pain

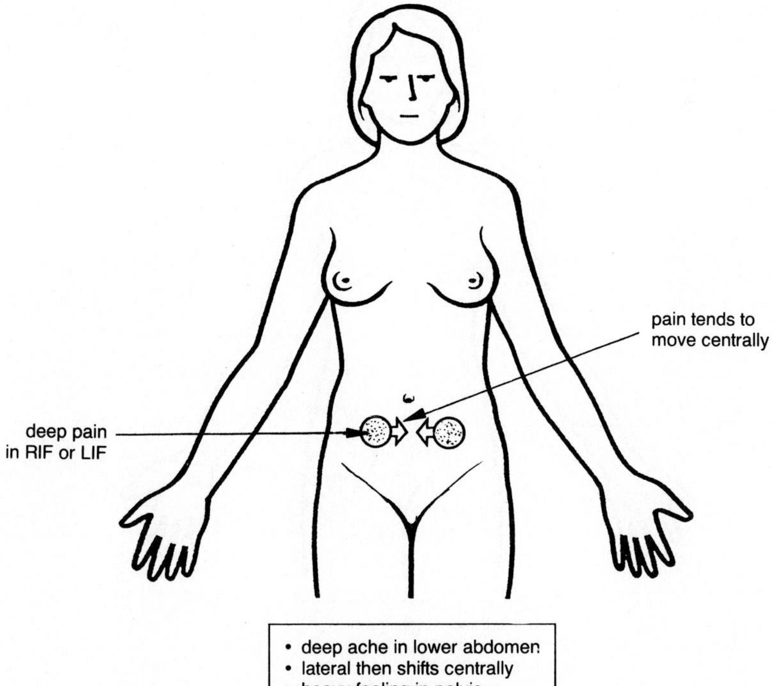

Fig. 76.3 *Typical clinical features of a ruptured Graafian follicle (mittelschmerz)*

- needle vaginal drainage by ultrasonography for a simple cyst
- laparoscopic surgery
  - — complex cysts
  - — large cysts
  - — external bleeding

Acute torsion of ovarian cyst

Torsions are mainly from dermoid cysts and may be difficult to distinguish from acute pelvic appendicitis.

Clinical features

- severe cramping lower abdominal pain (Fig. 76.4)
- diffuse pain
- pain may radiate to the flank or thigh
- repeated vomiting
- exquisite pelvic tenderness
- patient looks ill

Signs

- smooth, rounded, mobile mass palpable in abdomen
- may be tenderness and guarding over the mass, especially if leakage

Diagnosis

- ultrasound

Treatment

- laparotomy and surgical correction

Malignant ovarian tumours

Ovarian cancer has an incidence of 10 cases per 100 000 women per year and accounts for 5% of all cancers in women and 20% of all genital cancers. It is responsible for more genital cancer deaths because the tumour is often well advanced at the time of clinical presentation.[4] Earlier discovery may sometimes be made on routine examination or because of investigation of non-specific pelvic symptoms.

Ovarian cancer tends to remain asymptomatic for a long period. No age group is spared but it becomes progressively more common after 45 years.

Clinical features

- ache or discomfort in lower abdomen or pelvis
- gastrointestinal dysfunction, e.g. epigastric discomfort

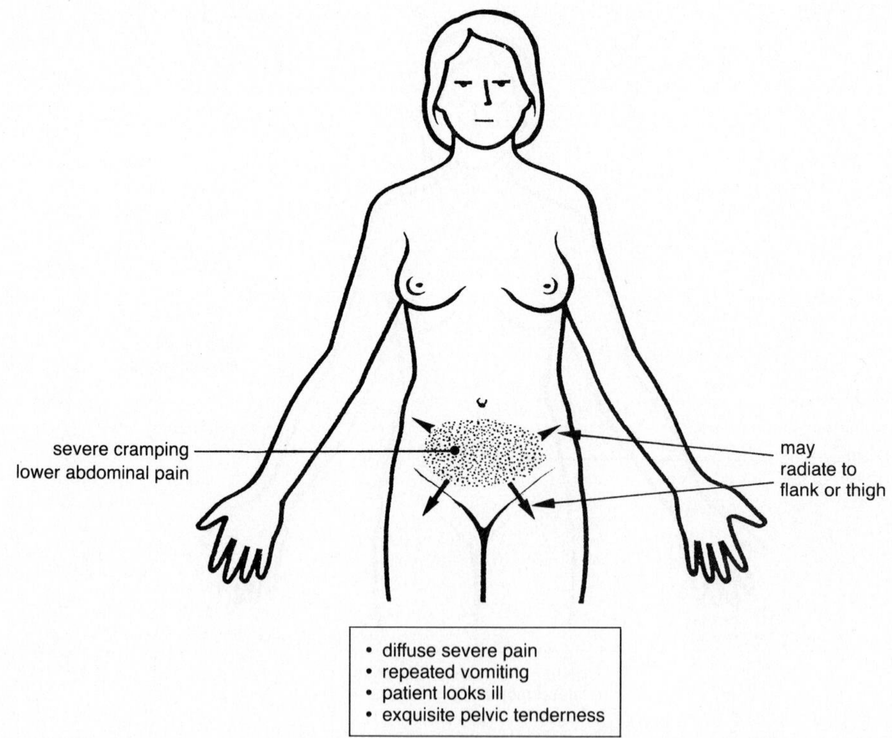

Fig. 76.4 *Typical clinical features of acute torsion of an ovarian cyst*

- sensation of pelvic heaviness
- ± menstrual dysfunction
- dyspareunia and/or dysmenorrhoea (10–20%)
- a combined vaginal–rectal bimanual examination assists diagnosis

Note Any ovary that is easily palpable is usually abnormal (normal ovary rarely > 4 cm).

Diagnosis

- ultrasound might be useful
- tumour markers such as CA 125, HCG (choriocarcinoma) and alpha fetoprotein are becoming more important in diagnosis and management

Dysmenorrhoea

Dysmenorrhoea (painful periods) may commence with the onset of the menses (menarche) when it is called primary dysmenorrhoea, or later in life when the term secondary dysmenorrhoea is applied.

Primary (functional) dysmenorrhoea

This is menstrual pain associated with ovular cycles without any pathologic findings. The pain usually commences within 1–2 years after the menarche and become more severe with time up to about 20 years.

Clinical features

- low midline abdominal pain
- pain radiates to back or thighs (Fig. 76.5)
- varies from a dull dragging to a severe cramping pain
- maximum pain at beginning of the period
- may commence up to 12 hours before the menses appear
- usually lasts 24 hours but may persist for two or three days
- may be associated with nausea and vomiting, headache, syncope or flushing
- no abnormal findings on examination

Management

- full explanation and appropriate reassurance
- promote a healthy lifestyle
  — regular exercise
  — avoid smoking and excessive alcohol
- recommend relaxation techniques such as yoga
- avoid exposure to extreme cold
- place a hot water bottle over the painful area and curl the knees onto the chest

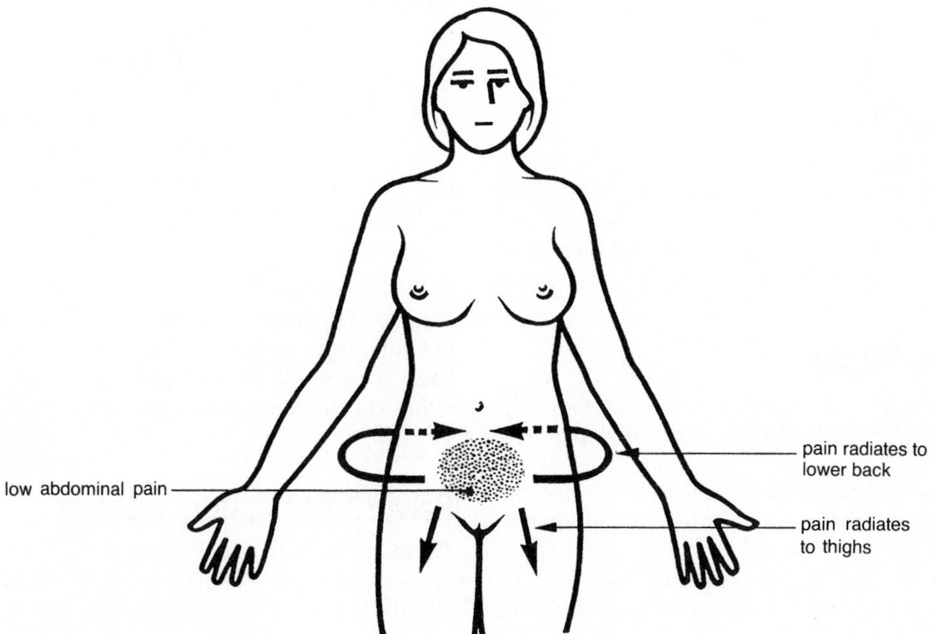

Fig. 76.5 *Typical pain of dysmenorrhoea*

Medication

Options include (trying in order):

- simple analgesics, e.g. aspirin or paracetamol (acetaminophen)
- prostaglandin inhibitors, e.g. mefenamic acid, 500 mg tds at first suggestion of pain (if simple analgesics ineffective)
- combined oral contraceptive (low-oestrogen triphasic pills preferable)

Secondary dysmenorrhoea

Secondary dysmenorrhoea is menstrual pain for which an organic cause can be found. It usually begins after the menarche after years of pain-free menses; the patient is usually over 30 years of age. The pain begins as a dull pelvic ache three to four days before the menses and becomes more severe during menstruation.

Commonest causes

- endometriosis } the major causes
- PID } the major causes
- IUCD
- submucous myoma
- intrauterine polyp
- pelvic adhesions

Investigations

Investigations include laparoscopy, ultrasound and (less commonly) assessment of the uterine cavity by dilation and curettage, hysteroscopy or hysterosalpingography.

Management involves treating the cause.

Pelvic adhesions

Pelvic adhesions may be the cause of pelvic pain, infertility, dysmenorrhoea and intestinal pain. They can be diagnosed and removed laparoscopically when the adhesions are well visualised and there are no intestinal loops firmly stuck together.

Endometriosis

Endometriosis is the condition where ectopically located endometrial tissue (usually in dependent parts of the pelvis and in the ovaries) responds to female sex hormone stimulation by proliferation, haemorrhage, adhesions and ultimately dense scar tissue changes.

Patients experience varying degrees of symptoms and loss of gynaecological function according to the site and severity of the endometriosis deposits.

Clinical features

- 10% incidence[5]
- puberty to menopause, peak 25–35 years
- secondary dysmenorrhoea
- infertility
- dyspareunia
- non-specific pelvic pain
- menorrhagia
- acute pain with rupture of endometrioma

Possible signs

- fixed uterine retroversion
- tenderness and nodularity in the pouch of Douglas/retrovaginal septum
- uterine enlargement and tenderness

Differential diagnosis

- pelvic inflammatory disease (PID)—see Table 76.4
- ovarian cysts or tumours
- uterine myomas

Diagnosis

- can be made only by direct visual inspection at laparoscopy or laparotomy

Treatment

- basic analgesics
- treatment can be surgical or medical

Medical: to induce amenorrhoea (only two-thirds respond to drugs)

- danazol (Danocrine)—current treatment of choice
- combined oestrogen-progestogen oral contraceptive: once daily continuously for about six months
- progestogens, e.g. medroxyprogesterone acetate (Depo-Provera)

Surgical Surgical measures depend on the patient's age, symptoms and family planning. Laser surgery and microsurgery can be performed either via laparoscopy or laparotomy.

Pelvic inflammatory disease

There are great medical problems in the serious consequences of PID, namely tubal obstruction, infertility and ectopic pregnancy. PID may be either acute, which causes sudden severe symptoms, or chronic, which can gradually produce milder symptoms or follow an acute episode. Acute PID is a major public health problem and is the most important complication of sexually transmitted disease among young women. The majority are young (less than 25 years) sexually active young women who are also nulliparous.

Some patients may experience no symptoms but others may have symptoms that vary from mild to very severe. The clinical diagnosis can be difficult as signs and symptoms can be non-specific and correlate poorly with the extent of the inflammation.

Table 76.5 *Diagnostic criteria for acute PID*

All three of the following should be present:
1. Lower abdominal tenderness (with or without rebound)
2. Cervical motion tenderness
3. Adnexal tenderness (may be unilateral)

plus

One of the following should be present:
1. Temperature ≥ 38°C
2. White blood cell count ≥ 10 500/mm^2
3. Purulent fluid obtained via culdocentesis
4. Inflammatory mass present on bimanual pelvic examination and/or sonography
5. ESR ≥ 15 mm/hr or C-reactive protein > 1.0 mg/dL
6. Evidence for presence of *N.gonnorhoeae* and/or *C.trachomatis* in the endocervix. Gram stain reveals Gram-negative intracellular diplococci. Monoclonal antibody stain for *C.trachomatis*.
7. Presence of > 5 white blood cells per oil immersion field on Gram stain of endocervical discharge.

Clinical features

Acute PID
- fever ≥ 38°C
- moderate to severe lower abdominal pain

Chronic PID
- ache in the lower back
- mild lower abdominal pain

Both acute and chronic
- dyspareunia
- menstrual problems (e.g. painful, heavy or irregular periods)
- intermenstrual bleeding
- abnormal, perhaps offensive, purulent vaginal discharge
- painful or frequent urination

The diagnostic criteria for acute PID are presented in Table 76.5.[6]

Examination

- In acute PID there may be lower abdominal tenderness ± rigidity.
- Pelvic examination: in acute PID there is unusual vaginal warmth, cervical motion tenderness and adnexal tenderness. Inspection usually reveals a red inflamed cervix and a purulent discharge.

Causative agents

These can be subdivided into two broad groups:

1. *Exogenous organisms*: those which are community acquired and initiated by sexual activity. They include the classic STDs, *Chlamydia trachomatis* and *Neisseria gonorrhoeae*. This usually leads to salpingitis.
2. *Endogenous infections*: these are normal commensals of the lower genital tract, especially *Escherichia coli* and *Bacteroides fragilis*. They become pathogenic under conditions that interrupt the normal cervical barrier such as recent genital tract manipulation or trauma, e.g. abortion, presence of an IUCD, recent pregnancy or a dilatation and curettage. The commonest portals of entry are cervical lacerations and the placental site. These organisms cause an ascending infection and can spread direct or via lymphatics to the broad ligament, causing pelvic cellulitis (Fig. 76.6).

Investigations

A definitive diagnosis is difficult since routine specimen collection has limitations in assessing the organisms. Definitive diagnosis is by laparoscopy but this is not practical in all cases of suspected PID.

- cervical swab for Gram stain and culture (*N.gonorrhoeae*)
- cervical swab and special techniques for *C.trachomatis*

Treatment of PID

Note Any IUCD or retained products of contraception should be removed at or before the start of treatment.
Sex partners of women with PID should be treated with agents effective against *Chlamydia trachomatis* and *Neisseria gonorrhoeae*.

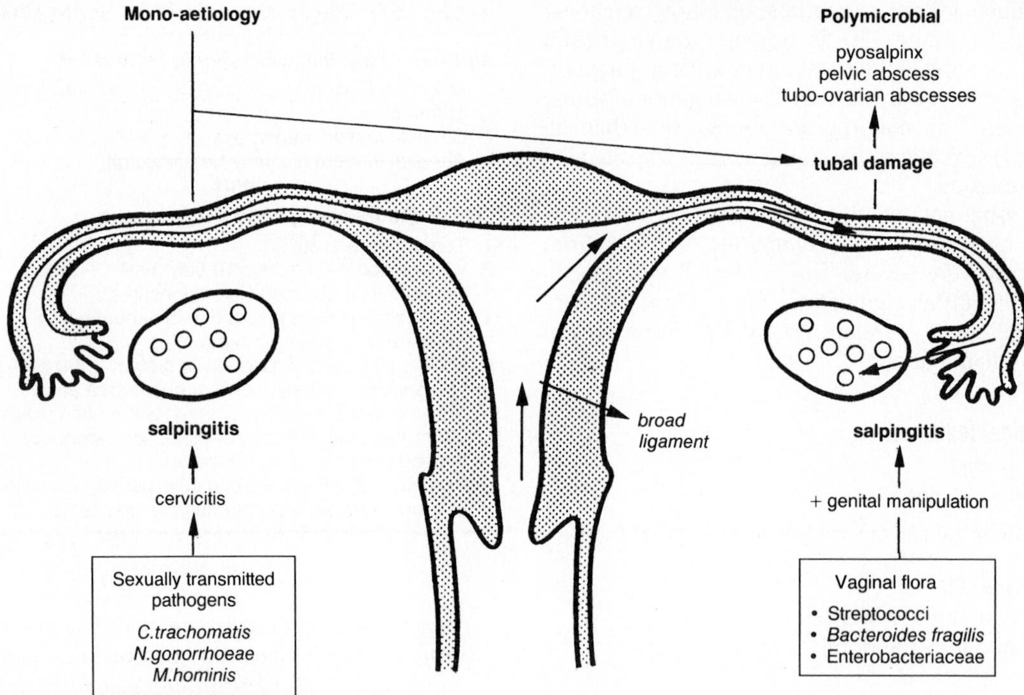

Fig. 76.6 *The pathogenesis of PID*

Sexually acquired infection[7]

Mild infection (treated as an outpatient):

doxycycline 100 mg (o) 12 hourly for 14 days

plus either

metronidazole 400 mg (o) 12 hourly with food for 14 days

or

tinidazole 500 mg (o) daily with food for 14 days

Where penicillinase-producing *Neisseria gonorrhoeae* (which is often tetracycline-resistant) is suspected or proven, add:

ciprofloxacin 500 mg (o) 12 hourly for 14 days

Severe infection (treated in hospital):

cefoxitin 2 g IV 8 hourly or cefotetan 2 g IV 12 hourly

plus

doxycycline 100 mg (o) 12 hourly

plus

metronidazole 500 mg IV 12 hourly

until there is substantial clinical improvement, when the oral regimen above can be used for the remainder of the 14 days. If the patient is pregnant or breast-feeding, doxycyline should be replaced by

erythromycin 500 mg IV or (o) 6 hourly

Infection non-sexually acquired (related to genital manipulation)

Mild infection

amoxycillin 500 mg (o) 8 hourly for 10 days

plus either

metronidazole 400 mg (o) 12 hourly with food for 10 days

or

tinidazole 500 mg (o) daily with food for 10 days

or (as a single agent)

amoxycillin/potassium clavulanate (500/125 mg) (o) 8 hourly for 10 days

Severe infection (including septicaemia)

(amoxy)ampicillin 1 g IV 6 hourly

together with

gentamicin 1.5 mg/kg IV 8 hourly

together with

metronidazole 500 mg IV 12 hourly

or (as single agents)

cefoxitin 2 g IV 8 hourly or cefotetan 2 g IV 12 hourly

until there is substantial clinical improvement, when the oral regimen above can be used for the remainder of the 14 days.

If infection with *Streptococcus pyogenes* or *Clostridium perfringens* is suspected or proven, then benzylpenicillin 2.4 g IV 4 hourly is the drug of choice.

When to refer

- All cases of 'unexplained infertility'.
- All teenagers with dysmenorrhoea sufficient to interfere with normal school, work or recreational activities, and not responding to prostaglandin inhibitors.
- Patients with dysmenorrhoea reaching a crescendo mid menses.
- Patients with dysmenorrhoea and unexplained bowel or bladder symptoms.
- Patients with positional dyspareunia.
- Patients with cyclic pain or bleeding in unusual sites.

Note Pelvic disease which can be treated by advanced laparoscopy surgery includes ectopic pregnancy, ovarian cysts, endometriosis and endometriomas, fibromyomata, pelvic adhesions and hydrosalpinx.

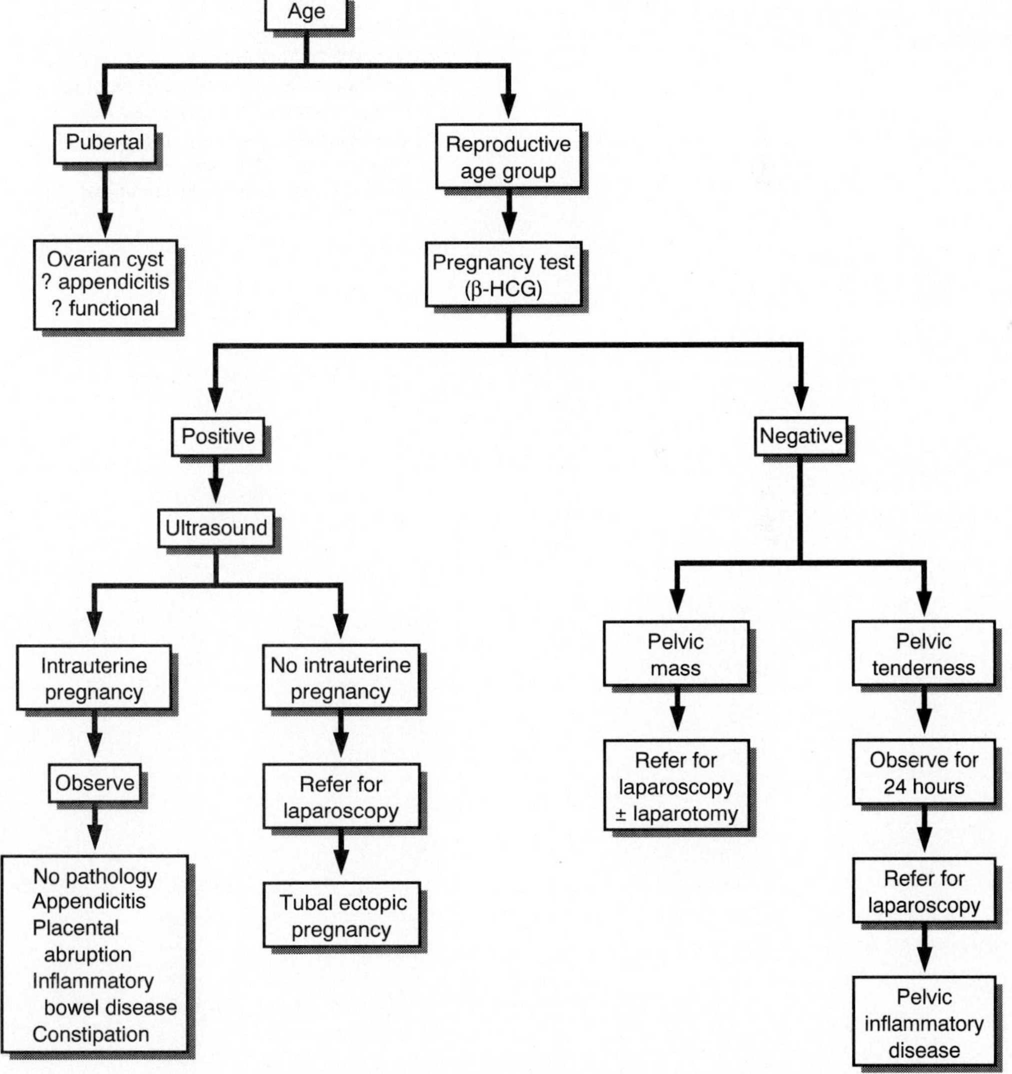

Fig. 76.7 *An approach to management of acute abdominal and pelvic pain in premenopausal women* AFTER FORBES

Practice tips

- Think of endometriosis and ovarian cysts in any woman with lower abdominal pain.
- In any woman whose normal activities are disturbed by dysmenorrhoea unrelieved by NSAIDs, endometriosis should be suspected.
- If an ectopic pregnancy is suspected and there are no facilities for resuscitation digital vaginal examination should be deferred for it may provoke rupture.[2]
- Acute abdominal and pelvic pain in the presence of a negative β-HCG is most often due to an ovarian cyst.
- A positive β-HCG plus an empty uterus and an adnexal mass are the classic diagnostic features of ectopic pregnancy.

References

1. Foy A, Brown R. Chronic lower abdominal pain in gynaecological practice. Update, 27 March 1987, 19–25.
2. Forbes KL. Lower abdominal and pelvic pain in the female: a gynaecological approach. Mod Medicine of Australia, September 1991, 24–31.
3. Soo Keat Khoo. Lower abdominal pain in women. Patient management supplement, August 1990, 13–23.
4. Mackay EV et al. *Illustrated textbook of gynaecology* (2nd edition). Sydney: WB Saunders, Bailliere Tindall, 1992, 514–524.
5. O'Connor DT. Endometriosis. In: MIMS Disease Index. Sydney: IMS Publishing, 1991–2, 175–177.
6. Hager WD, Eschenbach DA et al. Criteria for diagnosis and grading of salpingitis. Obstet Gynecol 1983; 61:113–114.
7. Mashford ML et al. *Antibiotic guidelines* (8th edition). Melbourne: Victorian Medical Postgraduate Foundation, 1994–95: 118–119.

77

Premenstrual syndrome

Premenstrual syndrome (PMS) is defined as a group of physical, psychological and behavioural changes which begin from 2 to 14 days before menstruation and are relieved immediately the menstrual flow begins.[1]

These symptoms occur in the luteal phase of the menstrual cycle yet the pathogenesis of PMS is still uncertain. Among the proposed causes are pyridoxine deficiency, excess prostaglandin production and increased aldosterone production in the luteal phase.[2] However, PMS is most probably a disorder of ovarian function with a relative excess of oestrogen the main determinant.[3]

Key features

- PMS increases in incidence after 30 years, with a peak incidence in the 30–40 year age group.
- PMS also occurs in the 45–50 year age group when it may alternate with menopausal symptoms, causing clinical confusion.[4]
- The symptoms of PMS decrease in severity just before and during menstruation.
- The symptoms cannot be explained by the presence of various psychological or psychiatric disorders.

Incidence

Up to 95% of women may experience premenstrual symptoms, which can vary from minor to severe. Interestingly, up to 15% of women can feel better premenstrually.[5] Statistics from countries such as Sweden, the United States and the UK indicate that up to 40% of women are significantly affected.[6] About 5–10% of women experience such severe symptoms that PMS disrupts their quality of life.

Aetiology

Various aetiological factors have been identified in contributing to PMS.[2]

Predisposing factors:

- mental illness
- alcoholism
- sexual abuse
- family history
- stress

Precipitating factors:

- hysterectomy
- tubal ligation
- cessation of the oral contraceptive

Sustaining factors:

- diet containing caffeine, alcohol, sugar
- smoking
- stress
- sedentary lifestyle

Symptoms

Various symptoms from among the 150 reported are summarised in Figure 77.1.

The most common symptoms are depression 71%, irritability 56%, tiredness 35%, headache 33%, bloatedness 31%, breast tenderness 21%, tension 19% and aggression/violence 13%.[7] Other important symptoms include weight gain, lowered performance, decreased libido and feeling out of control.

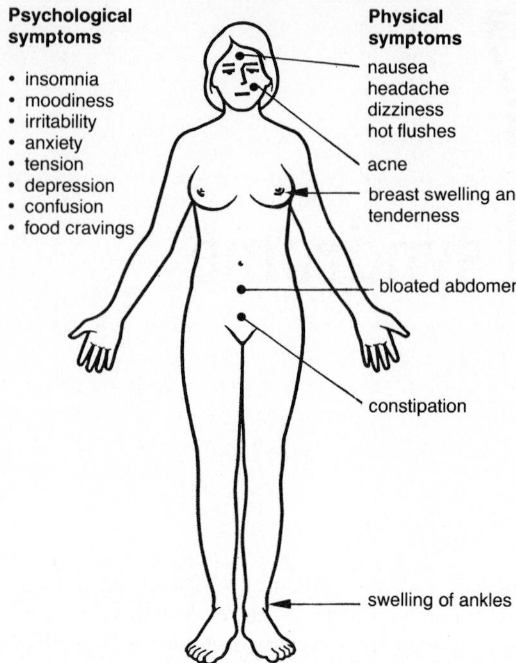

Fig. 77.1 *Symptoms of premenstrual tension*

Classification of PMS

It is convenient to classify PMS in terms of severity of symptoms.[4]

1. *Mild*: symptoms signal onset of menstruation. No medical advice sought or needed.
2. *Moderate*: symptoms annoying but insufficient to interfere with function at home or work. Medical advice sought in about one third.
3. *Severe*: symptoms are such that functions at work or home are disrupted. Medical advice is usually sought.

Differential diagnosis[4]

- menopause syndrome
- mastalgia
- other causes of fluid retention—renal or adrenal
- thyroid disorder (hyper or hypo activity)
- polycystic ovary syndrome (PMS may be a feature of oestrogen excess)
- psychiatric disorders: depression, mania

Diagnosis

- Thorough history—including diet, exercise habits, psychosocial background, emotional influences and family history.
- Menstrual calendar—for three months, showing timing of the three main symptoms.[4]
- Physical examination to exclude gynaecological, endocrine or other systemic disease; and also include:
  - — breast examination
  - — vaginal examination and Papanicolaou smear
- Investigations (if considered appropriate perform one or more serological tests):
  - — thyroid function tests
  - — serum progesterone and oestradiol in mid luteal phase of three representative cycles
  - — electrolytes and creatinine
  - — prolactin—if galactorrhoea or oligomenorrhoea present

Management

The basic aim of management is to reassure and treat the woman in such a way that she makes changes in her lifestyle to cope with the hormonal dysfunction rather than rely on medication. The management strategies include the following.

Explanation, reassurance and insight[8]

It is very helpful for the patient to understand the nature of her symptoms and to receive appropriate support and rapport. Advise her to be open about her problem and inform her family and close friends about her symptoms.

Keeping a diary[4]

Advise the patient to keep a daily diary of all her symptoms and when they occur over a 2–3 month period. This information should help her to plan around her symptoms: for example, avoid too many social events and demanding business appointments at the time when PMS symptoms are worst.

Dietary advice[4]

Advise the patient to eat regularly and sensibly; eat small rather than large meals and aim for ideal weight (if necessary).

Increase: complex carbohydrates (whole grains, vegetables and fruit), leafy green vegetables, legumes.

Decrease or avoid: refined sugar, salt, alcohol, caffeine (tea, coffee, chocolate), tobacco, red meat and excessive fluid intake during PM phase. Decrease total protein to 1 g/kg/day and fats.

Exercise

Recommend a program of regular exercise such as swimming, aerobics, jogging or tennis. Such exercise has been proven to decrease depression, anxiety and fluid retention premenstrually.[9]

Relaxation

Advise patients to plan activities that they find relaxing and enjoyable at the appropriate time. Consider stress reduction therapy including appropriate counselling.

Appropriate dress

Advise sensible dressing to cope with breast tenderness and a bloated abdomen, such as a firm-fitting brassiere and loose-fitting clothes around the abdomen.

Medication

Pharmaceutical agents that have been used with success in some patients and little or no relief in others include diuretics (e.g. spironolactone), vitamins and minerals (e.g. pyridoxine and evening primrose oil), antiprostaglandin preparations (e.g. mefenamic acid, indomethacin), bromocriptine, danazol (suppresses ovulation) and hormone preparations such as the oral contraceptive, progestogens and oestradiol implants. A combination of agents may have to be used.

- Oral contraceptives are the ideal first choice if contraception is needed. Select a moderate dose combined OC containing 50 μg ethinyl oestradiol.

Mild to moderate symptoms

- pyridoxine (Vitamin B_6) 100 mg daily if ineffective after 3 cycles try
- evening primrose oil capsules (gamma lineoleic acid) 1000 mg bd with food (day 12 to first day of next cycle)

A progestogen may be tried after or with evening primrose oil[4]

e.g. dydrogesterone 5 mg bd (day 12 to day 25) after 2 months increase to 10 mg bd

Severe symptoms

- fluoxetine 20 mg daily for 7–10 days before menstruation.

Individualised therapy

- PMS + fluid retention—use spironolactone 100 mg daily with previous agents
- PMS + severe mastalgia—consider bromocriptine
- PMS + dysmenorrhoea—mefenamic acid 500 mg tds

No matter what medication is taken, up to 70% of women will report an improvement in the early months of treatment, suggesting that a strong placebo factor is involved in management.[10]

When to refer[4]

- Refer to a gynaecologist if underlying disease is suspected or proven, e.g. polycystic ovary disease, endometriosis.
- Consider referral if prescribing of danazol is contemplated.
- Refer to an endocrinologist if an endocrine disorder such as adrenal, pituitary or thyroid is suspected or proven.
- Consider referral if depression or psychosis worsens or is not cyclical.

Practice tips

- Keeping a daily diary of symptoms is very helpful for both patient and clinician.
- Aim for lifestyle changes and common-sense non-pharmacological management.
- Triphasic oral contraceptives do not appear to be as effective as a monophasic OC.[10]
- Allow at least three cycles of treatment to provide a reasonable time for a particular medication.
- Drugs such as danazol or bromocriptine are second-line drugs with significant side effects and should be used with caution.
- High doses of pyridoxine, such as 500 mg a day, are associated with peripheral neuropathy so the dosage should be kept at around 100 mg/day.
- Be careful of overdiagnosing PMS and overlooking disorders such as depression, which may be exacerbated in the premenstrual phase.

References

1. Shreeve CM. *The premenstrual syndrome.* Thorson Publishers Ltd, 1983, 23–24.
2. Smith MA, Yong Kin EQ. Managing the premenstrual syndrome. Clinical Pharm, 1986; 5:788–797.
3. Brush MG. Pharmacological rationale for the management of PMS. Journal of Psychosomatic Obstetrics and Gynaecology, 1983; 2-1:35–39.
4. Smith M. Premenstrual syndrome. In: MIMS Disease Index. Sydney: IMS Publishing, 1991-92:439–441.
5. Farrell E. How to treat menstrual disorders. Australian Dr Weekly, 25 May 1990, IV–VI.
6. Labrum AH. Hypothalamic, pineal and pituitary factors in the premenstrual syndrome. Journal of Reproductive Medicine, 1983; 28(7):438–445.
7. Dalton K. *The premenstrual syndrome and progesterone therapy.* London: Heinemann, 1984, 3.
8. Murtagh J. Premenstrual syndrome. In: *Patient education.* Sydney: McGraw-Hill, 1992, 42.
9. Shroeder SA et al. *Current medical diagnosis and treatment.* East Norwalk: Appleton and Lange, 1990, 481–482.
10. Abraham S. The premenstrual syndrome. Modern Medicine of Australia, Sept. 1992, 80–86.

78

The menopause and osteoporosis

Definitions

The menopause is the cessation of the menses for longer than 12 months. In most western women it occurs between the ages of 45 and 55, with an average age of 50 years.

The World Health Organisation has defined the menopause as signifying the permanent cessation of menstruation, resulting from the loss of ovarian follicular activity.[1] However, the term is used in a broader sense to include the perimenopausal phase when ovarian function waxes and wanes and the periods become irregular. This may last 2–5 years and sometimes longer and involves the premenopausal and menopausal phases.

The postmenopause is the period following the menopause but cannot be defined until after 12 months of spontaneous amenorrhoea, except in women who have had an oöphorectomy.

Surgical menopause is known as bilateral oöphorectomy.

Summary

The climacteric can be subdivided into three phases:

Phase 1 Premenopausal: up to five years before the last menstrual period.

Phase 2 Menopausal—the last menstrual period.

Phase 3 Postmenopausal—approximately five years after the menopause.

Osteoporosis

Osteoporosis, which literally means porous bone, is reduced bone mass per unit volume. Osteoporosis is usually addressed in the context of the menopause because it is found mainly in postmenopausal middle-aged and elderly women and can be largely prevented by correcting oestrogen deficiency.

Physiology of the menopause

Inspection of Figure 78.1 provides an overview of how menopausal symptoms are related to ovarian follicular activity and hormonal activity.

The number of ovarian primary follicles declines rapidly as the menopause approaches, with few if any being identifiable following the cessation of menstruation. In the postmenopause phase FSH rises to levels 10–15 times that of the follicular phase of the cycle, while LH levels rise about threefold. The ovary secretes minimal oestrogen but continues to secrete significant amounts of androgens.

An uncomfortable effect of oestrogen withdrawal, often not appreciated by medical practitioners, involves urogenital problems where the epithelium of the vagina, vulva, urethra and the base of the bladder becomes thin and dry, leading possibly to dysuria and frequency, itching, dyspareunia and atrophic bleeding.

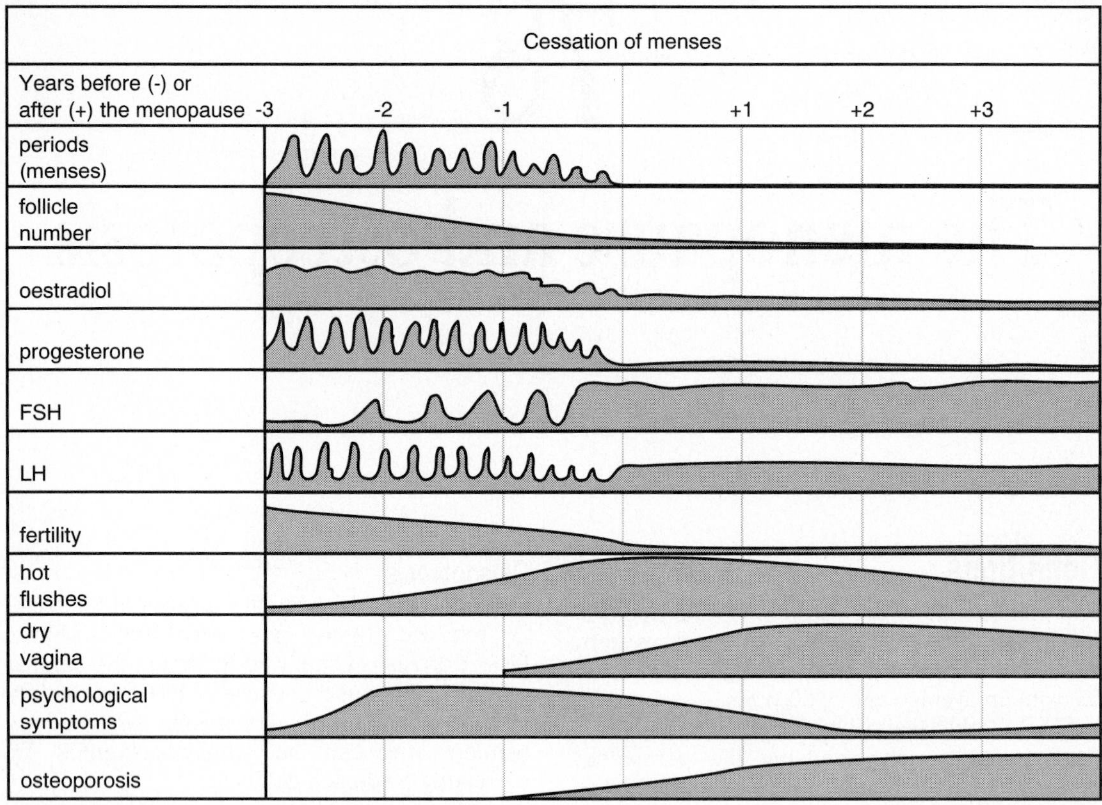

Fig. 78.1 *Schematic representation of some clinical, biological and endocrinological features of the perimenopausal and postmenopausal phases* AFTER BURGER

Clinical features

Due to small amounts of oestrogen being produced in the adrenal glands, symptoms other than cessation of periods may be mild or absent.

Symptoms

Vasomotor:[2]

- hot flushes (80%)
- night sweats (70%)
- palpitations (30%)
- lightheadedness/dizziness
- migraine

Psychogenic:

- irritability
- depression
- anxiety/tension
- tearfulness
- loss of concentration
- poor short-term memory
- unloved feelings
- sleep disturbances
- mood changes
- loss of self-confidence

Urogenital (60%):

- atrophic vaginitis
- vaginal dryness (45%)
- dyspareunia
- decline in libido
- bladder dysfunction, e.g. dysuria
- stress incontinence/prolapse

Musculoskeletal:

- non-specific muscular aches
- non-specific joint aches and pains

Skin and other tissue changes:

- dry skin
- formication (10%)
- new facial hair
- breast glandular tissue atrophy

Other:

- unusual tiredness
- headache

Clinical approach

A thorough evaluation of the patient is important, including a good history.

History

Enquire about any symptoms related to oestrogen deficiency and about other related symptoms, with an emphasis on the menstrual history and hot flushes. Enquire about mental state symptoms such as anger, irritability, depression, moodiness, loss of self-esteem and other such problems. Ask about sexual history, contraception, micturition and social history, including relationships.

Information on family history of osteoporosis, cancer and cardiovascular disease should be sought.

Physical examination

The general examination should include measurement of blood pressure, weight and height, breast palpation, abdominal palpation, vaginal examination and Pap smear. Note the texture of the vaginal epithelium.

Investigations[2]

Apart from a Papanicolaou smear, the following tests should be considered:

- urinalysis
- full blood count, lipids including HDL
- liver function tests
- mammography (all women, preferably after three months on HRT)
- diagnostic hysteroscopy and endometrial biopsy if undiagnosed vaginal bleeding
- bone density study (if risk factors)

If diagnosis in doubt, e.g. perimenopause; younger patient < 45 years; hysterectomy:

- serum FSH } Diagnostic
- serum oestradiol } Diagnostic

Differential diagnosis of menopause syndrome

- depression
- anaemia
- thyroid dysfunction
- hyperparathyroidism
- gynaecological disorders
  — dysfunctional uterine bleeding

Management

Education and lifestyle

Patients should receive adequate understanding, support and explanation with the emphasis being that the menopause is a natural fact of life. Emphasise the importance of leading a healthy lifestyle.

- correct diet
- avoid obesity
- adequate relaxation
- adequate exercise
- reduced smoking
- reduced caffeine intake
- reduced alcohol intake

Sexual activity

Advise that it is normal and appropriate to continue sexual relations, using a vaginal lubricant for a dry vagina. Contraception is advisable for 12 months after the last period.

Hormone replacement therapy

There is now convincing evidence that hormone replacement therapy at the menopause not only reduces climacteric symptoms and enhances the quality of life but also prevents osteoporosis and fractures, and reduces ischaemic heart disease and strokes.[3]

HRT has to be tailored to the individual patient and depends on several factors including the presence of a uterus, individual preferences and tolerance.[4]

The hormones to consider are:

- oestrogen
- progestogen, and
- testosterone

Oestrogen

Oestrogen comes in various preparations: oral, patches, implants, injections and topical vaginal preparations (Table 78.1). Injectables are not very effective so the common modes of administration are oral, implants or skin patches. Transdermal patches are the most favoured mode world-wide.

Vaginal creams or tablets are usually restricted to women who have mild menopausal symptoms and a dry vagina or urethra, or who cannot tolerate parenteral medication. Most women find the use of vaginal pessaries and creams messy, but the new oestradiol tablet, Vagifem, is a very effective topical therapy. The oral oestrogens in common use are Premarin, Ogen and Progynova. Implants of 50–100 mg (usually 50 mg) of oestradiol are given 3–12 monthly; patches (usually 50 μg) are applied every three and a half days, for example on Monday morning and Thursday night. Continuous daily oestrogen use is recommended; there is no reason to stop therapy for one week.

Table 78.1 *Oestrogens used in the menopause*[4]

Generic name	Proprietary name/s	Daily dose range	Usual daily protective dose
Oral			
Conjugated equine oestrogen	Premarin	0.3-2.5 mg	0.625 mg
Ethinyl oestradiol	Estigyn	0.01-0.03 mg	0.02 mg
Oestradiol valerate	Progynova	1.0-4.0 mg	2.0 mg
Oestriol	Ovestin	1.0-4.0 mg	2.0 mg
Piperazine oestrone sulphate	Ogen	0.625-5 mg	1.25 mg
Implants			
Oestradiol	Oestradiol implants	20-100 mg	50 mg
Skin patch			
Oestradiol	Estraderm TTS	2-8 mg every 3½ days	4 mg
Vaginal preparations			
Creams			
Conjugated equine oestrogen 0.0625%	Premarin	2-4 g	4 g
Ethinyl oestradiol 0.01%	Dienoestrol	2.5-10 g	5 g
Oestriol 1 mg/g	Ovestin	0.5 g	0.5 g
Tablets			
Oestradiol	Vagifem	25 μg	1 tablet (25 μg)
Pessaries			
Oestrone	Kolpon	100 μg-1 mg	1 mg

Note Vaginal therapy is usually given continuously for two weeks, then twice weekly.

Progestogen

Progestogen is given to women with a uterus and may be given continuously or cyclically. If it is not given, many women will develop hyperplasia of the uterus. If given cyclically (postmenopausal) it is given for the first to the twelfth day of the calendar month, generally as Provera or Primolut N (Table 78.2). A withdrawal bleed will occur and many elderly women find this unacceptable and thus may find continuous therapy more appropriate.

Progestogens should be given in the smallest possible dose, to prevent endometrial hyperplasia.

Testosterone

Testosterone is reserved for women whose libido does not improve with HRT. It is given as an implant of 50 mg and will last 3–12 months. An oestrogen implant of 50 mg should be given concurrently.

Contraindications to HRT

Important contraindications to HRT are listed in Table 78.3. The main absolute contraindications are oestrogen-dependent neoplasms such as endometrial and breast carcinoma, uncontrolled hypertension, severe active liver disease and active SLE.

Table 78.2 *Progestogens used in the menopause*[4]

Generic name	Proprietary name/s	Daily dose range	Usual daily protective dose
Levonorgestrel	Microlut Microval	0.03-0.9 mg	0.03 mg
Medroxyprogesterone acetate	Provera	2.5-20 mg	10 mg
Norethisterone	Primolut N	1.25-5 mg	2.5 mg

Table 78.3 *Contraindications to HRT*

(Absolute or relative)

Oestrogen-dependent tumour
- endometrial cancer
- breast cancer

Recurrent thromboembolism
Uncontrolled hypertension
Undiagnosed vaginal bleeding
Active liver disease
Active SLE
Otosclerosis
Acute intermittent porphyria

HRT regimens

Some commonly used regimens are presented in Table 78.4 and Figure 78.2. Regimens A and B are in common use. The transdermal system appears to be the most favoured although some women find it unsuitable. A useful regimen, especially for irregular bleeding in the perimenopausal phase, is the combined sequential pill (oestradiol and norethisterone) which can be continued for several years if necessary.

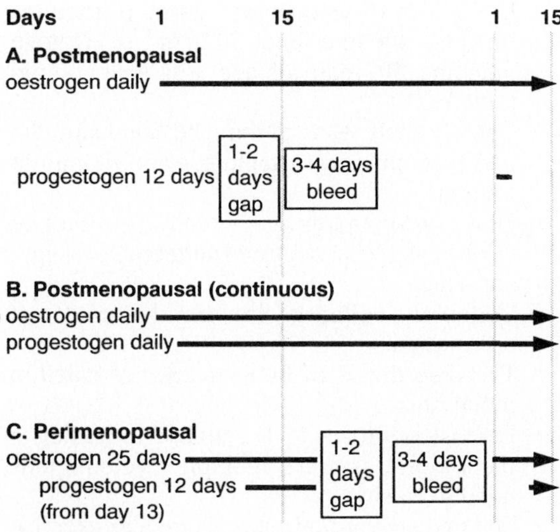

Fig. 78.2 *Possible HRT regimens for women with a uterus* AFTER FARRELL

Informed consent

HRT should be prescribed only after the woman has been informed of the regimens available, their relative benefits and risks and side effects.[3] It must be emphasised that HRT, especially the combined sequential formulation, is not a contraceptive.

Side effects of therapy[5]

In the first 2–3 months the woman may experience oestrogenic side effects, but these usually resolve or stabilise. Starting with a lower dose may minimise these side effects.

Table 78.4 *A summarised regimen for HRT*[4]

Oestrogen
Oral medication
- conjugated oestrogen (Premarin) 0.625 mg
  or
- piperazine oestrone (Ogen) 1.25 mg
  or
- oestradiol valerate (Progynova) 2 mg

Dosage
- half tablet for 7 days initially, then one tablet daily continuous

Transdermal patches
- oestradiol (Estraderm) 4 mg patch

Progestogen
- medroxyprogesterone (Provera) 10 mg
  or
- norethisterone (Primolut N) 5 mg, one tablet for first 12 days of month

To induce amenorrhoea
Give progestogen continuously daily, instead of cyclically
- medroxyprogesterone 2.5 mg
  or
- norethisterone 1.25 mg

Uterus present
Oestrogen and progestogen

No uterus (hysterectomy)
Oestrogen only

Perimenopausal regimen
Combined oestrogen and progesterone sequential therapy, e.g. Trisequens, Menoprem

Coming—the future
Combination patch
- oestrogen plus progestogen (first half of cycle)
- oestrogen only (second half of cycle)

Premenstrual syndrome (in 15%)

Action: decrease progestogen dose
or
change to alternative progestogen

Nausea and breast disorders

Cause: initial sensitivity to oestrogen
Action: reduce oestrogen to starting dose

Bleeding problems

Heavy bleeding
  Action: decrease oestrogen

Breakthrough bleeding
  Action: increase progestogen

Irregular bleeding
  Action: investigate + endometrial sampling

Intolerance of bleeding
  Action: use continuous regimen

No bleeding
  Action: reassure that this is not a problem

Leg cramps

Action: decrease oestrogen

Follow-up after commencing HRT[6]

- 3 months (ideal time for mammography)
- then 6 monthly

Allow 6 months to stabilise therapy.

Duration of treatment

The duration of treatment depends on several factors including the severity of symptoms, the response to therapy and the long-term aims, such as the desire for cardioprotection and osteoporosis prevention (at least 10 years) (Fig. 78.3). However, long-term therapy should be an informed decision made by the patient in consultation with the doctor. A useful working rule is to aim for treatment for 5 years and then review.

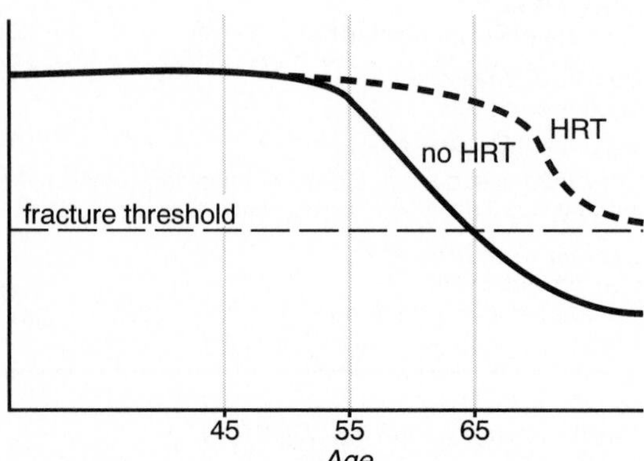

Fig. 78.3 *Graphic illustration of the effects of HRT on the fracture threshold of ageing women*

Osteoporosis

Osteoporosis refers to the increased bone fragility that accompanies ageing and many illnesses. Following the menopause, women begin to lose calcium from their bone at a much faster rate than men, presumably as a direct response to low levels of oestrogen. Within 5–10 years of the menopause, women can be seen to suffer from osteoporosis and by the age of 65 the rate of fractures in women has increased to 3–5 times that of men (Fig. 78.4).

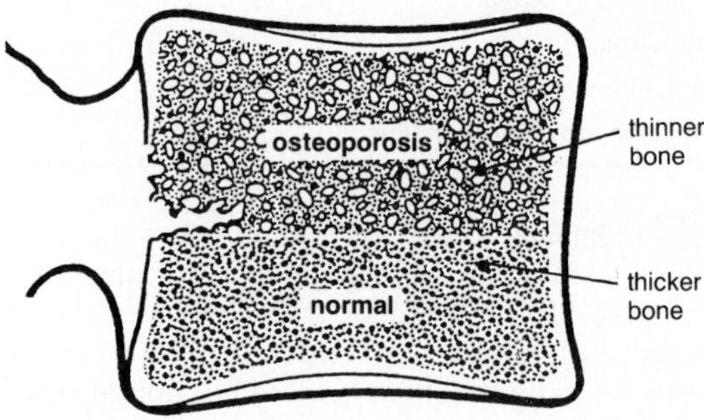

Fig. 78.4 *Osteoporosis is reduced bone mass per unit volume*

Facts and figures

- Osteoporosis is commonest in postmenopausal women.
- Up to 15% of women will develop fractures in their lifetime and 30% of all women reaching 90 years of age will suffer a hip fracture.[7]
- Osteoporosis leads to reduced bone strength and susceptibility to fracture, even with minor trauma.
- First presentation is usually a fracture (Colle's, femoral neck and vertebra) or height shrinkage.
- Vertebral collapse is the hallmark of osteoporosis.
- The disorder is of bone mass, not calcium metabolism.
- For osteoporosis in a vertebra including a pathological fracture, multiple myeloma may need exclusion.
- The first step in prevention is regular exercise and an adequate dietary intake of calcium (1000 mg per day).

Classification of osteoporosis

Primary

Type 1: postmenopausal (vertebral or distal forearm fractures within first 20 years of menopause)

Type 2: senile osteoporosis (fracture of proximal femur usually 20–30 years after menopause)

Secondary
To various endocrine disorders, malabsorption and malignancies. Various causes and risk factors are presented in Table 78.5.

Table 78.5 *Osteoporosis: risk factors or causes*

Risk factor or cause	
Female	
Thin build	
Race: Asian, Northern European	
Family history	
Premenopausal oestrogen deficiency e.g. amenorrhoea	
Early menopause < 45 (natural or surgical)	
Cigarette smoking	can be modified
High caffeine intake > 4 cups per day	can be modified
High alcohol intake > 2 standard drinks per day	can be modified
Low calcium intake	can be modified
Physical inactivity	can be modified
Chronic corticosteroid use	can be modified
Endocrine disorders • Cushing's disease • diabetes mellitus • hyperparathyroidism • thyrotoxicosis • hypogonadism • acromegaly	
Chronic renal failure	

Investigations

- Plain radiography is of limited value. Osteoporosis is not detectable until 50% of bone is lost.
- Plasma calcium, phosphate and alkaline phosphatase are all usually normal.
- Consider tests for multiple myeloma in an osteoporotic area.
- Densitometry can predict an increased risk of osteoporosis.

Treatment for osteoporosis

The goal of treatment is to prevent osteoporosis or reduce further loss. No treatment has been shown to replace lost bone effectively. Anabolic agents such as nandrolone deconate may reduce further loss but the side effects are problematic.

Medication of value in decreasing further loss
The following medication may be valuable in preventing further bone loss, possibly reversing the osteoporosis process and preventing further fractures.

- HRT

or

- calcitrol (a vitamin D metabolite)—avoid calcium supplements during therapy

or

- etidronate disodium (a biphosphonate)

The choice depends on the clinical status, such as the age of the patient and the extent of disease, the patient's tolerance of drugs and further clinical trials of these drugs. The one preferable solution is to give prophylaxis for individuals identified as high risk and the only widely accepted proven therapy is oestrogen therapy.

Recommendations for prevention

- HRT within two years of the onset of menopause
- Adequate dietary intake of calcium
  800–1000 mg per day—premenopause
  1500 mg per day—postmenopausal
  Calcium-rich foods include low-fat calcium-enriched milk (500 ml contains 1000 mg), other low-fat dairy products (e.g. yoghurt or cheese), fish (including tinned fish such as salmon with the bone), citrus fruits, sesame and sunflower seeds, almonds, brazil nuts and hazel nuts.
  Calcium supplements will be necessary in postmenopausal women (except if taking calcitrol).
- Exercise: moderate exercise against gravity, e.g. walking (brisk walking for 30 minutes four times a week), jogging or tennis, may make a small contribution to retarding bone loss.
- Lifestyle factors: stop smoking and limit alcohol and caffeine intake.

When to refer

- A problem arises in establishing the correct regimens for HRT.
- Complications not corrected by routine measures develop with HRT.
- Osteoporosis appears to be secondary to an underlying illness.
- Advice is required about the management of a patient with pathological osteoporotic fractures or loss of height.

Practice tips on the menopause

- Careful pretreatment assessment is important.
- Encourage conservative self-help management with an emphasis on lifestyle if symptoms are mild.
- Explain benefits and risks and get informed consent.
- Individualise HRT therapy.
- Regular follow-up is essential.
- Allow about six months to stabilise with HRT.
- The prime treatment for an oestrogen deficiency disorder is oestrogen.
- Use oestrogen-only therapy for women without a uterus.
- If a uterus is present give combined oestrogen-progestogen therapy (cyclical or continuous).
- Avoid giving progestogen in the presence of continuing ovarian activity.
- Severe side effects of progestogen may necessitate oestrogen-only therapy, with regular yearly endometrial biopsy.
- Always start with a low dose of oestrogen.
- Women who have experienced side effects such as migraine with the combined oral contraceptive may have the same problem with HRT.
- HRT is not a contraceptive so contraception is advisable in perimenopausal women for 12 months after the last period.
- Problematic loss of libido can be treated with testosterone in the short term, e.g. as a single parenteral dose or as a short course of oral tablets.
- Oestrogen deficiency results in a loss of elasticity and dryness of the vagina which can be partially helped with HRT.
- HRT does not always restore the sex drive but does help make sexual intercourse easier and more pleasant.
- The most practical solution in managing osteoporosis is prevention through HRT and adequate calcium intake. Calcium supplementation by itself is inadequate but appears to have a synergistic effect with HRT.
- HRT needs to be maintained for at least 10 years to achieve full benefit.
- Advantages of long-term HRT:
  — improvement in the quality of life
  — prevention of bone fractures, especially of wrist, hip and spine
  — reduction in coronary artery disease and cerebrovascular disease mortality

References

1. World Health Organisation Technical Report Series 670. WHO Scientific Group (1981): Research on the Menopause.
2. Wren B. Menopause. In: MIMS Disease Index, Sydney: IMS Publishing, 1991–92, 331–334.
3. Silberberg S, Burger H. Management of the menopause from an Australian perspective. Mod Medicine of Australia, May 1989, 14–18.
4. Rosenblatt J, Murtagh J. Hormone replacement therapy. Aust Fam Physician, 1992; 21:1345–1346.
5. Murkies AL. Common problems with hormone replacement therapy. Aust Fam Physician, 1992; 21:217–225.
6. Farrell E. Treatment options and menopause regimens. Aust Fam Physician, 1992; 21:240–246.
7. Seeman E, Young N. Osteoporosis. In: MIMS Disease Index, Sydney, IMS Publishing, 1991–92, 383–387.

79

Vaginal discharge

Vaginal discharge is one of the commonest complaints seen by family physicians yet it is one of the most difficult to solve, especially if it is recurrent or persistent. It is present if the woman's underclothes are consistently stained or a pad is required. It is important to make a proper diagnosis, to differentiate between abnormal (physiological) discharge and to be aware of the considerable variation in secretion of vaginal fluid.

The differential diagnoses should include consideration of normal discharge; vaginitis, either infective or chemical; sexually transmitted diseases (STDs); and urinary tract infection.

Key facts and checkpoints

- A recent survey of a large family planning clinic found that 17% of women complained of vaginal discharge.[1]
- Vaginal discharge may present at any age but is very common in the reproductive years.
- Vaginal discharge is a common presentation of those STDs responsible for pelvic inflammatory disease.
- One of the simplest methods of making a proper diagnosis is a wet film examination. It saves expensive laboratory investigations.

A diagnostic approach

A summary of the safety diagnostic model is presented in Table 79.1.

Table 79.1 *Vaginal discharge: diagnostic strategy model*

Q. Probability diagnosis

A. Normal physiological discharge

Vaginitis

- bacterial vaginosis 40–50%
- candidiasis 20–30%
- trichomonas 10–20%

Q. Serious disorders not to be missed

A. Neoplasia

- carcinoma
- fistulas

STDs/PID

- gonorrhoea
- chlamydia

Sexual abuse, esp. children

Tampon toxic shock syndrome (staphylococcal infection)

Q. Pitfalls (often missed)

A. Chemical vaginitis, e.g. perfumes

Retained foreign objects, e.g. tampons, IUCD

Endometriosis (brownish discharge)

Ectopic pregnancy ('prune juice' discharge)

Poor toilet hygiene

Genital herpes (possible)

Q. Seven masquerades checklist

A.	
Depression	—
Diabetes	✓
Drugs	✓
Anaemia	—
Thyroid disease	—
Spinal dysfunction	—
UTI	✓ (association)

Q. Is the patient trying to tell me something?

A. Needs careful consideration; possible sexual dysfunction.

Probability diagnoses

The two most common causes of vaginal discharge are physiological discharge and infective vaginitis.

Physiological discharge

Normal physiological discharge is usually milky-white or clear mucoid and originates from a combination of the following sources:

- cervical mucus (secretions from cervical glands)
- vaginal secretion (transudate through vaginal mucosa)
- vaginal squamous epithelial cells (desquamation)
- resident commensal bacteria
- cervical columnar epithelial cells

With physiological discharge there is usually no odour or pruritus.

In addition, the egg-white discharge accompanying ovulation may be noted. The discharge may be aggravated by the use of the pill. The normal discharge usually shows on underclothing by the end of the day. Clear or white, it oxidises to a yellow or brown on contact with air. It is increased by sexual stimulation.

Management:

- reassurance and explanation
- wear cotton underwear (not synthetic)
- bath instead of showering
- avoid douching and feminine deodorants
- use tampons instead of pads

Infective vaginitis

The commonest cause of infective vaginitis is bacterial vaginosis (formerly bacterial vaginitis, *Gardnerella vaginalis* or *Haemophilus vaginalis*) which accounts for 40–50% of vaginitis.[2] *Candida albicans* is the causative agent in 20–30% while *Trichomonas vaginalis* causes about 20% in Australia. The comparable features are outlined in Table 79.2. Human papilloma virus infection of vaginal epithelium may cause excess discharge.

Serious disorders not to be missed

The 'not to be missed' group includes carcinoma of the vagina, cervix or uterus and sexually transmitted diseases, including pelvic inflammatory diseases caused by *Chlamydia trachomatis* and *Neisseria gonorrhoeae*. Vaginal discharge is the most common presenting symptom of both of these serious STDs. Occasionally, infections of the endometrium and endosalpinx will produce a discharge that gravitates to the vagina.[1] Benign and malignant neoplasia anywhere in the genital tract may produce a discharge. Usually it is watery and pink or blood-stained.

Inspection should include vigilance for fistulas that may be associated with malignancy, inflammation or postirradiation.

Pitfalls

It is common to overlook the problem caused by hygienic preparations. Apart from the vaginal tampon, which may be retained (knowingly or otherwise), there is a variety of preparations that can induce a sensitivity reaction. These include deodorant soaps and sprays and contraceptive agents, especially spermicidal creams. Ironically, the various preparations used to treat the vaginitis may cause a chemical reaction.

Endometriosis of the cervix or vaginal vault may cause a bloody or brownish discharge.

Seven masquerades checklist

Of this group, diabetes mellitus leading to recurrent 'thrush', drugs causing a local sensitivity, and urinary tract infection have to be considered (Table 79.1).

Psychogenic considerations

This question needs to be answered, especially if the discharge is normal. The problem could

Table 79.2 *Characteristics of discharge for common causes of infective vaginitis (after Weisberg)*

Infective organism	*Colour*	*Consistency*	*Odour*	*pH*	*Associated symptoms*
Candida albicans	White	Thick (cream cheese)		4	Itch, soreness, redness
Trichomonas	Yellow/green	Bubbly, profuse (mucopurulent)	Malodorous, fishy	5-6	Soreness
Bacterial vaginosis	Grey	Watery, profuse, bubbly	Malodorous, fishy	5-6	—

be related to sexual dysfunction or it may reflect a problematic relationship, and this issue may need to be diplomatically explored. Vaginal discharge is an embarrassing problem for the patient and any discussion needs to be handled thoroughly and sensitively. A relevant sexual history may satisfactorily solve the problem.

The clinical approach

History

The history is important and should include:

- nature of discharge: colour, odour, quantity, relation to menstrual cycle, associated symptoms
- exact nature and location of irritation
- sexual history: arousal, previous STDs, number of partners and any presence of irritation or discharge in them
- use of chemicals such as soaps, deodorants, pessaries and douches
- pregnancy possibility
- drug therapy
- associated medical conditions, e.g. diabetes.

Physical examination

Optimal facilities for the physical examination include an appropriate couch and good light, bivalve Sims' specula, sterile swabs (preferably with transport media), normal saline, 10% potassium hydroxide, slides and coverslips and microscope. Inspection in good light includes viewing the vulva, introitus, urethra, vagina and cervix. Look for the discharge and specific problems such as polyps, warts, prolapses or fistulas. To differentiate between vaginal and cervical discharge, wipe the cervix clear with a cotton ball and observe the cervix. Perform a pH test and a wet film.

Pitfalls to keep in mind include:

- The patient may have had a bath or a 'good wash' beforehand and may need to return when the discharge is obvious.
- A retained tampon may be missed in the posterior fornix, so the speculum should slide directly along the posterior wall of the vagina.
- Candida infection may not show the characteristic curds, 'the strawberry vagina' of trichomonas is uncommon and bubbles may not be seen.

Acetic acid 2% is useful in removing the discharge and mucus to enable a clearer view of the cervix and vaginal walls.

Investigations

- pH test with paper of range 4 to 6
- amine or 'whiff' test: add a drop of 10% KOH to vaginal secretions smeared on glass slide
- wet film microscopy of a drop of vaginal secretions

A culture is necessary if no diagnosis is made after this routine.

A full STD workup

- swabs from the cervix for chlamydia, *N. gonorrhoeae*
  - — swab mucus from cervix first
  - — swab endocervix
  - — place in transparent media
- Pap smear
- viral culture (herpes simplex)
  - — scrape base of ulcer or ideally deroof a vesicle
  - — immediately immerse in culture medium
  - — transport rapidly to laboratory

Preparation of a wet film

To make a wet film preparation[2] (Fig. 79.1), place one drop of normal saline (preferably warm) on one end of an ordinary slide and one drop of 10% potassium hydroxide (KOH) on the other half of the slide. A sample of the discharge needs to be taken with a swab stick, either directly from the posterior fornix of the vagina or from discharge that has collected on the posterior blade of the speculum during the vaginal examination. A small amount of the discharge is mixed with both the normal saline drop and the KOH drop. A cover slip is placed over each preparation. The slide is examined under low power to get an overall impression, and under high power to determine the presence of lactobacilli, polymorphs, trichomonads, spores, clue cells and hyphae. A summary of various findings on wet film examination is presented in Table 79.3. Lactobacilli are long, thin Gram-positive rods; clue cells are vaginal epithelial cells that have bacteria attached so that the cytoplasm appears granular and often the entire border is obscured. They are a feature of bacterial vaginosis. Trichomonads are about the same size as polymorphs and to distinguish between the two one needs to see the movement of the trichomonad and the beating of its flagella under high power of the microscope. Warming the slide will often precipitate movement.

Refer to Figure 79.2.

Table 79.3 *Wet film examination (after Weisberg)*

	Lactobacilli	*Polymorphs*	*Epithelial cells*	*Clue cells*	*Other*
Normal	+	None or occasional	+	–	
Candidiasis	+	none or occasional	+	–	Spores/hyphae
Trichomoniasis	Absent or scant	Numerous	+	–	Trichomonads
Bacterial vaginosis	Absent or scant	Numerous	+	2–50%	

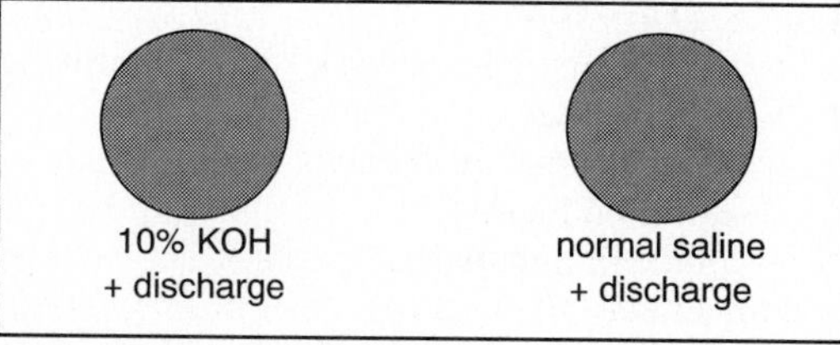

Examine for:

1. epithelial cells
2. polymorphs
3. lactobacilli
4. trichomonads
5. clue cells

Fig. 79.1 *Wet film method*

Other investigations

Gram-stain smear and culture should be contemplated only if a diagnosis cannot be made on wet film.

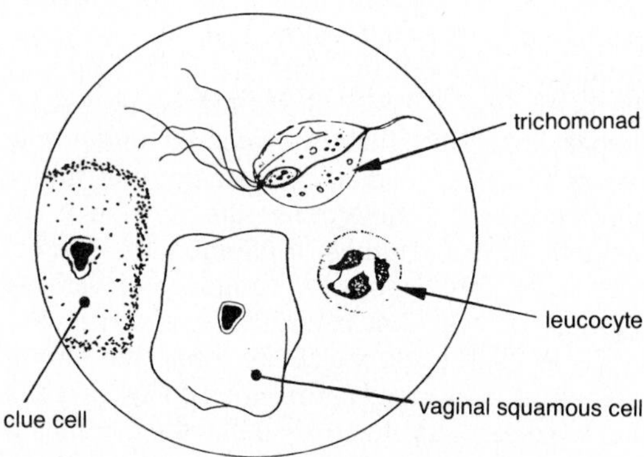

Fig. 79.2 *Relative sizes of various cells or organisms as seen in a wet smear*

Vaginal discharge in children

Staining on a child's underclothes may be due to excess physiological discharge, especially in the year before the menarche.[1] Vulvovaginitis is the most common gynaecological disorder of childhood, the most common cause being a non-specific bacterial infection.

Important causes to consider

- poor hygiene—usually a non-specific bacterial vaginitis, e.g. coliforms
- 'sandbox' vaginitis: little girls sitting and playing in sand or dirt may develop irritation from particulate matter trapped in the vagina[3]
- foreign body: consider if a bloody malodorous vaginal discharge
- candidiasis (moniliasis)—uncommon but consider if antibiotic therapy or possibility of diabetes
- sexual abuse (must not be missed)
- pinworm infestation (Enterobius)
- sexually transmissible organisms—usually postpubertal

Symptoms

- itching or burning
- may be a discharge that stains the underclothes
- ± dysuria

Examination

A careful general examination should be performed. In infants the best examination method is to place the child on her mother's lap with the legs held well abducted. Lateral traction applied to the labia allows the hymen orifice to be examined. Look for vulval or vaginal infection. Aspirate vaginal secretion with a medicine dropper for appropriate cultures. A Papanicolaou smear is advisable for a persistent problem since a sarcoma is a possibility. An older child can be placed in one of two suitable positions:

1. Supine, legs apart in a frog-leg position, with bottom of feet touching (generally preferred).
2. Prone, knee/chest position. This allows a better view of the hymenal orifice but many children do not like this position.

A rectal examination is performed to try to feel for foreign bodies in the vagina and to assess the pelvic anatomy.

Vaginal discharge in the elderly

Vaginal discharge can occur in the elderly from a variety of causes including infective vaginitis, atrophic vaginitis, foreign bodies, poor hygiene and neoplasia. It is important to exclude malignancy of the uterus, cervix and vagina in the older patient.

Atrophic vaginitis

In the absence of oestrogen stimulation the vaginal and vulval tissues begin to shrink and become thin and dry. This renders the vagina more susceptible to bacterial attack because of the loss of vaginal acidity. Rarely, a severe attack can occur with a very haemorrhagic vagina and heavy discharge:

- yellowish non-offensive discharge
- tenderness and dyspareunia
- spotting or bleeding with coitus
- the vagina may be reddened with superficial haemorrhagic areas

Treatment

- Oral hormone replacement therapy.
- Local oestrogen cream or tablet, e.g. Vagifem. The tablet is preferred as it is less messy.

Vaginal candidiasis

Infection with the fungus *Candida albicans* is a common and important problem with a tendency to recurrence.

Clinical features

- intense vaginal and vulval pruritus
- vulval soreness
- vulvovaginal erythema (brick red)
- vaginal excoriation and oedema
- white curd-like discharge
- discomfort with coitus
- dysuria

Factors predisposing to vaginal candidiasis[1]

Endogenous: diabetes mellitus
AIDS syndrome
pregnancy
debilitating diseases

Exogenous: oral contraceptives
antibiotics
immunosuppressants
carbohydrate-rich diet
orogenital/anogenital intercourse
IUCD
tight-fitting jeans
nylon underwear
humidity/wet bathing suit

Treatment

For the first attack of candidiasis it is appropriate to select one of the large range of vaginal imidazole therapies (clotrimazole, econazole, isoconazole, miconazole) for 1–7 days (Table 79.4). There appears to be no significant difference between imidazoles.[4] Nystatin is best reserved for recurrent cases or if there is local reaction to the imidazoles. Some therapists prefer creams to tablets and pessaries because cream can be applied to any tender vulval area, but a tablet and cream can be used simultaneously, especially for a heavy infection.

Gentian violet (0.5% aqueous solution) is useful for rapid relief.

A recommended initial regimen is:

clotrimazole 500 mg vaginal tablet as a single dose
clotrimazole 2% cream applied to vagina and vulva (for symptomatic relief)

An alternative regimen, especially for recurrent infections:

nystatin pessaries once daily for 7 days
and/or
nystatin vaginal cream (100 000 U per 4 g)

Advice to the patient

- Bathe the genital area gently two or three times a day for symptomatic relief. In preparing for the antifungal preparation, use 1–3% acetic acid or sodium bicarbonate solution (1 tablespoon to 1 litre of water). Thoroughly cleanse the vagina, including recesses between rugae and the fornices and also the folds around the vulva.
- Dry the genital area thoroughly after showering or bathing.
- Wear loose-fitting cotton underwear.
- Avoid wearing pantyhose, tight jeans or tight underwear or using tampons.
- Avoid having intercourse or oral sex during the infected period.
- Do not use vaginal douches, powders or deodorants.

Recurrent or recalcitrant infections

The reinfection might be occurring from the bowel. Check for predisposing factors including nail beds. Prescribe a course of oral medication, e.g. nystatin 500 000–1 000 000 U tds for 14 (or

Table 79.4 *Treatment of vaginal candidiasis*

Length of treatment	*Generic name*	*Vaginal therapy*	
		Tablets	***Cream 5 g***
Imidazoles			
1 day	clotrimazole	500 mg × 1	
(statim dose)	isoconazole	300 mg × 2	
3 days	clotrimazole	100 mg × 2	
	clotrimazole		2%
	econazole	150 mg	
	econazole		1.5%
	micronazole	200 mg	
6 days	clotrimazole	100 mg	
	clotrimazole		1%
7 days	miconazole	100 mg	2%
Nystatin			
14 days	nystatin	100 000 U	100 000 U
Oral therapy for recurrent recalcitrant infections			
14 days	ketoconazole	200 mg daily	
14 days	nystatin	500 000 U tds	

more) days. The treatment of partners is controversial but there seems to be no proven benefit in such treatment.[5]

Oral or topical nystatin treatment is recommended in pregnancy because of its relative low toxicity.

Vinegar and other acidic douches are not recommended as they tend to favour the growth of *Candida*. However, topical corticosteroid cream is most efficacious for the symptomatic relief of intense vulval pruritus.

If the woman is prone to recurrent infections it is advisable to keep the antifungal therapy on standby and use it when the problem first appears. Provide the patient with, for example, three or four clotrimazole 500 mg tablets and advise her to use one at the first sign of infection.

Trichomonas vaginalis

This flagellated protozoan, which is thought to originate in the bowel, infects the vagina, Skene's ducts and lower urinary tract in women and the lower genitourinary tract in men. It is transmitted through sexual intercourse and is relatively common in the female after the onset of sexual activity.

Clinical features

- profuse thin discharge (grey to yellow-green in colour)
- small bubbles may be seen in 20–30%
- pruritus
- malodorous discharge
- dyspareunia
- diffuse erythema of cervix and vaginal walls
- characteristic punctate appearance on cervix

Treatment

- oral metronidazole 2 g as a single dose (preferable) *or* 600 mg daily for 7 days

  or

  tinidazole 500 mg qid over 1 day (Table 79.5)
- use clotrimazole 100 mg vaginal tablet daily for 6 days during pregnancy
- attention to hygiene
- the sexual partner must be treated simultaneously
- the male partner should wear a condom during intercourse
- for resistant infections a 3–7 day course of either metronidazole or tinidazole may be necessary.

Table 79.5 *Oral treatment for bacterial vaginosis and trichomonas infections*

Length of treatment	*Generic name*	*Oral dosage*	*Trade name*
1 day (statim dose)	tinidazole	500 mg × 4	Fasigyn
	metronidazole	400 mg × 5	Flagyl
7 days (for recurrent)	tinidazole	500 mg daily	
	metronidazole	400 mg bd	

Bacterial vaginosis

Bacterial vaginosis is a clinical entity of mixed aetiology characterised by the replacement of the normal vaginal microflora (chiefly *Lactobacillus*) with a mixed flora consisting of *Gardnerella vaginalis*, other anaerobes such as *Mobiluncus* species, and *Mycoplasma hominis*.

Clinical features

- a grey, watery, profuse discharge
- malodorous
- no obvious vulvitis or vaginitis
- liberates an amine-like, fishy odour on admixture of 10% KOH
- ± dyspareunia and dysuria
- ± pruritus

Treatment

The same treatment (metronidazole or tinidazole) is used as for trichomonas vaginalis. Clindamycin 300 mg (o) bd for 7 days or 2% clindamycin cream can be used for resistant infections. Normal vaginal pH can be restored using a variety of topical douches such as povidone iodine solution (1 tablespoon per litre of water), vinegar (3–4 tablespoons per litre of water), topical Acigel or a milky solution of yoghurt to restore *Lactobacillus* levels.

There is no evidence that treatment of the male sexual partner reduces the recurrence rate or provides any significant benefit.[6] The STD treatment guidelines of the US Centers for Disease Control state explicitly that such treatment is of no proven benefit.[7]

Retained vaginal tampon

A retained tampon, which may be impacted and cannot be removed by the patient, is usually associated with an extremely offensive vaginal discharge. Its removal can cause considerable embarrassment to both patient and doctor.

Method of removal

Using good vision the tampon is seized with a pair of sponge-holding forceps and quickly immersed under water without releasing the forceps. A bowl of water (an old plastic ice-cream container is suitable) is kept as close to the introitus as possible. This results in minimal malodour. The tampon and water are immediately flushed down the toilet if the toilet system can accommodate tampons (Fig. 79.3). An alternative method is to grasp the tampon with a gloved hand and quickly peel the glove over the tampon for disposal.

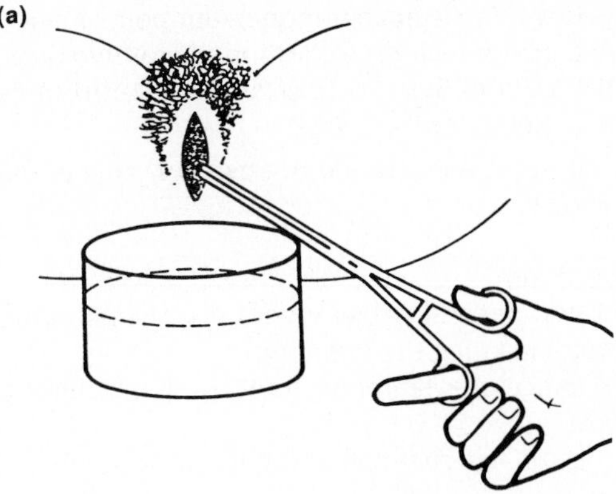

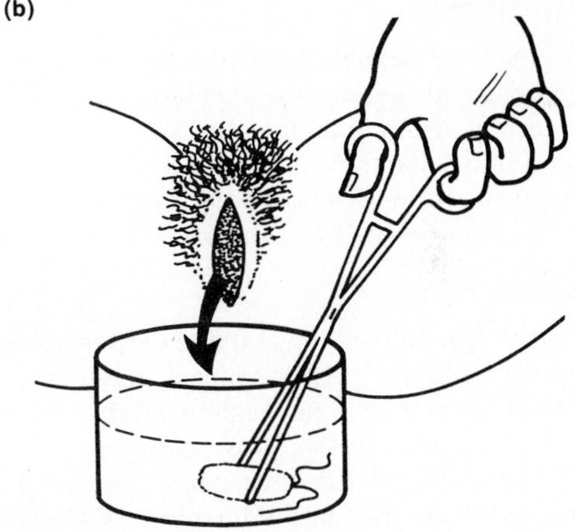

Fig. 79.3 *Removal of an impacted vaginal tampon*

Tampon toxic shock syndrome

Staphylococcal infection

This rare dramatic condition is caused by the production of staphylococcal exotoxin associated with tampon use for menstrual protection. The syndrome usually begins within five days of the onset of the period.

The *clinical features* include sudden onset fever, vomiting and diarrhoea, muscle aches and pains, skin erythema, hypotension progressing to confusion, stupor and sometimes death.

Management

Active treatment depends on the severity of the illness. Cultures should be taken from the vagina, cervix, perineum and nasopharynx. The patient should be referred to a major centre if 'shock' develops. Otherwise the vagina must be emptied, ensuring there is not a forgotten tampon, cleaned with a povidone iodine solution tds for two days, and methicillin or cloxacillin antibiotics administered for 8–12 days.

- These women should not use tampons in the future.

Prevention

- Good general hygiene with care in handling and inserting the tampons.
- Change the tampons three or four times a day.
- Use an external pad at night during sleep.

When to refer

- evidence of sexual abuse to children to an experienced sexual assault centre
- recurrent, recalcitrant infections
- presence of carcinoma or fistula
- staphylococcal toxic shock syndrome

Practice tips

- Failure of treatment may be due to diagnostic error, therapeutic error, sexual reinfection, chemical sensitivity to vaginal tablets, drug resistance or depressed host immunity.
- Patients with an infective cause appreciate the use of patient education material, especially that including preventive measures.
- Advise patients subject to vaginal infection about simple hygiene measures to keep the area dry and cool: avoid nylon underwear, pantyhose, tight jeans, wet swimsuits, perfumed soaps and vaginal deodorisers.
- A serious sequela is subsequent dyspareunia and vaginismus. The patient should be advised to have sufficient lubrication, such as KY jelly, to avoid distressing psychosexual problems.

References

1. Mackay EV et al. *Illustrated textbook of gynaecology* (2nd edition). Sydney: WB Saunder. Bailliere Tindall, 1992, 296–325.
2. Weisberg E. Wet film examination. Aust Fam Physician, 1991; 20:291–294.
3. Tunnessen WW. Jr. *Signs and symptoms in paediatrics* (2nd edition). Philadelphia: Lippincott, 1988, 458–460.
4. O'Neill S, Howard S. Recurrent vulvovaginal candidiasis. Aust Fam Physician, 1989; 18:102.
5. Sobel JD. Vulvovaginal candidiasis (chapter). In: Holmes KK et al (eds) *Sexually transmitted diseases*. New York: McGraw-Hill, 1990:515–523.
6. Vejtorp M, Bollreup AC, Vejtory L et al. Bacterial vaginosis: a double-blind randomised trial of the effect of treatment of the sexual partner. Br J Obst Gynecol, 1988; 95:920–6.
7. US Department of Health and Human Services, Public Health Service, Centers for Disease Control. *Sexually transmitted diseases; treatment guidelines*. MMWR, 1989; 38:S–8.

80

Domestic violence and sexual assault

Domestic violence basically means the physical, sexual or emotional abuse of one partner by the other, almost invariably abuse of a female by a male. However, the abuse can be of an elderly parent by the children or from some other member of the household to another member. It usually results from abuse and/or imbalance of power in close relationships. One person in the relationship consistently dominates or threatens with power and the abused victim gradually gives over more power.

A major problem in dealing with domestic violence is that it is hidden and the victims are reluctant to divulge the cause of their injuries when visiting medical practitioners.

Key facts and checkpoints[1]

- Between a quarter and one-third of relationships experience violence at some time.
- In 90–95% of cases the victims are women.
- 10% of women have been violently assaulted in the last year.
- 22% of homicides in Queensland in 1982–87 were spouse murders.
- In violent families with children, 90% of children witness the violence and 50% of children are victims of violence.
- 4% of relationships will experience chronic domestic violence (in 20% this occurs before marriage).
- Less than 20% of those who abuse their spouse abuse some other person.[2]
- Alcohol is a factor in 50% of domestic violence incidents (i.e. not the sole cause; it does make violence easier, and is used as an excuse). Other factors include work stress/pressure, financial stress and illness.
- Pregnancy is a high-risk time for victims of domestic battering.
- 50% of people know someone affected by domestic violence, but one-third refuse to speak about it or get involved in any way because they regard it as a 'private matter'.
- One in five people think that domestic violence is acceptable in certain circumstances.

We usually think of domestic violence in terms of physical violence but it can take many forms.[3] These include:

- physical abuse
- psychological abuse
- economic abuse
- social abuse (e.g. isolation)
- sexual abuse

Possible presentations

- Physical injuries: usually bruising caused by punching, kicking or biting; also fractures, burns, genital trauma
- Physical symptoms, e.g. back pain, headache, depression, sexual dysfunction, anxiety
- Psychological problems (both in the woman and her children)

A study by Stark et al[4] defines a three-stage sequence to the battering syndrome:

Stage 1: woman presents with injuries in the central anterior regions of the body (face, head and torso).
Stage 2: multiple visits to clinics, often with vague complaints.
Stage 3: development of psychological sequelae (alcohol, drug addiction, suicide attempts, depression).

Diagnosis

It is important to have a high index of suspicion and recognise and manage the problem to prevent further violence. If you suspect domestic violence—ASK! Talk to the woman alone:

- How are things at home?
- How are things with your spouse/children?
- Did anything unusual happen to bring about these injuries?'
- Has there been any violence?
- You seem to be having a hard time.

It is vital to believe the woman's story. Women are most likely to seek help from their family doctor in preference to any other agency.[5] The doctor has to take the initiative because patients rarely complain about the violence.[3] They may present up to 30 times before they take action to end the violence.[3]

Assessment

- Delineate the problem — pattern of violence
  — effect on the woman and her children
  — resources available to women
  — social/cultural environment
- Examine and investigate presenting symptoms.
- Check for coexisting injuries (common target areas are breast, chest, abdomen and buttocks). Inspect the ears, teeth and jaw.
- Check the patient's general health status.
- Look for signs of alcohol or drug abuse.
- Keep accurate records and consider taking photographs.
- X-rays are helpful and may show old fractures.

Victims

The victims come from all socioeconomic and cultural groups. As a rule they enter the relationship as normal, independent, competent women but gradually lose their coping ability and self-esteem and may become compliant victims.[1] This has been demonstrated by Hazelwood and workers in their investigations of sexual sadists.[2] Unfortunately, many victims believe that somehow they deserve their punishment.

Many would like to leave home but the move is not so simple. Some do love their husbands and live in hope that the marriage will eventually work. They may feel that they cannot cope with living alone nor with the guilt and perceived failure of moving out.

Perpetrators

Perpetrators generally have inner drives to be strong, protective and powerful but can only achieve this at home through an inappropriate show of strength. However, they are basically insecure with poor self-esteem, poor communication skills, learned violence from family origins and an inability to express appropriate emotions which tend to manifest as anger and violence.[1]

Although they usually control their violence outside the home, there is evidence that some perpetrators are guilty of violent behaviour in the community.

Violence can be triggered by factors such as alcohol, financial problems, frustrations at work and sexual problems.

Cycle of violence

A predictable pattern that is referred to as the 'cycle of violence' has been identified in many marriages. It is controlled by the perpetrator while the victim feels confused and helpless. The cycle repeats itself with a tendency for the violence to increase in severity (Fig. 80.1).

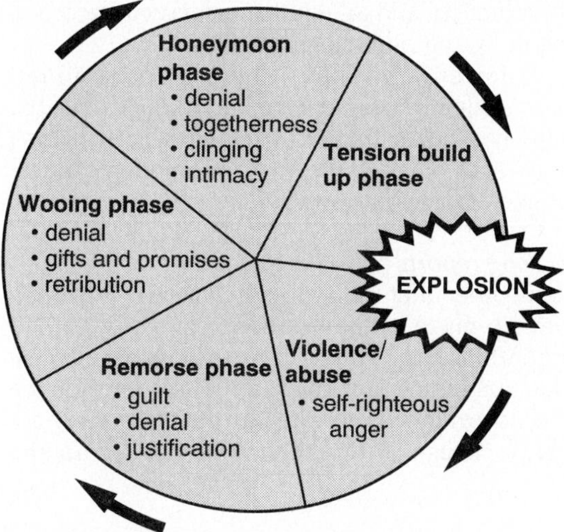

Fig. 80.1 *The cycle of domestic violence*

Table 80.1 *Management strategy for domestic violence*

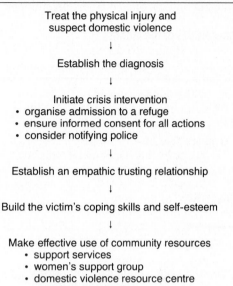

Treat the physical injury and suspect domestic violence

↓

Establish the diagnosis

↓

Initiate crisis intervention
- organise admission to a refuge
- ensure informed consent for all actions
- consider notifying police

↓

Establish an empathic trusting relationship

↓

Build the victim's coping skills and self-esteem

↓

Make effective use of community resources
- support services
- women's support group
- domestic violence resource centre
- social services/police
- social workers

Management

The key to successful management is initial recognition of the problem and establishment of empathetic caring and support for the victim and family. Do not try to fit the victims into the disease model. It must be emphasised that the perpetrators (as in most criminal activity) do not readily change their behavioural pattern and thus there is minimal prospect of the violence decreasing unless there is a dramatic reason to change. As with an alcohol problem, the person has to admit that he has a problem before effective counselling can begin. A management strategy is presented in Table 80.1.

Useful strategies

Do believe her:

- talk openly and explicitly about it
- express concern for her safety
- give information (i.e. about the course of action available to her; contacts for legal advice)
- respect her right to make her own decisions

Harmful strategies

Don't
- deny domestic violence
- minimise the importance of domestic violence
- blame the victim
- treat with tranquillisers
- refer to a psychiatrist
- refer to marriage guidance if the husband isn't interested
- set explicit criteria/rules (takes away her power yet again)

It is uncommon to get the co-operation of the perpetrator in the management process. If they do seek help they require counselling by a skilled and experienced practitioner, as treatment will be prolonged and complex.

As a general rule the most effective intervention in arresting the violence is to arrest the violent person.[3]

Sexual assault

Medical practitioners dealing with the difficult and distressing problem of alleged sexual assault should be trained in the subject and familiar with the laws applicable to sexual assault in their own state. Rape involves considerable violence and physical injury in 5–10% of cases, in which the victims fear for their lives.[6] Apart from the inevitable psychological consequences, the possibility of pregnancy or acquired STD should be considered. The inexperienced practitioner should refer the patient to the nearest available resource and then continue a caring involvement as the person's GP. Survivors of sexual assault should be allowed to accept or decline various treatment options offered by the practitioner.

Management of the victim

What you should do for the patient first is to offer and provide privacy, safety, confidentiality and emotional support. Believe them, listen to them and be non-judgemental.

Three important things to say initially to any victim:

- You are safe now.
- We are sorry this happened to you.
- It was not your fault.

Initial advice to the victim

If victim reporting to police:

1. Notify the police at once.
2. Take along a witness to the alleged assault (if there was a witness).
3. Do not wash or tidy yourself or change your clothing.
4. Do not take any alcohol or drugs.
5. Don't drink or wash out your mouth if there was oral assault.
6. Take a change of warm clothing.

If not reporting to police or unsure, contact any of the following:

1. a friend or other responsible person
2. Lifeline or Lifelink or a similar service
3. a doctor
4. a counselling service

Obtaining information

1. Obtain consent from the patient to record and release information.
2. Take a careful history and copious relevant notes.
3. Keep a record, have a protocol.
4. Obtain a kit for examination.
5. Have someone present during the examination (especially in the case of male doctors examining women).
6. Air-dry swabs (media destroy spermatozoa).
7. Hand specimens to police immediately.

Examination

If possible the patient should be clothed when seen. Have the patient undress while standing on a white sheet to collect debris, and note any injuries as each item is removed. Each part of the body should be examined, under good illumination, and all injuries measured, recorded carefully and on a diagram.

Injuries should be photographed professionally. Examine the body and genital area with a Wood's light to identify semen, which fluoresces. Palpate the scalp for hidden trauma. Collect appropriate swabs.

Making reports

Remember that as a doctor you are impartial. Never make inappropriate judgements to authorities (e.g. 'This patient was raped' or 'incest was committed'). Rather say: 'There is evidence (or no evidence) to support penetration of the vagina/anus' or 'There is evidence of trauma to __________ '.

Postexamination

After the medical examination a discussion of medical problems should take place with the patient. This should be done in private and kept totally confidential. A management plan for physical injuries and emotional problems is discussed.

Consider the possibility of STD and possible referral. Consider also the possibility of pregnancy and the need for postcoital hormone tablets. Organise follow-up counselling and STD screening.

References

1. Kerr A. Domestic violence. Treat it seriously. Aust Fam Physician, 1989; 18:1362–1369.
2. Hazelwood R, Warren J, Dietz P. Compliant victims of the sexual sadist. Aust Fam Physician, 1993; 22:474–479.
3. Knowlden S, Helman T. How to treat domestic violence. Australian Dr Weekly, 21 April 1989, I–VIII.
4. Stark E. et al *Wife abusing in the medical setting—an introduction to health personnel.* Rockville, Ma: National Clearing House for Domestic Violence, 1981, 7.
5. Western Australian Domestic Violence Task Force. *Break the silence.* Report to the Western Australian Government. Perth: Government Printer, 1986; 26–35:162–163.
6. Schroeder SA et al. *Current medical diagnosis and treatment.* East Norwalk. Appleton & Lange, 1990, 505–507.

81

Basic antenatal care

Pregnancy and childbirth are very important and emotional events in the lives of women and their families. Their care during and after pregnancy is one of the most satisfying aspects of the work of the family doctor, who generally chooses breadth of knowledge rather than depth of knowledge. The changing trend towards specialisation has meant a change of role for the city practitioner and now shared obstetric care is a commonly practised routine. The quality of care that can be given in family practice is often superior to that offered in the hospital antenatal clinic, partly because of the continuing personal care offered by the family doctor.[1]

Antenatal care presents preventive medicine opportunities *par excellence* and is the ideal time to develop an optimal therapeutic relationship with the expectant mother. The opportunities for anticipatory guidance should be seized and education about the myriad of possible sensations during pregnancy (such as heartburn, backache, leg cramps, various fears and anxieties) should be addressed. In other words, an optimal communication system should be established between the expectant couple and the health care system.

Early diagnosis of high-risk pregnancy is important but of little value unless followed by normal attendance for antenatal care.

The information presented here is a basis for the shared care strategy where family doctors share basic antenatal care with consultants and have a ready referral strategy for high-risk pregnancies.

The basic aim of antenatal care is to assess the risk of harm to mother and baby and apply the appropriate level of surveillance to minimise or eradicate harmful effects.

The initial visit

It is important to book the patient into hospital at the first visit and into the antenatal outpatient department if appropriate. It is mandatory to make an accurate estimation of the expected due date—this can be aided by the use of ultrasonography.

History checkpoints[2]

- Confirm the pregnancy by the menstrual history and by urine or serum human chorionic gonadotrophin if necessary.
- Previous obstetric history:
  - Gestation, length of labour, mode of delivery, birth weight of each baby.
  - Consider previous problems: foetal or neonatal abnormalities or deaths; preterm or growth-retarded infants.
  - Abortions: determine if there has been any termination of pregnancies or first or second trimester spontaneous abortions.
- Medical history:
  - Check for past evidence of diabetes, tuberculosis, anaemia, rubella, rheumatic fever, heart or renal disease, jaundice,

depression, transfusions and rhesus status.

- Family history:
  - — Features to consider are multiple pregnancies, hypertension and diabetes.
  - — If any of these pertain to first-degree relatives, consider a glucose screening or tolerance test.
- Psychosocial history:
  - — This is very important and includes an assessment of the emotional attitude.
- Drug history:
  - — Includes intake of nicotine, alcohol, aspirin, illicit drugs, OTC drugs and prescribed drugs.
- Important points to consider:
  - — Establish date of confinement (see obstetric calendar in Figure 81.1).
  - — If maternal age > 37 years, consider feasibility of amniocentesis or chorionic villus sampling (Down syndrome).
  - — Consider unusual causes for severe nausea and vomiting, e.g. hydatidiform mole, cerebral tumour.
  - — Investigate possible exposure to rubella.
  - — If vaginal bleeding: if Rh negative, send blood sample for Rh antibodies—if absent, give one ampoule anti-D gammaglobulin within 72 hours of first bleed.

The calculation is made from the first day of the last menstrual period

January	1	2	3	4	5	6	7	8	9	10	11	12	13	14	15	16	17	18	19	20	21	22	23	24	25	26	27	28	29	30	31	**January**
October	8	9	10	11	12	13	14	15	16	17	18	19	20	21	22	23	24	25	26	27	28	29	30	31	1	2	3	4	5	6	7	***November***
February	1	2	3	4	5	6	7	8	9	10	11	12	13	14	15	16	17	18	19	20	21	22	23	24	25	26	27	28				**February**
November	8	9	10	11	12	13	14	15	16	17	18	19	20	21	22	23	24	25	26	27	28	29	30	1	2	3	4	5				***December***
March	1	2	3	4	5	6	7	8	9	10	11	12	13	14	15	16	17	18	19	20	21	22	23	24	25	26	27	28	29	30	31	**March**
December	6	7	8	9	10	11	12	13	14	15	16	17	18	19	20	21	22	23	24	25	26	27	28	29	30	31	1	2	3	4	5	***January***
April	1	2	3	4	5	6	7	8	9	10	11	12	13	14	15	16	17	18	19	20	21	22	23	24	25	26	27	28	29	30		**April**
January	6	7	8	9	10	11	12	13	14	15	16	17	18	19	20	21	22	23	24	25	26	27	28	29	30	31	1	2	3	4		***February***
May	1	2	3	4	5	6	7	8	9	10	11	12	13	14	15	16	17	18	19	20	21	22	23	24	25	26	27	28	29	30	31	**May**
February	5	6	7	8	9	10	11	12	13	14	15	16	17	18	19	20	21	22	23	24	25	26	27	28	1	2	3	4	5	6	7	***March***
June	1	2	3	4	5	6	7	8	9	10	11	12	13	14	15	16	17	18	19	20	21	22	23	24	25	26	27	28	29	30		**June**
March	8	9	10	11	12	13	14	15	16	17	18	19	20	21	22	23	24	25	26	27	28	29	30	31	1	2	3	4	5	6		***April***
July	1	2	3	4	5	6	7	8	9	10	11	12	13	14	15	16	17	18	19	20	21	22	23	24	25	26	27	28	29	30	31	**July**
April	7	8	9	10	11	12	13	14	15	16	17	18	19	20	21	22	23	24	25	26	27	28	29	30	1	2	3	4	5	6	7	***May***
August	1	2	3	4	5	6	7	8	9	10	11	12	13	14	15	16	17	18	19	20	21	22	23	24	25	26	27	28	29	30	31	**August**
May	8	9	10	11	12	13	14	15	16	17	18	19	20	21	22	23	24	25	26	27	28	29	30	31	1	2	3	4	5	6	7	***June***
September	1	2	3	4	5	6	7	8	9	10	11	12	13	14	15	16	17	18	19	20	21	22	23	24	25	26	27	28	29	30		**September**
June	8	9	10	11	12	13	14	15	16	17	18	19	20	21	22	23	24	25	26	27	28	29	30	1	2	3	4	5	6	7		***July***
October	1	2	3	4	5	6	7	8	9	10	11	12	13	14	15	16	17	18	19	20	21	22	23	24	25	26	27	28	29	30	31	**October**
July	8	9	10	11	12	13	14	15	16	17	18	19	20	21	22	23	24	25	26	27	28	29	30	31	1	2	3	4	5	6	7	***August***
November	1	2	3	4	5	6	7	8	9	10	11	12	13	14	15	16	17	18	19	20	21	22	23	24	25	26	27	28	29	30		**November**
August	8	9	10	11	12	13	14	15	16	17	18	19	20	21	22	23	24	25	26	27	28	29	30	31	1	2	3	4	5	6		***September***
December	1	2	3	4	5	6	7	8	9	10	11	12	13	14	15	16	17	18	19	20	21	22	23	24	25	26	27	28	29	30	31	**December**
September	7	8	9	10	11	12	13	14	15	16	17	18	19	20	21	22	23	24	25	26	27	28	29	30	1	2	3	4	5	6	7	***October***

Or: (approximately) subtract three from months and add seven to days
e.g. 19/8/89
+7 − 3
26/5/90 Or: Naegele's rule—add seven days, nine months

Fig. 81.1 *Obstetric calendar to determine expected due date*

Physical examination

During the initial examination assess the patient's general physical and mental status. Examine the following:

- general fitness, colour (? anaemia)
- basic parameters: height, weight, blood pressure, pulse, urinalysis (protein and glucose)
- head and neck: teeth, gums, thyroid
- chest: including breasts/nipples
- abdomen: palpate for uterine size and listen to foetal heart (if indicated)

  Perform the four classic techniques of palpation (applies to later visits):

  1. Fundal palpation
  2. Lateral abdominal palpation
  3. Pawlik palpation
  4. Deep pelvic palpation
- legs: note oedema or varicose veins

Speculum examination: perform a Pap smear and swab (if indicated by abnormal vaginal discharge).

Pelvic examination: confirm uterus size and period of gestation by bimanual palpation.

Investigations

Standard antenatal investigations are outlined in Table 81.1 and a routine plan for antenatal care in Table 81.2.[3]

Visits during pregnancy

- initial in first trimester: 8–10 weeks
- up to 28 weeks: every 4–6 weeks
- up to 36 weeks: every 2 weeks
- 36 weeks–delivery: weekly

For each visit record:

- weight gain
- blood pressure
- urinalysis (protein and sugar); see Table 81.3
- uterine size/fundal height
- foetal heart (usually audible with stethoscope at 25 weeks and definitely by 28 weeks)
- foetal movements (if present)
- presentation and position of foetus (third trimester)
- presence of any oedema

Record day of first foetal movements (ask patient to write down the dates)

- primigravida: 17–20 weeks
- multigravida: 16–18 weeks

Fundal height

The relative heights of the uterus fundus are shown in Figure 81.2. The uterus is a pelvic organ until the twelfth week of pregnancy. After this time it can be palpated abdominally. At about

Table 81.1 *Standard antenatal investigations*

Essential	***Recommended or consider***
First visit	***First visit***
• full blood examination • blood grouping and rhesus typing • rhesus antibodies • cervical smear (if previous > 12 months) • midstream urine: microscopy and culture • HBs Ag (hepatitis surface antigen) • syphilis screen • haemoglobin electrophoresis (if indicated)	• HIV antibodies
Subsequent visits	***Subsequent visits***
• ultrasound 18-20 weeks (if doubt about foetal maturity) • midstream urine (M&C), 28 weeks (if high risk) • haemoglobin 30 weeks • Rh antibodies (negative mother), 28 weeks and 36 weeks	• glucose screening 28-30 weeks • cervical swab (group B haemolytic streptococcus) 32 weeks • test fetoplacental function (32-38 weeks)

For prenatal diagnosis of genetic abnormalities:
- amniocentesis (14-16 weeks)
- chorionic villus sampling (9-11 weeks)
- alpha-fetoprotein

Table 81.2 *A routine plan for antenatal care*

Week of pregnancy	Recorded observations									Checklist of reminders
	Date	Gestation (weeks)		BP	Weight (kg)	Urine		Foetus		
		date	size			protein	glucose	heart	position	
8–10										Confirm pregnancy and stage by examination Arrange basic investigations (Table 81.1) If Rh-negative arrange test for partner Consider psychosocial status Confirm hospital and medical arrangements Promote a healthy diet Discuss breast care
14										Discuss diet and general health Educate about recording first movements Arrange ultrasound 18 weeks to confirm dates, etc. Consider need for iron and folic acid
20										Record date of first movement Check that movements correspond with dates Confirm hospital booking Discuss coping abilities
26										Urinalysis, microscopy and culture Check foetal heart Reinforce value of breast-feeding Discuss antenatal classes and physiotherapy Check psychosocial issues Advise single mothers on available government benefits
28										Check haemoglobulin and film Repeat antibody screen if Rh-negative Consider glucose screening test
30										Check foetal position, presentation and heart Consider possibility of twins
32										Check breast care, diet, exercise program Consider special screening if necessary, e.g. repeated ultrasound
34										General check—health, breasts Check for signs of pre-eclampsia Check position ? breech
36										Check haemoglobin and film Arrange antibody test if Rh-negative Explain what to expect with onset of labour Check foetal position

(continues)

Table 81.2 *(continued)*

Week of pregnancy	Recorded observations									Checklist of reminders
	Date	Gestation (weeks)		BP	Weight (kg)	Urine		Foetus		
		date	size			protein	glucose	heart	position	
37										Check breast care, diet, coping ability Explain hospital admission procedures Check foetal position (? engaged)
38										Check breast care, state of legs, coping ability Check foetal position (? engaged head) Reaffirm understanding of when to go to hospital
39										Check any special concerns Discuss future family planning

Table 81.3 *Causes of proteinuria in pregnancy*

Urinary tract infection
Contamination from vaginal discharge
Pre-eclamptic toxaemia
Underlying chronic renal disease

20–22 weeks it has reached the level of the umbilicus and reaches the xiphisternum between 36 and 40 weeks. Palpation of the fundal height is affected by obesity and tenseness of the abdominal wall.

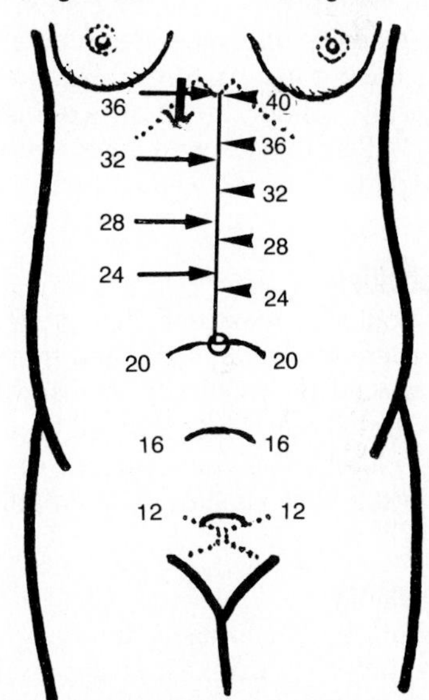

Fig. 81.2 *Fundal height in normal pregnancy (in weeks); the height of the fundus is a guide to the period of gestation. Nulliparas experience lightening at about 36 weeks when the fundal height usually reverts to the 34 week level*

Management of specific issues

Nutrition advice

A healthy diet is very important and should contain at least the following daily allowances:

1. Eat most:
   - fruit and vegetables (at least 4 serves)
   - cereals and bread (4–6 serves)
2. Eat moderately:
   - dairy products—3 cups (600 ml) of milk or equivalent in yoghurt or cheese
   - lean meat, poultry or fish—1 or 2 serves (at least 2 serves of red meat per week)
3. Eat least:
   - sugar and refined carbohydrates (e.g. sweets, cakes, biscuits, soft drinks)
   - polyunsaturated margarine, butter, oil and cream

Bran with cereal helps prevent constipation of pregnancy.

If the ideal diet is followed, iron, vitamin and calcium supplements should not be necessary. Do not diet to lose weight. Plan to gain about 12 kg during pregnancy.

Smoking, alcohol and other drugs[4]

Encourage patients to avoid all street drugs, alcohol, tobacco and caffeine (ideally). If they find this impossible, encourage the following daily limitations:

- 3–6 smokes
- 1 standard drink
- 1 cup of coffee or 2 cups of tea

Other household members should also stop smoking as passive smoking may be harmful to mother and child.

Breast-feeding

Mothers to be should be encouraged to breast-feed. Give advice and relevant literature. They can be directed to a local nursing mothers' group for support and guidance if necessary.

Antenatal classes

Referral to therapists conducting such classes can provide advice and supervision on antenatal exercises, back care, posture, relaxation skills, pain relief in labour, general exercises and swimming. Enrolment with the partner is recommended.

Normal activities

Mothers should be reassured that pregnancy is a normal event in the life cycle and that normal activities should be continued. Housework and other activities should be performed to just short of getting tired. The importance of getting sufficient rest and sleep should be emphasised.

Sex in pregnancy[5]

Coitus should be encouraged during pregnancy but with appropriate care, especially in the four weeks before delivery. Restriction would only seem necessary if there has been an adverse obstetric history and there are major complications in the current pregnancy.

The couple should be encouraged to be loving to each other and communicate their feelings freely, as the need for affection and physical contact is important. Coital techniques can be modified as the pregnancy progresses—posterior entry and the female superior position are quite suitable.

Travel

Pregnant women should avoid standing in trains. They should avoid international air travel after 28 weeks and travel after 36 weeks is usually not permitted. Patients should be counselled to wear a seat belt during car travel.

Psychosocial and emotional stress

Antenatal visits provide an ideal opportunity to become acquainted with the 'real' person and explore issues that help the patient. Provide whole person understanding with appropriate help and reassurance where necessary. Areas to be explored include support systems, attitudes of patient and partner to the pregnancy, sexuality, expectation of labour and delivery, financial issues, attitudes of parents and in-laws, and so on.

Weight gain in pregnancy

Although a standard weight gain is given as 12 kg over 40 weeks of pregnancy, it is common for some women in Australia to gain up to 20 kg without adverse effects.[2]

Normal weight gain is minimal in the first 20 weeks, resulting in a 3 kg weight gain in the first half of pregnancy. From 20 weeks onwards there is an average weight gain of 0.5 kg per week. From 36 weeks the weight gain usually levels off.[2]

Foetal movement chart

If daily foetal movements exceed ten and the pattern has not changed significantly, then usually the foetus is at no risk. However, if the movements drop to less than ten per day, then the patient should be referred to the hospital for foetal monitoring.

Possible exposure to rubella

When contact with a possible case of rubella occurs during pregnancy it is essential to establish the immune status of the patient. If she is already immune no further action is necessary. If her immune status is unknown, perform a rubella immunoglobulin G titre and immunoglobulin M and repeat the Ig G and Ig M titres in two or three weeks.

Threatened miscarriage

If a threatened miscarriage occurs, check the blood group and test for rhesus antibodies in maternal serum. If the mother is Rh negative and no antibodies are detected, give one ampoule of anti-D gammaglobulin intramuscularly. Assess her pelvis to rule out an ectopic pregnancy and, if indicated, perform pelvic scanning to confirm viability of the foetus or the presence of an extrauterine gestation.

Pregnancy sickness[6]

- nausea and vomiting occur in more than 50% of women
- almost always disappears by the end of first trimester
- mild cases can be dealt with by explanation and reassurance; it is preferable to avoid drug therapy if possible
- simple measures:
  - small frequent meals
  - a fizzy soft drink may help
  - avoid stimuli such as cooking smells
  - take care with teeth cleaning
  - avoid oral iron
- medication (for severe cases):
  - meclozine 25–50 mg bd, with pyridoxine 50–100 mg bd

Heartburn[6]

Gastro-oesophageal reflux is a major source of discomfort to women in the latter half of pregnancy. Non-pharmacological treatment such as frequent small meals, avoidance of bending over and elevation of the head of the bed are the mainstays of treatment. Smoking, alcohol and caffeine (coffee, chocolate, tea) intake should be avoided. Regular use of antacids is effective, e.g. alginate/antacid liquid (Gaviscon, Mylanta Plus) 10–20 ml before meals and at bedtime.

Cramps

Pregnant women are more prone to cramp. If it develops they should be advised simply to place a pillow at the foot of the bed so that plantar flexion of the feet is avoided during sleep. Prolonged plantar flexion is the basis of the cramps.

Varicose veins

These can be troublesome as well as embarrassing. Wearing special supportive pantyhose (not elastic bandages) is the most comfortable and practical way to cope, in addition to adequate rest.

Haemorrhoids

Haemorrhoids in the later stages of pregnancy can be very troublesome. Emphasising the importance of a high-fibre diet to ensure regular bowel habit is the best management. Painful haemorrhoids may be eased by the application of packs soaked in warm saline or perhaps haemorrhoidal ointments containing local anaesthetic.

Dental hygiene

Dental problems can worsen during pregnancy so special care of teeth and gums, including a visit to the dentist, is appropriate. Continuation of cleaning with a softer brush is recommended.

Back pain

Back pain, especially low back pain, is common during pregnancy and special back care advice can help women cope with this problem, which can become debilitating. Advice with lifting, sitting, and resting, using a firm mattress and avoiding high-heeled shoes will help.

Physical therapy administered by a skilled therapist can be extremely effective for pregnant patients but certain safety rules should be followed:

- *First trimester*: use normal physical therapy and advise exercises.
- *Second trimester*: use supine side lying rotation and sitting techniques only; advise exercises.
- *Third trimester*: avoid physical therapy (if possible); encourage exercises.

Guidelines for treatment

- Keep mobilisation and manipulation to a minimum.
- Use mobilisation in preference to manipulation.

- Safeguard the sacroiliac joints in the last trimester.
- Encourage active exercises as much as possible.
- Avoid medications wherever possible.
- Give trigger point injections (8 ml 1% lignocaine) around the SIJs if necessary.

Mineral supplements in pregnancy

Iron and folic acid are not routinely recommended for pregnant women who are healthy, following an optimal diet and have a normal blood test. Those at risk, e.g. with poor nutrition, will require supplementation.

Advice on when to seek medical help

- if contractions, unusual pain or bleeding occur before term
- if the baby is less active than usual
- if the membranes rupture (with fluid loss)
- the onset of regular contractions 5–10 minutes apart

References

1. Barker JH. *General practice medicine.* Edinburgh: Churchill Livingstone, 1984, 76–89.
2. Fung P, Morrison J. Obstetric share-care. Aust Fam Physician, 1989; 18:479–484.
3. Carson S, Gawthorn EC. A manual for primary health care. Sydney: Medical Observer, 1990, 3.1–3.20.
4. Smibert J. The principles of antenatal care. Aust Fam Physician, 1978; 9:1087–1094.
5. Beischer NA, Mackay EV. *Obstetrics and the newborn.* Sydney: Saunders, 1986.
6. Humphrey M. Pregnancy related disorders. In: MIMS Disease Index. Sydney: IMS Publishing, 1991–92, 435–438.

82

High-risk pregnancy

Definition[1]

A high-risk pregnancy is one in which the foetus is at increased risk of stillbirth, neonatal morbidity or death, and/or the expectant mother is at increased risk for morbidity or mortality.

High-risk pregnancies may be predicted before conception in some women, especially those with serious medical problems and a poor obstetric history. Other high risks can be identified at the first antenatal visit and others develop during the course of pregnancy. The first antenatal visit is the most important visit and demands time and care to make an accurate assessment.

Accurate determination of EDD

It is vital to determine the expected due date of confinement (EDD) based on the exact time of the last normal menstrual period (sometimes misleading), the fundal height, the time of first foetal movements and, if in doubt, ultrasound assessment.

High-risk obstetric patients

Guidelines for high-risk pregnancy are presented in Table 82.1. Recognition of these high-risk pregnancies is important for the family doctor involved in shared care. Common categories that require special surveillance are:

- elderly primigravida
- grand multipara (fifth or greater pregnancy, especially if > 35 years)
- those with a poor obstetric history
- previous caesarean section
- severely disadvantaged social problem, e.g. sole teenage parent with drug problem
- hypertension
- obesity
- short stature
- diabetes mellitus
- prolonged infertility or essential drug or hormone treatment
- heavy smoking or alcohol intake

The onset during pregnancy of the following:

- little or no weight gain during the first half of the pregnancy
- complications such as pre-eclampsia, multiple pregnancies and antepartum haemorrhage
- abnormal presentation
- abnormal foetal growth

Urinary tract infection

Acute pyelonephritis

This infection, usually due to *E. coli*, is one of the most common infective complications of pregnancy. Symptoms include fever, chills, vomiting and loin pain. Bladder symptoms such as frequency and dysuria are commonly absent. The patient should be hospitalised and may require intravenous fluid and antibiotic therapy.

Treatment of acute pyelonephritis

- amoxycillin 1 g IV 6 hourly for 48 hours, then 500 mg (o) 8 hourly (if bacteria sensitive) for 14 days [2,3]
- alternatives: cephalosporins, e.g. cephalothin IV and cephalexin 500 mg (o)

Table 82.1 *Guidelines for specialist obstetric consultation*

	Major risk factors Obstetric consultation mandatory	***Other risk factors Consultation should be considered***
Past problematic obstetric history	• previous caesarean section • incompetent cervical os • 2nd trimester spontaneous abortion • rhesus/other blood group incompatibility • thromboembolic disease • premature labour	• multiple spontaneous or elective abortions • premature delivery • previous stillbirth • neonatal death • grand multigravida
Problems related to pregnancy	• pre-eclampsia • rhesus/other blood group incompatibility • significant vaginal bleeding • placenta praevia • postmaturity at 42 weeks • multiple pregnancy • polyhydramnios • need for amniocentesis — genetic concerns — abnormal AFP — other	• recurrent urinary infections • abnormal uterine growth • inadequate maternal weight gain • hypertension
General factors		• age > 35 : < 18 • obesity > 110 kg • prepregnancy weight < 45 kg • psychosocial problems • short stature
Maternal disorders	• diabetes mellitus • systemic lupus erythematosus • sickle cell disease or other haemoglobinopathy	• anaemia: Hb < 10 g/dL • cardiovascular disease • chronic renal disease • alcohol or drug abuse • genital herpes
Perinatal problems	• premature labour • postmaturity (42 weeks) • disproportion • malpresentation • placental insufficiency	• non-vertex presentation (at term) • foetal arrhythmia • membranes ruptured > 18 hrs
Inadequate antenatal care		• late presentation (after 20 weeks) • no antenatal care • failed or poor attendance

Acute cystitis

Patients with acute cystitis typically have dysuria and frequency.

Treatment

- cephalexin 250 mg (o) 6 hourly[3]

  or
- amoxycillin/potassium clavulanate (250/125 mg) (o) 8 hourly

  or
- nitrofurantoin 50 mg (o) 6 hourly, if a beta-lactam antibiotic is contraindicated.

Note Nitrofurantoin is contraindicated in the third[2] trimester of pregnancy as it may lead to haemolytic diseases in the newborn. Cotrimoxazole and sulphonamides should be avoided.

- a high fluid intake should be maintained during treatment.

Asymptomatic bacteriuria[2]

- 5–10% of pregnant asymptomatic women have positive cultures during pregnancy.
- Ideally all women should be screened for bacteriuria at their first visit.
- Less than 1% will subsequently develop bacteriuria.

- Approximately 50% of such women subsequently develop pyelonephritis during pregnancy with an increased risk of preterm labour, mid-trimester abortion and pregnancy-induced hypertension.

Treatment

Treatment is recommended according to culture sensitivities. It is preferable to delay it until the first trimester has passed.[2]

Hypertensive disorders in pregnancy[4]

Hypertensive disorders complicate about 10% of all pregnancies. Pregnancy may induce hypertension in previously normotensive women or may aggravate pre-existing hypertension.

A classification of hypertensive disorders in pregnancy:

- **Pregnancy-induced hypertension**
  Definition:
  SBP > 140 mmHg and DBP > 90 mmHg, occurring for first time after 20th week of pregnancy and regressing postpartum.

> *Types:*
> Hypertension without proteinuria or oedema
> Pre-eclampsia
> - mild—generalised oedema
> - severe—proteinuria ± generalised oedema
>
> Eclampsia—proteinuria + generalised oedema + convulsions.

- **Essential (coincidental) hypertension**
  Chronic underlying hypertension occurring before the onset of pregnancy or persisting postpartum.
- **Pregnancy-aggravated hypertension**
  Underlying hypertension worsened by pregnancy.

Risk factors

The following are risk factors for pregnancy-induced hypertension:

- primigravidae
- family history of hypertension
- diabetes complicating pregnancy
- multiple pregnancy
- hydatidiform mole
- hydrops fetalis
- hydramnios
- renal disease

Clinical features include hypertension, weight gain, peripheral oedema and proteinuria (urinary protein > 0.3/24 hours). Late symptoms include headache (related to severe hypertension), epigastric pain and visual disturbances.

Management

The optimal treatment is delivery, and induction of labour needs to be timed appropriately—based on parameters such as the blood pressure level and the development of proteinuria. The BP level must be kept below 160/100 mmHg, because at this level intrauterine death is likely to occur.

Antihypertensive drugs[4]

Contraindicated drugs are ACE inhibitors and diuretics. There is no place for the use of diuretics alone unless cardiac failure is present.

Commonly used medications:

- Beta-blockers, e.g. labetalol, oxprenolol and atenolol (used under close supervision and after 20 weeks gestation)
- Methyldopa: good for sustained BP control

Guidelines for referral/admission to hospital

- When BP reaches 140/90 mmHg
- Development of proteinuria

Anaemias[2]

During the course of a normal pregnancy the haemoglobin should remain above 11 g/dL and the haematocrit above 33%. Levels below this, particularly less than 10 g/dL, require investigation. Iron demands during pregnancy are 725 mg, especially during the third trimester.

Types of anaemia in pregnancy:

- iron deficiency (approximately 50%)
- megaloblastic anaemia (usually due to folic acid deficiency)
- thalassaemia

Management

- If anaemia is found, measure serum ferritin, red cell folate and serum B12 as indicated
- Treatment is according to cause:
  - — iron deficiency: ferrous sulphate 1.8 g (o) daily
  - — megaloblastic anaemia: folic acid 10 mg (o) bd

Antepartum haemorrhage

If haemorrhage occurs under 24 weeks treat as for threatened miscarriage. If it occurs after 26 weeks admit to hospital for management. Remember to give anti-D if the mother is Rh negative. Do not perform a vaginal examination.

Trauma: motor vehicle accidents

Abdominal trauma in pregnancy is usually associated with seat belt restraints during motor vehicle accidents. However, these injuries are far less severe than those that occur when people are not wearing seat belts. Women should be encouraged to wear seat belts and should not be given certificates stating that seat belts should not be worn in pregnancy.

The incidence of placental abruption following accidents is related to the severity of the accident and the extent of the external injuries. Injured patients should be admitted to a unit where cardiotocography can be performed regularly for 48 hours and perinatal intensive care can be provided if needed.

Consideration for induction

Possible indications for induction:

- post-term (42 weeks or over)
- maternal hypertension
- pre-eclamptic toxaemia
- intrauterine growth retardation
- diabetes mellitus

Drugs in pregnancy

Drugs have to be used with great care during pregnancy. An Australian categorisation of drug risk is presented in summary in Table 82.2. It is worth noting that β_2-agonists used to treat asthma have a Category A rating.

Table 82.2 *Examples of medicines in pregnancy: an Australian categorisation of risk (Australian Drug Evaluation committee)*

	Category
Iron and haemopoietic agents	
• folic acid	A
• iron preparations (all types)	A
Antihistamines and antiemetics	
• phenothiazines, e.g. prochlorperazine	C
• meclozine, cyclizine	A
• other antihistamines	A or B2
Alimentary system agents	
• antacids	A
• H_2 receptor antagonists	B1
Cardiovascular	
• ACE inhibitor	D
• methyldopa	A
• calcium channel blockers	C
• beta-blockers	C
• digoxin	A
• diuretics (except spironalactone B3)	C
• glyceryl trinitrate	B2
Analgesics	
• aspirin	C
• paracetamol/acetaminophen	A
• codeine	A
• opioid analgesics	C
Hypnotics, sedatives, antipsychotic agents	
• barbiturates	C
• benzodiazepines	C
• chloral hydrate	A
• phenothiazines and butyrophenones	C
Antidepressants	
• tricyclics, e.g. amitriptyline	C
• tetracyclics, e.g. mianserin	B2
Anticonvulsants (all groups)	D
NSAIDs	C
Antimicrobials	
• penicillins	A
• cephalexin, cephalothin	A
• aminoglycosides	D
• nitrofurantoin	A
• tetracyclines	D
Corticosteroids	
• systemic	C
• inhalation	B3
Quinine	D

Code Category A—no harmful foetal effects recorded.
B—no harmful effects to date but limited experience (see ADEC guidelines for subgroups B1, B2, B3).
C—have caused or suspected of causing harmful effects on foetus or neonates without causing malformations (reversible).
D—have caused, are suspected to cause or may be expected to cause, an increased incidence of foetal malformation or irreversible damage. Also may have adverse pharmacological effects.

When to refer

If there is a possibility of cervical incompetence, refer for a specialist opinion before 14 weeks.

Referral to specialist centre[2]

The key to an optimal outcome is early identification of the high-risk pregnancy and early

Table 82.3 *Common indications for a glucose screening test*

Diabetes in first-degree relatives
Advancing maternal age > 35
Gross maternal obesity
Polyhydramnios
Glycosuria
Signs and symptoms suggestive of diabetes
Poor obstetric history, e.g. stillborn, large babies
Early pre-eclamptic toxaemia

referral to a specialist team to supervise the management of the remainder of the pregnancy. This has been shown to improve neonatal morbidity and mortality significantly. It is important that family physicians, obstetricians, perinatologists and neonatalogists work as a harmonious team.

References

1. Shires DB, Hennen BK, Rice DI. *Family Medicine.* New York: McGraw-Hill, 1987, 136–151.
2. Humphrey M. Pregnancy related disorders. In: MIMS Disease Index. Sydney: IMS Publishing, 1991–92, 435–438.
3. Mashford ML. *Antibiotic guidelines* (7th edition). Melbourne: Victorian Medical Postgraduate Foundation, 1992/3:31–36.
4. Michael CA. Hypertensive disease in pregnancy. In: MIMS Disease Index. Sydney: IMS Publishing, 1991–92, 272–275.

83

Postnatal care

Education for the puerperium and caring for the baby should begin during pregnancy so that a new mother is familiar with the basic principles of motherhood, especially infant feeding.[1]

Postnatal care really begins with the birth of the baby. Once the airways are cleared the baby should be given to the mother as soon as possible and not taken from her except for essential management.

Mother should remain in the labour ward (if delivered in hospital) for at least an hour after her birth and until she has passed urine. She should be inspected frequently to exclude the possibility of a silent postpartum haemorrhage and vital signs checked before transferring to a lying-in ward.

Guidelines for the lying-in ward[1]

- Every mother needs rest but should have full toilet and shower facilities.
- The baby should be in a bassinet beside the mother and may be taken into bed any time mother likes.
- Room in: the baby should not go to the nursery unless it is sick or the mother requests it.
- There should be no visiting restrictions on close relatives but restrictions should be put on other visitors for the first two or three days.
- Demand feed to appetite.
- No test weighing.
- No complementary feeding unless mother is empty and baby screaming.
- A golden rule is that breast-feeding and the supply of mother's milk is a classic case of 'supply and demand'.
- The doctor should listen carefully to what the mother is saying (and not saying) during visits.

Postnatal consultations

The two-week consultation

Mother:

- Assess the coping ability of the new mother
- Look for signs/symptoms of postpartum depression
- Provide encouragement and advice
- Check breast-feeding

Baby:

- Routine examination
- Perform a Phenistix test on the baby's napkin (in case the Guthrie test has been missed in hospital)

The six-week consultation

This is basically a repeat of the previous consultation and a checklist is presented in Table 83.1.

Contraception

Breast-feeding, when it is truly on demand, is an extremely good contraceptive, but in reality some supplement is necessary for about three months in the average lactating woman.

Table 83.1 *Checklist for postnatal check at 4–6 weeks*

The Mother
Pap smear (if not performed at first visit)
Check rubella status
Check for adequate contraception
Check if intercourse has been resumed and give advice (if appropriate)
Encourage abdominal and pelvic floor exercises
Check for back problems
Check weight, blood pressure and urine
Check breasts
Check perineum
Check psychological health, including coping ability
Check for postpartum thyroiditis
Discuss adequate diet, rest and personal care
Perform pelvic examination
Further follow-up if necessary
Give 'Personal Health Record' folder to mother
Baby
Routine examination
Check growth and feeding
Educate mother regarding immunisation schedule

Oral contraception

- The mini pill (progestogen only)
  - norethisterone 350 micrograms/day

    or
  - levonorgestrel 30 micrograms/day taken every night
- Transfer to combined OC when breastfeeding completed.

After-pains[1]

After-pains, which are more common and most intense after the second and subsequent pregnancies, are characterised by intermittent lower abdominal pains, like period pains, which are often worse during and after feeding. They are caused by oxytocin released from the posterior pituitary, which also causes the let-down reflex of nursing.

Treatment, after examination, is reassurance and analgesics in the form of paracetamol every four hours for three days or as long as necessary.

Breast-feeding

Insufficient milk supply

This is sometimes a problem in mothers who are under a lot of stress and find it hard to relax. A let-down reflex is necessary to get the milk supply going, and sometimes this reflex is slow. If there is insufficient supply, the baby tends to demand frequent feeds, may continually suck its hand and will be slow in gaining weight.[1]

There are three important factors in establishing breast-feeding:

1. positioning the baby on the breast
2. the 'let-down'
3. supply and demand

The breasts produce milk on the principle of supply and demand. This means that the more the breasts are emptied, the more milk is produced.

Advice to mother

- Try to practise relaxation techniques.
- Put the baby to your breast as often as it demands, using the 'chest to chest, chin on breast' method.
- Express after feeds, because the emptier the breasts, the more milk will be produced.
- Make sure you get adequate rest, but if you feel tired go to your doctor for a check-up.

Engorged breasts

Engorgement occurs when the milk supply comes on so quickly that the breasts become swollen, hard and tender. There is an increased supply of blood and other fluids in the breast as well as milk. The breasts and nipples may be so swollen that the baby is unable to latch on and suckle.

Advice to mother

- Feed your baby on demand from day 1 until the baby has had enough.
- Finish the first breast completely; maybe use one side per feed rather than some from each breast. Offer the second breast if the baby appears hungry.
- Soften the breasts before feeds or express with a warm washer or shower, which will help to get the milk flowing.
- Avoid giving the baby other fluids.
- Express a little milk before putting the baby to your breast (a must if the baby has trouble latching on) and express a little after feeding from the other side if it is too uncomfortable.
- Massage any breast lumps gently towards the nipple while feeding.
- Apply cold packs after feeding and cool washed cabbage leaves (left in the

refrigerator) between feeds. Change the leaves every two hours.

- Wake your baby for a feed if your breasts are uncomfortable or if the baby is sleeping longer than four hours.
- Use a good, comfortable brassiere.
- Remove your bra completely before feeding.
- Take paracetamol regularly for severe discomfort.

Point out that regular feeding and following demand feeding is the best treatment for engorged breasts.

Suppression of lactation[2]

Women may seek suppression of lactation for a variety of reasons such as weaning the baby, not wishing to breast-feed initially, or after still-birth.

Mechanical suppression

The simplest way of suppressing lactation once it is established is to transfer the baby gradually to a bottle or a cup over a three-week period. The decreased demand reduces milk supply, with minimal discomfort. If abrupt cessation is required, it is necessary to avoid nipple stimulation, refrain from expressing milk and use a well-fitting brassiere. Use cold packs and analgesics as necessary. Engorgement will gradually settle over a 2–3 week period.

Hormonal suppression

Hormonal suppression can be used for severe engorgement but only as a last resort. It is more effective if given at the time of delivery but may produce side effects.

- bromocriptine (Parlodel) 2.5 mg orally bd for 10–14 days[3]

Drugs and lactation

Drugs that can affect lactation or a breast-fed infant are listed in Table 83.2.

Table 83.2 *Drugs taken by nursing mother that can affect breast-fed infant or lactation*

Contraindicated drugs
Antibiotics: • aminoglycosides • chloramphenicol • nitrofurantoin • metronidazole • tetracycline • sulphonamides
Antihistamines
Antineoplastics/cytotoxics
Benzodiazepines
Bromocriptine
Combined oral contraceptive /oestrogens
Ergotamine
Gold salts
H_2 antagonists, e.g. cimetidine, ranitidine
Illicit drugs, e.g. cocaine, cannabis, LSD
Lithium
Quinidine
Thiouracil
Laxatives, e.g. cascara, senna
Alcohol (no harmful effects unless taken in excess)
Nicotine (increased respiratory distress in infants exposed)

Nipple problems with breast-feeding

Sore nipples

Sore nipples is a common problem, thought to be caused by the baby not taking the nipple into its mouth properly, often because of breast engorgement. The problem is preventable with careful attention to the position of the baby's sucking technique.

Management advice to mother

It is important to be as relaxed and comfortable as possible (with your back well supported) and for your baby to suck gently, so:

- Try to use the 'chest to chest, chin on breast' feeding position.
- Vary the feeding positions (make sure each position is correct).
- Start feeding from the less painful side first if one nipple is very sore.
- Express some milk first to soften and 'lubricate' the nipple. (Avoid drying agents such as methylated spirits, soap and tincture of benzoin, and moisturising creams and ointments, which may contain unwanted chemicals and germs.)
- Gently break the suction with your finger before removing the baby from the breast. (Never pull the baby off the nipple.)
- Apply covered ice to the nipple to relieve pain.
- Keep the nipples dry by exposing the breasts to the air and/or using a hair dryer on a low setting.

- If wearing a bra, try Cannon breast shields inside the bra. Do not wear a bra at night.

Cracked nipples

Cracked nipples are usually caused by the baby clamping on the end of the nipple rather than applying the jaw behind the whole nipple. Not drying the nipples thoroughly after each feed and wearing soggy breast pads are other contributing factors. Untreated sore nipples may progress to painful cracks.

Symptoms

At first, the crack may be so small that it cannot be seen. The crack is either on the skin of the nipple or where it joins the areola. A sharp pain in the nipple with suckling probably means the crack has developed. Feeding is usually very painful, and bleeding can occur.

Management advice to mother

Cracked nipples nearly always heal when you get the baby to latch onto the breast fully and properly. They usually take only 1–2 days to heal.

- Follow the same rules as for sore nipples.
- Do not feed from the affected breast—rest the nipple for 1–2 feeds.
- Express the milk from that breast by hand.
- Feed that expressed milk to the baby.
- Start feeding gradually with short feeds.
- A sympathetic expert such as an experienced nursing mother will be a great help if you are having trouble coping.
- Take paracetamol just before nursing to relieve pain.

Inverted nipples

An inverted nipple is one that inverts or moves into the breast instead of pointing outwards when a baby tries to suck from it. When the areola is squeezed, the nipple retracts inwards.

Treatment

During pregnancy, rolling and stretching the nipple by hand can be helpful. The partner can assist with gentle oral and manual stimulation.

A simple treatment, which should start at the beginning of the seventh month of pregnancy, is the Hoffman technique:

1. Draw an imaginary cross on the breast with the vertical and horizontal line crossing at the nipple.
2. Place the thumbs or the forefingers opposite each other at the edge of the areola on the imaginary horizontal line. Press in firmly and then pull the thumbs (or fingers) back and forth to stretch the areola.
3. In the vertical position, pull the thumbs or fingers upwards and downwards.

This procedure should be repeated about five times each morning. The nipple will become erect and is then easier to grasp, so that it can be slowly and gently drawn out.

Mastitis

Mastitis is basically cellulitis of the interlobular connective tissue of the breast. Usually restricted to lactating women it is caused mainly by a cracked nipple or poor milk drainage. The infecting organism is usually *Staphylococcus aureus* or more rarely *Escherichia coli* or *Candida albicans*. It is a serious problem and requires early treatment. Breast-feeding from the affected side can continue as the infection is confined to interstitial breast tissue and doesn't usually affect the milk supply.

NB Mastitis must be treated vigorously—it is a serious condition.

Clinical features

- a lump and then soreness (at first)
- a red tender area

possibly

- fever, tiredness, muscle aches and pains

Note: Candida infection usually causes severe breast pain—a feeling like a hot knife or shooting pains, especially during and after feeding. It may occur after a course of antibiotics.

Management

Prevention (in lactation)

- maintain free breast drainage
- attend to breast engorgement and cracked nipples

Treatment

- antibiotics: resolution without progression to an abscess will usually be prevented by antibiotics:

  flucloxacillin 500 mg (o) qid for 10 days

  or

  cephalaxin 500 mg (o) qid for 10 days

- therapeutic ultrasound ($2W/cm^2$ for 6 minutes) daily for 2–3 days
- aspirin or paracetamol for pain

Instructions to patients

- Keep the affected breast well drained.
- Keep breast-feeding: do it frequently and start with the sore side.
- Heat the sore breast before feeding, e.g. hot shower or hot face washer.
- Cool the breast after feeding: use a cold face washer from the freezer.
- Massage any breast lumps gently towards the nipple while feeding.
- Empty the breast well: hand express if necessary.
- Get sufficient rest.
- Keep to a nutritious diet and drink ample fluids.

Breast abscess

If tenderness and redness persist beyond 48 hours and an area of tense induration develops, then a breast abscess has formed. It requires surgical drainage under general anaesthesia, antibiotics, rest and complete emptying of the breast. Temporary weaning of breast-feeding from the affected side is necessary because of the surgical disruption.

For a description of surgical drainage refer to page 717.

Secondary postpartum haemorrhage[4]

Postpartum haemorrhage is any bright bleeding from the birth canal 24 hours or more after delivery. It may vary from very slight to torrential and may occur any time up to six weeks postpartum.

Causes

- retained products of conception
- infection, especially at placental site
- laceration of any part of the birth canal

Treatment

- ergometrine 0.5 mg IM injection
- exploration under GA if blood loss > 250 ml
  — gentle curettage required in the postpartum uterus
- antibiotics and blood as indicated

Note: Referral is necessary after the ergometrine injection. Occasionally a life-saving hysterectomy or ligation of the internal iliac arteries may be necessary.

Puerperal fever

The cause is genital infection in about 75% of patients. Other causes include urinary tract infection, mastitis and an intercurrent infection. Investigations include a vaginal swab for smear, culture and sensitivities (include anaerobic culture) and a midstream specimen of urine for microscopy and culture.

Treatment

- amoxycillin/potassium clavulanate plus metronidazole (while awaiting sensitivities)

Beware of severe puerperal sepsis such as Gram negative septicaemia or *Clostridium welchii* septicaemia.

Postnatal depression[2]

It is quite common for women to feel emotional and flat after childbirth; this is apparently due to hormonal changes and to the anticlimax after the long-awaited event. There are two separate important problems:

1. postnatal blues
2. postnatal (or postpartum) depression

Postnatal blues

'The blues' is a very common problem that arises in the first two weeks (usually from day 3 to day 5) after childbirth.

Clinical features

- feeling flat or depressed
- mood swings
- irritability
- feeling emotional (e.g. crying easily)
- tiredness
- insomnia
- lacking confidence (e.g. in bathing and feeding the baby)
- aches and pains (e.g. headache)

Fortunately 'the blues' is a passing phase and lasts only a few days.

Advice to mother

All you really need is encouragement and support from your partner, family and friends, so tell them how you feel.

- Avoid getting tired and rest as much as possible.
- Talk over your problems with a good listener (perhaps another mother with a baby).
- Accept help from others in the house.
- Allow your partner to take turns getting up to attend to the baby.

If 'the blues' lasts longer than four days, it is very important to contact your doctor.

Postnatal depression

Some women develop a very severe depression within the first 6–12 months (usually in the first six months) after childbirth. Agitation is a common symptom. Management involves counselling, support (refer to postnatal depression support group) and antidepressant medication. Appropriate antidepressants include amitriptyline (especially where anxiety is a major feature), dothiepin and fluoxetine.

Postpartum hypothyroidism

Postpartum hypothyroidism (postpartum thyroiditis) may be misdiagnosed as postpartum depression and should always be considered in the tired, apparently depressed woman in the first six months after delivery.

References

1. Smibert J. Practical postnatal care. Aust Fam Physician, 1989; 18:508–511.
2. Murtagh J. *Patient education*. Sydney: McGraw-Hill, 1992, 4–8.
3. Schroeder SA et al. *Current medical diagnosis and treatment*. East Norwalk: Appleton and Lange, 1990, 526–528.
4. Smibert J. Common puerperal complications. Aust Fam Physician, 18:824–827.

PART 6

MEN'S HEALTH

84

Scrotal pain

Scrotal pain in males can occur at all age groups but the child or adolescent with acute scrotal pain often poses a diagnostic challenge. Serious problems include testicular torsion, strangulation of an inguinoscrotal hernia, a testicular tumour and a haematocele, all of which require surgical intervention.

Key facts and checkpoints

- Torsion of the testis is the most common cause of acute scrotal pain in infancy and childhood.
- Torsion is also a feature of young men less than 25 years.
- Testicular pain can be referred to the abdomen.
- Torsion of the testis should form part of the differential diagnosis in a boy or young man who is vomiting and has intense pain in the inguinal region.
- The clinical picture of epididymo-orchitis can mimic torsion of the testis so closely that, in most children, the diagnosis should be made only at surgical exploration.[1]
- An abnormality predisposing to torsion of the testis is usually present bilaterally; the opposite testis should also be fixed to prevent torsion.
- Torsion must be corrected within four hours to prevent gangrene of the testis.

The clinical approach

History

It is important to determine whether there were any pre-existing predisposing factors or history of trauma.

Key questions

Have you noticed any burning of urine or penile discharge?
Have you had an injury to your scrotal region such as being struck by a baseball or falling astride something?
Have you travelled overseas recently?
Have you been aware of a lump in your testicle or groin?
Have you had an illness lately and have you noticed swelling of the glands in your neck or near your ear?
Do you have back pain or have you injured your back?

Examination

Both sides of the scrotum must be examined and contrasted. Inguinal and femoral hernial orifices, the spermatic cord, testis and epididymis must be checked on both sides. The patient should be examined standing and supine. The scrotum and its contents are examined systematically starting with the skin, which may include sebaceous cysts or rarely may exhibit thickening, sinuses or ulcers with inflammatory disorders such as filariasis and tuberculosis. A painful testis should be elevated gently to determine if the pain improves.

Investigations

Investigations that may help diagnose the painful testis in particular include:

- blood cell count
- urine analysis: micro and culture
- chlamydia antigen detection tests
- ultrasound
- technetium scan

Acute scrotal pain in children and adolescents

This problem is more likely to be encountered in the adolescent. A list of causes is presented in Table 84.1. Infants, however, can also have torsion of a testis or a testicular appendage, such as the hydatid of Morgagni.

Table 84.1 *Causes of scrotal pain or swelling*

Torsion of the testis
Torsion of a testicular appendage
Epididymo-orchitis
Mumps orchitis
Acute hydrocele
Idiopathic scrotal oedema
Haematoma/haematocele
Neoplasm
Henoch-Schönlein purpura
Strangulated inguinoscrotal hernia
Referred pain
Scrotal skin conditions

Clinical problem

A 15 year old teenager presents with the relatively acute onset of pain in his lower right abdomen and scrotum. He has vomited several times. On examination the right testicle is tender, red and swollen.

Discussion

The two main differential diagnoses are acute epididymo-orchitis (which requires little more than conservative treatment) or torsion of the testis, which demands emergency surgical intervention (Fig. 84.1). Less commonly the problem would be a haematoma or an acute hydrocele mimicking testicular torsion. This patient, however, must be regarded as having torsion of the testis. Early operation with torsion is imperative because, if the testis is deprived of its blood supply for more than a few hours, infarction is inevitable and excision becomes necessary. Excluding mumps, no youth under the age of 18 years should be diagnosed as suffering from acute epididymo-orchitis until the testis has been exposed at operation and torsion excluded.

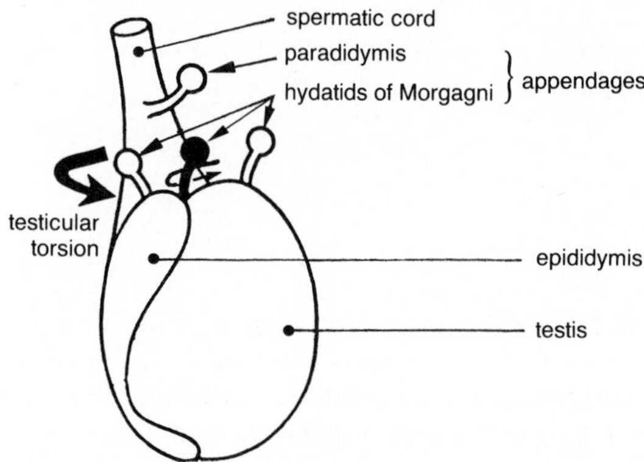

Fig. 84.1 *Torsion of the testis and an appendage: the 'black' hydatid of Morgagni is the one most likely to undergo torsion*

Torsion of the testis v epididymo-orchitis

With torsion of the testicle there is pain of sudden onset, described as severe aching sickening pain in the groin that may be accompanied by nausea and vomiting. With epididymo-orchitis the attack usually begins with malaise and fever. The testicle soon becomes swollen and acutely tender; however, elevation of the scrotum usually relieves pain in this condition while tending to increase it with a torsion.

A comparison of the clinical presentations is presented in Table 84.2.

Radiology as a diagnostic aid

Ultrasound is useful in distinguishing a cystic scrotal lump (such as a hydrocele) from a solid tumour. Its use to distinguish between a torsion and epididymo-orchitis is controversial as it cannot reliably detect changes that are diagnostic of early torsion. Since the investigation can involve unnecessary delay in treatment it is generally not recommended. A technetium scan can differentiate between the two conditions: in torsion the testis is avascular while it is hyperemic in epididymo-orchitis.

Table 84.2 *Clinical presentations of torsion of testis and acute epididymo-orchitis*

	Torsion of testis	*Epididymo-orchitis*
Typical age	Early teens, average range 5–15	Young adults Elderly
Onset	Usually sudden but can be gradual	Gradual
Severity of pain	Very severe	Moderate
Associated symptoms	Vomiting Possibly abdominal pain	Fever
Examination of scrotum	Very tender and red Testis high and transverse Scrotal oedema	Swollen, tender and red; can be tender on rectal examination
	Possible an acute hydrocele	Possibly an acute hydrocele
Effect of gentle scrotal elevation	No change to pain or worse pain	Relief of pain
Investigations	Technetium scan (if available, time permits and diagnosis doubtful)	Leucocytosis Possibly pyobacteria of urine

Time factor in surgical intervention

The optimal time to operate for torsion of the testis is within four (4) hours of onset of pain. About 85% of torsive testes are salvageable within six (6) hours but by ten (10) hours the salvage rate has dropped to 20%.[2]

At surgery the testicle is untwisted and if viable an orchidopexy is performed. A gangrenous testicle is removed. The opposite testis should be fixed by orchidopexy.

Torsion of a testicular appendage

Vestigial remnants to the testis or the epididymis are present in 90% of the male population.[1] Torsion of the testicular appendage, the pedunculated hydatid of Morgagni, has a similar presentation to that of torsion of the testis but is less severe (see Fig. 84.1).

It can be diagnosed by the appearance of a dark blue nodule at the upper pole of the testis (provided that it is not masked by an associated hydrocele). Surgical exploration is advisable.

Scrotal pain at various ages

Acute epididymo-orchitis

Apart from mumps, acute epididymo-orchitis is usually caused by sexually transmitted pathogens in males under 30 years old and by urinary tract pathogens in patients over 30 years old. In older men it usually follows urinary tract obstruction and infection or instrumentation of the lower genitourinary tract.

Investigations

Blood cell count:	leukocytosis
Urine micro and culture:	pyuria, bacteria and possibly *E. coli.* A sterile culture suggests chlamydia infection[3]
Tests for chlamydia:	antigen detection kits
Ultrasound:	can differentiate a swollen epididymis from testicular tumour

Treatment

- bed rest
- elevation and support of the scrotum
- analgesics
- antibiotics

  Sexually acquired

  amoxycillin/clavulanate 500/125 mg (o) 8 hourly for 10–14 days

  plus

  doxycycline 100 mg (o) 12 hourly for 10–14 days

  Associated with urinary infection

  amoxycillin/clavulanate 500/125 mg (o) 8 hourly for 10–14 days

  or

  trimethoprim 300 mg (o) daily for 10–14 days

  or

  cephalexin 500 mg (o) 6 hourly for 10–14 days

Orchitis

Acute orchitis is invariably due to mumps and occurs during late adolescence. It is usually unilateral but may be bilateral.

Chronic orchitis may be due to syphilis, tuberculosis, leprosy or various helminthic infections such as filariasis. The majority are tuberculous in origin.

Testicular neoplasm

Testicular tumours can occur at all ages but are more common in young men aged 20–30 (seminoma) and 30–40 years (teratoma). Sometimes they can mimic an acute inflammatory swelling and present with acute pain.

Strangulated inguinoscrotal hernia

It is possible that a supposed testicular torsion is found to be a strangulated inguinoscrotal hernia, usually an indirect inguinal hernia extending into the scrotum. It can be detected by careful palpation of the base (neck) of the scrotum.

Trauma and haematoceles

A diffuse haematoma into the scrotum which causes no significant problems can follow surgery to the inguinal area, a blow to this area or a fracture of the pelvis. These conditions cause extravasation of blood distally. However, a haematocele of the tunica vaginalis can be either acute or an 'old clotted haematocele' following injury, such as a blow to the testis or the drainage of a hydrocele.[5] Sometimes it can arise spontaneously. All types of haemotoceles require surgical exploration to exclude testicular rupture or a tumour.

Trauma to the scrotum may produce urethral injury and extravasation of urine into the scrotum. This problem requires urgent surgery.

Problems of scrotal skin

Sebaceous cysts are common and may be infected and require drainage.

Fournier's gangrene (idiopathic gangrene of the scrotum) is an acute fulminating cellulitis affecting the scrotal skin. It usually develops suddenly and without any apparent cause. Gangrene of the scrotal skin appears early if the infection is not quickly checked with broad spectrum antibiotics. The end result is sloughing of the scrotal coverings, leaving the testes exposed.[5]

Referred pain

Pain can be referred to the scrotal region from ureteric colic and quite commonly from disorders of the thoracolumbar spine, notably a disc disruption at the T12-L1 level involving the L1 nerve root. The pain therefore may be referred or radicular.

When to refer

- Any suspicion of torsion of the testis.
- Sudden onset of acute scrotal pain at any age.
- A history of recurrent transient testicular pain in a young man.
- Presence of a tender testicular lump.
- Presence of a haematocele surrounding the testis.

Note: Referral should be most urgent, using the critical four-hour guideline.

Practice tips

- Acute scrotal pain in infancy and adolescence should be regarded as torsion of the testis until proved otherwise.
- A history of recurrent transient pain (with or without swelling of the testis) in a young person means recurrent torsion. Urgent referral is essential.
- Although torsion usually occurs in the fully descended testis it can occur in an undescended testis.
- A pitfall is the phenomenon of 'testis redux' in which the descended testis undergoes torsion, is pulled into the superficial inguinal pouch by the cremasteric reflex and then becomes fixed by oedema.
- The development of acute hydrocele should be regarded with suspicion.
- Beware of the strangulated inguinoscrotal hernia presenting as a testicular torsion.

References

1. Jones PG. *Clinical paediatric surgery.* Sydney: Ure Smith, 1970, 231–236.
2. Gledhill T. Testicular torsion. Update, 1984;2:136–140.
3. Berger RE. Urethritis and epididymitis. Semin Urol, 1983;1:139.
4. Mashford L et al. *Antibiotic guidelines* (8th edition). Melbourne: Victorian Medical Postgraduate Foundation, 1994–95, 126–27.
5. Fry J, Berry H. *Surgical problems in clinical practice.* London: Edward Arnold, 1987, 87–88.

85

Inguinoscrotal lumps

Lumps in the groin are common to both sexes but males are likely to have a greater variety of swellings in this area and several may be associated with scrotal lumps.

Lumps in the groin

The commonest swellings encountered in the groin or inguinal area are herniae (also known as 'ruptures') and enlarged lymph nodes. The diagnosis of a hernia is usually straightforward but it must be differentiated from other swellings, including Malgaigne's bulgings; these are not true herniae but diffuse swellings in both inguinal regions seen in people with poor lower abdominal musculature.[1] Table 85.1 lists the differential diagnoses of groin lumps.

Table 85.1 *Differential diagnoses of a groin mass*

Hernia—femoral, inguinal
Malgaigne's bulgings
Lipoma
Undescended testis
Spermatic cord swelling—encysted hydrocele, lipoma
Lymph node—localised, generalised
Haematoma (postfemoral artery puncture)
Neoplasm—lipoma, others
Psoas abscess
Vascular anomalies • saphenous varix • femoral aneurysm

Herniae

The commonest types of herniae in the groin are inguinal, femoral and a combination of the two. Rare herniae in the region are obturator, Spigelian (low abdominal), preperitoneal inguinal and prevascular femoral. The basic parts of a hernia are shown in Figure 85.1 and important anatomical landmarks in Figure 85.2. An indirect inguinal hernia is a hernia through the deep inguinal ring, originating lateral to the inferior epigastric vessels, following the path of the processus vaginalis, and can traverse the whole length of the inguinal canal (Fig. 85.3). In the male it closely approximates the spermatic cord and may enlarge as it passes through the superficial inguinal ring into the scrotum—an inguinoscrotal hernia.

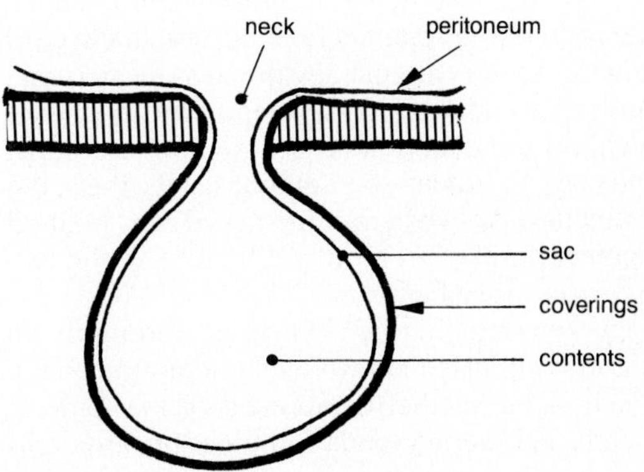

Fig. 85.1 *Basic components of a hernia*

Because of their narrow neck and oblique path in the inguinal canal such herniae are often irreducible and are prone to lead to strangulation of entrapped bowel.

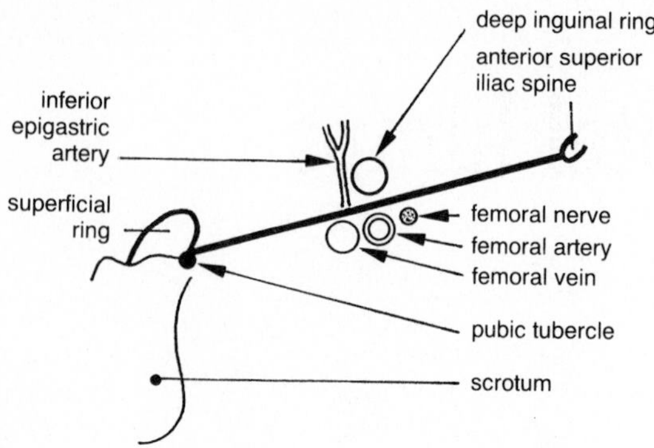

Fig. 85.2 *Key landmarks in the inguinal region: the deep inguinal ring lies above the mid-inguinal point (between the ASIS and the pubic tubercle); the femoral artery lies below this point*

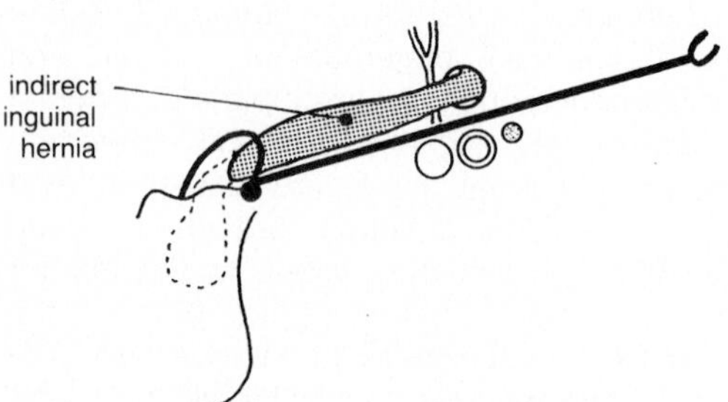

Fig. 85.3 *Indirect inguinal hernia: it emerges lateral to the inferior epigastric artery and passes into the scrotum medial to the pubic tubercle*

A direct inguinal hernia originates medial to the inferior epigastric vessels and protrudes through the posterior wall of the inguinal canal, and is therefore separate from the spermatic cord (Fig. 85.4). It is almost always seen in men and rarely descends into the scrotum.[2] Due to a wider neck, strangulation and obstruction are most unusual. It must be emphasised that the distinction between a direct and an indirect inguinal hernia can be very difficult and the two may occur together.

A femoral hernia herniates through the femoral ring (also known as the femoral canal), which is the medial component of the femoral sheath. The hernia tends to bulge forwards and then upwards as it becomes larger. The neck is lateral to the pubic tubercle (Fig. 85.5).

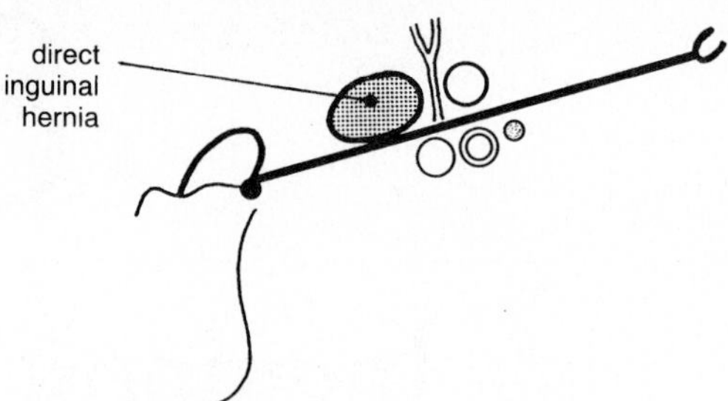

Fig. 85.4 *Direct inguinal hernia: it emerges medial to the inferior epigastric artery and bulges forward*

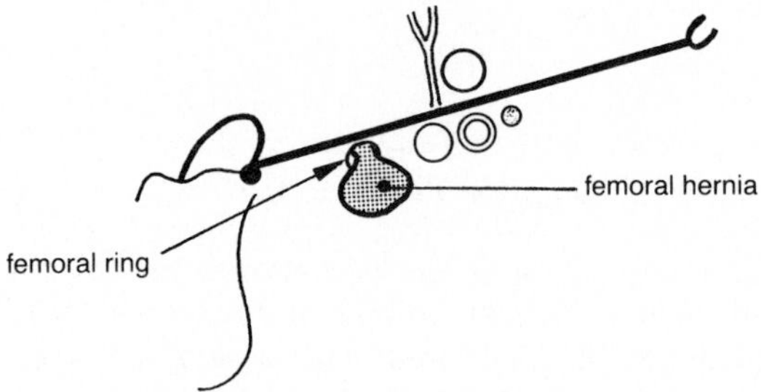

Fig. 85.5 *Femoral hernia: its neck is lateral to the pubic tubercle and it lies below the inguinal ligament*

Femoral herniae are often small, usually occur in females and may be unnoticed by the patient. They are particularly liable to produce bowel obstruction or strangulation.[2]

Guidelines with herniae

Acquired hernia

- always examine the scrotum
- frequently bilateral
- result from muscular weakness
- commonest—direct inguinal and femoral
- predisposing factors
  - — age (more common with increasing age)
  - — obesity
  - — pregnancy
- precipitating factors (related to above factors)
  - — increased intra-abdominal pressure
    - difficulty of micturition (prostatism)
    - straining at stool (constipation)
    - chronic cough, e.g. bronchitis
    - straining or lifting heavy objects
  - — nerve damage, e.g. post appendicectomy
- complications
  - — intestinal obstruction (Table 85.2)
  - — incarceration
  - — strangulation
  - — sliding

Table 85.2 *Symptoms and signs of hernial obstruction*

Colicky abdominal pain
Nausea and vomiting
Constipation and failure to pass flatus
Local tenderness and swelling
Abdominal distension
High-pitched tinkling bowel sounds
No expansile cough impulse

Clinical features

The main symptoms and signs:[1]

- lump
- discomfort or pain
  - a dragging pain
  - worse after standing or walking
  - referred to testicle (indirect inguinal)
- testicular pain—referred or with compression of the spermatic cord
- expansile impulse on coughing

Note: In over 50% of strangulated obturator herniae, pain is referred along the geniculate branch of the obturator nerve to the knee.[1]

A femoral hernia is easily missed in obese patients.

Larger femoral hernia are often irreducible.

Always attempt reduction in the recumbent position (direct herniae usually reduce easily).

Treatment of herniae

Surgery[3]

All symptomatic herniae require repair and all femoral herniae should be repaired. Obstructed and strangulated herniae require urgent surgery. The risk of strangulation is greatest with femoral herniae, moderate with indirect inguinal herniae and least with direct inguinal herniae.

Conservative

Asymptomatic inguinal herniae in patients with associated medical conditions, and who pose a significant operative risk, can be treated conservatively. A suitable truss to control a small inguinal hernia is a rat-tailed spring truss with a perineal band to prevent slipping.[1] Such a truss must be used with care and patients well instructed in its proper use. Trusses must always be applied over the inguinal canal with the patient lying flat and with the hernia reduced. Difficult reduction can be aided by a warm moist towelette.

Scrotal lumps

The scrotum contains the testes and distal parts of the spermatic cords, covered by layers of fascia and the dartos muscle. The testes are invested with tunica vaginalis derived from the peritoneal cavity during their descent.[1]

Disorders of the scrotum may be acute or chronic and bilateral or unilateral. Lumps may be cystic, solid or otherwise such as a varicocele, oedema and hernia. Solid lumps include a testicular tumour, epididymo-orchitis, and torsion of the testes. Cystic lumps include hydroceles, epididymal cysts and spermatoceles, and resolving extravasation. A comparison of scrotal lumps appears in Figure 85.7 and Table 85.3. Lumps in the scrotum usually develop from deeper structures, particularly the testes and its coverings, rather than scrotal skin.[1] Refer to Figure 85.6 for a comparison of scrotal lumps.

The cardinal sign of a true scrotal mass is that it is possible to get above it.

The patient usually presents with pain or a lump. Scrotal lumps are invariably gradual in onset and often go unnoticed until they are well developed.

Examination of the scrotum

The scrotum should be examined with the patient supine and then standing. The left testis usually hangs lower than the right. On inspection note any sebaceous cysts in the scrotal skin (very common), scabies if there are very pruritic nodules and scrotal oedema which causes taut pitting skin. Careful palpation will elicit the relevant structures in the scrotum. Gently palpate each testis and epididymis between the thumb and the first two fingers. The spermatic cord is palpable as it enters the scrotum after passing through the superficial ring and the testis and epididymis are readily palpable.

After palpation test for translucency of any swelling in a darkened room by shining the beam of a strong torch from behind the scrotum through the swelling. Transilluminable swellings that light up with a red glow include hydroceles and cysts of the epididymis. Swellings that contain blood or other tissue such as testicular tumours and most herniae do not illuminate.

Unilateral scrotal swelling

It is important to determine if the lump is inguinoscrotal or scrotal. It is scrotal if it is

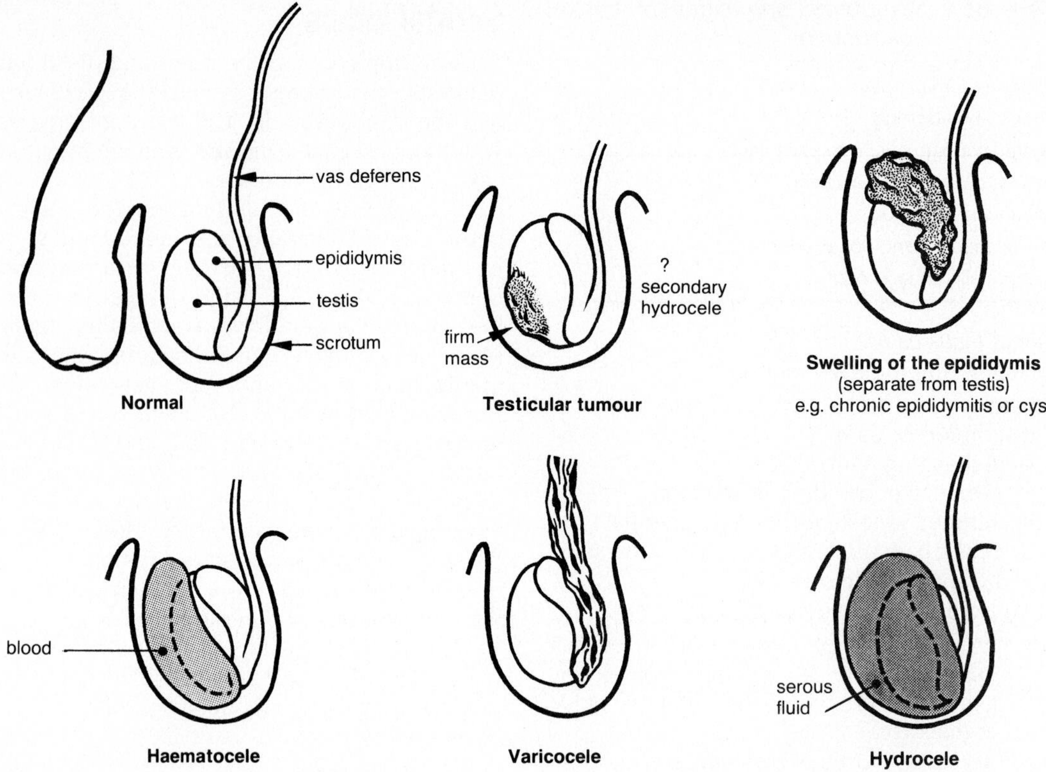

Fig. 85.6 *Basic comparison of scrotal lumps*

possible to get above the lump. If it is not possible to get above the lump then it is a large inguinal hernia or a combined hernia and hydrocele. (Fig. 85.7). The next feature to determine is whether the testis and/or epididymis can be palpated or whether they are obscured by a swelling such as a hydrocele.

Small testes

Testes are considered small in adults if less than 3.5 cm long. Small firm testes, 2 cm long or less, are a feature of Klinefelter's syndrome. Small soft testes indicate atrophy which may follow mumps orchitis, oestrogen therapy, hypopituitarism, cirrhosis and other related conditions.

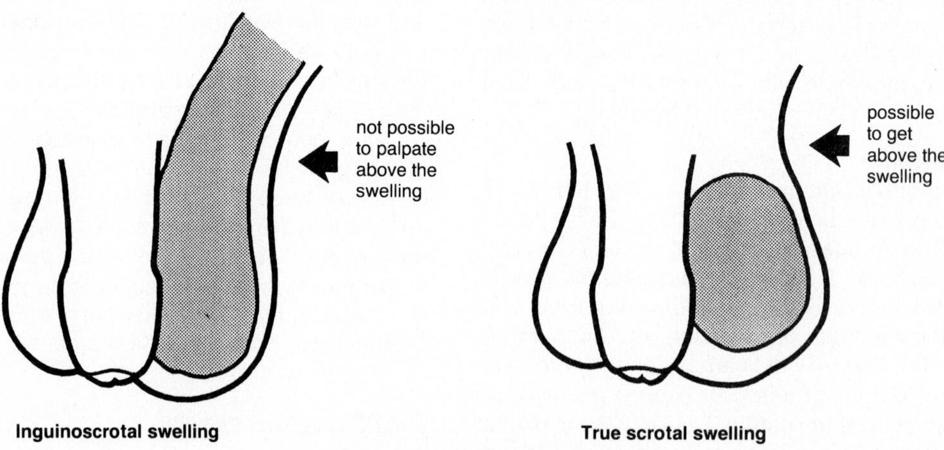

Fig. 85.7 *Difference between a true scrotal swelling and an inguinoscrotal swelling*

Table 85.3 *Features of scrotal lumps*

	Possible clinical setting	*Position*	*Palpation*	*Trans-illumination*
Hydrocele	Any age Primary or secondary • tumour • infection • torsion	Confined to scrotum Anterior: surrounds testis except posteriorly	Smooth, pear-shaped Lax or tense Testis impalpable, non-tender	Yes
Cyst of epididymis *Epididymal cysts and spermatoceles clinically similar	Asymptomatic or dragging sensation	Behind and above testis	Smooth and tense Multilocular swelling Testis easily palpable Appears separate from testis	Yes
Chronic epididymo-orchitis	90% cases tuberculosis Usually associated hydrocele	Behind and above testis	Firm swelling Hard and craggy (TB) Normal testis	No
Varicocele	Dragging discomfort	Usually left-sided Along line of spermatic cord Above testis	Soft like bunch of worms or grapes Collapses when patient supine and testis elevated Testis often smaller	No
Carcinoma	Young men 20-40 Painless lump Loss of testicular sensation	In body of testis Usually felt anterior May be hydrocele	Enlarged firm testis Feels heavy if large Normal epididymis (palpable)	No

Hydrocele

A hydrocele is a collection of clear amber fluid in the tunica vaginalis and can be primary or secondary. If a hydrocele develops it is important to rule out intrascrotal disease such as a tumour or infection. Ultrasound examination of the scrotum is helpful in assessing the state of the testis in the presence of a hydrocele. Hydroceles may be symptomless or cause dragging discomfort in the scrotum and groin.

Treatment of a primary hydrocele

Surgery is the most effective long-term treatment. A primary hydrocele can be treated by simple aspiration but the fluid usually reaccumulates and there is risk of bleeding or infection with repeated procedures.[4] However, aspiration followed by injection of a sclerosant agent (e.g. dilute aqueous phenol or STD) can prevent fluid accumulation and after two or three times can often cure the problem. This sclerotherapy may be complicated by pain and inflammatory reaction to the sclerosant.

Method

1. Inject LA into the scrotal skin down to the sac.
2. Insert an 18 or 19 gauge intravenous cannula through this site into the sac and remove the stilette, leaving the soft cannula in the sac (Fig. 85.8).
3. Remove the serous fluid initially by free drainage, possibly aided by manual compression on the sac and then by aspiration with a 20 ml syringe.
4. Record the volume.
5. Inject 2.5% or 3% sterile aqueous phenol or STD into the empty sac (10 ml for 200 ml of fluid removed, 15 ml for 200–400 ml and 20 ml for over 400 ml).

The procedure can be repeated after six weeks.

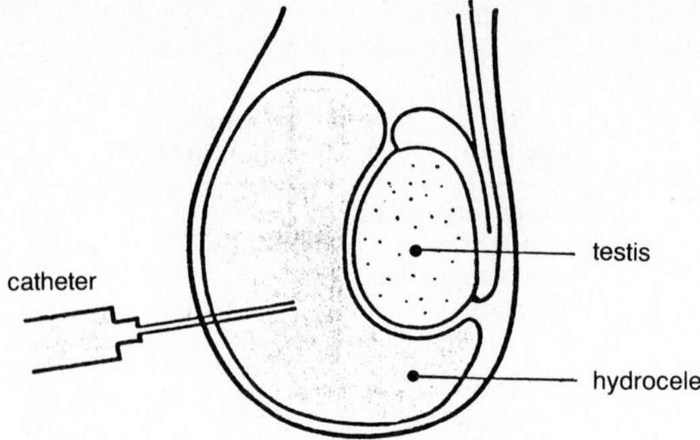

Fig. 85.8 *Aspiration of hydrocele*

Encysted hydrocele of the cord

This is a localised fluid-filled segment of the processus vaginalis within the spermatic cord. It is palpable as a cystic lump in the upper scrotum. It characteristically moves down with traction on the testis.

Epididymal cysts

The majority of epididymal cysts contain a clear colourless fluid. If the cysts communicate with the vasa efferentia a spermatocele filled with whitish fluid containing spermatazoa may form.

Epididymal cysts may be asymptomatic or may cause discomfort and cosmetic embarrassment and should be excised. Fertility may be impaired in patients undergoing bilateral cyst excision.

Aspiration and injection of sclerosant agents can also be used for epididymal cysts.[4]

Varicoceles

A varicocele is a varicosity of the veins of the pampiniform plexus. It is seen in 8% of normal males and occurs on the left side in 98% of affected patients, due to a mechanical problem in drainage of the left renal vein. A relationship with infertility has been observed but its nature is controversial.

Most varicoceles are asymptomatic and incidental findings. They can cause a dragging discomfort in the scrotum. Treatment is only indicated if it is symptomatic or perhaps for infertility. A scrotal support or even firm-fitting underpants may be all that is required to relieve discomfort.[1] Otherwise surgical treatment is by venous ligation.

Haematoceles

These can be either acute, resulting from trauma such as a fall astride, sports injury or tapping of a hydrocele, or chronic, where there is no obvious history of injury. Haematoceles are anterior to the testis and not transilluminable. As a rule, referral for possible surgical intervention is required: with acute injury there is a possibility of testicular rupture (associated urethral injury has to be considered); and a tumour has to be excluded with the chronic type. Pressure atrophy of the testis can occur with injury.

Testicular tumours

A mass that is part of the testis, and solid, is likely to be a tumour. Malignant testicular tumours account for about 2% of malignant tumours in men. They mainly affect fit young men and represent the commonest neoplasm in men aged 20–34 (Table 85.4).

Table 85.4 *Testicular tumours*[1, 4]

Tumour	*Incidence (%)*	*Peak incidence (years)*
Seminoma	40	30–40
Teratoma	32	20–30
Mixed seminoma/ teratoma	14	20–40
Lymphoma	7	60–70
Other tumours e.g. interstitial (Leydig) gonadoblastoma	uncommon	variable

Clinical features

- young men 20–40 years
- painless lump in body of testis (commonest feature)
- loss of testicular sensation
- associated presentations (may mask tumour)
  - — hydrocele
  - — varicocele
  - — epididymo-orchitis
  - — swollen testis with trivial injury
  - — gynaecomastia (teratoma)

Golden rules

- All solid scrotal lumps are malignant until proved otherwise and must be surgically explored.

- Beware of hydroceles in young adults.
- Tumours can mimic acute epididymo-orchitis—the so-called 'inflammatory' or 'flash fire' presentation.[3]

Metastases

Testicular tumours spread by direct infiltration via the lymphatics and the bloodstream. Metastases typically occur in the para-aortic nodes so it is advisable to palpate carefully from the umbilical area upwards. Metastases also occur in the neck, liver and chest.

Investigations

Useful investigations to aid diagnosis include:[3]

- ultrasound of the testis: can detect and diagnose with considerable precision underlying testicular lumps plus any invasion of the tunica
- tumour markers: alpha fetoprotein and human chorionic gonadotrophin
- chest and abdominal X-ray
- CT scanning of abdomen to assess para-aortic node involvement

Treatment

The initial treatment is orchidectomy with high division of the spermatic cord. Specialised treatment that depends on the staging of the tumour gives good results for seminoma, which is very sensitive to radiotherapy. The results for teratoma are not as satisfactory as for seminoma.

Prognosis is good for most testicular tumours with five year cure rates of 85–90%.[3]

Early detection and testicular self-examination

Studies of testicular cancer have shown the benefits of early detection.[5] Common errors that caused a delay of diagnosis included incorrect diagnosis, neglecting to examine the testes, and failure to achieve a specific diagnosis to explain the symptoms. Delay on the part of the patient was the major determinant of total delay. It is important that we promote secondary preventive measures by encouraging testicular self-examination (TSE) as a simple procedure that all young men, especially those at risk, should learn to do.

Information for patients on TSE

- Examine the testicles yourself when warm and relaxed, e.g. after a warm bath or shower, when the scrotal skin is most relaxed, or in bed.
- Explore each testicle individually.
- Using both hands, gently roll the testicle between the thumb and the index and middle fingers (Fig. 85.9).
- If pain is experienced, too much pressure is being applied.
- The normal testicle is egg-shaped, firm to touch and should be smooth and free of lumps.
- Feel for any changes in size, shape or consistency.
- If you do find something abnormal, it is most likely it will be an area of firmness, or a small lump on the front or side of the testicle.
- If you find something you think is abnormal, you should see your doctor as soon as possible.
- Remember that not all lumps are due to cancer.

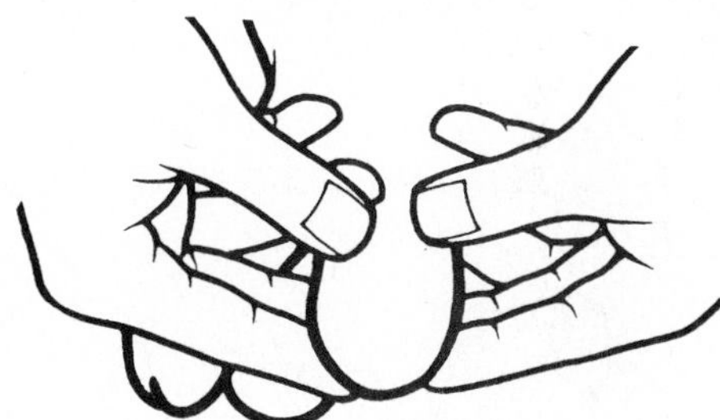

Fig. 85.9 *Testicular self-examination technique*

Undescended testes

A testis that is not in the scrotum may be ectopic, absent, retractile or truly undescended. The incidence is 2% in full-term males, 20% in premature male births and 1% at one year. More than two-thirds of undescended testes are located in the superficial inguinal pouch, that is, they are palpable in the groin.

Undescended testis

An undescended testis is one that cannot reach the bottom of the scrotum despite manual manipulation. After an indirect inguinal hernia it is the most common problem in paediatric surgery. The testis is usually normal but may become secondarily dysplastic if left outside the scrotum.

A truly undescended testis is one that has stopped in the normal path of descent and can occupy intra-abdominal, inguinal canal, emergent (just outside the external ring), high scrotal and midscrotal positions.[4] The cause of maldescent is probably mechanical.

Retractile testis

A retractile testis is one that can be manipulated into the scrotum irrespective of the position in which it is first located. It is a common condition. The testis can be present in the scrotum under circumstances such as a warm bath but retracted out of the scrotum when cold. Cremasteric contraction is absent in the first few months after birth and is maximal between 2 and 8 years.[1]

Ectopic testis

An ectopic testis is one that has left the normal path of descent and cannot be manipulated into the scrotum. It can be found in the perineum, upper thigh (femoral), base of the penis (prepubic), anterior abdominal wall or in the superficial inguinal pouch (Fig. 85.10a). True ectopic testes form only about 5% of all undescended testes (Fig. 85.10b).

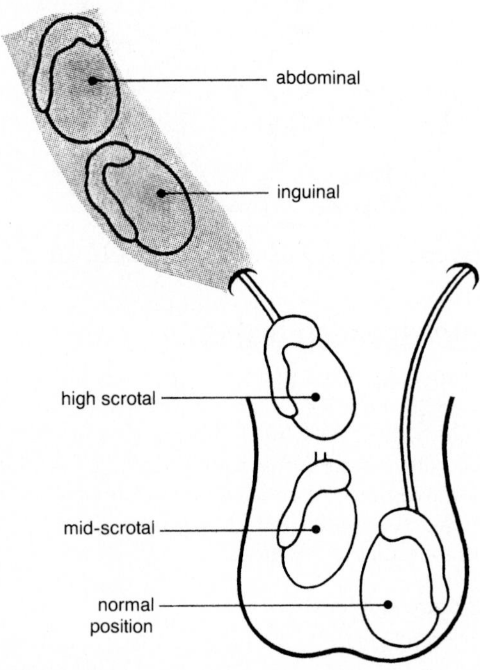

Fig. 85.10a *Undescended testis: arrested in the line of descent*

Ascending testis

An 'ascending' testis is one that was in the scrotum in infancy but subsequently moved back to the groin because the spermatic cord failed to elongate at the same rate of body growth.

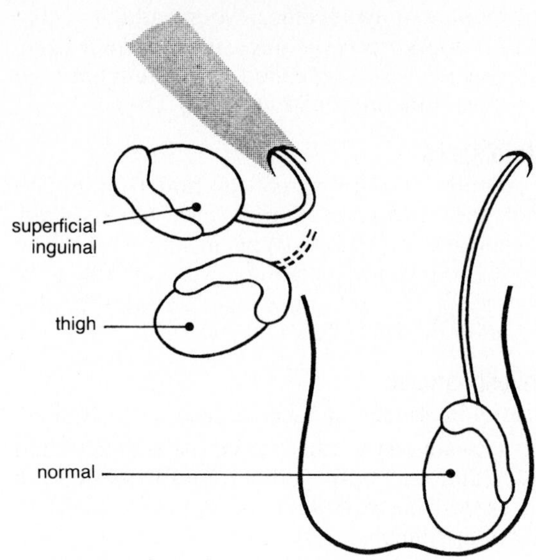

Fig. 85.10b *Undescended testis: ectopic*

Examination[6]

The examination of the testes should take place in a warm room and relaxed environment. Begin by placing one finger on each side of the neck of the scrotum to prevent the testes from being retracted out of the scrotum by the other hand. The scrotum is then carefully palpated for a testis. If impalpable the fingertips of one hand are placed just medial to the anterior superior iliac spine and moved firmly towards the pubic tubercle where the other hand waits to entrap the testis should it appear. The diagnosis then depends on carefully determining the range of movement.

The problem of non-descent

- testicular dysplasia
- susceptible to direct violence (if in inguinal region)
- risk of malignant change (seminoma) is 5–10 times greater than normal

Optimal time for surgery

The optimal time for orchidopexy is 12–18 months of age.[6] The production of spermatozoa is adversely affected in undescended testes from the age of two years onwards.[6] Exploration for the uncommon impalpable testis is worthwhile:

50% salvage rate, while in the other 50% either there is no testis or an abnormal and potentially neoplastic testis is removed.[6]

The advantages of early orchidopexy are summarised in Table 85.5.

Table 85.5 *Advantages of early orchidopexy (1 year)*[4]

Provides optimal chance of fertility
Corrects indirect inguinal hernias (coexists in 90%)
Reduces risk of trauma
Reduces risk of torsion
Reduces psychological consequences
Probably lessens the risk of malignancy (seminoma)

Hormone injections

Injections of chorionic gonadotrophic hormones are generally not recommended. They are ineffective except for borderline retractile testes.

References

1. Fry J, Berry H. *Surgical problems in clinical practice*. London: Edward Arnold, 1987,79–92.
2. Davis A, Bolin T, Ham J. *Symptom analysis and physical diagnosis* (2nd edition). Sydney: Pergamon Press, 1990, 212–220.
3. Hunt P, Marshall V. *Clinical problems in general surgery*. Sydney: Butterworths, 1991, 329–342.
4. Bullock N, Sibley G, Whitaker R. *Essential urology*. Edinburgh: Churchill Livingstone, 1989, 287–318.
5. Bolse J, Vogelzang NJ, Goldman A et al. Impact of delay in diagnosis on clinical stage of testicular cancer. Lancet, 1981;2:970–972.
6. Hutson J, Beasley S, Woodward A. *Jones clinical paediatric surgery*. Oxford: Blackwell Scientific Publications, 1992, 162–164.

86

Disorders of the penis

The most common penile disorders are those of psychosexual dysfunction and sexually transmissible diseases, but there are many other problems and these are most often related to the foreskin.

Disorders affecting the foreskin and glans

Phimosis

Phimosis is tightness of foreskin (prepuce), preventing its free retraction over the glans penis. The foreskin can be adherent to the glans penis even up to 5–6 years of age. It gradually separates until it becomes non-adherent usually by the age of six. Forcible retraction of the foreskin of any boy should be discouraged.

True congenital narrowing of the preputial orifice is rare. If the foreskin cannot be retracted by the age of seven years and is causing symptoms such as balanitis then circumcision is recommended. Ballooning of the foreskin during micturition can be a feature.

Treatment

Inflammatory phimosis can be treated by local corticosteroid cream. True scarring requires circumcision.[1] Some patients with true phimosis may have problems once they start to have intercourse. They require circumcision.

Paraphimosis

In paraphimosis the foreskin is retracted, swollen and painful. This is because it has been pulled back over the glans and cannot be pulled forwards again. This problem occurs in older boys, especially if a mild degree of phimosis is already present. Typically it occurs when the penis is erect or after catheterisation.

Management

Urgent manual reduction should be attempted first. It is usually performed without anaesthesia but a penile block (never use adrenaline in LA) may be appropriate.

Method 1

The glans penis and oedematous tissue distal to the constricting ring of foreskin are gently squeezed for several minutes to reduce the oedema. Manual reduction can then be performed by trying to advance the prepuce over the glans with the index fingers while gently compressing the glans with both thumbs (Fig. 86.1).

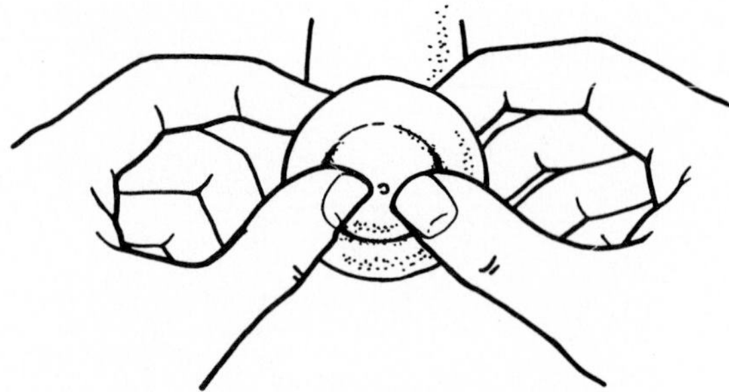

Fig. 86.1 *Acute paraphimosis: method of manual reduction*

Method 2

- Take hold of the oedematous part of the glans in the fist of one hand and squeeze firmly. A gauze swab or warm towelette will help to achieve a firm grip (Fig. 86.2).
- Exert continuous pressure until the oedema passes under the constricting collar to the shaft of the penis.
- The foreskin can then usually be pulled over the glans.

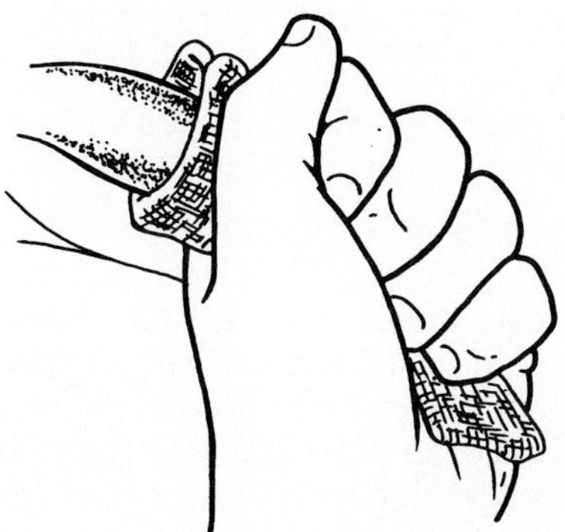

Fig. 86.2 *Acute paraphimosis: squeezing with a swab method*

Method 3

If manual reduction methods fail, a dorsal slit incision should be made in the constricting collar of skin under local or general anaesthetic (Fig. 86.3). The incision allows the foreskin to be advanced and reduces the swelling. Circumcision should be performed some days later when the inflammation has settled.[2]

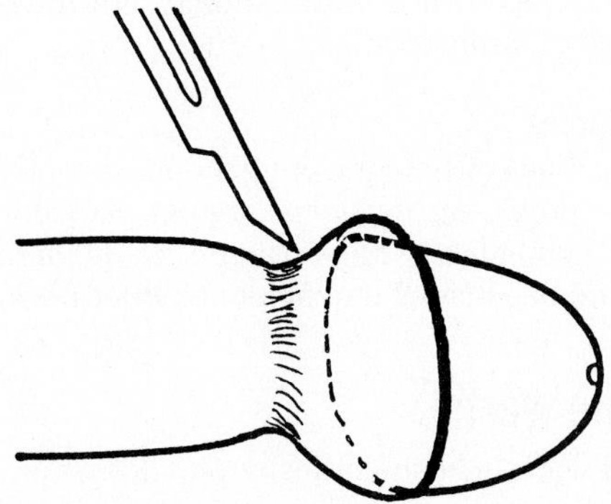

Fig. 86.3 *Acute paraphimosis: dorsal slit incision in the constricting collar of skin*

Balanitis (balanoposthitis)

Balanitis is inflammation of the foreskin which usually affects the glans penis and tissues behind the foreskin (balanoposthitis). The inflammation may simply be redness or irritation of the glans and foreskin or bacterial infection. This quite common problem may be due to *Candida albicans* infection, but in infants may be caused by wet nappies and in the elderly by diabetes with an associated organism.

Men presenting with balanitis should be screened for:

- diabetes
- Reiter's disease (especially if asymptomatic)

Treatment

- take swabs for culture
- careful washing behind foreskin

if yeasts present
 — topical nystatin or miconazole or clotrimazole cream

if trichomonads present
 — metronidazole or tinidazole (oral treatment)

if bacteria present
 — appropriate antibiotic, e.g. chloramphenicol or chlortetracycline

Thickening of the foreskin with skin pallor suggests balanitis xerotica obliterans which responds to corticosteroid cream if it is mild. Circumcision is indicated for recurrent problems.

Foreskin hygiene

The normal foreskin in infants and children does not need special care and should not be retracted for cleaning from birth to five years of age. However, from the age of six or seven, males should practise proper hygiene by gently retracting the foreskin and washing the area at least once a week.

Instructions to patients

- During a shower or bath slide the foreskin back towards your body (Fig. 86.4).
- Wash the end of the penis and foreskin with soap and water.
- After washing the area dry the end of your penis and foreskin and then replace the foreskin.
- If the foreskin has a tendency to become irritated and smelly, slide the foreskin back sufficiently to allow free urination.

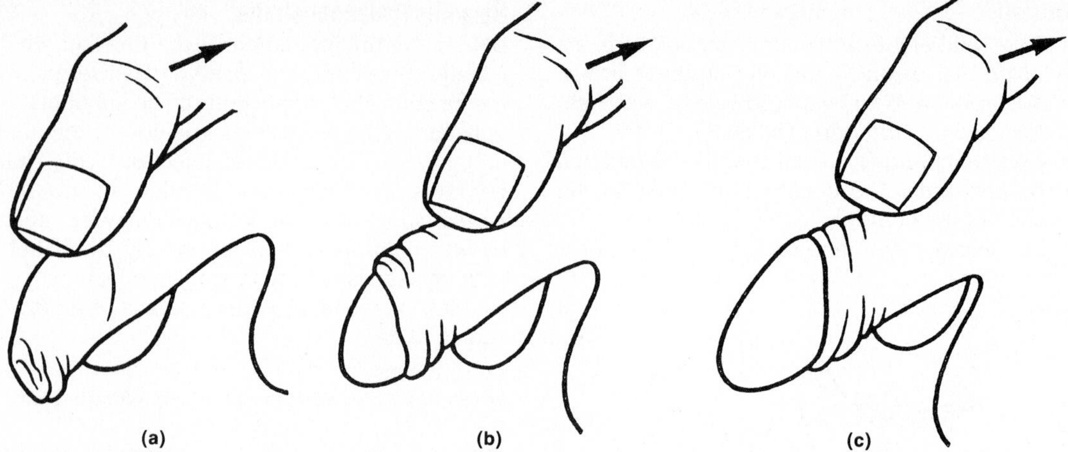

Fig. 86.4 *Foreskin hygiene: sliding foreskin back for washing*

Circumcision

Apart from abnormalities of the foreskin and religious reasons, circumcision for social reasons is generally discouraged. Arguments against circumcision include that it is not natural, unnecessary, carries a small but significant risk of morbidity and mortality, and is associated with meatal stenosis. Circumcision is now performed less frequently and most practitioners do not appear to favour it for social reasons. Proponents, however, argue that it reduces the risk of periurethral bacterial colonisation, systemic infections such as septicaemia, carcinoma of the penis, and STDs. Indications for circumcision include phimosis, paraphimosis and recurrent balanitis. Boys with hypospadias should never be circumcised, since the foreskin may be a vital source of skin for subsequent repair.[2]

Using a dorsal slit of the foreskin as an alternative to routine circumcision produces a cosmetically unacceptable result and should only be used as an emergency measure.

Disorders affecting the urethral meatus

Meatal stenosis

Meatal stenosis or stricture may be congenital or acquired. It may be acquired in the circumcised child, due to abrasion and ulceration of the tip of the glans. The incidence can be reduced by the application of Vaseline on the glans after circumcision.[1] Uncommon causes are direct trauma during circumcision and irritation from ammoniacal dermatitis. Meatal ulceration predisposes to meatal stenosis. It usually presents as pain during micturition or as slight bleeding on the napkin. In the child with mild meatal stenosis gentle dilation can be applied. Severe cases require surgical correction by meatotomy.

Catheterisation trauma is the usual cause in adults.

Hypospadias

Hypospadias is where the urethra opens on the underside or ventral aspect of the penis. It occurs in 1 in 300 males.[1] Congenital hypospadias may be glandular (most common), coronal, penile or perineal.[3]

Hypospadias may cause the stream of urine to be deflected downwards or splash or drip back along the penile shaft. Unless it is glandular, surgical repair is usually advised, using the available foreskin. Cordee is corrected at the same time. These boys should not undergo routine circumcision.

Epispadias

Epispadias is where the urethra opens at the base of the penis, on its dorsal aspect. It occurs in 1 in 30 000 males.[1] Most patients are incontinent of urine because of a deficient bladder neck.

Penile warts

Penile warts are usually fleshy, papillomatous and multiple outgrowths, commonly found around the coronal sulcus, the adjacent prepuce and the meatus. They are caused by human papilloma virus and usually transmitted sexually. Treatment includes keeping the affected areas cool and dry and applying with extreme care 10–25% podophyllin solution or podophyllotoxin 0.5% paint to the warts (only) as directed. Alternative treatments include liquid nitrogen, 5-fluorouracil cream, diathermy under general anaesthetic and alpha interferon injections into the lesions.

Penile ulcers

A common cause related to sexual activity is trauma to the frenulum if it is congenitally tight. Such traumatic ulcers may be slow to heal and the frenulum may neeed surgical division. The ulcers may resemble a venereal ulcer, e.g. syphilitic chancre, herpes simplex or AIDS. Another important (although rare) cause is carcinoma of the penis. Various causes are listed in Table 86.1.

Table 86.1 *Causes of penile lesions*

Non-ulcerative
- Balanitis
  - *Candida albicans*
  - Reiter's syndrome
  - diabetes mellitus
  - poor hygiene
- Skin desease
  - psoriasis
  - lichen planus
- Venereal warts

Ulcerative
- Trauma (tender)
- Carcinoma (non-tender)
- Herpes simplex (tender)
- Syphilis (non-tender)
- Chancroid (tender)
- Behçet's syndrome

Carcinoma of the penis

Carcinoma of the penis is rare, occurring at a rate of 1 in 100 000 of the male population.[2] There is an association with the non-circumcised person, the theory being that smegma may be carcinogenic.

Carcinoma usually starts as a nodular warty growth (or ulcer) on the glans penis or in the coronal sulcus. Initially it may resemble a venereal wart. The presenting symptom may be a bloodstained or foul-smelling discharge as the lesion is usually hidden by the foreskin. It is usually seen in elderly patients with poor hygiene.[3] Associated lymphadenopathy, which is present in 50% of patients on presentation, may be infective or neoplastic.

Priapism

Priapism is a persistent painful erection not associated with appropriate sexual stimulation. The corpora cavernosa are engorged and painful, but the corpus spongiosum and glans remain flaccid.[2] The cause is usually poor venous drainage. Priapism should be regarded as an emergency; if prolonged it may lead to thrombosis of the veins, resulting in impotence.

Although the aetiology is usually idiopathic, priapism may be associated with medical treatment of impotence with prostaglandin injections for impotence, haematological disorders such as sickle cell anaemia and leukaemia, metastatic malignant infiltration, spinal cord injuries, and drugs such as anticoagulants, marijuana, phenothiazines and some antihypertensives. Local intracavernous injections, especially papaverine, are probably the most common cause.

Management is an immediate urological referral where an urgent blood film should be ordered to exclude polycythemia and leukaemia; possibly dilute aramine 1 mg will be injected into the corpus cavernosum followed by massage. A poor response may require a second aramine injection or venous bypass surgery.

Peyronie's disease

Peyronie's disease is a fibrotic process, sometimes associated with Dupuytren's contracture, that affects the shaft of the penis and results in discomfort and deformity on erection. Typically the patient presents with painful 'crooked' erections. There is abnormal curvature of the erect penis. The penile deformity may prevent satisfactory vaginal penetration. On examination a non-tender hard plaque may be palpable just beneath the skin along the dorsum of the penis. Mild cases require reassurance and vitamin E cream to reduce discomfort. The problem may increase, remain static or spontaneously lessen over 1–2 years. Surgical treatment by penile tuck is indicated if the patient's erection is so deformed that sexual intercourse is difficult, or by penile implant if the patient is impotent.[2]

Haematospermia

Haematospermia, which is blood in the semen, presents as a somewhat alarming symptom. It is sometimes encountered in young adults and middle-aged men. The initial step is to determine that the blood is actually in the semen and not arising from warts inside the urethral meatus or from the orifice of the partner.

It usually occurs as an isolated event but can be secondary to urethral warts or prostatitis, or with prostatomegaly or prostatic tumour (especially in elderly patients).

References

1. Hutson J, Beasley S, Woodward A. *Jones clinical paediatric surgery*. Oxford: Blackwell Scientific Publications, 1992, 175–179.
2. Bullock N, Sibley G, Whitaker R. *Essential urology*. Edinburgh: Churchill Livingstone, 1989, 287–299.
3. Hunt P, Marshall V. *Clinical problems in general surgery*. Sydney: Butterworths, 1991, 365–368.

87

Disorders of the prostate

—

The main function of the prostate gland is to aid in the nutrition of sperm and keep the sperm active. It does not produce any hormones so there is usually no alteration in sexual drive following prostatectomy.

Prostatitis

Prostatitis embraces a group of conditions with pain in the prostate and typically affects men aged 30–50. Prostatitis usually occurs in the absence of identifiable bacterial growth, when it is termed non-bacterial prostatitis. The prostate may develop acute or chronic bacterial infection.

Prostatitis is usually caused by *E.coli* (commonest), *Streptococcus faecalis*, *Pseudomonas* or *Staphylococcus*. Some chronic infections have been shown to be associated with *Chlamydia trachomatis*.[1]

Prostatodynia means the presence of symptoms typical of prostatitis but without objective evidence of inflammation or infection (Table 87.1).

It is preferable to use the term 'prostatitis syndromes' to embrace these four terms (Table 87.1).

Clinical features of acute prostatitis

Symptoms

- fever, sweating, rigors
- pain in perineum (mainly), back and suprapubic area
- urinary frequency, urgency and dysuria
- variable degrees of bladder outlet obstruction
- ± haematuria

Signs

- fever
- rectal examination: prostate exquisitely tender, swollen, firm, warm, indurated

Table 87.1 *Classification of prostatitis syndromes*

	Prostatic pain	Prostatic rectal examination	Positive bladder culture	Positive prostatic secretion culture
Acute bacterial prostatitis	Yes	Abnormal	Yes	Yes
Chronic bacterial prostatitis	Often	Normal	Occasionally	Low counts
Non-bacterial prostatitis	Often	Normal	Occasionally	No
Prostatodynia	Often	Normal	No	No

Complications

- abscess
- recurrence
- epididymo-orchitis
- acute retention
- bacteraemia/septicaemia

Chronic prostatitis

Chronic prostatitis is diagnosed by a history of mild irritative voiding with perineal, scrotal and suprapubic pain. Ejaculatory pain can occur. The gland may be normal on clinical examination or tender and boggy. It should be suspected in men with recurrent UTI (refer Table 87.2).

Table 87.2 *Features of chronic bacterial prostatitis*

Difficult to treat
Relapsing infection
Perineal pain
Some leucocytes in expressed prostatic secretion

Investigations

- Fractional urine specimens and expressed prostatic secretions (EPS) obtained after prostatic massage can show excess white cells.
- Culture of the urine or ejaculate may be negative or give low counts.
- Prostatic stones (demonstrated by plain X-ray or transrectal ultrasound) may prevent successful treatment.

Treatment

Acute prostatitis

amoxycillin (or ampicillin) 1 g IV 6 hourly

+

gentamicin 120–160 mg IV 12 hourly to maximum 5 mg/kg/day

until there is substantial improvement, when therapy may be changed to an appropriate oral agent, based on the sensitivity of the pathogen(s) isolated, for the remainder of 14 days.[2]

For milder infection, oral treatment with amoxycillin/potassium clavulanate, trimethoprim or norfloxacin is suitable. Urinary retention or abscess formation almost always requires endoscopic surgery for relief.

Chronic bacterial prostatitis

Treatment of this condition is difficult. Avoid overtreatment with antibiotics. Reassurance is important and it is worth suggesting frequent ejaculation and hot baths. Massage only for recalcitrant cases.

doxycycline 100 mg (o) daily for 1 month

or

trimethoprim 300 mg (o) daily for 1 month

or

norfloxacin 400 mg (o) 12 hourly for 1 month

or

ciprofloxacin 500 mg (o) 12 hourly for 1 month[2]

Non-bacterial prostatitis

The symptoms may reflect retrograde passage of urine into prostatic tissue. Treat empirically with doxycycline 100 mg (o) 12 hourly or erythromycin 500 mg (o) 4 times daily, for 14 days. Emphasise good voiding habits.[2] Encourage normal sexual activity, stress management and a good diet.

Prostatodynia

Perform a thorough genitourinary tract investigation including urodynamic studies. Some patients have urethral sphincter spasm and may respond to diazepam or the alpha-blocking agent minipress 0.5 mg bd. Psychological counselling may be appropriate. Occasionally alcohol and caffeine induce flares of prostatodynia which may often be regarded as synonymous with non-bacterial prostatitis.

Rare causes of prostatitis include tuberculosis, gonorrhoea, parasites and fungi.

Bladder outflow obstruction

The symptoms of bladder outflow obstruction are usually classified as obstructive (primary) or irritative (secondary). Irritative symptoms may be caused by a bladder problem only. Obstructive symptoms are usually caused by benign prostatic hyperplasia, which can also cause irritative symptoms.

Obstructive symptoms:

- hesitancy
- weak stream
- postmicturition dribble
- straining
- urinary retention
- paradox incontinence

Irritative symptoms:

- urgency
- urge incontinence
- frequency
- nocturia
- dysuria
- suprapubic pain

Prostatism

This term is used to describe the clinical symptoms of hesitancy, a slow interrupted flow with terminal dribbling, frequency, urgency and nocturia.

Benign prostatic hyperplasia

Symptoms of benign prostatic enlargment (BPH) are present in most men after the age of 60, although the process begins about the age of 40. In the UK, 75% of men have significant hyperplasia by the age of 70 but only 10–15% require surgery for relief of obstructive symptoms.[1] The exact aetiology is unknown.

Clinical features of BPH:

- frequency of micturition
- urgency
- nocturia

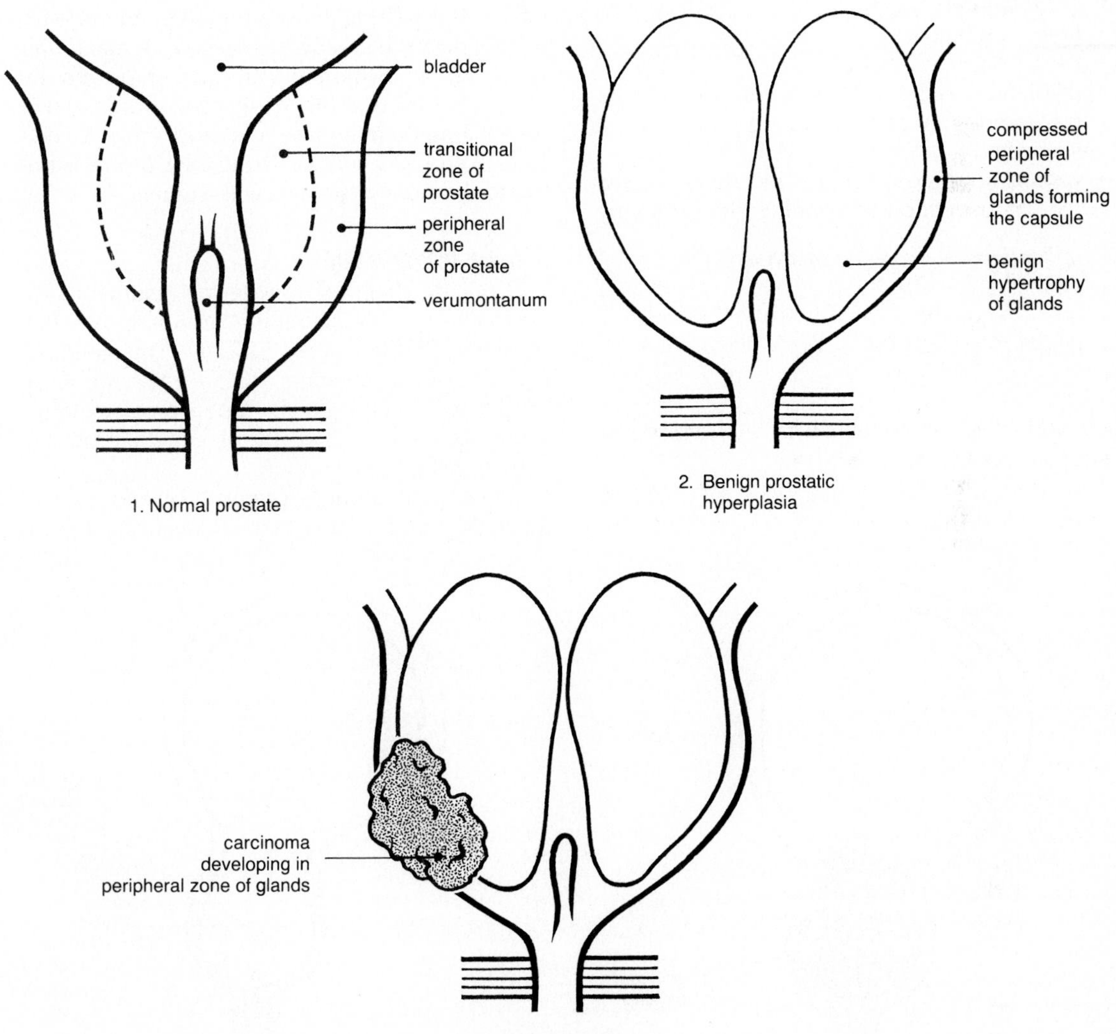

Fig. 87.1 *Diagrammatic comparison of prostatic tumours*

- hesitancy
- slow interrupted flow
- terminal dribbling
- acute retention (the presenting problem in 15% of patients)
- retention with overflow incontinence (less common)
- haematuria from ruptured submucosal prostatic veins can occur
- rectal examination usually detects an enlarged prostate

Note: Small glands can also cause outlet obstruction.

Investigations

These include

- urine culture
- renal function
- prostate specific antigen
- prostatic needle biopsy (with or without transrectal ultrasound) if carcinoma suspected
- voiding flow rate to confirm that the symptoms reflect obstruction and not bladder irritability

Complications of prostatic obstruction

- retention
- urinary infection
- bladder calculus formation
- uraemia

Self-help advice for patients with mild symptoms (after cancer excluded)

- Avoid certain drugs, especially OTC cough and cold preparations.
- Avoid fluids before bed-time.
- Urinate when you need to (do not hang on).
- Wait 30 seconds after voiding to ensure your bladder is empty.

Aims of treatment

- reduce urethral resistance
- improve detrusor function

Medical treatment

Patients with mild symptoms may be helped with alpha-adrenergic blocking drugs such as phenoxybenzamine, terazosin and prazosin to inhibit contraction of the muscle in the bladder neck and urethra.[1] A typical dose is prazosin 0.5 mg bd, or 1 mg nocte after commencing with 0.5 mg nocte. It can be increased to a maximum of 2 mg bd. Symptoms are not improved by increasing beyond this dose. Newer drugs such as the 5 alpha reductase inhibitors (finasteride) reduce prostatic volume. Urine flow improves but not to the same degree as with surgery.

Surgical management

The most effective long-term treatment for obstruction is transurethral resection of the prostate (TURP) (Fig. 87.2). Transurethral incision of the prostate (TUIP) gives identical results with small glands. Open prostatectomy accounts for less than 1% of benign prostatic surgery today.

Permanent springs (stents) placed in the prostatic urethra under local anaesthesia are an

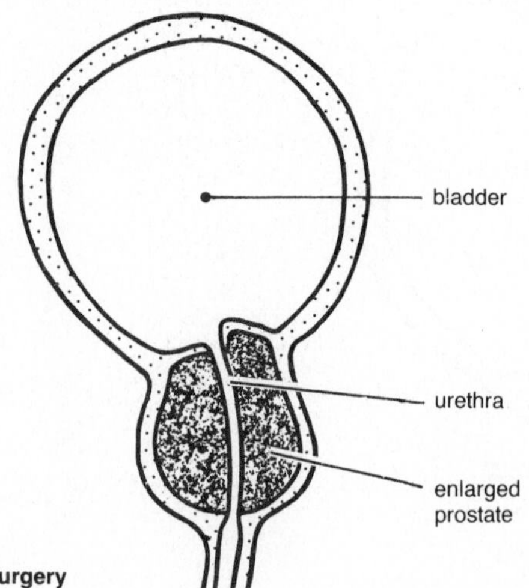

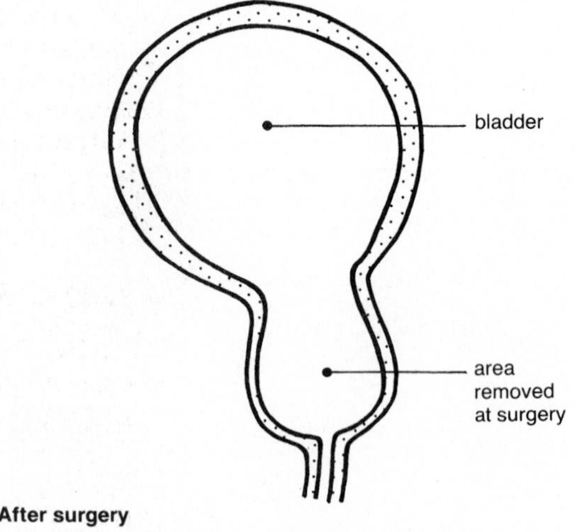

Fig. 87.2 *The process of prostatectomy*

option for the very frail patient. Laser, microwave and heat treatment are new methods that need long-term evaluation.

Absolute indications for prostatectomy include deterioration in renal function, the development of upper tract dilatation, and retention (following drainage and assessment). Eighty per cent of patients have surgery for symptoms.

Postoperative guidelines for the patient

- There may be urgency even to the point of incontinence for a few days.
- Bleeding can occur intermittently for three weeks, so increase fluid intake.
- Erectile function is usually unchanged (neither better nor worse) but loss of erection probably occurs in 5% of patients.
- Avoid intercourse for three weeks.
- Orgasms continue but there is usually no emission with ejaculation. The semen is ejaculated back into the bladder.
- If obstructive problems recur early there may be a stricture.

Note: Persisting postoperative frequency bothers about 15% of patients.

Drugs and prostatism

Certain drugs can cause symptoms of prostatism due to the effect of the drug on the bladder. It is very important for the family doctor to enquire about these drugs when evaluating such a patient. The problem is mainly an adverse effect of drugs with anticholinergic activity.

Anticholinergics

- atropine and hyoscine compounds
  e.g. disopyramide
  mazindol
  phenothiazines
  dicyclomine
  propantheline
  other belladonna alkaloids
- antidepressants
  especially tricyclic compounds
- antiParkinson agents
  e.g. amantadine
  benzhexol
  benztropine
  biperiden
  orphenadrine
  procyclidine

Beta-adrenoceptor agonists

- ephedrine
- salbutamol
- terbutaline
- OTC preparations (mainly for coughs and colds)
  e.g. sympathomimetics including ephedrine

Carcinoma of the prostate

Prostate carcinoma is the commonest malignancy in men and the third commonest cause of death from malignant disease in Australia. It is rare before the age of 50. By the age of 80 years 80% of men have histologic carcinoma within the gland but most appear to lay dormant.[3] Prostatic carcinoma may be asymptomatic, even when it has extended beyond the prostate. It usually commences in the posterior part of the gland. There are dramatic racial differences that tend to change with migration, which indicates that the conversion from histologic to clinical cancer reflects environmental influences.

Clinical features

Unsuspected carcinomas are often detected histologically by TURP. Clinical prostatic carcinoma presents typically with rapidly progressive symptoms of lower urinary tract obstruction or of metastatic spread, especially to bone (pelvis and vertebrae).[3] Symptoms include bladder outflow problems (prostatism) 70%, acute retention 25%, back pain 15%, haematuria 5% and uraemia 5%.[1] Other symptoms include tiredness, weight loss and perineal pain.

Digital rectal examination (DRE) may reveal a nodule (50% are not carcinoma). Locally advanced disease typically reveals a hard, nodular and irregular gland. The tumour may be large enough to obliterate the median sulcus. The borders may lack definition. On the other hand, there may be no evidence of the tumour (Table 87.3).

Table 87.3 *Comparison of findings on rectal examination of the prostate*

Benign hyperplasia	*Carcinoma*
Firm consistency	Hard and irregular
Smooth, convex, elastic lateral lobes	Rough contour
Smooth lateral border	Obliterated median sulcus
Mobile rectal mucosa	Mucosa may be fixed

Investigations to detect carcinoma

Blood analysis

- prostate specific antigen (PSA)
  - normal level less than 4 ng/mL
  - can be elevated without cancer
  - is prostate specific, not prostate cancer specific
  - can be 'normal' in 5% of cancers[4]
  - it is not changed by rectal examination
  - levels between 4 and 10 are equivocal
  - levels > 10 are only suggestive of cancer
- prostatic acid phosphatase
  - rarely needed
  - occasionally high in cancer patients with normal PSA

Biopsy

Consider biopsy (with or without transrectal ultrasound) if the DRE is positive or if the PSA is elevated.

Correlations:

PSA 4–10 with positive DRE—38% have a positive biopsy

PSA >10 with normal DRE—30% have a positive biopsy

PSA >10 with positive DRE—65% have a positive biopsy[4]

Investigations to stage disease

- radionuclide scan (not necessary if PSA <20)

Treatment

Many patients, particularly the elderly, have no symptoms and require no treatment. The treatment depends on the age of the patient and the stage of the disease.

For tumours that are potentially curable, radical prostatectomy or radiotherapy are the options.

For metastatic or locally advanced disease, androgen deprivation is the cornerstone of treatment, the options being:

- bilateral orchidectomy

  or
- daily antiandrogenic tablets

  e.g. cyproterone acetate (Androcur)
  flutamide (Eulexin)

  or
- monthly depot injections of luteinising hormone releasing hormone (LHRH) agonists

  e.g. goserelin (Zolodex)
  leuprorelin acetate (Lucrin)
  buserelin

Treatment combinations for small volume advanced prostatic carcinoma:

e.g.
- orchidectomy plus flutamide
- LHRH agonists plus flutamide may be advantageous—LHRH agonists cause an initial surge of testosterone so a preliminary antiandrogenic agent is necessary to prevent a flare.

References

1. Bullock N, Sibley G, Whitaker Q. *Essential urology*. Edinburgh: Churchill Livingstone, 1989, 287–299.
2. Mashford ML. *Antibiotic guidelines* (7th edition). Melbourne: Victorian Medical Postgraduate Foundation, 1992/3, 89–90.
3. Kumar PJ, Clark ML. *Clinical medicine* (2nd edition). London: Bailliere Tindall, 1990, 486–488.
4. Lawson P. *Disorders of the prostate*. Seminar proceedings notes (adapted from the Australian Prostate Health Council's information notes). Box Hill Hospital, Melbourne, 1993.

PART 7

SEXUALLY RELATED PROBLEMS

88

The infertile couple

—

Definition

Infertility is defined as the absence of conception after a period of 12 months of normal unprotected sexual intercourse.[1] It can be a very distressing and emotional problem for the couple who need considerable care, empathy and relatively rapid investigation of their problem. In assessing a couple with the problem of subfertility (this term is a preferable way of describing the condition to the patients) it is appropriate to involve both partners in the consultation. In determining the cause of the subfertility, three basic fertility parameters should be investigated.[2]

1. The right number of sperm has to be placed in the right place at the right time.
2. The woman must be ovulating.
3. The tubes must be patent and the pelvis sufficiently healthy to enable fertilisation and implantation.

Key facts and checkpoints

- Infertility affects 10–15% of all cohabitating couples.[3]
- This incidence increases with age.
- After the age of 32 fertility decreases by 1.5% per year.
- About 14% of couples who do not use contraception fail to achieve a pregnancy within 12 months.[4]
- More than 10% remain unsuccessful after 2 years.[4]
- About 50% of couples will seek medical assistance.[3]
- The main factors to be assessed are ovulation, tubal patency and semen analysis.
- About 30% of couples have an identifiable male factor.
- Female factors account for about 45%: tubal problems account for about 20% and ovulatory disorders about 20%.
- About 15–18% of cases have no apparent explanation.
- A significant number (25%) have combined male and female problems.
- Current specialised treatment helps 60% of subfertile couples to achieve pregnancy.[5]

Physiological factors[5]

Male fertility

Fertility in the male requires:

- normal hypothalamic function producing gonadotrophin-releasing hormone (GnRH)
- normal pituitary function producing the gonadotrophic hormones follicle stimulating hormone (FSH) and luteinising hormone (LH)
- normal seminiferous tubule and Leydig cell function
- normal sperm transport and delivery

Facts about sperm viability

- The maximum number of viable sperm is found in the ejaculate after a 48 hour abstinence.
- After entering receptive cervical mucus, sperm are capable of fertilising an egg for at least 48 hours.
- sperm survive for less than 30 minutes in the vagina.

Female fertility

Fertility in the female requires:

- normal function of the ovulatory cycle, which requires:
  - — normal hypothalamic-pituitary function producing the hormones GnRH, FSH and LH
  - — normal ovarian function with follicular response to FSH and LH (Fig. 88.1)
  - — appropriate prolactin levels (which are normally low); excessive prolactin secretion (hyperprolactinaemia) causes anovulation
- normal tubal transport and access of the ovum to incoming sperm
- receptive cervical mucus
- normal uterus to permit implantation of the fertilised ovum

Causes of infertility

Significant causes of infertility are summarised in Table 88.1 and illustrated in Figure 88.2.

Probabilities of pregnancy

Around 50% of normal couples having unprotected intercourse at least twice a week will probably achieve pregnancy in six months, 80% in one year and 90% in two years.[5]

A diagnostic approach

It is important to see both partners, not just the woman.

History

The following basic facts should be ascertained:

The man

- sexual function
- previous testicular problems/injury, e.g. orchitis, trauma, undescended testes
- medical problems: diabetes, epilepsy, tuberculosis, renal disorders
- past history (PH) of sexually transmitted diseases
- PH of mumps
- PH of urethral problems
- genitourinary surgery, e.g. hernia
- recent severe febrile illness
- occupational history (exposure to heat, pesticides, herbicides)
- drug intake (possible adverse effects from)
  - — alcohol
  - — chemotherapy
  - — anabolic steroids
  - — aminoglycoside antibiotics
  - — sulphasalazine
  - — cimetidine/ranitidine
  - — colchicine
  - — spironolactone

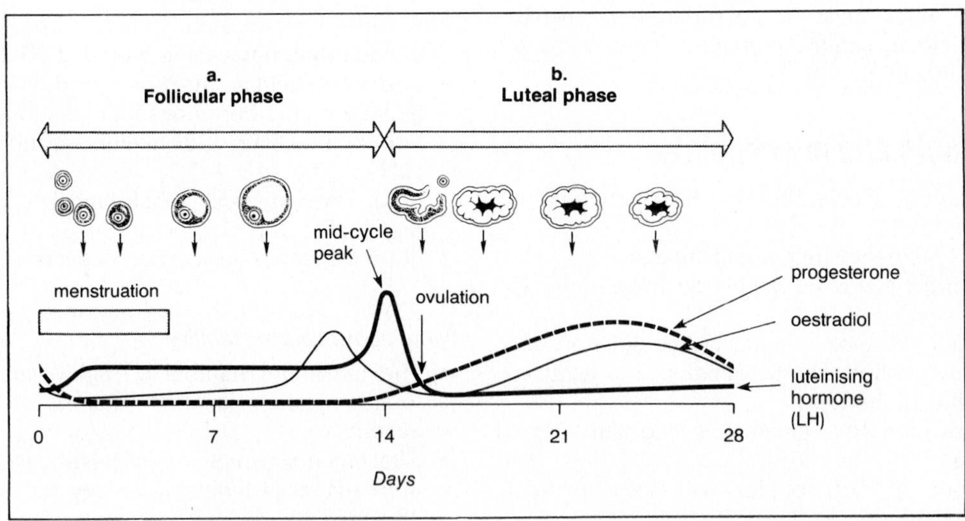

Fig. 88.1 *The normal ovulatory cycle: the midcycle peak of LH and FSH is at 14 days and ovulation occurs shortly afterwards*

Table 88.1 *Significant causes of infertility*

Female factors

Ovulation disorders
- ovarian failure
- stress
- polycystic ovary syndrome
- weight-related ovulation disorders
- hyperprolactinaemia
- other endocrine disorders
- idiopathic eugonadotropic anovulation

Tubal disease
- pelvic inflammatory disease
- endometriosis
- previous ectopic pregnancy
- previous tubal ligation
- previous peritonitis

Uterine and cervical abnormalities
- congenital
- acquired

Endometriosis

Male factors

Reduced sperm production
- congenital cryptorchidism (maldescent)
- inflammation, e.g. mumps orchitis
- antispermatogenic agents
  — chemotherapy
  — drugs
  — irradiation
  — heat
- idiopathic
- Klinefelter's syndrome

Hypothalamic pituitary disease
- hypogonadotropic disorder

Disorders of coitus
- erectile dysfunction
- psychosexual ejaculatory failure
- retrograde ejaculation
  — genitourinary surgery
  — autonomic disorders, e.g. diabetes
  — congenital abnormalities

Ductal obstruction

Couple factors

Joint subfertility
Psychosexual dysfunction

— antihypertensive agents
— narcotics
— phenytoin
— nitrofurantoin
— nicotine
— marijuana

The woman

- evidence of previous fertility
- onset of menarche
- menstrual history
- symptoms of ovulation
- symptoms of endometriosis
- PH of sexually transmitted disease and pelvic infection
- previous IUCD
- PH of intra-abdominal surgery, e.g. appendicitis
- PH of genitourinary surgery, including abortions
- obstetric history
- body weight: eating disorders (anorexia, obesity)
- drug intake
  — alcohol
  — smoking
  — oral contraception
  — anabolic steroids
  — major tranquillisers

Combined history

- frequency and timing of intercourse
- adequate penetration with intercourse
- use of lubricants
- attitudes to pregnancy and subfertility
- expectations for the future

Physical examination

A general assessment of body habitus, general health including diabetes mellitus, and secondary sexual characteristics should be noted in both man and woman. Urinalysis should be performed on both partners.

The man

- secondary sexual characteristics; note any gynaecomastia
- genitalia
  — size and consistency of the testes
    - normal size 3.5 to 5.5 cm long; 2 to 3.5 cm wide
    - small testes < 3.5 cm long
    - Klinefelter's 2 (or less) cm long (typical)
  — palpate epididymis and vas (present and non-tender is normal)
  — evidence of varicocele
  — PR: check prostate
  — note penis and location of urethra

The woman

- secondary sexual characteristics
- thyroid status
- genitalia and breasts

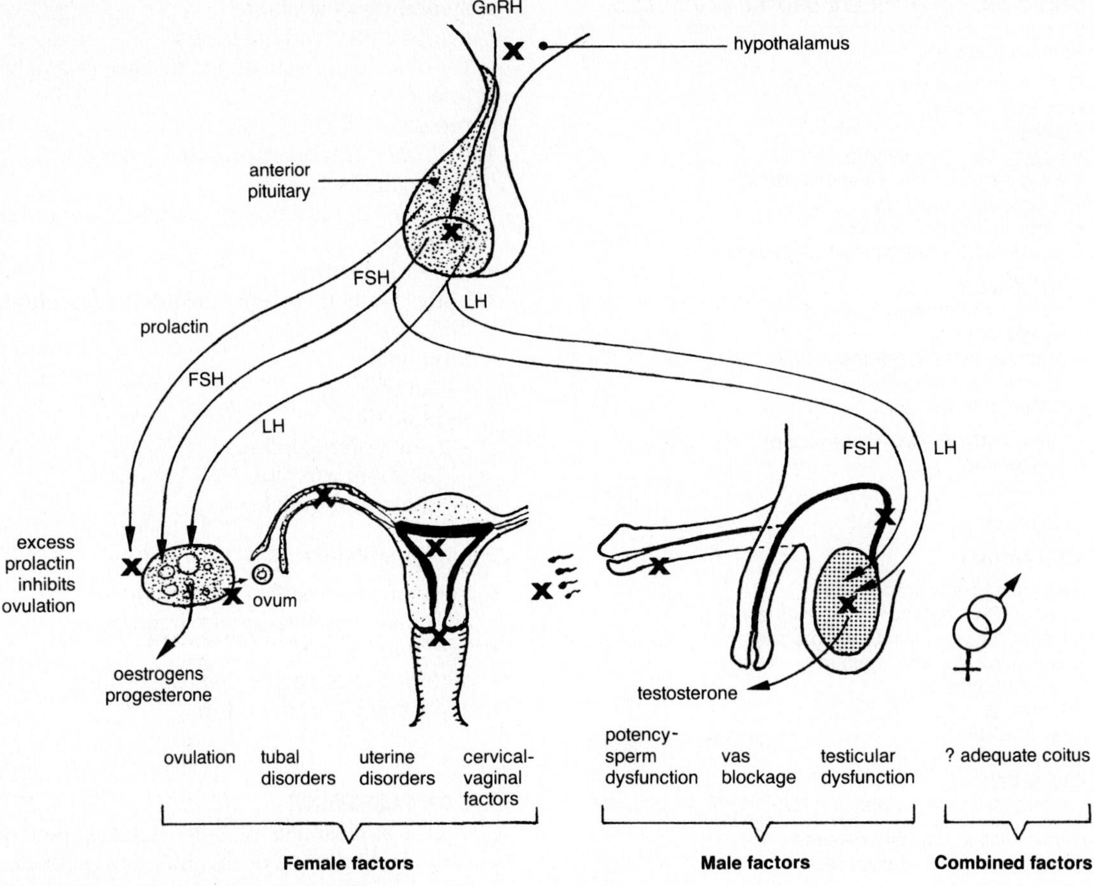

Fig. 88.2 *The major factors involved in subfertility* ADAPTED FROM KUMAR AND CLARKE

- vaginal and pelvic examination
  - assess uterus and ovaries (normal—present, mobile and non-tender)
  - the adnexae (any masses)

Investigations

These are usually performed after referral but the family doctor should organise initial investigations to assess where to refer, e.g. andrologist, endocrinologist, microsurgeon.

Initial investigations

Male—semen analysis:

It is advisable to obtain at least two or three samples over 2–3 months. It requires a complete ejaculation, preferably by masturbation, after at least three days sexual abstinence. Use a clean, dry wide-mouthed bottle; condoms should not be used. Semen should be kept warm and examined within one hour of collection.[6]

Normal values: volume > 3 ml
concentration > 20 million sperm/ml
motility > 60% after 2 hours
normal forms > 60%

Female—ovulation status:

- educate about temperature chart and cervical mucus diary, noting time of intercourse (take temperature with thermometer under tongue before getting out of bed in the morning)
- mid-luteal hormone assessment (21st day of cycle), i.e. serum progesterone and prolactin

Subsequent investigations

Diagnostic laparoscopy:

- direct visualisation corpus luteum, tubes; check tubal patency by insulfating blue dye from the cervix through tubes to peritoneal cavity

Further investigations (if necessary)

Both partners:

- postcoital or sperm cervical mucus contact test to test abnormalities in sperm transport through cervical mucus

Male

If azoospermia or severe oligospermia:

- serum FSH (if 2.5 times normal, indicates irreversible testicular failure)—this is the most important endocrine test in the assessment of male infertility
- antisperm antibodies (in semen or serum)

Female (other investigations may be necessary):

- thyroid function tests: ? hypothyroidism
- hysterosalpingogram
- endometrial biopsy
- ultrasound of pelvis
- computerised tomography of the pituitary fossa
- chlamydia (cervical culture)

Note: Ovulation or its absence is best demonstrated by using serial LH, progesterone and oestradiol levels in conjunction with ultrasonic imaging of the ovaries and their follicles.

Essential investigations are outlined in Table 88.2.

Table 88.2 *Essential investigations of the subfertile couple*

Basal body temperature chart and cervical mucus diary
Semen analysis
Serum progesterone and prolactin (day 21) in female
Laparoscopy and/or hysterosalpingogram

Management principles[3]

- Both partners should be involved in management decisions since fertility is a couple's problem.
- Infertility can cause considerable emotional stress, including the taking or placing of blame by one partner or the other, and subsequent guilt feelings; hence sensitive and empathetic support is essential. This may include marital counselling.
- Since recent advances have helped this problem so much, there is no place for guesswork or for empirical therapy and early referral is necessary.

Counselling the subfertile couple[7]

The counselling of subfertile couples has to be adapted to the level reached by the couple along the infertility pathway. The needs of each individual couple may be very different depending on their innate emotional nature, their lifestyle, moral, religious and ethical beliefs. However, their suffering can run very deep and deserves attention, time and opportunities for free expression of feelings and concerns.

The medical counselling model developed by Craig and Colagiuri[7] (Fig. 4.1) is very useful as it empowers patients to make their own decision through facilitation as opposed to the directive and advisory medical model.

The couple are provided initially with accurate and appropriate information. Anxiety is alleviated by reassurance and by dispelling myths such as an unfavourable position for intercourse, leakage of excess semen from the vagina or previous use of the pill causing their problem.

The facilitation process enables the couple to ventilate any feelings of guilt, anxiety, fear, anger and sexuality. The style of questioning should aim to explore the influence that the problem has had on the couple and then the influence they have over it. These processes then lead to decision making by the couple about further management strategies.

A graph of emotional responses to the infertility (Fig. 88.3) can be used to help the couple explore their current and past emotional responses to their problem. Apart from helping them realise that their problem is not unique, it provides opportunities for ventilation of important feelings that can act as a basis for counselling.

Treatment

If the problem has been identified, specific treatment needs to be prescribed by the consultant, e.g.

- Anovulation can be treated with ovulation induction drugs such as clomiphene, bromocriptine, gonadotrophins or GnRH.
- Endometriosis can be treated medically or surgically (peritubal adhesions).
- Male problems—little can be done to enhance semen quality. Corticosteroids may help if sperm antibodies are present. Consider IVF and related technology for male factor infertility.

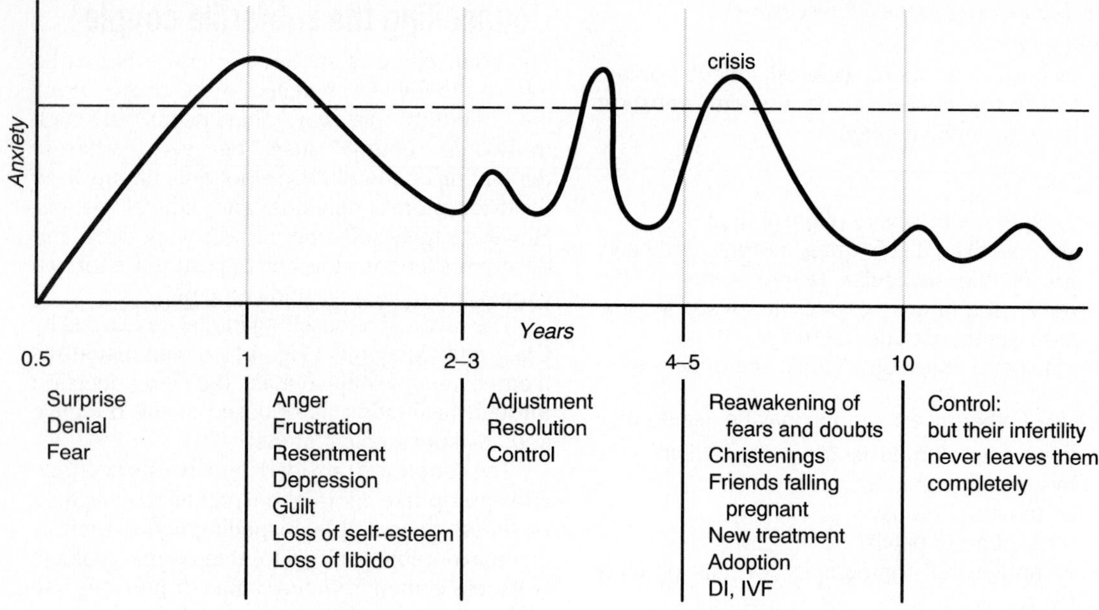

Fig. 88.3 *Emotional responses to infertility* COLAGIURI AND CRAIG[6], REPRINTED WITH PERMISSION

- Severe tubal disease—use in-vitro fertilisation and embryo transfer (IVF-ET).
- Unexplained subfertility—consider gamete intrafallopian transfer (GIFT), a modification of IVF. This method, in which eggs and sperm are placed into the Fallopian tubes, is best used in the treatment of infertility of unknown aetiology and carries a pregnancy rate of about 30% per couple.[2]

When to refer

- A family doctor should perform the initial investigations of a couple with infertility, including temperature chart, semen analysis and hormone levels, to determine whether it is a male or female problem and then organise the appropriate referral.

References

1. Kumer PJ, Clark ML. *Clinical medicine* (2nd edition). London: Bailliere Tindall, 1990, 792–794.
2. Kovacs G. Infertility: Who has the problem? Box Hill Hospital Seminar Course Notes, 1991.
3. Jequier AM. Infertility. In: MIMS Disease Index. Sydney: IMS Publishing, 1991–92, 292–295.
4. Smith H. Female infertility. Modern Medicine Australia, August 1990, 98–106.
5. Knowlden S, Helman T. How to treat infertility. Australian Dr Weekly, 25 August 1989, I–VII.
6. DeKrester D. Female infertility. Modern Medicine Australia, July 1990, 98–109.
7. Craig S. A medical model for infertility counselling. Aust Fam Physician, 1990;19:491–500.

89

Sexual dysfunction

Family doctors are often asked to provide advice and help for sexual concerns and are continually challenged to detect such problems presenting in some other guise. Since we deal with so much illness, including debilitating problems and prescribe so many drugs we must be aware and sensitive to the possible implications of their various effects on sexual health.

Sexual disorders can be considered in three major groups: sexual dysfunction, sexual deviation and gender role disorders. This chapter will confine itself to a discussion of sexual dysfunction.

Sexual dysfunction

Sexual dysfunction in men refers to persistent inability to achieve normal sexual intercourse while in women it refers to a persistent lack of sexual satisfaction.[1]

Several studies have demonstrated that sexual concerns and problems are common with a prevalence ranging from 10–70% of the population.[2] Difficult problems are summarised in Table 89.1. These studies have also indicated that patients are certainly willing to discuss their sexuality and wish their family doctors to become involved in counselling and management of their problems. Between 25 and 30% of sexual difficulties have an organic cause, while the remainder are emotional or psychogenic in origin.[3] The unique place of general practice and the family doctor provides ideal opportunities to address the sexual concerns of patients.

Table 89.1 *Sexual dysfunction: difficult problems*

Sexual desire
- low libido

Sexual arousal
- erectile impotence
- failure of arousal in women

Sexual orientation/activity
- homosexuality
- fetishism

Orgasm
- premature ejaculation
- retarded ejaculation
- orgasmic dysfunction in women

Male problems
- low libido
- erectile difficulties
- premature ejaculation
- failure to ejaculate, or retarded ejaculation

Female problems
- low libido
- failure of arousal
- vaginismus
- orgasmic difficulties

The most common problem influencing an effective outcome is difficulty in communication between doctor and patient, which prejudices effective history taking and counselling. The problem is not content-related, much of which is based on common sense, but the ubiquitous problem of communication.

If, as a practitioner, you counsel on the assumption that there is still astounding ignorance on sexuality in our society, then you will be amazed at the results and at how relatively simple it is to help so many confused people.

Opportunistic sexuality education

The family doctor has many opportunities to provide education in sexuality throughout the lifelong care of the patient and it is wise to have a strategy that matter of factly incorporates enquiries and information about sexual health.

Examples include:

- antenatal and postnatal care
- contraceptive requests
- parents concerned about their children's sex play
- serious illness—medical and surgical
- adolescent problems
- menopause problems

Presentations of sexual concerns

Although some patients may present directly with a complaint of sexual dysfunction, many will be less direct and use some other pretext or complaint as a 'ticket of entry' for their sexual concerns. Despite a seemingly terse approach the issue must be recognised and treated with considerable importance. This may mean scheduling an appropriate time to discuss the concerns.

Sometimes patients are unaware of an association between their medical problem and underlying sexual issues.[2] Doctors may recognise such an association and initiate a tactful psychosocial history that includes questions about sexuality. Examples are chronic backache, pelvic pain, vaginal discharge, tiredness, insomnia and tension headache (see Table 89.2).

Table 89.2 *How sexual issues may present in family practice*[2]

Minor non-sexual complaint—'entry ticket'
Specific sexual concern
Marital or relationship problem
Non-sexual problem (as perceived by the patient)
Sexual enquiry and counselling as part of illness management
Sexual enquiry as part of total health check-up
Infertility
Menopausal problems

The effect of illness on sexual function

Doctors seldom enquire about the impact of an illness on the sexual function of patients and their partners and tend to be unaware of the sexual needs of elderly people (Table 89.3). It is most appropriate to enquire about these issues in our patients, e.g. the postmyocardial infarction patient, the postprostatectomy patient, the patient taking antihypertensives or other drugs, and the postmastectomy or posthysterectomy patient (Table 89.4). Diabetes deserves special attention as 27–55% of diabetic men reported some erectile difficulties.[2]

Table 89.3 *Medical conditions affecting sexual performance*

Cardiovascular
- previous myocardial infarction
- angina pectoris
- peripheral vascular disease
- hypertension and its treatment

Respiratory
- asthma
- chronic obstructive airways disease

Endocrine
- diabetes mellitus
- hypothyroidism
- hyperthyroidism
- Cushing's syndrome

Neurological
- multiple sclerosis
- neuropathy
- spinal cord lesions
- Parkinson's disease

Musculoskeletal
- arthritis

Renal
- renal failure

Urological problems
- prostatectomy
- phimosis
- Peyronie's disease
- priapism

Hepatobiliary
- cirrhosis

Surgical
- vaginal repair
- hysterectomy
- others

Trauma
- motor vehicle accidents

Other
- Klinefelter's syndrome

Table 89.4 *Drugs affecting sexual arousal and function*

Male	*Female*
Alcohol	Alcohol
Narcotics	Narcotics
Marijuana	Marijuana
Anticholinergics	Combined oral contraceptive
Antihypertensives	CNS depressants
Antihistamines	Antihypertensives (selected)
Benzodiazepines	
Disulfiram	
Psychotherapeutic drugs	
Oestrogens	
Cytotoxic drugs	

Taking a sexual history

It is important to be alert for psychiatric disorders and situational factors and not to predict a person's sexual disposition. Avoid being too formal or too familiar but aim to display a wise, matter-of-fact, empathic, common-sense rapport. Tactfully explore the patient's attitude to sexuality and examine his or her relationship. As a practitioner, you have to be comfortable with your own sexuality and learn to be relaxed, confident and understanding when dealing with sexual concerns.

Probing questions for a suspected sexual problem

Do you have any trouble passing urine or any vaginal discharge (women)?
Are you sexually active?
What is the physical side of your marriage/relationship like?
Do you have any pain or discomfort during intercourse?
Is your relationship good?
Do you communicate well? Generally? Sexually?
Do you have any difficulties in your sexual relationships?
What is your sexual preference?
Are you attracted to men, women or both?
What drugs are you taking?
Do you take recreational drugs: alcohol, marijuana, nicotine?

Specific questions about sexuality

Do you get aroused/turned on? What turns you on?
Do you look forward to making love?
Do you spend much time on love play?
Does love making make you feel happy and relaxed?
Do you worry about getting pregnant (women)?
What do you do about contraception?
Do you worry about getting an STD?
Do you worry about getting AIDS?
How often do you reach a climax during love making?
How often do you have intercourse or have sexual activity without intercourse?
Do you 'come' together?

Female

Do you have enough lubrication? Are you wet enough?
Do you find intercourse uncomfortable or painful?

Male

Do you have trouble getting a full erection?
How long does it take you to 'come' after you insert your penis?
Do you 'come' too quickly?

Background history for an admitted problem

Can you think of any reasons why you have this problem?
What sex education did you have as a child? At home or at school?
Were your parents happily married?
Were sexual matters something that could be discussed in the home?
Did you come from a religious family?
Did you receive warnings or prohibitions as a child?
What was the family attitude to masturbation, extramarital sex, menstruation, contraception, etc.?
What is your attitude to masturbation?
Were you fondled or sexually abused by an adult, especially a member of the family?
Were there healthy shows of affection such as touching or hugging between family members?
Did you have any upsetting sexual experiences during childhood and adolescence?
What was your first sexual experience like?

Exploring sexual myths

The acceptance in part or in total of many sexual myths that have prevailed in our society may have affected the relationship of a couple, especially in the context of the modern trend towards openness in discussing sexuality. It is worthwhile to help patients identify whether any of these myths have influenced their concerns by exploring common myths and their significant consequences to the individual or couple.

Sexual myths that could be explored include:[2]

- men need sex, women need love
- men need more sex than women
- men must be the instigators
- men know all about it
- sex = intercourse
- in this enlightened age everyone understands sexual issues

Sexual myths in the male[4]

- A hard erection is essential for good sex.
- A man should not show his feelings.
- A real man is always horny and ready for sex.
- As a person gets older there is no change in sexual interest, response or performance.
- As a person gets older there is a loss of interest in sex.
- Sexual performance is what really counts.
- Men are responsible for their partner's sexual pleasure.
- Sex must lead to orgasm.
- A man and his partner must reach orgasm simultaneously.

Basic sexual counselling

The family doctor can learn to be an effective sex counsellor. Sex counselling can be emotionally demanding and, while good interviewing skills, interest, support and basic advice are important, additional skills are needed to be an effective counsellor.

The fundamental methods involve:

- good communication and allowing a 'comfortable' exchange of information
- giving the patient 'permission' to talk openly about sexual matters
- providing basic 'facts of life' information
- dispelling sexual myths, correcting other misunderstandings
- gentle guidance for appropriate insight
- de-emphasising the modern-day obsession with performance and orgasm and emphasising the value of alternate forms of sexual expression, e.g. caressing, kissing, and manual and oral stimulation
- reducing the patient's anxiety
- bolstering self-images affected by feelings of rejection, avoidance, guilt, resentment or incompetence
- reassuring the patient that he or she is normal (where appropriate)

Inappropriate doctor behaviour is presented in Table 89.5.

An interesting realisation after counselling families in sexuality is that most of the problems are not difficult and often spring from basic ignorance of normal sexual function; it's simply a matter of setting the record straight. The greatest hurdle is 'getting started' with delineating the problem. Once that barrier is crossed, satisfactory results appear to follow.

Table 89.5 *Sexual counselling: inappropriate doctor behaviour*

Overfamiliarity
Being too formal
Being too talkative
Blunt questioning
Being judgemental
Making assumptions about the other's sexuality
Imposing one's own beliefs and standards
Dogmatism
Tackling problems beyond one's experience

Another significant realisation is that sexual problems can be grossly underestimated. Human beings generally have a basic craving for intimacy, touching, stroking and loving sex. Apparently 'good' harmonious relationships can lack this type of intimacy, which may lead to various psychosomatic manifestations.

Ideally the family doctor should undertake a course in sexual counselling to promote confidence in the counselling process. Complex problems, especially those involving impotence, infertility and sexual deviations or perversions, demand referral to an expert.

The PLISSIT counselling model

The PLISSIT counselling model developed by Annon[5] can be used to build the skills needed in dealing with sexual problems, especially if there is a psychological element.[3]

The mnemonic PLISSIT stands for:

- P is for permission giving
- LI is for limited information

- SS is for specific suggestion
- IT is for intensive therapy

Permission giving allows patients to talk about sex, ask questions, feel guilty and so on. Their problems are shared with a reflective listening confidant.

Most medically trained people can probably provide the limited information required about sexual physiology and behavioural patterns.[3] Specific suggestion provides ideas for self-help and may include key reference books, and relevant audiotapes or videotapes (Table 89.6). The latter can certainly arouse interest, ideas and motivation for a renewal of sexual activity. With a little support and permission, the patient can take simple action to remedy or improve a problem.

Table 89.6 *Educational aids for sexual dysfunction*

Recommended books
- Comfort A. *The joy of sex.* London: Mitchell Beazley, 1987.
- Zilbergeld B. *Men and sex. A guide to sexual fulfilment.* Medindie SA: Souvenir Press, 1979.
- Castleman M. *Making love* (mainly for men.) Penguin.
- Crooks R, Baur K. *Our sexuality.* Menlo Park, Ca: Benjamin/Cummings Publishing Co. 1984.
- Williams W. *It's up to you—a self-help book for the treatment of erectile problems.* Sydney: Williams and Wilkins, 1989.
- Rickard-Bell R. *Loving sex: happiness in mateship.* Brighton Le Sands. Wypikaninkie Publications, 1992.
- Gochros, Fischer. *Treat yourself to a better sex life.* Simon and Schuster.
- Kitzinger S. *Women's experience of sex.* Penguin.

Recommended videos
- The lovers guide I and II. Andrew Stanway.
- The language of love.

Intensive therapy, whether psychiatric or emotional, calls for deeper involvement and can be a dangerous area for the inexperienced. Referral to the appropriate practitioner is usually advisable.[3]

Analogous roles of the penis and clitoris

An explanation of the analogous roles of the penis and clitoris (proposed by Cohen and Cohen) is a very useful strategy for educating patients and helping them to understand the relationship of intercourse and penile and clitoris stimulation with orgasm. The simple model (Fig. 89.1) can be shown to patients to explain, for example, the reasons why some women are unable to achieve orgasm by intercourse alone, especially using the conventional missionary position.[2, 6] It can readily be explained that clitoral stimulation in women is analogous to penile stimulation in men. Such information is very helpful for women and also to men who may perceive themselves as inadequate lovers. The use of such explanatory aids greatly facilitates the educational process and makes it more 'comfortable' for all concerned.

Impotence

Impotence (erectile dysfunction) is the inability to achieve or maintain an erection of sufficient quality for satisfactory intercourse. It doesn't refer to ejaculation, fertility or libido. Patients often use the term to refer to a problem of premature ejaculation, hence careful questioning is important.

Impotence is a common problem affecting 2% of males at 45 years and 25% of males aged 65.[7]

The most effective and practical approach to the man with impotence is to determine the response to an intrapenile injection where prostaglandin E_1 is preferred to papaverine.

Causes of impotence

- Psychogenic: related to stress, interpersonal or intrapsychic factors, e.g. depression, marital disharmony
- Neurogenic: disorders affecting the parasympathetic sacral spinal cord, e.g. multiple sclerosis; it usually develops gradually
- Vascular
- Hormone disorder
  - — androgen deficiency, e.g. testicular disease
  - — hypothyroidism
  - — hyperprolactinaemia (rare) → impotence and loss of libido due to secondary testosterone deficiency
- Drug-induced
  - — alcohol
  - — nicotine (four times the risk by age 50)
  - — pharmaceutical preparations
- Unknown

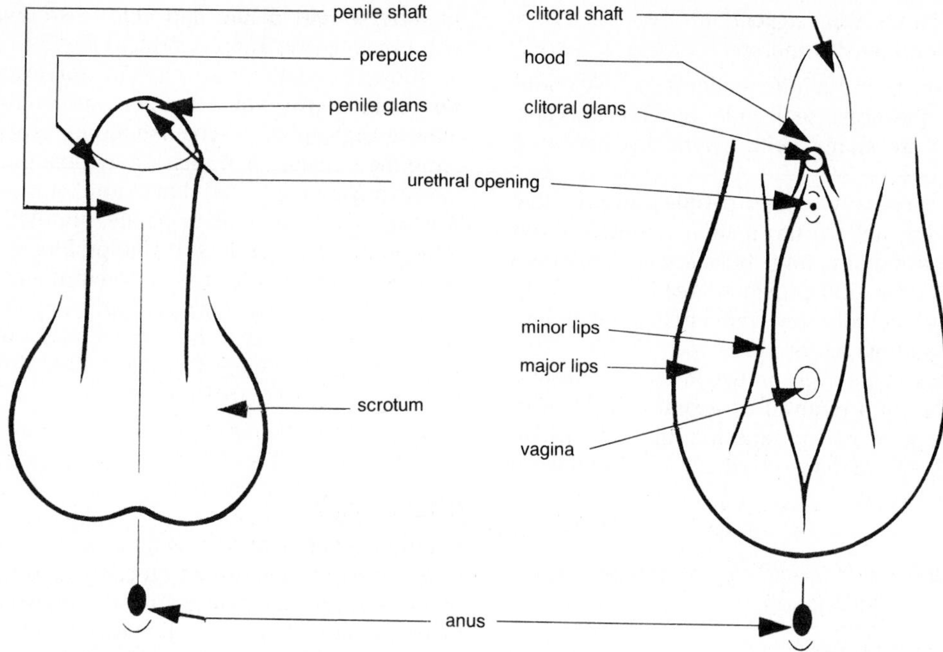

Fig. 89.1 *Analogous structures in male and female genitals* REPRODUCED WITH PERMISSION FROM G. AND M. COHEN, *CANADIAN FAMILY PHYSICIAN*, 852; 31:767–71

History

The nature of the onset of impotence is very important and this includes the nature of the relationship. Of particular importance is a drug history including alcohol, nicotine, street drugs and pharmaceutical agents. Ask about nocturnal and early morning erections.

Examination

This should include a rectal examination and examination of the vascular and neurological status of the lower limbs and the genitalia, especially the testicles and penis. Check the cremaster and bulbocavernosus reflexes.

Investigations

First-line blood tests:

- testosterone ? androgen deficiency
- thyroxine ? hypothyroidism
- prolactin ? hyperprolactinaemia
- glucose

Other blood tests to consider

- LFTs, especially gGT (alcohol effect)

Nocturnal penile tumescence

This is an electronic computerised test used to detect and measure penile erections during REM sleep. Normally there are three to five spontaneous erections lasting 20–35 minutes. It acts as a guide to differentiate between psychogenic (normal studies) and organic (poor function).

Dynamic tests of penile function[7]

These tests include injections of drugs into the corpus cavernosum (which is the simplest method) to assess function. If the patient does not have overt psychogenic impotence and the diagnosis is uncertain, the response to intracavernosal injections of prostaglandin E (PGE) can be tested. A good response to PGE indicates that the patient has psychogenic or neurogenic impotence (e.g. due to pelvic nerve division during colon resection). Responses at higher doses indicate an incomplete organic disorder, e.g. partial arterial occlusion, venous leak, or diabetic neuropathy (early). Total failure to respond suggests arterial occlusion or an idiopathic disorder of the corpora cavernosa.

Management

This should comprise appropriate patient education including a videotape of the specific recommended treatment and technique. The partners should be included in the discussions and general management process with an emphasis on bolstering their self-image which may have been affected by feelings of rejection or avoidance.

Psychogenic disorders

This will involve psychotherapy and sex behavioural modification as outlined under sexual counselling. Referral to a consultant may be appropriate.

Hormonal disorders

- testosterone for androgen deficiency: primary testicular disease (e.g. Klinefelter's syndrome) or gonadotrophin deficiency
  Step-wise trial:
  1. Oral: testosterone undecanoate (Andriol)
  2. IM: testosterone enanthate (Primoteston Depot) or testosterone esters (Sustanon)
  3. Subcutaneous implantation: testosterone implants (last 5–6 months)
- thyroxine for hypothyroidism
- bromocriptine for hyperprolactinaemia

Intrapenile injection

- PGE intracavernosal injections
  — self-administered after supervised teaching
  — maximum of three a week
  — may be a stop-gap measure prior to implant surgery

Vacuum constriction

- vacuum constriction devices may have a place in management

Surgery

- malleable penile prosthesis
- inflatable penile prosthesis (Fig. 89.2)
- vascular surgery where appropriate

Female orgasmic difficulties

It is necessary to determine whether the woman has been anorgasmic or can experience orgasms from other activities such as masturbation, manual or oral stimulation, even though she is non-orgasmic during intercourse.

The use of the Cohen model (Fig. 89.1) is very helpful in emphasising the importance of clitoral stimulation.

Therapy includes:

- sensate focus exercises[8]
- advice on the most appropriate positions for intercourse
- permission to use
  — sexual aids: books, magazines
  — visual tapes
  — self-stimulation

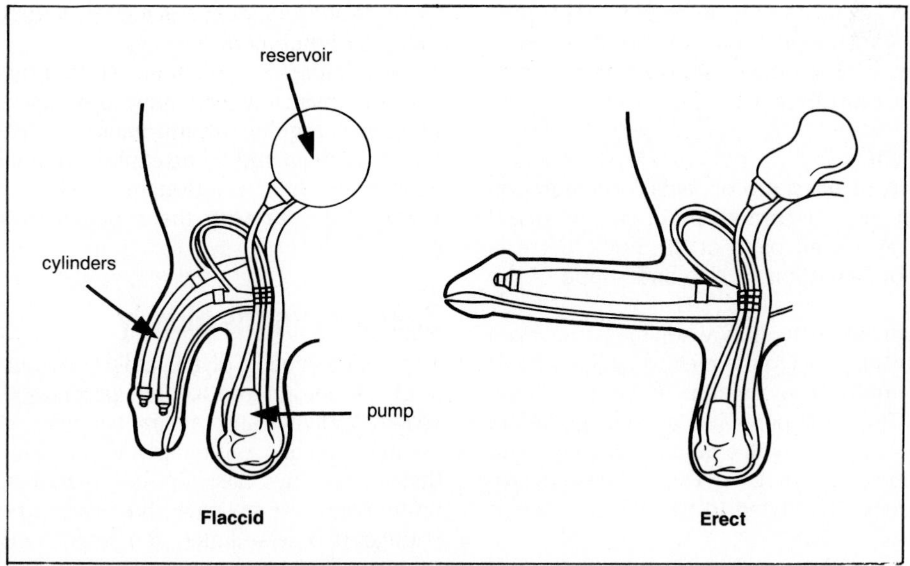

Fig. 89.2 *An inflatable prosthesis, showing positioning of the components*

Premature ejaculation

Premature ejaculation is a common problem that may not be clearly described by the patient so a careful history is necessary to define the problem. Both patient and partner may complain about the problem.

There are many approaches to treatment but they are aimed either at prolonged ejaculatory control or at satisfactory sexual activity without preoccupation with ejaculation and anticipation of better control with time and experience.

The standard management strategies to enhance ejaculatory control include a combination of three techniques:[8]

- graded sensate focus
- Masters and Johnson's squeeze technique[9]
- Semans' technique[10]

The small penis syndrome

In general practice it is not uncommon to counsel men and adolescent males for anxiety, sometimes pathological, about the relatively small size of their penis and its possible impact on sexual adequacy. Some males appear to be preoccupied with the size of their penis, especially when reaching the sexually active phase of their life. It is a manifestation of abnormal body image perception.

This attitude is related to the myth that a man's sexual performance depends on the size of his penis. The patient may present with minor (often trivial) non-sexual complaints as a 'ticket of entry' into the consulting room or perhaps as a manifestation of anxiety or depression related to preoccupation with penile size.

Measurement

Irrespective of physique or facial configuration most men are concerned about penile size.[11] However, as for all parts of the body, there is considerable variation in size and shape of the penis.

The average adult penis, when measured from the symphysis pubis to the meatus, is 3–4 inches (7.5–10.5 cm) long when flaccid (Table 89.7)[11, 12]. The erect penis has an average length of 6 inches (15 cm) with a range of slightly more than one inch (2.5 cm).[11, 12] This increase in size is not necessarily related to the original flaccid state.

Masters and Johnson[13] point out that a penis that is larger in its flaccid state does not increase in length proportionately during erection.

Table 89.7 *Average penile size*

		Flaccid	***Erect***
Length	inches	3–4	5–7
	centimetres	7.5–10.5	12–18
Circumference	inches	2.5–4	4–6
	centimetres	6–10	8–12

Psychological factors

Virility and performance are not related to the size of the penis.[11] Orgasm in the female does not depend on deep vaginal penetration. Penile size was found to have little relationship to a partner's satisfaction from sexual intercourse. The vagina, which is 4 inches (10 cm) long in the unstretched state, tended to accommodate itself to the size of the penis.

Counselling

Counselling the male with fears about sexual inadequacy related to penile size is based on providing reassuring information about the preceding anatomical and physiological facts. The reasons for the patient's concerns should be explored. It should be pointed out that the feeling of inadequacy often follows comparisons with unreal images of macho men portrayed in the media.

If a potential problem is suspected, a useful strategy is to raise the issue subtly by using the third person; in a casual matter-of-fact manner, say something like 'It's interesting how many men worry about such things as their performance and the size of their penis'.

It is important to emphasise that there is no way of physically enlarging a penis, and this includes regular masturbation and coitus. Furthermore, it should be explained that size has absolutely no relationship with physical serviceability or with the capacity to satisfy a partner.

Sexuality in the elderly

The sexual needs of the elderly in our society tend to be ignored or misunderstood. While sexual activity and sexual interest generally decline with age, our elderly are not asexual and their sexuality has to be recognised and understood. They have the same needs as younger people—namely, the need for closeness, intimacy and body contact.[14] The same studies have shown that significant numbers of elderly people continue to enjoy both sexual interest and activity throughout their lives. Their activity is determined by factors such as marital status, knowledge about sexuality, prior patterns of sexual expression, privacy and physical health.

A common problem is that termination of sexual activity stems from the belief that people feel they are 'over the hill' and have a performance anxiety. This applies particularly to people who have invariably experienced orgasm with intercourse and then start failing to maintain this pattern.

Many women require additional lubrication and need advice about the use of oestrogen cream or lubricating jelly.

The application of the PLISSIT model applies to the elderly with an emphasis initially on permission.

References

1. Kumar PJ, Clark ML. *Clinical medicine* (2nd edition). London: Bailliere Tindall, 1990, 997–998.
2. Cohen M, Cohen G. The general practitioner as an effective sex counsellor. Aust Fam Physician, 1989;18:207–212.
3. Richardson JD. Sexual difficulties: a general practice speciality. Aust Fam Physician, 1989;18:200–204.
4. Williams W. *It's up to you—a self-help book for the treatment of erectile problems*. Sydney: Williams and Wilkins, 1985, 16–34.
5. Annon JS. *Behavioural treatment of sexual problems. Brief therapy.* Hagerstown, Maryland: Harper and Rowe, 1976, 45–119.
6. Hite S. *The Hite report: a nationwide study of human sexuality*. New York: Dell Publishing Co, 1976, 229.
7. Keogh EJ. Medical management of impotence. Mod Medicine Australia, Feb 1991, 52–65.
8. Ross MW, Channon-Little LD. *Discussing sexuality*. Sydney: MacLennan & Petty, 1991:42–66.
9. Masters WH, Johnson VE. *Human sexual inadequacy*. Boston: Little, Brown and Company, 1970.
10. Semans JH. Premature ejaculation. A new approach. South Med J, 1956;49:353.
11. Green R. *Human sexuality*. Baltimore: Williams and Wilkins, 1975, 22–23.
12. Katchadourian HA, Lunde DT. *Fundamentals of human sexuality*. New York: Holt, Rinehart and Winston, 1975, 44.
13. Masters WH, Johnson VE. *Human sexual response*. Boston: Little, Brown, 1966, 191–193.
14. Cohen M. *Sex after sixty*. Can Fam Physician, 1984;30:619–624.

90

Sexually transmitted diseases

Sexually transmitted diseases (STDs) are a group of communicable diseases, usually transmitted by sexual contact. Their incidence has been of widespread significance during the past 30 years and they are a major public health problem in all countries.

The STDs have developed a high profile in modern society with the advent of HIV infection, hepatitis B, *Chlamydia trachomatis* as a major cause of pelvic inflammatory disease, the emergence of penicillin-resistant gonorrhoea and the increasing frequency of the human papilloma (wart) virus infection with its association with carcinoma of the cervix. STDs are summarised in Table 90.1.

Key facts and guidelines

- In western society most patients with STDs are in the 15–30 year age group.[1]
- Gonorrhoea and syphilis are no longer the commonest STDs.
- Chlamydial infection, hepatitis B, human papilloma virus and genital herpes are now common infections.
- Not all STDs are manifest on the genitals.
- Not all genital lesions are STDs.
- The 5% rule[2]
  - — 5% of urethritis (STD) in males is lower UTI
  - — 5% of lower UTI in females is urethritis (STD)
- *Chlamydia trachomatis* is now the commonest cause of urethritis.
- NSU typically causes dysuria in men but may be asymptomatic. It usually causes no symptoms in women.
- Gonorrhoea may cause no symptoms, especially in women.
- STDs such as donovanosis, lymphogranuloma venereum and chancroid occur mainly in tropical countries.
- The presentation of STD in children, especially vaginitis, should make practitioners consider sexual abuse.
- HIV infection, which is predominantly sexually transmitted, should be considered in any person at risk of STD as well as IV drug users. It must be appreciated that it can present as an acute febrile illness (similar to Epstein-Barr mononucleosis) before going into a long asymptomatic 'carrier' phase.

Collection of specimens

It is mandatory to collect the appropriate specimens before treatment, because of the epidemiological implications.

Material requirements (obtainable from laboratories):

- standard swabs
- stiff wire swabs
- glass slides
- teflon-coated slides for viral or chlamydial microscopy

Table 90.1 *Sexually transmitted diseases: causative organisms and treatment*

STD	Causative organism/s	Treatment
Bacterial		
Gonorrhoea	*Neisseria gonorrhoeae*	Amoxycillin or ceftriaxone Doxycycline
Non-specific urethritis	*Chlamydia trachomatis* *Ureaplasma urealyticum* *Mycoplasma hominis*	Doxycycline
Cervicitis and PID	*Neisseria gonorrhoeae* *Chlamydia trachomatis* mixed 'vaginal' flora	Mild: doxycycline + metronidazole or tinidazole Severe: add cephalosporins (IV use in hospital)
Syphilis	*Treponema pallidum*	Benzathine penicillin: best to refer
Bacterial vaginosis	*Gardnerella vaginalis* other anaerobes	Tinidazole or metronidazole
Granuloma inguinale (Donovanosis)	*Calymmatobacterium granulomatis*	Doxycycline
Chancroid	*Haemophilus ducreyi*	Erythromycin: best to refer
Lymphogranuloma venerum	*Chlamydia trachomatis*	Doxycycline: best to refer
Viral		
AIDS	HIV_1, HIV_2	Azidothymidine
Genital herpes	Herpes simplex virus	Acyclovir
Genital warts	Papilloma virus	Podophyllotoxin paint or other
Hepatitis	HBV, HCV	Immunoglobulin/interferon
Molluscum contagiosum	Pox virus	Various simple methods, e.g. deroofing with needle
Fungal		
Vaginal thrush (possible) Balanoposthitis	*Candida albicans*	Any antifungal preparation
Protozoal		
Vaginitis, urethritis Balanoposthitis	*Tricomonas vaginalis*	Tinidazole or metronidazole
Arthropods		
Genital scabies	*Sarcoptes scabiei*	Lindane 1% lotion
Pediculosis pubis	*Phthirus pubis*	Lindane 1% lotion

- transport media (three types)
  - — Stuart's (or Amies or similar)
  - — chlamydial
  - — viral

Your laboratory will advise on the most appropriate test kits and methods of collection.

Presenting conditions[2]

Most STDs fit into one (or sometimes more) of the easily definable categories of clinical presentation:

- urethritis—discharge and/or dysuria
- vaginitis—discharge + irritation + odour + dyspareunia
- cervicitis/pelvic inflammatory disease (PID) (possible symptoms)
  - — pelvic pain/lower abdominal pain (PID)
  - — backache (PID)
  - — mild discharge
  - — mucopurulent cervical discharge
  - — dyspareunia (PID)
  - — dysuria
- ulcer
- lump
- pruritus
- rash with — secondary syphilis
  - — HIV infection
  - — hepatitis B

Vaginitis

Vaginitis is presented in more detail in Chapter 79. The common pathogens are:

- *Candida albicans* → vaginal thrush
- *Trichomonas vaginalis*
- *Gardnerella vaginalis* → bacterial vaginosis

Of the three common pathogens, only *Trichomonas* is considered to be sexually transmitted and the only vaginitis requiring routine treatment of partners.

Gardnerella is more a marker of the condition rather than a true pathogen. Bacterial vaginosis (also termed anaerobic vaginosis) is really an altered physiological state rather than an infection or inflammation. The hallmark of the condition is the absence of lactobacilli. It is important to note that anaerobic vaginosis is frequently asymptomatic and found by accident when vaginal swabs are made for other purposes. In these circumstances treatment is not warranted.

Collection of specimens

Make two slides:

- one smear for air-drying and Gram stain
- one wet film preparation, under a cover slip, for direct inspection for the
  — pseudophyphae of *Candida*
  — 'clue cells' of *Gardnerella*
  — motile *Trichomonas*

Treatment (in summary)[1, 2]

- *Candida* on Gram stain: any antifungal preparation
  e.g. clotrimazole 500 mg vaginal tablets statim and clotrimazole 1% cream daily for symptomatic relief
- *Gardnerella* on Gram stain:
  e.g. metronidazole 2 mg (o) statim or 400 mg (o) bd for 7 days
  Acijel topically bd
- *Trichomonas* on wet film
  e.g. tinidazole 2 g (o) statim and treat partner

Urethritis

The important STDs that cause urethritis are gonorrhoea and non-specific urethritis (NSU: also termed non-gonococcal urethritis), which is three times more common than gonorrhoea.[2] NSU is commonly due to *Chlamydia trachomatis* but may also be caused by *Ureaplasma* and other unknown organisms.

Symptoms of urethritis

In males

The main symptoms (if present) are:

- a burning sensation when passing urine (dysuria)
- a penile discharge or leakage (clear, white or yellow)

Sometimes there is no discharge, just pain. Sometimes the infection is asymptomatic. Most often the symptoms are trivial with NSU. Although a creamy pus-like discharge is typical of gonorrhoea, and a less obvious milky-white or clear discharge typical of NSU, it is often difficult to differentiate the causes from the discharge. In some males the only complaint is spots on the underpants or dampness under the foreskin. Epididymo-orchitis in the young male should be presumed to be a complication of an STD urethritis.

In females

Gonorrhoea often causes no symptoms but can produce vaginal discharge or dysuria or pelvic inflammatory disease (PID). NSU usually causes no symptoms but may cause vaginal discharge, dysuria or PID. NSU is the commonest form of PID, which can result in infertility.

Gonococcal infection of anus and throat

In both sexes, gonorrhoea may infect the anus or oropharynx. Anorectal gonorrhoea may be asymptomatic or may present as a mucopurulent anal discharge (a feeling of dampness) and anal discomfort.

Oropharangeal gonorrhoea may be asymptomatic or present as a sore throat or dysphagia.

Collection of specimens

Take two swabs:

- standard swab for *Gonococcus* (into the urethral meatus): place into Stuart's transport medium
- wire swab for *Chlamydia* (2–4 cm into the urethra and twist around), after wiping away frank pus and exudate (Fig. 90.1). Place into *Chlamydia* transport medium.

Note: A wire swab and dedicated chlamydia transport medium is essential for *Chlamydia* diagnosis, as sap from wooden swabs and chemicals from some plastics kill *Chlamydia*.

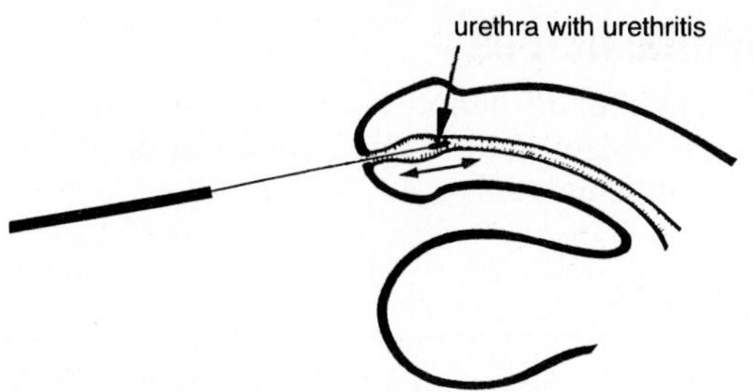

Fig. 90.1 *Taking a urethral swab*

In males direct immunofluorescence or ELISA will usually provide the diagnosis of chlamydial infection and culture is less important for the initial diagnosis.

Special notes

- Take an MSU in males who have dysuria but no discharge.

  or

  Take urethral swabs from females who have dysuria but not frequency. The presence of large numbers of coliform in a urethral swab culture is suggestive of bacterial cystourethritis (lower UTI).
- If gonococci on Gram stain, treat with amoxycillin; if no gonococci on Gram stain, treat with tetracycline; and if microscopy unavailable give both antibiotics.

Non-specific urethritis

Incubation period

The symptoms appear 1–2 weeks after intercourse, although the incubation period can be as long as 12 weeks or as short as five days (compare with IP of gonorrhoea—about 2–3 days).

Treatment

doxycycline 100 mg (o) 12 hourly for 10 days[3]

A second course may be required if the symptoms persist or recur (about one in five cases). Second-line treatment is erythromycin 500 mg qid for 7 days. All sexual partners, even if asymptomatic, need to be treated in the same way. If a female partner has proven cervicitis the treatment must be as for PID. Sexual intercourse must be avoided until the infection has cleared up in both partners. The importance of compliance must be stressed.

Prevention

Using condoms for vaginal and anal sex provides some protection.

Gonorrhoea

Incubation period

Gonorrhoea has a short incubation period of 2–3 days and symptoms usually appear 2–7 days after vaginal, anal or oral sex. The incubation period can be as long as three weeks.

Other manifestations of gonorrhoea

- Epididymo-orchitis and prostatitis (males)
- Urethral stricture is not uncommon in males

Treatment

amoxycillin 3 g (o) statim[3]
plus probenecid 1 g (o) statim
plus doxycycline 100 mg (o) bd for 10 days

If there is infection with penicillin-resistant gonococci due to β-lactamase (penicillinase) production, a problem prevalent in South-East Asia and Eastern Australia, the following should be used:[3]

ceftriaxone 250 mg IM (with lignocaine 1%) as a single dose

or

spectinomycin 2 g IM as a single dose
Each together with
doxycycline 100 mg (o) 12 hourly for 10 days

Sexual partners must be examined and treated and sexual intercourse must be avoided until the infection has cleared.

Prevention

Using condoms for vaginal, anal and oral sex provides good protection. Sexually active men and women (especially those at risk) need at least annual checks.

Cervicitis and PID

Pelvic inflammatory disease is covered in more detail in Chapter 76. It is not always an STD. The intrauterine device is also a common cause. Often multiple pathogens are involved in the infection.

Common pathogens are *Neisseria gonorrhoeae* and *Chlamydia trachomatis*. Swabs from the cervical os frequently underestimate the organisms involved and thus treatment needs to be directed to all possible pathogens.

Mucopurulent cervicitis is now known to be an early sign of PID, usually due to *Chlamydia*.[2]

Specimen collection

Cervical and urethral swabs for urethritis for *N.gonorrhoeae* and *C.trachomatis*.

Treatment

Therapy for cervicitis/PID is deliberately vigorous because the major aim is to prevent infertility and the consequent need for IVF in the long term. The detailed treatment is outlined on pages 743–744.

Summary[2, 3]

Cervicitis only (mucopus at cervix without pelvic pain or tenderness)

a 14 day course of doxycycline 100 mg bd, and

metronidazole 400 mg bd or tinidazole 500 mg (o) daily

Cervicitis + PID: add cephalexin 500 mg qid

Severe PID: hospitalise for IV therapy

Ulcers

STD causes of genital ulcers are presented in Table 90.2. Most genital ulcers are herpes—any small genital ulcer which is superficially ulcerated, scabbed, red-edged, multiple and painful is invariably herpes.

Syphilis is uncommon and may get overlooked, especially with anal chancres.

Chancroid is almost always an imported disease.

Table 90.2 *STD causes of anogenital ulcers*

	Pain	Specimen collection
Common		
Herpes simplex virus	Yes	Scraping for direct immunofluorescence Swab for antigen detection and culture into viral transport medium
Uncommon		
Treponema pallidum (primary chancre)	No	Exudate for dark ground microscopy and serum for leutic screen (reagin or treponemal tests)
Haemophilus ducreyi	Yes	Scraping for Gram stain and special culture
Calymmatobacterium granulomatis (granuloma inguinale)	No	Scraping for special stains

Genital herpes

The incubation period is usually 3–6 days but can be longer. A firm microbiological diagnosis is recommended.

Symptoms

With the first attack there is a tingling or burning feeling in the genital area. A crop of small vesicles then appears; these burst after 24 hours to leave small, red, painful ulcers. The ulcers form scabs and heal after a few days. The glands in the groin can become swollen and tender, and the patient might feel unwell and have a fever.

The first attack lasts about 2 weeks.

Males

The virus usually affects the shaft of the penis, but can involve the glans and coronal sulcus, and the anus (Fig. 90.2).

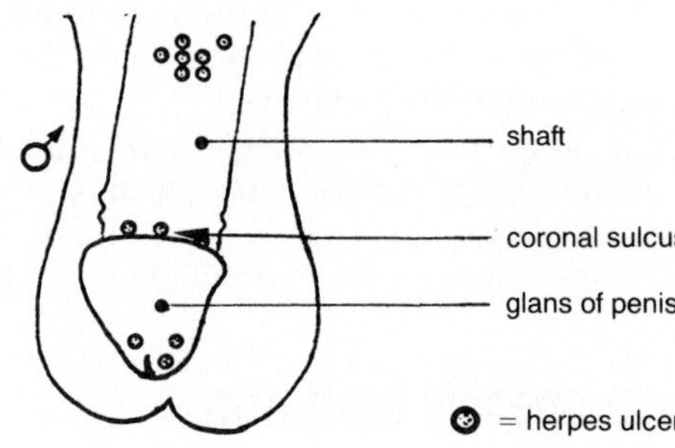

Fig. 90.2 *Usual sites of vesicles/ulcers in males*

Females

Vesicles develop around the opening of, and just inside, the vagina and can involve the cervix and anus (Fig. 90.3). Passing urine might be difficult, and there can be a vaginal discharge. In about 25%, the cervix is the only site of lesions and these cases may be asymptomatic.

In both sexes, it can affect the buttocks and thighs. A serious but uncommon complication, especially in females, is the inability to pass urine.

Transmission

It can be caught by direct contact through vaginal, anal or oral sex. Rarely is it transferred to the genitals from other areas of the body by the fingers.

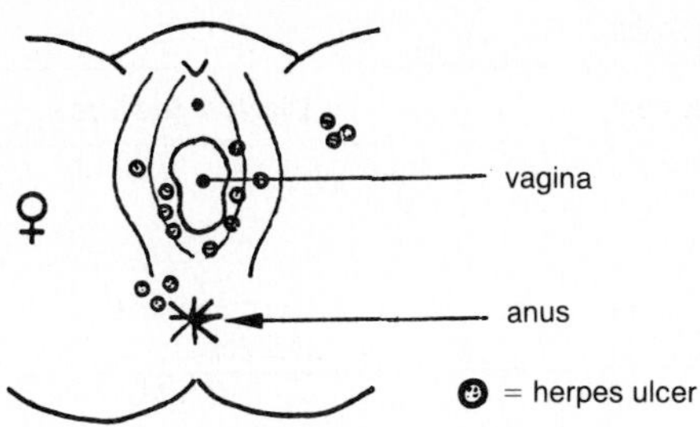

Fig. 90.3 *Usual sites of vesicles/ulcers in females*

Recurrence

Half of those who have the first episode have recurrent attacks; the others have no recurrence. Fortunately attacks gradually become milder, less frequent, last 5–7 days and usually stop eventually. Recurrences after many months or years can be precipitated by menstruation, sexual intercourse, masturbation, skin irritation and emotional stress.

Treatment of genital herpes

Antimicrobial therapy

Topical treatment

The proven most effective topical therapy is topical acyclovir (not the ophthalmic preparation). Other topical preparations provide relief but do not alter significantly the course of the infection; they should be applied as soon as the symptoms start.

Alternatives:

10% silver nitrate solution applied with a cotton bud to the raw base of the lesions, rotating the bud over them to provide gentle debridement. Repeat once or twice. This promotes healing and spreading.

or

10% povidone-iodine (Betadine) cold sore paint on swab sticks for several days.

Pain relief can be provided in some patients with topical lignocaine.

Oral treatment

Acyclovir for the first episode of primary genital herpes.

Dosage: 200 mg 5 times a day for 7–10 days or until resolution of infection.[2]

This appears to reduce the duration of the lesions from 14 days to 5–7 days.[2] Acyclovir is not usually used for recurrent episodes, which last only 5–7 days. Very frequent recurrences (six or more attacks in six months) benefit from low-dose acyclovir for six months (200 mg 2–3 times per day).

Supportive treatment (advice to the patient)

- Rest and relax as much as possible. Warm salt baths can be soothing.
- Icepacks or hot compresses can help.
- Painkillers such as aspirin or paracetamol give some relief.
- If urination is painful, pass urine under water in a warm bath.
- Keep the sores dry; dabbing with alcohol or using warm air from hairdryer can help.
- Leave the rash alone after cleaning and drying; do not poke or prod the sores.
- Wear loose clothing and cotton underwear. Avoid tight jeans.

Counselling

Since genital herpes is distressing and recurrent, patients are prone to feel stressed and depressed and can be assisted by appropriate counselling and support. Sexual abstinence should be practised while lesions are active. Consider referral to a self-help/support group.

Prevention

Spread of the disease can be prevented by avoiding sexual contact during activity of the lesions. Condoms offer some protection (not absolute) and patients should wash their genitals with soap and water immediately after sex. Condoms should always be used where a partner has a history of this infection.

Syphilis

In Australia syphilis usually presents either as a primary lesion or through chance finding on positive serology testing (latent syphilis).

It is important to be alert to the various manifestations of secondary syphilis. The classification and clinical features of syphilis are presented in Table 90.3 (see also Chap. 24).

Table 90.3 *Classification and clinical features of syphilis*

Type	*Time period*	*Infectivity*	*Clinical features*
Acquired			
Early (within first 2 years of infection)			
Primary	10-90 days, average 21	Infectious	Hard chancre Painless Regional lymphadenopathy
Secondary	6-8 weeks after chancre	Infectious	Coarse non-itchy maculopapular rash Constitutional symptoms (may be mild) Condylomata lata Mucous membrane lesions
Early latent	months to 2 years	Infectious	No clinical features but positive serology
Late (after the 2nd year of infection)			
Late latent	2 years plus	Non-infectious	
Tertiary (now rare)		Non-infectious	Late benign: gummas or Cardiovascular or Neurosyphilis
Congenital			
Early	within first 2 years of life	Infectious	Stillbirth or failure to thrive Nasal infection: 'snuffles' Skin and mucous membrane lesions
Late	after second year of life	Non-infectious	Stigmata, e.g. Hutchinson's teeth Eye disease CNS disease Gummas

Transmission

- sexual intercourse (usual common mode)
- transplacental to foetus
- blood contamination: IV drug users
- direct contact with open lesions

Management

The management of syphilis has become quite complex and referral of the patient to a specialist facility for diagnosis, treatment and follow-up is recommended.

Recommended anti-microbial therapy

Early syphilis (primary, secondary or latent) of not more than one year's duration:[3]

benzathine penicillin 1.8 g IM as a single dose
For patients hypersensitive to penicillin
doxycycline 100 mg (o) 12 hourly for 14 days
or
erythromycin 500 mg (o) 6 hourly for 14 days

Late syphilis: more than one year or indeterminate duration

benzathine penicillin 1.8 g IM once weekly for 3 doses

Cardiovascular and neurosyphilis and congenital syphilis are also treated with penicillin but require special regimens.

Lump

Common pathogens

- Wart (papilloma) virus—condylomata acuminata, venereal 'warts'
- Molluscum contagiosum (pox) virus

Uncommon

- *Treponema pallidum*—condylomata lata

Diagnosis

Warts and molluscum contagiosum have a distinctive appearance and are readily diagnosed by inspection. Removal of these for diagnosis is usually not required. Condylomata acuminata are multiple lesions that resemble warts superficially but are covered by abundant exudate. They occur in secondary syphilis and luetic screen is positive.

Treatment of warts

Counselling and support are necessary. Not all genital warts are sexually transmitted.

Warts may be removed by chemical or physical means, or by surgery. Treatment needs to be individualised. For small numbers of readily accessible warts the simplest treatment is:[3]

- podophyllin 25% solution in tinct benz co
  - apply with a cotton wool swab to each wart
  - wash off in 4 hours, then dust with talcum powder
  - repeat once weekly until warts disappear

or

- podophyllotoxin 0.5% paint (a more stable preparation)
  - apply bd with plastic applicator for 3 days
  - repeat in 4 days if necessary

Note: The normal surrounding skin should be spared as much as possible.
Avoid this treatment in pregnancy on cervical, meatal or anorectal warts.

Cryotherapy (liquid nitrogen) or laser or diathermy under general anaesthetic can be used for multiple lesions. Intralesional injection of alpha interferon is a treatment of the future.

All females (including partners of males with warts) should be referred to a specialised clinic where colposcopy is available, because of the causal link of warts to cervical cancer.

Treatment of molluscum contagiosum

These lesions often resolve spontaneously. There are many treatment choices to provoke resolution. These include:

- deroofing aseptically with a needle or sharp-pointed stick and expressing the contents (recommended)
- lifting open the tip with a sterile needle inserted from the side and applying 10% providone-iodine (Betadine) solution
- liquid nitrogen (for a few seconds)
- application of 25% podophyllin in tinc benzoin co
- application of 30% trichloroacetic acid
- destruction with electrocautery or diathermy

Itch

Common pathogens

Sarcoptes scabiei (scabies)

Phthirus pubis (pubic lice)

Candida albicans
- vulvovaginitis—females
- balanitis—males

Non-STD itchy rashes on genitals include dermatitis and psoriasis.

Diagnosis

Scabies: inspection on scraping and microscopy

- Inspection: scabies is diagnosed by a very itchy, lumpy rash. It is rare to find the tiny mites, but it may be possible to find them in the burrows, which look like small wavy lines.

Pubic lice: inspection for moving lice and nits (eggs) on hair shaft.

Candida albicans: swab for Gram stain and *Candida* culture.

Treatment

Scabies

Lindane (gammabenzene hexachloride) 1% lotion.[3] Apply to whole body from jawline down (include every flexure and area), leave overnight, then wash off. Wash clothing and linen after treatment.

or

(Especially in children, or during pregnancy or lactation): benzyl benzoate 25%, left for 24 hours before washing off. The whole family and close contacts must be treated regardless of symptoms which can take weeks to develop. One treatment is usually sufficient. It can be repeated in a week if necessary.

Note: Persistence of the itch after treatment is common. If the itch has not abated after seven days, re-treat. After this, reassurance is usually all that is required. Also prescribe a topical antipruritic, e.g. crotamiton cream and an oral antihistamine for the itch.

Pubic lice

Lindane 1% lotion (avoid during pregnancy and lactation). Apply to the affected area (only), leave overnight and then wash off. Bed clothes and underwear should be washed normally in hot water after treatment. Repeat the treatment after seven days. Sometimes a third treatment is necessary. Sexual contacts and the family must be treated (young children can be infested from heavily infested parents). Where the lice or the nits are attached to eyelashes, insecticides should not be used: apply Vaseline liberally to the lashes.

Candidiasis

topical imidazole, e.g. clotrimazole 1% applied 2-3 times daily

Extragenital STDs

Viral hepatitis

Sexual activity is a factor in the transmission of hepatitis B (in particular), hepatitis A (where faecal-oral contact is involved), hepatitis C (probably) and hepatitis D.[1]

Hepatitis B[1]

In western societies, sexual transmission of HBV is a common mode of spread and there is a higher prevalence in homosexual men and prostitutes. HBV prevalence in homosexual men is correlated with insertive and receptive anogenital contact and oroanal contact.

There is no specific therapy for hepatitis B, so prevention is important.

Prevention[1]

Several prevention strategies are available, including:

- immunisation
- prevention of infection in health care establishments
- management of exposure (needlestick injuries, etc)
- management of infants of mothers who are hepatitis B carriers
- condoms which offer some reduction of risk of sexual transmission
- personal hygiene

Immunisation

Immunisation should be encouraged in hepatitis B marker-free people at risk of acquiring this infection. At risk groups include sexual partners of carriers, institutional individuals, homosexuals, prostitutes, promiscuous homosexuals and drug addicts. Some health workers are exposed to risk.

Management of exposure

Sexual partners of acute cases and chronic carriers who are negative for surface antigen (HBsAg) and antibody can be offered hepatitis B immunoglobin, and routine hepatitis B immunisation should be commenced.

Hepatitis C

Although there have been doubts about the potential for sexual transmission of hepatitis C, Tedder et al in 1991[4] have demonstrated strong evidence for the sexual transmission of HCV. Significantly, more homosexual subjects than heterosexuals were positive for HCV antibody.

Human immunodeficiency virus infection

HIV infection (colloquially called AIDS, although this represents only the severe end of the disease spectrum) is predominantly sexually transmitted in the community. In Australia about 95% of current AIDS cases are sexually transmitted, 80–90% in homosexual or bisexual men.[1] The important risk factors in these men are receptive anal intercourse and multiple sexual partners.

Sexual transmission to women[1]

Although the heterosexual partners of infected men are at risk of infection, spread to and from women has been relatively uncommon in developed countries, but now appears to be increasing significantly. In central Africa, heterosexual spread appears to be an important means of transmission. Genital ulcerative diseases such as syphilis and genital herpes may be associated with an increased risk of heterosexual transmission.

HIV infection is considered in more detail in Chapter 22.

The full STD check-up[5]

Family doctors may be consulted by a prostitute or other sexually active female requesting a thorough check-up. Such people require certificates from time to time and may not have access to a public STD clinic. The visit should provide an opportunity for counselling and education about her health risks.

The screening program includes:

- Full sexual history.
- Physical examination: genital appearance, skin, breasts, oropharynx, lymph nodes, abdomen, careful anogenital examination.
- Investigations (guide only):
  1. Pap smear: 6–12 monthly
  2. Endocervical swabs for chlamydia and gonorrhoea 1–3 monthly (depending on risk)
  3. High vaginal swab and 'wet film prep' for vaginal pathogens 1–3 monthly
  4. HIV antibody test (with informed consent)—not ordered more often than every 3 months.
  5. Syphilis screening test: RPR/VDRL (as for 4)
  6. Hepatitis B screening: if negative, organise hepatitis B vaccination
  7. Rubella IgG as base line test: if negative, advise Rubella vaccination.

Consider

8. Throat swabs for gonorrhoea (if oral sex without condoms)
9. Urethral swab for gonorrhoea and chlamydia if urinary symptoms
10. Anorectal swab for gonorrhoea if sexual history indicates need

When to refer

Syphilis

- probably all suspected or confirmed cases but certainly for suspected tertiary syphilis
- HIV-positive patients, and
- suspected treatment failure

Pubic lice and scabies

- unresolved rash or itch despite apparently appropriate treatment

Genital warts

- urethral or cervical warts
- associated cervical HPV changes on cytology
- refractory warts

Gonorrhoea or non-specific urethritis: if complications develop, pelvic spread or extragenital problems develop, or symptoms persist after two courses of antibiotics.

Practice tips

- Do not presume that the patient or his/her partner has acquired an STD outside their relationship.
- The itch of scabies or pubic lice can be distressing: prescribe the topical antipruritic (crotamiton cream) and/or an oral histamine.
- Reassure the patient that the itch will gradually subside over a few weeks (especially with scabies). This allays anxiety that may lead to overzealous self-medication.
- Make every attempt to confirm or exclude genital herpes, using the appropriate investigations.
- Use acyclovir for first episodes of genital herpes and when recurrences are either frequent or painful.
- Twelve golden rules of management are presented in Table 90.4.

Table 90.4 *STDs: Twelve golden rules of management (Venereology Society of Victoria)*

1. An STD can only be diagnosed if the possibility is considered.
2. An adequate sexual history is paramount.
3. A proper history and careful examination must precede laboratory investigations.
4. Remember the sexual partner(s)!
5. Treatment consists of the appropriate antibiotic in correct dosage for an adequate period of time.
6. A patient concerned about STDs is probably an 'at risk' patient.
7. Counselling and education are fundamental to STD management.
8. Penicillin will not cure NSU.
9. *Not* all vaginal discharges are thrush.
10. Multiple, painful genital ulcers are most often due to herpes simplex.
11. Prompt, accurate treatment of PID is necessary to preserve fertility.
12. Remember the three Cs—Consent, Confidentiality and Counselling—of HIV antibody testing.

Acknowledgement

Part of this text, on hepatitis B, is reproduced from the *Handbook on sexually transmitted diseases*. 'Commonwealth of Australia copyright, reproduced by permission'. Professor John Turnidge has given permission to adopt his categories of presenting conditions.

References

1. NH&MRC Handbook on sexually transmitted diseases. Canberra: Department of Community Services and Health, 1990, 1–55.
2. Turnidge J. Sexually transmitted diseases.CHECK Programme. Melbourne: RACGP, 1989, Unit 210/211.
3. Mashford ML. *Antibiotic guidelines* (8th edition). Melbourne: Victorian Medical Postgraduate Foundation, 1994/5, 115–127.
4. Tedder RS, Gilson RJC, Briggs M et al. Hepatitis C virus: evidence for sexual transmission. Br Med J, 1991; 302:1299–1302.
5. Bradford D. Sexually transmitted disease. CHECK Programme. Melbourne: RACGP, 1993; Unit 252/253, 7–8.

PART 8

PROBLEMS OF THE SKIN

91

A diagnostic and management approach to skin problems

The diagnosis of skin problems depends on astute clinical skills based on a systematic history and examination and, of course, experience. If the diagnosis is in doubt it is appropriate to refer the patient to a skilled co-operative consultant, as the referral process is an excellent educational opportunity for the GP. Another opinion from a colleague/s in a group practice is also very educative. At least, cross-referencing the skin lesion with a colour atlas facilitates the learning process.

Terminology of skin lesions

Primary lesions

Macule — circumscribed area of altered skin colour < 1 cm diameter (Fig. 91.1)

Patch — macule of > 1 cm diameter (Fig. 91.1)

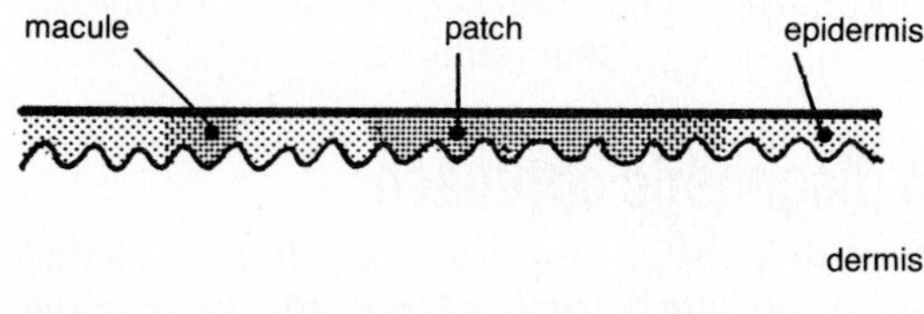

Fig. 91.1 *Macule and patch*

Papule — palpable mass on skin surface < 1 cm diameter (Fig. 91.2)

Maculopapule — a raised and discoloured circumscribed lesion

Nodule — circumscribed palpable mass > 1 cm diameter (Fig. 91.2)

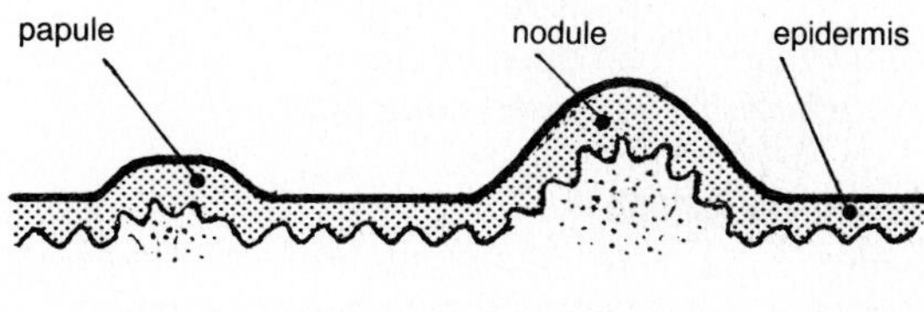

Fig. 91.2 *Papule and nodule*

Plaque — a flat-topped palpable mass > 1 cm diameter

Wheal — an area of dermal oedema (can be any size)

Angio-oedema — a diffuse area of oedema extending into subcutaneous tissue

Vesicle — a fluid-filled blister < 1 cm in diameter

Bulla — a vesicle > 1 cm diameter (Fig. 91.3)

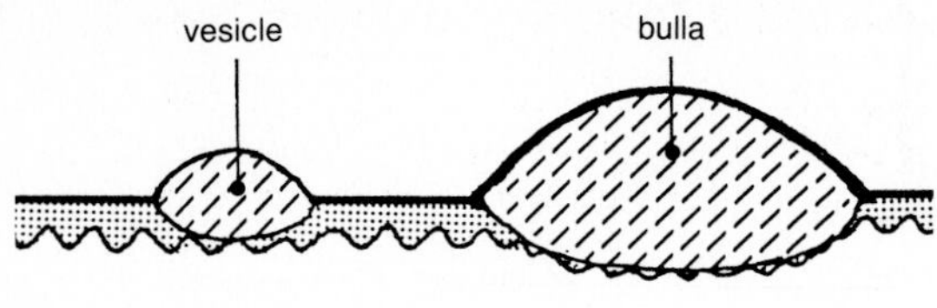

Fig. 91.3 *Vesicle and bulla*

Pustule	a visible collection of pus in the skin < 1 cm diameter
Abscess	a localised collection of pus in a cavity > 1 cm diameter
Furuncle	a purulent infected hair follicle; includes: • folliculitis—small furuncles • boils—larger furuncles
Carbuncle	a cluster of boils discharging through several openings
Purpura	bleeding into the skin appearing as multiple haemorrhages
Petechiae	purpuric lesions 2 mm or less in diameter
Ecchymosis	larger purpuric lesion
Haematoma	a swelling from gross bleeding
Telangiectasia	visible dilatation of small cutaneous blood vessels
Comedo	a plug of keratin and sebum in a dilated sebaceous gland
'Blackhead'	an open comedo
'Whitehead'	a closed comedo

Secondary lesions

Scales	an accumulation of excess keratin that presents as flaking
Crust	superficial dried secretions (serum and exudate)
Ulcer	a circumscribed deep defect with loss of all the epidermis and part or all of the dermis (Fig. 91.4); they usually heal with scarring
Erosion	a skin defect with complete or partial loss of the epidermis; they heal without scarring (Fig. 91.4)
Fissure	a linear split in the epidermis and dermis (Fig. 91.4)
Atrophy	thinning or loss of epidermis and/or dermis with loss of normal skin markings
Sclerosis	thickening of the dermis with induration of subcutaneous tissue; resembles a scar but may arise spontaneously, e.g. scleroderma
Scar	a healed dermal lesion where normal structures are replaced by fibrous tissue
Hypertrophic scar	rises above the skin surface
Atrophic scar	settles below the skin surface
Keloid	overgrowth of dense fibrous tissue extending beyond the original wound
Excoriation	scratch marks causing an erosion or an ulcer (loss of epidermis)
Lichenification	thickening secondary to chronic scratching or rubbing (in dermatitis)

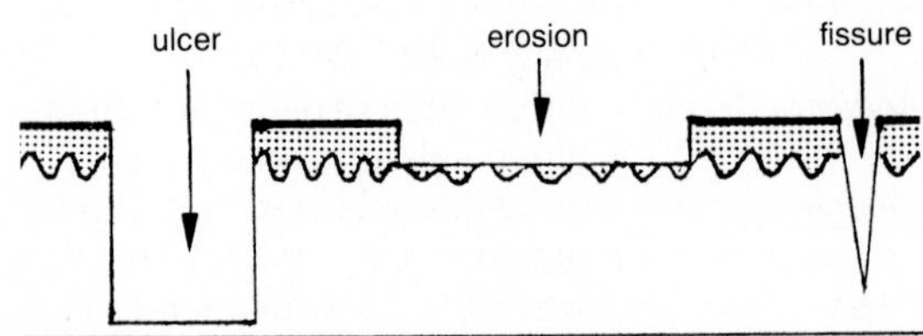

Fig. 91.4 *Ulcer, erosion and fissure*

Defining terms

Terms that are continually referred to in skin disease include:

nummular	= coin-like	} interchangeable
discoid	= disc-like	
annular	= ring-like	
circinate	= circular	
arcuate	= curved	
reticulate	= net-like	
pityriasis	= (pityron = bran): fine bran-like scaly desquamation	
guttate	= 'dew drop'	
rosea	= rose-coloured	
morbilliform	= like measles	
morphoea	= circumscribed scleroderma or skin infiltrate	

A diagnostic approach

The diagnostic approach of Robin Marks[1] presented here helps to achieve order in the midst of confusion. He describes the importance of simplifying the diagnostic process by being a 'lumper' rather than a 'splitter'. Most common dermatological problems fall into one of seven categories (Table 91.1). A problem that does not fit into one of these seven groups is either an unusual condition or an unusual presentation of a common condition and probably merits a consultant's opinion.

Table 91.1 *Common dermatological conditions*

Infections		
	bacterial	• impetigo
	viral	• warts
		• herpes simplex, herpes zoster
		• exanthemata
	fungal	• tinea
		• candidiasis
Acne		
Psoriasis		
Atopic dermatitis (eczema)		
Urticaria		
	acute and chronic	
	papular	• pediculosis
		• scabies
		• insect bites
Sun-related skin cancer		
Drug-related eruptions		

History

The three basic questions are:[1]

1. Where is the rash and where did it start?
2. How long have you had the rash?

   The split into three time zone groups (Table 91.2) is very useful. This question leads onto the next question regarding itch, as the patient is unlikely to tolerate an itchy eruption.
3. Is the rash itchy?

   If so, is it mild, moderate or severe? The nature of the itch is very helpful diagnostically. A severe itch is one that wakes the patient at night and leads to marked excoriation of the skin, while a mild itch is one that is only slightly upsetting for the patient and may not be noticeable for significant periods during the day.

Further questions

Do you have contact with a person with a similar eruption?
What medicines are you taking or have taken recently?
Have you worn any new clothing recently?
Have you been exposed to anything different recently?

Table 91.2 *How long has the rash been present?*

Acute (hours-days)	urticaria atopic dermatitis (allergic contact dermatitis particularly) insect bites drugs herpes viral exanthemata
Acute → chronic (days-weeks)	atopic dermatitis impetigo scabies pediculosis drugs pityriasis rosea psoriasis tinea candida
Chronic (weeks-months)	psoriasis atopic dermatitis tinea warts cancers skin infiltrations (such as granulomata, xanthomata)

Do you have a past history of a similar rash or eczema?
Do you have an allergic tendency? Asthma, hay fever?
Is there a family history of skin problems?

The nature of itching[1]

The characteristics of the itch are very useful in dividing up the diagnoses: an eruption that is not itchy is unlikely to be scabies and one that is very itchy is unlikely to be a skin tumour (Table 91.3).

However, nothing is absolute and variations to the rule will occur; for example, tinea, psoriasis and pityriasis versicolor are sometimes itchy and sometimes not. Chickenpox can vary from being intensely itchy, especially in adults, to virtually no itching.

Relieving or aggravating factors of the itch provide useful diagnostic guidelines; for example, Whitfield's ointment applied to an itchy eruption for a provisional diagnosis of ringworm would make the itch worse if it were due to eczema.

Physical examination[1]

There are two basic stages in the physical examination of a rash. The first is an assessment of the characteristics of the individual lesion and the second is the distribution or pattern of the lesions.

Table 91.3 *Is the rash itchy?*

Very	urticaria atopic dermatitis scabies, pediculosis insect bites chickenpox (adults) dermatitis herpetiformis
Mild to moderate	tinea psoriasis drugs pityriasis rosea candida stress itching/lichen simplex
Often not	warts, tinea impetigo, psoriasis cancers viral exanthemata seborrhoeic dermatitis

Characteristics of the individual lesion

The single most important discriminating feature is whether it involves the dermis alone or the epidermis as well (Table 91.4). If the lesion involves the epidermis there will be scaling, crusting, weeping, vesiculation or a combination of these (Fig. 91.5). The epidermal disorders are known as papulosquamous diseases. If the dermis alone is involved the lesion is by definition a lump, a papule or a nodule (Fig. 91.6). Characteristic features are non-scaly macules, papules or plaques. No lesion ever involves the epidermis without involving the dermis as well.

Table 91.4 *Appearance of individual lesions*

Epidermal	atopic dermatitis psoriasis tinea pityriasis rosea impetigo, herpes, warts cancers scabies solar keratoses
Dermal	urticaria insect bites, pediculosis, scabies drugs skin infiltrations viral exanthemata

Other characteristics of individual lesions which must be sought are the colour, the shape and the size. It is important to feel the skin during the physical examination and to note the consistency of the lesion (is it firm or soft?). The activity of the lesion may also be useful: does it have a clearing centre and an active edge?

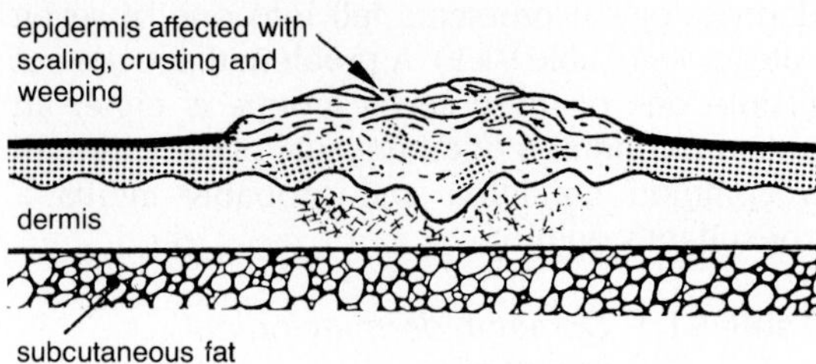

Fig. 91.5 *Epidermal skin lesion*

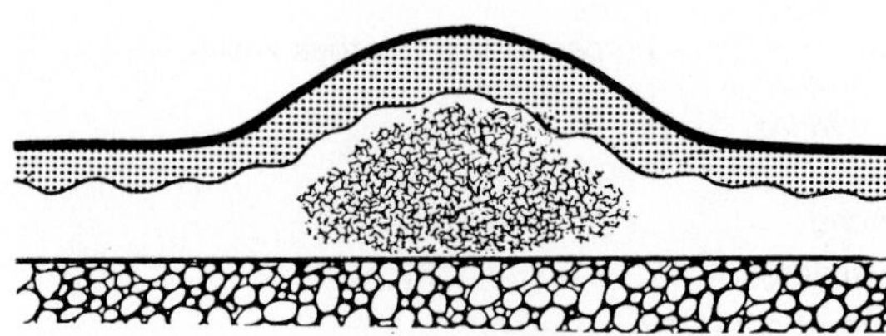

Fig. 91.6 *Dermal skin lesion*

Distribution of the lesions

The clinician must decide whether the lesions are localised or widespread. If they are widespread, are they distributed centrally, peripherally, or both? (Table 91.5). Diagnosis is often helped when the skin lesions are in a specific area (Table 91.6 and Figs 91.7 and 91.8). Itchy papules on the penis associated with a widespread pruritus is likely to be scabies. However, care has to be taken because many misdiagnoses are made instinctively on the distribution, e.g. anything in the flexures is dermatitis or anything on the feet is tinea.

Table 91.5 *Distribution of the rash*

Widespread	atopic dermatitis psoriasis scabies drugs urticaria
Central trunk	tinea versicolor pityriasis rosea herpes zoster viral exanthemata
Peripheral	atopic dermatitis tinea psoriasis warts insect bites

Another feature of an eruption which should be sought on examination is whether the lesions are all at the same stage of evolution.

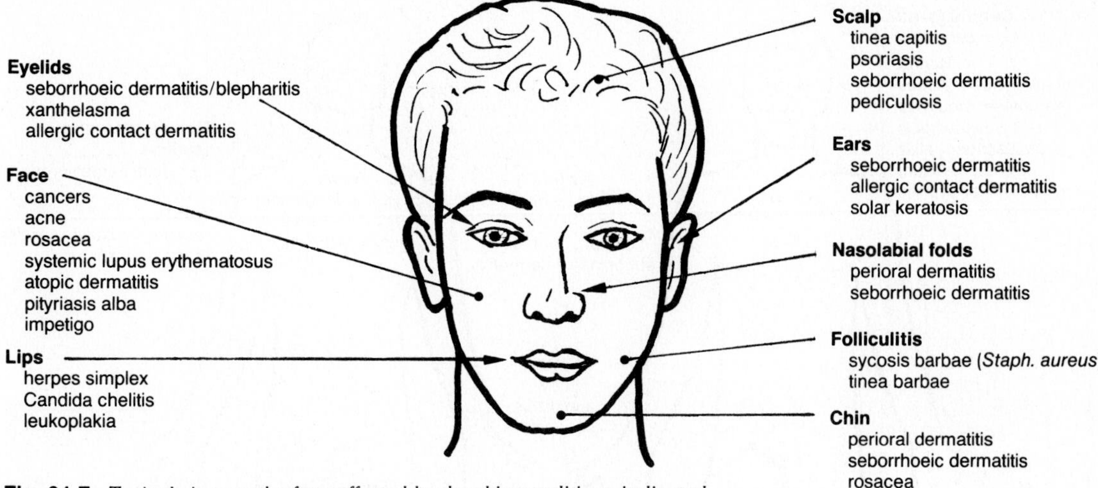

Fig. 91.7 *Typical sites on the face affected by the skin conditions indicated*

Table 91.6 *Specific areas affected*

Face	impetigo atopic dermatitis psoriasis photosensitive, e.g. drugs herpes simplex acne cancers viral exanthemata
Scalp	psoriasis seborrhoeic dermatitis pediculosis tinea chickenpox
Flexures	atopic dermatitis psoriasis seborrhoeic dermatitis tinea candida pediculosis
Mouth	aphthous ulcers herpes simplex candida measles
Nails	psoriasis tinea
Penis	scabies

Tables 1 to 6 have been prepared by Dr Robin Marks[1] and are reproduced with his permission.

It is necessary to perform a complete physical examination as well. There is after all no such thing as a skin disease but rather disease affecting the skin. The clinician must always bear this in mind when managing patients complaining of a skin eruption. Disease does not affect the skin in isolation and it is unforgivable to look only at the skin and ignore the patient as a whole.

Diagnostic tools

Appropriate diagnostic tools include:

- a magnifying lens
- a diascope, which is a glass slide or clear plastic spoon that is used to blanch vascular lesions in order to determine their true colour
- a 'maggylamp', which is a hand-held fluorescent light with an incorporated magnifier; it allows shadow-free lighting and magnification
- a dermatoscope—very valuable in the diagnosis of pigmented tumours but it does require skill and familiarity to achieve effective use
- Wood's light

Office tests and diagnostic aids

Wood's light

Wood's light examination is an important diagnostic aid for skin problems in general practice. It has other uses, such as examination of the eye after fluorescein staining. (A new, low-cost, small ultraviolet light unit called 'the black light' is available.)

Method

Simply hold the ultraviolet light unit above the area for investigation in a dark room.

Limitations of Wood's light in diagnosis

Not all cases of tinea capitis fluoresce, because some species that cause the condition do not produce porphyrins as a by-product. See Table

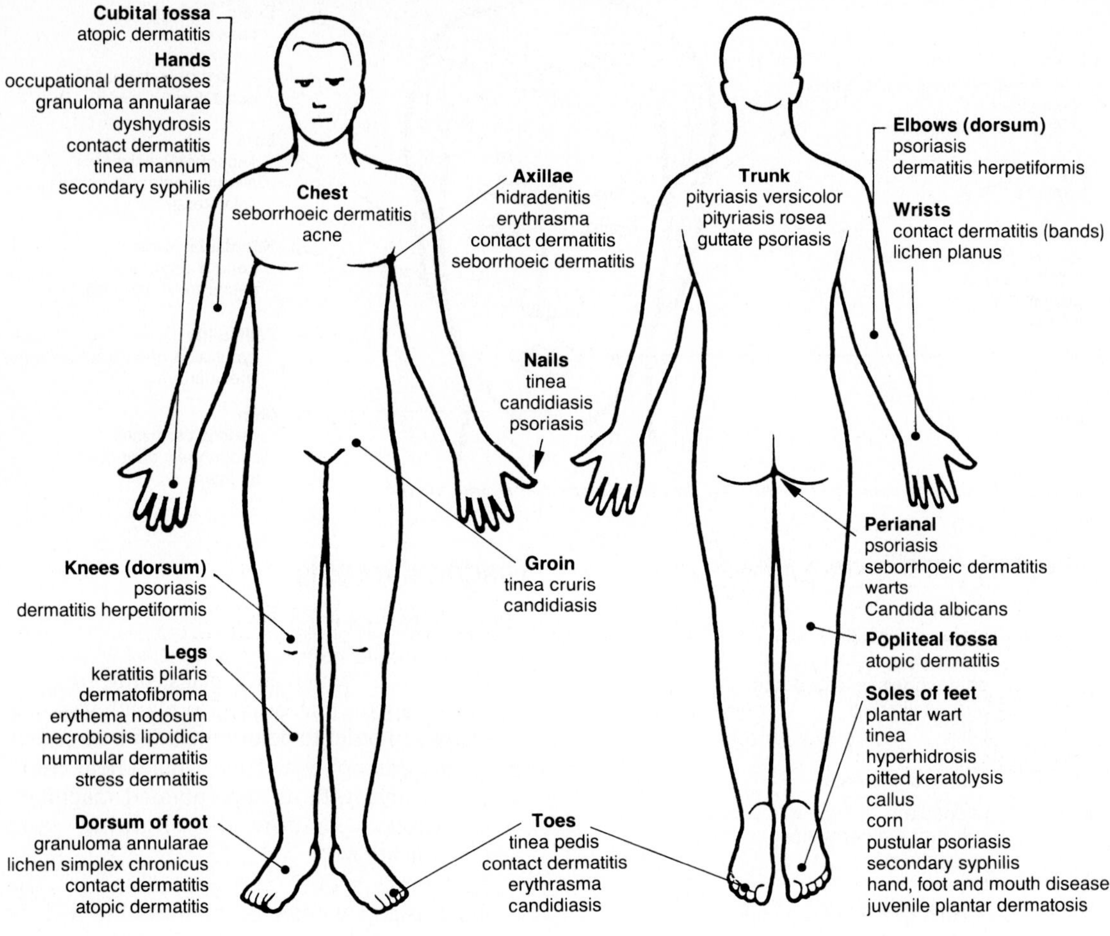

Fig. 91.8 *Typical regional location of various skin conditions*

91.7 for a list of the skin conditions that do fluoresce. Wood's light is really only useful for hair-bearing areas.

Table 91.7 *Skin conditions that produce fluorescence in Wood's light*

Tinea capitis	green
Erythrasma	coral pink
Pityriasis versicolor	pink-gold
Pseudomonas pyocyanea	yellowish-green
Porphyria cutanea tarda	red (urine)
Squamous cell carcinoma	bright red

Porphyrins wash off with soap and water, and a negative result may occur in a patient who has shampooed the hair within 20 hours of presentation. Consequently, a negative Wood's light reading may be misleading. The appropriate way of confirming the clinical diagnosis is to send specimens of hair and skin for microscopy and culture.

Skin scrapings for dermatophyte diagnosis

Skin scrapings is an excellent adjunct to diagnosis of fungal infections. Requirements are a scalpel blade, glass slide and cover slip, 20% potassium hydroxide (preferably in dimethylsulfoxide) and a microscope.

Method

- Scrape skin from the active edge.
- Scoop the scrapings onto the glass microscope slide.
- Cover the sample with a drop of potassium hydroxide.

- Cover this with a cover slip and press down gently.
- Warm the slide and wait at least five minutes for 'clearing'.

Microscopic examination

- Examine at first under low power with reduced light.
- When fungal hyphae are located, change to high power.
- Use the fine focus to highlight the hyphae (Fig. 91.9).

Note Some practice is necessary to recognise hyphae.

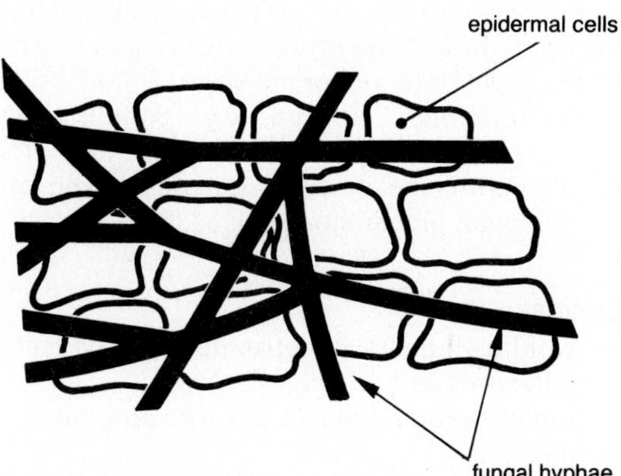

Fig. 91.9 *Diagrammatic representation of microscopic appearance of fungal hyphae*

Other uses of microscopy

Detection of the scabies mite: the burrow of the scabies mite is found (can be difficult!) and the epidermis is decisively scraped with a No. 15 scalpel blade, and transferred to a slide after adding a drop of liquid paraffin. The mite is very distinctive.

Patch testing

Patch testing is used to determine allergens in allergic contact dermatitis.

Biopsies

Punch or shave biopsies can be useful (see Figs 96.10 and 96.11).

Hair

Send hair samples for microscopy and root analysis.

Terminology of topical skin preparations

Bases or vehicles are a mixture of powders, water and greases (usually obtained from petroleum). The relative blending of these compounds determines the nature of the base, e.g. lotion, cream, ointment, gel or paste.

An *emollient* is a topical agent that is softening or soothing to the skin. It also acts as a skin moisturiser and is therefore used on dry skin or dermatoses related to dry skin, e.g. atopic dermatitis. Examples are:

- mineral oil
- white petrolatum (Vaseline)

An *astringent* is a topical agent that has styptic or binding properties with an ability to stop secretions from skin or tissues. An example is aluminium acetate solution (Burow's solution); the aluminium acetate acts as a protein precipitator and is a very effective soothing agent and antipruritic.

A *keratolytic* is an agent that softens or breaks up keratin. Examples are:

- urea 10%: for xerosis or keratosis pilaris
- urea 20%: cracked palms and soles
- salicylic acid 4–10%

An *antipruritic* agent is one that relieves itching. Examples are:

- menthol (0.25%)
- phenol (0.5%)
- coal tar solution (2–10%)
- camphor (1 or 2%).

A *lotion* is a suspension of an insoluble powder in water. Modern lotions use an emulsifying agent, which eliminates the need to shake the lotion. An example is calamine lotion (zinc oxide 5, calamine 15, glycerine 5, water to 100).

Paints and *tinctures* are rapidly drying liquid preparations which are very useful for intertriginous areas, especially between the toes and natal cleft. 'Tincture' is the preparation when alcohol is the vehicle. Example: podophyllin in tinct benz co (for genital warts).

Cream is a suspension of a powder in an emulsion of oil and water.

Ointment is a suspension of a substance in an oily vehicle.

Gels are substances with a greaseless, water-miscible base.

Pastes are similar to ointments in composition but are more viscid. They consist of an ointment to which another agent such as starch has been added.

Emulsions are mixtures of two immiscible liquids, one being dispersed throughout the other in small droplets.

Table 91.8 gives guidelines for choosing a topical vehicle.

Table 91.8 *Guidelines for choosing a topical vehicle*

Disorder	Topical vehicle
Acute inflammation: erythema, weeping	wet dressing solution lotions
Subacute inflammation: erythema, scaling	creams gels
Chronic inflammation: scaling, dryness, thickening	ointments impregnated tapes

Traditional chemicals used in extemporaneous preparations[2]

Salicylic acid: produces painless destruction of epithelium, thereby facilitating absorption. Consider its use for psoriasis, neurodermatitis, tinea of palms and feet, seborrhoeic dermatitis.

Resorcinol: a topical keratolytic with bactericidal and fungicidal properties. Consider its use for psoriasis, acne, rosacea, seborrhoeic dermatitis.

Tar: the three commonly found tar preparations are used for their anti-inflammatory, soothing and antimitotic properties. Consider their use for psoriasis, atopic dermatitis, seborrhoeic dermatitis and neurodermatitis.

Menthol and *phenol*: added to various preparations for their soothing and cooling effects. Consider for use in pruritic problems such as varicella, urticaria and atopic dermatitis.

Sulphur: of benefit in dermatoses, due mainly to its keratolytic properties. The other actions of sulphur are scabicidal, parasiticidal and fungicidal. Consider its use for acne, rosacea, seborrhoeic dermatitis, psoriasis and tinea.

Selection of corticosteroid preparations

- Class I and class II preparations are appropriate for most problems.
- Creams or lotions are used for 'weeping' lesions, the face, flexures and hair-bearing areas.
- Use ointments for dry and scaly skin.
- Use ointments and occlusive vehicles for dry and chronic skin surfaces.
- Ointments should not be used on weeping surfaces.
- Stubborn dermatoses such as hand eczema and psoriasis respond better to preparations under occlusion, such as plastic wrap applied overnight with appropriate securing in place.
- Use a gel or lotion for the scalp.
- For *Candida* infection, e.g. complicating seborrhoeic napkin dermatitis, mix 1% hydrocortisone in equal quantities with an antifungal preparation such as nystatin.

Cautions

- Avoid high-potency preparations on the face, in flexures and on infants.
- Corticosteroids can mask or prolong an infection.
- Long-term use can cause striae and skin atrophy, perioral dermatitis, 'steroid acne' and rosacea.
- Excessive use of more potent preparations can cause adrenal suppression; predispositions include use > 2 weeks, and use on thinner skin such as face, genitalia and intertriginous areas.
- Avoid sudden cessation: alternate with an emollient or a milder preparation.

The relative clinical potency of topical corticosteroids is given in Table 91.9.

Skin tips

- Do no harm. Introduce the mildest possible preparation to alleviate the problem.
- Creams tend to be drying.
- Ointments tend to reduce dryness and have greater skin penetration. If wet—use a wet dressing (wet soaks and a lotion). If dry—use an ointment (salve).
- Occlusive dressings with plastic wraps permit more rapid resolution of stubborn dermatoses.

Table 91.9 *Relative clinical potency of topical corticosteroids*

Mild (class I)
Hydrocortisone 0.1-1%
Moderate (class II)
Alcometasone dipropionate 0.05%
Betamethasone valerate 0.02-0.05%
Fluocortolone pivalate/hexanoate 0.25%
Triamcinolone 0.02-0.05%
Potent (class III)
Betamethasone dipropionate 0.05%
Betamethasone valerate 0.1%
Fluclorolone acetonide 0.025%
Flucinolone acotonide 0.025%
Fluocortolone pivalate/dexonate 0.5%
Halcinonide 0.1%
Very potent (class IV)
Halobetasol propionate 0.05% (USA)
Clobetasol propionate 0.05%

- Most toilet soaps use alkaline and are very drying; they should not be used on dry skin or dermatitis with dry skin. Soap substitutes include neutral soaps (Dove, Neutrogena), superfatted soaps (Oilatum) and non-soap cleanser (Cetaphil).
- Bath additives can be useful for dermatoses such as psoriasis, atopic dermatitis and for pruritus. For some people it may be better not to add it to the bath (diluting effect; accident from slipping) but to massage the oil into the dry itchy skin after the bath.
- Always give careful instructions to the patient regarding application of preparations: use a prepared handout if available.
- Alter the treatment according to the response.
- Explain the costs involved, especially where a preparation is expensive.

Rules for prescribing creams and ointments

How much cream?[3]

On average, 30 g of cream will cover the body surface area of an adult. Ointments, despite being of thicker consistency, do not penetrate into the deeper skin layers so readily, and the requirements are slightly less. Pastes are applied thickly, and the requirements are at least three to four times as great as for creams.

The 'rule of nines', used routinely to determine the percentage of body surface area affected by burns (Fig. 91.10), may also be used to calculate the amount of a topical preparation that needs to be prescribed.

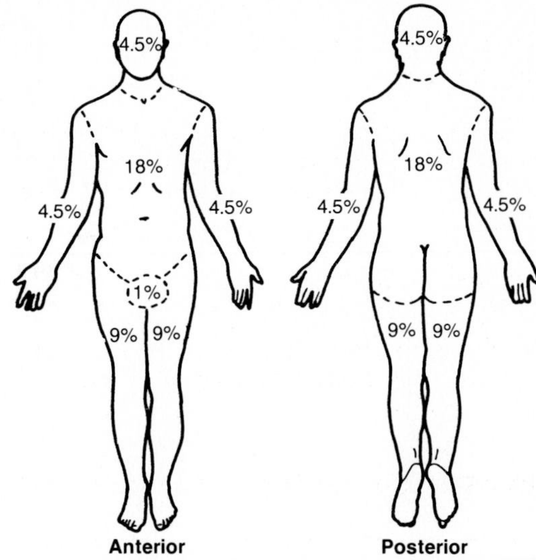

Fig. 91.10 *'Rule of nines' for body surface area*

For example:

- if 9% of the body surface area is affected by eczema, approximately 3 g of cream is required to cover it
- 9 g of cream is used per day if prescribed three times daily
- a 50 g tube will last 5–6 days

One gram of cream will cover an area approximately 10 cm × 10 cm (4 square inches), and this formula may be used for smaller lesions.

Some general rules

Remember:

1. to use cream or lotions for acute rashes
2. to use ointments for chronic scaling rashes
3. that a thin smear only is necessary
4. that 30 g
   - will cover the adult body once
   - will cover hands twice daily for two weeks
   - will cover a patchy rash twice daily for one week
5. that 200 g will cover a quite severe rash twice daily for two weeks

References

1. Marks R. A diagnostic approach to common dermatological problems. Aust Fam Physician, 1982, 11:696–702.
2. Kelly B. Extemporaneous preparations. Aust Fam Physician, 1993; 22:842–844.
3. Gambrill J. How much cream? Aust Fam Physician, 1982; 11:350.

92

Pruritus

Pruritus (the Latin word for itch) is defined simply as the desire to scratch.

It is one of the most important dermatological symptoms and is usually a symptom of primary skin disease with a visible rash. However, it is a subjective symptom and diagnostic difficulties arise when pruritus is the presenting symptom of a systemic disease with or without a rash. An associated rash may also be a manifestation of the underlying disease.

The broad differential diagnoses of pruritus are:

- skin disease
- systemic disease
- psychological and emotional disorders

Physiology[1]

Itch arises from the same nerve pathway as pain, but pain and itch are distinct sensations. The difference is in the intensity of the stimulus. Unrelieved chronic itch, like unrelieved pain, can be intolerable and cause suicide. There are many similarities: both are abolished by analgesia and anaesthesia; subdued by counter-irritation, cold, heat and vibration; and referred itch occurs just like referred pain. Antihistamines which act on the HI receptor are often ineffective, suggesting that histamine is not the only mediator of itch.[1]

Localised pruritus

Pruritus may be either localised or generalised. Localised itching is generally caused by common skin conditions such as atopic dermatitis (Table 92.1). Scratch marks are generally presented. Pruritus is a feature of dry skin. An intense localised itch is suggestive of scabies, also known as 'the itch'.

Itching of the anal and vulval areas is a common presentation in general practice.

Table 92.1 *Primary skin disorders causing significant pruritus*

Atopic dermatitis (eczema)
Urticaria
Dermatitis herpetiformis
Scabies
Pediculosis
Asteatosis (dry skin)
Lichen planus
Chickenpox
Contact dermatitis
Insect bites

A careful examination is necessary to exclude primary skin disease; a detailed history and examination should be undertaken to determine if one of the various systemic diseases is responsible.

The history may provide a lead to the diagnosis; for example, the itching of polycythaemia may be triggered by a hot bath which can cause an unusual prickling quality that lasts for about an hour.[2] On the other hand the itching may be caused by a primary irritant such as a 'bubble bath' preparation.

Generalised pruritus

Pruritus may be a manifestation of systemic disease. It can accompany pregnancy, especially towards the end of the third trimester (beware of cholestasis), and disappear after childbirth. These women are then prone to pruritus if they take the contraceptive pill.[3]

Systemic causes are summarised in Table 92.2 and a summary of the diagnostic strategy model is given in Table 92.3.

Table 92.2 *Systemic conditions that can cause pruritus*

Pregnancy

Chronic renal failure

Liver disorders:
- cholestatic jaundice, e.g. carcinoma of head of pancreas
  - primary biliary cirrhosis
  - drugs: chlorpromazine, antibiotics
- hepatic failure

Malignancy
- lymphoma: Hodgkin's disease
- leukaemia, esp. chronic lymphatic leukaemia
- disseminated carcinoma

Haematological disorders
- polycythaemia rubra vera
- iron deficiency anaemia
- pernicious anaemia (rare)

Endocrine disorders
- diabetes mellitus
- hypothyroidism
- hyperthyroidism
- carcinoid syndrome
- hyperparathyroidism

Malabsorption syndrome
- gluten sensitivity (rare)

Tropical infection/intestinal parasites
- filariasis
- hookworm

Drugs
- alkaloids
- opiates, cocaine
- quinidine
- chloroquine
- CNS stimulants

Senile pruritus

Polyarteritis nodosa

Irritants
- fibreglass
- others

Psychological and emotional causes
- anxiety/depression
- psychosis
- parasitophobia

Table 92.3 *Generalised pruritus: diagnostic strategy model*

Q. *Probability diagnosis*
A. Psychological/emotional[3]
Old dry skin

Q. *Serious disorders not to be missed*
A. Neoplasia
- lymphoma/Hodgkin's
- leukaemia: CLL
- other carcinoma

Chronic renal failure
Primary biliary cirrhosis

Q. *Pitfalls*
A. Pregnancy
Tropical infection/infestation
Polycythaemia
Generalised sensitivity, e.g. fibre glass, bubble bath

Q. *Seven masquerades checklist*
A.

Depression	✓	
Diabetes	✓	
Drugs	✓	
Anaemia	✓	iron deficiency
Thyroid	✓	hyper and hypo
Spinal dysfunction	—	
UTI	—	

Q. *Is the patient trying to tell me something?*
A. Quite likely: consider anxiety, parasitophobia.

Guidelines

- The prevalence of itching in Hodgkin's disease is about 30%. The skin often looks normal but the patient will claim that the itch is unbearable.[2]
- Pruritus can be the presenting symptoms of primary biliary cirrhosis and may precede other symptoms by 1–2 years.[3] The itch is usually most marked on the palms and soles.
- Pruritus can occur in both hyperthyroidism and hypothyroidism, especially in hypothyroidism where it is associated with the dry skin.

Investigations to consider

- urinalysis
- pregnancy test
- FBE and ESR
- renal function tests
- liver function tests
- random blood sugar
- stool examination (ova and cysts)
- chest X-ray
- lymph node biopsy (if present)
- immunological tests for primary biliary cirrhosis

Treatment

The basic principle of treatment is to determine the cause of the itch and treat it accordingly. Itch of psychogenic origin responds to appropriate therapy, such as amitriptyline for depression.[1]

If no cause is found:

- apply cooling measures, e.g. air-conditioning, cool swims
- avoid rough clothes
- avoid known irritants
- avoid overheating
- avoid vasodilatation, e.g. alcohol, hot baths/ showers
- treat dry skin with appropriate moisturisers, e.g. propylene glycol in aqueous cream
- topical treatment
  — emollients to lubricate skin
  — local soothing lotion such as calamine, including menthol or phenol (avoid topical antihistamines)
- sedative antihistamines (not very effective for systemic pruritus)
- non-sedating antihistamines during day
- antidepressants or tranquillisers (if psychological cause)

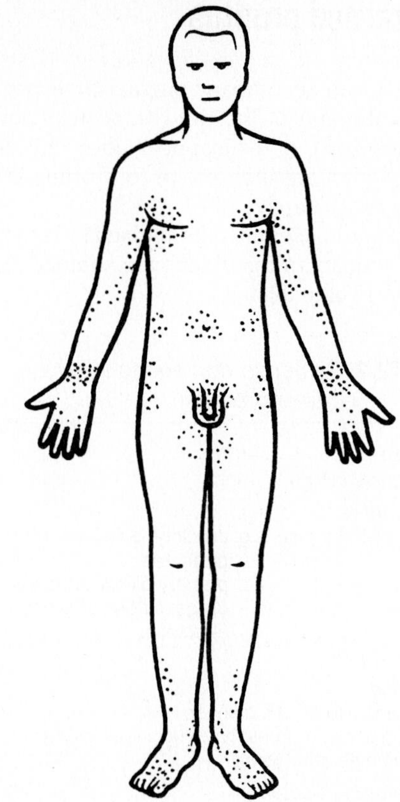

Fig. 92.1 *Typical distribution of the scabies rash*

Pruritic skin conditions

Scabies

Scabies is a highly infectious skin infestation caused by a tiny mite called *Sarcoptes scabiei.* The female mite burrows just beneath the skin in order to lay her eggs. She then dies. The eggs hatch into tiny mites, which spread out over the skin and live for only about 30 days. The excreta of the mites cause an allergic rash.

Clinical features

- intense itching (worse with warmth and at night)
- erythematous papular rash
- usually on hands and wrists
- common on male genitalia (see Chap. 90)
- also occurs on elbows, axillae, feet and ankles, nipples of females (Fig. 92.1)

Spread

The mites are spread from person to person through close personal contact (skin to skin), including sexual contact. They may also be spread through contact with infested clothes or bedding, although this is uncommon. Sometimes the whole family can get scabies. The spread is more likely with overcrowding and sexual promiscuity.

Treatment

Adults: lindane (gamma benzene hexachloride) 1% lotion

Children and pregnant women: benzyl benzoate 25% solution

Apply to the entire body from the jawline down (including under nails, in flexures and genitals), leave for 24 hours, then wash off thoroughly. Wash clothing and linen after treatment as usual in hot water. One treatment is usually sufficient. The whole family must be treated at the same time even if they do not have the itch.

Dermatitis herpetiformis

This extremely itchy condition is a chronic subepidermal vesicular condition in which the herpes simplex-like vesicles erupt at the dermoepidermal junction. The vesicles are so pruritic that it is unusual to see an intact one on presentation.

Some consider that it is always caused by a gluten-sensitive enteropathy. Most patients do have clinical coeliac disease.

Clinical features

- most common in young adults
- vesicles mainly over elbows and knees (extensor surfaces)
- also occurs on trunk, especially buttocks and shoulders (Fig. 92.2)
- vesicles rarely seen by doctors
- presents as excoriation with eczematous changes
- masquerades as scabies, excoriated eczema or insect bites
- typically lasts for decades
- associated with gluten-sensitive enteropathy
- skin biopsy shows diagnostic features

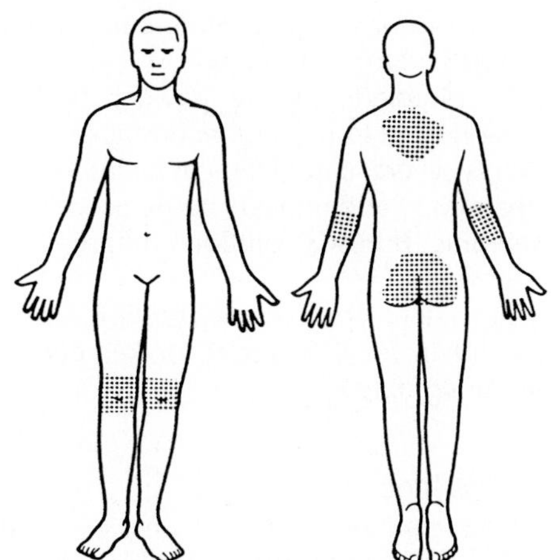

Fig. 92.2 *Typical distribution of dermatitis herpetiformis*

Treatment

- gluten-free diet
- dapsone (usually dramatic response)

Lichen planus

Lichen planus is an epidermal inflammatory disorder of unknown aetiology characterised by pruritic violaceous flat-tipped papules, mainly on the wrists and legs.

Clinical features

- young and middle-aged adults
- small, shiny, lichenified plaques
- symmetrical and flat-tipped
- violaceous
- flexor surfaces: wrists, forearms, ankles
- can affect oral mucosa—white streaks or papules or ulcers
- can affect nails and scalp

Management

- explanation and reassurance
- usually resolves over months, leaving discoloured marks without scarring
- recurrence rare
- asymptomatic lesions require no treatment
- topical moderately potent corticosteroids (may use occlusive dressing)
- intralesional corticosteroids for hypertrophic lesions

Pruritus ani

The generalised disorders causing pruritus may cause pruritus ani. However, various primary skin disorders such as psoriasis, dermatitis, contact dermatitis and lichen planus may also cause it, in addition to local anal conditions. It is covered in more detail in Chapter 30.

Pruritus vulvae

Causes of an itchy vulva to consider are:

- candidiasis (rash, cottage cheese discharge)
  - broad spectrum antibiotics
  - diabetes mellitus
  - contraceptive pill
- poor hygiene and excessive sweating
- tight clothing
- sensitivity to soaps, cosmetics and contraceptive agents
- overzealous washing
- local skin conditions
  - psoriasis
  - dermatitis/eczema (uncommon cause)
- post anal conditions, e.g. haemorrhoids
- infestations
  - threadworms (children)
  - scabies
  - pediculosis pubis
- infections
  - trichomonas
  - urinary tract infection
  - genital herpes
- menopause: due to oestrogen deficiency
- topical antihistamines
- vulval carcinoma
- psychological disorder, e.g. psychosexual problem, STD phobia

Treatment is according to the causation.

Jock itch

Jock itch is a term used to describe a common infection of the groin area in young men, usually athletes, that is commonly caused by a tinea infection, although there are other causes of a groin rash (Table 92.4). The dermatophytes responsible for tinea cruris (Dhobie itch) are *Trichophyton rubrum* (60%), *Epidermophyton floccosum* (30%) and *Trichophyton mentagrophytes*.[4] The organisms thrive in damp, warm, dark sites. The feet should be inspected for evidence of tinea pedis. It is transmitted by towels and other objects, particularly in locker rooms, saunas and communal showers.

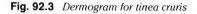

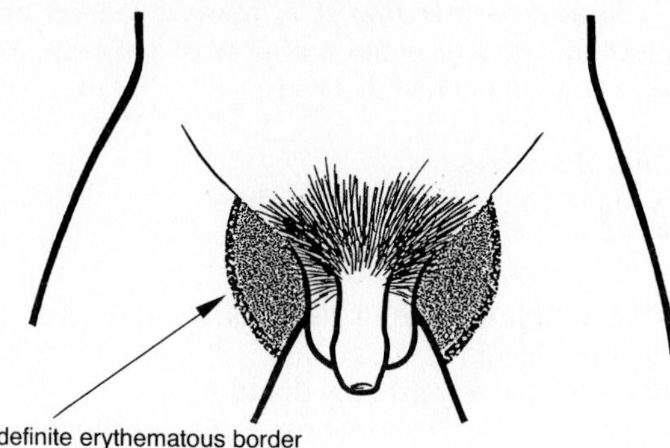

Fig. 92.3 *Dermogram for tinea cruris*

Table 92.4 *Common causes of a groin rash (intertrigo)*

Simple intertrigo
Skin disorders
• psoriasis
• seborrhoeic dermatitis
• dermatitis/eczema
Fungal
• candida
• tinea
Erythrasma
Contact dermatitis

Clinical features of tinea cruris

- itchy rash
- more common in young males
- strong association with tinea pedis (athlete's foot)
- usually acute onset
- more common in hot months—a summer disease
- more common in physically active people
- related to chafing in groin, e.g. tight pants, and especially nylon 'jock straps'
- scaling, especially at margin
- well-defined border (Fig. 92.3)

If left untreated the rash may spread, especially to the inner upper thighs, while the scrotum is usually spared. Spread to the buttocks indicates *T.rubrum infection.*

Diagnostic aids

- Skin scrapings should be taken from the scaly area for preparation for microscopy (see page 853).
- Wood's light may help the diagnosis, particularly if erythrasma is suspected.

Management of tinea cruris

- Soak the area in a warm bath and dry thoroughly.
- Apply an imidazole topical preparation, e.g. miconazole or clotrimazole cream; rub in a thin layer bd for 3–4 weeks.
- Apply tolnaftate dusting powder bd when almost healed to prevent recurrence.
- If itch is severe, a mild topical hydrocortisone preparation (additional) can be used.[4]
- If weeping: Burow's solution compresses dry the area.
- For persistent or recurrent eruption, use oral griseofulvin for 6–8 weeks, or ketoconazole (but more toxic).

Candida intertrigo

Candida albicans superinfects a simple intertrigo and tends to affect obese or bedridden patients, especially if incontinent.[5]

Clinical features

- occurs equally in men and women
- erythematous scaly rash in groin
- less well-defined margin than tinea (Fig. 92.4)
- associated satellite lesions
- yeast may be seen on microscopy

Treatment

- Treat underlying problem.
- Apply an imidazole preparation such as miconazole or clotrimazole.
- Use Burow's solution compresses to dry a weeping area.
- Use short-term hydrocortisone cream for itch or inflammation (long-term aggravates the problem).

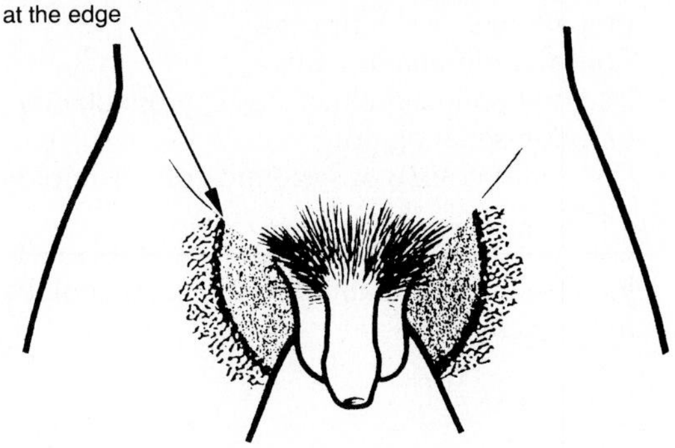

indefinite border with satellite macular lesions at the edge

Fig. 92.4 *Dermogram for candidiasis of crural area*

Erythrasma

Erythrasma, a common and widespread chronic superficial skin infection, is caused by the bacterium *Corynebacterium minutissimum*, which can be diagnosed by coral pink fluorescence on Wood's light examination. Itch is not a feature.

Clinical features

- superficial reddish-brown scaly patches
- enlarges peripherally
- mild infection but tends to chronicity if untreated
- coral pink fluorescence with Wood's light
- common sites: groin, axillae, submammary, toe webs (Fig. 92.5)

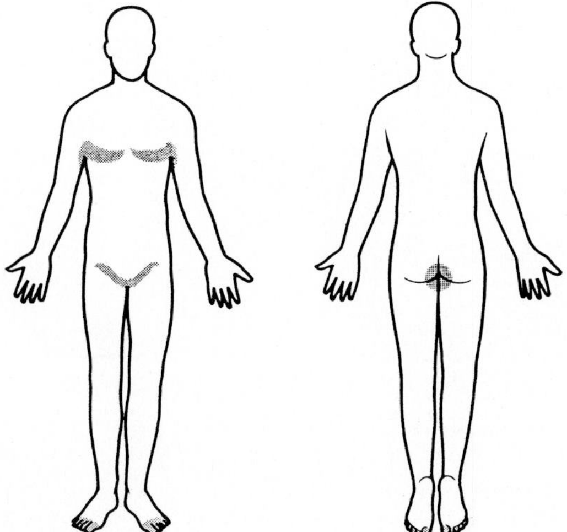

Fig. 92.5 *Typical sites of erythrasma*

Treatment

- erythromycin or tetracycline (oral)
- topical imidazole

Asteatotic eczema (winter itch)

This often unrecognised problem, which can be very itchy, is a disorder of the elderly. It is a form of eczema that typically occurs on the legs of the elderly, especially if they are subjected to considerable scrubbing and bathing. Other predisposing factors include the low humidity (winter, central heating) and diuretics. The problem may be part of a malabsorption state.

Clinical features

- dry skin
- fine scaling and red superficial cracking
- 'crazy paving' appearance
- occurs on legs, especially shins
- also occurs on thighs, arms and trunk

Treatment

- avoid scrubbing with soaps
- use aqueous cream and a soap substitute
- apply topical steroid diluted in white soft paraffin

Lichen simplex

Lichenification is a form of dermatitis caused by repeated scratching or rubbing, which results in epidermal thickening. Lichen simplex is the term used when no primary dermatological cause can be found.

Urticaria

Urticaria is a common condition that mainly affects the dermis. It can be classified as acute (minutes to weeks) or chronic (lasting more than two months).

The three characteristic features are:

- transient erythema
- transient oedema
- transient itch

Classification according to site

1. *Superficial*: affecting superficial dermis = urticaria; occurs anywhere on body, especially the limbs and trunk.
2. *Deep*: affecting subcutaneous tissue = angio-oedema; occurs anywhere but especially periorbital region, lips and neck.

Checklist of causes[3]

- Allergies (acute allergic urticaria is dramatic and potentially very serious)
  - azo dyes
  - drugs: penicillin and other antibiotics
  - foods: eggs, fish, cheese, others
  - infections: bacteria, parasites, protozoa, yeasts
- Pharmacological
  - drugs: penicillin, aspirin, codeine
  - foods: fish, shellfish, nuts, strawberries, artificial food colourings
  - plants: nettles, others
- Systemic lupus erythematosus
- Physical
  - cholinergic: response to sweating induced by exercise and heat, e.g. young athletes
  - heat, cold, sunlight
- Pregnancy (last trimester)
- Unknown (idiopathic)—80%; possible psychological factors

Investigations

- full blood examination—look for eosinophilia of parasites
- ANF and DNA binding—consider SLE
- challenge tests

Treatment

- Avoid any identifiable causes.
- Avoid salicylates and related food preparations, e.g. tartrazine.
- Consider elimination diets.
- Use oral antihistamines, e.g. cyproheptadine, or a non-sedating drug.
- Give short course of systemic corticosteroids if severe.
- Use topical soothing preparation if relatively localised, e.g. crotamiton 10%, or phenol 1% in oily calamine.

References

1. Walsh TD. *Symptom control.* Oxford: Blackwell Scientific Publications, 1989, 286–294.
2. Hunter JAA, Savin JA, Dahl MV. *Clinical dermatology.* Oxford: Blackwell Scientific Publications, 1989, 216.
3. Fry L et al. *Illustrated encyclopedia of dermatology.* Lancaster: MTP Press, 1981, 313–315 and 485–488.
4. Gin D. Tinea infection. In: MIMS Disease Index. Sydney: IMS Publishing, 1991–92, 545–547.
5. Cowen P. Intertrigo of the groin and toes. Aust Fam Physician, 1988; 17:947–948.

93

Common skin problems

Skin disorders are very common in general practice. According to Fry, 13% of the population (UK)[1] will be treated for skin disorders each year with the most common conditions being acute infections, dermatitis (eczema), warts, urticaria, pruritus, acne and psoriasis. According to Bridges-Webb et al[2], 13% of the problems managed in Australian general practice will be skin problems with the most common problems (in order of frequency) being dermatitis/eczema, solar/hyper keratosis, laceration, malignant neoplasm, bruise, skin ulcer, dermatophytosis, boil/carbuncle, naevus, mole and warts.

This chapter will focus on the common dermatoses.

Dermatitis/eczema

The terms 'dermatitis' and 'eczema' are synonymous and denote an inflammatory epidermal rash, acute or chronic, characterised by vesicles (acute stage), redness, weeping, oozing, crusting, scaling and itch.

Dermatitis can be divided into *exogenous* causes (allergic contact and primary irritant) and *endogenous*, which implies all forms of dermatitis not directly related to external causative factors. Endogenous types are atopic, nummular (discoid), dyshydrotic, pityriasis alba, lichen simplex chronicus, seborrhoeic.

The meaning of atopy

The term 'atopic' refers to a hereditary background or tendency to develop one or more of a group of conditions such as allergic rhinitis, asthma, eczema, skin sensitivities and urticaria. It is not synonymous with allergy.

An estimated 10% of the population are atopics with allergic rhinitis being the most common manifestation.[3]

Atopic dermatitis

Features of classical atopic dermatitis:[4]

- itch (often acute or chronic)
- usually a family history of atopy
- about 3% of infants are affected, signs appearing between three months and two years and manifest by five years
- often known trigger factors (Table 93.1) are evident
- lichenification may occur with chronic atopic dermatitis

Criteria for diagnosis

- itch
- typical morphology and distribution
- dry skin
- history of atopy
- chronic relapsing dermatitis

Dryness is a feature—the drier the skin the worse the dermatitis.

Distribution

The typical distribution of atopic dermatitis changes as the patient grows older. In infants the rash appears typically on the cheeks of the face, the folds of the neck and scalp. It may then spread to the limbs and groins. The change from infancy through to adulthood is presented in Figures 93.1a, b, c.

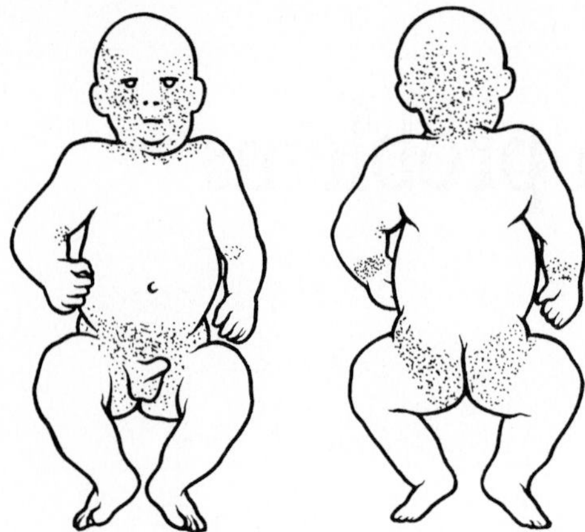

Fig. 93.1a *Relative distribution of atopic dermatitis in infants*

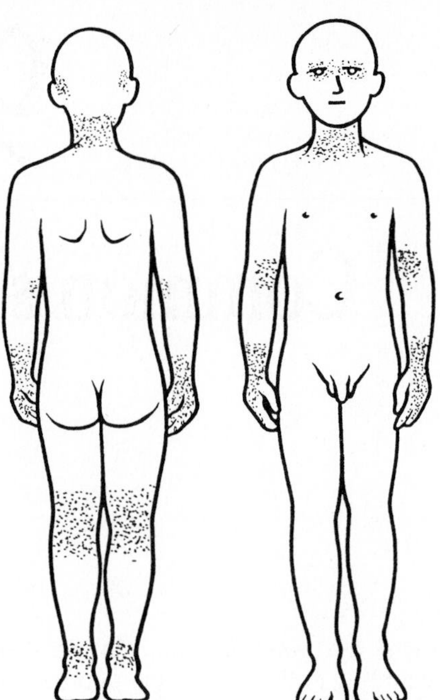

Fig. 93.1b *Atopic dermatitis in children*

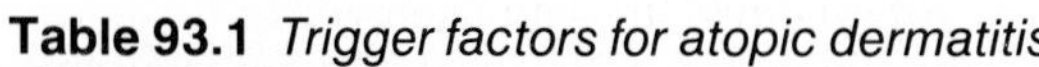

Table 93.1 *Trigger factors for atopic dermatitis*

Sweating: because it is drying
Sand, e.g. sand pits
Extremes of hot and cold
Rapid temperature changes
Soap and water/frequent washing, especially in winter
Chlorinated water
Bubble baths
Infection (viral, bacterial, fungal)
Allergy
Stress/emotional factors
Skin irritants
- wool, e.g. sheepskin covers
- brushed nylon or silk clothing
- chemical disinfectants
- detergents
- petrochemical products
- pollens

Scratching and rubbing
Perfumes
Poor general health
Foodstuffs (consider)
- cow's milk
- beef
- chicken
- nuts
- eggs
- food colourants
- oranges
- wheat

Note The relationship to food is controversial and uncertain. Rash testing is misleading. Consider eliminating the foodstuffs and reintroducing one at a time. If sensitive, the children go bright red a few minutes after feeding.

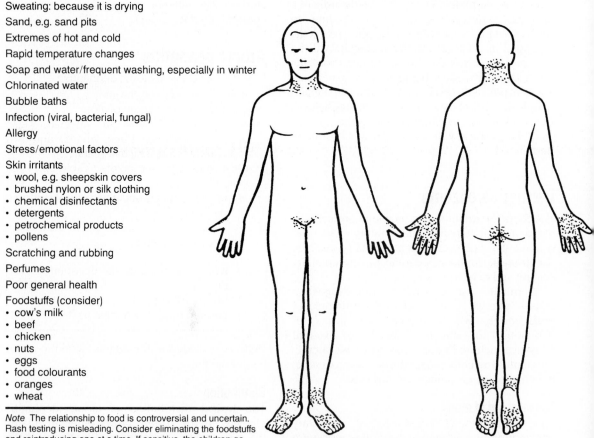

Fig. 93.1c *Atopic dermatitis in adults*

During childhood a drier and thicker rash tends to develop in the cubital and popliteal fossae and on the hands and feet, which may be dry, itchy, fissured and painful.

Prognosis

It is generally correct that children tend to 'grow out of' the problem as the function of their oil and sweat glands matures. The skin becomes less dry, less overheated and irritable.[5] About 60% of patients have virtually normal skin by six years and 90% by puberty.[5]

Treatment

Advice to parents of affected children:

- Avoid soap and perfumed products. Use a bland bath oil in the bath and aqueous cream as a soap substitute.
- Older children should have short, tepid showers.
- Avoid rubbing and scratching—use gauze bandages with hand splints for infants.
- Avoid sudden changes of temperature, especially those that cause sweating.
- Wear light, soft, loose clothes, preferably made of cotton. Cotton clothing should be worn next to the skin.
- Avoid wool next to the skin.
- Avoid dusty conditions and sand, especially sandpits.
- Avoid contact with people with 'sores', especially herpes.

Education and reassurance

Explanation, reassurance and support are very important. Emphasise that atopic dermatitis is a superficial disorder and will not scar or disfigure under normal circumstances. The child should be treated normally in every respect. Counselling is indicated where family stress and psychological factors are contributing to the problem.

Medication

Mild atopic dermatitis

- soap substitutes, such as aqueous cream
- emollients (choose from)
  - aqueous cream
  - sorbolene with 10% glycerol
  - bath oils, e.g. Alpha-Keri
- 1% hydrocortisone (if not responding to above)

Moderate atopic dermatitis

- as for mild
- topical corticosteroids (twice daily)
  - vital for active areas
  - moderate strength, e.g. fluorinated, to trunk and limbs
  - weaker strength, e.g. 1% hydrocortisone, to face and flexures
- oral antihistamines at night for itch

Severe dermatitis

- as for mild and moderate eczema
- potent topical corticosteroids to worse areas (consider occlusive dressings)
- consider hospitalisation
- systemic corticosteroids (rarely used)

Weeping dermatitis (an acute phase)

This often has crusts due to exudate. Burow's solution diluted to 1 in 20 or 1 in 10 can be used to soak affected areas.

General points of dermatitis management

Acute weeping	→	wet dressings (saline or Burow's)
Acute	→	creams
Chronic	→	ointments, with or without occlusion
Lichenified	→	ointments under occlusion

Other types of atopic dermatitis

Nummular (discoid) eczema

- chronic, red, coin-shaped plaques
- crusted, scaling and itchy
- mainly on the legs, also buttocks and trunk
- often symmetrical
- common in middle-aged patients
- may be related to stress
- tends to persist for months

Treatment as for classical atopic dermatitis.

Pityriasis alba

- these are white patches on the face of children and adolescents
- very common mild condition
- more common around the mouth
- can occur on the neck and upper limbs, occasionally on trunk
- it is a subacute form of atopic dermatitis
- full repigmentation occurs eventually

Treatment

- reassurance
- simple emollients
- restrict use of soap and washing
- may prescribe hydrocortisone ointment (rarely necessary)

Lichen simplex chronicus

- circumscribed thick plaques of lichenification
- often a feature of atopic dermatitis
- caused by repeated rubbing and scratching of previously normal skin
- due to chronic itch of unknown cause
- at sites within reach of fingers, e.g. neck, forearms, thighs, vulva, heels, fingers
- may arise from habit

Treatment

- explanation
- refrain from scratching
- fluorinated corticosteroid ointment with plastic occlusion

Dyshydrotic dermatitis (pompholyx)

- typically aged 20–40
- itching vesicles on fingers
- may be larger vesicles on palms and soles
- commonly affects sides of digits and palms
- lasts a few weeks
- tends to recur
- possibly related to stress

Treatment

- as for atopic dermatitis
- potent fluorinated corticosteroids topically
- oral corticosteroids may be necessary

Asteatotic dermatitis

This is the common very itchy dermatitis that occurs in the elderly, with a dry 'crazy paving' pattern, especially on the legs (see page 861).

Cracked (fissured) hands/fingers

This common cause of disability is usually due to dermatitis of the hands, or a very dry skin. It is usually part of the atopic dermatitis problem and it is important to consider allergic contact dermatitis.

Management of hand dermatitis

Hand protection:

- Avoid domestic or occupational duties that involve contact with irritants and detergents.
- Wear protective work gloves; cotton-lined PVC gloves.
- Avoid toilet soaps—use a substitute, e.g. Dove, Neutrogena.
- Cetaphil lotion is a useful soap substitute.
- Apply emollients, e.g. 2% salicylic acid in white soft paraffin (at night).
  If necessary:
  - hydrocortisone 1% ointment (not cream), or
  - stronger fluorinated preparation, or
  - tar preparation (at night).

Cracked heels

Cracked painful heels are a common problem, especially in adult women. It is a manifestation of very dry skin.

Treatment

- Soak the feet for 30 minutes in warm water containing an oil such as Alpha-Keri or Derma oil.
- Pat dry, then apply an emollient foot cream, e.g. Nutraplus (10% urea).

Contact dermatitis

Acute contact (exogenous) dermatitis can be either *irritant* or *allergic*.

Features:

- itchy, inflamed skin
- red and swollen
- papulovesicular

Irritant contact dermatitis

Caused by primary irritants, e.g. acids, alkalis, detergents, soaps.

Allergic contact dermatitis

Caused by allergens that provoke an allergic reaction in some individuals only—most people can handle the chemicals without undue effect. This allergic group also includes photo-contact allergens. Contact dermatitis is due to delayed hypersensitivity, with a long time of days to years. It is common in industrial or occupational situations where it usually affects the hands and forearms.

Common allergens

- ingredients in cosmetics, e.g. perfumes, preservatives

- topical antibiotics, e.g. neomycin
- topical anaesthetics, e.g. benzocaine
- topical antihistamines
- plants: rhus, grevillea, primula, poison ivy
- metal salts, e.g. nickel sulphate, chromate
- dyes
- perfumes
- rubber
- resins
- coral

Clinical features[4]

- dermatitis ranges from faint erythema to 'water melon' face oedema
- worse in periorbital region, genitalia and hairy skin; least in glabrous skin, e.g. palms and soles

Diagnostic hallmarks[4]

- site and shape of lesions suggest contact
- allergic causes found by patch testing
- improvement when off work or on holiday

Diagnosis

- careful history and examination
- consider occupation; family history; vacation or travel history; clothes, e.g. wetsuits, new clothes, Lycra bras; topical applications, e.g. medicines, cosmetics
- refer to a dermatologist for patch testing

Management

- determine cause and remove it
- if acute with blistering, apply Burow's compresses
- oral prednisolone for severe cases
- topical corticosteroid cream
- oral antihistamines

Seborrhoeic dermatitis

Seborrhoeic dermatitis is a very common skin inflammation that usually affects areas abundant in sebaceous glands or intertriginous areas. It is therefore common in hair-bearing areas of the body, especially the scalp and eyebrows. It can also affect the face, neck, axilla and groins, eyelids (blepharitis), external auditory meatus and nasolabial folds. The presternal area is often involved.

There are two distinct clinical forms: seborrhoeic dermatitis of infancy; and the adult form, which mainly affects young adults.

Studies have indicated that it is caused by a reaction to the yeast *Pityrosporum ovale*. It is also associated with HIV infection.

Principles of treatment

- Topical sulphur, salicylic acid and tar preparations are first-line treatment: they kill the yeast.
- Ketoconazole is most effective as topical (preferred) or oral treatment.
- Topical corticosteroids are useful for inflammation and pruritus and best used in combination. Avoid corticosteroids if possible.

Seborrhoeic dermatitis of infancy

This rash may be known as 'cradle cap' if it affects the scalp, or nappy rash/diaper dermatitis if it involves the napkin area.

It can be difficult to differentiate the rash from that of atopic dermatitis but seborrhoeic dermatitis tends to appear very early (before atopic dermatitis), even in the first month of life and mostly within the first three months, when androgen activity is most prevalent. The different features are summarised in Table 93.2 and the distribution is presented in Figure 93.2.

Table 93.2 *Differential diagnosis of seborrhoeic dermatitis and atopic dermatitis in infancy*

	Seborrhoeic dermatitis	***Atopic dermatitis (eczema)***
Age of onset	mainly within first 3 months	usually after 3 months
Itchiness	nil or mild	usually severe
Distribution	scalp, cheeks, folds of neck, axillae, folds of elbows and knees	starts on face elbow and knee flexures
Typical features	cradle cap red and scaly	vesicular and weeping
Napkin rash	common prone to infection with *Candida*	less common
Other features	may become generalised	

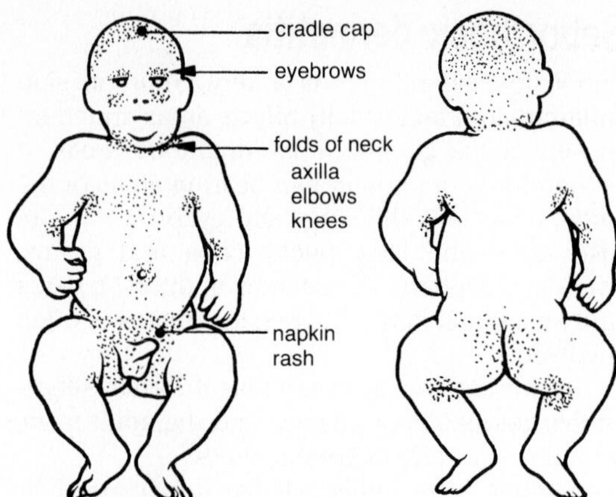

Fig. 93.2 *Seborrhoeic dermatitis: typical distribution in infants*

Seborrhoeic dermatitis usually appears as red patches or blotches with areas of scaling. This becomes redder when the baby cries or gets hot. Cradle cap may appear in the scalp. A flaky, scurf-like dandruff appears first, and then a yellowish, greasy, scaly crust forms. This scurf is usually associated with reddening of the skin.

The dermatitis can become infected, especially in the napkin area, and this becomes difficult to treat. If untreated, it often spreads to many areas of the body. It is said that cradle cap and nappy rash 'may meet in the middle'.

Treatment

Simple basic methods:

- Keep areas dry and clean.
- Bathe in warm water, pat areas dry with a soft cloth.
- Keep skin exposed to air and sun as much as possible.
- Avoid toilet soaps for washing (use emulsifying ointment or Cetaphil lotion).
- Rub scales of cradle cap gently with baby oil, then wash away loose scales.
- Change wet or soiled nappies often.
- For mild areas on body, apply a thin smear of zinc cream.

Medication

Scalp

- 1% sulphur and 1% salicylic acid in sorbolene cream
- apply overnight to scalp, shampoo off next day with a mild shampoo
- use 3 times a week

Face, flexures and trunk

- 2% sulphur and salicylic acid in aqueous or sorbolene cream
- hydrocortisone 1% (irritation on face and flexures)
- betamethasone 0.02–0.05% (if severe irritation on trunk)

Napkin area

- mix equal parts 1% hydrocortisone with nystatin or ketoconazole

Prognosis

Most children clear by 18 months (rare after two years).

Adult seborrhoeic dermatitis

Clinical features:

- any age from teenage onwards
- the head is a common area: scalp and ears, face, eyebrows, around eyes (blepharitis), nasolabial folds (Fig. 93.3)
- other areas: centre of chest, centre of back, scapular area, intertriginous areas, especially perianal (Fig. 93.4)
- red and scaly rash
- often very itchy
- secondary monilial infection common in flexures
- dandruff a feature of scalp area
- worse with stress and fatigue

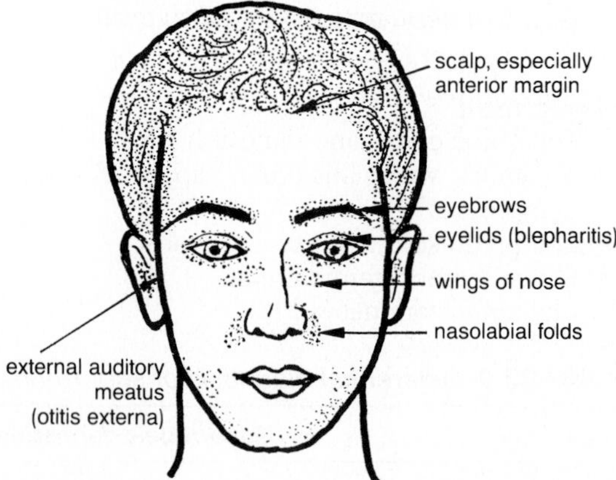

Fig. 93.3 *Seborrhoeic dermatitis: facial distribution in adults*

Treatment

Scalp

Options

1. salicylic acid 2% + sulphur 2% in aqueous cream overnight—shampoo off next day using

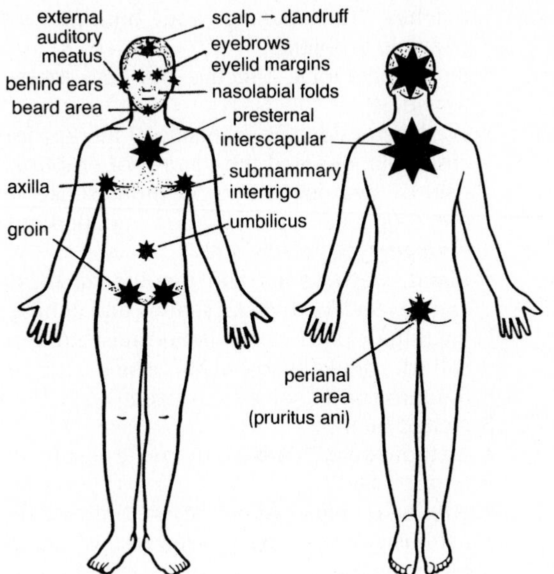

Fig. 93.4 *Seborrhoeic dermatitis: possible distribution in adults*

selenium sulphide or zinc pyrithione shampoos (apply 3 times a week)
2. ketoconazole shampoo
3. dexamethasone gel to scalp (if very itchy)

Face and body

- wash regularly using bland soap
- salicylic acid 2% + sulpur 2% (± tar) in aqueous cream

  or

  ketoconazole cream
- hydrocortisone 1% bd (if inflamed and pruritic)

Psoriasis

Psoriasis is a chronic skin disorder of unknown aetiology which affects 2–3% of the population. It appears most often between the ages of 10 and 30, although its onset can occur any time from infancy to old age. It has a familial predisposition although its mode of inheritance is debatable. If one parent is affected there is a 25% chance of developing it; this rises to 65% if two parents are affected.[3]

The feature of psoriasis is the increased frequency of mitosis and synthesis of DNA (suppressed by tar and dithranol) combined with enzyme and immune abnormalities. The result is overproduction of skin cells leading to thickening of the skin and overscaling.

Types of psoriasis	*Differential diagnosis*
infantile	seborrhoeic dermatitis, atopic dermatitis
plaque (commonest)	seborrhoeic dermatitis, discoid eczema, solar keratoses, Bowen's disease
guttate	pityriasis rosea, secondary syphilis, drug eruption
flexural	tinea, candida intertrigo, seborrhoeic dermatitis
scalp (sebopsoriasis)	seborrhoeic dermatitis, tinea capitis
nail	tinea, idiopathic onycholysis
pustular (palmoplantar)	tinea, infected eczema
exfoliative	severe seborrhoeic dermatitis

Factors that may worsen or precipitate psoriasis

- infection, especially Group A streptococcus
- trauma and other physical stress
- emotional stress
- sunburn
- puberty/menopause
- drugs
  - — antimalarials, e.g. chloroquine
  - — beta-blockers
  - — lithium
  - — NSAIDs
  - — oral contraceptives (especially exfoliative)

The typical patient

- older teenager or young adult
- possible family history
- onset may follow stress, illness or injury
- rash may appear on areas of minor trauma—the Kobner phenomenon
- rash improves on exposure to sun but worse with sunburn
- worse in winter
- itching not a feature
- lesions are most unlikely to appear on the face

Arthropathy

About 5% can develop a painful arthropathy (fingers, toes or a large joint) or a spondyloarthropathy (sacroiliitis).[6]

The rash

The appearance depends on the site affected. The commonest form is plaque psoriasis which begins with red lesions that enlarge and develop silvery scaling. The commonest sites are the extensor surfaces of the elbows and knees; then the scalp, sacral areas, genitals and nails are affected (Fig. 93.5).

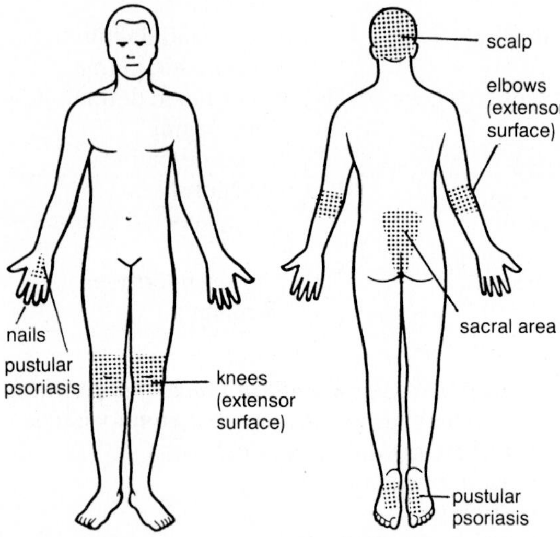

Fig. 93.5 *Psoriasis: typical skin distribution*

Diagnosis

Psoriasis is a clinical diagnosis but biopsy may be needed for confirmation. No laboratory test (including blood testing) is available.

Principles of management

While realising there is no cure for psoriasis the aim of treatment is to relieve discomfort, slow down the rapid skin cell division and work in consultation with a specialist to achieve these aims.[6]

- Provide education, reassurance and support.
- Promote general measures such as rest, and holidays preferably in the sun.
- Advise prevention, including avoidance of skin damage and stress if possible.
- Tailor treatment (including referral) according to the degree of severity and extent of the disease.

Treatment options

1. Topical therapy
   - dithranol (anthralin): concentrations range from 0.05 to 5%—effective on difficult thick patches but staining and burning are possible problems
   - tar preparations: effective but also messy to use
   - corticosteroids: the mainstay of therapy for small plaques and the control of eruption; use 1% hydrocortisone on more sensitive areas (genitals, groin, face) and perhaps stronger types elsewhere
   - bland preparations and emollients: these can be used for dryness, scaling and itching, e.g. liquor picis carbonis and menthol (or salicylic acid) in sorbolene base
   - 5-fluorouracil (sometimes used)
2. Systemic therapy
   - methotrexate: can have dramatic results in severe cases
   - etretinate: effective in severe intractable psoriasis (never used in females of child-bearing age)
   - cyclosporin
3. Physical therapy
   - phototherapy (UVB ultraviolet light): needs careful supervision as several whole body treatments daily required
   - UVB plus coal tar (Goeckerman regimen): reserved for severe psoriasis; UVB given after coal tar application.
   - photochemotherapy (PUVA = psoralen + UVA)—reserved for non-responders to UVB treatment or other therapies. A variation is REPUVA = retinoid + psoralen + UVA
   - intralesional corticosteroids—an excellent and effective treatment for isolated small or moderate-sized plaques that can be readily given by the family doctor

Method of injection

Mix equal parts of triamcinolone acetonide 10 mg/mL and plain local anaesthetic or normal saline and, using a 25 g or 23 g needle, infiltrate the psoriatic plaque intradermally to cover virtually all of the plaque. A small plaque can be covered by a single insertion while a larger plaque may require separate insertions (Fig. 93.6).

Stable plaque psoriasis

A recommended regimen for stable plaque psoriasis on limbs and/or trunk uses the following method.[7]

Apply dithranol 0.1% (Dithrocream) to affected area at night, leave for 20 minutes and then wash off under a shower:

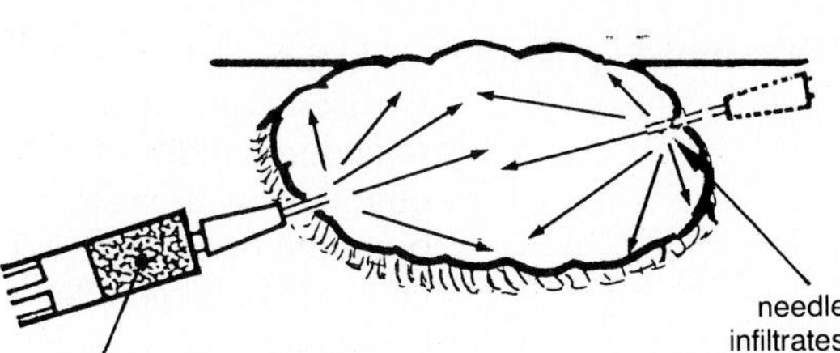

Fig. 93.6 *Intralesional corticosteroid injection technique for psoriatic plaque (requiring double injection—small plaques need only one infiltration)*

- increase the strength every five days
- avoid inflamed plaques, flexures or the face

then apply a bland emollient or a topical fluorinated corticosteroid.[7]

For a resistant localised plaque, consider an intralesional injection with triamcinolone.

An alternative to dithranol is tar, e.g. crude coal tar 1–4% plus salicylic acid 3–5% in sorbolene cream. It can be left on overnight and washed off in the morning.

Maintenance for milder stabilised plaque psoriasis

Egopsoryl TA (allantoin 2.5%, sulphur 0.5%, phenol 0.5%, coal tar solution 5%, menthol 0.75%, glycerol 18%).

Nappy rash

Nappy rash (or diaper dermatitis) is an inflammatory contact dermatitis occurring in the napkin area and can be a common presentation of mild or moderate underlying skin disease. It is found in children up to two years old and has a peak incidence between 9 and 12 months.[8]

Most children will develop nappy rash at some stage of infancy with an estimated 50% having it to a significant extent. The commonest type is *irritant dermatitis* but consider also

- seborrhoeic dermatitis
- *candida albicans* (tends to superinfect seborrhoea)
- atopic dermatitis
- psoriasis

Causes of nappy rash

The main predisposing factor in all types is dampness due to urine and faeces. Other causes or aggravating factors are:

- a tendency of the baby to eczema
- a tendency of the baby to seborrhoea
- infection, especially monilia (thrush)
- rough-textured nappies
- detergents and other chemicals in nappies
- plastic pants (aggravates wetness)
- excessive washing of the skin with soap
- too much powder over the nappy area (avoid powders)

Irritant dermatitis

This is a type of contact dermatitis with the erythema and scaling conforming to the napkin area. The flexures are usually spared. It is related to the activity of faecal proteases and lipases and probably not to the activity of ammonia (from urea) as previously promoted. The problem can vary from mild erythema to a severe blistering eruption with ulceration. Ultrabsorbent disposable nappies appear to be better than cloth nappies.[9] Diarrhoea is a causative factor of irritant dermatitis. If the eruption extends further than the points of contact with the nappy an underlying skin disease such as seborrhoeic or atopic dermatitis must be suspected.

Seborrhoeic dermatitis (SD)

This affects mainly the flexures of the natal cleft and groin. It is important to look for evidence of SD elsewhere, such as cradle cap and lesions on the face and axillae.

Atopic dermatitis

Atopic dermatitis can involve the napkin area. Pruritus is a feature and the child will be observed scratching the area. There may be evidence of atopic dermatitis elsewhere, such as the face.

Candidiasis (monilia nappy rash)

Superinfection of intertrigo or napkin dermatitis will result in a diffuse, red, raw, shiny or dry type of rash that will involve the flexures and extend beyond the napkin area as 'satellite lesions'. *Candida* tends to invade the skin folds and the foreskin of male babies.

Uncommon causes

Psoriatic nappy rash

This presents as a dry scaling eruption, primarily on the napkin area, but can extend to the flexures, trunk and limbs. The edge of the rash is sharply demarcated. The typical psoriatic scale is absent. It tends to occur in the first weeks of life. There is usually a family history.

Impetigo
If there is staphylococcus superinfection, bullae and pus-filled blisters will be present.

Histiocytosis X (Letterer-Siwe disease)
There is a similar rash to seborrhoeic dermatitis but the lesions are purpuric. In this serious disease the child is very ill and usually lymphadenopathy and hepatosplenomegaly may be found.

Management of nappy rash

Basic care (instructions to patients):

1. Keep the area dry. Change wet or soiled nappies frequently and as soon as you notice them. Disposable nappies are helpful.
2. After changing, gently remove any urine or moisture with diluted sorbolene cream or warm water.
3. Wash gently with warm water, pat dry (do not rub) and then apply any prescribed cream or ointment to help heal and protect the area. Vaseline or zinc cream applied lightly will do.
4. Expose the bare skin to fresh air wherever possible. Leave the nappy off several times a day, especially if the rash is severe.
5. Do not wash in soap or bath too often—once or twice a week is enough.
6. Avoid powder and plastic pants.
7. Use special soft nappy liners that help protect the sensitive skin.
8. Thoroughly rinse out any bleach or disinfectants.

Medical treatment

Some principles:

- The cornerstone of treatment is prevention.
- Emollients should be used to keep skin lubricated, e.g. mixture of zinc oxide and castor oil or Vaseline.
- Be careful of excessive use of corticosteroids, especially fluorinated steroids.
- If infection is suspected, confirm by swab or skin scraping.

Treatment

Atopic dermatitis	1% hydrocortisone
Seborrhoeic dermatitis	1% hydrocortisone + ketoconazole ointment
Candida	topical nystatin at each nappy change
Widespread (possible candida present)	1% hydrocortisone ointment mixed in equal quantities with nystatin ointment or clotrimazole cream (apply qid after changes)
Psoriatic dermatitis	tar and sulphur preparation, or 1% hydrocortisone

Facial rashes

Common facial skin disorders include acne, rosacea, perioral dermatitis and seborrhoeic dermatitis. These conditions must be distinguished from SLE.

Acne

Acne is inflammation of the sebaceous (oil) glands of the skin. At first there is excessive sebum production due to the action of androgen. These glands become blocked (blackheads and whiteheads) due to increased keratinisation of the sebaceous duct. The bacteria in the sebum produced lipases with the resultant free fatty acids, provoking inflammation.

Types of acne[10]

- *Infantile*: Occurs in the first few months of life, mainly on the face. Affects mainly boys and is a self-limiting minor problem. Reassurance only is required in most cases. Some are severe and may scar.
- *Adolescent*: The most common type, occurring around puberty. Acne is rare under 10 years; ages 13–16 are commonest and it is worse in males aged 18–19. It is slightly less common in girls and worse around 14 years with premenstrual exacerbations.
- *Cosmetica*: In females, associated with the prolonged use of skin care products, e.g. moisturiser, foundation cream and heavy make-up.
- *Oil*: Occurs mainly on the legs of workers exposed to petroleum products.

Taking a history

Enquire about use of any skin preparations—therapeutic or cosmetic; exposure to oils; possible diet relationships and drug intake.

Drugs which aggravate acne:[10]

- corticosteroids

- chloralhydrate
- iodides or bromides
- lithium
- phenytoin
- quinine
- oral contraceptives

Management

Support and counselling

Adolescents hate acne; they find it embarrassing and require the sympathetic care and support not only of their doctor but also of their family. It should not be dismissed as a minor problem.

Education

People with acne should understand the pathogenesis of acne and be given leaflets with appropriate explanations. Myths that must be dispelled include:

- It is not a dietary or infectious disorder.
- It is not caused by oily hair or hair touching the forehead.
- Ordinary chemicals (including chlorine in pools) do not make it worse.
- Blackheads are not dirt, and will not dissolve in hot, soapy water.

Reassure the patient that acne usually settles by the age of 20.

General factors

- Diet is considered not to be a factor but if there is a causal relationship with any foods, e.g. chocolate, avoid them.
- Special soaps and overscrubbing are unhelpful. Use a normal soap and wash gently.
- Avoid oily or creamy cosmetics and all moisturisers. Use cosmetics sparingly.
- Avoid picking and squeezing blackheads.
- Exercise, hair washing and shampoos are not of proven value.
- Ultraviolet light such as sunlight may help improve acne.

Principles of treatment

1. Unblock the pores (follicular ducts) with keratolytics such as sulphur compounds, salicylic acid (5–10%); with benzoyl peroxide (2.5%, 5% or 10%) or retinoic acid (tretinoin) 0.01% gel, 0.05% cream, lotion or liquid.
2. Decrease bacteria in the sebum with systemic antibiotics—tetracyclines or erythromycin—or with topical antibiotics such as clindamycin.
3. Decrease sebaceous gland activity with oestrogens, spironolactone, cyproterone acetate, or isotretinoin (note: isotretinoin is teratogenic).

Oral antibiotics

Use for inflammatory acne:

- tetracycline 1 g per day/doxycycline 100 mg per day
- use half this dose if mild
- reduce dosage according to response
  e.g. tetracycline 250 mg per day or every second day
  or
  doxycycline 50 mg per day
- use minocycline in resistant cases
- erythromycin or cotrimoxazole are alternatives

Some topical treatment regimens

Mild acne (mainly comedo type):

- Salicylic acid, sulphur and resorcinol preparations, e.g. salicylic acid 1%, resorcinol 0.5%, spirit to 100%.
- Night solution: 2% sulphur, 2% resorcinol in calamine lotion.

Mild to moderate acne:

- Basic regimen (benzoyl peroxide and retinoic acid)
  1. Use tretinoin 0.01% gel or 0.05% cream; apply each night.
  2. After two weeks, add benzoyl peroxide 2.5%, 5% or 10% gel once daily (in the morning). That is, maintenance treatment is:
     — tretinoin gel or cream at night
     — benzoyl peroxide gel mane
  3. Maintain for two months and review.
- An alternative regimen, if recalcitrant
  1. Use clindamycin HCI 600 mg in 60 ml of 70% isopropyl alcohol. Apply with fingertips twice daily.
  2. Alternative bases for clindamycin, especially if the alcohol is too drying or irritating:
     — Cetaphil lotion (Alcon) 100 ml, or
     Dermatech liquid 100 ml

  Clindamycin is particularly useful for pregnant women and those who cannot tolerate antibiotics or exfoliants.[10]

Other therapies

Severe cystic acne (specialist care)

- isotretinoin (Roaccutane)

Females not responding to first-line treatment

- combined oral contraceptive pill, e.g. ethinyloestradiol/cyproterone acetate (Diane-35 ED)

A new agent for mild to moderate acne

- azelaic acid

Rosacea

Rosacea is a common persistent eruption of unknown aetiology. It is typically chronic and persistent with a fluctuant course.

Clinical features

- mainly 30–50 years
- on forehead, cheeks, nose and chin (Fig. 93.7)
- periorbital and perioral areas spared
- vascular changes—erythema and telangiectasia
- inflammation—papules and pustules

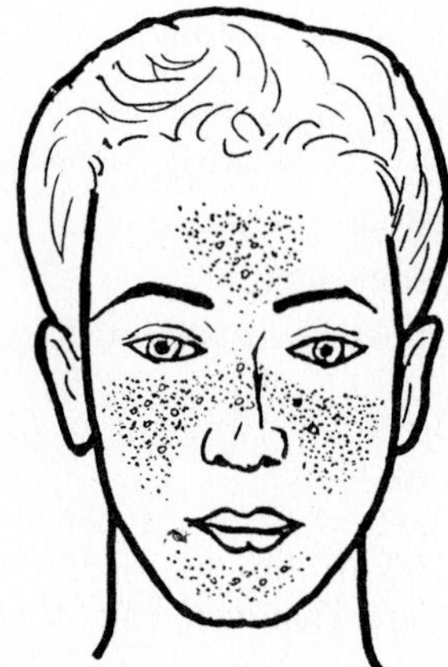

Fig. 93.7 *Rosacea: typical facial distribution*

Complications

- blepharitis
- conjunctivitis, sometimes keratitis and corneal ulcer
- associated rhinophyma in some cases

Management

- Apply cool packs if severe.
- Avoid factors that cause facial flushings, e.g. excessive sun exposure, heat, alcohol, spicy foods, hot drinks.

Systemic antibiotics

- tetracycline (first choice)
  erythromycin (second choice)
  e.g. 500–1000 mg daily, then 250 mg daily when controlled, for a total of 8–10 weeks. Repeated for recurrences: avoid maintenance. If using doxycycline, start with 100 mg then 50 mg daily.
- metronidazole 200 mg bd for resistant cases

Topical agents

- 2% sulphur in aqueous cream (milder cases)
  or
  metronidazole gel bd (more severe cases)
- hydrocortisone 1% cream is effective, but steroids are best avoided and strong topical steroids should not be used because of severe rebound vascular changes.

Perioral dermatitis

Clinical features:

- acne-like dermatitis of lower face
- usually young women
- around mouth and on chin, sparing adjacent perioral area (Fig. 93.8)
- frequently begins at the nasolabial folds
- multiple small red pustules and papules
- on a background of erythema and scaling
- may be related to pregnancy and oral contraception
- may be related to repeated topical corticosteroid (especially fluorinated) use

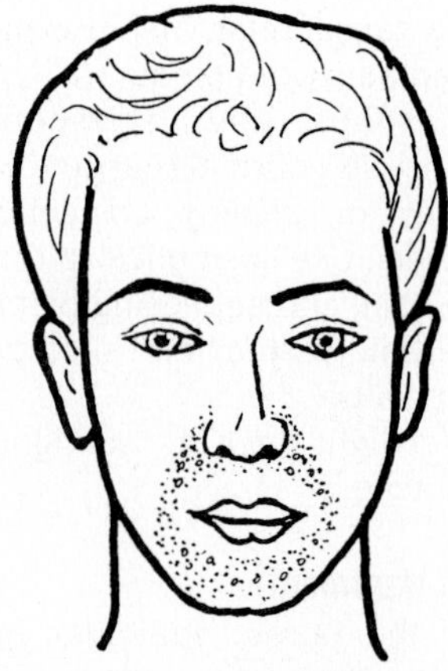

Fig. 93.8 *Perioral dermatitis: typical distribution*

Treatment

- Tetracycline 250 mg bd for 6–8 weeks.
- Discontinue any topical corticosteroid therapy.

Tinea

Tinea, or ringworm infections, are caused mainly by three major classes of dermatophytic organisms that have the ability to invade and proliferate in keratin of the skin, nails and hair. It is most useful to perform skin scrapings and microscopy to look for encroaching septate hyphae.[11] Confirm the diagnosis by fungal culture. Tinea cruris is presented on page 860.

Tinea pedis (athlete's foot)

Tinea pedis is usually caused by *Trichophyton rubrum* and is the commonest type of fungal infection in humans. Candida intertrigo and erythrasma are important differential diagnoses.

Symptoms

The commonest symptoms are itchiness and foot odour. Sweat and water make the top layer of skin white and soggy. There is scaling, maceration and fissuring of the skin between the fourth and fifth toes and also third and fourth toes.

Management

Advice to the patient:

- Keep your feet as clean and dry as possible.
- Carefully dry your feet after bathing and showering.
- After drying your feet, use an antifungal powder, especially between the toes.
- Remove flaky skin from beneath the toes each day with dry tissue paper or gauze.
- Wear light socks made of natural absorbent fibres, such as cotton and wool, to allow better circulation of air and to reduce sweating. Avoid synthetic socks.
- Change your shoes and socks daily.
- If possible, wear open sandals or shoes with porous soles and uppers.
- Go barefoot whenever possible.
- Use thongs in public showers such as at swimming pools (rather than bare feet).

Medication

Clotrimazole 1%, ketoconazole 2% or miconazole 2% cream or lotion, applied after drying, bd or tds for 2–3 weeks. If severe and spreading, prescribe oral griseofulvin or terbinafine after confirming the diagnosis by fungal culture.

Tinea corporis

Tinea corporis (ringworm infection of the body) is usually caused by *Trichophyton rubrum* (60%) or *Microsporum canis*.[11]

Clinical features

- spreading circular erythematous lesions
- slight scaling or vesicles at the advancing edge
- central areas usually normal
- mild itch
- may involve hair, feet and nails

Management

- clotrimazole 1% or miconazole 2% cream or ketoconazole 2% cream, applied bd for 3–4 weeks
- oral terbinafine or griseofulvin if no response

Tinea manuum

Tinea manuum is ringworm infection of the hand, usually presenting with scaling of the palms and plantar aspects of the fingers. The differential diagnoses are atopic dermatitis and contact dermatitis of the hands.

Clinical features

- usually unilateral
- spreading edge
- erythematous; fine scaling
- may be associated with tinea pedis

Treatment

- topical clotrimazole 1%, ketoconazole 2% or miconazole 2% cream for 4 weeks or, if resistant, terbinafine 250 mg or griseofulvin 500 mg daily for 4 weeks.

Tinea capitis

In Australia tinea capitis is usually due to *Microsporum canis* acquired from cats and dogs.

Clinical features

- usually in children
- patches of partial alopecia
- scaly patches
- small broken-off hair shafts
- hairs fluoresce yellow-green with Wood's light (not invariably, e.g. with *T. tonsurans* infection)

Treatment

- griseofulvin (o) Adults: 500–1000 mg daily
Children: 10 mg/kg/day
6 week course

Kerion

Kerion of the scalp and beard area may present like an abscess—tender and fluctuant. Usually occurs on the scalp, face or limbs. A fungal cause is possible if the hairs are plucked out easily and without pain (if painful and stuck, bacterial infection is likely).

Tinea incognito

This is the term used for unrecognised tinea infection due to modification with corticosteroid treatment. The lesions are enlarging and persistent, especially on the groins, hands and face.

The sequence is initial symptomatic relief of itching, stopping the ointment or cream and then relapse.

Tinea unguium (toe-nails and fingernails)

These onychomycosis problems are chronic and very resistant to treatment:

- usually associated with tinea pedis
- nails show white spots
- may be yellow-brown and crumbling
- starts from edge (periphery) and spreads towards base

Treatment

Fingernails: terbinafine 250 mg (o) daily for 4 weeks, or griseofulvin 500 mg daily (o) for 6 months

Toe-nails: terbinafine 250 mg (o) daily for 12 weeks, or griseofulvin for 12–18 months

New treatments: consider Naftin gel

Griseofulvin treatment: significant side effects include headaches and (long-term) bone marrow suppression or liver toxicity. Regular screening with FBE and LFTs advisable.

Pityriasis versicolor (tinea versicolor

Pityriasis versicolor is a superficial yeast infection of the skin (usually on the trunk) caused by *Pityrosporum orbiculare* (*Malassezia furfur*). The old name, tinea versicolor, is inappropriate because the problem is not a dermatophyte infection. It occurs world-wide but is more common in tropical and subtropical climates. There are two distinct presentations:

1. reddish brown, slightly scaly patches on upper trunk
2. hypopigmented area that will not tan, especially in suntanned skin

The term versicolor means variable colours.

Clinical features

- mainly young and middle-aged adults
- brown on pale skin or white on tanned skin
- trunk distribution (Fig. 93.9)
- patches may coalesce
- may involve neck, upper arms, face and groin
- scales removed by scraping show characteristic short stunted hyphae with spores on microscopy

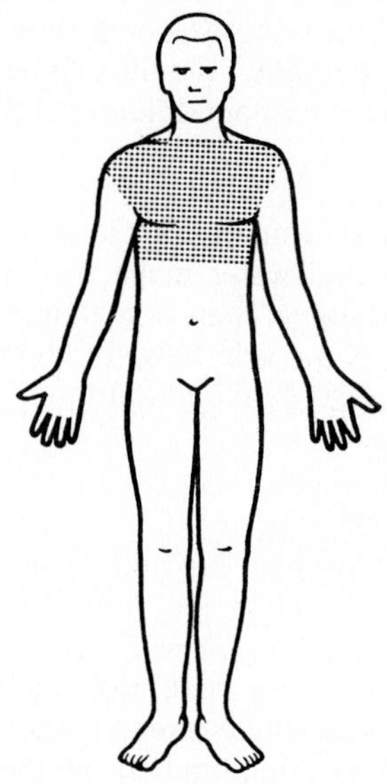

Fig. 93.9 *Pityriasis versicolor: typical truncal distribution (corresponding area on back)*

Differential diagnosis

Seborrhoeic dermatitis of trunk (more erythematous), pityriasis rosea, vitiligo, pityriasis alba (affects face).

Treatment

- Selenium sulfide (Selsun shampoo). Wash area, leaving on for 5–10 minutes, then wash off. Do this daily for two weeks (at night), then every second day for two weeks, then monthly for 12 months. Shampoo scalp twice weekly.

and/or

- Clotrimazole, miconazole or ketaconazole cream/lotion nocte for 2–4 weeks.

or

- Sodium thiosulphate 25% solution bd for 4 weeks (wash off after 10 minutes)

  or

  (for persistent or recurrent problems)
- Ketoconazole 200 mg daily for 7–10 days or 400 mg single dose[12]

Note Ketoconazole may be hepatotoxic. Always perform LFTs first (do not use long-term). Griseofulvin is inappropriate because the rash is not a fungal infection.
Warn patients that the patches may take a while to disappear and that cure does not equate with disappearance.

Dry skin

Disorders associated with scaling and roughness of the skin include:

- atopic dermatitis—all types, e.g. pityriasis alba, nummular eczema, asteatotic dermatitis
- ageing skin
- psoriasis
- ichthyotic disorders
- keratosis pilaris

Itching may be a feature of dry skin (but is not inevitable).

Aggravating factors:

- low humidity, e.g. heaters, air-conditioners
- frequent immersion in water
- heat/hot water
- toilet soaps

Management

- Ensure humidification if there is central heating.
- Reduce bathing.
- Bathe or shower in tepid water.
- Use a soap substitute, e.g. Dove or Neutrogena/Cetaphil lotion.
- Pat dry—avoid vigorous towelling.
- Rub in baby oil after bathing (better than adding oil to the bath).
- Avoid wool next to the skin (wear cotton).
- Drink plenty of water.
- Use emollients, e.g. Alpha-Keri lotion, QV skin lotion.
- Use moisturisers, e.g. Nutraplus; Calmurid.

Sunburn

Sunburn is normally caused by ultraviolet B (UV-B) radiation which penetrates the epidermis and superficial dermis, releasing substances such as leukotrienes and histamines which cause redness and pain. Severe sunburn may develop on relatively dull days because thin clouds filter UV-B poorly.

Clinical presentations:

Minor sunburn Mild erythema with minimal discomfort for about three days.

Moderate Moderate to severe erythema within a few hours; worse the following day—red, hot and moderately painful. Settles in 3–4 days with some desquamation.

Severe Classic signs of inflammation—redness, heat, pain and swelling. Skin develops vesicles and bullae. Systemic features develop with very severe burns, e.g. fever, headache, nausea, delirium, hypotension. May require IV fluids.

Differential diagnosis

- general photosensitivity: consider drugs, e.g. thiazide diuretics, tetracyclines, sulphonamides, phenothiazines, griseofulvin, NSAIDs
- acute systemic lupus erythematosus may present as unexpectedly severe sunburn
- photocontact dermatitis

Treatment

Hydrocortisone 1% ointment or cream for severe sunburn, early. Repeat in 2–3 hours and then the next day. Hydrocortisone is not useful after 24 hours and should be used for unblistered erythematous skin, not on broken skin.

Oral aspirin eases pain. Oil in water baths may help and wet applications such as oily calamine lotions may give relief.

Prevention

Avoid exposure to summer sunlight 10 am to 2 pm (or 11 am to 3 pm summer time saving). Use natural shade—beware of reflected light from sand or water and light cloud. Use a sunscreen with a minimum of SPF 15 +. Wear broad-brimmed hats and protective clothing.

References

1. Fry J. *Common diseases* (4th edition). Lancaster: MTP Press Limited, 1985, 337–339.
2. Bridges-Webb C. Morbidity and treatment in general practice. Med J Australia: Supplement, 19 October 1992, 26–27.
3. Berger P. *Skin secrets*. Sydney: Allen and Unwin, 1991:93–170.
4. Lane-Brown M. Dermatitis/eczema. In: MIMS Disease Index. Sydney: IMS Publishing, 1991–2, 137–140.
5. Millard LG. Irritable papular rashes. Medicine International, 1988; 49:2007–2011.
6. Lane-Brown M. Psoriasis. In: MIMS Disease Index. Sydney: IMS Publishing, 1991–92, 448.
7. Buxton PK. *ABC of dermatology*. London: British Medical Association, 1989, 40.
8. Gallachio V. Nappy rash. Aust Fam Physician, 1988; 17:971–972.
9. Aldridge S. Nappy rash. Australian Paediatric Review, 1991; Vol. 2, No. 1:2.
10. Berger P. Acne—pathogenesis and treatment. Modern Medicine Australia, September 1990, 83–89.
11. Gin D. Tinea infections. In: MIMS Disease Index. Sydney: IMS Publishing, 1991–92, 545–547.
12. Hunter JAA, Savin JA, Dahl MV. *Clinical dermatology*. Oxford: Blackwell Scientific Publications, 1989, 162–163.

94

Acute skin eruptions

The sudden appearance of a rash, which is a common presentation in children (Chap. 67), usually provokes patients and doctors alike to consider an infectious aetiology, commonly of viral origin. However, an important cause to consider is a reaction to a drug.

A knowledge of the relative distribution of the various causes of rashes helps with the diagnostic methodology. Many of the eruptions are relatively benign and undergo spontaneous remission. Fortunately, the potentially deadly rash of smallpox is no longer encountered.

Serious eruptions that demand accurate diagnosis and management include:

- primary HIV infection
- secondary syphilis
- Stevens-Johnson syndrome
- purpuric eruption of meningococcal septicaemia, typhoid, measles, other septicaemia

A list of important causes of acute skin eruptions is presented in Table 94.1.

Table 94.1 *Important causes of acute skin eruptions*

Maculopapular
- measles
- rubella
- scarlet fever
- viral exanthem (fourth disease)
- erythema infectiosum (slapped face syndrome or fifth disease)
- roseola infantum (sixth disease)
- Epstein-Barr mononucleosis (primary or secondary to drugs)
- primary HIV infection
- secondary syphilis
- pityriasis rosea
- guttate psoriasis
- urticaria
- erythema multiforme (may be vesicular)
- drug reaction
- scabies

Maculopapular vesicular
- varicella
- herpes zoster
- herpes simplex
- eczema herpeticum
- impetigo
- hand, foot and mouth disease
- drug reaction

Maculopapular pustular
- pseudomonas folliculitis
- staphylococcus aureus folliculitis
- impetigo

Purpuric (haemorrhagic) eruption
- purpura, e.g. drug-induced purpura, severe infection
- vasculitis (vascular purpura)
  - — Henoch-Schönlein purpura
  - — polyarteritis nodosa

The diagnostic approach

The diagnostic approach to skin eruptions presupposes a basic knowledge of the causes, and then a careful history and physical examination should logically follow.

The history should include:
site and mode of onset of the rash; mode of progression; drug history; constitutional

disturbance, e.g. pyrexia, pruritus; respiratory symptoms; herald patch?; diet—unaccustomed food; exposure to irritants; contacts with infectious disease; bleeding or bruising tendency.

The examination should include:
skin of whole body; nature and distribution of rash; soles of feet; mucous membranes; oropharynx; conjunctivae and the lymphopoietic system (? lymphadenopathy ? splenomegaly).

Laboratory investigations may include:

a full blood examination; syphilis serology; Epstein-Barr mononucleosis test; HIV test; rubella haemagglutination tests (x 2); viral and bacterial cultures.

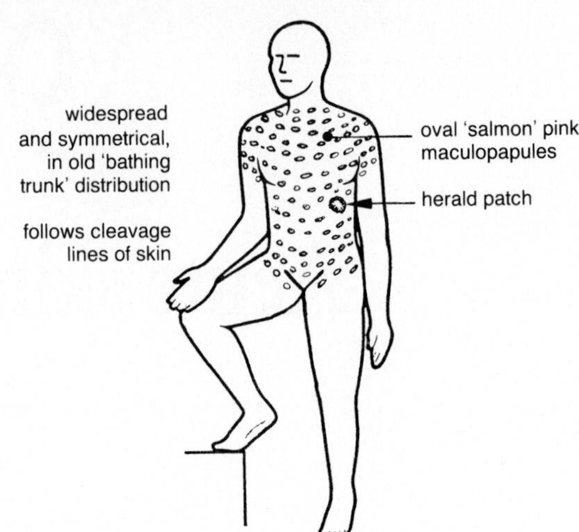

Fig. 94.1 *Pityriasis rosea: typical distribution*

Acute skin eruptions in children

The following skin eruptions (some of which may also occur in adults) are outlined in childhood infectious diseases (Chap. 67).

- measles (page 673)
- rubella (page 674)
- viral exanthem (fourth disease) (page 675)
- erythema infectiosum (fifth disease) (page 675)
- roseola infantum (sixth disease) (page 676)
- Kawasaki's disease (page 676)
- varicella (page 671)
- impetigo (page 679)

Pityriasis rosea

Pityriasis rosea is a common but mild acute inflammatory skin disorder. Although a viral agent is suspected to be the cause, no infective agent has been demonstrated.

Clinical features

- any age, mainly young adults (aged 15–30)
- preceding herald patch (1–2 weeks)
- oval, salmon-pink or copper-coloured eruption
- coin-shaped patches with scaly margins
- follows cleavage lines of trunk (Fig. 94.1)
- on trunk ('T-shirt' distribution)
- occurs also on upper arms, upper legs, neck, face (rare) and axillae
- patients not ill
- itch varies from nil to severe (typically minor itching)

Differential diagnosis

Herald patch	tinea corporis
Generalised rash	seborrhoeic dermatitis (slower onset), guttate psoriasis, drug eruption (Table 94.2), secondary syphilis

Table 94.2 *Drugs that cause eruptions suggestive of pityriasis rosea*[2]

Main drugs
- gold salts
- penicillamine
- captopril

Others
- arsenicals
- barbiturates
- bismuth
- clonidine
- metoprolol
- metronidazole

Prognosis

A mild self-limiting disorder with spontaneous remission in 4–10 weeks. It does not appear to be contagious.

Management

- Explain and reassure with patient education handout.[1]
- Bathe and shower as usual, using a neutral soap, e.g. Neutrogena.

- For bothersome itch: apply mild topical corticosteroid ointment or calamine lotion with 1% phenol or urea cream.
- Ultraviolet therapy is good but, like psoriasis, sunburn must be avoided. Expose rash to sunlight or UV therapy (if florid) three times a week.

Secondary syphilis

The generalised skin eruption of secondary syphilis varies and may resemble any type of eruption from psoriasiform to rubelliform to roseoliform. The rash usually appears 6–8 weeks after the primary chancre.

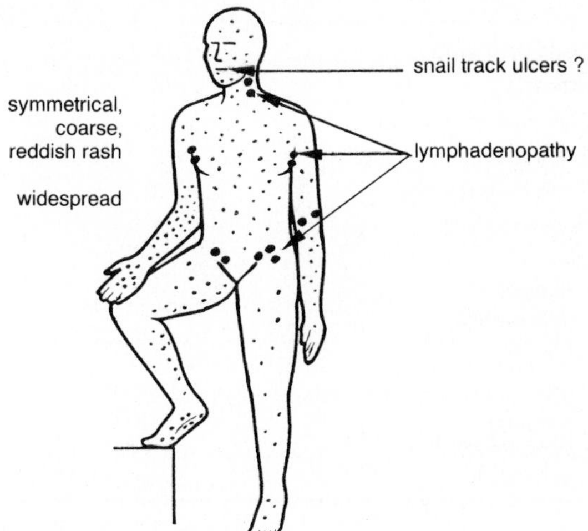

Fig. 94.2 *Secondary syphilis: typical features*

Features of the rash

- initially faint pink macules
- then becomes maculopapular
- can involve whole of body (Fig. 94.2)
- palms and soles involved
- dull red in colour and round
- more prolific on flexor surfaces
- symmetrical and relatively coarse
- asymptomatic

Associations (possible)

- mucosal ulcers: 'snail track'
- lymphadenopathy
- patchy hair loss
- condylomata lata

Treatment

- as for primary syphilis (Chap. 90)

Primary HIV infection

A common manifestation of the primary HIV infection is an erythematous, maculopapular rash, although other skin manifestations such as a roseola-like rash and urticaria can occur.

Clinical features

- symmetrical
- may be generalised
- lesions 5–10 mm in diameter
- common on face and/or trunk
- can occur on extremities including palms and soles (Fig. 94.3)
- non-pruritic

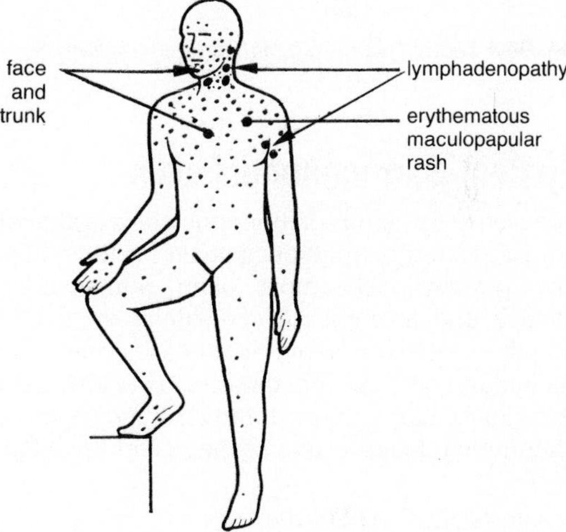

Note: mimics glandular fever

Fig. 94.3 *Primary HIV infection: typical features*

If such a rash, accompanied by an illness like glandular fever occurs, HIV infection should be suspected and specific tests ordered.

Guttate psoriasis

Guttate psoriasis is the sudden eruption of small (less than 5 mm) round red papules of psoriasis on the trunk (Fig. 94.4). The rash may extend to the limbs.

It is usually seen in children and adolescents and often precipitated by a streptococcal throat infection. The rash soon develops a white silvery scale. It may undergo spontaneous resolution or enlarge to form plaques.

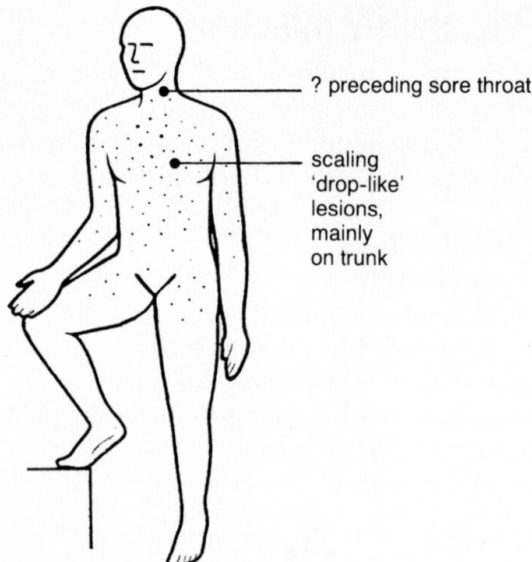

Fig. 94.4 *Guttate psoriasis: small, drop-like lesions, mainly on trunk*

Epstein-Barr mononucleosis

The rash of Epstein-Barr mononucleosis is almost always related to antibiotics given for tonsillitis. The primary rash, most often non-specific, pinkish and maculopapular (similar to that of rubella), occurs in about 5% of cases only. The secondary rash, which can be extensive and sometimes has a purplish-brown tinge, is most often precipitated by one of the penicillins (Fig. 94.5).

- ampicillin } 90–100%
- amoxycillin } association
- penicillin up to 50%

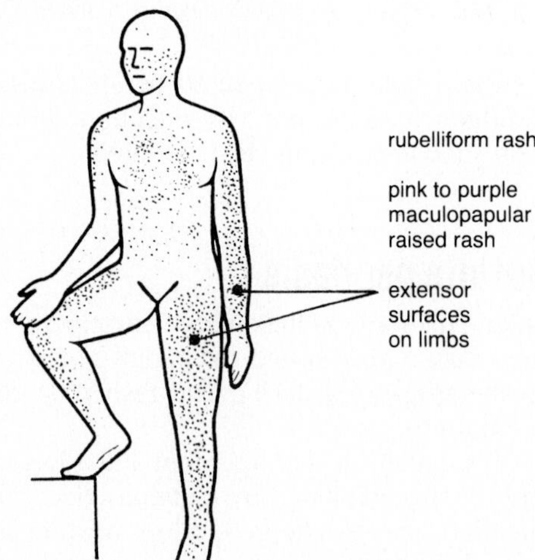

Fig. 94.5 *Epstein-Barr mononucleosis: typical rash induced by penicillin, amoxycillin or ampicillin*

Drug eruptions

A rash is one the most common side effects of drug therapy, which can precipitate many different types of rash; the most common is toxic erythema (Table 94.3). Most drug-evoked dermatoses have an allergic basis with the eruption appearing approximately 10 days after administration, though much sooner if previously sensitised.[3] The most common drugs that cause skin eruptions are summarised in Table 94.4.

Table 94.3 *Most common types of drug eruptions (after Thomas)*[3]

	Relative frequency **%**
Toxic erythema	45
Urticaria	25
Erythema multiforme	7
Eczematous dermatitis	5
Fixed drug reaction	3
Photosensitivity	3
Others • acne form • psoriasiform • pigmentation • erythema nodosum • toxic epidermal necrolysis • purpuric • pigmentary • exfoliative	

The most important fact to realise about drug reactions is that their appearances are so variable—they may mimic almost any cutaneous disease and, in addition, create unique appearances of their own.

When taking a history it is appropriate to enquire about medications or chemicals that may be overlooked such as aspirin, vitamins, toxins, laxatives and medicated toothpaste.

Toxic erythema

The maculopapular erythematous eruption is either morbilliform or scarlatiniform. It is more pronounced on the trunk than on the limbs and face but may become confluent over the whole body.

Drugs that typically cause toxic erythema include:

- antibiotics — penicillin/cephalosporins
  — sulphonamides
- thiazides
- carbamazepine

Table 94.4 *Most common drugs that cause skin eruptions*

Antimicrobials	• penicillin/cephalosporins • sulphonamides • tetracyclines • nitrofurantoin • streptomycin • griseofulvin • metronidazole
Diuretics	• thiazides • frusemide
Anticonvulsants	• carbamazepine • phenytoin
Tranquillisers	• phenothiazines • barbiturates • chlordiazepoxide
Anti-inflammatory and analgesics	• gold salts • aspirin/salicylates • codeine/morphine • pyrazolones, e.g. BTZ • other NSAIDs
Hormones	• combined oral contraceptive • stilboesterol • testosterone
Others	• phenolphthalein • serum • amiodarone • cytotoxic drugs • quinidine/quinine • bromides and iodides • sulphonylureas • allopurinol • warfarin • amphetamines

- barbiturates
- allopurinol
- gold salts

Photosensitivity

Several antibiotics increase the sensitivity of the skin to ultraviolet light and may lead to a rash with a distribution according to sunlight exposure. The photosensitive rash may be erythematous, resembling sunburn; eczematous; or vesicular.

Typical drugs: tetracyclines
sulphonamides/sulphonylureas
thiazides and frusemide
phenothiazines
retinoids
amiodarone
griseofulvin
antihistamines, especially promethazine
antimalarials
psoralens

Fixed drug eruption

The mechanism of fixed drug eruption is unknown. The most commonly affected areas are the face, hands and genitalia. The lesions, which are usually bright red but can have other characteristics, are fixed in site and appearance within hours of the drug's administration.

Typical drugs: phenolphthalein
tetracyclines
sulphonamides
salicylates
the oral contraceptive pill
barbiturates
chlordiazepoxide

Treatment of any drug reaction

The important aspect of management is to recognise the offending agent and withdraw it. The rash should be treated according to its nature.

There is a therapeutic impulse to prescribe antihistamines but they should be reserved for the treatment of urticarial drug eruptions. They may actually delay healing in purpuric, erythematous and vesiculobullous reactions. Antihistamines may act as allergens and show cross-sensitivity with phenothiazines, sulphonamides and topical antihistamines.

Table 94.5 lists drugs with the highest skin reaction rates.

Table 94.5 *Drugs with the highest reaction rates*

- penicillin and derivatives
- sulphonamides
- thiazide diuretics
- barbiturates
- quinidine
- anticonvulsants
- blood products
- gold salts

Erythema multiforme

Erythema multiforme is an acute eruption affecting the skin and mucosal surfaces.

Clinical features:

- mainly in children, adolescents, young adults
- symmetric
- erythematous papules
- mainly backs of hands, palms and forearms (Fig. 94.6)
- also on feet and toes, mouth
- occasionally on trunk and genitalia

- polymorphic
- vesicles and bullae may develop
- self-limiting (up to two weeks)

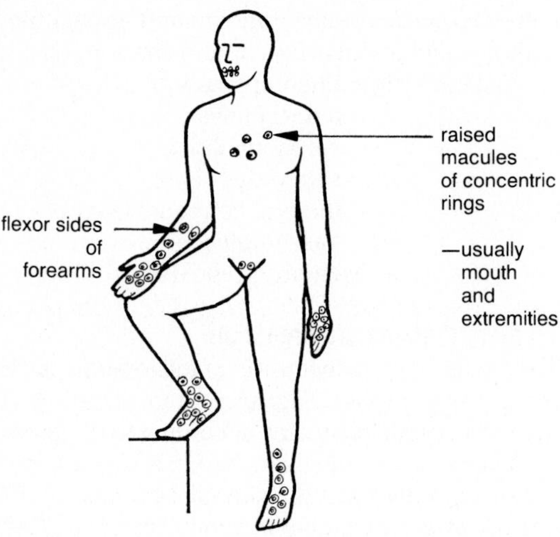

Fig. 94.6 *Erythema multiforme: typical distribution*

Stevens-Johnson syndrome

A very severe and often fatal variant. Sudden onset with fever and constitutional symptoms.

Causes and associations

Erythema multiforme is a vasculitis affecting the skin and mucosa. Herpes simplex virus (usually type I) is the commonest known association .

Associations include:

- unknown 50%
- herpes simplex virus 33%
- other infections, e.g.
  - — mycoplasma pneumonia
  - — tuberculosis
  - — streptococcus
- connective tissue disorders, e.g. SLE
- neoplasia
  - — Hodgkin's disease
  - — myeloma
  - — carcinoma
- deep X-ray therapy
- drugs
  - — barbiturates
  - — penicillin
  - — sulphonamides
  - — phenothiazines
  - — phenytoin

Treatment

Identify and remove cause, e.g. withdraw drugs.

Symptomatic treatment, e.g. antihistamines for itching.

Refer severe cases.

Erythema nodosum

Erythema nodosum is characterised by the onset of bright red, raised, tender nodules on the shins. The nodules may appear on the thighs and the arms. Adult females are typically affected. An arthritic reaction can affect the ankles and knees.

Causes/associations

- Sarcoidosis (commonest known cause)
- Infections
  - — Streptococcal infections
  - — tuberculosis
  - — leprosy
  - — fungal infections
- Inflammatory bowel disorders
- Drugs
  - — sulphonamides
  - — oral contraceptives
  - — bromides and iodides
- Unknown

Investigations

Tests include FBE, ESR, chest X-ray (the most important), Mantoux test.

Treatment

Identify the cause if possible. Rest and analgesics for the acute stage. Systemic corticosteroids speed resolution if severe episodes.

Prognosis

There is a tendency to settle spontaneously over 3–4 weeks.

Herpes zoster

Herpes zoster (shingles) is caused by reactivation of varicella zoster virus (acquired from the primary infection of chickenpox) in the dorsal root ganglion. The term comes from the Greek *herpes* (to creep) and *zoster* (a belt or girdle). Shingles is from the Latin *cingere* (to gird) or *cingulum* (a belt). In most instances the reason for reactivation is unknown, but occasionally it is related to an underlying malignancy, usually leukaemia or a lymphoma, to immunosuppression, or to a local disease or disturbance of the spine or spinal cord, such as a tumour or radiotherapy.

The incidence is 3.4 cases per 1000 population per year. A person of any age can get herpes zoster but it is more common in people over 50 years.

Clinical features

The main features are:

- the condition is preceded by several days of radicular pain with hyperaesthesia
- unilateral patchy rash in one or two contiguous dermatomes
- intense erythema with papules in affected skin
- later crusting and separation of scabs after 10–14 days, often with depigmentation, and
- regional lymphadenopathy

Distribution

Any part of the body may be affected, but thoracic and trigeminal dermatomes are the most common. It follows the distribution of the original varicella rash (worse on the face and trunk).

Cranial nerve involvement

The trigeminal nerve: 15% of all cases.

- ophthalmic branch—50% affects nasociliary branch with lesions on tip of nose and eyes (conjunctivae and cornea)
- maxillary and mandibular—oral, palatal and pharyngeal lesions

The facial nerve: lower motor neurone facial nerve palsy with vesicles in and around external auditory meatus (notably posterior wall)—the Ramsay Hunt syndrome.

Complications

Rare: meningoencephalitis
Uncommon: motor paralysis
Common:

- postherpetic neuralgia; increased incidence with age and debility, with duration greater than six months:

less than 50 years	1%
50 to 59 years	7%
60 to 69 years	21%
70 to 79 years	28%

- the neuralgia resolves within one year in 70–80% of these patients but in others it may persist for years
- eye complications of ophthalmic zoster including keratitis, uveitis and eyelid damage

Management

- Appropriate detailed explanation and reassurance. Dispel myths: namely, that it is not a dangerous disease, the patient will not go insane nor die if the rash spreads from both sides and meets in the middle.
- Explain that herpes zoster is only mildly contagious but children can acquire chickenpox after exposure to a person with the disorder. It is advisable to avoid contact with infants and young children who have never had chickenpox and avoid contact with the immunocompromised and those undergoing chemotherapy. Consider giving varicella zoster immunoglobulin to those immunocompromised contacts who have no history of varicella.
- Treating the rash: Instruct the patient to avoid overtreating the rash, which may become infected. Calamine lotion may be soothing but removal of the calamine can be painful. For a hot painful rash tepid water compresses are soothing and a drying lotion, e.g. menthol in flexible collodion, is most suitable. Acyclovir ointment can be used, although some authorities do not favour its use because of stinging.[4]
- Oral medication
  - — Analgesics such as aspirin or paracetamol with or without codeine should be first-line therapy.
  - — Acyclovir may reduce the duration of the disease and the infectivity of the rash. It should be used in all immunocompromised patients and also in the elderly (over 60 years) with significant pain, provided the rash has been present for less than 72 hours.[5]
  - — Dose: acyclovir 800 mg five times daily for seven days.
  - — An alternative to acyclovir in these patients is corticosteroids, although there is doubt about their efficacy.

Week 1	50 mg (o) daily
Week 2	25 mg (o) daily
Week 3	12.5 mg (o) daily[6]

Prevention

Consider giving varicella zoster immune globulin to contacts of patients who are immunosuppressed and have no history of varicella.

Postherpetic neuralgia

This pain is usually severe and varies in quality from paroxysmal stabbing pain to burning or aching. Spasms of pain upon light brushing of the skin is a feature.

Treatment options[6]

- Simple analgesics
- Transcutaneous electrical nerve stimulation (TENS) as often as necessary, e.g. 16 hours/ day for two weeks[6]

  plus

  tricyclic antidepressants
  e.g. amitriptyline 10–50 mg (o) nocte

  or

  doxepin 10–50 mg (o) nocte

  This is a starting trial dose in view of the patient's age.
- Carbamazepine (for lancinating pain)
  100 mg (o) bd initially, increasing the dose gradually to avoid drowsiness (up to 400 mg bd)
- Topical capsaicin 0.025% (Capsig) cream, apply four times a day (application of local anaesthetic cream 20 minutes beforehand may prevent a burning sensation).

Physical treatments

- Local corticosteroid and anaesthetic injections.
- Nerve blocks, e.g. supraorbital nerve.
- Excision of painful skin scar. If the neuralgia of four months or more is localised to a favourable area of skin, a most effective treatment is to excise the affected area, bearing in mind that the scar tends to follow a linear strip of skin. This method is clearly unsuitable for a large area.

Method

- Mark out the painful area of the skin.
- Incise it with its subcutaneous fat, using an elongated elliptical excision (Fig. 94.7).
- Close the wound with a subcuticular suture or interrupted sutures.

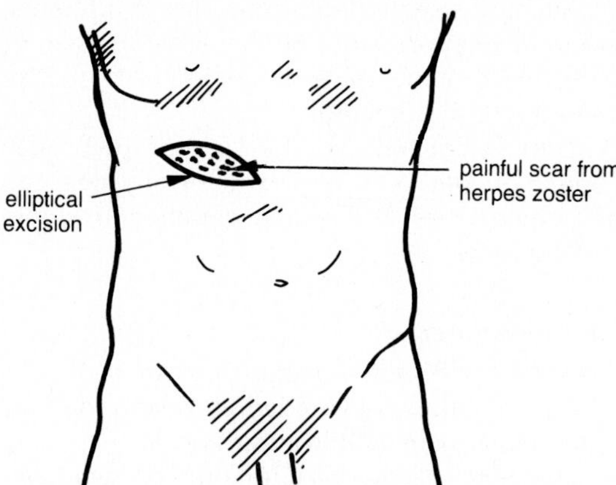

Fig. 94.7 *Postherpetic neuralgia: example of type of excision for severe problem*

Herpes simplex

Herpes simplex is a common infection caused by the large DNA herpes simplex virus (HSV) which can cause a vesicular rash anywhere on the skin or mucous membranes. There are two major antigenic strains of HSV:

- HSV 1, which commonly involves the lips and oral mucosa
- HSV 2, which basically affects the genitalia (common in adolescents and young adults)

Epidemiology

HSV has a world-wide distribution and is spread orally or genitally by infected secretions. Primary HSV infection is usually a disease of childhood, characteristically causing acute gingivostomatitis in a preschool child (page 679).

Table 94.6 summarises the major manifestations of HSV and possible complications.

Table 94.6 *Herpes simplex virus: manifestations and complications*

Examples of manifestations
- Herpes labialis (synonyms: fever blisters, cold sores)
- Keratoconjunctivitis, including dendritic ulcer
- Genital infection
- Other areas of skin such as buttocks

Complications
- Eczema herpeticum
- Erythema multiforme (3–14 days postinfection), often recurrent
- Myeloradiculopathy with genital herpes
- Pneumonia
- Encephalitis

Recurrent infection
Recurrences range from weeks to months and appear due to reactivation rather than reinfection. The cause is not clear but there are several known precipitating factors. These are fever, sunlight, respiratory infections, menstruation, emotional stress, local trauma and, with genital lesions, sexual intercourse.

Fatalities
HSV infections can be potentially fatal. Reactivated HSV can cause a focal destruction encephalitis. The untreated case fatality rate is as high as 70%, but this can be greatly reduced with the use of acyclovir. Neonates exposed to HSV can develop fatal disseminated infection. In compromised patients the disease can be severe.

Diagnosis
If the clinical picture is uncertain, immunofluorescence of, or culture from, vesicle fluid can aid diagnosis.

Genital herpes

see pages 838–839.

Herpes labialis (classical cold sores)

The objective is to limit the size and intensity of the lesions. At the first sensation of the development of a cold sore:

- apply an ice cube to the site for up to 5 minutes every 60 minutes (for first 12 hours)
- topical applications include

  idoxuridine 0.5% preparations (Herplex D liquifilm, Stoxil topical, Virasolve) applied hourly

  or

  povidone-iodine 10% cold sore paint: apply on swab sticks four times a day until disappearance

  or

  10% silver nitrate solution: apply the solution carefully with a cotton bud to the base of the lesions (deroof vesicles with a sterile needle if necessary). May be repeated.[7]

  or

  acyclovir cream (if available) five times daily for four days.

Oral medication
- acyclovir 200 mg five times daily or 800 mg twice daily for 7–10 days or until resolution (reserve for severe cases).

Zinc treatment
This empirically based treatment is favoured by some therapists. Zinc sulphate 220 mg tds, half an hour before meals, and large amounts of coffee during the day.

Topical zinc treatment
Zinc sulphate solution 0.025–0.05%, apply five times a day for cutaneous lesions and 0.01–0.025% for mucosal lesions.[4]

Prevention
If exposure to the sun precipitates the cold sore, use a 15+ sun protection lip balm, ointment or solastick. Zinc sulphate solution can be applied once a week for recurrences. Oral acyclovir 200 mg bd (6 months) can be used for severe and frequent recurrences.[4]

Advice to the patient
Herpes simplex is contagious. It is present in saliva and can be spread in a family by the sharing of drinking and eating utensils and toothbrushes or by kissing. It is most important not to kiss an infant if you have an active cold sore.

Hand, foot and mouth disease

This is a mild vesicular eruption caused by a Coxsackie A virus (usually A_{16}). HFM disease affects both children and adults but typically children under the age of ten.

Clinical features
- incubation period 3–5 days
- initial fever, headache and malaise
- sore mouth
- vesicles lead to shallow ulcers on buccal mucosa, gums and tongue
- greyish vesicle with surrounding erythema
- on hands, palms and soles (usually lateral borders)
- lesions resolve in 3–5 days
- healing without scarring

Management
- reassurance and explanation
- symptomatic treatment

Folliculitis

A generalised acute erythematous maculopapular rash can be a manifestation of bacterial folliculitis, typically caused by *Staphylococcus aureus* and *Pseudomonas aeruginosa.*

Pseudomonas folliculitis can cause confusion, the typical features being:

- rapidly spreading rash
- mainly on trunk, buttocks and thighs
- itchy
- small pustules surrounded by circular red-purple halo
- follows immersion in a hot spa bath or tub

Treatment is based on the sensitivity of the cultured organisms, e.g. ciprofloxacin.

References

1. Murtagh J. *Patient education*. Sydney: McGraw-Hill, 1992, 43.
2. Hunter JAA, Savin JA, Dahl MV. *Clinical dermatology*. Oxford: Blackwell Scientific Publications, 1989:55.
3. Thomas RM. Drug eruptions. Medicine International, 1988; 49:2038–2042.
4. Russo GJ. *Herpes simplex and herpes zoster*. Glendale: Audio Digest: Family Practice, 1991; 39:38.
5. Newton-John H, Murtagh J. Herpes zoster. Aust Fam Physician, 1986; 15:1343–1344.
6. Moulds RFW. *Analgesic guidelines* (2nd edition). Victorian Medical Postgraduate Foundation, 1992, 60–62.
7. Pollack A. Treatment of herpes simplex: A practice tip. Aust Fam Physician, 1982; 11:952.

95

Skin ulcers

An ulcer is a localised area of necrosis of the surface of the skin or mucous membrane. It is usually produced by sloughing of inflamed necrotic tissue. Ulcers of the skin are common, particularly on the legs and feet, on areas exposed to the sun, and on pressure areas such as the sacrum in older people.

The national morbidity survey (UK) showed that 2–3 per 1000 patients per annum consulted their general practitioner with 'chronic ulcers of the skin'.[1]

A clinical approach

It is useful to keep in mind the various causes of ulcers (Table 95.1). The commonest causes or types are venous and ischaemic ulcers of the leg, pressure ulcers (decubitus) and trauma. It is important not to misdiagnose malignant ulcers, including 'Marjolin's ulcer', which is squamous cell carcinoma developing in unstable chronic scars or ulcers, e.g. burns, venous ulcers, tropical ulcers, of longstanding duration. Amelanotic melanoma is a specific trap.

Table 95.1 *Types and causes of skin ulcers*

Traumatic

Decubitus (related to trauma)

Vascular
- Venous
  - varicose veins
  - post thrombophlebitis
- Arterial insufficiency
- Skin infarction (thrombolitic ulcer)
- Vasculitis
  - rheumatoid arthritis

Infective
- Tropical ulcer
- Tuberculosis
- *Mycobacterium ulcerans*
- Post cellulitis
- Chronic infected sinus

Malignant
- Squamous cell carcinoma
- Marjolin's ulcer (SCC)
- Basal cell carcinoma (rodent ulcer)
- Malignant melanoma
- Ulcerating metastases

Neurotrophic
- Peripheral neuropathy, e.g. diabetes
- Peripheral nerve injuries, e.g. leprosy

Haematological
- Spherocytosis
- Sickle cell anaemia

Miscellaneous
- Artefactual
- Pyoderma gangrenosum
- Insect and spider bites

History

A careful history helps determine the cause of the ulceration. Relevant history includes previous deep venous thrombosis or pulmonary embolism, diabetes, rheumatoid arthritis, inflammatory bowel disease, chronic skin ulcers and arterial insufficiency, including a history of intermittent claudication and ischaemic rest pain.

A drug history is important, considering especially beta-blockers and ergotamine which can compromise the arterial circulation, corticosteroids and NSAIDs which affect healing, and nifedipine which tends to aggravate ankle oedema.

Examination of the ulcer[2]

Any ulcer should be assessed for the following characteristics:

- site
- shape
- size
- edge: consider consistency
- floor
- base
- discharge
- surrounding skin
  - — colour (? signs of inflammation)
  - — sensitivity
- mobility in relation to underlying tissue
- regional lymph nodes

Site of ulcer

Venous ulcers typically occur on the medial side of the leg in relation to incompetent perforating veins in the traditional gaiter area (Fig. 95.1).

Ischaemic ulcers tend to occur on the lateral side and anterior part of the leg.

Trophic ulcers, which are associated with neuropathy, occur on parts subject to repeated pressure and trauma such as the 'ball' of the foot or the pulps of the fingers.

Solar-induced ulcers such as SCCs and BCCs occur on such parts exposed to the sun. It should be noted if the ulcer is related to old scars, including burns and chronic ulcers.

Fig. 95.1 *Area typically affected by varicose eczema and ulceration (the 'gaiter' area)*

Size, shape and edge

The classic appearances of various ulcers are presented in Figures 95.2a,b. These are general guidelines only. Infective ulcers due to mycobacterium species, and bed sores, tend to have an undermined edge while a trophic ulcer is punched out and typically round in surface shape. A raised firm ulcer edge may indicate malignancy.

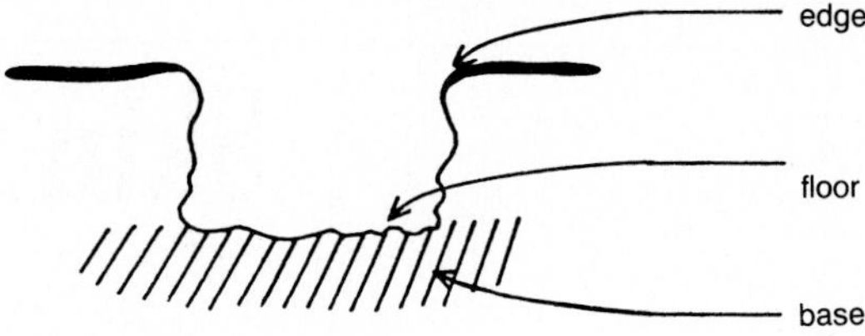

Fig. 95.2a *Parts of an ulcer*

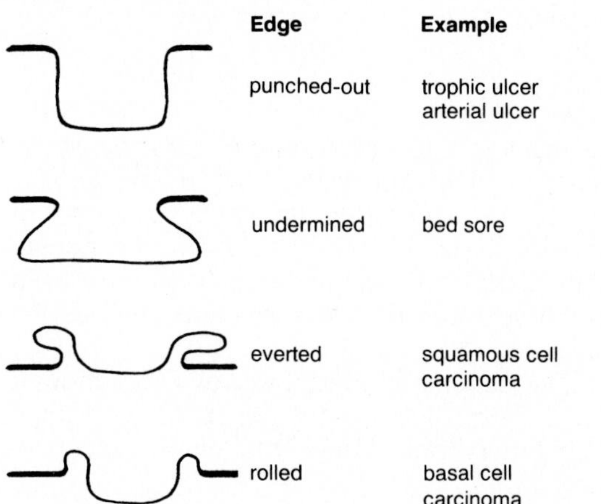

Fig. 95.2b *Types of ulcer*

Floor of the ulcer

The floor or base of the ulcer provides useful clinical information. A dry or extended base or necrotic eschar in the floor implies ischaemia. Venous ulcers on the other hand are often superficial and tend to have fibrinous exudate and ooze, sometimes purulent fluid.

Investigations

The following should be considered, according to the clinical findings:

- full blood count
- ESR
- random blood sugar
- rheumatoid factor tests
- duplex doppler studies
- swab for specific organisms

- biopsy, especially if SCC suspected (avoid biopsy if melanoma: amelanotic melanomas are a trap)

Lower limb ulceration

The most common causes of lower limb ulceration are venous disease, arterial disease and diabetes.

Differentiating between leg ulcers (85%) and foot ulcers (15%) is very important since they present two very different problems.[3] According to the survey by Stacey, venous disease is present in two-thirds of leg ulcers, while arterial disease occurs in 28% (Table 95.2). Ulceration on the foot frequently has an arterial aetiology (72%), with many of these patients also having diabetes, whereas venous disease is present in only 6%.[3]

Table 95.2 *Causes of chronic ulceration of the leg and foot*[3]

The leg	
Venous disease	52%
Mixed venous and arterial disease	15%
Arterial disease	13%
Others	20%
The foot	
Arterial disease	72%
Mixed venous and arterial disease	2%
Venous disease	4%
Others	22%

The differential characteristics are presented in Table 95.3.

A general examination, including the leg, is very important. This includes examining the venous drainage (pages 573–576), the arterial pulses and the sensation of the leg, and checking for the presence of diabetes.

Appropriate investigations (if required) include:

- full blood count
- blood sugar
- duplex doppler studies for arterial circulation

To swab or not to swab

A routine ulcer swab is not considered to be of significant value. If specific organisms such as *Mycobacterium ulcerans* are suspected, then cultures are necessary.

Venous ulceration

Venous ulceration (synonyms: 'varicose', 'stasis' and 'gravitational' ulcers) accounts for the majority of leg ulcers. Chronic venous insufficiency is one of the most common medical problems in the elderly, with an estimated incidence of 5.9%.[4]

The problem is invariably secondary to deep venous thrombophlebitis. The subsequent chronic venous hypertension produces trophic changes such as hyperpigmentation, fibrotic thickening, induration and oedema. The end point of this process is ulceration, which affects 3% of those with varicose veins and 30% of those with trophic changes.[5]

Table 95.3 *Comparison of typical features of venous and arterial ulceration of the leg*

	Venous	***Arterial***
Site	Around ankle and lower third of leg (gaiter area) Just above medial malleoli	Distal to ankle Upper two-thirds of leg
Pain	Nil to mild	Usually moderate to severe
Oedema	Usually present	Usually absent
Ulcer features	'Ragged' edge Often superficial Ooze +++	'Punched out' Often deep, involving deep fascia Dry
Associated limb features	Varicosities Varicose dermatitis Haemosiderin deposits Atrophie blanche	'Cold' extremities Ischaemic changes Diminished or absent peripheral pulses
History	Limb oedema Past DVT Failed graft	Peripheral vascular disease—claudication, rest pain Diabetes Smoker

Based on a table prepared by Dr Denise Findlay; reproduced with permission

Clinical features of venous ulcers[6]

- occur in same area as venous eczema
- shallow (but can reach periosteum)
- more common medial than lateral
- sometimes circumferential
- granulating floor sometimes with surrounding cellulitis
- notoriously slow in healing
- generally not tender but can be painful
- associated pain is usually relieved by raising the leg

On examination superficial varicosities are usually but not invariably present. Pitting oedema may be present early but with time fibrosis and firm induration develop. Other clinical features include dermatitis (eczema), punctuate capillary proliferation, haemosiderin, hyperpigmentation and 'atrophie blanche'.[7]

Arterial (ischaemic) ulcers

Ischaemic ulcers are generally localised to the most peripheral areas such as the tips of the toes and the point of the heel or to pressure points such as the heels, malleoli or head of the first metatarsal.

Clinical features:

- painful
- punched out
- minimal granulation tissue

Management of leg ulcers

A major advance in the management of venous ulcers has been the finding that wounds heal better in an occluded or semi-occluded state.[7]

Principles of optimal management

- explanation about the cause, and promotion of patient compliance
- promote clean granulation tissue to permit healing
- meticulous cleaning and dressing (avoid sensitising preparations)
- prevention and control of infection antibiotics if cellulitis (cephalexin or erythromycin)
- firm elastic compression bandage—use a minimal stretch bandage from base toes to just below the knee
- bed rest with elevation (if severe, 45–60 minutes twice a day and at night)
- encourage early ambulation
- appropriate modification of lifestyle including weight reduction

Note Firm compression is the single most important factor in the healing of venous ulcers.[5] Options include elastic stockings, elastic bandages, Unna's boots and legging orthoses.[8]

Cleansing/debridement agents

There are many cleansing agents, including: EUSOL (dilute—one-quarter strength), N saline, fibrinolysin co ointment (Elase), benzoyl peroxide, silver sulphadiazine (Silvazine) cream, Intra Site Gel.

A good combination is N saline cleansing followed by Intra Site Gel for debridement. Hydrogels such as Intra Site Gel, which have been found to be effective at debridement (including black necrotic areas), have generally replaced enzyme dressings. Simple formulations suggested by some practitioners for wound cleaning are honey or sugar or a paste of sugar and povidone iodine.

Medicated occlusive bandages

There are several suitable occlusive bandages which ideally should be left on for one week. All contain zinc oxide with the indicated additives, e.g. Acoband (paraffin), Calaband (calamine), Ichthaband (ichthamol), Quinaband (clioquinol + calamine), Tarband (coal tar), Zincaband (zinc oxide only).

Pitfalls and other factors to be considered

- Treat the primary cause by surgery or other means, e.g. varicose veins, vascular insufficiency.
- If oedema, elevate legs and prescribe diuretics. An ulcer will not heal in the presence of significant ankle oedema.
- Be careful of allergy to local applications.
- Be careful of irritation from local applications.
- Never apply corticosteroid preparations directly to ulcers.
- Avoid heavy packing of the wound.
- Consider grafting (pinch skin or split thickness).
- Consider oxpentifylline 400 (Trental) for chronic occlusive arterial disease.

Post-healing and prevention of ulcers

- Encourage preventive measures such as regular walking, good nutrition, no smoking,

elevation of leg when resting, great care to avoid trauma.
- Apply emollients for varicose eczema.
- Wear a compression grade elastic stocking for varicose ulcers, e.g. Jobst Fast-Fit, Tensor Press.

A recommended treatment routine for a leg ulcer is presented in Table 95.4. It is desirable (for the outpatient) to leave the dressings and bandages in place for one week, perhaps two weeks, depending on the state of the dressing.

Table 95.4 *A recommended leg ulcer treatment method*

- Clean with normal saline
- If slough, apply Intra Site Gel
- Dressing
  Silver sulphadiazine (Silvazine) cream covered with paraffin gauze
  or
  Povidone-iodine (Betadine) gauze
- Occlusive paste bandage, e.g. Icthaband (7 days), from base of toe to just below knee
  or
  Elastocrepe or Eloflex bandage to just below knee
- Tubigrip stockinette cover

Unna's boots

Unna's boots have an important place in the management of severe ulceration despite the discomfort and inconvenience for the patient. They appear to provide excellent fixed compression and healing and one particular study showed the superiority to elastic stockings (7.3 weeks compared to 18.4 weeks).[9]

Decubitus ulcers (pressure sores)

Pressure sores tend to occur in elderly immobile patients, especially those who are unconscious, paralysed or debilitated. The cause is skin ischaemia from sustained pressure over a bony area, particularly the heels, sacrum, hips and buttocks. Poor general health, including anaemia, are predisposing factors.

Clinical features:

- preliminary area of fixed erythema at pressure site
- relative sudden onset of necrosis and ulceration
- ulcer undermined at edges
- possible rapid extension of ulcers
- necrotic slough in base

Management

Prevention

- Good nursing care including turning patient every two hours.
- Regular skin examinations by the nursing and medical staff.
- Special care of pressure areas, including gentle handling.
- Special beds, mattresses (e.g. air-filled ripple) and sheepskin to relieve pressure areas.
- Good nutrition and hygiene.
- Control of urinary and faecal incontinence.
- Avoid the donut cushion.

Treatment of ulcer

Use above measures, plus:

- Clean base with saline solution (applied gently via a syringe) or Intra Site Gel.
- General guidelines for dressings:
  — deep ulcers: alginates, e.g. Tegagel
  — shallow ulcers: hydrocolloids, e.g. Duoderm, Cutinova Hydro
  — dry or necrotic ulcers: hydrogels, e.g. Intra Site
  — heavy exudative ulcers: foams, e.g. Lyofoam
- Give vitamin C, 500 mg bd.
- Give antibiotics for spreading cellulitis (otherwise of little use).
- Healing is usually satisfactory but, if not, surgical intervention with debridement of necrotic tissue and skin grafting may be necessary.

Undressing wounds

Removal of dressings from ulcerated wounds is very important. The contact layer should be removed slowly to prevent detachment of fragile epthelial surface cells and trauma to healthy granulation tissue.[10]

Trophic ulcers

Trophic ulcers are due to neuropathy causing loss of sensation (invariably diabetic) and usually follow an injury of which the patient was unaware.

A feature is a deep punched-out lesion (similar to ischaemic ulcers) over pressure points. A common site is the ball of the foot under the first metatarsal head, but the heel or a bunion may also be affected.

The ulcers may extend to the bone and into joints. They are prone to secondary infection.

Treatment is based on controlling the diabetes and clearing infection with appropriate antibiotics, but referral for surgical management is usually essential.

Dermatitis artefacta and neurotic excoriations

These self-inflicted ulcerated or erosive skin lesions have a psychological basis.

Dermatitis artefacta

In this condition the patients deny self-trauma and may have deep-seated psychological problems; or they may be malingering or manipulative for secondary gain.

Neurotic excoriations

These lesions, which are usually identical to the artefactual lesions, are caused by patients who admit to scratching, picking or digging at their skin. It occurs at times of stress and treatment is seldom successful. Treatment consists of counselling and topical antipruritics such as:

- liquor picis carbonis and menthol in sorbolene cream

or

- menthol (0.25%), salicylic acid (2.5%), glycerine (15%), emulsifying wax (15%), aqua ad 100 g cream.

References

1. Cormack J, Marinker M, Morrel D. In: *Practice. A handbook of primary health care.* London: Kluwer-Harrap Handbooks, 1980; 3:01–09.
2. Davis A, Bolin T, Ham J. *Symptom analysis and physical diagnosis* (2nd edition). Sydney: Pergamon Press, 1990, 380–389.
3. Stacey MC. Chronic venous ulcers. Sydney: Medical Observer, 29 March 1991, 31–32.
4. Beauregard S, Gilchrest BA. A survey of skin problems and skin care regimens in the elderly. Arch Dermatol, 1987; 123:1638–1643.
5. Fry J, Berry HE. *Surgical problems in clinical practice.* London: Edward Arnold, 1987, 115–117.
6. Buxton P. *ABC of dermatology.* London: British Medical Journal, 1989, 34–39.
7. Fitzpatrick JE. Stasis ulcers: update on a common geriatric problem. Mod Medicine of Australia, June 1990, 81–88.
8. Vernick SH, Shapiro D, Shaw FD. Legging orthosis for venous and lymphatic insufficiency. Arch Phys Med Rehab, 1987; 68:459–461.
9. Hendricks WM, Swallows RT. Management of stasis leg ulcers with Unna's boots versus elastic support stockings. J Amer Acad Dermatol, 1985; 12:90–98.
10. Rowland J. Pressure ulcers: a literature review and a treatment scheme. Aust Fam Physician, 1993; 22:1819–1827.

96

Common lumps and bumps

Lumps and bumps are very common presentations with the skin being a very common site for neoplastic lesions. Most of these lesions only invade locally, with the notable exception of malignant melanoma. Pigmented skin tumours thus demand very careful consideration, although only a very few are neoplastic. The optimum time to deal with the problem and cure any skin cancer is at its first presentation. The family doctor thus has an important responsibility to screen these tumours and is faced with two basic decisions: the diagnosis and whether to treat or refer.

Most skin lumps are benign and can be left *in situ*, but the family doctor should be able to remove most of these lumps if appropriate and submit them for histological verification. The main treatment options available in family practice are: biopsy, cryotherapy, curette and cautery, excision or intralesional injections of corticosteroid.[1] A list of common and important lumps is presented in Table 96.1.

Table 96.1 *Important lumps and their tissue of origin*[3]

Skin and mucous membranes
- fibroepithelial polyp (skin tag)
- sebaceous cyst
- implantation cyst
- mucocele
- hypertrophic scar and keloid
- warts and papillomas
- pox virus lumps
  - molluscum contagiosum
  - orf
  - milker's nodules
- seborrhoeic keratoses
- granuloma annularae
- dermatofibroma
- solar keratoses
- keratoacanthoma

malignant tumours
- basal cell carcinoma (BCC)
- squamous cell carcinoma (SCC)
- Bowen's disease
- malignant melanoma
- Kaposi's sarcoma
- secondary tumour

Subcutaneous and deeper structures
- lipoma
- neurofibroma
- soft fibroma
- lymph node

musculoskeletal
- ganglion

Skin cancer

The three main skin cancers are the non-melanocyctic skin cancers (basal cell carcinoma—BCC; squamous cell carcinoma—SCC) and melanoma. The approximate relative incidence is BCCs 80%, SCCs 15–20%, and melanomas less than 5%.[2] The incidence of non-melanotic skin cancer is approximately 800 new cases per 100 000 population per year, and 25 per 100 000 for melanoma. About 80% of skin cancer deaths are due to melanoma and the rest mainly due to SCC.[2]

A diagnostic approach to the lump

As with any examination, the routine of *look, feel, move, measure, auscultate* and *transilluminate* should be followed.

The lump or lumps can be described thus:

- number
- shape: regular or irregular
- size (in metric units)
- position
- consistency (very soft, soft, firm, hard or stony hard)
- mobility
- surface or contour
- special features
  - — exact anatomical site
  - — relation to anatomical structures
  - — colour
  - — temperature (of skin over lump)
  - — tenderness
  - — pulsation (transmitted or direct)
  - — impulse
  - — reducibility
  - — percussion
  - — fluctuation (? contains fluid)
  - — bruit
  - — transilluminability
  - — special signs
    - slipping sign
    - emptying sign of cavernous haemangioma
  - — regional lymph nodes
  - — ? malignancy (is it 1° or 2° ?)

Relation of the lump to anatomical structures[3]

The question 'In what tissue layer is the lump situated?' needs to be addressed.

Is it in the skin?

The lump moves when the skin is moved, e.g. sebaceous cyst.

Is it in subcutaneous tissue?

The skin can be moved over the lump. The slipping sign: if the edge of the lump is pushed, the swelling slips from beneath the finger, e.g. lipoma.

Is it in muscle?

The lump is movable when the muscle is relaxed but on contraction of the muscle this movement becomes limited.

Is it arising from a tendon or joint?

Movement of these structures may cause a change in the mobility or shape of the tumour.

Is it in bone?

The lump is immobile and best outlined with the muscles relaxed.

Fibroepithelial polyps

Synonyms: skin tags, acrochordon, benign squamous papilloma.

Clinical features:

- benign skin overgrowth
- increased incidence with age
- commonest on neck, axilla, trunk, groins
- no malignant potential
- can be irritating or unsightly to patient

Management

- can leave or remove
- snip off with scissors or bone forceps (Figs. 96.1a,b)

or

- tie base with fine cotton or suture material

or

- diathermy base

or

- apply liquid nitrogen (Fig. 96.2)

These methods do not require local anaesthetic.

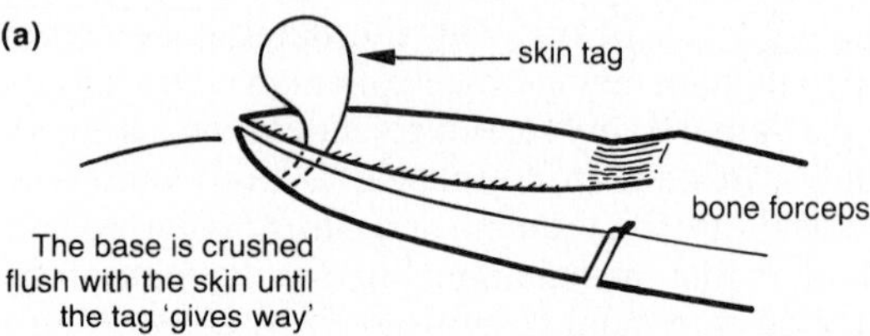

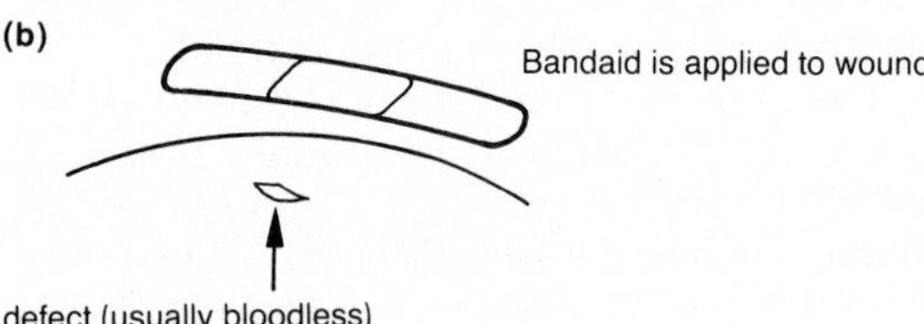

Fig. 96.1 *Removal of skin tags using bone forceps method*

Sebaceous cyst

Synonyms: 'pilar' cysts, wens, epidermoid cysts (similar in appearance)

Clinical features:

- firm to soft regular lump
- fixed to skin but not to other structures (Fig. 96.3a)
- found mainly on scalp—then face, neck, trunk, scrotum
- contains sebaceous material
- may be a central punctum containing keratin
- tendency to inflammation

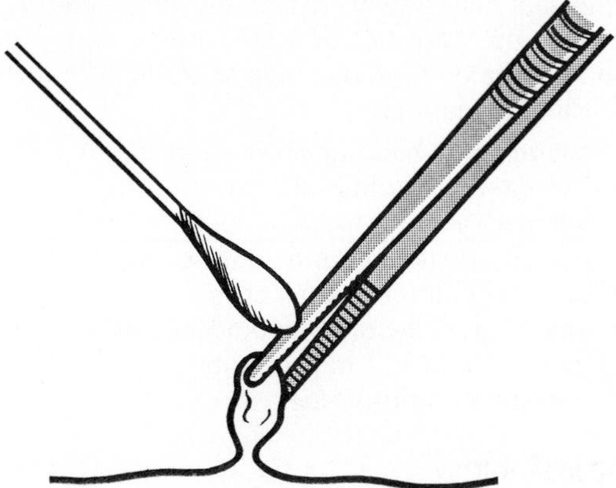

Fig. 96.2 *Removal of skin tag by liquid nitrogen: a cotton bud soaked in liquid nitrogen is applied to the forceps, which grasp the tag firmly*

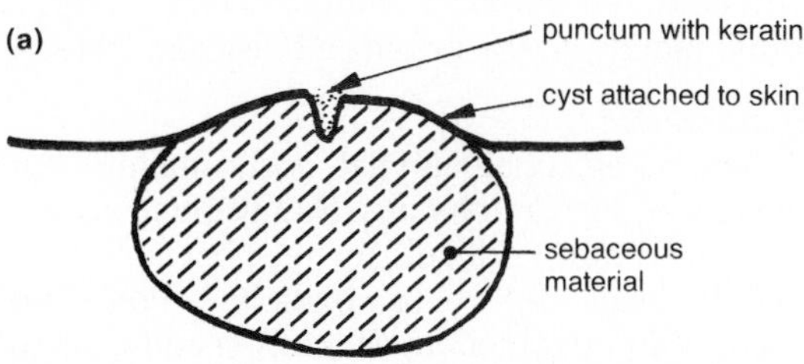

Fig. 96.3a *Configuration of a sebaceous cyst*

Management

- can leave if small and not bothersome

Surgical removal methods

There are several methods of removal of sebaceous cysts after infiltration of local anaesthetic over and around the cyst. These include:

Method 1 Incision into cyst

Make an incision into the cyst to bisect it, squeeze the contents out with a gauze swab and then avulse the lining of the cyst with a pair of artery forceps or remove with a small curette.

Method 2 Incision over cyst and blunt dissection

Make a careful skin incision over the cyst, taking care not to puncture its wall. Free the skin carefully from the cyst by blunt dissection. When it is free from adherent subcutaneous tissue, digital pressure will cause the cyst to 'pop out'.

Method 3 Standard dissection

Incise a small ellipse of skin to include the central punctum over the cyst (Fig. 96.3b). Apply forceps to this skin to provide traction for dissection of the cyst from the adherent dermis and subcutaneous tissue. Ideally, forceps should be applied at either end. The objective is to avoid rupture of the cyst. Inserting curved scissors (e.g. McIndoe's scissors), free the cyst by gently opening and closing the blades (Fig. 96.3c). Bleeding is not usually a problem. When the cyst is removed, obliterate the space with subcutaneous catgut. The skin is sutured with a vertical mattress suture to avoid a tendency to inversion of the skin edges into the slack wound. Send the cyst for histopathology.

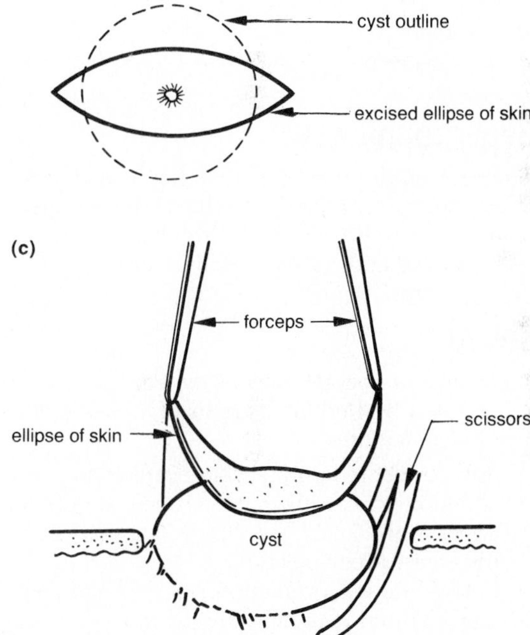

Fig. 96.3b, c *Standard dissection of a sebaceous cyst*

Treatment of infected cysts

Incise the cyst to drain purulent material. When the inflammation has resolved completely the cyst should be removed by Method 1 or Method 3.

Implantation cyst

Synonym: implantation dermoid

Clinical features:

- small cystic swelling
- may be tender

- usually follows puncture wounds
- especially on finger pulp, e.g. hairdressers, sewers
- contains mucus

Management
- incision removal (similar to sebaceous cyst)

Mucocele

A mucous retention cyst.

Clinical features:
- a benign tumour
- cyst containing mucus
- appears spontaneously
- common on lips and buccal mucosa
- smooth and round
- yellow or blue colour

Management
- incision removal

Hypertrophic scar

A hypertrophic scar is simply a lumpy scar caused by a nodular accumulation of thickened collagen fibres. It does not extend beyond the margins of the wound and regresses within a year.

Keloid

A keloid is a special type of hypertrophic scar that extends beyond the margins of the wound.

Clinical features:
- firm, raised, red-purple, skin overgrowth
- common on ear lobes, chin, neck, shoulder, upper trunk
- hereditary predisposition
- follows trauma, even minor, e.g. ear piercing
- may be burning or itchy and tender

Management
- prevention (avoid procedures in keloid-prone individuals)
- intradermal injection of corticosteroids in early stages (2–3 months) or X-ray treatment of surgical wounds within two weeks of operation.[4]

Warts and papillomas

Warts are skin tumours caused by the human papilloma virus (HPV). The virus invades the skin, usually through a small abrasion, causing abnormal skin growth. Warts are transmitted by direct or fomite contact and may be autoinoculated from one area to another.[5]

Clinical features:
- average incubation period—four months
- increased incidence in children and adolescents
- peak incidence around adolescence
- occurs in all races at all ages
- about 25% resolve spontaneously in six months[5] and 70% in two years
- present as various types

Types of warts

These include common warts, plane warts, filiform warts (fine elongated growths, usually on the face and neck), digitate warts (finger-like projections, usually on scalp), genital and plantar (Fig. 96.4).

Common warts

Skin-coloured tumours with a rough surface, found mainly on the fingers, elbows and knees.

Plane warts

Skin-coloured, small and flat, occurring in linear clusters along scratch lines. Mainly occur on the face and limbs. Difficult to treat because they contain very few virus particles. Prone to Koebner's phenomenon, which is seeding when a scratch passes through a plane wart.

Treatment options for warts

Topical applications:[5]
- salicylic acid, e.g. 5–20% in flexible collodion (apply daily or bd)
- formaldehyde 2–4% alone or in combination
- cantharadin 0.5–1% in equal parts collodion (available in USA), applied with care and occluded for 12 hours
- podophyllin 10–25% in tinct benz co *or* podophyllotoxin 0.5% (better) for anogenital warts—it is good on mucosal surfaces but does not penetrate normal keratin
- cytotoxic agents, e.g. 5-fluorouracil: very good for resistant warts such as plane warts and periungal warts

Cryotherapy

Carbon dioxide (−56.5°C) or liquid nitrogen (−195.8°C) destroys the host cell and stimulates an immune reaction.

Note Excessive keratin must be pared before freezing.
Results often disappointing.

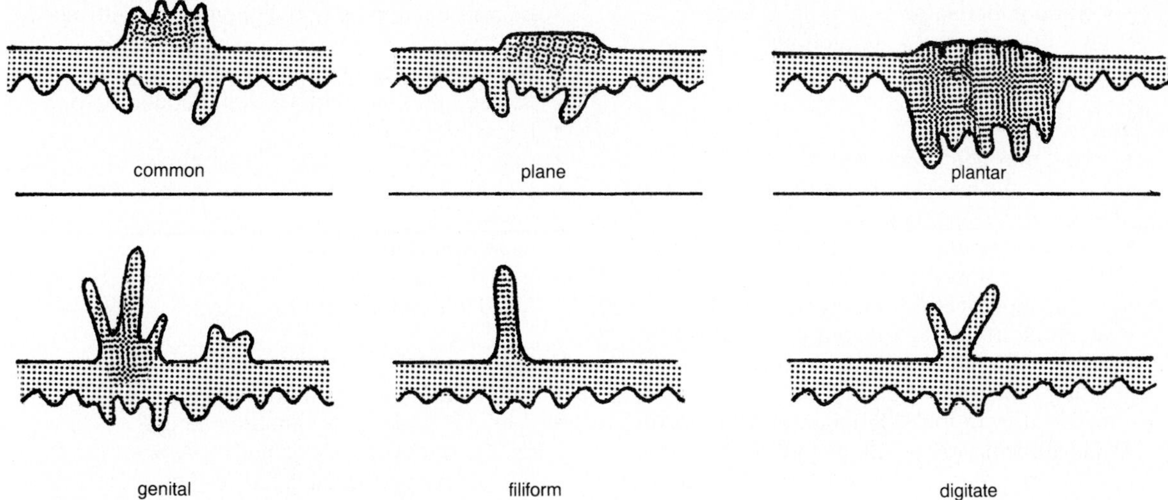

Fig. 96.4 *Configuration of various types of warts*

Curettage

Most common treatment; some plantar warts can be removed under LA with a sharp spoon curette. The problem is a tendency to scar so avoid over a pressure area such as the sole of the foot.

Electrodissection

A high-frequency spark under LA is useful for small, filiform or digitate warts. A combination of curettage and electrodissection is suitable for large and persistent warts.

Vitamin A and the retinoids

- topical retinoic acid, e.g. tretinoin 0.1% cream (Retin A) is effective on plane warts
- systemic oral retinoid, etretinate (Tigason) for recalcitrant warts

Specific wart treatment

The method chosen depends on the type of wart, its site and the patient's age.

Plantar warts: refer Chapter 57.

Genital warts: podophyllotoxin 0.5% paint (see Chap. 90).

Filiform and digitate warts: liquid nitrogen or electrodissection.

Plane warts: liquid nitrogen; salicylic acid 20% Co, e.g. Wartkil; consider 5-fluorouracil cream or Retin-A.

Common warts: a recommended method:

1. Soak the wart/s in warm soapy water.
2. Rub back the wart surface with a pumice stone.
3. Apply the paint (only to the wart; protect the surrounding skin with Vaseline). The paint: formalin 5%, salicylic acid 12%, acetone 25%, collodion to 100%.[4]

Do this daily or every second day. Carefully remove dead skin between applications.

Periungal warts (fingernails): consider 5-fluorouracil or liquid nitrogen. Always use a paint rather than ointment or paste on fingers.

Pox virus lumps

Skin tumours can be caused by pox viruses, some of which result from handling infected sheep, cows and monkeys and other animals such as deer. Hence they are usually found in sheep shearers, farmers and zookeepers.

Molluscum contagiosum

This common pox virus infection can be spread readily by direct contact, including sexual contact (page 841).

Clinical features:

- common in school-aged children
- single or multiple (more common)
- shiny, round, pink-white papule
- hemispherical up to 5 mm

- central punctum gives umbilical look
- can be spread by scratching and use of steroids

Treatment options

- liquid nitrogen (a few seconds)
- pricking the lesion with a pointed stick soaked in 1% or 2.5% phenol
- application of 15% podophyllin in friar's balsam (compound benzoin tincture)
- application of 30% trichloracetic acid
- destruction by electrocautery or diathermy
- ether soap and friction method
- lifting open the tip with a sterile needle inserted from the side (parallel to the skin) and applying 10% povidone iodine (Betadine) solution (parents can be shown this method and continue to use it at home for multiple tumours)

Orf

Orf is due to a pox virus and presents as a single papule or group of papules on the hands of sheep-handlers after handling lambs with contagious pustular dermatitis. The papules change into pustular-like nodules or bullae with a violaceous erythematous margin. It clears up spontaneously in about 3–4 weeks without scarring and no treatment is usually necessary.

Practice tip: Rapid resolution (days) can be obtained by an intralesional injection of triamcinolone diluted 50 : 50 in normal saline.[6]

Milker's nodules

In humans 2–5 papules appear on the hands about one week after handling cows' udders or calves' mouths. The papules enlarge to become tender grey nodules with a necrotic centre and surrounding inflammation. The patient can be reassured that the nodules are a self-limiting infection and spontaneous remission will occur in 5–6 weeks without residual scarring. One infection gives lifelong immunity.

Practice tip: Intralesional corticosteroid injection (as for orf).

Seborrhoeic keratoses

Synonyms: seborrhoeic wart, senile wart, senile keratoses (avoid these terms).

Clinical features:

- very common
- increasing number and pigmentation with age > 40 years
- sits on skin, appears in some like a 'sultana' pressed into the skin, i.e. well-defined border
- has a 'pitted' surface
- may be solitary but usually multiple
- common on face and trunk, but occurs anywhere
- usually asymptomatic
- usually causes patients some alarm (confused with melanoma)

Management

- usually nil apart from reassurance
- does not undergo malignant change
- can be removed for cosmetic reasons
- light cautery to small facial lesions
- freezing liquid nitrogen (especially if thin) decolours the tumour
- may drop off spontaneously
- if diagnosis uncertain, remove for histopathology

Granuloma annularae

Granuloma annularae are a common benign group of papules arranged in an annular fashion.

Clinical features:

- most common among children and young adults
- firm papules grouped in a 'string of pearls' pattern
- dermal nodules
- may be associated with minor trauma
- associated with diabetes
- usually on dorsum or sides of fingers (knuckle area), backs of hands, the elbows and knees

Management

- check urine/blood for sugar
- give reassurance (they usually subside in a year or so)
- cosmetic reasons: intradermal injection of triamcinolone (equal volume 10% with N saline)

Dermatofibroma

Synonyms: sclerosing haemangioma; histiocytoma.

This is a common pigmented nodule arising in the dermis due to a proliferation of fibroblasts, believed to develop as an abnormal response to minor trauma. The nodule gives a characteristic button-like feel and dimpling when laterally compressed (pinched) from the side with the fingers.

Clinical features:

- usually multiple
- firm, well-circumscribed nodules
- oval, 0.5–1.5 cm in diameter
- freely mobile over deeper structures
- slightly raised in relation to skin
- mainly on limbs, especially legs
- may itch
- mainly in women
- variable colour, pink or brown, tan or grey or violaceous
- characteristic 'dimple' sign on pinching margins

Treatment

- reassurance
- simple excision if requested

Solar keratosis

Solar keratoses are reddened, adherent, scaly thickenings occurring on light-exposed areas, with a potential for malignant change, especially on the ears.

Clinical features:

- sun-exposed fair skin
- mainly on face, ears, scalp (if balding), forearms, dorsum of hands (especially) and feet
- dry, rough, adherent scale
- discomfort on rubbing with towel
- scale can separate to leave oozing surface
- a small proportion undergo malignant change

Management

- reduced exposure to sunlight
- can disappear spontaneously
- liquid nitrogen if superficial

or

- 5-fluorouracil 5% cream daily for 3–4 weeks
- surgical excision for suspicious and ulcerating lesions
- biopsy if doubtful

Keratoacanthoma

Keratoacanthomas (KA) occur singly on light-exposed areas. The major problem is differentiation from squamous cell carcinoma (SCC), especially if on the lip or ear. The relative growth rates of three types of skin tumours are shown in Figure 96.5.

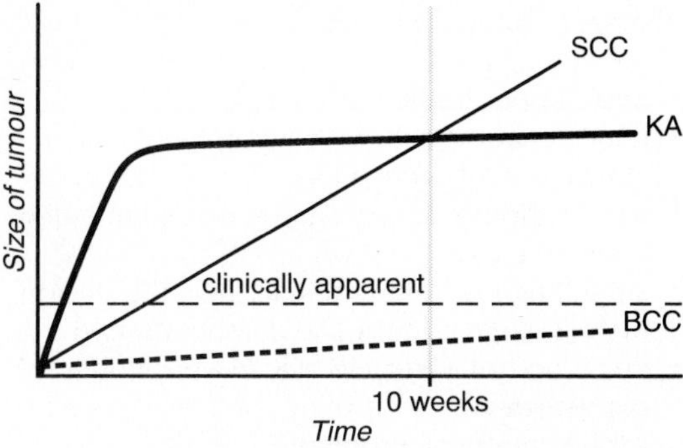

Fig. 96.5 *Relative growth rates of three types of skin tumours: keratoacanthoma, squamous cell carcinoma and basal cell carcinoma*

Clinical features:

- rapidly growing lesion on sun-exposed skin
- raised crater with central keratin plug (Fig. 96.6)
- grows to 2 cm or more
- arises over a few weeks, remains static, then spontaneously disappears after about six months; can leave a big scar
- can be confused with SCC

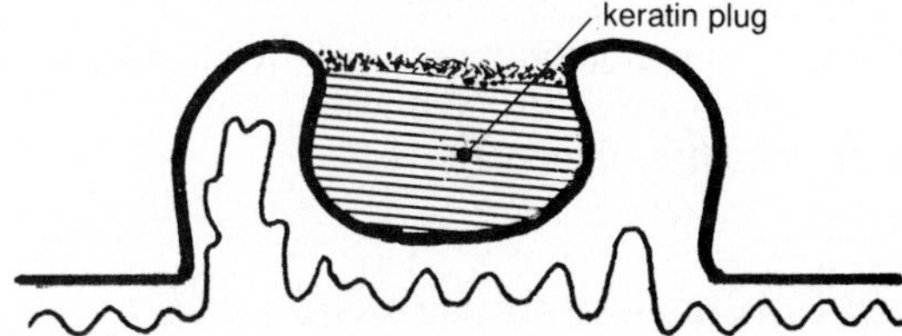

Fig. 96.6 *A typical keratoacanthoma*

Management

- remove by excision—perform biopsy
- if clinically certain—curettage/diathermy
- treat as SCC (by excision) if on lip/ear

The recommended treatment is surgical excision and histological examination. Ensure a 2–3 mm margin for excision. Most patients will not tolerate a tumour for six months on an exposed area such as the face while waiting for a spontaneous remission. Also, if it is an SCC, a potentially lethal cancer has remained *in situ* for an unnecessarily long period.

Basal cell carcinoma (BCC)

Clinical features:

- most common skin cancer (80%)
- age: usually > 35 years
- more frequent in males
- mostly on sun-exposed areas: face (mainly), neck, upper trunk, limbs (10%)
- may ulcerate easily = 'rodent ulcer'
- slow-growing over years
- has various forms: nodular, pigmented, ulcerated, etc.
- stretching the skin demarcates the lesion, highlights pearliness and distinct margin
- does not metastasise via lymph nodes or bloodstream
- local spread is a problem
- can spread deeply if around nose or ear

Clinical types

1. cystic nodular
2. ulcerated
3. pigmented
4. superficial
5. morphoeic

Management

- excision (5 mm margin) is best
- if not excision, do biopsy before other treatment
- radiotherapy is an option
- Moh's chemotherapy—a new form of treatment where the tumour removal is microscopically controlled.

Squamous cell carcinoma (SCC)

SCC is an important malignant tumour of the epidermis; it is also found on sun-exposed areas, especially in fair-skinned people. It tends to arise in premalignant areas such as solar keratoses, burns, chronic ulcers, leukoplakia and Bowen's disease, or it can arise *de novo*.

Clinical features:

- usually > 50 years
- initially firm thickening of skin, especially in solar keratosis
- surrounding erythema
- the hard nodules soon ulcerate
- occurs on the hands and forearms and the head and neck
- ulcers have a characteristic everted edge
- capable of metastases and may involve regional nodes
- SCCs of ear, lip, oral cavity, tongue and genitalia are serious and need special management

Management

- Early excision of tumours < 1 cm with 5–10 mm margin.
- Referral for specialised surgery and/or radiotherapy if large, in difficult site or lymphadenopathy.
- SCCs of the ear and lip, which have considerably more malignant potential, can be excised by wedge excision.

Bowen's disease

Bowen's disease begins as a slowly enlarging, sharply demarcated, thickened red plaque, especially on the lower legs of females. It may resemble solar keratosis or a patch of psoriasis. It remains virtually unchanged for months or years. It may become very crusty, ulcerate or bleed. It has a great potential for malignant change since it is a full thickness squamous cell carcinoma *in situ*.

Management

- biopsy first for diagnosis
- wide surgical excision if small
- skin grafting may be required

Note Biopsy a single patch of suspected psoriasis or dermatitis not responding to topical steroids.

Malignant melanoma

These are usually enlarging pigmented lesions with an irregular notched border. Refer to Chapter 97, on pigmented skin lesions.

Secondary tumour

These complex tumours may metastasise from the lung, melanoma or bowel and may arise in surgical scars, e.g. for carcinoma of the breast.

Kaposi's sarcoma

Kaposi's sarcoma presents as brownish-purple papules on the skin and mucosa. Apart from the well known presentation in immunocompromised individuals, it is seen as a primary tumour mostly in elderly men of central or eastern European origin.

Lipoma

Lipomas are common benign tumours of mature fat cells situated in subcutaneous tissue.

Clinical features:

- soft and may be fluctuant
- well defined; lobulated
- rubbery consistency
- may be one or many
- painless
- most common on limbs (especially arms) and trunk
- can occur at any site

Management

- reassurance about benign nature
- removal for cosmetic reasons or to relieve discomfort from pressure

Surgical excision

Many lipomas can be enucleated using a gloved finger, but there are a few traps: some are deeper than anticipated, and some are adjacent to important structures such as large nerves and blood vessels. Others are tethered by fibrous bands, and can recur. Recurrence is also possible if excision is incomplete.

Method

1. Outline the extent of the lipoma and note its anatomical relationships.
2. Infiltrate the area with 1% lignocaine with adrenaline (include the deepest part of the lipoma).
3. Make a linear incision (Fig. 96.7a) in the overlying skin, preferably in a natural crease line for about two-thirds of its length. The lipoma should bulge through the wound. For large lipomas, incise an ellipse of skin (Fig. 96.7b).
4. Insert a gloved finger between the skin and fatty tumour to determine whether it will shell out. It is important to seek the outer edge of each lobule, dissect it and bring it to the surface (Fig. 96.7c).
5. If necessary, insert curved scissors and use a blunt opening action to free any fibrous bands tethering the lipoma (Fig. 96.7d).
6. Ensure that all the fatty tissue is removed. Send it for histological examination.
7. Use a gauze swab to control bleeding and remove debris from the dead space.
8. Close the dead space with interrupted catgut sutures.
9. Close the skin with interrupted or subcuticular sutures.

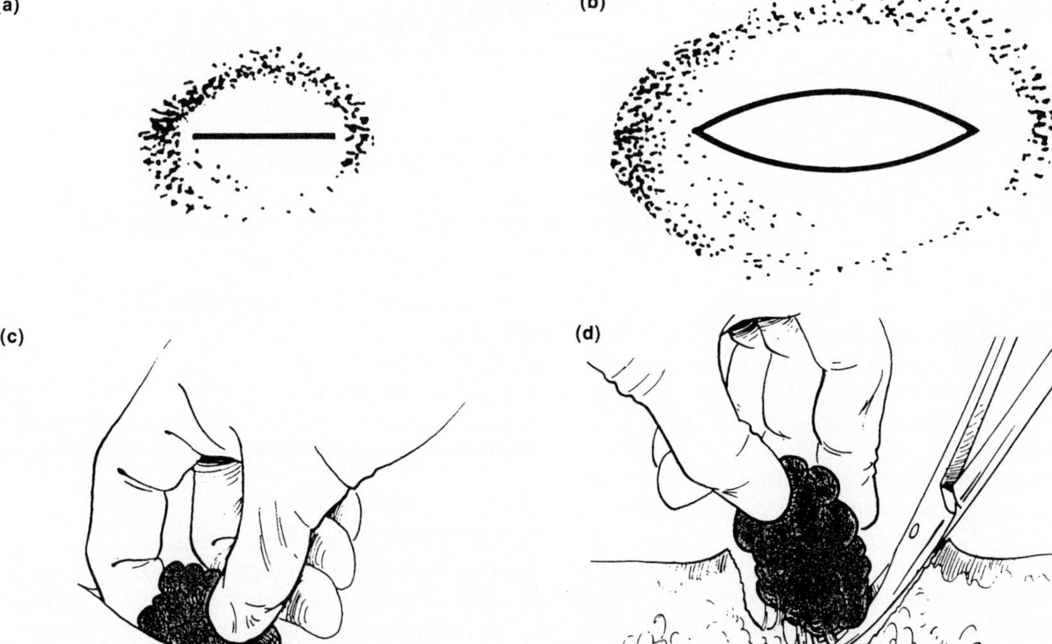

Fig. 96.7 **(a)** *Linear incision for small lipomas;* **(b)** *elliptical incision for large lipomas;* **(c)** *gloved-finger dissection to bring the lipoma to the surface;* **(d)** *blunt scissors dissection to free the lipoma from tethering fibrous bands*

Neurofibroma

These benign tumours are firm (sometimes soft) painless subcutaneous lumps aligned lengthwise in the long axis of the limb in relation to peripheral nerves. The lumps are more mobile from side to side than along the long axis. Some are tender to pressure with associated pain and paraesthesia on the nerve distribution.

Ganglion

Ganglia are firm cystic lumps associated with joints or tendon sheaths.

Clinical features:

- deep subcutaneous lumps
- around joints or tendon sheaths
- mostly around wrists, fingers, dorsum of feet
- immobile, fixed to deep tissues
- translucent
- contain viscid gelatinous fluid
- associated with arthritis and synovitis
- may disappear spontaneously
- recurrences common

Management

- can be left—wait and see
- do not 'bang with a Bible'
- needle aspiration and steroid injection

  or
- surgical excision (can be difficult)

Injection treatment of ganglia

Ganglia have a high recurrence rate after treatment, with a relapse of 30% after surgery. A simple, relatively painless and more effective method is to use intralesional injections of long-acting corticosteroid, such as methyl-prednisolone acetate.[7]

Method

1. Insert a 21 gauge needle attached to a 2 ml or 5 ml syringe into the cavity of the ganglion.
2. Aspirate some (not all) of its jelly-like contents, mainly to ensure the needle is *in situ*.
3. Keeping the needle exactly in place, swap the syringe for an insulin syringe containing up to 0.5 ml of steroid.
4. Inject 0.25–0.5 ml (Fig. 96.8).
5. Rapidly withdraw the needle, pinch the overlying skin for several seconds and then apply a light dressing.
6. Review in seven days and, if still present, repeat the injection using 0.25 ml of steroid.

Up to six injections can be given over a period of time, but 70% of ganglia will disperse with only one or two injections.

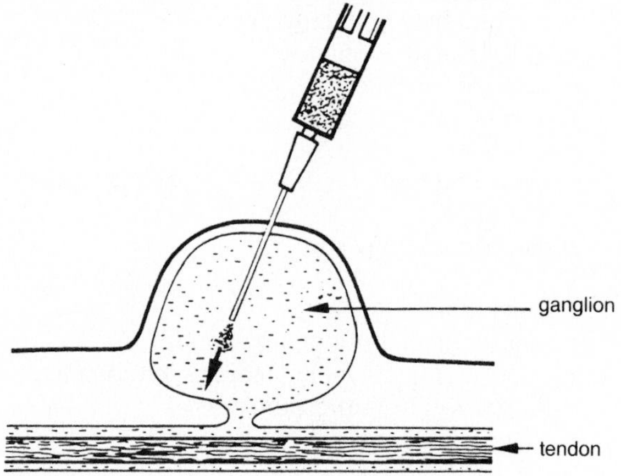

Fig. 96.8 *Injection treatment of ganglion*

Some preferred therapeutic options

Liquid nitrogen therapy

Ideally, liquid nitrogen is stored in a special, large container and decanted when required into a small thermos flask or spray device.

The easiest method of application to superficial skin tumours (Table 96.2) is via a ball of cotton wool rolled rather loosely on the tip of a wooden applicator stick. This should be slightly smaller than the lesion, to prevent freezing of the surrounding skin.

Table 96.2 *Superficial skin tumours suitable for cryotherapy*

Warts (plane, periungual, plantar, anogenital)
Skin tags
Seborrhoeic keratoses
Molluscum contagiosum
Solar keratoses

Method (basic steps)

1. Inform the patient what to expect.
2. Pare excess keratin with a scalpel.
3. Use a cotton wool applicator slightly smaller (not larger—see Fig. 96.9a) than the lesion.
4. Immerse it in nitrogen until bubbling ceases.
5. Gently tap it on the side of the container to remove excess liquid.

6. Hold the lesion firmly between thumb and forefinger.
7. Place applicator vertically (Fig. 96.9b) on tumour surface.
8. Apply with firm pressure: do not dab.
9. Freeze until a 2 mm white halo appears around the lesion.

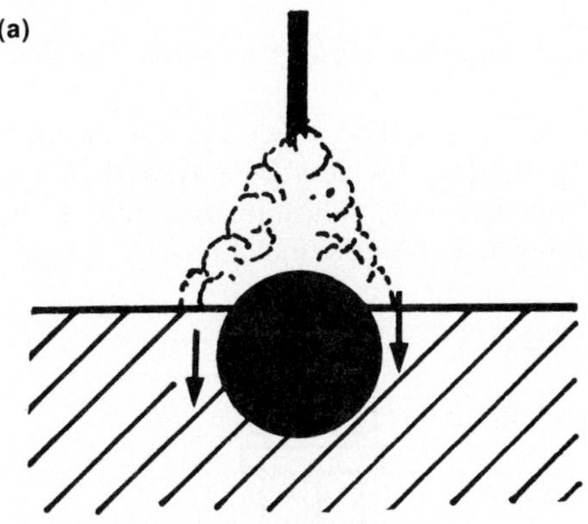

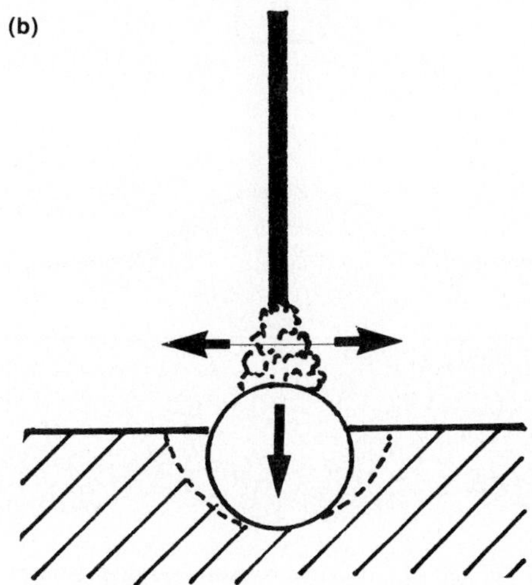

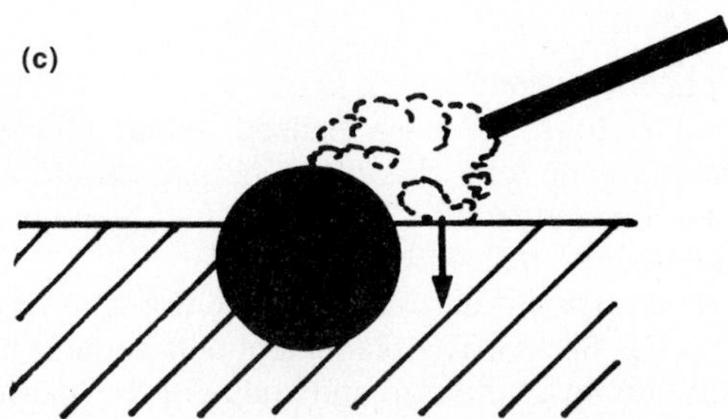

Fig. 96.9 *Application of liquid nitrogen:* **(a)** *applicator too large;* **(b)** *correct size and approach of applicator;* **(c)** *correct size but wrong position of applicator*

Explain likely reaction to patient, such as the appearance of blisters (possibly blood blisters). The optimal time for retreatment of warts is in 2–3 weeks (not longer than three weeks).

Biopsies

There are various methods for taking biopsies from skin lesions. These include scraping, shaving and punch biopsies, all of which are useful but not as effective or safe as excisional biopsies.

Shave biopsies

This simple technique is generally used for the tissue diagnosis of premalignant lesions and some malignant tumours, but not melanoma.

Method

1. Infiltrate with LA.
2. Holding a number 10 or 15 scalpel blade horizontally, shave off the tumour just into the dermis (Fig. 96.10).
3. Diathermy may be required for haemostasis.

The biopsy site usually heals with minimal scarring.

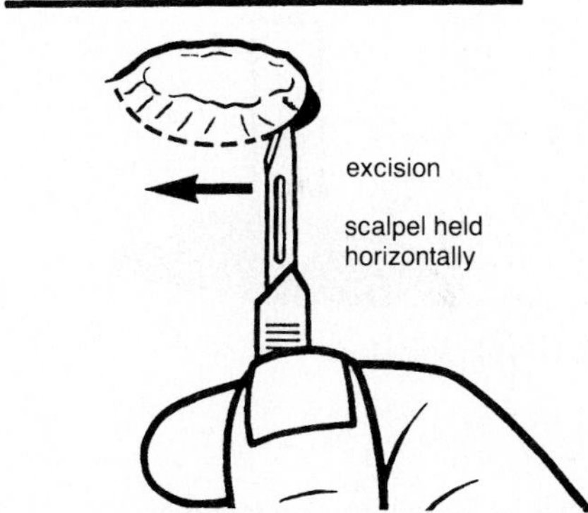

Fig. 96.10 *Shave biopsy*

Punch biopsy

This biopsy has considerable use in general practice, where full-thickness skin specimens are required for histological diagnosis. (Good quality disposable biopsy punches are available from Dermatech.)

Method

1. Clean the skin.
2. Infiltrate with LA.
3. Gently stretch the skin between the finger and thumb to limit rotational movement.

4. Select the punch (4 mm is the most useful size) and hold it vertically to the skin.
5. Rotate (in a clockwise, screwing motion) with firm pressure to cut a plug about 3 mm in depth (Fig. 96.11). Remove the punch.
6. Use fine-toothed forceps or a tissue hook to grip the outer rim of the plug.
7. Exert gentle traction and undercut the base of the plug parallel to the skin surface, using fine-pointed scissors or a scalpel.
8. Place the specimen in fixative.
9. Secure haemostasis by firm pressure or by diathermy.
10. Apply a dry dressing or a single suture to the defect.

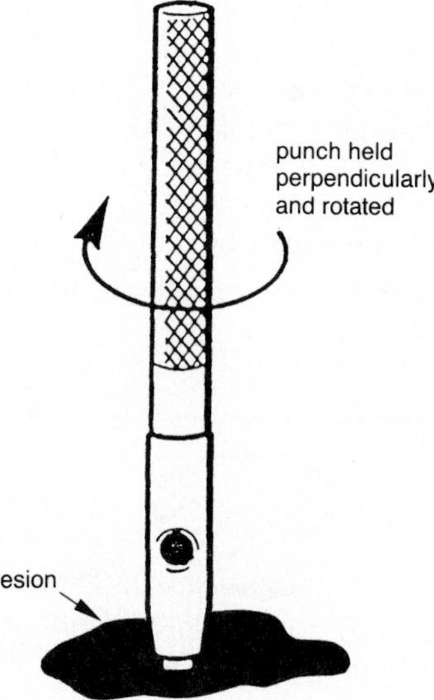

Fig. 96.11 *Punch biopsy*

Steroid injections into skin lesions

Suitable lesions for steroid injections are:

- plaque psoriasis
- granuloma annulare
- hypertrophic scars (early development)
- keloid scars (early development)
- alopecia areata
- lichen simplex chronicus
- necrobiosis lipoidica
- hypertrophic lichen planus

Triamcinolone is the appropriate long-acting corticosteroid (10 mg/mL). It may be diluted in equal quantities with saline.

Method

1. The steroid should be injected into the lesion (not below it).
2. Insert a 25 or (preferably) 27 gauge needle, firmly locked to a small insulin-type 1 ml syringe, into the lesion at the level of the middle of the dermis (Fig. 96.12).
3. High pressure is required with some lesions (e.g. keloid).
4. Inject sufficient steroid to make the lesion blanch.
5. Several sites will be needed for larger lesions, so preceding LA may be required in some instances. Avoid infiltration of steroid in larger lesions: use multiple injections.

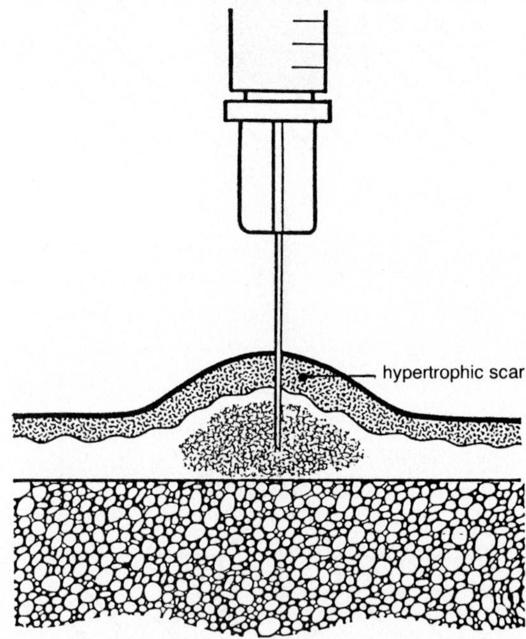

Fig. 96.12 *Injection of corticosteroid into mid-dermis*

Elliptical excisions

Small lesions are best excised as an ellipse. Generally, the long axis of the ellipse should be along the skin tension lines identified by natural wrinkles.

The intended ellipse should be drawn on the skin (Fig. 96.13). The placement will depend on such factors as the size and shape of the lesion, the margin required (usually 2–3 mm) and the skin tension lines.

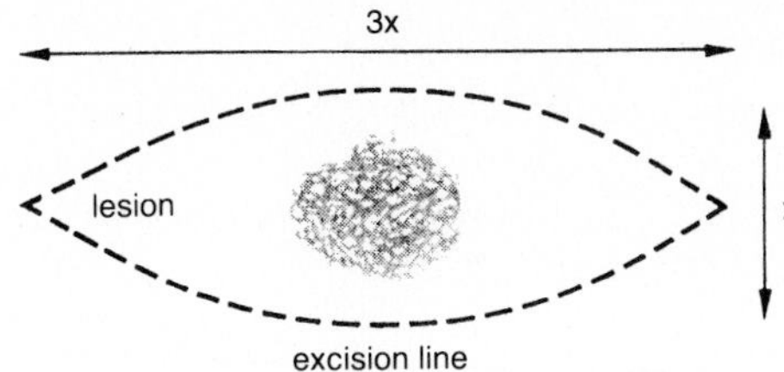

Fig. 96.13 *Ellipse excision*

General points

- The length of the ellipse should be three times the width.
- This length should be increased (say, to four times) in areas with little subcutaneous tissue (dorsum of hand) and high skin tension (upper back).
- A good rule is to obtain an angle at each end of the excision of 30° or less.
- These rules should achieve closure without 'dog ears'.

Excisions on the face

It is important to select optimal sites for elliptical excisions of tumours of the face. As a rule it is best for incisions to follow wrinkle lines and the direction of hair follicles in the beard area. Therefore, follow the natural wrinkles in the glabella area, the 'crow's feet' around the eye, and the nasolabial folds (Fig. 96.14). To determine non-obvious wrinkles, gently compress the relaxed skin in different directions to demonstrate the lines.

For tumours of the forehead make horizontal incisions, although vertical incisions may be used for large tumours of the forehead. Ensure that you keep your incisions in the temporal area quite superficial, as the frontal branch of the facial nerve is easily cut.

When to refer

Referral should be considered for:

- suspicion of melanoma
- tumours larger than 1 cm
- recurrent tumours, despite treatment
- incompletely excised tumours, especially with poor healing
- doubts about appropriate treatment
- recommended treatment beyond skills of practitioner

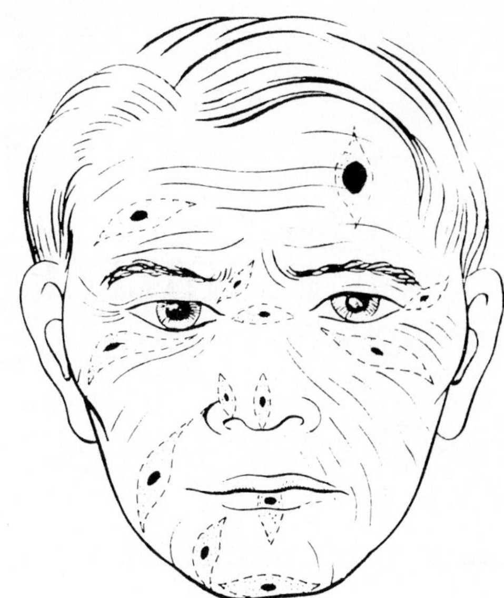

Fig. 96.14 *Recommended lines for excisions on face*
ADAPTED FROM J.S. BROWN *MINOR SURGERY: A TEXT AND ATLAS*, CHAPMAN AND HALL, LONDON, 1986

References

1. Paver R. The surgical management of cutaneous tumours in general practice. Modern Medicine Australia, 1991; March; 43–51.
2. Marks R. Skin cancer. In: MIMS Disease Index. Sydney: IMS Publishing, 1991–92, 490–493.
3. Davis A, Bolin T, Ham J. *Symptom analysis and physical diagnosis* (2nd edition). Sydney: Pergamon Press, 1990, 302–306.
4. de Launey WE, Land WA. *Principles and practice of dermatology* (2nd edition). Sydney: Butterworths, 1984, 280–281.
5. Berger P. Warts: how to treat them successfully. Modern Medicine Australia, August 1990, 28–32.
6. Reddy J. Intralesional injection for orf: a practice tip. Aust Fam Physician, 1993; 22:65.
7. La Villa G. Methylprednisolone acetate in local therapy of ganglion. Clinical Therapeutics, 1986; 47:455–457.

97

Pigmented skin lesions

The management of pigmented skin lesions is a constant concern for all practitioners and requires careful evaluation based on the natural history of these lesions and the increasing incidence of malignant melanoma in particular.

Most pigmented lesions are benign and include simple moles or melanocytic naevi, seborrhoeic keratoses, freckles and lentigines. Reassurance is all that is necessary in the management of these problems.

However, one-third of all melanomas arise in pre-existing naevi, many of which are dysplastic, and it is the recognition and removal of such naevi that is so important in the prevention of melanoma.[1]

Malignant melanoma is doubling in incidence each decade, which is an alarming statistic considering the public education programs about the hazards of sun exposure. Of equal interest is the fact that the 5 and 10 year survival rates for melanoma have doubled over the past decade, reflecting earlier diagnosis and treatment.[2]

A classification of pigmented skin lesions is given in Table 97.1.

Table 97.1 *Classification of pigmented skin lesions*

Non-melanocytic
- pigmented basal cell carcinoma
- seborrhoeic keratoses (page 900)
- solar keratoses (page 901)
- dermatofibroma (page 900)
- pyogenic granuloma
- foreign body granuloma
- talon noir (black heel)
- tinea nigra
- Becker's naevus

Melanocytic

Non-melanoma:
- freckles
- lentigines
- naevi
  1. congenital
  2. acquired
     - junctional → compound → intradermal
     - dysplastic
     - halo
     - blue
     - Spitz

Melanoma:
1. lentigo maligna (Hutchinson's melanotic freckle)
2. superficial spreading melanoma
3. nodular melanoma
4. acral lentiginous melanoma

Key facts and checkpoints

- The incidence of melanoma is greatest in white caucasians and increases with proximity to the equator.
- The early diagnosis and treatment of melanoma profoundly affects the prognosis.
- Melanoma is extremely rare before puberty.
- Some moles, particularly junctional naevi, have the potential to undergo malignant change.
- Most people have 5–10 melanocytic naevi on average.
- Multiple dysplastic naevi carry a higher risk of malignant change, which may occur in young adults. Such patients require regular observation (with photography).

Pyogenic granuloma

Synonyms: granuloma, granuloma telangiectaticum, acquired haemangioma

A pyogenic granuloma is a vascular lesion (without pus) due to a proliferation of capillary vessels. It is considered to be an abnormal reaction to minor trauma.

Clinical features:

- common in children and young adults
- usually on hands and face
- bright red 'raspberry'-like lesion
- raised, sometimes pedunculated
- friable—bleeds easily

Management

It must be distinguished from a melanotic melanoma or anaplastic SCC. Shave biopsy with electrocautery of base. The specimen must be sent for histological examination. They are prone to recur.

Talon noir ('black heel')

Talon noir is a black spotted appearance on the heel and is common in sports people. A similar lesion (probably smaller) is often found on the other heel.

'Black heel' is formed by small petechiae caused by the trauma of the sharp turns required in sport: shearing stress on the skin of the heel produces superficial bleeding. The diagnosis can be confirmed by gentle paring of the callus to reveal the multiple small petechial spots in the epidermis; these are then pared away. If there is doubt about the diagnosis (malignant melanoma is the main differential diagnosis), the lesion should be excised.

Tinea nigra

Tinea nigra is characterised by solitary black macular lesions on the palm or sole. The simple technique of taking skin scrapings to reveal fungal elements will allow easy differentation from malignant melanoma.

Becker's naevus

Becker's naevus is a faint, brown, diffuse pigmented area with a component of coarse hairs and is usually found on the shoulder and upper trunk. It occurs mainly in boys around puberty. It is not a birthmark, it is benign and reassurance is appropriate.

Freckles

Freckles are small brown macules (usually $<$ 0.5 cm), coloured by excessive epidermal melanin without any increase in the number of naevus cells (melanocytes). They occur mainly on light-coloured skin and tend to darken in summer and fade in winter. Cosmetic improvement can be achieved through use of sunscreens.

Lentigines

Lentigines are small rounded, brown to black macular areas ranging from 1 mm to 1 cm or more across. They are very common and usually appear in childhood as a few scattered lesions, often on areas not exposed to the sun. They may erupt during pregnancy. In the elderly, lentigines often develop on sun-damaged skin, usually on the backs of the hands (so-called 'liver spots') and on the face.

Unlike freckles they have increased numbers of melanocytes.

Management

Treatment is usually unnecessary. Liquid nitrogen or excision can be used for cosmetically unacceptable lesions. Sunscreens are needed to prevent further darkening of existing lesions.

Congenital melanocytic naevi

These moles are present at birth and are sometimes large.

Clinical features:

- variable colour: brown to black
- tend to be hairy and protruding
- increased risk of malignant change (especially in larger ones)

Common acquired naevi

These are the common moles for which an opinion is so often sought. The moles are localised benign proliferation of naevus cells. There may be a sharp increase in numbers during pregnancy. New lesions appear less frequently after the age of 20. The types are junctional, compound and intradermal. Naevi in children are usually the junctional type with proliferating naevus cells clumped at the dermoepidermal junction. With time the naevus cells 'move' into the dermis. A compound naevus has both junctional and dermal elements. With maturation all the naevus cells move into the dermis. Refer to Figure 97.1.

Clinical features

Junctional

- usually < 5 mm
- circular-shaped macules
- may be slightly elevated
- colour usually brown to black
- may be 'fuzzy' border with brownish halo

Most naevi of the palms, soles and genitals are junctional but there is no evidence to support the traditional view that naevi in these sites have more malignant potential.[2]

Compound

- dome-shaped, slightly raised pigmented nodules
- up to 1 cm in diameter
- colour varies from light to dark brown/black, but lighter than junctional naevi
- most are smooth but surface can be rough or verrucoid
- larger ones may be hairy, especially after puberty
- become 'flesh'-coloured in time

Intradermal

- look like compound but less pigmented
- often skin-coloured
- may evolve to pink or brown senile nodules or to soft pedunculated tags

Malignant potential of common acquired melanocytic naevi

Junctional: have significant potential to undergo malignant change (as long as junctional activity is present)

Compound: very rarely undergo malignant change

Intradermal: these are totally benign lesions

Management

- Provide appropriate reassurance.
- Observe.
- If lesion is changing or there is uncertainty, perform surgical excision (2-3 mm margin) for histopathology.

Halo naevus

A halo naevus consists of a depigmented halo around a central melanocytic naevus. It is the result of an autoimmune reaction. The central naevus gradually involutes. It tends to occur around puberty.

Management

Measure the lesion. Reassure and do nothing, as it usually disappears over the next few years; if doubtful at all, remove and obtain histological diagnosis.

Blue naevus

A blue naevus presents as a solitary slate-grey-blue dermal lesion. Blue naevi usually present in childhood and adolescence on the lower back

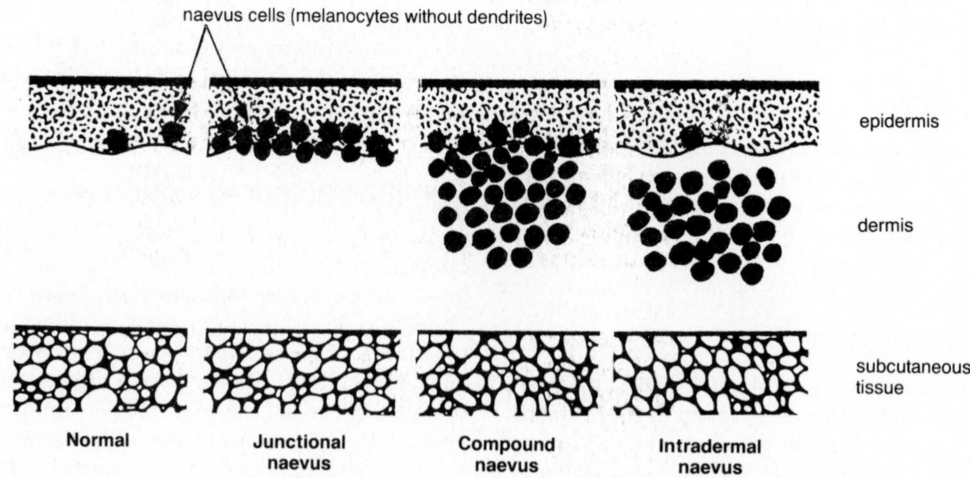

Fig. 97.1 *Comparison of melanocyte (naevus cell) distribution in various common acquired naevi*

and buttocks and the limbs, especially dorsa of the hands and feet. Malignant change is rare. Often excised for cosmetic reasons.

Spitz naevus (benign juvenile melanoma)

Spitz naevi, which are a type of junctional naevus, are also called benign juvenile melanomas or spindle cell naevi.

Clinical features:

- solitary pigmented or erythematous nodules
- occur in children, usually 4–8 years
- develop over 1–3 months
- well circumscribed, dome-shaped lesions

Management

- Reassure that there is no malignant potential.
- Surgical excision is treatment of choice (because of rapid growth and best 'reassurance' policy).

Dysplastic melanocytic naevi

These are large irregular moles which appear predominantly on the trunk in young adults. They can be familial or sporadic and are markers of an increased risk of melanoma, rather than necessarily being premalignant lesions. Even so, melanoma may arise within these lesions more frequently than would be expected by random chance.[3]

They are considered to be intermediate between benign naevi and melanoma.

Clinical features:

- age: adolescence onwards
- large > 5 mm (variable size)
- most common on trunk
- irregular and ill-defined border
- irregular pigmentation
- background redness
- variable colours: brown, tan, black, pink
- variation of colours within the naevus
- most are stable and do not progress to melanoma

Dysplastic naevus syndrome

The presence of multiple, large, irregular pigmented naevi, mainly on the trunk, presents a difficult management problem, especially if there is a family history of melanoma. The lifetime risk of melanoma may approach 100% for such patients.

Management

Use a follow-up program (similar to excised early melanoma) of six monthly review for two years (three monthly if family history of melanoma) and yearly thereafter, provided no lesions become malignant during the first two years. During this time the patient and family should become well versed in surveillance. Apart from measurement, good professional quality photographs of areas of the body or specific lesions of concern may also be helpful.

Any suspicious lesions should be excised for histological examination.

Advice to patients

To decrease your chances of getting a melanoma, you should protect yourself from the sun. These rules should be followed:

- Try to avoid direct sunlight when the sun is at its strongest (from 10 am to 3 pm).
- Always wear a broad-brimmed hat and T-shirt in the sun.
- Use a factor 15^{+} sunscreen on exposed skin and renew the sunscreen regularly.
- Sunbaking might give you a good tan but it is also going to increase your chances of getting a melanoma, so you should avoid it.

Melanoma

The early diagnosis of melanoma is vital to outcome. Thickness of a melanoma when it is removed is the major factor determining prognosis: it is vital to detect melanomas when they are in the thin stage and look like an unusual freckle.

In Australia, only 20–30% of melanomas develop in pre-existing melanocytic naevi (moles).[2] The majority arise in apparently normal skin. Initially the tumour tends to spread laterally in many cases and it should be removed at this stage when it is easily cured. An irregular border or margin is characteristic of the tumour.

Clinical features

- typical age range 30–50 years (average 40)
- can occur anywhere on the body
  more common — lower limb in women
  — upper back in men
- often asymptomatic
- can bleed or itch

Change
The sign of major importance is a recent change in a 'freckle' or mole

- change in size: at edge or thickening
- change in shape
- change in colour: brown, blue, black, red, white, including combinations
- change in surface
- change in the border
- bleeding or ulceration
- other symptoms, e.g. itching
- development of satellite nodules
- lymph node involvement

Types of melanoma

Lentigo maligna[3]
Lentigo maligna (Hutchinson's melanotic freckle) is a slow-growing form of intraepidermal melanoma which occurs on areas exposed to light (usually the face), predominantly in the elderly. If allowed to remain it may become invasive and the prognosis will be similar to that for other invasive melanomas. These lesions have all the variations in size, shape and colour of superficial melanomas.

Superficial spreading melanoma
Like lentigo maligna, the initial growth is in a lateral or radial intraepidermal manner, rather than in an invasive downward or vertical manner. It accounts for 70% of melanomas.

Nodular melanoma
Nodular melanoma, which accounts for 20% of melanomas, has no radial growth phase. It is typically found on the trunk and limbs of young to middle-aged individuals. Prognosis is determined by thickness at the time of excision.

Acral lentiginous melanoma
These typically occur on palms, soles and distal phalanges. They have a poorer prognosis than other types.

Variations
Amelanotic melanomas are flesh-coloured papules that increase in size or change shape. These lesions can be extremely difficult to diagnose and the poor prognosis associated with them is due to late diagnosis rather than an increased malignancy.

The features and associations of melanoma subtypes are presented in Table 97.2.

Prognosis

Determinants of prognosis include:[3]

- thickness (Breslow classification)
- level or depth (worse in level 4 or 5) (Fig. 97.2)
- site (worse on head and neck, trunk)
- sex (worse for men)
- age (worse > 50 years)
- amelanotic melanoma
- ulceration

Vertical growth is associated with invasion and the prognosis worsens with depth. The chance of cure is greater than 90% if a melanoma is removed when it is less than 0.75 mm thick. If the lesion is allowed to invade to a thickness of 4 mm or more, the likelihood of a cure is reduced to less than 30%.[3]

The influence of tumour thickness on five-year survival rates is shown in Table 97.3.

Staging is based on the tumour level (depth) shown in Figure 97.2:

Level 1—confined to the epidermis (*in situ*)
Level 2—tumour cells extend into the superficial (papillary) dermis
Level 3—tumour cells fill up the superficial dermis
Level 4—tumour cells extend into the deeper (reticular) layer
Level 5—invasion of subcutaneous tissue

Table 97.2 *Features and associations of melanoma subtypes (after Kelly[4])*

Melanoma subtype	*Frequency %*	*Radial growth phase*	*Location*	*Average age*	*Occupation profile*
Superficial spreading	70	+	Trunk, limbs	Middle-aged	Indoor worker
Nodular	20	–	Trunk, limbs	Middle-aged	Indoor worker
Lentigo maligna	7.5	+	Head, neck	Elderly	Outdoor worker
Acral lentiginous	2.5	+	Palms, soles mucosae	Not known	Not known

Reproduced with permission of J. Kelly[4]

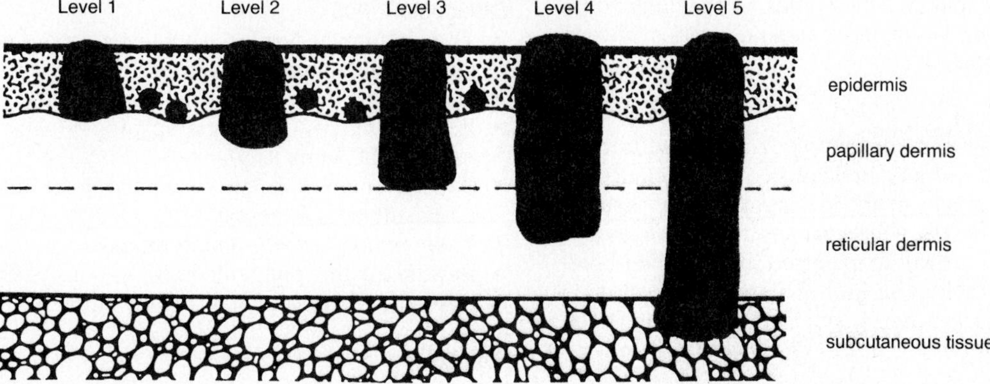

Fig. 97.2 *Assessment of tumour level: the levels of melanoma invasion* REPRODUCED BY PERMISSION J. KELLY[4]

Table 97.3 *The influence of tumour thickness on five-year survival rates (after Kelly[4])*

Range of tumour thickness (mm)	*Five-year survival rates %*
< 0.76	95–100
0.76–1.5	70–98
1.51–4.0	55–85
> 4.0	30–60

Reproduced with permission of J. Kelly[4]

Differential diagnosis

There are several common skin lesions that may be mistaken for melanoma.[1] They are:

1. Haemangioma (thrombosed)
2. Dermatofibroma (sclerosing haemangioma)
3. Pigmented seborrhoeic keratosis
4. Pigmented basal cell carcinoma
5. Junctional and compound naevi
6. Blue naevi
7. Dysplastic naevi
8. Lentigines

The diagnosis of melanoma can be made by exclusion of these lesions or direct recognition of the melanoma.

Facilitating early diagnosis of melanoma

An adequate light source without shadows is essential. Refer to page 851 for use of the 'maggylamp' and the dermatoscope.

Clinical examination of the skin[1]

It is important to examine the entire skin and not just the lesion presented by the patient. Comparison of pigmented skin lesions is very helpful in differentiating between benign and malignant. One satisfactory routine is:

- Starting at the head, examine the hairline, backs of ears, neck, back, and backs of the arms. Pull down the underwear to expose the buttocks; examine the backs of the legs.
- With the patient facing you, examine the anterior hairline, the front of the ears, the forehead, cheeks and neck, moving downwards to the anterior chest. Move bra straps as required to achieve complete coverage. Then examine the abdomen, pulling down the underwear to examine as far as the pubic hairs.
- Then examine the anterior surfaces of the legs. The 'maggylamp' is very useful for this examination.

After scanning the entire skin surface and comparing and contrasting naevi, specific lesions may be examined with the dermatoscope. Compare suspicious lesions with similar lesions elsewhere on the patient's skin.

Applying the ABCDE system[1]

A = **A**symmetry
Melanoma is almost always asymmetrical. Most non-melanoma lesions are symmetrical, oval or round.

B = **B**order
The border of the melanoma is usually well-defined, especially in the more malignant, compared with the dysplastic naevus which is almost always indistinct with a fading out

'shoulder' effect. The border of the melanoma is irregular while most benign lesions have a regular edge.

C = **C**olour
The classic blue-black colour is helpful but the *variety* of colours present in most melanomas is the most helpful. Magnification usually visualises greys, whites, violets, reds, oranges and shades of brown interspersed in the darker blue-black pigmentation. Early melanomas developing in dysplastic naevi do not have this deep pigmentation.

D = **D**iameter
The majority of melanomas when first seen are at least 7 mm in diameter, especially if arising from a pre-existing naevus. However, it is possible to diagnose small nodular melanomas < 5 mm.

E = **E**levation
Elevation indicates invasion and is a sign of more advanced disease.

Diagnosis by exclusion

In the diagnostic process consider the lesions outlined in the differential diagnosis and check out the various characteristics. Haemangiomas have an emptying sign when pressed with a finger. Pigmented BCCs can be difficult if they are fully pigmented but this is uncommon. The characteristic pearly-grey look and the telangiectasia are usually still visible on magnification with the 'maggylamp'. The most useful feature of dysplastic naevi is that they are usually multiple and lesions for comparison can generally be found elsewhere. Dysplastic naevi also have greater breadth and height and often a darker nodule in the centre—the 'target' sign.

Management points for naevi and melanomas

- Do not inject local anaesthetic directly into the lesion.
- Incisional biopsy of a melanoma or suspicious mole is best avoided.
- Accurate clinical diagnosis, with the definitive treatment performed in one stage, is optimal, rather than excision biopsy with follow-up surgery.

Management tips[1]

- The solitary dysplastic naevus has no significant malignant potential.
- Multiple excision of naevi is not justified.
- If in doubt, perform excision biopsy with a margin of 0.5 cm.
- If melanoma is strongly suspected, referral to a consultant is necessary.
- There is no place for punch biopsy.
- Beware of the pigmented BCC—it is easily missed but it usually has a shiny surface.

Counselling

An encouragingly positive and supportive approach can realistically be taken for most patients, as the overall survival for melanoma in Australia is more than 80%.[1]

Even with tumours greater than 4 mm thickness, 50% of patients will survive.

Follow-up

Follow-up tends to be based on the tumour thickness:[1]

1 mm	six monthly review for two years
1–2 mm	four monthly for two years, six monthly for next two years, then yearly for ten years
> 2 mm	review by both specialist and GP, regularly, for ten years

The first sign of metastasis is usually to the lungs so a yearly chest X-ray is advisable.

References

1. McCarthy W. The management of melanoma. Aust Fam Physician, 1993; 22:1177–1186.
2. Lauritz B. Pigmented skin lesions. In: Monash University Medical School's Annual Update Course for GPs. Course Proceedings, 1992, 33–34.
3. Marks R. Malignant melanoma. Aust Fam Physician, 1986; 15:584–585.
4. Kelly J. The management of early skin cancer in the 1990s. Aust Fam Physician, 1990; 19:1714–1729.

PART 9

COMMON CONTINUING MANAGEMENT PROBLEMS

98

Alcohol problems

Excessive drinking of alcohol is one of the most common and socially destructive problems in Australia. One survey found that 5% of Australian men and 1% of women were alcohol-dependent. It also showed that 84% of men and 80% of women drink alcohol, with 22% of the population drinking alcohol every day.[1]

Skinner refers to the prevalence of 'alcoholism' in North America as about 5–7% of the adult group, with a much larger group (20–30%) of individuals having drinking problems without major symptoms of alcoholism.[2]

Excessive and harmful drinking

People are said to be dependent on alcohol when it is affecting their physical health and social life yet they do not seem to be prepared to stop drinking to solve their problems.

For men, excessive drinking is more than four standard drinks of alcohol a day. For women, drinking becomes a serious problem at lesser amounts—two standard drinks a day. This level can also affect the foetus of the pregnant woman. High-risk or harmful drinking occurs at more than six drinks a day for men and four drinks a day for women.

Extent of the problem

- Alcohol is estimated to have a harmful effect on about 1 in 10 people.
- At least 15% of all patients admitted to hospital have an alcohol-related illness.
- About 50% of fatal traffic accidents involve alcohol.
- The author's study[3] identified alcohol dependence in 9.7% of the population studied and a further group of problem drinkers that included the 'explosive' or binge drinker (Fig. 98.1). Problem drinkers represent about 15–20% of the population.

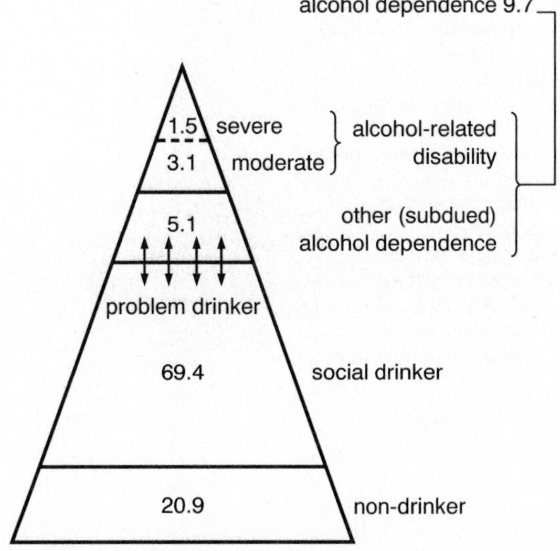

Fig. 98.1 *Prevalence of alcohol drinking patterns in the adult population (figures expressed as a percentage)*

Identifying the problem

As a profession we generally seem to be very slow in recognising the problem drinker; we need to train ourselves to have a sixth sense in early detection of the heavy or problem drinker.

Clinical pointers

Alcohol abuse should be suspected in any patient presenting with one or more of the physical or psychosocial problems presented in Table 98.1. Target areas for clinical scrutiny are outlined in Table 98.2. The facial features of the patient can be a helpful pointer, albeit of the more advanced drinker. These include:

- plethoric facies
- puffy 'greasy' facies
- telangiectasia
- rosacea + rhinophyma
- suffused ('bloodshot') conjunctivae
- prominent lower lip with chelitis of corners of mouth
- smell of stale alcohol or very 'minty' sweet breath (masking effect)

Table 98.2 *Target areas for clinical scrutiny*

Young and middle-aged bachelors
Divorced or separated individuals
Alcoholic beverage trade: bar trade, hotel staff
Professionals: politicians, doctors and others
Travelling professions, e.g. seamen, salesmen, truck drivers
Armed forces, especially returned servicemen
Authors, journalists and related workers
Social club patrons, e.g. sporting clubs

Taking a drinking history

This requires tact and skill and it must be noted that many problem drinkers considerably understate the level of their intake.

Useful strategies

- Ask questions as part of a matter-of-fact enquiry into health risk factors such as smoking and diet.

Table 98.1 *Adverse clinical effects of alcohol*

Psychological and social effects	*Physical effects*
• loss of self-esteem • irritability • devious behaviour • anxiety and phobias • depression • paranoia • stress • relationship breakdown • child abuse • poor work performance • memory disturbances • financial problems • accidents • driving offences • crime–violence • personal neglect • attempted suicide • pathological jealousy	• brain damage (if severe) • depression • epilepsy • Wernicke-Korsakoff syndrome • insomnia–nightmares • hypertension • heart disease — arrhythmias — cardiomyopathy — beri-beri heart disease • liver disease • pancreatic disease • dyspepsia (indigestion) • acute gastritis • stomach ulcers • sexual dysfunction • hand tremor • peripheral neuropathy • myopathy • gout • obesity • other metabolic/endocrine effects — hyperlipidaemia — pseudo-Cushing's syndrome — osteoporosis — osteomalacia • haemopoiesis — macrocytosis — leucopenia — thrombocytopenia

- Place the onus of denial on the patient by asking questions such as 'When did you last drink alcohol?' rather than 'Do you ever drink alcohol?'
- Record your patient's intake quantitatively in terms of standard drinks or grams of alcohol.
- Confirm the history by enquiring about the time spent drinking per day and expenditure on alcohol.

Useful questions

When did you last drink alcohol?
Do you like alcohol?
What is your usual intake each day? Each week?
What type of alcohol do you prefer to drink?
Do you take a drink in the morning?
Do you eat breakfast?
When was the last time you felt nauseated or 'off-colour' in the morning?
When do you get heartburn?
Do you drink with your mates or family or at the club?
How long do you usually go without alcohol?
When was the last time you were drunk?
When was the last time you cannot remember a drinking session?
About how much alcohol can you take before it affects you?
Has alcohol had any effects on you?
Does it give you the shakes?
Do you ever need to take alcohol to help you get to sleep?
Do you need it to steady your nerves?

Questionnaires

There are several questionnaires that can be most helpful, assuming the patient is fully co-operative. Two or more positive replies for the CAGE questionnaire[4] are suggestive of a problem drinker.

1. Have you ever felt you should CUT down on your drinking?
2. Have people ANNOYED you by criticising your drinking?
3. Have you ever felt bad or GUILTY about your drinking?
4. Have you ever had a drink first thing in the morning to steady your nerves or get rid of a hangover? (an EYE-OPENER)

Laboratory investigations

The following blood tests may be helpful in the identification of excessive chronic alcohol intake.

- blood alcohol
- serum gamma glutamyl transpeptidase (GGT): elevated in chronic drinkers (returns to normal with cessation of intake)
- mean corpuscular volume (MCV) : > 96fl

Other changes:

- abnormal liver function tests (other than GGT)
- high-density lipoproteins elevated
- low-density lipoproteins lowered
- serum uric acid elevated

Measuring alcohol intake

One standard drink contains 10 g of alcohol, which is in one middy (or pot) of standard beer (285 ml), two middies of low-alcohol beer or five middies of super-light beer. These are equal in alcohol content to one small glass of table wine (120 ml), one glass of sherry or port (60 ml) or one nip of spirits (30 ml) (Fig. 98.2).

1 stubby or can of beer	=	1.3 standard drinks
1 × 750 ml bottle of beer	=	2.6 standard drinks
1 × 750 ml bottle of wine	=	6 standard drinks

Fig. 98.2 *Standard drinks*

The 0.05 level

To keep below the 0.05 blood alcohol level drinking and driving limit, a 70 kg man or woman should not exceed:

2 standard drinks in 1 hour
3 standard drinks in 2 hours
4 standard drinks in 3 hours

The rule is that one standard drink is eliminated per hour so it is important to spread drinking time.

Approach to management

The challenge to the family doctor is early recognition of the problem. There are specific target areas which should be considered carefully by the general practitioner (Table 98.2). Several studies have shown that early intervention and brief counselling by the doctor are effective in leading to rehabilitation.[5] Some of the results are very revealing:

- Patients expect their family doctor to advise on safe drinking levels.[6]
- They will listen and act on our advice.[7]
- Treatment is more effective if offered before dependence or chronic disease has developed.[7,8]

Patients tend to have little insight into their problem and often need the development of unpleasant sequelae to make them aware of their alcohol-related problem. Furthermore, patients are not likely to offer concern about their drinking problem spontaneously but are often receptive to the initiative coming from their doctor.

The family doctor is ideally placed to identify and treat the problem of alcohol because the individual who abuses alcohol will tend to surface at some point in the provision of primary health care.

Of particular concern are teenage and early adult drinking patterns, often influenced by environmental factors including the home and sporting clubs. Fortunately many young people are able to control their drinking as they mature, provided they survive the risk-taking behaviour period. However, those who remain single tend to adopt drinking as part of their lifestyle. When the duration of excessive drinking increases to 10 or 15 years, patients tend to present with classic alcohol-related diseases.[2] According to Skinner, alcohol dependency usually develops in individuals in their early twenties, yet most patients admitted to alcohol treatment programs have a history of heavy drinking of 10–20 years with associated alcohol-related morbidity.

Alcohol-sensitising drugs

Drugs that cause a most unpleasant reaction when taken with alcohol include disulfiram and calcium carbimide. Their role is controversial and they should be restricted to a co-operative and highly motivated patient who gives informed consent.

The reaction causes nausea, vomiting, flushing, dizziness and dyspnoea.

Management

The best results are obtained with early recognition of the problem and prompt intervention to resolve it; the patient's admission of the problem and a resolve to face it; firm support and interest by the medical team and appropriate support from family and friends.

A brief practical management plan[9]

Giving patients feedback about their level of alcohol consumption, presenting objective evidence of harm and setting realistic goals for reducing alcohol intake induces many to change their drinking behaviour.

A six-step management plan, which has been employed in a general-practice early intervention program, is as follows:

1. *Feed back* the results of your assessment and specifically the degree of risk associated with their daily alcohol intake and bout drinking. Emphasise any damage that has already occurred.
2. *Listen* carefully to their reaction. They will need to ventilate their feelings and may respond defensively.
3. *Outline the benefits* of reducing drinking:
   - save money
   - less hassles from family
   - sleep better
   - have more energy
   - be less depressed
   - lose weight
   - better physical shape
   - lessen the risk of:
     - — hypertension
     - — liver disease
     - — brain disease
     - — cancer
     - — accidents

4. *Set goals* for alcohol consumption which you both agree are feasible. In most cases this will involve reduction to below certain 'safe limits'.
   For men: *no more than* 3–4 drinks 3–4 times per week (aim for less than 12 per week).
   For women: *no more than* 2–3 drinks 2–3 times per week (aim for less than 8 per week). Pregnant women should not have more than one drink 2–3 times per week. Some authorities recommend total abstinence.
   These are the *upper safe limits* and are *not* amounts that patients should be recommended to drink if their intake is normally lower.
   For patients who have already experienced some physical damage or substantial psychosocial problems, it is best to advise a period of total abstinence. For patients who are physically dependent on alcohol, long-term abstinence is advisable.
5. *Set strategies* to keep below the upper safe limits:
   - Quench thirst with non-alcoholic drinks before having an alcoholic one.
   - Have the first alcoholic drink *after* starting to eat (avoid drinking on an empty stomach).
   - Switch to low-alcohol beer.
   - Take care which parties you go to: avoid constant parties and other high-risk situations.
   - Think of a good explanation for cutting down on your drinking.
   - Have a physical workout when bored or stressed.
   - Explore new interests—fishing, cinema, social club, sporting activity.
6. *Evaluate* progress by having patients monitor their drinking by using a diary; check that any abnormal blood test results are returning to normal. Make a definite appointment for follow-up and give appropriate literature such as *Alcohol and health*. Obtain consent for a telephone follow-up. A useful minimum intervention plan is presented in Table 98.3.

The use of disulfiram

In compliant patients, disulfiram 250–500 mg daily can be used—such treatment has hazards and the patient requires intensive supportive therapy.

Table 98.3 *Minimum intervention technique plan (5–10 minutes)*

1. Advise reduction to safe levels
2. Outline the benefits
3. Provide a self-help pamphlet
4. Organise a diary or other feedback system
5. Obtain consent for a telephone follow-up
6. Offer additional help, e.g. referral to an alcohol and drug unit or to a support group.

Follow-up (long consultation one week later)

Review the patient's drinking diary. Explore any problems, summarise, listen and provide support and encouragement. If appointment is not kept, contact the patient.

Specialist services

According to progress and the patient's wishes and consent, specialist treatment units, group therapy and attendance at meetings of Alanon or Alcoholics Anonymous are potential sources of help to keep the alcohol-dependent person abstinent and coping.

Withdrawal symptoms

Symptoms of a 'hangover' include headache, nausea, irritability, malaise and a mild tremor. Withdrawal from alcohol in a chronic problem drinker includes:

- agitation
- prominent tremor
- sweating
- insomnia
- seizures
- delirium tremens

Treatment for moderate symptoms includes chlormethiazole (Hemineurin), chlordiazepoxide (Librium) or diazepam. The aim is to prevent development of delirium tremens. Maintain fluid, electrolytes and nutrition. Add vitamin B complex including thiamine because the patients are invariably thiamine deficient.

Recommended treatment for early withdrawal symptoms[10]

- diazepam 5–20 mg (o) every 2–6 hours (up to 120 mg (o) daily) titrated against clinical response (taper off after seven days)
- thiamine 100 mg IM or IV daily for 3–5 days, then 100 mg (o) daily
- vitamin B group supplement (o) or IM daily.

Delirium tremens

DTs is a serious life-threatening withdrawal state. It has a high mortality rate if inadequately treated and hospitalisation is always necessary.

Clinical features:

- may be precipitated by intercurrent infection or trauma
- 1–5 days after withdrawal
- disorientation, agitation
- clouding of consciousness
- marked tremor
- visual hallucinations, e.g. spiders, pink elephants
- sweating, tachycardia, pyrexia
- signs of dehydration

Treatment[10]

- hospitalisation
- correct fluid and electrolyte imbalance with IV therapy
- treat any systemic infection
- thiamine (vitamin B_1) 100 mg IM or IV daily for 3–5 days, then thiamine 100 mg (o) daily
- diazepam 10 mg as a single dose by slow IV injection (over several minutes) for sedation

  Repeat every 2–4 hours (up to 120 mg daily) titrated against clinical response

  or

  diazepam 20 mg (o) every 2–6 hours (up to 120 mg daily)

  This dose is usually required for 2–3 days, then should be gradually reduced till finished.

  If psychotic features, e.g. hallucinations and delusions,

  add

  haloperidol 2.5–5 mg (o) bd.

Note Chlormethiazole is not recommended because of its potential to produce excessive CNS depression and dependency.[10]

References

1. Rankin JS. The size and nature of the misuse of alcohol and drugs in Australia. In: Proceedings of 29th International Congress of Alcoholism and Drug Dependence, Sydney, February 1970, 10–20.
2. Skinner HA. Early detection and basic management of alcohol and drug problems. Australian Alcohol and Drug Review, 1985, 4:243–249.
3. Murtagh JE. Stigmata of alcohol dependence. Australian Family Physician, 1985, 14:204–205.
4. Mayfield D, McLeod G, Hall P. The CAGE questionnaire. Am J Psych, 1974; 131:1121–1123.
5. Skinner HA. Early intervention for alcohol and drug problems: core issues for medical education. Australian Alcohol and Drug Review, 1986; 5:69–74.
6. Cockburn J, Killer D, Campbell E, Sanson-Fisher RW. Measuring general practitioners' attitudes towards medical care. Family Practice, 1987; 3:192–199.
7. Wallace P, Cutler S, Haines A. Randomised controlled trial of general practitioner intervention in patients with excessive alcohol consumption. British Medical Journal, 1988; 297:663–668.
8. Saunders JB. The WHO project on early detection and treatment of harmful alcohol consumption. Australian Drug and Alcohol Review, 1987; 6:303–308.
9. Saunders JB, Roche AM. One in six patients in your practice. NSW medical education project on alcohol and other drugs. Sydney: A drug offensive pamphlet 1989: 1–6.
10. Mashford L et al. *Psychotropic drug guidelines* (2nd edition). Victorian Medical Postgraduate Foundation: 1993–4, 58–61.

99

Anxiety

Anxiety is an uncomfortable inner feeling of fear or imminent disaster. The criterion for anxiety disorder as defined at the International Classification of Health Problems in Primary Care (ICHPPC-2-Defined) (WONCA, 1985)[1] is:

generalised and persistent anxiety or anxious mood, which cannot be associated with, or is disproportionately large in response to a specific psychosocial stressor, stimulus or event.

Anxiety is a normal human emotion and most of us experience some temporary degree of anxiety in our lives as a normal reaction to stress and misfortune. Table 99.1 presents the scale formulated by psychologists to quantify life's main stresses. However, some people are constantly anxious to the extent that it is abnormal and interferes with their lives. They suffer from an anxiety disorder, a problem that affects 5–10% of the population.

The symptoms of anxiety, which are psychological or physical in manifestation, can vary enormously from feeling tense or tired to panic attacks.

Classification of anxiety

The following list represents approximately the categories of anxiety disorders recognised by the DSM-III-R:[2,3]

- generalised anxiety disorder
- panic disorder
- phobic disorder

Table 99.1 *Life change and stress survey of recent experiences*

Life event	***Life change units***
Death of spouse	100
Divorce	73
Marital separation	65
Jail term	63
Death of close family member	63
Personal injury or illness	53
Marriage	50
Fired at work	47
Marital reconciliation	45
Retirement	45
Change in health of family member	44
Pregnancy	40
Sex difficulties	39
Business readjustment	39
Death of close friend	37
Change to different line of work	36
Mortgage (large)	31
Change in responsibility at work	29
Son or daughter leaving home	29
Outstanding personal achievement	28
Wife begins or stops work	26
Begin or end school	26
Trouble with boss	23
Change in work hours or conditions	20
Change in residence	20
Change in schools	20
Mortgage or loan (modest)	17
Change in sleeping habits	16
Vacation	13
Christmas	12

Adapted from the Journal of Psychomatic Research, 1967: Vol 11; 216.

- obsessive compulsive disorder
- post-traumatic stress disorder

Generalised anxiety disorder

Generalised anxiety comprises excessive anxiety and worry about various life circumstances and is not related to a specific activity, time or event such as trauma, obsessions or phobias.

General features:

- persistent unrealistic and excessive anxiety
- worry about two or more life circumstances for six months or longer
- excessive worry about trifles
- at least six of the symptoms in the following list of clinical features
- about one-third present with mainly neurological symptoms, one-third with cardiovascular symptoms and one-third with mainly gastrointestinal symptoms[2]

Clinical features

Psychological

- apprehension/fearful anticipation
- irritability
- exaggerated startle response
- sleep disturbance and nightmares
- impatience
- panic
- sensitivity to noise
- difficulty concentrating or 'mind going blank'

Physical

- Motor tension
  - muscle tension/aching
  - tension headache
  - trembling/shaky/twitching
  - restlessness
  - tiredness/fatigue
- Autonomic overactivity
  - dry mouth
  - palpitations/tachycardia
  - sweating/cold clammy hands
  - flushes/chills
  - difficulty swallowing or 'lump in throat'
  - diarrhoea/abdominal distress
  - frequency of micturition
  - difficulty breathing/smothering feeling
  - dizziness or lightheadedness

Note Psychological disturbances are also referred to as disturbances of vigilance and scanning.

Symptoms and signs according to systems

Neurological: dizziness, headache, trembling, twitching, shaking, paraesthesia

Cardiovascular: palpitations, tachycardia, flushing, chest discomfort

Gastrointestinal: nausea, indigestion, diarrhoea, abdominal distress

Respiratory: hyperventilation, breathing difficulty, air hunger

Cognitive: fear of dying, difficulty concentrating, 'mind going blank', hypervigilance

Diagnosis of anxiety

The diagnosis is based on:

- the history: it is vital to listen carefully to what the patient is saying
- exclusion of organic disorders simulating anxiety by history, examination and appropriate investigation
- exclusion of other psychiatric disorders, especially depression

Main differential diagnoses

Note that this conforms to the seven masquerades list. Refer to Table 99.2.

- depression
- drug and alcohol dependence/withdrawal
- benzodiazepine dependence/withdrawal
- hyperthyroidism
- angina and cardiac arrhythmias
- iatrogenic drugs

> *Important checkpoints*
>
> Five self-posed questions should be considered by the family doctor before treating an anxious patient:[1]
>
> - Is this hyperthyroidism?
> - Is this depression?
> - Is this normal anxiety?
> - Is this mild anxiety or simple phobia?
> - Is this moderate or severe anxiety?

Management of anxiety

The management applies mainly to generalised anxiety as specific psychotherapy is required in other types of anxiety. Much of the management can be carried out successfully by the family doctor using brief counselling and support.[2]

Table 99.2 *Significant differential diagnoses of anxiety*

Psychiatric disorders
- depression
- drug and alcohol dependence/withdrawal
- benzodiazepine dependence/withdrawal
- schizophrenia
- acute or chronic organic brain disorder
- presenile dementia

Organic disorders
- drug-related
  - — amphetamines
  - — bronchodilators
  - — caffeine excess
  - — ephedrine
  - — levodopa
  - — thyroxine
- cardiovascular
  - — angina
  - — cardiac arrhythmias
  - — mitral valve prolapse
- endocrine
  - — hyperthyroidism
  - — phaeochromocytoma
  - — carcinoid syndrome
  - — hypoglycaemia
  - — insulinoma
- neurological
  - — epilepsy, especially complex partial seizures
  - — acute brain syndrome
- respiratory
  - — asthma
  - — acute respiratory distress
  - — pulmonary embolism

Management principles

- The aim is to use non-pharmacological methods and avoid the use of drugs if possible.
- Give careful explanation and reassurance
  - — explain the reasons for the symptoms
  - — reassure the patient about the absence of organic disease (can only be based on a thorough examination and appropriate investigations)
  - — direct the patient to appropriate literature to give insight and support (Table 99.3).
- Provide practical advice on ways of dealing with the problems.
- Advise on the avoidance of aggravating substances such as caffeine, nicotine and other drugs.
- Advise on general measures such as stress management techniques, relaxation programs and regular exercise and organise these for the patient (don't leave it to the patient).
- Advise on coping skills, including personal and interpersonal strategies, to cope with difficult circumstances and people (in relation to that patient).

Table 99.3 *Recommended reading for the anxious patient*

Herbert Benson	*The Relaxation Response*, Collins, London, 1984.
Dale Carnegie	*How to Stop Worrying and Start Living*, Rev. edn, ed. Dorothy Carnegie, Angus and Robertson, Sydney, 1985.
Ainslie Mears	*Relief without Drugs*, Fontana, Glasgow, 1983.
Norman Peale	*The Power of Positive Thinking* Cedar, London, 1982.
Claire Weekes	*Peace from Nervous Suffering*, Angus and Robertson, London, 1972.
Claire Weekes	*Self-help for your Nerves*, Angus and Robertson, London, 1976.

Patient education material

The author has found the following handout material to be invaluable in helping to manage less severe cases of generalised anxiety.[4]

Self-help

It is best to avoid drugs if you can; instead look at factors in your lifestyle that cause you stress and anxiety and modify or remove them (if possible). Be on the lookout for solutions. Examples are changing jobs and keeping away from people or situations that upset you. Sometimes confronting people and talking things over will help.

Special advice

Be less of a perfectionist: do not be a slave to the clock; do not bottle things up; stop feeling guilty; approve of yourself and others; express yourself and your anger. Resolve all personal conflicts. Make friends and be happy. Keep a positive outlook on life, and be moderate and less intense in your activities.

Seek a balance of activities, such as recreation, meditation, reading, rest, exercise and family/social activities.

Relaxation

Learn to relax your mind and body: seek out special relaxation programs such as yoga and meditation.

Make a commitment to yourself to spend some time every day practising relaxation. About 20 minutes twice a day is ideal, but you might want to start with only 10 minutes.[5]

- Sit in a quiet place with your eyes closed, but remain alert and awake if you can. Focus your mind on the different muscle groups in your body, starting at the forehead and slowly going down to the toes. Relax the muscles as much as you can.
- Pay attention to your breathing: listen to the sound of your breath for the next few minutes. Breathe in and out slowly and deeply.
- Next, begin to repeat the word 'relax' silently in your mind at your own pace. When other thoughts distract, calmly return to the word 'relax'.
- Just 'let go': this is a quiet time for yourself, in which the stresses in body and mind are balanced or reduced.

Medication

Doctors tend to recommend tranquillisers only as a last resort or to help you cope with a very stressful temporary period when your anxiety is severe and you cannot cope without extra help. Tranquillisers can be very effective if used sensibly and for short periods.

Pharmacological treatment

Acute episodes

The following drugs are recommended for patients who have intermittent transient exacerbations not responding to other measures.[6]

diazepam 2–5 mg (o) as a single dose
repeated bd as required

or

diazepam 5–10 mg (o) nocte

or

oxazepam 15–30 mg (o) as a single dose
repeated bd as required

Special notes:

- Recommended (if necessary) for up to two weeks, then taper off to zero over next four weeks.
- Reassess in seven days.
- Oxazepam is preferred in women patients; middle-aged men generally respond well to short-term diazepam.
- Be wary of drug-seeking behaviour, e.g. unfamiliar patients, especially if they request a specific benzodiazepine.
- Consider beta-blockers in patients with sympathetic activation such as palpitations, tremor and excessive sweating, e.g. propranolol 10–40 mg (o) tds.[6] They do not relieve the mental symptoms of anxiety, however.

Long-term treatment

If non-pharmacological treatment is ineffective for persisting disabling anxiety, the drug of choice is:

buspirone 5 mg (o) tds[6]

- increase if necessary to 20 mg (o) tds
- continue for several weeks after symptoms subside
- mean effective dose is 20–25 mg daily
- response takes 7–10 days
- does not appear to cause sedation

The alternatives to buspirone are the benzodiazepines:

diazepam 2–5 mg (o) bd or tds (or 5–10 mg nocte)

or

oxazepam 15–30 mg (o) bd

Try to wean the patient off medication each 6–12 months.

Panic disorder

Patients with panic disorder experience sudden, unexpected, short-lived episodes of intense anxiety. These tend to be recurrent and occur most often in young females.

The DSM-III-R diagnostic criteria for panic disorder include:

- the attack was unexpected and not triggered by the person being the focus of attention
- four attacks within a four week period

  or

  one or more attacks followed by at least one month of persistent fear of having another attack
- at least four of the following symptoms during at least one of the attacks:
  - shortness of breath (dyspnoea) or smothering sensations
  - dizziness, unsteady feelings or faintness
  - palpitations or accelerated heart rate (tachycardia)
  - trembling or shaking
  - sweating
  - choking
  - nausea or abdominal distress
  - depersonalisation or derealisation
  - numbness or tingling sensations (paraesthesias)

— flushes (hot flashes) or chills
— chest pain or discomfort
— fear of dying
— fear of going crazy or of doing something uncontrolled

Organic disorders that simulate a panic attack are hyperthyroidism, phaeochromocytoma and hypoglycaemia.

Management

Reassurance, explanation and support (as for generalised anxiety).

Cognitive behaviour therapy

This aims to reduce anxiety by teaching patients how to identify, evaluate, control and modify their negative, fearful thoughts and behaviour. If simple psychotherapy and stress management fails then patients should be referred for this therapy.

If hyperventilating, breathe in and out of a paper bag.

Pharmacological treatment[6]

Acute episodes:
diazepam 5 mg (o)
or
oxazepam 15–30 mg (o)
or
alprazolam 0.25–0.5 mg (o)

Prophylaxis[6]

imipramine 50–75 mg (o) nocte
increasing every 2–3 days to 150 mg nocte by day 7
dosage can be increased further depending on response and/or adverse effects
or
benzodiazepines
alprazolam 0.25–6 mg (o) daily in divided doses
or
clonazepam 0.5–6 mg (o) daily in divided doses

Note Medication should be withdrawn slowly. Medication for panic disorder may need to be continued for 6–12 months.

Phobic disorders

In phobic states the anxiety is related to specific situations or objects. Patients avoid these situations and become anxious when they anticipate having to meet them. A list of phobias is presented in Table 99.4.

Table 99.4 *Phobias*

Name of phobia	*Fear of*
Acrophobia	heights
Aerophobia	draughts
Agoraphobia	open spaces
Aichmophobia	sharp objects
Ailurophobia	cats
Algophobia	pain
Androphobia	men
Anthophobia	flowers
Anthropophobia	people
Arachnophobia	spiders
Aquaphobia	water
Astraphobia	lightning
Aviatophobia	flying
Bacteriophobia	bacteria
Bathophobia	depth
Brontophobia	thunder
Cancerophobia	cancer
Cardiophobia	heart disease
Claustrophobia	closed spaces
Cynophobia	dogs
Demonophobia	demons
Dromophobia	crossing streets
Equinophobia	horses
Genophobia	sex
Gynophobia	women
Haptephobia	being touched
Herpetophobia	creeping, crawling things
Hypsophobia	falling
Hypnophobia	going to sleep
Mysophobia	dirt, germs, contamination
Necrophobia	death
Neophobia	anything new
Numerophobia	numbers
Nyctophobia	darkness
Ochlophobia	crowds
Pyrophobia	fire
Taphophobia	being buried alive
Scotophobia	blindness
Sociophobia	social situations
Theophobia	God
Xenophobia	strangers
Zoophobia	animals

The three main types of phobic states are:

- simple phobias
- agoraphobia
- social phobias

The ten most common phobias (in order) are spiders, people and social situations, flying, open spaces, confined spaces, heights, cancer, thunderstorms, death and heart disease.[7]

Simple phobias

These are common among normal children and include fear of specific things such as snakes, spiders, thunder, darkness, dogs and heights. The problem is seldom encountered in practice and there is usually no call for drug therapy.

Agoraphobia

Avoidance includes the many situations involving the issues of distance from home, crowding or confinement. Typical examples are travel on public transport, crowded shops and confined places. The patients fear they may lose control, faint and suffer embarrassment.

The condition is commonly associated with depression, obsessions, marital and family disharmony, or drug and alcohol abuse.[8]

Social phobias

Social phobias include anxiety-provoking social gatherings when the person feels subject to critical public scrutiny, e.g. canteens, restaurants, staff meetings, speaking engagements. The sufferer may be a shy, self-conscious, premorbid personality.[2] Social phobias, including performance anxiety and symptoms, are often related to sympathetic overactivity.

Management

The basis of treatment for all phobic disorders is psychotherapy that involves behaviour therapy and cognitive therapy.

Pharmacological treatment[6]

This should be used only if non-pharmacological measures fail.

Agoraphobia with panic: use medications as for panic attacks.

Social phobia with performance anxiety: propranolol 10–40 mg (o) 30–60 minutes before the social event or performance.

Obsessive compulsive disorder

Anxiety is associated with obsessive thoughts and compulsive rituals.

The obsessions are recurrent and persistent intrusive ideas, thoughts, impulses or images that are usually resisted by the patient, e.g. a religious person having recurrent blasphemous thoughts.

Compulsions are repetitive, purposeful and intentional behaviours conducted in response to an obsession to prevent a bad outcome for the person, e.g. excessive washing of the genitals.

Mild obsessional or compulsive behaviour can be regarded as normal in response to stress.

Management

Optimal management is a combination of psychotherapeutic and pharmacological treatment, namely:

- cognitive behaviour therapy for obsessions
- exposure and response prevention for compulsions
- clomipramine 50–75 mg (o) nocte increasing gradually to 150–250 mg (o) nocte[6]

An alternative agent to clomipramine (if not tolerated or ineffective) is fluoxetine.

Post-traumatic stress disorder

This term describes the various symptoms and behaviour that follow a psychologically distressing event or experience outside the range of usual human experience, e.g. violent crime such as an armed hold-up, warfare, or natural disasters such as bushfires. The symptoms usually develop immediately after the event but can be delayed for months or years.

Typical symptoms and features:

- recurrent and intrusive distressing recollections
- recurrent distressing dreams of the event
- acting or feeling as if the event were recurring
- intense distress on exposure to resembling events
- persistent avoidance of events that symbolise or resemble the trauma
- increased arousal symptoms, e.g. insomnia, hypervigilance, exaggerated startle response, poor concentration, moodiness

Treatment

This is difficult and involves counselling, the basis of which is facilitating abreaction of the experience by individual or group therapy.[6] The aim is to allow the patient to face up openly to memories. Persistent symptoms are an indication for referral.

Pharmacological treatment

There is no specific indication for drugs but medication can have benefit in the treatment of panic attacks, generalised anxiety or depression.[6] Long-term use of benzodiazepines is not recommended but short-term use for their antianxiety and hypnotic effects may be appropriate for the very anxious patient.

Hyperventilation

Hyperventilation syndrome can be a manifestation of anxiety. The main symptoms are:

- lightheadedness, faintness or dizziness

- breathlessness
- palpitations
- sweating
- dry mouth with aerophagy
- agitation
- fatigue and malaise

Other symptoms include paraesthesia of the extremities, perioral paraesthesia and carpopedal spasm.

Management

- reassurance
- encourage patients to identify the cause and then control their rate and depth of breathing
- first aid management is to raise the carbon dioxide level by rebreathing from a paper (not plastic) bag or from cupped hands (if a bag is unavailable)

Benzodiazepine usage

The use of benzodiazepines as anxiolytics should be restricted and they should be used discretely. Markus et al[9] recommend reserving benzodiazepines to the following clinical situations.

1. Self-perpetuating anxiety following a precipitating event and not responding to non-pharmacological management. Give a short course for 2–4 weeks.
2. Situational anxiety affecting lifestyle, e.g. plane travel, dental appointments. Intermittent use only.
3. Emergency short-term use for agoraphobia and panic attacks.

They should not be used to treat depression, obsessional neuroses or chronic psychoses and should be used with caution in bereavement and crisis situations.

Problems associated with benzodiazepine use include:[1]

- impaired alertness, oversedation
- dependence
- increased risk of accidents
- adverse effects on mood and behaviour
- interaction with alcohol and other drugs
- potential for abuse and overdose
- risks during pregnancy and lactation
- muscle weakness
- sexual dysfunction
- diminished motivation
- lowered sense of competency
- lower self-esteem

Prescribing policy

It is appropriate to have a firm benzodiazepine prescribing policy; determine a clear-cut agreement for long-term users about the duration of the prescribed tablets, as well as information about the benefits versus risks. Long-term use should be avoided where possible and care should be taken with 'new patients' requesting a prescription.

Benzodiazepine withdrawal syndrome

This syndrome is usually relatively delayed in its onset and may continue for weeks or months.[1] Withdrawal features include:

- anxiety (rebound)
- depression
- insomnia
- nausea
- loss of appetite
- tremor
- confusion
- intolerance of loud noise, bright light or touch
- visual hallucinations
- epileptic seizures

There are several strategies to help the consenting patient to stop benzodiazepines, ranging from stopping completely to very gradual withdrawal. An effective method is to withdraw the drug very slowly while providing counselling and support, including referral to a self-help group. Antidepressants can be substituted if there is evidence of depression, while beta-blockers may help the withdrawal syndrome if other measures have failed.

When to refer

- if the diagnosis is doubtful
- if drug and alcohol dependence or withdrawal complicate the management
- if depression or a psychosis appears to be involved
- failure of response to basic treatment

Practice tips

- Be careful about confusing depression with anxiety.
- For anxiety, especially with cardiovascular symptoms (palpitations and/or flushing), always consider the possibility of hyperthyroidism and order thyroid function tests.

- Always try non-pharmacological measures to manage anxiety whenever possible.
- Be careful with use of benzodiazepines: aim at short-term treatment only.

References

1. Wilkinson G. *Anxiety: recognition and treatment in general practice*. Oxford: Radcliffe Medical Press, 1992, 5–62.
2. Vine RG, Judd FK. Anxiety disorders and panic states. In: MIMS Disease Index. Sydney: IMS Publishing, 1991–92, 51–55.
3. Gelder M. Diagnosis and management of anxiety and phobic states. Medicine International, 1988; 45:1857–1861.
4. Murtagh J. *Patient education*. Sydney: McGraw-Hill, 1992, 105.
5. Beattie R. Anxiety: patient education. Aust Fam Physician, 1985; 14:901.
6. Mashford ML. *Psychotrophic drug guidelines* (2nd edition). Melbourne: Victorian Medical Postgraduate Foundation, 1993/94, 87–100.
7. Anonymous author. Making it to the top ten. Melbourne: The Sun, 3 March 1990, 67.
8. Fryer AJ. Agoraphobia. Modern problems in pharmacopsychiatry, 1987; 22:91–126.
9. Markus AC, Murray Parker C, Tomson P et al. *Psychological problems in general practice*. Oxford: Oxford University Press, 1989, 12–43.

100

Asthma

Asthma may be defined as a disorder characterised by wide variations over short periods of time in resistance to airflow in intrapulmonary airways.[1] It can also be defined as a cough or wheeze associated with heightened airway responsiveness to inhaled histamine.[2] Asthma is a common and potentially fatal disorder; it is now regarded as an inflammatory disorder of the airways, which are hyperactive in the asthmatic patient.

Chronic asthma is an inflammatory disease with the following pathological characteristics:

- infiltration of the mucosa with inflammatory cells (especially eosinophils)
- oedema of the mucosa
- damaged mucosal epithelium
- hypertrophy of mucus glands with increased mucus secretion
- smooth muscle constriction (Fig. 100.1)

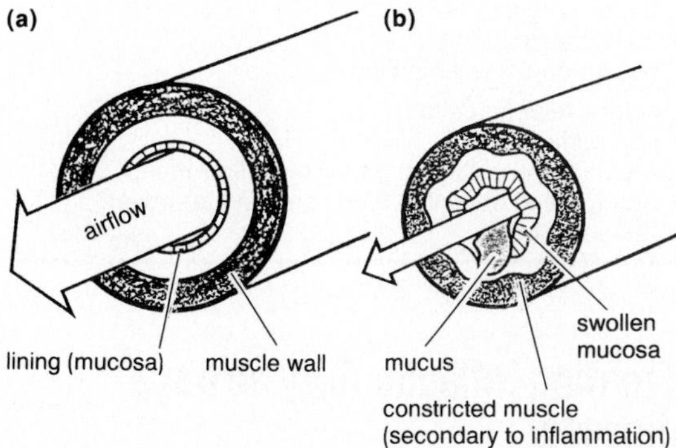

Fig. 100.1 *Airway changes in asthma:* **(a)** *normal airway;* **(b)** *airway in asthma*

Key facts and checkpoints

- Asthma continues to be underdiagnosed and undertreated.[1]
- It has an unacceptable mortality rate of approximately 5 per 100 000 of the population.
- About one child in four or five has asthma (usually in a mild form).
- It tends to develop between the ages of two and seven.
- Most children are free from it by puberty.
- About one adult in ten has asthma.
- All family doctors should keep abreast of developments in asthma management to achieve best possible control at all times in their patients.
- Three valuable home 'gadgets' to help the asthmatic are the mini peak flow meter, the large volume spacing device and the pump with nebuliser.
- The focus of management should be on prevention; an acute asthmatic attack represents failed treatment.
- Measurement of function is vital as 'objective measurement is superior to subjective measurement'.

Causes of asthma

No single cause for asthma has been found, but a variety of factors may trigger an attack. These include specific factors such as viruses and allergens and non-specific factors such as weather changes and exercise. A checklist of trigger factors is:

- infections, especially colds
- allergies, e.g. to animal fur, feathers, grass pollens, mould
- allergy to house dust, especially the dust mites
- cigarette smoke, other smoke and fumes
- sudden changes in weather or temperature
- occupational irritants, e.g. wood dust, synthetic sprays, chemicals
- drugs, e.g. aspirin, NSAIDs, beta-blockers (oral, parenteral or topical)
- certain foods and food additives may trigger asthma
  e.g. monosodium glutamate
  metabisulphites/sulphite preservatives/
  food colouring agents
  seafood
  nuts
- exercise, especially in a cold atmosphere
- emotional upsets or stress

Additional points

- Patients with asthma should not smoke.
- Atopic patients should avoid exposure to furred or feathered domestic animals if they have problems.
- About 90% of children with atopic symptoms and asthma demonstrate positive skin prick responses to dust mite extract. Total eradication of house dust mite from the home is difficult.

Clinical features

The classic symptoms are:

- wheezing
- coughing (especially at night)
- tightness in the chest
- breathlessness

Note Asthma should be suspected in children with recurrent nocturnal cough and in people with intermittent dyspnoea or chest tightness, especially after exercise.

Severe symptoms and signs are presented under the section on dangerous asthma later in this chapter.

Investigations

- Measurement of peak expiratory flow rate (PEFR): demonstrates variation in values over a period of time.
- Spirometry: a value of $< 75\%$ for FEV_1/VC ratio indicates obstruction.
- Measurement of PEFR or spirometry before and after bronchodilator: has a characteristic $> 20\%$ improvement.
- Inhalation challenge tests: airway reactivity is tested in a respiratory laboratory to inhaled histamine, methacholine, hypertonic saline and exercise.

Four big advances in the management of asthma

1. The realisation that asthma is an inflammatory disease. Therefore the appropriate first or second line treatment in moderate to severe asthma is inhaled sodium cromoglycate or corticosteroids.
2. The regular use of the mini peak flow meter.
3. The use of spacers attached to inhalers/puffers.
4. Improved and more efficient inhalers, such as Turbuhalers.

Reasons for suboptimal asthma control are presented in Table 100.1.

Table 100.1 *Reasons for suboptimal asthma control*[1,3]

Poor compliance
Inefficient use of inhaler devices
Failure to prescribe preventive medications, particularly inhaled corticosteroids for chronic asthma
Using bronchodilators alone and repeating these drugs without proper evaluation
Patient fears • inhaled or oral corticosteroids • concern about aerosols and the ozone layer • overdosage • developing tolerance • embarrassment • peer group condemnation
Doctor's reluctance to • use corticosteroids • recommend obtaining a mini peak flow meter • recommend obtaining a compressed air-driven nebuliser unit

Treating inflammatory airways disease

If inflammatory airways disease is undertreated there is the risk of irreversible airways obstruction from submucosal fibrosis. One of the most common mistakes in medical practice is to fail to introduce inhaled corticosteroids for the management of patients with moderately severe asthma.

Measurement of peak expiratory flow (PEF)

Patients with moderate to severe chronic asthma should be encouraged to obtain a PEF meter and measure their PEFR. PEF meter objective readings are more useful than subjective symptoms in assessing asthma control. They allow the establishment of a baseline of the 'patient's best'; they monitor changes; they allow the assessment of asthma severity and response to treatment.

Anyone older than six or seven years can usually test PEFR accurately. The PEFR should be measured in the morning and at night before inhaling the bronchodilator and then 10 minutes later. Ideally it should be performed three times for each test and the best reading recorded. The predicted normal values are a most useful guide. At some stage the patients best PEFR should be compared with the gold standard, namely FEV_1.

Warning signs when using PEF are:

- falling of PEFR and poor control
- readings less than 70% of normal best
- more morning dipping than normal
- erratic readings
- less response to bronchodilator than normal

Figure 100.2 shows a typical PEF recording of worsening asthma.

Large volume spacers

Some people who have trouble using inhalers can have a special 'spacer' fitted onto the mouthpiece of the inhaler. One or two puffs of the aerosol are put in the spacer. The patient breathes in from its mouthpiece, taking one deep inhalation, then one to two normal breaths, or four to six normal-sized breaths. This method is useful for adults having trouble with the puffer and for younger children (older than three). Spacers are very efficient, overcome poor technique and cause less irritation of the mouth and throat (Fig. 100.3). They allow increased airway deposition of inhalant and less oropharyngeal deposition.

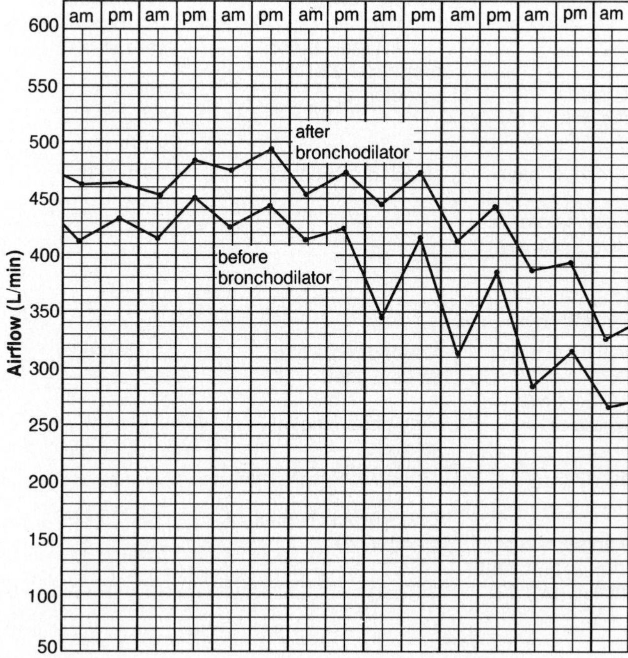

Fig. 100.2 *Typical peak expiratory flow record showing signs of worsening asthma*

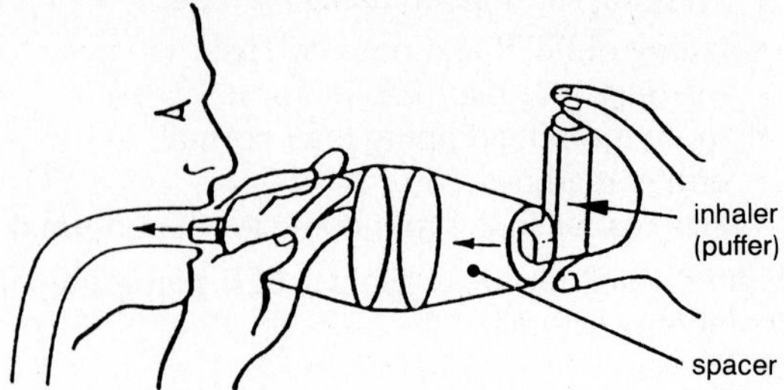

Fig. 100.3 *Using a spacer device. Rules: children—all puffs in at once, then inhale; adults—single puff, single breath*

Management principles

Aims of management:

- Abolish symptoms and restore normal airway function.[2]
- Maintain best possible lung function at all times—keep asthma under control.
- Reduce morbidity.
- Control asthma with the use of regular anti-inflammatory medication and relieving doses of $beta_2$ agonist when necessary.

Long-term goals:

- Achieve use of the least drugs, least doses and least side effects.
- Reduce risk of fatal attacks.
- Reduce risk of developing irreversible abnormal lung function.

Definition of control of asthma

- no cough, wheeze or breathlessness most of the time
- no noctural waking due to asthma
- no limitation of normal activity
- no overuse of $beta_2$ agonist
- no severe attacks
- no side effects of medication

The six step asthma management plan

The National Asthma Campaign of Australia has developed this plan, which can be summarised for both patient and doctor in the following point form. An important underlying theme for the plan is careful attention to educating the patient and family.

Table 100.2 *Assessment of asthma severity*[1,2]

Grade	*History*	*Medication use (bronchodilator)*	*Lung function*	
			Best PEFR (% predicted)	***PEFR % variability***
Mild	Episodic Mild occasional symptoms with exercise	Occasional use of bronchodilator for symptoms	Normal 100%	10–20%
Moderate	Symptoms most days Virtually asymptomatic on effective treatment Several known triggers apart from exercise	Needed most days	70–100%	20–30%
Severe	Symptoms most days Wakes at night with cough/wheeze Chest tightness on waking Hospital admission or emergency department attendance in past 12 months Previous life-threatening episodes	Needed more than 3 times a day or High dose inhaled steroids >800–1200 mcg daily or Oral steroids in past 12 months	≤ 70%	30%

1. Assess the severity of the asthma (Table 100.2)
   - Establish the peak expiratory flow rate (PEFR).
   - Both doctor and patient should agree on severity and common goals of treatment.
   - Consider symptoms and effect on living.
   - Consider medication requirements.
2. Achieve best lung function
   - Prescribe drug therapy to keep PEFR at best and to minimise symptoms.
   - Maintain the 'best' PEFR.
   - If PEF remains below predicted PEF level, treatment with high-dose inhaled steroids achieves optimal lung function in about 66% of patients.[3] (Appendix V).
3. Avoid trigger factors
   - Note any domestic or occupational 'triggers'.
   - Triggers can be inhaled or ingested.
   - If an allergen is clearly identified, avoid it, e.g. get rid of the cat, don't smoke, house dust mite avoidance strategies.
4. Stay at your best
   (keep patient at best lung function)
   - Organise an optimal medication program.
   - Consider inhaled medications, monitored with PEF, with as few drugs, doses and side effects as possible.
5. Know your action plan
   (prepare an easy-to-follow action plan)
   - This must cover three points:
   — recognition that asthma is deteriorating
   — patient initiates own extra medication
   — getting access to medical attention
6. Check your asthma regularly
   (review and educate the patient regularly and provide continuing care, even when the asthma is mild)

Patient (and family) education

This aspect is vital and patients can be referred to an asthma education resource centre. However, the family doctor should be continually educating and encouraging the patient to follow the six step asthma management plan.

Asthmatics tend to use 'denial' as a coping mechanism and are generally 'non-attenders' when well.

Prevention of attacks is the best treatment, and all asthmatics and their families should aim to know the disorder very well and become expert in it.

Know your asthma (advice for patients)

- Read all about it.
- Get to know how severe your asthma is.
- Try to identify trigger factors such as tobacco smoke and avoid them. There is an 80% increase in asthma incidence in children whose parents smoke.
- Become expert at using your medication and inhalers. A big problem is incorrect inhaler technique (35% of patients).
- Use your inhalers correctly and use a spacer if necessary.
- Know and recognise the danger signs and act promptly.
- Have regular checks with your doctor.
- Have physiotherapy: learn breathing exercises.
- Keep fit and take regular exercise.
- Work out a clear management plan and an action plan for when trouble strikes.
- Get urgent help when danger signs appear.
- Learn the value of a peak expiratory flow meter (for anyone over six).
- Get a peak flow meter to help assess severity and work out your best lung function.
- Keep at your best with suitable medications.
- Always carry your bronchodilator inhaler and check that it is not empty (learn about the water flotation test).

Pharmacological agents to treat asthma

It is useful to teach patients the concept of the 'preventer' and the 'reliever' for their asthma treatment. The pharmacological treatment of asthma is summarised in Table 100.3.

'Preventer' drugs or anti-inflammatory agents

These medications are directed toward the underlying abnormalities—bronchial hyper-reactivity and associated airway inflammation.

Corticosteroids

Inhaled:	Types	beclomethasone, budesonide
	Coming	fluticasone
	Dose range	400 μg–2000 μg (adults) aim to keep below 1600 μg (if possible)
	Availability	• metered dose inhaler • Turbuhaler • Rotacaps

Table 100.3 *Pharmacological treatment of bronchial asthma*

			Vehicle of administration				
	Generic types	***Examples***	***Nebulising solution***	***Oral***	***Aerosol (metered dose inhalation)***	***Dry powder (inhalation)***	***Injection***
Bronchodilators							
1. β_2-adrenoceptor agonists	Salbutamol	Ventolin	✓	✓	✓	✓	✓
	Terbutaline	Bricanyl	✓	✓	✓	✓	✓
	Fenoterol	Berotec	✓		✓		
	Adrenaline				✓		✓
2. Methylxanthines	Theophylline	Brondecon		✓			
		Nuelin		✓			
		Theo-dur		✓			
	Aminophylline						✓
3. Anticholinergics	Ipratropium bromide	Atrovent	✓		✓		
Mast cell stabilisers	Sodium cromoglycate	Intal	✓		✓	✓	
Corticosteroids	Beclomethasone	Aldecin			✓	✓	
		Becotide (50, 100)			✓	✓	
		Becloforte (250)			✓	✓	
	Budesonide	Pulmicort (100,200,400)	✓		✓	✓	
	Prednisolone			✓			
	Hydrocortisone	Solu-cortef					✓

Frequency: twice daily (helps compliance)

Side effects: oropharyngeal candidiasis, dysphonia (hoarse voice)
bronchial irritation: cough
adrenal suppression (doses of 2000 μg/daily sometimes as low as 800 μg)

Note Rinse mouth out with water and spit out after using inhaled steroids.

Oral: Prednisolone is used mainly for exacerbations. It is given with the usual inhaled corticosteroids and bronchodilators.

Dose: up to 1 mg/kg/day for 1–2 weeks

Side effects: these are minimal if drug is used for short periods

Oral corticosteroids can be ceased abruptly.

Long-term use: osteoporosis, glucose intolerance, adrenal suppression, thinning of skin and easy bruising.

Sodium cromoglycate (SCG)

This is available as dry capsules for inhalation, metered dose aerosols or as a nebuliser solution. The availability of the metered aerosol and spacer has helped the use of SCG in the management of asthma in children. Side effects are uncommon; local irritation may be caused by the dry powder. Systemic effects do not occur.

'Reliever' drugs or bronchodilators

The three groups of bronchodilators are:

- the β_2-adrenoceptor agonists (β-agonists)
- methylxanthines—theophylline derivatives
- anticholinergics

β_2-agonists

The inhaled route of delivery is the preferred route and the vehicles of administration include metered dose inhalation, a dry powder, and nebulisation where the solution is converted to a mist of small droplets by a flow of oxygen or air through the solution (Fig. 100.4).

Oral administration of β_2-agonists is rarely required. The inhaled drugs produce measurable bronchodilatation in 1–2 minutes and peak

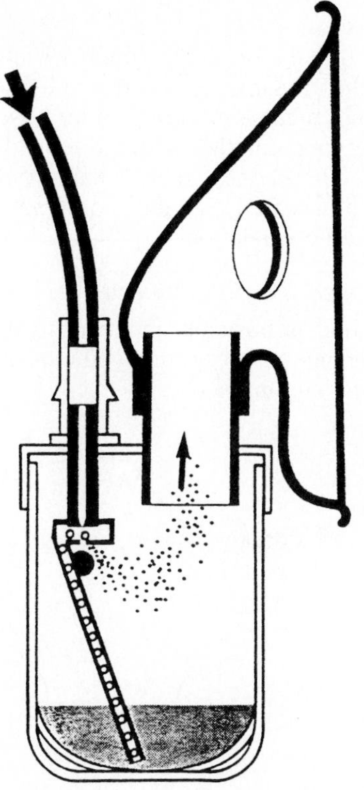

Fig. 100.4 *Demonstration of the mechanism of the jet nebuliser*

effects by 10–20 minutes. The traditional agents such as salbutamol and terbutaline are short-acting preparations. The new longer-acting agents include salmeterol and formoterol.

Theophylline derivatives

These oral drugs may have complementary value to the inhaled agents but tend to be limited by side effects and efficacy.

Prophylactic agents

This term is reserved for those medications that are taken prior to known trigger factors, particularly exercise-induced asthma.

Exercise-induced asthma

- β_2-agonist inhaler (puffer); two puffs immediately before exercise last 1–2 hours. New longer-acting agents such as salmeterol are more effective.
- Sodium cromoglycate, two puffs.
- Combination β_2-agonist + sodium cromoglycate.
- Paediatricians often recommend a non-drug warm-up program as an alternative to medication.

A general management plan for chronic asthma is summarised in Figure 100.5.

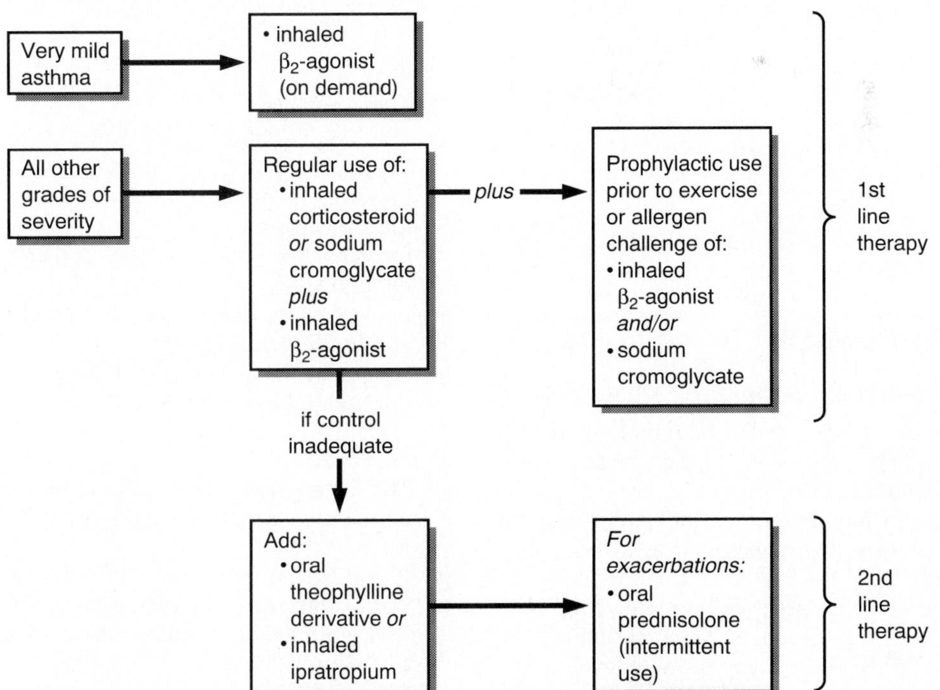

Fig. 100.5 *Management plan for chronic asthma* REPRODUCED FROM SEALE JP *ASTHMA*[2] WITH PERMISSION OF *MIMS DISEASE INDEX*

Correct use of the asthma metered dose inhaler (puffer)

Did you know that . . . ?

- faulty use of inhaler technique occurs in at least one-third of users
- 90% of the medication sticks to the mouth and does not reach the lungs
- it is the inhalation effort—not the pressure from the aerosol—that gets the medication to the lungs
- it is important to instruct patients properly and check their technique regularly

The two main techniques

The open-mouth technique and the closed-mouth technique are the main methods, and both are effective. The patient and doctor should choose the technique that suits them best. Both techniques are suitable for most adults. Most children from the age of seven can learn to use puffers quite well.

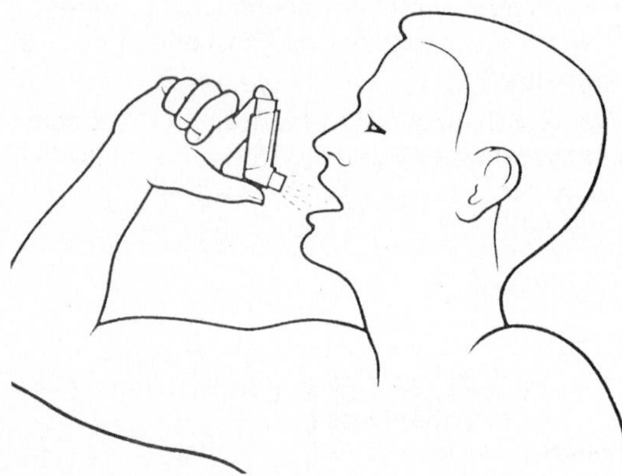

Fig. 100.6 *Using the metered dose inhaler: the open-mouth technique*

Instructions for patients

The open-mouth technique (Fig. 100.6)

1. Remove the cap. Shake the puffer vigorously for 1–2 seconds. Hold it upright (canister on top) to use it (as shown).
2. Hold the mouthpiece of the puffer 4–5 cm (about three finger-breadths) away from your mouth.
3. Tilt your head back slightly with your chin up. Open your mouth and keep it open.
4. Slowly blow out to a comfortable level.
5. Just as you start to breathe in (slowly) through your mouth, press the puffer firmly, once. Breathe in as far as you can over 3–5 seconds. (Do not breathe in through your nose.)
6. Close your mouth and hold your breath for about 10 seconds; then breathe out gently.
7. Breathe normally for about one minute, then repeat the inhalation.

The closed-mouth technique (Fig. 100.7)

The method is basically identical to the open-mouth technique except that you close your lips around the mouthpiece.

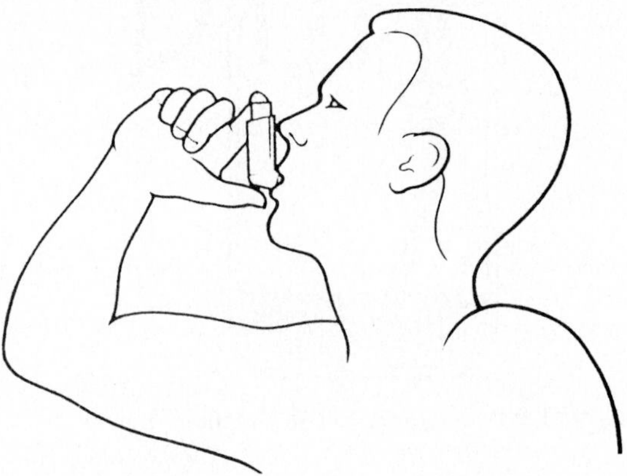

Fig. 100.7 *Using the metered dose inhaler: the closed-mouth technique*

Common mistakes

- holding the puffer upside down
- holding the puffer too far away
- pressing the puffer too early and not inhaling the spray deeply
- pressing the puffer too late and not getting enough spray
- doing it all too quickly: not breathing in slowly and holding the breath
- squeezing the puffer more than once
- not breathing in deeply

Extra points

1. The usual dose of standard metered dose aerosol is one or two puffs every 3–4 hours for an attack.
2. If you do not get adequate relief from your normal dose, you should contact your doctor.
3. It is quite safe to increase the dose, such as to 4–6 puffs.

4. If you are using your inhaler very often, it usually means your other asthma medication is not being used properly. Discuss this with your doctor.

The Turbuhaler

The Turbuhaler is a delivery system that is now widely used as an alternative to the metered dose inhaler.

Dangerous asthma

Failure to recognise the development of a severe attack has cost the lives of many asthmatics. The severe attacks can start suddenly (even in mild asthmatics) and catch people by surprise.

High-risk patients

People who have experienced one or more of the following are more likely to have severe attacks:

- a previous severe asthma attack
- previous hospital admission, especially if to intensive care
- hospital attendance in the past 12 months
- long-term oral steroid treatment
- carelessness with taking medication
- night-time attacks, especially with severe chest tightness
- recent emotional problems

Early warning signs of severe asthma or an asthma attack:

- symptoms persisting or getting worse despite adequate medication
- increased coughing and chest tightness
- poor response to two inhalations
- benefit from inhalations not lasting two hours
- increasing medication requirements
- sleep being disturbed by coughing, wheezing or breathlessness
- chest tightness on waking in the morning
- low peak expiratory flow readings

Dangerous signs

- marked breathlessness, especially at rest
- sleep being greatly disturbed by asthma
- asthma getting worse quickly rather than slowly, despite medication
- feeling frightened
- difficulty in speaking; unable to say more than a few words
- exhaustion
- drowsiness or confusion
- chest becoming 'silent' with a quiet wheeze, yet breathing still laboured
- cyanosis
- chest retraction
- respiratory rate greater than 25 (adults) or 50 (children)
- pulse rate > 120
- peak flow < 100 L/min

Asthma action plans

Examples of action plans for patients are presented below.

Action plan

If you are distressed with severe asthma:

- Call an ambulance and say 'severe asthma attack' (best option)
  or
- Call your doctor
  or
- If you are having trouble finding medical help, get someone to drive you to the nearest hospital

Keep using your bronchodilator inhaler continuously if you are distressed.

The following is an example of an asthma action plan that the patient keeps on a card for easy reference.

Asthma Action Plan

Name ....

Contact Dr .... Tel. ....

Hospital tel. ....

Measure peak flow before reliever

Best peak flow: 600 (example)........................

Peak flow	***Treatment***
1. Below 480 (or 80% of best)	double dose of preventer
2. Below 360 (or 60% of best)	start prednisolone and contact doctor
3. Below 240 (or 40% of best)	continue reliever and dial 000 for ambulance

The acute asthma attack

Summary (adult dosage)[3]

- continuous nebulised salbutamol (or terbutaline) if nebuliser available (if not: 6–10 puffs of β_2-agonist inhaler, preferably with spacer, using two loading puffs at a time followed by 4–6 breaths)

  Ipratopium bromide may be mixed with β_2-agonist for concurrent nebulisation
- parenteral β_2-agonist, e.g. salbutamol 500 μg IM, SC
- corticosteroids, e.g. prednisolone 50 mg (o) statim then daily

  or

  hydrocortisone 250 mg IV or IM
- monitor PEF

The management of status asthmaticus is presented on pages 981–983.

Asthma in children

The prevalence of asthma is increasing in childhood and the management (especially in infants) is always a concern for the family doctor.

Key checkpoints

- Bronchodilators, inhaled or oral, are ineffective under 12 months.
- The delivery method is a problem in children and Table 100.4 gives an indication of what systems can be used at various levels.
- In the very young, e.g. 1–2 years old, a spacer with a face mask can deliver the aerosol medication.
- The PEF rate should be measured in all asthmatic children older than six years. Children under six years generally cannot cope with the meters and those with mild asthma don't usually need PEF measurement.
- The Turbuhaler is usually not practical under 7–8 years.

Prophylaxis in children

Sodium cromoglycate (SCG) by inhalation is the prophylactic drug of choice in childhood chronic asthma of mild to moderate severity.

- SCG has no significant side effects
- a symptomatic response occurs in about 1–2 weeks (can take up to 4–6 weeks)
- SCG (Forte) is an alternative to low-dose inhaled corticosteroids once the asthma is stable, especially if there are steroid side effects

If there is no clinical response to SCG, use inhaled corticosteroids, but the risks versus benefits must always be considered. Any dose equal to or greater than 400 μg in children can have possible side effects, including growth suppression and adrenal suppression. Aim for a maintenance of 100-400 μg, which keeps the child symptom-free. One or two attacks only is not an indication to start corticosteroids.

Guidelines for the management of asthma in children (1–4 years) are summarised in Table 100.5. Delivery systems for children are presented in Table 100.4.

When to refer

- If you are doubtful about the diagnosis.
- For problematic children.
- For advice on management when asthmatic control has failed or is difficult to achieve.

Table 100.4 *Delivery systems for asthma in children*

Vehicle of administration	***Age in years***			
	Less than 2	***2–4***	***5–6***	***7 and over***
Inhaler alone			*	✓
Inhaler + spacer		✓	✓	✓
Inhaler + spacer + face mask/aerochamber	✓	✓		
Turbuhaler			*	✓
Nebuliser/air compressor/face mask	✓	✓	✓	✓
Spincaps				✓
Rotacaps				✓

* possible in some individual children

Table 100.5 *Management plan for children 1-4 years*

Grade of asthma	*Agent*	*Vehicle*
Mild	β_2-agonist	Inhaler + spacer Nebuliser
Moderate	β_2-agonist	Inhaler + spacer or Nebuliser
	sodium cromoglycate if unresponsive ↓ corticosteriod	Inhaler + spacer or Nebuliser
Severe	β_2-agonist ↓	Inhaler + spacer or Nebuliser
	corticosteroid	
	theophylline	Sprinklers (oral)
	ipratopium bromide	Nebuliser
	prednisolone	Oral

Note Improvised 'spacer' with paper cup or plastic soft-drink bottle: an aerosol may be administered to children by plunging the mouthpiece of the inhaler through the base of the cup and then holding the open end of the cup over the child's mouth, or by cutting out the base of a plastic soft-drink bottle and holding this over the mouth while the inhaler is inserted into the open top of the bottle.

Practice tips

- Reassure the patient that 6–10 inhaled doses of a β_2-agonist is safe and appropriate for a severe attack of asthma.
- It is important to achieve a balance between undertreatment and overtreatment.
- Beware of patients, especially children, manipulating their peak flow.
- Get patients to rinse out their mouth with water and spit it out after inhaling corticosteroids.
- Patients who are sensitive to aspirin/ salicylates need to be reminded that salicylates are present in common cold cure preparations and agents such as Alka-Seltzer.[1]
- Possible side effects of inhaled drugs can be reduced by always using a spacer with the inhaler, using the medication qid rather than bd, rinsing the mouth, gargling and spitting out after use, and using corticosteroid sparing medications.

References

1. Rees J, Price J. *ABC of asthma* (2nd edition). London: British Medical Journal, 1989, 1–34.
2. Seale JP. Asthma. In: MIMS Disease Index. Sydney: IMS Publishing, 1991–92, 59–65.
3. Rubinfeld AR. How to treat asthma. Aust Dr Weekly, 1 February 1991, I–VIII.

101

Epilepsy

Epilepsy is defined as a 'tendency to recurrence of seizures'. It is a symptom, not a disease. A person should not be labelled 'epileptic' until at least two attacks have occurred.[1] Epilepsy is common and affects about one person in 50. Both sexes are about equally involved, and it seems to run in some families. Famous people who have had epilepsy include Julius Caeser, Agatha Christie, Thomas Edison and Handel.

The most important factors in the management of epilepsy are the accurate diagnosis of the type of seizures; identification of the cause and appropriate investigation; the use of first-line drugs as the sole therapy of some weeks; and adjustment of the dose, according to clinical experience and plasma levels, to give maximum benefit.

To be accurate in diagnosing seizures the diagnosis must be based on:

- the observation of a witness to the seizures
- a general and neurological examination
- an electroencephalogram (EEG), although this has considerable limitations
- a computerised tomography (CT) scan or MRI (especially if the EEG is focal and a tumour is suspected)

Long-term ambulatory EEG recording now provides more information and, coupled with video monitoring, it will make a permanent record of the seizure which can be reviewed at will. The CT scan or MRI scan is necessary to exclude a focal cause (such as a cyst, tumour, malformation or abscess) which might be treatable by surgery.

It will also identify mesotemporal sclerosis (an abnormality in the hippocampus due to birth hypoxia), thereby making some 'idiopathic' seizures into secondary seizures from a known cause.

An underlying organic lesion becomes more common in epilepsy presented for the first time in patients over the age of 25 and thus more detailed investigation is required.[1]

Optimal management includes adequate psychosocial support with education, counselling, advocacy and appropriate referral.

Types of epilepsy

Epileptic seizures are classified in general terms as generalised and partial (Table 101.1). Partial seizures are about twice as common as generalised seizures and usually due to acquired pathology.[2]

Generalised seizures

The epileptic discharge affects both cerebral hemispheres simultaneously from the outset. The seizure may be primary or secondary due to acquired cerebral pathology.

The main features are:

- abrupt impairment or loss of consciousness
- possible bilateral symmetrical motor events

Types

- Tonic clonic (formerly called grand mal) seizure: this is the classic convulsive seizure with muscle jerking (page 625)

Table 101.1 *Classification of epileptic seizures*

1. Generalised seizures
Convulsive
tonic clonic (previously called grand mal)
tonic
clonic
atonic
Non-convulsive
absence (petit mal)
atypical absence
myoclonic

2. Partial seizures
Simple partial (consciousness retained)
with motor signs (Jacksonian)
with somatosensory symptoms
with psychic symptoms
Complex partial (consciousness impaired)

3. Secondary generalised seizures
Simple partial seizures evolving to tonic clonic seizures
Complex partial seizures evolving to tonic clonic seizures
Simple partial seizures evolving to complex partial seizures and then to tonic clonic seizures

- Tonic seizure: stiffness only, often with a 'drop'
- Clonic seizure: jerks only
- Atonic seizure: loss of tone, and 'drops'
- Absence seizure (formerly called petit mal): involves loss of consciousness with no or only very minor bilateral muscle jerking, mainly of the face[2] (page 438)
- Myoclonic seizure: bilateral discrete muscle jerks, which may be very severe, and loss of consciousness

Partial seizures

In partial seizures the epileptic discharge begins in a localised focus of the brain and then spreads out from this focus. The clinical pattern depends on the part of the brain affected.

- simple partial seizures: consciousness is retained (page 438)
- complex partial seizures: consciousness is clouded so that the patient does not recall the complete seizure (page 438).

Both these types of partial seizure can evolve into a bilateral tonic clonic seizure; this is termed a secondary generalised seizure and is usually due to diffuse brain pathology.[1]

Investigations

Standard minimum investigations are:

- serum calcium
- fasting glucose
- EEG (usually with sleep deprivation)
- syphilis serology

Other tests may include:

- chest and skull X-ray
- brain scan
- video EEG (limited mainly to frequent seizures) or to diagnostic dilemmas
- magnetic resonance imaging (MRI)
- CT scanning

A patient presenting with the first seizure after the age of 25 will require more detailed investigation.

Table 101.2 *Antiepileptic drugs*

The following antiepileptic drugs (with brand names) are available

Benzodiazepines
clonazepam (Rivotril)
diazepam (various)

Carbamazepine (Tegretol, Teril)

Corticotrophin

Phenobarbitone and related drugs
methylphenobarbitone (Prominal)
primidone (Mysoline)

Phenytoin (Dilantin)

Sodium valproate (Epilim)

Succinimides
ethosuximide (Zarontin)
methosuximide (Celontin)
phensuximide (Milontin)

Sulthiame (Ospolot)

New drugs (probably as 'added on' therapy)
Lamotrigine

Vigabatrin (Sabril)

Gabapentin

Felbamate

Approaches to management

- An accurate diagnosis of the seizure type is essential.
- An underlying brain disease has to be investigated and treated.
- A decision has to be made about whether drug therapy is appropriate. Most seizures require long-term antiepileptic (anticonvulsant) drug therapy aimed at suppressing the underlying seizure activity in the hope that it may subside, so that 'cure' ultimately occurs and treatment may be ceased. A summary of antiepileptic drugs is presented in Table 101.2.
- The choice of drug depends on the seizure type, on consideration of the age and sex of

the patient and on efficacy in relation to toxicity.

- Treatment should be initiated with one drug and pushed until it controls the events or causes side effects, irrespective of the medication blood level. The disorder can usually be controlled by one drug provided adequate serum or plasma concentrations are reached.[3]
- If a maximum tolerated dosage of this single drug fails to control the seizures, replace it with an alternative agent. Add the second drug and obtain a therapeutic effect before removing the first drug.
- It is important to review the need for anticonvulsants every 12 months. Consider drug withdrawal if the patient has been free of seizures for several years (best under specialist supervision).
- Special attention should be given to the adverse psychological and social effects of epilepsy. Emotional and social support is important and advice about epilepsy support groups is appropriate.

Drug therapy

The following are important specific considerations:

- It is best to select the most effective recommended drug for a specific seizure type (Table 101.3).
- Young women prefer carbamazepine to phenytoin because of the adverse effects of gingival hypertrophy and hirsutism.
- Each drug has specific adverse effects (Table 101.4) while all drugs tend to be sedating, especially phenobarbitone and its derivatives.
- Twice daily dosage is usually practical.
- Phenytoin should be increased in small increments (25–50 mg) above a dose of 300 mg daily.
- Phenytoin or carbamazepine will bring about control in at least 80% of patients with tonic clonic seizures.[1]

Adverse drug reactions

Patients should be warned about significant side effects:

- Nausea, dizziness, ataxia, visual disturbance or excessive tiredness/fatigue indicate excessive dosage of carbamazepine or phenytoin.
- Most drugs can cause a rash.
- Gingival hyperplasia is a classic effect of phenytoin.
- Hirsutism can occur with phenytoin while hair loss can occur with sodium valproate.
- Sodium valproate has rare but potentially serious toxic effects
  - — liver toxicity
  - — dysmorphogenic effects (specifically spina bifida) on foetus during pregnancy

Table 101.3 *Recommended selection of antiepileptics in epilepsy*

Type of seizure	*First-line therapy*	*Second-line therapy*
Tonic/clonic	Sodium valproate In young women (still reproductive) use carbamazepine	Phenytoin or Phenobarbitone
Absence (petit mal)	Sodium valproate	Ethosuximide or Clonazepam
Myoclonic	Sodium valproate	Clonazepam
Simple partial (Jacksonian)	Carbamazepine	Phenytoin or Sodium valproate
Complex partial	Carbamazepine	Sodium valproate or Clonazepam or Phenytoin

Table 101.4 *Commonly used antiepileptics: usual dose and adverse reactions*

	Usual starting adult dose	***Average satisfactory adult dose (mg/kg/day***	***Therapeutic plasma concentration range (µmol/L)***	***Significant adverse reactions***
Carbamazepine	100-200 mg daily or bd, increasing gradually to control (max: 2 g/day)	30	25-50 free level 6-13	Anorexia, nausea, vomiting, dizziness, drowsiness, skin rashes, tinnitus, ataxia, diplopia Small risk of spina bifida in foetus Drug interactions, e.g. COC, warfarin, other anticonvulsants
Clonazepam	0.25 mg bd increasing to control	0.1-0.2		Drowsiness, fatigue, muscle weakness, ataxia, dizziness Respiratory problems Interacts with alcohol
Ethosuximide (used only in absence seizures)	20-30 mg/kg/day in 2 divided doses	30	300-700	Anorexia, nausea, vomiting Diarrhoea Drowsiness, ataxia, headache Beware of blood dyscrasias
Phenobarbitone	30-90 mg bd	2-4	45-130	Drowsiness Dizziness, ataxia Skin rashes Mood changes, e.g. excitable Interacts with warfarin, COC, other anticonvulsants
Phenytoin	5 mg/kg/day in 2 divided doses	5-6	40-80 free level 4-8	Drowsiness, fatigue, mental confusion, ataxia, nystagmus, slurred speech, anorexia, dizziness, nausea, vomiting Skin reactions Gum hypertrophy, hirsutism Foetal malformations, e.g. cleft lip and palate, congenital heart disorders
Sodium valproate	500 mg bd, increasing to achieve control (up to 2-3 g/day)	20-30 Standard dose: 500 mg mane 1000 mg nocte	300-750 free level 30-75	Drowsiness, tremor, hair loss Platelet effect Risk of neural tube defects in foetus Hepatic failure Interacts with other anticonvulsants To be avoided in pregnancy

(therefore it is a risk in women of child-bearing age, especially if inadvertent pregnancy occurs due to pill failure related to antiepileptic interaction).

- LFTs should be performed every two months for six months after starting sodium valproate.[1] Liver toxicity is much more common in the under 2 years old age group.

Patient education

Points worth emphasising:

- Most patients can achieve complete control of seizures.
- Most people lead a normal life—they can expect to marry, have a normal sexual life and have normal children.
- Patients need good dental care, especially if they are taking phenytoin.
- A seizure in itself will not cause death or brain damage unless in a risk situation such as swimming.
- Patients cannot swallow their tongue during a seizure.
- Take special care with open fires.
- Encourage patients to cease intake of alcohol.
- Adequate sleep is important.

Driving

One has to be very careful about driving. Most people with epilepsy can drive. Applicants for learner's licence need to be seizure-free for two years, with an annual medical review for five years following receipt of the licence. Restrictions range from one month to two years, depending on the circumstances of the seizures.

Employment

People with epilepsy can hold down most jobs, but if liable to seizures they should not work close to heavy machinery, in dangerous surroundings, at heights (such as climbing ladders) or near deep water. Careers are not available in some services, such as the police, military, aviation (pilot, traffic controller) or public transport (e.g. bus driver).

Sport and leisure activities

Most activities are fine, but epileptics should avoid dangerous sports such as scuba diving, hang-gliding, parachuting, rock climbing, car racing and swimming alone, especially surfing.

Table 101.5 outlines contraindications for sporting activities. These apply to patients who suffer from very frequent seizures, especially the complex partial seizures with prolonged postictal states.[4]

Table 101.5 *Sporting activities: contraindications*[4]

Absolute contraindications

- flying and parachuting
- motor racing
- mountain and rock climbing
- high diving
- scuba diving
- underwater swimming, especially competitive
- hang-gliding
- abseiling

Relative contraindications

- aiming sports such as archery and pistol shooting
- contact sports such as boxing, rugby, football, including soccer, where heading the ball is involved
- competitive cycling for children with absence epilepsy
- bathing and swimming
- gymnastics, especially activities such as trampolining and climbing on bars
- ice skating and skiing
- javelin throwing

Avoid trigger factors

- fatigue
- lack of sleep
- physical exhaustion
- stress
- excess alcohol
- prolonged flashing lights, e.g. video games (this applies to those with a proven response to a proper EEG with photic stimulation)

Photosensitive epilepsy in children

Some children suffer from photosensitive epilepsy related to prolonged exposure to computer and video games. There is some evidence that such children may not have seizures if they keep one eye covered. If television provokes seizures, strategies such as watching it with ambient lighting and using the remote control rather than approaching the set will minimise the problem.

Pregnancy and epilepsy[5]

Although the outcome is successful for more than 90% of epileptic women, there is a slightly increased risk of prematurity, low birth weight, mortality, defects and intervention. About 45% of women have an increased number of seizures, due mainly to a fall in antiepileptic drug levels.

All antiepileptic drugs are potentially teratogenic, with different drugs being related to different defects: phenytoin has been related to cleft lip and palate and congenital heart disease, while sodium valproate (in particular) and carbamazepine have been associated with spina bifida. All antiepileptic drugs are expressed in breast milk but in such reduced concentrations as not to preclude breast-feeding.

Pitfalls in management of epilepsy[3]

Misdiagnosis

The main pitfall associated with seizure disorders and epilepsy is misdiagnosis. It should be realised that not all seizures are generalised tonic clonic in type. The most common misdiagnosed seizure disorder is that of complex partial seizures (an underdiagnosed disorder) or the variations of generalised tonic clonic seizures (tonic, clonic or atonic separately).

The diagnosis of epilepsy is made on the history rather than the EEG so a very detailed description of the events from eye witnesses is important.

The features of complex partial seizure (described on pages 438–39) have many variations, the commonest being a slight disturbance of perception or consciousness. The complex partial seizure may evolve to a generalised tonic clonic seizure. A simple partial seizure may also do this.

In tonic clonic seizures the patient may become momentarily rigid or fall to the ground and perhaps have one or two jerks only.

Misdiagnosing behavioural disorders

It is important to differentiate between a fit and a behavioural disorder, but it can be difficult. About 20% of apparently intractable 'seizures' are considered to be pseudoseizures, i.e. emotionally based.[6] Ancillary testing, especially with video EEG recording, can help overcome these diagnostic problems but the differentiation may be difficult as the most common situation for pseudoseizures is in the person who has real fits.

Overtreatment

Polypharmacy

Polypharmacy is counterproductive for the patient and the seizure disorder. This is especially applicable to drugs with a high incidence of side effects. If a patient is taking several medications, management of the case needs questioning and perhaps reconsidering with a consultant's help.

Seizure control may be improved by reducing polypharmacy. When initiating treatment it is best to select one drug and increase its dose until its maximum recommended level, the onset of side effects or appropriate control. If control is not obtained, it should be replaced with an alternative agent but a cross-over period is essential. Combination therapy should only be tried when all appropriate antiepileptics have failed as monotherapy.[1]

Prolonged treatment

The question should be asked at some stage 'Does this patient really need medication?' Some patients are kept on antiepileptics for too long without any attempt being made to wean them off medication or to transfer them onto antiepileptics less prone to side effects. Patients should not be left on inappropriate drugs for too long, especially if side effects and drug interactions are a problem.

Drug interactions

Drug interactions with antiepileptics should always be kept in mind. The most serious of all is the interaction with the oral contraceptive pill, because pregnancy can occur.

Management of status epilepticus

Focal status

- a high index of suspicion is needed to diagnose
- oral medication usually adequate
- avoid overtreatment

Generalised status

Absence attack (petit mal)

- hospitalisation
- IV diazepam

Tonic clonic (dangerous!)

- ensure adequate oxygenation: attend to airway (e.g. Guedel tube); give oxygen
- IV diazepam 5–20 mg (rate not exceeding 2 mg/min)—beware of respiratory depression and other vital parameters
- IV phenytoin (if severe status): 1 g over 20–30 minutes

Other drugs to consider instead of diazepam:

- clonazepam (next choice); phenobarbitone; thiopentone; paraldehyde

Diazepam can be given rectally. In an adult 10 mg is diluted in 5 ml of isotonic saline and introduced via the nozzle of the syringe into the rectum.

DOs and DONTs for the onlookers of a seizure

- Don't move the person (unless necessary for safety).
- Don't force anything into the person's mouth.
- Don't try to stop the fit.
- Do roll the person on to his or her side with the head turned to one side and chin up.
- Do call for medical help if the seizure lasts longer than 10 minutes or starts again.
- Do remove false teeth and help clear the airway once the fit is over.

When to refer[2]

Specialist referral is advisable under the following circumstances:

- uncertainty of diagnosis
- at onset of seizure disorder to help obtain a precise diagnosis
- when seizures are not controlled by apparent suitable therapy ? wrong drug ? suboptimal dose ? progressive underlying disorder
- when the patient is unwell, irrespective of laboratory investigation
- when a woman is considering pregnancy (preferable) or has become pregnant: to obtain therapeutic guidance during a difficult phase of management
- for assessment of the prospects for withdrawing treatment after some years of absolute seizure control

Practice tips

- The EEG has considerable limitations in diagnosis. It is diagnostic in less than 50%,[1] although more diagnostic if conducted under sleep deprivation. An accurate eye witness account of the seizure is the most reliable diagnostic aid.
- During evaluation look for evidence of neurofibromatosis.
- Beware of interactions between antiepileptics and the oral contraceptive pill
- Interactions between erythromycin and carbamazepine can cause toxicity.
- Always aim to achieve monotherapy.
- An important toxic reaction can occur with phenytoin and carbamazepine.
- Patients should not drive while medication is being adjusted, particularly if weaning is being attempted.
- The development of sophisticated surgical techniques means that surgery can be used in selected patients with poor control. Evaluation for surgery is a very specialised area.

References

1. Scott AK. Management of epilepsy. In: *Central nervous system*. London: British Medical Journal, 1989, 1–2.
2. Eadie MJ. Epilepsy. In: MIMS Disease Index. Sydney:IMS Publishing, 1991–92, 179–182.
3. Ianseck R. *Pitfalls in neurology*. Proceedings Handbook: Annual Update Course for General Practitioners. Monash University Medical School, 1992, 1–4.
4. Cordova F. Epilepsy and sport. Aust Fam Physician, 1993; 22:558–562.
5. Kilpatrick C. Epilepsy poses special problems. Aust Dr Weekly, 19 February 1993, 48.
6. Theodore HR. Neurotrek. A PC based system for automated recording of epileptic seizures and similar events. Patient Management, 1992; 16:15–16.

102

Rhinitis/hay fever

Rhinitis is inflammation of the nose causing sneezing, nasal discharge or blockage for more than an hour during the day. Rhinitis is subdivided into various types:

- According to time span:
  - seasonal rhinitis: occurs only during a limited period, usually spring time
  - perennial rhinitis: present throughout the year
- According to pathophysiology:
  - allergic rhinitis: an IgE mediated atopic disorder
  - vasomotor rhinitis: due to parasympathetic overactivity

Both allergic and vasomotor rhinitis have a strong association with asthma.

The classification can be summarised as:

- seasonal allergic rhinitis = hay fever
- perennial rhinitis
  - allergic (usually due to house dust mites)
  - non-allergic = vasomotor
    - eosinophilic
    - non-eosinophilic

Clinical features of rhinitis

Nasal symptoms:

- sneezing
- nasal obstruction and congestion
- hypersecretion: watery rhinorrhoea, postnasal drip
- reduced sense of smell
- itching nose (usually allergic)

Throat symptoms:

- dry and sore throat
- itching throat

Irritated eyes (allergic)

Abnormal nasal mucous membrane—pale, boggy, mucoid discharge. A transverse nasal crease indicates nasal allergy, especially in a child.

Allergens

- pollens from trees (spring) and grass (in summer)
- moulds
- house dust mites (perennial rhinitis)
- hair, fur, feathers (from cats, dogs, horses, birds)
- some foods, e.g. cow's milk, eggs, peanuts, peanut butter

Diagnosis

Allergic rhinitis—nasal allergy:

- detection of allergen specific IgE antibodies (not specific)
- RAST test or skin testing for specific allergens (can get false negatives)

Vasomotor rhinitis—a diagnosis of exclusion.

Other causes of rhinitis

- Chronic infection (viral, bacterial, fungal)
- Rhinitis of pregnancy

- Rhinitis medicamentosa—following overuse of OTC decongestant nasal drops or sprays
- Drug-induced rhinitis
  - various antihypertensives
  - aspirin
  - phenothiazines
  - oral contraceptives
  - cocaine, marijuana
- Chemical or environmental irritants (vasomotor rhinitis)
  - smoke and other noxious fumes
  - paints and sprays
  - cosmetics

Factors aggravating rhinitis (vasomotor)

- emotional upsets
- fatigue
- alcohol
- chilly damp weather
- air-conditioning
- sudden changes in temperature and humidity

Allergic rhinitis

Allergic rhinitis may be seasonal or perennial. Its prevalence varies from 5–10% with a peak prevalence in children and young adults up to 20%.[1] The symptoms are caused by release of powerful chemical mediators such as histamine, serotonin, prostaglandins and leukotrienes from sensitised mast cells.[1]

Seasonal allergic rhinitis (hay fever)

This is the most common type of allergic rhinitis and is invariably initiated by pollen allergens. The allergens responsible for perennial allergic rhinitis include inhaled dust, dust mite, animal dander and fungal spores.

Most cases of hay fever begin in childhood with one half having the problem by the age of 15 and 90% of eventual cases by the age of 30.[2] Approximately 20% suffer from attacks of asthma.

While patients with hay fever tend to have widespread itching (nose, throat and eyes), those with perennial rhinitis rarely have eye or throat symptoms but mainly sneezing and watery rhinorrhoea.

Nasal polyps

Nasal polyps are round, soft, pale peduculated outgrowths arising from the nasal or sinus mucosa. They occur in patients with all types of rhinitis, especially allergic rhinitis. Symptoms include nasal obstruction and loss of smell.

Simple polyps can be readily snared and removed, but referral to a specialised surgeon is advisable since the aim is to remove the polyp with the mucosa of the sinuses (often ethmoid cells) from which it arises. This reduces the incidence of recurrence.

Management

- Appropriate explanation and reassurance with an understanding and supportive approach.
- Advise on methods of avoiding and reducing exposure to various allergens and irritants.
- Where food intolerance is suspected, food elimination regimens should be considered.

Advice to the patient

- Keep healthy, eat a well-balanced diet, avoid 'junk food' and live sensibly with balanced exercise, rest and recreation. If your eyes give you problems, try not to rub them, avoid contact lenses and wear sunglasses.
- Avoid using decongestant nose drops and sprays: although they soothe at first, a worse effect occurs on the rebound.
- Avoidance therapy: avoid the allergen, if you know what it is (consider pets, feather pillows and eiderdowns).
- Sources of the house dust mite are bedding, upholstered furniture, fluffy toys and carpets. Seek advice about keeping your bedroom or home dust-free, especially if you have perennial rhinitis.
- Pets, especially cats, should be kept outside.
- Avoid chemical irritants such as aspirin, smoke, cosmetics, paints and sprays.

Pharmacological management

Therapy can be chosen from:

1. oral antihistamines (not so effective for vasomotor rhinitis)
2. decongestants
3. sodium cromoglycate
   - intranasal: powder insufflation or spray
   - ophthalmic drops for associated conjunctivitis
4. corticosteroids
   - intranasal (not so effective for non-eosinophilic vasomotor rhinitis)
   - oral and parenteral (very effective if other methods fail)
   - ophthalmic drops for allergic conjunctivitis

5. hyposensitisation/immunotherapy: consider when specific allergens are known and conventional response is inadequate

Antihistamines

Antihistamines are the first-line treatment for allergic rhinitis. The newer generation antihistamines that do not cross the blood-brain barrier and avoid sedation are used in preference to the first generation antihistamines which cause variable degrees of drowsiness. Available non-sedating antihistamines are presented in Table 102.1.

Intranasal therapy

Intranasal decongestants should be used for limited periods only because of the problem of rebound congestion. They are effective for both forms of rhinitis. Adverse problems occur in the elderly and in patients with prostatic hypertrophy and glaucoma.

Intranasal sodium cromoglycate acts by preventing mast cell degranulation and is effective without serious side effects. However, patient compliance is a problem as it needs to be used 4–6 times a day.

Intranasal corticosteroid sprays are the most effective agents for treating allergic rhinitis.[3] Side effects are minimal and adrenal suppression is not a problem. Patients should be informed that the spray won't give immediate relief (about 10 days for symptom control) and must be used throughout the hay fever season.

Table 102.2 lists intranasal preparations for rhinitis, and Table 102.3 gives a summary of recommended treatment steps.

Allergic conjunctivitis

Itching of the eyes can be a most uncomfortable problem with hay fever and a most effective symptomatic treatment is with sodium cromoglycate (Opticrom) drops instilled as required.

When to refer

Where surgical intervention is required, such as with nasal obstruction from polyps, bulky nasal turbinates and deviated septum.

Table 102.1 *Non-sedating antihistamines (oral regimens)*

Generic name	***Onset***	***Dosage***
Astemizole	Relatively slow	10 mg daily
Loratadine	Very rapid	10 mg daily
Terfenadine	Rapid	60 mg bd

Table 102.2 *Intranasal preparations for rhinitis*

	Brand name	***Dosage***	***Comments***
Sodium cromoglycate	Rynacrom powder (capsules)	Insufflate 1 capsule, qid	Compliance a problem
	Rynacrom nasal spray	Spray 4-6 times daily	
Beclomethasone dipropionate	Aldecin nasal Beconase nasal	Spray once or twice daily according to instructions	
Budesonide	Rhinocort nasal		
Flunisolide	Rhinalar nasal		
Tramazoline + dexamethasone	Tobispray	Spray once tds	Use for short periods only
Ipratropium bromide	Atrovent	2, 3 or 4 times daily	Useful for vasomotor rhinitis Care needed with elderly
Various sympathomimetics e.g. phenylephrine		2, 3 or 4 times daily	Short-term use only Care with elderly, prostatic hypertrophy

Table 102.3 *Summary of recommended treatment steps for rhinitis*

Allergic rhinitis
- patient education
- allergen avoidance (if possible)
- non-sedating antihistamines
- inhaled sodium cromoglycate
  or
- inhaled corticosteroids
- immunotherapy if applicable

Vasomotor rhinitis
- patient education
- trigger avoidance (if possible)
- inhaled corticosteroids
- anticholinergics, e.g. ipratropium bromide
- nasal surgery if necessary

Practice tips

- Avoid long-term use of topical decongestant nasal drops.
- Avoid topical antihistamine preparations
- Prescribe sodium cromoglycate eye drops for the hay fever patient with itchy eyes.
- Be careful of severe systemic reactions that can occur with intradermal skin testing and with immunotherapy. Resuscitation facilities should be available.

References

1. Scoppa J. Rhinitis (allergic and vasomotor). In: MIMS Disease Index. Sydney: IMS Publishing, 1991–92, 463–465.
2. Fry J. *Common diseases* (4th edition). Lancaster: MTP Press, 1985, 134–138.
3. Avery J. Allergic rhinitis. Current Therapeutics, February 1988, 75–83.

103

Hypertension

Hypertension is a serious community disorder and the most common condition requiring long-term drug therapy in Australia. It is a silent killer as most people with hypertension are asymptomatic and unaware of their problem. Epidemiological studies have demonstrated the association between hypertension and stroke, coronary heart disease, renal disease, heart failure and atrial fibrillation.

Definitions and classification

- The various categories of blood pressure are arbitrarily defined according to blood pressure values for both diastolic and systolic readings (Table 103.1).[1,2]

> For adults aged 18 years and older hypertension is:
> diastolic pressure > 90 mmHg
> systolic pressure > 140 mmHg

- Isolated systolic hypertension is that > 160 mmHg in the presence of a diastolic pressure < 90 mmHg.
- Hypertension is either essential or secondary (Table 103.2).
- Essential hypertension is the presence of sustained hypertension in the absence of underlying, potentially correctable renal, adrenal or other factors.
- Malignant hypertension is that with a diastolic pressure > 120 mmHg and exudative vasculopathy in the retinal and renal circulations.
- Refractory hypertension is BP > 140/90 and > 160/90 if aged more than 60 despite maximum dosage of two drugs for 3–4 months.

Table 103.1 *Classification of blood pressure in adults aged 18 years and older measured as sitting blood pressure (mmHg)*[1,2]

Range (mmHg)	*Category*
Diastolic	
< 85	Normal blood pressure
85-89	High normal blood pressure
90-104	Mild hypertension
105-114	Moderate hypertension
> 115	Severe hypertension
Systolic (assumes 'normal' or 'high normal' diastolic blood pressure)	
< 140	'Normal' systolic blood pressure
140-159	Borderline isolated systolic hypertension
⩾ 160	Isolated systolic hypertension

- Adapted from the 1988 Report of the Joint National Committee on Detection, Evaluation and Treatment of High Blood Pressure.
- The classification is based on the average of two or more readings on at least three or more occasions.
- In subjects aged 50 or less the diastolic level always takes precedence over the systolic level.
- Before diagnosis is made the variation between readings should not exceed 10 mm of mercury for systolic blood pressure or 6 mm of mercury for diastolic blood pressure.

Table 103.2 *Classification of hypertension*

Essential (90–95%)

Secondary (approximately 5–10%)

Renal (3–4%)
- glomerulonephritis
- reflux nephropathy
- renal artery stenosis
- other renovascular disease

Endocrine
- primary aldosteronism (Conn's syndrome)
- Cushing's syndrome
- phaeochromocytoma
- oral contraceptives
- other endocrine factors

Coarctation of the aorta

Drugs

Key facts and checkpoints

- In the United States, 15% of 18–24 year olds and 60% of 65–74 years olds have hypertension.[3]
- In the US, studies show that only 54% of all hypertensives are aware of their disease and only 11% are being treated adequately. Similar figures have been shown in the UK.[4]
- The risk of cardiovascular disease rises significantly with increasing blood pressure.
- If both parents have hypertension there is a 50% chance of the offspring developing hypertension and if one parent has HT there is a 25% chance.
- Headache may occur in hypertensive patients (most are asymptomatic): it is typically early morning, occipital and throbbing: it appears to be related to severity of blood pressure.
- Any dizziness in hypertensive patients is usually due to postural hypertension from treatment.
- Reductions in blood pressure are associated with a reduced incidence of stroke and pressure-related events such as heart failure, but not of coronary artery disease.
- Target organs (including some specific examples) that can be damaged by hypertension include the heart (failure, LVH, ischaemic disease), the kidney (renal insufficiency), the retina (retinopathy), the blood vessels (peripheral vascular disease, dissecting aortic aneurysm) and the brain (cerebrovascular disease).
- Deaths in hypertensive patients have been shown to be due to stroke 45%, heart failure 35%, renal failure 3% and others 17%.[4]
- Factors increasing chances of dying in hypertensive patients are: male patient; young patient; family history; increasing diastolic pressure.[4]

Secondary hypertension

Secondary hypertension may be suggested in patients below 40 by the history (Table 103.3), physical examination, severity of hypertension or the initial laboratory findings. It is also more likely in patients whose blood pressure is responding poorly to drug therapy, patients with well-controlled hypertension whose blood pressure begins to increase, and patients with accelerated or malignant hypertension.[2]

The most common causes of secondary hypertension are various renal diseases, such as chronic glomerulonephritis, chronic pyelonephritis (often associated with reflux nephropathy) and analgesic nephropathy.[1] There will often be no physical findings to indicate the existence of such renal diseases, but an indication will generally be obtained by the presence of one or more abnormalities when the urine is examined. Clinical pointers include general atheroma, smokers, proteinuria and abdominal bruit.

Table 103.3 *Clinical features suggesting secondary hypertension*[5]

Clinical features	*Likely cause*
Abdominal systolic bruit	Renal artery stenosis
Proteinuria, haematuria, casts	Glomerulonephritis
Bilateral renal masses with or without haematuria	Polycystic disease
History of claudication and delayed femoral pulse	Coarctation of the aorta
Progressive nocturia, weakness	Primary aldosteronism (check serum potassium)
Paroxysmal hypertension with headache, pallor, sweating, palpitations	Phaeochromocytoma

Physical findings that may suggest secondary hypertension include epigastric bruits (indicating possible renal artery stenosis) and abdominal aortic aneurysm. Less common findings include abdominal flank masses (polycystic kidneys), delayed or absent femoral pulses (coarctation of the aorta), truncal obesity with pigmented striae (Cushing's syndrome), and tachycardia, sweating and pallor (phaeochromocytoma).

Further investigation will be required to confirm or reveal secondary hypertension.

Conn's syndrome: clinical features

- weakness due to hypokalaemia
- polyuria and polydypsia
- Na ↑, K ↓, alkalosis
- aldosterone ↑ (serum and urine)
- plasma renin ↓

Phaeochromocytoma: clinical features

(paroxysms or spells of)

- hypertension
- headache (throbbing)
- sweating
- palpitations
- pallor/skin blanching
- rising sensation of tightness in upper chest and throat (angina can occur)

24 hour urinary catecholamines ↑ (VMA)

Detection of hypertension[1]

Hypertension can only be detected when blood pressure is measured. Therefore every reasonable opportunity should be taken to measure blood pressure.

Diagnosis should not be made on the basis of a single visit. Initial raised blood pressure readings should be confirmed on at least two other visits within the space of three months; average levels of 90 mmHg diastolic or more, or 140 mmHg systolic or more, are needed before hypertension can be diagnosed. This will avoid the possibility of an incorrect diagnosis, committing an asymptomatic normotensive individual to unjustified, lifelong treatment.

Measurement[1]

Blood pressure varies continuously and can be affected by many outside factors. Care should therefore be taken to ensure that readings accurately represent the patient's usual pressure. The essential steps in this process are outlined below.

Position

Patients should be seated with their bare arm supported and positioned at heart level. Any sleeve should be loose above the sphygmomanometer cuff.

Cuff size and placement

A cuff size that will completely occlude the brachial artery is essential for accurate measurement. Cuffs that are too short or too narrow may give falsely high readings. The cuff's rubber bladder should have a width of at least 40% of the circumference of the patient's arm and a length at least double that. The commonly used cuffs are often shorter than this recommendation. Suitable cuffs are made by Trimline (PyMaH) and Accosan. Several sizes, including cuffs for children and the obese, should be available. The bladder of the cuff deteriorates over about two years and should be replaced at intervals.[6]

A preferable cuff placement is to have the tubes emerging from the bladder point proximally (Figure 103.1) thus leaving the cubital fossa free.[6]

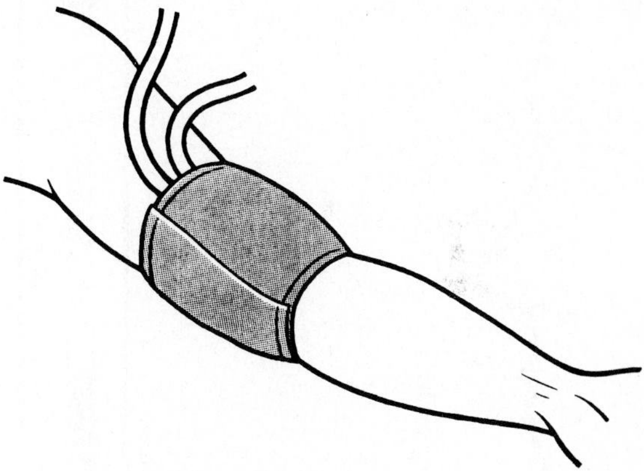

Fig. 103.1 *Correct placement of the cuff*

Equipment

Ideally, measurement should be taken with a reliable and properly maintained sphygmomanometer. Otherwise, a recently calibrated aneroid manometer or a calibrated electronic instrument can be used. It is essential that all equipment is maintained regularly. All tubing connections should be airtight.

Palpation

Initially, systolic blood pressure should be recorded by the palpatory method at the radial or brachial artery (the brachial artery is felt just medial to the biceps tendon in the cubital fossa). This will prevent low auscultatory systolic pressures caused by a 'silent gap'.

Note this reading and add 30 mmHg to it as the upper level to which to inflate the cuff, while accurately measuring the BP with the bell of the stethoscope over the brachial artery.

Taking the reading

While the BP is being measured, the cuff should be deflated at a rate no greater than 2mm of mercury for each beat. One of the commonest errors is to allow the column of mercury to fall too rapidly.

Pressure should be recorded to the nearest 2 mm of mercury (it should not always end in 0 or 5). Parallax errors should be avoided when reading levels (Figure 103.2).[6,7] Wait 60 seconds and repeat the BP measurement.

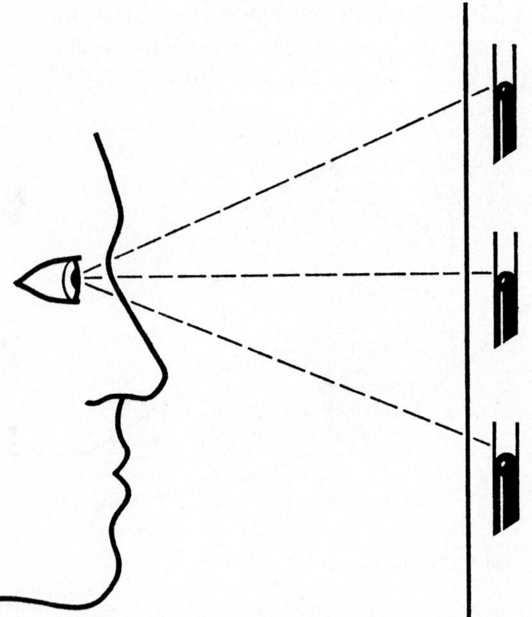

Fig. 103.2 *Correct eye level: the observer should be within 1 metre of the manometer, so the scale can be easily read to avoid a parallax error—the eye should be on the same horizontal level as the mercury meniscus*

Recording

On each occasion when BP is taken, two or more readings should be averaged. If the first two readings differ by more than 6 mmHg systolic or 4 mmHg diastolic, more readings should be taken.

Both systolic and diastolic levels should be recorded. For the diastolic reading the disappearance of sound (Phase 5)—that is, the pressure when the last sound is heard and after which all sound disappears—should be used.[8] This is more accurate than the muffling of sounds (Phase 4) (Fig. 103.3).

Heart rate and pulse

At the same time the BP is measured, the heart rate and rhythm should be measured and recorded. A high heart rate may indicate undue stress that is causing the associated elevated BP reading. An irregular heart rhythm may cause difficulty in obtaining an accurate BP reading.

BP modifying factors

Apprehension:	Patient should be rested for at least five minutes and made as relaxed as possible.
Caffeine:	Patients should not take caffeine for 4–6 hours before measurement.
Smoking:	Patients should also avoid smoking for two hours before measurement.
Eating:	Patients should not have eaten for 30 minutes.

Strategies for high initial readings

If the initial reading is high (DBP > 90, SBP > 140) repeat the measures after five minutes of quiet rest. The 'white coat' influence in the medical practitioner's office may cause higher readings so measurement in other settings such as the home or the workplace should be managed whenever possible.

Confirmation and follow-up[1]

Repeated blood pressure readings will determine whether initial high levels are confirmed and need attention, or whether they return to normal and need only periodic checking. Particular attention should be paid to younger patients to ensure that they are regularly followed up.

Initial diastolic blood pressure readings of 115 mmHg or more, particularly for patients with target organ damage, may need immediate drug therapy.

Once an elevated level has been detected, the timing of subsequent readings should be based on the initial pressure level, as shown in Table 103.4.

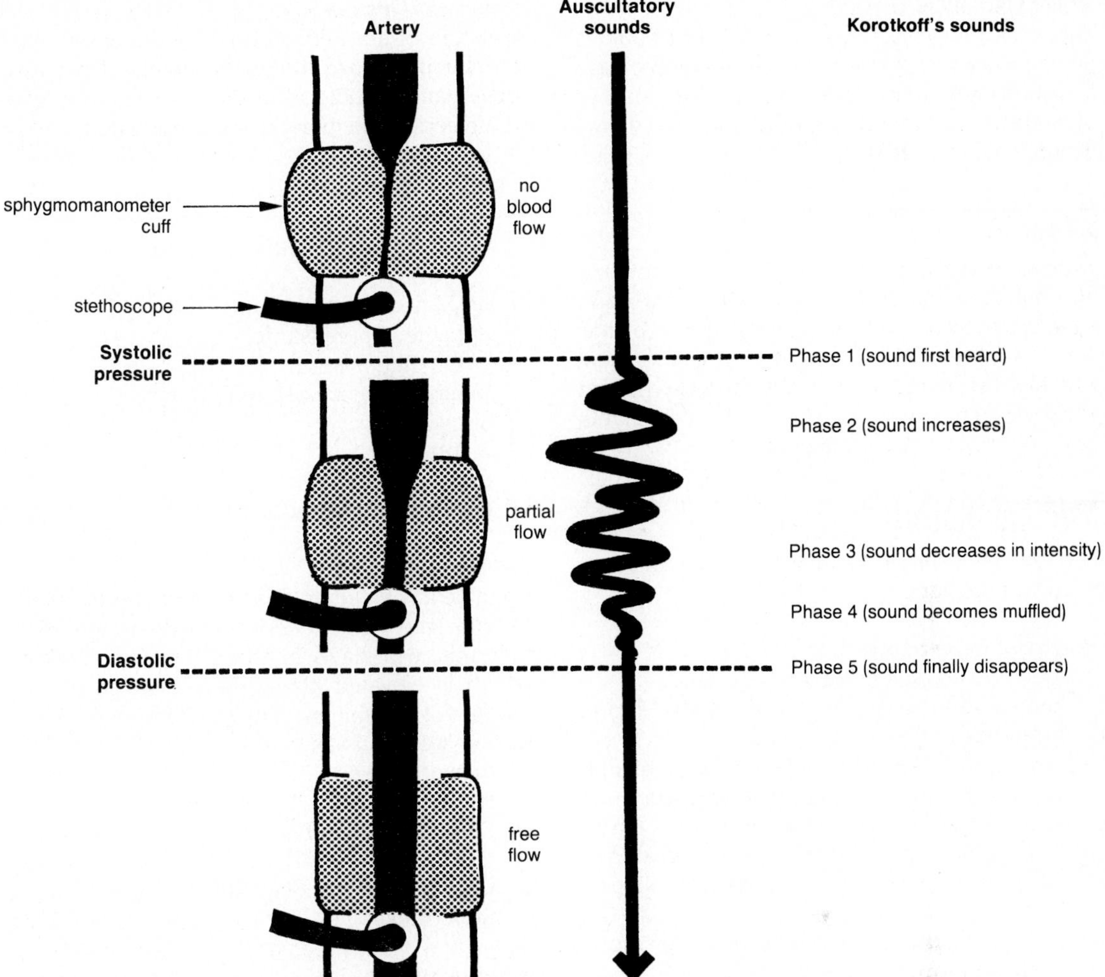

Fig. 103.3 *Illustration of blood pressure measurement in relation to arterial blood flow, cuff pressure and auscultation*

Table 103.4 *Follow-up criteria for initial blood pressure measurement for adults 18 years and older*[1,2]

Range (mmHg)	*Recommended follow-up**
Diastolic	
< 85	Recheck within 2 years
85–89	Recheck within 1 year
90–104	Confirm within 2 months
105–114	Evaluate or refer within 2 weeks
> 115	Evaluate or refer immediately
Systolic, when diastolic is < 90	
< 140	Recheck within 2 years
140–199	Confirm within 2 months
> 200	Evaluate or refer within 2 weeks

* If recommendations for follow-up of diastolic and systolic blood pressure are different the shorter recommended time for recheck and referral should take precedence.[2]

If mild hypertension is found, observation with repeated measurement over 3–6 months should be followed before beginning therapy. This is because levels often return to normal.

Ambulatory 24 hour monitoring

This is not required for the diagnosis and follow-up of most hypertensive patients but in some patients with fluctuating levels, borderline hypertension or refractory hypertension (especially where the 'white coat' effect may be significant) ambulatory monitoring has a place in management. Studies have shown that this method provides a more precise estimate of blood pressure variability than casual recordings. This has implications for the timing of drug therapy in individual patients.

'White coat' hypertension

This group may comprise up to 25% of patients presenting with hypertension. These people have a type of conditioned response to the clinic or office setting and their home BP and ambulatory BP profiles are normal.

Evaluation

As well as defining the blood pressure problem, the clinical evaluation for suspected hypertension should also determine whether the patient has potentially reversible secondary hypertension, whether target organ damage is present, and whether there are other potentially modifiable cardiovascular risk factors present.

Medical history

The following should be included in the medical history of the patient:

History of hypertension

- method and date of initial diagnosis
- known duration and levels of elevated blood pressure
- symptoms that may indicate the effects of high blood pressure on target organ damage, such as headache, dyspnoea, chest pain, claudication, ankle oedema and haematuria
- symptoms suggesting secondary hypertension (Table 103.3)
- the results and side effects of all previous antihypertensive treatment

Presence of other diseases and risk factors

- a history of cardiovascular, cerebrovascular or peripheral vascular disease, renal disease, diabetes mellitus or recent weight gain
- other cardiovascular risk factors, including obesity, hyperlipidaemia, carbohydrate intolerance, smoking, salt intake, alcohol consumption, exercise levels and analgesic intake
- other relevant conditions, such as asthma or psychiatric illness (particularly depressive illness)

Family history

Particular attention should be paid to the family history of hypertension, cardiovascular or cerebrovascular disease, hyperlipidaemia, obesity, diabetes mellitus, renal disease, alcohol abuse and premature sudden death.

Medication history

A history of all medications, including over-the-counter products, should be obtained because some can raise blood pressure or interfere with antihypertensive therapy. These include:

- oral contraceptives
- hormone replacement therapy
- steroids
- non-steroidal anti-inflammatory agents (NSAIDs)
- nasal decongestants and other cold remedies
- appetite suppressants
- amphetamines
- monoamine oxidase inhibitors
- analgesics
- ergotamine
- cyclosporin
- carbenoxolone and licorice

Caffeine intake[1]

Caffeine has an acute dose-related pressor effect. People who have recently ingested significant amounts will have a blood pressure reading which is elevated above their usual level. The amount of caffeine in a cup (225 ml) in common dietary sources is as follows:

Instant coffee	90 mg
Brewed coffee	125 mg
Decaffeinated coffee	4.5mg
Tea	60 mg
Chocolate drinks (e.g. hot chocolate)	5 mg
Cola drinks	25 mg

Alcohol intake[1]

Alcohol has a direct pressor effect that is dose-related. An assessment of the average daily number of standard drinks is important—more than two standard drinks (20 g alcohol) a day is significant.

Physical examination

The approach to the physical examination is to examine possible target organ damage and possible causes of secondary hypertension. The main features to consider in the physical examination are Illustratred in Figure 103.4.

The four grades of hypertensive retinopathy are illustrated in Figure 103.5.

Leg pulses and pressure

To assess the remote possibility of coarctation of the aorta in the hypertensive patient, perform at least one observation comparing:

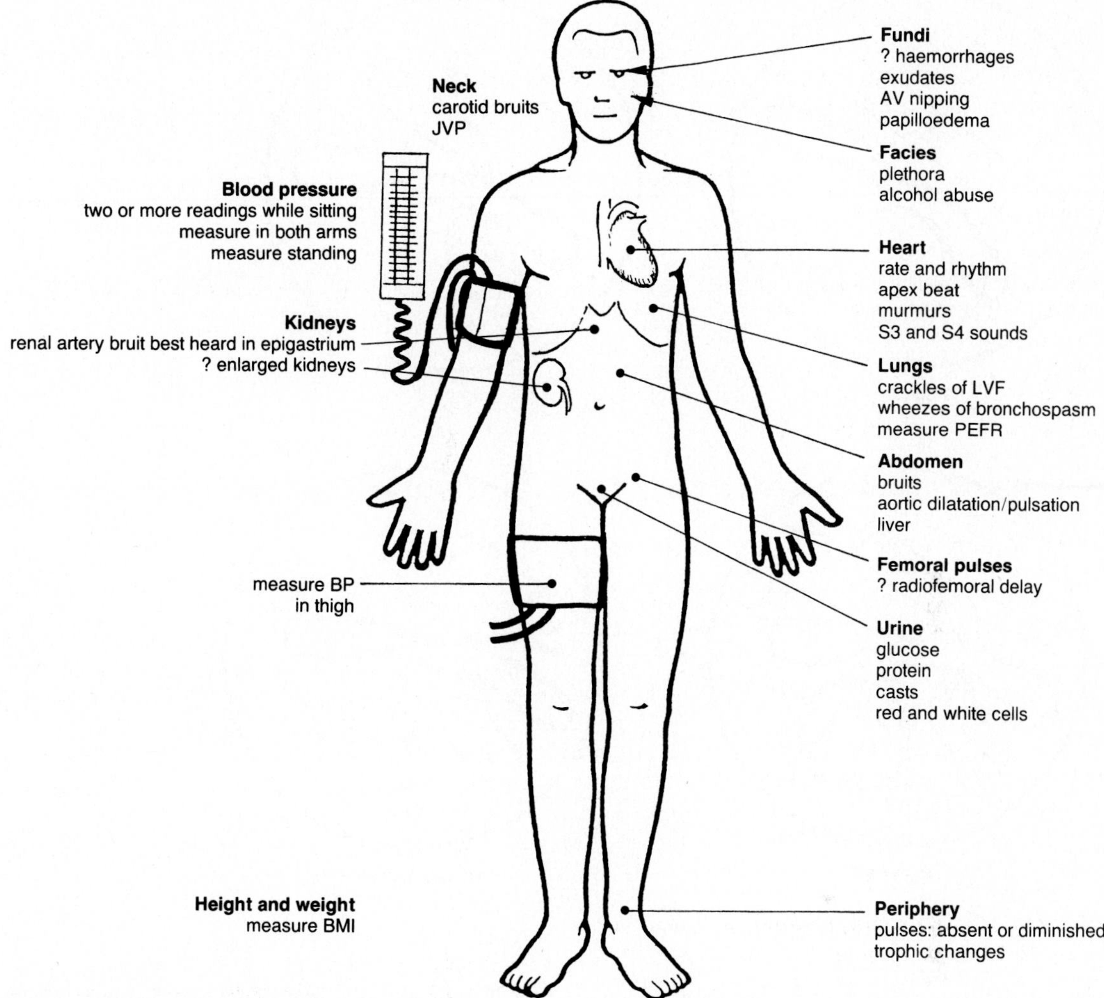

Fig. 103.4 *Physical examination of patient with hypertension: what to look for*

1. the volume and timing of the radial and femoral pulses
2. the blood pressure in the arm and leg

Blood pressure measurement in the leg

- Place the patient prone.
- Use a wide, long cuff at mid-thigh level.
- Position the bladder over the posterior surface and fix it firmly.
- Auscultate over the popliteal artery.

Investigations

The following are the basic screening tests recommended for all patients:

- Urine tests
  — urinalysis (for protein and glucose)
  — micro-urine (casts, red and white cells)
  — urine culture (only if urinalysis abnormal)
- Biochemical tests
  — potassium and sodium
  — creatinine and urea
  — uric acid
  — cholesterol
- ESR
- ECG

Other investigations, such as renal imaging studies (especially renal ultrasound), vanillyl mandelic acid (VMA) and plasma renin, are not routine and should be done only if specifically

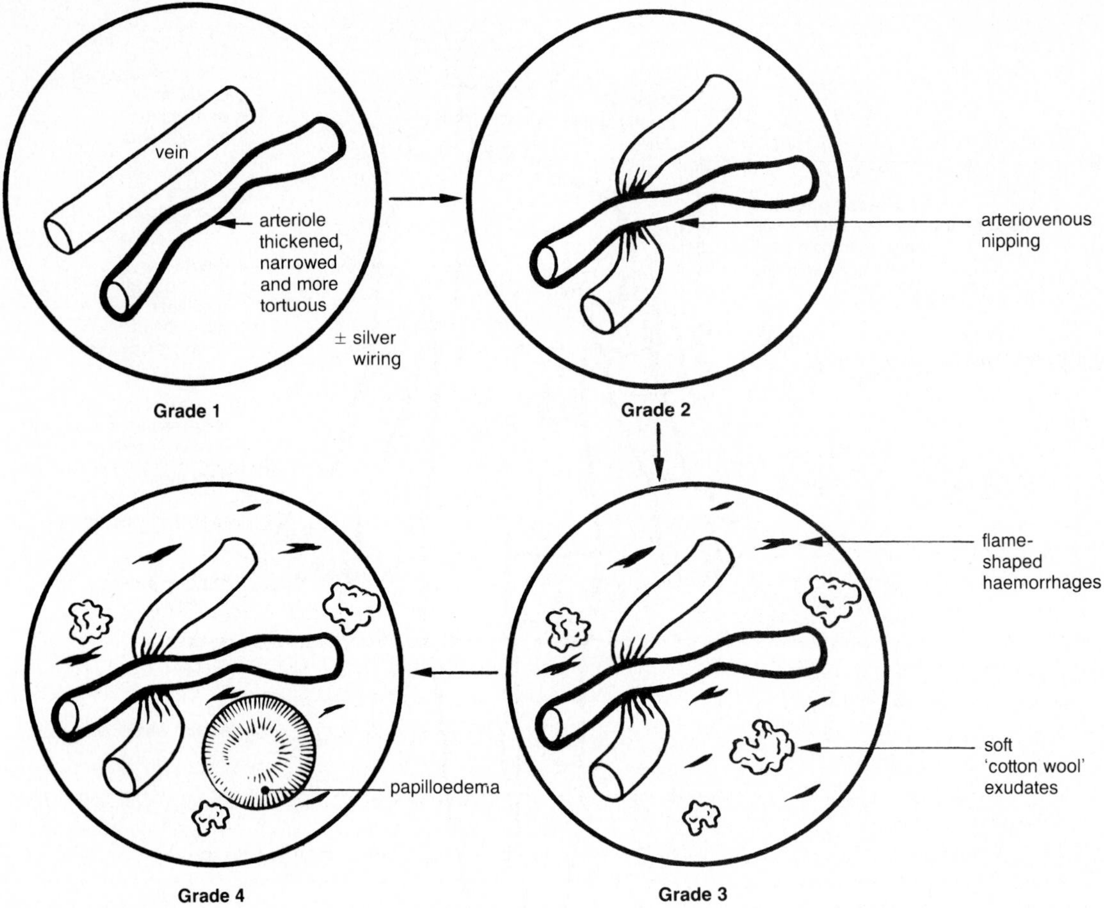

Fig. 103.5 *The four grades of hypertensive retinopathy*

indicated. A chest X-ray may serve as a baseline against which to measure future changes. However, if a chest X-ray shows the heart is enlarged, it is more likely to represent chamber dilatation than increased ventricular wall thickness.[1] Specific renal studies now favoured include isotope scans, doppler studies of renal arteries and renal arteriography.

Treatment

A correct diagnosis is the basis of management. Assuming that the uncommon secondary causes are identified and treated, treatment will focus on essential hypertension.

Management principles

- The overall goal is to improve the long-term survival and quality of life.
- Promote an effective physician–patient working relationship.
- Aim to reduce the levels to 140/90 mmHg or less (ideal).
- Undertake a thorough assessment of all cardiovascular risk factors.
- Instruct all patients in the use of non-drug treatment strategies and their potential benefits.
- In patients with mild to moderate hypertension and no target organ damage, consider ambulatory or home BP monitoring.
- Drug therapy should be given to those with:
  - sustained high initial readings, e.g. DBP $>$ 95 mmHg
  - target organ damage
  - failed non-drug measures.
- Make a careful selection of an antihypertensive drug and an appraisal of the side effects against the benefits of treatment.

- Avoid drug-related problems such as postural hypotension.
- Avoid excessive lowering of blood pressure.
- Aim to counter the problem of patient non-compliance.
- Be aware of factors that may contribute to drug resistance.

Patient education

Patient education should include appropriate reassurances, clear information and easy-to-follow instructions. It is important to establish patients' understanding of the concept of hypertension and its consequences by quizzing them about their knowledge and feelings.

Correction of patients' misconceptions[1]

Patients are likely to have several misconceptions about hypertension which may adversely affect their treatment.

For example, they might believe that:

- hypertension can be cured
- they do not need to continue treatment once their BP is controlled
- they do not have a problem because they do not have symptoms
- they need to take additional pills, or stop treatment, in response to symptoms they believe are caused by high or low blood pressure levels
- they need not take prescribed pills if they attend to lifestyle factors such as exercise and diet
- they can gauge their blood pressure by how they feel

Tips for optimal compliance

- Establish a good caring rapport
- Give patients a card of their history with BP readings.
- Give advice about pill-taking times.
- Set therapeutic goals.
- Establish a recall system.
- Provide patient education material.

On review:

- Ask if any pills were missed by accident.
- Attempt to reduce waiting time to a minimum, e.g. direct a patient to a spare room upon arrival.
- Review all cardiovascular risk factors.
- Enquire about any side effects.

Non-pharmacological treatment modalities

If the average diastolic BP at the initial visit is between 90 and 100 mmHg, and there is no evidence of end-organ damage, non-pharmacological therapy is indicated for a three month period without use of antihypertensive drugs. Remember to remove, revise or substitute drugs which may be causing hypertension, e.g. NSAIDs, corticosteroids, oral contraceptives, hormone replacement therapy.

Behaviour intervention measures include:

- *Weight reduction*
  There is considerable evidence that weight loss and gain are linked to a corresponding fall and rise in BP. Hovell has estimated that for every 1 kg of weight lost, blood pressure dropped by 2.5 mmHg systolic and 1.5 mmHg diastolic.[9] The BMI should be calculated for all patients and where required a weight loss program organised to reduce the BMI to between 20 and 25.
- *Reduction of alcohol intake[1]*
  The direct pressor of alcohol is reversible. Drinking more than 20 g of alcohol a day raises blood pressure and makes treatment of established hypertension more difficult. People with hypertension should limit their alcohol intake to one or two standard drinks (10 g) per day. Reduction or withdrawal of regular alcohol intake reduces BP by 5–10 mmHg.
- *Reduction of sodium intake*
  Some individuals seem to be more sensitive to salt restriction. Advise patients to put away the salt shaker and use only a little salt with their food. Reduction of sodium intake to less than 100 mmol sodium per day is advised.
- *Increased exercise*
  Regular aerobic or isotonic exercise helps to reduce BP.[10] Hypertensive patients beginning an exercise program should do so gradually. Walking is an appropriate exercise. Weights and other forms of isometric exercises should be avoided because they will significantly elevate blood pressure in the hypertensive subject.
- *Reduction of particular stress*
  If avoiding stress or overwork is difficult, recommend relaxation and/or meditation therapy.

- *Other dietary factors*
  There is evidence that lactovegetarian diets and magnesium supplementation can reduce BP.[11,12] A diet high in calcium, and low in fat and caffeine, may also be beneficial. Avoid licorice and licorice-containing substances.
- *Smoking*
  Smoking causes acute rises in blood pressure but does not appear to cause sustained hypertension. However, the elimination of smoking is important as it is a strong risk factor for cardiovascular disease and continuing to smoke may negate any benefits of antihypertensive therapy.[1]

Pharmacological therapy

The benefits of drug therapy appear to outweigh any known risks to individuals with a persistently raised diastolic pressure > 95 mmHg. Although the ideal antihypertensive drug has yet to be discovered there are many effective antihypertensive drugs available.[13] Deciding which one to use first involves an assessment of the patient's general health, the medication's known side effects, the simplicity of its administration and its cost. A useful plan is outlined in Figure 103.6.

Various disorders such as diabetes, asthma, chronic obstructive airways disease, Raynaud's phenomenon, heart failure, and elevated serum urate and/or lipid levels may restrict the use of some classes of drugs.

Guidelines

- Start with a single drug.
- A period of 4–6 weeks is needed for the effect to become fully apparent.
- If ineffective, consider increasing the drug to its maximum recommended dose, or add an agent from another compatible class, or substitute with a drug from another class.
- Use only one drug from any one class at the same time.
- A summary of first-line therapy options and the uses of the various pharmacological agents is shown in Table 103.5.

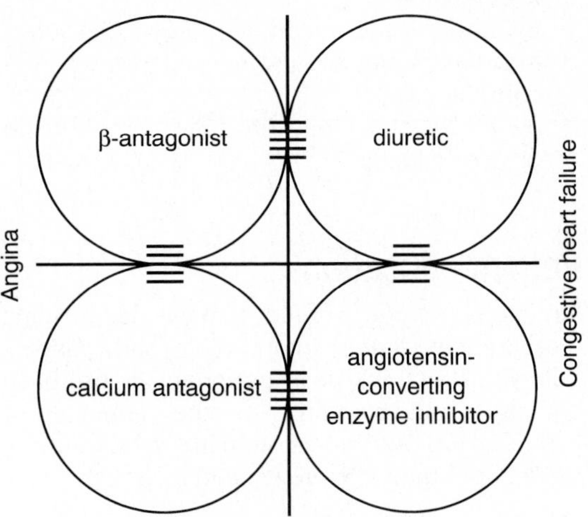

Fig. 103.6 *Choice of therapy in mild hypertension: adjacent groups of drugs can be usefully combined. Drugs in the upper half of the diagram (β-antagonist and thiazide agents) are the basis of stepped care regimens used to treat hypertension for the past two decades and used in the major trials. These drugs are cheap, but have metabolic effects. Newer drug groups (lower half) lack metabolic effects. β-antagonist and calcium channel antagonist agents (left side) are indicated in patients with coexisting ischaemic heart disease. Diuretics and angiotensin-converting enzyme inhibitor agents (right side) are particularly useful in heart failure. α_1-antagonist agents are also candidates for initial therapy* FROM G. L. JENNINGS AND K. SUDHIR, INITIAL THERAPY OF PRIMARY HYPERTENSION *MED J AUST* 1990; 152:198–203

Starting regimens

The traditional method has been to use stepwise therapy until ideal control has been reached, commencing with:

1. thiazide diuretic or β-blocker (cardioselective)
2. combination of diuretic and β-blocker
3. add a vasodilator (ACE inhibitor)

Table 103.5 *First-line pharmacological options for the management of hypertension*[7]

Drug class					
Diuretic	***Beta-blocker***	***Calcium channel antagonist***	***ACE inhibitor***	***Central-acting agent***	***Alpha-blocker***
Typical examples and starting dose (oral therapy)					
chlorothiazide 250 mg daily	atenolol 50–100 mg daily	verapamil 40 mg bd	captopril 6.25 mg bd	methyldopa 125 mg bd	prazosin 0.5 mg nocte
hydrochloro-thiazide 12.5 mg daily	metoprolol 50 mg daily	felodipine 2.5 mg bd	enalapril 2.5 mg daily		terazosin 0.5 mg nocte
indapamide 2.5 mg daily	pindolol 5 mg daily propranolol 40 mg daily	nifedipine 20 mg bd diltiazem 90 mg bd	lisinopril 2.5 mg daily ramipril 2.5 mg daily	clonidine 50 mcg, bd	*Note*: labetalol (100 mg bd) is a combined α and β blocker
Recommended in					
Heart failure (mild) Older patients	Anxious patient Young patients Angina Postmyocardial infarction Migraine	Asthmatics Angina PVD	Heart failure PVD	Asthmatics	Asthmatics PVD Heart failure
Contraindications					
Maturity onset diabetics Hyperuricaemia	Asthma COAD History of wheeze Heart failure Heart block (2°,3°) PVD Brittle IDDM	Heart block 2nd & 3rd degree (verapamil)	Bilateral renal artery stenosis	Liver disease (methyldopa)	Heart failure (mechanical obstruction)
Precautions					
Hypokalaemia Thiazides + ACE inhibitors Renal failure	Avoid abrupt cessation with angina Use with verapamil Use with NSAIDs Use in smokers	With β-blockers and digoxin CCF	Chronic renal disease With K sparing diuretics and NSAIDs	Depression	Elderly patients
Important side effects					
Rashes Sexual dysfunction Weakness Blood dyscrasias Muscular cramps Hypokalaemia Hyperuricaemia Hyperglycaemia Lipid metabolism effect	Fatigue Insomnia Vivid dreams Bronchospasm PVD/cold extremities Sexual dysfunction Lipid metabolism effect	Headache Flushing Ankle oedema Palpitations Dizziness Nausea Constipation (verapamil)	Cough Weakness Rash Dysgeusia (taste) Hyperkalaemia First dose hypotension	Sedation Dry mouth Bowel disturbances Fatigue Orthostatic hypotension Sexual dysfunction Haemolytic anaemia (methyldopa)	First dose syncope Orthostatic hypotension Weakness Palpitations Sedation Headache

However, the newer classes of drugs can be used as first-line agents.

The following are useful combinations:[1,5]

Initial agent	*Additional drugs*
Diuretic	β-blocker ACE inhibitor or α-blocker
β-blocker	Diuretic Calcium antagonist (except verapamil)
α-blocker	Diuretic β-blocker
ACE inhibitor	Diuretic Calcium antagonist
Calcium antagonist	β-blocker ACE inhibitor
Diuretic	Central acting agent ACE inhibitor

Relatively ineffective combinations[1]

Diuretic and calcium antagonist
Beta-blockers and ACE inhibitors

Undesirable combinations[1]

More than one drug from a particular pharmacological group: beta-blockers and verapamil (heart block, heart failure); potassium-sparing diuretics and ACE inhibitors (hyperkalaemia).

Diuretics[1,5]

- Thiazides are good first-line therapy for hypertension.
- Hypokalaemia is more common in patients treated with thiazide diuretics than loop diuretics, e.g. frusemide, bumetanide.
- Hypokalaemia can be corrected with potassium-sparing diuretics or changing to another first-line drug.
- Loop diuretics are less potent as antihypertensive agents but are indicated where there is concomitant cardiac or renal failure and in resistant hypertension.
- Thiazides are less effective where there is renal impairment.
- Thiazides may precipitate acute gout.
- NSAIDs may antagonise the antihypertensive and natriuretic effectiveness of diuretics.
- A diet high in potassium and magnesium should accompany diuretic therapy, e.g. lentils, nuts, high fibre.

Beta-blockers

- NSAIDs may interfere with the hypotensive effect of beta-blockers.
- If blood pressure is not reduced by one beta-blocker it is unlikely to be reduced by changing to another.
- Verapamil plus a beta-blocker may unmask conduction abnormalities causing heart block.
- In patients with ischaemic heart disease, or susceptibility to it, treatment must not be stopped suddenly—this can precipitate angina at rest.

Calcium antagonists

- These drugs reduce blood pressure by vasodilatation.
- The properties of individual drugs vary, especially their effects on cardiac function.
- The dihydropyridine compounds (nifedipine and felodipine) tend to produce more vasodilatation and thus related side effects.
- Unlike verapamil or diltiazem (which slows the heart), dihydropyridine drugs can be used safely with a beta-blocker.
- Verapamil is contraindicated in second and third degree heart block.
- Verapamil and diltiazem should be used with caution in patients with heart failure.
- These drugs are efficacious with ACE inhibitors, beta-blockers, prazosin and methyldopa.

ACE inhibitors

Angiotension-converting enzyme is responsible for converting angiotension I to angiotension II (a potent vasoconstrictor and stimulator of aldosterone secretion) and for the breakdown of bradykinin (a vasodilator). ACE inhibitors are effective in the elderly; improve survival and performance status in cardiac failure; are protective of renal function in diabetes; and cardioprotective in postmyocardial infarction. For patients with normal renal function, the dose should not exceed 150 mg daily for captopril, 40 mg daily for enalapril or lisinopril, 10 mg daily for ramipril, and 8 mg daily for perindopril.

Disturbance in taste is usually transitory and may resolve with continued treatment. Cough, which occurs in about 15% of patients, may disappear with time or a reduction in dose but it often persists and requires a change in drug in some patients. Angioedema, a potentially life-threatening condition, may occur in 0.1–0.2% of subjects.

Prazosin

A specific problem is the 'first dose phenomenon' which can cause acute syncope about 90 minutes after the first dose, hence treatment is best initiated at bed time. Prazosin potentiates beta-blockers and works best if used with them. It is a useful first-line therapy in patients who are unsuitable for diuretic or beta-blocker therapy, e.g. those with diabetes, asthma or hyperlipidaemia.

Vascular smooth muscle relaxants

(other than calcium channel antagonists)

These include hydralazine, minoxidil and diazoxide, which are not used for first-line therapy but for refractory hypertensive states and hypertensive emergencies.

Mild hypertension[1]

Mild hypertension in adults is defined as a diastolic pressure (Phase 5) persistently between 90 and 104 mmHg, without target organ damage.[14] This group includes those with 'white coat' hypertension.

Mildly hypertensive people have almost twice the risk of vascular disease compared to normotensive people, and evidence shows that morbidity and mortality rise with an increase in blood pressure.[1]

Patients treated appropriately have fewer stokes and pressure-related cardiovascular complications than those not treated. Drug treatment has potential side effects which cannot be ignored; sometimes the risks from this form of treatment could exceed those if the patient remains untreated.[14] Therefore, the initial approach to the management of mild hypertension should be based on non-drug measures and should focus on behaviour change. Consequently, overt side effects are avoided and risk prevention measures enhanced.

Often the success of this approach is improved by using people with particular skills, such as dietitians. If after six months or more these methods have not succeeded, then drug therapy may be necessary.[14]

Practical guidelines for patients with persistent diastolic blood pressure between 90 and 104 mmHg are shown in Figure 103.7.

Moderate hypertension[1]

If diastolic pressure is between 105 and 114 mmHg then a more aggressive approach is necessary, particularly for patients with target organ damage. Appropriate non-pharmacological measures should be tried in all subjects, especially where likely success is possible, e.g. obesity, high alcohol intake. This will fail in the majority, who will require drug therapy. If there is poor response to initial therapy a second drug may be prescribed after a short time. The interval between the changes in treatment may also be reduced. Combination therapy may be more effective than maximum doses of any single agent.

Severe hypertension[5]

For people with severe hypertension, their blood pressure may be life-threatening. Patients with an average diastolic pressure of over 115 mmHg should be checked immediately for hypertensive complications, particularly marked fundoscopic changes, proteinuria or cardiac failure. They are more likely to have an underlying cause, e.g. renovascular disease. Hospitalisation may be necessary for these patients.

In such cases the opinion of a specialist is important, because of the likely risk of serious illness or death.

Hypertensive emergencies

A hypertensive emergency occurs when high blood pressure causes the presenting cardiovascular problem. Typical presentations of hypertensive emergencies (which are rare) include hypertensive encephalopathy, acute hypertension, heart failure, dissecting aortic aneurysm and eclampsia.

In all such cases referral to a specialist is essential and the patient should be hospitalised immediately for monitoring and treatment. Treatment must be individualised, mindful of the nature of the underlying problem and associated disorders.

Such treatment may include nifedipine capsules 10 mg taken orally (capsule bitten then swallowed) every hour until there is a response. Otherwise, sodium nitroprusside in an intensive care setting is the optimal treatment.

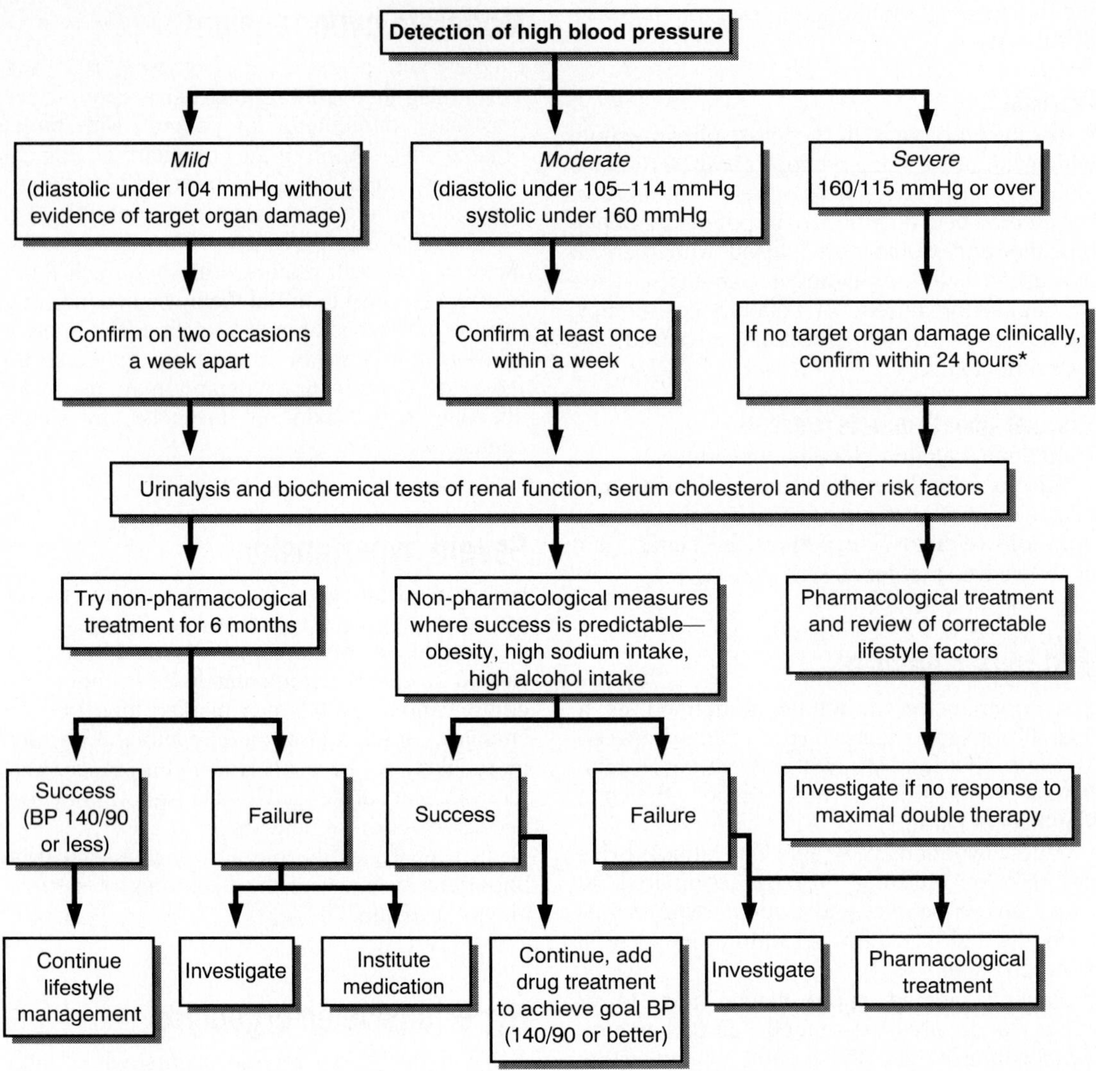

Fig. 103.7 *Decision tree for managing hypertension* AS RECOMMENDED BY THE NATIONAL HEART FOUNDATION

Isolated systolic hypertension[1]

Isolated systolic hypertension is most frequently seen in elderly people.

Definition: systolic BP $>$ 160 mmHg with a DBP $<$ 90 mmHg

Patients with isolated systolic hypertension should be treated in the same way as those with classic systolic/diastolic hypertension. Evidence that reducing isolated systolic blood pressure decreases the mortality and morbidity risk has been demonstrated by the SHEP (systolic hypertension in the elderly) study.[16]

Non-pharmacological therapy should be commenced as is relevant to the patient. If drugs are used the SBP should be cautiously lowered to between 140 and 160 mmHg. The drugs of choice are diuretics, calcium channel-blocking agents and ACE inhibitors.

Refractory hypertension

Refractory hypertension exists where control has not been achieved despite reasonable treatment for three or four months. A review of a possible secondary cause is appropriate.

Checklist of possible reasons[1]

- drug-related causes: doses too low; inappropriate combinations; effects of other drugs, e.g. antidepressants, adrenal steroids, NSAIDs, sympathomimetics, nasal decongestants, ergotamine, oral contraceptives, psychotropics
- poor compliance with therapy
- renovascular hypertension
- nicotine; licorice; caffeine (strong coffee)
- obesity
- excessive alcohol intake
- excessive salt intake
- renal insufficiency and other undiagnosed causes of secondary hypertension
- volume overload, e.g. inadequate diuretic therapy
- illicit substances, e.g. amphetamines, cocaine, anabolic steroids

When adequate control is not possible and the cause is not obvious, the patient should be referred to a specialist. Measurement outside the clinic may help such people, as may 24 hour ambulatory monitoring; this will help to avoid 'white coat' hypertension.

Hypertension in children and adolescents

The recording of blood pressure should be part of the normal examination in children and used in their continuing care. Blood pressure should be measured in all children who are unwell. Blood pressure is less frequently measured in children for a number of reasons, such as an appropriately sized cuff being unavailable or difficulty in measuring BP in the infant or toddler.

The children of parents with hypertension should be closely watched. Those at risk of secondary hypertension, e.g. renal or cardiovascular disease, urological abnormalities and diabetes mellitus, should have routine measurements Those children with visual changes, headache or recurrent abdominal pain or seizures, and those on drugs such as corticosteroids or the pill, should have their blood pressure checked regularly.

Although secondary causes of hypertension are more common in children than in adults, young people are still more prone to developing essential rather than secondary hypertension. Renal parenchymal disease and renal artery stenosis are the major secondary causes.

The upper limits of normal BP for children in different age groups are:[1]

Age (in years)	*Arterial pressure (mmHg)*
14–18	135/90
10–13	125/85
6–9	120/80
5 or less	110/75

The proper cuff size is very important to avoid inaccurate readings and a larger rather than a smaller cuff is recommended. The width of the bladder should cover 75% of the upper arm. In infants and toddlers use of an electronic unit may be necessary. Although cessation of sound (Phase 5) is the better reflection of true diastolic pressure, there is often no disappearance of sound in children and so estimation of the point of muffling has to be recorded.

Diagnostic evaluation and drug treatment for children are similar to those for adults. When a child is obese, reduction in weight may adequately lower BP. ACE inhibitors or calcium channel-blocking agents are preferable in the young hypertensive, with diuretics a second agent. ACE inhibitors should be avoided in postpubertal girls.

Hypertension in the elderly

Blood pressure shows a gradual increasing linear relationship with age.

Guidelines for treatment

- Isolated systolic hypertension is worth treating.[16]
- Older patients may respond to non-pharmacological treatment.
- Reducing dietary sodium is more beneficial than with younger patients.
- If drug treatment is necessary, commence with half the normal recommended adult dosage. 'Start low and go slow.'
- Patients over 70 and in good health should be treated the same as younger patients.
- Treatment is probably of no benefit to patients > 80 years with uncomplicated hypertension.
- A gradual drop in blood pressure is recommended.

- Drug reactions are a limiting factor.
- Drug interactions are also a problem: these include NSAIDs, antiParkinson drugs and phenothiazines.

Specific treatment

1st line choice: thiazide diuretic (low dose)[1]; if hypokalaemia develops add a K-sparing diuretic rather than K supplements. Use a combination thiazide and K-sparing diuretic. Diuretics may aggravate bladder difficulties, e.g. incontinence.

2nd line choice: beta-blockers (low dose) where diuretic cannot be prescribed or if angina.

Other effective drugs (especially for isolated systolic hypertension):

- ACE inhibitors (especially with heart failure)
- calcium channel antagonists

Both these groups are generally well tolerated but constipation is a constant problem with verapamil.

Special management problems

Diabetes mellitus

The causes of hypertension are the same for diabetics as for non-diabetics. Diabetic nephropathy can be a significant cause. Diabetic autonomic neuropathy can cause orthostatic hypotension. Diabetics with persistent or sustained DBP > 90 mmHg and proteinuria need treatment. The threshold for treatment of hypertension in the diabetic is lower than in the non-diabetic.

Treatment

- Use basic non-pharmacological treatments, especially weight reduction, if applicalbe.
- ACE inhibitors and calcium channel blockers are useful initial drugs because they do not affect insulin and diabetes control.
- Other suitable drugs are prazosin, hydralazine and methyldopa.
- Diuretics added to an ACE inhibitor are effective but caution is required because they can aggravate glucose control.
- Proteinuria and renal function need to be monitored.

Pregnancy

Hypertension in pregnancy can be either pre-eclampsia (pregnancy-induced hypertension) or essential hypertension. Blood pressure levels normally drop during the second trimester and rise in the third. A DBP > 80 mmHg in late pregnancy is considered unacceptable. All treatments except for diuretics and ACE inhibitors can be used. Hypertensive pregnant women should be supervised in association with a specialist unit.

Surgical patients

Patients whose BP is under control before surgery should continue the same treatment. If oral medication is affected by the surgery, parenteral treatment may be needed to avoid rebound hypertension. This is a particular problem with clonidine and possibly methyldopa. Withdrawal of other drugs, such as beta-blockers, may have adverse consequences.

Renal disease

Renal function is not adversely affected by the treatment of severe or malignant hypertension. Use a loop diuretic, e.g. frusemide, initially. Beta-blockers, calcium antagonists, prazosin and methyldopa can be used, while caution is needed with ACE inhibitors, particularly if there is underlying renovascular disease.

Heart failure

First-line treatment for associated hypertension includes ACE inhibitors and diuretics. Other suitable drugs are a hydralazine-nitrate combination and methyldopa. Calcium antagonists should be used with care and verapamil and beta-blockers should be avoided.

Ischaemic heart disease

Recommended drugs are beta-blockers and calcium antagonists.[7] Verapamil should be used with care with a beta-blocker but nifedipine is quite safe.

Obstructive airways disease

Apart from beta-blockers, all other routine antihypertensives can be used.

Impotence

It is prudent to avoid antihypertensives that are possibly associated with impotence, e.g. thiazide diuretics, methyldopa, resperine and beta-blockers. Suitable agents to use are ACE inhibitors and calcium blockers.

Can hypertension be overtreated?[17]

Yes. Excessive blood pressure reduction, particularly if acute, can seriously compromise perfusion in vital organs, especially if blood flow is already impaired by vascular disease. Careful monitoring of the patient, including standing BP measurement, is important.

There is also evidence that lowering DBP < 85 mmHg, particularly for patients with ischaemic heart disease, may be detrimental.[18]

Step-down treatment of mild hypertension[17]

This is an important concept that recognises that drug treatment need not necessarily be lifelong. If blood pressure has been well controlled for several months to years it is often worth reducing the dosage or the number of drugs.

A 'drug holiday' (cessation of treatment) can be hazardous, however, because satisfactory control is usually temporary and hypertension will re-emerge. Careful monitoring under such circumstances is mandatory.

When to refer[5]

- Refractory hypertension—adequate control not possible and cause not obvious.
- Suspected 'white coat' hypertension—for ambulatory blood pressure monitoring.
- Severe hypertension—diastolic BP > 115 mmHg.
- Hypertensive emergency.
- If there is evidence of ongoing target organ impairment.
- If there is severe renal impairment (serum creatinine > 0.2 mmol/L).
- If a treatable cause of secondary hypertension is found.

Practice tips

- Hypertension should not be diagnosed on a single reading.
- At least two follow-up measurements with average systolic pressure > 140 mmHg or diastolic pressures > 90 mmHg are required for the diagnosis.
- Beware of using beta-blockers in a patient with a history of wheezing.
- Add only one agent at a time and wait about four weeks between dosage adjustments.
- Excessive intake of alcohol can cause hypertension and hypertension refractory to treatment.
- If hypertension fails to respond to therapy, an underlying renal or adrenal lesion may have been missed.
- The low-pitched bruits of renal artery stenosis are best heard by placing the diaphragm of the stethoscope firmly in the epigastric area.
- Older patients may respond better to diuretics, calcium antagonists and ACE inhibitors.
- Younger patients may respond better to beta-blockers or ACE inhibitors.

References

1. Hypertension Guideline Committee, 1991 report. *Hypertension: diagnosis, treatment and maintenance*. Adelaide: Research Unit RACGP (South Australian Faculty), 1991.
2. The 1988 Report of the Joint National Committee on Detection, Evaluation and Treatment of High Blood Pressure. National High Blood Pressure Education Program. Bethesda, Maryland: National Heart, Lung and Blood Institute, National Institute of Health, May 1988. NIH Publication No. 88–1088.
3. Sloane PD, Slatt PD, Baker RM. *Essentials of family medicine*. Baltimore: Williams and Wilkins, 1988, 149–153.
4. Sandler G. High blood pressure. In: *Common medical problems*. London: Adis Press, 1984:61–106.
5. Stokes G. Essential hypertension. In: MIMS Disease Index. Sydney: IMS Publishing, 1991–2, 265–271.
6. Fraser A. Measurement of blood pressure. Aust Fam Physician, 1989; 18:355–359.
7. *ABC of hypertension*. London: British Medical Association. 1989, 1–50.
8. Bates B. *A guide to physical examination and history taking* (5th edition). Philadelphia: Lippincott, 1991, 284.
9. Hovell MF. The experimental evidence for weight loss treatment of essential hypertension. A critical review. Am J Public Health, April 1982; 72(4):359–368.
10. Blair SN, Goodyear NN, Gibbons LW, Cooper KH. Physical fitness and incidence of hypertension in healthy normotensive men and women. JAMA, 1984; 252 (4):487–490.

11. Rouse IL, Beilin LJ. Vegetarian diet and blood pressure. Editorial review. J Hypertension, 1984; 2:231–240.
12. Kestlefoot H. Urinary cations and blood pressure—population studies. Ann Clin Research, 1984; 16 Supp (43):72–80.
13. Jennings G, Sudhir K. Initial therapy of primary hypertension. Med J Australia, 1990; 152:198–202.
14. Guidelines for the treatment of mild hypertension. Memorandum from a WHO/ISH meeting. Endorsed by Participants at the Fourth Mild Hypertension Conference. Bulletin of the World Health Organisation, 1986; 64(1):31–35.
15. Moulds RFW. *Cardiovascular drug guidelines* (1st edition). Melbourne: Victorian Medical Postgraduate Foundation, 1991–2, 21–28.
16. SHEP Co-operative research group. Prevention of stroke by antihypertensive drug treatment in older persons with isolated systolic hypertension. J Amer Med Assn, 1991; 265:3255–3264.
17. Vandongen R. Drug treatment of hypertension. Aust Fam Physician, 1989; 18:345–348.
18. Cruickshank JM, Thorp JM, Zacharias FJ. Benefits and potential harm of lowering high blood pressure. Lancet, 1987; 1:581–584.

PART 10

ACCIDENT AND EMERGENCY MEDICINE

104

Emergency care

When Elisha arrived, he went alone into the room and saw the boy lying dead on the bed. He closed the door and prayed to the Lord. Then he lay down on the boy, placing his mouth, eyes and hands on the boy's mouth, eyes and hands. As he lay stretched out over the boy, the boy's body started to get warm—the boy sneezed seven times and then opened his eyes.'

II Kings 4: 32-5
(A miracle or successful artificial resuscitation?)

Definition of the emergency

'An event demanding immediate medical attention'.

The demand is determined by patients, relatives, neighbours, nurses, police and others, but is sometimes modified by the doctor or his/her staff.

The common concept of emergencies is an organic one, but the cause is often emotional, or of social origin. The general practitioner has to learn to understand the patient's feeling of urgency and the cure by reassurance may not be simple at all, but can require great skill and understanding. Despite this, the general practitioner must be available and organised to cope with the medically defined emergency when it comes. Emergency care outside the hospital represents one of the most interesting and rewarding areas of medical practice. City doctors will have to modify their degree of availability, equipment and skills according to paramedical emergency services, while others, especially remote doctors, will need total expertise and equipment to provide optimal circumstances to save their patients' lives.

In dealing with a specific emergency, the doctor adopts a different approach. Instead of taking a history and performing an examination in the usual way, he or she replaces this with a technique of rapid assessment and immediate management. In fact the diagnosis may be possible on the information available over the telephone.

Key facts and figures

- The commonest emergency calls in a survey of a typical community were[1] accidents and violence (50.7%), abdominal pain (9.9%), dyspnoea (7.2%), chest pain (5.8%), syncope/blackout (5.2%), other acute pain (5.0%).
- The prevalence of emergency calls was 2.6 per 1000 population per week.
- The commonest specific conditions in this study were lacerations 19%, fractures 11%, injuries from transport accidents 11%, bronchial asthma 4%, ischaemic heart pain 3.5%, appendicitis 3%.
- The commonest causes of sudden death were myocardial infarction 67%, accidents 10%, cerebrovascular accidents 7%, pulmonary embolism 6%, suicide 4%.
- The main vital emergency procedures were cardiopulmonary resuscitation, intubation and ventilation, intravenous access including cutdown, intravenous (or rectal) dextrose and arrest of haemorrhage.

Principles of management

The important principles of management of the emergency call can be summarised as follows:

1. The practitioner must be aware of life-threatening conditions.
2. It is important to 'get up and go' when the call signals danger.
3. The provisional diagnosis should follow the telephone call.
4. The practitioner should be prepared mentally and physically:
   PLAN, EQUIP and PRACTISE
5. Chest pain/collapse/myocardial infarction (collectively) represents *the* premium emergency call.
6. Beware of children with respiratory distress and traumatic injuries.
7. The most savable patients are those with blood loss. Hence IV fluids for intravascular volume expansion and blood availability are essential.
8. The necessary basic skills to cope with most emergencies involve ABC—airway, breathing, circulation.
9. Have the equipment and the skills to handle potentially HIV-contaminated body fluids[2].
10. Carrying a defibrillator is ideal for the doctor attending emergencies: 70% of cardiac arrests occur in the home.

Vital basic skills

1. Rapid intravenous access: direct or cutdown (including 50% Dextrose).
2. Cardiopulmonary resuscitation including upper airway relief, intubation and ventilation, treatment of cardiac arrhythmias and defibrillation.
3. Cricothyroidotomy.
4. Arrest of haemorrhage.
5. Knowledge of usage of common emergency drugs.

When to get up and go

Typical emergency calls to be prepared for are summarised in Table 104.1. The following symptoms and signs make attendance at the emergency mandatory:

- unconsciousness
- convulsions
- chest pain in an adult, especially associated with pallor and sweating
- pallor and sweating in any patient with pain, collapse or injury
- collapse, especially at toilet
- significant haemorrhage
- breathlessness, including bronchial asthma
- the agitated patient threatening homicide or suicide (take a policeman for company)
- serious accidents
- asthmatic patients

Table 104.1 *Emergencies to consider being prepared for*

Cardiovascular	chest pain, esp. myocardial infarction arrhythmias aneurysms—dissecting or ruptured pulmonary embolism peripheral vascular obstruction, e.g. common femoral artery haemorrhage and shock acute pulmonary oedema bacterial endocarditis
Respiratory	acute asthma obstruction, e.g. foreign body tension pneumothorax surgical emphysema epiglottitis, croup and bronchiolitis (children) acute lobar pneumonia
CNS	fits/faints/funny turns collapse and blackout meningitis/encephalitis cerebrovascular accidents subarachnoid haemorrhage subdural/extradural haematomas
Eyes	foreign body, esp. penetrating other trauma acute glaucoma 'flashburns' at night
ENT	severe epistaxis severe earache acute sinusitis barotrauma
Gastrointestinal	acute abdominal pain acute gastroenteritis incarcerated/strangulated hernia rectal bleeding
Genitourinary	ruptured ectopic pregnancy renal colic haemorrhage (bleeding PV) acute retention acute paraphinosis torsion of testicle
Skin	burns
Musculoskeletal	dislocations and fractures spinal fractures—trauma or pathological acute back pain/sciatica
Endocrine	diabetic coma/hypoglycaemia Addisonian crisis myxoedemic madness/coma severe thyrotoxicosis/thyroid 'storm'

(continued)

Table 104.1 *(continues)*

Haemopoietic	haemolytic crisis septicaemia
Psychogenic	delirium and dementia psychotic episodes hyperventilation suicide/parasuicide hysteria breath-holding attacks
Others	multiple trauma electrocution hypothermia/hyperthermia overdosage/poisoning severe vomiting bites and stings anaphylaxis high fever/rigors severe drug reactions • oculogyric crises • MAOI reaction • anaphylaxis street drug effects drowning/near drowning

Don't forget the value of oxygen

Ideally, the doctor who attends emergency calls should carry an oxygen delivery unit or at least rely on the simultaneous arrival of an ambulance with resuscitation equipment. Most cases require a high flow rate of 8–10 L/minute.

Typical medical emergencies requiring oxygen:

- bronchial asthma
- acute pulmonary oedema
- acute anaphylaxis
- myocardial infarction
- cardiopulmonary arrest
- collapse

Twelve golden rules

Twelve important rules for the diagnostic approach to the emergency call.

1. Always consider the possibility of hypoglycaemia in the unconscious patient.
2. Consider intra-abdominal bleeding first and foremost in a patient with abdominal pain who collapses at toilet.
3. Acute chest pain represents myocardial infarction until proved otherwise.
4. Exclude acute epiglottitis in a child with a sudden onset of respiratory distress and pallor.
5. Consider the possibility of a ruptured intra-abdominal viscus in any person, especially a child, with persistent post-traumatic abdominal pain.
6. Always consider the possibility of acute anaphylaxis in patients with a past history of allergies.
7. Always consider the possibility of depression in a postpartum woman presenting with undifferentiated illness or problems in coping with the baby.
8. Always consider ectopic pregnancy in any woman of child-bearing age presenting with acute abdominal pain.
9. If a patient is found cyanosed always consider upper airway obstruction first.
10. Beware of the asthmatic who is cyanosed with a 'silent chest' and tachycardia.
11. Consider ventricular fibrillation or other arrhythmia foremost in an adult with sudden collapse or dizziness.
12. The sudden onset of severe headache adds up to subarachnoid haemorrhage.

Emergencies in children

Important serious emergencies in children include:

- trauma, especially head injuries and intra-abdominal injuries
- swallowed foreign bodies
- respiratory problems
  - — bronchial asthma
  - — epiglottitis
  - — croup
  - — inhaled foreign body
  - — acute bronchiolitis
- severe gastroenteritis
- septicaemia, e.g. meningococcal septicaemia
- myocarditis
- immersion
- poisoning
- bites and stings
- seizures
  - — tonic-clonic epilepsy
  - — febrile convulsions
- sudden infant death syndrome (SIDS)
- child abuse
  - — emotional
  - — physical
  - — sexual
- psychogenic disturbances
  - — anxiety/hyperventilation
  - — suicide/parasuicide

Survey by age group

The author's study analysed emergencies into two groups,[1] preschool (0–5 years), primary school (6–12), adolescence (13–17).

The commonest emergency calls in the 0–5 years group were poisoning, accidents and violence, dyspnoea, fever/rigors, convulsions, abdominal pain, earache, vomiting.

In the 6–12 age group—accidents and violence, dyspnoea, abdominal pain, vomiting, acute allergy, bites and stings, earache.

In the 13–17 age group—accidents and violence, abdominal pain, psychogenic disorders, acute allergy, bites and stings, epistaxis.

Identifying the very sick child

The busy general practitioner will see many sick children in a day's work, especially in the winter months with the epidemic of upper respiratory tract infections. It is vital to be able to recognise the very sick child who requires special attention, including admission to hospital. It is unlikely that the commonplace robust, lustily crying, hot, red-faced child is seriously ill but the pale, quiet, whimpering child spells danger. These rules are particularly helpful in the assessment of babies under six months of age.[3]

> The signs of a very sick infant include:
> - generalised pallor
> - lying quietly/inactive
> - whimpering
> - uninterested
> - languid, maybe floppy
> - eyes (in a still body) follow people around room
> - sunken eyes
> - chest wall recession—moderate/severe rib retraction

Preceding 24 hour history

- reduced feeding (less than 50% of normal intake)
- less than four wet nappies.

Predictive combinations

- pallor + drowsiness + fever = meningitis
- drowsiness + chest wall recession = pneumonia or severe bronchiolitis
- pallor + inactivity = intussusception

Collapse in children

Collapse in children is a very dramatic emergency and often represents a life-threatening event. It is important to remember that the child's brain requires two vital factors:

oxygen and glucose

There is only a two minute reserve once cerebral blood flow stops.

Important causes of collapse are presented in Table 104.2. Keep in mind child abuse as a cause of collapse.

Table 104.2 *Collapse in children: causes to consider*

Anaphylaxis	penicillin injection stings
Asphyxia	near drowning strangulation
Airways obstruction	asthma epiglottitis croup inhaled foreign body
CNS disorders	convulsions meningitis encephalitis head injury
Severe infection	gastroenteritis → dehydration septicaemia myocarditis
Hypovolaemia	dehydration, e.g. heat blood loss, e.g. ruptured spleen
Cardiac failure	arrhythmias cardiomyopathy
Metabolic	acidosis, e.g. diabetic coma hypoglycaemia hyponatraemia
Poisoning	drug ingestion envenomation
SIDS	near miss
Functional	breath-holding attacks conversion reaction vasovagal

Note Consider child abuse.

Initial basic management[4]

1. lay child on side
2. suck out mouth and nasopharynx
3. intubate or ventilate (if necessary)
4. give oxygen 8–10 L/min by mask
5. pass a nasogastric tube
   0–3 years 12FG
   4–10 years 14FG
6. attention to circulation
   ? give blood, SPPS, Haemaccel or N saline
7. take blood for appropriate investigations
8. consider 'blind' administration of IV glucose

Note: Once an endotracheal tube is in place drugs used in paediatric CPR can be given by this route (exceptions are calcium preparations and sodium bicarbonate).

Adrenaline, lignocaine and atropine are readily absorbed. The doses should be at least twice IV dosage and diluted in N saline. Drugs can also be administered by the intraosseous route.[3]

Poisoning

Poisoning in children is a special problem in toddlers (accidental) and in adolescents (deliberate). Children of 1–2 years old are most prone to accidental poisoning. The most common cause of death in comatose patients is respiratory failure.

The common dangerous poisons in the past were kerosene and aspirin. Excluding household chemicals, camphor/moth balls, pesticides, insecticides and opiates, the dangerous drugs are:

- antidepressants, especially tricyclics
- antihypertensives
- anxiolytics, e.g. benzodiazipines
- chloral hydrate
- digoxin
- iron tablets
- Lomotil (diphenoxylate)
- paracetamol/acetaminophen
- potassium tablets
- quinine/quinidine
- salicylates, e.g. aspirin

In a UK study[5] the main cause of deaths from poisoning were (in order) tricyclics, salicylates, opiates including Lomotil, barbiturates, digoxin, orphenadrine, quinine, potassium and iron.

Principles of treatment[6, 7]

- Identify the poison
- Support vital functions—ABCD
  Airway — relieve obstruction
  Breathing — ventilate with oxygen
  Circulation — treat hypotension/arrhythmias
  Dextrose — avoid severe hypoglycaemia
- Dilute the poison — give a cupful of milk or water to drink
- Remove the poison
  - induce emesis:
    1. rub back of child's throat with spoon or spatula
    2. give syrup of ipecac (see Table 104.3); avoid common salt

  Note: The modern swing is away from emesis which is only useful for very recent ingestion (< 30 minutes) or for iron/slow K poisoning where concretions form in the stomach.
  - gastric lavage: within 4 hours (refer Table 104.4 for guidelines)
  - gastric aspiration

Table 104.3 *Guidelines for syrup of ipecacuanha*

Dosage:

< 1 year:	do not give
1 year:	15 ml
2 years:	20 ml
3 years:	25 ml
4 years:	25 ml
> 4 years:	30 ml

Follow with 100-200 ml water
Optimal time: within 30 minutes
Mean time to emesis—20 minutes (range 15-60 minutes)
If ineffective—repeat with ½ dose after 20 minutes

Contraindications:
> 3 hours since ingestion
rapidly acting convulsants
acid
alkali
strychnine
petroleum products
- kerosene
- petrol

patient cannot sit up and hold a vomit bowl
impaired consciousness
- actual
- anticipated

Table 104.4 *Guidelines for gastric lavage*

Do within 4 hours ingestion
Within 6 hours for analgesics, tricyclics, iron and digoxin

Contraindications:
- stuporose or comatose
- absent gag reflex (unless endotracheal tube in situ)
- acid
- alkali

Method:
- child on left side
- head of bed tilted down
- insert orogastric tube (lubricated)

< 2 years	12-14 size FG
2 - 4	14-18 size FG
5 - 12	18-22 size FG
> 12	22-30

- check in stomach by aspiration
- instil 50-100 ml lukewarm tap water or saline via large syringe or funnel
- brief pause then drain into bucket
- repeat often until washings clear
- use about 2-3 litres
- restrict the total volume to 40 ml/kg
- be careful of water intoxication

- Delay absorption
  - activated charcoal (the preferred method)
    1 g/kg orally or via gastric tube (best)
    before emesis or lavage/aspiration (refer Tables 104.5 and 104.6)
    (multiple dose charcoal, 5–10 g every 4 to 8 hours, is effective)
  - evaporated milk
    aspirin and petroleum products
  - sodium bicarbonate
    iron and salicylates

Table 104.5 *Drugs not absorbed by active charcoal*

Acids	Ethanol
Alkalis	Iron
Boric Acid	Iodines
Bromides	Lithium
Cyanide	Other heavy metals

Table 104.6 *Drugs successfully treated by repeated doses of activated charcoal*

Chlorpropamide
Cyclosporin
Dextropropoxephene
Digoxin
Methotrexate
Phenobarbital
Phenytoin
Salicylate
Theophylline
Tricyclic antidepressant

- Increase secretion
  (intensive care unit)
- Administer antidote early (see Table 104.7)
- Treat any complications
  - respiratory failure
    - hypoventilation
    - apnoea
  - pulmonary aspiration of gastric contents
  - arrhythmias
  - hypotension
  - seizures
  - delayed effects,
    e.g. paracetamol (hepatotoxicity)
    tricyclics (arrhythmia)

Table 104.7 *Important antidotes for poisons*

Poison	***Antidote***
Benzodiazepines	flumazenil
Carbon monoxide	oxygen 100% hyperbaric oxygen
Cyanide	dicobalt edetate sodium nitrite sodium thiosulphate
Heavy metals, e.g. Pb, As, Hg, Fe	dimercaprol
Iron	desferrioxamine
Isoniazid	pyridoxine
Methanol, ethylene glycol	ethanol (ethyl alcohol)
Narcotics/opiates	naloxone (Narcan)
Organophosphates	atropine pralidoxamine (2-PAM)
Paracetamol (acetaminophen)	acetylcysteine (IV) (effective within 12 hours) consider up to 36 hours
Phenothiazines	benztropine

Investigations

- drug levels, e.g. paracetamol, aspirin, iron
- blood gas analysis
- X-ray
  - chest
  - abdomen, e.g. radiopaque iron tablets
  - skull
- ECG

Psychosocial care

The reasons for the poisoning need to be carefully evaluated and proper support and advice given.

Swallowed foreign objects

A golden rule

The natural passage of most objects entering the stomach can be expected.

This includes:

- coins
- buttons
- sharp objects
- open safety pins
- glass (e.g. ends of thermometers)

Special cases are:

- very large coins: watch carefully
- hair clips (usually cannot pass duodenum if under 7 years)

Management

- Manage conservatively.
- X-ray all children (mouth to anus) on presentation.
- Investigate unusual gagging, coughing and retching with X-rays of the head, neck, thorax and abdomen (check nasopharynx and respiratory tract).
- Watch for passage of the foreign body in stool (usually three days).
- If not passed, order X-ray in one week.
- If a blunt foreign body has been stationary for one month without symptoms, remove at laparotomy.

Febrile convulsions

Features:

- The commonest cause is an upper respiratory infection, e.g. the common cold or similar viral syndrome.
- About 5 per 100 incidence in children.
- Rare under six months and over five years.
- Commonest age range 9–20 months.
- Recurrent in up to 50% of children.
- Perform lumbar puncture after first convulsion if less than two years or cause of fever not obvious.
- Epilepsy develops in about 2–3% of such children.

Management of the convulsion (if prolonged)

- undress the child to singlet and underpants to keep cool
- maintain the airway and prevent injury
- place patient chest down with head turned to one side
- give diazepam by one of two routes:
  IV 0.25 mg/kg, undiluted or diluted (10 mg in 20 ml N saline)
  or
  rectally 0.4 mg/kg (dilute with saline or in pre-prepared syringe)
  Note: Although the IV route is preferred, the rectal route is ideal in a home or office situation; e.g. consider a two year old child (weight 12 kg) with a persistent febrile convulsion. The dose of diazepam injectable is 0.4 mg/kg so 5 mg (1 ml) of diazepam is diluted with isotonic saline (up to 10 ml of solution) and the nozzle of the syringe pressed gently but firmly into the anus and injected slowly.
- rectal paracetamol 15 mg/kg statim

Meningitis or encephalitis

Diagnosing meningitis and encephalitis requires a high level of clinical awareness and watchfulness for the infective problem that appears more serious than normal. *Bacterial meningitis* is basically a childhood infection. Neonates and children aged 6–12 months are at the greatest risk. Most cases begin as septicaemia, usually via the nasopharynx.

Clinical presentations (typical)

Infancy:

- fever, pallor, vomiting, ± altered conscious state
- lethargic
- refusing to feed, indifferent to mother
- neck stiffness
- Kernig's sign unreliable
- may be bulging fontanelle

Children over 3 years:

- meningeal irritation more obvious, e.g. headache, fever, vomiting, neck stiffness.
- later: delirium, altered conscious state

Note: Antibiotics may mask symptoms.

Fulminating:

- dramatic sudden onset shock, purpura ± coma
- usually due to meningococcal septicaemia, also *Haemophilus influenzae* type B, *Streptococcus pneumoniae*

Treatment

If meningitis suspected, admit to hospital for lumbar puncture and ongoing management.

Meningococcaemia

Note: treatment is urgent once suspected

- take blood culture if time and facilities permit then
- benzylpenicillin 60 mg/kg IV statim and 4 hourly 5–7 days
  or (if uncertain)
- third generation cephalosporin (better option)
- admit to hospital

Acute epiglottitis

Acute epiglottitis due to *Haemophilus influenzae* is a life-threatening emergency in a child. A toxic febrile illness, with sudden onset of inspiratory stridor, should alert one to this potentially fatal condition. A high index of suspicion of epiglottitis is always warranted in such presentations.

Differential diagnosis

The main alternative diagnosis is viral laryngotracheobronchitis (croup). There are however significant clinical differences.

Epiglottitis is characterised by fever, a soft voice, lack of a harsh cough, a preference to sit quietly (rather than lie down) and especially by a soft stridor with a sonorous expiratory component (Fig. 104.1).

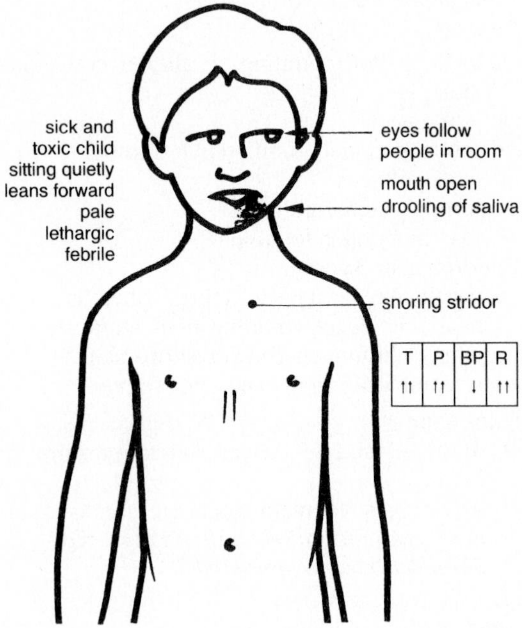

Fig. 104.1 *Typical features of acute epiglottitis*

Croup is distinguished by a harsh inspiratory stridor, a hoarse voice and brassy cough.

Other differential diagnoses include tonsillitis, infectious mononucleosis and bacterial tracheitis. The clinical features of croup and epiglottitis are compared in Table 104.8.

Diagnostic tip

The child with epiglottitis usually sits still and the eyes follow you around the room because limited head movement protects the compromised airway.

Physical examination

DO NOT EXAMINE THE THROAT.

A swollen cherry-red epiglottis recognised on examination of the nasopharynx confirms the diagnosis. However, the initial diagnosis should be made on the clinical history and appearance of the child.

Direct examination using a spatula and torch should not be performed in the office but only where there are appropriate facilities for suction, endotracheal intubation and tracheostomy, as this procedure can precipitate laryngeal obstruction.

Almost all children with epiglottitis require nasotracheal intubation.

Management

Transporting the patient to hospital: After ringing the hospital to warn about the emergency the practitioner should escort the child to hospital in an ambulance (with the child sitting propped up on mother's knee) prepared to perform cricothyroidotomy using a large bore cannula in the unlikely event of sudden obstruction.

The primary objective, during transportation, is to keep the child calm. This is enhanced by having mother nurse the child during transfer.

If the child's condition deteriorates administer 100% oxygen by mask. Most obstructed patients can be bagged and masked which is sufficient to maintain oxygenation. If obstruction occurs, use the cannula to provide an airway.

Method of emergency cricothyroidotomy (last resort)

- Lay the child across your knees with neck fully extended
- Insert a number 14 needle or angiocath through the cricothyroid membrane.

Always try to intubate once before resorting to cricothyroidotomy.

Hospital treatment

Intubation: in theatre suck away profuse secretions and perform nasotracheal intubation

Antibiotics: chloramphenicol 80 mg/kg/day IV (max. 4 g in 4 divided doses) 5 days (only if severe penicillin hypersensitivity)

or (preferable)

cefotaxime 100–150 mg/kg/day IV (max. 6 g/day in 3 divided doses)

or

ceftriaxone 100 mg/kg to max. 1 g/day IV as single daily dose

Note: Continue therapy for 5 days. Early transfer to oral therapy, e.g. Augmentin, is desirable.

Table 104.8 *Comparison of clinical features of croup and acute epiglottitis*

	Croup	*Epiglottitis*
Epidemiology		
Periodicity	winter months, late autumn	any time of the year
Age	6 months to 6 years occasionally older	6 months to 6 years
Incidence	common	infrequent
Clinical		
Onset	prodrome of URTI or coryza two days	rapid 2–6 hours
Fever	variable, rarely above 39°C	usually above 39°
Toxicity	often not anorexic drinking fluids looks like URTI	very lethargic looks ill, pale, drooling
Stridor	loud inspiratory, increased if upset harsh brassy cough	soft stridor, often barely audible expiratory 'flutter'
Pathology		
Causative organism	viral - mostly Parainfluenza 1	bacterial, mostly *H.influenzae* some B haemolytic streptococcus
Site	larynx, trachea, bronchi	epiglottis
Laboratory		toxic FBC, increased WCC +ve blood culture +ve epiglottis culture
Treatment	mild cases: • at home with moist air moderate: • admit to hospital • cool humified air in mist tent • observe severe: • nurse in intensive care • low oxygen concentration • dexamethasone IV 0.2 mg/kg • nebulised adrenaline 1:1000 solution (max. 5 ml) • facilities for artificial airway ? endotracheal tube for 48 hours	• airway support with nasotracheal intubation, e.g. 48 hours • blood culture Antibiotic: 3rd generation cephalosporin, e.g. cefotaxime or ceftriaxone Prevention • Hib vaccine

Very severe asthma

Very severe asthma in children should be referred to an intensive care unit.

- continuous nebulised 0.5% salbutamol via mask[4]
- oxygen flow 4 L/min through the nebuliser
- IV infusion of
  salbutamol 5 mg/kg/min
  hydrocortisone 4 mg/kg IV statim then 6 hourly

Common mistakes

- using assisted mechanical ventilation inappropriately (main indications are physical exhaustion and cardiopulmonary arrest—it can be dangerous in asthma)
- not giving high flow oxygen
- giving excessive fluid
- giving submaximal bronchodilator therapy

Breath-holding attacks

This is a dramatic emergency. There are two types: one is related to a tantrum (description follows) and the other is a simple faint.

Clinical features

- age group—usually six months to six years (peak 2–3 years)

- precipitating event (minor emotional or physical)
- children emit a long loud cry, then hold their breath
- they become pale and then blue
- if severe, may result in unconsciousness or even a brief tonic-clonic fit
- lasts 10–60 seconds

Management

- Reassure the parents that attacks are self-limiting, not harmful and are not associated with epilepsy or mental retardation.
- Advise parents to maintain discipline and to resist spoiling the child.
- Try to avoid incidents known to frustrate the child or to precipitate a tantrum.

Note: Important childhood emergency drugs with dosages are presented in Table 104.9.

Emergencies in the elderly

Elderly patients suffer from a different spectrum of emergency problems.

The commonest problems encountered were:

- chest pain, especially ischaemic heart disease
- syncope/blackout, e.g. arrhythmias, sudden death, TIAs, CVAs.
- dizziness/giddiness, e.g. arrhythmias, postural hypotension
- dyspnoea, e.g. acute cardiac failure, asthma
- abdominal pain, e.g. biliary colic, bowel obstruction

Table 104.9 *Important childhood emergency drugs (after Pitt)*

Drug	*Route*	*Dose*	*Notes*
Adrenaline 1:10 000	IV	0.1 ml/kg/dose	Anaphylaxis, asystole (repeat every five minutes until response)
Adrenaline 1:1000	Nebuliser	0.5 ml/kg/dose (maximum 5 ml)	LTB (patient must be admitted)
Aminophylline	IV slowly	5 mg/kg loading	Moderate to severe asthma
Atrophine	IV	0.02 mg/kg	Bradycardia producing shock
Dextrose 50%	IV	1 ml/kg	Hypoglycaemia
Diazepam	IV or PR	0.25 to 0.4 mg/kg	Seizures
Glucagon	IV or IM	0.1 mg/kg (maximum 1 mg)	Hypoglycaemia
Hydrocortisone	IV	4 to 8 mg/kg	Anaphylaxis, asthma
Morphine	IV or IM	0.1 to 0.2 mg/kg	Sedation, pain relief
Paraldehyde	PR	0.3 ml/kg (dilute 1:2 in peanut oil)	Seizures
Paracetamol	O	15 to 20 mg/kg loading	Fever
Salbutamol	Nebuliser	0.3 ml/kg	Asthma
Salbutamol	IV	5 mg/kg	
Sodium bicarbonate 8.4%	IV	2 ml/kg	Titrate against blood gases
Soluble insulin	IV infusion	0.1 u/kg/hr	Only if glucose > 14 mmol/l

IV: intravenous injection
PR: per rectum
IM: intramuscular injection
O: orally
LTB: laryngotracheal bronchitis (croup)

Note: 1. Volume resuscitation: IV fluid bolus 20 mg/kg statim of crystalloid, e.g. N saline.
2. Endotracheal tube sizes: $\frac{\text{age}}{4} + 4$

Special problems in the elderly include:

- fractures from falls, e.g. neck of femur, radius, humerus
- cerebrovascular accidents
- ruptured aneurysms
- problems of dementia and delirium
- abdominal colic syndromes, e.g. renal colic, biliary colic

Important medical emergencies in adults

This section includes summarised protocols for management of emergencies.

Acute anaphylaxis

Common causes: bee stings, wasp stings, other bites, parenteral antibiotics especially penicillin

Other causes: allergic extracts, blood products, antivenom, radiological contact materials, anaesthetic agents

Note: The danger symptom is itching of the palms of hands and soles of the feet.

Differential diagnosis: syncope

First-line treatment

- oxygen 8–10 L/min
- salbutamol aerosol inhalation
- adrenaline 0.5 mg 1:1000 IM or SC—best given in upper body, e.g. deltoid (repeat in 5 minutes if necessary)
- insert IV line and give colloid solution
- promethazine 10 mg IV slowly (or 25 mg IM)

  or

  diphenhydramine 10 mg IV (or 25 mg IM)
- admit to hospital (observe at least 4 hours)

If not responding:

- adrenaline 0.5 ml 1:1000 IM (repeat every 5–10 minutes as often as necessary)
- hydrocortisone 500 mg IV
- establish airway (oral airway or endotracheal intubation) if required
- nebulised salbutamol if bronchospasm

Acute pulmonary oedema

- keep the patient propped up in bed
- oxygen by mask or intranasally (4 L/min)
- insert IV line
- morphine 1 mg/min IV (up to 5–10mg) + metoclopramide 10 mg IV
- frusemide 20–60 mg IV
- glyceryl trinitrate (nitroglycerin) 300–600 μg sublingual

Note: keep in mind underlying cause
e.g. myocardial infarction (? silent)
arrhythmia
cardiomyopathy
anaemia

Status asthmaticus

Status asthmaticus is a life-threatening condition that is resistant to standard treatment. It requires intensive medication because of marked obstruction to the air passages, due to severe smooth muscle spasm and inflammation, producing mucosal oedema and mucous impaction.

Initial treatment

- oxygen 8–10 L/min by mask
- continuous nebulised 0.5% salbutamol (or terbutaline) by face mask—using compressed (8 L/min) oxygen for nebulisation

  NB: can use salbutamol with ipratropium (0.025%)—2 ml of each with 2 ml saline
- insert IV line
- hydrocortisone 4 mg/kg (e.g. 200–250 mg) IV statim

If no response in 30 minutes (or deterioration):

- chest X-ray to exclude complications
- arterial blood gases
- IV administration of

  salbutamol 125–500 μg (over 2 min) statim

  or

  adrenaline 1:10 000 (1 ml over 30 seconds) if on monitor

  then

  IV infusion of

  salbutamol 7.5 μg/kg/hr
  hydrocortisone

Note: Aminophylline 250 mg over 5 minutes can be given as a loading dose (if patient not taking prior oral theophylline, if failing to respond and on a cardiac monitor).

If not responding, exhausted and moribund:

- intubation with IPPV
- hydration with IV fluids

Consider isoflurane or halothane inhalation to 'break' bronchospasm.

Hypoglycaemia

- 50% dextrose, 20–50ml IV
  (if IV line difficult, administer rectally by pressing the nozzle of a large syringe into the anus and inject slowly)
  or
  glucagon, 1 ml, IM
  then oral glucose

Myocardial infarction (refer to page 313)

First-line management:

- arrange ambulance and hospitalisation
- oxygen (face mask)
- insert IV line
- glyceryl trinitrate (nitroglycerin) 300mg (½ tab) SL
- aspirin 300 mg (1 tab)
- morphine 1 mg per minute IV
  until pain relief (up to 15 mg)
  ± metoclopramide 10 mg IV for vomiting

Note: Avoid IM injections.

Hyperventilation

Rebreathe slowly from a paper (not plastic) bag
or
Into cupped hands

Status epilepticus and serial seizures

Status epilepticus = repeated convulsions without regaining consciousness after initial tonic-clonic seizure

Serial seizures = repeated convulsions after regaining consciousness

Management

diazepam 5–20 mg IV
followed by
phenytoin 15–18 mg/kg over 30 mins (1–1.25 g in most adults); further diazepam can be given
Other drugs to consider: clonazepam, lorazepam
phenobarbitone
thiopentone
midazolam (can use 1 IM)

Bites and stings

Bites and stings from animals, spiders and insects in Australia and the United States are commonplace but fatal bites are uncommon.

Snake bites

Snake bites are more common and severe in those handling snakes and in those trying to kill the snake. Snakes are more aggressive when mating or sloughing their skin (about four times a year). They strike for one-third of their length at 3.5 metre/second. Over 70% of bites are on the legs.

First aid

1. Keep the patient as still as possible.
2. Do not wash, cut, manipulate the wound, apply ice or use a tourniquet.
3. Immediately bandage the bite site firmly (not too tight). A crepe bandage is ideal: it should extend above the bite site for 15 cm, e.g. if bitten around the ankle the bandage should cover the leg to the knee.
4. Splint the limb to immobilise it: a firm stick or slab of wood would be ideal.
5. Transport to a medical facility for definitive treatment. Do not give alcoholic beverages or stimulants.
6. If possible, the dead snake should be brought along.

Note: A venom detection kit is used to examine a swab of the bitten area or a fresh urine specimen (the best) or blood.

Envenomation

Not all patients become envenomated and the antivenom should not be given unless there is evidence of this. Envenomation is more likely when the snake has a clear bite, such as in snake handlers or barefooted people or hands placed in burrows.

Important early symptoms of snake bite envenomation include:

- nausea and vomiting (a reliable early symptom)
- abdominal pain
- perspiration
- severe headache
- blurred vision

Refer to Figure 104.2 for detailed effects.

Treatment of envenomation

- set up a slow IV infusion of N saline
- give IV antihistamine cover (15 minutes beforehand) and 0.3 ml adrenaline 1:1000 SC (0.1 ml for a child)
- dilute the specific antivenom (1 in 10 in N saline) and infuse slowly over 30 minutes via the tubing of the saline solution
- have adrenaline on standby
- monitor vital signs

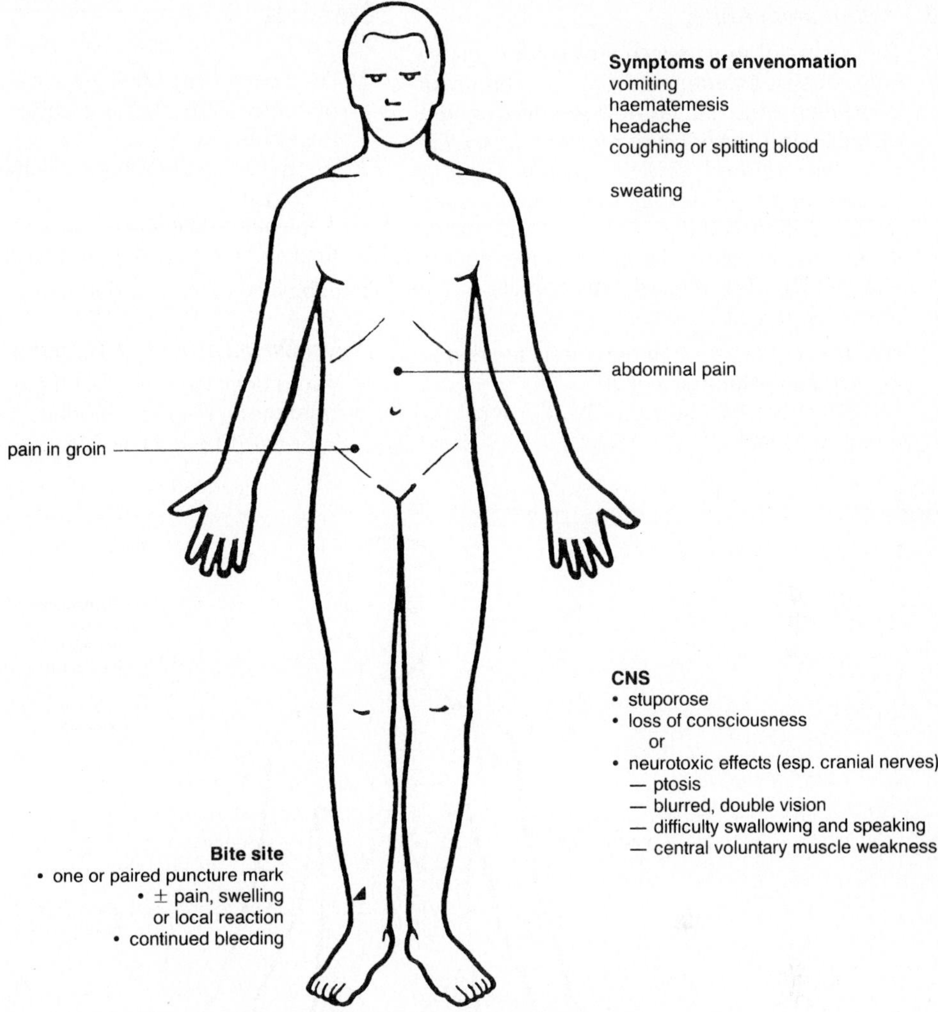

Fig. 104.2 *How to recognise snake bite envenomation*

Note: Do not give antivenom unless clinical signs of envenomation or biochemical signs, e.g. positive urine, or abnormal clotting profile.

Spider bites

The toxin of most species of spider causes only localised pain, redness and swelling, but the toxin of some, notably the deadly Sydney funnel-web spider (*Atrax robustus*), can be rapidly fatal.

First aid

Sydney funnel-web: as for snake bites.
Other spiders: apply an ice pack, do not bandage.

Treatment

1. *Sydney funnel-web*

Signs of envenomation (in order):

- muscle fasciculation—limb → tongue/lip
- marked salivation or lacrimation
- piloerection
- dyspnoea
- neurological symptoms, e.g. disorientation, coma

Treatment — specific antivenom
— resuscitation and other supportive measures

2. Other spider bites

The toxins of most species of spiders cause only localised symptoms but the venom of a selected few, namely the red-back spider of Australia (*Latrodectus mactans hasseltii*) and its related black widow spider (*Latrodectus mactus*), can cause envenomation which is rarely fatal but is more serious in the young, the frail and the elderly. The clinical features of envenomation are presented in Figure 104.3.

Treatment of envenomation (rarely needed)
— give antihistamine, e.g. IM
— antivenom IM injection (IV if severe) 15 minutes later

Bee stings

First aid

1. Scrape the sting off sideways with a fingernail or knife blade. Do not squeeze it with the fingertips.
2. Apply 20% aluminium sulphate solution (Stingose).
3. Apply ice to the site.
4. Rest and elevate the limb that has been stung.

If anaphylaxis (treat as outlined).

Preventive measures (if hypersensitive)

- Avoid bees (and wasps) if possible.
- Immunotherapy to honey bee (or wasp venom). There is no cross-allergy between

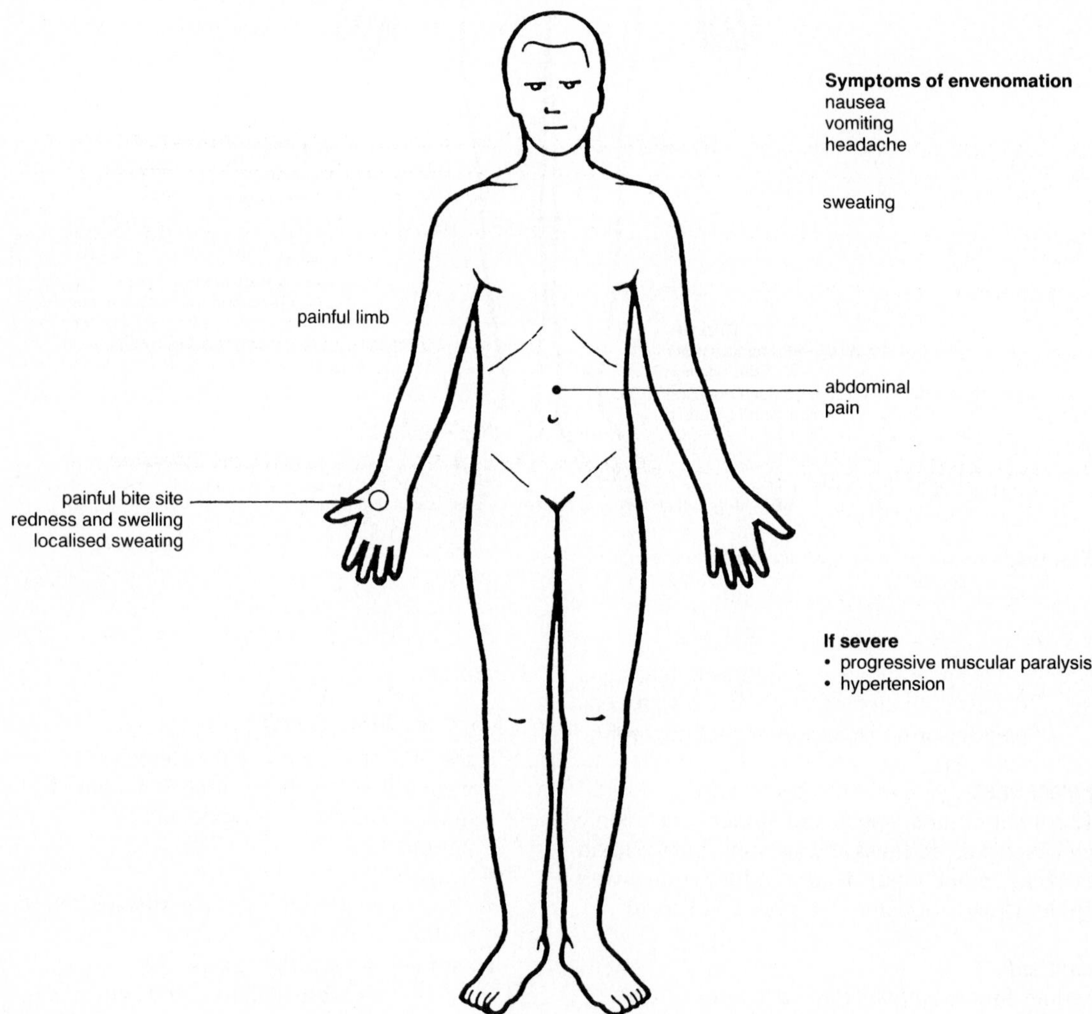

Fig. 104.3 *How to recognise* Latrodectus mactus *envenomation*

the honey bee, the 'yellow jacket wasp' and the paper wasp. Specific hyposensitisation against the Vespula species is required and for the bee use pure venom antigen.

- Immunotherapy should be offered to those:
  - — with a history of asthma who have had a single severe reaction to a bee sting
  - — who have had a minimum of three stings with serial crescendo reactions
  - — occupationally exposed who manifest severe reactions
  - — with elevated venom-specific IgE (RAST) antibodies, or positive venom prick tests.

Centipede and scorpion bites

The main symptom is pain, which can be very severe and prolonged.

First aid

1. Apply local heat, e.g. hot water with ammonia (household bleach)
2. Clean site.
3. Local anaesthetic, e.g. 1–2 ml of 1% lignocaine infiltrated around the site.
4. Check tetanus immunisation status.

Other bites and stings

This includes bites from ants, wasps, jellyfish, scorpions and centipedes.

First aid

1. Wash the site with large quantities of cool water.
2. Apply vinegar (liberal amount) or aluminium sulfate 20% solution (Stingose) to the wound for about 30 seconds.
3. Apply ice for several minutes.
4. Use soothing anti-itch cream or 5% lignocaine cream or ointment if very painful.

Medication is not usually necessary.

Box jellyfish or sea wasp (*Chironex fleckeri*)

This is the most dangerous jellyfish in Australian waters and has been responsible for at least 80 extremely painful and sudden deaths.[8] Death can occur in minutes due to cardiopulmonary failure. It is limited to tropical waters north of the Tropic of Capricorn and is found in coastal waters during the summer.

Prevention

- Avoid swimming, paddling and wading in 'jellyfish alert' areas in unsafe months.
- Otherwise, use a 'stinger suit'.

Treatment

- The victim should be removed from the water to prevent drowning.
- Inactivate the tentacles by pouring vinegar over them for 30 seconds (do not use alcohol)—use up to 2 litres of vinegar at a time.
- Check respiration and the pulse.
- Start immediate cardiopulmonary resuscitation.
- Give box jellyfish antivenom by IV injection.
- Provide pain relief if required (ice, lignocaine and analgesics).

Stinging fish

The sharp spines of the stinging fish have venom glands which can produce severe pain if they spike or even graze the skin. The best known of these is the stonefish. The toxin is usually heat-sensitive.

Treatment

- Bathe or immerse the affected part in very warm to hot (not scalding) water—this may give instant relief.[8]
- If pain persists, give a local injection/infiltration of lignocaine 1% or even a regional block. If still persisting, try pyridoxine 50 mg intralesional injection.
- A specific antivenom is available for the sting of the stonefish.

The embedded tick

Some species of ticks can be very dangerous to human beings, especially to children. If they attach themselves to the head and neck, a serious problem is posed. As it is impossible to distinguish between dangerous and non-dangerous ticks, early removal is mandatory. The tick should be totally removed, and the mouth-parts of the tick must not be left behind. Do not attempt to grab the tick by its body and tug. This is rarely successful in dislodging the tick, and more toxin is thereby injected into the host.

As an office procedure, many practitioners grasp the tick's head as close to the skin as possible with fine forceps or tweezers, and pull the tick out sideways with a sharp rotatory action. This is acceptable, but not as effective as the methods described here.

First aid outdoor removal method

- Saturate the tick with petrol or kerosene and leave for three minutes.

- Loop a strong thin thread around the tick's head as close to the skin as possible, and pull sharply with a twisting motion.

Office procedure

- Infiltrate a small amount of LA in the skin around the site of embedment.
- With a number 11 or 15 scalpel blade make the necessary very small excision, including the mouth parts of the tick, to ensure total removal (Fig. 104.4).
- The small defect can usually be closed with a bandaid (or Steri-strips).

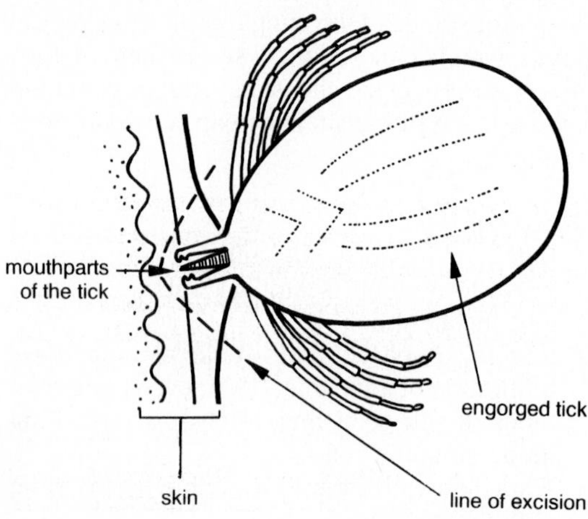

Fig. 104.4 *Removing the embedded tick*

Human bites and animal bites

These bites can cause problems of suppurative infection and management in general. They are outlined in Chapter 105.

A pot pourri of emergency calls

Electric shock

Useful facts:

- Direct current (DC) from welding machines or lightning produce more electrolyte tissue damage and burns than AC (domestic supply).
- Injuries occur at distant sites from entry or exit.
- Severe muscle contractions can cause bone fracture.
- Household shocks tend to cause cardiac arrest (ventricular fibrillation) and myocardial damage is common.
- Ischaemic necrosis of a limb is a common effect.
- Apparent minor initial injuries may be very misleading (Fig. 104.5).
- Neurological deficits and psychoneurotic sequelae are common in survivors.

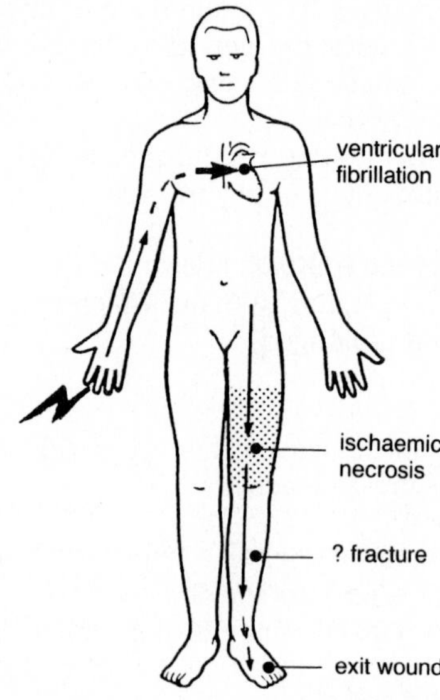

Fig. 104.5 *Effect of electric shock passing through the body*

Principles of management

- Make the site safe: switch off the electricity. Use dry wool to insulate rescuers.
- 'Treat the clinically dead'.
- Attend to ABC.
- Give a praecordial thump in a witnessed arrest.
- Consider a cervical collar (? cervical fracture).
- Provide basic cardiopulmonary resuscitation, including defibrillation (as required).
- Give a lignocaine infusion (100 mg IV) after cardiac arrest.[9]
- Investigate and consider
  - — careful examination of all limbs
  - — X-ray of limbs or spine as appropriate
  - — check for myoglobinuria and renal failure
  - — give tetanus and clostridial prophylaxis
- Get expert help—intensive care unit, burns unit.

Lightning strike

Prevention (during an electrical storm):

- Don't shelter under trees (splash phenomenon—Fig. 104.6).[10]

- Avoid using telephone.
- Avoid holding metal objects, e.g. golf clubs.
- Keep as low to ground as possible.

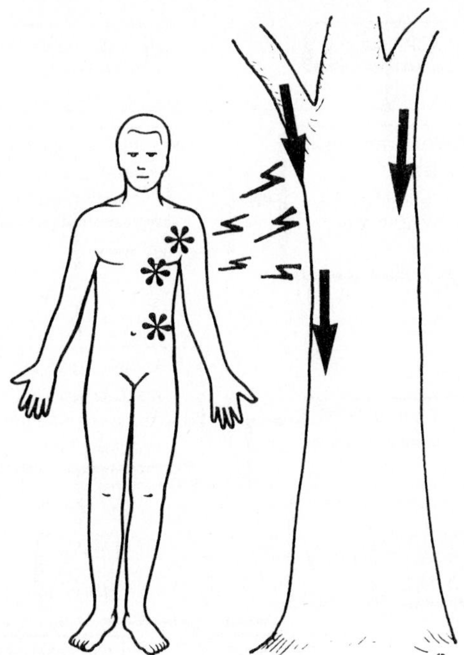

Fig. 104.6 *'Splash effect' where current is reflected from tree*

Clinical effects:

- Burn injury (90%): the 'flashover' phenomenon—clothing disintegrates
- Blast injury, e.g. ruptured spleen, subdural, ruptured eardrum
- Electrical injury as for household shock (uncommon)

Diagnosing the hysterical 'unconscious' patient

One of the most puzzling problems in emergency medicine is how to diagnose the unconscious patient caused by a conversion reaction. These patients really experience their symptoms (as opposed to the pretending patient) and resist most normal stimuli, including painful stimuli.

Method

1. Hold the patient's eye or eyes open with your fingers and note the reaction to light. Now hold a mirror over the eye and watch closely for pupillary reaction. The pupil should constrict with accommodation from the patient looking at his or her own image.

or

2. Hold the patient's fist above their nose and drop it. The 'hysterical' patient will usually just miss hitting the nose.

Petrol sniffing

The three main acute problems:

1. Fitting: give diazepam IV (as for convulsions). May require paraldehyde IM.
2. Agitation/aggressive behaviour: try to calm patient in a well lit room. Give sedation with diazepam. Give haloperidol for hallucinations or delusions.
3. General debilitation: this may include acute infections, e.g. chest infection or anaemia. Investigation and referral for breaking the habit is necessary.

Near drowning

The rule to remember is that victims can respond to resuscitation after considerable immersion time (up to 30 minutes) and that mouth-to-mouth resuscitation should always be attempted even if pulseless or with fixed dilated pupils. The usual routine of basic life support and CPR apply.

Artificial surfactant given via an endotracheal tube has been used successfully in the UK.

There is no significant difference in outcome and management between salt water and fresh water drowning.

Vital emergency skills

Cardiopulmonary resuscitation (CPR)

Cardiopulmonary arrest (CPA): it is essential that all doctors are familiar with the protocol for instituting basic life support in such an eventuality. Sick patients do visit our offices daily and the potential for sudden collapse including a cardiac arrest is ever present. About 75% of arrests are due to ventricular fibrillation and over 75% of victims have severe coronary artery disease.[11] After three (3) minutes of CPA (unconsciousness, no pulse, no respiration) there will be permanent cerebral dysfunction.

Important causes of sudden death are outlined in Table 104.10.[12]

The ABC basic life support for cardiac arrest should be followed, but ideally DABC is best (defibrillation first if a defibrillator is available—the outcome appears to be directly related to the speed of defibrillation).

Table 104.10 *Causes of sudden death*

Cardiac arrhythmias
- ventricular fibrillation (75%)
- ventricular tachycardia
- torsade de pointes VT (? drugs)
- sick sinus syndrome
- severe bradycardia

Sudden pump failure
- acute myocardial infarction
- cardiomyopathy

Cardiovascular rupture
- myocardial rupture
- dissecting aneurysm aorta
- subarachnoid haemorrhage

Acute circulatory obstruction
- pulmonary embolism

Others include
- pulmonary hypertension
- mitral valve prolapse
- elecrolyte abnormalities
- glue sniffing

Basic life support

The following represents a logical ABC plan for the adult patient who collapses or is found apparently unconscious.

1. Shake and shout at the patient.
2. Check breathing.
3. Check pulse (feel carotid adjacent to thyroid cartilage).
4. Call for help (if no pulse).
5. Finger sweep oropharynx (clear it).
6. Place victim on back on firm surface.
7. Thump precordium (if arrest witnessed).
8. Tilt head back (to maximum).
9. Lift chin (use airway if available).
10. Commence basic life support:
    Expired air resuscitation (EAR)—5 quick breaths
    External chest compression
    One rescuer: 15:2 (compressions/breaths) 80 beats/min
    Two rescuers: 5:1 60 beats/min

The basic schedule for cardiopulmonary resuscitation is presented in Table 104.11 and a flow chart for basic life support in Figure 104.7.

Method of expired air resuscitation

With the victim's head in the 'sniffing the morning air' position (head totally tilted back and chin pulled forward) the rescuer takes a deep breath and seals his or her lips around the mouth or nose of the victim. Pinch the victim's nose if using mouth-to-mouth resuscitation. Four or five quick

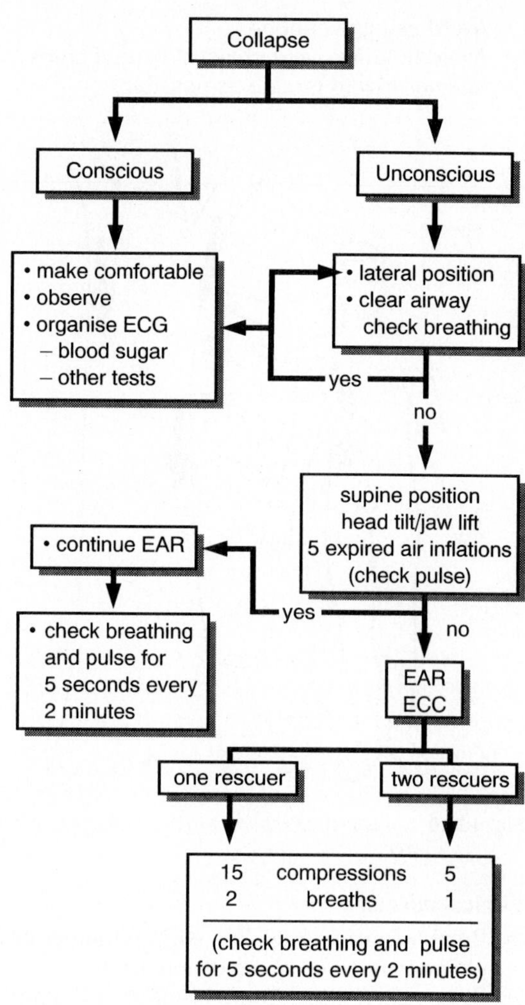

Fig. 104.7 *Algorithm for basic life support: CPR in the collapsed patient*

Table 104.11 *Basic schedule for CPR*

	Infant <1 year	***Child***	***Adult***
Compression (rate per min)	100	80	60
Depth of compression (cm)	1-2	3	4-5
Position of compression	centre sternum	centre sternum	4 cm above xiphisternum
Method	2 fingers	1 hand	2 hands
Ventilation (rate per minute)	20	16	12
Head tilt	Nil	Mid	Full

full puffs are given within 10 seconds (Figs. 104.8 and 104.9). EAR is the only method of artificial respiration that successfully ventilates the patient.[11] If the chest does not move easily, obstruction is present. If available a sucker should be used to clear the oropharynx. Firmly fitting dentures should be left in place as they make artificial respiration easier. A resuscitube or Laerdal pocket mask (which should be in the doctor's bag) is ideal for EAR and saves mouth-to-mouth contact.

For optimal airway patency:

1. Clear foreign matter
   - from mouth: use finger sweep
   - from airway: blow between shoulder blades
   - consider a Heimlich manoeuvre
2. Lay patient supine on flat, firm surface (A). Note how the soft tissue of the pharynx can obstruct the airway by falling backwards.

(A)

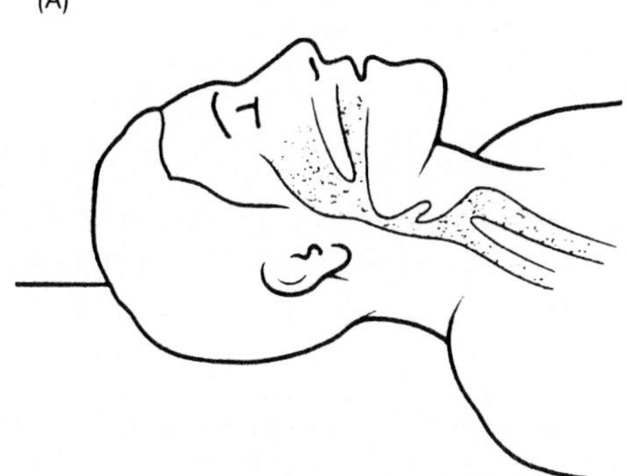

3. In order to overcome this, apply a head tilt (B) plus a chin lift (C) or jaw thrust manoeuvre.
   (*Note*: avoid excessive movement of the neck if spinal injury is suspected, but clearing the airway has first priority.)

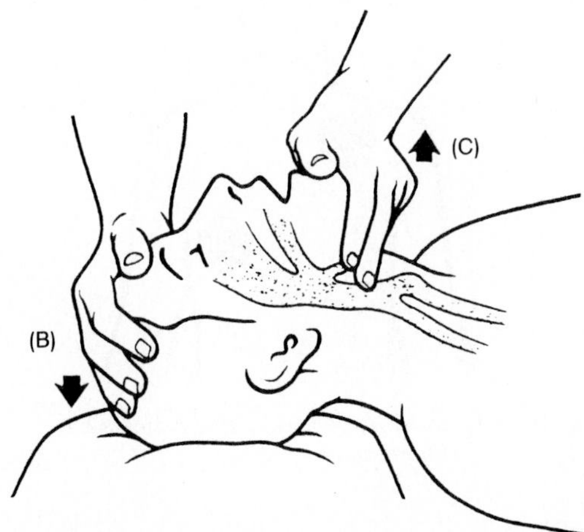

Slight flexion of the neck with small cushion

Fig. 104.8 *Basic life support: A = Airway*

Expired air resuscitation:

1. Five full breaths within 10 seconds.
2. Observe rise of chest, not of abdomen.
3. Look, listen and feel for exhalation.
4. Check the carotid pulse.
5. If no pulse, commence full cardiopulmonary resuscitation.

In a two operator CPR, the person ventilating is best situated on the opposite side of the patient from the person performing chest compression.

Fig. 104.9 *Basic life support: B = Breathing*

External chest compression

Compressions are safely performed by finding the xiphisternal notch then placing the broad heel of one hand over the lower half of the sternum (in adults) with the heel of the second hand placed over the first with the fingers interlocked. Remember to keep the arms and elbows straight as the sternum is rhythmically depressed for 4–5 cm. Try to keep to this position as 'wandering' causes fractured ribs or worse. The fingers must be kept off the chest.

Maintain the compression for 0.5 second, then relax—compressions should be smooth, regular and uninterrupted.

Check pupil size and reaction to light and the carotid or femoral pulse. The compressions should ideally produce an impulse in the femoral pulse. Another person can check for carotid or femoral pulsation during CPR (Fig. 104.10).

Maintenance of CPR

Consider ceasing CPR if there is no improvement in 30 minutes. Exceptions where prolonged CPR can be successful are cold water drowning, marine envenomation, snake bite, and cyanide and organophosphate poisoning.

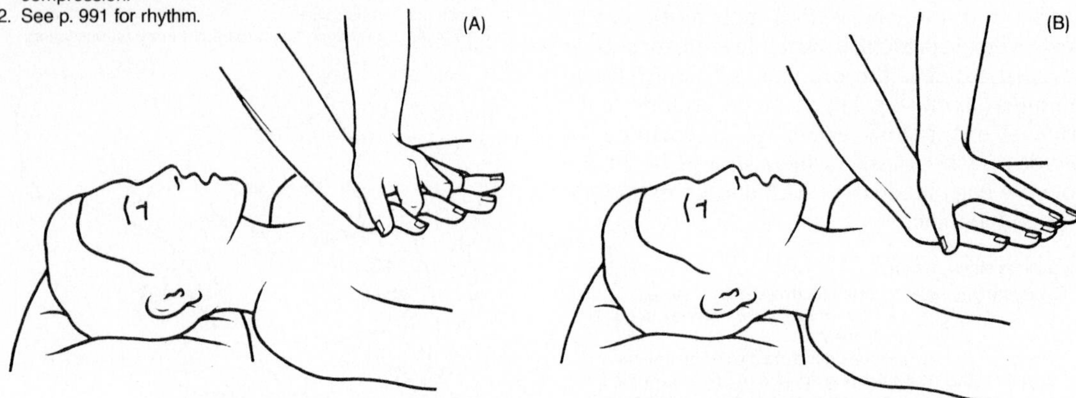

1. If carotid or femoral pulse is weak or absent, immediately commence external cardiac compression.
2. See p. 991 for rhythm.
(A)
(B)

External cardiac compression with fingers locked (A), and with fingers extended (B). Heel of one hand placed on lower sternum 2 finger-breadths above the xiphoid sternal junction. Heel of second hand placed on first. Ensure fingers don't exert pressure. The patient should be lying on a firm surface, the operator level with shoulder.

Fig. 104.10 *Basic life support: C = Circulation*

Note: Ventilation of the patient in the first minutes is the key to success especially if a bag and mask are available to perform this. It must not be neglected during basic or advanced cardiorespiratory life support.

Advanced cardiac life support

Advanced life support depends on the availability of skilled personnel and appropriate equipment. Optimal initial support involves:

- endotracheal intubation (otherwise bag and oxygen)
- ECG monitoring
- intravenous access (large peripheral or central vein)

Optimal initial therapy involves:

- defibrillation
- oxygen
- cardioactive drugs, especially adrenaline

If an ECG recording is unavailable the best course of action is:

- defibrillation
  if unsuccessful
- adrenaline IV

Defibrillation

The ideal defibrillator is an automatic machine, e.g. Heartstart, which automatically delivers regulated shocks, e.g. 200J → 200J → 360J over about 1 minute.

For defibrillation, two paddles should be placed correctly on the chest wall, using one of two positions:

- one to right of upper sternum and the other over the apex of the heart (Fig. 104.11)
- one over anterior wall of chest and the other under tip of left scapula

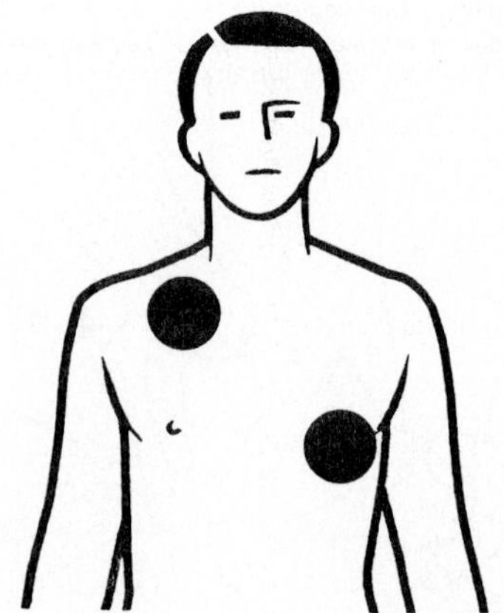

Fig. 104.11 *Standard position of two paddles for defibrillation*

Hairs on the chest should be shaved to accommodate the paddles.

A protocol for advanced cardiac life support is presented in Fig. 104.12.[13]

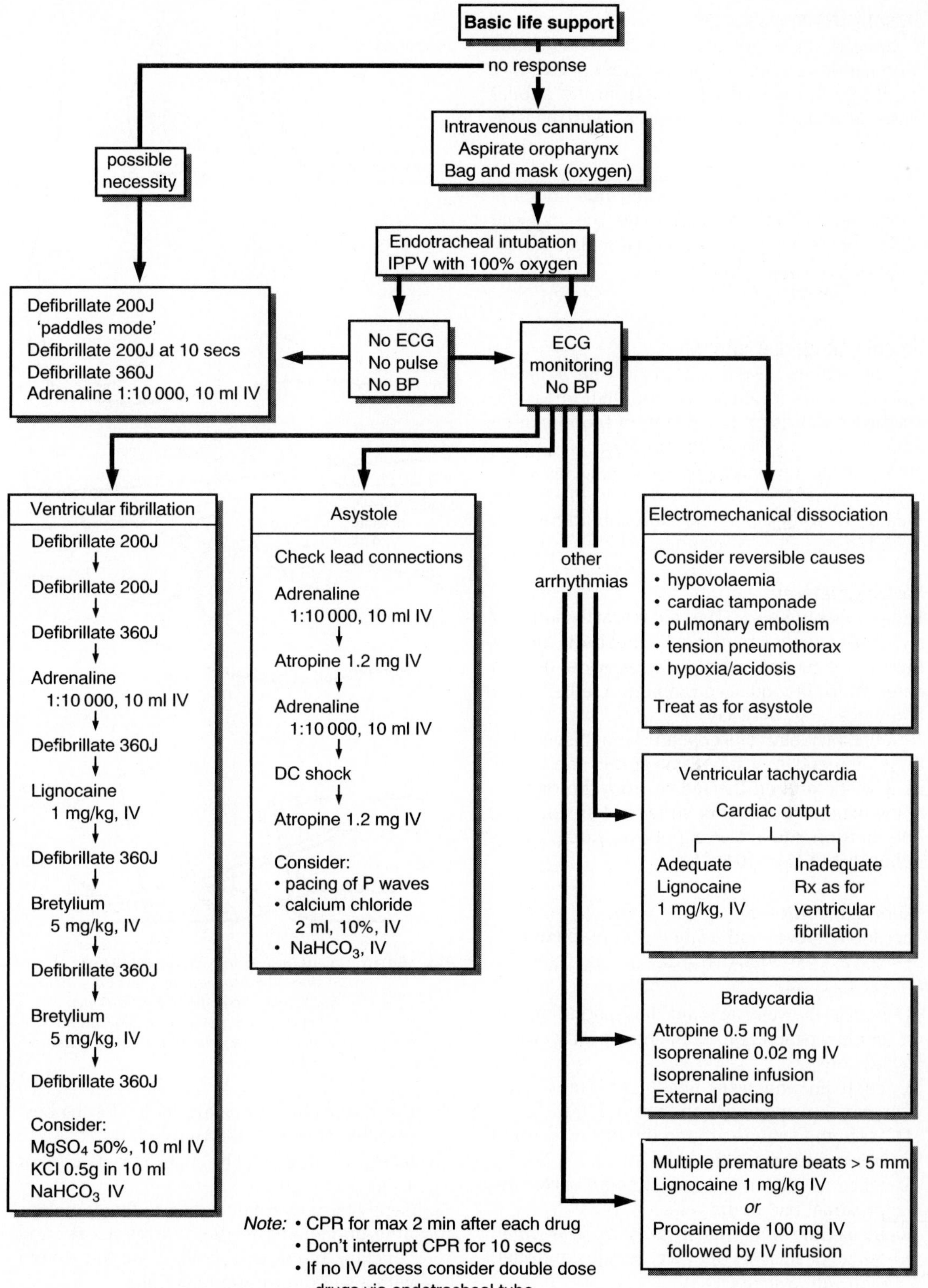

Fig. 104.12 *Protocol for advanced cardiac life support*

Urgent intravenous access

It is preferable to aim for transcutaneous cannulation of veins initially so a peripheral line should be introduced into a vein in the cubital fossa. Several lines may be required with massive blood loss.

Alternative routes:

- central venous cannulation: most doctors should be able to cannulate the external jugular vein with a standard cannula
- peripheral venous cutdown
- interosseous infusion

Urgent intravenous cutdown

In emergencies, especially those due to acute blood loss, transcutaneous cannulation for the infusion of fluids or transfusion of blood can be difficult. For the short-term situation, a surgical cutdown into the long saphenous vein at the ankle or the cephalic vein at the wrist is life-saving. Ideally, the long saphenous vein should be used in children.

Surface anatomy

Long saphenous vein: The vein lies at the anterior tip of the medial malleolus. The best site for incision is centred about 2 cm above and 2 cm anterior to the most prominent medial bony eminence (Fig. 104.13a).

Cephalic vein: The cephalic vein 'bisects' the bony eminences of the distal end of the radius as it winds around the radius from the dorsum of the hand to the anterior surface of the forearm. The incision site is 2–3 cm above the tip of the radial styloid (Fig. 104.13b).

Method of cutdown

After fitting gloves and using a skin preparation:

1. Make a 1.5–2 cm transverse skin incision over the vein.
2. Locate the vein by blunt dissection (do not confuse the vein with the pearly white tendons).
3. Loop an aneurysm needle or fine curved artery forceps under and around the vein.
4. Place the ligature around the distal vein and use this to steady the vein.
5. Place a loose knotted ligature over the proximal end of the vein.
6. Incise the vein transversely with a small lancet or scissors or by a carefully controlled stab with a scalpel.

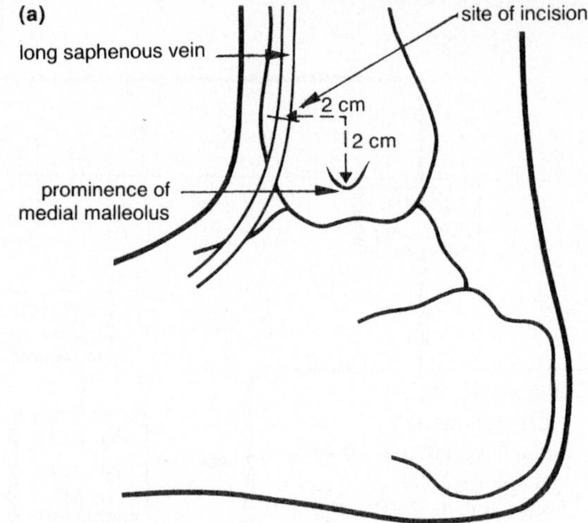

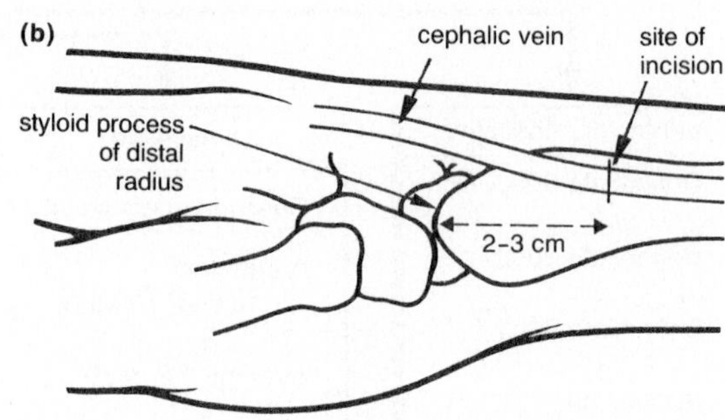

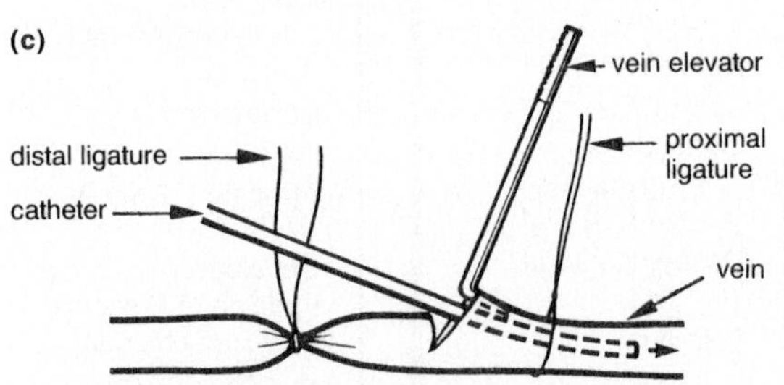

Fig. 104.13 *Urgent intravenous cutdown:* **(a)** *site of incision over long saphenous vein (medial perspective);* **(b)** *site of incision over cephalic vein at wrist (radial or lateral perspective);* **(c)** *method of introduction of catheter into vein*

7. Use a vein elevator (if available) for the best possible access to the vein.
8. Insert a catheter (Fig. 104.13c); use 14 or 16 g.
9. Gently tie the proximal vein to the catheter.
10. After connecting to the intravenous set and checking the flow of fluid, close the wound with a suitable suture material.

Intraosseous infusion

In an emergency situation where intravenous access in a collapsed person (especially children) is difficult, parenteral fluid can be infused into the bone marrow (an intravascular space). Intraosseous infusion is preferred to a cutdown in children under five years. It is useful to practise the technique on a chicken bone.

Site of infusion

- adults and children over 5: distal end of tibia
- children under 5: proximal end of tibia
- the distal femur: 2–3 cm above condyles in mid-line is an alternative

Method for proximal tibia (Fig. 104.14)

Note: Strict asepsis is essential (skin preparation and sterile gloves).

- Inject local anaesthetic (if necessary).
- Choose 16 g intraosseous needle (Dieckmann modification) or a 16–18 g lumbar puncture needle.
- Hold it at right angles to the anteromedial surface of the proximal tibia about 2 cm below the tibial tuberosity (Fig. 104.14). Point the needle slightly downwards, away from the joint space.

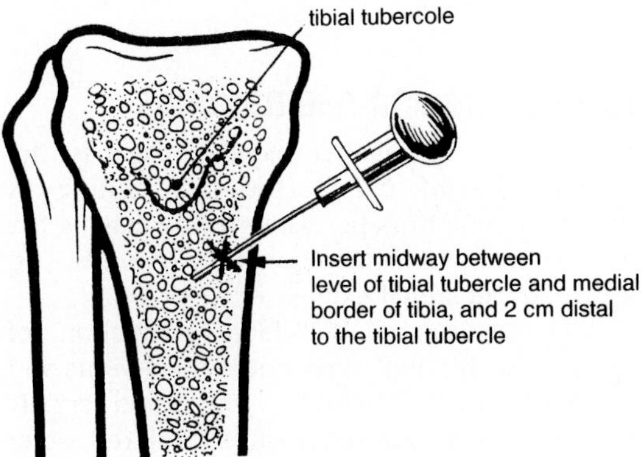
tibial tubercole
Insert midway between level of tibial tubercle and medial border of tibia, and 2 cm distal to the tibial tubercle

Fig. 104.14 *Intraosseous infusion*

- Carefully twist the needle to penetrate the bone cortex; it enters bone marrow with a sensation of giving way.
- Remove the trocar, aspirate a small amount of marrow to ensure its position.
- Hold the needle in place with a small POP splint.
- Fluid can be infused with a normal IV infusion—rapidly or slowly.
- The infusion rate can be markedly increased by using a pressure bag at 300 mmHg pressure.

References

1. Murtagh J. The anatomy of a rural practice. Aust Fam Physician, 1981;10:564–567.
2. Hogan C. The management of emergencies in general practice. Aust Fam Physician, 1989;19:1211–1219.
3. Tibballs J. Endotracheal and intraosseous drug administration for paediatric CPR. Aust Fam Physician, 1992;21:1477–1480.
4. Robinson M. *Practical paediatrics.* Melbourne: Churchill Livingstone, 1990:251–255.
5. Fraser NC. Accidental poisoning deaths in British children 1958–77. Br Med J, 1980;280:1595.
6. Stevenson N. Drug overdose. Aust Fam Physician, 1989;18:1235–1238.
7. Yuen A. Accidental poisoning in children. Patient Management, Nov. 1991,39–45.
8. Sutherland SK. Venomous bites and stings. In: MIMS Disease Index. Sydney: IMS Publishing, 1991–2, 587–591.
9. Walpole BG. Electric shock. Aust Fam Physician, 1989;18:1252–1258.
10. Crocker B, Thomson S. Lightning injuries. Patient Management, Nov. 1991, 51–55.
11. Kumer PJ, Clarke MC. *Clinical ı ıedicine* (2nd edition). London: Bailliere Tindall, 1990:541.
12. Schroeder SA. *Current medical diagnosis and treatment.* East Norwalk: Appleton and Lange, 1990:280.
13. Young S. Cardiopulmonary resuscitation in VMPF. 'Emergency management—in the first hour', Course proceedings, 1991, 8–9.

105

Common skin wounds and foreign bodies

Injuries to the skin, including simple lacerations, abrasions, contusions and foreign bodies, are among the commonest problems encountered in general practice. To manage these cosmetically important injuries well is one of the really basic and enjoyable skills of our profession.

Key guidelines

- A well-prepared treatment room with good sterilisation facilities, instruments, sterile dressings and an assistant facilitates management.
- With lacerations check carefully for nerve damage, tendon damage and arterial damage.
- Beware of slivers of glass in wounds caused by glass—explore carefully and X-ray (especially with high-resolution ultrasound) if in doubt.
- Beware of electrical or thermal wounds because marked tissue necrosis can be hidden by slightly injured skin.
- Beware also of roller injuries such as car wheels.
- Beware of pressure gun injuries such as oil and paint. The consequences can be disastrous.
- Avoid suturing the tongue, and animal and human bites, unless absolutely necessary.
- Keep records of drawings or photographs of wounds in your medical records.
- Have a management plan for puncture wounds, including medical needlestick injuries.
- Gravel rash wounds are a special problem because retained fragments of dirt and metal can leave a 'dirty' tattoo-like effect in the healed wound.

Contusions and haematomas

A contusion (bruise or ecchymosis) is the consequence of injury causing bleeding in subcutaneous or deeper tissue while leaving the skin basically intact. It might take weeks to resolve, especially if extensive.

A haematoma is a large collection of extravasated blood that produces an obvious and tender swelling or deformity. The blood usually clots and becomes firm, warm and red; later (about 10 days) it begins to liquify and becomes fluctuant.

Principles of management

- Explanation and reassurance
- RICE (for larger bruises/haematomas)—48 hours
  R: rest
  I: ice (for 20 minutes every 2 waking hours)
  C: compression (firm elastic bandage)
  E: elevation (if a limb)
- Analgesics: paracetamol/acetaminophen

- Avoid aspiration (some exceptions)
- Avoid massage
- Heat may be applied after 72 hours as local heat or whirlpool baths
- Consider possibility of bleeding disorder if bleeding out of proportion to injury

Problematic haematomas

Some haematoma in certain locations can cause deformity and other problems.

Haematoma of nasal septum[1]

Septal haematoma following injury to the nose can cause total nasal obstruction. It is easily diagnosed as a marked swelling on both sides of the septum when inspected through the nose (Fig. 105.1). It results from haemorrhage between the two sheets of mucoperiosteum covering the septum. It may be associated with a fracture of the nasal septum.

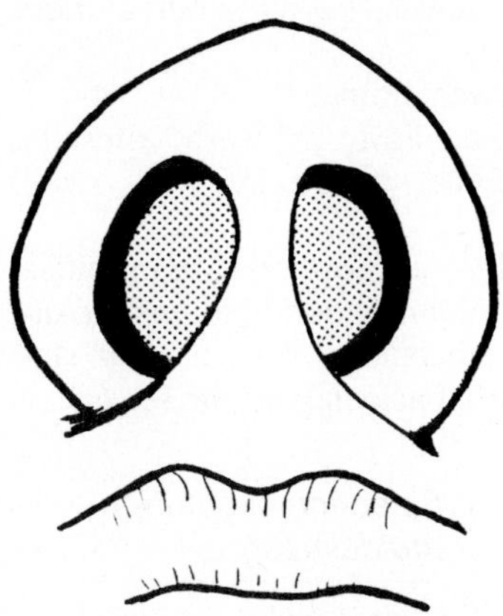

Fig. 105.1 *Inferior view of nasal cavity showing bilateral swelling of septal haematoma*

Note: This is a most serious problem as it can develop into a septal abscess. The infection can pass readily to the orbit or the cavernous sinus through thrombosing veins and may prove fatal, especially in children. Otherwise it may lead to necrosis of nasal septal cartilage followed by collapse and nasal deformity.

Treatment

- Remove blood clot through an incision, under local anaesthetic.
- Prescribe systemic (oral) antibiotics, e.g. penicillin or erythromycin.
- Treat as a compound fracture if X-ray reveals a fracture.

Haematoma of the pinna[1]

When trauma to the pinna causes a haematoma between the epidermis and the cartilage, a permanent deformity known as 'cauliflower ear' may result. The haematoma, if left, becomes organised and the normal contour of the ear is lost.

The aim is to evacuate the haematoma as soon as practical and then to prevent it re-forming. One can achieve a fair degree of success even on haematomas that have been present for several days.

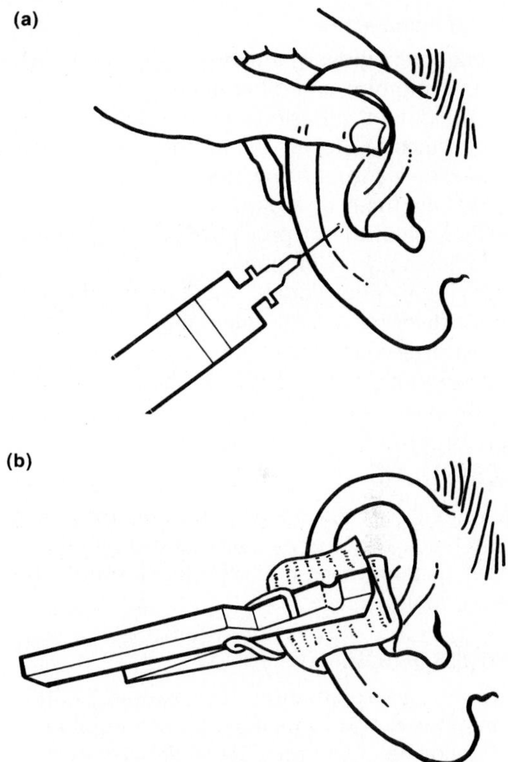

Fig. 105.2 *Treatment of haematoma of the pinna*

Method

Under aseptic conditions insert a 25 g needle into the haematoma at its lowest point and aspirate the extravasated blood (Fig. 105.2a). Apply a padded test tube clamp to the haematoma site and leave on for 30–40 minutes (Fig. 105.2b). Generally, daily aspiration and clamping are sufficient to eradicate the haematoma completely.

Pretibial haematoma

A haematoma over the tibia (shin bone) can be persistently painful and slow to resolve. An efficient method is, under very strict asepsis, to inject 1 ml lignocaine 1% and 1 ml hyaluronidase and follow with immediate ultrasound. This may disperse or require drainage.

Abrasions

Abrasions vary considerably in degree and potential contamination. They are common with bicycle or motorcycle accidents and skateboard accidents. Special care is needed over joints such as the knee or elbow.

Rules of management

- Clean meticulously, remove all ground in dirt, metal, clothing and other material.
- Scrub out dirt with sterile normal saline under anaesthesia (local infiltration or general anaesthesia for deep wounds).
- Treat the injury as a burn.
- When clean apply a protective dressing (some wounds may be left open).
- Use paraffin gauze and non-adhesive absorbent pads such as Melolin.
- Ensure adequate follow-up.
- Immobilise a joint that may be affected by a deep wound.

Lacerations

Lacerations vary enormously in complexity and repairability. Very complex lacerations and those involving nerves or other structures should be referred to an expert.

Principles of repair

- Good approximation of wound edges minimises scar formation and healing time.
- Pay special attention to debridement.
- Avoid deep layers of suture material in a contaminated wound—consider drainage.
- Inspect all wounds carefully for damage to major structures such as nerves and tendons and for foreign material:
  — shattered glass wounds require careful inspection and perhaps X-ray.
  — high energy wounds, e.g. motor mowers, are prone to have metallic foreign bodies and associated fractures.
- Be prepared to readily take X-rays of wounds to look for foreign objects or fractures (compound fractures).
- Trim jagged or crushed wound edges, especially on the face.
- All wounds should be closed in layers.
- Avoid leaving dead space.
- Do not suture an 'old' wound (greater than 8 hours) if it is contaminated with primary closure: leave four days for suturing if not infected.
- Take care in poor healing areas such as backs, necks, calves and knees; and in areas prone to hypertrophic scarring such as over the sternum of the chest and the shoulder.
- Use atraumatic tissue-handling techniques.
- Everted edges heal better than inverted edges.
- Practise minimal handling of wound edges.
- A suture is too tight when it blanches the skin between the thread—it should be loosened.
- Avoid tension on the wound, especially in fingers, lower leg, foot or palm.
- The finest scar and best result is obtained by using a large number of fine sutures rather than a fewer thicker sutures more widely spread.
- Avoid haematoma.
- Apply a firm pressure dressing when appropriate, especially with swollen skin flaps.
- Consider appropriate immobilisation in wounds. Many wound failures are due to lack of immobilisation from a volar slab on the hand or a back slab on the leg.

Table 105.1 *Selection of suture material (guidelines)*

Skin	nylon 6/0 nylon 3/0 nylon 5/0	face back, scalp elsewhere
Deeper tissue (dead space)	catgut 4/0 Dexon/Vicryl 3/0 or 4/0	face elsewhere
Subcuticular	catgut 4/0	
Small vessel ties	plain catgut 4/0	
Large vessel ties	chromic catgut 4/0	

Practical aspects

Suture material (Table 105.1)

- Monofilament nylon sutures are generally preferred for skin repair.
- Use the smallest calibre compatible with required strains.

- The synthetic, absorbable polyglycolic acid or polyglactin sutures (Dexon, Vicryl) are stronger than catgut of the same gauge, but do not use these (use catgut instead) on the face or subcuticularly.

Instruments

Examples of good quality instruments:

- locking needle holder (e.g. Crile-Wood 12 cm)
- skin hooks
- iris scissors

Holding the needle

The needle should be held in its middle; this will help to avoid breakage and distortion, which tend to occur if the needle is held near its end (Fig. 105.3).

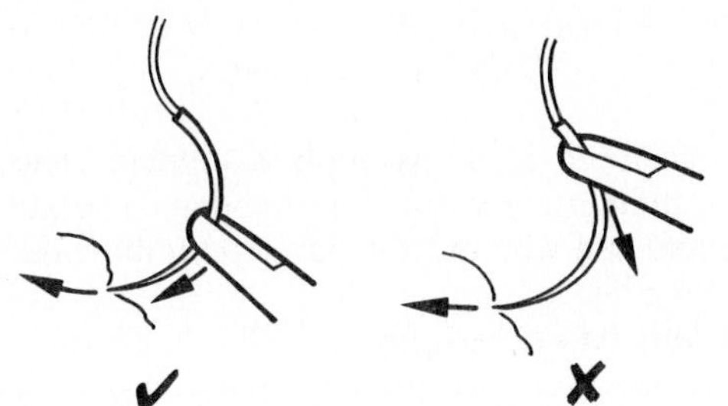

Fig. 105.3 *Correct and incorrect methods of holding the needle*

Dead space

Dead space should be eliminated to reduce tension on skin sutures. Use buried absorbable sutures to approximate underlying tissue. This is done by starting suture insertion from the fat to pick up the fat/dermis interface so as to bury the knot (Fig. 105.4).

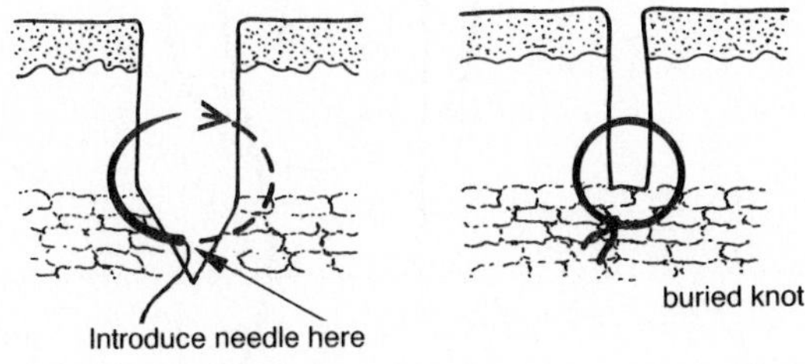

Fig. 105.4 *Eliminating dead space*

Everted wounds

Eversion is achieved by making the 'bite' in the dermis wider than the bite in the epidermis (skin surface) and making the suture deeper than it is wide. Shown are:

- simple suture (Fig. 105.5a)
- vertical mattress suture (Fig. 105.5b)

The mattress suture is the ideal way to evert a wound.

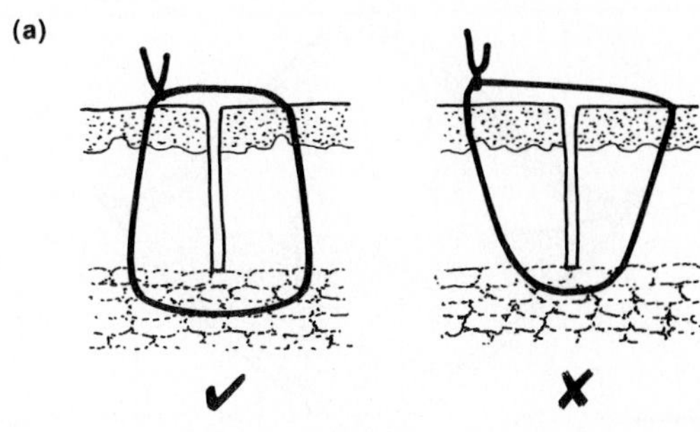

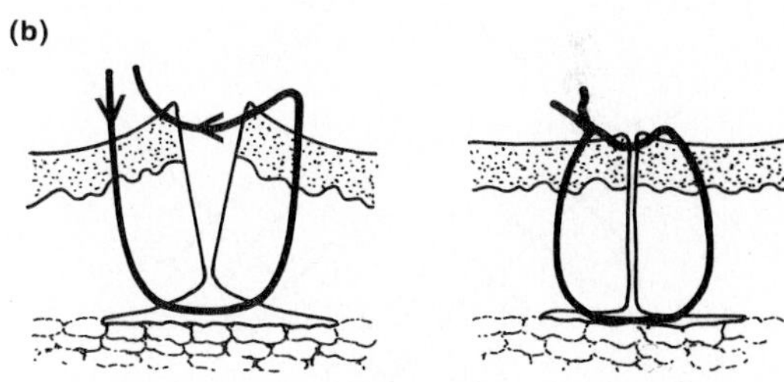

Fig. 105.5 *Everted wounds:* **(a)** *correct and incorrect methods of making a simple suture;* **(b)** *making a vertical mattress suture*

Number of sutures

One should aim to use a minimum number of sutures to achieve closure without gaps but sufficient sutures to avoid tension. Place the sutures as close to the wound edge as possible.

Special techniques for various wounds

The three-point suture

In wounds with a triangular flap component, it is often difficult to place the apex of the flap accurately. The three-point suture is the best way to achieve this while minimising the chance of strangulation necrosis at the tip of the flap.

Method

1. Pass the needle through the skin of the non-flap side of the wound.

2. Pass it then through the subcuticular layer of the flap tip at exactly the same level as the reception side.
3. Finally, pass the needle back through the reception side so that it emerges well back from the V flap (Fig. 105.6).

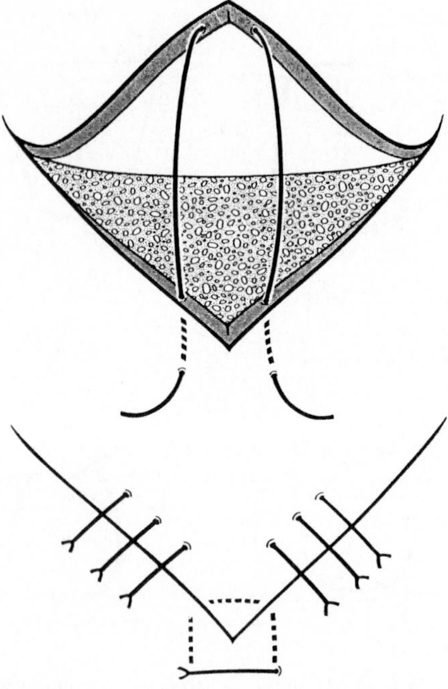

Fig. 105.6 *The three-point suture*

Triangular flap wounds on the lower leg

Triangular flap wounds below the knee are a common injury and are often treated incorrectly. Similar wounds in the upper limb heal rapidly when sutured properly, but lower limb injury will not usually heal at first intention unless the apex of the flap is given special attention.

Proximally based flap

A fall through a gap in flooring boards will produce a proximally based flap; a heavy object (such as the tailboard of a trailer) striking the shin will result in a distally based flap.

Often the apex of the flap is crushed and poorly vascularised; it will not survive to heal after suture.

Treatment methods (under infiltration with LA)

1. Preferred method: To attempt to salvage the distal flap, scrape away the subcutaneous tissue on the flap and use it as a full-thickness graft.
2. An alternative is to excise the apex of the flap, loosely suture the remaining flap and place a small split-thickness graft on the raw area (Fig. 105.7).

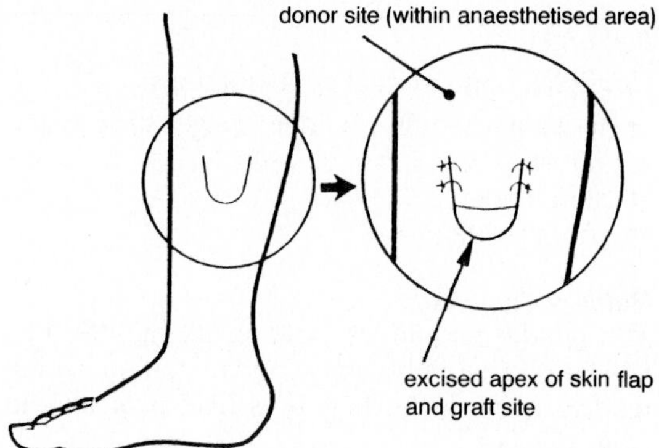

Fig. 105.7 *Triangular flap wound repair: proximally based flap*

For both methods apply a suitable dressing and strap firmly with a crepe bandage. The patient should rest with the leg elevated for three days.

Distally based flap (Fig. 105.8)

This flap, which is quite avascular, has a poorer prognosis. The same methods as for the proximally based flap can be used. Trimming the flap and using it as a full thickness graft has a good chance of repair in a younger person but a poor chance in the elderly.

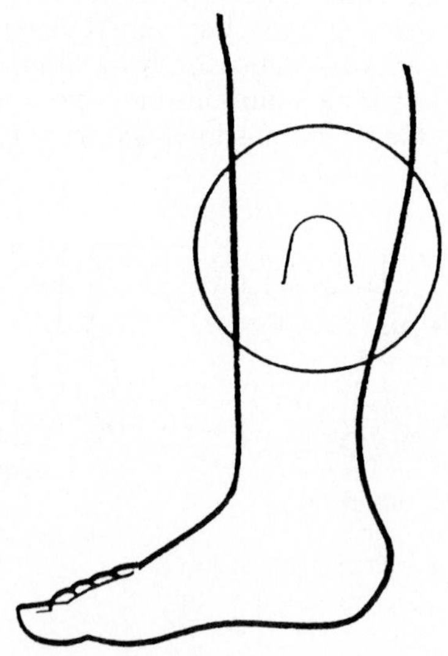

Fig. 105.8 *Triangular flap wound repair: distally based flap*

Repair of cut lip

While small lacerations of the buccal mucosa of the lip can be left safely, more extensive cuts require careful repair. Local anaesthetic infiltration may be adequate, although a mental nerve block is ideal for larger lacerations of the lower lip.

For wounds that cross the vermilion border, meticulous alignment is essential. It may be advisable to premark the vermilion border with gentian violet or a marker pen. It is desirable to have an assistant.

Method

1. Close the deeper muscular layer of the wound using 4/0 CCG. The first suture should carefully appose the mucosal area of the lip, followed by one or two sutures in the remaining layer.
2. Next, insert a 6/0 monofilament nylon suture to bring both ends of the vermilion border together. The slightest step is unacceptable (Fig. 105.9). This is the key to the procedure.
3. Close the inner buccal mucosa with interrupted 4/0 plain catgut sutures.
4. The outer skin of the lip (above and below the vermilion border) is closed with interrupted nylon sutures.

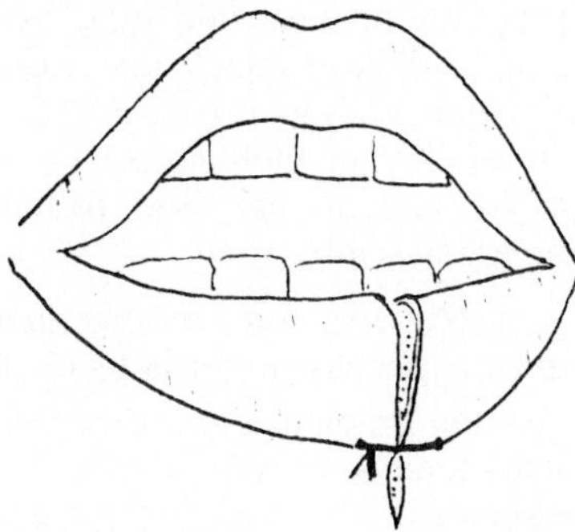

Fig. 105.9 *The lacerated lip: ensuring meticulous suture of the vermilion border*

Post repair

1. Apply a moisturising lotion along the lines of the wound.
2. Remove nylon sutures in 3–4 days (in a young person) and 5–6 days (in an older person).

Repair of lacerated eyelid

General points:

- Preserve as much tissue as possible.
- Do not shave the eyebrow.
- Do not invert hair-bearing skin into the wound.
- Ensure precise alignment of wound margins.
- Tie suture knots away from the eyeball.

Method

1. Place an intermarginal suture behind the eyelashes if the margin is involved.
2. Repair conjunctiva and tarsus with 6/0 catgut.
3. Then repair skin and muscle (orbicularis oculi) with 6/0 nylon (Fig. 105.10).

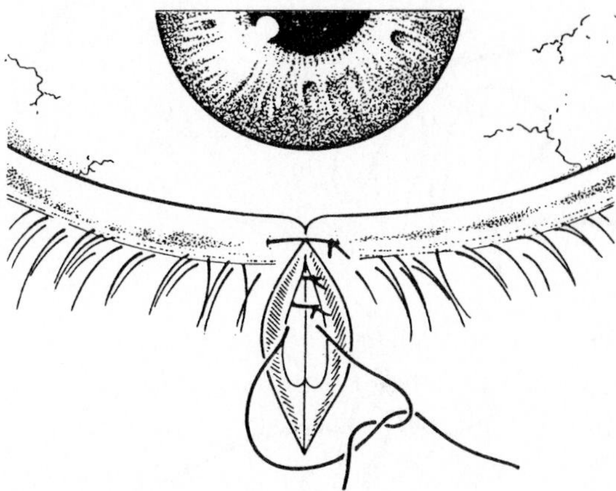

Fig. 105.10 *The lacerated eyelid*

Repair of tongue wound

Wherever possible, it is best to avoid repair to wounds of the tongue because these heal rapidly. However, large flap wounds to the tongue on the dorsum or the lateral border may require suturing. The best method is to use buried catgut sutures.

Method

1. Get patient to suck ice for a few minutes, then infiltrate with 1% lignocaine LA and leave 5–10 minutes.
2. Use 4/0 or 3/0 catgut sutures to suture the flap to its bed, and bury the sutures (Fig. 105.11).

It should not be necessary to use surface sutures. If it is, 4/0 silk sutures will suffice.

The patient should be instructed to rinse the mouth regularly with salt water until healing is satisfactory.

The amputated finger

In this emergency situation, instruct the patient to place the severed finger directly into a fluid tight sterile container, such as a plastic bag or sterile specimen jar. Then place this 'unit' in a bag containing iced water with crushed ice.

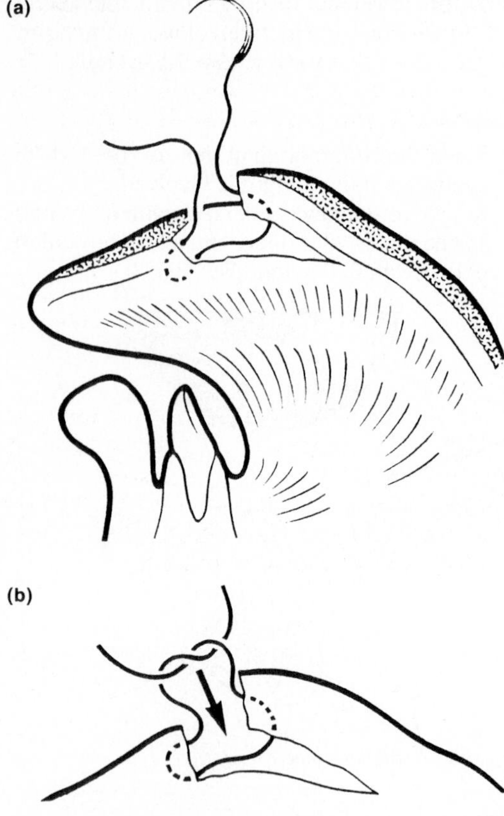

Fig. 105.11 *Repair of tongue wound*

Note: Never place the amputated finger directly in ice or in fluid such as saline. Fluid makes the tissue soggy, rendering microsurgical repair difficult.

Care of the finger stump

Apply a simple, sterile, loose, non-sticky dressing and keep the hand elevated.

Bite wounds

Human bites

Human bites can present a serious problem of infection. Anaerobic organisms in the oral cavity, e.g. Vincent's, can penetrate the damaged tissue and form a deep-seated infection. Streptococcal organisms are a common pathogen. Complications of the infected wounds include cellulitis, wound abscess and lymphangitis.

Principles of treatment

- Clean and debride the wound carefully, e.g. aqueous antiseptic solution or hydrogen peroxide.
- Give prophylactic penicillin if a severe or deep bite.
- Avoid suturing if possible.
- Tetanus toxoid (although minimum risk).
- Consider rare possibility of HIV and hepatitis B,C or D infections.
- If infected give procaine penicillin IM and Augmentin.

Dog bites

1. Non-rabid

Dog bites typically have poor healing and carry a risk of infection with anaerobic organisms, including tetanus, staphylococci and streptococci. Puncture wounds are more prone to infection than laceration.

Principles of treatment

- Clean and debride the wound with aqueous antiseptic, allowing it to soak for 10–20 minutes.
- Aim for open healing—avoid suturing if possible (except in 'privileged' sites with an excellent blood supply such as the face and scalp).
- Apply non-adherent, absorbent dressings (paraffin gauze and Melolin) to absorb the discharge from the wound.
- Tetanus prophylaxis: immunoglobulin or tetanus toxoid.
- Give prophylactic penicillin for a severe or deep bite: 1.5 million units procaine penicillin IM statim then orally for five days. Tetracycline or flucloxacillin are alternatives.
- Inform the patient that slow healing and scarring are possible.

Rabid or possibly rabid dog (or other animal)

(not currently applicable in Australia)

- wash the site immediately with detergent or hydrogen peroxide or soap
- do not suture
- if rabid: human rabies immune globin (passive)
antirabies vaccine (active)
- uncertain: capture and observe animal
consider vaccination

Cat bites

Cat bites can have the most potential for suppurative infection. The same principles apply as for the management of human or dog bites, but use flucloxacillin. It is important to clean a deep and penetrating wound. Another problem is cat-scratch disease, presumably caused by a Gram-negative bacterium.

Clinical features of cat-scratch disease

- an infected ulcer or papule pustule at bite site (30% of cases) after three days or so[2]
- 1–3 weeks later: fever, headache, malaise regional lymphadenopathy (may suppurate)
- intradermal skin test positive
- benign self-limiting course
- sometimes severe symptoms for weeks

Scalp lacerations in children

If lacerations are small but gaping use the child's hair for the suture, providing it is long enough.

Method

Make a twisted bunch of the child's own hair on each side of the wound. Tie a reef knot and then an extra holding knot to minimise slipping. Ask an assistant to drop compound benzoin tincture solution (Friar's balsam) on the hair knot. Leave the hair suture long and get the parent to cut the knot in five days.

Forehead and other lacerations in children

Despite the temptation, avoid using reinforced paper adhesive strips (Steri-strips) for children with open wounds. They will merely close the dermis and cause a thin, stretched scar. They can be used only for very superficial epidermal wounds in conjunction with sutures.

Adhesive glue for wound adhesion

A tissue adhesive glue can be used successfully to close superficial smooth and clean skin wounds, particularly in children. A commercial preparation Histoacryl (active ingredient enbucrilate) is available, but Superglue also serves the purpose. The glue should be used only for superficial, dry, clean and fresh wounds. No gaps are permissible with this method.

Wound anaesthesia in children

New topical preparations which provide surface anaesthesia are being used for wound repair in children. They include lignocaine and prilocaine mixture (EMLA cream) and tetracaine, adrenaline and cocaine (TAC) liquid.

Removal of skin sutures

Suture marks are related to the time of retention of the suture, its tension and position. The objective is to remove the sutures as early as possible, as soon as their purpose is achieved. The timing of removal is based on common sense and individual cases. Nylon sutures are less reactive and can be left for longer periods. After suture removal it is advisable to support the wound with micropore skin tape (e.g. Steri-strips) for 1–2 weeks, especially in areas of skin tension.

Method

1. Use good light and have the patient lying comfortably.
2. Use fine, sharp scissors which cut to the point or the tip of a scalpel blade, and a pair of fine, non-toothed dissecting forceps that grip firmly.
3. Cut the suture close to the skin below the knot with scissors or a scalpel tip (Fig. 105.12a).
4. Gently pull the suture out towards the side on which it was divided—that is, *always towards the wound* (Fig. 105.12b).

(a)

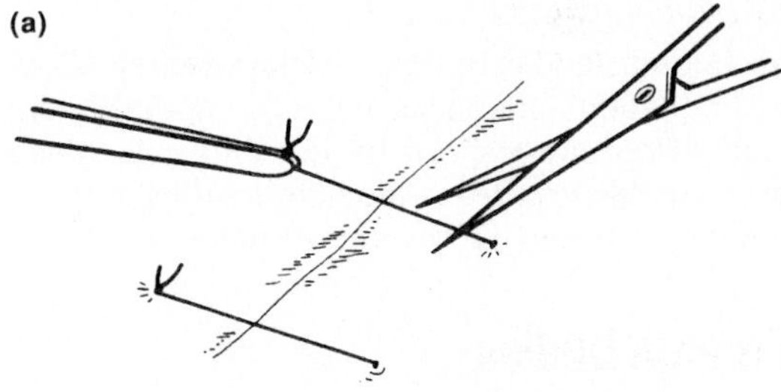

(b)

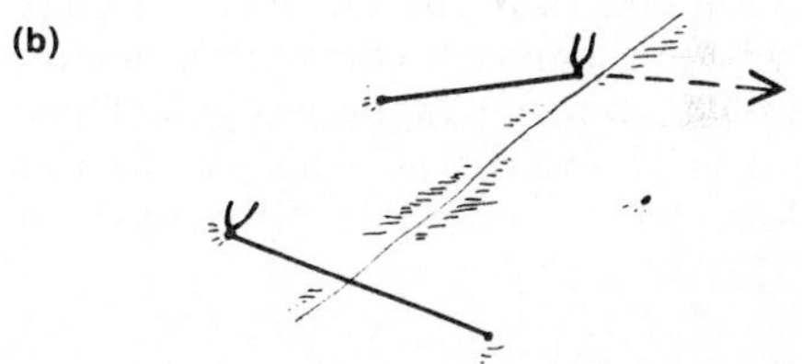

Fig. 105.12 *Removal of skin sutures:* **(a)** *cutting the suture;* **(b)** *removal by pulling towards wound*

When to remove non-absorbable sutures

For removal of sutures after non-complicated wound closure in adults, see Table 105.2. *Note*: Decisions need to be individualised according to the nature of the wound and health of the patient and healing. In general take sutures out as soon as possible. One way of achieving this is to remove alternate sutures a day or two earlier and remove the rest at the usual time. Steri-strips can then be used to maintain closure and healing.

Table 105.2 *Time after insertion for removal of sutures*

Area	Days later
Scalp	6
Face	3 (or alternate at 2, rest 3–4)
Ear	5
Neck	4 (or alternate at 3, rest 4)
Chest	8
Arm (including hand and fingers)	8–10
Abdomen	8–10 (tension 12–14)
Back	12
Inguinal and scrotal	7
Perineum	2
Legs	10
Knees and calf	12
Foot (including toes)	10–12

Additional aspects

In children, tend to remove 1–2 days earlier. Allow additional time for backs and legs, especially the calf. Nylon sutures can be left longer because they are less reactive. Alternate sutures may be removed earlier (e.g. face in women).

Foreign bodies

Penetrating gun injuries

Injuries to the body from various types of guns present decision dilemmas for the treating doctor. The following information represents guidelines, including special sources of danger to tissues from various foreign materials discharged by guns.

Gunshot wounds

Airgun

The rule is to remove subcutaneous slugs but to leave deeper slugs unless they lie within and around vital structures (e.g. the wrist). A special common problem is that of slugs in the orbit. These often do little damage and can be left alone, but referral to an ophthalmologist would be appropriate.

0.22 rifle (the pea rifle)

The same principles of management apply but the bullet must be localised precisely by X-ray. Of particular interest are abdominal wounds, which should be observed carefully, as visceral perforations can occur with minimal initial symptoms and signs.

0.410 shotgun

The pellets from this shotgun are usually only dangerous when penetrating from a close range. Again, the rule is not to remove deep-lying pellets—perhaps only those superficial pellets that can be palpated.

Pressure gun injuries

Injection of grease, oil, paint and similar substances from pressure guns (Fig. 105.13) can cause very serious injuries, requiring decompression and removal of the substances.

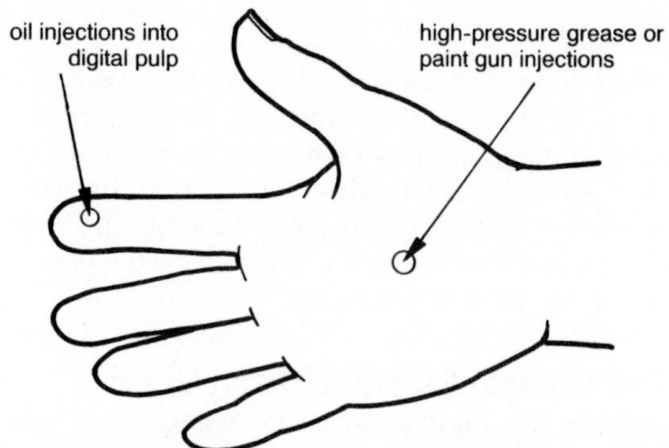

Fig. 105.13 *Dangerous accidental injections into the hand*

Grease gun and paint gun

High pressure injection of paint or grease into the hand requires urgent surgery if amputation is to be avoided. There is a deceptively minor wound to show for this injury, and after a while the hand feels comfortable. However, ischaemia,[1] chemical irritation and infection can follow, with gangrene of the digits, resulting in, at best, a claw hand due to sclerosis. Treatment is by immediate decompression and meticulous removal of all foreign material and necrotic tissue.

Oil injection

Accidental injection of an inoculum in an oily vehicle into the hand also creates a serious problem with local tissue necrosis. If injected into the digital pulp, this may necessitate amputation. Such injections are common on poultry farms, where many fowl-pest injections are administered.

Splinters under the skin

The splinter under the skin is a common and difficult procedural problem. Instead of using forceps or making a wider excision, use a disposable hypodermic needle to 'spear' the splinter (Fig. 105.14) and then use it as a lever to ease the splinter out through the skin.

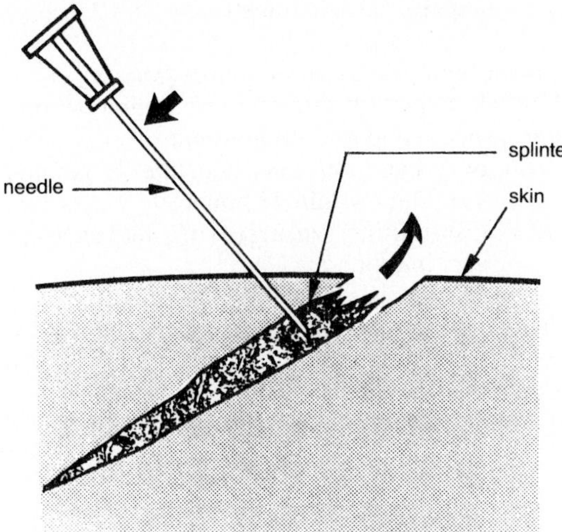

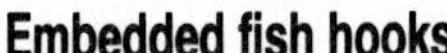

Fig. 105.14 *Removal of splinters in the skin*

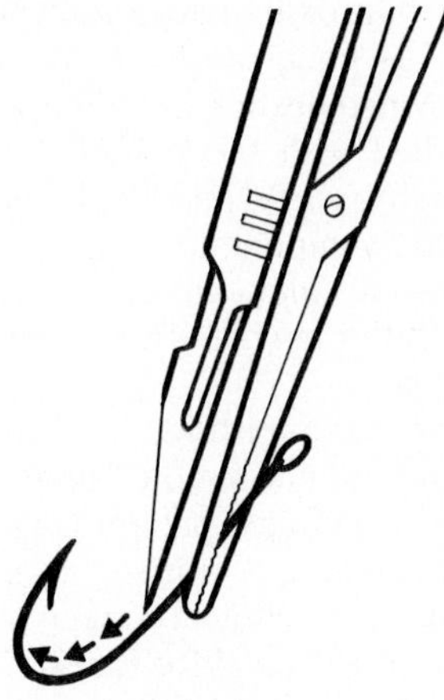

Fig. 105.15 *Removal of fish hooks by cutting a path in the skin*

Embedded fish hooks

Two methods of removing fish hooks are presented here, both requiring removal in the reverse direction, against the barb. Method 2 is recommended as first-line management.

Method 1

1. Inject 1–2 ml of LA around the fish hook.
2. Grasp the shank of the hook with strong artery forceps.
3. Slide a D11 scalpel blade in along the hook, sharp edge away from the hook, to cut the tissue and free the barb (Fig. 105.15)
4. Withdraw the hook with the forceps.

Method 2

This method, used by some fishermen, relies on a loop of cord or fishing line to forcibly disengage and extract the hook intact. It requires no anaesthesia and no instruments—only nerves of steel, especially for the first attempt.

1. Take a piece of string about 10–12 cm long and make a loop. One end slips around the hook, the other hooking around one finger of the operator.
2. Depress the shank with the other hand in the direction that tends to disengage the barb.
3. At this point give a very swift, sharp tug along the cord.
4. The hook flies out painlessly in the direction of the tug (Fig. 105.16).

Note: You must be bold, decisive, confident and quick—half-hearted attempts do not work.

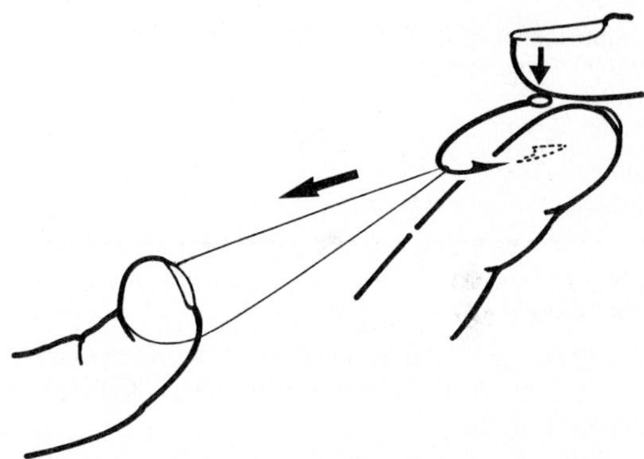

Fig. 105.16 *Fisherman's method of removing a fish hook intact*

For difficult cases, some local anaesthetic infiltration may be appropriate. Instead of a short loop of cord, a long piece of fishing line double looped around the hook and tugged by the hand, or flicked with a thin ruler in the loop, will work.

Needlesticks and sharps injuries

Accidental skin puncture by contaminated 'sharps', including needles (with blood or blood-stained body fluids), is of great concern to all health care workers. Another problem that occurs occasionally is the deliberate inoculation of some people such as police from angry sociopathic individuals. A needlestick accident is the commonest incident with the potential to transmit infections such as HIV and hepatitis B,C or D. The part of the venipuncture that is most likely to cause the accident is the recapping or resheathing of the needle. This practice should be discouraged.

Infections transmitted by needlestick accidents are summarised in Table 105.3. The risk from a contaminated patient is greatest with hepatitis (10–30%), while the risk of seroconversion or clinical infection after a needlestick with HIV positive blood[3] is very low (probably about 1 in 300–1000).

Table 105.3 *Infections transmitted by needlestick accidents*

Viruses
Human immunodeficiency virus (HIV)
Hepatitis B,C,D
Herpes simplex
Herpes varicella-zoster
Bacteria
Streptococcal infections
Staphylococcal infections
Syphilis
Tuberculosis
Other
Malaria

Prevention

- Avoid physically struggling with overdose victims or high-risk patients for lavage or venipuncture.
- Needles should not be recapped.
- Dispose of needles immediately and directly into a leakproof, puncture-proof sharps container.
- Avoid contact with blood.
- Wear protective gloves (does not prevent sharps injury).

Management

- Squeeze out and wash under running tap water with soap and/or dilute sodium hypochlorite solution, e.g. Milton.
- Encourage bleeding.
- Obtain information about and blood from the sharps victim and the source person (source of body fluid). A known carrier of hepatitis B surface antigen or an HIV-positive source person will facilitate early decision making.

Note: It takes three months to seroconvert with HIV so the patient may be infected but negative on initial tests.

Known hepatitis B carrier source person

If injured person immune — no further action

If non-vaccinated and non-immune

— give hyperimmune hepatitis B gamma-globulin (within 48 hours)

— commence course of hepatitis B vaccination

Known HIV-positive source person

Refer to consultant about relative merits of drug prophylaxis and serological monitoring.

Options

zidovudine (AZT) prophylaxis within 72 hours

300 mg qid for 6 weeks

or

serological monitoring 0,4,6,12,24 and 52 weeks[4]

Unknown risk source person

Take source person's blood (if consent is given) and sharps victim blood for hepatitis B (HBsAg and anti-HBs) and (if high risk for HIV) HIV status tests. Commence hepatitis B vaccination if not vaccinated.

Note: Informed consent for testing and disclosure of test results for involved person should be obtained.

Tetanus prophylaxis

Tetanus is a very serious disease but completely preventable by active immunisation. It should be universal, especially if the childhood immunisation program is followed. However, all patients with wounds should be assessed for their tetanus status and managed on their merits. For severe wounds the possibility of gas gangrene should also be considered.

For the primary immunisation of adults, tetanus toxoid (singly or combined with diphtheria if primary childhood course not given) is given as two doses six weeks apart with a third dose six months later. Booster doses of tetanus toxoid are given every ten years or at the time of major injury occurring five years after previous dose.

Table 105.4 *Guide to tetanus prophylaxis in wound management*

	Clean, minor wounds		*All other wounds*	
History of active tetanus immunisation	***Tetanus toxoid[1]***	***Tetanus immune globulin***	***Tetanus toxoid[1]***	***Tetanus immune globulin***
Uncertain, or less than 3 doses	yes	no	yes	yes
3 doses or more	no[2]	no	no[3]	no[4]

1. Adult or child 8 years and over—use tetanus toxoid or ADT. Child 7 years or less, use tetanus toxoid or CDT or DTP (if due, on routine immunisation schedule.
2. Yes, if more than 10 years since last dose.
3. Yes, if more than 5 years since last dose.
4. Yes, if more than 10 years since last dose and tetanus-prone wound.

Passive immunisation

Passive immunisation, in the form of tetanus immune globulin 250 units by IM injection, is reserved for non-immunised individuals or those of uncertain immunity wherever the wound is contaminated or has devitalised tissue. Wounds at risk include those contaminated with dirt, faeces/manure, soil, saliva and other foreign material; puncture wounds; wounds from missiles, crushes and burns.

The guide is outlined in Table 105.4.

- Give tetanus immune globulin if patient is not immunised or if wound is grossly contaminated.
- Never send a patient home before thoroughly washing their hair and carefully examining for other lacerations.
- Any laceration in the cheek, mandible or lower eyelid may damage the facial nerve, parotid duct or lacrimal duct respectively.
- When a patient falls onto glass it takes bone to halt its cutting path. Assume all structures between skin and bone are severed.

Practice tips

- Have the patient lying down for suturing and parents of children sitting down.
- Avoid using antibiotic sprays and powders in simple wounds—resistant organisms can develop.
- Consider tetanus and gas gangrene prophylaxis in contaminated and deep necrotic wounds.
- Give a tetanus booster if patient has not had one within five years for dirty wounds or within ten years with clean wounds.

References

1. Hansen G. *Practice tips.* Aust Fam Physician, 1982; 11:867.
2. Schroeder SA et al. *Current medical diagnosis and treatment.* East Norwalk: Appleton and Lange, 1990, 957.
3. Spelman D. Transmission of infection by needlesticks, sharps and splashes. Aust Fam Physician, 1988;17:681.
4. Hammond L. AIDS and hepatitis B protection strategies. Aust Fam Physician, 1990;19:657–661.

106

Common fractures and dislocations

—

Common fractures and dislocations usually apply to the limbs and the shoulder girdle, and their management requires an early diagnosis to ensure optimum treatment and to prevent irretrievable bad results. Early diagnosis depends on the physician being vigilant and on having knowledge of the less common conditions so that a careful search for the diagnosis can be made.

The diagnosis is dependent on a good history followed by a careful examination, good-quality routine X-rays and, if necessary, special investigations. The golden rule is: if in doubt—X-ray. The family doctor should develop the habit of looking at a patient's X-rays. Such a back-up to the radiologist's report can help avoid many embarrassing missed diagnoses.

There are many pitfalls involved in managing fractures and dislocations. Many injuries such as fractures of the arm and hand seem trivial but they can lead to long-term disability. This chapter presents guidelines to help avoid these pitfalls.

General guidelines

- A fracture usually causes deformity but may cause nothing more than local tenderness over the bone.
- The classic signs of fracture are:
  — pain
  — tenderness
  — loss of function
  — deformity
  — swelling/bruising
  — crepitus
- X-ray examination of the affected area of the upper limb should include views of joints proximal or distal to the site of the injury.
- If an X-ray is reported as normal but a fracture is strongly suspected, an option is to splint the affected limb for about ten days and then repeat the X-ray.
- As a rule, displaced fractures must be reduced whereby bone ends should be placed in proper alignment and then immobilised until union occurs.
- Clinical union is the absence of pain on movement at the fracture site.
- Bony union is the presence of trabeculae crossing the fracture site on X-ray.
- Non-union is caused by factors such as inadequate fixation, excessive distraction, loss of healing callus, infection or avascular necrosis.
- Stiffness of joints is a common problem with immobilisation in plaster casts, so the joints must be moved as early as possible. Early use is possible if the fracture is stable.
- A stress fracture is an incomplete fracture resulting from repeated small episodes of trauma, which individually would be insufficient to damage the bone. Stress

fractures, especially in the foot, are most likely to result from sport, ballet, gymnastics and aerobics. Their incidence rises sharply at times of increased activity.[1]

- A dislocation is a complete dislocation of one bone relative to another at a joint.
- A subluxation is a partial displacement such that the joint surfaces are still in partial contact.
- A sprain is a partial disruption of a ligament or capsule of a joint.
- Always consider associated soft-tissue injuries such as neuropraxia to adjacent nerves, caused by bleeding.

Testing for fractures[2]

This method describes the simple principle of applying axial compression for the clinical diagnosis of fractures of bones of the forearm and hand, but also applies to bones of the limbs.

Many fractures are obvious when applying the classic methods of diagnosis but it is sometimes more difficult if there is associated soft-tissue injury from a blow or if there is only a minor fracture such as a greenstick fracture of the distal radius.

If the bone is compressed gently from end to end, a fracture will reveal itself and the patient will feel pain. A soft-tissue injury of the forearm will show pain, tenderness, swelling and possibly loss of function. It will, however, not be painful if the bone is compressed axially—that is, in its long axis.

Walking is another method of applying axial compression, and this is very difficult (because of pain) in the presence of a fracture in the weight-bearing axis or pelvis. Hence, every patient with a suspected fracture of the lower limb should be tested by walking.

Method

1. Grasp the affected area both distally and proximally with your hands.
2. Compress along the long axis of the bones by pushing in both directions, so that the forces focus on the affected area (fracture site; Fig. 106.1a). Alternatively, compression can be applied from the distal end with stabilising counterpressure applied proximally (Fig. 106.1b).
3. The patient will accurately localise the pain at the fracture site.

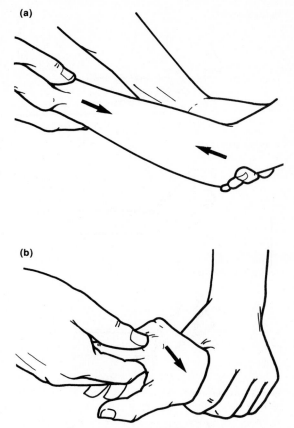

(a)

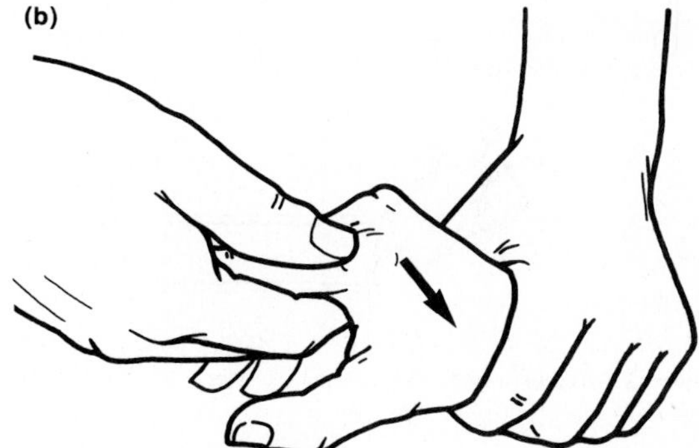

Fig. 106.1 *Testing for fractures:* **(a)** *axial compression to detect a fracture of the radius or ulna bones;* **(b)** *axial compression to detect a fracture of the metacarpal*

Principles of treatment of limb fractures

To reduce any fracture properly, the following steps must be undertaken (Fig. 106.2a).[3]

1. Disimpact the fragments, usually by increasing the deformity.
2. Re-establish the correct length of the bone.
3. Re-establish the correct alignment by proper reduction of the fracture.

Adequate anaesthesia, analgesia and relaxation are important. Maintenance of the reduction depends upon the moulding which utilises the intact periosteal bridge to hold the fracture fragments in a reduced position. Figure 106.2b illustrates the principle of moulding to maintain reduction.[3]

fracture (impacted)

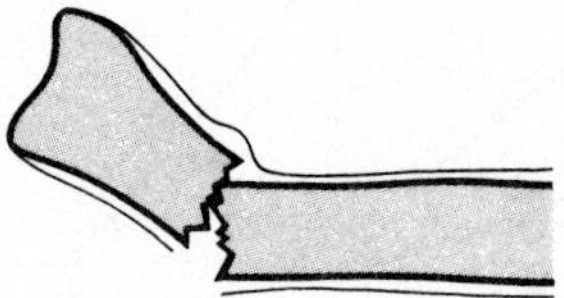

Step 1. Disimpaction

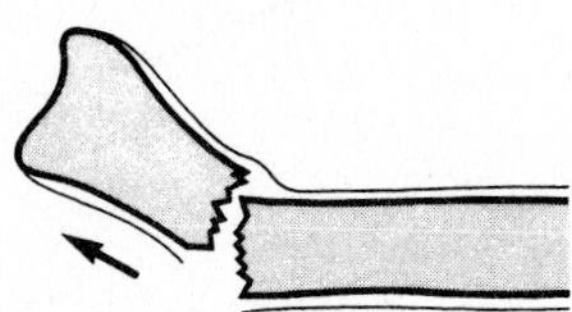

Step 2. Establish length

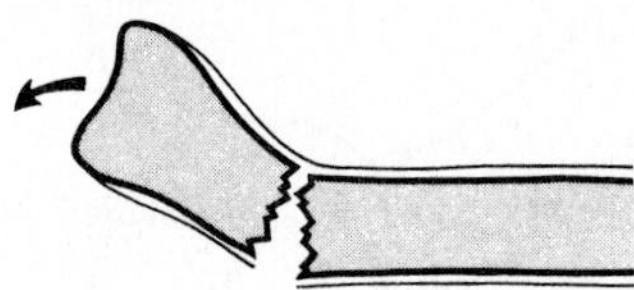

Step 3. Establish alignment

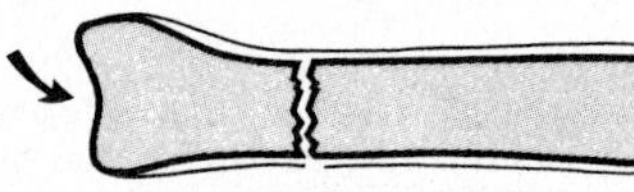

Fig. 106.2a *Principles of reduction of fractured bones*

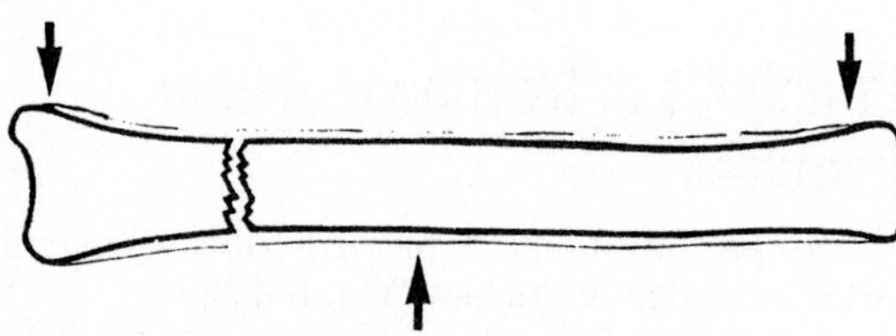

Fig. 106.2b *Principles of moulding to maintain reduction: the arrows indicate three point pressure areas required to maintain reduction*

Fractures and dislocations of the face and skull

Skull fractures

Closed fractures without any neurological symptoms do not require active intervention. Depressed fractures may require elevation of the depressed fragment. Compound fractures of the vault require careful evaluation and referral. Special care is required over the midline as manipulation (usually by elevation) of any depressed fragment can tear the sagittal sinus, causing profuse and fatal bleeding.[4]

Base of skull fractures

These fractures are difficult to diagnose on radiography but their presence is indicated by bleeding from the nose, throat or ears. CSF may be observed escaping, especially through the nose, if the dura is also torn.

Treatment of basal fractures is based on prevention of intracranial infection and avoidance of excessive interference with the nose or ear, such as with packing and nasogastric tubes. An appropriate antibiotic is cotrimoxazole.[4]

'Malar' fracture

A fractured zygomaticomaxillary complex (malar) is a common body contact sports injury or injury resulting from a fight.

Clinical features:

- swelling of cheek
- circumocular haematoma
- subconjunctival haemorrhage
- palpable step in infraorbital margin
- flat malar eminence when viewed from above
- paraesthesia due to infraorbital nerve injury
- loss of function, i.e. difficulty opening mouth

Management

- head injury assessment
- exclude 'blowout' facture of the orbit
- exclude ocular trauma
  - — remove contact lenses if worn
  - — check visual acuity
  - — check for diplopia
  - — check for hyphaema
  - — check for retinal haemorrhage
- persuade patient not to blow nose (can cause surgical emphysema)
- if fracture displaced, refer for reduction under GA

Reduction methods

- elevation by temporal or intraoral approach—healing can be expected in 3–4 weeks
- some require interosseous wiring or plating or pinning

Fracture of mandible

A fracture of the mandible follows a blow to the jaw. The patient may have swelling (which can vary from virtually none to severe), pain, deformity, inability to chew, malalignment of the jaw and teeth and drooling of saliva. Intraoral examination is important as submucosal ecchymosis in the floor of the mouth is a pathognomonic sign.

A simple office test for a suspected fractured mandible is to ask patients to bite on a wooden tongue depressor (or similar firm object). Ask them to maintain the bite as you twist the spatula. If they have a fracture they cannot hang onto the spatula because of pain.[5]

X-rays: AP views and lateral obliques
an orthopantomogram provides a global view

First aid management

- check the patient's bite and airway
- remove any free-floating tooth fragments and retain them
- replace any avulsed or subluxed teeth in their sockets
  NB Never discard teeth.
- first aid immobilisation with a four-tailed bandage (Fig. 106.3)

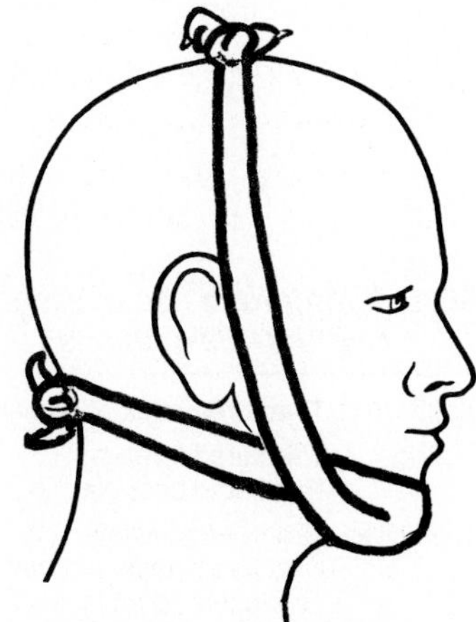

Fig. 106.3 *Immobilisation of a fractured mandible in a four-tailed bandage*

Treatment

Refer for possible internal fixation.

A fracture of the body of the mandible will usually heal in 6–12 weeks (depending on the nature of the fracture and fitness of the patient).

Dislocated jaw

The patient may present with unilateral or bilateral dislocation. The jaw will be 'locked' and the patient unable to articulate or close the mouth.

Method of reduction

- Get the patient to sit upright with the head against the wall.
- Wrap a handkerchief around both thumbs and place the thumbs over the lower molar teeth, with the fingers firmly grasping the mandible on the outside.
- Firmly thrusting with the thumbs, push downwards towards the floor.

This action invariably reduces the dislocation, but the reduction can be reinforced by the fingers rotating the mandible upward as the thumbs thrust downwards.

Fractured vertebrae/spinal column

Cervical fractures, especially atlas (C1), axis (C2) and odontoid process, require early referral with the neck immobilised in a cervical collar.

Thoracolumbar fractures

Fractures or fracture dislocations of the thoracic and lumbar vertebrae, without neurological deficit, are classified as either stable or unstable.

Stable fractures

- compression fractures of vertebral body with $< 50\%$ loss of vertical height
- minor fractures
- laminar fractures

Treatment: rest on firm-to-hard bed for 10–28 days depending on symptoms, followed by a brace.

Special problems:

- retroperitoneal haematoma
- paralytic ileus
- associated kidney rupture with L_1 fractures

Unstable fractures

Burst fractures and shearing fractures are usually unstable. They are often associated with partial or complete paraplegia and require referral.

Fractures of sacrum and coccyx

No treatment apart from symptomatic treatment is required. Manual reduction per rectum can be attempted for significant forward displacement of the coccyx. Advise the use of a rubber ring or special cushion (such as a Sorbo cushion) when sitting. Excision of the coccyx may be considered for persistent discomfort.

Fractured rib

Features:

- pain over the fracture site especially with deep inspiration and coughing
- localised tenderness and swelling
- pain in the site upon whole chest compression
- X-ray confirms diagnosis and excludes underlying lung damage, e.g. pneumothorax. There is a high incidence of false negative fractures on X-ray, so caution is necessary.

Treatment

A simple rib fracture can be extremely painful. The first treatment strategy is to prescribe analgesics, such as paracetamol, and encourage breathing within the limits of pain. If pain persists in cases of single or double rib fracture with no complication, application of a rib support is most helpful.

The universal rib belt

A special elastic rib belt can provide thoracic support and mild compression for fractured ribs (Fig. 106.4). Despite its flexibility it gives excellent support and symptom relief while permitting adequate lung expansion. The elastic belt is 15 cm wide and has a Velcro grip fastening, so it can be applied to a variety of chest sizes.

Fig. 106.4 *Method of application of a universal rib belt*

Healing time

3–6 weeks.

Fractures of the clavicle

There is a history of a fall onto the outstretched hand or elbow. The patient has pain aggravated by shoulder movement and usually supports the arm at the elbow and clasped to the chest. The most common fracture site is at the junction of the outer and middle thirds, or in the middle third.

Treatment

- St John elevated sling to support arm—for three weeks
- figure of eight bandage (used mainly for severe discomfort)
- early active exercises to elbow, wrist and fingers
- active shoulder movements as early as possible

Special problem

Fracture at the lateral end of the bone. Consider referral for open reduction.

Healing time

4–8 weeks.

The appropriate use of slings for fracture–dislocations is presented in Table 106.1.

Table 106.1 *Appropriate use of slings for fracture-dislocations*

Collar and cuff	Fractured shaft of humerus
Broad arm sling	Fractured forearm Fractured scapula
St John's high sling	Fractured clavicle Fractured neck of humerus Subluxed acromioclavicular joint Dislocated acromioclavicular joint Subluxed sternoclavicular joint

Fractures of the scapula

Fractures of the scapula may include:

- body of scapula: due to a crushing force, considerable blood loss, may be rib fractures

- neck of scapula (may involve joint)
- acromion process } due to a blow or fall on
- coracoid process } the shoulder

Treatment

- broad-based triangular sling for comfort
- early active exercises for shoulder, elbow and fingers as soon as tolerable
- a large glenoid fragment usually requires surgical reduction

Healing time

Several weeks to months.

Fractures of the sternum

These are treated symptomatically with analgesics but careful evaluation of thoracic injuries, including cardiac tamponade, is essential. A significantly depressed fracture should be referred.

Acromioclavicular joint dislocation/ subluxation

A fall on the shoulder, elbow or outstretched arm can cause varying degrees of separation of the acromioclavicular joint, causing the lateral end of the clavicle to be displaced upwards.

Grades I & II	partial separation, involving tearing of the acromioclavicular capsule and ligaments
Grade III	complete tearing, also affecting the coracoclavicular ligaments

Treatment

- Analgesics.
- St John arm sling (suitable for all injuries).
- Mobilisation exercises as soon as possible

  and (for Grade III)
- a compression bandage (or long straps of adhesive low-stretch strapping) with padding at pressure points—elbows, clavicle and coracoid. The clavicle should be manipulated into its correct position and the forearm elevated: applying pressure from above (clavicle) and below (elbow) to achieve compression, apply a bandage over the outer end of the clavicle and round the elbow joint which is flexed to 90°. The bandage or strapping is worn for 2–3 weeks.[6]
- The issue of internal fixation versus conservative treatment for a complete dislocation is controversial, but reduction and internal fixation is a favoured method of treatment.

Sternoclavicular joint dislocation/ subluxation

This uncommon injury is caused by a fall or very heavy impact on the shoulder, causing the medial end of the clavicle to move forwards (making it prominent) or backwards. The injury can be very painful for several months.

Special problem

Backward (inward) displacement of the clavicular end with danger to major blood vessels: an urgent reduction is essential if complications develop. Plain X-rays are difficult to interpret but a CT scan is the ideal diagnostic method.

Treatment

If forward subluxation occurs and the patient is prepared to accept a small lump, a sling is worn for about seven days. Early exercises are encouraged. If there is total dislocation, open surgical reduction is recommended.

Dislocation of the shoulder

Dislocations of the shoulder joint can be caused by an impact on the arm by falling directly on the outer aspect of the shoulder, or by a direct violent impact, or by a forceful wrenching of the arm outwards and backwards.

Types of dislocation:

- anterior (forward and downward)—95% of dislocations
- posterior (backward)—difficult to diagnose
- recurrent anterior dislocation

Anterior dislocation of the shoulder

Management

An X-ray should be undertaken to check the position and exclude an associated fracture. Reduction can be achieved under general anaesthesia (easier and more comfortable) or with intravenous pethidine ± diazepam. The following methods can be used for anterior dislocation.

Kocher method

- elbow flexed to 90° and held close to the body
- slowly rotate arm laterally (externally)
- adduct humerus across the body by carrying point of elbow
- rotate arm medially (internally)

Hippocratic method

Apply traction to the outstretched arm by a hold on the hand with countertraction from stockinged foot in the medial wall of the axilla. This levers the head of the humerus back. It is a good method if there is an associated avulsion fracture of the greater tuberosity.

Milch method (does not require anaesthesia or sedation)

- Patient reclines at 30° and with guidance slowly bends the elbow to 90°.
- The patient is asked to lift the arm up slowly with the elbow bent so that they can pat the back of their head (requires considerable reassurance and encouragement).
- At this position, traction along the line of the humerus (with countertraction) achieves reduction.

Postreduction

- Reduction is complete if the hand can rest comfortably on the opposite shoulder.
- Confirm reduction by X-ray.
- Keep the arm in a sling for two weeks.
- Apply a swathe bandage to the chest wall.
- After immobilisation, begin pendulum and circumduction exercises.
- Combined abduction and lateral rotation should be avoided for three weeks.

Posterior dislocation of the shoulder

This rare problem accounts for the most commonly misdiagnosed major joint dislocation.[7] It is caused by a fall onto the outstretched hand with the arm internally rotated, or by a direct blow to the front of the shoulder. The shoulder contour may look normal but the major clinical sign is painful restriction of external rotation which is usually completely blocked. Beware of the problem of pain in the shoulder after a convulsion. An 'axillary shoot through' X-ray view should be routinely ordered following shoulder trauma (Fig. 106.5).

Reduction of posterior dislocation

Using appropriate analgesia or anaesthesia, apply traction to the shoulder in 90° of abduction (with the elbow at right angles) and laterally (externally) rotate the limb.

Recurrent anterior dislocation

A simple procedure for reducing recurrent anterior dislocation

- Get the patient to sit comfortably on a chair with legs crossed.
- The patient then interlocks hands and elevates the upper knee so that the hands grip the knee.
- The knee is gradually lowered until its full weight is taken by the hands. At the same time the patient has to concentrate on relaxing the muscles of the shoulder girdle. This method usually effects reduction without the use of force.

Recurrent dislocation requires definitive surgery.

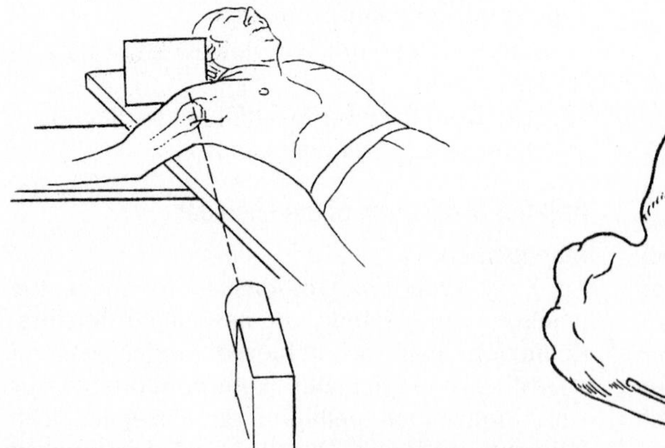

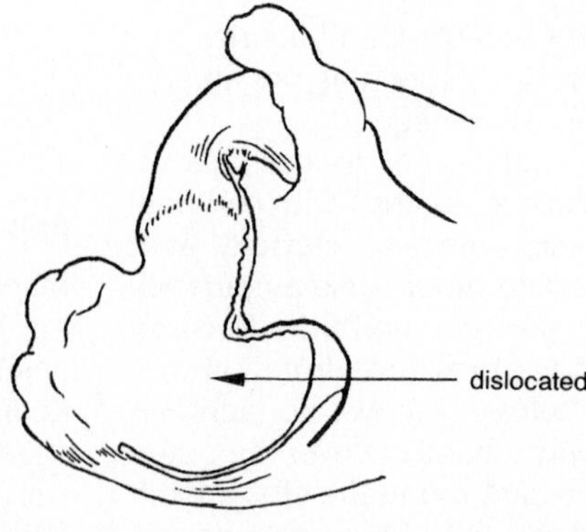

Fig. 106.5 *X-ray (axillary view) illustrating posterior dislocation of the shoulder; the femoral head is pushed backwards with an impaction fracture anteriorly*

Pitfalls

- nerve injury, especially axillary (circumflex) nerve
- a fractured neck of the humerus, especially in the elderly, may mimic a dislocation
- associated fractures (greater tuberosity, head of radius, glenoid) may require internal fixation
- great difficulty with some reductions
- failing to X-ray all suspected dislocations; failing to obtain an axillary view to show posterior displacement or fractures of the humerus or glenoid.

Orthopaedic problems that cause difficulties in diagnosis and management are outlined in Table 106.2.

Table 106.2 *Important orthopaedic problems that cause difficulties in diagnosis and management*

Shoulders
• Posterior dislocation of the shoulder
• Recurrent subluxations
• Unstable surgical neck fractures of humerus
• The avascular humeral head
Elbow
• Supracondylar fractures with forearm ischaemia
• Fracture of the lateral humeral condyle in children
• Fractured neck of radius in children
• The Monteggia fracture with dislocation of radial head
Wrist
• Scaphoid fractures
• Scapholunate dislocation
• The unstable Colles' fracture
Fingers
• Phalangeal fractures
• Intra-articular fractures
• Penetrating injuries of the metacarpophalangeal joint
• Gamekeeper's thumb (MCP joint)
The hip
• Congenital dislocation of the hip
• Septic arthritis
• Slipped upper femoral epiphysis
• Subcapital fractures
• Stress fractures of the femoral neck in athletes
Foot and ankle
• Stress fractures of the navicular
• Intra-articular fractures

Fractured greater tuberosity of humerus

Treat with a combination of immediate mobilisation and rest in a sling unless grossly displaced, when surgical reduction is advisable. Shoulder stiffness can be a disabling problem, so early movement is encouraged with review in seven days.

Fractured surgical neck of humerus

This usually occurs in the elderly due to a fall onto the outstretched hand. The fragments may be impacted. The greater tuberosity may also be fractured. Watch out for associated dislocation. In adolescents, fracture-separation of the upper humeral epiphysis occurs.

Treatment (no displacement or impaction)

- triangular sling
- when pain subsides (10–14 days) encourage pendulum exercises in the sling
- aim at full activity within 8–12 weeks post injury

Healing

Union usually occurs in four weeks and consolidation at six weeks

Pitfalls with fractures of the surgical neck

Minimally displaced fractures of the surgical neck of the humerus are usually managed conservatively, but overzealous early mobilisation can lead to non-union.[7] If there is a communication of this fracture with joint fluid, movement washes away the fracture haematoma and leads to the development of true pseudoarthrosis. Judicious early immobilisation will avert this complication.

Always remember the cardinal fracture management rule: 'First ensure that stability of the fracture is sufficient to allow healing before prescribing rehabilitation exercises or early use of the extremity'.[7]

The management of various humeral fractures is summarised in Figure 106.6.

Fracture of shaft of humerus

Humeral shaft fractures may be:

- spiral—due to a fall on the hand
- transverse or slightly oblique—fall on elbow with arm abducted
- comminuted—heavy blow

Caution: watch for radial nerve palsy.

Treatment

- Perfect bony opposition is not necessary; some over-riding is acceptable but distraction of the fragments is not.

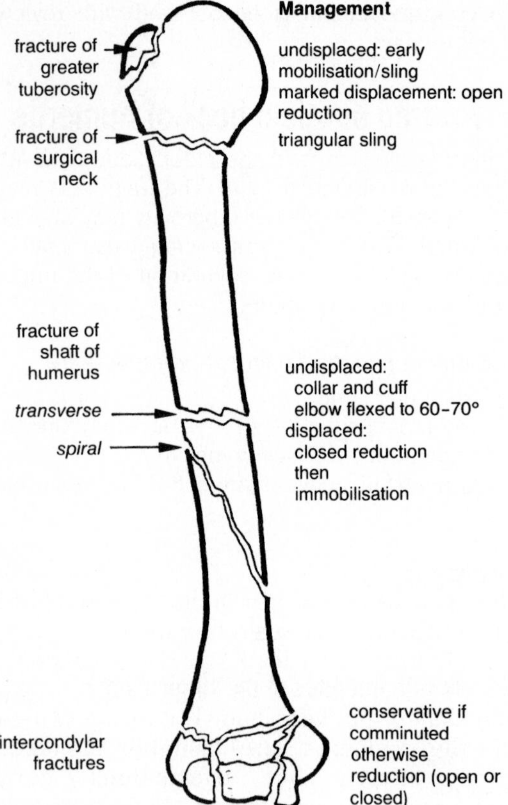

Fig. 106.6 *Various fractures of the humerus in adults*

- Undisplaced fracture: collar and cuff with elbow flexed to 60–70°.
- Displaced fracture: use closed reduction under general anaesthetic followed by immobilisation for 4–6 weeks in an arm-to-chest bandage (sling and swathe)[4] or in a U-shaped plaster slab with a triangular sling.

Intercondylar fractures in adults

Intercondylar fractures, which may be T-shaped or Y-shaped, are usually caused by a fall on the point of the elbow which drives the olecranon process upwards, splitting the condyles apart. Fractures involving the joint can cause long-term problems. Referral for reduction (closed or open) is appropriate. Conservative treatment with a collar and cuff can be used for comminuted fractures.

Fractures and avulsion injuries around the elbow joint in children

Potentially severe deforming injuries include:

- supracondylar fractures
- fracture of the lateral humeral epicondyle
- fracture of medial humeral epicondyle (Fig. 106.7)
- fracture of neck of radius

Fractures around the elbow in children require referral to consultants experienced in radiology and fracture management.

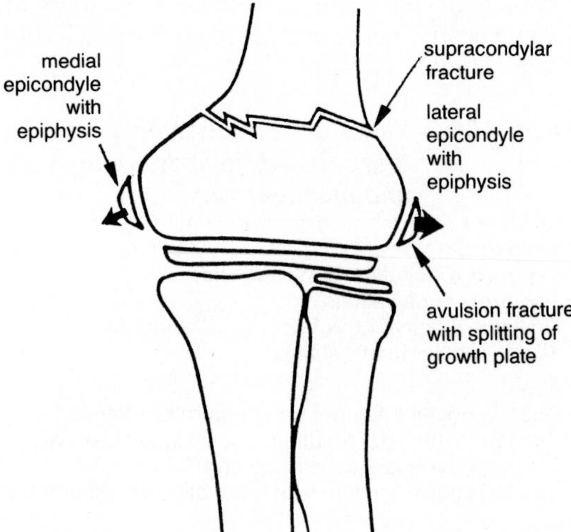

Fig. 106.7 *Fractures and avulsion injuries around the elbow joint in children*

Supracondylar fractures with forearm ischaemia

Supracondylar fractures represent about half of all elbow fractures in children; and most are extension fractures following falls onto the outstretched arm.

Pressure of the displaced bony fragments causing impingement on the brachial artery leads to impending forearm flexor compartment ischaemia and muscle death. Severe forearm pain is the most significant and important sign of ischaemia.

This diagnosis must always be assumed in displaced supracondylar fractures in children. Therefore, it is the general practitioner's responsibility to ensure treatment is expedited.

The fracture is reduced by hyperflexion of the elbow during traction (after lateral displacement has been corrected) and then immobilised in flexion in a plaster cast from the shoulder to the wrist for six weeks. The tragedy is that Volkmann's ischaemic contracture of the forearm is still occurring in children and is preventable.[7]

Fracture of the lateral humeral epicondyle

Fractures of the lateral humeral epicondyle also result from a fall onto the outstretched arm in children (Fig. 106.7). It appears that a varus component of force with the elbow in extension leads to avulsion of the lateral half of the distal humeral growth plate.

Severe late complications due to splitting of the growth plate into halves can result from even minimally displaced fractures if unrecognised. Unfortunately, they remain the most frequently overlooked yet the most easily treated of all major growth plate disturbances in children. The end result is non-union, a valgus deformity and ulnar nerve palsy.

Early open reduction and internal fixation with wires close the separation of the growth plate. Suspect the injury if there is pain and swelling around the outside of the elbow in children following falls. Careful review of comparative elbow X-rays are required to make the diagnosis.

Fracture of the medial humeral epicondyle

This problem occurs typically in adolescents following a fall onto the outstretched hand. The medial epicondyle may be avulsed by massive flexor pronator muscle contraction together with abduction stresses on the forearm. Avulsion of the epicondyle occurs in the young patient before the epiphysis is united. If untreated or incorrectly treated it may result in distressing elbow pain and restriction of extension.

Fractured neck of radius

This is caused by a child falling on the outstretched hand. The fracture line is transverse and is situated immediately distal to the epiphysis.

The degree of tilt is critical. Up to 15° of tilt is acceptable but, beyond that, reduction (preferably closed) will be necessary. The head of the radius must never be excised in children.

Dislocated elbow

A dislocated elbow is caused by a fall on the outstretched hand, forcing the forearm backwards to result in posterior and lateral displacement (Fig. 106.8). The peripheral pulses and sensation in the hand must be assessed carefully. Check the function of the ulnar nerve before and after reduction.

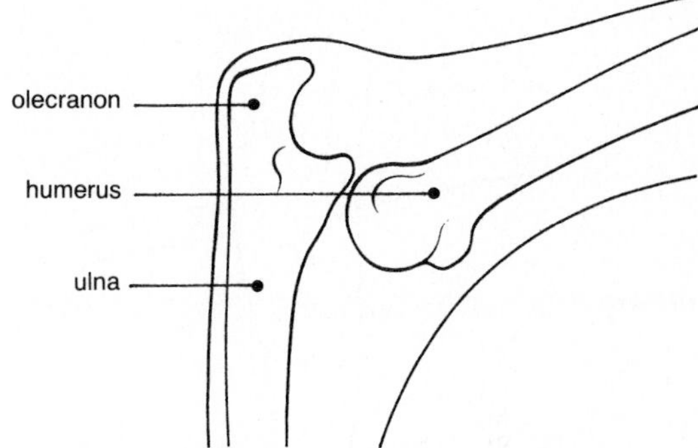

Fig. 106.8 *Dislocated elbow: uncomplicated posterior dislocation*

Treatment

Attempt reduction with patient fully relaxed under anaesthesia. It is important to apply traction to the flexed elbow but allowing it to extend approximately (20–30°) to enable correction of the lateral displacement and then the posterior displacement.

Follow-up

Encourage early mobilisation with gentle exercises in between resting the elbow for 2–3 weeks in a collar and cuff with the elbow flexed above 90°, avoiding passive movements. This will minimise the possibility of myositis ossificans. Recurrent dislocation of the elbow is uncommon.

A simple method of reduction

This method reduces an uncomplicated posterior dislocation of the elbow without the need for anaesthesia or an assistant. The manipulation must be gentle and without sudden movement.

Method

1. The patient lies prone on a stretcher or couch, with the forearm dangling towards the floor.

2. Grasp the wrist and slowly apply traction in the direction of the long axis of the forearm (Fig. 106.9).
3. When the muscles feel relaxed (this might take several minutes), use the thumb and index finger of the other hand to grasp the olecranon and guide it to a reduced position, correcting any lateral shift.

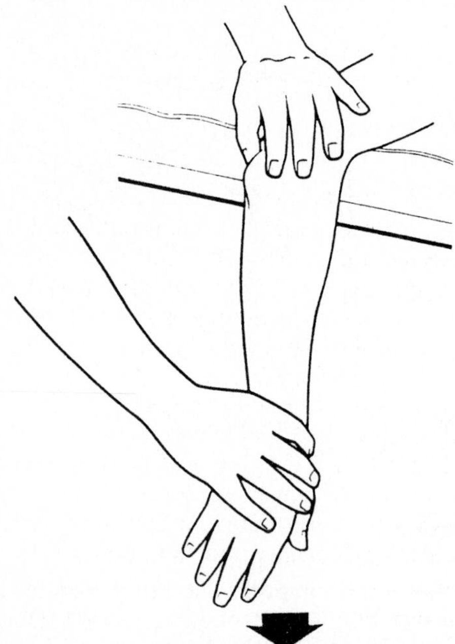

Fig. 106.9 *Dislocated elbow: method of reduction by traction on the dependent arm*

Pitfalls

- incomplete reduction: ulna articulates with capitellum and not the trochlea
- injury to ulnar nerve (spontaneous recovery usually occurs after 6–8 weeks)
- associated fractures, e.g. coronoid process, which may cause instability

Fractured head of radius (adults)

If the fracture is very slight and undisplaced, treat conservatively with the elbow at right angles in a collar and cuff for three weeks or with a plaster back slab. However, most fractured heads of radius require excision of the entire radial head.

Fractured olecranon

- Comminuted fracture (with little displacement): sling for three weeks and active movements.
- Transverse (gap) fracture: open reduction with screw or wire.

Monteggia fracture-dislocation of the radial head

Fractures of the proximal third of the ulna with dislocation of the radial head (Monteggia fracture–dislocation) (Fig. 106.10) have a treacherous history during treatment.

Redislocation or subluxation of the radial head is common.

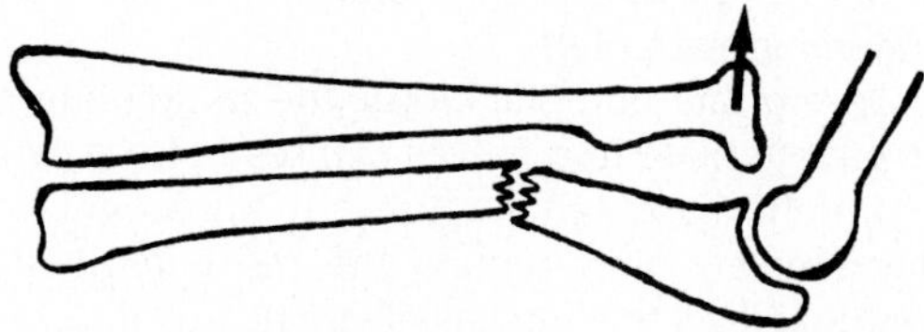

Fig. 106.10 *Monteggia fracture–dislocation of the radial head; it is important not to miss a dislocated head of radius with a fracture of the proximal third of the ulna*

Since surgical intervention is advisable, referral of displaced forearm fractures for early surgery is recommended. In adults Monteggia fractures are usually treated by internal fixation. Follow up X-rays are mandatory to ensure that there has not been a late redislocation of the radial head.

Fracture-dislocation in the lower forearm (Galeazzi injury)

This injury is usually caused by a fall on the hand and is a combination of a fractured radius (at the junction of its middle and distal thirds) and subluxation of the distal radioulnar joint. The patient should be referred, as open reduction is often required.

Fractures of the radius and ulna shafts

General features

It is more common to have both bones broken; a fracture of one bone alone is uncommon and usually caused by a direct blow. For a fracture of one bone alone look for evidence of an associated dislocation. In children greenstick fractures are common. Fractured radial shafts tend to slip and ulna fractures heal slowly. When a patient has a fracture of only one forearm bone or with limited pronation or supination, think of dislocation. Dislocation of the head of the radius or inferior radioulnar joint can be missed if X-rays do not include the elbows and wrist joints.

Reduction

- A greenstick fracture is readily straightened by firm pressure.
- A complete fracture (spiral or transverse) is reduced by traction and rotation.
- A slight overlap and angulation is permissible in children but perfect reduction is essential in adults.
- A plaster cast should include both the elbow and the wrist joints.

Healing time: (adults) spiral fracture—6 weeks
transverse fracture—12 weeks

Colles' fracture of lower end of radius

A Colles' fracture, probably the most common of all fractures, is a supination fracture of the distal 3 cm of the radius, caused by a fall onto the outstretched hand.

Clinical features

- usually an elderly woman
- osteoporosis is common
- fall on dorsiflexed hand
- fracture features
  - impaction
  - posterior displacement and angulation
  - lateral displacement and angulation
  - supination
  - dinner fork deformity (Fig. 106. 11)

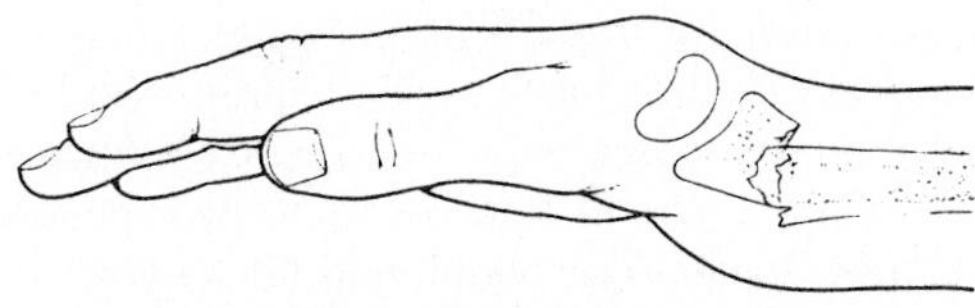

Fig. 106.11 *Dinner fork deformity of Colles' fracture: a fracture of the distal head of the radius showing impaction and posterior displacement and angulation*

Treatment

- if minimal displacement—below-elbow plaster for four weeks, then a crepe bandage
- if displaced: meticulous reduction under anaesthesia
  - set in flexion 10°, medial rotation 10° and pronation
  - below-elbow plaster 4–6 weeks (six weeks maximum time)

Problems associated with Colles' fracture:

- watch for ruptured extensor pollicus longus tendon
- stiffness of the elbow, MCP joints and IP joints
- discomfort at inferior radioulnar joint due to disruption
- reflex sympathetic dystrophy

Pitfall: the unstable Colles' fracture[7]

With the advent of modern imaging techniques and power equipment it has become a simple procedure to pin unstable Colles' fractures percutaneously, even in the elderly. Thus severe deformities are now unacceptable. An early percutaneous pin is much simpler than a late osteotomy. Colles' fractures deserve more respect than they received in the past.

Remember the basic classification into intra-articular and extra-articular fractures. Restoring reasonable joint surface alignment is an important part of the treatment and fortunately is usually relieved with simple traction under local or general anaesthesia. Confirmation of maintenance of reduction with X-rays at one week and two weeks is very important.

Smith's fracture of lower end of radius

This is often referred to as a 'reverse Colles''. It is caused by a fall on the back of the hand. The lower fragment is flexed and impacted on the upper fragment. It is reduced and immobilised for six weeks in a cast as for Colles' fracture but with the wrist extended.

Ulna styloid fracture

Treat symptomatically.

Radial styloid fracture

Undisplaced: plaster slab for three weeks
Displaced: closed reduction and plaster slab for six weeks
if fails—open reduction

Scaphoid fractures

Scaphoid fractures account for almost 75% of all carpal injuries, but are rare in children and the elderly.[8] If a scaphoid fracture is suspected in the presence of a normal X-ray of wrist, a follow up X-ray should be arranged in two weeks. For undisplaced fractures, eight weeks in a below-elbow scaphoid cast usually suffices. Displaced fractures of the scaphoid require reduction (either open or closed) and, if unstable, internal fixation.

All scaphoid fractures require late X-ray evaluation of treatment to diagnose non-union before they become symptomatic from late degenerative changes. Early bone grafting of a non-union can prevent fragment collapse and radioscaphoid degenerative changes.

Scapholunate dislocation

This not uncommon carpal injury results from disruption of the scapholunate interosseous ligament and palmar radiocarpal ligaments. It results in a gap appearing between the scaphoid and lunate bones (the so-called 'Terry-Thomas' sign on plain anterior-posterior X-rays of the wrist) and the scaphoid rotating into a vertical position on lateral X-rays. It is associated with pain in the wrist on dorsiflexion.

Early diagnosis with referral simplifies treatment. This injury has only been recognised in recent times.

Fractures of the hands and fingers

Thumb fractures

The thumb's special function renders injuries more difficult than other digits. Fractures well clear of the joints in the proximal and distal phalanges are treated in a similar way to other digits. However intra-articular injuries are more common and internal fixation is more likely on the thumb than other digits.[9]

Bennett's fracture

This is a fracture dislocation of the first carpometacarpal joint. The larger fragment of the first metacarpal dislocates proximally and laterally (Fig. 106.12).

Treatment

Under anaesthesia the thumb is reduced using the forces indicated (Fig. 106.12). A scaphoid

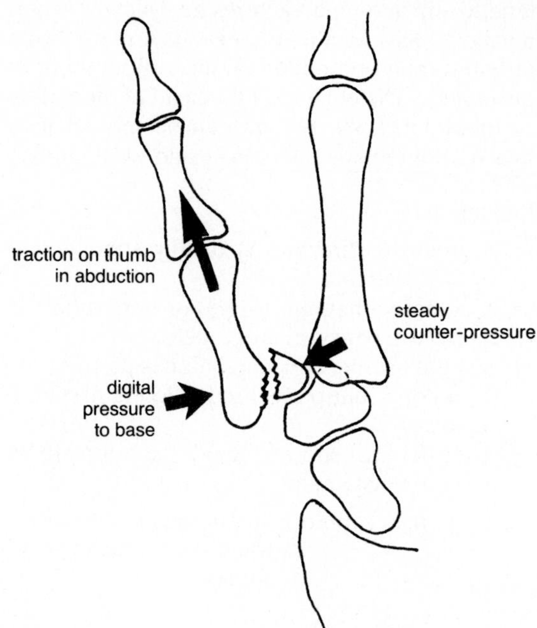

Fig. 106.12 *Method of reduction of a Bennett's fracture—dislocation of the first carpometacarpal joint*

plaster is applied with the thumb in the open grasp position. If anatomical reduction cannot be achieved by closed means then open reduction and internal fixation is indicated; if in doubt it is preferable to operate.

Gamekeeper's thumb

This problematic injury of the metacarpophalangeal joint is presented in more detail on page 1047.

Metacarpal fractures

Metacarpal fractures can be stable or unstable, intra-articular or extra-articular, and closed or open. They include the 'knuckle' injuries resulting from a punch which is prone to cause a fracture of the neck of the fifth metacarpal. As a general rule, most metacarpal (shaft and neck) fractures are treated by correcting marked displacements with manipulation (under anaesthesia) and splinting with a below-elbow, padded posterior plaster slab that extends up to the dorsum of the proximal phalanx and holds the metacarpophalangeal joints in a position of function (Fig. 106.13).[4] There is often a tendency for metacarpal fractures to rotate and this must be prevented. This is best achieved by splinting the MCP joints at 90° which corrects any tendency for malrotation. If there is gross displacement, shortening or rotation then surgical intervention is indicated. A felt pad acts as a suitable grip. The patient should exercise free fingers vigorously. Remove the splint after three weeks and start active immobilisation.

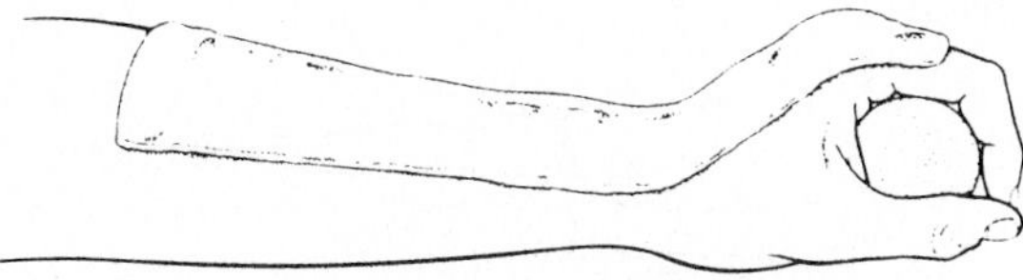

Fig. 106.13 *Fracture of the metacarpal: showing position of function with posterior plaster slab and the hand gripping a roll of felt padding*

Phalangeal fractures

These fractures result from either direct trauma causing a transverse or a comminuted fracture or a torsional force causing an oblique fracture. The tendency to regard fractures of phalanges (especially middle and proximal phalanges) as minor injuries (with scant attention paid to management and particularly to follow-up care) is worth highlighting. These fractures require as near perfect reduction as possible, careful splintage and, above all, early mobilisation once the fracture is stable—usually in two or three weeks.

Nevertheless, overzealous mobilisation can be as dangerous as prolonged immobilisation. Early operative intervention should be considered if the fracture is unstable.

Angulation is usually obvious but it is most important to check for rotational malalignment, especially with torsional fracture. A simple method is to get the patient to make a fist of the hand and check the direction in which the nails are facing. Furthermore each finger can be flexed in turn and checked to see if the fingertips point toward the tubercule of the scaphoid (palpable halfway along the base of the thenar eminence and 1.5 cm distal to the distal wrist crease).

The phalanges

- distal phalanges: usually crush fractures; generally heal simply unless intra-articular
- middle phalanges: tend to be displaced and unstable—beware of rotation
- proximal phalanges: are the greatest concern, especially of little finger; intra-articular fractures usually need internal fixation

Treatment

Non-displaced phalanges with no rotational malalignment Strap the injured finger to the adjacent normal finger with an elastic garter or adhesive tape for 2–3 weeks, i.e. 'buddy strapping' (Fig. 106.14). Start the patient on active exercises.

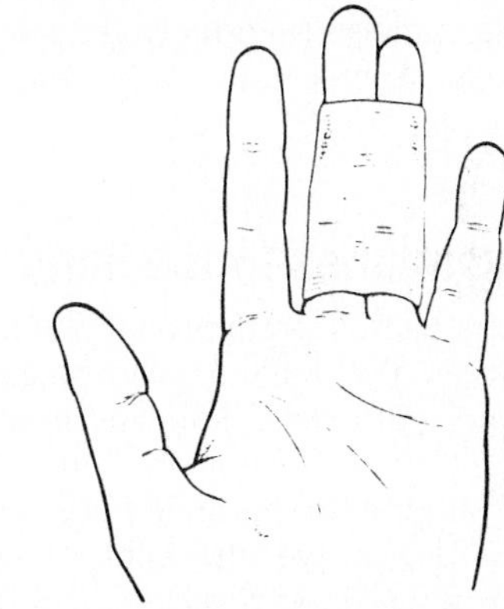

Fig. 106.14 *Treatment of non-displaced phalanges by 'buddy' strapping: the fractured finger is strapped to an adjacent healthy finger*[4]

or

If pain and swelling is a problem, splint the finger with a narrow dorsal or anterior slab (a felt-lined strip of malleable aluminium can be used)(Fig. 106.15). An alternative is to bandage the hand while the patient holds a tennis ball or appropriate roll of bandage in order to maintain appropriate flexion of all interphalangeal joints.

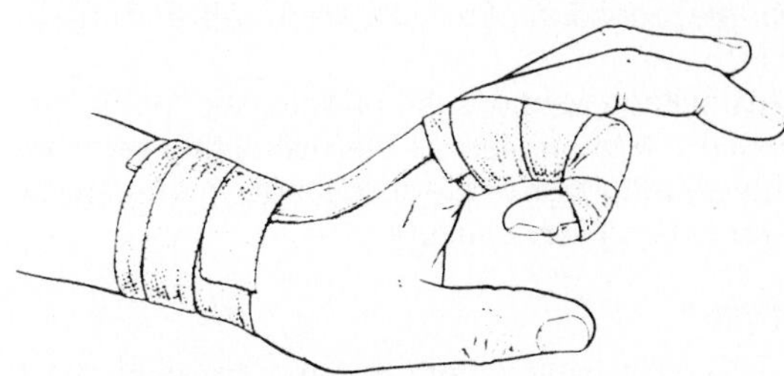

Fig. 106.15 *Method of splinting a phalangeal fracture of the index finger by a posterior plaster slab*[4]

Displaced interphalangeal fractures (usually proximal and middle) With suitable anaesthesia correct the deformity by traction and direct digital pressure. Maintain correction by splintage for 2–3 weeks. Ensure flexion at the interphalangeal joints with a dorsal padded plaster slab from above the wrist to the base of the finger nail (Fig. 106.15).

Intra-articular phalangeal fractures

Intra-articular phalangeal fractures are a great problem in management as subsequent stiffness of even a single interphalangeal joint can be a significant disability. Subsequent degenerative changes are common.

Wherever possible, displaced intra-articular fractures should be anatomically reduced and percutaneously pinned or openly reduced and internally fixed. Appropriate early referral is recommended.

Penetrating injuries to the hand

Assessing these injuries requires a careful history and examination. The pugilist who sustains a seemingly minor cut over a 'knuckle' may have a tooth-penetrating injury to the metacarpophalangeal joint. In the flexed position the dorsal hood is drawn over the joint. The point of penetration of the hood retracts as the finger extends and 'locks' saliva into the joint. This injury invariably results in a severe septic arthritis unless aggressively treated with surgical debridement and high-dose antibiotics.

Dislocated fingers

For dislocated fingers immediate reduction is advisable. Test for an associated fracture and X-ray if appropriate. General anaesthesia may be necessary for reduction of a dislocated thumb.

Simple reduction of a dislocated interphalangeal joint

This method employs the principles of using the patient's body weight as the distracting force to achieve reduction of the dislocation. It is relatively painless and very effective.

Method

1. Face the patient, both in standing positions.
2. Firmly grasp the distal part of the dislocated finger. A better grip is achieved by wrapping simple adhesive tape around the end of the finger.
3. Request the patient to lean backward, while maintaining the finger in the fixed position (Fig. 106.16).
4. As the patient leans back, sudden, painless reduction should spontaneously occur.

Splint the joint for three weeks to allow soft tissue healing.

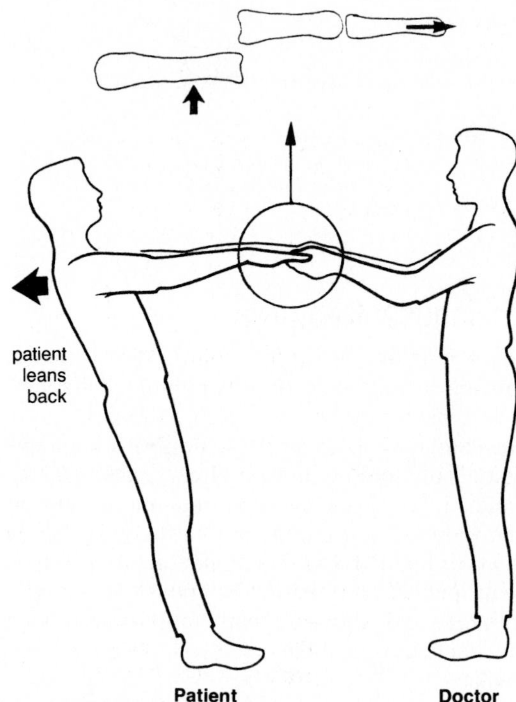

Fig. 106.16 *Reduction of a dislocated finger*

Pitfalls

- instability—torn collateral ligaments: unstable in lateral direction
- interposed volar plate—postreduction full flexion absent
- fractures of base of phalanx

These problems may need surgical reduction.

Fractures of the pelvis

Fractures of the pelvic ring are either:

1. stable: a single fracture
2. unstable: a break at two sites or association with disruption of the symphysis pubis or sacroiliac articulation

Treatment

Stable pelvic fracture:

- symptomatic, especially analgesics
- bed rest on a firm-to-hard bed for 2–6 weeks
- attempt walking with an aid as soon as comfortable

Unstable fractures: these are usually serious with possible associated visceral damage or blood loss. Patients should be referred for expert help.

Femoral fractures

Femoral neck fractures include:

- subcapital fractures
- intertrochanteric fractures
- stress fractures in the young

Subcapital fractures are usually treated by a pin or a primary prosthesis or maybe even simple traction, while intertrochanteric fractures are treated with a plate and pins.

A trap can be the impacted subcapital fracture which may permit partial weight bearing, thus making radiological investigation essential in elderly patients complaining of hip pain. The displaced subcapital fracture has at least a 40% incidence of avascular necrosis and usually requires prosthetic replacement.

Beware of the teenage athlete who complains of hip pain after running. Exclude a slipped upper femoral epiphysis and then a stress fracture. A technetium bone scan will detect the fracture which can cause avascular necrosis of the femoral head. This problem may be prevented with early cessation of weight-bearing activities.

A summary of the management of other femoral fractures is presented with Figure 106.17.

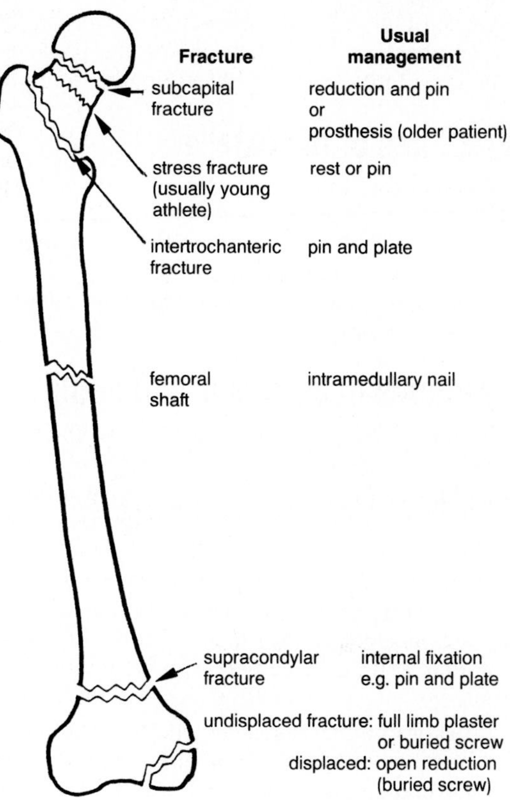

Fig. 106.17 *Management of basic fractures of the femur*

Dislocations of the lower limbs

Posterior dislocation of the hip

This causes a very painful shortened leg which is held adducted, medially rotated and slightly flexed.

Management

- adequate analgesia, e.g. IM pethidine
- X-rays to confirm diagnosis and exclude associated fracture
- reduction of the dislocated hip under relaxant anaesthesia
- follow-up X-ray to confirm reduction and exclude any fracture not visible on the first X-ray

Dislocated patella

The dislocated patella is always displaced laterally. Immediate reduction can be attempted by placing the thumb under the lateral edge of the patella and pushing it medially as the knee is extended. This may be attempted without anaesthesia or by using pethidine and intravenous diazepam as a relaxant.

X-rays with anteroposterior, lateral, skyline and intracondylar views should be taken to exclude an associated osteochondral fracture.

The usual RICE treatment should be given initially and crutches provided. Rest of the injured knee is achieved using a knee splint with the knee held in extension and crutches for 4–6 weeks.

Weight bearing is permitted when the swelling has subsided and the patient is gradually taken off the crutches. Introduce quadriceps exercises with the knee in extension.

Recurrent dislocation/subluxations in young females (14 to 18 years): requires surgery—combined tibial tubercle transfer with lateral release of the capsule. Immediate surgery in the acute phase is undertaken only in the presence of haemarthrosis with an osteochondral fracture.

Fractures of the patella

- Fractures without displacement: walking plaster cylinder four weeks.
- Displaced single transverse fracture: surgical reduction with Kirschner wires.
- Displaced and comminuted fracture: refer for patellectomy.

Fractures of both tibia and fibula

The nature and management of these fractures varies considerably. Some fractures are caused by blunt injuries, such as a blow from a motor car bumper, while twisting forces cause a spiral fracture of both bones at different levels. As a general rule referral of patients to a specialist is necessary, especially where soft-tissue damage is significant. Management of fractures with minimal soft-tissue damage can be summarised thus:

- No or minimal displacement: full length cast as for isolated fracture of tibia.
- Displacement: reduction under general anaesthesia, then application of cast as above (meticulous alignment essential).
- Period of immobilisation: adults 16 weeks, children 8 weeks.

Fracture of fibula[8]

An isolated fracture of the fibula is usually due to stress or to a direct blow. The patient is generally able to stand and move the knee and ankle joints. However, most spiral fractures are associated with injuries of the ankle or knee. The ankle in particular should be examined and X-rayed.

Treatment is usually with analgesics to control the pain and no more than a crepe bandage or a walking stick is necessary. A below-knee walking plaster for about three weeks will help those with severe discomfort.

Fracture of the tibial shaft

A fracture of the tibia alone is uncommon in adults but more common in children, due to a twisting injury. Reduction may not be necessary in some patients. Many can be reduced to a satisfactory position in the anaesthetised patient by letting the fractured leg hang over the edge of the table with the knee at a right angle.

A padded cast from the groin to the metatarsal necks is applied with the knee joint at 10° of flexion, and the ankle at a right angle. This should be maintained for 3–4 months.

Fracture around the ankle

The ankle is one of the areas liable to fractures. The commonest mechanism is forceful inversion of the foot, which can cause fracture of the fibula on a level with the joint line and tearing of the lateral collateral ligament. Other injuries can also occur such as fracture of the medial malleolus and tearing of the tibiofibular syndesmosis. At least three views on X-ray are needed: anteroposterior, lateral and a half oblique 'mortise' view.

Undisplaced, uncomplicated fractures are treated with a plaster cast from just below the knees to the toes for 6–8 weeks. The foot must be plantigrade, i.e. with the foot at 90° to the leg and neither in varus nor in valgus.[8] Fractures that are displaced or cause instability of the ankle joint require surgery to achieve stability followed by a longer period of immobilisation.

Stress fractures of the foot

Stress fractures of the navicular, calcaneus and metatarsal bones can be found in otherwise healthy people from the age of seven onwards. Long-distance runners and high-performance athletes are also susceptible.
Clinical features:

- localised pain during weight-bearing activity
- localised tenderness and swelling (not inevitable)
- plain X-rays are necessary but show no fracture in about 50% of cases[6]
- this can be repeated in 2–3 weeks if suspected
- a nuclear bone scan may confirm the diagnosis

Navicular

This hitherto unrecognised stress fracture has become apparent with the advent of CT scanning, which shows up the fracture better than nuclear scanning. It is seen in athletes involved with running sports and presents as poorly localised mid-foot pain. Plain X-ray is usually normal. The fracture, like the scaphoid fracture, is difficult to manage since delayed union and non-union are common. Cast immobilisation for eight weeks may prevent the need for an operation.

Metatarsal bones

The second metatarsal is probably the most common site of all for stress fracture because it is invariably the largest metatarsal and absorbs a greater load than the others.[1]

Treatment

- rest is the basis of treatment
- resting the foot with crutches for 6 weeks provides optimal healing
- healing usually takes 6–8 weeks
- gradual slow resumption of activity

Fractures of the toes

Most toe injuries are easy to treat but, like the fingers, the great and little toes demand special attention. Intra-articular injuries of the great toe (unless undisplaced) should be treated by internal fixation.

Buddy strapping can be used for many uncomplicated fractured phalanges of the toes, which tend to angulate and rotate more readily and are often harder to control than finger fractures. Strapping them to their adjacent toes on both sides simultaneously tends to counteract this problem.

Like the little finger, the little toe is injured by forceful abduction and if allowed to heal in that position may leave difficulties in wearing shoes.[9]

Approximate average immobilisation times for various fractures are given in Table 106.3.

Table 106.3 *Healing of uncomplicated fractures (adults)*

Fracture	***(Approximate) average immobilisation time (weeks)***
Rib	3–6 (healing time)
Clavicle	4–8 (2 weeks in sling)
Scapula	weeks to months
Humerus	
• neck	3–6
• shaft	8
• condyles	3–4
Radius	
• head of radius	3
• shaft	6
• Colles'	4–6
Radius and ulna (shafts)	6–12
Ulna—shaft	8
Scaphoid	8–12
Metacarpals	
• Bennett's #	6–8
• Other MCs	3–4
Phalanges (hand)	
• proximal	3
• middle	2–3
• distal	2–3
Pelvis	rest in bed 2–6
Femur	
• femoral neck	according to surgery
• shaft	12–16
• distal	8–12
Patella	3–4
Tibia	12–16
Fibula	0–6
Both T and F	16
Pott's fracture	6–8
Lateral malleolus avulsion	3
Calcaneus	
• minor	4–6
• compression	14–16
Talus	12
Tarsal bones (stress #)	8
Metatarsals	4
Phalanges (toes)	0–3

Important principles

- Children under 8 years usually take half the time to heal.
- Have a check X-ray in 1 week (for most fractures).
- Radiological union lags behind clinical union.

Dislocation of toes

Dislocations occur mainly at the metatarsophalangeal joint and are rare; they require special care because of the strong tendons crossing the joint. Perfect reduction of the dislocated great toe is essential and it should be supported by a below-knee plaster cast extending beyond the toes. Temporary internal fixation with a Kirschner wire or open ligamentous repair may be required.[9]

Plastering tips

Plaster of Paris

The bucket of water

- Line the bucket with a plastic bag for easy cleaning.
- The water should be deep enough to allow complete vertical immersion.
- Use cold water for slow setting.
- Use tepid water for faster setting.
- Do not use hot water: it produces rapid setting and brittle plaster.

The plaster rolls

- Do not use plaster rolls if water has been splashed on them.
- Hold the roll loosely but with the free end firm and secure (Fig. 106.18).
- Ensure that the centre of the plaster is fully wet.
- Drain surface water after removal from the bucket.
- Gently squeeze the roll in the middle: do not indent.

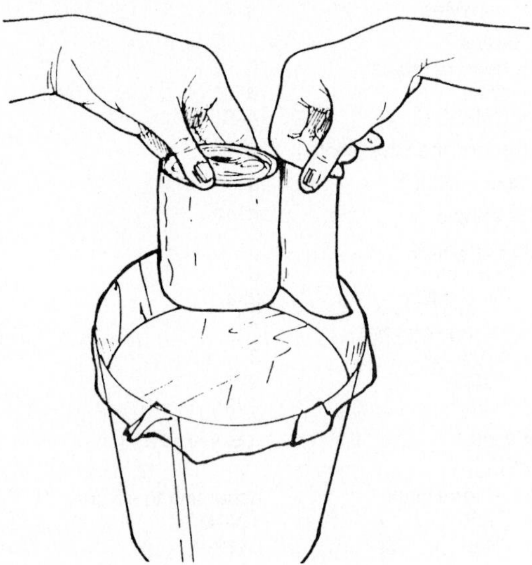

Fig. 106.18 *Holding the plaster roll*

Padding

- Use Velband or stockinet under the plaster.
- With Velband, moisten the end of the roll in water to allow it to adhere to the limb.
- For legs, make extra padding around the ankle and heel.
- Avoid multiple layers of padding.

Method

- Use an assistant to support the limb where possible (e.g. hold the arm up with fingers of stockinet).
- Lay the bandage on firmly but do not pull tight.
- Lay it on quickly.
- Overlap the bandage by about 25% of its width.

References

1. Quirk R. Stress fractures. Aust Fam Physician, 1993;22: 300–307.
2. Brentnall E. Diagnosing a fracture. Aust Fam Physician, 1990;19:948.
3. McMenimen PJ. Management of common fractures of the upper limb. Aust Fam Physician, 1987;16:783–791.
4. Cook J, Sankaran B, Wasunna A. *Surgery at the district hospital: obstetrics, gynaecology, orthopaedics and traumatology*. Geneva: World Health Organisation, 1991:75–162.
5. Brentnall E. Spatula test for fracture of mandible. Aust Fam Physician, 1992;21:1007.
6. Peterson L, Renström P. *Sports injuries: their prevention and treatment*. Sydney: Methuen, 1986, 179–181.
7. Young D, Murtagh J. Pitfalls in orthopaedics. Aust Fam Physician, 1989;18:645–660.
8. Apley AG, Solomon L. *Apley's system of orthopaedics and fractures*. Oxford: Butterworth–Heinemann, 1993; 601–604.
9. Carter G. Fractures and dislocations of fingers and toes. Aust Fam Physician, 1993;22: 310–317.

107

Major trauma

Major trauma, which is the third leading cause of death in Australia, is where one or more areas of the body (head and neck, chest, spine, abdomen and pelvis, limbs) is damaged by severe external trauma.

Critical injury is the situation where damage leads to failure of one or more of the vital systems (nervous, cardiovascular, respiratory, urinary, gastrointestinal).

About 50% of deaths from major trauma occur within seconds to minutes and 35% occur in 1–2 hours. These are the so-called golden hours where early intervention can be lifesaving.

Death is usually caused by:

- airway obstruction
- hypotension due to blood loss
- head injury

The early management of severe trauma is now a specialised part of accident and emergency training.

Important guidelines

- For each death in a motor vehicle accident 30 people sustain injuries.[1]
- Almost two-thirds of road accident deaths occur before arrival at a hospital.
- All patients with multiple injuries should receive high flow oxygen.
- Another simple and important measure is to elevate the legs of a patient with signs and symptoms of significant blood loss.
- Having cleared the airway in a trauma victim, the restoration of effective breathing takes the highest priority.
- Deterioration in conscious level may be due to hypoxia or hypoperfusion rather than primary brain injury.
- Remember the possibility of myocardial infarction in a middle-aged or elderly patient presenting with major trauma and shock.
- The normal circulatory blood volume is five litres.
- Bleeding from superficial lacerations such as the scalp must not be ignored: the blood loss may be sufficient to tip the patient with multiple trauma into 'shock'.

The information in this chapter is a guide to help practitioners cope with major trauma when working in circumstances relatively remote from a major trauma centre. Emergency lifesaving measures may have to be taken before stabilising the victim or victims for evacuation to an appropriate management facility.

Assessment and management priorities[2]

The following step-wise approach is recommended. It is very important to wear gloves, an apron and eye protection during this process.

1. Rapid primary survey and resuscitation of vital functions
   - A Airway maintenance with protection of the cervical spine
   - B Breathing and ventilation
   - C Circulation and haemorrhage control
   - D Dysfunction of the central nervous system
   - E Exposure: completely undress the patient

Resuscitation of vital functions involves simultaneous attention to the airway with high-flow oxygenation and insertion of an intravenous line.

2. Detailed secondary survey.
3. Definitive care, including evacuation (if necessary).

The three basic X-rays for blunt trauma are presented in Table 107.1.

Table 107.1 *Three basic X-rays for blunt trauma*

Chest
Cervical spine (lateral view)
Pelvis

Airway management

During the process of airway management it is vital to protect the cervical spine which should be stabilised with the hands and kept in a neutral position. Ideally a conforming hard cervical collar should be used.

If the patient cannot reply to commands or questions, open the mouth and check the upper airway.

- Clear debris and remove liquid vomit with a rigid sucker.
- Remove dentures or solid foreign objects with Magill forceps.
- Lift the chin and ventilate with bag and mask using high-flow oxygen.
- A Guedel airway may be needed to maintain the airway.
- Intubation may be necessary if the gag reflex is absent and if there is a flail segment of the chest—a cuffed endotracheal tube is the safest method. An orotracheal tube is preferred to nasotracheal intubation.
- If endotracheal intubation is not possible, perform a cricothyroidotomy.

Cricothyroidotomy

Emergency surgical access to the upper airway is a rare necessity but it can be a simple lifesaving procedure.

Adults

- patient supine and neck extended
- palpate the groove between the cricoid and thyroid cartilage
- make a short (2–3 cm) transverse incision through the skin and cricothyroid membrane (Fig. 107.1)
  — ensure the incision is *not* made above the thyroid cartilage
- insert an endotracheal or tracheostomy tube.

  If unavailable, any piece of plastic tubing will do or even the shell of a ball point pen.

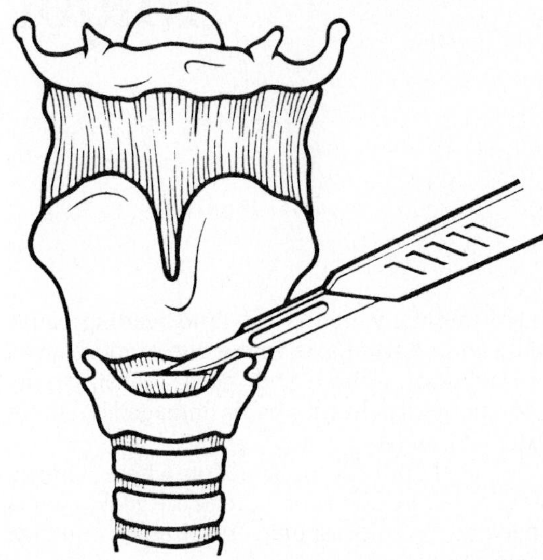

Fig. 107.1 *Cricothyroidotomy (in adult)*

Children

- do not perform a stab wound in children because of poor healing
- use a 14–15 g intravenous cannula
- pierce the cricothyroid membrane at an angle of 45°
- free aspiration of air confirms correct placement
- a 3.0 mm endotracheal tube connector fits into the end of the cannula or a 7.0 mm connector into a 2 ml or 5 ml syringe barrel connected to the cannula
- the connector is attached to the oxygen circuit; this system will allow oxygenation for about 30 minutes but carbon dioxide retention will occur

Breathing

Ensure the endotracheal tube is placed in the trachea. Auscultate in three areas: epigastrium, left lateral chest, right lateral chest. Check movement on both sides of chest. The respiratory rate should be noted.

If the upper airway has been cleared but respiratory distress is still present, possible causes include pneumothorax and/or haemothorax. If respiration is not markedly embarrassed, a chest X-ray should be taken with a view to insertion of a thoracostomy tube.

Tension pneumothorax

If respiratory distress is developing rapidly a tension pneumothorax could be responsible. Such symptoms include dyspnoea, cyanosis and a tympanitic expanded hemithorax. A lifesaving procedure is the insertion of an intercostal catheter or needle in the second intercostal space in the mid-clavicular line and connecting it to an underwater seal. The site is at least two finger-breadths from the edge of the sternum, so that damage to the internal mammary artery is avoided.

Ruptured diaphragm

The possibility of rupture of the diaphragm should be kept in mind, especially if there is chest and abdominal trauma, although it is often very difficult to diagnose at first presentation. This condition can manifest itself at a variable time after injury, whether it be by persistent symptoms such as vomiting and respiratory distress or by signs of the presence of the stomach in the left hemithorax.

Chest drain insertion[3]

Thoracostomy tubes are usually inserted for combined haemopneumo-thoraces, that is, to clear blood and/or air from the pleural cavity. A preliminary X-ray should be taken to ensure that either blood or air is interposed between the chest wall and the lung.

Position: 4th or 5th intercostal space
mid-axillary line

Note The diaphragm is often raised to a surprising degree so assume it is at the level of the nipple and make the site of insertion at or above this level.

Method

With a scalpel a 2 cm incision is made through the skin and the underlying muscle in an intercostal space, sufficiently deep to be somewhere near the pleura. A skin incision alone is not suitable, as excessive force will then be required to introduce the tube. The tube can be inserted in the usual manner mounted on a trocar, but a less traumatic method is to incise through the pleura and insert the index finger to ensure entry into the pleural cavity. The end of the tube is then grasped with a larger artery forceps and placed in the pleural cavity, fed in several inches and secured (see Figs 107.2 and 107.3).

Some air may enter the pleural cavity using this method, but it is expelled once the tube is connected to underwater seal drainage. If underwater seal drainage is not available, a flap valve can be fashioned by tying a cylinder of surgical rubber glove onto the open end of the tube. Similar devices are available commercially and are present in most emergency departments; however, they can easily get blocked with blood if a haemothorax is present.

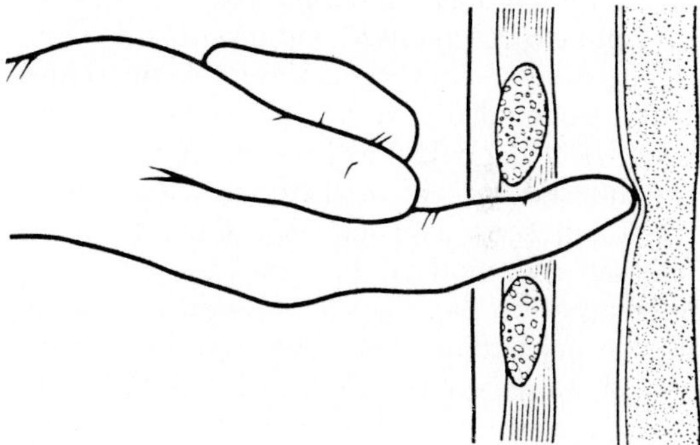

Fig. 107.2 *Thoracostomy: a finger is introduced into the pleural cavity*

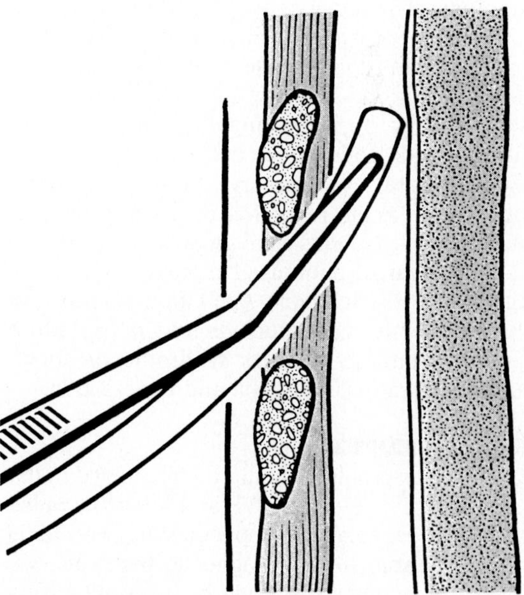

Fig. 107.3 *Thoracostomy: the drainage tube is introduced into the pleural cavity with a large artery forceps*

Circulation and haemorrhage control

A rapid assessment is made of the circulation and possible blood loss. Haemostasis should be achieved with direct pressure rather than the use of tourniquets. Multiple packs into wounds should be avoided. Two important monitors are a cardiac monitor and a central venous line.

To replace blood loss two peripheral lines should be inserted into the cubital fossa, if possible. The larger the needle gauge the better; for example, the rate of flow in ml per minute for a 14 g cannula is 175–220 and for a 16 g cannula is 100–150. Flow rates are improved by using pressure bags to 300 mmHg.

Cutdown can be used and if problems occur an interosseous infusion is a suitable alternative (refer page 995). A colloid solution (e.g. Haemaccel) should be used initially with one litre infused rapidly. If there are two lines a crystalloid solution such as normal saline or Hartman's solution can be used on one side and Haemaccel on the other line. Blood is required after a major injury or where there has been a limited response to two litres of colloid.[2] Blood should be warmed before use. The pneumatic antishock suit has been shown to be useful in 'shocked' patients, especially those suspected of having fractures of the pelvis and legs. Massive amounts of blood loss can be associated with these fractures. It must be remembered that young patients can compensate well for surprising degrees of blood loss and maintain normal vital signs simply by increasing the cardiac stroke volume. Such patients can collapse dramatically.

Peripheral circulatory failure (shock) signifies an acute reduction of tissue perfusion and seriously affects vital organs such as the kidneys. It can be minimised or prevented by early aggressive resuscitation. Apart from blood and fluid loss other causes include respiratory failure (adult respiratory distress syndrome or shock lung), myocardial infarction and pancreatitis.

Cardiac tamponade

This serious problem should be diagnosed in the presence of an elevated JVP and a narrow pulse pressure, especially if a penetrating wound is present (Table 107.2). Diagnostic percutaneous needle paracentesis is made by inserting a long wide-bore needle and syringe (which can be connected to a three-way tap) into the epigastrium just between the xiphisternum and the left costal margin. It is advanced slowly towards the heart by aiming it towards the tip of the left scapula. The pericardium is reached after advancing 3–4 cm. If the ventricular wall is struck there is a scraping, moving sensation transmitted to the hand.

Table 107.2 *Signs of pericardial tamponade*

Beck's triad 1. JVP elevated 2. muffled heart sounds 3. hypotension
Narrowed pulse pressure
Tachycardia
Pulsus paradoxicus
Treatment 1. oxygen 2. relieving paracentesis 3. thoracotomy

Head injury

Head injury is the major cause of death in major trauma. A Glasgow coma scale (page 624) can be used to assess cerebral status. A useful simplified method of recording the conscious state is to use a five-level system rating.

1. awake
2. confused
3. responds to shake and shout
4. responds to pain
5. unresponsive coma

Unequal pupils

It is worth noting that relatively minor blunt trauma to the eye region will cause a traumatic mydriasis.[3] Unequal pupils in a conscious patient whose conscious level is not deteriorating is usually not significant in patients with head injury.

The single physical sign that outweighs all others in head injury assessment is the level of consciousness. If this is satisfactory, there is little cause for concern.

Emergency exploratory burr hole[3]

After a head injury, a rapidly developing mass lesion is heralded by a deteriorating conscious level (e.g. Glasgow coma scale 15 to 3); a rising blood pressure (e.g. 140/70 to 160/100); slowing respirations (16 to 10); a slowing pulse (70 to 55) and a dilating pupil. In such conditions an urgent burr hole is indicated even in the absence of a plain X-ray and a CT scan of the head. Even elevating a depressed fracture may be sufficient to alleviate the pressure.

Method (in absence of neurosurgical facilities)

- Ideally performed in an operating theatre.
- The patient is induced, paralysed, intubated and ventilated (100% oxygen).
- Dehydrating dose of mannitol (1 g/kg IV in one hour) administered.
- After shaving the scalp, a mark is made over the site of external bruising, especially if a clinical fracture is obvious. A 5 cm long incision is made over the site of external bruising or swelling. Otherwise the burr hole is made in the low temporal area. A vertical incision is made above the zygoma, and the skull is trephined 2–3 cm above it (Fig. 107.4). This is the site of the classical middle meningeal haemorrhage.
- The clot is gently aspirated and the skin is loosely sutured around the drain.
- If there are difficulties controlling the bleeding, the intracranial area is packed with wet balls of Gelfoam or similar material.
- Other areas that can be explored in the presence of subdural haematoma include:
  - frontal region: a suspicion of an anterior fossa haematoma, e.g. a black eye
  - parietal region: haematoma from the posterior branch of the middle meningeal artery (Fig. 107.4).

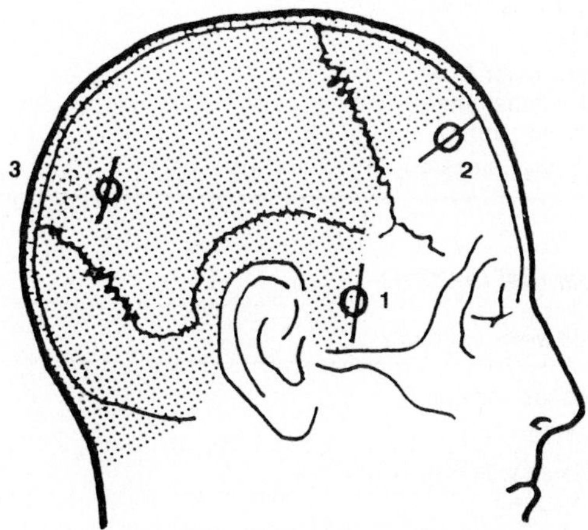

Fig. 107.4 *Three sites suggested for burr holes:* **(1)** *low in the temporal region will disclose a classical middle meningeal artery bleed; on division of the muscle, haematoma should be found between the muscle and the fracture line;* **(2)** *frontal region;* **(3)** *parietal region*

Spinal injuries

Severe injuries of the upper cervical spine are immediately fatal. Patients with quadriplegia from cervical spine injury and paraplegia from thoracic or lumbar spine injuries require transfer to a spinal injury unit.

Remarkable recovery from quadriplegia due to cervical spine injury may follow prompt reduction of flexion-rotation injuries with bilateral facet dislocation in a spinal unit. Open reduction may be required.[4]

If these problems are present, insert an indwelling catheter and aim to avoid pressure sores by frequent (two hourly) turning.

Signs of spinal injury include:[3]

- priapism in the male patient
- hypotension with bradycardia
- decreased motor power and sensation below the lesion
- decreased anal sphincter tone

Urinary catheterisation

A catheter should be inserted to measure the patient's rate of urine output. A perurethral approach is used if there is no contraindication, such as evidence of urethral injury. Contraindications include: blood at the meatus; perineal bruising; impalpable or high-riding prostate; inability to pass urine; inability to pass a catheter; or simply clinical suspicion of major clinical pathology.

If a patient has a ruptured urethra, attempted insertion of a catheter can convert a partial tear into a complete tear, or may introduce infection.

Nasogastric intubation

Nasogastric intubation can be both therapeutic (especially with pronounced gastric distension) and diagnostic.

Special caution is required in the presence of a maxillary fracture or a fracture of the cribriform plate.

Diagnostic peritoneal lavage

Intra-abdominal bleeding has to be considered according to the nature of the trauma and stability of the circulation. The ideal investigation is a CT scan to detect injuries. Peritoneal lavage is a reliable bedside test to demonstrate haemoperitoneum. It requires minimal equipment. The only relative contraindications are previous intra-abdominal surgery (except uncomplicated appendicectomy or cholecystectomy) and pregnancy.

Method[3]

- Empty bladder, by catheterisation if necessary.
- Inject local anaesthetic with a 23 g, 32 mm needle just below the umbilicus at an angle of 45° towards the pelvis.
- A stab incision is made at this site at the same angle so that it extends through the linea alba.
- Insert the trocar of the peritoneal dialysis kit.
- Pass the catheter into the peritoneal cavity and withdraw the trocar.
- Attach a syringe and aspirate for blood.
- If negative: infuse 1L of normal saline.
- Cut the drip tubing and place the end in a transparent container below the bed to allow the lavage fluid to drain by gravity.
- If the fluid is clear or lightly bloodstained, the test is negative.
- If the fluid is heavily bloodstained, the test is positive.
- Bile-stained fluid is an absolute indication for urgent laparotomy.

Think of associations

When certain injuries, especially bony fractures, are found it is important to consider associated soft-tissue injuries. Table 107.3 presents possible associated injuries with various fractures, while Table 107.4 outlines possible associated injuries with various physical signs or symptoms.

Table 107.3 *Associated injuries related to specific fractures*

Fracture	***Associated injuries to consider***
Ribs	Pneumothorax Haemothorax Ruptured spleen (lower left 10–11) Ruptured diaphragm (lower left 10–11)
Sternum	Ruptured base of heart with tamponade Ruptured aorta
Lumbar vertebra	Ruptured kidney (L_1, L_2) and other viscera, e.g. pancreas (L_2)
Pelvis	Heavy blood loss Ruptured bladder Ruptured urethra Fractured femur
Temporal bone of skull	Cerebral contusion Extradural haematoma Subdural haematoma
Femur	Blood loss, possible >1 L

Table 107.4 *Associated serious injuries and typical clinical features*

Physical sign or symptom	***Associated serious injury***
Subconjunctival haematoma with no posterior limit	Fractured base of skull
Sublingual haematoma	Fracture of mandible
Surgical emphysema	Pneumothorax with pleural tear Ruptured trachea
Unequal pupils	Cerebral compression, e.g. extradural haematoma Trauma to II and III cranial nerves Eye injuries, including traumatic mydriasis Brainstem injuries
Shoulder tip pain without local injury	Intra-abdominal bleeding, e.g. ruptured spleen Intra-abdominal perforation or rupture, e.g. perforated bowel
Bluish-coloured umbilicus	Intra-abdominal bleeding, e.g. ruptured ectopic pregnancy

Roadside emergencies

The first two hours after injury can be vital: proper care can be lifesaving, inappropriate care can be damaging. Proper acquaintance with resuscitation procedures is important. The first step is for someone to notify the police and ambulance or appropriate emergency service. The site of an accident should be rendered safe by eliminating as many hazards as possible, e.g. turning off the ignition of a vehicle, warning people not to smoke, moving victims and workers out of danger of other traffic.

Attention should be given to:

- the airway and breathing
- the cervical spine: protect the spine
- circulation: arrest bleeding
- fractured limbs (gentle manipulation and splintage)
- open wounds, especially open chest wounds, should be covered by a firm dressing

Major haemorrhage is a common cause of death in the first few hours. Lacerated organs and multiple fractures can lose 250ml of blood a minute; pressure should be applied to control haemorrhage where possible. Colloids that can be administered intravenously for blood loss include Haemaccel.[5]

Most convulsions after trauma are due to hypoxia and will subside when it is corrected by adequate care of the airway; if not, IV anticonvulsant medication may be given.

Intramuscular narcotic injections (morphine, pethidine) and alcohol 'to settle the victim's nerves' must be avoided. When the patient is under control, he or she should be shifted into the coma position (Fig. 107.5).

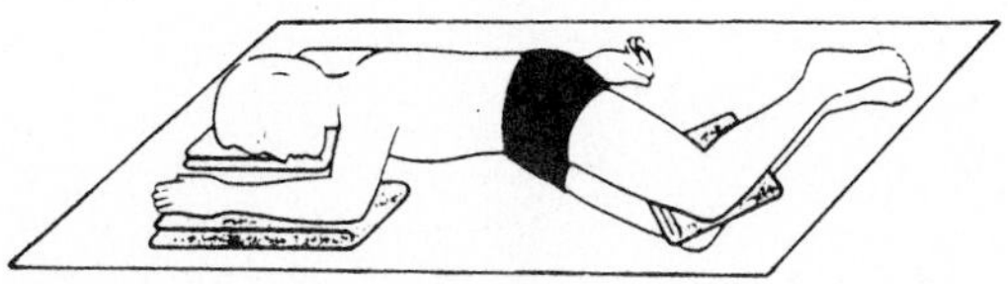

Fig. 107.5 *The coma position*

Administration of first aid to the injured at the roadside

A simple guide is as follows:

1. Check airway and breathing (being mindful of cervical spine)
   a. Check oral cavity
      ? tongue fallen back
      ? dentures or other foreign matter in mouth
      Clear with finger and place in oral airway if available, or hold chin forward.
   b. Check breathing
      if absent, commence artificial respiration if feasible.
2. Check circulation
   If pulse absent, commence external cardiac massage if possible.
3. Check for haemorrhage, especially bleeding from superficial wounds. Apply a pressure bandage directly to the site.
4. Check for fractures, especially those of the cervical spine.

   Rules to remember
   - Immobilise all serious fractures and large wounds before shifting.
   - Always apply traction to the suspected fracture site.
   - Splint any fractured limbs with an air splint, wooden splint or to body, e.g. arm to chest, leg to leg.
   - For a suspected or actual fractured neck, apply a cervical collar, even if made out of newspaper; or
     Keep the head held firmly in a neutral position with gentle traction (avoid flexion and torsion).
   - Lay the patient on his or her back with head supported on either side.
5. Shifting the patient
   - Immobilise all fractures.
   - Lift the casualty without any movement taking place at the fracture site, using as much help as possible.
   - Always support the natural curves of the spine.
   - Protect all numb areas of skin (e.g. remove objects such as keys from the pockets).
6. The unconscious patient
   - Transport the casualty lying on the back if a clear airway can be maintained.
   - If not, gently move into the coma position.
7. Reassure the patient (if possible)
   - Reassurance of the casualty is most important.
   - Conduct yourself with calmness and efficiency.
8. Help the medical team
   Take notes of your observations at the accident, e.g. record times, colour of casualty, conscious level, respiration, pulse, blood pressure.

References

1. Trinca G, Murtagh JE. Road accident trauma—facts and trends. Aust Fam Physician, 1984; 13:239.
2. Skinner D, Driscoll P, Earlam R. *ABC of major trauma*. London: British Medical Journal, 1991, 1-13.
3. Webster V. *Trauma*. Melbourne: RACGP, CHECK Programme, 1986; Unit 176:3–14.
4. Ryan P. *A very short textbook of surgery* (2nd edition). Canberra: Dennis and Ryan, 1990, 75–77.
5. Walpole BG. Roadside emergencies. Aust Fam Physician, 1984; 13:249–253.

108

The doctor's bag and other emergency equipment

Almost everyone who goes to bed counts upon a full night's rest: like a picket at the outposts, the doctor must be ever on call.

Karl F. Marx (1796–1877)

General practitioners who perform home visits and nursing home visits require the traditional doctor's bag that includes the basic tools of trade, drugs (including those for emergency use), stationery and various miscellaneous items. Country doctors will by necessity use their bag for more emergency home and roadside calls.[1] These recommended contents are simply a guide for cross-checking.

Essential requirements for the bag

- sturdiness
- lockable, e.g. combination lock
- ready interior access
- uncluttered
- disposable single-use items
- light, portable equipment
- regular checks to ensure non-expired drugs
- storage in a cool place (not boot of car)

Stationery (checklist)

- Practice letterhead and envelopes
- Prescription pads
- Hospital admission forms
- Sickness/off-work certificates
- X-ray, pathology referral forms
- Accounting forms
- Dangerous drugs record books
- Continuation notes
- Large adhesive labels to record visit (attach later to patient's history)
- Tie-on labels for emergencies
- Recommendation forms (to psychiatric/mental hospitals)
- Pens

Miscellaneous items

Quick reference cards

- the Doctor's Bag checklist[1,2,3]
- dosage details of drugs, all age groups
- important telephone numbers

Local map
Phonecard or coins for public telephone use
Handbook of emergency medicine

Equipment

Sphygmomanometer (aneroid)
Stethoscope
Diagnostic set (auriscope + ophthalmoscope)
Tongue depressors
Tourniquet

Small needle disposal bottle
Scissors
Syringes 2, 5, 10 ml
Needles 19, 21, 23, 25 g
Scalp veins (butterfly) needles
IV cannulae 16 g, 18 g, 20 g
Alcohol swabs
Micropore tape
Thermometer
Artery forceps
Urine testing sticks
Pathology specimen bottles
Skin swabs, throat swabs
Torch
Patellar hammer
Oral airway, e.g. Revivatube, Resuscitube (Fig. 108.1), Guedel
Scalpel (disposable)
File (for glass ampoules)
Examination glove

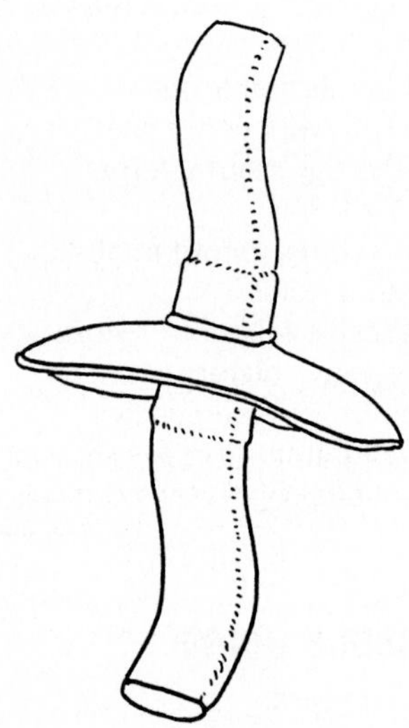

Fig. 108.1 *The two-way Resuscitube*

Drugs

Drugs (oral)

Samples of commonly used:

- analgesics
- antibiotics
- antidiarrhoeal agents
- antiemetics
- antihistamines
- sedatives

Glyceryl trinitrate (nitroglycerin)
Soluble aspirin (myocardial infarction)
Emetic: syrup of ipecachuana

Drugs (inhaled)

Salbutamol aerosol

Drugs (topical)

Anaesthetic eyedrops

Drugs (injectable)

Refer to Tables 108.1 and 108.2.

The country doctor's bag

Country doctors, especially in isolated areas, usually carry additional equipment in their motor vehicles when called to the scene of an accident or other emergency. The equipment will vary according to geographic factors, the ambulance service and the special interests and enthusiasm of the practitioner.

Accident kit

The following list represents the contents of an isolated country doctor's kit; it will occupy a standard briefcase only.

Flashlight and spare batteries
Sterile compression bandages
Steristrips (large and small)
Plastic container of antiseptic
Wide bore needle
Sterile suture set
Gillies' forceps
Small scissors
Large scissors (for cutting clothing)
Artery forceps × 2
Laerdal pocket mask (Fig. 108.2)
Medium-sized torch
Cervical collar
Triangular bandages × 2
Crepe bandages × 2
Air splints × 2
Disposable scalpel with blade
Safety pins
Sterile gauze
Urinary catheter
Blood alcohol sampling kit
Makeshift hook to suspend IV fluid pack
1 litre IV fluid (N saline)

Table 108.1 *Injectable drugs (ideal kit)*

Drug	*Presentation*	*Indications*
Adrenaline	1 mg/mL	hypersensitivity reactions and anaphylactic shock; * bronchial asthma; ventricular asystole; * hypoglycaemia
Atropine sulphate	0.6 mg/1 mL	bradycardia (after myocardial infarction); * ureteric colic; organophosphate poisoning (Malathion)
Benztropine	Cogentin 2 mg/2 mL	acute phenothiazine-induced extrapyramidal reactions
Diazepam	Valium 10 mg/2 mL	status epilepticus and other convulsions such as eclampsia; sedation in acute anxiety and severe tension headache
Ergometrine maleate	0.25 mg/1 mL	uterine bleeding; abortion or postpartum haemorrhage
Frusemide	Lasix 20 mg/2 mL	left ventricular failure, including acute pulmonary oedema
Glucagon	1 mg + 1 mL solvent	hypoglycaemia
Glucose 50%	5 g/10 mL	hypoglycaemic coma
Haloperidol	Serenace 5 mg/1 mL	psychiatric emergencies such as severe agitation, psychoses
Hydrocortisone sodium succinate	Solu-cortef 100 mg/2 mL 250 mg/2 mL	anaphylactic shock; status asthmaticus, Addisonian crisis; thyrotoxic crisis; acute allergies
Hyoscine butylbromide	Buscopan 20 mg/1 mL	* ureteric and biliary colic; acute pancreatitis
Lignocaine	Xylocard 100 mg/5 mL (IV) 321 mg/3 mL (IM)	myocardial infarction ventricular arrhythmias, especially ventricular extrasytoles
Morphine sulphate	15 mg/1 mL	acute pulmonary oedema; relief of severe pain (not due to muscular spasm) such as myocardial infarction
Naloxone (more than one ampoule)	Narcan 0.4 mg/ mL	opiate respiratory depression
Penicillin	Procaine 1.5 g injection	severe life-threatening infections (after blood has been taken for culture) such as meningococcal septicaemia, bacterial endocarditis, gas gangrene, quinsy
Pethidine	100 mg/2 mL	severe pain such as ureteric and biliary colic; (beware of drug addicts simulating renal colic or migraine)
Phytomenadione (vitamin K)	Konakion	anticoagulant overdose with haemorrhage
Prochlorperazine *or* Metoclopramide	Stemetil 12.5 mg/ mL Maxolon 10 mg/2 mL	severe vomiting (examples: Meniere's disease and gastritis), acute labyrinthitis, migraine
Promethazine	Phenergan 50 mg/2 mL	acute allergic conditions, * antiemetic
Salbutamol	Ventolin 0.5 mg/mL	bronchial asthma, other bronchospasm
Water	5 ml	dilutant

* May be useful as an alternative drug

The contents of this bag provide the equipment to cope with common accidents, including:

- bleeding wounds, e.g. arterial bleeders
- tension pneumothorax
- fractured cervical spine
- fractured limbs
- fractures of the shoulder girdle
- snake bites

In addition, some country doctors carry a trephine to cope with the extradural haematoma.

Table 108.2 *Additional cardiopulmonary drugs (optional)*

Injectable drugs	*Presentation*	*Indications*
Aminophylline	250 mg/10 ml	bronchial asthma; acute pulmonary oedema
Isoprenaline	Isuprel 1 mg/mL	bradycardia unresponsive to atropine; asystole
Metaraminol bitartarte	Aramine 10 mg/mL	non-hypovolaemic shock; anaphylactic, drug-induced, associated with spinal anaesthesia, ? cardiogenic
Terbutaline	Bricanyl 0.5 mg/mL	bronchospasm; asthma, bronchitis, smoke inhalation
Verapamil	Isoptin 5 mg/2 mL	supraventricular tachycardia, atrial flutter and fibrillation with rapid ventricular response
Heparin	5000 U/mL	thromboembolism, myocardial infarction

Note The author recommends the MIN-I-JET syringe packs for ideal emergency use. The range includes Naloxone 5 ml, aminophylline, atropine, adrenaline, dextrose, lignocaine, isoprenaline, sodium bicarbonate.

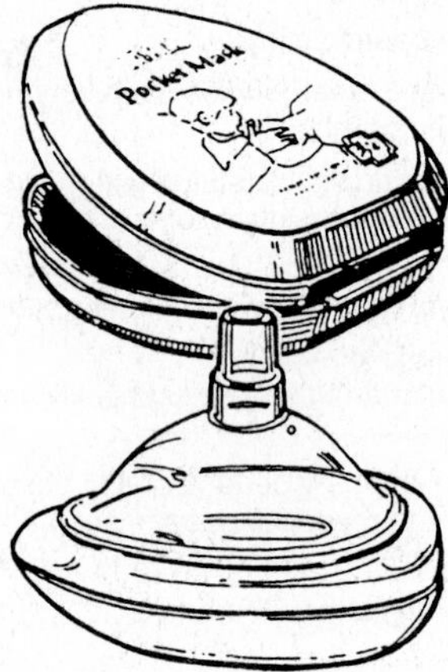

Fig. 108.2 *The Laerdal pocket mask*

Resuscitation kit

The country doctor can carry an oxyresuscitator unit with the following standard items:

Oxygen
Suction
Laryngoscopes
Endotracheal tubes
Oropharyngeal airways, e.g. Guedel
Endotracheal adaptor
Face mask, e.g. Laerdal pocket mask (with one-way valve), or Concorde mask

The base of the unit contains:

Paediatric tracheostomy tube
Self-retaining tourniquet
Intravenous infusion needle
Intravenous infusion tubing
Haemaccel 500 ml
Disposable scalpel, Chromic catgut, Mosquito forceps } for intravenous cutdown
Magill's forceps

Other equipment that could be carried:

A balloon resuscitator and sucker + oxygen cylinder (instead of the oxyresuscitator)
Normal saline or Hartman's solution
Sodium bicarbonate (100 mL)
Portable ECG and defibrillator, e.g. Heartstart

Precautions at the scene of the accident[4,5]

- Don't become a casualty yourself.
- Do not speed to the accident.
- Be alert for other traffic, hazardous material, HIV contamination, power lines, petrol and other inflammable material, jagged edges.
- Turn ignition off as first measure.
- Ensure proper triage: check airways of all victims first, attend to cervical spine injuries and arrest bleeding.
- Recruit bystanders for simple tasks.
- Control the accident scene: stop traffic with proper lights and signs.

Practice tips

- Check your doctor's bag every month for drugs that may be expired, damaged or in short supply (your practice nurse can do this).
- Replace any used drugs or materials the day after use.

- Always have your bag handy but don't carry it in the car in hot weather. It is best to be able to grab it from a safe accessible spot when you leave for an emergency.
- Drugs of addiction (pethidine and morphine) may be kept separate and then taken from their secure place when their use is anticipated, e.g. myocardial infarction, severe biliary or renal colic.
- Keep a spare kit in your surgery if you or your assistants or locums perform a lot of emergency work.
- Familiarise yourself with the layout of your bag (including ampoule files) so that using it in urgent circumstances is efficient.
- Use a large intravenous cannula wherever possible if rapid infusion is required.

References

1. Murtagh J. The doctor's bag: emergency equipment. Aust Fam Physician, 1982; 11:279–280.
2. Hogan C. The management of emergencies in general practice. Aust Fam Physician, 1989; 18:1211–1219.
3. Troller J. The doctor's bag. Essential requirements. Current Therapeutics, August 1990, 64–65.
4. Walpole BG. Roadside emergencies. Aust Fam Physician, 1984; 13(4):249–253.
5. Murtagh J. *Medical emergencies.* Melbourne, RACGP CHECK Programme, 1987; 189:19–22.

109

The treatment room and equipment

The French physician, René Laënnec, who first described cirrhosis of the liver, was the very same whose aversion to applying his naked ear to the perfumed but unbathed bosoms of his patients inspired him to invent the stethoscope . . . The entire medical world continues to pay homage to Laënnec for his gift of space interpersonel.

Richard Selzer (1928—)

Planning

A treatment room is best planned by those who will run and use it, including the nursing sister of the practice. It is wrong to assume that an architect knows best. The function of the room has to be considered: is it to be used exclusively for minor surgery and accidents and emergencies; or is it a general purpose room that can act as the sister's room or as a second consulting room?

Some practitioners may choose to install expensive equipment such as X-ray units, special sterilisers, microscopes, ECG units, electrotherapeutic units such as ultrasonography or interferential machines, and portable defibrillators; others can cope with the simplest equipment.

The room

The function of the room will determine some of the requirements. Access is important if the room is used as an emergency room: can a patient in a wheelchair, or on crutches or on a stretcher be moved comfortably in and out of the treatment room? How close is the room to the ambulance access for transfer of the critically ill?

Some doctors prefer a mobile couch; others prefer a couch placed in the centre of the room.

The room does not need a desk: one option is to use a mobile tray that can hold records and other writing material and can also be used as a dressing table.

Floor space is important, hence most equipment should be stored on accessible shelves or bench tops. The floors should be washable and non-slip (not carpeted) and the walls should be washable.

A mobile overhead light is ideal. A central theatre light, however, is too expensive and an alternative is to use angle-poise lamps at each end of the couch.

An intravenous drip stand and bottle doubles for intravenous fluids and eye irrigation, but it is preferable to have a hook from the ceiling or wall to support an intravenous drip.

Other important practical questions include:

- Are there enough lights, power sockets and taps?
- Can taps be turned off by the elbow after scrubbing?
- Is there adequate ventilation for a steriliser?
- Is there ready access from the main consulting room to the treatment room?
- Is a push button 'intercom' practical?

Resuscitation equipment

Sick people attend surgeries and unfortunately they sometimes have an unpredictable habit of 'collapsing', occasionally with a cardiopulmonary arrest. Any injection of local anaesthetic has the potential to produce a convulsion. Thus it is imperative to have resuscitation equipment available to cope with emergencies such as:

- bronchial asthma
- cardiac arrest
- acute blood loss and continuing haemorrhage
- convulsions, including febrile convulsions

Resuscitation equipment ideally should include:

- an oxygen unit
- suction
- a compressed air pump, nebuliser, solutions and masks
- intravenous equipment and fluids
- an oral airway (Resuscitube or Guedel airway)
- a doctor's bag with standard drugs
- a defibrillator
- Ambubag or Air-viva

Commercially available resuscitation (air or oxygen and suction) units include the oxy-viva (CIG), Modulaide oxygen (Laerdal) and Dr Blue Bag (CIG).

Basic equipment

When equipping the practice do not purchase more than you need. It should be remembered that many hospitals replace instruments at a stage when they are still useful, and these, as well as adequate trolleys, couches and instrument or suture trays, tables and microscopes can be purchased inexpensively.

Standard surgical instruments include scalpels and blades (disposable items available), artery forceps, Gillies' forceps, Allis' forceps, dissecting forceps, splinter forceps, scissors, Magill's forceps, bone forceps, probes and sponge-holding forceps. Important accessories include syringes, needles, suture material, local anaesthesia, float bowls, gauze and swabs.[1]

Dressing and suture materials are important considerations. Dressing kits, already prepacked and sterilised, are available commercially or can be obtained through the local hospital, especially for country practitioners.

Sharps disposable containers are essential to eliminate as far as possible the risk of accidental puncture from used needles.

The microscope is an invaluable item of equipment in the practice.

Special equipment

Practitioners exhibit varying skills and interest in the different surgical disciplines. Recommended equipment to manage basic problems includes:

Ear, nose and throat—auriscope, head mirror, aural specula, laryngeal mirror, nasal specula, nasal packing, nasal packing forceps, BIP (bismuth iodoform paraffin) paste, spirit burner, topical anaesthesia, ear syringe, wax curette, Waxsol drops, dental broach, small Foley catheter, cupped alligator forceps, foreign body remover, eustachian catheter, Epistat nasal catheter, Merocel ear wick and nasal pack.

Eyes—binocular loupe, dental burr, meibomian clamp, eye stream, Minims (for example, fluorescein and amethocaine), eye testing charts (46 cm and 305 cm), multiple pin holes, sterile cotton buds, non-allergenic tape, eye pads, eyebrow tweezers.

Skin—liquid nitrogen, electrodiathermy unit, small dermatome, punch biopsy punches (disposable), Wood's light, e.g. 'the black light', 20% potassium hydroxide (for dermatophyte diagnosis).

The cryosurgical unit, complete with cylinder of gas and cryoprobe, is an excellent though expensive unit.

A wide-bore trocar and cannula (with expellor) is needed for subcutaneous insertion of hormone implants.

Musculoskeletal—plaster, open toe cast shoe (to allow walking on leg plaster), plaster cutters, air splints, aluminium-backed foam splints. Soft cervical collars, lumbar supports (for example, McKenzie roll), crutches. Special electrotherapy equipment, e.g. ultrasound.

Genitourinary—specula, uterine sound, intrauterine contraceptive devices, tenaculum, urinary catheter.

Anorectal—proctoscope, gloves, haemorrhoid ligatures, suppositories, enemas (e.g. Microlax). Haemorrhoid (Gabriel) injection syringe and needle with ampoules of 5% phenol in almond oil.

Respiratory—vitalograph, peak flow meter, air pump, nebuliser and accessories. Hand-held nebulisers and spacers for inhaler technique demonstration.

Pharmaceutical preparations

The emergency injectable drugs such as adrenaline, morphine and diazepam can be located in locked cupboards or in the doctor's bag.

Many topical preparations have a multiplicity of uses. These include various antiseptics, topical freezing preparations such as ethyl chloride, ether, trichloractic acid, podophyllin paint, silver nitrate, phenol of various strengths, salicylic acid paste, ethanolamine 5%, and Stingose.

Syrup of ipecacuanha is essential to cope with the ingestion of various poisons.

Office sterilisation

Sterilisation of office equipment is a very important issue, especially with items and instruments that breach the body surface. These must be sterile, that is, free from all infections and potentially infectious matter[2,3] including bacteria, viruses, chlamydia, rickettsia, mycoplasma, protozoa and spores. Endoscopy equipment in particular requires special attention. The practitioner is responsible for preventing cross-infection in the practice and hence careful attention to correct decontamination of medical instruments is essential.

Distinctions between main techniques

- *Decontamination*—a general term to cover methods of cleaning, disinfection and sterilisation for removal of microbial contamination from medical equipment such as to render it safe.[2]
- *Disinfection*—inactivation of vegetative bacteria, viruses and fungi, but not necessarily of bacterial spores.
- *Sterilisation*—complete destruction or removal of micro-organisms and their spores from materials.

Many doctors still use the misnomer 'steriliser' when referring to a hot water disinfector, which does not kill all bacterial spores. The principal methods of decontamination are steam under pressure (autoclaves), dry heat (hot air ovens), boiling water and chemical disinfectants. The use of sterile single-use instruments and other equipment removes the need for any procedures to decontaminate instruments.

Sterilisation techniques[2]

Heat disinfectants

1. Steam under pressure (autoclave)

This is the most reliable method of sterilising instruments. However, if the instruments were not cleaned properly beforehand they would not necessarily be rendered sterile. The steam steriliser should have a drying cycle.

Recommended sterilisation times and temperatures for autoclaves are:

Temperature (°C)	*Time (minutes)*
121	15
126	10
134	3

2. Hot air ovens

Recommended times and temperatures for dry heat are:

Temperature (°C)	*Time (minutes)*
160	60
170	40
180	20

3. Hot water disinfectors

To ensure destruction of the HIV virus it is important to boil the instruments for 10–30 minutes. The recommended time is 30 minutes. If another instrument is added to the load, timing must start anew.

Cold or chemical disinfectors

Chemical disinfection is an uncertain process and should only be used when more effective heat treatment is inappropriate. It is suitable for medium-risk items such as thermometers or flexible endoscopes which can be damaged by heat or steam.

1. *Alcohol*: e.g. ethyl or isopropyl alcohol as 70% v/v in water. Alcohol does not kill spores.

Note Surgical spirit should be avoided for routine disinfection purposes.

2. *Glutaraldehyde*: a 2% solution of alkaline glutaraldehyde is suitable for disinfection of fibreoptic equipment, which should be thoroughly washed in water and detergent immediately after use.
3. *Hypochlorite*: hypochlorites as a solution of sodium hypochlorite, e.g. 'Milton' bleach, or as sodium dichloroisocyanurate (NaDCC) tablets or granules have a wide microbicidal activity.

Table 109.1 summarises categories of risk and types of instruments decontaminated in general practice.[2]

Table 109.1 *Risk categories and types of instrument decontamination*[2]

	Risk instruments	
High risk	***Medium risk***	***Low risk***
Surgical scissors Metal/plastic forceps Stitch cutters Intrauterine device sets Uterine sounds Tenacula Hypodermic needles Vaginal specula used for inserting IUDs	Vaginal specula for vaginal examination Ring pessaries Ring diaphragms Proctoscopes Nasal specula Tongue depressors Laryngeal mirrors Thermometers	Ear syringe nozzles Skin thermometer
	Recommended method of decontamination	
Sterilise or single-use (presterile)	Sterilise by autoclaving or dry heat or single-use (non-presterile)	Sterilise or boil (nozzles) especially if skin breaks or infection suspected
	Alternatives	
None	Boil if suitable or none	Chemical disinfection or wash

Note All scrubbing brushes and bottle brushes used for cleaning purposes must themselves be autoclaved or disinfected regularly. Reprinted with permission from *A code of practice for sterilisation of instruments and control of cross-infection*, published by the BMA.

Summary

The recommendations about the contents of the treatment room are not intended to be complete or a mandatory survival package. Some practitioners manage comfortably with basic equipment such as an Air-viva, a standard doctor's bag and a handful of instruments. Others have very advanced rooms with equipment compatible with their special interests and geographical location. The medical equipment can be obtained from suppliers, and some equipment has been designed by doctors who market their own concepts.

An autoclave is undoubtedly the most efficient method of sterilising reusable medical instruments[3], although great diligence must be exercised in the cleaning of the equipment beforehand and in the care of the autoclave. General practitioners should consider using single-use presterilised material wherever possible and employing the services of nearby hospital sterilising departments for sterilisation of instruments.

The efficiently managed treatment room should have an accurate record of procedures and list of current stock (including expiry dates, service dates and faulty equipment). There is no doubt patients and therapists benefit from an efficient treatment room.

References

1. Murtagh J, Troller J. Establishing a treatment room. Aust Fam Physician, 1989; 18:22–24.
2. Dawson J. *A code of practice for sterilisation of instruments and control of cross-infection*. London: British Medical Association, 1989:31–52.
3. Hammond L. Office sterilisation. Aust Fam Physician, 1990; 19, 693.

110

Common sporting injuries

Although there is considerable overlap between injuries occurring during everyday activities and sporting and recreational activities, there are many injuries that are characteristic to sports people. Many of these injuries are the result of trauma of various degrees and include the many varieties of fractures, dislocations and soft tissue injuries.

Injuries to the eye

Blunt injuries to the eye are common in sport. Examples include tennis and squash balls, cricket balls and baseballs and fists and fingers associated with body contact sports. Haemorrhage is the most common problem and occurs throughout the eye: subconjunctivally; in the anterior chamber (hyphaema); into the vitreous; and underneath the retina or choroid.

Another common problem is a corneal abrasion where a small wound can be caused by a foreign body, a fingernail or a contact lens. It needs to be treated with great respect.

Hyphaema

With hyphaema, bleeding from the iris collects in the anterior chamber of the eye. The danger is that, with exertion, a secondary bleed from the ruptured vessel could fill the anterior chamber with blood, blocking the escape of aqueous humour and causing a severe secondary glaucoma. Loss of the eye can occur with a severe haemorrhage. It is likely to happen between the second and fourth day after the injury.

Management

- First, exclude a penetrating injury.
- Avoid unnecessary movement: vibration will aggravate bleeding. (For this reason, do not use a helicopter if evacuation is necessary.)
- Avoid smoking and alcohol.
- Do not give aspirin (can induce bleeding).
- Prescribe complete bed rest for five days and review the patient daily.
- Apply padding over the injured eye for four days.
- Administer sedatives as required.
- Beware of 'floaters', 'flashes' and field defects.

Arrange ophthalmic consultation after one month to exclude glaucoma and retinal detachment. No sport before this time.

Generally, recovery runs an uneventful course. If secondary bleeding occurs (usually the second, third or fourth day) the patient should be transported immediately to the nearest eye hospital. Evacuate by air (not by helicopter) only if the cabin altitude can be kept below 1300 metres (4000 feet). It is important to prevent vomiting and expansion of air within the eye.

Protective spectacles should always be worn when playing squash. People with monocular vision should be advised not to participate in this sport.

Knocked out or broken teeth

If a permanent (second) tooth is knocked out it can be saved by immediate proper care. Likewise, a broken tooth should be saved and urgent dental attention sought.

The knocked out tooth

- Place the tooth in its original position, preferably immediately (Fig. 110.1): if dirty, put it in milk before replacement or, better still, place it under the tongue and 'wash it' in saliva. Do not use water, and do not wipe or touch the root.
- Fix the tooth by moulding strong silver foil (e.g. a milk bottle top or cooking foil) over it and the adjacent teeth.
- Refer the patient to his or her dentist or dental hospital as soon as possible.

Note Teeth replaced within half an hour have a 90% chance of successful reimplantation.

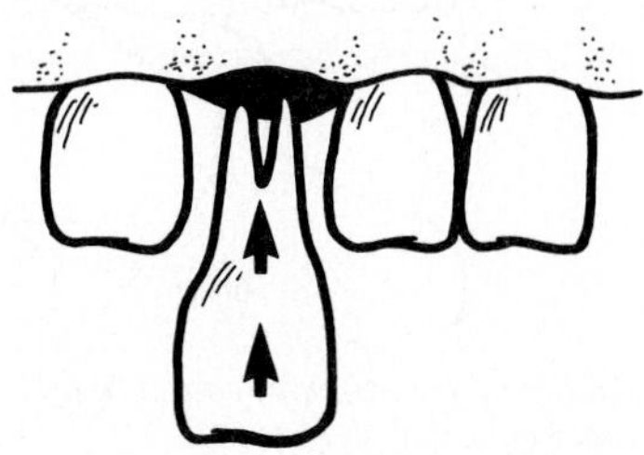

Fig. 110.1 *Replacement of a knocked-out tooth*

Injuries to the nose

Common injuries to the nose include epistaxis and fractures of the nasal bones.

Epistaxis

First aid is simple tamponade, which is invariably effective. The soft cartilaginous part of the nose should be pinched between the finger and thumb for 5–10 minutes. The head should be kept bent slightly forward. Packing of the nose may be required.

Fracture of the nose

If deformity is present the patient should be referred for reduction within seven days.

Septal haematoma

Special care has to be taken of a septal haematoma, which has a tendency to become infected (page 997).

Shoulder injuries

Common shoulder injuries acquired in sporting activities include:

- dislocated or subluxed acromioclavicular joint (page 1013)
- fractured clavicle (page 1012)
- dislocated shoulder (page 1013)
- supraspinatus tendinitis (page 528)

Swimmer's shoulder

Painful shoulders occur in about 60% of elite level swimmers during their career. The basic disorder is rotator cuff tendinitis, particularly supraspinatus tendinitis, which is considered to be associated with abnormal scapular positioning and cervicothoracic dysfunction. The best treatment is prevention, which aims at rotator cuff strengthening exercises, better scapulothoracic control, including correction of thoracic extension if it is decreased, and scapular stabilisation exercises.[1]

Elbow injuries

Soft-tissue disorders of the elbow are extremely common. Two types of tennis elbow are identifiable. 'Backhand' tennis elbow or lateral epicondylitis (page 539) and 'forehand' tennis elbow or medial epicondylitis, which is also known as golfer's elbow or baseball pitcher's elbow. These common problems, often unrelated to sporting activity, are presented in more detail in Chapter 54.

Hand injuries

Hand and finger injuries are very important in sporting activities and include fractures and dislocations of phalanges and metacarpals. A mallet finger is a common injury and can result from overuse.

Ligamentous disruption of finger joints can cause instability and require early referral. An example is gamekeeper's thumb, often encountered in skiers, where there is complete tearing of the medial ligament of the metacarpophalangeal joint.

Mallet finger

A mallet finger is a common sports injury caused by the ball (football, cricket ball or baseball) unexpectedly hitting the finger tip and forcing the finger to flex. Such a forced hyperflexion injury to the distal phalanx can rupture or avulse the extensor insertion into its dorsal base. The characteristic swan neck deformity is due to retraction of the lateral bands and hyperextension of the proximal interphalangeal joint.

The 45° guideline

Without treatment, the eventual disability will be minimal if the extensor lag at the distal joint is less than 45°; a greater lag will result in functional difficulty and cosmetic deformity.

Treatment

Maintain hyperextension of the distal interphalangeal joint for six weeks, leaving the proximal interphalangeal joint free to flex.

Equipment

- Friar's balsam (will permit greater adhesion of tape)
- Non-stretch adhesive tape, 1 cm wide: two strips approximately 10 cm in length

Method

1. Paint finger with Friar's balsam (compound benzoin tincture).
2. Apply the first strip of tape in a figure of eight configuration. The centre of the tape must engage and support the pulp of the finger. The tapes must cross dorsally at the level of the distal interphalangeal joint and extend to the volar aspect of the proximal interphalangeal joint without inhibiting its movement (Fig. 110.2a).
3. Apply the second piece of tape as a 'stay' around the midshaft of the middle phalanx (Fig. 110.2b).

Reapply the tape wherever extension of the distal interphalangeal joint drops below the neutral position (usually daily, depending on the patient's occupation). Maintain extension for six weeks.

Surgery

Open reduction and internal fixation are reserved for those cases where the avulsed bony fragment is large enough to cause instability, leading to volar subluxation of the distal interphalangeal joint.

Tenpin bowler's thumb

Tenpin bowler's thumb is a common stress syndrome in players. It usually presents as a soft-tissue swelling at the base of the thumb web, with associated pain and stiffness of the digits used for bowling. It may cause a traumatic neuroma of the digital nerve at this site with associated hyperaesthesia.

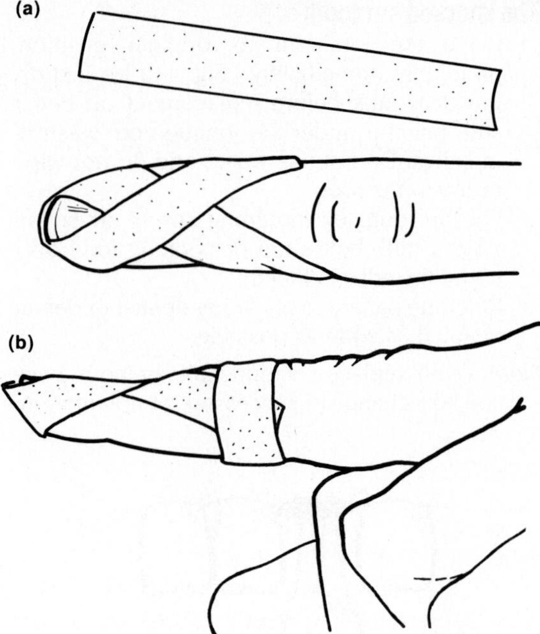

Fig. 110.2 *Mallet finger:* **(a)** *application of first tape;* **(b)** *application of 'stay' tape*

Management

- rest
- massage
- bevel the bowling ball holes to reduce friction
- an intralesional injection (Fig. 110.3) of 0.25 mL of long-acting corticosteroid mixed with local anaesthetic (resistant cases)

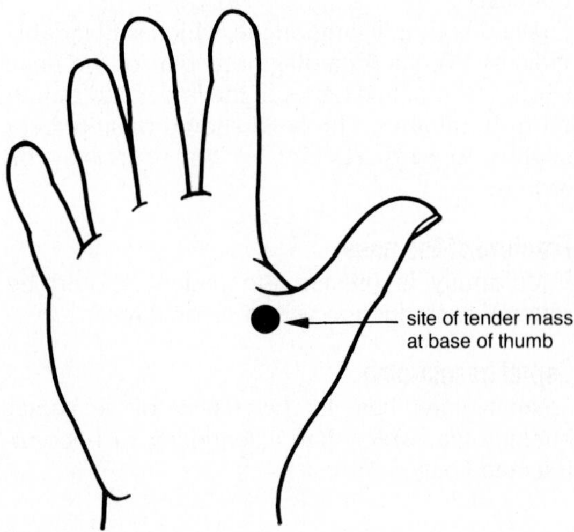

Fig. 110.3 *Tenpin bowler's thumb*

Snow skiing injuries

The most common injuries encountered in snow skiing are soft-tissue injuries and fractures and dislocations.

A study by Robinson showed that the six most common skiing injuries were: strains to the medial collateral ligament of the knee 24.3%; contusions of soft tissue (excluding head and neck) 17.6%; lacerations 15.5%; neck and back injuries 7.8%; fractures 7.6%; and dislocations.[2]

There has been a large decrease in injuries relative to participation in the past decade because of improved equipment and attention to safety. The most common fractures in skiers are those involving the tibia and fibula, especially spiral fractures. Other common fractures are of the clavicle, wrist and humerus. Dislocation of the shoulder region (glenohumeral joint and acromioclavicular joint) are due to falls on hard impacted snow.

Skier's thumb[3]

A special injury is skier's thumb (also known as gamekeeper's thumb) in which there is ligamentous disruption of the metacarpophalangeal joint with or without an avulsion fracture of the base of the proximal phalanx at the point of ligamentous attachment. This injury is caused by the thumb being forced into abduction and hyperextension by the ski pole as the skier pitches into the snow.

Diagnosis is made by X-ray with stress views of the thumb. Incomplete tears are immobilised in a scaphoid type of plaster for three weeks, while complete tears and avulsion fractures should be referred for surgical repair.

Spinal problems

Spinal dysfunction, particularly of the neck and low back, are very common problems in sport, as for the general population.

Serious problems include pars interarticularis fractures, spondylolisthesis, disc disruptions with prolapse and, rarely, vertebral body fracture. The common problems are the various facet joint syndromes and musculoskeletal strains, which are managed conservatively as outlined in Chapters 31 and 52. The key to management is a conservative approach with a back education and exercise program.

Injuries to the lower limbs

Injuries due to trauma and overuse of the lower limbs comprise the most frequent group of sports-related disorders requiring medical attention.

The three main causes of overuse trauma are:

- friction, e.g. peritendinitis
- stress or overload, e.g. hamstring tear, tibial stress fracture
- ischaemia, e.g. anterior compartment syndrome

Overuse leg syndromes

Increased community participation in physical activity, including running and jogging, has resulted in a concomitant increase in overuse leg injuries, especially in the lower leg with its weight-bearing load. The common cause is repetitive trauma where the forces involved overwhelm the tissue's ability to repair adequately. Common causes of chronic leg pain include hamstring injuries and injuries to the lower leg.

Principles of management

Prevention:

- maintain ideal weight
- good nutrition
- adequate preparation
- warm-up exercises for the legs
- proper footwear
- proper activity planning

Treatment of injury

- Rest, or relative rest: the patient is allowed to perform activities that do not aggravate the injury.
- Ice: apply an ice pack for 20–30 minutes every two hours while awake during the first 48–72 hours post injury.
- Compression: keep the injured muscle or tissue firmly bandaged for at least 48 hours.
- Elevation: rest the leg on a stool or chair until the swelling subsides.
- Correction of predisposing factors (intrinsic or extrinsic), e.g. orthotics for malalignment, correction of training errors.
- NSAIDs for painful inflammatory response.
- Physical therapy, e.g. stretching, mobilisation when acute phase settled.

Groin pain

Groin pain is a particularly common condition among athletes.

Acute groin pain

Acute conditions such as muscle and musculotendinous strains[4], and overuse injuries such as tendinitis and tendoperiostitis, are generally readily diagnosed and treated. Diagnostic difficulties can arise because of referred pain from the lumbosacral spine, hip and pelvis. More common acute groin injuries include injuries to the following muscles and their tendons (Fig. 110.4).

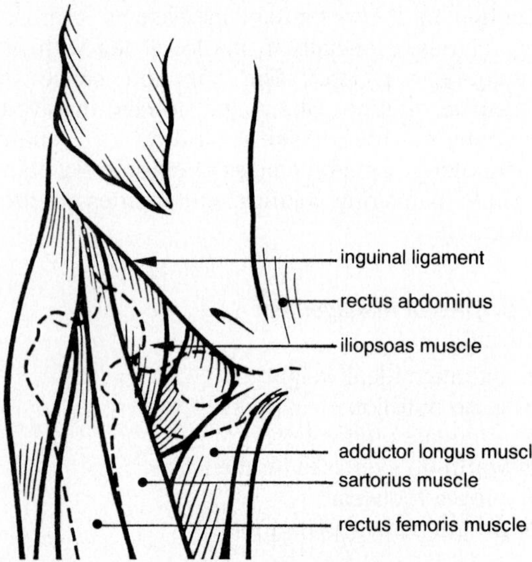

Fig. 110.4 *Muscles in the groin region subject to musculotendinous injuries in the athlete*

- adductor longus, e.g. musculotendinous strains
- rectus femoris
- sartorius
- iliopsoas

Other injuries include:

- SUFE in adolescents
- avulsion fractures in adolescents, e.g. rectus femoris and sartorius on the iliac spines

Chronic groin pain

There are many causes of chronic groin pain, with bone and joint abnormalities being more likely causes. Important causes include:

- muscle and musculotendinous lesions, e.g. adductor longus tendoperiostitis
- bursitis, e.g. iliopsoas bursitis
- osteitis pubis (pubic symphysis)
- stress fractures, e.g. femoral neck and pubic rami
- sacroiliac and hip joint disorders, e.g. osteoarthritis hip/tumour
- lumbar spine: L1/L2 or L2/L3 disc
- 'occult' inguinal or femoral hernia

Investigations

- X-ray of pelvis (AP, lateral, oblique)
- tomography of pubic symphysis (to detect osteitis pubis and pubic instability)
- bone scan to detect stress fractures or osteitis pubis
- herniography
- CT scan or ultrasound (increasing potential)

Jock itch

Jock itch, or tinea cruris, is a common infection in the groin area of young men, especially athletes, who are subjected to chaffing in the groins from tight shorts and nylon 'jock straps'. The feet should be inspected for evidence of tinea pedis. The dermatophyte is transmitted by towels and other objects, particularly in change rooms and communal showers (page 860).

Hamstring injuries

Hamstring strains are common in athletes. The short head of biceps femoris is the most commonly strained component of the hamstring group.

Clinical features:

- a history of a 'pull', 'twinge', 'tear' or 'twang' in the back of the thigh
- a soreness and lump develops (with a severe tear a person can collapse)
- localised tenderness
- limitation of straight leg raising
- pain on resisted or active knee flexion or hip extension
- bruising (usually in popliteal fossa) may be present

Management

The immediate goals of treatment of the acute injury are to relieve pain and minimise swelling.

- RICE for 72 hours
- NSAIDs, e.g. aspirin or indomethacin
- stretching exercises
  - — passive stretching after ice treatment
  - — then active stretching
  - — then isometric contraction exercises

Haematomas in muscle ('corked thigh')

Haematomas can be intramuscular or intermuscular or interstitial and usually result from a sharp blow, e.g. knee to the thigh or kick in the anterior compartment of the leg.

An intramuscular haematoma can cause an acute compartment syndrome which may require urgent decompression. One objective of treatment is to prevent excessive scarring. Other complications include infection, cyst formation, thrombophlebitis and myositis ossificans.

Management

- RICE treatment with emphasis on cooling
- non-weight-bearing, using crutches initially
- consider admission to hospital or a day surgical unit to check progress
- referral for expert advice may be appropriate because of the potentially serious nature of the injury

Injuries to the knee

Knee injuries are common, have multiple clinical disorders and are potentially disastrous to the athlete. The various injuries and overuse syndromes are presented in considerable detail in Chapter 50, on the painful knee.

Acute injuries

Acute injuries (pages 485–88) include:

- meniscal tears
- ligamentous tears and strains (of varying degrees)
  - — anterior cruciate ligament
  - — posterior cruciate ligament
  - — medial collateral ligament
  - — lateral collateral ligament

Overuse syndromes

The knee is very prone to overuse disorders (pages 488–90). The pain develops gradually without swelling, is aggravated by activity and relieved with rest. It can usually be traced back to a change in the sportsperson's training schedule, footwear, technique or related factors. It may be related also to biomechanical abnormalities ranging from hip disorders to disorders of the feet.

Overuse injuries include:

- patellofemoral pain syndrome (jogger's knee/runner's knee)
- patellar tendinitis (jumper's knee)
- synovial plica syndrome
- infrapatellar fat-pad inflammation
- anserinus bursitis/tendinitis
- biceps femoris tendinitis
- semimembranous bursitis/tendinitis
- quadriceps tendinitis/rupture
- popliteus tendinitis
- iliotibial band friction syndrome (runner's knee)
- the hamstrung knee

A careful history followed by systematic anatomical palpation around the knee joint will pinpoint the specific overuse syndrome.

Overuse injuries to lower leg

A summary of the clinical and management aspects of various injuries is presented in Table 110.1 and in Figure 110.5.

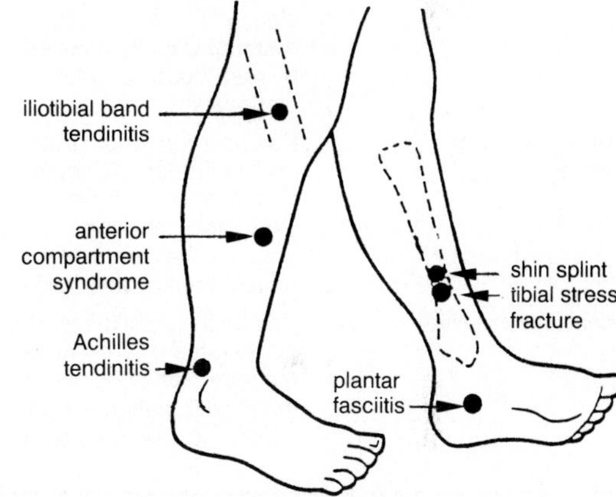

Fig. 110.5 *Common sites of overuse injuries in the lower leg*

Common causes of chronic lower leg pain in sports people include:[5]

- medial tibial stress syndrome (previously called shin splints)
- stress fractures (Fig. 110.6)
- exertional compartment syndrome, especially anterior compartment
- tibialis anterior tenosynovitis (Fig. 110.7)
- chronic muscle strains

These problems are invariably due to excessive physical demands in athletes striving for the ultimate performance or in the occasional athletes who have made inadequate preparation for their activity. Training errors contribute to a large proportion (60%) of overuse injuries.[5]

Table 110.1 *Clinical comparisons of overuse syndromes in lower leg*

Syndrome	*Symptoms*	*Cause*	*Treatment*
Anterior compartment syndrome	Pain in the anterolateral muscular compartment of the leg, increasing with activity. Difficult dorsiflexion of foot, which may feel floppy	Persistent fast running (e.g. squash, football, middle-distance running).	Modify activities. Surgical fasciotomy is the only effective treatment.
Iliotibial band tendinitis	Deep aching along lateral aspect of knee or lateral thigh. Worse running downhill, eased by rest. Pain appears after 3-4 km running.	Running up hills by long-distance runners and increasing distance too quickly.	Rest from running for 6 weeks. Special stretching exercises. Correct training faults and footwear. ? injection of LA and corticosteroids deep into tender areas.
Tibial stress syndrome or shin splints	Pain and localised tenderness over the distal posteromedial border of the tibia. Bone scan for diagnosis.	Running or jumping on hard surfaces.	Relative rest for 6 weeks. Ice massage. Calf (soleus stretching). NSAIDs. Correct training faults and footwear.
Tibial stress fracture	Pain, in a similar site to shin splints, noted after running. Usually relieved by rest. Bone scan for diagnosis.	Overtraining on hard (often bitumen) surfaces. Faulty footwear.	Rest for 6-10 weeks. Casting not recommended. Graduated training after healing.
Tibialis anterior tenosynovitis	Pain, over anterior distal third of leg and ankle. Pain at beginning and after exercise ± swelling, crepitus. Pain on active or resisted ankle dorsiflexion.	Overuse—excessive downhill running.	Rest, even from walking. Injection of LA and corticosteroid within tendon sheath.
Achilles tendinitis	Pain in the Achilles tendon aggravated by walking on the toes. Stiff and sore in the morning after rising but improving after activity.	Repeated toe running in sprinters or running uphill in distance runners.	Relative rest. Ice at first and then heat. 10 mm heel wedge. Correct training faults and footwear. NSAIDs.

Principles of treatment

1. rest or relative rest
2. exercise program (where appropriate)
3. correction of predisposing factors, e.g.
   — training errors
   — proper footwear
   — inadequate warm-up
   — malalignment
4. analgesics: use NSAIDs only if true inflammatory pain (pain at rest)

Stress fractures

Stress fractures are an important cause of lower leg pain and foot pain in sport, accounting for 5–15% of injuries.[5] Stress fractures occur in the tibia and fibula and in the foot (navicular, calcaneus and metatarsals). The important clinical factor is to keep stress fractures in mind and X-ray the tender area. If the X-ray is negative and there is a high index of suspicion, a radionuclide scan should be ordered.

In the tibia, stress fractures occur mainly in the proximal metaphysis and the junction of the middle and distal thirds of the shaft. In the fibula they usually occur 5–7 cm above the tip of the lateral malleolus (Fig. 110.6).

These stress fractures usually occur after prolonged and repeated heavy loading such as long-distance running and repeated jumping.

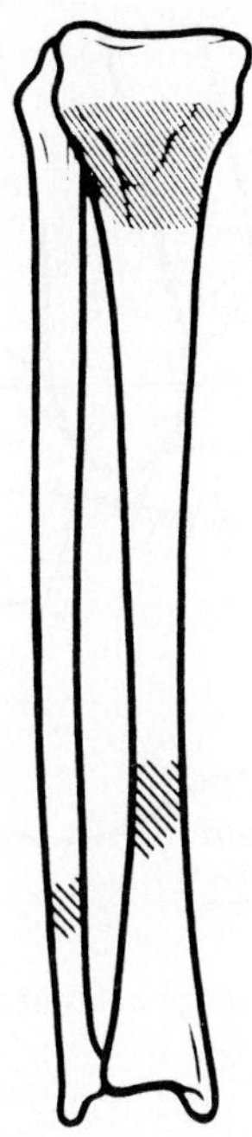

Fig. 110.6 *Typical sites of stress fractures in athletes in the tibia and fibula*

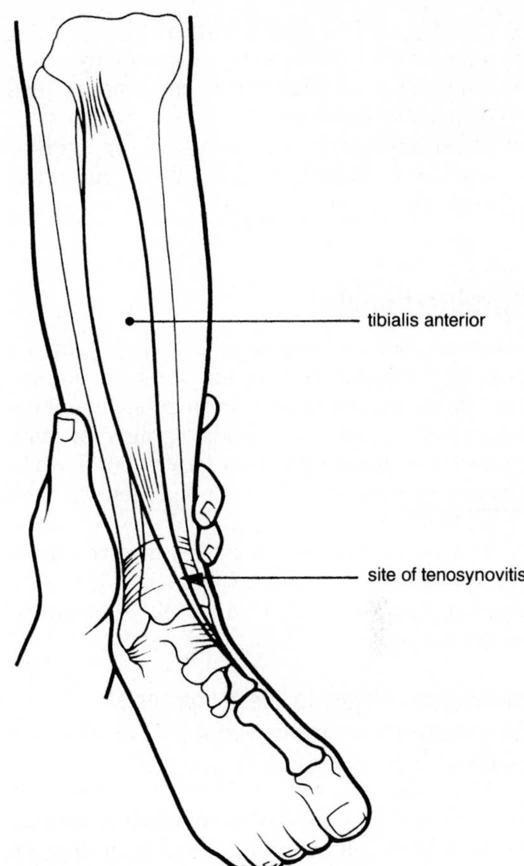

Fig. 110.7 *Site of tibialis anterior tenosynovitis*

Torn 'monkey muscle'

The so-called torn 'monkey muscle', or 'tennis leg', is actually a rupture of the medial head of gastrocnemius at the musculoskeletal junction where the Achilles tendon merges with the muscle (Fig. 110.8). It is not a torn plantaris muscle as commonly believed. This painful injury is common in middle-aged tennis and squash players who play infrequently and are unfit.

Clinical features:

- a sudden sharp pain in the calf (the person thinks he/she has been struck from behind, e.g. a thrown stone)
- unable to put heel to ground
- walks on tip toes
- localised tenderness and hardness
- dorsiflexion of ankle painful
- bruising over site of rupture

Management

- RICE treatment for 48 hours
- ice packs immediately for 20 minutes and then every two hours when awake (can be placed over the bandage)
- a firm elastic bandage from toes to below the knee

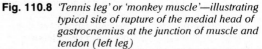

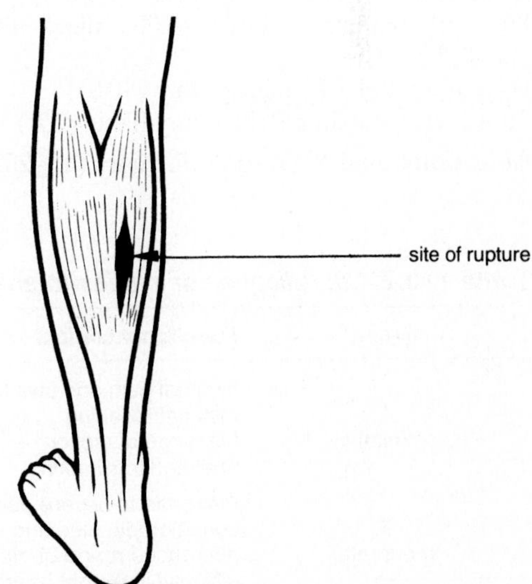

Fig. 110.8 *'Tennis leg' or 'monkey muscle'—illustrating typical site of rupture of the medial head of gastrocnemius at the junction of muscle and tendon (left leg)*

- crutches can be used if severe
- a raised heel on the shoe aids mobility
- commence mobilisation after 48 hours rest, with active exercises
- physiotherapist supervision for gentle stretching massage and then restricted exercise

Sprained ankle

There are two main ligaments that are subject to heavy inversion or eversion stresses, namely the lateral ligaments and the medial ligaments respectively. Most of the ankle 'sprains' or tears involve the lateral ligaments (up to 90%) while the stronger tauter (deltoid) ligament is less prone to injury.

The lateral ligament complex involves three main bands: the anterior talofibular (ATFL), the calcaneofibular (CFL) and the posterior talofibular ligament (PTFL) (Fig. 110.9).

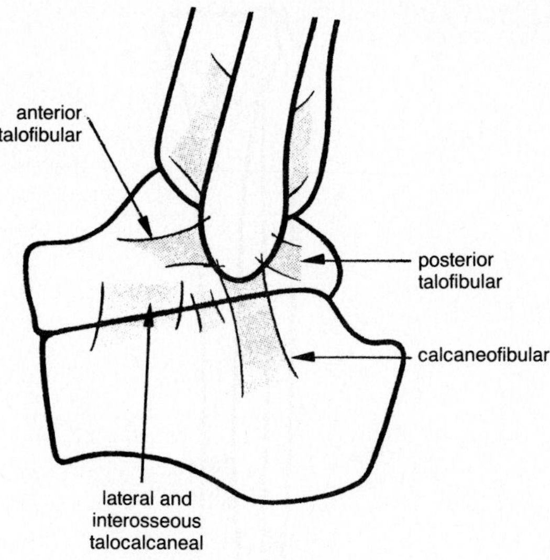

Fig. 110.9 *Lateral ligaments of the ankle*

Mechanism of injury to lateral ligaments[6]

Forced inversion causes about 90% of all ankle injuries.

Most sprains occur when the ankle is plantarflexed and inverted such as when landing awkwardly after jumping or stepping on uneven ground.

Inversion

Foot in plantar flexion: ATFL injury likely (50–60%)
Foot in neutral: CFL injury likely (10%)
Foot in dorsiflexion: PTFL injury likely (5%)

Note Combined ATFL and CFL injury (15–25%).

Eversion

Foot in plantar flexion or neutral: medial ligament (mainly anterior part)

The classification of ankle injuries is presented in Table 110.2.

Clinical features of sprained lateral ligaments

Common features

- ankle 'gives way'
- difficulty in weight bearing
- discomfort varies from mild to severe
- bruising (may take 12–24 hours) indicates more severe injury
- may have functional instability: ankle gives way on uneven ground

Table 110.2 *Classification of injuries to ankle ligaments (adapted from Litt)[6]*

Grade	Functional/clinical	Ligamentous stability
I (mild)	minimal pain and swelling minimal bleeding full range of motion heel and toe walking	minor ligamentous injury with only a partial tear of the ligament stable ankle joint
II (moderate)	moderate to severe pain and swelling considerable bleeding decreased range of motion difficulty in weight bearing and ambulation	similar to Grade I only more severe partially unstable joint
III (severe)	minimal to severe pain and swelling pronounced bleeding minimal range of motion unable to weight bear	complete ligamentous rupture with unstable joint

Physical examination (perform as soon as possible)

- note swelling and bruising
- palpate over bony landmarks and three lateral ligaments
- test general joint laxity and range of motion
- a common finding is rounded swelling in front of lateral malleolus (the 'signe de la coquille d'oeuf')
- test stability in A-P plane (anterior draw sign)

Is there an underlying fracture?[7]

For a severe injury the possibility of a fracture—usually of the lateral malleolus or base of fifth metatarsal—must be considered. If the patient is able to walk without much discomfort straight after the injury, a fracture is unlikely.

Indications for X-ray include:[7]

- inability to weight bear immediately after injury
- marked swelling and bruising soon after injury
- marked tenderness over the bony landmarks
- marked pain on movement of the ankle
- crepitus on palpation or movement
- point tenderness over the base of the fifth metatarsal
- special circumstances, e.g. litigation potential

Management

The treatment of ankle ligament sprains depends on the severity of the sprain. Most grade I and II sprains respond well to standard conservative measures and regain full, pain-free movement in 1–6 weeks, but controversy surrounds the most appropriate management of grade III sprains.

Grade I sprain

R rest the injured part for 48 hours, depending on disability
I ice pack for 20 minutes every 3–4 hours when awake for the first 48 hours
C compression bandage, e.g. crepe bandage
E elevate to hip level to minimise swelling
A analgesics, e.g. paracetamol ± codeine
R review in 48 hours, then 7 days
S special strapping

Use partial weight bearing with crutches for the first 48 hours or until standing is no longer painful, then encourage early full weight bearing and a full range of movement with isometric exercises.[7] Use warm soaks, dispense with ice packs after 48 hours. Walking in sand, e.g. along the beach, is excellent rehabilitation. Aim towards full activity by two weeks.

Special strapping

A firm support for partial tears in the absence of gross swelling provides excellent symptomatic relief and early mobilisation.

Method

- Maintain the foot in a neutral position (right angles to leg) by getting patient to hold the foot in that position by a long strap or sling.
- Apply small protective pads over pressure points.
- Apply one or two stirrups of adhesive low-stretch 6–8 cm strapping from halfway up medial side, around the heel and then halfway up the lateral side to hold foot in slight eversion (Figs 110.10 a,b).
- Apply an adhesive bandage, e.g. Acrylastic (6–8 cm) which can be rerolled and reused.
- Reapply in 3–4 days.
- After seven days remove and use a non-adhesive tubular elasticised support until full pain-free movement is achieved.

Grade II sprain

RICE treatment (as above) for 48 hours but ice, e.g. ACE wrap, should be every 2–3 hours and no weight bearing, using crutches, for 48 hours. Then permit partial weight bearing with crutches and begin the active exercise program. Follow-up and supportive strapping as for Grade I. Note that the ice packs can be placed over the strapping.

Grade III

It would be appropriate to refer this patient with a complete tear. Initial management includes RICE and analgesics and an X-ray to exclude an associated fracture. The three main treatment approaches appear to be equally satisfactory.

Surgical repair

Some specialists prefer this treatment but it is usually reserved for the competitive athlete who demands absolute stability of the ankle.

Plaster immobilisation

This is reserved usually for patients who are unable actively to dorsiflex their foot to a right angle and those who need to be mobile and protected in order to work. The plaster is maintained until the ligament repairs, usually 4–6 weeks. The patient can walk normally when comfortable with a rockered sole or open cast walking shoe.

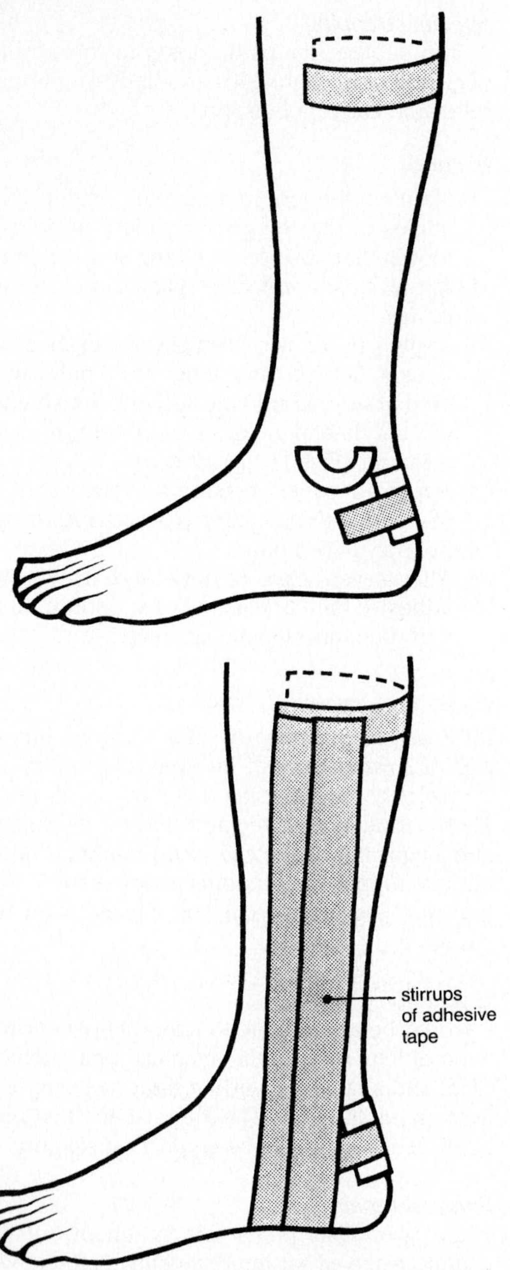

Fig. 110.10a, b *Supportive strapping for a sprained ankle:* **Step 1** *apply protective pads and stay tape;* **Step 2** *apply stirrups to hold foot in slight eversion*

Strapping and physiotherapy
This approach is generally recommended. After the usual treatment for a Grade II repair, including the strapping as described, a heel lock (Fig. 110.10c) should be used. The patient continues on crutches and appropriate physiotherapy is given with care so that the torn ends are not distracted. Strengthened balance is achieved by the use of elastic bands, swimming and cycling.

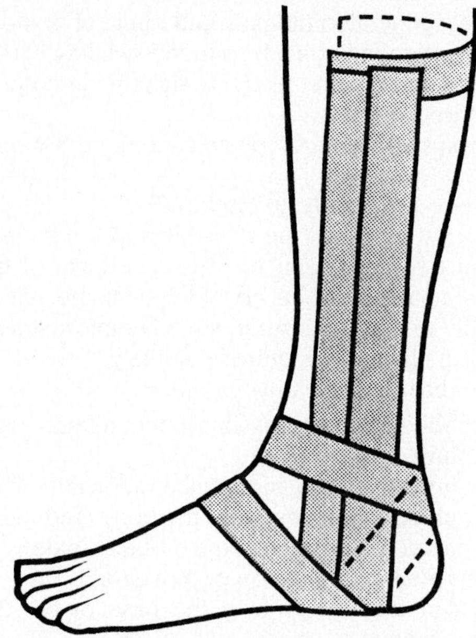

Fig. 110.10c *Supportive strapping for a sprained ankle:* **Step 3** *apply an ankle lock tape*

Non-response to treatment
There are some patients who, despite an apparently straightforward ankle sprain, do not respond to therapy and do not regain a full range of movement. In such patients alternative diagnoses in addition to ligament tearing must be considered (Table 110.3). These require careful clinical assessment and further investigation such as bone scans.

Heel disorders

Important causes of heel pain and other disorders resulting from overuse sporting activities include:

- Achilles tendon disorders
  — tendinitis/peritendinitis
  — tear: partial or complete
- bruised heel
- 'pump bumps'/bursitis
- calcaneal apophysitis
- plantar fasciitis (page 585)
- talon noir
- blisters

Table 110.3 *Unstable ankle injuries to be considered in delayed healing (after Brunker[7])*

Osteochondral fracture of the talar dome
Dislocation of the peroneal tendons
Sinus tarsi syndrome
Anteroinferior tibiofibular ligament injury
Post-traumatic synovitis
Anterior impingement syndrome
Posterior impingement syndrome
Anterior lateral impingement
Rupture of posterior tibial tendon
Reflex sympathetic dystrophy
Other fractures • base 5th metatarsal (avulsion) • lateral process of talus • anterior process of the calcaneus • tibial plafond • stress fracture navicular

Achilles tendinitis/peritendinitis

The inflammation that occurs as a combination of degenerative and inflammatory changes due to overuse may appear either in the tendon itself or in the surrounding paratendon. The latter is called peritendinitis rather than tenosynovitis because there is no synovial sheath.

Clinical features:

- history of unaccustomed running or long walk
- common in runners who change routine
- usually young to middle-aged males
- aching pain on using tendon
- tendon feels stiff, especially on rising
- tender thickened tendon
- palpable crepitus on movement of tendon

Preventive measures

- warm-up and stretching exercises in athletes
- good quality shoes
- 1 cm heel raise

Treatment

- Rest: ? crutches in acute phase, plaster cast if severe
- Cool with ice in acute stage, then heat
- NSAIDs
- 1–2 cm heel raise under the shoe
- ultrasound and deep friction massage
- mobilisation, then graduated stretching exercises

Note Ensure adequate rest and early resolution because chronic tendinitis is persistent and very difficult to treat.
Avoid corticosteroid injection in acute stages and never give into tendon. Can be injected *around* the tendon if localised and tender.

Partial rupture of Achilles tendon

Clinical features:

- a sudden sharp pain at the time of injury
- sharp pain when stepping off affected leg
- usually males >30 sporadically engaged in sport
- history of running, jumping or hurrying up stairs
- a tender swelling palpable about 2.5 cm above the insertion
- may be a very tender defect about size of tip of little finger

Treatment

If palpable gap—early surgical exploration with repair.

If no gap, use conservative treatment:

- initial rest (with ice) and crutches
- 1–2 cm heel raise inside shoe
- ultrasound and deep friction massage
- graduated stretching exercises

Convalescence is usually 10–12 weeks.[8] A poor response to healing manifests as recurrent pain and disability, indicates surgical exploration and possible repair.

Complete rupture of Achilles tendon

This common problem in athletes occurs in a possibly degenerated tendon subjected to a sudden increased load, e.g. a skier with foot anchored and ankle dorsiflexed.

Clinical features:

- sudden onset of intense pain
- patient usually falls over
- feels more comfortable when acute phase passes
- development of swelling and bruising
- some difficulty walking, especially on tip toe

Diagnosis

- palpation of gap (best to test in first 2–3 hours as haematoma can fill gap)
- positive Thompson's test (Figs 110.11 a,b)

Note The injury may be missed because the patient is able to plantar flex the foot actively by means of the deep long flexors to the foot.

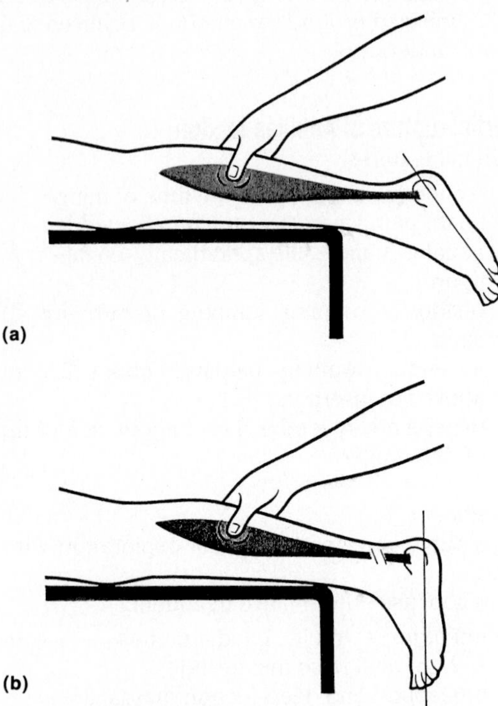

Fig. 110.11 *Thompson's calf squeeze test for ruptured Achilles tendon:* **(a)** *intact tendon, normal plantar flexion;* **(b)** *ruptured tendon, foot remains stationary*

Treatment

Early surgical repair (within three weeks).

'Pump bumps'

A 'pump bump' is a tender bursa over a bony prominence lateral to the attachment of the Achilles tendon. This is caused by inflammation related to poorly fitting footwear irritating a pre-existing enlargement of the calcaneus. Treatment is symptomatic and attention to footwear.

Talon noir

Talon noir or 'black heel', which has a black spotted appearance on the posterior end of the heel, is common in sportsmen and women, especially squash players. It tends to be bilateral and is caused by the shearing stresses of the sharp turns required in sport. The diagnosis is confirmed by gentle paring away of the hard skin containing old blood.

Disorders of the feet and toes

Common problems include:

- fractures of toes
- foot strain
- ingrowing toe-nails
- 'black' nails
- bony outgrowth under the nail (subungual exostosis)
- calluses
- athlete's foot (tinea pedis)
- plantar warts

Black nails ('soccer toe')

Black or 'bruised' nails are due to subungual haematoma caused by trauma. The problem can be acute or chronic and is seen in the great toes. Acute cases are usually the result of the toe being trodden on, while chronic cases are the result of wearing ill-fitting shoes (too narrow or loose) or the toe-nails being left too long.

The problem is encountered commonly in sports that involve deceleration forces and include running (especially cross-country with downhill running), netball, basketball, tennis, football and skiing.

Treatment

An acute subungual haematoma should be decompressed with a hot needle or other procedure through the nail. A chronic non-painful problem should be left to heal. The toe-nails will become dystrophic and be replaced by 'new' nails.

Attention should be paid to the footwear either by changing it or by placing protective padding in the toes of the running shoes or boots.

Injuries in adolescents

If an adolescent engaged in sport presents with pain in the leg it is important to consider the following problems.

- slipped upper femoral epiphysis (page 556)
- avulsion of epiphyses, e.g. ischial tuberosity (hamstring)
- stress fracture
- Osgood-Schlatter's disorder
- Scheuermann's disorder
- idiopathic scoliosis

References

1. Fitzpatrick J. Shoulder pain a real wet blanket. Australian Dr Weekly, 5 February 1993, 56.
2. Robinson M. Hazards of alpine sport. Aust Fam Physician, 1991; 20:961–970.
3. Elliott B, Sherry E. Common snow skiing injuries. Aust Fam Physician, 1984; 13:570–574.
4. Zimmermann G. Groin pain in athletes. Aust Fam Physician, 1988; 17:1046–1052.
5. James T. Chronic lower leg pain in sport. Aust Fam Physician, 1988; 17:1041–1045.
6. Litt J. The sprained ankle. Aust Fam Physician, 1992; 21:447–456.
7. Brukner P. The difficult ankle. Aust Fam Physician, 1991; 20:919–930.
8. Sloane PD, Slatt LM, Baker RM. *Essentials of family medicine*. Baltimore: Williams and Wilkins, 1988, 253–259.

PART 11

EVERYDAY PRACTICE TIPS

111

Nitty gritty problems A-Z (a summary)

Acne (mild to moderate)

(refer page 872)

Topical

tretinoin 0.01% gel or 0.05% cream nocte for two weeks, then add
benzoyl peroxide 2.5%, 5% or 10% mane

Systemic

tetracycline 1 g per day or doxycycine 100 mg per day for 10 days, then reduce according to response, e.g. doxycycline 50 mg per day for 4–6 weeks

Alopecia areata (patchy hair loss)

Potent topical cortiosteroids (class III or IV).

Intradermal injections of triamcinolone (Kenacort A10)

or

Minoxidil 2% (Regaine)

1 ml bd applied to scalp (for 4 or more months)

Anal fissure (persistent)

External sphincterotomy

Angina

(refer page 309)

- Modification of risk factors
- Regular exercise (e.g. walking 20 minutes a day) to threshold of angina
- Relaxation program

Mild and stable

- aspirin 100 mg (o) daily
- glyceryl trinitrate (sublingual prn)

Moderate and stable

- as above

+

- beta-blocker, e.g. atenolol 50–100 mg (o) daily
- glyceryl trinitrate (ointment and patches) daily (12 hours only)

or

isosorbide trinitrate 60 mg (o) SR tablets mane (12 hour span)

Anorexia (simple) in children and infants

Acid or alkaline gentian mixture (preferably alkaline)

5–10 ml 30 to 60 minutes before meals, tds

Acid or alkaline gentian mixture (for infants)

4 ml 30 to 60 minutes before feeds

or

Incremin mixture

$<$ 2 years: 2.5 ml daily

$>$ 2 years: 5 ml daily

Antibiotics (when to take)

(refer Table 111.1)

Aphthous ulcers (canker sores)

Precautions: consider blood dyscrasia, denture pressure, Crohn's disease, pernicious anaemia

Treatment methods (use early when ulcer worse)

Consider applying a wet, squeezed-out, black teabag directly to the ulcer regularly (the tannic acid promotes healing).

Symptomatic relief

Apply topical lignocaine, e.g. 2% jelly or 5% ointment with cotton bud: after two minutes apply lignocaine gel or paint, e.g. SM-33 adult paint formula or SM-33 gel (children) every three hours.

Healing

Tetracycline suspension rinse

- empty contents of 250 mg capsule into 20–30 ml of warm water and shake it
- swirl this solution in the mouth for 5–10 minutes every three hours or apply the solution soaked in cotton wool wads to the ulcers (has a terrible taste)

or

Triamcinolone 0.1% (Kenalog in orobase) paste
apply 8 hourly and nocte (preferred method)

or

10% chloramphenicol in propylene glycol
apply with cotton bud for one minute (after drying the ulcer) 6 hourly for 3–4 days

or

Beclomethasone spray onto ulcer tds

Asthma

(refer pages 934–41)

Athlete's foot (tinea pedis)

(refer page 895)

- Keep feet clean and dry at all times.
- Wear cotton or woollen sockettes (avoid synthetics).
- Charcoal inner soles (in every shoe).
- Clotrimazole 1% or miconazole 2% cream or lotion (after drying) bd or tds for 2–3 weeks (an alternative to the imidazoles is topical ketoconazole or terbinafine).

Back pain

Low back pain (refer Chap. 31)
Thoracic back pain (refer Chap. 32)

Table 111.1 *Ingestion of oral antibiotics in relation to food*

Antibiotic	*Advice with respect to food*
Amoxycillin	May be taken with food but not essential
Amoxycillin/clavulanic acid	Take with food
Ampicillin	As above
Cefaclor	As above
Cephalexin	As above
Ciprofloxacin	As above
Clindamycin	As above
Cloxacillin	Take on an empty stomach
Cotrimoxazole	Take with food
Doxycycline	Take with food or milk
Erythromycin base	Take on an empty stomach
Erythromycin estolate and ethylsuccinate	Take with food but not essential
Erythromycin stearate	Take on an empty stomach
Flucloxacillin	Take on an empty stomach
Griseofulvin	Take with food
Ketaconazole	Take with food
Metronidazole	Take on an empty stomach
Minocycline	Take with food or milk
Penicillins	Take on an empty stomach
Tetracycline	Take on an empty stomach
Tinidazole	Take with food
Trimethoprim	Take with food

Note: 'Take on an empty stomach' means about 1 hour before food.

Bed sores (pressure sores)

(refer page 893)

- good nursing care—regular turning of patient
- air-filled ripple mattress and/or sheepskin over pressure areas
- good nutrition and hygiene
- vitamin C 500 mg bd
- clean base with saline or Intra Site Gel
- consider simple alternatives, e.g. honey or sugar + povidone iodine paste bd
- dressings as required

Bee stings

- scrape off stinger (if still present)—don't squeeze it
- apply cold packs
- apply vinegar, Stingose or methylated spirits
- oral antihistamines (if necessary)

Belching (aerophagia)

(patient swallows air without admitting it)

- make patient aware of excessive swallowing
- avoid fizzy (carbonated) soft drinks
- avoid chewing gum
- don't drink with meals
- don't mix proteins and starches
- eat slowly and chew food thoroughly before swallowing
- eat and chew with the mouth closed

If persistent

Simethicone preparation, e.g. Mylanta II, Phazyme

If desperate

Place one small cork between the back teeth after meals for 30 minutes.

Bell's palsy

Prednisolone 60 mg daily for 3 days then taper to zero over next 7 days (start within 3 days of onset)

- adhesive tape or patch at night over eye if corneal exposure
- consider artificial tears if eye dry
- massage and facial exercises during recovery
- about 90% spontaneous recovery

Bladder dysfunction (in women during night)

Women with urethral syndrome constantly wake at night with urge to micturate but produce only a small dribble of urine.

- instruct patient to perform a pelvic lift exercise by balancing on upper back, lifting her pelvis with knees flexed and holding position for 30 seconds
- squeeze pelvic floor inwards (as though holding back urine or faeces)
- repeat a few times

Blepharitis

Precautions: corneal ulceration, recurrent staphylococcal infections

Treatment

- eyelid hygiene—clean with a cotton bud dipped in 1:10 dilution of baby shampoo, once or twice daily
- artificial tears, e.g. hypromellose 1%
- tetracycline 1% ointment to lid margins 3–6 hourly
- control scalp seborrhoea with medicated shampoos

Body odour

Cause: poor hygiene, excessive perspiration and active skin bacteria
axilla and groin main focus

Precautions: consider uraemia, vaginitis

Treatment method

- scrub body, especially groins and axillae, with deodorant soap at least morning and night
- try an antibacterial surgical scrub
- keep clothes clean, regular laundry
- choose suitable clothes—natural fibres, e.g. cotton, not synthetics
- use an antiperspirant deodorant
- alternative soap—pine soap
- diet: avoid garlic, fish, curry, onions, asparagus
- reduce caffeine (coffee, tea and coca cola drinks), which stimulates sweat activity
- shave axillary hair
- axillary wedge resection for excessive perspiration

Breath-holding attacks

(refer page 981)

- reassure parents
- advise firm discipline
- try to avoid precipitating incidents

Bruxism (teeth grinding)

- Practise keeping teeth apart.
- Slowly munch an apple before retiring.
- Practise relaxation techniques, including meditation, before retiring (bruxism is related to stress).
- Place a hot face towel against the sides of the face before retiring to achieve relaxation.
- If this fails and bruxism is socially unacceptable during the night, use a mouthguard.

Burning feet syndrome

Anterior burning pain in forefoot—consider tarsal tunnel syndrome (refer page 570) or peripheral neuropathy, e.g. from diabetes or vascular insufficiency.

Burns

Management depends on extent and depth (burns are classified as superficial or deep).

Small burns should be immersed in cold water immediately, e.g. tap water for 20 minutes.

Chemical burns should be liberally irrigated with water.

Refer the following burns to hospital:

- > 10% surface area, especially in a child (see rules of 9, page 855)
- all deep burns
- burns of difficult or vital areas, e.g. face, hands, perineum/genitalia, feet
- burns with potential problems, e.g. electrical, chemical, circumferential.

Treatment of superficial burns

Most scalds cause partial thickness (superficial) burns. Smear the clean burnt or scalded area with silver sulfadiazide (Silvazine) cream with a sterile gloved hand or spatula (3 mm thick layer).

Exposure (open method)

- keep open without dressings (good for face, perineum or single surface burns)
- renew coating of cream every 24 hours

Dressings (closed method)

- suitable for circumferential wounds
- cover creamed area with non-adherent tulle, e.g. paraffin gauze
- dress with an absorbent bulky layer of gauze and wool
- use a plaster splint if necessary

Burns to hands

A first aid method for partial thickness burns to hands is to place the hand in a suitable plastic bag containing a liberal quantity of silverazine. If a sterile plastic bag is unavailable a standard household bag will suffice.

Then apply a crepe bandage around the hand, leaving the fingers and thumb free so that the fingers can move freely in the bag. Consider placing the arm in a sling. Change the bag every day or second day to review the wound.

Calluses

- Remove the cause.
- Proper footwear is essential, with cushion pads over callosities.
- Pare with a sterile sharp scalpel blade.

'Cellulite'

The best way to overcome 'cellulite' is to keep to ideal weight. If overweight, lose it slowly and exercise to improve the muscle tone in the buttocks and thighs.

Chickenpox

(refer page 671)

- rest in bed until feeling well
- give paracetamol for fever
- drink ample fluids
- calamine lotion to relieve itching
- daily bathing with sodium bicarbonate (half a cup added) or Pinetarsol (preferable) in bath water

Chilblains

Precautions: think Raynaud's
protect from trauma and secondary infection
do not rub or massage injured tissues
do not apply heat or ice

Physical Rx: elevate affected part
warm gradually to room temperature
Drug Rx: apply glyceryl trinitrate vasodilator spray or ointment or patch (use plastic gloves and wash hands for ointment)
Other Rx: rum at night
nifedipine

Chloasma

see Melasma

Cold sores

- apply an ice cube to site for 5 minutes every 60 minutes (first 12 hours)
- apply idoxuridine 0.5% preparation hourly at onset

  or

  povidone-iodine 10% cold sore paint: on swab stick 4 times a day until disappearance

Common cold

- rest 24–48 hours if feeling weak
- aspirin or paracetamol (up to 8 tablets a day for adults)
- steam inhalations using menthol or Friar's balsam
- gargle aspirin in lemon juice for a sore throat
- vitamin C—2 g a day for 5–7 days
- increase fluid intake
- stop smoking (if applicable)
- use cough drops or syrup for a dry trouble-some cough

Conjunctivitis

(refer page 411)

Constipation (idiopathic)

- patient education, including 'good habit'
- adequate exercise
- plenty of fluids, e.g. water, fruit juice
- avoid laxatives and codeine compounds
- optimal bulk diet
- unprocessed bran, e.g. 15–30 g/day

If unsuccessful

- isphagula (Fybogel), e.g. adults: 1 sachet in water bd

Corns on feet

- Remove cause of friction and use wide shoes.
- Use corn pads.
- Soften corn with a few daily applications of 15% salicylic acid in collodion, then pare.

'Cracked' and dry lips

- Use a lip balm with sunscreen, e.g. Sunsense 15 lip balm.
- Women can use a creamy lipstick.
- Vaseline helps.

'Cracked' hands and fingers

- Wear protective work gloves: cotton-lined PVC gloves.
- Use soap substitutes, e.g. Cetaphil lotion, Dove.
- Apply 2–5% salicylic acid and 10% liq picis carb in white soft paraffin ointment.

  or

- Corticosteroid ointment: class II–III.

'Cracked' heels

- Soak feet for 30 minutes in warm water containing an oil such as Alpha-Keri or Derma Oil.
- Pat dry, then apply a cream such as Nutraplus (10% urea) or Eulactol heel balm.

Cramps (nocturnal cramps in legs)

Precautions: treat cause (if known), e.g. tetanus, drugs, sodium depletion, hypothyroidism.

Physical

- muscle stretching and relaxation exercises: stretch calf for three minutes before retiring (Figure 111.1) then rest in chair with the feet out horizontally to the floor with cushion under tendoachilles (10 minutes)
- massage and heat to affected muscles
- try to keep bedclothes off feet and lower part of legs—use a doubled-up pillow at the foot of the bed

Drugs

- quinine sulphate 300 mg nocte

  or

- biperiden 2–4 mg nocte

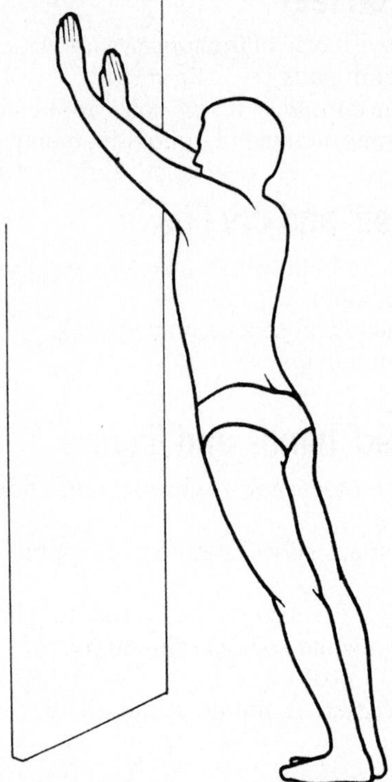

Fig. 111.1 *Leg-stretching exercise for cramp*

Croup

(refer page 981)

- get child to inhale humidified steaming air, e.g. in bathroom with hot water taps running (minor obstruction usually resolves after 30–60 minutes)
- special nebulisers can be hired
- paracetamol mixture 4–6 hourly
- no place for cough medicine
- support child on pillows
- keep child calm

If significant laryngeal obstruction:

- nebulised adrenaline 1:1000 solution (0.05 ml/kg/dose)
  ↓
- dexamethasone IM 0.2 mg/kg
  ↓
- artificial airway (nasotracheal intubation or tracheostomy)

Crying baby

Checklist: hunger; wet or soiled nappy; teething; colic; infection; loneliness; or seeking attention.

Dandruff

Dandruff (pityriasis capitis) is mainly a physiological process, the result of normal desquamation of scale from the scalp. It is most prevalent in adolescence and worse around the age of 20.

Treatment

Shampoos:

zinc pyrithione, e.g. Dan-Gard
or
selenium sulphide, e.g. Selsun
Method: massage into scalp, leave for 5 minutes, rinse thoroughly—twice weekly

Persistent dandruff with severe flaking and itching indicates seborrhoeic dermatitis or psoriasis.

Treatment

coal tar + salicylic acid compound (Sebitar) shampoo
or
Ionil T plus shampoo
Method: as above, followed by Sebi Rinse

If persistent, especially itching, use a corticosteroid, e.g. betamethasone scalp lotion.

Dizzy turns in elderly women

If no cause such as hypertension is found, advise them to get up slowly from sitting or lying and to wear firm elastic stockings.

Dizzy turns in girls in late teens

- common due to blood pressure fluctuations
- give advice related to stress, lack of sleep, or excessive activity
- reassure that it settles with age (rare after 25 years)

Dry hair

- Don't shampoo every day.
- Use a mild shampoo (labelled for 'dry or damaged hair').
- Use a conditioner.
- Snip off the split or frayed ends.
- Avoid heat, e.g. electric curlers, hair dryers.
- Wear head protection in hot wind.
- Wear a rubber cap when swimming.

Dry skin

- Reduce bathing and frequency and duration of showering.
- Bathe and shower in tepid water.
- Use a soap substitute, e.g. Dove, Neutrogena or Cetaphil lotion.
- Rub in baby oil after patting dry.
- Avoid wool next to skin (e.g. wear cotton).
- Use emollients, e.g. Alpha-Keri lotion.
- Use moisturisers, e.g. Calmurid, Nutraplus.
- Use dilute corticosteroid ointment if resistant local patches.

Dysmenorrhoea (primary)

Mild: explanation
healthy lifestyle
practise relaxation, e.g. yoga
pelvic floor exercises
apply warmth to area (hot water bottle)

Medication for moderate to severe pain: simple analgesics, e.g. paracetamol
prostaglandin inhibitors
e.g. mefenamic acid 500 mg tds
combined oral contraceptive pill
low oestrogen triphasic pill

Ectropion

- requires surgical repair (local anaesthetic)
- use a mild ointment prior to surgery

Entropion

If unsuitable for surgery, use a strip of hypo-allergenic, non-woven surgical tape (1 cm × 3 cm) to evert lid and secure to cheek (Fig. 111.2).

Enuresis (bedwetting)

(refer page 633)

Epistaxis

Simple tamponade

- pinch 'soft' part of nose between thumb and finger for five minutes
- apply ice packs to bridge of nose (Fig. 111.3)

Simple cautery of Little's area (under local anaesthetic)

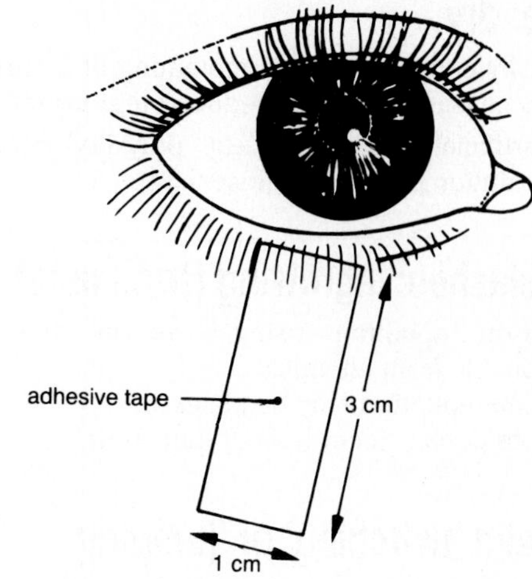

Fig. 111.2 *Treatment of entropion*

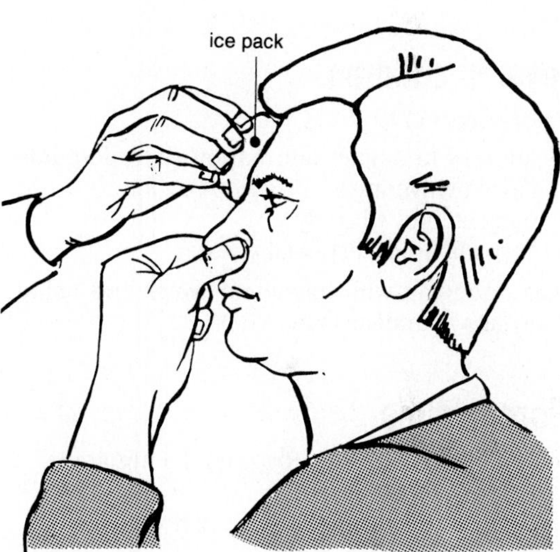

Fig. 111.3 *First-line treatment for epistaxis*

use one of 3 methods: electrocautery
trichloracetic acid or
silver nitrate stick

Persistent anterior bleed:
Merocel (surgical sponge) nasal tampon

'Trick of the trade' for recurrent anterior epistaxis:

- apply topical antibiotic, e.g. Aureomycin ointment, bd or tds for 10 days
  or (better option) Nasalatenose cream tds for 7–10 days

Severe posterior epistaxis

Use a Foley's catheter or an Epistat catheter.

Eye: dry

Usually elderly patient complaining of a chronic gritty sensation—due to reduced tear secretion.

- artificial tear drops, e.g. polyvinyl alcohol solution or hypromellose 0.5%

Eyelashes: ingrowing (trichiasis)

Perform epilation using eyebrow tweezers (available from chemists).
Regular epilation may be necessary.
Severe cases: electrolysis of hair roots

Eyelid 'twitching' or 'jumping'

Advise that cause is usually stress or fatigue.
Reassure and counsel.
Consider prescribing clonazepam if severe.

Fever in children

(refer page 431)

- undress to singlet and nappy or underpants (avoid shivering)
- paracetamol 4 hourly
- copious fluids, especially water

Note Sponging with lukewarm water and using fans is unnecessary.

Fibromyalgia

Consider: clonazepam (Rivotril) 0.5 mg nocte
or
amitriptyline 50–75 mg nocte

Flashburns to eyes

Cause: intense ultraviolet light burns to corneas (keratitis), e.g. arc welding, UV lamps, snow reflection

Precautions: foreign bodies
continued use of topical anaesthetics (once only)

Treatment

- topical long-acting LA drops, e.g. amethocaine, statim
- homotropine 2% eye drops, 1–2 drops statim
- broad spectrum antibiotic eye ointment, bd in lower fornix (48 hours)
- analgesics, e.g. codeine + paracetamol
- eye padding for 24 hours

Folliculitis: of groin

Folliculitis of the groin area is common in women who shave and tends to recur.

- Use tea tree lotion daily for folliculitis.
- Prior to shaving apply 'tea tree wash'.
- If persistent, use povidone-iodine or chlorhexidine (Hibiclens) solution.
- If severe, use mupirocin 2% (Bactroban) ointment

Folliculitis: of trunk from spa baths

Due to pseudomonas or *Staphylcoccus aureus*

- Rx—ciprofloxacin 500 mg (o) bd for seven days

Foot ache

- Avoid wearing high heels.
- Wear insoles to support the foot arch.
- Perform foot exercises.
- Soak the feet in a basin of warm water containing therapeutic salts (Epsom salts is suitable).
- Massage feet with baby oil followed by a special ribbed wooden foot massager.

Foot odour (smelly and sweaty feet)

Includes pitted keratolysis secondary to hyperhidrosis (common in teenagers)

Treatment

- education and reassurance
- wear cotton or woollen socks
- aluminium chloride 20% in alcohol solution (Driclor, Hidrosol)—apply nocte for one week, then 1–2 times weekly as necessary
- shoe liners, e.g. 'Odor eaters'; charcoal inner soles
- apply undiluted Burow's solution after a shower or bath
- the teabag treatment (if desperate)
  - prepare 600 ml of strong hot tea (from two teabags left in water for 15 minutes)
  - pour the hot tea into a basin with 2 litres of cool water
  - soak the feet in this for 20–30 minutes daily for 10 days, then as often as required

Freckles and lentigines (sun spots)

- Reassure the patient.
- Use a sunscreen.

- Otherwise, rather than use 'fade cream', use fresh lemon juice. Squeeze lemon juice (½ lemon) into a small bowl and apply the juice with a cotton ball to the spots daily. Continue for eight weeks.
- Apply tretinoin 0.05% cream daily at night, if necessary.

Frostbite

Treatment depends on severity.

Precautions: watch for secondary infection, tetanus, gangrene

Physical Rx:
- elevate affected limb
- rewarm in water just above body temperature 40°C (104°F) or use body heat, e.g. in axillae
- avoid thawing or refreezing
- surgical debridement
- don't debride early (wait until dead tissue dried)
- don't drink alcohol or smoke
- for blistering, apply warm water compresses for 15 minutes every 2 hours

Drug Rx:
- analgesics

Gastroenteritis

(refer pages 356–59)

Genital herpes

(refer page 838)

Genital warts

(refer page 841)

Geographical tongue

- explanation and reassurance
- no treatment if asymptomatic
- Cepacaine gargles, 10 ml tds, if tender

Gingivitis

- use dental floss regularly (twice a day)
- brush carefully at gumline with Sensodyne (pink) toothpaste
- perform gum massage between thumb and index finger
- use Listerine mouthwash or dilute hydrogen peroxide
- take Vitamin C—2 g daily

Gout (acute attack)

- bed rest
- keep weight of the bedclothes off the foot with a bed cradle or pillow under bedclothes
- avoid aspirin (it may exacerbate gout)
- indomethacin 100 mg (o) statim, 75 mg 2 hours later, then 50 mg (o) 8 hourly; relief can be expected in 24–48 hours
- add an antiemetic, e.g. maxalon 10 mg (o)
- consider an intra-articular injection of corticosteroid, e.g. 1 ml of triamcinolone under a digital nerve block

Haemorrhoids

(refer page 252)

Halitosis

- Exclude dental disease, malignancy, pulmonary TB, nasal and sinus infection.
- Consider drugs as a cause.
- Avoid onions, garlic, peppers, spicy salami and similar meats.
- Avoid strong cheeses.
- Avoid smoking and excessive nips of alcohol.
- Brush teeth regularly during day—immediately after a meal.
- Rinse mouth out with water after meals.
- Avoid fasting for long periods during the day.
- Gargle with mouthwash, e.g. Listerine.
- Use dental floss regularly to clean the teeth.

Tip: use an oil/water wash, e.g. equal volumes of aqueous Cepacol and olive oil, gargle a well-shaken mixture and spit out, qid.

Hangover

Preventive advice:

- Drink alcohol on a full stomach.
- Select alcoholic drinks that suit you: avoid champagne.
- Avoid fast drinking—keep it slow.
- Restrict the quantity of alcohol.
- Take two soluble aspirin before retiring.
- Drink three large glasses of water before retiring.

Treatment

- Drink ample fluids because of relative dehydration effect of alcohol.
- Take soluble aspirin, e.g. Aspro Clear (600 mg).
- Drink orange juice or tomato juice, with added sugar.
- A drink of honey in lemon juice helps.
- Coffee and tea are suitable beverages.
- Have a substantial meal but avoid fats.

Hay fever (allergic rhinitis)

(refer page 950)

- patient education
- allergen avoidance (if possible)
- non-sedating antihistamines
  - — astemizole 10 mg daily, or
  - — loratadine 10 mg daily, or
  - — terfenadine 60 mg bd

If ineffective

- inhaled sodium cromoglycate

  or
- inhaled corticosteroids
- use sodium cromoglycate (Opticrom) drops for eye irritation

Head banging or rocking in toddlers

This is common < 4 years when going to sleep, especially in 3 year olds. Reassure parents that problem settles by 4–5 years.

Heartburn (dyspepsia)

(refer page 377)

- patient education
- lifestyle changes
  - — maintain ideal weight (very important)
  - — stress management
  - — reduce or cease smoking
  - — reduce or cease alcohol intake
  - — reduce or cease coffee and chocolate
  - — avoid fatty foods, e.g. pastries
- antacids (alginate/antacid mixture)
  - — Gaviscon liquid or Mylanta plus liquid 10–20 ml, on demand or two hours after meals
    20–30 ml at bed time

Hiccoughs (hiccups)

Simple brief episodes:

- rebreathing air in paper bag (as for hyperventilation)
- breath holding
- sucking ice/swallowing iced water
- catheter inserted quickly in and out of nose
- pressure on the eyballs

Persistent (assuming exclusion of organic diseases):

- chlorpromazine orally or IV

  or
- valproic acid

Consider acupuncture, hypnosis or phrenic nerve block.

Hirsuitism

- Exclude adrenal or ovarian pathology.
- Use bleaching, waxing or depilatory creams, or shave.
- Do not pluck hairs, especially around the lips and chin.
- Plucking stimulates hair growth but shaving appears to have no effect.
- Electrolysis may help.
- Drug treatment: spironolactone 100–200 mg daily; takes 6–12 months to respond.

Hyperventilation

- Get patient to breathe in and out of a paper bag.
- If a paper bag is unavailable, rebreathe air from cupped hands over nose and mouth.
- Encourage them to learn to slow down breathing.
- Investigate the possibility of phobias.
- Advise cutting out caffeine and nicotine.

Impetigo

(refer page 679)

- If mild and limited: antiseptic cleansing and removal of crusts with mupirocin (Bactroban) or chlorhexidine or povidone-iodine
- If extensive: flucloxacillin or erythromycin (orally)

Impotence

(refer page 829)

Incontinence of urine

- Search for a cause: refer to a consultant.
- Avoid various drugs, e.g. diuretics, psychotropics, alcohol.

In women:

- bladder retraining and pelvic floor exercises (mainstay of treatment)
- physiotherapist referral

Consider incontinence aids:

- absorbent pads and special pants
- condoms and catheters; urinary drainage bags
- absorbent sheeting

Infantile colic

Usually an infant 2–16 weeks old
(refer page 218)
Avoid medications if possible but consider:

simethicone preparations, e.g. Infacol wind drops

or

dicyclomine, e.g. Infacol-C syrup or Merbentyl syrup

Influenza

- Rest in bed until fever subsides and patient feels better.
- Codeine compound tablets (helps cough and discomfort).
- Drink as much water and fruit juice as possible; freshly squeezed lemon juice and honey preparations help.
- Consider vitamin C 2 g daily.

Ingrowing toe-nails

- Correct nails properly: cut across so that the cut slopes towards the centre of the nail and do not cut towards the edges (Fig. 111.4).
- Fashion the toe-nails so that the corners project beyond the skin.
- Wear good-fitting shoes (avoid tight shoes).
- Keep toe area clean and dry.

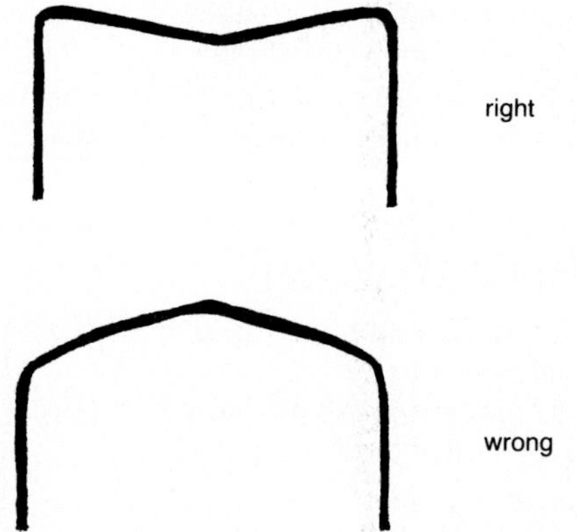

Fig. 111.4 *Correct method of cutting toe-nails*

Insect stings

- Wash site with large quantities of cool water.
- Apply vinegar (liberal amount) or aluminium sulfate 20% solution (Stingose) for about 30 seconds.
- Apply ice for several seconds.
- Use soothing anti-itch cream or 5% lignocaine ointment if very painful.

Insomnia

- Give explanation and reassurance (treat cause if known).
- Try to recognise what helps patient to settle best, e.g. warm bath, listening to music.
- Establish a routine before going to bed.
- Avoid alcohol and drinks containing caffeine in evening.
- Try a warm drink of milk before retiring.
- Organise a comfortable quiet sleep setting.
- Sex last thing at night is usually helpful.
- Try relaxation therapy, meditation.
- Consider hypnosis.
- If all conservative means fail, try temazepam 10–20 mg (o) at night (limit to 2 weeks).

Intertrigo (due to *Candida albicans*)

- Treat underlying problem, e.g. obesity, diabetes.
- Apply clotrimazole or miconazole or nystatin preparation.
- Apply Burow's solution compresses if weeping.
- Keep area dry and skin folds apart (if possible).

Irritable bowel

- reassurance and patient education
- stress management/relaxation
- avoid foods that 'irritate', smoking, alcohol, laxatives, codeine
- high-fibre diet (2 teaspoons unprocessed bran daily)
- medications to consider:

  metamucil 1 teaspoon bd

  or

  mebeverine HCl (Colofac) 125 mg tds

Jet lag

(refer page 89)

Jitters

(pre-occasion jitters/performance anxiety)
Propranolol 10–40 mg (o) 30–60 minutes before the event or performance.

Jock itch

see Tinea cruris

Keloid or hypertrophic scar

Various methods (refer page 898)
Multiple pressure injections:

- Spread film of corticosteroid solution over scar.
- Apply multiple pressure through solution with a 21 g needle held tangentially (about 20 superficial stabs per cm^2).
- Avoid bleeding.
- Repeat in 6 weeks

or

Intralesional injection of triamcinolone.

or

Topical class III–IV corticosteroid ointment with occlusion.

Keratoacanthoma

Surgical excision and histology
(refer page 901)

Keratoses (solar and seborrhoeic)

Options:

- liquid nitrogen (repeat in 3–4 weeks if necessary)

  or
- 6% salicylic acid in petroleum alba

  or
- 5-fluorouracil 5% cream bd (3 weeks on face or 6 weeks on hands)

  or
- PMC paint

podophyllin resin	10%
salicylic acid	20%
SVI add	100

- some may require diathermy or biopsy

Lactation suppression

- avoid nipple stimulation
- refrain from expressing milk
- use well-fitting brassiere
- bromocriptine (Parlodel) 2.5 mg (o) bd for 10–14 days
- avoid oestrogens

Laryngitis

- avoid talking
- drink ample fluids
- avoid cigarettes
- use steam inhalations (5 minutes bd)

Leg ulcer

(refer page 892)

Lice

(refer page 679)

Head lice

maldison (malathion) 5% lotion
apply once a week for 2–3 weeks

Pubic lice

lindane 1% lotion
apply to affected area, leave overnight then wash off
repeat after 7 days (maybe third treatment)

Lichen planus

(troublesome, e.g. itching)

- topical fluorinated steroids under plastic occlusion
- consider intralesional injections of triamcinolone for hypertrophic areas

Mastalgia (cyclical)

- vitamin B complex with B_6 (100 mg) daily } try first
- evening primrose oil 4–6 g (o) daily } try first
- mefenamic acid 500 mg tds

Consider:

norethisterone 5 mg daily (2nd half of cycle)
bromocriptine 2.5 mg bd
danazole 200 mg daily

Melasma (chloasma)

2% hydroquinone in sorbolene cream

Ménière's disease

- explanation and advice
- avoid coffee and smoking
- low-salt diet
- sodium depleting diuretic
- oral urea 20–30 g in orange juice (with warning of attack)

Consider: betahistine, diazepam or meclozine.

Menopause syndrome

(refer pages 754–55)

Migraine attack

(refer page 453)

First signs of attack:

1st line: soluble aspirin 2–3 tablets (o)
+
metoclopramide 10 mg (o)

2nd line: sumatriptan 100 mg (o) or 6 mg (SC) injection
repeat in 2 hours if necessary

Established attack:
metoclopramide 10 mg (2 ml) IM or IV

Migraine prophylaxis

(for > 2 attacks per month)

- propranolol 40 mg (o) bd increasing up to 320 mg daily if necessary
  or
- pizotifen 0.5 mg (o) nocte increasing to 3 mg if necessary

Molluscum contagiosum

Refer pages 841 and 899 for various treatments. The best in the surgery is application of liquid nitrogen.

Monkey muscle tear

(refer page 1051)

- RICE treatment for 72 hours
- compress with firm elastic bandage (toes to below knee)
- crutches if necessary
- raised heel on shoe
- physiotherapist referral
- active exercises after 48 hours

Morning-after pill

(must be used within 72 hours)

- use high oestrogen pill:
  50 μg EO + 250 μg LNG (Nordiol) × 2 pills (or equivalent dose in other pills)
- repeat in 12 hours
- add an antiemetic, e.g. maxalon 10 mg (o)

Morning sickness

- invariably disappears by end of first trimester
- explanation and reassurance
- simple measures
  - small frequent meals
  - fizzy soft drinks
  - avoid stimuli such as cooking smells
  - avoid oral iron
  - be careful cleaning teeth

Medication (for severe cases):

- meclozine 25–50 mg bd with
- pyridoxine 50–100 mg bd

Mouth: angular fissures

- check dentures and hygiene
- apply dimethicone cream for protection
- if persistent and/or for suspected candida, use antifungal cream

Mouth: bad taste

- look for cause, e.g. teeth, gums, depression
- consider Ascoxal tablets, 1–2 tabs dissolved in 25 ml warm water as mouthwash for two rinses up to five times daily

Mouth ulcers

(as for aphthous ulcers)

Nappy rash

The main factor is dampness due to urine and faeces.

Irritant dermatitis

- Keep the area dry.
- Change wet or soiled napkins often—disposable ones are good.
- Wash gently and pat dry (do not rub).

- Avoid excessive bathing and soap.
- Avoid powders and plastic pants.
- Use emollients to keep skin lubricated e.g. zinc oxide and castor oil cream

  or

  nappy rash cream formula

sol. al. acetate	16%
wool fat	33%
camphor	1%
boric acid	1%
zinc cream	add 100

  sig: apply each change

If: atopic dermatitis: 1% hydrocortisone
seborrhoeic dermatitis: 1% hydrocortisone and ketoconazole ointment
Candida albicans: topical nystatin at each nappy change
widespread nappy rash: 1% hydrocortisone and nystatin ointment or clotrimazole cream (qid after changes)

Neck pain

(refer Chap. 52)

Nipples: cracked

(refer page 787)

- Get baby to latch onto breast fully and properly.
- Do not feed from the affected breast—rest the nipple for 1–2 feeds.
- Express the milk from that breast by hand.
- Start feeding gradually with short feeds.
- Take paracetamol 1 g just before feeding to relieve the pain.
- Avoid drying agents such as spirits, creams and ointments.

Nipples: sore

- Use a relaxed feeding technique.
- Try to use the 'chest to chest, chin on breast' feeding position.
- Start feeding from the less painful side first if one nipple is very sore.
- Express some milk first to soften and 'lubricate' the nipple.
- Never pull the baby off the nipple: gently break the suction with your finger.
- Apply covered ice to the nipple to relieve pain.
- Keep the nipples dry (exposure to air or to hair dryer).
- Do not wear a bra at night.
- If wearing a bra by day, try Cannon breast shields.

Nose: offensive smell from

Ensure no foreign body present.

- mupirocin 2% nasal ointment
  instil 2 or 3 times a day

  or
- kenacomb ointment
  instil 2 or 3 times a day

Nose: stuffy, running

- blow nose hard into disposable paper tissue or handkerchief until clear
- nasal decongestant for 2–3 days only
- steam inhalations with Friar's balsam or menthol preparations—use 1 teaspoon to 500 ml boiled water in old container (Fig. 111.5)

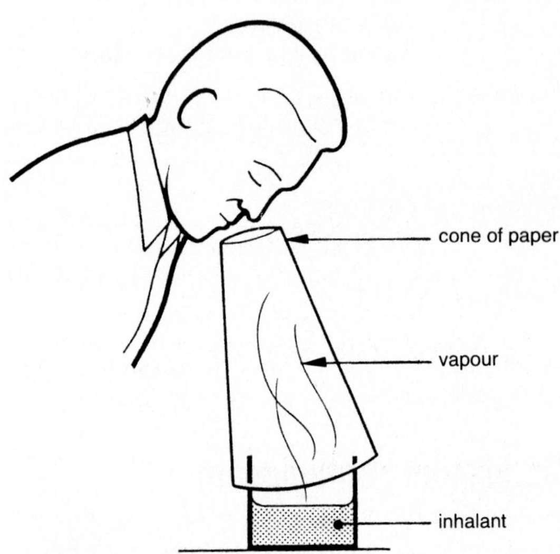

Fig. 111.5 *Steam inhalation*

Obesity

(refer pages 651–54)

Obsessive compulsive disorder

- refer for group therapy
- clomipramine (Anafranil)
  50–75 mg (o) nocte, increasing every 2 to 3 days to 150–250 mg orally (o) nocte

Oily hair

- Shampoo daily with a 'shampoo for oily hair'.
- Massage the scalp during the shampoo process.
- Leave the shampoo on for at least five minutes.
- Avoid hair conditioners.
- Avoid overbrushing.
- Attend to lifestyle factors: relaxation and balanced diet are important.

Otitis externa

- aural toilet—dry mopping
- dressing with insertion of 4 mm Nufold gauze
- topical kenacomb ointment or drops
- consider wick insertion

See Tropical ear.

Otitis media

(refer pages 401–403)

Children

- rest patient in warm room with adequate humidity
- paracetamol suspension of pain (high dosage)
- decongestants only if nasal congestion
- amoxycillin (1st choice) 40–50 mg/kg/day in three divided doses for 10 days; cephalosporin, e.g. cefaclor (2nd choice)
- follow-up: evaluate hearing at 10 days

Adults

- analgesics
- nasal decongestants only for nasal congestion
- antibiotics:
  - first choice: amoxycillin 750 mg (o) 12 hourly for five days, or Augmentin
  - second choice: doxycycline or cefaclor

Panic attack

(refer page 926)

- general support, explanation and reassurance
- stress management
- rebreathe into a paper bag if hyperventilating
- initial treatment

  oxazepam 15–30 mg (o)
  or
  alprazolam 0.25–0.5 mg (o)

Prophylaxis

Consider:

- tricyclic antidepressants

  or
- alprazolam 0.25–6 mg (o) in 2–4 divided doses

Paronychia: acute

Uncomplicated with localised pus:

- simple elevation of nail fold (Fig. 111.6) or puncture the fold close to the nail to drain pus
- advice on hygiene
- antibiotics rarely necessary
- exclude diabetes

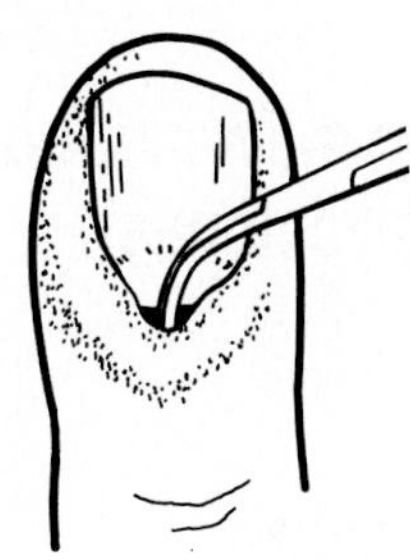

Fig. 111.6 *Treatment of paronychia by elevating the nail fold*

Complicated with subungual extension:

- small vertical excision alongside the nail

  or
- removal of nail in part or totally
- exclude diabetes

Paronychia: chronic

- usually due to a secondary invading organism
- culture organisms
- exclude diabetes

Attend to causation

- Minimise contact with water, soap, detergents, lipid solvents and other irritants.
- Keep hands dry (avoid wet work if possible).
- Wear cotton lined gloves for maximum of 15 minutes.

Topical medications to nail folds

2% thymol in alcohol qid
or
10% sulphacetamide in alcohol

For Candida (if cultured)
tincture Daktarin bd
or
clotrimazole topical preparations

Perianal haematoma

Within 24 hours of onset:

- simple aspiration of blood
  or
- surgical drainage under LA

Within 24 hours to 5 days of onset:

- express thrombus through small incision under LA

Day 6 onwards:

- leave alone unless very painful or infected

Periodic limb movement disorder (nocturnal myoclonus)

clonazepam 50–75 mg (o) nocte increasing to 150–250 mg (o) nocte

Perioral dermatitis

- tetracycline 250 mg bd for 6–8 weeks
- consider topical 2–4% sulphur and 2% salicylic acid in aqueous or sorbolene cream
- consider ketoconazole 2% cream
- avoid corticosteroids

Perspiration: excessive

- use an antiperspirant deodorant
- reduce caffeine intake
- avoid known aggravating factors
- refer for axillary wedge resection

Photoageing/wrinkles

Prevention

- Avoid exposure to the sun.
- Use an SPF 15+ sunscreen during the day.
- Wash with a 'neutral' mild soap, e.g. Neutrogena (maximum twice daily) and pat dry.

Treatment

- tretinoin (Retin-A) cream
  apply once daily at bedtime (on dry skin)
  test for skin irritation by gradual exposure, e.g. 5 minutes at first (wash off), then 15 minutes until it can be left overnight
- Lac-Hydrin (USA)
  12% solution may be effective alternative; other lactic acid preparations may be useful

Pityriasis rosea

- explanation and reassurance
- bathe and shower as usual—use a neutral soap, e.g. Neutrogena, Dove
- use a soothing bath oil, e.g. QV bath oil, Hamilton bath oil
- for itching: urea cream or calamine lotion with 1% phenol
- expose rash to sunlight (avoid sunburn)

Pityriasis versicolor (tinea versicolor)

(refer page 876)
selenium sulfide (Selsun shampoo) (see page 876 for instructions)
or
econazole 1% (Pevaryl) foaming solution

- apply to wet body (after shower)
- rub in from head to toe
- do not rinse, allow to dry
- shower off next morning
- apply for 3 consecutive days once weekly for 3 weeks

or
clotrimazole, miconazole, or econazole cream/lotion applied nocte for 2–4 weeks
Ketoconazole cream for 10 days in severe or resistant cases.

Plantar warts

(refer pages 589–90)

- pare wart with a 21 g scalpel blade
- apply Upton's paste to wart each night and cover (after paring)
  or
- apply paste of 70% salicylic acid in raw linseed oil after paring occlude for one week; review; pare; apply liquid nitrogen, review
  or
- apply liquid nitrogen
  repeat in one week, then as necessary

Premenstrual tension

- explanation and reassurance
- advise recording a daily symptom diary for 2–3 months
- attend to lifestyle factors
  - diet
  - exercise
  - relaxation
- medication (refer pages 748–49)

  moderate dose COC with 50 μg ethinyl oestradiol

  otherwise

  pyridoxine 100 mg/day

  or

  evening primrose oil capsules 1 g bd (day 12 to day 1 of next cycle)
- severe PMT
  - fluoxetine 20 mg daily, 7–10 days

Prickly heat (miliaria/heat rash)

- Keep the skin dry and cool, e.g. fan, air conditioner.
- Dress in loose-fitting cotton clothing.
- Reduce activity.
- Avoid frequent bathing and overuse of soap.

Rx: Lotion: salicylic acid 2%, menthol 1%, chlorhexidine 0.5% in alcohol.

Proctalgia fugax

Use salbutamol inhaler, two puffs, when awakened by pain.

Prostate: benign prostatic hypertrophy

Initial trial:

- avoid caffeine
- avoid wheat, dairy and yeast products
- zinc and vitamin C tablets, e.g. Zinvit-C 250 tds

Consider:

- minipress 0.5 mg (o) bd for 3–7 days

  adjust to maintenance dose 2 mg (o) bd

Pruritis ani

(refer page 254)

Treat cause, e.g. dermatitis.

General measures

- Stop scratching.
- Bathe carefully: avoid hot water, excessive scrubbing and soaps.
- Use bland aqueous cream, Cetaphil lotion or Neutrogena soap.
- Keep area dry and cool.
- Keep bowels regular and wipe with cotton wool soaked in warm water.
- Wear loose-fitting clothing and underwear.
- Avoid local anaesthetics and antiseptics.

If still problematic and a dermatosis probably involved use:

hydrocortisone 1% cream

or

hydrocortisone 1% cream with clioquinol 0.5 to 3% (most effective)

If isolated area and resistant:

infiltrate 0.5 ml triamcinolone intradermally

If desperate:

fractionated X-ray therapy

Pruritus vulvae

(refer page 859)

Management depends on cause, e.g. candidiasis

General measures

- Attend to hygiene and excessive sweating.
- Keep genital area dry and wash thoroughly at least once a day.
- Avoid overzealous washing.
- Do not wear pantyhose, tight jeans or tight underwear, or use tampons.
- Do not use vaginal douches, powders or deodorants.
- Use aqueous cream or Cetaphil lotion rather than toilet soap.

Psoriasis

General:

- tar baths, e.g. Pinetarsol or Polytar
- sunlight (in moderation)

For stable plaques on limbs or trunk:

- apply dithranol 0.1% cream (Dithrocream) to affected area at night, leave 20–30 minutes, wash off under shower and increase strength every 5 days to 1% (up to maximum 2 hours)
- then apply topical fluorinated corticosteroid in the morning

For milder stabilised plaques:
- Egopsoryl TA—apply bd or tds
  or
  topical fluorinated corticosteroids

For resistant plaque:
- topical fluorinated corticosteroids (II–III class) with occlusion
- intralesional injection of triamcinolone mixed (50:50) with LA or normal saline (Fig. 111.7)

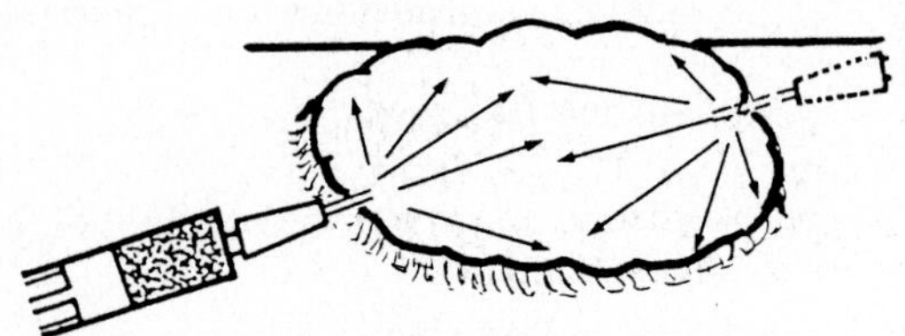

Fig. 111.7 *Intralesional injection for psoriasis*

Renal (or ureteric) colic

- pethidine and metoclopramide (10 mg) injection statim:
  give IM or by IV titration
- indomethacin suppositories (take home for any further pain)
  limited to two a day

Anecdotal: jump up and down vigorously on the leg of the affected side.

Restless legs

Exclude diabetes, uraemia, hypothyroidism, anaemia.

It is mainly a functional disorder affecting the elderly.

- diet: eliminate caffeine and follow a healthy diet
- exercises: gentle stretching of legs, particularly of hamstrings and calf muscles, for at least five minutes before retiring (Fig. 111.8)

Medication

1st choice: clonazepam 1 mg, one hour before retiring
2nd choice: diazepam
May help: codeine, levodopa, baclofen, propranolol
Generally unhelpful: carbamazepine, quinine, antipsychotics and antidepressants

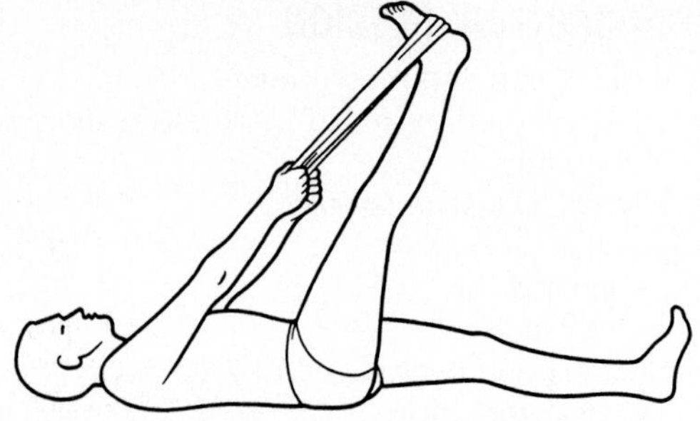

Fig. 111.8 *Stretching exercise for restless legs*

Ringworm (tinea corporis)

- clotrimazole 1%, miconazole 2% or ketoconazole 2% cream; apply bd for 5–6 weeks (ensure 4 weeks past apparent cure)
- may require griseofulvin

Rosacea

- tetracycline 250 mg bd or qid
  (doxycycline 100 mg)

until improved, then
- tetracycline 250 mg daily
  (doxycycline 50 mg)
  for total of about 8–10 weeks

Second line: erythromycin (in similar dose)

Topical agents
- 2% sulphur in aqueous cream (milder cases)
  or
- metronidazole gel bd (more severe cases)

Roundworms (acariasis)

- pyrantel (various preparations)
  10 mg/kg as single dose

Scabies (all types)

- lindane 1% lotion
  apply to whole body from jawline down
  leave overnight and wash off
- use benzyl benzoate 25% in children, pregnancy, lactation

Seborrhoeic warts/keratoses

- explanation and reassurance
- can be left alone
- liquid nitrogen applications for cosmetic improvement

Shingles (herpes zoster)

(refer pages 884–85)

- use menthol in flexible collodion for the rash
- for severe cases (within 48 hours of development of rash) acyclovir 800 mg 5 times daily for 7 days

Postherpetic neuralgia

- consider topical capsaicin cream (Capsig); apply 3–4 times a day

Sinusitis: acute

(refer page 422)

- look for nasal pathology such as polyposis and dental problems
- analgesics
- steam inhalations (Fig. 111.5)
- pseudoephedrine tablets
- antibiotics (1st choice)—for 7–10 day course
  amoxycillin
  or
  amoxycillin/potassium clavulanate (if amoxycillin-resistant)
  or
  doxycycline

Sinusitis: chronic

Sinusitis persisting longer than two weeks, despite repeated antibiotic and decongestant therapy, is common in general practice. Postnasal drip with cough, especially at night, is a feature.

- steam inhalations with Friar's balsam or menthol (best is menthol Co APF inhalation)
- vitamin C (sodium ascorbate) 2–4 g daily (a powder can be obtained and mixed with orange juice)

Snoring

If abnormal, refer to a sleep laboratory for assessment and management of obstructive sleep apnoea syndrome and other abnormalities.

If functional, give the following advice to consider:

- Obtain and maintain ideal weight.
- Avoid drugs, e.g. sedatives, hypnotics.
- Avoid sleeping on the back—consider sewing tennis balls on back of nightwear or wear bra (with tennis balls) back to front.
- Keep neck extended with a soft collar at night.
- Provide partner with appropriate ear plugs!

Stinging fish

Injury due mainly to sharp spines, e.g. stone fish.

- bathe or immerse part in very warm to hot water
- consider infiltration with local anaesthetic

Stitch in side

A stitch in the epigastric or hypochondrium is sharp pain due to cramping in the diaphragm.

- Stop and rest when the pain strikes during activity. Then walk—don't run.
- Apply deep massage to the area with the pulps of the middle three fingers.
- Perform slow deep breathing.

Prophylaxis

- undertake a program of abdominal breathing prior to activity.

Stuttering

Recommend medical hypnotherapy if no contraindications.

Stye in eye

- Apply heat with direct steam from a thermos (Fig. 111.9) onto the closed eye or by a hot compress (helps spontaneous discharge).
- Perform lash epilation to allow drainage (incise with a D_{11} blade if epilation doesn't work).
- Only use topical antibiotic ointment, e.g. chloramphenicol, if infection spreading locally, and systemic antibiotics if distal spread noted by preauricular adenitis.

Fig. 111.9 *Steaming a painful eye*

Subconjunctival haemorrhage

- Patient explanation and reassurance is necessary.
- It absorbs over two weeks.
- Although no local therapy is necessary, bathing with a weak salt solution twice daily helps.

Sunburn

(refer page 877)

- aspirin (for pain)
- promethazine (for sedation/itching) only if necessary

Topical:

- hydrocortisone 1% ointment or cream for unblistered severe cases (early)
  repeat in 2–3 hours, then next day (not after 24 hours)
  or
- bicarbonate of soda paste, applied 2 hourly
  or
- oily calamine lotion

Sweating (excessive)

General hyperhidrosis

- explanation and reassurance
- trial of probanthine aluminium chloride 20% in alcohol solution if localised area

Axillary hyperhidrosis

Treatment:

- explanation and reassurance
- *see* treatment of body odour
- aluminium chloride 20% in alcohol solution (Driclor, Hidrosol); apply nocte for one week, then 1–2 times weekly or as necessary

Surgery

Wedge resection of a small block of skin and subcutaneous tissue from axillary vault. Define sweat glands with codeine starch powder. The area excised is usually about 4 cm × 2.5 cm.

Tearduct (nasolacrimal duct) blockage in child

- if conjunctivitis present
  chloramphenicol eye drops
- perform regular massage from inner canthus to base of nose (teach mother) at least twice daily
- if persistent in infant: requires nasolacrimal probing at 4 months—otherwise leave to 6 months or so as it may resolve

Teething

Precautions: exclude other possible causes of irritability in a teething child, e.g. UTI, meningitis, otitis media. Teething doesn't cause fever.

Treatment:

- paracetamol
- trimeprazine or antihistamine (o) nocte
  or
- combined mixture, e.g. Polaramine Infant Co

Chewing

- teething ring (kept cold in the refrigerator)
  or
- baby can chew on a clean, cold, lightly moistened facewasher (a piece of apple can be placed in the facewasher)
  or
- parent can massage gum with forefinger wrapped in a soft cloth or gauze pad (Oro-sed gel can be massaged into gums every 3 hours if extremely troublesome)

Temporomandibular joint dysfunction

Refer to the various exercise techniques on page 423. Most effective and simplest method is placing a piece of soft wood, e.g. carpenter's pencil, firmly against back molars and biting rhythmically on the object with a grinding movement for 2–3 minutes at least 3 times a day.

Tennis elbow

(refer page 539)

Tension headache

- explanation and reassurance
- remove source of anxiety (if possible)
- counselling
- relaxation techniques/meditation
- consider cervical spine as factor and treat any dysfunction with mobilisation, massage and exercises
- aspirin or paracetamol for pain

Threadworms

- explanation and reassurance
- pyrantel (various oral preparations) 10 mg/kg as a single dose

Thrush (moniliasis)

In infants: nystatin oral drugs 1 ml held in mouth as long as possible 4 times daily

In adults: amphotericin, 1 lozenge (10 mg) dissolved slowly in mouth, 6 hourly for 10 days

or

nystatin, 1 lozenge (100 000 units) dissolved slowly in mouth, 6 hourly for 10 days

Vaginal thrush

(refer page 763)

Tick bites

(refer page 987)

Tinea capitis

Griseofulvin 500 mg (o) for 8 weeks

Also — take hair plucking and scale for culture
— Selsun shampoo twice weekly
— topical clotrimazole or miconazole

Tinea cruris (jock itch)

- Soak the area in a warm bath and dry thoroughly.
- Apply clotrimazole 1% or miconazole 2% cream; rub in a thin layer bd for 3–4 weeks.
- When almost healed, apply tolnaftate dusting powder bd for 3–4 weeks.
- If itch severe: add 1% hydrocortisone cream.
- If weeping: apply Burow's solution compresses.

Tinea pedis (athlete's foot)

(refer page 875)

- patient education
- keep feet clean and dry
- use antifungal powder between toes after drying
- wear socks of natural absorbent fibres (avoid synthetics)
- wear open sandals and shoes with porous soles and uppers (if possible)
- use thongs in public showers
- keep toe spaces separated if interdigital

Rx: clotrimaxole 1% or miconazole 2% cream or lotion; apply bd or tds for 2–3 weeks

or

ketoconazole 2% cream bd

if widespread or smelly vesiculobullous (take scrapings), use griseofulvin (Griseostatin) 330 mg (o) daily for 6 weeks

Tinea of toe-nails and fingernails (tinea unguium)

- usually associated with tinea pedis
- nails show white spots; may be yellow and crumbling
- starts at the edge of periphery and spreads towards base

Treatment:

- terbinafine (Lamisil) 250 mg (o) daily
  - fingernails 4 weeks
  - toe-nails 12 weeks
- consider nail avulsion and systemic treatment

Tinnitus

Precautions:

- exclude drugs including marijuana, vascular disease, depression, aneurysm and vascular tumours
- beware of lonely elderly people living alone (suicide risk)

Management

- educate and reassure the patient
- relaxation techniques
- background 'noise', e.g. music playing during night
- tinnitus maskers
- hearing aids

Drug trials to consider (limited efficacy)

- betahistine (Serc) 8–16 mg daily (max. 32 mg)
- carbamazepine (Tegretol)
- antidepressants
- sodium valproate

Tongue problems

- geographical tongue: reassurance and Cepacaine gargles 10 ml tds if tender
- black or hairy tongue: this is basically a harmless condition related to smoking and antibiotic treatment
  Rx (if patient pressure):
  — brush with toothbrush using sodium bicarbonate paste
  or
  — suck fresh pineapple pieces

Torticollis (acute wry neck)

Muscle energy therapy, which is simple to use and highly effective, is described on page 516.

Travel sickness

Oral preparations:

- dimenhydrinate (Andrumin, Dramamine, Travs)
  or
- promethazine theoclate (Avomine)
  or
- hyoscine (Kwells)

Take 30–60 minutes before the trip
repeat 4–6 hourly during trip (maximum 4 doses in 24 hours)

Dermal:

- hyoscine dermal disc (Scop)
  apply to dry hairless skin behind ear 5–6 hours before travel, leave on for 3 days

Tropical ear

For severe painful otitis media in tropics:

- prednisolone (orally) 15 mg statim, then 10 mg 8 hourly for 6 doses followed by
- Merocel ear wick
- topical Kenacomb or Sofradex drops for 10 days

Umbilical discharge

Usually infected (fungal or bacterial) dermatitis, often with offensive discharge.

Precautions: consider umbilical fistula, carcinoma, umbilical calculus.

Management:

- swab for micro and culture
- toilet—remove all debris and clean
- keep dry and clean—daily dressings
- consider Kenacomb ointment

Umbilical granuloma in infants

Apply a caustic pencil gently daily for about 5 days.

Urticaria (hives)

- search for cause, e.g. drugs, food, infestation
- food check: nuts, chocolate, cheese, fish, eggs

Rx: antihistamines: cyprohepadine 16–32 mg daily
astemizole or terfenadine

- lukewarm baths with Pinetarsol or similar soothing bath oil
- topical 0.5% hydrocortisone—apply every 4 hours for itching

Vaginal thrush (monilial vaginitis)

- Bathe genital area bd or tds with sodium bicarbonate (especially before using treatment).
- Dry area thoroughly.
- Wear loose-fitting cotton underwear.
- Avoid wearing tight clothing or using tampons.
- Avoid vaginal douches, powders or deodorants.

Rx: can use amphotericin, clotrimazole, econazole, isoconazole, miconazole or nystatin.
Examples:

- clotrimazole 500 mg vaginal tablet statim, and clotrimazole 2% cream applied to vagina and vulva (for symptomatic relief)
  or (especially if recurrent or recalcitrant)
- nystatin pessaries, once daily for 7 days and/or nystatin vaginal cream, 4 g once daily for 7 days

Varicose ulcers

(refer pages 891–92)

Whiplash

(refer page 517)

Wrinkles

(refer page 1076)

Writer's cramp

- education and reassurance
- avoid holding pen too tight
- clonazepan 0.5 mg bd (if persisting)

Ionizing radiation illness

Although this is fortunately not an everyday problem and hopefully never will be to readers, it is worthwhile to conclude with an overview of the clinical consequences of radioactive fallout. The nuclear disasters in Eastern Europe highlighted the paucity of knowledge available to the general practitioner about the known clinical effects of the radioactive elements (mainly iodine and caesium) that are discharged into the atmosphere.

Apart from nuclear accidents, the effects of excessive ionising radiation can follow accidental exposure in hospitals and industry, and in the use of atomic weaponry. Ionising radiation can be either penetrating (X-rays, gamma rays, neutrons) or non-penetrating (alpha or beta particles).

The revised *Système International* (SI) nomenclature uses the Sievert (SV) as the unit of radiation dose to body tissue. It is the absorbed dose weighted for the damaging effect of the radiation. As a guideline the annual background radiation is approximately 2.5 millisievert and a typical X-ray is 0.5 millisievert.

The general principles of radiation exposure are:

- The closer to the focus of radiation, the more devastating the injury.
- Radiation illness can vary from mild vomiting to acute leukaemia.
- The most sensitive tissues are the brain, the gastrointestinal mucosa and bone marrow.
- The dividing (mitotic) cells of blood, the gastrointestinal tract, skin, lenses and gonads are especially vulnerable.

Severe acute radiation sickness

The extent of the radiation damage depends on the dose of radiation. The typical clinical effects are presented in Table 111.2. The acute effects include the cerebral or CNS syndrome, haemopoietic syndrome, gastrointestinal syndrome and the skin and mucous membrane syndrome (radiation dermatitis).

Table 111.2 *Clinical effects of radioactive fallout from a nuclear accident (using Chernobyl as a reference)*

*Radiation dose expressed in sieverts**	*Distance from focus (approximate)*	*Typical clinical effects (variable time of onset)*	*Mortality risk*
10–50	1 km	Nausea, vomiting, diarrhoea, Cerebral syndrome Fever Fluid and electrolyte imbalance Acute leukaemia	100% Rapidly fatal
6–10	2–3 km	Nausea, vomiting, diarrhoea Rash Acute leukaemia/agranulocytosis	80–100%
2–6	4–6 km	Nausea, vomiting Rash Leukaemia/agranulocytosis Alopecia Cataracts	50%
1–2	7–8 km	Nausea, vomiting Agranulocytosis (mild)	Not immediate Long-term cancer risk
0–1	9 km and over	Nausea, vomiting	Not fatal

* 1 sievert = 10 REM (older unit)
typical X-ray = 0.5 millisievert

Acute lethal injury

The lethal problems that can result from acute exposure to radiation are due to haemopoietic failure, gastrointestinal mucosa damage, central nervous system damage and widespread vascular injury (Figure 111.10).

Death is usually due to haemorrhage, anaemia or infection secondary to haemopoietic failure (mainly leukaemia). Lymphocytes are the most sensitive cells, then leucocytes, erythrocytes and platelets. Where death doesn't occur, recovery of cells can take months.

High doses of radiation produce irradiation of the brain, leading to the cerebral syndrome. This is characterised by nausea, vomiting, listlessness and drowsiness followed by convulsions, ataxia and, usually quickly, death.

The gastrointestinal syndrome, which is maximal three to five days after exposure, is caused by destruction of the crypt cells in the mucosa. It is characterised by intractable nausea and vomiting (which responds poorly to antiemetic drugs) and diarrhoea with subsequent severe fluid and electrolyte imbalance.

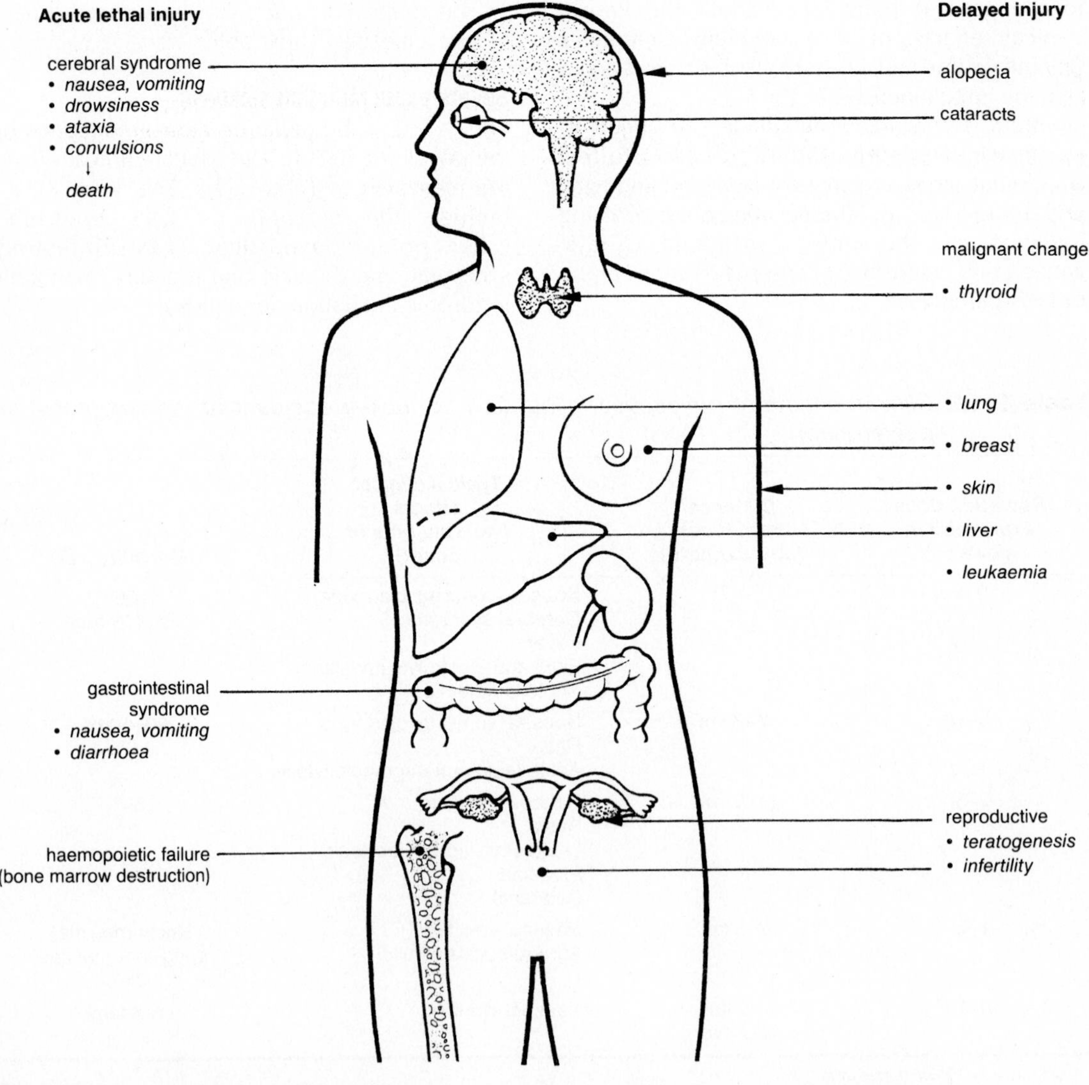

Fig. 111.10 *Clinical effects of radiation illness*

The acute effects on the skin and mucous membrane include erythema, epilation, blistering, purpura, destruction of fingers and secondary infection. Total loss of body hair, particularly alopecia, is a serious prognostic sign.

Mild acute radiation sickness

The main symptoms are malaise, weakness, anorexia, nausea and vomiting. The blood film is affected with diminished production of the blood cells. Lymphocytes are the most sensitive and lymphopenia develops within several days with a fall in all white cells and platelets within another three weeks.

Delayed effects

Other organs with a tendency to absorb radiation do not show immediate effects but will undergo malignant change. The thyroid gland is the most vulnerable. Others include the lungs, kidney, liver and breast, skin and salivary glands.

Acute myeloid leukaemia is a common sequela. Other late sequelae include infertility, teratogenesis, skin changes and cataracts.

Management

Acute radiation sickness is a medical emergency and arrangements must be made for immediate referral to hospital. Contaminated clothing should be removed and substituted with protective clothing.

The response to treatment is obviously dependent on the extent, degree and localisation of tissue damage.

For distressing nausea and vomiting use:
metoclopramide 10 mg IM or IV (slowly) injections

or

chlorpromazine 25–50 mg IM 4–6 hourly

Treatment might include:

- fluid and electrolyte replacement
- ultra isolation techniques to prevent infection
- antibiotics are necessary
- bone marrow transplantation
- platelet or granulocyte transfusion

APPENDICES

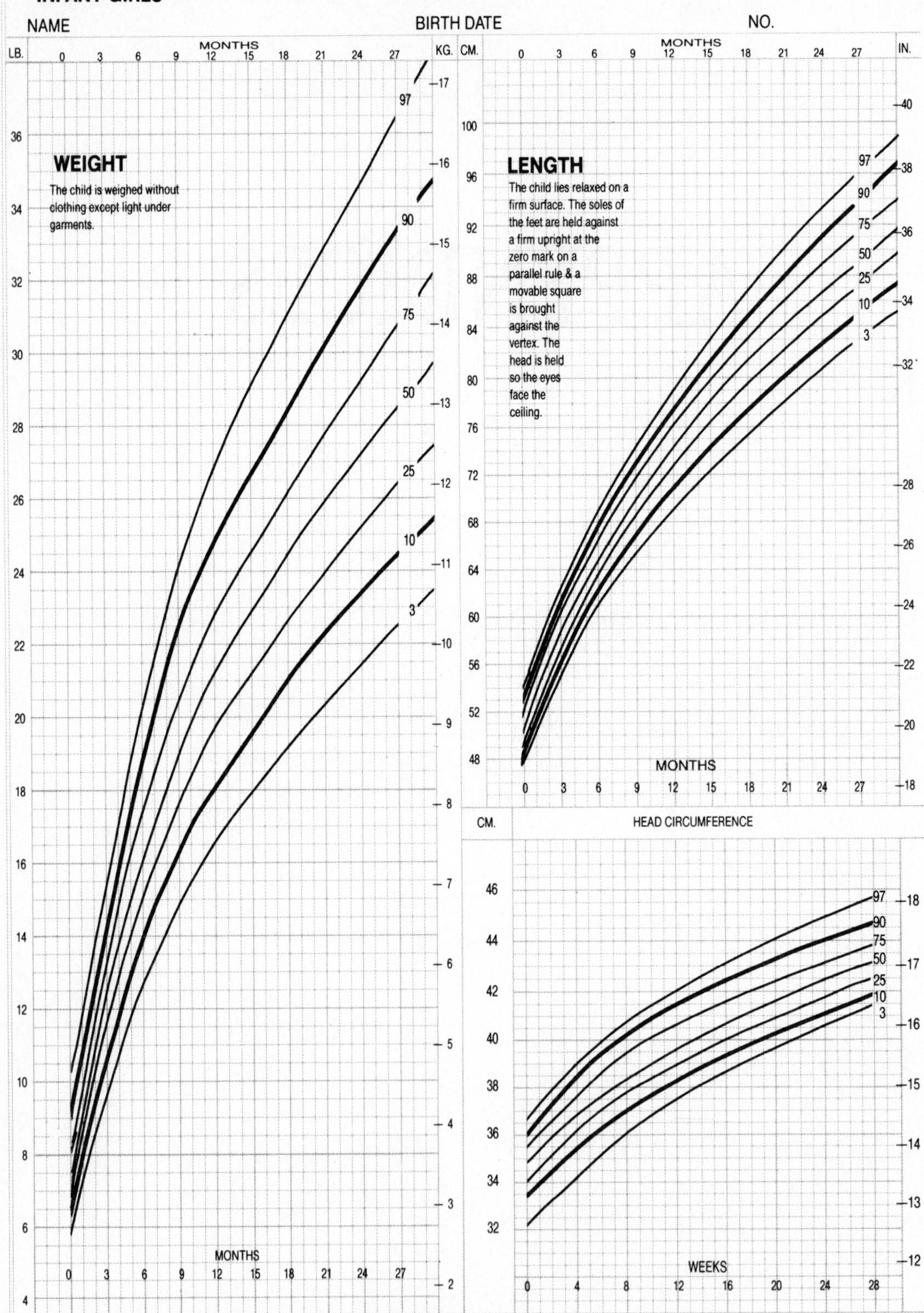
INFANT GIRLS
NAME
BIRTH DATE
NO.
LB.
MONTHS
KG.
CM.
IN.
WEIGHT
The child is weighed without clothing except light under garments.
LENGTH
The child lies relaxed on a firm surface. The soles of the feet are held against a firm upright at the zero mark on a parallel rule & a movable square is brought against the vertex. The head is held so the eyes face the ceiling.
97
90
75
50
25
10
3
HEAD CIRCUMFERENCE
WEEKS

INFANT BOYS

NAME BIRTH DATE NO.

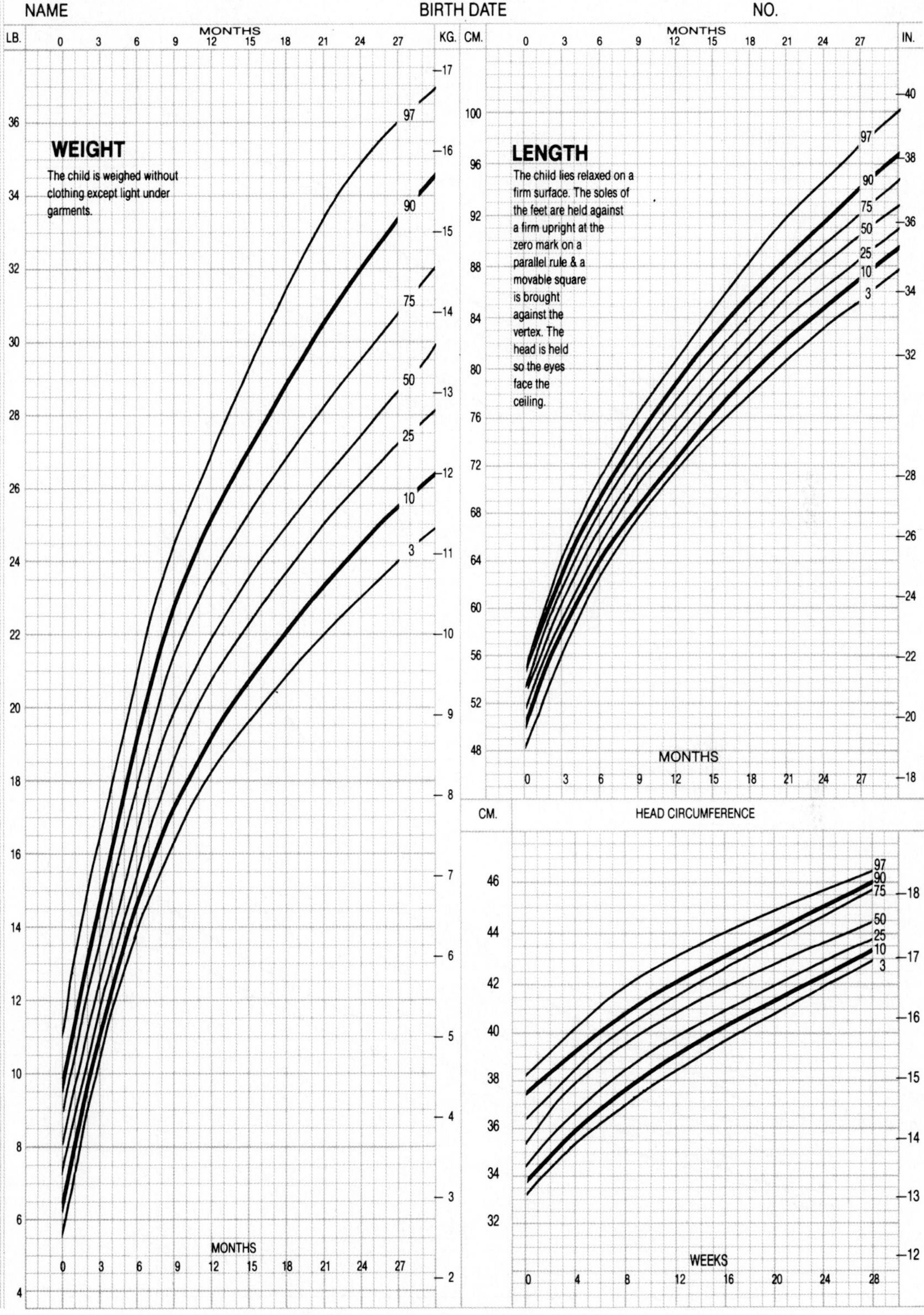
WEIGHT
The child is weighed without clothing except light under garments.
LB.
KG.
MONTHS
0 3 6 9 12 15 18 21 24 27
97
90
75
50
25
10
3
LENGTH
The child lies relaxed on a firm surface. The soles of the feet are held against a firm upright at the zero mark on a parallel rule & a movable square is brought against the vertex. The head is held so the eyes face the ceiling.
CM.
IN.
HEAD CIRCUMFERENCE
WEEKS
0 4 8 12 16 20 24 28

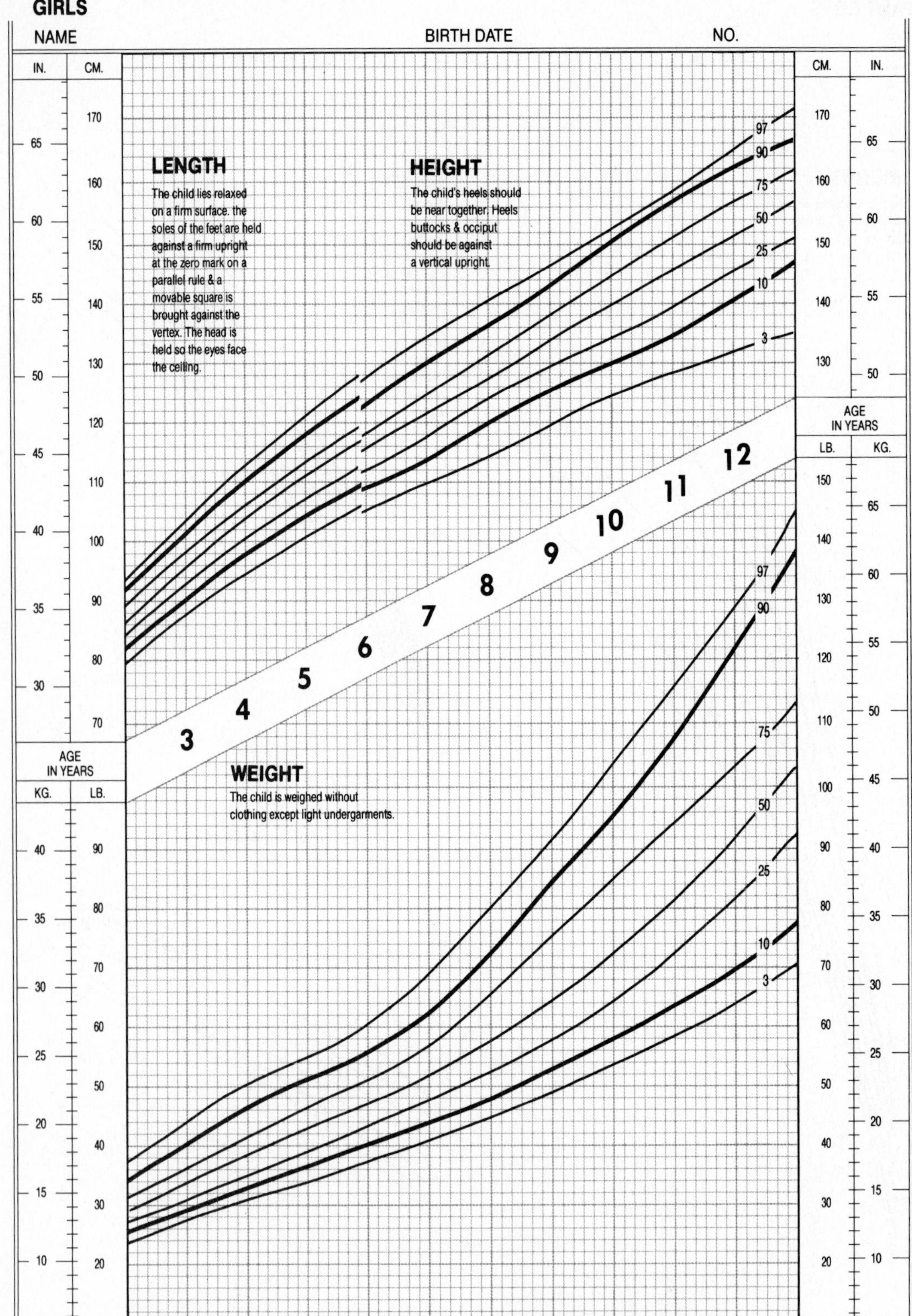
GIRLS
NAME
BIRTH DATE
NO.
IN.
CM.
LENGTH
The child lies relaxed on a firm surface. the soles of the feet are held against a firm upright at the zero mark on a parallel rule & a movable square is brought against the vertex. The head is held so the eyes face the ceiling.
HEIGHT
The child's heels should be near together. Heels buttocks & occiput should be against a vertical upright.
AGE IN YEARS
KG.
LB.
WEIGHT
The child is weighed without clothing except light undergarments.
3
4
5
6
7
8
9
10
11
12
97
90
75
50
25
10
3

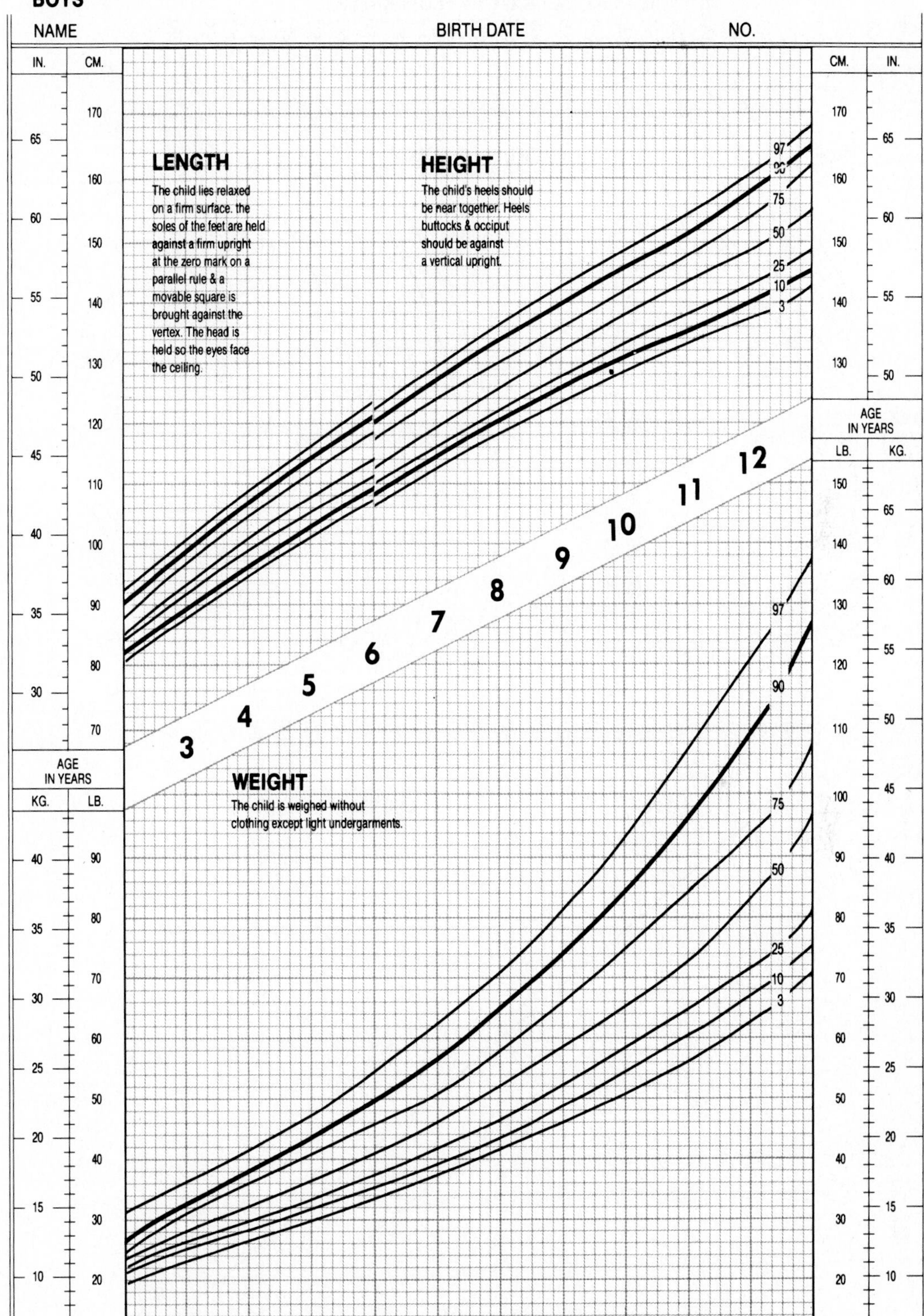
BOYS
NAME
BIRTH DATE
NO.
IN.
CM.
LENGTH
The child lies relaxed on a firm surface. the soles of the feet are held against a firm upright at the zero mark on a parallel rule & a movable square is brought against the vertex. The head is held so the eyes face the ceiling.
HEIGHT
The child's heels should be near together. Heels buttocks & occiput should be against a vertical upright.
97
90
75
50
25
10
3
AGE IN YEARS
3
4
5
6
7
8
9
10
11
12
KG.
LB.
WEIGHT
The child is weighed without clothing except light undergarments.

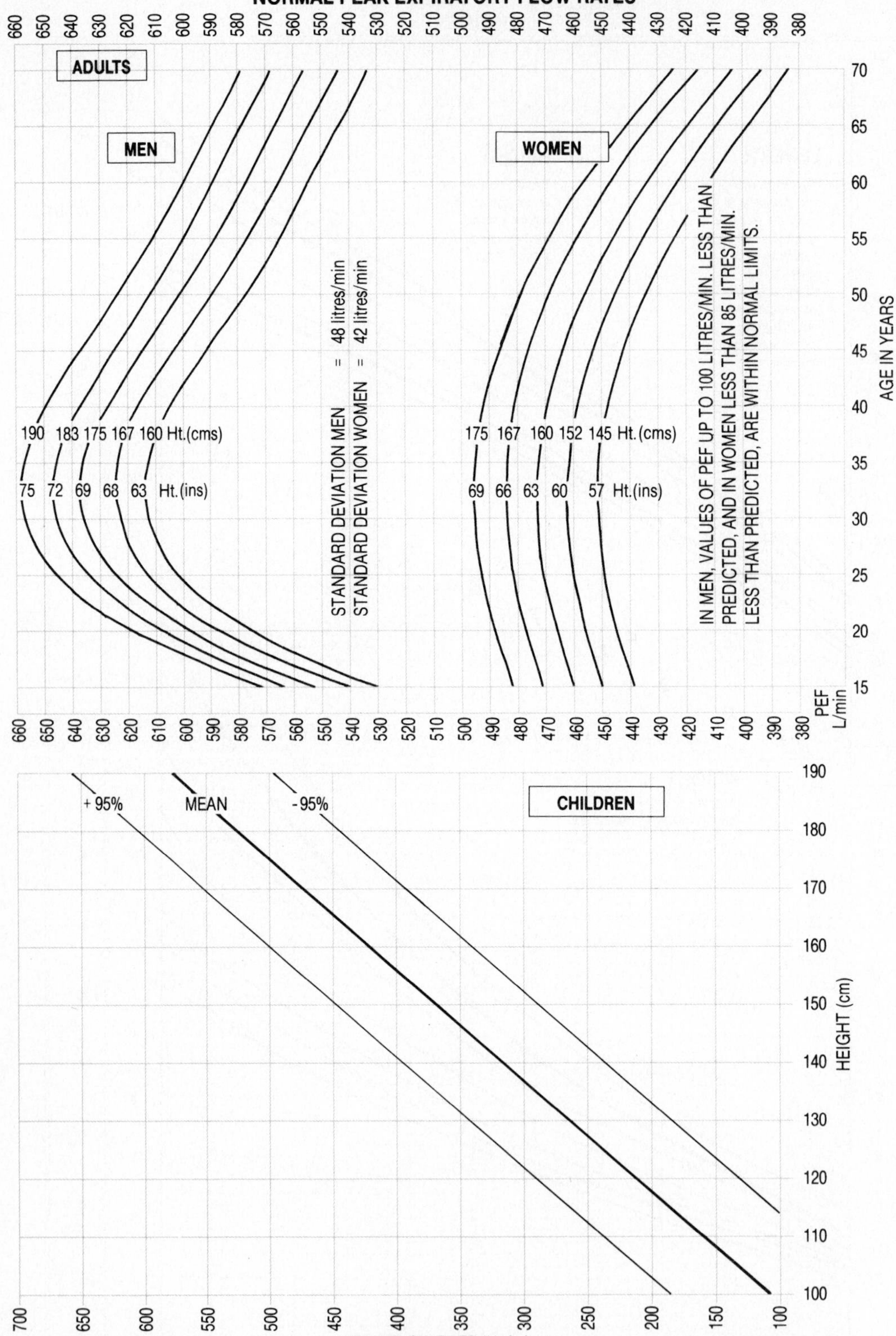
NORMAL PEAK EXPIRATORY FLOW RATES
ADULTS
MEN
WOMEN
190 183 175 167 160 Ht.(cms)
75 72 69 68 63 Ht.(ins)
175 167 160 152 145 Ht.(cms)
69 66 63 60 57 Ht.(ins)
STANDARD DEVIATION MEN = 48 litres/min
STANDARD DEVIATION WOMEN = 42 litres/min
IN MEN, VALUES OF PEF UP TO 100 LITRES/MIN. LESS THAN PREDICTED, AND IN WOMEN LESS THAN 85 LITRES/MIN. LESS THAN PREDICTED, ARE WITHIN NORMAL LIMITS.
AGE IN YEARS
PEF L/min
CHILDREN
+ 95%
MEAN
- 95%
HEIGHT (cm)
PEAK FLOW RATE (l/min.)

THE AUSTRALIAN NUTRITION FOUNDATION

Weight For Height Chart

(For Men and Women from 18 years onward)

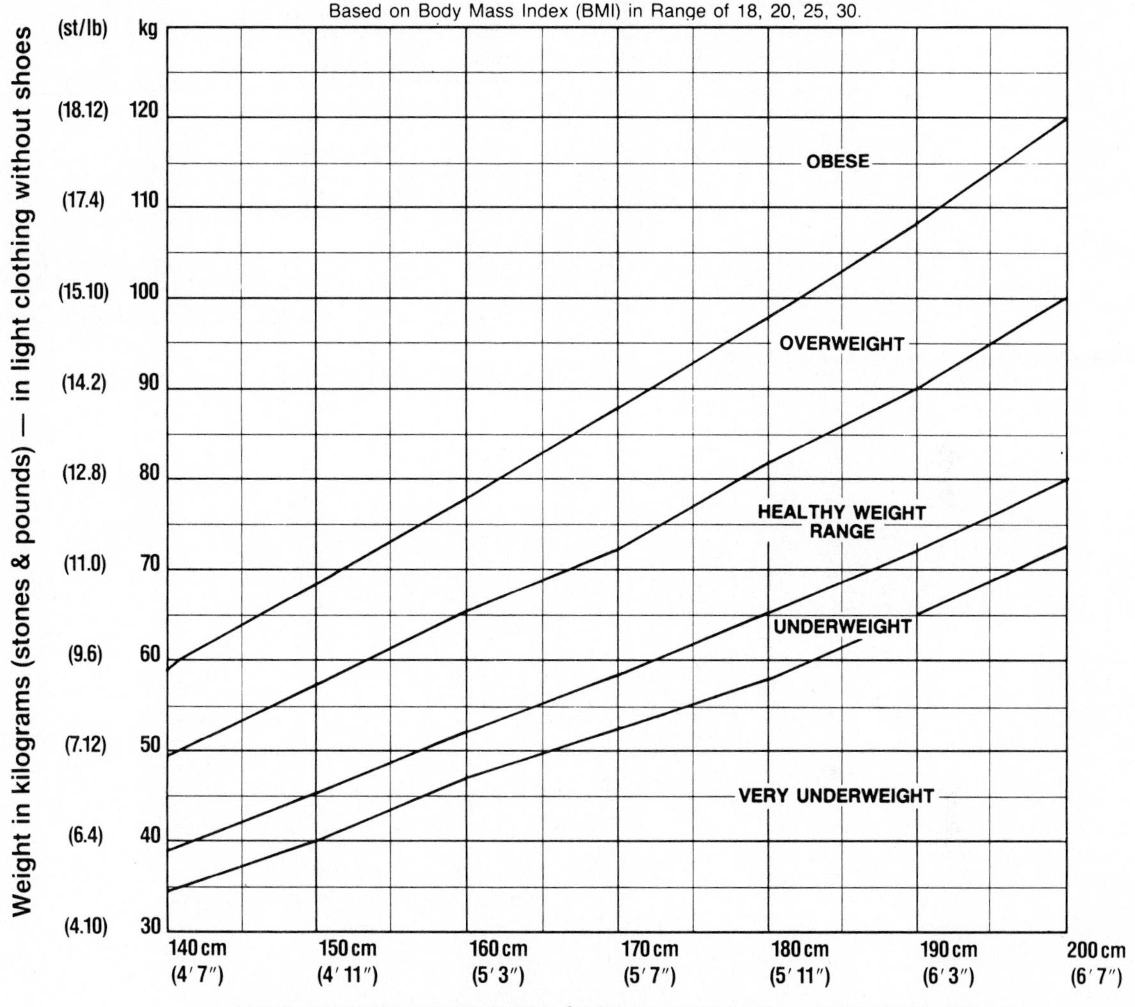

Index